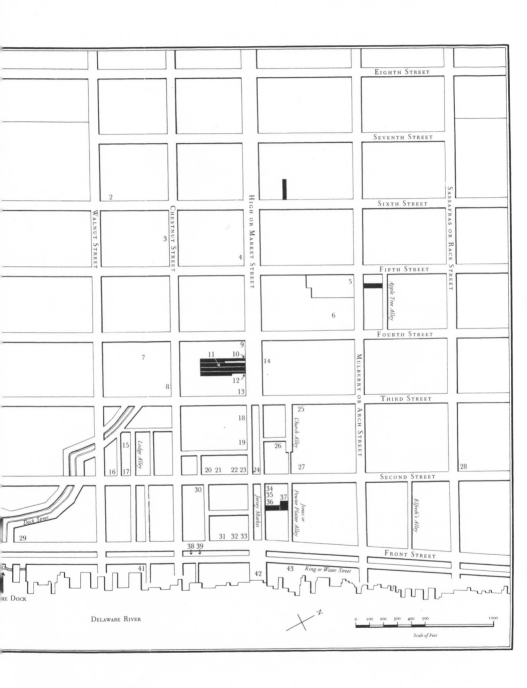

EIGHTH STREET

SEVENTH STREET

SIXTH STREET

FIFTH STREET

FOURTH STREET

THIRD STREET

SECOND STREET

FRONT STREET

WALNUT STREET

CHESTNUT STREET

HIGH OR MARKET STREET

MULBERRY OR ARCH STREET

SASSAFRAS OR RACE STREET

Apple Tree Alley

Church Alley

Lodge Alley

Jersey Market

Jones or Pewter Platter Alley

Elfreth's Alley

Dock Street

King or Water Street

THE DOCK

DELAWARE RIVER

0 100 200 300 400 500 1000

Scale of Feet

The Life of Benjamin Franklin   VOLUME 3

The Life of
Benjamin Franklin

VOLUME 3

~

Soldier, Scientist, and Politician
1748–1757

J. A. Leo Lemay

PENN

University of Pennsylvania Press
Philadelphia

Published by
University of Pennsylvania Press
Philadelphia, Pennsylvania 19104–4112

Printed in the United States of America on acid-free paper

10 9 8 7 6 5 4 3 2 1

Library of Congress Cataloging-in-Publication Data

Lemay, J. A. Leo (Joseph A. Leo), 1935–
    The life of Benjamin Franklin / J. A. Leo Lamay.
        p.   cm.
    Includes bibliographical references and index.
    Contents: v. 1. Journalist, 1706–1730—v. 2. Printer and publisher, 1730–1747—v. 3. Soldier, scientist, and politician, 1748–1757
    ISBN 0-8122-3854-0 (v. 1 : acid-free paper).—ISBN 0-8122-3855-9 (v. 2 : acid-free paper).—ISBN 978-0-8122-4121-1 (v. 3 : acid-free paper)
    1. Franklin, Benjamin, 1706–1790.   2. Statesmen—United States—Biography.
3. Scientists—United States—Biography.   4. Inventors—United States—Biography.
5. Printers—United States—Biography.   I. Title.
E302.6.F8L424   2005
973.3′92—dc22
[B]   2004063130

Frontispiece: Benjamin Franklin, mezzotint by Edward Fisher after Mason Chamberlain. Courtesy, National Portrait Gallery.

Endpapers: Map of Franklin's Philadelphia with key places of interest indicated. Reprinted from *The Papers of Benjamin Franklin*, ed. Leonard W. Labaree et al. (New Haven, Conn.: Yale University Press, 1959–), vol. 2, facing p. 456. Courtesy, Ellen R. Cohn.

Contents

Illustrations

Franklin's Philadelphia *endpapers*
Benjamin Franklin, mezzotint by Benjamin Martin, after Mason
Chamberlain *frontispiece*

FIGURES

Preface

AT THE BEGINNING OF 1748, Franklin was known in Pennsylvania as clerk of the Pennsylvania Assembly and in the Middle Colonies as the printer and editor of *Poor Richard's Almanac* and the *Pennsylvania Gazette* (the best colonial newspaper). By the middle of 1757, however, he had become famous in Pennsylvania as a public-spirited citizen and a soldier; well-known throughout America as a writer, politician, and the most important theorist of the American empire; and renowned in the western world as a natural philosopher. This volume tells the story of that transformation.

In late 1747, Britain's war with Spain and France had been under way since 1741 and 1744, respectively. French and Spanish ships were raiding up and down the colonies' Atlantic coast and even in the Delaware Bay. With an organized force of fewer than several hundred, enemy troops could have plundered the entire city of Philadelphia. The Pennsylvania Assembly, dominated by the Quaker Party, refused to provide defense. Franklin proposed a volunteer militia, aroused the public, and raised more than ten thousand volunteer troops in Pennsylvania. He organized a successful lottery that raised funds to buy cannon and build fortifications to defend Philadelphia. When peace was proclaimed in August 1748, he was the most popular person in Pennsylvania.

During the same period, Franklin devoted whatever time he could spare to electricity. News concerning its inexplicable marvels had appeared in popular magazines in 1745. In 1746 European electrical experimenters created the Leyden jar, an early capacitor. It could build up and store an electric charge that would be released when the inside and outside of the bottle were connected. Its effects were astonishing. Two hundred Swiss guards, with hands joined, would all be shocked and jump instantaneously upon receiving the electric charge. No one understood how the Leyden jar worked. Franklin offered the first good explanation, based partly on the atomic theories of the Greeks. He theorized that electricity was not created; rather, it separated existing elements into positive and negative charges. He also suggested that atmospheric electricity existed; hypothesized that lightning was an electrical discharge; and experimented to test the hypothesis. During the first several years of his electric experiments, English electricians ridiculed him. Then, following Franklin's directions, the French tested and proved correct his theories that clouds could contain electric charges and that lightning was electrical in nature. He quickly became the best-known living natural philosopher, and the Royal Society of London awarded him its Copley medal in 1753—the most prestigious existing scientific award, comparable to today's Nobel Prize.

Franklin was also interested in weather, and like all almanac makers, he wondered if one could go beyond the comments on the seasons and prediction of eclipses. Almost by accident, he tracked the progress of hurricanes and found that although the winds in the great storms blew from the northwest, the storms actually moved up from the southeast. Having established the southeast-to-northwest direction in which the storms moved, he hypothesized why and where they started and why they traveled in a northwest direction. Taking into account the effects of trade winds, the Appalachian Mountains, and the behavior of hot and cold air, his hypotheses were simple, crude, and brilliant. So too were his ruminations on tornadoes, whirlwinds, and waterspouts. They were the best explanations, thought Captain James Cook, that existed. Franklin was America's first scientific weatherman.

In 1749 Franklin started the Academy and College of Philadelphia (now the University of Pennsylvania). Franklin's basic idea for the academy was to educate youths who were approximately thirteen to eighteen in ways that would prepare them either for further study or for a career in business. Franklin projected a radically different education as an alternative to the apprenticeship system and to the existing elite academic schools. The latter taught youths Latin and a little Greek, which were the requirements for entrance into the colleges of the day—Harvard, Yale, and William and Mary—where one further studied Latin and Greek. The apprenticeship system taught a youth a specific trade, which he then practiced for the remainder of his life. Franklin's Academy of Philadelphia would be primarily an English, mathematical, and agricultural school, with an emphasis on the study of modern languages (French, Spanish, and German) rather than Latin and Greek. But the major financial contributors to the academy wanted the traditional curriculum; Latin and Greek at first supplemented and then gradually superseded Franklin's proposed curriculum.

While the academy was taking shape, Dr. Thomas Bond came to Franklin with a project for starting a hospital "for the Reception and Cure of poor sick Persons." Bond was finding it impossible to interest enough people to contribute funds. Franklin subscribed £25 and wrote "on the Subject in the Newspapers." Despite their joint efforts, the money was insufficient, so Franklin appealed to the legislature. When the proposal ran into trouble there, Franklin came up with the idea of the first matching grant. Partially because the assemblymen doubted that Franklin and Bond would be able to raise the necessary amount, the House unanimously passed the bill on 1 February 1750/1, granting £2,000 if the projectors first raised £2,000 privately. Years later, Franklin wrote: "I do not remember any of my political Manoeuvres, the Success of which gave me at the time more Pleasure. Or that in after-thinking of it, I more easily excus'd myself for having made some Use of Cunning" (A 123).

Although Franklin planned to add a college to the academy, when the Academy and College of Philadelphia was officially chartered in 1754, it featured, to Franklin's chagrin, the traditional subjects. It was even in danger of becoming primarily a school for ministers, like Harvard and Yale. It remained nonsectarian, however, and within a few years two medical students, whom Franklin had encouraged, started a medical school. That began the transformation of the Academy and College of Philadelphia into a university. The medical school offered superior training, partly because of the Pennsylvania Hospital. In it, the students could attend the doctors on their rounds of the patients and learn about various illnesses and possible remedies. The first medical school in the colonies, it featured empirical training comparable to the best anywhere in the world.

In imitation of the Union Fire Company (which Franklin had started in 1736), six other fire companies were founded in Philadelphia, and by 1751 they met together quarterly to practice fire fighting. That year, Franklin used these companies as a base for projecting an insurance company that would protect against loss by fire. Franklin served as its president for two years, but after it became successful and financially sound, he left it to its fortune.

While increasingly more of a national and international figure because of his improvements to the common stove and especially because of his electrical experiments, Franklin also took a greater interest in politics. Like numerous Americans, he was irritated by English condescension to Americans and by the English assumption of superiority. In the spring of 1751, his frequent rumblings of discontent with English attitudes erupted. England's dumping of felons into the American colonies, and the Board of Trade's sneering comment that transporting felons provided for "the better peopling of America," outraged him. In the most furious attack on the English authorities before the Stamp Act, Franklin compared the British transporting of criminals to dumping toilets on the dining tables of Americans. "Jakes on our Tables!" became the first widely reprinted editorial in American journalism. A month later, May 1751, Franklin reinforced his news reports and editorial with a savage satire, "Rattlesnakes for Felons," which proposed sending rattlesnakes to England as a suitable return for the English criminals.

Earlier that year, in January 1751, Franklin had proposed a plan for the union of the colonies. The farsighted proposal became a blueprint for Franklin's Albany Plan of 1754. Before the end of 1751, Franklin drafted the fundamental document of the American Revolution, "Observations Concerning the Increase of Mankind, Peopling of Cities, etc." It showed that within every twenty-five years, America's population doubled, whereas England's and Europe's population would not double in one thousand years. Thus, within a century, America's population would be larger than England's, and if the colonies remained within the British empire, an American city would likely become the empire's capital. "Observations Concerning the Increase of Mankind" circulated widely in manuscript in England and America, but it was not published until 1755. All the major revolutionaries—Washington, Jefferson, Adams, and others—knew "Observations," and all of them, in part because Franklin had proven it, believed in the future greatness of America. As the most significant study of the influence of the frontier on American history, "Observations" influenced not only the future American rebellion but also the succeeding intellectual achievements of Richard Price, Adam Smith, Thomas Malthus, Charles Darwin, and Frederick Jackson Turner.

Franklin officially entered politics in his annus mirabilis, 1751. Though he had been clerk of the Pennsylvania Assembly since 1736, and though he had—as a writer, reporter, and editor—influenced votes and elections ever since his *Modest Enquiry into the Nature and Necessity of a Paper-Currency* (1729), he himself had no vote in the assembly. But in May 1751, after the death of a Philadelphia representative, he was elected to the Pennsylvania House. He quickly became its most active assemblyman, serving on more committees than anyone and writing the reports for the committees on which he served.

Though Governor James Hamilton and other Proprietary Party members hoped that Franklin might join them, the Proprietary Party tended to believe more in social hierarchy, in the privileges of the elite, and in the authority of the proprietors and of Great Britain than did the Quaker or Popular Party. In one area, defense, Franklin agreed with the Proprietary Party. He thought Pennsylvania should support troops for its defense on the Pennsylvania frontier and the Delaware Bay and should even contribute to colonial military expeditions like the one to Cape Breton in 1745. But in all other ways, Franklin's views were closer to those of the Quaker Party. The Proprietary Party could be regarded as Pennsylvania's version of England's Tory Party, and the Quaker Party as Pennsylvania's Whigs. Franklin was a radical egalitarian all his life. Not all Quaker Party members were Quakers, but many were, and some were pacifists. Nevertheless, he identified with the Quaker Party and immediately became its leader. The moderate Quaker Isaac Norris remained in the most powerful position, Speaker of the Pennsylvania Assembly, but Franklin became the Quaker Party's driving force.

In Franklin's first assembly session (which was the third and last for the assembly of 1750–51), Speaker Norris assigned him to a committee that focused on the expense entailed in conducting Indian affairs. As they had become increasingly expensive, the proprietors, who were the primary beneficiaries of the treaties, refused to bear any of the cost. For the assembly, Franklin wrote a message reminding Governor James Hamilton that the assembly had previously asked whether the proprietors would not contribute part of the expense of Indian treaties. Hamilton replied that the proprietors did not intend to pay for any part of the expenses and that they would prefer not to hear again about the matter. Franklin promptly drafted a series of resolves blasting the proprietors for their parsimony, unfairness, and arrogance. The assembly unanimously approved the resolves on 22 August 1751. It should have become clear at that time to anyone who was aware of the assembly's actions that Franklin had become a Quaker Party leader.

The chief proprietor of the Proprietary Colony of Pennsylvania, Thomas Penn, had resolved to raise all the money for himself that he could. He did so primarily by controlling the land: he sold land at a high price to Pennsylvania settlers and charged them a comparatively small quitrent thereafter. Though his grandfather William Penn had been given the land by King Charles II, William Penn had also bought the land that would be settled from the Indians. He then sold land to the colonists at a profit. Thomas Penn continued that practice but took greater advantage of the Indians and the colonists.

Believing that the Pennsylvania Assembly was becoming too powerful, Thomas Penn decided that he or his primary deputy, the lieutenant governor of Pennsylvania (in practice, the lieutenant governor in Pennsylvania was called the governor), would control the funds the assembly raised. Further, Penn forbade the governor to pass any act of assembly that taxed his estate in Pennsylvania. Penn demanded a £5,000 bond from his governors to observe the secret instructions.

Though Franklin had retired as a printer at the beginning of 1748, he remained active in selecting the contents of the *Pennsylvania Gazette*, and he annually compiled *Poor Richard's Almanac.* His income as postmaster of Philadelphia and comptroller of the postal service in America supplemented his income from his printing partnership. As comptroller, he improved the routines, routes, and schedules of the post office by traveling north to New England in the late summer of 1753. Because of his electrical experiments, he was granted an honorary master of arts degree by Harvard and then by Yale. Later in 1753, he was appointed joint deputy postmaster general of the American post office. He had previously, as postmaster of Philadelphia and then as comptroller of the American post office, designed a short and simple post office form that systemized postal accounting, and now he determined to improve the frequency and the geographical extent of the postal system. The American post office had never been profitable, but Franklin made it so.

In the early 1750s, the French began to build a series of forts from Lake Erie down the Allegheny River to present-day Pittsburgh. They claimed the land from the Great Lakes to the Ohio River and from it to the Mississippi River and to New Orleans. The French and the English colonists carried on an unofficial war, mainly on the western side of the Appalachian Mountains. While the colonists unofficially fought the French, the individual colonies competed with one another. Thus the Ohio Company of Virginia set up a post at what became Pittsburgh and indirectly claimed that part of Pennsylvania as its own. On 17 April 1754, a large French force ousted the small party of Virginians at that location and set up Fort Duquesne. Strategically, it was the key to the Ohio Valley and to the rivers that flowed from the northeast into the Mississippi. Encouraged by the French, Indians who were allied with them began to kill settlers on Britain's frontier. The settlers asked for protection, and the Pennsylvania Assembly, despite its pacifist members, passed money supply bills—which Frank-

lin wrote—to provide funds for armaments and troops. But the governor, following Thomas Penn's secret instructions, rejected the bills of 1753 and 1754 for two
reasons: (1) he was not given control of all the funds raised, and (2) the bills
would draw interest from the Loan Office, with which the assembly could finance
the state. Later, when the bills became a direct tax, the governor rejected them
because they would also tax the proprietors' Pennsylvania estates. Since the governor did not reveal to the legislature the real reasons for rejecting the bills, the
assemblymen were not certain why the money bills were continually rejected, but
they suspected it was because of Penn's secret instructions.

In the early fall of 1753, Isaac Norris and Franklin, representing the assembly,
and Richard Peters, representing the governor, attended an Indian treaty at Carlisle, Pennsylvania, attempting to renew friendship with the Indians along the
Ohio River whose lands the French were invading. The treaty was the first in
which Franklin had an active role, but the treaty was inconclusive. One result
was that Franklin wrote an Indian trade bill that would eliminate the whiskey-
trading whites and supply the Indians with goods at less expensive prices. The
assembly passed it, but the governor rejected it because the bill would lessen the
proprietors' profits.

Although the English colonists vastly outnumbered the French in America,
they were politically divided, while the French were united. The French military
was stronger than that of any single English colony. The solution recommended
by friendly Indians of the Six Nations (the great league of the Iroquois) was that
the English colonies unite. On 4 May 1754, reporting news of the French taking
the Virginians' fort at Pittsburgh, Franklin dramatized the English predicament
with America's most famous cartoon: a drawing of a cut snake over the words
"JOIN, or DIE." Initials of the various colonies appeared under the parts of the
cut snake. Most American newspapers of the day copied the cartoon, and they
resurrected it after the Stamp Act passed (1765) to urge colonial unity and, later,
independence.

Alarmed by news that some of the Six Nations were dissatisfied with the
behavior of the English, the British authorities recommended that the various
colonies renew their friendship with the Iroquois and that the colonies join
together to fight the French and hostile Indians. A meeting was called at Albany.
Delegates came from Massachusetts, Rhode Island, Connecticut, Pennsylvania,
and Maryland. Franklin was one of the four councillors appointed from Pennsylvania. On the way to Albany, he revised his 1751 scheme of union and presented it at the Albany Conference. The Indian treaty went hand in hand with
the meetings on the union of the colonies. The delegates presented other plans
of union, but Franklin's was preferred. It was modified and subsequently approved on 10 July 1754 by a majority of the councillors present at Albany.

The Albany Plan, however, failed to win the approval of a single colony.
Most colonies feared they would lose some portion of their autonomous power.
By the time the British authorities received it, they believed they had settled the

immediate problem by sending General Edward Braddock with an army to attack the French. The British authorities were also concerned that a united America might become a completely different entity than a group of separate, weak colonies. The Albany Plan did not recommend a political unification of the colonies, but it did call for their united defense and for a single policy for their future growth. Franklin no doubt hoped the colonies would gradually develop into a political federation. Most of the delegates who drew up the Articles of Confederation of the Continental Congress were familiar with the Albany Plan. Further, most members of the Constitutional Convention of 1788 were aware of both the Albany Plan and the Articles of Confederation when they wrote the constitution creating the United States. Perhaps the Albany Plan had no influence on later developments; perhaps it had some.

In January and February 1754, Franklin and William Hunter, joint deputy postmasters general of North America, went to Maryland to improve the mail service south of Philadelphia, and in the fall, they journeyed north as far as Maine. Franklin renewed old friendships in Boston and made new ones. The most amazing revelation was the frank Americanism of Franklin's letters to Massachusetts governor William Shirley. In December 1754, Franklin condemned English mercantilism, especially the Acts of Trade and Navigation; censured the English authorities for favoring small groups of English merchants over the thousands of American colonists; said that Americans would not accept representation in Parliament unless they were granted a fair number of seats and unless Parliament first repealed all the old anti-American acts; criticized English attitudes toward America; and claimed that if any group deserved favor, it should not be the stay-at-home English but the adventurous Americans. Governor Shirley must have been dumbfounded at Franklin's opinions. Bits and pieces of Franklin's Americanism had appeared earlier, but these statements were stronger than previous ones, partly because they were, comparatively, gathered together, and unlike Franklin's earlier anonymous or pseudonymous writings, these were not only signed by Franklin but directed to, arguably, the most important English official in America.

In the first days of January 1755, Franklin journeyed from Boston to Rhode Island with Catharine ("Katy") Ray, the first of several younger women who became infatuated with the fun-loving, flirtatious, famous American. Opinions differ, but I do not believe that they had sex. She was, however, evidently in love with him, and he was fond of her. Their letters are delightful and intriguing— Franklin's, in particular, are simply fun. They remained friends throughout their lives.

Back in Philadelphia (1755), Franklin found that Pennsylvania's new governor, Robert Hunter Morris, had already become embroiled with the Pennsylvania Assembly. Though Franklin remained the strongest advocate of a militia and of taxes for defense, the Quaker Party was reluctant to grant more than token amounts of money, and the governor rejected whatever money bills the House passed. Outraged by the inaction of the government, frontier settlers delivered the bodies of killed and scalped settlers to the steps of the statehouse (Independence Hall) in Philadelphia. When General Edward Braddock arrived in America, he was furious that Pennsylvania had done nothing (so he had been told by Thomas Penn before leaving England and by Governor Morris after coming to America) to help the war effort.

Unofficially, the Pennsylvania Assembly asked Franklin to see Braddock and to explain that the governor consistently vetoed their bills for defense. With his son, Franklin visited Braddock's camp on the frontier in the late spring of 1755, set up a mail route for the British army, had the Pennsylvania legislature send food and supplies to the British officers, and secured wagons to haul Braddock's cannons and supplies to Fort Duquesne. Braddock celebrated Franklin's help. But the general was "shamefully defeated" (George Washington's words) near Fort Duquesne and died of his wounds. In the late summer of 1755, the defense of the Pennsylvania frontier was in greater disarray than before Braddock arrived.

The assembly had passed bills for defense in 1752, 1753, and 1754, only to see them vetoed by Governors Hamilton and Morris. In 1755, however, Franklin crafted and the House passed two small measures for defense: one lent money that the House borrowed on its own credit, and the other raised money from the General Loan Office. Another new governor, William Denny, arrived late in 1755 with the same secret instructions from Thomas Penn. As the Pennsylvania Assembly passed bills for defense and Denny refused them, public opinion became aroused against the proprietors and their governors—not only in Pennsylvania and in England but even within the ranks of the British authorities. Therefore, Thomas Penn decided to give a "free gift" of £5,000 toward the defense of the province. Upon that news, the legislature promptly passed a £55,000 bill for defense. With money forthcoming, Franklin ushered a militia bill through the legislature on 25 November 1755 and wrote a dialogue urging the bill's acceptance. The militia and the supply bills passed. As one of the commissioners in charge of spending the money, he journeyed with the governor and others to the frontier in December 1755.

Penn's "free gift" turned out to be funds raised from past-due quitrents, many of which were owed by settlers in or near the frontier. Raiding by hostile Indians left many settlers unable to farm. Penn ordered his receiver-general of rents to be merciless—pay or lose the land. In consequence, Franklin and others assailed Penn and the governor. Franklin thought Penn proud, avaricious, and despicable; Penn thought Franklin a rabble-rousing, contemptible leader of the poor and "lower sort" of people.

Hostile Indians had wiped out the Moravian town of Gnadenhütten, on the frontier in Northampton County, on 24 November 1755. Governor Denny and the commissioners sent a militia force there in December, but Indians attacked and killed the troops. Knowing that Franklin was the most popular commissioner, Denny asked him to take charge of the military in Northampton County.

(This was a win-win situation: if Franklin succeeded, good; if he failed, the governor would be rid of the most popular opposition leader—permanently!) Franklin accepted. In January 1756, "General" Franklin went to Bethlehem, marched to Gnadenhütten in the miserable January weather, built a fort there, and sent out troops to build other forts. While at Gnadenhütten (and whenever he was away from Philadelphia for more than a week or so), Franklin wrote Deborah and she wrote him. Their letters are loving exchanges, none more so than those Franklin managed to pen while on the frontier.

In February, Franklin returned to Philadelphia and to the assembly sessions where a revised version of his former bill for improving the police passed. In March he traveled to Virginia to inspect postal routes from Philadelphia and, while in Williamsburg, received an honorary master's degree (his third) from the College of William and Mary. From 16 June to 28 July, he conferred in New York with America's new commander in chief, Lord Loudoun, on post office communications and Pennsylvania politics. In the fall, Governor Denny, James Hamilton, and he made a military inspection tour of the frontier, returning on 14 October for the new assembly's opening.

Governor Denny and the commissioners rode to Easton early in November 1756 for a treaty with Teedyuscung and the Delaware/Lenape Indians. Franklin wrote Governor Denny's Indian treaty speeches and inquired into the reasons why the Indians had become disaffected with the Pennsylvanians. The Delaware Indians suggested that fraud in land dealings and in trade were underlying causes, but they said the immediate cause was simply the war between France and England, with each side succeeding in getting some Indians to fight with them. After their return, Franklin and Isaac Norris renewed their attempts to pass an Indian trade bill. Their former one had passed the assembly on 11 November 1755, but the proprietary authorities had stalled, then suggested revisions for the bill, and then stalled on the revised bill. It never passed.

By November 1756 fighting on the frontier exhausted the funds. Only a little more than £1,000 of Thomas Penn's £5,000 "gift" had come in, and Governor Denny continued to veto the assembly's money bills because they either taxed the proprietors or did not grant the governor complete control of the funds. Franklin wrote the assembly's rallying cry: "Those who would give up essential Liberty, to purchase a little temporary Safety, deserve neither Liberty nor Safety." But as the French and their Indian allies killed more people on the frontier, Franklin and the assembly submitted and passed a tax bill that did not tax the proprietors. The governor vetoed it, however, because he would not entirely control its funds. Refusing to concede further, the assembly instead voted to send Franklin as its agent to petition the British authorities. The assembly believed that it should have the right to tax Thomas Penn's holdings along with all others and that it should control how the money was spent.

Having agreed on 3 February 1757 to sail to England as the Pennsylvania Assembly's agent, Franklin prepared to go to New York to embark, but Lord

Loudoun intended to come to Philadelphia to confer with various governors and asked Franklin to remain there, perhaps in part to discuss postal routes but certainly to discuss Pennsylvania politics. Franklin remained and conferred with Lord Loudoun, who finally advised Governor Denny to sign the assembly's tax bill. Franklin went to New York in March but had to wait until June before the indecisive Lord Loudoun finally allowed a packet to sail. At sea, the ever-curious Franklin began his observations on the effect of oil on water, and on the relation between the temperature of the sea and the course of the Gulf Stream. It was at sea, too, that he wrote one of his best-known but often misunderstood efforts, *The Way to Wealth.*

We may make these Times better if we bestir ourselves.

—*The Way to Wealth*, 7 July 1757 (7:342)

As yet, the Quantity of Human Knowledge bears no Proportion to the Quantity of Human Ignorance.

—To William Shipley, 27 November 1755 (6:276)

For my own Part, at present I pass my time agreably enough. I enjoy (thro' Mercy) a tolerable Share of Health; I read a great deal, ride a little, do a little Business for my self, more for others; retire when I can, and go [into] Company when I please; so the Years roll round, and the last will come; when I would rather have it said, *He lived usefully*, than, *He died rich*.

—Franklin to his mother, 12 April 1750 (3:475)

ONE

The Association, 1747–1748

'Tis designed to mix the Great and Small together, for the sake of Union and
Encouragement. Where Danger and Duty are equal to All, there should be no
Distinction from Circumstances, but All be on the Level.
—"Remarks" on the Association, 1747, 3:209

FRANKLIN TOOK PRIDE IN AMERICA and being an American. His writings for the
militia Association, especially the pamphlet *Plain Truth*, more openly combined
Americanism with criticism of the British authorities than any previous writing.
Plain Truth also demonstrated the political power of the press. By expertly using
the *Pennsylvania Gazette*, broadsides, and pamphlets, Franklin created a militia
of more than ten thousand men, despite the semi-pacifist position of the Pennsylvania Assembly.[1] Though some contemporary Pennsylvanians condemned
him, most praised him for an amazing and desirable accomplishment.

THE GATHERING STORM

Before 1747, England's war with Spain (1739–48) seemed distant and insignificant to most Pennsylvanians. Clashes occurred on the seas and in the West
Indies. The only fighting in North America took place in Georgia and Florida.
Even after France joined Spain against England in 1744, fighting continued,
though mainly in Canada, along the New England frontier, and in upstate New
York. The American success in taking the "impregnable" French fortress of Louisbourg on Cape Breton on 16 June 1745 marked the high point of American
military achievement before the Revolution. Franklin had been disgusted with
the Pennsylvania legislature for not helping with that effort (*Life* 2:350). Despite
appeals by Pennsylvania's governor and numerous individuals like Franklin, the
Quaker-dominated Pennsylvania Assembly refused to contribute significantly to
the war. With friendly Indians on the frontier and with no coast on the Atlantic,
Pennsylvanians felt secure.

That changed. French and Spanish privateers waylaid Pennsylvania's shipping, and its trade dramatically declined. At the same time, the enemy privateers
increased their activity outside the Delaware Bay. In response, a number of
Philadelphia merchants fitted out a well-armed ship. Franklin reported the news
in the *Pennsylvania Gazette* on 14 May: "We hear that the *Warren*, Privateer,

Captain [Alexander] Katter, is to sail Tomorrow or Next-day, on a Month's Cruise, between the Capes of Virginia and the Neversinks, to guard our Trade from the Enemy Privateers, who have chaced several Vessels lately near the Capes." Several of Franklin's Quaker friends—William Coleman (an original Junto member), Isaac Griffitts (a merchant, whose store was on Water Street), Reese Meredith (a Union Fire Company member), Amos and Robert Strettel (Amos was later a director of the Philadelphia Contributionship, and Robert later a trustee of the Philadelphia Academy)—financed the ship. Other Quakers objected to their action. The Friends appointed committees (one including John Smith, James Logan's son-in-law) to talk with them about their mistake in supporting warfare, but the ship financers would not concede that they were in error. The Quakers subsequently disowned them.

Finances dictated that the *Warren* could not just be kept cruising in the Delaware Bay. It left on what the owners hoped would be a profitable voyage to Lisbon in July, not returning until 12 November. Richard Peters, clerk of the Pennsylvania Council and secretary to the governor, wrote to Thomas Penn on 29 November 1747 that the investigation of the Quakers who contributed to the *Warren* made "moderate Friends . . . disoblig'd at these imperious Measures of the Meeting . . . [and] it has rais'd an Universal Odium in the Members of all the other Congregations" (3:215).

On 4 July 1747 Pennsylvania's Provincial Council forbade Pennsylvania pilots to escort foreign ships above Marcus Hook, which is about twenty miles south of Philadelphia, without a special license. A week later, when a sloop appeared off Cape May, New Jersey, a pilot went to it and was seized. It proved to be a French privateer. Franklin's *Gazette* reported on 16 July that the previous Sunday, "the French put all the Hands they had (except three Men and a Boy) on board the Pilot Boat, and sent her up the Bay." The boat went as far up the Delaware as Bombay-Hook (about halfway between the mouth of the Delaware and Philadelphia) and "landed at the plantation of Mr. Liston, from whom they took four Negroes, and rifled his House of several Things to considerable Value: They then went to the House of James Hart, and carried off a Negroe Wench; and upon his Wife's shutting the Door against them, one of them fired through it, and wounded her slightly in the Thigh." The French took two more pilot boats and captured the ship *Mary* near the mouth of the Delaware Bay, wounding the American captain who resisted the boarding party.

Receiving the news on 13 July 1747, the council called on the assembly members in town for their advice. John Kinsey, Speaker of the House, told the council that he did not believe the House would support funds for defense, but he added that although the House might refuse to vote the funds, "yet they . . . would make Compensation" in some way.[2] On 18 August 1747, the acting executive of Pennsylvania, council president Anthony Palmer, asked the assembly to protect Philadelphia. He said the city was helpless: "The Terror and Confusion, the Ruin of vast numbers of Families, the Destruction of Trade, the Bloodshed,

Cruelty, and other fatal Consequences which must unavoidably attend the plundering or burning this City, are too obvious to need a Description." The Quaker-controlled assembly responded on 25 August that "Accidents" like the plundering of isolated plantations and seizing of pilots were to be expected. Threats to invade Philadelphia were "so many Bravados," and the assembly chided the council for alarming the citizens. The assembly also claimed that the council encouraged invasion by publicizing Philadelphia's lack of defenses. The House, ever mindful that no one wanted to pay taxes, added that it was unnecessary to worry about the Indians joining the war and, though gifts to the Indians were in order, the Indians' loyalty to the English was assured without them.[3]

Richard Peters wrote the proprietors, summarizing the origin of Franklin's militia Association. He reported that on 29 November 1747, "some Merchants and Captains of Ships in the French Islands . . . actually concerted a Scheme to be executed by Six Privateers of Force against the City some time next Year" (3:214). Amid such rumors, William Kelly, who had been taken prisoner in August off the North Carolina coast by a French privateer commanded by Captain Lehay, arrived in Philadelphia. On 21 September 1747, Kelly testified before magistrate Thomas Hopkinson that he had been a passenger on the sloop *Elizabeth*, bound for Philadelphia from Providence, when captured by Lehay, who had previously seized three English prizes. As the French privateer continued up the coast, it took several more prizes before arriving near the Delaware Bay. There it seized a sloop about fifteen leagues outside the bay, and two more ships within the bay. When the privateer approached Cape May, it hoisted English colors and seized the first pilot, William Flower, who came onboard, and similarly seized another pilot, Luke Shields. When Lehay left the bay, he allowed the English prisoners to go ashore in the pilot boats.[4]

After the new Pennsylvania Assembly for 1747–48 met, President Anthony Palmer warned on 16 October 1747 that the French and Spanish privateers "will continue their Depredations in the Spring, and in all likelyhood block up the Trade of this flourishing Colony—a Loss which . . . will be sensibly felt" (3:214–18). The next day the assembly merely replied that it hoped Philadelphia was in no danger and adjourned. With the assembly abdicating responsibility, the Pennsylvania government was powerless.

FRANKLIN'S PRESS CAMPAIGN

The situation was desperate. The council and acting governor had repeatedly presented the necessity of defense to a noncompliant, Quaker-controlled assembly. Franklin believed something had to be done. No one unconnected with government before Franklin had attempted to arouse the general population to take a political position through the power of the press. In his *Autobiography*, Franklin wrote that he decided "to try what might be done by a voluntary Association of the People" (A 92). The Association resulted from Franklin's realization of the possibilities inherent in the press and especially in that relatively new vehicle, the newspaper. He waged a publicity campaign to awaken Pennsylvanians to danger. Richard Peters correctly observed that Franklin "thought he cou'd by some well wrote Papers improve this opportunity, take an advantage of their Fears and spirit them up to an Association for their Defence" (3:215).

On 22 October 1747, Franklin opened the campaign in the *Pennsylvania Gazette.* He published verses complimenting Robert Barclay's *Apology*. The *Apology*, a standard exposition of Quakerism, justified defensive war. About the same time, Franklin reprinted as a broadside Matthew Green's *A Copy of Verses . . . Occasion'd by his Reading Robert Barclay's Apology*, which also took a moderate Quaker position.[5] Franklin followed up the poems with an anonymous piece (which I believe he wrote) in the 5 November *Gazette* saying that the verses on Barclay's *Apology* made him read the book. The *Gazette* author pointed out that Barclay and many other Quakers were not against defensive war. He also cited the opinions of Friends in England. Meanwhile, Franklin was writing a pamphlet and consulted his friends Tench Francis, William Coleman, and Thomas Hopkinson about a voluntary militia. They encouraged him but urged him to try to keep politics out of the proposal. Franklin replied that he intended to castigate both the Quaker Party and the Proprietary Party but that if William Allen, the leader of the Proprietary Party, cared to, he and his friends could then publish a vindication of themselves and join in the Association. Franklin offered to publish all such papers for free. If they were too voluminous for the newspaper, he would print them gratis as pamphlets and send them along with the newspaper to every Pennsylvania customer.

Before Franklin's major pamphlet *Plain Truth* appeared, Indians from the Ohio River arrived in town on the evening of 11 November bringing news about "Affairs relating to the War betwixt the English and French in those Parts." Led by the Oneida chief Scarouady, they met with the Pennsylvania Council on 13 November, requesting guns, powder, and supplies to fight the French.[6] The council consulted Indian expert Conrad Weiser. On the morning of 16 November, he advised giving the Indians a small present immediately and sending a large one to the Ohio in the coming summer. That afternoon, the council met again with the Indians, assured them of their friendship and affection, and followed Weiser's advice.[7] Franklin asked Richard Peters for a copy of the council's minutes on the Indian negotiations. The *Pennsylvania Gazette* published the news about Scarouady and the Ohio Indians on 12 November 1747 and featured another Indian development, as we will see, on 3 December. Since Franklin was printing war news in the *Gazette* for the next month, he held off printing the council's exchanges with the Ohio Indians until 12 January—by which season few ships and little news were coming into Philadelphia.

PLAIN TRUTH

Plain Truth: or, Serious Considerations on the Present State of the City of Philadelphia, and Province of Pennsylvania by a "Tradesman of *Philadelphia*" had a "sudden and surprising effect." The title implied that the author would give an objective, blunt appraisal. The words *Plain Truth* suggested that the "Tradesman of *Philadelphia*" would be a version of a popular persona, the "plain dealer," a colloquial or homely figure who spoke the perhaps unwelcome truth. The bluff, truthful speaker was a well-known character type before William Wycherly featured it in his popular Restoration play, *The Plain Dealer* (1677); many newspapers still use that title.

The pamphlet appeared on 17 November 1747. The title page quoted an excerpt from Sallust's *Bellum Catilinae*. Four lines from the bottom of the quotation, Franklin set in capitals a key clause: "NON VOTIS, NEQUE SUPPLICIIS MULIEBRIBUS, AUXILIA DEORUM PARANTUR." Two days later, he published a translation in the *Gazette*: "Divine Assistance and Protection are not to be obtain'd by timorous Prayers and womanish Supplications." The translation from Sallust continued, "To succeed, you must join salutary Counsels, Vigilance, and couragious *Actions*." The Latin on the title page appealed to the learned, and on the verso, Franklin appealed to everyone by featuring the first American political cartoon. The woodcut from a children's book illustrated Aesop's fable of Hercules and the wagoneer: next to a wagon stuck in the mud, a wagoneer kneeling on the ground called out for Hercules to help him. Underneath the cut, the printed text read "NON VOTIS, &c." Aesop's well-known fable said: "As a Waggoneer was driving his Team, his Waggon sank into a Hole, and stuck fast. The poor Man immediately fell upon his Knees, and prayed to Hercules that he would get his Waggon out of the Hole again. Thou Fool, says Hercules, whip thy Horses, and set thy Shoulder to the Wheels; and then if thou wilt call upon Hercules, he will help thee."[8]

Poor Richard had voiced the moral in 1736: "God helps them that help themselves." Franklin had cited the Aesop fable in his "Queries on a Pennsylvania Militia," 6 March 1733/4, when he pointed out that the French had settled from the Great Lakes to the mouth of the Mississippi and would in the future want to control the rivers in Pennsylvania and New York that ran "far back toward their present Settlements." Franklin urged in the 1734 "Queries" that Pennsylvania should be prepared for possible war.[9] He may have foreseen this additional use for the woodcut when, earlier in 1747, he had it made (or made it himself) for a children's reader. It was an American woodcut, for it portrayed a Conestoga wagon.

Like Franklin's *Modest Enquiry into the Nature and Necessity of a Paper Currency* (1729), *Plain Truth* was modeled on the four-part structure of the puritan sermon—text, doctrine, reasons, and uses. Superimposed upon the puritan sermon structure were elements of the classical oration, with Franklin paying special attention to ethos, or the speaker's character, and pathos, or the speaker's appeals to the audience's emotions.

Plain Truth opened with a brief paragraph on the English character: "It is said the wise Italians make this proverbial Remark on our Nation, viz. *The*

Non Votis, &c.

Figure 1. The earliest American political cartoon, "Hercules and the Wagoneer." Verso of title page of Benjamin Franklin, Plain Truth *(1747). Franklin's woodcut of "Hercules and the Wagoneer" was originally made for a schoolbook that Franklin printed early in 1747 depicting a fable by Aesop. His illustrations of Aesop's fables were the first ones printed in America. The moral of the print is that the wagoner (shown here on the bottom right) should get in the mud behind the wagon, yell for his horses to go—and push.*

The woodcut, like the classical allusion from Sallust on the title page, echoed the thesis of Franklin's 6 March 1733/4 essay concerning the French threat to America. In that Pennsylvania Gazette *essay, he asked, "Whether the ancient Story of the Man, who sat down and prayed his Gods to lift his Cart out of the Mire, hath not a very good Moral?" Poor Richard's version of the moral said, "God helps them that help themselves" (2:140).*

Franklin or a local Philadelphia craftsman made the woodcut, for the wagon has the unique design of the Pennsylvania Conestoga wagon. The background of Fable Ten, "Of the Good Natur'd Man and the Adder," which portrays Franklin's distinctive Pennsylvania fireplace (Life 2:397, fig. 26b), confirms the local Americanism of Franklin's 1747 Aesop's fables. Courtesy, Library Company of Philadelphia.

English FEEL, *but they do not SEE.*"[10] Corresponding to the puritan sermon's structure, a brief explication followed the text: "That is, they are sensible of Inconveniencies when they are present, but do not take sufficient Care to prevent them: Their natural Courage makes them too little apprehensive of Danger, so that they are often surpriz'd by it, unprovided of the proper Means of Security. When 'tis too late they are sensible of their Imprudence: After great Fires, they provide Buckets and Engines." Many Franklin readers knew that he referred to the Philadelphia fire of 24 April 1730, after which the Philadelphia Common Council purchased fire engines. "After a Pestilence they think of keeping clean their Streets and common Shores." Most Philadelphians recognized that Franklin here referred to his environmental fight to clean up Dock Creek—a controversy he had initiated in 1739 and had thus far lost, even though Dock Creek was widely blamed for a contagious disease that struck Philadelphia during the summer of 1747 (3:228n).

Matching the opening, Franklin closed the first paragraph with a proverb: "And when a Town has been sack'd by their Enemies, they provide for its Defence, etc. This Kind of AFTER-WISDOM is indeed so common with us, as to occasion the vulgar, tho' very significant Saying, *When the Steed is stolen, you shut the Stable Door.*" The proverbs reinforce the feeling of common sense and plain truth present throughout the pamphlet. The New England Congregational ministers of Franklin's youth commonly cited additional biblical passages to prove the "text"; similarly, Franklin quoted a second proverb with the same import to prove the first. The second saying anticipated the doctrine or thesis drawn from the "text": persons should attempt "to think of some Means of Avoiding or Preventing the Mischief before it be too late" (3:191).

Plain Truth: The Dilemma

The reasons or proofs began with the dilemma: "War, at this Time, rages over a great Part of the known World. . . . Pennsylvania, indeed, *situate* in the Center of the Colonies, has hitherto enjoy'd profound Repose; and tho' our Nation is engag'd in a bloody War, with two great and powerful Kingdoms, yet, defended, in a great Degree, from the French on the one Hand by the Northern Provinces, and from the Spaniards on the other by the Southern . . . our People have, till lately, slept securely in their Habitations." Note that Franklin did not thank the crown; the northern colonies had defended Pennsylvania from the French and the southern colonies had defended it against the Spanish. An undercurrent of criticism of the British authorities runs throughout *Plain Truth*. His readers knew that the one major victory in North America occurred in 1745, when the New Englanders with the help of the British Navy had taken the French fortress of Louisbourg on Cape Breton. Though other American colonies had provided for defense, Pennsylvania had not because "The Length and Difficulty of our Bay and River has been thought" an effectual security (3:191).

Pennsylvanians, however, were fooling themselves in their sense of security.

Franklin devoted three paragraphs to the state of affairs: (1) in Philadelphia, (2) on the frontier, and (3) to those living near the Delaware Bay. The enemy had informants who knew all three areas. Spying "has been the Practice of all Nations in all Ages, whenever they were engaged, or intended to engage in War." Though no believer in the Bible, Franklin used it to appeal to his audience. The Book of Judges (18:2) said, "That *the Children of Dan sent of their Family five Men from their Coasts to spie out the Land, and search it, saying, Go, search the* LAND." He had quoted the same passage in his 1734 "Queries" on a Pennsylvania militia (W 223–24). He also used the popular anti-Catholic prejudice (which had intensified in 1746 because Catholics generally supported Charles Stuart's invasion of Great Britain) by reminding Philadelphians that Roman Catholic priests lived among them.[11]

Like Philadelphia, the frontier settlements were threatened. "We have, 'tis true, had a long Peace with the Indians: But it is a long Peace indeed, as well as a long Lane, that has no Ending. The French know the Power and Importance of the Six Nations, and spare no Artifice, Pains or Expence, to gain them to their Interest." Here for the first time in *Plain Truth*, he anticipated the French and Indian War. From prophecy, however, he descended to glib propaganda: "By their Priests they have converted many to their Religion, and these have openly espoused their Cause. The rest appear irresolute" (4:193–94). Conditions were deteriorating. Pennsylvania's former Indian allies were now mainly neutral and would probably shortly become enemies.

After more than a year of inactivity at Albany, the English military forces there were being disbanded "by Orders from the Crown." Franklin implicitly cried out, "What imbecility!" Two weeks earlier on 9 November, the *Pennsylvania Gazette* published the news that the duke of Newcastle had canceled the projected expedition against Canada. The four companies of soldiers from Pennsylvania at Albany, which included Ensign William Franklin, were discharged. "When our boasted Expedition is laid aside, thro' want (as it may appear to them [i.e., their former Indian allies]) either of Strength or Courage; when they see that the French, and their Indians, boldly and with Impunity, ravage the Frontiers of New York, and scalp the Inhabitants; when those few Indians that engaged with us against the French, are left exposed to their Resentment: When they consider these Things, is there no Danger that, thro' Disgust at our Usage, joined with Fear of the French Power, and greater Confidence in their Promises and Protection than in ours, they may be wholly gained over by our Enemies and join in the War against us?" (3:194). Franklin implied that the crown cared little for America and less for the lives of Americans. The devastation of Pennsylvania's frontier must follow.

It would have been treason to criticize the crown more openly. At about the time that he composed *Plain Truth*, Franklin wrote *Poor Richard* for 1748, where, among the sayings, he put in the following traitorous sentiment: "Robbers must exalted be, / Small ones on the Gallow-Tree, / While greater ones ascend to

Thrones, / But what is that to thee or me?" (3:248). Thirteen years later, when David Hume defended his patron, the duke of Bedford, from Franklin's criticisms concerning the 1746–47 Albany expedition, Franklin documented his reasons for the criticism, though he knew that Hume did not want to acknowledge Great Britain's lack of concern about American affairs. Franklin wrote Hume on 27 September 1760 that perhaps Bedford was "hearty in the Scheme of the Expedition" but said that "others" in the administration were not: "It is certain that after the Duke of Newcastle's first Orders to raise Troops in the Colonies, and Promise to send over Commissions to the Officers, with Arms, Clothing, & c. for the Men, we never had another Syllable from him for 18 Months; during all which time the Army lay idle at Albany for want of Orders and Necessaries" (9:228–29).

From criticizing the British authorities, the tradesman persona moved on to the foolish selfishness of some Pennsylvanians: "Perhaps some in the City, Towns and Plantations near the River, may say to themselves, An Indian War on the Frontiers will not affect us; the Enemy will never come near our Habitations . . . And others who live in the Country, when they are told of the Danger the City is in from Attempts by Sea, may say, *What is that to us? The Enemy will be satisfied with the Plunder of the Town, and never think it worth his while to visit our Plantations: Let the Town take care of itself.* These are not mere Suppositions, for I have heard some talk in this strange Manner. But are these the Sentiments of true Pennsylvanians, of Fellow-Countrymen, or even of Men that have common Sense or Goodness?"

Franklin asked his audience to unify for the good of the whole: When the French and Indian War broke out on the frontiers less than half a dozen years later, Franklin urged a similar argument. Pennsylvania must unite to protect the whole body politic: "Is not the whole Province one Body, united by living under the same Laws, and enjoying the same Priviledges? Are not the People of City and Country connected as Relations both by Blood and Marriage, and in Friendships equally dear? Are they not likewise united in Interest, and mutually useful and necessary to each other?" He then carried the body metaphor to a logical conclusion: "When the Feet are wounded shall the Head say, *It is not me; I will not trouble myself to contrive Relief!* Or if the Head is in Danger, shall the Hands say, *We are not affected, and therefore will lend no Assistance!* No. For so would the Body be easily destroyed: But when all Parts join their Endeavours for its Security, it is often preserved" (3:194–95). Later, Franklin applied the body metaphor to relations between Great Britain and the colonies. Throughout the pre-Revolutionary period, he stressed that the empire was a single body and that the authorities should run it for the good of the whole.[12] Franklin repeatedly criticized the British authorities for harming the colonies in order to benefit a group of English merchants. In *Plain Truth*, the "Tradesman"/Franklin reminded his audience that the Pennsylvania Assembly had previously provided funds for defense: on 24 July 1745, it had voted £4,000 to help provision the garrison after Cape Breton was taken, and on 21 October 1741, it had voted £3,000 for the English war effort. "Shall Country and Town join in helping Strangers (as those comparatively are) and yet refuse to assist each other?" (3:194–95).

Turning to the war's effect on Pennsylvania's economy, Franklin said that the successful voyages of the enemy's privateers in the Delaware Bay guaranteed their return, "the Profit being always Certain, and the Risque next to nothing." Trade would decline and the price of all foreign goods would rise: "As long as the Enemy cruize at our Capes, and take those Vessels that attempt to *go out*, as well as those that endeavour to *come in*, none can afford to trade, and Business must be soon at a Stand." The "Stand" implies that trade will turn to other ports that can be entered with less danger, like New York, and that Pennsylvania would be left with "A Lessening of Business to every Shopkeeper, together with Multitudes of bad Debts; the high Rate of Goods discouraging the Buyers, and the low Rates of their Labour and Produce rendering them unable to pay for what they had bought: Loss of Employment to the Tradesman and bad Pay for what little he does: And lastly, Loss of many Inhabitants, who will retire to other Provinces not subject to the like Inconveniencies; whence a Lowering of the Value of Lands, Lots, and Houses."

The "Tradesman" said that the French and Spanish have been told that Pennsylvanians are Quakers, "against all Defence." He acknowledged that some Pennsylvanians were pacifists but maintained that they constituted only a small part "of the Inhabitants." Their enemies believed the false report because nothing was "done by any Part of the People towards their Defence." Since refusing to defend "one's self or one's Country, is so unusual a Thing among Mankind," the French and Spanish possibly might not believe it "till by Experience they find, they can come higher and higher up our River, seize our Vessels, land and plunder our Plantations and Villages, and retire with their Booty unmolested." He then asked: "Will not this confirm the Report, and give them the greatest Encouragement to strike one bold Stroke for the City, and for the whole Plunder of the River?" (3:196–97).

Some persons claimed that the expense of a vessel to guard the Delaware Bay would be greater than the enemy could take from Pennsylvania. They said it would be cheaper to open an insurance office to pay all losses. Franklin refuted such reasoning: "What the Enemy takes is clear Loss to us, and Gain to him; encreasing his Riches and Strength as much as it diminishes ours, so making the Difference double; whereas the Money paid our own Tradesmen for Building and Fitting out a Vessel of Defence, remains in the Country, and circulates among us; what is paid to the Officers and Seamen that navigate her, is also spent ashore, and soon gets into other Hands; the Farmer receives the Money for her Provisions; and on the whole, nothing is clearly lost to the Country." On the other hand, "should the Enemy, thro' our Supineness and Neglect to provide for the Defence, both of our Trade and Country, be encouraged to attempt this City, and after plundering us of our Goods, either *burn it*, or put it to Ransom; how great would that Loss be! Besides the Confusion, Terror, and Distress, so many Hundreds of Families would be involv'd in!" (3:197).

The "Tradesman"/Franklin proceeded from the economy of Pennsylvania to the devastation resulting from an enemy attack. He appealed to the prejudices and fears of his audience. Since the city had no organized defense, "on the first Alarm, *Terror* will spread over All." Without a united force, most persons would flee. "The Man that has a Wife and Children, will find them hanging on his Neck, beseeching him with Tears to quit the City, and save his Life, to guide and protect them in that Time of general Desolation and Ruin. All will run into Confusion, amidst Cries and Lamentations, and the Hurry and Disorder of Departers, carrying away their Effects. The Few that remain will be unable to resist. *Sacking* the City will be the first, and *Burning* it, in all Probability, the last Act of the Enemy." Such would be the case if the Philadelphians had timely notice. "But what must be your Condition, if suddenly surprized, without previous Alarm, perhaps in the Night! Confined to your Houses, you will have nothing to trust to but the Enemy's Mercy. Your best Fortune will be, to fall under the Power of Commanders of King's Ships, able to controul the Mariners; and not into the Hand of *licentious Privateers*." The latter must endure having their "Wives and Daughters . . . subject to the wanton and unbridled Rage, Rapine and Lust, of *Negroes, Molattoes*, and others, the vilest and most abandoned of Mankind" (3:197–98).

To racial, Franklin added economic prejudice. The rich, he said, would probably not suffer greatly: "The Means of speedy Flight are ready in their Hands; and with some previous Care to lodge Money and Effects in distant and secure Places, tho' they should lose much, yet enough may be left them, and to spare." But the tradesmen, shopkeepers, and farmers would suffer. They could not run away with their families—and if they did, how would they subsist? "What little we have gained by hard Labour and Industry, must bear the Brunt . . . Tho we are numerous, we are quite defenceless, having neither Forts, Arms, Union, nor Discipline." Philadelphia and the countryside could be easily defended if proper measures were taken, but who would do so? And who would pay? (3:198–99).

PLAIN TRUTH: BOTH PARTIES CONDEMNED

After portraying the possible devastation, Franklin blamed both the Quaker and the Proprietary parties for the defenseless situation. The maneuver actually gained him support from most elements of both parties, for it suggested that the independent speaker was of neither party—and yet the Quaker Party leaders could read with pleasure the condemnation of the Proprietary Party leaders and vice versa. Everyone knew that Franklin wrote *Plain Truth*. The Quaker assemblymen could of course fire him as printer and as clerk of the assembly. Franklin risked his lucrative offices when he suggested that the Quaker members who opposed war should resign their positions: "Should we intreat them to consider, if not as Friends, at least as Legislators, that *Protection* is as truly due from the Government to the People, as *Obedience* from the People to the Government; and that if on account of their religious Scruples, they themselves could do no Act for our Defence, yet they might retire, relinquish their Power for a Season, [and] quit the Helm to freer Hands during the present Tempest." That would happen during 1755 and 1756.

The doctrine that "*Protection* is as truly due from the Government to the People, as *Obedience* from the People to the Government" cut both ways. It also condemned the governor, council, and proprietor—and, to carry out the implication to its logical conclusion, the doctrine also condemned the British authorities and the king. Franklin implicitly threatened the proprietary government: if it did not protect the people, then it did not deserve obedience. Thomas Penn, as we will see, objected to the doctrine. Franklin also charged that the Quaker legislators had spent "large Sums" opposing the petitions to the British authorities for military defense and had engaged expensive lawyers to represent them against the majority of Pennsylvanians (3:199). The information must have shocked many citizens, and Franklin's saying it must have angered a number of Quaker legislators.

Franklin suggested that the Quakers employ their usual subterfuge in voting funds for defense, saying it was for the "King's Use." Though the treasury was "at present empty, it may soon be filled by the outstanding Public Debts collected; or at least Credit might be had for such a Sum, on a single Vote of the assembly: That tho' *they* themselves may be resigned and easy under this naked, defenceless State of the Country, it is far otherwise with a very great Part of the People; with *us*, who can have no Confidence that God will protect those that neglect the Use of rational Means for their Security; nor have any Reason to hope, that our Losses, if we should suffer any, may be made up by Collections in our Favour at Home!" (3:199).

In this passage, Franklin rebuked the wealthy Quakers who would probably receive help from the English Quakers if they did suffer. Using his knowledge of rhetoric, he condemned the Quaker legislators with a series of epistrophes— sentences made more effective by concluding with the same words: "Should we conjure them by all the Ties of Neighbourhood, Friendship, Justice and Humanity, to consider these Things; and what Distraction, Misery and Confusion, what Desolation and Distress, may possibly be the Effect of their *unseasonable* Predominancy and Perserverance; yet all would be in vain: For they have already been by great Numbers of the People petitioned in vain. Our late Governor [George Thomas] did for Years solicit, request, and even threaten them in vain. The Council have since twice remonstrated to them in vain. Their religious Prepossessions are unchangeable, their Obstinacy invincible. Is there then the least Hope remaining, that from that Quarter any Thing should arise for our Security?" (3:199–200).

Franklin's censure of the proprietarians was even more severe. He used class resentment in attacking "those Great and rich Men, Merchants and others, who are ever railing at Quakers for doing what their Principles seem to require, and what in Charity we ought to believe they think their Duty, but take no one Step themselves for the Public Safety? They have so much Wealth and Influence if they would use it, that they might easily, by their Endeavours and Example, raise a military Spirit among us, make us fond, studious of, and expert in Martial Discipline, and effect every Thing that is necessary, under God for our Protection." He declared that envy had seized their hearts and had eaten out and destroyed every generous, noble, public-spirited sentiment. The proprietary partisans, like the Quakers, were blind to the good of the whole. "*Rage at the Disappointment of their little Schemes for Power, gnaws their Souls, and fills them with such cordial Hatred to their Opponents, that every Proposal, by the Execution of which those may receive Benefit as well as themselves, is rejected with Indignation. What, say they, shall we lay out our Money to protect the Trade of Quakers? Shall we fight to defend Quakers? No; Let the Trade perish, and the City burn; let what will happen, we shall never lift a Finger to prevent it*" (3:200).

At least the Quakers had conscience to plead for their position. The proprietary partisans seemed to have no conscience: "*Conscience* enjoins it as a DUTY on you (and indeed I think it such on every Man) to defend your Country, your Friends, your aged Parents, your Wives, and helpless Children: And yet you resolve not to perform this Duty, but act *contrary* to *your own* Consciences, because the Quakers act *according* to *theirs*." Franklin told an anecdote illustrating his favorite moral that all should strive for the common good: "'Till of late I could scarce believe the Story of him who refused to pump in a sinking Ship, because one on board, whom he hated, would be saved by it as well as himself." (At the end of 1756, he used a variation of this anecdote in advocating a militia act [6:305].) The "Tradesman"/Franklin sardonically observed of human nature "that our Passions, when violent, often are too hard for the united Force of *Reason, Duty* and *Religion*" (3:201).

Having set forth the dilemma and condemned both the Quaker and the Proprietary parties, Franklin turned to the "middling People, the Farmers, Shopkeepers and Tradesmen of this City and Country," and appealed to them: "Thus unfortunately are we circumstanc'd at this Time, my dear Countrymen and Fellow-Citizens . . . Thro' the Dissensions of our Leaders, thro' *mistaken Principles* of *Religion*, join'd with a Love of Worldly Power, on the one Hand; thro' *Pride, Envy* and *implacable Resentment* on the other; our Lives, our Families and little Fortunes, dear to us as any Great Man's can be to him, are to remain continually expos'd to Destruction, from an enterprizing, cruel, now well-inform'd, and by Success encourag'd Enemy." Both parties engaged in foolish and mischievous contentions "for *little Posts* and *paltry Distinctions*. . . . It seems as if our greatest Men, our *Cives nobilissimi* of both Parties, *had sworn the Ruin of the Country, and invited the French, our most inveterate Enemy, to destroy it*." He asked the rhetorical question, "Where then shall we seek for Succour and Protection?" He repeated the biblical citation that implied Great Britain would be no help: "we are *far from* ZIDON, *and there is no Deliverer near*" (3:202, cf. 193).

PLAIN TRUTH: THE APPEAL

Franklin's appeal for action corresponded to the application section of the puritan sermon: "perhaps there is yet a Remedy, if we have but the Prudence and the Spirit to apply it" (3:201–2). Ordinary citizens could bear arms and defend the province. Excluding the Quakers, Pennsylvania had at least "60,000 fighting men, acquainted with fire-arms, many of them hunters and marksmen, hardy and bold." All Pennsylvania really needed was order, discipline, and a few cannon: "At present we are like the separate Filaments of Flax before the Thread is form'd, without Strength because without Connection; but UNION would make us strong and even formidable." Even if the great merchants of both parties did not help, and even if they opposed the union, the people could unite to defend themselves. Franklin appealed to their patriotism. He granted that "the fierce fighting Animals of those happy Islands [Britain] are said to abate their native Fire and Intrepidity when removed to a Foreign Clime, yet with the People 'tis not so." (Franklin had ironically cited the same belief concerning the degeneration of English dogs in America on 9 October 1729; *Life* 1:419.) He reminded his audience that New Englanders had demonstrated their extraordinary bravery and skill in the astounding 1745 victory at Fort Louisbourg (3:202).

Franklin also celebrated Pennsylvania's Germans as fighters: "Nor are there wanting amongst us, Thousands of *that Warlike Nation*, whose Sons have ever since the Time of Caesar maintained the Character he gave their Fathers, of joining the most *obstinate Courage* to all the other military Virtues." Franklin said that many Germans had been soldiers "in the Service of their respective Princes; and if they fought well for their Tyrants and Oppressors, would they refuse to unite with us in Defence of their *newly acquired* and most precious *Liberty* and *Property*?" (3:203).

If Pennsylvanians organized, they could defend themselves. Having prepared for their own safety, "we might then, *with more Propriety*, humbly ask the Assistance of Heaven, and a Blessing on our lawful Endeavours"—clearly alluding to the Latin epigraph and the cartoon prefacing *Plain Truth*. As in his 1734 "Queries on a Pennsylvania Militia," Franklin argued that the mere knowledge that Pennsylvania possessed an effective militia would keep enemies from attacking them. He cited the "wise and true Saying, that *One Sword often keeps another in the Scabbard*." The use of the proverb (as in the opening of the pamphlet) strengthened the commonsense appeal of the argument and the plain-dealer persona. Franklin reinforced the saying with his own sententia: "The Way to secure Peace is to be prepared for War" (3:202). The "Tradesman"/Franklin said that if the "Hints" met with approval, he would propose "a Form of an ASSOCIATION for the Purposes herein mentioned," and a plan for raising the money "necessary for the Defence of our Trade, City, and Country, without laying a Burthen on any Man" (3:202–4).

Calling again on religion, Franklin appended a prayer condemning divisions in this time of danger and asking for unity not only between the political parties and religions but also between the different national groups (alluding not only to the Germans but also to traditional hostilities among the English, Irish, Welsh, and Scots): "*May the* GOD *of* WISDOM, STRENGTH *and* POWER, *the Lord of the Armies of Israel, inspire us with Prudence in this Time of* DANGER; *take away from us all the Seeds of Contention and Division, and unite the Hearts and Counsels of all of us, of whatever* SECT *or* NATION, *in one Bond of Peace, Brotherly Love, and generous Public Spirit; May he give us Strength and Resolution to amend our Lives, and remove from among us every Thing that is displeasing to him; afford us his most gracious Protection, the Designs of our Enemies, and give* PEACE" (3:204).

Plain Truth: Reception

The pamphlet was a sensation. Franklin printed a thousand copies—about three times as many as the usual pamphlet or sermon—and he gave them away. Skyrocketing demand for the pamphlet made him print another thousand copies two weeks later. He also had a thousand copies in German printed.[13] Richard Peters called *Plain Truth* "a strong and pathetick appeal to the People." The public awaited the proposal.

Plain Truth initiated a supposed literary war. An advertisement in the *Pennsylvania Gazette* on 19 November said the pamphlet contained injurious reflections "on a Number of Persons, who the Writer calls the Party opposite to the Quakers, as if they were utterly regardless of the Publick Good, and from mean and unjustifiable Motives, would refuse to do any Thing for the Defence of their Country." In fact, said the author, several of these persons had spent six hundred pounds each to fit out the privateer *Warren* to guard the Delaware River and Bay. The penultimate sentence noted that though the persons pointed at had reason to resent "the abusive and unjustifiable Treatment given them by that Writer, yet they wave every Thing of the Kind, in Consideration of his appearing to mean well." Further, the advertiser promised that if the author of *Plain Truth* could propose a scheme "by which the Inhabitants of this Province may be united and disciplined, and the Country and City put into a State of Defence, none shall enter into the same more heartily than they." I suspect that this advertisement was also by Franklin, who had, said Richard Peters, discussed the strategy of blaming both parties with Tench Francis, William Coleman, and Thomas Hopkinson—all members of the Proprietary Party—before writing *Plain Truth* (3:215). Blaming wealthy persons for not taking on themselves the expense of defending the whole province did not, as the historian Alan Tully has pointed out, make good sense.[14] It was a rhetorical ploy to appear politically impartial. Always conscious of the besetting sin of vanity, Franklin would have been ironically amused that the penultimate sentence concluded with a compliment, even though a minor one ("appearing to mean well"), to himself.[15]

The Quaker pacifists became angry and wrote several replies. Two are noted below, when discussing the Fast Day of 7 January. A third tract, the anonymous *Treatise Shewing the Need we Have to rely upon God as the soul Protector of this Province*, claimed in its advertisement in the *Pennsylvania Journal* for 23 June that it answered *Plain Truth* and contained "*Remarks* on the Author's Irreligion." Though the author announced on the title page that he was "one that wisheth well to all Mankind," he not only made an ad hominem attack on Franklin, he also roundly condemned the moderate Quakers, the Proprietary Party members, and everyone except pacifists. He charged that those who favored the Association really desired a "change in Government" and called them "warlions" who would raise taxes "to gratify their ambitious Minds." He fulfilled the advertisement's charge merely by claiming that the author of *Plain Truth* was "a Man wholly given up to *Irreligion*."[16]

CALL TO ACTION

By word of mouth and no doubt by a handbill, Franklin called a meeting for Saturday, 21 November 1747, of Philadelphia's "middling people" at Walton's schoolhouse, which was held in Chancellor's sail loft on Arch Street. According to Richard Peters, Franklin notified the Library Company members and members of the various fire companies. He probably also invited all the tradesmen (save for the pacifist Quakers) who lived in the area. About 150 people showed up, mostly artisans and Franklin's friends. After calling them "the first Movers in every useful undertaking that had been projected for the good of the City," Franklin "pull'd a Draught of an intended Association out of his Pocket and read it" (3:216).

It contained a preamble and eight short sections. The preamble continued the undercurrent of criticism of the "Mother Country." The French and Spanish know "that this Colony is in a naked defenceless State, without Fortifications or Militia of any Sort, and is therefore exposed daily to Destruction from the Attacks of a very small Force: That we are at a great Distance from our Mother Country, and cannot, on any Emergency, receive Assistance from thence." The use of "Mother Country" was ironic, for not only was the "Mother Country" unable to help the colonies in case of enemy attack, but the "Mother Country" did not care about America. "That thro' the Multiplicity of other Affairs of greater Importance (as we presume) no particular Care hath hitherto been taken by the Government at Home of our Protection, an humble Petition to the Crown for that purpose, sign'd by a great Number of Hands, having yet had no visible Effect."[17] In effect, Franklin again suggested that the "Mother Country" did not think America or American lives important.

Looking back at Pennsylvania's history, Franklin wrote that "the Assemblies of this Province, by reason of their religious Principles, have not done, nor are likely to do any Thing for our Defence, notwithstanding repeated Applications to them for that Purpose." Therefore, "for our mutual Defence and Security, and for the Security of our Wives, Children and Estates, and the Preservation of the Persons and Estates of others, our Neighbours and Fellow Subjects" (3:205–6), the signers were now forming a militia Association based on eight provisions.

1) Arms: by 1 January, each signer would provide himself with "a good Firelock, Cartouch Box, and at least twelve Charges of Powder and Ball," and as many as conveniently could, "with a good Sword, Cutlass or Hanger, to be kept always in our respective Dwellings, in Readiness, and good Order."

2) Local groups: before 1 January, the signers would form themselves into companies of fifty to one hundred men each, consisting of persons "situated most conveniently for meeting together."

3) Local organization: at the first meeting, three persons were to be chosen "by Ballot out of, and by each Company, to be Captain, Lieutenant and Ensign of the same." In order for the Association to have the blessing of the government, those elected would have "to obtain Commissions" from the governor.

4) Higher organization: the officers of the city and each county would meet and elect colonels, lieutenant colonels, and majors, whose names they would submit to the governor or his delegate to receive commissions for a year. The officers and men would serve gratis. The signers agreed to pay due obedience to them. Further, the superior officers would meet in Philadelphia on the third Monday in March to frame general regulations for the Association, which would be observed until a meeting of the General Military Council.

5) Training: the signers agreed to meet with their companies to train in military discipline at the times and places the officers appointed, "not exceeding four Times in one Year, unless called together on some Emergency by the Governor," and on the third Monday in August all regiments in each county would meet at the county seat for a general exercise and review.

6) The General Military Council: at the annual meetings, the regiments would choose by ballot four deputies from each county who were members of the Association "of most Note for their Virtue, Prudence and Ability, who shall meet together at Philadelphia in fourteen Days after their Election, at their own Expence, and form a GENERAL MILITARY COUNCIL, to consult upon and frame such *regulations* as shall be requisite for the better ordering our military Affairs, improving us in military Knowledge, and uniting and ordering our Strength, so as to make it of the most Service for our common Security." The Associators agreed to obey the council's orders and regulations.

7) No taxes, fines, or punishments: the General Military Council will not "subject us to any Pecuniary Mulcts, Fines, or Corporal Penalties, on any Account whatever; We being determined, in this whole Affair, to act *only* on Principles of REASON, DUTY and HONOUR." The council will leave all expenses for batteries or fortifications to voluntary subscription.

8) Duration: the Association will continue until a more effectual provision is made to answer the same ends "or until Peace shall be established between Great Britain, and France and Spain, and no longer" (3:206–8).

When asked about cannons and other expensive fortifications for the protection of the town from ships in the Delaware River, Franklin answered that he proposed to raise the funds through a lottery and that he thought they could also secure cannons either through the proprietaries from England or by borrowing them from neighboring governments.

The plan instantly succeeded. Everyone at the Saturday evening meeting agreed to it and offered to join the proposed militia Association. No, not yet, said Franklin, "let us offer it at least to the Gentlemen and if they come into it, well and good, we shall be the better able to carry it into Execution." He planned a meeting with the gentlemen and wealthy merchants two days later, Monday evening, and a meeting of both groups and all other supporters the following day. Franklin knew his chances of success were greater if he appealed to the hierarchical beliefs of the leaders in the colonial society, but he also knew that they would learn of the success of the meeting with the tradesmen and that they would be all the more willing to come into the plan if the majority of the citizens were for it.

THE ASSOCIATION ORGANIZED

On Monday night, 23 November 1747, Franklin offered the "Form of Association for our common Security and Defence against the Enemy" to the "principal Gentlemen, Merchants and others, at Roberts's Coffee-House," on the northeast corner of Chestnut and Front streets, "where after due Deliberation, it was unanimously approv'd." Franklin said he would print copies the next day and called for another meeting that evening, 24 November, at the New Building to begin signing. He printed the "Form of Association" on both sides of a broadside, leaving plenty of room for signatures. That evening, the New Building "was pretty full. I had prepared a Number of printed Copies, and provided Pens and Ink dispers'd all over the Room." Franklin wrote that he "harangu'd them a little on the Subject, read the Paper & explain'd it, and then distributed the Copies, which were eagerly signed, not the least Objection being made" (3:208).

Since Franklin printed comments about each section of the "Form of Association" in the *Gazette* of 3 December, we know roughly what he said on 24 November. His remarks explained and justified the articles and suggested actions that others who were not joining the Association could take to help. The remarks also document further Franklin's values and his wide reading. He commented on arms and said that *use* was to be more regarded than *uniformity*, and therefore he used the general word *firelock* rather than *musket* (which had no rifling in the bore). Revealing his familiarity with military manuals, Franklin said that some writers advised that one-fourth the weight of the ball was sufficient powder and that more powder made the gun violently recoil, rendering the shot less certain. The military writers added that the bullets should slip down the bore with ease, otherwise both time and rapid fire were lost. Franklin advised that though bayonets were not required, it would be good for some to have them; they were "useful against a violent Onset from irregular Foot, as against Horse." He suggested that older or infirm citizens who could not perform the training could nevertheless help if they kept arms and ammunition ready: if occasion called, they could either use them or lend them to others who were unprovided (3:208–9).

Concerning article 2, local groups, Franklin remarked that the organization was intended to prevent people from "sorting themselves into Companies, according to their Ranks in Life, their Quality or Station." He had already appeased the normal hierarchical expectations of his society, and now he affirmed his personal egalitarianism: " 'Tis designed to mix the Great and Small together, for the sake of Union and Encouragement. Where Danger and Duty are equal to All, there should be no Distinction from Circumstances, but All be on the Level" (3:209).[18]

Franklin's egalitarianism also appeared in the election, rather than the appointment, of officers. Knowing that it contradicted the English and European practices, Franklin attempted to justify the procedure. He said that when the governor appointed the officers, it sometimes happened that "Persons absolutely disagreeable to the People are impower'd to command them. This is attended with very ill Consequences, rendering the Meetings for military Exercise, instead of a Pleasure, a most grievous Burthen, and by Degrees discouraging them even to a total Disuse." But where the militia choose their officers, "it is to be presumed the Choice will naturally fall on Men of the best Character for their military Skill; on such too, from whose Prudence and Good-nature there may be no Fear of Injustice or military Oppression." He thought that voting would prevent resentments against those chosen and that annual elections would "excite an Emulation in All to qualify themselves for being chosen in their Turn" (3:209).

Franklin's further commentary on article 3 testified to his reading of classical history: Though the rotation of offices was contrary to modern use, the "wonderful Success of the Old Romans proves it absolutely right. The Romans, without Doubt, affected Glory and Command as much as other People; but yet they disdained not to obey in their Armies the same Persons whom they had formerly commanded; and to serve as private Soldiers, where they had been formerly Generals." He added that the application to the governor for commissions preserved the prerogative, and at the same time the annual elections secured the liberty of the people. He concluded his remarks on the local officers: "What can give more Spirit and martial Vigour to an Army of FREEMEN, than to be led by those whom they have the best Opinion?" (3:209–10).

The remarks on article 4, higher organization, said that if it was reasonable for the people to choose their officers, it was appropriate for the officers to choose their commanders: "The whole Choice, indeed, may, in one Sense, be said to be in the People, as it takes its Rise from them. Without some general Regulations for uniting our Force, or such Part of it as may be requisite, our general arming would be to little Purpose. And as every Neighbourhood would be glad of Assistance if attacked, so it ought to be willing to give Assistance where it is needed. The great Number of Horses in this Province are in this Respect a vast Advantage; for tho' perhaps we may not form Regiments of Horse, yet those who are to fight on Foot, may, by *their* Means, be suddenly assembled in great Numbers where wanted, even from very distant Places." He again cited classical history: "The Romans, in sudden Expeditions, sometimes put two Men to a Horse. One on Foot was greatly assisted in his March by holding on the Horse's Mane, while the other rid; and they alternately relieved each other." So too modern calvary, on similar occasions, sometimes carry infantrymen with them (3:210).

In article 5, training, Franklin returned to the roles that older or infirm persons might fulfill. Those not able to undergo the military exercise should nevertheless attend the training days and observe them so that they might be able to help if called upon. Besides, "Their Presence and Approbation may encourage younger Men; and the gravest and wisest among us need not be ashamed to countenance Exercises so manifestly tending to the public Good." Since the article limited the meetings to four a year, people would not often be called from their jobs; at the same time, four trainings a year was enough to keep what had been learned in mind, though more frequent meetings could be useful until the militia became "expert." In an emergency, that is, an actual invasion by enemies, the militia agree to assemble on the governor's call; "but when 'tis known that we are all prepared, well armed and disciplined, etc. there is Reason to hope such an Emergency may never happen." There should be meetings of regiments as well as of companies, for in a major engagement, it would be necessary for regiments to act together (3:210–11).

Franklin's ostensible reasons for choosing the third Monday in August for the date of the general annual training seem odd. He said it was the time of "most Leisure, being after Harvest, the Days of middling Length, and the Heats chiefly over." Did he mean to write that planting was over? Aren't most crops harvested later? In Philadelphia, the average July high is 87° and August, 85°. The heat is not much less in August. But people in the eighteenth century, as in the twenty-first, liked a break in the summer. Militia trainings were a traditional time of revelry. I suspect that Franklin chose the time because he thought it would be popular. Franklin also suggested that to make the trainings "more entertaining and useful, Prizes may be set up for the best Marksmen, and others most expert in any of the martial Exercises." As we saw earlier (*Life* 1:14–15), trainings featured prizes for marksmanship.

Commenting on article 6, the General Military Council, Franklin said that the regulations necessary could not easily be specified in a few articles and that, as circumstances changed, the regulations should be altered or amended. Therefore, a General Military Council, "compos'd of prudent, good and able Men," would be established. Again Franklin found a use for persons who could not do the trainings: "The old and wise . . . may here be of Service." The General Military Council would unite all the whole Association in one body (3:211).

Article 7 stressed that "In worthy Minds, the Principles of *Reason, Duty* and *Honour*, work more strongly than the Fears of Punishment." Franklin allowed an exception, however, if the volunteers in local companies wanted to make a temporary agreement to pay small fines if they were late for trainings "or the like," which could be applied to purchasing drums, colors, and so forth, or to be given in prizes, or to refresh themselves after exercise; "they are not hereby restrain'd from doing so." The last article, 8, duration, said that the Association would continue only so long as the war continued "and 'tis heartily to be wish'd, that a safe and honourable Peace may the very next Year render it useless." Franklin ended with an appeal to the volunteers to treat the conscientious objectors well (3:211–12).

According to Franklin's *Autobiography*, at the end of his "harangue" on Tuesday evening, 24 November 1747, nobody objected to the plan, and "above Twelve hundred persons signed the *Form of Association* (A 109). Franklin misremembered. At the time, he reported in the *Pennsylvania Gazette* that "upwards of Five Hundred Men of all Ranks subscribed their Names; and as the Subscription is still going on briskly in all Parts of the Town, 'tis not doubted but that in a few Days the Number will exceed a Thousand, in this City only, exclusive of the neighbouring Towns and Country." Five days later on 29 November, when Richard Peters reported on the Association to the proprietors, he said that Franklin told him "there will be a thousand" signatures to it by that night (3:216). Franklin's article in the *Gazette* on 26 November summarized the events concerning the formation of the Association and urged men to join. Franklin editorialized: "'Tis hop'd the same laudable Spirit will spread itself throughout the Province; it being certain that we have Numbers more than sufficient, to defeat (with the Blessing of God) any Enterprize our Enemies can be suppos'd to form against us." Before summer, over ten thousand men had signed the articles (3:470).

The Pennsylvania Authorities Approve

On the same Thursday, 26 November, that Franklin editorialized about the initial success of the Association, the Common Council of Philadelphia (on which Quakers were a minority) met, rehearsed the recent developments, and added their own appeal to the proprietors for cannon, arms, and ammunition. Franklin had lobbied his friends on the Philadelphia Corporation to sponsor the lottery to raise money for arms and cannons for the Association. The corporation noted that if the lottery for the Association "was approved of by this Board, and some persons appointed by them to oversee & inspect the Management thereof, it might give a Sanction and Credit" to it. The board approved the idea and decided at the next meeting to appoint a committee to support the lottery.[19] Some historians have said that the proprietary leader William Allen opposed the militia.[20] He was, however, in the second most important position on the Philadelphia Council (recorder), supported the motion, became a manager of the Association lottery, and donated his lottery winnings (the large sum of £312) to the Association. James Logan considered Allen, after Franklin, the most important leader of the Association movement (3:472). Meeting on the same Thursday, 26 November, the governor's Pennsylvania Council summarized the recent events and "resolv'd to give all due Protection & Encouragement to the Members of the Association, it being the only Method thought on likely to preserve the Lives & Properties of their Fellow-Citizens in case of a Descent; and likewise to give the Proprietors an account of what was propos'd to be done for the Defence of the Place, and to bespeak their favourable Reception of the several Addresses which would go by this Conveyance."[21]

The next day, Franklin wrote his scientific friend Cadwallader Colden, now lieutenant governor of New York, sending along a copy of *Plain Truth* and "Form of Association." Franklin said, "Tho' *Plain Truth* bore somewhat hard on both Parties here, it has had the Happiness not to give much Offence to either. It has wonderfully spirited us up to defend our selves and Country, to which End great Numbers are entring into an Association." He told Colden that "we" were starting a lottery to raise £3,000 to erect a battery of cannon on the Delaware River below the city, that "we" had petitioned the proprietors Thomas and Richard Penn to send cannon from England and ordered their correspondents to send cannon from there if the proprietors refused to supply them. "We" was no doubt really Franklin, though he knew enough of politics and human nature not only to consult with a group of leaders about these moves but also to suggest that not all the ideas were his own. As he remarked in the *Autobiography* concerning his "Manner of acting to engage People in" the Library Company and "future Undertakings," he "put myself as much as I could out of sight, and stated it as a Scheme of a *Number of Friends*" (A 72, 74).

After the budget of news, Franklin came to his real purpose in writing Colden: "I am desired to write to you, and desire your Opinion, whether if our Government should apply to Governor Clinton, to borrow a few of your spare Cannon, till we could be supply'd, such Application might probably meet with Success" (3:212–13). Colden's reply is not extant, but he probably was ambivalent. Colden knew that most New York authorities felt that Pennsylvania had hitherto done nothing to help New York, almost nothing for the other colonies, and little for its own defense. Nevertheless, he and Franklin were friends who respected one another, and Colden may have tried to help.

Since Franklin and proprietary supporters like William Allen knew that the chief proprietor, Thomas Penn, would be concerned about the Associators as a possible threat to his own prerogative powers, they enlisted the support of Richard Peters, his secretary and primary Pennsylvania correspondent. In a letter of 29 November to the proprietaries (really to Thomas Penn), Peters assured Penn that Franklin and other leaders of the movement had kept him (and, by implication, the proprietors) informed of all developments. They had "nothing in view but the Security of their Lives and Properties," and believed that "they were at the same time doing the Proprietaries true Service in defending the Country by a voluntary association which the Legislature had refus'd to do." They had told Peters they depended on him "to make their regards to the Proprietors Family known . . . in such a manner as to induce them [the Penns] to believe the Associators were heartily in their Interest." Since numerous persons would join the Association, it would be to the proprietors' advantage to encourage them "by a generous Supply of Cannon and small Arms." Peters reported on the past activities for defense of the province: the petition to the Pennsylvania Assembly, the petition from the merchants to the Lords of the Admiralty for a man-of-war,[22] the addresses to Penn from the governor's council and from the Philadelphia common council, and the scheme to raise £3,000 by a lottery of £20,000 (3:217).

In his letter to Penn, Peters said that Tench Francis, William Coleman, and Thomas Hopkinson were partly responsible for the "Scheme" to make the speaker "a Tradesman of Philadelphia." Peters also reported that the pamphlet *Plain Truth* was "mostly" by Franklin. If one takes Peters literally, others who helped write *Plain Truth* suggested the persona.[23] Peters, however, knew Thomas Penn well and was pretty certain Penn would object. Peters also reported that the Proprietary Party leader William Allen told him about Franklin's plan "before it was reduc't to any settled Form" because Franklin wanted Peters to know everything about the evolving militia Association so that he could reassure the proprietors that it was for the general good. I think that Peters, like Allen, Franklin, and others, believed that Thomas Penn, a stickler for prerogative, would see the militia Association as a possible threat to the rights of the authorities. Peters was informing Penn that good proprietary supporters like Allen, Francis, Coleman, Hopkinson, and himself all agreed that such an Association was necessary, as well as beneficial to the proprietaries. At the same time, Peters assured Penn that he had "had no hand in it neither privately nor publickly myself" (3:217).

Foreseeing that Thomas Penn would probably object to the militia Association, Franklin sought out the support of the principal proprietarians who would be likely to support him. When he made the governor (or the president and council) the authority who actually commissioned the officers (3:206), he was attempting to forestall Penn's probable objections. Franklin may have been thinking of the Association by late September 1747. He suggested in *Poor Richard* for 1748 that Pennsylvanians (and Franklin) esteemed the proprietors. Poor Richard celebrated William Penn for "securing the *liberty*, and endeavouring the *happiness* of his people." The almanac praised the current proprietors: "Let no envious mind grudge his posterity those advantages which arise to them from the wisdom and goodness of their ancestor; and to which their own merit, as well as the laws, give them an additional title" (3:259).

Thomas Penn, however, was not appeased by Poor Richard's praise. Despite the assurances of Peters and the addresses of the governor's council, Penn was aghast when he heard about the Association.

FRANKLIN'S PUBLICITY CAMPAIGN

Though the form of Association and the remarks on it were the major item in the 3 December *Gazette*, it was not the only piece publicizing the Association. The front page contained a letter addressed to Franklin (and, I believe, written by him) describing the sacking of Portobello by English privateers under the command of Henry Morgan. Translated from the French (the author/Franklin modestly said, "as well as I can"), the description vividly portrayed the confusion and distress of a city like Philadelphia when attacked and alluded to *Plain Truth*'s "lively Picture" of such a possibility. It suggested that if even Englishmen had proven themselves unspeakable rapists and murderers in sacking cities, what could one expect from the French or the Spanish?

In the same newspaper, Franklin featured a letter from Pennsylvania's Indian authority Conrad Weiser, who said that the French had induced two Indian tribes living near the Mississippi to make war on Pennsylvania and the neighboring provinces. On their way to Pennsylvania, the tribes met with the Miami (or Twightwee) Indians, who told them that the English were friends of the Six Nations, and that if they attacked the English, the Six Nations would set upon them. So the two tribes returned home. Franklin commented, "By this Instance we see of what Importance the Friendship of the *Six Nations* is to us, and the Mischiefs that may attend their present Dissatisfaction at the *English* management of the War, if proper Measures are not taken to remove it, and prevent their being gained over by the *French*."

However, since the Indians could have terrorized the frontier, Franklin called for a force to be ready to defend it: "How necessary therefore is it, that we should be every where armed and provided for Defence." Another Association item in the 3 December paper appeared as an advertisement dated "Chester County, Dec 1." Though the dateline suggests that someone in Chester County wrote it, I suspect that Franklin did so with the advice and input of some Chester County residents. The ad stated that since persons in Chester County lived remote from one another, it was advisable to appoint times and places for them to meet to sign the Association's "Form of Association." Six dates and places were specified. The same paper advertised both Franklin's 1746 edition of a standard military handbook by General William Blakeney, *The New Manual Exercise*, and a second edition of *Plain Truth*.

Firearms and Cannons

When projecting the Association, Franklin knew funds would be needed to buy cannons and to build batteries on the Delaware River. He thought of a lottery before proposing the Association. In the 3 December 1747 paper, he announced that the scheme of the lottery for raising money for defense would be published that Saturday, 5 December, "and may be had gratis . . . at the *Post-Office*." That same 3 December, James Logan wrote him that he "most heartily" wished success to Franklin's Association, but he had some doubts about it, "partly for want of arms for some of the common people." Now a semi-invalid, Logan had hoped his friend Franklin would visit but realized that the Association was taking all his time: "But I request to be informed, as soon as thou hast any leisure, what measures are proposed to furnish small arms, powder, and ball to those in the country; and particularly what measures are taken to defend our river . . . where there ought not to be less than forty guns, from six to twelve pounders. What gunners are to be depended on?" In concluding, Logan praised Franklin's scheme for a lottery and promised to contribute (3:219–20).

Though no record exists of a Philadelphia Common Council meeting between 26 November 1747 and 18 January 1747/8, one must have been held before 5 December to appoint the lottery managers and others who would help. By 5 December, Franklin had printed 1,000 copies of a small broadside called the *Scheme of the Philadelphia Lottery* and 30,000 lottery tickets. One set of 10,000 numbered tickets were sold. When the drawing started, a second set of 10,000 numbered tickets were put into hollow wheels and turned about, so that the selection of a particular ticket was at random. A third set of 10,000 tickets was in another hollow wheel. The last set was mainly blank but contained 2 tickets with £500 written on them; 3 tickets with £300 written on them; 5 with £200; 10 with £100, and so forth, down to 2,080 tickets with £3 written on them. A boy chose a ticket from the first hollow wheel. The holder of the ticket with that same number on it was about to have his chance. Another boy chose a ticket from the second hollow wheel. If that ticket contained a prize, then the owner of the numbered ticket won. Records were kept of the winning and losing tickets, and Franklin later published the winning ticket numbers.

Printing the tickets, like printing *Plain Truth*, was at Franklin's personal expense. On 5 December he gave away the lottery handbills at the post office and had them posted around Philadelphia and in the counties. The advertisement announced that lottery tickets were for sale at the homes of the lottery managers: William Allen, Joshua Maddox, William Masters, Samuel M'Call, senior, Edward Shippen, Thomas Leech, Charles Willing, John Kearsley, William Clymer, senior, Thomas Lawrence, junior, William Coleman, and Thomas Hopkinson. Six were members of the Philadelphia Common Council; four (Masters, Leech, Kearsley, and Clymer) were not. But these four were also leading citizens: Leech and Clymer were Philadelphia representatives in the legislature; William Masters was later chosen a representative to replace a conscientious Quaker pacifist; and Dr. John Kearsley had represented Philadelphia in the Pennsylvania Assembly for nineteen consecutive terms (1722–40).

In addition to the lottery managers, ten persons were added who, with the managers, would decide how to dispose of the £3,000 raised by the lottery. They were William Wallace, John Stamper, Samuel Hazard, Philip Syng, John Mifflin, James Coultas, William Branson, Reese Meredith, Thomas Lloyd, and Franklin. Of this group, only Stamper and Mifflin were Philadelphia councilmen, both having just been elected in 1747. All the others were well-known local Philadelphians. William Wallace, a sugar baker, had businesses at the north end of Front Street and at the upper end of Second Street. Samuel Hazard was a merchant on Second Street and later on Arch Street and a trustee for the use of George Whitefield's New Building. Philip Syng, an Anglican and a silversmith, was Franklin's close friend and participated in his electrical experiments and in all of his civic activities. James Coultas, an original member of a social club called the Schuylkill Company (formed on 1 May 1732), became a captain of Philadelphia's company #9 of the Association and later was elected sheriff of Philadelphia County. Judging by the 1756 tax evaluation of Philadelphia property, William Branson was the second richest person in Philadelphia. Franklin bought steel and stoves from Branson when he began experimenting with the Pennsylvania fireplace in 1738 (*Life* 2:468). Reese Meredith, a merchant and Oxford graduate, was among the Friends disowned for funding the privateer *Warren*. And Thomas Lloyd (d. 1754), merchant, was a member of Franklin's Union Fire Company. Franklin published the scheme for the lottery in the 12 December paper and reprinted it weekly through 5 January 1748.

At noon on Monday, 7 December, Franklin replied to Logan, saying he was "heartily glad" Logan approved of the Association. To Logan's questions, Franklin replied that the Association would have "arms for the poor in the spring, and a number of battering cannon." The Germans were "as hearty as the English, 'Plain Truth' and the '[Form of] Association' are in their language, and their parsons encourage them." Franklin said that the Association leaders "proposed to breed gunners by forming an artillery club, to go down weekly to the battery and exercise the great guns. The best engineers against Cape Breton were of such a club, tradesmen and shopkeepers of Boston." Franklin's brother John belonged to Boston's Artillery Company: "I was with them at the Castle [the island, Castle William, which commanded the approach to Boston's harbor] at their exercise in 1743" (3:224–25). Franklin reported that nearly eight hundred persons had already signed the "Form of Association," with more signing hourly, and that one company of Dutch was complete.

THE ASSOCIATORS MEET

That afternoon, 7 December 1747, nearly six hundred Associators met with their arms at the statehouse (now Independence Hall, on Chestnut between Fifth and

Sixth streets) and marched down to the courthouse (on High/Market Street at Second Street). For the first time in Pennsylvania, a large military force met—no doubt to the disapproval of the Quaker pacifists. As yet, they had no organized command structure, though they had agreed to Franklin's proposed scheme. Anthony Palmer, president of the Pennsylvania Council and acting governor, and several council members were present when Secretary Richard Peters read an announcement to the group that the government did not disapprove of their proceedings. If they chose officers according to the articles, the government would grant them commissions. The council already knew Franklin's plan for dividing the Associators into companies. Now Franklin informed the Associators. Because persons from all parts of Philadelphia had signed the "Form of Association" "promiscuously," Franklin asked two inhabitants of each ward to divide the signers into companies. They had gone around their respective wards and taken down the names of persons from each ward in separate lists in order to see whether there were enough members in a ward to form a company. Some wards contained more than enough. Franklin read off the names of signers, arranged according to wards. Since Philadelphia's Mulberry Ward was large enough for two companies and since the Germans there, "who are as hearty and as forward" as any Associators, desired to have their own company, one was accordingly German and the other English. If the Associators approved the division by wards, Franklin would give the lists of each company to some member within the company who would call the volunteers together on 1 January to elect the officers.

"In the mean time, if each Company shall think fit to meet by itself one Evening in a Week or oftner, to improve in the Exercise of Arms, those who have the Lists will look out for and provide convenient Rooms in different Parts of the Town to accommodate the several Companies." By meeting and training, "we shall not only improve in the Discipline, but become acquainted with each other, and so be better able to judge, when the Day of Election comes, who among us are fittest to be our Officers." Franklin hoped that the Associators would make "a noble Appearance" by 1 January (3:226). The Associators approved Franklin's plan. Reporting the meeting in the *Pennsylvania Gazette* on 12 December, Franklin added: "'Tis not doubted but on the first of *January*, the Day of Election, there will be a very full Appearance of the Associated in this City, all Hands being busy in providing Arms, putting them in Order, and improving themselves in military Discipline."

CALLING IN RELIGION'S AID

On 8 December 1747, the Pennsylvania Council met and appointed Abraham Taylor and Thomas Hopkinson to draft a proclamation for a general fast, to be announced the following day. The idea was Franklin's. He recorded in the *Autobiography* that the Pennsylvania Council approved his activity in organizing the Association and that they consulted him in every measure concerning it:

"Calling in the Aid of Religion, I propos'd to them the Proclaiming a Fast, to promote Reformation & implore the Blessing of Heaven on our Undertaking. They embrac'd the Motion, but as it was the first Fast ever thought of in the Province, the Secretary had no Precedent from which to draw the Proclamation." Franklin wrote it. "This gave the Clergy of the different Sects an Opportunity of Influencing their Congregations to join in the Association" (A 110–11).

The following day, Wednesday, 9 December, the Pennsylvania Council approved the proclamation for a public fast day to take place on 7 January 1747/8. Franklin printed it in the 12 December *Gazette*. The ministers did not wait. The Reverend Robert Jenney, rector of Christ Church, preached "an excellent Sermon on the Lawfulness of Self-Defence, and of Associating for that Purpose" to a large audience on Friday, 11 December. Franklin continued his news blitz for defense by publishing in the 15 December *Gazette* the exchanges between the governor's council and the representatives: President Palmer's message of 16 October, telling of the danger to Philadelphia and to Pennsylvania and asking for funds to protect the city and province; the assembly's answer refusing to give funds; Palmer's message of 24 November reporting the king's request that the legislature pay the troops that had been raised from the province; Palmer's message of 25 November requesting gifts for the Six Nations who were meeting with the Ohio Indians in the spring; and finally the assembly's lame reply putting off voting any funds. On 22 December, after giving "An Account of the Manner of Drawing a Publick Lottery," he listed the persons who were selling the lottery tickets. In addition to all the lottery managers, he added "and by B. Franklin, at the Post-Office," which remained until 1752 at Robert Grace's house, 131 Market Street.

Like the Anglican minister Jenney, the Presbyterian minister Gilbert Tennent did not wait for the fast day. On Thursday, 24 December, he "preached an excellent Sermon in the New Building, on the Lawfulness of War, and on the Usefulness of the Association." In his news report about the sermon, Franklin said that "great Numbers of the Inhabitants of this Province" had entered the Association and more were signing up. Though Jenney did not publish his sermon, Tennent did. It appeared on 1 January, in time for the first great Association meeting. Tennent's *The Late Association for Defense, Encourag'd, or the Lawfulness of Defensive War* had two editions, both published by young William Bradford (1722–91), nephew of Franklin's former rival Andrew Bradford (d. 1742). In it, Tennent praised *Plain Truth* as "a late ingenious excellent *Performance*."[24] Since Franklin's 1746 edition of General Blakeney's handbook of militia exercises had sold out, Franklin advertised on 22 December a forthcoming edition, and noted in the 29 December *Gazette* that he would publish it "To-Morrow."

"THE NECESSITY OF SELF-DEFENCE"

The Postscript to the *Pennsylvania Gazette* of 29 December 1747 contained an anonymous letter to "Mr. Franklin," the editor. Franklin wrote it to promote the militia Association.[25] In it, the author adopted a minister's persona and explicated a biblical passage often cited by pacifists. Though appearing in the paper as a letter or periodical essay, its organization, like *Plain Truth* and *A Modest Enquiry into the Nature and Necessity of a Paper Currency*, followed the puritan sermon structure. Franklin began with a brief statement of the text (which, in this case, was also the doctrine), "The absolute and obvious Necessity of Self-Defence, in the present Conjuncture." He had considered "attentively several Passages in the New Testament, from whence some have endeavoured to shew the Unlawfulness of Christians bearing Arms on any Account." Though he had intended to write an examination of them, "Mr. *Tennent's* Sermon last *Thursday*" was "so full and clear on the Subject, so well supported by Strength of Argument, and carried on with such masterly Judgment and Address, that I am of Opinion, the Publication thereof may sufficiently answer the most material Purposes in my View; wherefore I only now present you a few Thoughts which lay ready, on one particular Passage, as an Amusement to your Readers, till the above Sermon appears in Print."

Franklin pointed out that "some Kinds of War were held lawful amongst the primitive Christians, as appears evidently from many of the ancient Martyrs, who suffered Torture and Death, for their Faith in Jesus, and Constancy to the Christian Religion." At their martyrdom, they were soldiers of Christ. Further, said Franklin, that time was "in the early Ages of Christianity, while the Streams flow'd pure from the Fountain, 'ere the Apostacy had crept in, or the holy Doctrines of Jesus and his Apostles, were exchanged for the corrupt Traditions of Men, being only a few Centuries from Christ." Such expressions of religious primitivism were standard in New England Congregationalism.[26] In view of the constant warfare carried on by the early martyrs, the essayist found it surprising that any Christians should now deny the lawfulness of defensive war. But pacifists often cited "our Saviour's Answer and Command to the Disciple who drew a Sword in his Defence" as proof of their position. From it they concluded "that the Use of Arms is in all Cases forbid by Christ." Moving from some general considerations, Franklin proceeded to explicate Matthew 26:51–54.

"For the better understanding this Matter, observe what" the four Evangelists report concerning the actions of the persons with Jesus when Judas betrayed him and he was arrested. He quoted and commented on Mark 14:47, Luke 20:49–51, and John 18:10, before turning to Matthew: "And behold one of them which were with Jesus, stretched out his Hand, and drew a Sword, and struck a Servant of the High Priest's, and smote off his Ear. Then said Jesus unto him, Put up again thy Sword into his Place; for all they that take the Sword, shall perish with the Sword. Thinkest thou that I cannot now pray to my Father, and he shall presently give me more than twelve Legions of Angels. But how then shall the Scripture be fulfilled, that thus it must be?"

What conclusion, asked the anonymous minister/Franklin, can be drawn from this? It does not "follow that the Use of Arms is prohibited, since it must be granted, the Words, *All they that take the Sword, shall perish with the Sword,* cannot be understood in an absolute literal Sense, as to Individuals; it being evident that all Men who have taken the Sword, have not perished by the Sword, but many of them died in the common Course of Nature, by Diseases, or old Age: Nor will any, 'tis presum'd, be so uncharitable to suppose, this can be meant of the Souls of all those who have taken the Sword. The Passage therefore by no Means determines this Point, whether to use a Sword on any Occasion, be right or wrong."

The letter writer/Franklin instead maintained that Matthew warned people against "attempting to propagate the Christian Religion by Fire or Sword." He thought it also attempted to convince Jews of their "great Mistake, in expecting the Messiah with outward Pomp and Regal Authority." Mainly, however, the biblical text should be understood "to illustrate the great Difference between Christ's Kingdom and those of Princes." If God desired, He could have commanded "an invincible Army of Angels" that was not "liable to Change, or subject to Dissolution." To reinforce the point, Franklin, in the manner of ministers, cited another biblical passage: "The Word of the Lord endureth for ever; and this is the Word which by the Gospel is preached unto you" (1 Peter 1:24, 25).

The minister/Franklin considered other possible interpretations: "the above quoted Words of Christ may either generally relate to the Revolutions and Periods of States, or in a more limited Sense (as in this Case of the Disciples) only signify, that all who persist in opposing their Swords, as private Men against the Legal Authority of the Magistracy, shall perish with the Sword." He said that additional explications could be advanced, "all *agreeing* to demonstrate no Inconsistency in the Passage, unless taken in an absolute literal Sense, and without which, a total Prohibition or Discouragement of bearing Arms will not follow." The speaker claimed that the words "Put up again thy Sword into his Place" conveyed "an Idea very different to laying it aside for ever as unlawful." Instead the words suggest that "The Sword, when in its proper Place, is ready against a suitable Occasion. The Passage might be enlarged upon; but, in my Apprehension, no Construction appears more clear and easy, that the Text simply pointing out a Contradistinction between the Kingdom of Christ, and those of temporal Princes." Weapons, though "useful and necessary in the latter, are not only unlawful, but improper and ineffectual for establishing the former."

The speaker voiced Franklin's actual belief in freedom of religion. No force should be used to make persons change their opinions, so long as those opinions—no matter how improbable they appeared to others—did no harm. As he wrote his parents on 13 April 1738: "Opinions should be judg'd of by their Influences and Effects; and if a Man holds none that tend to make him less Virtuous or more vicious, it may be concluded he holds none that are dangerous" (*Life* 2:295–99).

Franklin then rewrote the Bible in order to make its meaning more explicit.

Not many persons in the eighteenth century took such freedom: "If Liberty may be taken to vary the concise, comprehensive Stile of Scripture into a familiar Way of Speech, the Sense of those Verses appears much the same as if Christ had said, '*Peter*, put up thy Sword on this Occasion, it is no Time now to use carnal Weapons; My Kingdom is not of this World, is neither capable of being supported, or liable to be subverted by the Sword, to the Dangers of which all earthly Kingdoms are continually exposed: Mine stands on a more sure Foundation, in the Defence whereof, if Force availed, a most powerful Army of Angels would now descend to my Assistance.'"

In Mark 14:54 "an immediate Reason is given why our Saviour did not admit any kind of Defence to be made in his Behalf." Franklin did not again cite the verse ("But how then shall the Scriptures be fulfilled, that thus it must be?"), for his audience knew the Bible well. He went on, "It would frustrate the End of his Coming, and prevent the fulfilling of the Scriptures, which agrees with that given by St. *John*; and the whole Passage appears plainly to have no Relation to the Lawfulness or Unlawfulness of using the Sword in any other Case than on the Score of Religion, but most particularly in preventing Christ being delivered to the *Jews*." The essayist observed that it was obvious that "since Swords were by Christ commanded to be procured, yet forbidden to be used on this Occasion, they were certainly intended for some other Purpose."

Though ministers not infrequently quoted classical authors in their reasons or proofs (the third and usually longest division of a puritan sermon), Cicero was so notorious a skeptic that puritan ministers rarely cited him. Nevertheless, Franklin did: "we may here well use an Expression of *Cicero* with redoubled Energy, *Quid Gladii volunt? quos habere certi non liceret, si uti illis nullo pacto liceret.*" ("What is the meaning of the swords we carry? We should certainly not be permitted to have them, were we never to be permitted to use them.")[27]

The persona/Franklin reinforced his proof that Christ believed in the necessity of arms by citing a slightly later passage in Luke (22:35) where "we find very plainly Christ's Opinion of the Necessity of having Swords in these Words, *When I sent you without Purse, and Scrip, and Shoes, lacked ye any Thing? And they said, Nothing.* This was when our Lord sent his Disciples, [Luke] Chapter x. 1. *Before his Face, into every City, and Place, whither he himself would come.* But now, when the Lord is about to be offered up, and his Disciples are to remain in the World, it seems they are not to expect a miraculous Support and Defence: For Christ says, [Luke] Chapter xxii. 36. *But now, he that hath a Purse, let him take it, and likewise his Scrip, and he that hath no Sword, let him sell his Garment, and buy one.*" Franklin observed that money and provisions or food were lawful and necessary "in the tedious Journey of human Life," thus assuming a common religious attitude toward life. The key statement, however, came last: "*And he that hath no Sword, let him sell his Garment, and buy one.*" The text, according to Franklin, said that "a Sword was lawful, and still more necessary, even of greater Consequence than our very Clothes; and the Experience of

Christians from that Time down to the present, may be appealed to, Whether Money and Provisions have not been found very useful, and in many Cases, the Defence of Mens Lives and Liberties of greater Consequence than Food or Raiment; agreeable to our Saviour's Words in another Place, *Is not the Life more than Meat, and the Body than Raiment?* Matth. 6:25."

The minister/Franklin moved from the reasons or proofs part of the puritan sermon to the application, implicitly applying his commentary on Luke to Philadelphia's Quakers: "Yet how punctually do some Christians perform the first and second Parts of this Injunction? Very diligently they provide Purse, and Scrip, yet neglect that most necessary Provision, the Sword, notwithstanding Food and Raiment are represented by Christ of so much less Consequence than Life, which, under Providence, is protected and defended by the Sword, and (on Account of its signal Use, no Doubt) is commanded to be purchased at the Expence of our Garments."

It was plain, said the anonymous essayist, that "some Use was to be made of Swords; but it has been already shewn that Christianity was not to be forced upon People by the Sword: What better Use then remains, than the Defence of our Country, and the Protection of the Helpless and Innocent?" The speaker/ Franklin then applied the moral to the situation of Philadelphia and challenged the pacifists: "If any can be shewn more consistent with Christianity, or beneficial to Mankind, it would be kind in the *Quakers* to inform those, whose present Measures of using Arms they condemn." Finally, the anonymous writer concluded, like many puritan sermon authors, with another biblical quotation and a brief comment on it: "Should some object, that on the Answer, [Luke 22] Verse 38, *Lord, Behold here are two Swords,* Christ said, *It is enough.* Let them remember, that the same Proportion which was adjusted for the Disciples, is enough in most well peopled Countries." Each soldier should have two weapons (firearm and bayonet?).

The essay probably failed to sway any pacifists, but Franklin meant to reassure those persons who believed in self-defense but were troubled by the passage "All they that take the Sword, shall perish with the Sword."

The Associators Organize

On Friday, 1 January 1747/8, the companies of the Associators met and elected the ensigns, lieutenants, and captains. The elected officers then went to the statehouse, where President Anthony Palmer and the Pennsylvania Council awaited. Secretary Richard Peters and Palmer had prepared and signed commissions at the previous board meeting on 29 December, leaving the officers' names blank. The council now instructed Peters to fill in the names and to countersign the commissions. Then the officers of the eleven Philadelphia companies withdrew "into a Room by themselves" and elected Franklin colonel. Franklin knew that the proprietary partisans and the Quaker Party would resent both him and the Associators if he were the colonel. It was good politics for the Association and for him to refuse. He declined the offer, giving as his excuse the lack of any military experience. The *Autobiography* continued the charade: "conceiving myself unfit, I declin'd that Station, and recommended Mr. Lawrence, a fine Person and Man of Influence, who was accordingly appointed" (A 110). Franklin misremembered. He was so little impressed with the abilities of the general officers that he had forgotten who was the colonel and who the lieutenant colonel. Franklin actually nominated Abraham Taylor, who was elected colonel; Thomas Lawrence was then elected lieutenant colonel. Both were members of the Pennsylvania Council—and Proprietary Party stalwarts.

After the company officers elected the regimental officers, the entire regiment assembled at the statehouse and marched through the town to the courthouse on Market Street, "where it was drawn up in three Divisions, and after three general Discharges from each Division, separated, each Captain leading off his own Company." Franklin further reported in the *Gazette*: "The whole was performed with the greatest Order and Regularity, and without occasioning the least Disturbance. Some of the Companies exceed 100 Men each, and most of them fall but little short of that Number." Franklin printed the names of the officers of the eleven Philadelphia companies thus far organized. Though other Associator companies had met on 1 January, the *Gazette* had not yet received their reports.

Thereafter, the news reports of the election of Association officers appeared every week through 5 May, and news of reviews and other information relating to the Association continued into the summer.

SUPPORT FOR THE LOTTERY: THE UNION FIRE COMPANY

Well-off persons who believed in the Association patronized the lottery by buying its tickets. They did not care about winning. James Logan, William Allen, and Franklin showed that they supported the Association and the lottery. Like these three, others turned back their winnings. Though the tickets sold briskly, it might take months rather than weeks to sell them all. Franklin therefore tried to persuade various organizations to buy tickets, and he considered the Union Fire Company a possibility. When it met at Henry Pratt's (on High/Market Street, near Second Street) on Monday, 28 December, Franklin requested that at the next meeting (before money could be spent, company rules required that members be notified at the prior meeting), the Union Fire Company buy lottery tickets to support the Association. The funds on hand amounted to £63.1.9.

Franklin told two anecdotes concerning Quaker pacifism and the Union Fire Company's support for the lottery: "My being many Years in the Assembly, the Majority of which were constantly Quakers, gave me frequent Opportunities of seeing the Embarrassment given them by their Principle against War, whenever Application was made to them by Order of the Crown to grant Aids for military Purposes." Since the moderate Quakers were unwilling to refuse the authorities directly and unwilling to offend the pacifists, they employed a variety of evasions

Friday laſt Nine Companies of the Aſſociators of thi
City, and one of *Myamenſing*, having choſen their Offi
cers for the enſuing Year, marched up, and met at th
State-Houſe ; where the PRESIDENT and COUNCIL
were ſitting, who immediately granted the Commiſ
ſions. The Officers then withdrawing into a Room by
themſelves, elected ABRAHAM TAYLOR, Eſq; Co
lonel ; THOMAS LAWRENCE, Eſq; Lieutenant Colo
nel ; and SAMUEL M'CALL, Eſq; Major of th
Regiment ; which ſoon after began its March throug
the Town, to the Court-Houſe, in *Market-Street*
where it was drawn up in three Diviſions, and afte
three general Diſcharges from each Diviſion, ſeparated
each Captain leading off his own Company. The whole
was performed with the greateſt Order and Regularity,
and without occaſioning the leaſt Diſturbance. Some of
the Companies exceed 100 Men each, and moſt of them
fall but little ſhort of that Number. On the ſame Day
the *Kingſeſs* Company met at *Jenkins*'s Ferry, and choſe
their Officers. Several other Companies of Aſſociators
in the neighbouring Towns met alſo ; but the Accounts
of their Elections are not yet come to hand.

*ORDER of the ſeveral Companies, determined by
Lot, with the Names of the Officers, viz.*

NUMBER I.

Charles Willing, Captain ; *Atwood Shute*, Lieutenant ; *James Claypole*, Enſign.

NUMBER II.

Thomas Bond, Captain ; *Richard Farmer*, Lieutenant
Plunkett Fleeſon, Enſign.

NUMBER III.

John Inglis, Captain ; *Lyn-Ford Lardner*, Lieutenant ; *Thomas Lawrence*, jun. Enſign.

Figure 2. The militia Association elections. Pennsylvania Gazette, *5 January 1747/8. On Friday, 1 January 1747/8, eleven Philadelphia Association companies met and elected officers. The officers proceeded to the statehouse (Independence Hall), where President Anthony Palmer and the Pennsylvania Council instructed Secretary Richard Peters to sign their commissions. Withdrawing "into a Room by themselves," the officers elected Franklin colonel. He declined, saying he lacked military experience. Actually, he knew that if he accepted the office, the Pennsylvania authorities would resent him and the association—whereas they would think it just and suitable if the officers chose a leading Proprietary Party member. Subsequently, Abraham Taylor, a member of the governor's council, was elected colonel.*

From the statehouse (#3, endpapers), the Association officers marched through the town to the courthouse (#24, endpapers), where the companies were "drawn up in three Divisions, and after three general Discharges from each Division, separated, each Captain leading off his own Company." Franklin reported in the Pennsylvania Gazette *of 5 January 1747/8 that "The whole was performed with the greatest Order and Regularity, and without occasioning the least Disturbance. Some of the Companies exceeded 100 Men each, and most of them fall but little short of that Number."*

Franklin printed the officers' names of the eleven Philadelphia companies organized up to that point. Every subsequent issue of the Gazette *through 5 May printed the names of the newly elected officers from different towns and counties. For many colonial Pennsylvanians, it was the only time their names ever appeared in print. Every issue of the* Gazette *from November 1747 through May 1748 featured news of the Association. Courtesy, Library Company of Philadelphia.*

to avoid complying with the authorities, but when it became necessary to do so, they used various disguises in complying. The common evasion was to grant money under the phrase of its being *"for the King's Use*, and never to enquire how it was applied." When the request, however, was not directly from the crown, "that Phrase was found not so proper, and some other was to be invented. As when Powder was wanting, (I think it was for the Garrison at Louisburg,) and the Government of New England solicited a Grant of some from Pennsylvania, which was much urg'd on the House by Governor Thomas, they could not grant Money to buy Powder, because that was an Ingredient of War, but they voted an Aid to New England, of Three Thousand Pounds, to be put into the hands of the Governor, and appropriated it for the Purchasing of Bread, Flour, Wheat, *or other Grain*. Some of the Council desirous of giving the House still farther Embarrassment, advis'd the Governor not to accept Provision, as not being the Thing he had demanded. But he replied, 'I shall take the Money, for I understand very well their Meaning; *Other Grain*, is Gunpowder,' which he accordingly bought; and they never objected to it."[28]

Franklin feared that the vote in the fire company might fail, and he privately proposed to Philip Syng that if so, "let us move the Purchase of a Fire Engine with the Money; the Quakers can have no Objection to that: and then if you nominate me, and I you, as a Committee for that purpose, we will buy a great Gun, which is certainly a *Fire-Engine*: I see, says he, you have improv'd by being so long in the Assembly; your equivocal project would be just a Match for their Wheat *or other grain*" (A 114–15). Though he was not elected to the Pennsylvania Assembly until 1751, Franklin had been its clerk since 1734 and was present on 24 July 1745 when the assembly voted £4,000, not £3,000, for the "Flour, Wheat or other Grain." He probably meant to check the date and amount; for in the manuscript of the *Autobiography*, he made a note to himself, "See the Votes," but never did.

The second anecdote described the Union Fire Company meeting on Monday, 4 January 1747/8. The minutes record, "Pursuant to a Minute of the last Meeting the Clerk left Notice in writing at the Houses of all the Members" that a vote on spending would be taken. In the *Autobiography*, Franklin wrote: "The Company consisted of Thirty Members, of which Twenty-two were Quakers, and Eight only of other Persuasions. We eight punctually attended the Meeting; but tho' we thought that some of the Quakers would join us, we were by no means sure of a Majority. Only one Quaker, Mr. James Morris, appear'd to oppose the Measure. He express'd much Sorrow that it had ever been propos'd, as he said *Friends* were all against it, and it would create such Discord as might break up the Company. We told him, that we saw no Reason for that; we were the Minority, and if *Friends* were against the Measure and outvoted us, we must and should, agreeable to the Usage of all Societies, submit."

The company met at 6:00 P.M. "When the Hour for Business arriv'd [7:00 P.M.], it was mov'd to put the Vote. He allow'd we might then do it by the Rules, but as he could assure us that a Number of Members intended to be present for the purpose of opposing it, it would be but candid to allow a little time for their appearing. While we were disputing this, a Waiter came to tell me two Gentlemen below desir'd to speak with me. I went down, and found they were two of our Quaker Members. They told me there were eight of them assembled at a Tavern just by; that they were determin'd to come and vote with us if there should be occasion, which they hop'd would not be the Case; and desir'd we would not call for their Assistance if we could do without it, as their Voting for such a Measure might embroil them with their Elders and Friends. Being thus secure of a Majority, I went up, and after a little seeming Hesitation, agreed to a Delay of another Hour. This Mr. Morris allow'd to be extremely fair."

The members waited until 8:00 P.M. to vote. "Not one of his opposing Friends appear'd, at which he express'd great Surprise; and at the Expiration of the Hour, we carried the Resolution Eight to one; And as of the 22 Quakers, Eight were ready to vote with us and, Thirteen by their Absence manifested that they were not inclin'd to oppose the Measure, I afterwards estimated the Proportion of Quakers sincerely against Defense as one to twenty-one only. For these were all regular Members of the Society, and in good Reputation among them, and had due Notice of what was propos'd at that Meeting" (A 112–13).

Franklin told a good story, but this part of the *Autobiography* was written in 1788, over forty years after the event. The autobiographer had forgotten exactly how many persons were present and who they were, so he supplied details to make it seem realistic—and dramatic. Four years earlier (March 1784), he had told the story to John Jay. There he also said that twenty-two of the thirty members were Quakers but attributed the opposition to the pacifist Anthony, not James, Morris.[29] Anthony Morris (1682–1763), a Quaker brewer and assemblyman from Philadelphia, was well-known to Franklin but, unlike James Morris, was not a member of the Union Fire Company. Its minutes record that on 4 January 1747/8, ten persons were present, not eight, and James Morris was not among them. Present were Thomas Lawrence, Edward Shippen, Benjamin Franklin, William Parsons, Philip Syng, William Plumsted, Richard Sewell, Thomas Hatton, Samuel Neave, and Hugh Roberts. It was natural for Franklin to recall James Morris as opposed, for he was a member of the Pennsylvania Assembly from Philadelphia County and a pacifist leader. Along with John Armitt and John Dilwyn, James Morris resigned on 29 February from the Union Fire Company because it supported the lottery. So three Quaker members of the company strongly opposed the military, though one, Dilwyn, wavered, and attended a meeting on 25 April before requesting again, on 30 May, that he be dropped as a member.

Did any member present on 4 January oppose the measure? It could hardly have been William Parsons, William Plumsted, or Philip Syng, all of whom were Anglicans and close friends of Franklin. It was not the Anglican Thomas Lawrence, a member of the council and newly elected lieutenant colonel of the

Philadelphia City Associators; nor the Presbyterian Edward Shippen (1703–81), later of Lancaster. That leaves Thomas Hatton (c. 1718–72), Samuel Neave (1707– 74), Hugh Roberts (1706–86), and Richard Sewall [Sewell]. Neave and Sewall seem unlikely, for Neave was a founding member of the Schuylkill Fishing Company, a social group; and Sewall was a sheriff of Philadelphia. Though Hugh Roberts was a good Quaker, he was among Franklin's best friends and it seems unlikely that he would have opposed the Association; he did, however, affirm pacifist principles twelve years later, in 1760. If anyone at the 4 January meeting opposed voting the money for the lottery, it was probably the Quaker merchant Thomas Hatton. The 4 January minutes simply record that the company voted to support the lottery. The "Clerk was then ordered to draw an Order on Benjamin Shoemaker the Companies Treasurer for the Sum of Sixty pounds payable to Edward Shippen for thirty Lottery Tickets." Hugh Roberts, the clerk for that evening, signed the order.[30]

Support for the Lottery: The Philadelphia City Corporation

Two weeks later, on Monday, 18 January, Mayor William Atwood and the Philadelphia Common Council noted that a number of lottery tickets had not yet been sold and voted to buy two thousand tickets. The City Corporation added that if, after the remaining lottery tickets were sold, any prospective purchasers wanted to buy more, the treasurer "shall be & is hereby impower'd to sell out at the Prime Cost" the tickets purchased by the corporation. The next day, Franklin reported and praised the decision in the *Pennsylvania Gazette*, probably exaggerating when he wrote that only a few tickets were left. The *Gazette* further said that the batteries to be erected on the Delaware River were "preparing with all Diligence . . . and such is the *Zeal* and *industry* of all concern'd, that 'tis not doubted they will be in good Condition very early in the Spring." Franklin noted that in the country "the Association goes on with great Success, notwithstanding the Season." The managers of the lottery gave notice that the drawing would begin on Monday, 8 February. By early February, the managers had sold all the lottery tickets and the demand for them was continuing. Therefore, the Philadelphia City Corporation sold some that they had bought, "which may be had at the Post-Office till Saturday," 6 February.

Even the Quaker James Logan supported the lottery. Franklin told an anecdote concerning the pacifist principles of Friends:

> The honorable and learned Mr. Logan, who had always been of that Sect, was one who wrote an Address to them, declaring his Approbation of defensive War, and supporting his Opinion by many strong Arguments: He put into my Hands Sixty Pounds, to be laid out in Lottery Tickets for the Battery, with Directions to apply what Prizes might be drawn wholly to that Service. He told me the following Anecdote of his old Master William Penn respecting Defense. He came over from England, when a young Man, with that Proprietary, and as his Secre-

tary. It was War Time, and their Ship was chas'd by an armed Vessel suppos'd to be an Enemy. Their Captain prepar'd for Defense, but told William Penn and his Company of Quakers, that he did not expect their Assistance, and they might retire into the Cabin; which they did, except James Logan, who chose to stay upon Deck, and was quarter'd to a Gun. The suppos'd Enemy prov'd a Friend; so there was no Fighting. But when the Secretary went down to communicate the Intelligence, William Penn rebuk'd him severely for staying upon Deck and undertaking to assist in defending the Vessel, contrary to the Principles of *Friends*, especially as it had not been required by the Captain. This Reproof being before all the Company, piqu'd the Secretary, who answer'd, *I being thy Servant, why did thee not order me to come down: but thee was willing enough that I should stay and help to fight the Ship when thee thought there was Danger.* (A 113)

The drawing began at the statehouse on Monday, 8 February, and ended on Wednesday, 17 February. Franklin published the winning numbers in three pages of the *Pennsylvania Gazette* on 23 February, where he announced that payment of the prizes would begin on Thursday, 25 February, at William Allen's house, from 9 to 12 and 3 to 5. The winners included William Allen, £312; the Philadelphia City Corporation, £262; and Franklin, £12. They gave their prize money to the lottery managers for the Association.

Publicity and the Fast Day

On the appointed fast day, Thursday, 7 January 1747/8, many ministers preached in favor of the Association. Two sermons were subsequently published. The Reverend William Currie, minister of St. David's Anglican church, echoed parts of Franklin's *Plain Truth* in *A Sermon Preached in Radnor Church*, which Franklin and Hall published on 16 January. Gilbert Tennent's usual Philadelphia publisher, young William Bradford, printed *A Sermon Preached at Philadelphia, January 7, 1747/8*. Meanwhile, the Quaker pacifist, merchant, and intellectual John Smith composed a reply to Tennent's 24 December sermon, *The Late Association for Defense, Encourag'd*. Smith submitted the reply to several Friends, including the Quaker Speaker of the House, John Kinsey, and to the Quaker board of overseers, who approved it. Franklin and Hall published it on 30 January as *The Doctrine of Christianity Vindicated*. The Quakers subsidized it and gave it away at Franklin and Hall's printing shop and at Smith's home. Smith recorded in his diary: "the printer's house & indeed my own was like a fair— people came so thick to get them. D. Hall told me that he never saw a pamphlet in so much Request at first coming out in London."[31] Franklin and Hall published a second edition on 2 February.

Before Smith's pamphlet appeared, Gilbert Tennent preached two more sermons on defensive warfare on Sunday, 24 January, his third and fourth supporting the Association. Subsequently, he wrote a preface, dated 19 March, to these two and published them under the title *The Late Association for Defence Farther*

DEVICES and MOTTOES painted on some of the Silk Colours of the Regiments of ASSOCIATORS, in and near *Philadelphia*.

I. A Lion erect, a naked Scymeter in one Paw, the other holding the *Pennsylvania* Scutcheon. Motto, PRO PATRIA.

II. Three Arms, wearing different Linnen, ruffled, plain and chequed; the Hands joined by grasping each the other's Wrist, denoting the Union of all Ranks. Motto, UNITA VIRTUS VALET.

III. An Eagle, the Emblem of Victory, descending from the Skies. Motto, A DEO VICTORIA.

IV. The Figure of LIBERTY, sitting on a Cube, holding a Spear with the Cap of Freedom on its Point. Motto, INESTIMABILIS.

V. An armed Arm, with a naked Faulchion in its Hand. Motto, DEUS ADJUVAT FORTES.

VI. An Elephant, being the Emblem of a Warrior always on his Guard, as that Creature is said never to lie down, and hath his Arms ever in Readiness. Motto, SEMPER PARATUS.

VII. A City walled round. Motto, SALUS PATRIÆ, SUMMA LEX.

VIII. A Soldier, with his Piece recover'd, ready to present. Motto, SIC PACEM QUERIMUS.

IX. A Coronet and Plume of Feathers. Motto, IN GOD WE TRUST.

X. A Man with a Sword drawn. Motto, PRO ARIS ET FOCIS. &c. &c.

Most of the above Colours, together with the Officers Half-Pikes and Spontons, and even the Halberts, Drums, &c. have been given by the good Ladies of this City, who raised Money by Subscription among themselves for that Purpose.

Figure 3. Flags of the first Associator companies, Pennsylvania Gazette, 12 January 1747/ 8. Franklin supplied "Devices and Mottos" for the Associator companies (A 110). No flag is extant from the 120 companies, but we know twenty of the devices and mottos. He published ten in the Pennsylvania Gazette *on 12 January 1747/8 and ten more on 16 April 1748. These twenty devices and mottos constitute the largest number of original heraldic emblems created by a single person in colonial America. (No doubt he also supplied one hundred more for the additional companies.) Typical of the traditional devices, the first depicts "A Lion erect, a naked Scymeter in one Paw, the other holding the Pennsylvania Scutcheon. Motto, Pro Patria." The shield and the lion are found on the Penn family coat of arms and on the official seal of Pennsylvania. Franklin evidently intended both the "body" (or figure on the device) and the "soul" (or motto, "Pro Patria") to reassure the Penns and the English government that the Associators, which became an army of more than ten thousand men existing outside any official government structure, were loyal to the Penns, Pennsylvania, and England.*

The bodies on the flags are generally standard heraldic figures. Five are military symbols (nos. V, VII, VIII, IX, and X). The iron armor of number V emphasizes the traditional nature of the figures. Number IX, "A Coronet and Plume of Feathers," is the attribute of the Prince of Wales. Of the other five figures, three portray standard heraldic animals: a lion (I), an eagle (III), and an elephant (VI). One (IV) is a common personification: "The Figure of LIBERTY, sitting on a Cube, holding a Spear with the Cap of Freedom on its Point. Motto, INESTIMABILIS."

Finally, number II is original: "Three arms, wearing different Linnen, ruffled, plain, and chequed; the Hands joined by grasping each the other's Wrist, denoting the Union of all ranks. Motto, Unita Virtus Valet." The three kinds of cloth symbolize the main classes of colonial American society: the gentlemen, with ruffled lace; the merchants, with plain linen (the adjective "plain" especially suggests Quakers); and the common workmen, with checked gingham. In this device, Franklin created an egalitarian symbol of the union of three classes.

One motto, or soul, appears to be original. According to the conventions of emblem literature, the soul was supposed to be in a learned language—or at least in a language other than the native tongue. But Franklin violated the rule with "In God We Trust" (IX), which testifies to his genius for creating proverbs and sententiae. It is the earliest recorded usage of the phrase that appeared on U.S. coinage in 1865 and was adopted as the official motto of the United States in 1956. Courtesy, Library Company of Philadelphia.

Encourag'd: or, the Consistence of Defensive War with True Christianity. Earlier in January he had preached a communion sermon, *Brotherly Love Recommended. A Sermon Preached . . . before the Sacramental Society,* recommending love and tolerance to the entire community of Philadelphia, especially to Quakers and Presbyterians bitterly opposed to each other concerning the Association. It appeared on Thursday, 11 February. By that date both Currie and Tennent were writing replies to Smith's *Doctrine of Christianity Vindicated.* Tennent's rejoinder, advertised as "Just Published" on 5 April, again began with the title *The Late Association for Defence Farther Encouraged* but then continued with a subtitle, *in a Reply to . . . "The Doctrine of Christianity."* Currie titled his reply to Smith *A Treatise on the Lawfulness of Defensive War,* which appeared about 9 June. Later in the year, John Smith's brother, Samuel Smith, wrote *Necessary Truth,* which tried to answer Franklin's *Plain Truth* (Smith 1–11), Franklin's piece in the *Gazette* of 5 November 1747 on Barclay's *Apology* (Smith 11–12), and his essay of 19 November 1747 on the non-pacifism of the famous Quaker William Edmondson (Smith 12–13). Franklin and Hall also published on 26 November 1748 [Benjamin Gilbert], *Truth Vindicated, and the Doctrine of Darkness Manifested,* another pacifist reply to Tennent's answer to John Smith.

THE ASSOCIATOR FLAGS

Franklin designed flags for the militia companies and enlisted the aid of patriotic women to make them. "The Women, by subscriptions among themselves, provided Silk Colours, which they presented to the Companies, painted with different Devices and Mottos which I supplied." He relegated his role to a dependent clause at the end of the sentence, an example of his attempting to avoid vanity in the *Autobiography.*[32] He published descriptions of ten flags in the 12 January *Gazette* and ten more in the 16 April 1748 paper. These twenty devices and mottos are the largest number of original heraldic emblems created by a single individual in colonial America. Though we only know the substance of twenty flags, Franklin probably suggested devices and mottos for most of the 120 companies.

All colonial printers worked with watermarks and other symbolic devices. Franklin is distinguished from other colonial printers by his artistic creativity and his interest in—and scholarly knowledge of—symbols. His first teacher in visual symbols (after such schoolbooks as the *New England Primer*) was his older brother James, an expert illustrator who made wood engravings. Throughout his life, Franklin collected books and manuscripts on the arts, heraldry, and emblems, and made numerous designs, including cartoons and the illustrations on the colonial and Revolutionary paper currency.[33] Like these other figures, almost all the devices on the Associator flags are traditional. Number I depicts "A Lion erect, a naked Scymeter in one Paw, the other holding the *Pennsylvania* Scutcheon. Motto, Pro Patria." The shield and the lion are found on the Penn family coat of arms and on the official seal of Pennsylvania. Franklin probably chose this as his first flag as part of his attempt to reassure the proprietors that the Associators, an army of more than ten thousand men, were loyal to the Penns, to the province of Pennsylvania, and to Great Britain.

Attempting to be absolutely clear to his audience, Franklin avoided the specialized diction of heraldry. He wrote "A Lion erect" rather than "A Lion rampant guardant." The normal heraldic description would be: "A Lion rampant guardant, holding in the dexter forepaw a naked Scymeter, hilted and pommelled, and in his sinister the Pennsylvania Scutcheon." But such a description would not immediately be understandable to all his readers, so he used the common language; since no other words were so precise and succinct as *Scymeter* (a short, curved sword; more commonly spelled *scimiter*) and *Scutcheon*, he used them.

In flag number XVI, Franklin was not so careful and began with the standard heraldic diction and used a Latin motto: "A Lion rampant, one Paw holding up a Scymiter, another on a Sheaf of Wheat; Motto, Domine Protégé Alimentum." The motto, "Owners Protect Provisions," implied that local militia, protecting their own homes and families, were superior to hired or professional soldiers. In number XVII, he again avoided heraldic diction. Instead of "A Lion dormant," he wrote: "A sleeping Lion; Motto, Rouze me if you dare." Though Franklin used clear and simple diction for his audience, he probably also took pleasure in undercutting heraldry's formal, aristocratic traditions.[34]

Franklin's original symbols/emblems reveal his egalitarian American aesthetic. Number II is "Three Arms, wearing different Linnen, ruffled, plain, and chequed; the Hands joined by grasping each the other's Wrist, denoting the Union of all ranks. Motto, Unita Virtus Valet." Two clasped hands are a common emblem of friendship. Franklin knew it, among other sources, from the seal of the city of Philadelphia. But Franklin changed the symbol by making it three hands and wrists, by strengthening the holds by having each grasp another's wrist, and by capturing the idea of three different classes joined together. The shirt sleeves symbolize the three main classes of colonial American society: the gentlemen, with ruffled lace; the clerks and common merchants, with plain linen (*plain* may especially suggest Quakers); and the common artisans, with checked gingham. This original device created a dramatic symbol of the union of the classes, which Franklin reinforced with the motto "Unity makes us stronger."

A second original figure also has an egalitarian moral: "Three of the Associators marching with their Muskets shoulder'd, and dressed in different Clothes, intimating the Unanimity of the different Sorts of People in the Association; Motto, Vis Unita Fortior." ("Strength united is more powerful.") Two of the souls, or mottos, on the flags are also original. According to the rules of emblem literature, the soul was supposed to be in a learned language, usually Latin—or at least in a language other than the native tongue. Franklin violated the rule for his original mottos. They are in English, though they echo common heraldic sentiments. Number XVII, "Rouze me if you dare," contains the sentiment of a common Renaissance motto, "Nemo me impune lacessit" ("No one provokes me with impunity"). Finally, number IX, "In God We Trust," echoes religious appeals to God from ancient times. But the words show Franklin's genius for sententiae. It is the earliest recorded usage of the phrase that first appeared on U.S. coinage in 1865 and was adopted as the official motto of the United States in 1956.

The souls or mottos are among the many indications that Franklin knew Latin well. Although most of the Latin mottos are traditional,[35] seven are not. Number II, *unita virtus valet* (unity makes us stronger), is above; Franklin modified the traditional *deus adjuvat* (God assists) in number V by adding *fortes* (the strong); number VII, *salus patriae, summa lex* (a safe homeland, the highest law); VIII, *sic pacem querimus* (thus I pacify quarrels); XVI, *domine protégé alimentum* (nourishment protected by the Lord); XVIII, *spero per deum vincere* (I hope to conquer by God); and XIX, the easiest one, *pro deo & georgio rege* (for God and King George).

Though none of the flags survives, a quilt in the Chester County Historical Society, which was probably made in 1748, has the word "Association" repeated on it, material evidence of a patriotic lady's support.[36]

THE WAR SCARE

John Bartram wrote Peter Collinson on 30 January that Pennsylvania expected "A visit from the French early in the spring." In preparation for the possible invasion, Association volunteers were "daily exercising & learning the Martial discipline." They were also preparing "forts & bateries to stop any vessels that come in a hostile manner." In general, "the clergy exercises thair talents with all thair force of eloquence to persuade thair hearers to defend thair country, liberties & families by the sword and the blessing of god but our [Quaker] society like fools or something worse opposeth them by pamphlets persuasion & threats of reading them out of our meetings for breach of our discipline in takeing up the carnal weapon which unreasonable proceeding I suppose hath made one hundred hypocretes to one convert for thay cant bind the freedom of thought."[37] Bartram's sentiment proves Franklin's advertising campaign succeeded. He had convinced Bartram and no doubt many other persons to be prepared if an enemy attacked.

On 25 March 1748, Richard Peters wrote Thomas Penn: "And now the people are hastening to erect a Battery which when done their Fears will subside for the City, tho' the Trade will be absolutely destroyed. There are now highly Associated Companys who behave very orderly. Signals and words of Command are settled all over the Country, and the Alarms are as far as I can deduce well contrived. I shall send you the general Disposition with Lists of the Officers and Numbers of them in Each Company by the London Ship." Though Peters's support for the Association at the beginning had been unenthusiastic, he had

Figure 4. An Association quilt, 1748?, 1774? The 86 x 77–inch quilt has a linen face and backing with a cleaned wool filling. The face or top is made up of six segments of linen plain-weave fabric stitched together. After stitching, the top of the quilt was block-printed in reds and blues. The center medallion is 20⅜ x 9⅜ inches. Adjacent to the center medallion is a textile block-print impression of the word "Association" under a crown. The word "Association" measures 6⅝ inches and from the bottom of the word "Association" to the top of the crown measures 3½ inches. The "Association and crown" image is repeated fifteen times on the longer side of the quilt and fourteen times on the shorter. Quarters of the circular floral medallion are block-printed in the four corners of the central spandrels between the central field and the borders.

The quilt dates from the eighteenth century, perhaps from the 1748 voluntary militia Association. Dr. Patricia J. Keller, who called the quilt to my attention and provided the description, suggested that it alluded to the 1774 Continental Congress "Association" for non-importation. Provenance supports her theory. An ancestor of the family who donated the quilt to the Chester County Historical Society belonged to the committee charged with enforcing the 1774 non-importation association. Although Keller believes the quilt was created as a tangible demonstration of support for non-importation and domestic manufacture, I suspect it was made to sell for funds to help build batteries, buy cannon, and purchase guns and ammunition for the 1748 militia Association. The textile block print of "Association and crown" would have been expensive to make and was probably meant to be used hundreds of times. The crown/king symbol in the print seems more appropriate to 1748 than 1774. Courtesy, Chester County Historical Society.

become convinced that it was good for Pennsylvania and would also serve the political interests of the proprietors with the British authorities: "I begin to see this Affair in a different Light from what I did at first, and I think it may be exceedingly for the Proprietary Interest, for the Ease of Government and the Preservation of the place under the Blessing of divine Providence." Peters said that he had been afraid that the Quaker pacifist principles would endanger the constitution of the province if the war continued, but now the Association and "Batteries on the River, may reconcile the Province better to His Majesty and his Ministers, and save them the trouble and the Quakers the Shame of an Act of Parliament to incapacitate them for sitting in Assembly."[38]

Cannon

Franklin met the problem of providing cannon to protect Philadelphia with three methods: begging, borrowing, and buying. He presented the methods to the Pennsylvania Council on 26 November 1747, which supported them.[39] The council begged for cannon from the proprietors, the English authorities, and those available in Philadelphia. The proprietors hemmed and hawed and finally, long after the crisis was over, contributed fourteen 18-pounders, which Franklin noted in the *Pennsylvania Gazette* on 15 November 1750. The Pennsylvania Council tried to borrow cannon from Massachusetts and New York. Governor William Shirley of Massachusetts had none to spare. Governor George Clinton of New York said on 5 January 1747/8 that he awaited an engineer from England to survey the province's defenses. He added that New York would like to help but had to wait for the expert's opinion to "Judge whether & how far I can comply." With the lottery becoming a success, the Associators were also able to buy cannon. The military commanders proposed to erect two batteries on the Delaware River, and requested the lottery managers meet with them on 7 March "to determine the Places where to fix them."[40]

When Franklin announced the forthcoming construction of batteries in the *Pennsylvania Gazette* on 1 March, he said that the commanders and lottery managers "would be glad to receive the Advice of those that have Judgment or Experience in such Affairs." He knew human nature well enough to realize that numerous persons might come forward whose advice was worthless, and therefore he asked that persons with "Judgment or Experience" in military affairs "reduce their Sentiments to Writing, with their Reasons, and communicate them to the managers for their Consideration at the *said* Meeting." No doubt few persons wrote out their sentiments and reasons, and Franklin and others in charge probably personally asked experts for advice.

In a letter to Franklin of 3 December 1747, James Logan had suggested that two batteries were necessary, one at "Red Bank, on the Jersey side" and another on the Pennsylvania side. The committee decided to erect them there, evidently at its 7 March meeting. Red Bank was opposite the mouth of the Schuylkill River, where several islands on the Pennsylvania side made the passage narrow.

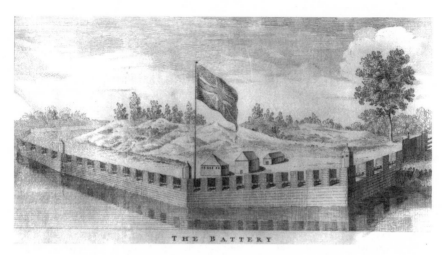

THE BATTERY

Figure 5. The Association battery at Wicaco. A detail in Scull and Heap's Map of Phila-delphia, 1750. In December 1747, Franklin devised a lottery to raise £3,000 to build batter-ies and to buy cannon to defend Delaware and Pennsylvania from enemy Spanish and French privateers. The lottery sold out in six weeks and the Pennsylvania Gazette *an-nounced the winners from 8 to 17 February.*

A month later, on 25 March 1748, Richard Peters, secretary of the province, wrote Thomas Penn, chief proprietor: "And now the people are hastening to erect a Battery." Franklin and the lottery managers oversaw the construction of the largest battery. It was built on William Allen's land at Wicaco, just a few hundred yards south of Dock Street, Philadelphia. Franklin begged, borrowed, and bought cannon for several batteries. On 28 April, the Gazette *reported the Wicaco battery was "near finished" and that installing the heavy cannon borrowed from New York would begin "next Week." By May, Franklin "regularly took my turn of Duty there as a common soldier" (A 110). Courtesy, Pennsylva-nia Historical Society.*

A battery at Red Bank would command the river channel. The major battery was erected at Wicaco, on the Delaware River just a quarter mile south of Phila-delphia.

At the Pennsylvania Council meeting on 8 March 1747/8, informants re-ported that Mr. Armstrong, "his Majestie's Engineer," had arrived in New York. The council decided to renew their application to Governor Clinton "for a Loan of Cannon, & to add the greater weight thereto, they thought that sollicitations shou'd be made by two of their Members, & Mr. Lawrence & Mr. Taylor were requested to undertake the Journey." A group of five of Pennsylvania's best-known citizens, Richard Peters, William Allen, Abraham Taylor, Thomas Law-rence, and Franklin, journeyed overland to New York to borrow cannon. They evidently left early on 9 March and arrived on 10 or 11 March. Richard Peters reported to Thomas Penn on 25 March that the Pennsylvanians "met with an ill-natur'd Disposition" in most New Yorkers who said "Pennsylvania deserv'd nothing" because the Quakers did not join them in defending the frontiers. Pennsylvania spent little or nothing on defense "tho' it cost New york Government the annual Sum of forty five thousand Pounds." Peters continued that at first Chief Justice James DeLancey "from his love of Popularity or rather a regard to his Interest among the People, prov'd averse but soon came to think of the Application in another Light."

Franklin attributed the change to sociability and Madeira: "Governor Clinton . . . at first refus'd us peremptorily: but at a Dinner with his Council where there was great Drinking of Madeira Wine, as the Custom at that Place then was, he soften'd by degrees, and said he would lend us Six. After a few more Bumpers he advanc'd to Ten. And at length he very good-naturedly conceded Eighteen. They were fine Cannon, 18 pounders, with their Carriages" (A 110). Franklin did not remember the details of what had happened all those years before (he wrote this in 1788), but he gave specifics to tell a good story. At the time, Richard Peters reported that they borrowed "Twelve Pounders and two Eighteen Pounders." He also noted that "Mr Allen and the other Gentlemen have" given a bond for £1,000 "to return the Gunns within three months" of their being requested.[41]

The Pennsylvanians returned before 25 March. Their concern shifted from borrowing the cannon to the logistics of bringing them from New York to Philadelphia. The easiest way would have been by ship from New York to Philadelphia, but the Pennsylvania Provincial Council received a letter from Governor Clinton on 31 March that "Don Pedro is upon the Coast with one or two Vessels."[42] The cannon had to go by land. Ships took them from New York up the Raritan Bay, past Perth Amboy to Brunswick, New Jersey, where William Oake was paid £4.1.0 for landing them. The cannon were taken on the difficult overland route from Kingston past Princeton to Trenton, New Jersey, arriving before 16 April, whence they were loaded on ships and sent down the Delaware River to Philadelphia.

Thomas Penn Opposes the "Dangerous" Franklin

Despite the reassurances of proprietary partisans Richard Peters, William Allen, and members of the Pennsylvania Council, Thomas Penn was horrified by the Association. On 29 March 1748 he wrote Lynford Lardner, the receiver-general of the proprietors' quitrents, that Franklin's pamphlet *Plain Truth* "has done much mischief, as such a spirit raised in a people cannot be of any service, but under proper and legal regulations, and I am sure the people of America are too often ready to act in defiance of the Government they live in, without associating themselves for that purpose." The next day, in a letter to the president and council, Penn said that if the information was correct that the French intended to send a "considerable Force" against the city in the spring, the council had "great reason" for their fears and should do all they could to protect Pennsylvania. Nevertheless, he opposed the Association. Though its officers received commissions from the Pennsylvania Council, the soldiers bound themselves to obey the military, not Penn's government.

Penn claimed that the basic idea of the Association took away power from the king (i.e., himself and the British authorities) and gave it to the people, "which I fear will be esteemed greatly Criminal." He thought that the Association "cannot end in anything but Anarchy and Confusion. The People in General are so fond of what they call Liberty as to fall into Licenciousness, and when they know they may Act . . . by Orders of their own Substitutes, in a Body, and a Military manner, and independent of this Government, why should they not Act against it." Penn also disapproved of the artillery batteries, perhaps because the Association controlled them: "The erecting a Battery on such a Scheme was certainly a Wild project, the only thing you could have done was the fitting out two or three Ships the largest you had, which might have been of real Use 'til you had known what Success an Application to the Admiralty could meet with." At the same time, however, he promised that "Whenever any Law shall be made in Pennsylvania for establishing a Militia and erecting a Fort or Battery, we shall be very ready to Shew our concern for the Safety of the City by giving Cannon for such a Battery."[43] Penn meant that he would support a militia in which the governor appointed the officers.

Penn found Franklin dangerous. When Penn wrote Peters on 9 June 1748 and informed him that peace was shortly expected, he took up Franklin's role in the Association. Penn conceded that Franklin had achieved the purposes intended but objected to them and to Franklin. The doctrine, "tho very true in it self, that Obedience to Governors is no more due than Protection to the People, yet it is not fit to be always in the heads of the Wild unthinking Multitude." Besides, in the case of Pennsylvania it was not the government "properly Speaking that should be inveighed against, but the Assembly." Penn wrote that Franklin "is a dangerous Man and I should be very Glad he inhabited any other Country, as I believe him of a very uneasy Spirit. However as he is a sort of Tribune of the People, he must be treated with regard" (3:186). Though Penn's appraisal of Franklin seems uncannily accurate, Penn knew Philadelphia and Franklin well. Penn had spent nine years in Philadelphia (1732–41) and had been burned in effigy upon leaving (*Life* 2:226, 340). While Penn was in Pennsylvania, a supercilious opponent (probably Richard Peters) printed an attack on Franklin as a "Prince and Leader" of "the meaner sort." Penn's "Tribune of the People" reflects Peters's opinion (*Life* 2:431).

Penn's opposition surprised and chagrined his supporters. Franklin had foreseen such a possibility when he refused the offer of a colonel in the Philadelphia regiment. In their letter of 30 July (written before they received Penn's letter of 9 June), the councillors reassured the proprietors that since the "Principal Officers" are "under the immediate direction of this Board," the Association was under the proprietors' control. At the end of its letter, the council summarized, "On the whole, as the Association had no Power, nor pretended to have any but what they receiv'd from this Board, and as we granted none but such as we think are well warranted by the Charter, we hope you will be as well satisfied of the Legality of the proceeding as we assure ourselves you are of the usefulness and necessity of it."[44]

Preparations

Not waiting for the cannon to arrive before starting to build the batteries, the lottery managers purchased "Plank for the Platforms, and all other Materials, . . . and such is the *Zeal* and *industry* of all concern'd, that 'tis not doubted" the batteries "will be in good Condition very early in the Spring."[45] On 1 March, the Association officers met, drafted recommendations, and adjourned to 4 April. Besides borrowing and begging cannon from afar, the Associators surveyed those on the various wharves of Philadelphia, finding nearly seventy of different sizes, "fit for Service on Occasion." Franklin noted in the 28 April *Gazette* that the "committees appointed by the lottery managers to erect Fascine Batteries on the Wharves" had set the cannon in the most proper places. The same paper announced that the "Grand Battery at Wicaco below this Town is also near finished, and 'tis thought will be ready the Beginning of next Week to receive the heavy Cannon borrowed from N. York." Mayor William Atwood allowed the Associators to build a breastwork on his property, "8 to 10 Foot thick, compos'd of Timber and Plank fill'd in with Earth rammed down." Carpenters and laborers erected the defense "gratis, and perform'd the Work with the greatest Alacrity and surprizing Dispatch."

Despite Franklin's appeal to the Germans in *Plain Truth* and his paying Joseph Crellius to translate it into German, the Pennsylvania Germans did not, "in proportion to their numbers," join the Association. The German pacifist printer Christopher Saur replied with a pamphlet that he, like Franklin with *Plain Truth*, gave away. Franklin heard that Saur and other Germans claimed that if the Germans "were quiet," the French would not "molest them." They said further that "the trouble hazard and Expence of defending the Province" would be "a greater inconvenience than any that might be expected from a change of Government" (4:485). At the time, Franklin ignored these comments. The English generally joined, and every issue of the *Gazette* celebrated new companies. Deborah Franklin's brother, John Read, evidently became an Associator, for he borrowed 49 shillings from Franklin on 15 April 1748 to buy a musket.

On 11 May 1748, Richard Peters wrote the proprietors that there would soon be ten thousand men in the Association. The following week on 17 May, the Pennsylvania Provincial Council announced to the assembly that the "Province, which very lately was in a defenceless State, is now, thro the Zeal and Activity of some, who have the Love of their Country sincerely at Heart, render'd capable, with the Blessing of God, of defending itself against the Designs of our Enemies." In addition to the news of the formation of new companies and the names of the officers, the newspapers carried frequent notices of the reviews of the Associator companies and regiments. The *Pennsylvania Gazette* reported on 24 May that Colonel "Taylor's regiment of associators in this city, consisting of eleven companies, was under arms, and review'd by their honours the President and Council, in the field. Strangers who were present agree, that the progress this regiment has made in military discipline in so short a time, was truly extraordinary."

The preparations were not unnecessary. On 26 May, President Anthony Palmer and the council learned that a "Spanish Privateer of fourteen Carriage Guns, eight six Pounders & six four Pounders . . . a Brigantine of a hundred & sixty Men" was at "Elsenbourgh in the River," just ten miles south of Newcastle. Though the British Admiralty had sent a ship to Philadelphia, it was a small sloop, the *Otter*, Captain Ballet, which had few sailors and fewer guns. Ballet had arrived in Philadelphia four days earlier and had to set about making his sloop seaworthy: "his Guns were" now ashore and the *Otter* "unrigg'd." Captain Ballet said "the first & most serviceable thing to be done was for his Men quickly to raise a good Battery & place his Guns on it." The council approved a series of defenses and appointed their fellow member, Abraham Taylor, who was colonel of the Associated Regiment of Philadelphia, in charge. The council consulted Speaker John Kinsey, who assured the council members that if they spent money "for the Good of the Province" in defending Philadelphia, the assembly would repay them. Enemy ships sailed up the river, and the *Gazette* of 26 May reported that they were at "Bombay-Hook, and had taken two shallops there."

With enemy privateers just a few miles south of Philadelphia, some pacifist Friends briefly abandoned their principles. John Smith, James Logan's son-in-law, recorded in his diary on 26 May that "The town was alarmed with the news of a Spanish Brigadeer Privateer being at Ready Island, and much frightened were many people about it." Several days later on 31 May, Smith considered "what friends could do in the present circumstance." Reportedly, five or six privateers were at the entrance to the Delaware Bay. The assembly had made no provision for any emergencies, and the council either could not or would not borrow money upon the credit of the assembly's repaying it. Smith "thought if a Scheme could be drawn up reciting what J. Kinsey, the Speaker, had said in Council, viz., that he believed if they were put to any Expense in discharge of what they conceived to be their duty, that an adequate provision would be made by the Assembly in support of Government, and Binding the Subscribers to fulfil the Interest and meaning of that declaration—it would help to still the Clamour & noises of the people." So Smith drew up an instrument and pledged to give one hundred pounds to support any actions the council might take. He took it to "Jemmy" Pemberton (Israel Pemberton, Jr.), who likewise subscribed one hundred pounds. Then Smith had second thoughts, consulted older Friends who advised against the project, and so he canceled it. Nevertheless, rumors about the subscription spread.[46]

The Assembly Again Refuses

The president and council summoned the Pennsylvania Assembly to meet on 8 June. The next morning, the council said: "in this Time of general Calamity, we again press you on that disagreeable subject [protecting the river from privateers], in Hopes that the miserable Circumstances to which we are now reduced, may, at length prevail with you to provide a proper Remedy." Shortly before the assembly session began, a well-known itinerant Quaker minister, John Churchman (1705–75), arrived in Philadelphia. A few nights later, as Churchman lay in bed, "it came very weightily upon me to go to the house of Assembly, and lay before the members thereof the danger of departing from trusting in that divine arm of power which had hitherto protected the Inhabitants of our land in peace and safety." He wanted to do so "without giving just cause of offence to any," for a number of Quakers had declared "their willingness" to give money for the king's use "to shew our loyalty to him," even though "as a people, we had a testimony to bear against all outward wars and fightings."[47]

Churchman waited nearly a week, then called upon a Friend, asking if any Friends ever went to the assembly to speak before the legislators. The person replied, not recently, though formerly it was "a common practice for them to sit in silence a while, like solemn worship, before they proceeded to business." Churchman went to the statehouse, arriving just as Speaker Kinsey was entering. It was probably the morning of 10 or 11 June. Churchman asked that Kinsey admit him, "for I thought I had something to say to them which seemed to me of importance."

Kinsey tried to put Churchman off, saying that "it was a critical time, and they had a difficult affair before them." The politician suggested that it might be better to wait until the members were leaving and then the Quaker members could be asked to stay. Another Friend who had arrived said he "thought it would be best, and less liable to give offence, for there were divers members not of our society." But Churchman was not satisfied. "I had a particular desire that those members who were not of our society should be present; believing that it would be better for them to hear and judge for themselves than to have it at second hand, as it might be differently represented." Churchman then directly asked Speaker Kinsey to "go in and inform the members, that a countryman was in waiting who had a desire to be admitted, having something to communicate to them, and if they refused," he would be satisfied. Kinsey did and returned. The legislators were willing.

Churchman found "a great awe over my mind when I went in, which I thought in some measure spread, and prevailed over the members beyond my expectation." While awe spread over some members, perhaps the assembly clerk, Franklin, practiced making arithmetical magic squares and circles. "After a silence of perhaps ten or twelve minutes," Churchman felt as though "all fear of man was taken away, and my mind influenced to address them." He said that if those in authority "would seek unto God . . . for wisdom and counsel to ask singly for him that ordained the power . . . each will be a blessing under God to themselves and their country." But if they allow their "fears and the persuasions of others, to prevail with them to neglect such attention, and so make or enact laws in order to their own protection and defence by carnal weapons and fortifications, . . . he who is superintendant, by withdrawing the arm of his power, may permit those evils they feared to come suddenly upon them, and that in his heavy displeasure." He told the legislators that they had lived in peace and tranquillity for more than fifty years and that though they acted "for a mixed people of various denominations," yet they should not "oppress tender Consciences, for there are many of the Inhabitants whom you now represent, that still hold forth the same religious principles with their predecessors." At the conclusion of his speech, Churchman "acknowledged their kindness in hearing me with so much patience." Several members followed him out and thanked him.[48]

Naturally the clerk of the House, Franklin, made no note in the minutes of Churchman's speech, for the *Votes and Proceedings* were brief, limited to business, and were "corrected" by a committee of the house. Without taking any action, the assembly ignored the plea of the council and adjourned on 11 June, which was probably the day before or the very day that Churchman addressed them. The Pennsylvania Council met on 14 June, passed a series of resolves condemning the House, and said that since most of the House were Quakers and opposed to preparations for defense, "it may be reasonably supposed such an Assembly *are unfavourable* as well as incompetent Judges of the Expediency of any military Undertakings whatever." The council asserted that no one in the future would be induced to volunteer private funds for the support of the province. The council condemned the assembly and the Quakers for chastising its own members who contributed to fitting out the privateer *Warren*: "far from offering to repay" private persons who paid for the defense of the province, "the House has never so much as *thanked* those that by private Subscriptions fitted out a Vessel the last Year to scour our Coast; but instead publickly disapproved their Conduct, in a late former Message to this Board."

Franklin risked his position as clerk when he printed the exchange between the council and the assembly in the *Pennsylvania Gazette* for 16 June, for he knew that the publicity would embarrass and anger the Quaker Party. When Richard Peters wrote the proprietors on 16 June, Peters reported that even William Allen thought the resolves were too strong and disapproved of them. When the assembly next met on 25 August 1748, its members ordered that Franklin "lay before the House the Newspaper, containing certain Resolves of Council lately published, relating to the Proceedings of the House in their last sitting." Implicitly, the House was threatening to fire Franklin as clerk and printer. No doubt Franklin was unrepentant when he laid the offending *Gazette* before the House.[49]

Ready!

Enemy privateers sailed up the Delaware Bay and threatened Newcastle at the
end of May; the New Castle County Associators rushed out; Associator companies from nearby counties hurried to help; and the enemy privateers sailed back
down the river. Franklin used the occasion to praise the Associators. On 9 June,
the *Gazette* lamented that it had not "yet received an account of the Names of
those Companies of Associators who so readily and generously went in from
the Country for the Defence of Newcastle; otherwise it would be inserted." On
23 June, he published the information with an editorial note: "The Following
are the Companies of Associators, who so generously and readily went to the
Assistance of the People of Newcastle, when they were threaten'd by the Enemy's
Privateers, viz. Col. Armstrong's, Lieut. Col. Patterson's, Major M'Crea's, Capt.
Grey's, Capt. M'Mechan's, Captain Bush's, Capt. Crow's, Captain Danford's,
Captain Reese's, and Captain Porter's, all of Newcastle County. And Capt. Clinton's, and many others from Chester County, were also on their March to Newcastle, but on hearing that the Enemy were gone, they return'd home, at the
same time assuring them, that they might depend upon their Assistance on the
least Appearance of Danger. The generous and ready Disposition of the Country
shewn on this Occasion, sufficiently convinces the People of Newcastle, that
there are some Thousands of Men of good Courage, and well armed, always
ready to assist them on the shortest Notice."

Franklin continued propagandizing for the Association with the following
note in the same 23 June paper: "The Associators mount guard every night in
their turns, at the Great Battery, near this city. In case of any alarm in the night
all well disposed persons are desired to place candles in their lower windows
and doors, for the more convenient marching of the militia and other well-
affected persons who may join them." By the late spring of 1748, well-armed
batteries of cannon along the Delaware River protected Philadelphia from invasion by sea, and thousands of organized militia were prepared to come to the
aid of any place needing help.

Franklin served as a private patrolling the Wicaco battery. The first lottery
had been a success, but more cannons and fortifications were desirable. On 2
June 1748, Franklin published a scheme for a second Philadelphia lottery to raise
£9,375 for the Association, which was 12½ percent of the total lottery sale of
£75,000. Though slower than the first, it was successful, having drawings beginning 10 September.

The Coming of Peace

In England by the late spring of 1748, Spain, France, and England were negotiating peace. On 9 June, Thomas Penn wrote Richard Peters about "the prospect
of a speedy peace, Preliminarys having been long since signed on the Foot of
delivering up all places that have been taken during the War." Penn knew that
the news would be welcome in Pennsylvania, though the Americans in general

would be chagrined that France would regain Cape Breton. But considering France's victories in the Netherlands, Penn was surprised that France would consent to peace without adding some part of that land to its kingdom. There were, he said, no further preparations to pursue in Pennsylvania, "unless our Assembly would consent to Erect a Battery, or continue that already made, with about four Men to Attend it, which if they will consent to, it shall be furnished with Cannon when ever they will Apply for them." On Wednesday, 17 August, "In Pursuance of his Majesty's Command, signified to the Honourable the President and Council of this Province . . . his Majesty's Proclamation for a Cessation of Arms was published here."[50]

Despite the official end of fighting, the preparations in Pennsylvania continued, though with lessening vigor. The next day, the *Pennsylvania Gazette* announced that on Monday, 29 August, "a General Review of the City Regiment" would take place "at the usual Place of Parade, at 9 o'clock in the Forenoon; at which time the Artillery Company are to be at their respective Posts, at the GRAND BATTERY." The review took place accordingly, and the 1 September *Gazette* noted that the Associators marched to the "Great Battery . . . where they were saluted with One and Twenty Guns, and nam'd the Battery, The Association." The paper also contained "An Ode, humbly inscribed to the Associators of Pennsylvania" by "Philomusaeus," the Scotch physician Dr. Adam Thomson.[51]

With the signing of the Treaty of Aix-la-Chapelle on 18 October 1748, the War of the Austrian Succession (in America, King George's War) ended. The treaty restored the status quo ante in the colonies, thereby returning Cape Breton/Louisbourg to France. The incredible victory at Cape Breton had been fought for nought. New Englanders and others, like Franklin, who supported the Cape Breton expedition were disgusted with the treaty and Britain. It proved to Americans that Great Britain cared little about the colonies and the colonists. Pennsylvanians learned the preliminary articles of agreement for a general peace from a London proclamation of 4 August, which appeared in the 3 November 1748 *Pennsylvania Gazette*. Finally, on Wednesday, 17 May 1749, peace was proclaimed at Philadelphia: "The Governor & Council, preceded by the Sheriff and his Officers, and attended by the Supreme Judges, Mayor, Alderman, & Common Council of the City of Philadelphia, & a large company of Gentlemen, went in Procession to the Court House & there proclaim'd the Peace." Franklin was no doubt among the gentlemen present on the occasion, but he chafed at the outcome. In a brief Americanized chronology of the history of the world in *Poor Richard* for 1752, Franklin ended with the "Taking of *Cape-Breton*."

FRANKLIN THREATENED

The Association made Franklin temporarily unpopular with many members of the Quaker assembly. It blamed him, not unjustly, for a series of *Pennsylvania Gazette* notices critical of pacifists and the Quaker Party. The Pennsylvania

Council "took me into confidence, & I was consulted by them in every Measure wherein their Concurrence was thought useful to the Association" (A 110). Some Quaker Party members suspected that Franklin was becoming a proprietary supporter. The assembly had ordered Clerk Franklin on 25 August 1748 to bring in the 16 June *Pennsylvania Gazette* containing the Pennsylvania Council's resolves condemning the House. It was then, I believe, that James Read notified him that he had lost his interest in the House.[52] Read, who had "some friends in the House, and wish'd to succeed me as their Clerk, acquainted me that it was decided to displace me at the next Election, and he therefore in good Will advis'd me to resign, as more consistent with my Honour than being turned out."

James Read, who lived next door to Franklin, had, on 20 April 1745, married Susanna Leacock, daughter of John Leacock, a second cousin of Deborah (Read) Franklin. Franklin knew that Read, who had been a rival book-seller, owed considerable money to the London printer William Strahan. At the same time, Read was prosecuting Franklin's friend Robert Grace for a small debt. Franklin considered Read a bit of a blackguard and was irritated with him. Franklin explained to Strahan that he took Read's action "the more amiss," since "the Office could not have been of much Service to him, the Salary being small; but valuable to me; as a Means of securing the Publick Business to our Printing House" (3:377). In the *Autobiography*, Franklin wrote he told Read "that I had read or heard of some Public Man, who made it a Rule never to ask for an Office, and never to refuse one when offer'd to him. I approve, says I, of his Rule, and will practise it with a small Addition; I shall never *ask*, never *refuse*, nor ever *resign* an Office. If they will have my Office of Clerk to dispose of to another, they shall take it from me. I will not by giving it up, lose my Right of some time or other making Reprisals on my Adversaries." Less than two months after the assembly humiliated him, the assemblymen again, on 15 October, chose Franklin its clerk. "Possibly as they dislik'd my late Intimacy with the Members of Council who had join'd the Governors in all the Disputes about military Preparations with which the House had long been harass'd, they might have been pleas'd if I would voluntarily have left them; but they did not care to displace me on Account merely of my Zeal for the Association; and they could not well give another Reason" (A 111).

CONCLUSION

James Logan wrote Thomas Penn on 4 November 1749 that Franklin, by publishing *Plain Truth* and "his further private contrivances, occasioned the raising of ten Companies of near one hund'd men each in Philadelphia and above one hund'd companies in the Province and Counties." Logan said he "set on foot two Lotteries for Erecting of Batteries, purchasing great guns and to dispatch which he went himself to New York and borrowed there 14—which were brought thro' New Jersey by land . . . All this without much appearing in any part of it himself, unless in his going to New York himself in Company with others of whose going he was the occasion, for he is the principal Mover and very Soul of the Whole." Like the Pennsylvania Council, the members of Philadelphia's Common Council had learned to follow the advice and suggestions of Franklin. At their next election, they chose him a member. Though Thomas Penn had opposed the Association, on 21 February 1748/9 he actually seemed to brag to Governor Jonathan Belcher of New Jersey that the French and Spanish privateers would have taken Philadelphia "had it not been for our volunteer Militia."[53] That means, I am sure, that he made at least the same claim to the British authorities.

Franklin had established a reputation as a military expert and achieved fame with most Pennsylvanians. He had been well-known because of his writings and the design of the Pennsylvania fireplace, but the Association gave Franklin a run of popularity. He wrote Cadwallader Colden on 29 September 1748: "I have refus'd engaging further in publick Affairs; The Share I had in the late Association, &c. having given me a little present Run of Popularity, there was a pretty general Intention of chusing me a Representative for the City at the next Election of Assemblymen; but I have desired all my Friends who spoke to me about it, to discourage it, declaring that I should not serve if chosen." Having retired as a printer, Franklin hoped to have the leisure "to read, study, and make Experiments," ideally intending that he might "produce something for the common Benefit of Mankind" (3:318).

The Association succeeded because of Franklin's crafty diplomacy, his literary genius, and his use of the press—especially because of his use of that relatively new but powerful instrument of the press, the newspaper. The Association prefigured the American Revolution, for it was an organized body, existing outside the structure of Great Britain's authority, paying only lip service to that authority. Franklin's resentment of English condescension and his Americanism had appeared earlier but were stronger in his writings for the Association in 1747 and 1748. The themes that appear in the Association writings anticipate those in Franklin's pre-Revolutionary works. Egalitarianism, Americanism, and the good of the whole recur often from 1747 to 1776. As we have seen in Volumes 1 and 2 of *Life*, Americanism was not uncommon in Franklin's writings before *Plain Truth*, but it appears more directly and more frequently afterward. The idea of union, though primarily confined to the union of all classes of people within Pennsylvania and to all parts of the colony, was implicitly against the French and Spanish all along the East Coast of America, and against the French and their Indian allies all along the western frontier. He repeated these undercurrents directly in 1751 and again in 1754. His Americanism became ever stronger for the next twenty-five years—and so did a complementary quality: his resentment and antipathy toward Britain for its treatment of America and Americans.

TWO

Electricity

How many ways there are of kindling fire, or producing heat in bodies! By the sun's rays, by collision, by friction, by hammering, by putrefaction, by fermentation, by mixtures of fluids, by mixtures of solids with fluids, and by electricity. And yet the fire when produced, though in different bodies it may differ in circumstances, as in colour, vehemence, &c. yet in the same bodies is generally the same. Does not this seem to indicate that the fire existed in the body, though in a quiescent state, before it was by any of these means excited, disengaged, and brought forth to action and to view? May it not constitute part, and even a principal part, of the solid substance of bodies? If this should be the case, kindling fire in a body would be nothing more than developing this inflammable principle, and setting it at liberty to act in separating the parts of that body, which then exhibits the appearances of scorching, melting, burning, &c.
—*Franklin to Ebenezer Kinnersley, 29 February 1762, 10:49*

Franklin's Knowledge of Electricity before 1746

Scholars have often said that Franklin was able to make his early and best contributions to electricity because he was not burdened with past theories concerning the subject.[1] The opinion dates back at least to Pieter van Musschenbroek's assumption in 1759 that Franklin had not known and still did not know the work of the European electrical experimenters. Musschenbroek, a Dutch natural philosopher and a key figure in discovering the Leyden jar, hoped that Franklin would "go on entirely on your own initiative and thereby pursue a path entirely different from that of the Europeans, for then you shall certainly find many other things which have been hidden to natural philosophers throughout" the ages (8:329–30). Franklin's friend, the English minister and natural philosopher Joseph Priestley, best known as the discoverer of oxygen, wrote in 1767 that Franklin's "great discoveries were made intirely independent of any in Europe."[2]

Franklin himself is partly responsible for the belief. When he heard in 1770 that a biographical account of the deceased Peter Collinson was in preparation, Franklin wrote Michael Collinson, Peter's son, an appreciation of Collinson's numerous gifts and services to the Library Company of Philadelphia: "he transmitted to the Directors the earliest Accounts of every new European Improvement in Agriculture and the Arts, and every philosophical Discovery: Among which, in 1745, he sent over an Account of the new German Experiments in Electricity, together with a Glass Tube, and some Directions for using it, so as to repeat those Experiments. This was the first Notice I had of this curious Subject, which I afterwards prosecuted with some Diligence, being encouraged by the friendly Reception he gave to the Letters I wrote to him upon it."

Franklin's "small Testimony" to Peter Collinson's memory (17:66) was almost too generous. Collinson sent news of numerous "philosophical" discoveries to the Library Company members but hardly mentioned every one of them. Franklin himself wrote in the *Autobiography* that "Dr. Spence" introduced him to electricity in Boston in 1746 (A 152) but that, too, was too generous to Dr. Archibald Spencer.[3] Collinson was the major single conduit for information concerning natural philosophy to the Philadelphians, and he was more important to Franklin's early scientific publications than anyone else, but neither Spencer nor Collinson really introduced Franklin to the "curious Subject."

HALLER'S "HISTORICAL ACCOUNT OF . . . ELECTRICITY"

In the winter of 1744–45, the Swiss physiologist Albrecht von Haller published an up-to-date summary in French of the history of electricity, which was translated into English in the early spring of 1745. Peter Collinson sent the Library Company a copy together with a present of a glass tube (A 153). Like I. Bernard Cohen and John L. Heilbron, I had supposed in 1964 that Collinson sent the *Gentleman's Magazine* of April 1745, which contained Haller's "An historical account of the wonderful discoveries made in Germany, &c. concerning Electricity."[4] But reviewing Cohen's *Benjamin Franklin's Science* in 1991, I pointed out that what Collinson actually sent was a six-pence pamphlet that came out in March or April, at least several weeks before the *Gentleman's Magazine* for April, which appeared in mid-May. The pamphlet, *Acta Germanica, No. VI, Vol. II*, contained "a large account of electricity, with copper plate representations." The *Gentleman's Magazine* reprinted it without the illustrations. The pamphlet was not mentioned in the Library Company minutes nor recorded in the 1746 *Additions*[5] to the Library Company *Catalogue*, but it, together with Collinson's glass tube, started Franklin and a group of friends on their electrical experiments (*Life* 2:115).

Appreciating Collinson on 8 February 1770, Franklin recalled that with the glass tube, Collinson sent "Directions for using it." Around the same time he sent the present to Franklin and the Library Company, the London Quaker wrote his New York correspondent, Cadwallader Colden, on 30 March 1745 of the "Astonishing" effects of electricity. The mere rubbing of a glass tube could invest a person with "Electric Fire." The person need not be "touched by the Tube but the Subtile Effuvia that Flies from it pervades Every pore and renders him what Wee call Electrified for then Lett him touch Spirits of Wine & the Spark . . . from his finger on the touch will Sett the Spirits In flame." Collinson related others: "I have Seen oyle of Sevil-oriangs—& Camphire Sett on fire &

Gun powder mixt with oyl of Lemmons will take Fire—but what would you say to see Fire come out of a Piece of thick Ice & Sett the Spirits In flame or Electrical Fire drawn through Water & performe the same?"

Most of Collinson's experiments are found in Haller's "account," though he apparently saw some of them performed. I. Bernard Cohen commented that Collinson's letter to Colden was a "close paraphrase" of Haller's article.[6] Since the *Gentleman's Magazine* version of Haller's article did not appear until mid-May, Collinson, writing at the end of March, evidently reflected the pamphlet. When Collinson sent the glass tube and the pamphlet to the Library Company, he no doubt included information similar to that he sent Colden.

THE FRANKLIN/KINNERSLEY LECTURES

Franklin mentioned in the *Autobiography* that he encouraged his friend, "ingenious neighbour," and fellow investigator of electricity, Ebenezer Kinnersley, to give public lectures on the new experiments. Sometime before 10 May 1749, Franklin "drew up for him two Lectures, in which the Experiments were arranged in such Order and accompanied with Explanations, in such Method, as that the foregoing should assist in Comprehending the following." In procedure, Franklin followed Descartes's third maxim in his *Discourse on Method*.[7] I. Bernard Cohen found and printed a copy of "Lecture One" in 1941.[8] He noted that the spelling in the lecture followed Franklin's normal spelling, thus suggesting that the copy was an accurate version of Franklin's draft. Lecture One reveals information about Franklin's knowledge of electricity. The date of the lectures also shows that Franklin had learned about the contemporary English and European advances in electricity earlier than scholars have thought.

It had been assumed that Kinnersley first gave lectures on electricity in 1751, but in 1961 I showed that Kinnersley lectured in Annapolis, Maryland, and advertised a partial syllabus in the *Maryland Gazette* for 10 May 1749.[9] The introduction to Lecture One briefly sketched the history of electricity and referred to several electrical experimenters (the French electrician Charles Dufay and the German Georg Matthias Bose, among others) whom Joseph Priestley in 1767, followed by twentieth-century scholars, supposed Franklin did not know until after 1752. Though only the manuscript of Lecture One survives, the 10 May 1749 advertisement shows that it was the basis of Kinnersley's first lecture; and the printed 10 May 1749 partial syllabus also proves that Lecture Two presented Franklin's theories on the electrification of clouds and on the electrical nature of lightning. He did not send these theories to England until 1750, though he had published a brief summary of them in an engraved comment on the Lewis Evans map of 1749 (*Life* 2:483, fig. 32).

The manuscript of Lecture One is in an unknown hand (not Franklin's or Kinnersley's) and dated 1752, which I. Bernard Cohen interpreted as the date of composition of the Lecture. The manuscript notebook has other jottings in the back concerning electricity that reflect experiments performed after 1750, but the materials in Lecture One appear in Kinnersley's partial syllabus in May 1749. I believe Cohen was correct to judge Lecture One to be an accurate copy of the first of the two lectures that Franklin wrote for Kinnersley, and, as Cohen commented, it shows Franklin "had a thorough knowledge of the history of electricity." But the partial syllabus shows that Franklin and Kinnersley had that knowledge before May 1749 instead of "by 1752."[10]

ELECTRICITY TO 1730

Numerous persons in the early eighteenth century knew the history of electricity. Greek philosophers had observed electrical phenomena in ancient times. The Greek Thales of Miletus (ca. 640–546 B.C.) found that amber, after being rubbed by silk, attracted light bodies like bran, chaff, and so on. Franklin read about amber's surprising qualities in Pliny when he was a boy.[11] A touch of Franklin's whimsy comes out in the Franklin/Kinnersley lecture when Franklin explains that the word *electricity* comes from the Greek word for amber, and that the word for electricity might have been *Ambricity*, as having "the Property of Amber." He continued: "Had this Property been first discover'd in Glass," electricity would be called "*Vitricity* from *Vitrum* the name of Glass . . . for Glass has the same Property to Perfection."[12]

In the seventeenth century, the English natural philosopher William Gilbert (1540–1603) in *De Magnete* (1600) proved that, when rubbed, numerous substances in addition to amber attracted light bodies. In Italy, Niccolò Cabeo (1585–1650) discovered that when light matter touched something that had an electric charge, the matter was repulsed. Cabeo showed that repulsion, as well as attraction, characterized electricity. In the late seventeenth century, the German Otto von Guericke (1602–86) invented a rudimentary electric machine: a sulphur ball about eighteen inches in diameter mounted on a wooden axle that was rubbed by hand. The rubbed ball attracted light objects; for example, a feather would hover above the ball and stay there, always keeping the same side toward the ball while the experimenter walked around it. The ball felt warm and crackled and glowed in the dark. Von Guericke also found that a linen thread would conduct electricity, that is, attached to the ball at one end, it would attract chaff at the other. He published the observation that rubbed amber would attract some electrical materials but repel others. Von Guericke expanded on Cabeo's observation on electrical repulsion and noted amber would attract light objects again after touching a non-electrified object. In 1675, Sir Isaac Newton improved Von Guericke's machine by substituting glass for sulphur.[13]

The early eighteenth-century English experimenter Francis Hauksbee (d. 1713) found that a glass globe emptied of air and turned against his hand by a machine like a large grindstone would glow brightly within so that one could read a book in a dark room. He found that an iron rod hanging from the ceiling by silk ropes would accumulate an electrical charge. Hauksbee also first used a glass tube, about thirty inches long and an inch in diameter, to replace the glass globe. The glass tube became standard. Though less powerful, it was easier to use than the glass globe electrical machine. Hauksbee also described electricity's alternate attraction and repulsion.[14]

Following Hauksbee's experiments, Isaac Newton suggested that most phenomena appearing in the actions of small particles of bodies upon one another were caused by electrical attraction. In the second edition of the *Principia* (1713), Newton said a "certain most subtle spirit," which he later said was electrical in nature, caused the attraction.[15]

Franklin had gained some knowledge of electricity while in London in 1725–26, if not before. At the time, his Boston boyhood acquaintance Isaac Greenwood was assisting Jean Théophilus Desaguliers, the experimenter for the Royal Society of London. Desaguliers's 1725 syllabus for *A Course of Mechanical and Experimental Philosophy* distinguished the law of cohesion from electrical attraction and contained a heading titled "Experiments Relating to Electrical Attraction and Repulsion."[16] We do not know which experiments Desaguliers performed, but he knew the recent research. Whatever public lectures on experimental philosophy Desaguliers gave in 1725 Franklin likely knew.

Franklin addressed his earliest extant letter, 2 June 1725, to the naturalist Hans Sloane, the secretary of the Royal Society. They met, and Sloane showed Franklin "all his Curiosities" (A 44), but it is unlikely that they talked about electricity. It was still regarded as the property of attracting light bodies, but enough different observations about it were being made that the word *electricity* was gradually coming to mean the "*cause* underlying the observed electrical phenomena."[17]

FRANKLIN AND ELECTRICITY, 1732–45

The first books the Library Company of Philadelphia ordered in 1732 included *The Philosophical Transactions of the Royal Society*, which brought the *Transactions* down to 1720.[18] It contained Hauksbee's experiments. There were also books on Newton, chemistry, astronomy, mathematics, geology, and other sciences. By the time the 1741 *Catalogue* appeared, the Library Company had added J. T. Desaguliers, *System of Experimental Philosophy* (1719); Francis Hauksbee, *Physico-Mechanical Experiments* (1719); and Martin Clare, *Motion of Fluids* (1735). Franklin would have read these among other books on natural philosophy before 1741.[19] The English electrician Stephen Gray (d. 1736) experimented with conductivity, finding that wire carried electric currents well but that silk threads did not. He devised the "Dangling Boy" experiment, which became a staple of the scientific lecturers: on 8 April 1730, he suspended a boy by silk ropes, electrified him, and discovered that the human body could be a conductor.[20] More important, he created rudimentary insulated electrical systems by putting objects on glass and on cakes of resin.

As noted earlier (*Life* 2:488–89), Franklin followed the Harvard scientist Isaac Greenwood's career and acted as his agent when he arrived in Philadelphia in 1740. Franklin no doubt attended Greenwood's lectures, which included up-to-date scientific information. Greenwood had published an outline of his 1739 lectures as *An Experimental Course of Mechanical Philosophy,* which concluded with Stephen Gray's "new Discoveries as to Electricity."[21] The Franklin/Kinnersley lecture celebrated Gray's discovery "that Wax, Pitch, Silk & several other things, wou'd stop the Electric Virtue from running off, or dissipating in the Common Mass of Matter." Franklin called it a "single & very small Experiment" that paved the way for numerous ones that followed. After Gray, experimenters learned "to retain & consequently by Addition to encrease the Quantity of the Electric Matter, 'till it became sensible in the Strokes it gave, audible in Snaps or Cracks, & visible in Flame; and having this subtile, flying Fluid now confin'd, and as it were in their Power, they cou'd subject it to infinite Tryals in order to discover its Nature."[22]

Repeating Gray's experiment in France, Charles François de Cisternay Dufay (1698–1739) took the place of the boy. Instead of suspending himself by silk cords, Dufay insulated himself by standing on pitch, electrified himself, and when he reached out to touch a person standing on the floor, "heard a snap, felt a shock, and saw a spark between the end of his hand and the person."[23] Dufay's experiment caused Gray to repeat, confirm, and vary it. He found that a suspended iron bar (a device Hauksbee had used) would conduct electricity as well as a boy—and was easier to experiment with. He also discovered that the shape as well as the substance affected the result. A blunt iron rod gave the same snap and spark, but if it were pointed, it gave a glow when brought near a grounded electric substance. The snap occurred only with a blunt conductor, though the glow also came from a single body at each approach of the tube.[24] Von Guericke's observation that points attracted small objects better than blunt bodies may have inspired Gray's experiments with pointed versus blunt objects, and perhaps gave Franklin's friend Thomas Hopkinson the initial hint for his experiments with pointed conductors. Though Haller discussed Gray's and Dufay's experiments, he did not report the information concerning points, and neither did the 1749 Franklin/Kinnersley lecture.

Dufay theorized in 1733 that two kinds of electricity existed, vitreous and resinous, and that vitreous repelled all other objects charged from glass (which gave a positive charge) but attracted objects charged from resin (which gave a negative charge), whereas resinous electricity repelled all others charged from resin and attracted others charged from glass.[25] Though Joseph Priestley wrote that Franklin and his fellow experimenter Ebenezer Kinnersley were both "wholly unacquainted" with Dufay's contrary electricities of glass and sulphur until after 1752, Haller's 1745 essay discussed vitreous and resinous electricities and commented that "one body of the vitreous assisted the attraction of another which was of the resinous kind."[26] Franklin's humorous remarks about "Ambricity" and "Vitricity" in the Franklin/Kinnersley lecture probably alluded to Dufay's names for the supposedly different kinds of electricity.

In his *Autobiography*, Franklin attributed his introduction to electricity to "Dr. Spence's" lectures, which he attended in Boston (A 152). From Boston, "Spence" (Dr. Archibald Spencer) went to Philadelphia, where Franklin acted as his agent (*Life* 2:489). I. Bernard Cohen found two sets of notes on Spencer's 1744 Philadelphia lectures. No doubt the lectures were the same ones Franklin attended in Boston. Both sets say that "Fire [i.e., electricity] is Diffus'd through all Space, and may be produced from all Bodies." His generalizations about electricity and his performance of Stephen Gray's "Dangling Boy" experiment show that Spencer gave a fairly up-to-date introduction to electricity.

In 1738, Desaguliers introduced the terms *conductor* and *supporter*, that is, objects like silk ribbons, which would support conductors but not conduct electricity well. Then he defined *electrics per se* (conductors) and *non-electrics* ("a Body as cannot be made electrical by any Action upon the Body itself immediately; though it is capable of receiving that Virtue from an *Electrical per se*").[27] Franklin read Desaguliers's revised *Course of Mechanical and Experimental Philosophy* and cited volume 2 (which appeared in April 1744) in his *Account of the New Invented Pennsylvanian Fireplaces,* which appeared late in October 1744 (2:439). Desaguliers's first volume (1734) summarized Hauksbee's contributions on pages 17–21 and Gray's on pages 450–51, including Gray's early use of insulated electrical system in which a man stands on a cake of resin or glass to make experiments. Volume 2 appeared in April 1744 and reprinted Desaguliers's *Dissertation Concerning Electricity* (1742). In 1745 Haller summarized Desaguliers's work and his *Course of Mechanical and Experimental Philosophy*. Haller's report was up to date in electricity, at least through 1742. He included the English electrician Granville Wheler (1701–70), who took Hauksbee's observations on attraction and repulsion further and showed in 1739 that a thread may be attracted or repelled, repelled only, or attracted only according to whether it is insulated, electrified by communication, or grounded.[28]

I conclude that, before 1745, Franklin had a good knowledge of electricity from Greenwood's and Spencer's lectures and experiments, from reading Desaguliers's *Course of Mechanical and Experimental Philosophy* (1734–44), and from the current *Philosophical Transactions of the Royal Society*. He must have known at least selective numbers of the *Transactions* like the one in 1734 containing James Logan's description of Thomas Godfrey's improvement of the quadrant.[29] In the fall of 1747, he reprinted Christopher Middleton's account of Hudson Bay in *Poor Richard* from the *Transactions* for 1743 (3:245 n9). Evidently Franklin began buying the current *Transactions* by 1744; his extant personal file of the *Transactions* extends from 1744 through 1789.[30]

In addition to the *Transactions*, Peter Collinson sent books and other gifts to the Library Company. Though his 1745 gift of a glass tube is well-known, an earlier one, sent in 1742, is usually overlooked. By the ship *Constantine*, Captain Henry Elwes, Collinson sent glass tubes with which Library Company members could repeat the electrical experiments reported in the *Transactions*. On 8 July

1742, the *Pennsylvania Gazette* announced that the *Constantine* had entered inward, and Joseph Breintnall noted on 13 September 1742 that "The Trunk of Books, Glass Tubes &c . . . were come in good order." Glass tubes were both cheaper and easier to pack and ship than an electrical machine. No record exists of Franklin or anyone else in Philadelphia making use of this early gift of electrical apparatus, but the present may have drawn Franklin's attention to the electrical experiments.[31]

Franklin began the study of electricity in 1745 with Collinson's tube and Haller's pamphlet. He repeated the experiments he had seen Spencer and others perform, "and by much Practice acquir'd great Readiness in performing those also which we had an Account of from England, adding a Number of new Ones. I say much Practice, for my House was continually full for some time, with People who came to see these new Wonders. To divide a little this Incumbrance among my Friends, I caused a number of similar Tubes to be blown at our Glass-House, with which they furnish'd themselves, so that we had at length several Performers" (A 153). Franklin had the glass tubes made at Caspar Wistar's glass house in New Jersey.[32] On 25 May 1747, Franklin said that "electricity is so much in vogue" in Philadelphia that more than one hundred such tubes had "been sold within these four months past" (3:134).

FIRST EXPERIMENTS

Franklin's contributions to the theory of electricity began in 1746, when he was forty. As usual, Franklin attempted to impose a method on his undertaking. He kept "Electrical Minutes" in which he recorded the experiments he made, "with memorandums of such as I purposed to make, the reasons for making them, and the observations that arose upon them, from which minutes my letters were afterwards drawn" (5:523–24). Unfortunately, the electrical minutes do not survive. He referred to them in a 28 June 1750 letter to Cadwallader Colden and characterized and quoted from them in a letter to John Lining on 18 March 1755.

The invention of the condenser or capacitor can be attributed to Ewald Jürgen Von Kleist of Kammin in Pomerania (Prussia) in 1745 or, independently and slightly later, to Pieter van Musschenbroek and the lawyer Andreas Cuneaus in Leyden. Musschenbroek showed that when a person held a corked bottle, half filled with water, with a nail or chain going through the cork and into the water, and the nail or chain touched to an electrified prime conductor, it took on an electric charge. The jar became a capacitor (called at first a "condenser") and stored the electric charge. Later, if the person holding the bottle touched the nail, he received an electric shock. In 1746, the Leyden jar electrified the Western world. It was an inexplicable marvel. When Musschenbroek described his experiment, he said, "I've found out so much about electricity that I've reached the point where I understand nothing and can explain nothing."[33] News of the amazing Leyden jar appeared in various English and European newspapers in March 1746 and then in all the most popular English magazines for

March. Since the March issues appeared in mid-April, and since it took about six weeks for the average ocean voyage from London to Philadelphia, Franklin probably learned about the Leyden jar during June 1746.

Because of the power and portability of the Leyden jar, lectures and shows featuring electrical experiments quickly became a fad. The nineteenth-century English scientist Humphrey Davy said that "No single philosophical discovery, ever excited so much popular and scientific attention, as this of the Leyden phial."[34] Experiments appeared in newspapers and magazines from 1746 to 1755. The *London Evening Post* for 30 September 1746 advertised lectures on electricity for one shilling each. During that year, England's most popular magazine, the *Gentleman's Magazine*, carried seven articles about recent electrical discoveries. Perhaps the only important new experiment that it omitted was Georg Matthias Bose's letter describing his method of generating electricity and his experiments, but the letter appeared in both the *London Magazine* and the *Scots Magazine*.[35] The Franklin/Kinnersley lecture called the invention of the Leyden jar "another Capital Experiment on which many others are built." During the year, Franklin became "immersed in Electrical Experiments" (10:310).

Franklin's close friends joined him in the experiments and performed their own. The three most important were the lawyer and judge Thomas Hopkinson, an original Junto member; the silversmith Philip Syng, another Junto member; and, as we have seen, Ebenezer Kinnersley. They helped and spurred on one another. When the botanist John Bartram visited James Logan on 22 February 1746/7, he told Logan of a series of experiments that Franklin had devised, including one where a ball turned "many hours about an Electrified Body." That was probably a version of Gray's feather show but done with a small, light, cork ball. Logan, who kept up with the experiments published in the *Transactions*, wrote Franklin the next day, briefly rehearsed his knowledge of those devised by Francis Hauksbee, Stephen Gray, Gowin Knight, and the Comte de Buffon, and added, "But your own Experiments in my judgment exceed them all" (3:111).

On 6 March 1746/7, John Bartram told Cadwallader Colden about an electrical experiment, probably one that Franklin had performed: "I suppose thee hath allready heard of the Electrical experiments which thay can so efectualy apply to a man as well as to many other objects as to fill him so full of fire that if another man doth but put his finger to the electrified person the fire will fly out & strike that part which approacheth nearest. I take this to be the most Surpriseing Phoenomena that we have met with & is wholy incomprehensible to thy friend."[36] Evidently Franklin and his friends were experimenting with insulated electrical systems, anticipating experiments leading up to those he reported on 25 May 1747.

Before then, on 28 March 1747, Franklin wrote Peter Collinson: "Your kind present of an electric tube, with directions for using it, has put several of us on making electrical experiments, in which we have observed some particular phaenomena that we look upon to be new." Franklin said he would send an account of them, but added, "though possibly they may not be new to you, as among the numbers daily employed in those experiments on your side the water, 'tis probable some one or other has hit on the same observations." Electricity had, he told Collinson, absorbed him: "I never was before engaged in any study that so totally engrossed my attention and my time as this has lately done; for what with making experiments when I can be alone, and repeating them to my Friends and Acquaintance, who, from the novelty of the thing, come continually in crouds to see them, I have, during some months past, had little leisure for any thing else" (3:118–19).

Franklin's first published experiment demonstrated "the wonderful Effect of Points both in *drawing* off and *throwing* off the Electrical Fire" (3:127). He showed that a long, sharp needle would, at six or eight inches away, quietly draw off electricity from an electrified iron shot of three or four inches in diameter, whereas a blunt object would have to be brought within an inch and would draw off the electricity with a spark. Further, if one presented the needle in the dark, a light would appear at the end of the needle from a distance of a foot or more away: "The less sharp the Point, the nearer you must bring it to observe this Light." He also experimented with grounding (as opposed to insulating) the point or needle. "If you take the Blade of the Bodkin out of the wooden Handle, and fix it in a Stick of sealing Wax, and then present it" to the electrified iron shot, "no such Effect follows," because the bodkin/needle was insulated; "but slide one Finger along the Wax till you touch the Blade, and the Ball flies to the Shot immediately" (3:127). The finger would ground the electric charge and allow it to pass.

Though Franklin designed the experiment "drawing off" the electricity, his friend Thomas Hopkinson thought of one for "throwing off" the charge. Franklin also observed that a condenser could not build up an electrical charge if a pointed body were near it, for the charge was continually drawn away by the point (3:128). The leading English electrician, William Watson, made a similar discovery late in 1746,[37] but Franklin and Hopkinson had not heard of it when they made their observations.

The Fundamental Hypothesis

Dufay's theory was standard in 1747. Rubbing glass created vitreous electricity, and rubbing amber created resinous electricity. Franklin, however, hypothesized that "the Electrical Fire was not created by Friction, but collected, being an Element diffused among, and attracted by other Matter, particularly by Water and Metals" (3:130). Franklin's conclusion resulted from a series of experiments. His conjecture applied the atomism of the Greeks to electricity and echoed Lucretius's fundamental encapsulation of that philosophy, *ex nihilo, nihilo est* ("nothing can be created from nothing"). Though atomism was becoming more widely accepted throughout the seventeenth and eighteenth centuries, not all natural philosophers were atomists. Most persons in the eighteenth century believed in spontaneous generation, among them John Needham of the Royal Society and the French intellectuals Buffon and Diderot.[38] Many persons before and after Franklin thought electricity was created from nothing.

William Watson in London and Franklin in Philadelphia followed Stephen Gray and experimented with insulated electrical systems. Both men used wax rather than pitch to isolate the electrified person and both introduced a second person standing on another wax cake. In Watson's experiment, person "A" is electrified, then reaches toward "B," who receives the electricity in a snap. As the process is repeated, the snap diminishes with each repetition. Watson made and reported the experiment but drew no conclusions.[39]

Franklin reported his similar experiments to Collinson on 25 May 1747 using three people. He observed that a person standing on glass or wax could not electrify himself. The rubbed glass tube could not communicate to him any more electricity than it had received from him by rubbing. But if two persons stood on wax, with one rubbing the tube, and the other close enough to draw off the electricity, they would both become electrified. If one touched the other after the operation, a stronger spark occurred between them than if another person, not near them when the electrification was taking place, touched either one. It did not matter if the third person was grounded or was also standing on glass or wax. Further, after the two persons who were charged had touched one another, each had only the normal amount of electricity and there would be no spark when the third person touched either (3:130–31). Since that experiment took three persons, one wonders who the three people were. His son William Franklin and his co-experimenters, Kinnersley, Hopkinson, and Syng, are among the possibilities. Franklin, however, no doubt devised the experiment and probably was the "rubber."

Franklin then attempted "to account for" the experiment. All three persons had originally the same amount of electricity. When the person standing on wax rubbed the tube, he passed some electricity from himself to it. The person standing on wax with his hand near the end of the tube took off some of that electricity from the tube to himself. To a third person, both people standing on wax appear to be electrified because the first person has given part of his electricity to the glass tube, and therefore has less than the normal amount; the second person standing on wax has received part of the first person's electricity from the glass, and therefore has more than the normal amount. Thus either person standing on wax could shock a third person who still had the normal amount of electricity. Further, since the first person has less than the normal amount and the second person more, the shock was greater between them than between either of them and the person having the normal amount. The shocks would restore each person to the usual amount of electricity.

Writing to Peter Collinson on 25 May 1747, Franklin said that his reasoning on the experiments "might well enough be spared" (3:130), but the explanation gave his fundamental thesis. Perhaps Franklin made the experiment and then formulated his theory. I suspect, however, that as Franklin repeated the experiments of Gray, Bose, and others, he began to think that electricity was commonly found throughout matter and devised an experiment to test the hypothesis. Either way, the experiments and the thesis are a good example of the method that Francis Bacon attributed to the bee, as opposed to the ant or the spider: "The men of experiment are like the ant: they only collect and use; the reasoners resemble spiders, who make cobwebs out of their own substance. But the bee takes a middle course; it gathers its material from the flowers of the garden and of the field, but transforms and digests it by a power of its own." That was, said Bacon, "the true business of philosophy," combining experiments with understanding. Without the metaphors, Isaac Newton said the same in characterizing the scientific method when concluding his *Optics*.[40]

The experiment proved Franklin's theory "that the Electrical Fire was not created by Friction, but collected, being an Element diffused among, and attracted by other Matter, particularly by Water and Metals" (3:129–30). The experiment with insulated electrical systems proved that electricity existed in matter. The new hypothesis provided a fundamental insight into the nature of electricity. It was not necessarily two separate kinds of things, either resinous or vitreous. It seemed instead to be one substance with different qualities. The amount of electricity, Franklin claimed, remained the same: "the Equality is never destroyed, the Fire only circulating." The new theory called for new nomenclature: "Hence have arisen some new Terms[41] among us. We say *B* (and other Bodies alike circumstanced) are electrised *positively*; *A negatively*: Or rather *B* is electrised *plus* and *A minus*." He modestly added, "*These Terms* we may use till your Philosophers give us better" (3:131–32). Franklin's theory of electricity applied the law of conservation to electricity. It had elements that could be separated into positive and negative charges, but the amount of electricity remained the same.

The 1923 Nobel Prize winner in physics, Robert Andrews Millikan, said that Franklin's experiment, with its interpretation, "is probably the most fundamental thing ever done in the field of electricity." Franklin's single-fluid theory of electricity was, Millikin stated, the progenitor of the electron theory.[42] The English surgeon Dr. John Freke, like a few others, anticipated Franklin in the theory of the conservation of electrical "matter." He theorized that electricity "cannot arise from any of the Apparatus; because, nothing can send out of it a quantity of matter, but there must be less of that matter remaining." Freke grasped a fundamental idea of electricity. Unfortunately, he seemed not to understand the idea of insulated electrical systems, and his own hypothesis led him astray. His proof that electricity did not come from any apparatus was that "the ball of glass, &c. after every so many experiments, remains undiminished, and as fit for the same use as at first." Freke did not realize that electricity could also be in other materials and in the person who turned the ball. He believed that

electricity was gathered from air. His theory was, at least temporarily, a dead
end.[43]

REMARKS ON FRANKLIN'S THEORY

Less than two weeks after writing Collinson, Franklin addressed Cadwallader
Colden on 5 June 1747, repeating the information that electricity was a real
element or species of matter, not created by friction but collected. He added:
"In this Discovery they were before-hand with us in England; but we had hit on
it before we heard it from them." The statement raises several questions. First,
what did he mean by "this Discovery"? Second, when did Franklin originate the
theory? Third, did the English really precede him in the theory? Finally, was he
able to formulate his new theory because he did not know the current studies
in electricity?

First, "this Discovery" referred to the theory that electricity was not created
but redistributed in electrical experiments. Thus, the Leyden jar had no more
electricity in it after being charged than before. It was only separated, with one
part on the outside of the jar and the other on the inside. Franklin commented,
"When we use the Terms of *Charging* and *Discharging* the Phial, 'tis in Compliance with Custom, and for want of others more suitable: since We are of Opinion, that there is really no more electrical Fire in the Phial, after what is called
it's *charging* than before" (3:354). In his *Sequel to Experiments and Observations
on Electricity* (which appeared in November 1746),[44] William Watson, the chief
English electrician, published his experiment proving "The Impossibility of
Electrising one's self (tho' standing on Wax) by Rubbing the Tube and drawing
the Fire from it: and the Manner of doing it by passing the Tube near a Person,
or Thing standing on the Floor" (3:130). Neither Watson nor the author who
reviewed Watson's *Sequel* in the *Gentleman's Magazine* for November, however,
deduced anything from the experiment. The reviewer merely noted "That glass
tubes and globes have not the electrical power in themselves, for if the machine,
and the man who turns the wheel, are placed on pitch, the power is surprizingly
diminished, and sometimes there is none at all; but if any part of it has communication with the floor or wainscott, by means of a man or a piece of wire, &c.
touching both, the electrical power appears as usual."[45]

Like the reviewer, Watson regarded the experiment with insulated electrical
systems as an interesting one that made advances over those by Georg Matthias
Bose and the rector at Leiden, Jean N. S. Allamand. They gave no interpretation
of the phenomenon. Professor I. Bernard Cohen described Franklin's experiments and observations on the quantity of electricity in the Leyden jar as a
"beautiful example of reasoning" that "provides an illustration of the vast simplicity and superiority of Franklin's form of the theory to Watson's."[46]

Second, when did Franklin devise the theory? He probably received the November issue (published in mid-December) of the *Gentleman's Magazine*, which
reviewed Watson sometime during the week before 17 April 1747, when the *Wil-*

liam Gailey, Captain Henry Harrison, entered Philadelphia. The only previous ship to enter Philadelphia from London that might possibly have carried the November *Gentleman's Magazine* was the ship *Mary*, Captain Bernard Martin, who entered the week before 4 February, but Martin probably left London before the magazine was published. In the 25 May 1747 letter to Collinson, Franklin said, "We had for some Time been of Opinion, that the Electrical Fire was not created by Friction, but collected, being an Element difffused among, and attracted by other Matter" (3:129–30). One indication of "How long" ago it was may be gathered from Franklin's further statement that the Philadelphia group had performed experiments with different persons standing on insulated platforms "some Months before Mr. Watson's ingenious *Sequel* came to hand" (3:130). Collinson sent Watson's *Sequel* to Franklin in March 1747, but Franklin would have read that information in the November 1746 *Gentleman's Magazine* (published in mid-December, so probably in Philadelphia before March) before receiving Watson's booklet. Collinson's March letter is not extant and its exact date is unknown, but since the typical voyage took about six weeks, Franklin could not have had it for more than a few weeks at most before writing Collinson on 25 May. Franklin's hypothesis and his experiments to prove them were clearly the result of a long period of trial and error, no doubt taking months. As noted above, John Bartram wrote Cadwallader Colden about such experiments on 6 March 1746/7. Franklin had probably devised the theory in 1746, but certainly well before April 1747.

Third, did the English really precede him in the theory? No. Watson's experiments with insulated electrical systems were more complicated than previous ones, but he drew no conclusions. Franklin made his experiments before learning of Watson's, they were more thorough than Watson's, and the new theory was entirely Franklin's. He was, typically, overly generous to Watson, both in his 25 May 1747 letter to Collinson and in his 5 June letter to Cadwallader Colden. Finally, he did not make his experiments and conjectures in ignorance of what was going on in England and Europe. The *Gentleman's Magazine* and other popular English magazines of the day featured the new advances in electricity. Any interested person in America could keep up with almost all the important advances merely by reading the popular magazines. By 25 May 1747, Franklin knew Watson's *Sequel* and corrected an error by Watson (3:132).

The terms *vitreous* and *resinous* were well-known, but Franklin coined *plus* and *minus* because they better expressed what he thought happened in creating an excess or deficiency of electric charge. At the same time, he used the terms *electric per se* and *non-electrics* for the next few years. When Cadwallader Colden, however, asked him what was the difference between an electric and a non-electric, Franklin, on 31 October 1751, described the former understanding and the meaning of the terms but said that they should now "be laid aside as improper"; instead, Franklin recommended the words *conductor* and (instead of Desaguliers's term, *suspender*) *non-conductor* (4:203).

Franklin's single-fluid theory asserted that nothing was really created or destroyed; electrification merely rearranged the "Electrical Fire" so that when some things were electrified positively, others were electrified negatively. Normally, matter was in equilibrium. The principle underlying Franklin's new system of electricity was the conservation of matter. Matter could not be created or abrogated; it could merely be changed or rearranged. J. L. Heilbron noted: "Although Franklin did not 'discover' conservation, he was unquestionably the first to exploit the concept fruitfully."[47] To David Rittenhouse in 1788, Franklin said that the "power of man relative to matter seems limited to the separating or mixing the various kinds of it, or changing its form and appearance by different compositions of it; but does not extend to the making or creating new matter, or annihilating the old. . . . We cannot destroy any part of it, or make addition to it."[48]

Concluding the letter to Collinson of 25 May 1747, Franklin related several showmanship experiments that Kinnersley later used in his lectures. Some were new and some merely improvements. He also gave practical suggestions for performing electrical experiments. He filled the Leyden jar with granulated lead rather than water, for the lead was easily warmed and kept the vial warm and dry in damp air. William Watson in his *Sequel* had improved the Leyden jar by coating it with tinfoil. Both Franklin's and Watson's jars eliminated the water inside the jar and the moisture associated with it. Watson's jars weighed less than Franklin's and became standard.

Franklin explained that the Philadelphians rubbed the glass tubes with buckskin, always keeping the same side of the skin to the tube, and they never sullied "the Tube by Handling." Thus, rubbing the tube was done "readily and easily without the least Fatigue, especially if kept in tight Pasteboard Cases, lined with Flannel and fitting close to the Tube." Franklin said he mentioned the method, "because the European Papers on Electricity frequently speak of rubbing the Tube as a fatiguing Exercise." He also described Philip Syng's electrical machine, which was more convenient than the European ones: "Our Spheres are fixt on Iron Axels, which pass thro' them. At one End of the Axis there is a small Handle with which we turn the Sphere like a common Grind-Stone. This we find very commodious; as the Machine takes up but little Room, is portable, and may be enclosed in a tight Box, when not in Use. 'Tis true the Sphere does not turn so swift as when the great Wheel is used; but Swiftness we think of little Importance, since a few Turns will charge the Vial etc. sufficiently" (3:134).

The Leyden Jar Analyzed

Franklin no doubt started using the Leyden jar in 1746. He mentioned the improvement he made but did not give his analysis of the Leyden jar until writing Collinson on 28 July 1747. In the Franklin/Kinnersley lecture, Franklin said that the Leyden jar "has let great Light into this Part of Natural Knowledge."[49] In fact, the Leyden jar was an inexplicable phenomenon to all electricians. Franklin said that in electrifying the jar, "at the same Time that the" inside of the "Bottle &c. is electrised *positively* or *plus*," the outside, or the coating on the outside "of the Bottle is electrised *negatively* or *minus* in exact Proportion, i.e. whatever quantity of Electrical Fire is thrown in at the Top [inside], an equal Quantity goes out at the Bottom [outside]" (3:157). The glass, a non-conductor, separated the two charges and allowed them to build up. Charging the Leyden jar separated positive and negative electricity. Because the glass was a non-conductor, internal communication could not restore the separated positive and negative electricity of the charged jar; only external communication could do so, either from another grounded source or by connecting the inside and outside.

The explanation of how the Leyden jar worked and Franklin's terminology implied that the electric charge might be measurable.[50] "Suppose the common Quantity of Electricity in each Part [of the coating inside and outside] of the Bottle, before the Operation begins is equal to 20; and at every Stroke of the [glass] Tube [connected to the inside coating], suppose a Quantity equal to 1 is thrown in; then, after the first Stroke, the Quantity contained in the Wire and upper Part of the Bottle will be 21, in the Bottle 19. After the second, the upper Part will have 22, the lower 18, and so on, till after 20 strokes the upper Part will have a quantity of Electrical Fire equal to 40, the lower none; and then the Operation ends; for no more can be thrown into the upper Part when no more can be driven out of the lower Part. If you attempt to throw more in, it is spued back thro' the Wire, or flies out in loud Cracks *thro' the sides of the bottle*" (3:157–58).

On 28 July 1747, Franklin reported on experiments to test his hypothesis. In one experiment, a charged Leyden jar was placed on wax with a wire coming up from the outside of the bottom of the jar to about six inches from the wire on the top of the jar. A cork ball was suspended on a silk thread between them. The cork would play back and forth between the wire attached to the outside bottom of the jar and the wire at the top that went down into the inside (see fig. 15a). After the equilibrium was restored, the ball stopped. When the Leyden jar was electrified in the reverse way, the same thing would happen (3:159–60).[51] The experiment proved that in charging a Leyden jar, the inside gained approximately as much as the outside lost (and vice versa). I. Bernard Cohen noted that this was the first experiment in which a circuit was used in such a way that the "electrical 'fire' [i.e., the motion] was manifested by a means other than a spark, shock, or explosion." It began, he wrote, "the evolution of the electric current."[52]

Franklin devised methods to organize his data. In his 28 July 1747 letter, he numbered the theses and then the experiments, thus making the individual theses and experiments easier to cite. Franklin had employed a similar strategy in "An Essay on Paper-Currency, proposing a new Method for fixing its Value" (W 286–90; February 1741) and would do so later in "Observations Concerning the Increase of Mankind" (4:225–34; 1751).

At first, Franklin assumed that the electricity was in the coating (now usually

Figure 6. Charging the Leyden jar, 1746. Jean-Antoine Nollet, Essai sur l'éléctricité des corps (Paris: Guerin, 1746), facing p. 216. The amazing Leyden jar was first announced early in 1746. Later that year, the French electrical experimenter, Jean-Antoine Nollet, published a survey of electricity that included an illustration of charging the jar. On the right, the lady is rubbing the globe of an electric machine. Electric matter moves from the rubbed surface of the globe into a metal bar. The electric charge (a stream of sparks that looks like a short attachment in the illustration) is going into a metal bar suspended by silk ropes (the insulated bar was called a "prime conductor"). At the other end of the prime conductor, a man is holding a Leyden jar at the bottom. Its top has a metal ring hanging on the end of the prime conductor. The metal wire goes down from the metal ring through the cork and into the water, which fills about half of the jar's round bottom portion. The electric machine drives electrical matter ("charges") into the jar via the prime conductor. When the Leyden jar has as much as it can accept, a spark might flash from a corner of the bar.

Only the prime conductor and the inside of the Leyden jar are insulated. The electrical machine is gathering electricity from the floor and indirectly from the earth. The man is standing on the floor and is indirectly connected with the earth, so that he may be considered a grounding wire, a path for the discharge of the accumulated electrical matter to the ground. The jar thus acts as a condenser (its late eighteenth-century name), now (since the early twentieth century) called a capacitor, that is, a device that accumulates and stores an electric charge. Courtesy, Edgar Fahs Smith Collection, University of Pennsylvania Library.

tinfoil) or material in the inside and on the outside of the glass. He tested the hypothesis and found himself wrong. A note to Peter Collinson from 14 August 1747 said that some recent experiments made him doubt the principles he had advanced. He now was "a little diffident of my Hypothesis, and asham'd that I have express'd myself in so positive a manner." The embarrassed Franklin asked Collinson not to "expose those Letters; or if you communicate them to any

Friends, you would at least conceal my Name." He said that his conjectures outran his knowledge: "In going on with these Experiments, how many pretty Systems do we build, which we soon find ourselves oblig'd to destroy!" He concluded by mocking his vanity: "If there is no other Use discover'd of Electricity, this, however, is something considerable, that it may *help to make a vain Man humble*" (3:171).

On 13 July 1747 Franklin reported to the Library Company that he had received a letter from Proprietor Thomas Penn with a "compleat Electrical Apparatus," which he turned over to the Library Company. Penn may not have known that Franklin and others had been performing experiments. Since electrical demonstrations had become popular entertainments, Penn assumed that the Library Company members would be interested. No information exists about what he sent, but a "compleat Electrical Apparatus" probably contained at least one glass tube, a Leyden jar, an insulating stand, and a recent version of an electrical machine.

Cadwallader Colden learned of Penn's present and wrote Franklin on 3 August 1747 that some New York friends heard that Franklin had the whole apparatus. They would like to purchase similar ones "if they can be made at Philadelphia from what you have sent to you." Franklin quickly replied that Philadelphia's artisans could "make the Apparatus." He did not mention that he and his friends had improved the jar and made a more convenient machine. He merely said that he would have them priced and "if you shall conclude to have it done here, I will oversee the Work, and take Care that every Part be done to perfection, as far as the Nature of the Thing admits" (3:157–58, 168). Colden wanted the apparatus, and Franklin replied on 13 August that the charge would not exceed ten or twelve pounds. Caspar Wistar's New Jersey glassworks made the glass parts of the apparatus, and Benjamin Lockley/Loxley, a Philadelphia carpenter who made electrical machines for Lewis Evans in 1751, may have made the wooden parts.[53]

WHEREIN LIES THE ELECTRICITY?

Franklin did not report the results of his further experiments to Collinson for nearly two years. From the fall of 1747 until the summer of 1748, Franklin devoted all his time and energy to the military crisis of King George's War. Though he had retired as a printer at the beginning of 1748, he had numerous other duties, including being postmaster of Philadelphia, comptroller of the post office for North America, and clerk of the Pennsylvania Assembly. He had no time to spare. He remarked to Peter Collinson on 18 October 1748 that he hoped the "approaching peace" would allow the Philadelphians to "resume" their electrical experiments. Further, Franklin never rushed to publish, and the embarrassing mistakes no doubt confirmed that he should delay publication of his experiments. At the same time, he knew that mistakes in conjectures and in the interpretation of experiments were unavoidable—and that even mistaken theories could advance knowledge.

Finally, in a letter to Peter Collinson on 29 April 1749, Franklin described his "ingenious analysis" (Joseph Priestley's appraisal)[54] of the Leyden jar. He placed a charged Leyden jar upon glass, then took out the cork and the wire, and found that the water gave as strong a shock as when the wire was in it. Therefore, the electric force was not in the cork or wire. Again taking up the charged jar, he placed it on glass, drew out the wire and cork again, then decanted the water into an empty bottle, which likewise stood on glass. Taking up that second bottle, he tested it, but it had no charge. The water itself was not electrified. Either the charge was lost in decanting or it remained in the bottle. Filling the same bottle with fresh water, he found it gave a shock. Perhaps, however, the thin coating of moisture remaining in the Leyden jar when the water was poured out might contain the charge (3:356).

To determine whether glass had the property as glass or whether the shape mattered, Franklin took a pane of glass and, laying it on his hand, placed a plate of thin lead on its upper surface. He then electrified the plate and, bringing a finger to it, saw a spark and felt a shock. So the charge was not affected by the shape of the glass but in the use of conductors separated by a non-conductor. Then he found that the size of the plates of lead did not seem to affect the amount of electricity, for small lead plates had the same charge as large ones. Removing the lead from the glass, he found no electricity in the lead. Testing the glass without the lead, he found that "the glass being touched in the electrified Part with a Finger, afforded only very small pricking Sparks, but a great Number of them might be taken from different Places." Then placing the glass back between the plates of lead and completing a circuit between the two surfaces, "a violent Shock ensu'd. Which demonstrated the Power to reside in the Glass as Glass." The lead or non-electrics "served only like the Armature of the Loadstone, to unite the Forces of the several Parts, and bring them at once to any Point desired. It being a Property of a Nonelectric, that the whole Body instantly receives or gives what Electrical Fire is given to or taken from any one of its Parts" (3:356–57). Later, the marquis de Condorcet judged Franklin's analysis of the Leyden jar a "masterpiece at once of sagacity, of perspicuity, and of art."[55]

Franklin made further experiments. Since whatever a Leyden jar takes in at one surface it loses at the other, he tried charging several jars together by connecting the outside of one with the inside of another; the fluid that was driven out of the first would be received by the second, and what was driven out of the second would be received by the third, and so forth. The electrical force increased with the addition of each jar. Since the shape of the glass did not matter, and since flat planes of glass were easier to arrange and would do as well, with one side becoming charged positively and the other negatively, he created what he dubbed "an electrical battery." Electricians spoke of a Leyden bottle as being *charged* and the spark from it being *fired*; Franklin extended the possible cannon allusion to a "electrical battery." His use of the word "fir'd" when he first described the electric battery tends to confirm my hypothesis, as does his "Party of Pleasure," which concluded with the "Discharge of Guns from the Electrical Battery" (3:365). From his coinage, we have today in common usage such words as "flashlight *battery*."[56]

Franklin's electrical battery consisted of "eleven Panes of large Sash Glass, arm'd with thin leaden Plates," coated on each side, "placed vertically, and supported at two Inches Distance on Silk Cords, with Hooks of thick Leaden Wire one from each Side standing upright," connected so that charging one right-hand side would charge them all. Bringing the wire connected to all eleven right-hand sides together with the wire connected with all the left-hand sides created an electric force eleven times more powerful than the force created by one pane.[57] Today, such a arrangement is called eleven capacitors connected in parallel. The charge from his "electric battery" was powerful, for it could make a hole through a quire of paper. That amazed contemporaries, for a quire of paper was "thought good Armour against the Push of a Sword, or even against a Pistol Bullet" (3:357, 359).

Reporting the experiment, Franklin noted that, according to William Watson's most recent book, Dr. Bevis had previously used panes of glass rather than bottles to store electricity. (Franklin later was informed that John Smeaton, another Royal Society electrician, first used panes of glass.) The Philadelphians had not known the earlier experiments when they performed their own, which were different, and from which they "drew different Consequences" (3:358). One conclusion was that the electric charge was not on the coating but on the glass itself. Watson neither repeated the experiment nor accepted Franklin's conclusion.

Franklin described Kinnersley's parlor trick of a magical picture of a king with a "little moveable gilt crown" on his head. If a person (the "traitor") or group of persons (the "conspirators") tried to take off the crown, they could not without receiving a shock. Franklin next reported on his own "electrical Wheel, that turns with considerable Strength," and could be made to serve as an "Electrical Jack" and constantly turn a large fowl over a fire (3:358). (Was this the first chicken/turkey grilled by an electric rotating motor?) He then described a "Selfmoving Wheel, which would run for half an hour," and speculated that the wheels might be applied to the ringing of chimes and moving orreries. Since Kinnersley's 10 May 1749 advertisement included "Eight musical bells rung by an electrified Phial," the 29 April letter must have been composed a considerable time before Kinnersley devised the chimes. In *Experiments and Observations* (1751), Franklin noted that ringing chimes had been since done, and in the revised edition of 1769, he specified that Kinnersley had contrived the method (3:361).

Though Franklin hoped his electrical experiments might lead to something useful to "Mankind," by the spring of 1749 they still had only led to playful gadgets. He closed his long letter of 29 April 1749 to Peter Collinson with a plan for a celebration ending the season: "Chagrin'd a little that We have hitherto been able to discover Nothing in this Way of Use to Mankind, and the hot Weather coming on, when Electrical Experiments are not so agreable; 'tis proposed to put an End to them for this Season somewhat humorously in a Party of Pleasure on the Banks of SchuylKill. Spirits, at the same Time, are to be fired by a Spark sent from Side to Side through the River, without any other conductor than the water; an experiment which we some time since performed, to the amazement of many. A Turky is to be killed for our Dinners by the Electrical Shock; and roasted by the electrical Jack, before a Fire kindled by the Electrified Bottle; when the Healths of all the Famous Electricians in England, Holland, France and Germany, are to be drank in Electrified Bumpers, under the Discharge of Guns from the Electrical Battery" (3:364–65).

I hope they did it.

Three Franklin Students

Before Franklin's disciples began lecturing for pay, several persons gave courses on natural philosophy in America. As noted above, Isaac Greenwood and Dr. Archibald Spencer included electricity in their demonstrations of mechanics and natural philosophy (*Life* 2:488–90). After the invention of the Leyden jar, electrical demonstrations became dramatic, and advertisements for electrical lectures commonly appeared in English and European newspapers. In America, William Claggett, a Newport, Rhode Island, clockmaker, used the Leyden jar in his experiments and by December was able to set fire to spirits of wine with electricity. Early in 1747 Claggett began giving public lectures in Boston. Claggett inspired John Williams and Daniel King, who both lectured on electricity in Boston in 1747. Richard Brickell followed them, giving demonstrations in New York during May 1748. So far as is known, none of them devised any new electrical experiments.[58] Three persons, however, whom Franklin trained, demonstrated the Philadelphia experiments and theories: Samuel Dömjen in 1748, Ebenezer Kinnersley in 1749, and Lewis Evans in 1751.

Samuel Dömjen (fl. 1740–49)

Samuel Dömjen, a Greek Orthodox priest from Transylvania, left home in the early 1740s to travel around the world. After going through Germany, France, and Holland to England, he studied at Oxford for several years. When he sailed to America in 1747, he carried an affidavit from the vice-chancellor of Oxford, Euseby Isham, testifying to his character. He landed in Maryland, sailed to New England, and then journeyed overland to Philadelphia, arriving late in 1747. He stayed until sometime after 22 April 1748.[59] Franklin "taught him the use of the tube; how to charge the Leyden phial, and some other experiments," so that Dömjen could lecture on electricity.

In the spring of 1748, Dömjen toured Maryland, Virginia, and North and South Carolina giving lectures. In Charleston, he advertised his "many wonderful experiments in ELECTRICITY" in the 31 October 1748 *South Carolina Gazette* and promised to "electrise" anyone who pleased.[60] He wrote Franklin from Charleston that "he had lived eight hundred miles upon Electricity, it had been meat, drink, and cloathing to him." His last Charleston advertisement appeared on 26 December 1748, so he probably left there early in 1749. He went on to the West Indies, and Franklin never heard from him again. Dömjen had intended to continue on to South America and from there to the Orient, and so around the world back to Transylvania, presenting lectures on electricity to support himself (5:521–22).

Dömjen no doubt gave the usual 1740s parlor tricks, including those reported by Haller in 1745: Bose's electrical kiss from a lovely lady (which Franklin made more striking in an experiment reported in May 1747 [3:133]); sparks issuing out of cold water; electricity passing through a river; and Stephen Gray's experiment showing that electricity could travel through a long string. He probably also demonstrated the more recent experiments with Leyden jars and John Freke's representation of the sensitive plant, which had appeared in the *Gentleman's Magazine* in October 1746. Finally, he must also have shown the experiments that Franklin and his friends devised in Philadelphia before April 1748: he established that points attracted electricity more strongly than blunt bodies, explained the single-fluid theory, and probably gave the impressive artificial spider demonstration (3:133). In Charleston, Dr. John Lining attended Dömjen's lectures and became interested in electricity. Lining later repeated Franklin's kite experiments and in 1755 asked Franklin about Dömjen. Franklin replied that the last letter from Dömjen "was, I think, from Jamaica," desiring Franklin to send him more electrical apparatus. Since Franklin never heard from him again, he thought Dömjen had probably died (5:522).

Ebenezer Kinnersley (1711–78)

Franklin wrote two lectures on electricity for his co-experimenter Ebenezer Kinnersley before May 1749. Kinnersley "procur'd an elegant Apparatus for the purpose, in which all the little Machines that I had roughly made for myself, were nicely made by Instrument-makers." From 1749 to 1753, Kinnersley lectured on electricity throughout the mainland colonies and West Indies (A 153). In 1753, Franklin arranged for him to become master of the English school at the Philadelphia Academy. Thereafter, when not too busy with teaching, Kinnersley gave lectures in Philadelphia and elsewhere, often devising new experiments and always keeping up with the latest developments. When he retired as a lecturer, his electrical apparatus was considered the best in America and equal to the best in the world.⁶¹

Lewis Evans (ca. 1700–1756)

Evans, a scrivener, surveyor, and mapmaker, worked for Franklin in the post office and as a clerk from at least 1736 until at least 1753. He appeared frequently in Franklin's financial accounts, especially during the early 1740s. The Franklins no doubt attended his marriage to Martha Hoskins at Christ Church on 21 January 1743/4. When their daughter Amelia was christened on 23 November 1744, Deborah Franklin was the godmother. Evans filled in the blank spaces of his 1748 map with Franklin's hypotheses concerning natural philosophy (*Life* 2:483, fig. 32). When Boston's James Bowdoin and a group of his friends visited Philadelphia in late September and early October 1750, they saw Franklin's experiments and Bowdoin asked to buy copies of his electricity letters. Franklin evidently had him hire Evans for that purpose and said he would oversee the copies. On 25 October 1750, Franklin sent Bowdoin the 155-page manuscript, copied by Lewis Evans and illustrated with his wash drawings of Franklin's sketches (4:117).

Evans advertised a course of thirteen lectures on "Natural Philosophy and Mechanics, Illustrated by Experiments" in James Parker's *New York Gazette* on 29 July 1751. Evans gave the lectures at the home of the Reverend Ebenezer Pemberton, Franklin's childhood companion and his main opponent in the 1735 trial of the Reverend Samuel Hemphill. Franklin may have recommended Evans to Parker, Pemberton, and Colden, though Evans already knew Parker and Colden. The lectures included electricity. The advertisement said: "The Properties of . . . the Electrical Fluid . . . are explained by the Help of the best Machines and Instruments."

Evans presented Franklin's electrical theories, explaining "the Nature of Attraction and Repulsion, and of the several other grand phenomena beyond any Thing heretofore imagined." After performing in New York, he went to New Jersey and lectured at the College of New Jersey in Newark. On 11 September 1751, Edward Shippen, Philadelphia's former mayor, wrote his son Joseph Shippen, a student at the college (it moved from Newark to Princeton in 1756), that he was "glad to hear that Mr. Evans exceeds our Expectations; to be sure he took a vast deal of Pains to qualify himself for the business; and he had a daily Instruction for 6 Weeks before he set off, of Mr. Franklin, whom we account one of our Solomons."⁶² Evans spent the following winter lecturing in the South. By February 1752 he was in Charleston, South Carolina, advertising on 2 March and 20 April 1752 in the *South Carolina Gazette*.⁶³

Franklin repeatedly sponsored Evans. On 24 December 1753, Franklin had him paid for engrossing the articles for the Philadelphia Contributionship (the insurance company Franklin founded). In 1754, Evans returned to mapmaking, producing a *General Map of the Middle British Colonies* (1755), and joined

Thomas Pownall and Benjamin Franklin in planning a settlement on the Ohio. Franklin and Hall printed his *Geographical . . . Essays* (1755) and *Geographical Essays, No. II* (1756). Like his 1749 *Map of Pennsilvania, New Jersey, and New York*, Evans's *Geographical . . . Essays* reflected Franklin's facts and hypotheses (*Life* 2:481–87) (I will point out other echoes of Franklin in Evans's *Essays* (below, p. 260) when considering the influence of Franklin's "Observations Concerning the Increase of Mankind").

LIGHTNING AND ELECTRICITY

Early electricians frequently noted similarities between the small sparks of electricity and lightning. Francis Hauksbee in 1705 compared electrical sparks to "Flashes of Lightning."[64] In 1708 Dr. Samuel Wall thought the electric spark was like lightning and the noise it made resembled thunder. Stephen Gray also thought so in 1735.[65] In 1745 Albrecht von Haller gathered together a number of the earlier comments on lightning. Noting Gray's observation that electricity could be conducted by a cord, Haller asked, "Could it have been thought that the virtue, or current of the electric matter, so moveable and incapable of rest, could so tenaciously adhere to the silken cord, and not be dissipated, and lost in air?" He then shrewdly commented: "Lightening has pretty much the same qualities, for it generally runs over the whole length of the solid bodies which it strikes, and it has been seen to descend along the wire of a steeple-clock from top to bottom, and the threads of the wire have been found at the bottom of the steeple, melted into thousands of small bits." Haller continued, "This is not the only property which lightening has in common with electricity." Then, speaking of Hauksbee's experiments, Haller repeated that electricity produced flame and light, "in both respects resembling lightening."[66]

The *Pennsylvania Gazette* often featured accounts of lightning, not only reporting terrible storms at sea and on land but also giving news accounts of persons being struck by lightning. In the 10 July 1732 *Gazette*, Franklin wrote a detailed account of the result of lightning striking a house in Allentown (1:275). His first letter to Collinson (25 May 1747) on electrical experiments and theories incidentally noted the analogy of the electric spark with lightning: "We electrify upon Wax, in the Dark, a Book that has a double Line of Gold round upon the Covers, and then apply a Knuckle to the Gilding; the Fire appears every where upon the Gold like a Flash of Lightning" (3:134–35).

By the fall of 1748, Franklin theorized that clouds had electric charges. He wrote: "Thunder never happens, but with the Meeting of Sea and Land Clouds. The Sea Clouds coming freighted with Electricity, and meeting others less so, the Equilibrium is restored by Snaps of Lightning: and the more opposite the Winds, and the larger and compacter the Clouds, the more dreadful are the shocks." He first published the conjecture in Lewis Evans, *The Map of Pennsilvania, New Jersey, and New York* (1749), along with his thoughts on geology and on the course of hurricanes. What may be most striking about Franklin's hypothesis concerning atmospheric electricity is that it was so clearly a theory. Franklin was able to make his fundamental advances in electricity because of his imaginative attempts to account for facts that he, like everyone else, did not understand. He tried to find an explanation. Some theories were wrong, but he had to have a hypothesis before he could think of a way to test it.

On 29 April 1749, writing his "Observations and Suppositions towards form- ing a new Hypothesis for explaining the several Phaenomena of Thunder Gusts," Franklin conjectured that clouds were electrified and that lightning re- sulted from differently charged clouds either striking into one another or into the earth. He speculated that "As electrified Clouds pass over a Country, high Hills and high Trees, lofty Towers, Spires, Masts of Ships, Chimneys &c. as so many Prominences and Points, draw the Electrical Fire, and the whole Cloud discharges there" (3:374). Among Franklin's electrical papers, this one is un- usual, for it contains only a few experiments attempting to prove the hypotheses. That may be because Franklin originally addressed the letter to Kinnersley (A 153), who knew Franklin's experiments.

In the lecture Franklin drafted for Kinnersley at about the time (March 1749?) he wrote "Observations and Suppositions," he proposed an experiment to test his hypothesis that clouds might be electrified. Though "Water is reck- on'd a mortal Foe to Fire of all kinds," the "Electric Fire subsists in it without the least Inconvenience." One could draw sparks from water, and one could ignite alcohol and other substances from electricity drawn from water. The Franklin/Kinnersley lecture continued: "If the Fire of Lightning be of the same kind, we may cease to wonder at its subsisting in Clouds tho' loaden with Show- ers of Hail or Rain."[67]

Franklin conjectured that if an electrified cloud coming from the sea met a cloud "raised from the Land, and therefore not electrified, the first will flash it's Fire into the latter, and thereby both Clouds shall be made suddenly to deposit Water." Franklin's experiment tending to prove the theory began with two round pieces of pasteboard, two inches in diameter. Then, "from the Center and Circumference of each of them, suspend by fine silk Threads, 18 Inches long, 7 small Balls of Wood (or 7 Peas)" of the same size. The balls appended to each pasteboard will form "equal equilateral Triangles, one Ball being in the Center, and six at equal Distances from that and from each other; and thus they represent Particles of Air. Dip both Sets in Water, and some cohering to each Ball, they will represent Air loaded. Dextrously electrify one Sett, and it's Balls will repel each other to a greater Distance, enlarging the Triangles. Could the Water, supported by the seven Balls, come into Contact, 'twould form a Drop or Drops so heavy as to break the Cohesion it had with the Balls, and so fall" (3:370–71).

Then Franklin compared the experiment with thunderstorms. Let two sets of balls represent clouds, the one "a Sea Cloud electrified, the other a Land Cloud." When the balls are brought "within the Sphere of Attraction," they will fly toward each other and the separate balls will join together. "The first electrified Ball that comes near an unelectrified Ball by Attraction, joyns it, and gives it Fire." Instantly they separate, "and each flies to another Ball of it's own Party, one to give and the other to receive Fire, and so it proceeds thro both Sets, but so quick as to be in a Manner instantaneous. In the Collision they shake off and drop their Water which represents Rain" (3:371).

The microcosmic experiment seemed to illustrate Franklin's theory, but no one could be certain that the macrocosm would behave similarly. Franklin said that when a prime conductor had just a little electric fire in it, "you must approach it very near with your knuckle, before you can draw a Spark." If the conductor has more electricity, it will give a spark at a greater distance and make a loud snap." But "to what a great Distance may 10,000 Acres of Electrified Cloud strike and give its Fire, and how loud must be that Crack!" (3:372).

The most striking topic in Kinnersley's *Maryland Gazette* advertisement of 10 May 1749 (only twelve days after Franklin wrote "Observations") is in Lecture Two: "Various Representations of LIGHTNING, the Cause and Effects of which will be explained by a more probable Hypothesis than has hitherto appeared; and some useful Instructions given how to avoid the Danger of it." Could the "useful Instructions given how to avoid the Danger of" lightning in Kinnersley's lecture refer to the use of lightning rods? Probably not, though the notice of Franklin's *Experiments and Observations on Electricity* in the April 1751 *Gentleman's Magazine* evidently assumed so.[68] The "useful Instructions" were more likely the ones Franklin mentioned in his 29 April 1749 letter. Since high hills, high trees, lofty towers, spires, masts of ships, chimneys, and other high objects all tended to attract the electric fire, it was especially dangerous to take shelter under a lone tree in a meadow; it would attract lightning. It was much better to stand in the open and become wet. In 2005 E. Philip Krider, an authority on atmospheric electricity, wrote that Franklin's advice for attempting to avoid lightning "is still valid."[69] Water was so good a conductor that if one were wet, lightning might run over the water to the ground without harming the person struck, whereas if one were dry, there was a much greater chance of being seriously hurt. Evidently Franklin tested the theory: "Hence a wet Rat can not be kill'd by the exploding Electrical Bottle, when a dry Rat may" (3:374).

The experiments and hypotheses contained in the electrical letters must have been made over a period of more than six months before 29 April. Why then would Franklin address "Observations and Suppositions" to Kinnersley, his neighbor who made experiments with him? Franklin probably expected the letter to be published and addressed it to him as a compliment. Since the reasoning about the electrification of clouds is the same as in the engraving on Lewis Evans's map, Franklin evidently made these hypotheses and experiments before October 1748, when the Evans map was in "great forwardness." Further, the "new Hypothesis" written for Kinnersley on 29 April 1749[70] was one of two long letters on electricity of that date. The other, to Peter Collinson (3:352–65), re-

By a Number of Experiments, lately made in Philadelphia, *several of the principal Properties of the Electrical* Fire *were demonstrated, and its effects shewn.*

1. THAT it is a real *Element,* intimately united with all other matter, from whence it is *collected* by the tube, or sphere, and not *created* by the friction. 2. That tho' it will fire inflammable bodies, itself has no sensible heat. 3. That it doth not, like common matter, take up any perceptible time in passing thro' great portions of space. 4. That bodies replete with this fire strongly attract such as have less of it, and repel such as have an equal quantity. 5. That it will live in water, a river not being sufficient to quench the smallest spark of it. 6. That, contrary to other matter, it is more strongly attracted by slender sharp points, than by solid blunt bodies, &c. *Also among other curious particulars were shewn,* 1 A representation of the sensitive plant. 2. A small globe to revolve round a larger, as the earth does round the sun. 3. A representation of the seven planets, shewing a probable cause of their keeping at a distance. 4. An artificial spider, animated by electrical fire, to act like a living one, and endeavour to catch at a fly. 5. A leaf of the most weighty of metals, is suspended in the air, as is said of *Mahomet*'s tomb. 6. A perpetual shower of sand, which rises again as fast as it falls. 7. Various representations of *Lightning,* the cause and effects of which were explain'd by a more probable hypothesis than has hitherto appeared; and some useful instructions given how to avoid the danger of it. 8. The force of the electrical spark, making a fair hole thro' a quire of paper. 9. Small animals kill'd by it instantaneously, &c. &c.

Figure 7. Ebenezer Kinnersley's advertisement of Franklin's electrical theories. Gentleman's Magazine, *January 1750. Ebenezer Kinnersley was Franklin's friend and neighbor who assisted him in electrical experiments. Franklin encouraged him to give public lectures on electricity and drew up a syllabus. Kinnersley made highly successful lecture tours in the colonies beginning in the spring of 1749. The* Gentleman's Magazine *for January 1749/50 reprinted one of his advertisements. Its heading is similar and the content identical to Kinnersley's* Maryland Gazette *advertisement of 10 May 1749.*

When it originally appeared, the advertisement contained the earliest detailed explanations of what caused lightning and gave advice on how to avoid being struck by it (#6 in the first numbering and especially #7 in the second). Kinnersley knew all the experiments and hypotheses in the two documents that Franklin dated 29 April 1749: "Further Experiments and Observations in Electricity" (3:352–65) and "Observations and Suppositions towards forming a new Hypothesis for explaining the several Phaenomena of Thunder Gusts" (3:365–76).

Franklin's 1749 theories in the latter amplified the statements on atmospheric electricity that he had written in 1748 and published in the Lewis Evans map before 29 February 1749 (Life 2:483, fig. 32). Dr. John Mitchell submitted Franklin's "Observations and Suppositions" to the Royal Society, where it was read but "laught at by the Connoisseurs" (A 153).

When Edward Cave, the Gentleman's Magazine's *editor, reprinted Kinnersley's advertisement, he probably did not know that it had anything to do with Franklin. Since the notice appeared in both the* Gentleman's Magazine *and in the* Scots Magazine *in January 1750, the two magazines likely took it from some British newspaper of January. When he published Franklin's* Experiments and Observations *fifteen months later (April 1751), Cave recalled the advertisement and mentioned it in the publication announcement. Instead of featuring the novelty of Franklin's proposed experiment to prove that lightning was electrical, Cave implied that the* Experiments and Observations *merely repeated materials like this advertisement that had appeared earlier. Perhaps Cave wanted to deemphasize Franklin's lightning rod suggestion because he knew that the Royal Society experts considered the idea implausible. Courtesy, Library Company of Philadelphia.*

ported experiments that Franklin had made in 1748 (P 3:352). Merely to copy these two long letters would have taken nearly a day, and he wrote a third letter the same day (3:377–79).

Before late 1749, Franklin was fairly sure that clouds were electrified and that lightning was an electrical phenomenon. On 7 November 1749, he listed twelve similarities between electricity and lightning. All of them were well-known by electricians. He jotted them down in his electrical minutes: "1. Giving light. 2. Colour of the light. 3. Crooked direction. 4. Swift motion. 5. Being conducted by metals. 6. Crack or noise on exploding. 7. Subsisting in water or ice. 8. Rending bodies it passes through. 9. Destroying animals. 10. Melting metals. 11. Firing inflammable substances. 12. Sulphureous [i.e., ozone] smell." Franklin stated in conclusion: "The electric fluid is attracted by points. We do not know whether this property is in lightning. But since they agree in all the particulars wherein we can already compare them, is it not probably they agree likewise in this?" Then he added the key proposition: "Let the experiment be made!" (5:524).

The theory was complete; but how could it be tested?

THE LIGHTNING ROD

Within four months, Franklin thought of lightning rods. Writing Peter Collinson on 2 March 1750, Franklin said that "houses, ships, and even towns and churches may be effectually secured from the stroke of lightening by pointed rods erected on their highest points." He thought that "Electrical fire would . . . be drawn out of a cloud silently, before it could come near enough to strike," and then he broke off. The idea would surprise Collinson, so Franklin added: "This may seem whimsical, but let it pass for the present, until I send the experiments at large" (3:472–73). A month before Franklin wrote this letter, Collinson informed him on 5 February 1749/50 that he was "collecting all" Franklin's "tracts" on electricity "to putt them into some printers Hand to be communicated to the publick" (3:460).

Slightly over a year later, on 27 March 1751, Collinson wrote that Edward Cave, the publisher of the *Gentleman's Magazine*, had "been ready for some time past" to issue the pamphlet and "only wants the small Engraving of the Instruments" (3:460, 4:122).

Some students have suggested that Franklin had not at this date thought it necessary that the rods should be grounded, but when he first suggested lightning rods, their primary purpose was not to draw electricity to an insulated stand but to draw it out of the clouds before lightning would strike.[71] To do so, the rods would have to be grounded, just as they would if lightning did strike. The longer statement in Franklin's 29 July 1750 "Opinions and Conjectures" specified that the rod should go "down into the Ground" (4:19). The brief 2 March 1750 letter to Collinson proposing lightning rods was printed in the *Gentleman's Magazine* for May 1750, which appeared about mid-June. It contained

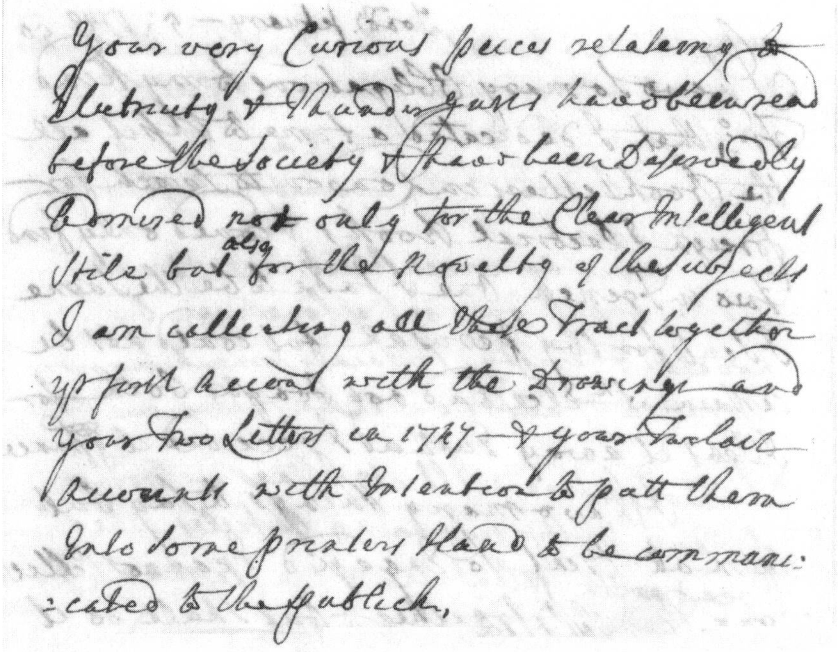
Your very Curious peices relateing to
Electricity & Thunder gusts have been read
before the Society & have been Deservedly
Admired not only for the Clear Intelligent
Stile but also for the Novelty of the Subjects
I am collecting all these Tracts together
yr first Accot with the Drawings and
your Two Letters in 1747—& your Two last
Accounts with Intention to putt them
Into some printers Hand to be communi:
:cated to the publick,

Figure 8a. Peter Collinson to Franklin, 5 February 1749/50, announcing his intention to publish Franklin's electrical experiments. Collinson, a wealthy Quaker merchant, botanist, and member of the Royal Society, wrote Franklin that his "very Curious peices" had been read at the Royal Society and were "Deservedly Admired" for their style and subject matter. However, he knew they had been slighted by not being printed in the Philosophical Transactions of the Royal Society. *Consequently, Collinson decided to publish them himself: "I am collecting all these Tracts together: your first Account with the Drawings and your Two Letters in 1747—and your Two last Accounts with Intention to putt them into some printers Hand to be communicated to the publick." Courtesy, American Philosophical Society.*

the earliest public suggestion of lightning rods, but Franklin's name was not mentioned. The author was "A Gentleman in America." In a note the editor mentioned that the "ingenious Letters" of the author would soon be published as a pamphlet. Collinson wrote Franklin on 25 April 1750 that Dr. John Fothergill, another intellectual London Quaker, had joined him in printing Franklin's letters, "which are now under the Press under the Inspection and Correction of our Learned and Ingenious Friend Doctor Fothergill for Wee thought it a great Pitty that the Publick should be deprived the benefit of so many Curious Experiments" (3:476).

Franklin's name finally appeared in the December 1750 *Gentleman's Magazine* in a note. Editor Edward Cave, giving an account of some electrical experi-

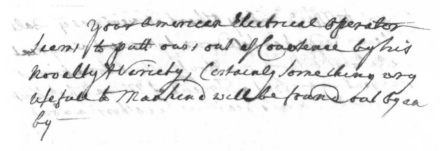

Figure 8b. In the same letter, Collinson revealed his pique at the English electricians. "Your American Electrical Operator seems to putt ours out of Countenance by his Novelty and Variety. Certainly something very usefull to Mankind will be found out by an by" (3:460). After reading Collinson's news and intentions, Franklin evidently resolved to gather together his various thoughts on electricity into a coherent whole titled "Opinions and Conjectures concerning the Properties and Effects of the Electrical Matter," 29 July 1750 (4:9–34). He must have hoped that Collinson would receive the comprehensive statement in time (as he did) to publish it with his earlier letters. Courtesy, American Philosophical Society.

ments now "in the press," mentioned that a certain "B. Franklin" had made a hole through a quire of paper with electricity. The note was, in effect, an advertisement for Franklin's forthcoming pamphlet.[72]

After receiving Collinson's letter of 5 February and probably that of 25 April telling him of the forthcoming publication of his collected letters on electricity, Franklin wrote "Opinions and Conjectures concerning the Properties and Effects of the Electrical Matter, arising from Experiments and Observations made in Philadelphia, 1749," as a capstone for the earlier communications. He began "Opinions" on 29 July 1750 by saying that electricity passes through common matter, and immediately added an ironic note: "If any one should doubt" whether electricity passes through bodies, "a Shock from an electrified large Glass Jar, taken thro' his own Body, will probably convince him" (4:10). One might see in Franklin's ironic remark a humorous version of Kant's grandiose battle cry of the Enlightenment—"Sapara aude!" (Dare to know!).[73] Franklin theorized that points attract and discharge electricity more easily than blunt objects: "the Force with which the electrified Body retains it's Atmosphere, by attracting it, is proportioned to the Surface over which the Particles are plac'd; i.e., four square Inches of that Surface retain their Atmosphere with 4 times the Force, that one square Inch retains it's Atmosphere." (Franklin's early idea of an "electrical atmosphere" was the immediate area around an electrified object that contained the electrical "effluvia.") Then he came up with one of those wonderful analogies that are absolutely simple but seemingly convincing: "as in Plucking the Hairs from the Horse's Tail, a Degree of Strength, insufficient to pull away a Handful at once, could yet easily strip it Hair by Hair, so a blunt

A curious Remark on ELECTRICITY; *from a Gentleman in* America ; *whose ingenious Letters on this Subject will soon be published in a separate Pamphlet, illustrated with Cuts.*

Extract of a Letter to Mr P. C. F. R. S.

I Was very much pleased with some ingenious papers in the late *Transactions* on the subject of electricity.

There is something however in the experiments of points, sending off, or drawing on, the electrical fire, which has not been fully explained, and which I intend to supply in my next. For the doctrine of *points* is very curious, and the effects of them truly wonderfull; and, from what I have observed on experiments, I am of opinion, that houses, ships, and even towns and churches may be effectually secured from the stroke of lightening by their means; for if, instead of the round balls of wood or metal, which are commonly placed on the tops of the weather-cocks, vanes or spindles of churches, spires, or masts, there should be put a rod of iron 8 or 10 feet in length, sharpen'd gradually to a point like a needle, and gilt to prevent rusting, or divided into a number of points, which would be better——the electrical fire would, I think, be drawn out of a cloud silently, before it could come near enough to strike; only a light would be seen at the point, like the sailors * corpu ante. This may seem whimsical, but let it pass for the present, until I send the experiments at large.†

Figure 9. Franklin proposes lightning rods, 2 March 1750: "A Curious Remark on Electricity," Gentleman's Magazine 20 *(May 1750): 208. Franklin's letter of 2 March 1750 to Collinson (3:472–73) contained his first published suggestion that lightning rods could protect buildings and ships. Although Franklin had conjectured, both in the Lewis Evans map of 1748/9 and in his "Experiments" of 29 April 1749, that electricity existed in the atmosphere, he had not previously suggested that lightning could either be prevented from striking or that, if it struck, it could be carried safely from the top of a structure into the ground (or sea). He does not specify grounding here, though I agree with I. Bernard Cohen that grounding is obviously implied. Only later did he think of collecting atmospheric electricity to test its charge. The "Gentleman in America" is anonymous, but contemporary electricians knew it was Franklin. His name did not appear in the* Gentleman's Magazine *until the end of 1750, and then in a footnote. Franklin incorporated a revised version of this letter into "Opinions and Conjectures concerning the Properties and Effects of the Electrical Matter," 29 July 1750 (4:19) immediately before he proposed the sentry box experiment to test the theory (see fig. 11). Courtesy, Library Company of Philadelphia.*

Body presented, cannot draw off a Number of Particles at once; but a pointed one, with no greater Force, takes them away easily, Particle by Particle" (4:16).

J. L. Heilbron, however, pointed out that Franklin "confused force and pressure in his analogy."[74] Shortly after his explanation and analogy of "the Power and Operation of Points," Franklin wrote that when he first theorized about them, his conjectures "appear'd perfectly satisfactory," but after writing the explanations, "I must own, I have some Doubts about them. Yet as I have at present Nothing better to offer in their Stead, I do not cross them out: for even a bad Solution read, and it's Faults discovered, has often given Rise to a good one in the Mind of an ingenious Reader" (4:17). Thus he asked future students to supply better explanations.

In his 29 July "Opinions," Franklin speculated that the "Power of Points may possibly be of some Use to Mankind, tho' we should never be able to explain it." The following experiment proved that miniature lightning rods worked: he made a tube of pasteboard nearly ten feet long and a foot in diameter and covered it with "Dutch embossed Paper almost totally gilt." It could collect "a much greater electrical Atmosphere than a Rod of Iron of 50 Times the Weight would do." He suspended the prime conductor on silk lines. "Let a Person standing on the Floor, present the Point of a Needle, at 12 or more Inches Distance from it; and while the Needle is so presented, the Conductor cannot be charg'd; the Point drawing off the Fire as fast as it is thrown on by the Electrifying Globe." If one charges the tube first and then presents "the Point at the same Distance," the tube "will suddenly be discharg'd." When done in the dark, "you see a Light on the Point" at the discharge. "If the Person, holding the Point, stands upon Wax, he will be electrified by receiving the Fire at 12 or more inches" from the tube. But if one attempts to "draw off the Electricity with a blunt Body," it must be brought within a distance of about two inches before the tube will discharge, which is accompanied by "a Stroke and Crack" (4:17–18).

Franklin created a miniature version of the action between an electrified cloud and a lightning rod: Hang "a Pair of large Brass scales" by silk cords from a beam of two or more feet. "Suspend the Beam" by a twisted "Packthread from the Cieling, so that the Bottom of the Scales may be about a Foot from the Floor. The Scales will move round in a Circle by the Untwisting of the Packthread." Set a blunt "Iron Punch on End upon the Floor, in such a Place, as that the Scales may pass over it, in making their Circle; then Electrify one Scale." As the scales move round, the electrified scale dips toward the iron punch when passing over it. When it comes close, the electrified "Scale will snap and discharge" its electricity into the iron punch. "But if a Needle be stuck on the End of the Punch," instead of the scale "drawing nigh to the Punch and snapping," it silently discharges its electricity "thro' the Point." Even if "the Needle be plac'd upon the Floor, near the Punch, it's Point upwards, the End of the Punch tho' so much higher than the Needle, will not attract the Scale and receive it's Fire, for the

Needle will get it and convey it away, before it comes nigh enough for the Punch to act" (4:18).

If electricity and lightning were the same, the pasteboard tube and the scales "may represent electrified Clouds. If a Tube only 10 Foot long, will strike and discharge it's Fire on the Punch at 2 or 3 Inches Distance; an electrified Cloud of perhaps 10,000 Acres may strike and discharge on the Earth at a proportionably greater Distance." The horizontal motion of the scales over the floor could represent the motion of the clouds over the earth, and the erect iron punch a hill or high building, "then we see how electrified Clouds passing over Hills or high Buildings, at too great a Height to strike, may be attracted lower till within their striking Distance." A needle fixed on the punch, with its point upright, or even on the floor, below the punch, will draw the fire from the scale silently at a much greater space than the striking distance and so prevent its descending toward the punch. Franklin speculated that an iron rod fixed on top of a building would do the same (4:18–19).

Franklin asked, "may not the Knowledge of this Power of Points be of Use to Mankind; in preserving Houses, Churches, Ships &c. from the Stroke of Lightning; by Directing us to fix on the highest Parts of those Edifices upright Rods of Iron, made sharp as a Needle and gilt to prevent Rusting, and from the Foot of those Rods a Wire down the outside of the Building into the Ground; or down round one of the Shrouds of a Ship and down her Side, till it reach'd the Water? Would not these pointed Rods probably draw the Electrical Fire silently out of a Cloud before it came nigh enough to strike, and thereby secure us from that most sudden and terrible Mischief!" (4:19). The primary idea was to conduct electricity safely into the ground (or the water) before it struck as lightning.

Another miniature way of demonstrating the effectiveness of lightning rods probably occurred to Franklin sometime later in 1750. He designed little houses and steeples with removable lightning rods.[75] Giving a house or steeple that did not have a lightning rod a strong electric shock, the house would burst apart, and if there were a bit of gunpowder within it, the electricity would ignite it. But if the house contained a grounded lightning rod, it would safely carry off the electric charge.

Kinnersley used such dollhouses in his lectures by the spring of 1751: to his earlier topics in his lectures on electricity, the *Pennsylvania Gazette* advertisement of 11 April 1751 added, "How to secure Houses, Ships, &c. from being hurt by its destructive Violence."

TESTING THE THEORY

When Franklin sent Cadwallader Colden a copy of his 29 April 1749 "Essay towards a new Hypothesis of the Cause and Effects of Lightning, &c.," he mentioned that Colden had seen "some Hints" of the essay "in my first Electrical Minutes." They are not extant. Had he briefly speculated on the identity of

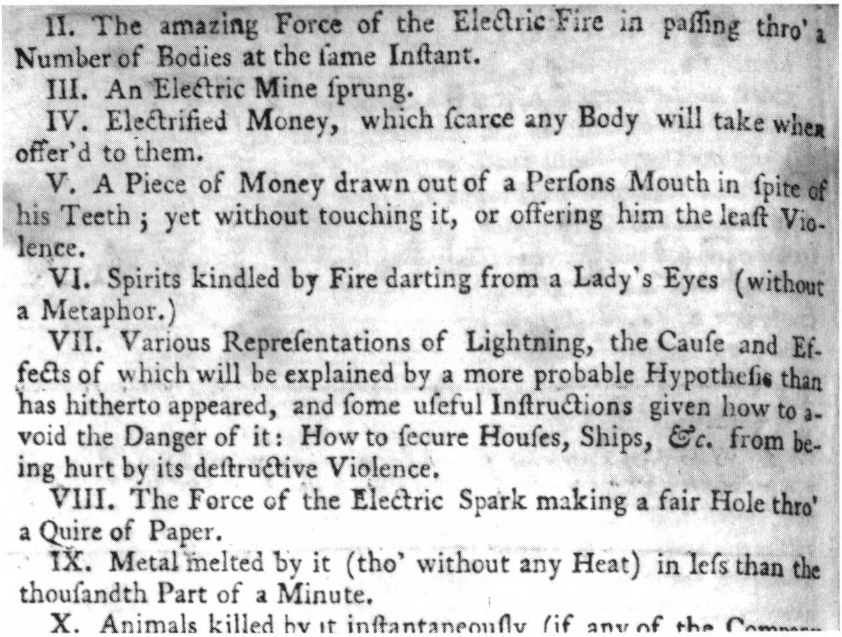

II. The amazing Force of the Electric Fire in paffing thro' a Number of Bodies at the fame Inftant.

III. An Electric Mine fprung.

IV. Electrified Money, which fcarce any Body will take when offer'd to them.

V. A Piece of Money drawn out of a Perfons Mouth in fpite of his Teeth ; yet without touching it, or offering him the leaft Violence.

VI. Spirits kindled by Fire darting from a Lady's Eyes (without a Metaphor.)

VII. Various Reprefentations of Lightning, the Caufe and Effects of which will be explained by a more probable Hypothefis than has hitherto appeared, and fome ufeful Inftructions given how to avoid the Danger of it: How to fecure Houfes, Ships, &c. from being hurt by its deftructive Violence.

VIII. The Force of the Electric Spark making a fair Hole thro' a Quire of Paper.

IX. Metal melted by it (tho' without any Heat) in lefs than the thoufandth Part of a Minute.

X. Animals killed by it inftantaneoufly (if any of the Comp---

Figure 10a. Kinnersley demonstrates Franklin's theory that lightning rods could protect structures, Pennsylvania Gazette, *11 April 1751. Kinnersley added at the end of #VII of his syllabus on electricity: "How to secure Houses, Ships, &c. from being hurt by its destructive Violence." The advertisement in the* Pennsylvania Gazette *shows that Kinnersley was demonstrating the effectiveness of lightning rods, though in miniature. As Franklin wrote in the* Autobiography: *"He procur'd an elegant Apparatus for the purpose, in which all the little Machines that I had roughly made for myself, were nicely form'd by Instrument-makers" (A 153). None of Kinnersley's props survives, but in addition to the standard gadgets like electric machines, Leyden jars, glass-plate batteries, and prime conductors, he added dollhouses and toy ships. The miniature structures without grounded lightning rods would burst apart when a small charge of electricity struck them. The same structures with grounded rods would carry the spark harmlessly through the structures to a table, the floor, or the ground. Courtesy, Library Company of Philadelphia.*

electricity and lightning in his electrical journal before 1749? It would not be surprising. Before April 1747, Franklin knew all twelve similarities that he listed on 7 November 1749. Now, however, Franklin had resolved to make an experiment to test the hypothesis.

In "Opinions and Conjectures," Franklin proposed an experiment that would "determine the Question, Whether the Clouds that contain Lightning are electrified or not." Franklin's first idea for testing atmospheric electricity called for a huge, cumbrous apparatus. Given the state of knowledge concerning electricity, the test was brilliant. In view, however, of Franklin's later kite experiment, the apparatus was an awkward, colossal behemoth. He proposed that "a

Figure 10b. A thunder house. Harvard College purchased this thunder house from the Reverend John Prince of Salem for nine shillings in 1789. It is 6 x 10 x 8 inches high to the ridgepole and 10½ inches high to the top of the rod. The top is separate and the sides are hinged at the bottom. In one side, a small square of wood with a wire running through it is removable. When in place, the wire connects the up and the down parts of the miniature lightning rod, so that the wire carries electricity harmlessly to the "ground." But when the block is removed, the square can be filled with a small charge of gunpowder, and then, when sparks of electricity are applied near the top of the lightning rod, the house blows apart.

Using such miniatures, Kinnersley lectured throughout the Middle Colonies and New England beginning in the spring of 1751. James Bowdoin, the Reverend Andrew Eliot, and Dr. John Perkins were among the Bostonians who judged that Kinnersley "most effectually" proved Franklin's "doctrine of Electricity" (4:191–92). Convincing testimonials to Kinnersley's demonstrations of the identity of lightning and electricity appeared in the New York Gazette on 1 June 1752. In August and September 1752, when Americans who had attended Kinnersley's lectures learned of the French proof of Franklin's theory, the news confirmed what they already believed.

The top of the lightning rod on this thunder house has threads so that one can screw a small ball into it. One could thus demonstrate the difference between a pointed and a blunt conductor. The point versus ball termination shows that this thunder house was constructed after the controversy over the shape of the lightning rods at the Royal Powder Magazine at Purfleet, England. King George III decided in 1778 that blunt conductors rather than Franklin's pointed conductors should be used. The king's position gave a political bias to the scientific dispute. The rebel Franklin advocated rods ending in a point; King George III, acting on the advice of Benjamin Wilson, advocated ones ending in a ball. Courtesy, Collection of Scientific Instruments, Harvard University, Cambridge, Massachusetts.

Figure 11. Franklin's projected sentry box experiment to prove lightning was electricity. Lewis Evans's manuscript copy for James Bowdoin. Sometime before 25 October 1750, Lewis Evans transcribed Franklin's key manuscripts for James Bowdoin, a wealthy Boston merchant and natural philosopher. Franklin had suggested a grounded lightning rod in a letter of 2 March 1750. He theorized that it would draw "electrical fire" out of a cloud and into the ground before the lightning could come near enough to a structure to strike. He said that the idea would surprise Collinson: "This may seem whimsical, but let it pass for the present, until I send the experiments at large" (3:472–73).

Then, in his 29 July 1750 "Opinions and Conjectures," he addressed the underlying question: did electricity exist in the atmosphere during lightning storms? If so, by means of a pointed rod one should be able to take some electricity from the atmosphere and store it in a Leyden jar.

Franklin wrote: "On the Top of some high Tower or Steeple, place a Kind of Sentry Box big enough to contain a Man and an electrical Stand. From the Middle of the Stand let an Iron Rod rise, and pass bending out of the Door, and then upright 20 or 30 feet, pointed very sharp at the End. If the Electrical Stand be kept clean and dry, a Man standing on it when such Clouds are passing low, might be electrified, and afford Sparks, the Rod drawing Fire to him from the Cloud. If any Danger to the Man should be apprehended (tho' I think there would be none) let him stand on the Floor of his Box, and now and then bring near to the Rod, the Loop of a Wire, that has one End fastened to the Leads; he holding it by a Wax-Handle. So the Sparks, if the Rod is electrified, will Strike from the Rod to the Wire and not affect him" (4:19–20).

Though it was unlikely that lightning would strike (and if it did strike, it was possible that it would travel through the wire to the sentry box without killing the experimenter), the experiment was dangerous—but it succeeded. No lightning bolt struck the rod, which drew its electricity from the charges often present in the atmosphere during a storm. Courtesy, the American Academy of Arts and Sciences.

Kind of Sentry Box big enough to contain a Man and an electrical Stand" should be constructed on the top of a high tower or steeple. From the middle of the electrical stand "let an Iron Rod rise, and pass bending out of the Door, and then upright 20 or 30 feet, pointed very sharp at the End. If the Electrical Stand be kept clean and dry, a Man standing on it when such Clouds are passing low, might be electrified, and afford Sparks, the Rod drawing Fire to him from the Cloud" (4:19–20). The reader is often surprised that Franklin did not think the chance of being struck by lightning was great. But the experiment was to test whether the dark clouds contained electricity, not to conduct lightning to the ground. Franklin wanted the iron rod to be insulated in order to test whether it contained electricity.

A lightning strike was possible, and he gave minimal directions on how to perform the sentry box experiment in order to keep safe from lightning: "If any Danger to the Man should be apprehended (tho' I think there would be none) let him stand on the Floor of his Box, and now and then bring near to the Rod, the Loop of a Wire, that has one End fastened to the Leads; he holding it by a Wax-Handle. So the Sparks, if the Rod is electrified, will Strike from the Rod to the Wire and not affect him" (4:20). Replying to a later query about the safety of the experiment, Franklin wrote on 10 March 1773 that though there was no connection between the iron rod on top of the sentry box and the earth, one would be safe in touching the iron rod "with the Ring of the Wire fastned to the Glass Phial by way of Handle, especially if the other End of that Wire went into the Earth. And if not, yet I think he could receive no greater Stroke than the Shock of so much charged Glass as his Hand was apply'd to" (20:104). Even after the death of Georg Wilhelm Richmann while performing a version of Franklin's sentry box experiment, Franklin mistakenly wanted to believe there was little chance for electrocution.

"Opinions and Conjectures" appeared in Franklin's *Experiments and Observations on Electricity*. Dr. John Fothergill's brief preface suggested that Franklin's theory belonged with the ether concepts of Descartes and Newton, "an invisible, subtle matter, disseminated through all nature." (That was one of the two standard previous ideas of the nature of electricity; the other was that it was created from nothing by the electric machine or by rubbing.) At the same time, Fothergill stressed the great power of electricity, "perhaps the most formidable and irresistible agent in the universe." He called attention to Franklin's thoughts on lightning: "From the similar effects of lightening and electricity our author has been led to make some probable conjectures on the cause of the former; and at the same time, to propose some rational experiments in order to secure ourselves, and those things on which its force is often directed, from its pernicious effects; a circumstance of no small importance to the publick, and therefore worthy of the utmost attention" (4:129).

The *Gentleman's Magazine* listed *Experiments and Observations* among the "Books Published this Month" in April 1751, advertising the ninety-two-page pamphlet for 2s 6d.—an expensive price even for an elegant quarto. The announcement, which did not mention Franklin's name, listed four contents. First, that the light of fire and of the sun produce different effects in electrical experiments. Second, that in the Leyden jar, the force is neither in the lead, the water (which was what Franklin had previously thought—and what William Watson still believed [3:358]), nor the shape of the jar, but on the opposite sides of the glass (e.g., the inside and outside of the jar). Third, the electrical battery could accumulate so great a degree of electricity that, when discharged, "the spark could make a hole thro' a quire of paper, which is thought to be pistol proof." Fourth, "Thunder gusts are also accounted for upon electrical principles," but it treated this, Franklin's most exciting thesis, as old news, citing two notices that had appeared in the *Gentleman's Magazine* in 1750. The first was Kinnersley's syllabus reprinted from the *Maryland Gazette* of 10 May 1749 in the *Magazine* for January 1750 (which, as I suggested above, probably did not actually refer to lightning rods) and the second was Franklin's suggestion for erecting lightning rods in the 2 March 1750 letter to Collinson, which had appeared in the *Gentleman's Magazine* for May 1750. The notice ignored the proposed experiment to test whether thunderclouds were electrified.

Before the sentry box experiment proved atmospheric electricity existed, Franklin had convinced a few persons that his theory was true. His letter of 29 April 1749 on thunderstorms presumably won over Collinson and Fothergill. Ebenezer Kinnersley's lectures convinced a number of New Englanders before June 1752. From Boston, James Bowdoin wrote Franklin on 21 December 1751 that he had attended Kinnersley's lectures and thought they proved "most effectually your doctrine of Electricity." Dr. John Perkins, who also attended the lectures, wrote on 17 February 1752: "Your Rationale on Clouds and Rain appears extreamly probable to me and so that of the *Aurora Borealis*. As to the *Fulmen* [lightning], it is demonstrable that it is the same Thing." Perkins, who had a reputation for "the least credulity in common philosophic opinions of any man of his times" (4:267n), believed that lightning was electricity. Two gentlemen from Newport, Rhode Island, wrote on 11 May that Kinnersley had convinced them that lightning was electricity.[76]

STIFLED AND RIDICULED

Letters on scientific matters sent to members of the Royal Society of London were usually forwarded to the secretary, Dr. Cromwell Mortimer; read or summarized at meetings of the society; and, if they were judged valuable, published in its *Philosophical Transactions*. The secretary generally turned over letters on electricity to William Watson, who described them to the society. Thus, on 21 May 1747, Watson summarized a paper on electricity by Dr. Johann Heinrich Winkler, professor of natural philosophy at Leiden, who confessed that his miniature imitation of the aurora borealis delighted the eyes but did not advance the knowledge of electricity. He remarked on "the difficulty there is in offering any thing upon this subject, that may be satisfactory to a truly philosophical understanding."[77] It seems surprising that such a letter, confessedly making no contribution, was printed.

Most historians have said Franklin's view of the English reception of his electrical theories was too sensitive. Franklin wrote that Collinson got the experiments "read in the Royal Society, where they were not at first thought worth so much Notice as to be printed in their Transactions. One Paper which I wrote for Mr. Kinnersley, on the Sameness of Lightning with Electricity, I sent to Dr. Mitchel, an Acquaintance of mine, and one of the Members also of that Society; who wrote me word that it had been read but was laught at by the Connoisseurs: The Papers however being shown to Dr. Fothergill, he thought them of too much value to be stifled, and advis'd the Printing of them. Mr. Collinson then gave them to Cave for publication in his *Gentleman's Magazine*; but he chose to print them separately in a Pamphlet, and Dr. Fothergill wrote the Preface. It was however some time before those Papers were much taken Notice of in England" (A 153–54).

Franklin was right. Only one snippet from his series of fundamental and revisionist hypotheses appeared in the *Philosophical Transactions* before the publication of the 1751 *Experiments and Observations on Electricity*. Most scholars have rejected Franklin's reaction because I. Bernard Cohen, followed by the 1961 editors of the *Papers* (4:125, 125 n9), pointed out that his theories were noticed three times in the *Gentleman's Magazine* in 1750.[78] The January notice reprinted Kinnersley's partial syllabus from the *Maryland Gazette* of 10 May 1749.[79] It contained no mention of Franklin or Kinnersley. On 5 February 1750, Collinson wrote Franklin that he intended to have his letters on electricity published, saying that Franklin's "Novelty and Variety" put the English electricians "out of Countenance" (3:460). He arranged for Edward Cave to bring them out. The second notice of Franklin's work appeared in the *Magazine* for May (which came out in mid-June) and printed a column devoted to Franklin's letter of 2 March 1750 suggesting lightning rods. Cave noted in the heading that he was going to publish a pamphlet containing the "ingenious" author's letters. Cave did not give Franklin's name. The third, a footnote in the magazine for December 1750, mentioned the forthcoming book and Franklin's name.

This skimpy recognition appeared in the wrong place. The *Philosophical Transactions* was the prestigious place to publish scientific papers. When the popular periodicals printed scientific papers, they were usually extracts from the *Transactions*, often printed carelessly. Though Cohen and others are right that Franklin's work was noticed in the *Gentleman's Magazine*, Franklin's reaction was justified.[80]

The foremost English electrician and the authorities at the Royal Society stifled Franklin's work. The minutes of the Royal Society's meetings, kept by Dr. Mortimer, first mention Franklin on 21 January 1747/8, when Watson read that part of Franklin's letter of 25 May 1747 relating to insulted electrical systems

(3:130–32). Watson later printed that part of Franklin's letter within his own seventy-one-page essay in the 1748 *Philosophical Transactions*. Introducing the quotation from Franklin, Watson condescendingly said that he "seems very conversant in this Part of Natural Philosophy." Watson quoted the four numbered experiments on insulated electrical systems and Franklin's analysis of them, repeating Franklin's new terms, *positive* and *negative* electricity. The English electrician ended with Franklin's complimentary reference to himself (3:132) and omitted the following sentence, which pointed out a mistake by Watson.

After quoting Franklin, Watson wrote: "The Solution of this Gentleman, in relation to this Phaenomenon, so exactly corresponds with that which I offer'd very early last Spring, that I could not help communicating it."[81] In other words, Watson printed Franklin in order to claim priority. As I pointed out above, however, Franklin's experiments were more thorough than Watson's, and only Franklin explained their significance. When Watson reported to the Royal Society on 21 January 1747/8, Dr. Mortimer echoed the electrician's opinion, recording that Franklin's experiments "appear to correspond exactly with what Mr. Watson had offer'd very early last spring." Those two pages (one-third of page 98 and just over half of page 100) are buried in Watson's article (pp. 49–120) and are the only words by Franklin published in the *Philosophical Transactions* before the French 1752 confirmation of his theory that storm clouds possessed electrical charges and that lightning was electricity.

Franklin's second major communication on electricity, 28 July 1747, which contained his analysis of what happens in the charging and discharging of the Leyden jar, and which cited errors by Watson (3:159), was ignored. Dr. John Fothergill evidently thought that it would be politic to omit Watson's errors, and therefore they are not in the eighteenth-century editions of Franklin's *Experiments and Observations*. They were, of course, in Franklin's originals and copied by Lewis Evans for James Bowdoin. Since Franklin edited the 1769 edition of his *Experiments and Observations*, he could have reintroduced his corrections of Watson but did not bother. Franklin's third and fourth major communications, both dated 29 April 1749, were read to the Royal Society. The more fundamental and inclusive one was "Observations and Suppositions." Originally addressed to Kinnersley, it was, surprisingly, not sent to Collinson but instead to Dr. John Mitchell, the Virginia naturalist and mapmaker who was also a member of the Royal Society. Perhaps the change indicates that Franklin hoped that Mitchell, unlike Collinson, would manage to have his letter printed in the *Philosophical Transactions*. Watson began to read the letter on 9 November 1749 but, it "being long," the rest of it was deferred to 16 November. Then Watson read the "New Theory of Thunder-Gusts" (the minutes later inserted "by Mr. Franklin"). The Journal Book recorded a one-sentence statement of Franklin's subject: "The Ingenious Author of this Essay endeavours to account for the several Phaenomena of Thunder and Lightning from Electricity." No publication, just a note in the minutes.

Dr. John Mitchell reported to Franklin that the English electricians laughed at the theory (A 153). Since Mitchell's letter is not extant and this part of Franklin's *Autobiography* was written in 1788, one could think that Franklin was overly sensitive in characterizing its reception, but Edward Wright also recorded the scientists' scorn. He wrote that he and his friends had "ridiculed Mr. *Franklin's* project for emptying clouds of their thunder, and . . . could scarce conceive him to be any other than an imaginary Being." Over a year later when a member of the academy in Paris told Wright that Franklin's experiment had succeeded, Wright at first thought his informant was putting him on, but soon began "to abate of my incredulity."[82] J. L. Heilbron has cautioned, however, that the idea that electricity could be emptied from the atmosphere "silently by trickles was neither plausible nor correct."[83]

One person who heard Franklin's theory at the Royal Society took it seriously. William Stukeley mentioned it in his diary. Although Franklin's letter on atmospheric electricity causing thunder and lightning was not published, Stukeley's foolish hypothesis citing Franklin, which maintained that electricity also caused earthquakes, appeared in the *Philosophical Transactions.*[84]

Franklin's second letter of 29 April 1749, addressed to Collinson, had analyzed where the charge lay in the Leyden jar. On 14 December 1749, Dr. Mortimer gave Watson the letter. He judged it "worthy of being read at the Society" and did so on 21 December, promising to make some written observations on it. On 11 January 1749/50, he unnecessarily paraphrased what Franklin wrote (Franklin's original is clearer), and he mentioned that he had read Franklin's "former Papers." His real purpose came out in two longer paragraphs quarreling with Franklin's observation that the electricity was on the glass. Watson thought that he had proven that the shock came from "the Electric matter in the water or other non-Electrics." One might argue that glass is a non-electric and that Watson was correct; but in saying that it was "in the water or" he showed he did not want to concede that Franklin was right. He rejected Franklin's theory without bothering to repeat the experiments proving it.[85] On 21 December 1750, the part of Franklin's letter of 25 May 1747 that claimed that electricity was not created by friction but collected from other matter (3:129–30) was read in the Royal Society, and then Franklin's theory about positive and negative electricity (which Watson had previously read and printed in the *Philosophical Transactions*) was orally presented a second time. Why more of the 25 May 1747 letter had not appeared previously is one mystery, and why the only part printed in the *Philosophical Transactions* was repeated at the 20 December meeting is another. Were some English electricians beginning to accept Franklin's theories?

Franklin appeared twice more in the Royal Society's minutes before *Experiments and Observations* was published in April 1751. A part of his letter (otherwise unknown) to Collinson of 6 December 1750[86] was read on 17 January 1750/1. Franklin said that a "piece of paper gilt on one side" was "placed between

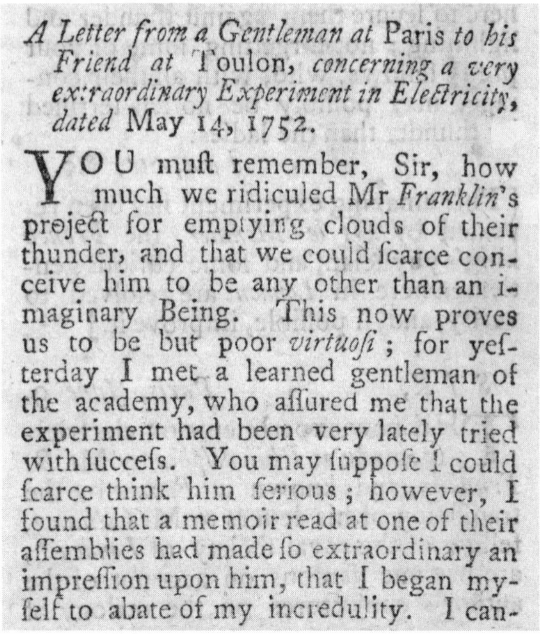

A Letter from a Gentleman at Paris *to his Friend at* Toulon, *concerning a very extraordinary Experiment in Electricity,* dated May 14, 1752.

YOU muft remember, Sir, how much we ridiculed Mr *Franklin's* project for emptying clouds of their thunder, and that we could fcarce conceive him to be any other than an imaginary Being. This now proves us to be but poor *virtuofi* ; for yefterday I met a learned gentleman of the academy, who affured me that the experiment had been very lately tried with fuccefs. You may fuppofe I could fcarce think him ferious ; however, I found that a memoir read at one of their affemblies had made fo extraordinary an impreffion upon him, that I began myfelf to abate of my incredulity. I can-

Figure 12. The establishment electricians jeer at Franklin's theories. Gentleman's Magazine, June 1752. Shortly after the French demonstration of Franklin's sentry box experiment proved that lightning was electrical, an anonymous letter reporting the news on 14 May 1752 recalled that electricians had jeered at the hypothesis. Franklin identified the author as Edward Wright (ca. 1729–61) of Kersey, Sterling County, Scotland. Since the well-connected Wright (a descendent of Robert II, king of Scots) contributed to the Philosophical Transactions of the Royal Society in 1750 and later became a member of the Royal Society, it seems likely that it was the Royal Society electricians who jeered at Franklin's theories. The letter supports the statements of Peter Collinson, Dr. John Mitchell, Dr. John Fothergill, and Franklin himself that the major electricians at first either ignored or ridiculed his theories. Courtesy, Library Company of Philadelphia.

two slips of Glass tyed together, and the shock from a large Glass Jar" was "sent thro'," which "deprived the paper of the gold and drove it into one of the glasses, which is stained with it." The paper was "discolored and seems scorched." The experiment reappeared in section 24 of Franklin's "Opinions and Conjectures" of 29 July 1750 (4:21–22). At the same meeting on 17 January 1751, the minutes cite an additional experiment, not mentioned elsewhere: Franklin attempted to gild a teacup with gold leaf by electricity, but the "stroke broke" the cup, though "part of the metalline stain appears on the broken pieces." Franklin sent the pieces of glass, the discolored paper, and pieces of the teacup to Collinson, and subsequently they "were shown to the members present" at the 17 January Royal Society meeting.

After Franklin's *Experiments and Observations* appeared in April, Watson, on

9 May 1751, reported on it and on "another Letter" from Franklin to Collinson, "containing a Supplement to the said Book." Watson continued on 6 June 1751 with "An Account of Mr. B.F.'s treatise lately published intitled, *Essays and Observations on Electricity*," a summary subsequently published in the *Philosophical Transactions*.[87] Though the letters were not printed, Franklin's name appeared—for only the second time—in the *Philosophical Transactions*. Watson begrudgingly reported that the booklet consisted of four letters that Franklin had sent to Collinson that have "in the whole or in part" been communicated to the society. In fact, when bits of three of the four letters had been orally mentioned, Watson said they either merely confirmed his theories or they were wrong. In addition to quickly dispensing with the four letters, Watson briefly described Franklin's grand summary ("Opinions and Conjectures") and the letter to Collinson of 4 February 1751, which had arrived too late to be included in *Experiments and Observations*. Watson overlooked the "Additional Experiment" sent to Collinson in September 1750 (4:111–13, 136 n6).

The reigning English electrician persevered in saying that Franklin's experiments and theories "coincide with and support those I some time since communicated to the Society" (4:138). Watson again ignored the three subjects that would most appeal to and surprise both ordinary persons and the expert electricians: Franklin's "doctrine of points," his suggestion for using lightning rods to protect buildings, and his proposed experiment to determine whether "Thunder-gusts" (i.e., thunderclouds) contain electricity.[88] Watson and the English electricians continued to ignore and stifle Franklin's findings. A few days before the French confirmation of Franklin's hypothesis that lightning was electrical, Watson reported on 11 June 1752 that the analogy between thunder and electricity was an observation that the best-known French electrician, abbé Jean Antoine Nollet, had "laid before the Public above four Years ago—before Mr. Franklin was heard of."[89] Of course Haller and numerous others had done so before Nollet. No one except Franklin listed so many similarities or, most important, proposed a test for the hypothesis.

After Franklin's pamphlet had been published in the spring of 1751, a letter of his finally appeared in the *Philosophical Transactions*. Franklin wrote it on 29 June 1751; it was read in the society on 14 November and published in the *Philosophical Transactions* for 1751–52. It commented on a ship captain's report of *comazants* (i.e., corposants or St. Elmo's fire) on the top mainmasts and on the lightning that struck the ship. Franklin explained that, in his opinion, when the captain saw the corona on the mainmasts, "the electrical fire was then drawing off, as by points, from the cloud; the largeness of the flame betokening the great quantity of electricity in the clouds." He said that if there had been a "good wire-communication," a lightning rod, from the top of the masts to the sea, it would have conducted the lightning "into the sea without damage to the ship." Franklin's explanation of St. Elmo's fire became standard.[90]

Vindicated!

In the fall of 1751, the French naturalist George-Louis Le Clerc, comte de Buffon, read Franklin's *Experiments and Observations* and asked his friend, the naturalist Thomas François Dalibard, to translate the booklet. As Dalibard read it, he decided he wanted to show the new "Philadelphia" experiments. He called upon a popular public lecturer in experimental philosophy, M. de Lor,[91] for help. During the winter, Dalibard repeated Franklin's experiments and publicly demonstrated them. He gained a reputation for the shows. King Louis XV heard about the exhibitions and asked to see the experiments. The duke d'Ayen offered his country house at St. Germain as an appropriate site, and on 3 February 1752, Buffon, Dalibard, and de Lor entertained Louis XV with the experiments. He enjoyed them and sent Franklin his compliments. That inspired Dalibard to conduct Franklin's proposed sentry box experiment. In March 1752,[92] his translation of Franklin's *Experiments and Observations* appeared.

Dalibard set up the sentry box in a garden at Marly-la-ville, a small village "seven or eight leagues from *Paris*, on the road to *Compeigne*." Following Franklin's suggestion, he erected an iron rod about an inch in diameter and forty feet long and improvised an insulated stand, consisting of three wine bottles supporting a wide plank. Inside the sentry box, silk cords held the rod and rested on glass bottles, "so that supposing it could be electrified, it would not part with its virtue." Since Dalibard was not going to be in the area constantly, he showed the parish priest, Father Raulet, and a former dragoon, who was now a local joiner, Coiffier, what to do if any thunderclouds appeared. At 2:20 P.M. on 10 May 1752, it began to thunder and hail. Coiffier ran to the sentry box and presented a brass wire stuck into a glass handle to the end of the iron bar. A spark came immediately to the wire. The brave Coiffier sent a child to summon the curé, Raulet, who came running with all his might through the hail. Alarmed by the sight, the villagers feared that lightning had killed Coiffier. Raulet arrived, followed by a crowd. Raulet repeated the experiment in the sentry box while the crowd, awed, stood in the hail watching. Each time he presented the wire to the jar, the sparks flew from the rod into it, for as long as it took to say "a *pater* and an *ave*." Raulet immediately wrote the news to Dalibard, and Coiffier rushed off with the letter. Three days later on 13 May 1752, Dalibard reported the experiment's success to the Paris Academy (4:302–10).[93]

When questioned twenty years later whether lightning could have killed Coiffier, Franklin thought the danger minimal. Coiffier "was safe in touching" the insulated wire to the iron rod, "especially if the other End of that Wire went into the Earth. And if not, yet I think he could receive no greater Stroke than the Shock of so much charged Glass as his Hand was apply'd to" (20:104). Franklin said that if there was a down conductor nearby that went into the earth, it would protect the experimenter, but there was no down conductor. If lightning had struck, perhaps, since Coiffier was standing on an insulated platform and handling an insulated conductor, a bolt of lightning would bypass him and descend through the wood of the sentry box. Perhaps. According to E. Philip Krider, the "chance of a direct lightning strike to a 40-foot iron rod under a small thunderstorm is roughly 1 in 5,000. If such a strike should happen, the best place to be standing is probably on the insulator—and hope that the inevitable side flash from the rod to ground does not pass through you. There would also be the chance of a smaller, upward discharge from the rod (in response to a nearby strike), and in that case, the odds could be as high as 1 in 100, but the threat of death or injury would not be as great."[94]

Informed of the sentry box experiment's success, Louis XV commanded abbé Guillaume Mazéas to send word to the Royal Society of London that he applauded Franklin and Collinson. Mazéas complied and sent a letter of 20 May to the Reverend Stephen Hales, a Royal Society member, reporting the experiment's success on 10 May, and the king's compliment (4:315–17). A similar letter from Paris, dated 26 May, described the experiments and was widely reprinted in the English newspapers and magazines. The experiments proved "that thunder clouds may be deprived of their fire, by iron bars."[95] That was Franklin's primary thesis (and a dangerous one, with an insulated lightning rod); the secondary one was that if lightning struck, a grounded rod would safely conduct the electricity into the ground.

Proof that lightning was electrical in nature made Franklin famous. For the next two years newspapers and magazines carried notices about experiments on atmospheric electricity. Perhaps Benjamin Wilson's confirmation was the most unusual one. On 22 August 1752, he was acting Shakespeare's *Henry IV* with friends near Chelmsford in Essex. A thunderstorm came up while he was playing the king. He rushed outside in his "Royal Robes" with a quart bottle in which he put a curtain rod. Standing in the bowling green, he collected electricity in the iron rod and drew out sparks. His fellow actors "not only saw the sparks, but caused sparks themselves, by approaching the rod with their fingers." John Bevis reported Wilson's account in the *Gentleman's Magazine* and Wilson later amplified the circumstances in his memoirs.[96] As the long review of Franklin's *Experiments and Observations on Electricity* in the *Monthly Review* for August 1753 (well over two years after its publication) commented, "This hypothesis has rendered our author very famous, a great number of experiments made in different parts, as well of *Europe* as *America*, having proved the similarity of lightening and electricical fire."[97]

The Kite Experiment

The *Gentleman's* and the *London* magazines for May 1752 reported the success of the sentry box experiment and said that it proved "that thunder clouds may be deprived of their fire" by lightning rods. If Dalibard, de Lor, Buffon, or someone else in France wrote Franklin of the experiment's success, the letter could not have reached Franklin before the middle of June, but no ships from

France arrived in Philadelphia in June or July 1752. Since the magazines for May were not printed until the middle of June or slightly later, and since the normal sailing time between London and Philadelphia was about six weeks (occasionally less but often more), news of the French success could hardly have reached Philadelphia before August. The only ship from London to arrive in Philadelphia in June, July, or August 1752 was the ship *Hibernia*, Captain William Child, which appeared in the "Inward Entries" on 27 August. The front page of the 27 August *Pennsylvania Gazette* featured news brought by Child, and page two reprinted the *London Magazine* report of the success of the sentry box experiment.[98] I suspect Franklin told Hall not to feature the news on the front page. Franklin learned sometime during the week before 27 August 1752 that French experimenters had confirmed his theory.[99]

The existence of atmospheric electricity and lightning's identity with electricity were not, however, news to Franklin, for he had performed the kite experiment in June. Franklin meant to carry out the sentry box experiment himself, but he supposed that a high structure would be necessary. About the time that he thought of the sentry box experiment (probably early in 1750, some months before he proposed it in a letter of 29 July 1750), he knew that parishioners wanted to build a steeple on Christ Church. That would be the highest point in Philadelphia. The vestry of Christ Church unanimously voted to build it on 11 March 1751. Franklin and his son William contributed to the building fund, and Franklin served as a manager of two lotteries to raise money for it. But construction on the steeple still had not started in June 1752. The statehouse was also building a wooden steeple to replace its small bell cupola. Franklin probably intended to use whichever steeple was finished first. Although the 1752 Scull and Heap map of Philadelphia shows a wooden steeple on the statehouse, it was not completed until March 1753.[100] Sometime in the late spring of 1752, Franklin speculated that a high steeple might not be necessary; he might be able to test the theory with a kite. That must have appealed to his impishness as well as to his admiration for simplicity, whenever practical.

Waiting for a thunderstorm, Franklin prepared a special kite, consisting of a cross made of two light strips of cedar, fastened at the middle and tied at the four ends to a large, thin, silk handkerchief. He chose silk rather than strong kite paper because it could bear the wind and rain of a thunderstorm without tearing. To the top of the cross he fixed a thin wire of more than a foot long that extended to the middle of the cross. There, he attached a hemp string. Franklin knew that the string, especially when wet, conducted electricity. At the other end, he tied a key[101] and a silk ribbon. Since the electricity could possibly dissipate if he grounded the conductor, Franklin assumed that, to test the atmosphere, he should insulate the conductor.

Only his son William, then about twenty-four years old, knew of the proposed experiment, for if he were wrong, he would be ridiculed.[102] One June day, storm clouds appeared. Franklin and William went to a field, taking their prepared kite and Leyden jars. William raised the kite, and then Franklin, standing in a shed, held the hempen string by the silk ribbon, which would not, when dry, conduct electricity. Silk would conduct electricity when wet, which was one reason for standing in the shed. Franklin was careful not to have the string touch the door of the shed, for if electricity came down the string, it would be grounded if it touched the wood. With the kite raised and Franklin waiting, one dark cloud passed, and nothing happened. Franklin must have been glad no one but William was watching. Perhaps his hypothesis was wrong. Then, as a second cloud drew near, the threads of the hempen string stood erect and avoided one another. The string was electrified! Joseph Priestley, describing the story from Franklin's telling, wrote: "let the reader judge of the exquisite pleasure he must have felt at that moment." He put his knuckle near the key and drew a spark. Again, another spark. Again, another. Then, as the rain started and wet the string, "he collected electric fire very copiously" into the Leyden jar.[103]

Describing the kite experiment on 19 October 1752, Franklin wrote: "when the Rain has wet the Kite and Twine, so that it can conduct the Electric Fire freely, you will find it stream out plentifully from the Key on the Approach of your Knuckle. At this Key the Phial may be charg'd; and from Electric Fire thus obtain'd, Spirits may be kindled, and all the other Electric Experiments be perform'd, which are usually done by the Help of a rubbed Glass Globe or Tube; and thereby the *Sameness* of the Electric Matter with that of Lightning compleatly demonstrated" (4:367).

When and where did Franklin fly the kite? Joseph Priestley, who received his information from Franklin, wrote that it happened in June 1752, a month after the French electricians had verified the same theory but before Franklin heard they had done so. Unfortunately, we have no weather diaries detailing the thunderstorms for Philadelphia in June 1752, or we might speculate which day Franklin flew the kite. Where? At least four possibilities have been suggested. Franklin had purchased a pasture from the brick maker William Coats on 31 July 1741, evidently as a place to keep a pony for William. By 30 April 1747 he had bought a horse named Jack for himself. In 1773, the pasture was described as in Hickory Lane, which a knowledgeable Philadelphian, Penrose R. Hoopes, said "ran west from the present Fifth Street and Fairmont Avenue to Ridge Avenue." Another suggested location was the Philadelphia commons. Dr. Henry Stuber, in his 1790–91 "Life of Franklin," reported that Franklin flew it in the commons, and his statement was often reprinted. In 1864 James Parton followed Stuber's identification and said that the site had been "about the corner of Race and Eighth streets, near a spot where there was an old cow-shed." I. Minis Hays, writing in 1924, said that according to tradition, "he flew it on a vacant lot about 10th and Chestnut streets." Finally, Ronald W. Clark followed a theory that located it "on the high ground near the junction of what are now Eighteenth and Spring Garden streets, a site where the wind was likely to be strong and where Franklin would have the seclusion he wanted." That seems rather far

PHILADELPHIA, October 19.

AS frequent Mention is made in the News Papers from *Europe*, of the Succefs of the *Philadelphia* Experiment for drawing the Electric Fire from Clouds by Means of pointed Rods of Iron erected on high Buildings, &c. it may be agreeable to the Curious to be inform'd, that the fame Experiment has fucceeded in *Philadelphia*, tho' made in a different and more eafy Manner, which any one may try, as follows.

Make a fmall Crofs of two light Strips of Cedar, the Arms fo long as to reach to the four Corners of a large thin Silk Handkerchief when extended ; tie the Corners of the Handkerchief to the Extremities of the Crofs, fo you have the Body of a Kite ; which being properly accommodated with a Tail, Loop and String, will rife in the Air, like thofe made of Paper ; but this being of Silk is fitter to bear the Wet and Wind of a Thunder Guft without tearing. To the Top of the upright Stick of the Crofs is to be fixed a very fharp pointed Wire, rifing a Foot or more above the Wood. To the End of the Twine, next the Hand, is to be tied a filk Ribbon, and where the Twine and the filk join, a Key may be faftened. This Kite is to be raifed when a Thunder Guft appears to be coming on, and the Perfon who holds the String muft ftand within a Door, or Window, or under fome Cover, fo that the Silk Ribbon may not be wet ; and Care muft be taken that the Twine does not touch the Frame of the Door or Window. As foon as any of the Thunder Clouds come over the Kite, the pointed Wire will draw the Electric Fire from them, and the Kite, with all the Twine, will be electrified, and the loofe Filaments of the Twine will ftand out every Way, and be attracted by an approaching Finger. And when the Rain has wet the Kite and Twine, fo that it can conduct the Electric Fire freely, you will find it ftream out plentifully from the Key on the Approach of your Knuckle. At this Key the Phial may be charg'd ; and from Electric Fire thus obtain'd, Spirits may be kindled, and all the other Electric Experiments be perform'd, which are ufually done by the Help of a rubbed Glafs Globe or Tube ; and thereby the *Samenefs* of the Electric Matter with that of Lightning compleatly demonftrated.''

Figure 13. Franklin announces the success of his kite experiment, Pennsylvania Gazette, *19 October 1752. After describing how to make a strong rain- and storm-resistant kite, Franklin wrote that a silk ribbon should be tied to the end of the twine string attached to the kite, and "where the Twine and the silk join, a Key may be fastened." When an electrical storm occurs, "the Person who holds the String must stand within a Door, or Window, or under some Cover, so that the Silk Ribbon may not be wet; and Care must be taken that the Twine does not touch the Frame of the Door or Window." As the electric storm comes near, "the pointed Wire will draw" down electricity, "and the Kite, with all the Twine, will be electrified, and the loose Filaments of the Twine will stand out every Way, and be attracted by an approaching Finger." After rain "has wet the Kite and Twine, so that it can conduct the Electric Fire freely, you will find it stream out plentifully from the Key on the Approach of your Knuckle. At this Key the Phial may be charg'd; and from Electric Fire thus obtain'd, Spirits may be kindled, and all the other Electric Experiments be perform'd, which are usually done by the Help of a rubbed Glass Globe or Tube; and thereby the Sameness of the Electric Matter with that of Lightning compleatly demonstrated" (4:367).*

In the following years, Dr. John Lining of Charleston, South Carolina, and a number of European natural philosophers successfully repeated Franklin's kite experiment. Courtesy, Library Company of Philadelphia.

away. No one knows where he flew the kite, but Franklin's pasture, which probably had a small barn for food and shelter for two horses, seems to me the most likely site.[104]

Was it dangerous? Yes. If lightning had struck the kite, Franklin might have been killed. He took the risk. I suspect that Franklin inspired Immanuel Kant's definition of the Enlightenment, "Supere Aude!" If not, its sentiment dovetails with Franklin's action. It was unlikely that lightning would strike, but it could have. He often demonstrated personal bravery, both before and after the kite experiment. Was the experimenter brave or foolhardy? All the early electrical experimenters gave themselves shocks. When Musschenbroek first experienced a shock from the Leyden jar, he said that he "would not take a second shock for the kingdom of France." But in the following years, electricians commonly shocked themselves and others with the Leyden jar. Bose, perhaps the best showman of the first experimenters, avowed that "he wished he might die by the electric shock, that the account of his death might furnish an article for the memoirs of the French Academy." Joseph Priestley praised Bose's "philosophical heroism" as "worthy of the renowned Empedocles." Georg Richmann, a German electrician in St. Petersburg, unfortunately proved the dangerous possibilities of conducting experiments with thunderclouds. On 6 August 1753, Richmann "prepared for making Electrical Observations, or the Means for averting the Effects of Thunder, according to the Method practised by Mr. Franklin, of Philadelphia." He erected the apparatus and, with a thunderstorm approaching, went to the apparatus by the end of the lightning rod.

Lightning struck with "an Explosion like that of a small Cannon." Richmann was electrocuted. When Franklin printed the account in the *Pennsylvania Gazette*, he added a paragraph saying that the accident proved the theory of the lightning rod: if the apparatus had gone from the top of the house into the ground, Richmann would have been safe. But he was using an insulated conductor, as in the sentry box experiment Franklin had described. Joseph Priestley called Richmann "justly envied" and claimed that he had gained fame as a martyr to science.[105] I suspect he would rather have lived. It has been said that Richmann had about one chance in 100,000 of being struck by lightning. E. Philip Krider, however, has revised that estimate: "Based upon what we know today, the odds were probably between 1 in 1,000 to 1 in 10,000."[106]

Publication: Kite Experiment

When Franklin finally published the kite experiment in the *Pennsylvania Gazette* on 19 October 1752, one might have supposed that it was something he had heard of, performed by someone else: "As frequent Mention is made in the News Papers from Europe, of the Success of the Philadelphia Experiment for drawing the Electric Fire from Clouds by Means of pointed Rods of Iron erected on high Buildings, &c. it may be agreeable to the Curious to be inform'd, that the same Experiment has succeeded in Philadelphia, tho' made in a different and more easy Manner, which any one may try." The account never mentioned Franklin. Of course, everyone who knew anything about electricity knew it was his experiment. Cadwallader Colden, who read its reprinting in the *New York Evening Post* on 23 October, asked Franklin to give "a more perfect & particular account" of the experiment, "in a manner to preserve it better & to give it more Credit than it can obtain from a common Newspaper."[107] Franklin did not. What would he add? It would only seem vainglorious. Anyone could repeat it, and numerous persons did, though the French sentry box experiments made repetitions superfluous.

After showing in June 1752 that some thunderclouds were electrified, Franklin had lightning rods erected on the statehouse, the Philadelphia Academy, and probably his own home. These would have been grounded rods, because he hoped to draw electricity out of the clouds before lightning actually struck. When he wrote Peter Collinson in October, he said he "was pleased to hear of the Success of my experiments in France, and that they there begin to Erect Points on their buildings. We had before placed them upon our Academy and Statehouse Spires" (4:364).

Though he told no one other than his son William (and possibly Deborah) that he intended to try to test the electrification of clouds with a kite, he must have told a number of people about its success shortly thereafter. He could hardly have erected the lightning rod on the statehouse without the permission of the Speaker of the House and at least the approval of a few other members, and though he was the president of the board of trustees of the academy, he would not have erected a rod there without the approval of some other trustees. From the House of Representatives, I would guess that at least Speaker Isaac Norris and Franklin's fellow representative from the city of Philadelphia, Hugh Roberts, knew about the kite experiment's success before August, and from the academy trustees, probably Richard Peters, Isaac Norris (a trustee as well as Speaker), Philip Syng, Dr. Thomas Bond, and others (the four named were among those present at a trustees' meeting on 11 August 1752) knew about the kite experiment before Franklin announced it on 19 October.[108]

Among the first persons Franklin probably told were his fellow experimenters in electricity, Philip Syng and Ebenezer Kinnersley. The third experimenter, Thomas Hopkinson, had died in 1751. It has been said that Kinnersley could not have known about the kite experiment's success because his lecture syllabus in the *Pennsylvania Gazette* in September 1752 was the same as that advertised in April 1751, but the 1751 syllabus included demonstrations of a miniature lightning rod and instructions on "How to secure Houses, Ships, &c. from being hurt by its destructive Violence." There was no reason to change the syllabus.[109] Moreover, after news of the sentry box experiment's success appeared in the *Pennsylvania Gazette* in late August, Kinnersley had to know that lightning was an electric discharge.

When did Franklin erect the first lightning rods? I speculate that it was after

Figure 14. Portions of the original (?) lightning rod in Independence Hall, Philadelphia. During the restoration of Independence Hall in 1960, the old paneling and plaster were removed from the tower stairwell, and under them, in the northwest corner, portions of the seemingly original lightning rod were discovered. Franklin installed the original lightning rod in August 1752. Either it or the lightning rod at the Philadelphia Academy (demolished in 1844) was the first lightning rod erected in the world. The few earlier rods in France were insulated and had no down conductor. The purpose of the earlier rods was to test whether atmospheric electricity existed, whereas the usual purpose of lightning rods is to conduct lightning safely into the ground. (As we will see, Franklin devised a way to combine the two purposes.)

The steeple on Independence Hall was erected during the reconstruction of the building in 1751. On 28 September 1754, while the Reverend Ezra Stiles was visiting Philadelphia, he recorded that Ebenezer Kinnersley took him to the steeple of the academy, from which Stiles "viewed the city of Philadelphia . . . [and] the rods & wires which defend the Academy House from lightning" (Stiles, "Diary" Proceedings Massachusetts Historical Society, 2nd ser., 7 [1891–92]: 340–41).

When E. Philip Krider first published an illustration of this lightning rod fragment, he thanked Penelope H. Batchelor of Independence National Historical Park for calling it to his attention. Courtesy, Independence National Historical Park, Philadelphia.

6 August but before Captain Child arrived from London during the week of 20–27 August. The 6 August *Pennsylvania Gazette* printed two news notes concerning electricity. One note was dated from Portsmouth, New Hampshire, 23 July: "The Main-Mast of a Schooner at the North-End, was struck by the Lightning; and altho' the Mast is shiver'd to Pieces by it (and the other Mast ruin'd by the Shock) till it came to a Ring that encompassed it (which it melted a little)

yet below that Ring there is no Effects of it." Franklin added to the news note, "A plain Proof of the Electrick Nature of Lightning." I. Bernard Cohen noted that the New Hampshire report did not actually prove the electrical nature of lightning.[110] If, however, Franklin wanted to erect lightning rods on the statehouse and the academy, his comment was propaganda for the purpose. But it would hardly be convincing unless his friends knew of the kite experiment.

The second news note appeared in the same paper: "Last Friday, early in the Morning, the Lightning struck two houses on Society Hill, and did them considerable damage, but burnt no person. It was very remarkable in both houses, that the Lightning in its passage from the Roof to the Ground, seem'd to go considerably out of a direct course, for the sake of passing thro' Metal; such as Hinges, Sash Weights, Iron Rods, the Pendulum of a Clock, &c. and where it had sufficient metal to conduct it nothing was damag'd; but where it pass'd thro' Plastering or Wood-work, it rent and split them surprizingly." In effect, Franklin reported that lightning, like electricity, followed the best conductors (the path of least resistance). This article, too, was good propaganda. It reaffirmed the danger from lightning in Philadelphia and at the same time asserted the truth of his theory concerning lightning—for those who knew of the success of the kite experiment. I suspect that shortly after 6 August but before 20 August, Franklin, with the consent of a few key persons, installed lightning rods on two major Philadelphia structures—the world's first lightning rods.

On 1 October, Franklin wrote the account quoted above of the kite experiment to Peter Collinson. Read in the Royal Society on 21 December, it was published in the *Philosophical Transactions*.[111] In *Poor Richard* for 1753 (advertised as in the press on 19 October and as "Just Published" on 16 November), Franklin gave directions for installing a lightning rod: erect "a small Iron Rod (it may be of the Rod-iron used by the Nailers) . . . six or eight Feet above the highest Part of the Building. To the upper End of the Rod fasten about a Foot of Brass Wire, the Size of a common Knitting-needle, sharpened to a fine Point; the Rod may be secured to the House by a few small Staples." The rod should . go down the house and three or four feet into the ground. Lightning would not damage a house with such a rod, for it would be "attracted by the Points" and would pass through "the Metal into the Ground without hurting any Thing." Ships too, with "a sharp pointed Rod fix'd on the Top of their Masts, with a Wire from the Foot of the Rod reaching down, round one of the Shrouds, to the Water, will not be hurt by Lightning" (4:408–9). Franklin's homey comparisons ("Knitting-needle") made the sizes clear and tended to disarm readers' possible fear.

Franklin's "Good Silk Garters"

The publicity attending his proof that lightning was electrical in nature delighted Franklin. He could not help but tell his friend Jared Eliot on 12 April 1753 about Louis XV's compliment: "The Tatler tells us of a Girl who was observ'd to grow suddenly proud, and none could guess the Reason, till it came to be known that she had got on a pair of new Silk Garters. Lest you should be puzzel'd to guess the Cause when you observe any thing of the kind in me, I think I will not hide my new Garters under my Petticoats, but take the Freedom to show them to you, in a Paragraph of our Friend Collinson's last Letter viz.—But I ought to mortify, and not indulge, this Vanity; I will not transcribe the Paragraph.—Yet I cannot forbear."

After teasing Eliot and himself concerning the warfare between pride and modesty, Franklin gave in to pride. He quoted Collinson's letter: "If any of thy Friends . . . should take Notice that thy Head is held a little higher up than formerly, let them know; when the Grand Monarch of France strictly commands the Abbé Mazeas to write a Letter in the politest Terms to the Royal Society, to return the Kings Thanks and Compliments in an express Manner to Mr. Franklin of Pennsilvania, for the useful Discoveries in Electricity, and Application of the pointed Rods to prevent the terrible Effects of Thunderstorms. I say, after all this, is not some Allowance to be made if the Crest is a little elevated." Collinson added: "I think now I have stuck a Feather on thy Cap, I may be allowed to conclude in wishing thee long to wear it."

Franklin next mocked himself and the honor: "On reconsidering this Paragraph, I fear I have not so much Reason to be proud as the Girl had; for a Feather in the Cap is not so useful a Thing, or so serviceable to the Wearer, as a Pair of good Silk Garters." Then, like Collinson, Franklin concluded his letter with a compliment to the addressee: "The Pride of Man is very differently gratify'd, and had his Majesty sent me a Marshal's Staff, I think I should scarce have been so proud of it as I am of your Esteem, and of subscribing my self with Sincerity Dear Sir, Your affectionate Friend and humble Servant" (4:466–67).

Honors and tributes followed: Harvard awarded Franklin a master of arts on 25 July 1753; Yale followed on 12 September 1753; and William and Mary conferred the degree on 20 April 1756. Distinguished societies elected him a member, including the Royal Society of London.[112] In the eighteenth century, the Royal Society's Copley medal was science's most distinguished prize, comparable to today's Nobel Prize. The Royal Society awarded Franklin the Copley medal in 1753. He wrote in the *Autobiography* that the members of the society "made me more than Amends for the Slight with which they had before treated me" (A 155–56).

Awarding the Copley medal on 30 November 1753, the earl of Macclesfield, president of the society, said that electricity was known "long ago" but that until recently, it "was thought to be of little importance." It seemed only to illustrate "the Being and Nature of Attraction and Repulsion," and nothing "much worth notice" was "expected to arise from it." Many people had noted the "Analogy between the effects of Lightning and Electricity; yet I take Mr. Franklin to be the first who, among other curious discoveries, undertook to shew from experiments, that the former owed it's origin entirely to the latter;

and who pointed out an easy method, whereby any one might satisfie himself" of its truth (5:130–32).

Though delighted with the honors and tributes, Franklin suggested that the lightning rod would have been invented without him. When the South Carolina physician Dr. John Lining asked him how he ever "came first to think of proposing the experiment of drawing down the lightning," Franklin replied on 18 March 1755 that "the thought was not so much 'an out-of-the-way one,' but . . . might have occurred to any electrician" (5:523–24).

ATMOSPHERIC ELECTRICITY

In September 1752 Franklin devised an easy method of learning more about atmospheric electricity. Wanting to perform "some Experiments" with electricity drawn from the skies, he thought of bells. Perhaps William Watson's *Sequel* (read to the Royal Society on 30 October 1746 and published in 1747) inspired him: it described a German electrician's demonstration of the ringing of bells with electricity,[113] but Franklin may have done so earlier, for the ringing of bells used the same technique as Franklin's proof of the conservation of matter in the charging and discharging of the Leyden jar.

Franklin fixed a pointed rod "to the top of my chimney, and extending about nine feet above it. From the foot of this rod, a wire (the thickness of a goose quill) came through a covered glass tube in the roof, and down through the well of the staircase; the lower end connected with the iron spear of a pump. On the staircase opposite to my chamber door, the wire was divided; the ends separated about six inches, a little bell on each end; [and] between the bells a little brass ball suspended by a silk thread, to play between and strike the bells when clouds passed with electricity in them." The apparatus in place, Franklin frequently heard the bells and then charged Leyden jars from the wire that went up to the lightning rod. One night an especially loud ringing in the hall awakened him: "Starting up and opening the door, I perceived that the brass ball, instead of vibrating as usual between the bells, was repelled and kept at a distance from both; while the fire passed sometimes in very large quick cracks from bell to bell; and sometimes in a continued dense white stream, seemingly as large as my finger, whereby the whole staircase was enlightened as with sunshine, so that one might see to pick up a pin" (19:247).

That winter, 1752–53, Franklin thought of an experiment to determine whether the clouds were electrified positively or negatively. He had conjectured in 1748 that sea clouds were positive and that when they came into contact with land clouds, which had less electricity, "the Equilibrium" was "restored by snaps of Lightning." Now he could charge a Leyden jar with electricity from the skies and then determine whether it was positive or negative. For several months he found the clouds always charged negatively. He abandoned his early hypothesis concerning a difference between clouds formed over the ocean and those

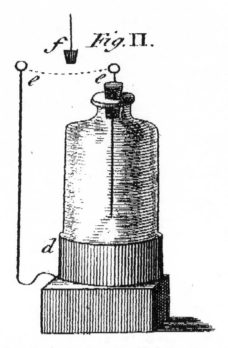

Figure 15a. *Discharging a Leyden jar. From Franklin's* Experiments and Observations on Electricity *(1751). A wire at the top of the Leyden jar goes down through a cork into the water inside the bottle, and the jar is charged through this wire. Another wire goes from the thin covering of metal on the outside bottom of the jar up to a position about five inches from the top wire. After charging the Leyden jar, a cork ball is suspended between the two ends of the metal wires. The cork ball will go back and forth, carrying small quantities of electricity until the amount of electricity inside and outside the bottle reaches an equilibrium. Courtesy, American Philosophical Society.*

formed over land. They all seemed to be charged negatively. That led to a new and surprising thought.

HERESY: THE DIRECTION OF LIGHTNING

Did lightning strike from the earth to the clouds? Crazy! Could it be? Franklin had thought that sparks passed from the positive charge to the negative. If clouds were charged negatively, did lightning come from the earth and strike into the clouds? Franklin continued gathering electricity in Leyden jars from the atmosphere and testing it. On 6 June 1753, between 5 and 7 o'clock, he finally found a cloud that tested positive, though several just before and after were negative. So clouds could strike from one to another. He had abandoned his earlier belief that the salt content affected whether the clouds were in a negative or positive state. But when lightning struck, was it coming from the earth to the clouds or, as everyone had always believed, from the clouds to the earth? Per-

Figure 15b. Testing atmospheric electricity, September 1752, a detail in Edward Fisher's mezzotint (frontispiece). A detail in the upper left of Edward Fisher's mezzotint of Franklin after Mason Chamberlain shows Franklin's apparatus, devised in September 1752 and erected on the house at 325 Market Street that he was renting from John Wistar. (The frontispiece is later, but the apparatus is basically the same.) It combined a lightning rod with a device for testing whether the atmosphere is electrified. A bell-shaped termination of an up-lightning rod is on the right and another bell-shaped termination of a down-lightning rod is on the left. A clapper hangs between the two. The clapper will function like the cork ball in figure 15a. When the electric atmosphere is greater or less than that of the earth, the clapper will swing back and forth, striking the metal-shaped bells, the cloud and the earth playing the parts of the inner and outer coatings of the Leyden jar, respectively.

From the inside of the bell-shaped metal termination on the right, two cork balls hang suspended by threads. They are apart, showing that the up-lightning rod currently has a charge so that the balls are repelling one another. When the clapper strikes the bell-shaped termination of the up-lightning rod, the two cork balls will, for at least a nanosecond, start to lose their charge (i.e., the difference between the charge in the atmosphere and in the earth) and fall back together. When the clapper strikes the bell-shaped termination of the down-lightning rod, the cork balls hanging down from the bell-shaped up-rod on the right will again be charged and therefore repel one another. If the electrical atmosphere is greatly different from that of the earth, electricity will arc between the up- and down-rods. Courtesy, National Portrait Gallery.

haps minute examination of the evidence from houses and other places where lightning had struck would confirm his new and strange hypothesis that lightning generally struck from the earth to the clouds.

The *Pennsylvania Gazette* for 21 June 1753 asked: "Those of our Readers in this and the neighbouring Provinces, who may have an Opportunity of observing, during the present Summer, any of the Effects of Lightning on Houses, Ships, Trees, &c. are requested to take particular Notice of its Course, and Deviation from a strait Line, in the Walls or other Matter affected by it, its different Operations or Effects on Wood, Stone, Bricks, Glass, Metals, Animal Bodies, & c. and every other Circumstance that may tend to discover the Nature, and compleat the History of that terrible Meteor." The observations would be "very thankfully accepted and acknowledged" by Benjamin Franklin.

While Franklin was in New England on post office business in the summer of 1753, lightning struck a vacant Philadelphia house about 3:00 A.M. on 8 July. William Franklin knew about his father's theory that lightning generally strikes from the earth to the sky, and he searched for and found evidence to confirm it. He examined the house at 6:00 that morning. In his detailed report of 12 July, William referred to the "general receiv'd Opinion" that lightning strikes from above, but he gave numerous details that suggested it came from the earth. The shingles on the roof had been "all thrown upwards, as if done by some Instrument forc'd underneath them. Splinters from the "wooden Moulding . . . were all drove upwards, as if occasion'd by a Bullet shot against it from below." Several shattered upright parts of the window frames were "broadest at the Bottom, and terminating almost to a Point at the Top, whereas the contrary might have been expected to have happen'd, if the Force which split them came from above."

Franklin replied on 23 July 1753, thanking William for the "circumstantial Account . . . which you think sufficient to establish my new Hypothesis of the Direction of Lightning." Kinnersley had also inspected the house and found a pane of glass that he thought suggested that the lightning stroke was upward. Franklin told William that he was writing Kinnersley a short report of the experiments he made before leaving home and referring him to William for the new hypothesis, "which I have not now time to give at length" (5:15).

Risking Ridicule

Franklin suggested to Peter Collinson on 28 August 1753 that generally "'*tis the Earth that strikes into the Clouds*, and not the Clouds that strike into the Earth." Collinson found it a "strange Doctrine" and kept it "a profound Secret," not wanting the mistake to embarrass Franklin (5:71, 233). In September 1753, writing Collinson, Franklin asked that everyone who had "an Opportunity of observing the recent Effects of Lightning on Buildings, Trees, &c. that they would consider them particularly with a View to discover the Direction." He then gave directions for examining the effects of lightning to determine direction: if, for example, the path of the lightning passed through wood, the splinters would fly off from the top if the lightning came up from the ground, but if the lightning struck from above, the splinters would fly off from the bottom (5:76).

Numerous previous electricians had anticipated Franklin's theory that lightning was electricity, but no one had ever thought that lightning struck from the earth to the clouds. Franklin was sensitive to the possible ridicule and criticism. He wrote to the English electrician William Watson on 19 April 1754 that he was advancing "a Doctrine so seemingly Paradoxical, Viz. That Clouds are most commonly Electrified Negatively, and the Strokes of Lightning therefore most frequently upwards from the Earth to the Cloud That I fear it will be thought whimsical . . . I hope however that you will not suffer it to be condemned too hastily; but procure it a fair and thorough Examination" (5:266). A month later, writing to Collinson on 28 May, Franklin said he was apprehensive that the notion would "appear so extravagantly whimsical, that none of your Electricians will give themselves the trouble of repeating and verifying the Experiment and the [Royal] Society will be half asham'd of the Honour [in awarding him the Copley medal] they have done me" (5:330). Writing on 29 July 1754, Franklin thanked Collinson for sending a recent pamphlet by the Italian electrician Giambatista Beccaria, "which pleases me much; and the more, as I find his Experiments and Observations on Lightning have led him to the same strange Opinion with me, Thunder-Strokes are sometimes upwards from the Earth to the Cloud; so that I hope the Paper I sent you last Spring on that Subject, will now be kept a little in Countenance, till your Philosophers have Opportunity of verifying the Experiments therein related" (5:395).

Earlier, Franklin had proven his theory that the electricity lay in the coating on the inside and outside of the Leyden jar was wrong. Now he knew that his 1748 theory that held that sea clouds were full of water and that they were charged positively was also wrong. Repeated tests had shown that almost all clouds were in a negative state. His mistake concerning sea clouds was based on another mistake. He had thought the sea "might possibly be the grand Source of Lightning" because of "the common Observation of its luminous Appearance in the Night on the least Motion; an Appearance never observ'd in fresh Water" (4:257). He had hypothesized that its "luminous Appearance" was caused by "Electric Fire, produced by Friction between the Particles of Water and those of Salt" (5:68). During the early summer of 1753, however, he found that seawater in a bottle would "appear luminous" when shaken, yet it would not do so after "a few hours." He concluded that "the luminous appearance in Sea Water must be owing to some other Principle." He tried another theory: in hard gales, would friction against various objects cause the air to become electrified? No. That experiment also failed. Later that year, his Boston correspondent James Bowdoin suggested that microscopic "animalcula" caused the luminosity (5:133), a theory that Franklin accepted and published.[114]

If the earth struck into the clouds, did that mean that the idea of lightning rods was faulty? No, he reassured Collinson in September 1753. The effects were the same. For all practical purposes, it did not matter if lightning struck from above or from below: "Those who are versed in electrical Experiments, will easily conceive that the Effects and Appearances must be nearly the same in either case; the same Explosion, and the same Flash between one Cloud and another, and between the Clouds and Mountains, &c. the same rending of Trees, Walls, &c. which the electric Fluid meets with in its Passage, and the same fatal Shock to animal Bodies; and that pointed Rods fixt on Buildings or Masts of Ships, and communicating with the Earth, or Sea, must be of the same Service in restoring the Equilibrium silently between the Earth and Clouds, or in conducting a Flash or Stroke, if one should be, so as to save harmless the House or Vessel: For Points have equal Power to *throw off*, as to *draw on* the electric Fire, and Rods will conduct up as well as down" (5:72).

Any student who has taken a basic course in electrical engineering learns that Franklin got positive and negative wrong, but the nomenclature is arbitrary. E. Philip Krider has explained that "Most cloud-to-ground lightning begins in the cloud, and initially the air breaks down and becomes conducting via a downward-propagating" leader stroke. "When the leader gets to within about 30 meters (100 feet) of the ground, an upward-propagating attachment process connects the leader to the ground. Once contact has been established, a very intense return stroke goes back to the cloud following the path established by the initial leader."[115] Franklin was right. Usually the main stroke is from the earth to the clouds.

Needed: A New Hypothesis

Though lightning rods and the effects of lightning might be the same whichever way lightning went, the new observations posed a difficulty and a challenge: "now we as much need an Hypothesis to explain by what means the Clouds become *negatively*, as before to show how they became *positively* electrify'd." Franklin came up with another theory. First, he apologized: "I cannot forbear venturing some few Conjectures on this Occasion; They are what occur to me at present; and tho' future Discoveries should prove them not wholly right, yet they may in the mean time be of some use, by stirring up the Curious to make more Experiments and occasion more exact Disquisitions" (5:72). He conjectured that all things contained "a Quantity of the Electric Fluid, just as much as they can contain, which I call the natural Quantity." The natural quantity was not the same in all kinds of common matter of the same dimensions: "a solid Foot, for instance, of one kind of common Matter may contain more of the Electric Fluid than a solid Foot of some other kind of common Matter; and a pound weight of the same kind of common Matter, may, when in a rarer State, contain more of the electric Fluid than when in a denser State." Thus, "When a Portion of Water is in its common dense State, it can hold no more electric Fluid than it has; if any be added, it spreads on the Surface." But "When the same Portion of Water is rarified into Vapour, and forms a Cloud, it is then capable of receiving and absorbing a much greater Quantity" and "there is room for each particle to have an electric Atmosphere" (5:73).

Water in a rarified state, "or in the form of a Cloud, will be in a negative State of Electricity." The cloud, coming close to the earth, would receive from it a flash of electricity. Franklin made an experiment showing that "a Body in different Circumstances of Dilatation and Contraction is capable of receiving and retaining more or less of the Electric Fluid on its Surface." He placed a clean wine glass on the floor and on top of it a small silver can.

> In the Cann I put about 3 yards of brass Chain, to one End of which I fastened a Silk Thread which went right up to the Cieling where it passed over a Pully, and came down again to my hand, that I might at Pleasure draw the Chain up out of the Cann, extending it 'till within a Foot of the Cieling and let it gradually sink into the Cann again. From the Cieling by another Thread of fine raw Silk, I suspended a small light Lock of Cotton, so as that when it hung perpendicularly, it came in Contact with the Side of the Cann. Then approaching the Wire of a Charged Vial to the Cann, I gave it a Spark which flowed round it in an electric Atmosphere; and the Lock of Cotton was repelled from the Side of the Cann to the distance of about 9 or 10 Inches. The Cann would not then receive another Spark from the Wire of the Vial; but as I gradually drew up the Chain, the Atmosphere of the Cann diminished by flowing over the rising Chain, and the Lock of Cotton accordingly drew nearer and nearer to the Cann; and then, if I again brought the Vial Wire near the Cann, it would receive another Spark and the Cotton fly off again to its first Distance; and thus, as the Chain was drawn higher, the Cann would receive more Sparks. (5:74–75)

The experiment proved that the can and the extended chain supported a greater amount of electrical atmosphere than the can "with the chain gathered up into its Belly." Franklin concluded that an "Increase of Surface makes a Body capable of receiving a greater Electric Atmosphere" (5:75). But he found, as we will see, difficulties with this theory. He applied the observation to the behavior of clouds. Water in its rarified state, or in the form of a cloud, will have less than its natural quantity of electricity and will be in a negative state. Such a cloud, coming near the earth, will receive from it a flash of the electric fluid. The quantity of the fluid will sometimes be extremely large "to supply a great extent of Cloud." A negative cloud being supplied from the earth "may strike into other Clouds that have not been supplied." He concluded that thunder-clouds, being full of water, were "generally in a negative State of Electricity compared with the Earth" (5:74).

The exception was the cloud in a positive state of electricity. Franklin conjectured that a cloud with its natural quantity might become "compressed by the driving Winds, or some other means, so that part of what it had absorbed was forced out, and formed an electric Atmosphere around it in its denser State" (5:73). He then performed an experiment showing that a body in different conditions of "Dilatation and Contraction" was capable of receiving and retaining more or less of the electric fluid on its surface.

Franklin noted an objection to his new hypothesis: if water in its rarified state as a cloud "requires and will absorb more of the electric Fluid than when in its dense State as Water, why does it not acquire from the Earth all it wants at the Instant of its leaving the Surface?" He confessed that he could not give a satisfying solution, but he said that he would state the conjecture and the problem "in its full Force" and "submit the whole to Examination" (5:76), hoping that someone would come up with a more satisfying explanation.

Impious and Dangerous Rods

From time immemorial, thunder and lightning had been thought to be acts of God, punishing human beings for their sins.[116] Franklin had heard this often in sermons as a boy in Boston. In the year that James Franklin started the *New-England Courant*, Cotton Mather wrote a survey of contemporary science, *The Christian Philosopher* (1721), in which he devoted Essay 16 to thunder and lightning. After briefly surveying the scientific theories (none of which mentions electricity, though a number of early electricians had already compared the "electric fire" to lightning), Mather claimed that thunder was "the Voice of God" and lightning "the Arrows of God." In thunderstorms, he said, God is calling for "a thorough Repentance."[117]

Jonathan Edwards, who was just three years older than Franklin, wrote in his "Personal Narrative" that he "felt God at the first appearance of a thunderstorm." As he saw "the lightnings play" and heard the "awful voice of God's thunder," he was led "to sweet contemplations of my great and glorious God."[118] Franklin reprinted the older religious ideas in various publications, including the *Pennsylvania Gazette* and *Poor Richard*. Even after theorizing that lightning was electricity, Franklin reprinted the following verses in *Poor Richard* for December 1751.

> Ere the Foundations of the World were laid,
> Ere kindling Light th'Almighty Word obey'd,
> Thou wert; and when the subterraneous Flame,
> Shall burst its Prison, and devour this Frame,
> From angry Heav'n when the keen Lightning flies,
> When fervent Heat dissolves the melting Skies,
> Thou still shalt be; still as thou wert before,
> And know no Change when *Time* shall be no more.

Local ministers called for reformation whenever lightning struck some colonial American town. Franklin and Kinnersley knew that some persons would think their electrical experiments impious, especially the theory that lightning was electrical in nature and that iron rods could safely conduct lightning. In the Franklin/Kinnersley electrical lectures in 1749, the Baptist minister Kinnersley emphasized that God was the cause underlying whatever natural causes man found. After suggesting two hypotheses concerning the actions of planets within the solar system, Kinnersley concluded: "by whatsoever natural Causes these glorious suspended Worlds are kept asunder in opposition to the great Force of mutual Gravity . . . that Cause is in the Hands of the great Maker & Governour of the Universe."[119]

Writing in private to friends, Franklin ironically joked about the implications of science for the older religious attitudes. After he proposed the use of lightning rods, he wrote Cadwallader Colden on 23 April 1752, " 'Tis well we are not, as poor Galileo was, subject to the Inquisition for Philosophical Heresy. My Whispers against the orthodox Doctrine in private Letters, would be dangerous; your Writing and Printing would be highly criminal. As it is, you must expect some Censure, but one Heretic will surely excuse another." Franklin was more sarcastic and even sacrilegious when writing David Hume on 19 May 1762 about lightning rods and a theological controversy in Neuchâtel (that letter will be considered in *Life*, Volume 4).

When he introduced lightning rods into his lectures in 1751, Kinnersley attempted to forestall religious objections. Two anonymous letters of 11 May 1752 from gentlemen in Newport, Rhode Island, to friends in New York provide evidence of the prejudice and testimony to the effectiveness of his demonstrations. One Newport writer said that he had thought any attempt to explain the cause of lightning was idle and vain, and that any attempt to avoid lightning was merely "Presumption." The demonstrations, however, were so clear and convincing that "all my former pre-conceived Notions . . . together with my Prejudices, immediately vanish'd." The author assured his correspondent that Kinnersley had the "highest Christian Character" and made electricity "subservient to the true Intent of all Knowledge, both natural and reveal'd, *viz.*, to lead us to the first Cause by refining, enlarging and exalting our Ideas of the great Author and God of Nature." The second Newport writer testified that the "Christian Philosopher" Kinnersley implanted in his lectures "the loftiest Ideas of the Almighty God and great Author of all Nature."[120]

A month later in June 1752, when Franklin succeeded in drawing "electric fire" (as sparks of electricity were usually called) from the sky, he realized that he had triumphed over ages of superstition regarding lightning. He tried to avoid the charge of presumption and blasphemy when he described lightning rods in *Poor Richard* for 1753.

Jealous electricians claimed that lightning rods were inadequate and dangerous. The renowned French electrician Nollet attempted to contradict Franklin's theories while at the same time claiming precedence in identifying lightning as electricity. Franklin read his book, and on 12 April 1753 wrote Cadwallader Colden that he was surprised and disappointed by the French savant: "In one or two Places," he appeals "to the superstitious Prejudices of the Populace, which I think unworthy of a Philosopher: He speaks as if he thought it Presumption in Man, to propose guarding himself against the *Thunders of Heaven*! Surely the Thunder of Heaven is no more supernatural than the Rain, Hail or Sunshine of Heaven, against the Inconveniencies of which we guard by Roofs and Shades without Scruple." Franklin ironically continued that he could now reassure Nol-

How to secure Houses, &c. from LIGHTNING.

IT has pleafed God in his Goodnefs to Mankind, at length to difcover to them the Means of fecuring their Habitations and other Buildings from Mifchief by Thunder and Lightning. The Method is this: Provide a fmall Iron Rod (it may be made of the Rod-iron ufed by the Nailers) but of fuch a Length, that one End being three or four Feet in the moift Ground, the other may be fix or eight Feet above the higheft Part of the Building. To the upper End of the Rod faften about a Foot of Brafs Wire, the Size of a common Knitting-needle, fharpened to a fine Point ; the Rod may be fecured to the Houfe by a few fmall Staples. If the Houfe or Barn be long, there may be a Rod and Point at each End, and a middling Wire along the Ridge from one to the other. A Houfe thus furnifhed will not be damaged by Lightning, it being at-tracted by the Points, and paffing thro the Metal into the Ground without hurting any Thing. Veffels alfo, having a fharp pointed Rod fix'd on the Top of their Mafts, with a Wire from the Foot of the Rod reaching down, round one of the Shrouds, to the Water, will not be hurt by Lightning.

Figure 16. *"How to secure Houses, &c. from Lightning,"* Poor Richard Improved *(1753). On the penultimate page of* Poor Richard Improved *for 1753, which was advertised as "Just Published" on 16 November 1752, Franklin gave instructions for erecting lightning rods and simultaneously tried to avoid the pitfall of seeming to deny that God caused lightning. He began by asserting "It has pleased God in his Goodness to Mankind, at length to discover to them the Means of securing their Habitations and other Buildings from Mischief by Thunder and Lightning." One should furnish structures with a small iron rod that extended above the structure into the ground. The upper end should be "six or eight Feet above the highest Part of the Building" with a further foot of brass wire at the end, and the down rod should go "three or four Feet in the moist Ground."*

Franklin wrote, "A House thus furnished will not be damaged by Lightning, it being attracted by the Points, and passing thro the Metal into the Ground without hurting any Thing." He still hoped that lightning rods might silently carry the atmospheric electricity down the rods into the earth, thus preventing lightning from actually striking a structure. If, however, lightning did strike, the lightning rod would conduct the electricity into the ground. Courtesy, American Philosophical Society.

let because it was usually lightning "from the Earth that strikes the Clouds," not lightning from the heavens striking the earth (4:463). Reviewing Nollet's *Letters* (1753) for the Royal Society of London on 17 May 1753, William Watson also seemed prejudiced. He endorsed Nollet's theories and agreed with Nollet's statement that "considering the electrification of pointed bodies as a proof of lessening the matter of thunder" is a "vain hope." Watson quoted Nollet approvingly that experiments with electrification of clouds were too dangerous to make and that "mischiefs arising from thunder" could not "be averted by the apparatus proposed."[121]

Twenty-three-year-old John Adams recorded a dramatic instance of prejudice. Sometime between 5 and 18 December 1758, he witnessed the railing of Ben Veasey, a Braintree, Massachusetts, neighbor, against "the Presumption of Philosophers in erecting Iron Rods to draw the Lightning from the Clouds." Adams ironically reported that Veasey's "Brains were in a ferment with strong Liquor and he railed, and foamed against those Points and the Presumption that erected them, in Language taken partly from Scripture and partly from the drunken Disputes of Tavern Philosophy, in as wild mad a manner as King Lear. . . . He talked of presuming upon God as Peter attempted to walk upon the Water, attempting to controul the Artilry of Heaven, an Execution that Mortal man cant Stay."[122]

Ephraim Chambers's *Cyclopaedia* had popularized the theory that explosions of sulphur caused both lightning and earthquakes, underground sulphur explosions bringing on earthquakes and sulphur explosions in the clouds causing lightning. After earthquakes shook England in February and on 8 March 1749/50, the Reverend William Stukeley, as noted above, replaced sulphur with electricity as the cause of earthquakes and lightning, citing Franklin's "Hypothesis." In the same number of the *Philosophical Transactions*, the Reverend Stephen Hales argued that lightning caused earthquakes.[123] An anonymous refutation of Stukeley's essay appeared in the *Gentleman's Magazine* in August 1751.

The great 1755 Lisbon earthquake caused Voltaire, Immanuel Kant, and others to question the usual theodicies. Boston had an earthquake on 18 November 1755, which inspired Boston's Reverend Thomas Prince to republish his 1727 sermon *Earthquakes the Works of God*. He added an appendix updating the earlier theories concerning earthquakes. Since "the sagacious Mr. Franklin" had proven that lightning was electricity, and since the earth sometimes struck into the clouds, was not an earthquake also caused by electricity? Prince claimed that lightning rods drew down electricity into the earth and thereby caused earthquakes. Lightning rods were unbalancing nature. Prince claimed: "The more *Points of Iron* are erected round the *Earth* to draw the *Electrical Substance* out of the *Air*, the more the *Earth* must needs be charged with it." Consequently, there would be more earthquakes. "In *Boston* are more erected than any where else in *New England*; and *Boston* seems to be more dreadfully shaken. Oh! there is no getting out of the mighty Hand of God! If we think to avoid it in the *Air*, we cannot in the *Earth*: Yea it may grow more fatal." Presumably Prince did not know that there were few, if any, lightning rods in Lisbon.

Prince's assessment irritated Franklin's friend and correspondent John Winthrop, a professor of natural philosophy at Harvard. Winthrop published *A Lecture on Earthquakes; Read in the Chapel of Harvard-College in Cambridge,*

N.E. November 26th 1755. The scientist observed that earthquakes had previously been described as either "horizontal, or from side to side" or "perpendicular, or right up and down." Winthrop validated both descriptions by comparing earthquake motion to the "undulating motion" of a wave, which indeed rolls up and down and from side to side (as many persons who have become seasick in boats can testify). He also observed that bricks from his thirty-two-foot-high chimney had fallen thirty feet away. He calculated that the speed of the tremor was twenty-one feet per second, and opined that the shorter in duration the earth's vibrations were, the quicker the pendulum effect: "Our buildings were rocked with a kind of angular motion, like that of a cradle; the upper parts of them moving swifter, or thro' greater spaces in the same time, than the lower; the natural consequence of an undulatory motion of the earth."[124] Winthrop's observations and measurements began the science of seismology.

Winthrop chastised Prince: "I should think, though with the utmost deference to superior judgements, that the pathetic exclamation . . . ["O! there is no getting out of the mighty Hand of God!"] might well enough have been spared." Winthrop commented, "I cannot believe, that in the whole town of *Boston*, where so many iron points are erected, there is so much as one person, who is so weak, so ignorant, so foolish, or to say in one word, so atheistical, as ever to have entertained a single thought, that it is possible, by the help of a few yards of wire, to 'get out of the mighty hand of GOD.'" Prince replied and Winthrop responded, leading to another round in the quarrel (6:404n).

John Adams knew Prince's sermon and purchased a copy of Winthrop's *Lecture*. He wrote in his copy of Winthrop that Prince's exclamation "Oh! there is no getting out of the mighty Hand of God!" was popular. Most people in Massachusetts, Adams wrote, "consider Thunder, and Lightening as well as Earthquakes, only as Judgments, Punishments, Warnings &c. and have no conception of any Uses they can serve in Nature. I have heard some Persons of the highest Rank among us, say, that they really thought the Erection of Iron Points, was an impious attempt to robb the almighty of his Thunder, to wrest the Bolt of Vengeance out of his Hand. And others, that Thunder was designed, as an Execution upon Criminals, that no Mortal can stay." He also found that even in instances of church steeples struck by lightning, "where Iron Bars have by Accident conveyed the Electricity as far as they reached without damage, which one would think would force Conviction, have no weight at all."

Adams generalized that most people rejected all novelties: "This Invention of Iron Points, to prevent the Danger of Thunder, has met with opposition from the superstition, affectation of Piety, and Jealousy of new Inventions, that Inoculation to prevent the Danger of the Small Pox, and all other usefull Discoveries, have met with in all ages of the World." He questioned whether the belief in lightning as divine retribution really was found in the Bible: "I am not able to satisfy myself, whether the very general if not universal apprehension that Thunder, Earthquakes, Pestilence, Famine &c. are designed merely as Punishments of sins and Warnings to forsake, is natural to Mankind, or whether it was artfully propagated, or whether it was derived from Revelation." He concluded, however, that such beliefs could not come from "real Revelation": "An Imagination that those Things are of no Use in Nature but to punish and alarm and arouse sinners, could not be derived from real Revelation, because it is far from being true, tho few Persons can be persuaded to think so."[125]

Franklin read Winthrop's pamphlets at the time and recalled them when writing to him over a dozen years later on 2 July 1768. Franklin mentioned the continuing practice of constructing high buildings without lightning rods and of the expressions against lightning rods even by Nollet: "It is perhaps not so extraordinary that unlearned men, such as commonly compose our church vestries, should not yet be acquainted with, and sensible of the benefit of metal conductors, in averting the stroke of lightning, and preserving our houses from its violent effects; or that they should be still prejudiced against the use of such conductors, when we see how long even philosophers, men of extensive science and great ingenuity, can hold out against the evidence of new knowledge that does not square with their preconceptions, and how long men can retain a practice that is conformable to their prejudices, and expect a benefit from such practice, though constant experience shows its inutility."

Pope Benedict XIV had recommended the use of lightning rods shortly after they were proven effective,[126] but the old practice of consecrating church bells and ringing them during thunderstorms continued. Franklin ironically alluded to it: "though for a thousand years past bells have been consecrated by priests of the Romish church, in expectation that the sound of such blessed bells would drive away those storms, and secure our buildings from the stroke of lightning; and during so long a period it has not been found by experience that places within the reach of such blessed sound are safer than others where it is never heard; but that on the contrary, the lightning seems to strike steeples of choice, and that at the very time the bells are ringing; yet still they continue to bless the new bells and jangle the old ones whenever it thunders" (15:169).

MEDICINE, ELECTRICITY, AND RELIGION

After the discovery of the Leyden jar, numerous experimenters treated various maladies with electric shocks. Speculative contributions on electricity for medicinal purposes appeared in the 1747 periodicals, some with illustrations. The *London Magazine* for June 1747 showed a complicated electrical machine, and the July issue portrayed a nude man taking an electrical bath inside a tank suspended by silk cords. D. Stevenson, writing from the "Office of Ordance, in the Tower of London," said that such enclosures should be installed in "all Places where People resort for Health, as Bath," and in all hospitals, where he expected the sick, lame, and wounded persons, as well as those with smallpox, to benefit. The periodicals reported numerous cures, especially in cases of palsy and partial paralysis. The *Gentleman's Magazine* reported the case of "a Gentleman who has entirely recovered his Speech by the use of the Electrical Machine alone, after having lost it above 20 months."[127]

After reading such accounts, persons with various ailments asked Franklin or Kinnersley to give them electric shocks. Franklin's friend and patron James Logan had suffered a stroke in 1740 that partially paralyzed his right side. When he suffered attacks of palsy in 1749 he had himself shocked, perhaps by Franklin, who supplied the apparatus. Franklin sent him news of the French experiments giving shocks to paralytic persons, and said that when he came out to "fetch the apparatus," he would be glad to perform whatever experiments Logan wanted "which you cannot well try yourself" (3:433). Governor Jonathan Belcher of New Jersey had palsy, read about the cures in the English magazines, consulted his physician, and wrote Franklin in the fall of 1752 about using electric shocks. Franklin replied that if Belcher wanted, he would come to Burlington and administer them. As it turned out, Franklin did not, but he sent the machinery to Belcher "with the particular directions how to use it." Belcher wrote on 18 November, thanking him, and concluded with a reference to their both being from Boston, "Your Friend and Countryman." The Reverend Aaron Burr, president of the College of New Jersey, electrified Belcher several times, but Belcher reported no improvement (4:255).[128]

Franklin relieved Joseph Huey's partial paralysis. Franklin wrote him on 6 June 1753 that he was "glad to hear that you increase in Strength; I hope you will continue mending till you recover your former Health and Firmness." Franklin also evidently advised him to "use the cold Bath," and asked him about its effect, but nothing more is known of Huey (cf. below, pp. 311–12). Another patient is mentioned in Franklin's early writings on electricity, but only because she inadvertently took an electric shock. A very tall young woman asked Franklin to electrify her feet. As he was preparing to do so, she stooped forward "to look at the placing of her feet" and inadvertently put her forehead "too near my prime-conductor" and received a shock. "She dropt, but instantly got up again, complaining of nothing" (5:525).

On 21 December 1757, Franklin summarized his experiences with the use of electricity for medical purposes. Many paralytics had come to Franklin asking him to electrify them, "which I did for them, at their Request." Normally he had the patients sit in a chair, electrified them, and drew large strong sparks from all parts of the affected limb or side. Franklin would then charge two six-gallon jars and send the united shock through the affected limb, repeating the stroke three times a day. The patients usually improved for several days. The affected limbs were more capable of motion and seemed stronger: "These Appearances gave great Spirits to the Patients, and made them hope a perfect Cure; but I do not remember that I ever saw any Amendment after the fifth Day." After the patients found their improvement ceasing, they stopped the shocks, and in a short time relapsed to their former condition, "So that I never knew any Advantage from Electricity in Palsies that was permanent."

Franklin suspected that electricity was not medically effective and that any improvement in the patient was a result of exercise and the patient's desire to believe in some improvement: "how far the apparent temporary Advantage might arise from the Exercise in the Patients Journey and coming daily to my House, or from the Spirits given by the Hope of Success, enabling them to exert more Strength in moving their Limbs, I will not pretend to say" (7:299). Nevertheless, various individuals often asked Franklin to use electricity to attempt to help cure them, and when he could, he tried to cooperate (12:29, 14:95).

The exception was a young woman evidently suffering from hysteria rather than palsy or paralysis: "C.B. was a 24-year old woman who had suffered from severe convulsive fits for ten years." She wrote Dr. Cadwalader Evans that she had gone to Philadelphia in the beginning of September 1752 to ask Franklin to cure her with electric shocks: "I receiv'd four shocks morning and evening; they were what they call 200 strokes of the wheel, which fills an eight gallon bottle, and indeed they were very severe." At the first shock she felt the fit coming on, but the second "effectually carry'd it off." That experience happened repeatedly, "yet the symptoms gradually decreased, 'till at length they intirely left me." She did this for two weeks, "and when I went home, B. Franklin was so good as to supply me with a globe and bottle, to electrify myself every day for three months." Five months later, she reported that she was cured. She lived a healthy life to age seventy-nine.[129]

Further Experiments on Atmospheric Electricity

In September 1753, Franklin suggested another miniature proof that lightning rods might either prevent or carry off lightning. When positioned to see "horizontally the under Side of a Thunder Cloud," he observed that it appeared "very ragged, with a Number of separate Fragments" or small "Clouds one under another, the lowest sometimes not far from the Earth." The clouds were like "so many Stepping Stones" and assisted "in conducting a Stroke between the Cloud and a Building." Based on the observation, Franklin devised an experiment, which Joseph Priestley judged "most ingenious and beautiful."[130] Franklin took several "Locks of fine loose Cotton" and connected one with a prime conductor by a slender thread of two inches, connected another with the first, and still another with the second. As one turned the globe producing electricity, the locks of fine loose cotton extended "themselves towards the Table (as the Lower small Clouds do towards the Earth) being attracted by it." Then, presenting an erect needle under the lowest, "it will shrink up to the second, the second to the first, and all together to the Prime Conductor, where they will continue as long as the Point continues under them." Franklin then applied the demonstration to thunderstorms: "May not in like manner, the small electrised Clouds, whose Equilibrium with the Earth is soon restored by the Point, rise up to the main Body, and by that means occasion so large a Vacancy, as that the grand Cloud cannot strike in that Place?" (5:78).

Johann Carl Wilcke, who translated Franklin's *Experiments and Observations* into German late in 1758, wrote that he saw Franklin's hypothesis confirmed on 28 August 1758. As he was observing a large fringed cloud passing over a forest of tall fir trees, the ragged, lower parts of the cloud were seemingly attracted lower and then "suddenly rose higher, and joined the larger cloud."[131]

Writing Kinnersley about lightning rods on 20 February 1762, Franklin noted that they had not been so widely adopted in England as in America. England had fewer thunderstorms than America and less lightning. He said that those who "calculate chances may perhaps find that not one death (or the destruction of one house) in a hundred thousand happens from that cause, and that therefore it is scarce worth while to be at any expence to guard against it." But some buildings were "more exposed than others to such accidents," and perhaps they especially should have lightning rods. But a psychological reason also existed for erecting lightning rods: "there are minds so strongly" fearful of lightning "as to be very unhappy every time a little thunder is within their hearing." Therefore, "it may . . . be well to render this little piece of new knowledge as general and as well understood as possible, since to make us *safe* is not all its advantage, it is some to make us *easy*. And as the stroke it secures us from might have chanced perhaps but once in our lives, while it may relieve us a hundred times from those painful apprehensions, the latter may possibly on the whole contribute more to the happiness of mankind than the former" (10:52). As we will see, Franklin made a similar point about learning to swim in his 1749 *Proposals Relating to the Education of Youth in Pennsylvania* (3:403n).

After the summer of 1752, Franklin installed lightning rods in his successive Philadelphia homes, including the final one he built in 1763–65. While in France during the American Revolution, lightning struck his home, "which was visible to the Neighbours, who immediately ran in to see if any Damage was done, or any Fire commenc'd which might by their Assistance be extinguish'd." They found nothing disturbed and his family only frightened by the extraordinary noise. Franklin returned to Philadelphia in 1785 and added a major addition to the house in 1786–87. When the old lightning rod was taken down, he found "that the Copper Point which had been nine Inches long, and in its thickest Part about one third of an Inch Diameter, had been almost all melted and blown away, very little of it remaining attach'd to the Iron Rod. . . . at length the Invention has been of some Use to the Inventor" (S 9:617).

PERSONAL NOTES

Deborah evidently was somewhat afraid of Franklin's experiments. Franklin's own experience probably confirmed her fear. On the evening of 23 December 1750, Franklin accidently "made an Experiment in Electricity that I desire never to repeat." He was about to kill a turkey by a shock from two large glass jars that contained "as much electrical fire as forty common Phials." On this social occasion, Franklin, talking with the company, became temporarily distracted. He was about to see if the two bottles were fully charged "by the Strength and Length of the stream issuing to my hands as I commonly used to do, and which I might safely eno' have done if I had not held the chain in the other hand." He "took the whole" electric charge "thro' my own Arms and Body, by receiving the fire from the united Top Wires with one hand, while the other held a Chain connected with the outsides of both Jars." A great flash and a crack as loud as a pistol ensued, "yet my Senses being instantly gone, I neither Saw the one nor heard the other; nor did I feel the Stroke on my hand." Afterward Franklin found the electricity had "raised a round swelling" on his hand "where the fire enter'd as big as half a Pistol Bullet." He concluded that electricity was quicker than "Sound, Light and animal Sensation."

The electrical shock felt like "an universal Blow thro'out my whole Body from head to foot . . . after which the first thing I took notice of was a violent quick Shaking of my body which gradually remitting, my sense as gradually return'd, and then I tho't the Bottles must be discharged but Could not conceive how, till at last I Perceived the Chain in my hand, and Recollected what I had been About to do: that part of my hand and fingers which held the Chain was left white as tho' the Blood had been Driven Out, and Remained so 8 or 10 Minutes after, feeling like Dead flesh, and I had a Numbness in my Arms and the back of my Neck, which Continued till the Next Morning but wore off." He added that on Christmas Day, two days later, "Nothing Remains now of this Shock but a Soreness in my breast Bone, which feels As if it had been Brused. I did not fall, but Suppose I should have been Knocked Down if I had Received the Stroke in my head: the whole was Over in less than a minute."

Franklin wrote that he was "Ashamed to have been Guilty of so Notorious A Blunder; A Match for that of the Irishman, Sister Told me of, who to Divert his Wife pour'd the Bottle of Gun Powder on the live Coal; or of that Other, who being About to Steal Powder, made a Hole in the Cask with a Hott Iron" (4:82–83). Other electricians must occasionally have made similar mistakes, but who else published his mistake and ridiculed himself? Ironically, everyone who writes about Franklin's electricity tells of his blunder (including me).

Deborah worried about Franklin's electrical apparatus while he was in England. No doubt she suppressed her concern while Franklin was with her. She may have enjoyed witnessing some experiments, but the occasional ringing of the bell and the flashes of sparks in her stairway scared her. She wrote him about it early in 1758. Franklin replied from London on 10 June 1758: "If the ringing of the Bells frightens you, tie a Piece of Wire from one Bell to the other, and that will conduct the lightning without ringing or snapping, but silently. Tho' I think it best the Bells should be at Liberty to ring, that you may know when the Wire is electrify'd, and, if you are afraid, may keep at a Distance" (P 8:94). I suspect she just tried to avoid that area of her stairway.

Starting Game for Philosophers

Commentators have often said that Franklin was typically American in being less concerned with philosophy and theory than with the practical and useful.[132] Some of Franklin's statements seem to confirm this opinion: "What signifies Philosophy that does not apply to some Use?" (9:251). The sententia is memorable. Ignoring its context, it seems to say that theoretical investigations are worthless. But Franklin made the statement after he carried out a series of experiments on the ability of different colors to absorb heat. Within its context, it justifies theoretical science. I. Bernard Cohen pointed out that when Franklin "made the experiments, he could hardly have known that there would be any possible practical application, since at the time the fact of varying absorption of heat as a function of color was not even known to exist."[133]

But even in the comparatively brief discussion of his experiments and conjectures given above, Franklin attempted to understand phenomena, made hypotheses trying to account for what he observed, and devised experiments to confirm or refute the hypotheses. As he said concerning a theory that failed, "how many pretty Systems do we build, which we soon find ourselves oblig'd to destroy" (3:171). Franklin judged that he had "too strong a penchant to the building of hypotheses," but he ventured to publish some that he did not find entirely satisfactory because they might lead others to think of better ones (4:341, 5:79). He suggested experiments and hypotheses for further research and experiments to Joseph Priestley, Jan Ingenhousz, and other natural philosophers. As Harvard's John Winthrop said, Franklin was "good at starting game for philosophers" (S 9:652).

When he introduced the theory that lightning rods would either carry off the electricity in the atmosphere silently or would, if lightning struck, convey it safely into the ground, he conceded that he did not know why points possessed such power or why metal conducted electricity: "Nor is it of much Importance to us to know the Manner in which Nature executes her Laws, 'tis enough, if we know the Laws themselves. 'Tis of real Use to know, that China left in the Air unsupported, will fall and break; but how it comes to fall, and why it breaks, are Matters of Speculation. 'Tis a Pleasure indeed to know them, but we can preserve our China without it." Thus, he said, "in the present Case, to know this Power of Points may possibly be of some Use to Mankind" is sufficient, "tho' we should never be able to explain it" (4:17).

One might suppose that Franklin was saying it was unimportant to understand gravity or electric atmosphere or the greater conductivity of metal and water compared to some other matter. In fact, he echoed Newton's statement in the "General Scholium" to book 3 of the *Principia* concerning gravity. Here, he aligned himself with Newtonian agnosticism as opposed to Cartesian omniscience. Who would claim that Newton was not interested in explanations for observed phenomena? Franklin cared about causes.[134] He was saying that for most people's daily lives, it may not be as important to know the causes as to know what will happen. Like Newton, however, Franklin found it a "Pleasure indeed" to know the causes—and he sought the reasons underlying various phenomena throughout his life. He was highly successful in discovering them and in encouraging research not only in electricity but in sciences from meteorology to the common cold. Perhaps no other person between Newton's death (1727) and Franklin's (1790) did more to advance and promote research than he. Adrienne Koch, a historian of ideas, observed: "Only the proper passion for theoretical understanding can explain Franklin's sustained and highly constructive inquiry into the nature of electrical phenomena—an inquiry that might or might not have had ultimate practical significance."[135]

Writing on 6 December 1753 of the causes and effects concerning attraction and repulsion in electricity, Franklin agreed with Cadwallader Colden that it seemed "absurd to suppose that a Body can act where it is not. I have no Idea of Bodies at a Distance attracting or repelling one another without the Assistance of some Medium, tho' I know not what that Medium is, or how it operates. When I speak of Attraction or Repulsion I make use of those Words for want of others more proper, and intend only to express *Effects*, which I see, and not *Causes*, of which I am ignorant." What could the medium be? Franklin cited an example that everyone could understand but that no one had yet satisfactorily explained: "When I press a blown Bladder between my Knees, I find I cannot bring its Sides together, but my Knees feel a Springy Matter pushing them back to a greater Distance, or repelling them. I conclude that the Air it contains is the Cause." And when he tried to compact air, he found he could not "force its Particles into Contact." He therefore supposed "there must be some Medium between its Particles that prevents their Closing, tho' I cannot tell what it is. And if I were acquainted with that Medium, and found its Particles to approach and recede from each other according to the Pressure they suffer'd, I should imagine there must be some finer Medium between them by which these Operations were performed" (5:146).

What was in air that human force could not compress? No one knew. So too there was attraction and repulsion. Franklin advanced the understanding of electric atmospheres around points and blunt bodies, but what was that atmosphere? No one knew. Franklin wanted to know and he hoped that if he did learn, he might be able to put what he learned to some use. But first, he was curious, what was in the air?

CHALLENGES

Phenomena that defied Franklin's theories especially interested him. In experiment #29 reported on 29 April 1749, he noted that he was surprised that negatively charged bodies repelled one another. The fact was "hitherto not satisfactorily accounted for" by his theories (3:363–64). Franklin published a later experiment, expressed his puzzlement, and asked others if they could account for it. As in the experiment reported in September 1753, quoted above (5:74–75), he used a silver can: "I electrified a silver pint cann, on an electric stand, and then lowered into it a cork ball, of about an inch diameter, hanging by a silk string, till the cork touched the bottom of the cann. The cork was not attracted to the inside of the cann as it would have been to the outside, and though it touched the bottom, yet, when drawn out, it was not found to be electrified by that touch, as it would have been by touching the outside." Why would the outside of the can be electrified and the inside not? He reported to Dr. John Lining on 18 March 1755: "The fact is singular. You require the reason; I do not know it. Perhaps you may discover it, and then you will be so good as to communicate it to me" (5:525–26).

Franklin generalized about his failures and his ignorance: "I find a frank acknowledgment of one's ignorance is not only the easiest way to get rid of a difficulty, but the likeliest way to obtain information, and therefore I practice it: I think it an honest policy. Those who affect to be thought to know every thing, and so undertake to explain every thing, often remain long ignorant of many things that others could and would instruct them in, if they appeared less conceited" (5:525–26). He told Priestley about the experiment, asking him to repeat it and "ascertain the fact." Priestley did so, and carried the experiment further. He believed he found that "the attraction of electricity is subject to the same laws with that of gravitation, and is therefore according to the squares of the distances."[136]

Priestley thought that the study of electricity afforded more "ingenious speculation" than any other science: "Here the imagination may have full play, in conceiving of the manner in which an invisible agent produces an almost infinite variety of visible effects." The progress of electricity, he thought, was based on theories: "Hypotheses, while they are considered merely as such, lead persons to try a variety of experiments, in order to ascertain them. In these experiments, new facts generally arise. These new facts serve to correct the hypothesis which gave occasion to them. The theory, thus corrected, serves to discover more new facts; which, as before bring the theory still nearer to the truth." According to Priestley, the progress of our understanding the nature of electricity had been based on hypotheses. He named Franklin its major single investigator and theoretician. Priestley concluded that if a person can frame the theory "so as really to suit all the facts, it has all the evidence of truth that the nature of things can admit."[137] Franklin failed to create a theory of electricity that explained all the facts, but his theory dramatically advanced the study of electricity and provided a starting point for future investigations.

Franklin's hypothesis of positive and negative electricity was, Priestley said, the most important one in electricity, and yet Franklin, "with a truly philosophical greatness of mind, to which few persons have ever attained, always mentions it with the utmost diffidence." Priestley quoted Franklin's statement that all the appearances he had seen, "in which Glass and Electricity are concern'd, are I think explain'd" by the theory. "Yet perhaps it may not be a true one, and I shall be obliged to him that affords me a better" (4:31–32). Priestley added, "It is no wonder, indeed, that this excellent philosopher should treat even his own hypothesis with such indifference, when he had so just a sense of the nature, use, and importance of all hypotheses."[138]

LOVELY SCIENCE

Franklin found science lovely. Stars through telescopes and tissues through microscopes presented startling and beautiful appearances. Franklin wrote in *Poor Richard* for 1751: "The Flesh of all Land and Sea Animals dried, and cut into very thin Slices, gives a beautiful View of the various Fibres, and their Convolutions. The Brain, the spinal Marrow, and even the Hairs of Animals, exhibit different Curiosities" (4:90). Joseph Priestley repeatedly revealed an aesthetic delight in Franklin's work. In his *History and Present State of Electricity,* Priestley wrote that Franklin's demonstration that "completely proved, that the coating on one side received just as much as was emitted from the discharge of the other" was "a beautiful experiment." He called the miniature demonstration of the action between electrified clouds and the earth "a most ingenious and beautiful experiment."[139]

Of course Franklin never commented that his own experiments were beautiful, but he obviously enjoyed his "philosophical amusements" (4:68, 340). When he retired from business at the beginning of 1748, he hoped to spend the rest of his life in "philosophical Studies and Amusements" (A 119). Franklin twice called an experiment of Ebenezer Kinnersley's "beautiful." Why? It demonstrated that electricity heated iron, thus proving "that the Fusion of Iron by a Stroke of Lightning may be a hot and not a cold Fusion as we formerly suppos'd" (11:97, 10:37). Elegantly refuting Franklin's former idea and proving a new one was "beautiful."

Perhaps what Franklin most enjoyed about it was that it led him to speculate about the nature of matter. Not only did it all contain electricity, but it also all seemed to contain fire.

How many ways there are of kindling fire, or producing heat in bodies! By the sun's rays, by collision, by friction, by hammering, by putrefaction, by fermentation, by mixtures of fluids, by mixtures of solids with fluids, and by electricity. And yet the fire when produced, though in different bodies it may differ in circumstances, as in colour, vehemence, &c. yet in the same bodies is generally the same. Does not this seem to indicate that the fire existed in the body, though in a quiescent state, before it was by any of these means excited, disengaged, and brought forth to action and to view? May it not constitute part, and even a principal part, of the solid substance of bodies? If this should be the case, kindling fire in a body would be nothing more than developing this inflammable principle, and setting it at liberty to act in separating the parts of that body,

which then exhibits the appearances of scorching, melting, burning, &c. . . .
When a single spark from a flint, applied to a magazine of gunpowder, is immediately attended with this consequence, that the whole is in flame, exploding
with immense violence, could all this fire exist first in the spark? We cannot
conceive it. And thus we seem led to this supposition, that there is fire enough
in all bodies to singe, melt, or burn them, whenever it is, by any means, set at
liberty, so that it may exert itself upon them, or be disengaged from them. This
liberty seems to be afforded it by the passage of electricity through them, which
we know can and does, of itself, separate the parts even of water; and perhaps
the immediate appearances of fire are only the effects of such separations? If so,
there would be no need of supposing that the electric fluid *heats itself* by the
swiftness of its motion, or heats bodies by the resistance it meets with in passing
through them. They would only be heated in proportion as such separation
could be more easily made. Thus a melting heat cannot be given to a large wire
in the flame of a candle, though it may to a small one; and this not because the
large wire resists *less* that action of the flame which tends to separate its parts,
but because it resists it *more* than the smaller wire; or because the force being
divided among more parts, acts weaker on each. (10:49–50)

Franklin loved hypothesizing.

Franklin found science lovely for at least five reasons. First, as he said in *Poor
Richard*, it could reveal surprising and aesthetically beautiful sights. Second, the
sequence of reasoning and experimental proof was often so simple and clear
that it was a pleasure. The sequence sometimes had the structure of a work of
art as defined by Edgar Allan Poe: no part of the experiment could be dispensed
with, and all the parts together necessarily led to the conclusion.[140] Like a su-
perbly constructed short story, Franklin's theses and logical steps often seem
inevitable. The original experiments as recorded in Franklin's "Electrical Minutes" could not have been so sequential and logical, but his final streamlined
presentation emphasized the rigorous and exact inevitability of the outcome.
The hypotheses and experiments proving them sometimes achieved the simplicity, beauty, and elegance of Euclidean geometry.

Third, the experiments often proved facts (whether concerning the nature
of electricity or the way it behaved) previously unknown. Such additions to
knowledge were gratifying. That lightning often struck upward from the earth
was an unimaginable new discovery. What surprise and great pleasure it gave
Franklin! Fourth, science often suggested that the mysteries of the world revealed a wonderful, complex order that was decipherable to human understanding. Whether caused by God or by natural forces, early electricity testified to a
fantastically complex but increasingly explainable universe. Electricity caused
and explained some of the most amazing and previously inexplicable actions in
nature.

Fifth and finally, that some electrical phenomena contradicted the generally accepted theories of electricity was a tantalizing pleasure. The puzzles challenged the theorists of physics and promised the possible thrill of new discoveries. The more one knew, the more there was to know. Franklin delighted in phenomena that contradicted his theories. He enjoyed advancing and receiving conjectures that might explain what he did not understand. Being wrong meant that there were more challenges. Being amazed was a challenge. After Thomas Jefferson replaced him as minister to France and Franklin, at age seventy-nine, set out to return home, he wrote his scientific friend Jan Ingenhousz on 29 April 1785, "Welcome again my dear Philosophical Amusements."

APPRECIATIONS

Joseph Priestley wrote that Franklin's experiment proving the identity of lightning and electricity was "the greatest, perhaps, that has been made in the whole compass of philosophy, since the time of Sir Isaac Newton" (4:368). In the *Old Farmer's Almanac* for 1755, Nathaniel Ames celebrated Franklin: "Who 'ere presum'd, till Franklin led the Way, / To climb the amazing Height of Heaven, / And rob the Sky of it's tremendous Thunder; / And leave the Clouds, with Winds and Tempests fraught, / But Breath enough to shake the trembling Trees, / And rock the Birds that pearch upon their Boughs."[141] In 1756, Immanuel Kant labeled Franklin "the Prometheus of modern times." In 1778 Turgot honored him with the most famous modern epigraph: "Eripuit coelo fulmen, sceptrumque tyrannis" (He seized the lightning from the skies and the scepter from the tyrants).[142] In 1849 Alexander von Humboldt appraised his achievement: "From this period the electric process passes from the domain of speculative physics into that of cosmical contemplation—from the recesses of the study to the freedom of nature."[143]

As we have seen, Robert A. Millikan thought Franklin's work was the most fundamental contribution ever made in electricity. He considered Franklin one of the six greatest scientists from the Renaissance to the nineteenth century. Those whom Millikan ranked with Franklin were Copernicus in the fifteenth century, Galileo in the sixteenth, Newton and Huyghens in the seventeenth, and Laplace in the eighteenth.[144] Millikan summarized Franklin's achievement: he forged the disparate facts known of electricity into a single, simple, and consistent system, based on his hypothesis of a single electric fluid (which we today call the electron theory) and the conservation of charge.[145]

Peter Kapitsa, Russian Nobel Prize winner in physics in 1978, compared the formulation of the Franklinian system of electricity in the eighteenth century to Ernest Rutherford's work with radioactivity in the early twentieth century: "Until Franklin's work made its appearance, a large quantity of experimental data had been gathered, but the facts had been separate from one another. The hypothesis offered by him not only united these facts into one harmonious picture but also showed the right path for further researches." In Kapitsa's opinion, the qualities demonstrated by Franklin and Rutherford were "great imagi-

Figure 17. A thunderstorm raging outside Franklin's study. A detail from Edward Fisher's mezzotint of Benjamin Franklin after Mason Chamberlain (frontispiece). When Ebenezer Kinnersley first introduced the idea of lightning rods to the public on 11 April 1751, he carefully tried to avoid anything that might seem like religious presumption. Electricity, he advertised, would help "give us more noble, more grand and exalted ideas of the Author of nature." Nevertheless, Kinnersley encountered religious prejudice, for many ministers continued preaching that lightning was God's punishment for mankind's sins. Kinnersley, like Franklin, was generally successful in convincing persons that their former notions resulted from traditional, incorrect knowledge. Two persons in Rhode Island wrote letters published in the New York Gazette of 1 June 1752 saying that Kinnersley's demonstrations overturned their former prejudices.

Chamberlain's painting and Fisher's mezzotint indirectly confront the warfare of science and religion. Franklin, like some impervious deity, sits inside his study, protected by a lightning rod, which is portrayed in the upper right of this detail. The dominant building outside is the large one on the left, being rent by lightning. Next to it is a building with a lightning rod running up from its chimney—and it rests as free from danger or injury as Franklin. To its right, lightning is toppling the steeple of a structure. Since the commonest structures with steeples are churches, the detail in the painting suggests the warfare of science and religion—and the triumph of science. Courtesy, National Portrait Gallery.

nation, perspicacity, and daring." Kapitsa thought Franklin was the greatest American scientist. Selecting one preeminent scientist from various modern nations, Kapitsa said that Russia can be proud of having given "Lomonosov to mankind; the English brought forth Newton; the Italians contributed Galileo; the Dutch produced Huyghens; the French, Descartes; the Germans, Leibniz; and the Americans, Franklin." Kapitsa believed that "The accomplishments of these great savants are the pride of all mankind.[146]

Perhaps such scientists as Joseph Priestley, Humphrey Davy, Ernest Rutherford, Robert A. Millikan, and Peter Kapitsa, as well as modern historians of science like I. Bernard Cohen and J. L. Heilbron, have exaggerated Franklin's achievements. I doubt it, but I do not have enough science to judge. But for his age and for the future, Franklin evidently added a new quality to physical matter. Everything seemingly had some kind of electric charge.

What was Franklin's own attitude toward his achievement as an electrician? When his friend and former collaborator Ebenezer Kinnersley wrote Franklin on 12 March 1761 concerning experiments that deviated from Franklin's "Electrical Orthodoxy," Franklin replied that the Franklinian theory was believed by some at present but not by everyone; "and, perhaps, it may not always be orthodoxy with anybody. Opinions are continually varying. . . . Nor is that variation without its use, since it occasions a more thorough discussion, whereby error is often dissipated, true knowledge is increased, and its principles better understood and more firmly established" (9:285, 10:46–47). He hoped he had made a contribution toward an understanding of one more finally inexplicable marvel.

THREE

Astronomy, Weather, and the Northwest Passage: Natural Philosopher, 1748–1757

"The improvement of geography and astronomy is the common concern of all polite nations."
—Franklin to James Bowdoin, 28 February 1753, 4:446

FRANKLIN'S CONTRIBUTIONS TO NATURAL PHILOSOPHY in electricity, weather, and demography are well-known, but he also wrote on astronomy, geophysics, meteorology, and geography (the northwest passage). The topics recorded by the visiting naturalist Pehr Kalm (1716–79) suggest the breadth of Franklin's interests. Kalm, a student of Linneaus, came to America in the fall of 1748 to collect plants and animals for the Swedish natural philosopher. He arrived in Philadelphia on 15 September 1748, carrying letters of introduction to Franklin from Peter Collinson and Dr. John Mitchell (3:323). Most topics discussed with Kalm continue Franklin's earlier interests (*Life* 2:452–99), but the range of subjects from hickory tea and paleontology to such practical matters as stoves and how to prevent candles from dripping (3:53–63) reflect Franklin's omnivorous curiosity—and knowledge.

Franklin's early scientific correspondents were James Logan, John Bartram, and Cadwallader Colden. Franklin wrote Logan about linguistics in 1749 (3:393). He published Bartram's preface, notes, and appendix on *Medicina Britannica*, a medical treatise on plants (1751) by the English physician Thomas Short.[1] And he exchanged thoughts with Colden about light, radiation, and physics (4:299–300). In the late 1740s, Peter Collinson became his frequent correspondent. Besides writing him on electricity, the practical handyman Franklin suggested ways of making and packaging barometers so they would not break so easily (5:331–32). In the 1750s, favorite new correspondents were Charleston's Dr. John Lining and Boston's James Bowdoin and Dr. John Perkins. With Lining, Franklin continued to explore the subjects that he also discussed with Colden: electricity, cold, heat, and light. He theorized to Lining that the same materials that conducted electricity well were also the best conductors of heat (7:184–90). Bowdoin and a group of his friends visited Franklin and Philadelphia in order to learn more about electricity and about Franklin's other interests. With Perkins, Franklin discussed weather, waterspouts, and—since Perkins knew his sister Jane Mecom and brother John well—family matters.

ASTRONOMY

Franklin's interest in astronomy began when he was a boy. One of his earliest books was *The Surprizing Miracles of Nature and Art* (*Life* 1:46), which discussed meteors, comets, and eclipses. By 1748, he was a minor expert on astronomy: every year *Poor Richard* listed the forthcoming eclipses of the sun and moon. In 1743, 1746, and 1747, Franklin illustrated the path of the eclipses for the future year. The illustrations continued during 1748–57 (1750, two in 1751, 1752, and 1753). The 1748 almanac celebrated Copernicus and compared the Copernican and Ptolemaic systems. In the two pages devoted to January, Franklin wrote: "On the 19th of this Month, *Anno* 1493, was born the famous Astronomer Copernicus, to whom we owe the Invention, or rather the Revival (it being taught by Pythagoras near 2000 Years before) of that now generally receiv'd System of the World which bears his Name, and supposes the Sun in the Center, this Earth a Planet revolving round it in 365 Days, 6 Hours, &c. and that Day and Night are caused by the Turning of the Earth on its own Axis once round in 24h. &c." Franklin explained that the former system, "which prevail'd before Copernicus, suppos'd the Earth to be fix'd, and that the Sun went round it daily." Franklin then thought of an analogy to explain the Copernican system's superiority: "Ptolomy is compar'd to a whimsical Cook, who, instead of Turning his Meat in Roasting, should fix That, and contrive to have his whole Fire, Kitchen and all, whirling continually round it" (3:248–49).

To prepare the readers for the change in September 1752 from the Julian to the Gregorian calendar, Franklin explained their differences in the preface to *Poor Richard* for 1752. Tongue-in-cheek, he also noted that the Gregorian calendar was not perfect, "for we have shewn, that, in four Centuries, the *Julian Year* gains three Days, One Hour, twenty Minutes: But it is only the three Days are kept out in the *Gregorian Year*; so that here is still an Excess of one Hour, twenty Minutes, in four Centuries; which in 72 Centuries will amount to a whole Day" (4:246). The humor is Franklin's but the statistic may be copied.

In 1752, Theophilus Grew (*Life* 2:172) or, possibly, Franklin, mistakenly predicted the time of an eclipse of the sun. Grew/Franklin wrote that on 2 May, "about Two a Clock in the Afternoon," the sun "will appear eclipsed almost 7 Digits." The eclipse would begin, he said, at 12:38, reach the middle at 1:50, and end at 2:59. Franklin illustrated the path of the eclipse. The *Pennsylvania Gazette* for 30 April 1752, however, carried a correction by "T. Fox, carpenter," who had calculated the beginning would be at 12:20, the "greatest Obscuration" of the sun would occur at 1:35, and the end at 2:46.

On *Saturday* next (if the Air be clear) will be vifible, an *E-clipfe* of the *Sun*, the greateft Obfcuration will be at 35 Min. paft One a Clock, *Apparent Time*, when the *Sun* will be eclipfed 7 *Digits*, that is, nearly Half the *Sun's Difk* will be darkened on the *South* Side. The Beginning will be at 20 Min. paft Twelve, and the End at 46 Min. after Two.

N. B. *Halley's Tables*, from which thefe Numbers are calculated, put the *Moon's* Place at this Time 6 Min. of a Degree forwarder than *Brent's Tables*, and hence arifes the Difference between this Account, and that publifhed in *Poor Richard's* Almanack.

The Conftruction of this *Eclipfe*, and its Appearance in divers Parts of the *Earth*, may be feen in the *Mathematical School*, at the *Academy*.

Figure 18. *T. Fox, carpenter, corrects Poor Richard, Pennsylvania Gazette, 30 April 1752. In the fall of 1751, Poor Richard's Almanac predicted that on 2 May 1752, "about Two a Clock in the Afternoon," the sun "will appear eclipsed almost 7 Digits." Franklin (or, more likely, Theophilus Grew, whom Franklin sometimes employed to do the calculations for the almanac) wrote that the eclipse would begin at 12:38 P.M., reach its most obscuring position at 1:50, and end at 2:59. On 30 April, however, the Pennsylvania Gazette corrected that calculation. Instead, the eclipse would begin at 12:20 P.M., the "greatest Obscuration" of the sun would occur at 1:35, and depart from the sun at 2:46. "T. Fox, carpenter," who sent in the information, explained that Halley's tables, "from which these Numbers are calculated," put the moon's place at this time six "minutes of a degree forwarder than Brent's Tables, and hence arises the Difference between this Account, and that published in Poor Richard."*

The incident is a credit to Fox, Grew, and Franklin. At the academy's mathematical room, interested persons could view carpenter Fox's version of an orrery that illustrated the progress of the eclipse from "divers Parts of the Earth." Evidently Theophilus Grew, a highly successful mathematics teacher at the academy since 1751, invited Fox to display the machine there. Grew was generous in his treatment of Fox. In turn, Fox was generous in explaining how the error occurred. When Fox sent in the correction of Poor Richard to the Pennsylvania Gazette, David Hall no doubt checked with Franklin to see if he should print it. Franklin said yes; or, perhaps, Franklin learned of Fox's machine and of his correction to Poor Richard, and asked him to send it in to the Gazette. Either way, Franklin was generous. It was good publicity for the academy—but a criticism of Poor Richard.

Unfortunately, no description of Fox's orrery or other references to it are known. Courtesy, Library Company of Philadelphia.

THE TRANSIT OF MERCURY

Astronomers knew there would be a transit of Mercury in 1753, and *Poor Richard* (which was advertised as "Just published" on 16 November 1752) gave the exact Greenwich times for the transit. Local astronomers who knew the latitude and longitude of their towns could then determine when the eclipse would occur. Comparisons of the results could confirm the earth's distance from the moon, but the main purpose of making accurate observations in 1753 was to practice for the transits of Venus that would occur in 1761 and 1769. If made in the East Indies as well as in America, the results could establish the distance of the earth both from the sun and from other planets in the solar system. The information had been impossible to obtain during Isaac Newton's lifetime and remained a chief desideratum in Newtonian science.[2]

Franklin gave mathematical calculations and the exact times concerning the forthcoming transit of Mercury in Philadelphia, probably from Grew's calculations; but the prose is Franklin's. He wrote that Mercury would go off the sun's disk at 7:31 A.M.: "The Sun rises at 1 min. past Five, and if you get up betimes, and put on your Spectacles, you will see Mercury rise in the Sun, and will appear like a small black Patch in a Lady's Face" (4:408). *Poor Richard* printed an illustration of the course of Mercury across the sun. Evidently Grew (or Franklin?) again used Brent's *Tables*, for Franklin appended a note: "Dr. Halley puts this Conjunction an Hour forwarder than by this Calculation" (4:408). On 3 May, however, the *Pennsylvania Gazette* published carpenter T. Fox's calculation from Halley that the beginning egress would be visible in Philadelphia at 5:17; that it would be in the center at 5:39; and that it would end at 5:41. Fox had it emerge two hours and ten minutes earlier than did Grew/Franklin.

Mercury's transit caused international cooperation. The French astronomer, geographer, and mapmaker Joseph-Nicolas Delisle sent directions for observing the transit of Mercury to New York's governor, asking him to forward them overland to Joseph-Pierre de Bonnécamps, S.J., at Quebec.[3] Delisle also wrote the Jesuits in the East Indies to make observations. New York's James Alexander translated the letter and sent it to Franklin on 29 January, saying that "It Would be a great honour to our young Colleges in America if they forthwith prepared themselves with a proper apparatus for that Observation and made it." Alexander said that Franklin had "on so many Occasions Demonstrated Your Love To Literature and the good of Mankind in General" that no person could better "think of the ways and means of perswading these Colledges to prepare themselves for taking that Observation" (4:417).

Having checked the available literature, Alexander stated that the transit would end at New York at 5:03 A.M. Franklin or Grew, however, had published in *Poor Richard* that the sun would rise at 5:01 and that the transit would end at 7:31 A.M. Either Franklin or Alexander corrected the emergence at New York to 6:18 A.M. (4:408; cf. 418n5). Alexander stressed the importance of making accurate observations, for after the 1760s, the eighteenth-century astronomers thought it would be 2004 before another good opportunity of ascertaining distances within the solar system would occur.[4] Alexander concluded by saying that since several colonies were starting colleges, "all ways Should be thought of To Induce each of those [colleges] To provide a proper apparatus for makeing such

Observations" so that in 1761 "they May be Expert at Takeing Observations of that Kind."

Franklin immediately printed fifty copies of Alexander's letter and Delisle's directions in a four-page folio pamphlet with an inserted hand-drawn illustration. Evidently Franklin did not wait for a decent woodcut to be made and instead paid a scrivener to copy the illustration. Franklin sent the pamphlet to those he knew would be interested, like Dr. Samuel Johnson in Stratford, Connecticut, and sent others to various correspondents to distribute. Sending James Bowdoin a copy on 28 February, he wrote, "The Improvement of Geography and Astronomy is the common Concern of all polite Nations, and I trust our Country will not miss the Opportunity of Sharing in the Honour to be got on this Occasion." We can be sure that by "our Country" Franklin meant America, for he hoped that "we may not be excell'd by the American French, either in Diligence or Accuracy." Weather permitting, Franklin intended to observe the transit "at our Academy." He also enclosed a copy of *Poor Richard* for 1753, competitively asserting, "You will see by our Almanack, we have had this Transit under Consideration before the Arrival of these French Letters."

Franklin wrote Cadwallader Colden the same day that "we" were preparing "to make accurate Observations on the approaching Transit of Mercury." Colden replied on 20 March giving some "Hints concerning our Observation of the Transit," for which Franklin thanked him on 12 April and remarked, "I see it is not without Reluctance that the Europeans will allow that they can possibly receive any Instructions from us Americans." In the *Pennsylvania Gazette* on 5 April, Franklin published a request from London's Royal Society to observe the transit. The ingenious carpenter T. Fox replied in the 3 May paper, giving the correct times and course of the transit for Philadelphia.

Alas, Franklin's hopes were dashed. All up and down the East Coast, clouds hid the transit. Not a single observation was made. He informed Peter Collinson of his disappointment in a letter of 1 June (which is not extant). Collinson replied on 20 July 1753 that he was sorry, "Yett Wee much applaud your Ingenuity and Industry to Instruct your Neighbours on the Transit" (4:14).

Franklin's efforts were not entirely in vain. He had also sent half a dozen copies to his nephew Benjamin Mecom in Antigua, who gave one to the Reverend William Shervington. With a clear sky in Antigua on 6 May, Captain Richard Tyrell, with Shervington in attendance, made observations of the transit. Shervington sent the results to Franklin in a letter of 20 June 1753. He received them in Boston and forwarded copies to James Alexander in New York and Collinson in London. Collinson had the letter read in the Royal Society and published in the *Philosophical Transactions*. After Franklin returned to Philadelphia, he printed Shervington's letter in the *Pennsylvania Gazette* for 6 September 1753. The episode was "yet another example of Franklin's general interest in all branches of science and his zeal in advancing the cause of science by his personal efforts whenever the occasion offered."[5]

WEATHER

Like astronomy, weather was a major subject of *Poor Richard*. Franklin often spoofed weather predictions, even when he was emerging as the most notable weatherman that America had ever had and as one of the foremost weather experts of the eighteenth century. In the preface to the 1753 *Poor Richard* almanac, Franklin wrote: "I am particularly pleas'd to understand that my *Predictions of the Weather* give such general Satisfaction; and indeed, such Care is taken in the Calculations, on which those Predictions are founded, that I could almost venture to say, there's not a single One of them, promising *Snow, Rain, Hail, Heat, Frost, Fogs, Wind*, or *Thunder*, but what comes to pass *punctually* and *precisely* on the very Day, in some Place or other on this little Globe of ours" (4:403). Since the scientific study of weather chronologically followed the study of astrology, Franklin as Poor Richard claimed to be the heir to an ancient learned tradition—but at the same time he ridiculed Poor Richard as a person who did not know the common facts of history. He slyly concluded the next sentence with a howler: "our Art has been cultivated in great Cities, and even in the Courts of Princes; witness History, from the Days of King Nebuchadnezzar I. of Babylon, to those of Queen [!] James I. of England" (5:181).

Franklin observed that although the winds in "Norwesters" blew from the northwest, the course of the great storms moved up from the southwest to the northeast. He then added a comment revealing that the observation was, at least in part, based on nautical observations—"all our great Storms begin to Leeward." He amplified the nautical diction in a letter of 13 February 1749/50: "N East Storms begin to Leeward; and are often more violent there than farther to Windward." Every sailor knew that the wind generally blew from the south to the northeast along the coast. That's why "Down East" became a cant term for Maine: if one set out from Boston, the wind generally blew the sailing ships downwind, toward the east, toward Maine. Earlier, Franklin had theorized about high and low pressure systems and the possible effect of the long ridge of mountains in North America that ran northeast to southwest (*Life* 2:481–85). Might not the mountains also affect the course of the storms? Though Franklin restated these thoughts later, in 1748 he "anticipated thermal theories of cyclone formation" by scientists in the second half of the nineteenth century.[6]

Franklin popularized geophysics and meteorology in the 1749 *Poor Richard*. Citing William Whiston's *New Theory of the Earth*, Franklin gave the diameter and circumference of the earth and the velocity at which it rotates on its axis and revolves around the sun (3:338). His 1751 "Physical and Meteorological Observations, Conjectures, and Suppositions" (4:235–43) gathered together his meteorological speculations. Approaching such questions as how the earth's rotation affected its wind patterns, Franklin began with the simple characteristics and nature of air. Air and water mutually attract each other, and just as salt will dissolve in water, so water will dissolve in air. Even earth will "dissolve or mix" with air. He gave a microcosmic example of a macrocosmic theory: "A Stroke of a Horse's Hoof on the Ground in a hot dusty Road, will raise a Cloud of Dust, that shall, if there be a light Breeze, expand every way till perhaps near as big as a common House." Most eighteenth-century persons had probably observed it, but who before Franklin tried to fit it into a theory concerning the world's weather? He explained, "'Tis not by mechanical Motion communicated to the Particles of Dust by the Hoof, that they fly so far, nor by the Wind that they spread so wide; But the Air near the Ground, more heated by the hot Dust struck into it, is rarified and rises, and in rising mixes with the cooler Air, and communicates of its Dust to it, and it is at length so diffus'd as to become invisible" (4:236–37). Thus dust is carried up into the air in hot, dry seasons; later, showers bring it down, "For Water attracting it stronger, it quits the Air and adheres to the Water" (4:236–37). Since the air's temperature is continually changing, air is in "continual Motion." From this fact, Franklin conjectured how fogs, mists, clouds, and summer hail were created.

His "Physical and Meteorological Observations" echoes English meteorologist George Hadley's 1735 article "Concerning the Cause of the General Trade Winds" in the *Philosophical Transactions*. Hadley had commented on hot air becoming lighter than the air around it and theorized that the earth's rotation caused the trade winds to move from east to west, rather than simply to come in toward the lighter air equally from all directions. When Franklin wrote the meteorological essay he did not recall where he had read Hadley, but he evidently chanced across Hadley's article later, and in the fourth edition (1769) of his *Experiments and Observations on Electricity*, Franklin noted his debt in the copy he gave to the Royal Society. He added a footnote on his indebtedness to Hadley in the fifth edition (1774). E. Philip Krider, who called my attention to Franklin's annotation and subsequent footnote, wrote that Franklin's account of the phenomena is simpler and easier to understand than Hadley's.[7] Further, Franklin added his own theories. After hypothesizing that the earth's rotation affected its major wind patterns, Franklin proved that air attracts and supports "many other Substances," including dust and water (4:235–38). The "Physical and Meteorological Observations" answered his Junto question of 1732: "Whence comes the Dew that stands on the Outside of a Tankard that has cold Water in it in the Summer Time?" (1:260; *Life* 1:344, fig. 23a). He wrote, "Cold condenses and renders visible the Vapour" (4:239).

Franklin conjectured that "heavy cold air over a heated country, becoming by any means unequally supported, or unequal in its weight, the heaviest part descends first, and the rest follows impetuously. Hence gusts after heats, and hurricanes in hot climates. Hence the air of gusts and hurricanes cold, though in hot climes and seasons; it coming from above" (4:239). Clouds were formed, he theorized, by "cold air descending from above, as it penetrates our warm region full of watry particles, condenses them, renders them visible, forms a cloud thick and dark, overcasting sometimes, at once, large and extensive; sometimes, when seen at a distance, small at first, gradually increasing; the cold edge, or surface, of the cloud, condensing the vapours next it, which from smaller clouds that join it, increase its bulk, it descends with the wind and its acquired weight, draws nearer the earth, grows denser with continual additions of water, and discharges heavy showers" (4:239–40).

After remarking that the earth turned at about fifteen miles a minute at the equator and that, at the poles, it was effectually still, Franklin conjectured that the air near the tropics, being constantly heated, rose. Since "the earth and air had less motion" in more northern latitudes, it did not have "the quicker motion of the equatorial earth." Because the earth was turning from west to east, it made the wind blow west and slip under the rising southern air. Great bodies of water were colder in the summer and warmer in the winter than the continents because, Franklin suggested, seas and lakes, "agitated by the winds, continually change surfaces; the cold surface in winter is turned under, by the rolling of the waves, and a warmer turned up; in summer, the warm is turned under, and colder turned up. Hence the more equal temper of sea-water, and the air over it. Hence, in winter, winds from the sea seem warm, winds from the land cold. In summer the contrary" (4:241). "Hence . . . hence . . . hence"—the conjectures were all pie in the sky, for Franklin had no experiments to suggest (no lightning rod), but he hoped that observations over time would prove him right—or wrong.

Waterspouts and Whirlwinds

Taking up waterspouts and tornadoes, Franklin compared them with water in a funnel: "the water acquires a circular motion, receding every way from a center, and leaving a vacancy in the middle, greatest above, and lessening downwards, like a speaking trumpet, its big end upwards." Later, he chose a similar but more common analogy: the draining of water in a bathtub. Air, he thought, "may form the same kind of eddies, or whirlings, the parts of air acquiring a circular motion, and receding from the middle of the circle by a centrifugal force, and leaving there a vacancy; if descending, greatest above, and lessening downwards; if ascending, greatest below, and lessening upwards." That happened, he conjectured, in the forming of whirlwinds on land or waterspouts at sea (4:242).

Writing James Bowdoin on 24 January 1752, Franklin said that he intended to send a copy of his "Physical and Meteorological Observations" to Dr. John Perkins and would ask Perkins to show the conjectures to Bowdoin. Franklin noted, "By throwing our occasional Thoughts on Paper, we more readily discover the Defects of our Opinions, or we digest them better, and find new Arguments to support them. This I sometimes practice, but such Pieces are fit only to be seen by Friends" (4:259).

Perkins replied to Franklin's thoughts on 16 October 1752, questioning whether waterspouts really ascended. He imagined that they descended from

clouds. He supposed that if a whirlwind rose from water, "it would be too heavy
to continue the ascent beyond a considerable Height, unless parted into Small
Drops: And even then by its centrifugal Force from the Manner of Conveyance
it would be flung out of the Circle and fall scatter'd like Rain" (4:359). Spurred
on by Perkins's doubts, Franklin reread the *Philosophical Transactions* and wrote
friends who had told him of waterspouts, including Dr. William Mercer (d. ca.
1769) of New Brunswick, New Jersey. Mercer responded that when he was at St.
John's, Antigua, a waterspout came onto the land, which convinced him that
waterspouts were the same as whirlwinds. He was only about one hundred yards
from the waterspout as it approached the St. John's wharf: "There appeared in
the water a circle of about twenty yards diameter, which, to me, had a dreadful,
though pleasing appearance. The water in this circle was violently agitated, being
whisked about, and carried up into the air with great rapidity and noise, and
reflected a lustre, as if the sun shined bright on that spot, which was more
conspicuous, as there appeared a dark circle around it. When it made the shore,
it carried up with the same violence shingles, staves, large pieces of the roofs of
houses, &c." (4:378).

Having rechecked various bits of data, Franklin replied to Perkins on 4 February 1753. Franklin said he agreed "that by means of a Vacuum in a Whirlwind,
Water cannot be suppos'd to rise in large Masses to the Region of the Clouds:
For the Pressure of the surrounding Atmosphere could not force it up in a
continu'd Body or Column to a much greater Height than thirty feet: But if
there really is a Vacuum in the Center or near the Axis of Whirlwinds, then I
think Water may rise in such Vacuum to that Height or to less Height as the
Vacuum may be less perfect." One must admire Franklin's diplomacy. He disagreed while granting that Perkins was right. But if a strong perfect vacuum
existed of forty or fifty feet or higher, then the water in the waterspout could
rise to that height (4:429–30).

Franklin thought whirlwinds and waterspouts were basically the same. They
both attracted wind from a large space around them. That whirlwinds did so
was common knowledge; Franklin added that "an intelligent Whaleman of
Nantucket informed me" that three becalmed ships formed a triangle and that
when a waterspout appeared in their midst, each ship's officers testified that the
waterspout was to leeward: "So that in this Particular likewise, Whirlwinds and
Waterspouts agree." He generalized that "A Fluid moving from all Points horizontally towards a Center, must at that Center either ascend or descend." Franklin's comparison followed: "Water being in a Tub, if a Hole be open'd in the
Middle of the Bottom, will flow from all Sides to the Center, and there descend
in a Whirl."[8] But if the whirling motion toward a center were on the land or
water, whatever it caught up must ascend.

If some whirlwinds or waterspouts descended, Franklin reasoned they
"would press the Roof of a House inwards, or force in the Tiles, Shingles or
Thatch; force a Boat down into the Water, or a Piece of Timber into the Earth."

But the opposite usually happened (4:434). He portrayed the action of water-spouts and whirlwinds with three illustrations. The first figure was a cross-section of a whirlwind/waterspout. The arrows pointing inward toward the central vacuum indicated the direction of the wind toward the vacuum. The four letters "a" are just within the points of the arrows at the circumference. Next to the vacuum, Franklin shows the whirling motion by smaller arrows. And the four letters "b" are in the vacuum. He wrote: "Between aaaa and bbbb I suppose a Body of Air condens'd strongly by the Pressure of the Currents moving towards it from all sides without, and by its Centrifugal Force from Within; moving round with prodigious Swiftness" (4:434). The whirling body of air be-tween aaaa and bbbb "rises spirally." Its force "tears Buildings to Pieces, twists up great Trees by the Roots, &c. and by its spiral Motion raises the Fragments so high till the Pressure of the surrounding and approaching Currents diminish-ing can no longer confine them to the Circle, or their own centrifugal Force encreasing grows too strong for such Pressure, when they fly off in Tangent Lines as Stones out of a Sling, and fall on all Sides and at great Distances" (4:437).

A second figure represented the elevation of a waterspout. The cone was identified at the bottom by "P P" (post?) and halfway up by "P." "At first it was a vacuum until "WW [water?] the rising Column of Water has fill'd so much of it." (One "W" is at the bottom of the cone and the second is about one-sixth of the way up.) "The Spiral Whirl of Air" surrounds the bottom of the vacuum and continues to nearly half the way up (to "P," which has an "S" [spiral?] on either side). The swirling air continues up until it reaches the "cool Region of the Air" (A, B, C, D; 4:437). The "B. B." at the bottom portrays the "Bush" of water surrounding the foot of the waterspout as described in 1703 by Alexander Stuart in the *Philosophical Transactions.*[9] Franklin thought that at first the "Whirl of Air" would be "as invisible as the Air itself tho' reaching in reality from the Water to the Region of cool Air in which our low Summer Thunder Clouds commonly float; but presently it will become visible at its Extremities" (4:437).

Stuart's "Bush" was formed by the swelling and rising of the water in the beginning vacuum, "which is at first a small low broad Cone whose Top gradu-ally rises and sharpens as the Force of the Whirl increases. *At its upper End*, it becomes visible by the Warm Air brought up to the cooler Region, where its Moisture begins to be condens'd into thick Vapour by the Cold . . . It seems easy to conceive, how by this successive Condensation from above the Spout appears to drop or descend from the Cloud, tho' the Materials of which it is composed are all the while ascending" (4:437–38). Franklin further cited Stuart on the color of waterspouts, dark on the sides and white in the middle.

To Stuart, Franklin added Cotton Mather's report in the *Philosophical Trans-actions* of a whirlwind as a dark cloud "with a pillar of light in it, about 8 or 10 foot diameter," which tore up "Trees by the Roots, blowing them up in the Air like Feathers" (4:439). Franklin showed why the middle of the vacuum looked

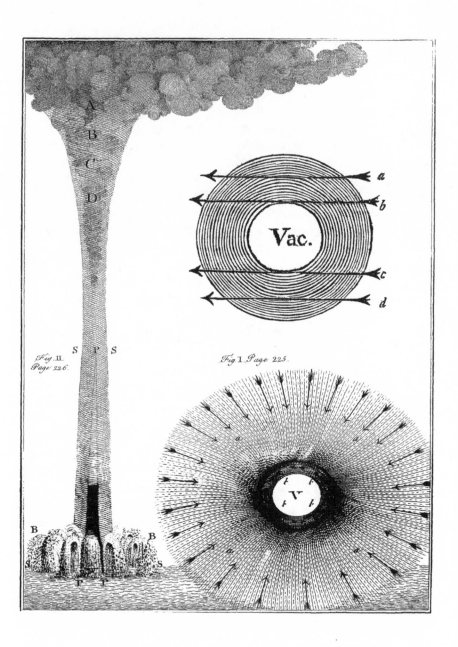

Fig. II.
Page 226.

Fig. I. Page 225.

Vac.

a
b
c
d

S P S

B B
S S
P T

Figure 19. The elevation, cross-section, and winds of a waterspout, Experiments and Observaions on Electricity *(1769). America's first scientific weatherman, Franklin drafted his "Physical and Meteorological Observations, Conjectures, and Suppositions" late in 1752 (4:235–43) and circulated it among his friends interested in natural philosophy. The Boston physician Dr. John Perkins challenged his theory that the water ascended in waterspouts. Perkins believed it descended from clouds (4:358–60). In replying on 4 February 1753, Franklin reexamined the evidence; referred to and quoted a pertinent article of half a century before in the* Philosophical Transactions of the Royal Society; *cited passages by William Dampier from his voyages; identified and quoted the person who had previously told him that when waterspouts move onto land they behaved like whirlwinds, picking up leaves, dust, and other objects; and theorized what happened and why in air or fluid currents in a whirlwind, whirlpool, or waterspout (4:429–42).*

The exchange and Franklin's procedure of collecting, interpreting, and analyzing evidence are excellent examples of his methodical approach. Once he had gathered all the evidence, he then posed hypotheses that would account for what happened in the phenomena, using such commonplace analogies as water draining from a tub.

When he printed the letter of 4 February 1753 in the fourth edition of Experiments and Observations on Electricity *(1769), he had the printer insert a large fold-out engraving representing the elevation and winds of a waterspout, and a magic square of 8. Since this magic square is well-known and since a magic square of 16 has been illustrated in* Life *2:477 (fig. 30), the magic square is replaced here by the engraving of the cross-section of the wind in a waterspout, which appeared a few pages later in* Experiments *(1769). Courtesy, University of Delaware Library.*

lighter with an illustration: "if we look at such a hollow Pipe in the Direction of the Arrows, and suppose opacous Particles to be equally mix'd in the Space between the two circular Lines, both the Part between the Arrows a and b and that between the Arrows c and d, will appear much darker than that between b and c; as there must be many more of those opaque Particles in the Line of Vision across the Sides than across the Middle." As usual, Franklin tried to think of a comparison: "It is thus, that a Hair in a Microscope evidently appears to be a Pipe, the Sides shewing darker than the Middle"(4:440).[10]

Franklin imagined that Dr. Perkins might argue that if water were drawn up into the clouds during waterspouts, why was there no salt rain? Franklin replied that God had so ordered it that, although particles of air would attract and hold water, they would not do so with salt. Though metals, even gold, could be rendered volatile by great heat, salt could not: "when Salt rises as it will a little Way into Air with Water, there is instantly a Separation made; the Particles of Water adhere to the Air, and the Particles of Salt fall down again, as if repell'd and forc'd off from the Water by some Power in the Air . . . Otherwise, our Rains would indeed be salt, and every Tree and Plant on the Face of the Earth be destroy'd, with all the Animals that depend on them for Subsistence." Thus Franklin gave air as an example of the Design Argument typical of scientific deism: "He who hath proportioned and given proper Qualities to all Things, was not unmindful of this. Let us adore him with Praise and Thanksgiving!" (4:441). That attitude is unusual for Franklin, who would have realized that life as we know it could never have developed if rain was commonly salty. But Franklin always bore in mind his particular audience. He was writing to Dr. John Perkins, a New England Congregationalist who, early in life, had been patronized by Cotton Mather. Franklin may have thought Perkins believed in the Design Argument.

In closing, Franklin said he had not tried to answer all Perkins's comments because he did not know any "Facts sufficient to make" a pertinent answer. Franklin said that the hypothesis of "descending Spouts" was ingenious and might be true. Franklin submitted what he had written "to your candid Examination. If my Hypothesis is not the Truth itself, it is least as naked: For I have not with some of our learned Moderns disguis'd my Nonsense in Greek, cloth'd it in Algebra, or adorn'd it with Fluxions" (4:442). Too bad he didn't. As Philip K. Krider noted, in the nineteenth century, Herman von Helmholtz described the phenomenon in mathematical terms.[11] In casting doubt upon his own hypotheses, Franklin's conclusion deliberately avoided the air of certainty associated, somewhat unjustly, with Descartes and mathematical reasoning. In its eighteenth-century context, Franklin's conclusion aligns him with the implicitly agnostic traditions of Aristotle and Newton as opposed to Cartesian mathematical absolutism.[12]

Franklin had, however, gathered together more material on whirlwinds and waterspouts than any previous writer. It is not surprising that Franklin's later disciple, Polly Stevenson, found his theses more probable than did Dr. Perkins. William Falconer inserted Franklin's discussion of waterspouts in his *Universal Dictionary of the Marine* (London: Cadell, 1769). Citing Falconer, Captain James Cook wrote that he thought "the ingenious Dr. Franklin" gave "the most rational account I have yet read of waterspouts."[13]

Chasing the Whirlwind

Franklin wrote about whirlwinds again in 1755. Though descriptive rather than theoretical, the account was both fun and a good example of Franklin's curiosity. On 9 April 1755, Franklin and his son William left Philadelphia for Annapolis, Maryland, with Governors William Shirley and Robert Hunter Morris. The governors journeyed on to Alexandria to meet General Braddock. After the governors left Annapolis, Colonel Benjamin Tasker, whom Franklin had met at Albany,[14] invited them to his plantation where they were treated "with great hospitality and kindness." On the way there, from the top of a small hill, "we saw in the vale below us, a small whirlwind beginning in the road, and shewing itself by the dust it raised and contained." The form was that of a funnel. It was "spinning on its point, moving up the hill towards us, and enlarging as it came forward." When it passed by, "its smaller part near the ground appeared not bigger than a common barrel, but widening upwards, it seemed, at 40 or 50 feet high, to be 20 or 30 feet in diameter."

They all stood watching the dust devil, but Franklin's "curiosity being stronger," he followed it, "riding close by its side, and observed its licking up, in its progress, all the dust" under it. Recalling the "opinion that a shot, fired through a waterspout, will break it, I tried to break this little whirlwind, by striking my whip frequently through it, but without any effect." Soon, it veered off the road and went into the woods, "growing every moment larger and stronger, raising, instead of dust, the old dry leaves with which the ground was thick covered, and making a great noise with them and the branches of the trees, bending some tall trees round in a circle swiftly and very surprizingly, though the progressive motion of the whirl was not so swift but that a man on foot might have kept pace with it, but the circular motion was amazingly rapid."

Carrying the leaves upward in a spiral, the land devil was plainly visible at a distance. When Franklin "saw the trunks and bodies of large trees invelop'd in the passing whirl, which continued intire after it had left them, I no longer wondered that my whip had no effect on it in its smaller state." Franklin chased after it for "about three quarters of a mile, till some limbs of dead trees, broken off by the whirl, flying about, and falling near me, made me more apprehensive of danger." He continued watching it from a distance. At its top, many leaves "got loose from the upper and widest part" and were scattered in the wind, but so great was their height in the air that they appeared no bigger than flies.

Franklin noted that the course of "the general wind then blowing" moved along with the Tasker party, but the "progressive motion of the whirlwind was in a direction nearly opposite, though it did not keep a strait line, nor was its progressive motion uniform, it making little sallies on either hand as it went, proceeding sometimes faster, and sometimes slower, and seeming sometimes for a few seconds almost stationary, then starting forwards pretty fast again." When he rejoined the company, Franklin found them "admiring the vast height of the leaves, now brought by the common wind, over our heads. These leaves accompanied us as we traveled, some falling now and then round about us, and some not reaching the ground till we had gone near three miles from the place where we first saw the whirlwind begin."

The anecdote ended with Franklin's social note on his host and on the addressee of the letter, Peter Collinson: "Upon my asking Col. Tasker if such whirlwinds were common in Maryland, he answered pleasantly, *No, not at all common; but we got this on purpose to treat Mr. Franklin.* And a very high treat it was, to, Dear Sir, Your affectionate friend, and humble servant, B. F." (6:167–68).

THE NORTHWEST PASSAGE

Franklin wanted to believe in a northwest passage, perhaps partly because a route from Hudson Bay to the Pacific would be a boon to the colonial economy. The Irish leader Arthur Dobbs (1689–1765), who was to become the governor of North Carolina, also hoped to find a northwest passage and helped finance a trip to search for it in 1741. The captain of his expedition, Christopher Middleton (d. 1770), returned to England convinced that no northwest passage existed, but Dobbs suspected the Hudson's Bay Company had bribed him to suppress information that would lead to commercial success for Dobbs and others. In the summer of 1744, Franklin read Dobbs's criticisms of Middleton's reports and believed Dobbs (2:410, 410n9). In an *Account of the Countries Adjoining to Hudson's Bay* (1744), Dobbs published the supposed letter of a Spanish admiral, Bartholomew De Fonte, who had gone from the Pacific Ocean up a series of rivers and lakes down toward Hudson's Bay in 1640, where he encountered a ship from Boston.[15] Dobbs took the account from a 1708 periodical edited by the naturalist James Petiver, who probably wrote the apocryphal voyage.[16] Franklin read the De Fonte narrative in Dobbs's volume and tried to learn about the Boston ship. In the same year that Dobbs's *Account* appeared, 1744, Parliament passed a reward of £20,000 for the discovery of the northwest passage. Dobbs financed another exploration in 1746. It also failed, but two sailors on the expedition, Henry Ellis (1721–1806) and Theodorus Swaine Drage (ca. 1712–74), believed in a northwest passage and wrote accounts of the voyage.[17]

Franklin read their reports. Late in 1747, he excerpted in *Poor Richard* parts of Captain Christopher Middleton's account from the *Philosophical Transactions* of the "Extraordinary Degrees and Surprising Effects of Cold in Hudson Bay." In addition to Middleton's and Dobbs's writings on the northwest passage (2:410), Franklin knew John Harris's collection of voyages and travels, which also printed the De Fonte account.[18] In June 1748, Peter Collinson sent Franklin the first volume of Theodorus Swaine Drage's book on the 1746 voyage (3:300). Drage, who often used the simpler name Charles Swaine,[19] moved to Chestertown, Kent County, Maryland, in 1749 or 1750. Perhaps Arthur Dobbs had put him in touch with Chestertown's Reverend James Sterling, who was writing an epic poem on Dobbs. Drage/Swaine interested Sterling and his friend Governor Samuel Ogle of Maryland in an exploring expedition for the northwest passage. Ogle gave him a permit for the trip on 3 November 1750.[20] Swaine (to adopt the name he commonly used during his time in Maryland and Pennsylvania) sought out the best-known money-raiser of the area, Benjamin Franklin, and found that Franklin believed that a northwest passage probably existed.

Perhaps Swaine asked Franklin to organize a subscription (or did Franklin suggest it?) for a voyage to explore Hudson's Bay. A ship from New England rather than from London would have an easier voyage and more time during the normal summer to explore. Swaine loaned Franklin his documents concerning the northwest passage, including Arthur Dobbs's account. Swaine also published the De Fonte letter in volume 2 of his *Account of a Voyage for the Discovery of a North-west Passage* (1749).[21] Since De Fonte told of meeting a ship from Boston commanded by Captain Shapley and owned by Major General Seimor Gibbons, Franklin investigated. He wrote Boston's Reverend Thomas Prince, who had published the first volume of his *Chronological History* of New England in 1736 and was working on the second. Prince reported that Admiral Peter Warren of the Royal Navy, who served in the Boston area off and on from 1730 to 1746, had earlier asked him the same question. Prince had told Warren that a Major Edward Gibbons existed about 1635 in the colony. Trying now to answer Franklin, Prince could not find a Captain Shapley but inquired of a very old man who recalled that when he was a boy, there was a famous Captain Shapley of Charlestown, Massachusetts. Prince went there and found Shapley's descendants and his will. Prince concluded that the account was true "in general, but suppos'd a Mistake as to" General Gibbons being onboard (10:96–97).

Wanting to believe the De Fonte account, Franklin wrote Prince back, speculating that the original Spanish account said "Seignior" Gibbons. Franklin said it was unlike the Spanish to give merely a first and last name; Quakers would, but not the Spanish. Therefore he guessed that the English copier of the account made a mistake. When Franklin learned that Gibbons lived near Charlestown, Massachusetts, Shapley's home, he thought they must have known one another. In that case, Gibbons might well have sailed with Shapley (10:97–98).

Franklin adduced another bit of evidence. Increase Mather's *Remarkable Providences* (1684) reported that, sailing from New England "*to some other Parts of America,*" Major Gibbons and his crew were becalmed for weeks, ran out of provisions, and cast lots to see who would first be eaten by the others. At the last minute, they spied another ship, which proved to be a French pirate. Its captain, however, knew Gibbons, who had treated him kindly in the past, and so he relieved Gibbons and the crew (10:98). Though Mather gave no date for the event, Franklin supposed it was from the mid-seventeenth century or before. It proved to him that, contrary to Prince, Gibbons sometimes sailed on his own ships. For Franklin, that made the De Fonte account seem true.[22]

Since the prose of the De Fonte narrative was clumsy, Franklin thought it was an "Abridgement and a Translation." Unlike most imaginary voyages, it contained nothing marvelous. Franklin supposed that some Spanish would deny the truth of the De Fonte account out of commercial jealousy, but others appeared to accept it (10:89). The De Fonte narrative seemingly anticipated and confirmed various accounts of the weather and Eskimos that Franklin had read. De Fonte described Eskimo hunting boats (kayaks) and "Iron Knives" used by the hunters. Eskimos could not make iron, so they must have traded for it, perhaps from the Hudson's Bay Company or from the "Danes at Greenland" (10:92). Franklin implied that the hardy seafaring Eskimos used kayaks throughout the northern waters and portions of the northwest passage. In his *Account of a Voyage*, Charles Swaine made the first known attempt to map De Fonte's voyage and discoveries. No doubt the material he loaned Franklin included either a printed (if he had printed copies by then) or a manuscript version of his map.[23]

By 1750 the Reverend James Sterling finished his epic poem, *An Epistle to the Hon. Arthur Dobbs*, and sailed back to Ireland and then to London, ostensibly to see it published. Sterling knew John Hanbury, the greatest tobacco merchant of the mid-eighteenth century. He contacted Hanbury and proposed that they meet with the Board of Trade and ask for an "exclusive right" to trade with Labrador. With several investors, they did so on 16 April 1752. After another meeting, the Board of Trade said that it disapproved of monopolistic grants and turned down the application with the comment that the Hudson Bay Company's charter precluded an exclusive grant of the Labrador trade. Meanwhile, on 12 May 1752, the perfidious Sterling secured the king's bounty for the second time, managed to obtain for himself a collectorship of customs for the northern Chesapeake Bay, which paid £80 a year, and happily sailed back to Maryland.[24]

That fall, Franklin raised £1,500 (4:448) to explore the northwest passage, and the group bought a schooner in Newbury, Massachusetts. It was probably Franklin who renamed the ship *Argo*. Evidently Charles Swaine journeyed to Massachusetts with letters from Franklin to Thomas Prince and others, and continued the search for evidence in Massachusetts of the De Fonte account.[25] Purchased and outfitted for a sixteen-month voyage at a cost of only £900, the *Argo*, according to the merchant and ship owner William Allen, cost only "a trifle when compared to the charge of those vessels sent from London." Franklin informed his New York friend Cadwallader Colden on 28 February 1753 that "she sails in a few days" (4:448). The 10 May *Pennsylvania Gazette* mentioned that the *Argo* had sailed on 4 March "for Hudson's-Bay, on the Discovery of the North-west Passage." After stopping "at the Hianna's, near Cape Cod, and at Portsmouth, in New England, to take in her Compliment of Hands, and some particular Necessaries, [the *Argo*] took her Departure from the latter Place on the 15th of April, all well on board, and in high Spirits."

Franklin reported the voyage's outcome in the 15 November 1753 *Gazette*. Captain Charles Swaine encountered "Ice off of Farewell; left the Eastern Ice, and fell in with the Western Ice in lat. 58. and cruiz'd to the Northward to Lat. 63. to clear it, but could not, it then extending to the Eastward." The winter was the coldest for decades, and ice blocked the entrance to Hudson's Straight. On the return south, Swaine met with "two Danish Ships bound to Ball River and Disco up Davis's Straits, who had been in the Ice fourteen Days off Farewell, and had then stood to Westward, and assured the Commander that the Ice was fast to the Shore all above Hudson's Straits to the Distance of 40 Leagues out."

Finding that he "could not get round the Ice," Swaine "press'd thro' it, and got into the Straits Mouth the 26th of June, and made the Island Resolution, but was forc'd out by vast Quantities of driving Ice, and got into a clear Sea the first of July." After "repeated Attempts to enter the Straits in vain," Swaine explored the Labrador coast, and found "no less than 6 Inlets, to the Heads of all which they went, and of which we hear they have made a very good Chart, and have a better Account of the Country, its Soil, Produce, &c. than has hitherto been published." John Patten, an Indian trader whom the French had captured and returned to Philadelphia, had drawn a good map of the Ohio country for the Pennsylvania Assembly in 1752. He sailed on the voyage as the "Draughtsman & Mineralist" and mapped the Labrador coast.[26]

Swaine thought that the country was "like Norway." He discovered, however, that though a pass through Labrador to Hudson's Bay had been thought probable, a "high Ridge of Mountains running North and South about 50 Leagues within the Coast" precluded the possibility. He found "a fine Fishing Bank, which lies but 6 Leagues off the Coast" of Labrador. Franklin concluded his news report: "No bad Accident happen'd to the Vessel, and the Men kept in perfect Health during the whole Voyage, and return all well."

In 1768, Swaine published *The Great Probability of a Northwest Passage*, which contained his account of explorations in Labrador from 1 August to 20 September 1753. Franklin may have helped publish the book: he bought at least ten copies to sell in America, plus at least one for himself and probably several others for friends. Two later sources shed light on the voyage. Swaine recorded that in one harbor the *Argo* encountered a snow, the *Hope*, Captain Elijah Goff, from London. He brought four Moravian missionaries, including the diarist Christian Frederick Post (1710?–85), all of whom planned to remain in Labrador. Financed by the London firm of Nisbet, Bell, and Grace, the *Hope* intended to set up trade and, evidently, to search for gold. On 5 August, the *Hope* was in Nisbet Harbour, where Captain Goff and the Moravians were building a house when the *Argo* entered the harbor. Patten boarded the *Hope*, explained that the *Argo* had intended to search for the northwest passage, was prevented by the ice, and so went on, according to instructions, to explore Labrador. The next day, Swaine and Patten went aboard the *Hope* and dined, and on Friday, 7 August, Captain Goff did the same aboard the *Argo*. On Sunday, the *Argo* sailed on.[27]

The Philadelphia 1753 expedition had failed, but Franklin and the others who had raised money for fitting out Captain Swaine did not fault him. Instead, on 23 November, they met at the Bull's-Head Tavern for dinner and "expressed a general Satisfaction with Captain *Swaine's* Proceedings during his Voyage." Though "he could not accomplish his Purpose," the subscribers "unanimously voted him a very handsome Present."[28] Two weeks later, Franklin wrote that Swaine had "made some Discoveries of the Harbours on the Labrador Coast that may be useful." He added that he thought the financers would "fit her out again in the Spring for a second Attempt" (5:148).

Not all the investors continued. Some wanted to sell the boat and provisions and recover part of their investment. An advertisement appeared in the *Pennsylvania Gazette* on 1 January 1754: "To be sold, By publick Vendue, at Stamper's Wharff, on the 28th of February next, the Schooner Argo, With all her Tackle, Apparel, Stores, Boats, &c. An Inventory to be seen at John Stamper's." Stamper had been listed among the Philadelphia investors who opposed the London merchants who were trying to secure a monopoly of the Labrador trade (4:384). But Franklin, William Allen, and some others evidently bought out Stamper and proceeded with a second expedition. Their interest was no doubt reaffirmed by the *Gentleman's Magazine* in 1754. It featured accounts of the northwest passage and the De Fonte account together with a version of Joseph-Nicolas Delisle's *Carte général des découvertes de l'Admiral De Fonte* (Paris, September 1752) showing De Fonte's supposed route.[29]

The *Pennsylvania Gazette* announced on 2 May 1754 that "The Schooner Argo, Captain Swaine, is sail'd on a second Attempt for the Discovery of the north-west passage." Nearly six months later, on 24 October, the newspaper announced that the *Argo* had returned "from a second Attempt . . . without Success." Franklin added that "The Particulars of the Voyage are not come to hand, but may be expected in a future Paper." He did not want to publish the depressing details; they never appeared in the *Gazette*. But William Bradford's *Pennsylvania Journal* of 24 October 1754 reported that the Indians killed three of Swaine's men "on the Labrador Coast." Franklin surely knew that information and more. Swaine had sent the mapmaker and mineralogist John Patten and two other men to explore the immediate area, but unknown to Swaine, Patten had been asked to look for a mine from which ore specimens had been collected "the Year before." Looking for gold, the three went farther than instructed, were killed by the natives, and their boat was taken. That left the *Argo* shorthanded. The unhappy crew wanted to go back, and Swaine, possibly fearing a mutiny, found it "most prudent to return."[30]

Despite the trip's brevity, Swaine had collected a number of Eskimo "Habits, wore by the Eskemkaux Indians, . . . instruments, with their Utensils, and other

Curiosities, belonging to that People," and on Saturday, 9 November 1754, in the name of the financers of the local North-west Company, donated them to the Library Company. I suspect that Franklin was responsible both for asking Swaine to collect the materials before the trip and later for asking the contributors to donate the collection.[31]

The 14 November *Pennsylvania Gazette* that told of the gift also indirectly announced the end of the Philadelphians' search for a northwest passage: "To be SOLD, BY publick vendue, at the London Coffee House, on Saturday the 23d instant, at ten a clock in the Morning, The Schooner, ARGO, with all her tackle, apparel boats, &c. An Inventory to be seen at the place of sale." The proceeds would have been divided among the contributors in proportion to their contributions.

Most of the investors presumably abandoned their hopes and interest in a northwest passage. Franklin, however, still thought it might exist. Eight years later in London, on 27 May 1762, Franklin wrote out for his good friend Dr. John Pringle the reasons he believed that the De Fonte account had some truth. Pringle was the physician of John Stuart, third earl of Bute, who was prime minister in 1762–63. Pringle probably asked Franklin for the account to give it to Bute.[32] Franklin mentioned the letters and papers he had in Philadelphia "together with the Journals of the two Voyages I promoted." Though the voyages were unsuccessful, the journals contain "valuable Information; and the Charts taken of the Coast, Harbours, and Islands of Labrador, for a considerable Extent, may be useful" (10:99).

Franklin persisted in believing in the De Fonte account: "there may probably be no practicable Passage for Ships," but he thought that a passage existed for boats "such as DeFonte found and has describ'd." He also thought that the country was habitable, "and would produce all the Necessaries of Life." He had intended to draw a map of "my Idea of De Fonte's Voyage" but found Delisle's map generally correct.[33] He ignored Swaine's early map. Franklin thought Delisle placed "the Entrance of Los Reyes too far South, which Entrance I conceive, by the Distance sailed, 866 Leagues from Cape Abel, ought to be near Lat. 60. and that it carries the Strait Ronquillo too far North, which I imagine should enter Hudson's Bay between Lat. 60 and 62, where I have made two crooked red Lines. The Bay North of Cape Elias discover'd by the Russians, is perhaps the Entrance of the Archipelago St. Lazarus, describ'd by DeFonte, leading to Rio Los Reyes" (10:99–100). In putting the entrance to Los Reyes at 60 degrees rather than 53 degrees, Franklin may partially reflect "Braddock Mead" [John Green], *Remarks in Support of the New Chart of North and South America* (1753). Green placed the mouth of Los Reyes at 63 degrees.[34]

Partially reflecting Franklin's continued belief, particularly the information in his 27 May 1762 letter to Pringle, Swaine's *Great Probability* (1768) gave numerous supporting speculations and traced the history of attempted explorations of the northwest from the late sixteenth century. Swaine also gave

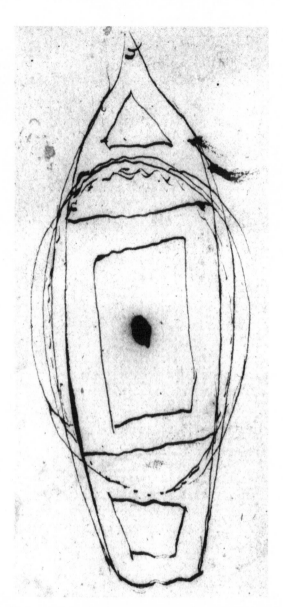

Figure 20. Franklin's rough sketch of an Eskimo kayak. Franklin made the rough sketch on a draft of a letter to George Whitefield, 19 June 1764. Perhaps Franklin made the drawing earlier or later than that date. We know he thought of kayaks when he wrote on 27 May 1762 his reasons for believing that the De Fonte account of a northwest passage was true (10:93–94).

The rough sketch may be based on some illustration that he had seen, or it may reflect an actual kayak. Captain Charles Swaine (Theodorus Swaine Drage) probably collected one among the Eskimo artifacts and "other Curiosities" that he brought back from Labrador in 1754. Franklin and other investors had financed Swaine's search for a northwest passage. If so, Franklin surely examined it. The investors in the expeditions, likely at Franklin's suggestion, donated the artifacts to the Library Company on 9 November 1754. Courtesy, American Philosophical Society.

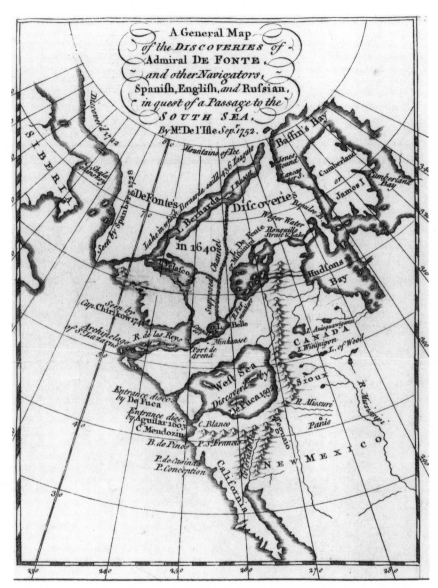

Map 1. Franklin's "correction" of Delisle's map of the De Fonte expedition. Thomas
Jeffries printed a version of Delisle's map in his edition of Gerhard F. Müller's Voyage
from Asia to America (London: Jeffreys, 1761) which Franklin thought roughly correct:
"I only think it places the Entrance of Los Reyes too far South, which Entrance I conceive,
by the Distance sailed, 866 Leagues from Cape Abel, ought to be near Lat. 60. and that it
carries the Strait Ronquillo too far North, which I imagine should enter Hudson's Bay
between Lat. 60 and 62, where I have made two crooked red Lines [just to the left of the
"H" in "Hudson's Bay"]. The Bay North of Cape Elias discover'd by the Russians, is
perhaps the Entrance of the Archipelago St. Lazarus, describ'd by DeFonte, leading to Rio
Los Reyes" (10:100).

anecdotes of Captain Nicholas Shapley ("Old Nick") that he said he had gathered from relatives in Kittery, Maine, including the hearsay that Shapley had been in the northwest passage. Swaine believed he established a connection between Major General Gibbons and Alexander Shapley, Nicholas Shapley's brother. Since Swaine's information seems more detailed than Franklin's, I suspect that Swaine actually did visit relatives and descendants of the Shapleys. On the other hand, Franklin investigated, but probably not in person. He knew Prince and no doubt wrote a letter of introduction for Swaine. Only Franklin said that Prince had earlier answered the same questions from Captain Peter Warren of the Royal Navy. Swaine's remarks on the Spanish language echo Franklin's. In 1762 Franklin had recorded the cannibalism story from Increase Mather's *Essay for Recording of Illustrious Providences*, and Swaine in 1768 recorded it from Cotton Mather's *Magnalia*, book 6. Franklin had read Mather's *Magnalia* and probably mentioned it, rather than Increase Mather's earlier and lesser-known work, to Swaine—perhaps because Increase Mather's title suggested the marvelous. Franklin and Swaine shared information before and after the expeditions.[35]

Franklin remained a believer in the De Fonte hoax. John Adams recorded that on the morning of 24 February 1783, Franklin said that the English version of the De Fonte letter was a translation "from the Spanish, and that the Translator or Printer put Seymour for Seignor." Franklin also repeated to Adams the information he had learned from Thomas Prince.[36]

How surprising that the normally skeptical Franklin was taken in by the De Fonte hoax. But, had Franklin not been wrong, we would have another reason to celebrate his extraordinary perspicacity. The qualities of intellectual independence and curiosity demonstrated in this mistaken belief were the same ones that enabled him to make contributions to so many fields. He would have been inhuman if he were not sometimes wrong.

FOUR

Clerk, Councilman, and Magistrate, 1748–1751

"The first Mistake in publick Business, is the going into it."
—Poor Richard, July 1758, 7:353

DURING THE FIRST HALF OF 1748, Franklin became the most popular man in the colony. His entry into elected political office resulted from his creation of the militia Association. Though the representatives elected him printer (1730) and clerk of the assembly (1736), these were primarily political appointments made through the patronage of the Speaker of the House. By 1739, when Speaker Andrew Hamilton retired, Franklin was well established in these positions, obviously doing a good job, and had many friends among the legislators. John Kinsey (Speaker, 1739–50) saw no reason to replace Franklin as printer or as clerk.

CLERK OF THE HOUSE, 1748–51

Franklin risked his position as clerk of the assembly in organizing the Association in 1747 and did so again on 16 June 1748. When the assembly met during 8–11 June 1748, the president (Anthony Palmer, senior member of the council and acting governor) and council asked the legislature for funds to defend Pennsylvania. The assembly refused and adjourned on 11 June. The council met on 14 June and passed a series of "Resolves" condemning the House for adjourning before the council could reply to its last message. The preamble to the resolves said that since most members of the House were Quakers and opposed to preparations for defense, "it may be reasonably supposed such an Assembly *are unfavourable* as well as incompetent Judges of the Expediency of any military Undertakings whatever." The council claimed that in the future, no one would be induced to volunteer private funds for the support of the province. It condemned the assembly and the Quakers for censuring its own members who contributed to fitting out the privateer *Warren*: "far from offering to repay" private persons who paid for the defense of the province, "The House has never so much as *thanked* those that by private Subscriptions fitted out a Vessel the last Year to scour our Coast; but instead publickly disapproved their Conduct, in a late former Message to this Board."[1]

Though he knew that the Quaker assemblymen would be outraged at him for doing so, Franklin printed the Pennsylvania Council's "Resolves" in the *Pennsylvania Gazette* on 16 June 1748. Franklin agreed with the council's condemning the assembly for doing nothing to defend the province. Though the House said on 1 September 1748 that it presumed Franklin printed the resolves by the council's order, Franklin probably printed them because he wanted to. As we will see, when Governor Robert Hunter Morris ordered him on 19 March 1755 not to print the letters of British secretary of state Thomas Robinson in the assembly's minutes, he did so anyway, claiming that he was the "immediate servant" of the assembly (5:535–36). The council's "Resolves" were surprisingly bold. When Richard Peters wrote Thomas Penn on 16 June 1748, Peters reported that William Allen was surprised at the "Resolves" and disapproved of them.[2]

At its next session, the House ordered Clerk Franklin on 25 August to lay before the assembly the 16 June *Pennsylvania Gazette* containing the council's "Resolves." Franklin was thus publicly, though indirectly, chastised for publishing them. Perhaps if King George's War was not winding down (the "Proclamation for a Cessation of Arms" was published in Philadelphia on 17 August 1748)[3] the Quaker-controlled assembly would not have publicly humiliated Franklin, but to many Quakers, the forthcoming peace justified their pacifism.

The House said on 1 September 1748 that the council's resolves were "so very extraordinary, as that without Breach of the Trust reposed in us by our Country, we cannot forbear to speak our Sentiments of them," and so the House made a long, tedious assertion of its rights, which appeared in the 8 September *Gazette*.[4] The president and council replied on 3 September: "Your Message, upon which our Resolves were made, we thought justly liable to be censured by every one who had Sense enough to see how they were deserted by their Representatives, whose Assistance they had a Right to expect." The message concluded by asking whether the House's conduct or the council's had "contributed most to the Public Service," and the council would leave the question to the public to decide.[5] The House retorted that "the Representative Body of the Province" could be more readily believed than the president and council.[6] Franklin published the answers and rejoinders in the 15 September *Gazette*. Neither any other colonial American newspaper nor any newspaper in Great Britain published as much or as timely local political news as Franklin's *Pennsylvania Gazette*.

As noted in Chapter 1, the public attack on Franklin probably encouraged James Read to warn him that some assembly members intended to vote against him as clerk for the following year, and Read evidently announced at this time that he would run against Franklin. After the new assembly convened, some members opposed Franklin as clerk, for the minutes only say that he was elected, whereas they often record that he was elected unanimously. Though the assemblymen knew that Franklin favored a strong defense, they also knew that in almost all other matters he agreed with the Quaker Party.

Speaker John Kinsey was known for a fierce temper. On Wednesday morning, 9 November 1748, his son John Kinsey, Jr., while on a ferry returning from a hunting trip, accidently shot himself and died. His friends brought the news to the Pennsylvania Assembly, which was in session with Speaker Kinsey presiding. Normally the assembly met at 10:00 A.M. and 3:00 P.M., but the 9 November minutes note only that the House met at 10:00 A.M. and adjourned to the next day. The reason for the extraordinary morning adjournment is not explained. But what happened was that young Kinsey's friends, who were probably somewhat afraid of Speaker Kinsey's possible reaction, informed Franklin about the young man's death. In a letter to Thomas Penn, Richard Peters noted that the news of young Kinsey's death was brought to the House while Kinsey was presiding and that Franklin was informed of the tragedy. "Franklin brought about an adjournment in a prudent manner & then broke the thing to the Father, who at first rav'd & was in a sad Condition, but he soon recover'd & had the Courage in Compliance with the Rules of the [Quaker] Meeting, to attend his Sons funeral the next Day."[7] One can only speculate about the "prudent manner."

A major change occurred in Pennsylvania politics when Speaker Kinsey himself died on 12 May 1750. The Quaker intellectual John Smith recorded, "The loss of this Great & Good man occasions a general Lamentation, and to present appearance is irreparable," but it later emerged that he had taken more than £3,000 from the General Loan Office for his own use. Lewis Evans commented in his *Brief Account of Pennsylvania* that the assembly members "were apt to distribute places of Profit amongst themselves especially the Loan Office, but the Instance of Mr. K[insey']s falling Short in his Account has lately induced them to act otherwise."[8]

The Pennsylvania Assembly elected Isaac Norris its Speaker at its next meeting, 6 August 1750. Norris continued Kinsey's moderate Quaker policies, giving money when necessary "for the king's use." The stalwart pacifist Israel Pemberton, however, succeeded Kinsey as clerk of the Pennsylvania and New Jersey Yearly Meeting and became the unofficial spiritual Quaker leader. Pemberton also won a seat in the assembly in the fall of 1750. Thus, the Quaker Party in the Pennsylvania Assembly became divided, with Pemberton the leader of the pacifist Friends and Norris the leader of the moderates.

Common Councilman, 1748–55

The Common Council of Philadelphia (also known as the Philadelphia Corporation) governed the city, with the mayor as the chief executive. Among its various duties, the council rented the stalls in the market, regulated the price of bread, decreed the proper measure of a cord of wood, licensed the sale of liquor, governed activity at the semi-annual fairs, leased ferries and wharves, provided some fire-fighting equipment, and heard appeals from the mayor's court. It was a self-perpetuating body; new members were elected by the existing ones. Its annual election was on the first Tuesday in October. As the 1748 election approached, the members had good reason to consider Franklin as a possible new member. Not only was he the most active Philadelphia citizen, but he had become well-known throughout the province when he organized the successful militia Association.

The Common Council had helped Franklin make the Associator movement a success by purchasing two thousand tickets at its first lottery. The "Cessation of Arms" proclaimed in Philadelphia on 17 August 1748 made the Associator movement seem almost like a personal victory for Franklin. Because of his efforts, Philadelphia had excellent defenses against invasion. As John Bartram noted, the citizens generally were unhappy with the pacifist Quakers who were in the process of censuring and disowning Septimus Robinson and Robert Strettell for investing in the *Warren*, a ship that would help protect the Delaware River and Bay from the French and Spanish privateers. Showing support for Robinson and Strettell, the Common Council promoted them from councilmen to aldermen for the coming year. And, in appreciation of Franklin, it elected him a councilman on 4 October 1748. In view of his support of the council's "Resolves" and his implicit criticism of the assembly, the Proprietary Party members probably hoped that Franklin was changing. Perhaps making him a member of the Common Council (which was dominated by proprietaries) would help convert him to the Proprietary Party.

Of the thirty-two members who elected Franklin, only six did not have some institutional connection with him. They were the mayor, William Attwood; the aldermen Samuel Hassell and William Till; and the councillors William Biddle, Nathaniel Allen, and Isaac Jones. The recorder, William Allen, was a fellow Freemason, a member of the Library Company, and a manager and treasurer of the Association. He had worked closely with Franklin throughout the previous year and would do so in several of Franklin's future projects. After the governor, Allen was the leading Proprietary Party member.

Six of the eight aldermen present on 4 October had connections with Franklin. William Plumsted, a close friend and Junto member, took part in every Franklin endeavor, including the Freemasons, Library Company, Union Fire Company, Association, and later the academy. Edward Shippen, also a member of the Union Fire Company, became mayor the following year and moved to Lancaster in 1752. Abraham Taylor was an Association officer, a Library Company member, and became a trustee of the academy. Joseph Turner, William Allen's partner, was a Union Fire Company member and became a supporter of the academy. And Charles Willing, a fellow Freemason, belonged to the Library Company, was an Association officer, and became a trustee of the academy. All were proprietaries, none more so than Franklin's old friend Plumsted.

Of the twenty-two councillors, three were close friends: Coleman, Francis, and Hopkinson. William Coleman, a fellow Junto member, also belonged to the Library Company and became involved with Franklin in the Philadelphia Academy and in the American Philosophical Society. Attorney General Tench Francis, who would become a key supporter in the Philadelphia Academy, was also a Library Company member. Thomas Hopkinson, who was currently performing electrical experiments with Franklin, was a member of the Junto, the Library Company, the Freemasons, and became a supporter of the Philadelphia Academy. He was also a member of the governor's council. John Inglis was an Association officer and a supporter of the Philadelphia Academy. William Logan, son of Franklin's patron James Logan, belonged to the Union Fire Company. Joshua Maddox contributed to the Philadelphia Academy. Samuel McCall, Jr., belonged to the Library Company, was an Association officer, and supported the Philadelphia Academy. Septimus Robinson was a fellow Freemason and an Association officer. Benjamin Shoemaker, a Union Fire Company member, also belonged to the Library Company. Several other councilmen were also Library Company members: the two Mifflins, Joseph Morris, Joseph Sims, John Sober, and John Stamper.

After his election, Franklin attended the next meeting of the Philadelphia Council on 16 November and took the usual oaths. The main business concerned the second Association lottery. Recorder William Allen noted that some tickets of the second class remained unsold and proposed that the corporation buy a number of them. The corporation agreed to buy up to four hundred tickets if "it should be necessary to prevent any Delay in the next Drawing." Though Franklin was absent from the 24 November meeting, the board assigned him to a committee to draft a congratulatory address for the new governor, James Hamilton, who was the son of Franklin's former patron, Andrew Hamilton. Franklin attended the next day when the draft was presented, slightly revised, approved, and presented to Hamilton.

The Common Council minutes record only two meetings in 1749: the election on 3 October and a meeting on 6 November. Franklin missed both (he was out of town for the second). In 1750 he attended all four meetings, 8 January, 30 and 31 July, and the election, 2 October. The 8 January meeting mainly concerned the nightly watch, Franklin's old Junto project (*Life* 2:404–8). The July meetings decided to grant funds for Franklin's new project, the Philadelphia Academy (see Chapter 7, below, 194–95).

Franklin's first political defeat occurred on Tuesday, 2 October 1750. William Allen had been chosen to replace John Kinsey as the chief justice of Pennsylvania and therefore had decided to relinquish his office as recorder of Philadelphia. The Philadelphia Common Council meeting on 2 October was well attended, partly because the new mayor would be chosen, but that had probably been decided upon already. The aldermen and common councillors no doubt knew that both Tench Francis and Benjamin Franklin would be candidates for the office of recorder. The Quaker intellectual John Smith recorded the outcome, together with his own opinion: "Heard that there was some Contest in the Common Council to-day about the choice of a Recorder. The Two Candidates were B. Franklin & Tench Francis, and notwithstanding the vast superiority of the former's Capacity and Character he had but 19 Votes when the other had

24."[9] Since Francis was the attorney general and, at that time, a good Proprietary Party member, the vote may well have been in part along party lines, for the Proprietary Party dominated the Philadelphia Corporation. Franklin's partisans probably included William Plumsted, Robert Strettell, Phineas Bond, Thomas Hopkinson, Thomas Bond, Samuel Rhoads, William Coleman, plus another twelve persons. Even among those whom I hypothesize supported Franklin, at least Plumsted and Hopkinson were proprietaries.

The corporation held nine meetings in 1751; Franklin attended eight. He was present on 21 March, when "a great Majority" approved Mayor Thomas Lawrence's proposal to bestow £100 on the academy instead of an entertainment for the corporation. The spate of council meetings in July (8, 15, 22, and 29) concerned rewarding the ferryman "for his extraordinary Expence" in buildings and improvements to the city's main ferry across the Delaware. Franklin also attended on 23 September, 1 October, and 10 December but was absent on 13 August. At the election on 1 October 1751 he was chosen an alderman, which meant that he automatically became a city magistrate and an associate justice of the mayor's court.

Although Franklin wrote that such offices flattered his ambition (A 120), his mother took a more realistic view. She wrote him on 14 October 1751: "I am glad to hear that you are so well respected in your toun for them to chuse you alderman alltho I don't know what it means nor what the better you will be of it beside the honer of it." When Franklin read that, it must have given him an ironic smile, for it was all too true. The higher one went, the more onerous the duties. The aldermen-elected mayor often refused to serve. In 1745, Alderman Abraham Taylor was elected mayor, refused to serve, and was fined £30. Then the council held a new election and chose Joseph Turner, who refused and instead happily paid his £30. Finally, Alderman James Hamilton did serve and did spend the usual amount of money, but instead of a feast for the board and principal citizens, he gave £150 toward erecting an exchange or some other useful public building. In 1746, Alderman William Attwood was elected mayor without incident. Alderman Joseph Morris was elected in 1747, even though he was absent, and when Charles Willing and Samuel Rhoads went to tell him he had been elected, they could not find him. The board met again that afternoon (6 October 1747) and sent two official messages, one to his home in the city and the other to his residence in Bucks County. At his home in Philadelphia, his wife would not accept the notice. The messenger, James Whitehead, had been hired to "go up into Bucks County, or where else he might be inform'd [that] Alderman Morris was gone, & endeavour to serve him personally with the said Notice, and bring his Answer to the Board at their Next meeting." At that meeting Whitehead said "he had used his utmost Endeavours" but had been unable to find him. The Common Council then held another election, and thus Morris escaped both the office and the £30 fine.

The council met four times in 1752, with Franklin present on 17 March, 16

May, and 3 October but absent on 17 November. For the six meetings in 1753, Franklin attended on 2 and 16 February, when the important issue of the Blue Anchor Dock came before the corporation, and missed those on 28 May, 23 July (he was in New England), 31 August, and 2 October (he was in Carlisle negotiating an Indian treaty).

THE BLUE ANCHOR LANDING

The Blue Anchor Landing (a landing on the Delaware River near the Blue Anchor Tavern, at the northwest corner of Front and Dock streets) occasioned a minor crisis while Franklin was on the Philadelphia Corporation. William Allen, recorder, had reported at a council meeting on 17 November 1746 that according to a deed he had found among the papers of the previous recorder, the corporation owned a lot that had been thought, by mistake, to belong to the city "and has been used as a free Landing." If it belonged to the corporation, the group could use the rent or fees from it as funds to run services in the city; if it belonged to the city as a free landing, it could not be rented, but presumably any upkeep or repairs would be paid by the corporation. After being mentioned again at meetings on 23 September and 10 December 1751 with Franklin in attendance, the corporation decided on 17 March 1752 that the lot might "be let for a considerable Yearly Rent" and desired Recorder Tench Francis (who had replaced Allen as recorder on 2 October 1750) to advertise the lot for rent. For some reason Francis did not, and the corporation again, on 2 February 1753, asked him to advertise it.

The advertisement appeared in the *Pennsylvania Gazette* on 6 February 1753 and stirred up opposition from the city assessors and others who had considered the ground a public landing. They requested a meeting to be informed by what right "or Pretence of right, the Mayor and Commonalty had published" the ad. The opposing parties met on 12 February, with Franklin present among the magistrates. Among the freeholders questioning the corporation's right to rent the Blue Anchor Landing were his close friends Thomas Leech and Samuel Rhoads (who, we have seen, was a member of the Philadelphia Corporation). Tench Francis produced a brief on the corporation title, which the protestors thought deficient. They said that "the Inhabitants have had the free uninterrupted Possession and use of the said Landing from the first Settlement of this city." One of the oldest inhabitants, Samuel Powell, who had arrived in Philadelphia in 1685, testified that Edward Shippen, while mayor of Philadelphia in 1701, had purchased the lot "for the use of the citizens of Philadelphia to be a free and common Landing Place forever."[10]

The next day, 13 February, a group of citizens and city assessors (the magistrates of the Philadelphia Corporation were not invited) met and decided to present a memorial to the corporation at its next meeting. They met the next evening to review the memorial and asked that the "City Burgesses, Overseers of the Poor, Assessors and Wardens" join them. Franklin and Hugh Roberts, as members of the Pennsylvania Assembly (the "City Burgesses"), joined the large number of citizens on 14 February 1753 who amended and approved the two memorials. They were ordered to be engrossed. The group met the next night, 15 February, at the courthouse and signed them. They presented them to the Common Council (Franklin present as alderman) at its meeting on the following day, 16 February 1753. The memorial was read and "order'd to lie on the Table." That was the last time the Blue Anchor Landing appeared in the minutes of the Philadelphia Corporation.[11]

The protesters prepared and placed with the recorder of deeds a document concerning the affair, asserting the public's right to the Blue Anchor Landing. Besides real estate documents and depositions, the document briefly described the 16 September meeting of the Philadelphia Common Council: "The Council after some debate concerning the Premises appointed a Committee to search the aforesaid Records on their behalf to discover if anything was to be found in favour of their Title." The notes on the meetings reveal that Franklin was one of the three aldermen appointed to investigate the records and report back. If the report was made, it was not entered in the minutes. The document concluded, "And we do not find that the Corporation proceeded any further in offering the said Landing for sale, being as we apprehend generally convinced of their mistake in attempting this Incroachment, on the right of the people."[12] The "Memorial of the Wardens, Commissioners, Assessors, and Overseers of the Poor," which was presented to the council, and the "Petition of the Inhabitants" both appeared in the *Pennsylvania Gazette* on 20 February 1753. Documents accompanying the petitions of 1691 and 1692 tended to confirm that the Blue Anchor Landing was meant for public use.

What was Franklin's role in the controversy? The Philadelphia Common Council's minutes are spare, recording disagreements by saying that "the majority voted." Since Franklin believed the public had the right of eminent domain, he would have supported the traditional use of the Blue Anchor Landing as a public landing. But the ownership of the landing may not have arisen at the first two meetings, 23 September and 10 December 1751, when the landing was mentioned in the council's meetings with Franklin present. Perhaps he did not question the council's ownership of the lot when it decided on 2 February 1753 to advertise it for rent. On the other hand, he must have known that the Blue Anchor Landing had, ever since he had arrived in Philadelphia in 1723, been used as a public landing. He probably also knew, however, that the public's right to it on the basis of past use or of eminent domain would not have convinced his fellow councilmen. They would have wanted to think that they were acting for the general good of Philadelphia.

As one of the two city burgesses present at the town meeting on 14 February 1753, Franklin supported and, on 15 February, signed the memorial to the city magistrates (which, of course, included himself as an alderman). Further, the *Pennsylvania Gazette*'s publication of the memorials and documents on 20 February indirectly affirmed his support for keeping the Blue Anchor Landing as a public convenience.

B. Franklin, Esquire

When appointed an alderman, Franklin automatically became a city magistrate and an associate justice of the mayor's court. When fulfilling these duties, he would be addressed as "Esquire" and would be expected to sign any official documents as "B. Franklin, Esquire" and to stamp them with his personal seal. He probably did so on some occasions in 1751 or 1752, but the earliest such document I have seen is from Wednesday, 16 May 1753, when John Frederick Ruhr and Anna Maria Ruhr appeared before "Benjamin Franklin Esqr one of the Justices" to record a deed: "in witness whereof I have hereunto set my Hand and Seal the Day and Year abovesaid. B. Franklin, Esq." This document may also be the earliest extant example of Franklin's seal, but it has been partially destroyed by having a bit of paper impressed upon it.[13] He was called "Esquire" in print when the *Boston Gazette* of 31 July 1753 reported that the corporation of Harvard College awarded "Benjamin Franklin, of *Philadelphia*, Esq; a Degree of *Master of Arts.*" The speech of the earl of Macclesfield bestowing upon him the Copley medal on 30 November gave the formal title of esquire. The notice of the prize in the *Gentleman's Magazine* for November 1753 mistakenly identified him as "Ben Franklyn, Esq; of Maryland," and the following number, for December, corrected itself: "Benjamin Franklin, Esq; of Philadelphia (not of Maryland)." The title page of part 3 of his *New Experiments and Observations on Electricity*, which appeared in London the following year, September 1754, called him "Esquire" (5:134, 433). Within a couple of years, old friends adopted the formal address—and the closest old friends, like John Bartram and Hugh Roberts, continued to call him "Dear Benjamin" and "Dear Ben" (6:465–66, 8:79, 449; cf. 7:246, 8:81).

Last Common Council Meetings

Franklin attended only the 31 August meeting of the Philadelphia Corporation in 1754; he missed 25 April, 1 and 4 October, and 4 December (he was in New England for the last three). In 1755, he was present on 1 March and 7 October, the annual election and presentation of the new mayor to the governor. He missed the meetings of 16 and 29 August and 4 November. The last meeting he attended before going to England in 1757 was on 7 October 1755. Though he was out of town for five months in 1756, he could have attended several of its meetings in the latter part of the year. But he chose not to, perhaps because the business of the Philadelphia Corporation was mainly routine, but probably because the majority of the Philadelphia Common Council were Proprietary Party members. Franklin had become widely recognized as the leading critic of the Proprietary Party and no doubt felt increasingly estranged from most members of the Philadelphia Corporation.

Appointment to the Philadelphia Common Council was for life, but Alderman Franklin never attended during his return to Philadelphia in 1763–64. He did, however, appear at the very last meeting of the superannuated Common Council of Philadelphia on 17 February 1776. After having ignored the most pressing political matters in the pre-Revolutionary period, the Philadelphia Corporation died of inbreeding and irrelevance.

FREEMASON

As Franklin knew, his friend William Allen, who was often kind and generous to deserving persons, was sometimes prickly, jealous, and resentful. After Allen learned that Boston's Thomas Oxnard, the provincial grand master of Masons in North America,[14] had appointed Franklin the provincial grand master of Pennsylvania's Masons on 10 July 1749, Allen displayed those qualities. Franklin's position became known before 29 August when Thomas Mullen of Philadelphia's Tun Tavern Lodge petitioned the Grand Lodge to ask for a "Deputation under its sanction." A committee was appointed but nothing further about the petition appeared in the Tun Tavern Lodge minutes.[15] When Franklin held the first regular meeting of the Grand Lodge on 5 September 1749, he appointed Dr. Thomas Bond the deputy grand master, Joseph Shippen the senior grand warden, Philip Syng the junior grand warden, William Plumsted the grand treasurer, and Daniel Byles the grand secretary. He surely invited Allen, who may not have attended. Franklin held the meeting at the Royal Standard, which was on the south side of Market Street east of Second Street and belonged to Henry Pratt, a fellow Freemason. The Grand Lodge also issued a warrant for a new lodge, which would be known as the "First Lodge," since its charter was the first to be granted by a Grand Lodge in Pennsylvania.[16]

The news upset William Allen. He had been a Freemason before Franklin and had appointed Franklin to his first Masonic office, junior grand warden, on St. John's Day, 24 June 1732 (*Life* 2:88). Allen wrote his influential and wealthy London friends, asking to be appointed provincial grand master of Pennsylvania. William Lord Byron, baron of Rochdale, England's grand master, appointed him grand master of Pennsylvania during the winter of 1749–50. Allen waited until the next meeting of the Grand Lodge of Pennsylvania before revealing his commission. On Tuesday, 13 March 1750, when the Grand Lodge met at the Royal Standard, Allen entered the meeting and presented his direct commission from the grand master of England as provincial grand master of Pennsylvania. Franklin immediately acknowledged Allen's authority. Allen, in turn, appointed Franklin deputy grand master and kept the other appointees, except Dr. Bond.[17]

Franklin and Allen no doubt thought that Franklin's immediately acknowledging Allen's authority would have ended any dispute. However, when the Boston Masons learned that their commission to Franklin had been overturned, they objected to the grand master of England in a "humble Remonstrance" of 7 October 1751. All the masters, senior wardens, and junior wardens of the four

Figure 21. William Allen by Robert Feke, ca. 1746. The richest man in Philadelphia, William Allen cooperated with Franklin and generously supported most of Franklin's public-spirited projects. Allen was a merchant, ship owner, lawyer, and major landholder, and later the chief justice of Pennsylvania. He became jealous, however, as Franklin received more attention and praise than he. When the Boston Freemasons named Franklin the grand master of Pennsylvania, Allen appealed to England and secured that title. He was also no doubt miffed by General Edward Braddock's praise of Franklin—and by Braddock's ignoring his own role in securing wagons for the British army. As a leading member of the Proprietary Party, Allen became Franklin's political enemy by 1755. Though Franklin attempted to remain cordial (as his naming the fort he built in 1756 Fort Allen shows), Allen had permanently turned against Franklin.

In a three-quarter-length portrait, the large, portly Allen is standing, his face three-quarters front, with his left shoulder toward the spectator. His left hand hangs down and he has a tricorner hat tucked under his arm; his right hand grasps a gold-tipped walking stick, an icon suggesting landed gentry. Wearing a shoulder-length white wig, a long coat, a waistcoat, a cravat, and a white blouse with ruffles at the sleeves, he is obviously a gentleman of importance and wealth.

Allen was a generous patron of promising artists. It is fitting that he was also painted by John Smibert as a young man in 1740 and by Benjamin West as an older man about 1763–64. Courtesy, Independence National Historical Park.

Boston lodges signed it. After pointing out that three successive grand masters of the Grand Lodge of Boston had been given the title "Grand Master of North America," they claimed that official masonry in North America "has wholly originated from us." They asked that the present grand master, Thomas Oxnard, and his successors be recognized "as Grand Master over all the Lodges" of North America, and that "all future Deputations or Constitutions be from him or his Deputy only." Charles Pelham, the grand secretary, signed the remonstrance and evidently drafted it.[18]

Perhaps the remonstrance was never sent. No record of it survives in the archives of the Grand Lodge of England. Franklin would not have wanted to make an issue of the Boston grand master's authority whereby Franklin was appointed. As he advised William Smith concerning insults, "The noblest Victory is obtained by Neglect and by Shining on" (4:475). And yet there is one more turn of the screw: at a Boston Masonic meeting six months later on 10 April 1752, "Bro. McDaniel appeared for the Lodge in Philadelphia and paid for its constitution thirty-one pounds and ten shillings." Hugh McDaniel had held a variety of offices in the St. John's Boston lodge, including being master in 1739 and 1740 and deputy grand master of the Grand Lodge in 1751. Confirmation that McDaniel paid the sum occurs on 11 October 1754 (when Franklin was visiting the Boston Grand Lodge). The minutes listed the lodges that had supposedly been started under the auspices of the Boston Grand Lodge. The first was the Philadelphia lodge, with McDaniel as the primary founder.[19] Thirty-one pounds and ten shillings was a large sum in 1752—more than many working people made in a year. Though I can speculate what happened, I nevertheless find the record mysterious and tantalizing.

MAGISTRATE, 1750–54

Like everyone the governor appointed to a public office, magistrates represented the Pennsylvania establishment. Most magistrates were Proprietary Party members. Quaker Party members often turned down appointments, for the position could be unpopular.[20] Governor James Hamilton probably appointed Franklin in part hoping that it might help make him a proprietary. Franklin's accepting the appointment may be regarded as an attempt to be a good citizen, or possibly as an effort to adjudicate between the Quaker and Proprietary parties. Also, as he said in the Autobiography, the promotion flattered his ambition (A 120).

Confirmation of the suspicion that Hamilton hoped to make Franklin a proprietary is found in a letter from Richard Peters to Thomas Penn in 1752: Peters commented that as an assemblyman Franklin "thinks it too soon to open as he is but a new member." Peters expected Franklin to reveal himself a proprietary follower. Peters added that since Franklin was a magistrate "he will most certainly be opposed by the people" and soon would become unpopular. Implicitly, Peters seems to confirm the general unpopularity of the Penns and their adherents.[21]

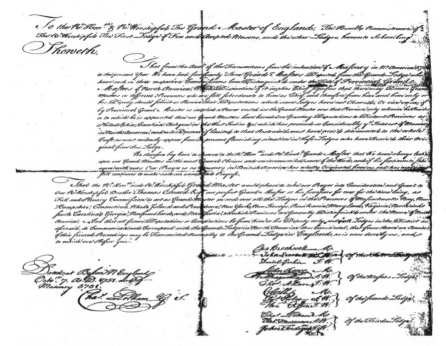

Figure 22. The Boston Freemasons' protest, 7 October 1751. Thomas Oxnard, the provincial grand master of Masons in North America, appointed Franklin the provincial grand master of Pennsylvania's Masons on 10 July 1749. Franklin held a meeting of the Grand Lodge on 5 September 1749 and appointed officers for the forthcoming year. Irritated by Franklin's being preferred, William Allen (who had been a Mason before Franklin) wrote his London friends asking to be appointed provincial grand master of Pennsylvania by England's grand master. Allen received the commission and revealed it at the next meeting of the Pennsylvania Grand Lodge on Tuesday, 13 March 1750. Franklin immediately acknowledged Allen's authority.

The Boston Masons, however, were irritated when they learned that their commission to Franklin had been overturned, and they objected. In a "humble Remonstrance" of 7 October 1751, the secretary of the Grand Lodge of Massachusetts, and the masters, senior wardens, and junior wardens of all four Boston lodges protested. For decades, the successive grand masters of the Grand Lodge of Boston had been given the title "Grand Master of North America." As such, the grand master of North America had chartered lodges in various American colonies. They asked that the present grand master, Thomas Oxnard, and his successors be recognized "as Grand Master over all the Lodges" of North America, and that "all future Deputations or Constitutions be from him or his Deputy only."

Perhaps the remonstrance was never sent. No record of it survives in the archives of the Grand Lodge of England or in Boston's Grand Lodge. Franklin would not have wanted to make an issue of the Boston grand master's authority. Nevertheless, on 10 April 1752, Hugh McDaniel, a mainstay of the Boston Freemasons, paid the Massachusetts Grand Lodge "thirty-one pounds and ten shillings" for the constitution of the "Lodge in Philadelphia." Franklin was present in Boston six months later when the Massachusetts Grand Lodge listed its subsidiary lodges: Pennsylvania's was first, with McDaniel as its founder. As with so many details in Franklin's biography, one is left with unanswered questions. Courtesy, University of Delaware Library.

Conflicting dates appear for Franklin's appointment as a justice of the peace. Governor Hamilton signed the commission appointing him and others as magistrates for Philadelphia city and county on Saturday, 3 June 1750. But on Friday, 30 June, Governor Hamilton and the Pennsylvania Council "agreed to appoint" Franklin and others as justices. Evidently, the practice was for the governor to make the appointment and then, often at a later time, for the Provincial Council to affirm it. The 3 June date therefore marks the beginning of Franklin's duties as a magistrate. In the *Autobiography*, Franklin wrote that he tried the office of justice of the peace "a little," attended a few courts, and sat "on the Bench to hear Causes" (A 120). When he was elected an alderman on 1 October 1751 and thereby automatically became a member of the mayor's court, he had already been serving as a justice of the peace for Philadelphia County for over a year.

Few court documents for Philadelphia city and county exist for the early 1750s, and Franklin's participation is recorded in only one. In the June 1750 term of the Court of Common Pleas, Lawrence Williams, represented by John Ross, brought an action to recover £3,794.19.10 against William Till, represented by Tench Francis. At the time (as in our Supreme Court today), several justices heard a case. These justices were Thomas Lawrence, Edward Shippen, Joshua Maddox, and Benjamin Franklin. David Paul Brown, the mid-nineteenth-century historian of Pennsylvania's courts, wrote that none of the four had either prosecuted or defended persons in court and none was "professionally educated" in the law. The case dragged on until 12 March 1752/3 when Franklin and the other judges signed the depositions to be given to the jury.[22]

Franklin wrote in the *Autobiography* that he found "more knowledge of the Common Law than I possess'd, was necessary to act in that Station with Credit." Therefore, he "gradually withdrew from it, excusing myself by my being oblig'd to attend the higher Duties of a Legislator in the Assembly" (A 101). Though he was, after the Speaker, the most active member of the House beginning with the assembly of 1751–52, Franklin did not withdraw from the magistrate's position until later. He evidently served faithfully as a magistrate through 1753. On 25 May 1752, when the "Justices for the City and County of Philadelphia" were appointed, Franklin was reappointed, moving up from twenty-seventh to seventeenth in the commission.[23] Had he not been discharging the magistrate's duties, the members of the Pennsylvania Council (four were fellow justices of Philadelphia city and county) would hardly have proposed and voted for him.

The scarce extant records show that Franklin performed various duties as a magistrate, including serving, on 5 June 1752, on the Orphans' Court for the City and County of Philadelphia. He probably began withdrawing from his position as a magistrate during 1754. The last time that we know he acted as a justice was 22 May 1754.[24] The reason he gave in the *Autobiography* for abandoning the position was not the only one—and probably not the major one. He had too little time to pursue his scientific and literary interests. Something had to give. Serving as a magistrate was time-consuming and sometimes boring. Further, the magistrates were almost all proprietary partisans, appointed to their positions by the governor, with the approval of the council and, at a distance, of the proprietors. It was not "the higher Dutys of a Legislator in the Assembly" that made Franklin stop being a magistrate (A 120) but his increasing aversion to the positions of the proprietors and the Proprietary Party.

FIVE

The Academy and College of Philadelphia

"The Idea of what is true Merit, *should also be often presented to Youth, explain'd and impress'd on their Minds, as consisting in an Inclination join'd with an* Ability *to serve Mankind, one's Country, Friends and Family; which* Ability *is (with the Blessing of God) to be acquir'd or greatly encreas'd by true Learning; and should indeed be the great* Aim *and* End *of all Learning."*
—*Franklin,* Proposals Relating to the Education of Youth *(1749), 3:419*

HOME SCHOOLING WAS AT LEAST as important for girls and boys in the eighteenth century as it is today. Three kinds of formal education for boys existed then. One was the elite school, where one primarily studied Latin and, later, a little Greek. Second, other elementary schools existed, like George Brownell's, which Franklin attended for his second year and final year of schooling, where boys and girls learned a smattering of everything, but one generally spent only a few years at such schools. The third kind of education was the apprenticeship system. Franklin found all three unsatisfactory. The formal school prepared the student to pass the Latin examination required for admittance to college about age seventeen or eighteen. At college, students primarily studied Latin and Greek to prepare them for the ministry or, perhaps, some other career, such as a merchant or a physician. Most boys became apprentices at about age twelve and learned the "mysteries" of one trade well until they were approximately twenty or twenty-one. Then they became journeymen, condemned to practice that trade for the rest of their lives. Of course the poorest people learned no craft or trade and spent their lives as servants or laborers.

In Volume 1 (*Life* 1:50–51), I described Franklin's education, his disappointment at being taken from the South Grammar School (present-day Boston Latin School), his dislike for his father's trade, his admiration for the handicrafts that he saw with his father, and his resentment at being condemned to the apprenticeship system. All his elder brothers were "put Apprentices to different Trades" (A 6). At age sixteen, the apprentice printer turned his early disappointment into a rejection of the value of a classical education. In Silence Dogood No. 4, the teenager expressed his resentment in a satire. The dream-vision of Harvard ridiculed the usual college curriculum and prefigured his radical reformist program of education. In the satire, a personified Learning sat "surrounded almost on every Side with innumerable Volumes in all Languages." On her right sat English, "with a pleasant smiling Countenance, and handsomely attir'd," but on her left "were seated several *Antique Figures* with their Faces veil'd." Franklin's early essay anticipated his later opinion that most of the useful knowledge was available in English, that other modern languages were valuable adjuncts, especially for merchants and for trade, but that Latin, Greek, and Hebrew contributed little to modern learning.[1]

Eleven years later, Franklin echoed Francis Bacon's theory on the development of civilization, writing in 1733 that "when Colonies are in their Infancy, the Refinements of Life, it seems, cannot be much attended to." Early colonists must devote their energy to encouraging agriculture, promoting trade, and establishing good laws. The "other Arts and Sciences, less immediately necessary, how excellent and useful soever, are left to the Care and Cultivation of Posterity. Hence it is that neither in this, nor in the neighbouring Provinces, has there yet been made any Provision for a publick generous Education."[2] After another decade, when Franklin's son William was about fifteen and had been studying with Alexander Annand for about five years, Franklin probably wished there were a nearby college he could attend. Franklin drew up a proposal "for establishing an Academy" and probably read it in the Junto, requesting suggestions and criticisms. He thought Richard Peters was "a fit Person to superintend such an Institution," but Peters intended to work for the proprietors, and Franklin, "not knowing another at that time suitable for such a Trust," let the project temporarily die (A 91–92).

THE FIRST PLAN: A GOOD ENGLISH EDUCATION

After retiring as a printer, Franklin became caught up in the practical necessities of war for nearly a year (November 1747 to August 1748) and then resurrected the academy project. He talked it over in the Junto, and in the summer of 1749 approached a number of wealthy civic leaders. Forty years later, in June 1789, when he made a final appeal for education primarily featuring the English language, he told of his original project. Just as he "had provided only for English Books" in projecting the Library Company, so too in the 1749 "Scheme my Ideas went no farther than to procure the Means of a good English Education." Franklin found, however, that some "Persons of Wealth and Learning, whose Subscriptions and Countenance we should need, being of Opinion that it ought to include the learned Languages, I submitted my Judgment to theirs." He included Latin and Greek in the curriculum. He resolved, however, "to preserve as much of" the original plan as he could "and to nourish the English School by every Means in my Power" (S 10:10). *Poor Richard* for 1749 (written in October 1748) stated Franklin's opinion of the standard education: "Most of the Learning in Use, is of no great Use" (3:347).

Franklin began to campaign for an educational institution in Pennsylvania in the summer of 1749. He talked privately to friends who might contribute to an academy and then published a letter, "On the Need for an Academy," in the *Pennsylvania Gazette* on 24 August 1749. Again echoing Bacon, Franklin said that at first Pennsylvanians had to attend to practical matters, but now that Americans were enjoying "times of more wealth and leisure," they should encourage arts and learning: "Numbers of our inhabitants are both able and willing to give their sons a good education if it might be had at home." Since *home* in colonial American usage generally referred to England, Franklin's usage asserted Americanism and appealed to local pride and indirectly to local economic interests. "It is thought" that "a proposal for establishing an Academy in this province, will not now be deem'd unreasonable." To give the proposal a classical attestation, Franklin quoted Pliny's letter urging the establishment of a local school, so that persons "may receive their education where they receive their birth" (3:386).

The Idea of the English School

At the request of the academy trustees, Franklin "sketch'd out" his *Idea of the English School* in the summer or fall of 1750. Sending a copy to Connecticut's Dr. Samuel Johnson on 25 October, Franklin claimed to be unfit to compose such a document, "having neither been educated myself (except as a Tradesman) nor ever concern'd in educating others." He asked Johnson to either amend it "or (which perhaps will be easier to do) give us a Compleat Scheme of your own" (4:72). Johnson replied with praise for the plan, only suggesting a few more models of the best English writers. Franklin thanked him on 22 November, claiming that Johnson's comments were too generous: "I find 'tis deficient in the main Thing [the additional models of English writing]; like the Man's excellent Race-Horse that had every good Quality, Courage excepted" (4:476). Franklin incorporated his suggestions for the study of additional English writers in the sixth and last year (except Shakespeare, who, as Franklin presumably realized, was inimitable), printed a slightly revised version of his draft, and gave it to the trustees, probably before classes started in January 1751. Later, when Franklin published Richard Peters' sermon on the opening of the academy in September 1751, he appended his *Idea of the English School* (4:101–2).

Every student admitted into the English school should "be at least able to pronounce and divide the Syllables in Reading, and to write a legible Hand." He told Johnson that he thought they should generally be between "8 years of Age and 16" so that when they left school, they still had time to learn whatever profession that did not require the "learned Languages" that they intended to study (4:72). Franklin was idealistic, for most boys would not know how to read and write until they were a year or two older than eight. In the "First or lowest Class," the students should learn grammar and spelling. Franklin suggested a competitive method for teaching: two students nearly equal in their spelling ability should each propose ten words every day to the other to be spelled. He who correctly spelled most of the other's words was "Victor for that Day; he that is Victor most Days in a Month" wins a prize, "a pretty neat Book of some Kind useful in their future Studies." Franklin thought this method would make the youths "good Spellers very early." He commented, "'Tis a Shame for a Man to be so ignorant of this little Art, in his own Language, as to be perpetually confounding Words of like Sound and different Significations; the Consciousness of which Defect, makes some Men, otherwise of good Learning and Understanding, averse to Writing even a common Letter."[3] Short pieces like "Croxall's Fables" should be read aloud and the difficult words explained (4:102–3).

In the second year, students would be taught reading aloud with "proper Modulations of the Voice according to the Sentiments and Subject." Suitable papers like the easier *Spectators* would be assigned as homework. The following day, the students would "give an Account, first of the Parts of Speech, and Construction of one or two Sentences," which would "oblige them to recur frequently to their Grammar, and fix its principal Rules in their Memory." Every student should have a dictionary. Students would discuss the author's intention and the meaning of every uncommon word, which "would early acquaint them with the Meaning and Force of Words, and give them that most necessary Habit, of Reading with Attention."

"The Youth" should be "made acquainted with good Stiles of all Kinds in Prose and Verse, and the proper Manner of reading each Kind. Sometimes a well-told Story, a Piece of a Sermon, a General's Speech to his Soldiers, a Speech in a Tragedy, some Part of a Comedy, an Ode, a Satyr, a Letter, Blank Verse, Hudibrastick, Heroic, &c. But let such Lessons for Reading be chosen, as contain some useful Instruction, whereby the Understandings or Morals of the Youth, may at the same Time be improv'd" (4:103–4). In the third year, the students should study rhetoric from "some short System, so as to be able to give an Account of the most usual Tropes and Figures." After reading aloud short speeches from the classics or parliamentary debates, they should memorize them and deliver them "with the proper Action, &c." Franklin suggested the students begin reading history with Charles Rollin's *Antient and Roman Histories*, and in subsequent years read "the best Histories of our own Nation and Colonies." He recommended "The Natural and Mechanic History contain'd" in Noel Antoine Pluche's *Spectacle de la Nature*, a popular encyclopedia of science and technology for young readers. Franklin said that "next to the Knowledge of *Duty*, this Kind of Knowledge is certainly the most useful, as well as the most entertaining."

Future merchants, artisans, and farmers would benefit from the study of works like Pluche: "The Merchant may thereby be enabled better to understand many Commodities in Trade; the Handicraftsman to improve his Business by new Instruments, Mixtures and Materials; and frequently Hints are given of new Manufactures, or new Methods of improving Land, that may be set on foot greatly to the Advantage of a Country." The study of science and technology should be continued in subsequent classes (4:104–5). Franklin professed in the *Autobiography* that "Prose Writing has been of great Use to me in the Course of my Life, and was a principal Means of my Advancement" (A 12). Though penmanship was the "Writing-Master's Business," style, grammar, and punctuation were responsibilities of the English master. The students in the fourth year "should be put on Writing Letters to each other on any common Occurrences, and on various Subjects, imaginary Business, &c. containing little Stories, Accounts of their late Reading, what Parts of Authors please them, and why. Letters of Congratulation, of Compliment, of Request, of Thanks, of Recommendation, of Admonition, of Consolation, of Expostulation, Excuse, &c. In these they should be taught to express themselves clearly, concisely, and naturally, without affected Words, or high-flown Phrases." The models Franklin recommended were the letters of Sir William Temple and Alexander Pope. During the same year, Dr. Johnson's *Ethices Elementa, or First Principles of Morality* would be taken up "to lay a solid Foundation of Virtue and Piety" (4:105–7).

Fifth-year students should continue writing letters and add essays and occasional poems, "not to make them Poets, but for this Reason, that nothing acquaints a Lad so speedily with Variety of Expression, as the Necessity of finding such Words and Phrases as will suit with the Measure, Sound and Rhime of Verse, and at the same Time well express the Sentiment." The essays "should all pass under the Master's Eye, who will point out their Faults, and put the Writer on correcting them." Franklin advocated the method that he had used in teaching himself to write: "let the Sentiments of a *Spectator* be given, and requir'd to be cloath'd in a Scholar's own Words." They would also study Dr. Johnson's *Noetica, or First Principles of Human Knowledge* (4:106–7; cf. A 13–14).

In the sixth and final year, "besides continuing the Studies of the preceding, in History, Rhetoric, Logic, Moral and Natural Philosophy, the best English Authors may be read and explain'd." From Dr. Johnson's suggestions, Franklin enumerated Milton, Addison, Pope, Swift, *Telemachus*, and the *Travels of Cyrus*. From his original list, Franklin kept Tillotson, "the higher Papers in the *Spectator* and *Guardian*," and "the best Translations of Homer, Virgil and Horace." Every day some classes could be with the writing master, some with the mathematical master "learning Arithmetick, Accompts, Geography, Use of the Globes, Drawing, Mechanicks, &c.," and the others "in the English School, under the English Master's Care." At the end of the school year, public ceremonies should be held before the trustees and citizens, with prizes awarded. Franklin concluded that the graduates "will come out of this School fitted for learning any Business, Calling or Profession, except such wherein Languages are required; and tho' unaquainted with any antient or foreign Tongue, they will be Masters of their own, which is of more immediate and general Use; and withal will have attain'd many other valuable Accomplishments; the Time usually spent in acquiring those Languages, often without Success, being here employ'd in laying such a Foundation of Knowledge and Ability, as, properly improv'd, may qualify them to pass thro' and execute the several Offices of civil Life, with Advantage and Reputation to themselves and Country" (4:107–8).

"*Any* business, *any* calling, *any* profession!" exclaimed the historian Bernard Bailyn.[4] He appreciated the radicalness of Franklin's plan. Instead of raising a boy in an apprenticeship, wherein the youth would spend seven to twelve years learning one craft, he would instead be prepared for a multitude of possibilities. He could then, at about age seventeen, choose what trade or profession he wanted to join. That was hardly the end, for groups like the Junto and subscription libraries were becoming common in colonial towns. In 1751 Franklin was still in the process of transforming himself from the chandler's son to whatever it was he would finally become. He wanted everyone to have that possibility.

Proposals Relating to the Education of Youth in Pennsylvania

Franklin followed up the 24 August 1749 newspaper essay with *Proposals Relating to the Education of Youth in Pennsylvania*, which he distributed on 23 October "with my Newspapers, gratis" (S 10:10). As soon after "as I could suppose their Minds a little prepared by the Perusal of it, I set on foot a Subscription for Opening and Supporting an Academy; it was to be paid in Quotas yearly for Five Years; by so dividing it I judg'd the Subscription might be larger, and I believe it was so, amounting to no less (if I remember right) than Five thousand Pounds." He said that "In the Introduction to these Proposals, I stated their Publication not as an Act of mine, but of some *publick-spirited Gentlemen*; avoiding as much as I could, according to my usual Rule, the presenting myself to the Publick as the Author of any Scheme for their Benefit" (A 117).

The primary audience for the proposals was wealthy Philadelphians who could afford to pledge and contribute to pay for buying a lot, building the school, and hiring teachers. In the *Proposals*, Franklin wrote that "some public-spirited Gentlemen, to whom" the *"Hints"* have been privately communicated, approved the project and "directed a Number of Copies to be" printed and distributed in order "to obtain the Sentiments and Advice of Men of Learning, Understanding, and Experience in these Matters." The same gentlemen "have determin'd to use their Interest and best Endeavours, to have the Scheme, when compleated, carried gradually into Execution." Franklin asked that "Those who incline to favour the Design with their Advice, either as to the Parts of Learning to be taught, the Order of Study, the Method of Teaching, the economy of the School, or any other Matter of Importance to the Success of the Undertaking, are desired to communicate their Sentiments as soon as may be, by Letter directed to B. Franklin, *Printer*, in Philadelphia" (3:397). Franklin had used a similar persona of a speaker giving only "Hints" and seeking advice in the founding document of the American Philosophical Society (14 May 1743) and in writings on the militia Association in late 1747 and early 1748. Though he had been retired as a printer for nearly two years, and though a printer might not seem to be an ideal person to found an academy, Franklin often used the artisan persona, not only in his fictions but also in his several wills and in his epitaph.[5]

"The good Education of Youth," Franklin wrote, "has been esteemed by wise Men in all Ages, as the surest Foundation of the Happiness both of private Families and of Common-wealths." He cited Milton, Locke, Rollin, Turnbull, and others who "generally complain, that the *old Method* of education is in many Respects wrong; but long settled Forms are not easily changed." Franklin often made similar statements about the perseverance of old forms—from the spelling of English, to the habits of individuals, to the customs of nations: "For us, who are now to make a Beginning, 'tis, at least, as easy to set out right as wrong." He flattered his audience by telling them that many "first Settlers" had received a good education in Europe and that by their good management, the present generation had attained prosperity. The "first Settler," however, could not do everything. The present youth are of equal ability, but "the best Capacities require Cultivation" (3:399).

After again calling the *Proposals* merely "*Hints*" toward forming a plan of education, Franklin revealed that he viewed education and the projected academy as a way for youths to achieve a better life. Since the English satires on America often portrayed it as a land of extraordinary opportunity because of the backwardness and ignorance of the Americans, he turned the American Dream on its head:[6] "Something seems wanting in America to incite and stimulate Youth to Study. In Europe the Encouragements to Learning are of themselves much greater than can be given here. Whoever distinguishes himself there, in either of the three learned Professions, gains Fame, and often Wealth and Power: A poor Man's Son has a Chance, if he studies hard, to rise, either in the Law or the Church, to gainful Offices or Benefices; to an extraordinary Pitch of Grandeur; to have a Voice in Parliament, a Seat among the Peers; as a Statesman or first Minister to govern Nations, and even to mix his Blood with Princes" (3:400).

In order to train Pennsylvania's future leaders, Franklin proposed that "some Persons of Leisure and public Spirit, apply for a CHARTER, by which they may be incorporated, with Power to erect an ACADEMY for the Education of Youth, to govern the same, provide Masters, make Rules, receive Donations, purchase Lands, etc. and to add to their Number, from Time to Time such other Persons as they shall judge suitable." The academy was to be different from previous colonial colleges, which religious groups sponsored to teach future ministers. Franklin suggested that the "boarding Scholars diet together, plainly, temperately, and frugally" and that in order "to keep them in Health, and to strengthen and render active their Bodies, they be frequently exercis'd in Running, Leaping, Wrestling, and Swimming, etc." To John Locke's comments about swimming as "a skill which may serve" a person in need, Franklin added a thought that he later expressed concerning the fear of lightning (10:52): "'Tis some Advantage besides, to be free from the slavish Terrors many of those feel who cannot swim, when they are oblig'd to be on the Water even in crossing a Ferry" (3:402, 403n).

Though it would be desirable if students "could be taught *every Thing* that is useful, and *every Thing* that is ornamental: But Art is long, and their Time is short." Franklin expected many readers to know that the sententiae originated with Hippocrates. After that nod to the classics, he continued with his common-sense observation: "It is therefore proposed that they learn those Things that are likely to be *most useful* and *most ornamental*. Regard being had to the several Professions for which they are intended" (3:404). One thinks, "Of course!"—but most people expect the traditional forms, and some fear novelty. The prefatory remarks also specified learning mathematics and studying the English classics—including, surprisingly, Algernon Sidney and *Cato's Letters*. Even more surprising, Franklin advocated a curriculum that offered the student choices. He suggested what courses would be most useful for particular professions, but the student would choose what courses to take.

The Curriculum

After Franklin found he could not convince the major sponsors to provide only an English education, he drew up a detailed syllabus that included the possibility of studying Greek and Latin. Nevertheless, his curriculum differed drastically from the standard education available in other colonial and English academies and colleges. He adopted two strategies to make the innovative program acceptable. First, he buttressed his work with quotations from the best authorities on education—Milton, Locke, and others—whose reputations he celebrated at the beginning of the pamphlet. If readers disagreed with the *Proposals*, they would seem to be contradicting not only the unnamed Philadelphians who supported the *Proposals* but also the best authorities from the past century. Franklin did not, of course, point out that he was selective in his quotations from the authorities or that he sometimes misrepresented them. Franklin's second strategy was to claim that the curriculum was founded on the study of history. He did not say so, but Franklin was following Bacon's opinion in *The Advancement of Learning*.[7] After all, studying Latin and Greek was studying the past. His curriculum, however, did not emphasize the classical languages but everything most useful that could be learned from the past and the present. Franklin's curriculum had thirteen areas.

1. Geography. An exposure to history would arouse students' curiosity in geography, "the places *where* the greatest Actions were done," and make them interested in chronology or when events happened. Maps of the world were unusual in Franklin's day, and he recalled in his last year of life that his father, Josiah, had four large maps of the world in his parlor, which Franklin studied while his father said long prayers before meals (*Life* 1:37).
2. Comparative anthropology (my anachronistic name). The second subject

anticipated today's comparative anthropology: history would introduce students to ancient customs, "religious and civil" (3:411). The comparative study of religion suggested skepticism concerning the absolute validity of any particular one. In the seventeenth and eighteenth centuries, a number of religious thinkers tried to prove that the American Indians descended from the lost ten tribes of Israel by comparing Old Testament customs to those of American Indians. Writers like the French Canadian Jesuit Joseph François Lafitau made elaborate use of the comparative method in trying to prove the thesis. A few skeptics, however, implied that the manners, customs, and religion of the American Indians were as valid as Christianity (*Life* 2:509–14). No college studied comparative religious and civil customs per se, though such subjects formed an incidental part of learning Greek and Latin. Franklin had in mind the comparative method and stage theory of history. A few seventeenth- and eighteenth-century theorists had hypothesized that mankind developed in four economic stages, and Franklin had applied the theory to the development of American civilization in his 1751 "Observations Concerning the Increase of Mankind" (4:225 – 34).[8]

3. Morality. The third use of history was common, though Franklin gave it his own characteristic stamp. History, or the study of famous individuals of the past, would make students interested in morality: "by descanting and making continual Observations on the Causes of the Rise or Fall of any Man's Character, Fortune, Power, &c. mentioned in History, the Advantages of Temperance, Order, Frugality, Industry, Perseverance, &c." would be apparent. Franklin described these qualities in his "Art of Virtue" in part 2 of the *Autobiography* (*perseverance* appears there as *resolution*). "Indeed," Franklin said, "the general natural Tendency of Reading good History, must be, to fix in the Minds of Youth deep Impressions of the Beauty and Usefulness of Virtue of all Kinds, Publick Spirit, Fortitude, &c" (3:412). The "Beauty" of virtue is a doctrine that Franklin, like Jonathan Edwards, took from Lord Shaftesbury's *Characteristics of Men, Manners, Opinions, Times* (1713), which also celebrated "Publick Spirit." The "usefulness" of virtue, however, is pure Franklin, here presented by a shrewd persona trying to win others to virtue. Alexis de Tocqueville could have had Franklin in mind when he wrote: "It is often difficult [to decide] . . . whether the main object of religion [for Americans] is to procure eternal felicity in the next world or prosperity in this."[9]

4. Oratory and Print. No one appreciated the importance of print more than Franklin. The new method of communication was a key to power. Franklin approached his insight in a traditional way. He declared that "History will show the wonderful effects of Oratory, in governing, turning and leading great Bodies of Mankind, Armies, Cities, Nations. When the Minds of Youth are struck with Admiration at this, then is the Time to give them the Principles of that Art, which they will study with Taste and Application. Then they

may be made acquainted with the best Models among the Antients, their Beauties being particularly pointed out to them." He seemed to be advocating the traditional study of the orations of Caesar, Cicero, and Demosthenes.

Then the cat escaped the bag: "Modern Political Oratory being chiefly performed by the Pen and Press, its Advantages over the Antient in some Respects are to be shown; as that its Effects are more extensive, more lasting, &c." (3:413). That belief explained his recommendation of the Whig political writers like Algernon Sidney and the authors of *Cato's Letters* as among the English "classics." The primary modern key to political ideals lay in writing, not oratory. That may, however, have been wish fulfillment on Franklin's part, for though he was a brilliant writer, he was not an especially good public speaker (A 90; *Life* 2:415). Technology gradually superseded Franklin's opinion. The telephone, radio, television, and the computer have made spoken communication at least as powerful a medium as it was before the age of print.

5. Religion. Franklin's fifth use of the past took up "the Advantage of a Religious Character among private Persons": "History will also afford frequent Opportunities of showing the Necessity of a *Publick Religion*." He gave four reasons, none of which had to do with truth, God, or theology: (1) "Its Usefulness to the Publick" because it helped make persons obey the laws; (2) "The Advantage of a Religious Character among private Persons"— people generally thought that if others were religious that meant they were trustworthy and virtuous;[10] (3) "The Mischiefs of Superstition, &c."—the ostensible meaning was that training in Christianity would lead one to see that other religions were superstitious (in an undercurrent, Franklin may have been questioning the validity of any religion); (4) "The Excellency of the Christian Religion above all others antient or modern" (3:413). For Franklin, that common belief had considerable irony.

Though Franklin regarded the last statement as an example of "Partiality" being "natural to Mankind" (4:234), he admired the Christian virtues. The Golden Rule, to "do unto others as you would have them do unto you," was Franklin's fundamental belief. Perhaps the best-known version is in the Sermon on the Mount, Matthew 7:12, "all things whatsoever ye would that men should do to you, do ye even so to them." Hebrews 10:24 also expressed the belief: "Let us consider one another to provoke unto love and good works." Franklin praised Christianity as greater than other religions because it preached that you love one another (3:413; cf. pp. 270, 518). In his 1751 "Appeal for the Hospital," Franklin celebrated charity as the virtue that most recommended us to God (4:148). Commenting in 1758 on his uncle Benjamin Franklin's acrostic poem, Franklin echoed 1 Corinthians 13:13, "Faith, hope, and charity, and the greatest of these is charity" (8:154).

6. Political science. "*History* will also give Occasion to expatiate on the Advantage of Civil Orders and Constitutions, how Men and their Properties are

protected by joining in Societies and establishing Government; their Industry encouraged and rewarded, Arts invented, and Life made more comfortable: The Advantages of *Liberty*, Mischiefs of *Licentiousness*, Benefits arising from good Laws and a due Execution of Justice, &c. Thus may the first Principles of sound *Politicks* be fix'd in the Minds of Youth" (3:413). Franklin echoed the Lockeian rather than the Hobbesian theory of the origin of government and politics. He probably thought it was better for people to believe the Lockeian theory. As we have seen, however, he tended to believe that the Hobbesian theory was more correct. Whatever the truth concerning the original rise of government, however, Franklin was a Lockeian in his personal life, believing in the advantages of "joining" together in voluntary associations for particular purposes, whether to fight fires, establish libraries, or encourage science.[11]

7. Rhetoric, logic, and composition. Franklin emphasized competition: "On *Historical* Occasions, Questions of Right and Wrong, Justice and Injustice, will naturally arise, and may be put to Youth, which they may debate in Conversation and in Writing. When they ardently desire Victory, for the Sake of the Praise attending it, they will begin to feel the Want, and be sensible of the Use of *Logic*, or the Art of Reasoning to *discover* Truth, and of Arguing to *defend* it, and *convince* Adversaries. This would be the Time to acquaint them with the Principles of that Art." Competition, he thought, made learning more interesting: "Publick Disputes warm the Imagination, whet the Industry, and strengthen the natural Abilities" (3:413–15).

8. Languages. Since the classics were to be part of the curriculum, Franklin wrote a splendid justification for learning them: "When Youth are told, that the Great Men whose Lives and Actions they read in History, spoke two of the best Languages that ever were, the most expressive, copious, beautiful; and that the finest Writings, the most correct Compositions, the most perfect Productions of human Wit and Wisdom, are in those Languages, which have endured Ages, and will endure while there are Men; that no Translation can do them Justice, or give the Pleasure found in Reading the Originals; that those Languages contain all Science; that one of them is become almost universal, being the Language of Learned Men in all Countries; that to understand them is a distinguishing Ornament, [—then] they may be thereby made desirous of learning those Languages, and their Industry sharpen'd in the Acquisition of them" (3:415).

Franklin's recommendation was partially tongue-in-cheek. The battle of the ancients versus moderns was a major seventeenth-century intellectual quarrel.[12] Almost everyone granted that in the sciences, the moderns excelled. Electricity, in which Franklin was currently making new discoveries and creating new hypotheses, was among the many sciences wherein the ancients were comparatively ignorant. Indeed, between the publication of the *Proposals* in mid-October and the writing of the "Constitutions of the

Academy" in mid-November, Franklin made his sustained comparison between electricity and lightning, and called for "the Experiment" to test it. When Franklin wrote "That those languages contain all Science," he was mocking the supposed necessity of studying Greek and Latin. Franklin knew that Latin and Greek were useful for some professions and said so, but he chafed at their being required. Modern foreign languages, he believed, were more useful for more people—and therefore should be studied in preference to the dead languages. That doctrine was heretical in the mid-eighteenth century, where the study of modern foreign languages in school was rare. As we have seen, Franklin taught himself German, French, Italian, and Spanish—and improved greatly his Latin. We know he read these five languages well and that he did not speak or write fluently in any (*Life* 2:17–20).

The curriculum should be suited to the student's goal. All who intended to become ministers should study Latin and Greek; those who intended to become doctors should take Latin, Greek, and French; the students of law should learn Latin and French; and the merchants (the most numerous class) should learn French, German, and Spanish. No one should be compelled to learn Latin, Greek, or the modern foreign languages, though none who desired to learn them should be refused. But English, arithmetic, and other studies were essential (3:415). Franklin had intended to make English the only language for everyone, but once he was forced to include the classical languages, he suggested that everyone in the academy should study at least two languages—and that future businessmen should learn three.

9. Modern history. The history of modern England and America was another subject that no college taught: "If the new *Universal History* were also read, it would give a *connected* Idea of human Affairs, so far as it goes, which should be follow'd by the best modern Histories, particularly of our Mother Country; then of these Colonies; which should be accompanied with Observations on their Rise, Encrease, Use to Great-Britain, Encouragements, Discouragements, &c. the Means to make them flourish, secure their Liberties, &c." (3:415). When Franklin wrote this in 1749, no text for such a course existed. He was purchasing the new volumes of the *Universal History* as they appeared,[13] but when he advertised the latest volume in the 9 July 1747 *Pennsylvania Gazette*, he complained that there was no general history of the world, for Sir Walter Raleigh's did not come down even to the seventeenth century, and that of Dr. William Howells, "the most General History extant in *English*," dealt only with the European nations.

In various publications Franklin had briefly sketched the history of the American colonies. His *General Magazine* (1741) contained materials on the politics and governments of the American colonies, and his *American Instructor* (1748) printed Franklin's brief histories of them. Though Boston's Dr. William Douglass began publishing a general history of the American colonies in 1749, it was large, diffuse, and had numerous errors—unsuitable for a textbook.[14] If Franklin had not become caught up in Pennsylvania politics in 1751 and then in imperial concerns in 1755, he might well have expanded his previous notes on the colonies and published them for the academy's students.

10. Agriculture. Franklin turned to the "best *Histories of Nature*" that would later be "of great Use to them, whether they are Merchants, Handicrafts, or Divines." The inclusion of artisans might have surprised some readers, though it is unlikely that even the best-educated among the trustees would have mentioned it to "B. Franklin, Printer" (3:416). "The Improvement of Agriculture being useful to all, and Skill in it no Disparagement to any," Franklin recommended that "*Gardening, Planting, Grafting, Inoculating* &c. be taught and practised." He suggested "Excursions . . . to the neighbouring Plantations of the best Farmers, their Methods observ'd and reason'd upon" (3:417). Agriculture and gardening as subjects of study appealed to Philadelphia's wealthiest citizens, like James Logan, Allen, and the proprietors, all of whom prided themselves upon their gardens. William Allen became the chief single contributor to the Philadelphia Academy. Franklin wrote the English merchant and naturalist Peter Collinson on 4 February 1751 that he would do his best to have natural history (i.e., the study of agriculture, plants, and animals) taught in the academy, for it was "a Science of more real Worth and Usefulness, [than] several of the others we propose to teach, put together" (4:113).

11. Trade and commerce. Franklin recommended something like modern business schools. "The History of *Commerce*, of the Invention of Arts, Rise of Manufactures, Progress of Trade, Change of its Seats, with the Reasons, Causes, &c. may also be made entertaining to Youth, and will be useful to all" (3:417–18). In 1749 there were no texts for such studies, only individual tracts like those by proto-economist Sir William Petty and early demographer Edmund Halley. The Scots intellectuals like David Hume, Adam Ferguson, and Adam Smith were beginning to write about and to teach such subjects, but few persons in 1749 had glimmerings of economics, statistics, and business as possible disciplines. The only colonial American to make a major original contribution to these topics was Franklin.

12. Technology. Franklin claimed that the study of history would arouse an interest in mechanics and engineering: "the Accounts in . . . History of the prodigious Force and Effect of Engines and Machines used in War, will naturally introduce a Desire to be instructed in *mechanics*, and to be informed of the Principles of that Art by which weak Men perform such Wonders, Labour is sav'd, Manufactures expedited, &c. This will be the Time to show them Prints of antient and modern Machines, to explain them, to let them be copied, and to give Lectures in Mechanical Philosophy" (3:418). Franklin's first fame came as a mechanical engineer. From 1738 to 1744, and thereafter off and on for the remainder of his life, Franklin experimented with heating

systems. By 1744 he had designed the most efficient stove in the world. It was sold throughout the colonies, Great Britain, and Europe (*Life* 2:468–74).
13. Natural philosophy/science. Few people in the mid-eighteenth century were capable of teaching such courses. Exceptions included the experimenter for the Royal Society of London, John Theophilus Desaguliers, and the Harvard scientist Isaac Greenwood. The normal lecturer on natural philosophy, like Dr. Archibald Spencer, had limited knowledge. Perhaps the only person in Pennsylvania who could have done it was Franklin. Early in 1751, he gave a daily private course in science for six weeks to his amanuensis, the map-maker Lewis Evans, who then went off to New York, the College of New Jersey (Princeton), and other places, giving lectures to college students and to general audiences in science and technology. Before the summer of 1751, Franklin offered his fellow electrical experimenter Ebenezer Kinnersley a position at the academy. Kinnersley, who became the English professor, also taught physics and science to the advanced students.[15]

Franklin closed his *Proposals* on a high note: Throughout the student's education, "Benignity of Mind," which he defined as a "*searching for* and *seizing* every Opportunity *to serve* and *to oblige*," should be constantly inculcated and cultivated. These are "the Foundation of what is called GOOD BREEDING; highly useful to the Possessor, and most agreeable to all." Further, the students should be taught "The Idea of what is *true Merit*." At this point, most writers would have brought in religion. Instead, Franklin defined "*true Merit*" as "an *Inclination* join'd with an *Ability* to serve Mankind, one's Country, Friends and Family; which *Ability* is (with the Blessing of God) to be acquir'd or greatly encreas'd by *true Learning*; and should indeed be the great *Aim* and *End* of all Learning." He referred to God again in a note near the end, where he wrote his credo: "*Doing good to Men* is the *only Service of God* in our Power" (3:419). No statement of the purpose of education is more noble.

Organization

After circulating the *Proposals*, Franklin collected subscription promises. He "met with but few Refusals in soliciting the Subscriptions; and the Sum was the more considerable, as I had put the Contribution on this footing that it was not to be immediate and the whole paid at once, but in Parts, a Fifth annually during Five Years" (S 10:10). He believed that many persons subscribed because the *Proposals* insisted on an English education. He told possible subscribers that they would elect twenty-four trustees. That is too large a number for an efficient management, but Franklin probably made the total large as a means to get more persons to contribute. Major subscribers no doubt expected to be elected trustees.

Franklin and Tench Francis, Pennsylvania's attorney general, drew up the "Constitutions of the Academy of Philadelphia" and presented it to the trustees on 13 November 1749. The "Constitutions" began with a seemingly bland statement of the reasons for education: "Nothing can more effectually contribute to the Cultivation and Improvement of a Country, the Wisdom, Riches, and Strength, Virtue and Piety, the Welfare and Happiness of a People, than a proper Education of Youth, by forming their Manners, imbuing their tender Minds with Principles of Rectitude and Morality, instructing them in the dead and living Languages, particularly their Mother-Tongue, and all useful Branches of liberal Arts and Science." Calling Latin and Greek "dead" languages and the modern languages "living Languages" suggests that Franklin had at least partially convinced Tench Francis of the superiority of studying English and other modern languages.

Though "the present State of our infant Country will" not be able to immediately create a great college, the proposers can still lay "a Foundation for Posterity to erect a Seminary of Learning more extensive, and suitable to their future Circumstances." To this end, Franklin proposed "An Academy for teaching the Latin and Greek Languages, the English Tongue, grammatically and as a Language, the most useful living foreign Languages, French, German and Spanish." Again, Franklin acceded to the ideas of others, for "Latin and Greek" are listed before English. Then he added a summary of his comprehensive plan of education: "As Matters of Erudition naturally flowing from the Languages, History, Geography, Chronology, Logick and Rhetorick, Writing, Arithmetick, Algebra, the several Branches of the Mathematicks, Natural and Mechanick Philosophy, Drawing in Perspective, and every other useful Part of Learning and Knowledge, shall be set up, maintained, and have Continuance, in the City of Philadelphia" (3:422).

Recalling in 1789 the erosion of his idea to make the English school dominant, Franklin said that the first instance of "Partiality in favor of the Latin Part of the Institution" appeared in the draft of the "Constitutions" in giving "the Title of Rector to the Latin Master, and no Title to the English one." More flagrant partiality appeared in the salaries. Franklin recorded (the concluding exclamation point is his) that the majority of the trustees, probably at the meeting approving the "Constitutions" on 13 November, voted "to give twice as much Salary to the Latin Master as to the English, and yet require twice as much Duty from the English Master as from the Latin, viz. 200£ to the Latin Master to teach 20 Boys; 100£ to the English Master to teach 40!" Franklin noted that the trustees who had contributed the most money insisted on that arrangement. Though the majority favored the idea of an English academy, they thought the major donors "had a kind of Right to predominate in Money matters." Therefore the majority submitted, "tho' not without Regret, and at times some little Complaining" (S 10:13).

Franklin wrote the passage as an old man, and I question whether the majority of the early supporters of the Philadelphia Academy really believed in his new curriculum. Since the trustees could not find "a proper Person" for an

English master "who would undertake the Office for so low a Salary," they voted nine months later on 27 July 1750 to increase the English master's salary to £150. Franklin unhappily emphasized that there were to be two separate schools. "The Latin Master was not to teach the English Scholars Logic, Rhetoric, &c.; that was the Duty of the English Master; but he was to teach those Sciences to the Latin Scholars" (S 10:13).

Franklin appealed to James Logan, perhaps the most learned man in Pennsylvania, to subscribe, but he was ill and hardly able to travel outside his home. Logan refused, thinking that his son William would contribute. After William Logan refused, the aged and sick Logan reconsidered on 8 January 1750, and Franklin then inserted his name as the first trustee, followed by Thomas Lawrence and William Allen (3:352, 456). At the initial trustees' meeting on 13 November 1749, Franklin was elected president. In the *Autobiography*, Franklin mistakenly recalled hiring a house, engaging masters, and opening the school—all within the next few months. Then, finding the house "too small," the trustees looked for another (A 117). Actually, at the meeting on 13 November, the trustees named a committee to meet with the New Building trustees to consider purchasing it and to receive estimates of the cost to remodel it. Though James Logan offered the trustees a lot for the academy on Sixth Street, they declined, saying George Whitefield's New Building was "in all respects better suited."

The New Building

In 1741, the New Building had been built at Fourth and Arch streets for George Whitefield, but after he returned to England at the year's end, it was rarely used. By 1747, the trustees responsible for the debt on the building and grounds were ready to give it up. They petitioned the Pennsylvania Assembly for permission to sell it, but the trustees responsible for its use asked for more time. Writing Whitefield on 6 July 1749, Franklin reported that nothing had been done about the building. He did not add what Whitefield and he both knew—the debt was mounting (*Life* 2:436–38).

During December and January, Franklin met several times with the New Building's trustees, who finally agreed to sell it for the price of the outstanding debts—£775.18.11, which was only about half of the original cost of construction.[16] The trustees of both the New Building and the academy met at Roberts Coffee House on Thursday, 1 February 1750, and executed the deed. Franklin explained in the *Autobiography*: as "a Member of both Sets of Trustees, that for the Building and that for the Academy, I had good Opportunity of negociating with both, and brought them finally to an Agreement, by which the Trustees for the Building were to cede it to those of the Academy, the latter undertaking to discharge the Debt, to keep forever open in the Building a large Hall for occasional Preachers according to the original Intention, and maintain a Free School for the Instruction of poor Children." Since the academy trustees did not have enough cash to pay for new construction as well as to buy the building, they voted to borrow £800 from the trustees of the second Association lottery. Franklin probably thought of and accomplished that too. He had been an organizer and trustee of the lottery, which had been projected before peace was proclaimed in the summer of 1748. Franklin arranged for the loan and no doubt the terms: it would be repaid with interest by the academy trustees after the subscriptions were collected.[17]

Then began the task of transforming the large assembly hall into rooms suitable for classes. "By dividing the great and lofty Hall into Stories, and different Rooms above and below for the several Schools, and purchasing some additional Ground, the whole was soon made fit for our purpose." The 100 x 70 feet rectangular building was separated into two stories, with the first floor split up into rooms for the different classes, and the second floor left as a large assembly hall for "publick examination," with a "beautiful Rostrum, or pulpit." In a rare mention of the effort that Franklin put into public projects, he noted: "The Care and Trouble of agreeing with the Workmen, purchasing Materials, and superintending the Work fell upon me" (A 118–19).

Writing his Connecticut minister friend Jared Eliot on 13 February 1749/50, Franklin said that the academy's "Subscription goes on with great Success." The trustees expected to raise more than £5,000 in Pennsylvania currency: "We have bought for the Academy, the House that was built for Itinerant Preaching, which stands on a large Lot of Ground capable of receiving more Buildings to lodge the Scholars, if it should come to be a regular Colledge. The House is 100 foot long and 70 wide, built of Brick; very strong; and sufficiently high for three lofty Stories: I suppose it did not cost less than £2000 building; but we bought it for £775.18.11 ³/₄: tho' it will cost us 3 or perhaps 400 more to make the Partitions and Floors, and fit up the Rooms." As the plans evolved, the trustees decided to have only two stories, perhaps because they could not afford three. Franklin sent along a copy of the "Constitutions," though "we expect a Charter from our Proprietaries this Summer, when they may prob'ly receive considerable Alterations." Keeping the project in the public eye, Franklin reported progress on the remodeling in the *Gazette* of 17 May 1750: "The brick partitions in the great New Building, to make Rooms for the Academy, are already carried up a considerable Height, and the Work will be finished with all Expedition."

To his natural philosopher friend Cadwallader Colden, Franklin expressed the hope on 28 June 1750 that an observatory would be built on top of the Academy building, and "as we shall have a mathematical Professor, I doubt not but we shall soon be able to send you some Observations accurately made." Finances, however, were lacking, and the trustees deemed the observatory an unnecessary expense. Franklin next proposed a steeple. On 9 April 1751, the trustees ordered that the steeple be finished and the rooms plastered but that no additional work be done without their approval. At the Union Fire Company on 30 March 1752, Franklin and Philip Syng suggested that the bell purchased by it and the Hand-in-Hand Fire Company (*Life* 2:374) be placed in the academy

Philadelphia Anno 1750

Account of the Buildings &c Dr to Benjamin
Franklin for Sundry Disbursements of his Acco't from
11 April to 15 June Viz.

paid Richard Arrel for Boards of Acco't £	21. 2. 2	
paid Thomas Atkinson for Ditto	26. 18. 8½	
paid Joseph Scull for Stone	3. 7. 6	
paid Nathan Bewley for Lime	6. —	
given the Bricklayers to drink	2. 3	
given ditto for drink	7. 6	
paid Joseph Campbell for Sand	1. 8. 6	
paid Edmond Wooley for Stone had of J. Scull	3. 7. 6	
paid R. Tatum for digging for a Foundation	15. 9	
paid Edmond Wooley towards his Work	20. —	
paid John Coates in part for Bricks	10. 10. 1½	£100

Figure 23. Renovating George Whitefield's New Building: The academy's first expenses, 1750. The trustees of the academy bought the New Building on 1 February 1750 for the bargain price of £775.18.11. They immediately began transforming the large meeting house into rooms suitable for classes. "By dividing the great and lofty Hall into Stories, and different Rooms above and below for the several Schools, and purchasing some additional Ground, the whole was soon made fit for our purpose." The 100 x 70 foot rectangular building was separated into two stories, with the first floor and part of the second split up into rooms for the different classes, and a large part of the second floor made into an assembly hall for "publick examination," with a "beautiful Rostrum, or pulpit."

While raising money for the academy, Franklin kept the public informed. The Pennsylvania Gazette of 17 May 1750 noted that "The brick partitions in the great New Building, to make Rooms for the Academy, are already carried up a considerable Height, and the Work will be finished with all Expedition." In a rare mention of the effort that he devoted to his various public projects, he noted: "The Care and Trouble of agreeing with the Workmen, purchasing Materials, and superintending the Work fell upon me" (A 118–19).

Acting as the treasurer, Franklin kept accounts of what he paid the various artisans. Here is the first (11 April to 13 June 1750) of a series of Franklin's disbursements. He paid Richard Arrel and Thomas Atkinson for boards, Joseph Scull for stone, Nathan Bewley for lime, the bricklayers (who presumably worked for free) for drinks, Joseph Campbell for sand, Edmund Wooley for stone from J. Scull, R. Tatum for digging a foundation, Edmund Wooley for various work, and John Coates for bricks. Courtesy, Archives, University of Pennsylvania.

"until the two Companys please to Remove it to another Place." The Hand-in-Hand Company agreed in April, and thereafter the bell served both for school purposes and for a fire alarm.

Fund-raising, 1750

The projectors appealed to Thomas Penn for his support. Penn's begrudging reply to Governor James Hamilton on 12 February 1750 said that the "proposal for the education of youth is much more extensive than ever I designed, and I think more so than the Circumstances of the Province render necessary, the best of our People must be people of business, which I do not think very great publick Schools or Universitys render youth fit for, and the additional Exercises are not fit accomplishments for many." Franklin had said that the academy would benefit Philadelphia by attracting students from the neighboring colonies. Penn disagreed. He also said that the people in England "think we go too fast with regard to these matters; and it gives an opportunity to those Fools who are always telling their Fears that the Colonies will set up for themselves." He wrote that he would think further about it. He concluded, however, with a comment against the projected academy: "I must confess my opinion at present is that there are few Children that want more than a good common School education and then for that you set out too great at first" (4:5n2).

Franklin also asked the Philadelphia Common Council for funds. He was a member of the corporation but shrewdly requested that William Allen, recorder of the Common Council, present the appeal. On 30 July 1750, Allen "acquainted the Board that there is a Design on Foot for the Erecting a Publick Academy and Charity School in this City." Though many people had contributed to its support, the building of an academy was "attended with a great Expence in the Beginning," and therefore "some further Assistance is necessary to carry it into Execution in the best Manner." Allen pointed out that the corporation had considerable money on hand, as well as an annual income of about three hundred pounds, and proposed that the academy was "worthy of some Encouragement from this Board, as their Circumstances may very well afford it." Since only a small number of the members were present, the board put off the consideration for a day and ordered "That the Members of this Board have notice to meet Tomorrow at four a Clock in the Afternoon, to consider a Proposal of contributing a Sum of Money for the Encouragement of the Academy & Charity School now erecting in this City."[18]

The next day, 31 July, Franklin presented a paper on the progress of the academy. He said that the trustees of the academy had already spent nearly £800 "and will probably expend near as much more in fitting up the Rooms for the Schools, and furnishing them with proper Books and Instruments." He listed four benefits expected from the institution. First, he emphasized that educating youths in Pennsylvania would save the country money and allow parents to conveniently oversee their morals. Second, the graduates would be qualified to become magistrates. Currently, there was a "great Want" of qualified persons in several counties. He added that the "vast Numbers of Foreigners" that immigrated to Pennsylvania annually, who were "totally ignorant of our Laws, Customs, and Language," made the schooling of native Pennsylvanians more necessary. Third, the school would train persons who could become schoolmasters in the country. Fourth, the school would attract students from the neighboring colonies and benefit Philadelphia's economy: "This Advantage is so considerable, that it has been frequently observed in Europe, that the fixing a good School or College in a little inland Village, has been the Means of making it a great Town in a few Years." He claimed that the "great Expence of such a Work is in the Beginning" and that within a few years, the school would be able to support itself. "Some Assistance," however, "from the Corporation is immediately wanted."[19]

At the request of Allen and Franklin (nine other academy trustees were council members), the Philadelphia Council voted by "a great Majority" to contribute £200 toward transforming the New Building into a school, voted unanimously to give £50 a year for five years for the Charity School, and voted "by a great Majority" to grant £50 a year for five years for sending one person from the Charity School to the academy.[20] That was the academy's first scholarship. Franklin publicized the council's gift in the *Pennsylvania Gazette* on 2 August 1750. The news was good advertising.

While Franklin was raising funds for transforming the New Building into a school, the Reverend Gilbert Tennent, who had occasionally preached in the New Building, went to Franklin and asked him to help raise money for a new Presbyterian church. Franklin, "unwilling to make myself disagreable to my fellow Citizens, by too frequently soliciting their Contributions . . . absolutely refus'd." Tennent then asked him for a list of persons who were generous and public-spirited. "I thought it would be unbecoming in me, after their kind Compliance with my Solicitations, to mark them out to be worried by other Beggars" and again refused. Then Tennent asked for his advice. "That I will readily" give: "in the first Place, I advise you to apply to all those whom you know will give something; next to those whom you are uncertain whether they will give anything or not; and show them the List of those who have given; and lastly, do not neglect those who you are sure will give nothing; for in some of them you may be mistaken." Tennent laughed, thanked him, and asked everybody—no doubt including Franklin, who testified that his "Mite for such purposes" as building "new Places of worship" was never refused (A 124, 77).

Preparations for Opening

The trustees set up a committee consisting of Franklin, William Allen, William Coleman, Richard Peters, Thomas Hopkinson, and Tench Francis to purchase £100 worth of Latin and Greek authors. Franklin named the purchase another instance of favoring the Latin school; nothing was given "for *English Books*" (S

10:13). As president of the board, Franklin suggested, interviewed, and hired the earliest faculty, with the approval of the other trustees. Richard Peters wrote Thomas Penn on 17 February 1750 that he "asked Mr. Franklin, who is the soul of the whole,[21] whether they would not find it difficult to collect masters. He said, with an air of firmness, that money would buy learning of all sorts, he was under no apprehensions about masters" (4:35). For head of the academy, Franklin and the trustees considered the Connecticut minister Dr. Samuel Johnson, whose *Ethices Elementa* (1746) was the first textbook of moral philosophy written and published in America, but they wanted to know more about him before offering the position. For rector, Franklin thought of David Martin, and the trustees offered him the position on 29 March 1750, hoping he would take it up by 13 May. Martin, the sheriff of Hunterdon County, New Jersey, accepted, moved to Philadelphia, and became Franklin's favorite chess opponent. He was successful in the position, but his tenure was short, for he died in December 1751.[22]

I suspect that Franklin approached Samuel Johnson about printing his *Elementa Philosophica* or the "First Principles of Metaphysics and Logic" as an indirect way to become acquainted with the clergyman. Franklin's letter is not extant, but on 10 May 1750, Johnson replied that he had thought of printing a revised edition of his *Ethices* with the *Noetica*. Having established contact with Johnson, Franklin and Tench Francis traveled to Stratford, Connecticut to meet him and to discuss the possibility of his becoming head of the Philadelphia Academy. The two trustees left Philadelphia after 1 July. Impressed with Johnson, they returned to Philadelphia and at the trustees' meeting on 27 July, recommended hiring him. The trustees agreed, and Franklin wrote Johnson on 9 August of the terms, which included a salary of £100 sterling a year. Franklin also pressed him to visit, being certain that Johnson would find Philadelphia to his liking. Richard Peters wrote Johnson on 6 August, offering to put Johnson up in his home during the visit.[23] Franklin wrote again on 23 August and 13 September, but by then Philadelphia was experiencing a minor smallpox epidemic.

By 25 October 1750 Franklin realized that Johnson was reluctant to come and gave him an easy way to refuse by saying that smallpox might be a "perpetual Bar" to Johnson, for Philadelphia had a smallpox epidemic every four or five years. Franklin wrote again on 24 December 1751 and 8 January urging Johnson to accept the offer, but the clergyman finally gave a definite refusal in a letter (not extant) evidently sent in late January 1752 (4:260–62). Franklin arranged for David Hall to publish Johnson's two books together, the *Elementa Philosophica* and a second edition of his *Ethices*.[24] Advertised in the *Pennsylvania Gazette* on 19 October 1752, the books sold poorly. Franklin printed 500 but sold no more than 50 in Pennsylvania (5:261). Johnson had said that he could sell 100 in Connecticut and perhaps another 100 in Boston. Evidently he could not. When Franklin wrote him on 15 April 1754, he told Johnson that even if he could not

Figure 24. The Philadelphia Academy's New Building, 1740, and its dormitory, 1761. Drawing attributed to Pierre Eugène Du Simitiére, ca. 1770. Edmund Wooley, the primary architect of George Whitefield's New Building, designed a large meeting house in 1740 where Whitefield and other Christian ministers would preach. The structure was the largest in Philadelphia (and probably in the English colonies) when it was built. The entrance in the middle of the long side of the structure was common for meeting houses of the day.

In 1750, the carpenter-architect Robert Smith (1722–77) remodeled the New Building, adding the partitions inside and the steeple on the roof. The elaborate two-story pedimented portico with segmented arches within it were, in the opinion of the architectural historian Damie Stillman, probably added later than 1740 or even 1750.

Smith designed and built the general purpose and dormitory building (30 x 70 feet) in 1761. Perhaps he was chosen partially because he had assisted in designing and building Princeton's Nassau Hall in 1754. Though in the Georgian style, the academy and college's dormitory and general purpose building lack the broad pedimented projecting central section found in the most fashionable (and more expensive) new buildings, like Harvard's Hollis Hall of 1762–63. Perhaps Smith reworked the entrance to the main academy and college building in 1761. Courtesy, Library Company of Philadelphia.

sell 200 copies, to "make yourself easy nevertheless, I shall be perfectly satisfy'd with your Endeavour." Twelve years later, at the dissolution of the Franklin-Hall partnership in 1766, Hall still had not sold enough to break even and charged Franklin £25 for its printing (13:90, 112).

On 17 December 1750, the trustees hired David James Dove as the English master, Theophilus Grew as the mathematics master, and Charles Thomson as a tutor in Latin and Greek. Dove had been giving lectures in experimental philosophy, but Franklin "prevailed" upon him to accept the position as English master (S 10:14). Franklin thought Dove "an excellent Master" and nearly a year later said that "his Scholars have made a surprizing Progress" (4:223). Dove, however, began teaching privately on the side and spent less time at the academy than the trustees had expected. On 10 October 1752, Franklin and Richard Peters were asked to speak to him about not attending during all the school hours. Dove desired to have time off to teach a school for girls, which he was holding in his home, but the trustees refused. At the following meeting he appeared and renewed his request, saying that otherwise he would give a quarter's notice and resign. On 13 February 1752/3, the trustees reaffirmed their decision and asked him to stay until they hired someone else, saying that they would give him a quarter's notice.

In Franklin's later opinion, the decision ruined the English school. Under Dove, it had gained more than ninety students. The boys performed extremely well at the monthly visitations, and large audiences attended. Now a new English teacher was needed. On Franklin's recommendation, the trustees hired Ebenezer Kinnersley. They then sent for Dove, said that they had found a new master of the English school, and gave him the quarter's notice stipulated. Dove, however, declared he would attend the school no longer. Kinnersley was promptly installed on 10 July 1753, at a salary of £150 annually.

Without naming Kinnersley, Franklin wrote in 1789 that Dove's successor was "a good Man," but he did not possess "the Talents of an English Schoolmaster in the same Perfection with Mr. Dove." The number of students declined. Monthly visitations became poorly attended and were "at length discontinued." Thus, by "injudiciously starving the English Part of our Scheme of Education," the trustees saved fifty pounds but "lost Fifty Scholars, which would have been 200£ a Year." And thereby, Franklin wrote, the trustees defeated "one great End of the Institution" (S 10:15–16). Classes started without a writing master, but three months before the Charity School for poor children opened, Franklin advertised in the *Pennsylvania Gazette* on 13 June 1751, "A single Man, that writes a fine round hand, is wanted as a school Teacher in the Academy. Enquire of Benjamin Franklin." Evidently the salary would be insufficient to support a man with a family.

At the 10 November 1750 meeting, the trustees decided to purchase two lots, one on each side of the academy, for possible future additions. When Franklin mentioned the acquisition to Dr. Samuel Johnson on 11 July 1751, he said that the purchase would prevent our "being crouded and our Air taken away by future neighbouring Buildings, so we have now a Front of 205 Foot, and our Ground is 200 foot deep, the House 100 foot front by 70 deep, standing the Middle of the Ground," all in "the Inhabited Part of the City" (4:146).

Classes Start

The trustees decided on 17 December 1750 to start classes on 7 January. That day, Governor James Hamilton led a procession of the trustees from his home to the remodeled New Building where the Reverend Richard Peters preached *A Sermon on Education*. Though Peters was one of the leaders interested in the traditional study of Greek and Latin in the academy, he celebrated at length the English school, saying that every language has its own unique idioms, phrases, copiousness, beauties, and elegance.[25] Since the classrooms were not quite ready, the students met for the time in William Allen's warehouse at Second and Arch streets. Within a few months, 145 students had enrolled and paid tuition. On 16 September 1751, the trustees opened the Charity School for boys, and on 17 November 1753, Franklin and William Shippen were asked to arrange for a school for girls to be taught reading, sewing, and knitting. Franklin reported on 11 December 1753 that Mrs. Frances Holwell agreed to teach thirty girls a year. Among other chores, the girls made samplers, for the minutes record the purchase of canvas and crewels. The school for girls was evidently successful: on 12 March 1755, Franklin wrote the trustees a letter saying that he and Shippen had agreed to raise the number of girls to fifty and to give Mrs. Holwell £15 per year for an assistant.

In *Poor Richard* for 1752, Franklin printed an excerpt from Richard Savage's poem "On Public Spirit," but he revised and added to it, making the poem applicable to Pennsylvania. The four lines concerning education were changed to reflect the creation and future hopes for the Philadelphia Academy:

> There too the Walls of rising Schools ascend,
> For Publick Spirit still is Learning's Friend,
> Where Science, Virtue, sown with liberal Hand,
> In future Patriots shall inspire the Land. (4:249)

The 26 October 1752 *Pennsylvania Gazette* printed an abstract of the academy's accounts from 27 December 1749 to 10 June 1752. The trustees had received a total of £2,586.14.7 and paid out a total of £3,402.17.6½ . Franklin explained that "the great Expence of Purchasing and Building, necessary for the speedy Accommodation and Establishment of the Academy," had occasioned the trustees to advance money "before the annual Subscriptions could be collected." He asked that, if possible, the third annual subscription, which was due on 25 November, be made early. He announced that the Charity School now had one hundred students, "most of which, tho' from eight to thirteen Years of Age, had never been sent to any School before; nor did it seem likely many of them would ever have been sent . . . if it had not been for this Institution." Franklin hoped that "further charitable Benefactions of well disposed and publick-spirited Persons, will enable the Trustees not only to continue, but to extend the good Effects of this great Foundation."

The trustees asked Attorney General Tench Francis on 9 June to draft a charter for the academy and send it to the proprietors. Ten months later, on 10 April 1753, they received word that the proprietors approved and were donating £500 to the academy. William Allen, Tench Francis, and Franklin were assigned to draft an "address of thanks" to them. They did, and on 13 July, while Franklin was in Boston, the academy's other trustees went to Governor Hamilton's house and received the engrossed charter.

FRANKLIN AND WILLIAM SMITH: EARLY RELATIONS

Franklin probably met William Smith (1727–1803) through his New York printing partner, James Parker. Smith, a tutor to the two sons of Colonel Joshua Martin in New York, wrote poems, essays, and tracts on education. When Parker was prosecuted in the summer of 1752 for reprinting *An Indian Speech* (*Life* 2:511–12), the twenty-five-year-old Smith wrote a letter for Parker on the freedom of the press. Though Smith no doubt intended for Parker to print it, the printer was "much in his Penitentials" (4:311), and, anxious to avoid further controversy, he did not. Parker may have given Franklin a copy of Smith's letter and probably gave Smith a copy of Richard Peters's *Sermon on Education*, which appended Franklin's *Idea of the English School*.

Early in 1753, Smith wrote *The College of Mirania* (published by Parker), which suggested that his projected New York school contained not only a traditional college but also a school for mechanics, that is, artisans and merchants. It would be similar to "the English School in *Philadelphia*, first sketch'd out by the very ingenious and worthy *Mr. Franklin.*" Like Franklin's English school, it would not teach Greek or Latin. "The Time thus spent is entirely thrown away" because mechanics would "never have any Occasion to make use of those Languages."[26] Trying to flatter Franklin, Smith sent him a copy.

Since Smith intended to go to England to take holy orders and settle there, he asked Franklin about the possibility of having his two students educated at the Philadelphia Academy. He also volunteered to interview any prospective teachers from England that the academy might want to hire. Replying on 19 April 1753, Franklin assured Smith that his two charges could be well educated at the Philadelphia Academy and that Francis Alison and Grew were successful teachers of the classics and of mathematics. Franklin also said that the "Mathematical School" was "pretty well furnished with Instruments," that the "English Library" was "a good one," and that there was a "middling Apparatus for Experimental Philosophy," which the trustees intended "speedily" to improve. He thanked Smith for the pamphlet, said he would soon read it and write him, and told him that he would be glad to see him if Smith visited Philadelphia (4:468–69).

Franklin wrote Smith again on 3 May and thanked him for *The College of Mirania*, though Franklin added it would be better without the "those Expressions of Resentment against your Adversaries." He said that instead of replying to criticism, "the Noblest Victory is obtained, by Neglect, and by *Shining on.*" He may have at that time been thinking of Smith as a possible rector of the academy, for he suggested that if Smith came to Philadelphia he bring a letter of introduction to William Allen (4:475–76). Franklin presumably thought that

Allen, the major single contributor to the Philadelphia Academy, would be better disposed toward Smith if he thought he had a major role in Smith's visiting the academy.[27] Smith came in late May and wrote *A Poem on Visiting the Academy of Philadelphia*, which he dated 5 June and dedicated to the trustees. Franklin and Hall printed it, advertising that it would be published on 16 June. Franklin's subsequent correspondence with Smith reveals that he spoke to him during this visit about establishing a college and about Smith's possible role in it. Peters wrote Thomas Penn on 5 June that the academy now had "sixty-five Boys from the neighbouring Colonies" and recommended Smith, who had spent ten days in Philadelphia.

As comptroller of the post office for North America, Franklin left Philadelphia in mid-June for New England. In New York he again saw Smith, who accompanied him to Connecticut, where they called on Dr. Samuel Johnson in Stratford. From New Haven, Franklin wrote Peter Collinson on 26 June 1753, introducing Smith, who intended to depart soon for England. Franklin told Collinson that the academy was flourishing but that it lacked someone to teach "the higher Parts of Learning." Franklin proposed to Collinson that the proprietor might endow a salary on the rector. Smith might "possibly be prevail'd on to engage in that Service, if proper Steps were taken with him." He suggested that if Collinson "should think with me as to the Expediency and Utility of this Matter, I know I need not urge your Goodness to take some early Opportunity of proposing it to the Consideration of the Proprietors" (4:512). Franklin had no reason to believe at the time that Smith was avaricious as well as ambitious. Toward the end of July 1753, Smith left for England to take holy orders. After meeting Smith, Collinson judged him to be "a Very Ingenious Man" but added in his letter to Franklin of 12 August 1753, "It's a Pitty but He was more Solid, and Less flighty" (5:120).

Franklin wrote Smith on 27 November 1753 that matters at the academy had not changed. Though most trustees "would be glad to see a Rector establish'd," they "dread entring into new Engagements 'till they are got out of Debt." Franklin thought a good professor of the higher branches of learning would draw enough new students to pay a "great Part if not the whole of his Salary," but he feared that it might be a few years before the other trustees would agree with him. Thus "all the Pleasure I promis'd myself in seeing you settled among us, vanishes into Smoke" (5:120). Collinson, however, had replied to him on 15 September 1753 that he would, "with the Archbishop's Assistance," try to convince the proprietor to endow a professorship at the academy. When Collinson wrote again on 26 January 1754, he repeated his praise of Smith's "great Abilities," yet he again suggested that his "Warmth and Fire of Youth" would need to be "Temper'd by your prudent and Cordial Advice" (5:59, 190, 193).

Richard Peters wrote Thomas Penn praising Smith and sending a copy of his *Mirania*; so Penn met with Smith. Penn at first objected that "liberal institutions" were not "useful in an infant Country," and then he inconsistently said that the academy interfered with his design for an educational institution, "of which he intended to be the Founder." Smith, however, wooed him, spent several days at his country estate, and dined with him once or twice every week. Penn relented and agreed to support the academy, giving annually a significant sum. He intended to return to Pennsylvania, and when he did, he would give "a manor to the Academy." Smith had not intended to return to America, but Thomas Herring, the archbishop of Canterbury, supported the project of an academy and told him that he would have the "opportunity of doing more good" in America than in England "and that the Encouragement would be better than I could expect at first setting out in England even if I had the greatest friends" (5:206–7, 213).

Smith took the archbishop's advice and resolved to go to Pennsylvania. The bishop of London ordained Smith a deacon on 21 December and priest on 23 December. After receiving the King's Bounty on 16 January 1754,[28] Smith wrote Franklin and Richard Peters a long letter in February, bragging of the "uncommon share" of confidence that Thomas Penn honored him with and proclaiming Penn "not only the *nominal* but the *real* father of his Country" (5:207, 212). Smith left London on 5 April. Franklin wrote him on 18 April. The letter is surprising because of the warm friendship Franklin expressed for Smith. Franklin had not heard from him for some time, "which I should tell you chagrins me not a little, were I not asham'd to own to my Pupil, that I do not always practise the Philosophy I endeavour'd to teach him" (5:263).

It was apparently the first and only time that Franklin called someone "my Pupil," and the other persons whose silence he ever complained about were his family and good friends. At the time, despite Collinson's warnings, Franklin considered Smith a friend and protégé. When Franklin wrote him on 18 April, he had not received Smith's long letter of February praising Penn. Franklin received Smith's letters on 29 April 1754 and wrote Richard Peters the next morning about them, "concerning which I shall be glad to talk with you when you have a little Leisure." The note gives a charming glimpse into Franklin's life: "If you are at liberty to dine where you please to day, I shall be glad of your Company; my Dame being from home, and I quite Master of the House" (5:269). Presumably a servant (his slaves Peter and Jemima?) prepared dinner.[29]

Smith arrived in Philadelphia on 23 May. No doubt he quickly called on Franklin. The trustees met two days later, on 25 May 1754. They agreed to hire an additional person to teach logic, rhetoric, ethics, and natural philosophy. The trustees then asked Franklin and Peters to speak to Smith, "lately arrived from London," to teach these subjects "upon Trial." The minutes mention no salary, but Smith accepted. On 11 July, his salary was set at £200 a year. Presumably Franklin and the trustees (except Peters) did not know at the time that Penn was privately paying Smith an additional £50 annually. Because of the payment, the historian Francis Jennings called Smith an "undercover agent and spy for

Thomas Penn, with Franklin as one of the primary objects of his spying."[30] There may be an element of truth in Jennings' accusation.

In February 1754, Smith wrote Franklin and Peters that "I shall always glory to prefer private to public good." The editors of the *Papers of Benjamin Franklin* query whether the comment is a private joke (5:207n5). Perhaps, though it may well have been a Freudian slip. Smith had great ability, and in many ways he was an excellent provost for the College of Philadelphia. He had additional ambitions, including wanting to become America's Anglican bishop.

The College

Though begun as an academy and charity school, the institution was also meant to become a college. Franklin referred to the "Academy or college" in his paper on the need for an academy in 1749 and again in his letter to Dr. Samuel Johnson of Connecticut of 9 August 1750 (3:386, 4:38). When Pehr Kalm visited Philadelphia in 1751, Franklin told him that the Philadelphia academy was "destined to be" a college. In his *Sermon on Education* preached at the opening of the Academy, Richard Peters said that though the "foundation is call'd an academy, yet it is more properly an assemblage of schools, under one roof," and predicted that it would become a collegiate "institution, and a seminary for every kind of science."

An abstract of Peters's sermon appeared in the *Gentleman's Magazine* in December 1753. The author (Peters) said that the English school would be secondary to the Latin and Greek school. In describing the Latin school, he gave it part of the charge that Franklin had assigned the English school. The author wrote: "In the *Latin* schools the masters will be particularly enjoined, to correct, refine, and beautify their mother tongue, so that the scholars may be enabled to understand it perfectly well, and write it with purity and elegance." The author paid some respect to Franklin's ideas. Learning Latin would not necessarily make students "masters of their mother tongue." From his sermon he repeated that English, like every other language, had its own grammar, "idioms and peculiarities, which render a separate set of rules and instructions necessary for the attainment of it."[31]

While Franklin was in New England on post office business from September 1754 to February 1755, Smith and Alison proposed on 10 December that the academy grant college degrees. The trustees agreed, and a new charter was prepared and approved on 11 February, with Franklin still away. At the 17 March meeting, with Franklin present, Smith was chosen provost and Alison vice provost and rector. On 14 May, Governor Robert Hunter Morris approved the new charter, and on 10 June 1755 the trustees accepted it. The academy thereupon became "The College, Academy and Charitable Schools of Philadelphia." At its 10 June meeting, the trustees appointed Franklin and several others to a committee to revise the "Rules and Statutes of the College, Academy, and Charity School" together with the "Laws and Statutes of the Trustees." The document, which the editors of the *Papers of Benjamin Franklin* thought Franklin "probably prepared," was adopted on 11 July 1755 (6:104).

Fund-raising, 1754–55

In 1754 the initial pledges of money annually for five years were about to expire, and the trustees knew that the college income must drop. Though Franklin had hoped that once built and staffed the institution could become self-supporting, it did not. Presumably at Franklin's suggestion, George Whitefield informed the trustees that he intended to preach sermons on Sunday, 22 September 1754, to collect money for the Charity School. Three trustees waited on him on 17 September "to settle the Manner of Collecting." His two sermons on 22 September raised £185.16s. Franklin then proposed a lottery. He had projected and carried through two successful lotteries for the Association in 1748 and served on the lottery committees to raise money for a steeple on Christ Church (2 November 1752 and 27 February 1753). Lottery tickets to benefit the College of New Jersey were currently selling in Pennsylvania. Though lotteries were outlawed in Pennsylvania, the fine for conducting one was only £100, with half the fine going to the governor and "the other moiety to any person that shall sue for the same."[32] If the governor approved the lottery, he would donate his £50 to the cause; so too could the other responsible citizen who sued.

Philip G. Nordell suggested that Franklin wrote the advertisement for the academy lottery, which was published in the *Pennsylvania Gazette* on 3 October 1755. Maybe not; he had left with William Hunter on 2 September 1754 for New York and New England on post office business. The advertisement concluded with a sentence alluding to the previous lotteries for the College of New Jersey and echoing Franklin's *Proposals* of 1749: "Those who . . . have lately contributed liberally to Matters of mere *external Ornament* to the City, will doubtless more chearfully encourage the Academy; an Undertaking which aims at *adorning* the Minds of our Youth with every Excellence, and rendering them really useful and serviceable Members of Society." The lottery's managers were all trustees and included Franklin.[33]

The Philadelphia Common Council met on 1 March 1755 with Franklin, William Plumsted, Tench Francis, William Allen, and other academy trustees present as councilmen. Since some lottery tickets remained unsold and since "the Time appointed for drawing the said Lottery is near at Hand, it was proposed, that to prevent any Delay, a Number of the said Lottery Tickets should be taken out on Account, and at the Risque of this Corporation." The board resolved "that five Hundred Tickets (in Case so many shall remain unsold at the Time appointed for drawing) be taken up by the Treasurer on account of this Corporation." The lottery was successful.[34]

After the college was established, more funds were needed. The *Pennsylvania Gazette* for 11 March 1755 announced a second academy lottery. Its purposes were to maintain and improve the New Building, to purchase scientific instruments (which Franklin would do), to buy ground rents as endowments for salaries, and to support the two charity schools. Franklin wrote this advertisement, which concluded with sentiments echoing his statements in *Proposals Relating to the Education of Youth in Pennsylvania*: "As therefore this Lottery is proposed for the most useful and charitable Purposes, it is hoped that it will meet with due Encouragement; for even its Blanks may be deemed Prizes, as the Satisfaction arising from a Consciousness of doing Good, is, to benevolent Minds, far more valuable than Money" (5:507). But times had changed. French and Indians were attacking the frontier; Braddock and his army were defeated on 9 July; and tickets sold slowly. Nevertheless, by June 1756, all had sold.

On Thursday, 12 February 1756, Charlotte Brown, the matron of the General Hospital with General Braddock's forces, attended a presentation at the academy with Deborah Franklin. Brown was surprised and "agreably entertain'd by hearing the Boys speak." Afterward she dined at William Smith's. Though Deborah Franklin had taken her to the academy, Brown did not mention Franklin. Since Franklin was still the president of the academy and no doubt attended the presentation, Smith probably invited him to dine, along with Deborah and Charlotte Brown. If so, it may have been their last friendly meeting.

Franklin and Provost Smith: Part Two

Smith won the support of Thomas Penn, but Penn won the support of William Smith. Early in 1755, Smith anonymously published *A Brief State of the Province of Pennsylvania*, attacking Pennsylvania's Quaker Party for refusing to support the war effort and charging that they dishonestly propagandized the Pennsylvania Germans in order to gain their votes. He demanded that all Pennsylvania Assembly members take the oath of allegiance to the king. Since Quakers would not take oaths, that would have prevented them from serving in the House. Smith also argued that Germans who did not understand English should not be allowed to vote. His recommendations would have destroyed the Quaker Party. Though Smith was rumored to be the author, Franklin did not want to think so, and by 7 October he still only suspected that Smith might have polished the pamphlet's style (6:170–71, 216).

Early the following year, Smith published *A Brief View of the Conduct of Pennsylvania*, repeating, adding to, and defending the previous pamphlet. "Humphrey Scourge" replied to Smith in "Mild Advice to a certain Parson" in the *Pennsylvania Journal* on 25 March 1756, calling him Penn's sycophant and a would-be Anglican bishop. Smith's political opponents charged that he was attempting to win over his students to his own political positions. If true, that would have ruined him, but several students (including Jacob Duché, Jr., Francis Hopkinson, and Hugh Williamson) testified on 21 June 1756 that his lectures had no party politics. On 5 July 1756 three trustees, Richard Peters, Abraham Taylor, and Alexander Stedman (Taylor, who was sometimes a member of the

Engraved by John Sartain, Phil.ᵃ

Figure 25. The Reverend William Smith, mezzotint by John Sartain, after Benjamin West. William Smith was a young man of great energy and ability who began as a disciple of Franklin but changed allegiances when he won the approval of Thomas Penn—who added to his academy salary an annual stipend of £50. After Smith became the provost of the Philadelphia Academy, he emerged as the chief penman for the Proprietary Party. Franklin was the main author for the Popular or Quaker Party. Smith became Franklin's opponent in other ways than politics, including their positions on the German charity schools and their ideas on the kind of education to be offered in the Academy and College of Philadelphia. Smith even accused Franklin of stealing electrical theories—a charge that Ebenezer Kinnersley, the supposed victim, refuted.

Benjamin West painted the three-quarter-length portrait of Smith, showing him in his clerical robe and without a wig. Standing by a table or desk with several books and a curled sheet of paper on it, Smith is posed with his right hand raised in a gesture and his left holding a book that is resting on other books on the table. Provost Smith appears to be lecturing to students at the College of Philadelphia. To judge from the identification of Smith as "Æt. 30," West painted the portrait in 1757 at age nineteen.

Unfortunately, West's original painting at the Historical Society of Pennsylvania was repainted incompetently in the nineteenth century. John Sartain's engraving of West's painting, made for Horace Wemyss Smith's 1880 biography of his great-grandfather, is a better image. Courtesy, Library Company of Philadelphia.

council, had difficulties with the proprietors, but the other two were stalwart Proprietary Party members), were asked to look into the matter. They reported on 13 July that the charges were unfounded. The trustees sent their report to the *Pennsylvania Gazette*. The trustees' minutes for 10 August noted that David Hall replied that since the innuendos against Smith had not appeared in the *Gazette*, he would not publish the committee's report there.

Smith's political affiliation alienated Franklin, who wrote Collinson on 15 June 1756 that Smith had become "universally odious," and on 5 November 1756 that Smith had "scribbled himself into universal dislike." Only the "Proprietary Faction" countenanced him a little. The academy "dwindles, and will come to nothing if he is continued." A few months later Franklin noted that the enrollment had declined from more than 200 paying students to 118 (6:457, 7:12, 50).

FRANKLIN REPLACED AS PRESIDENT, 11 MAY 1756

Franklin had been elected president of the Board of Trustees annually from its initial meeting on 13 November 1749 to 11 May 1756. He was, however, increasingly out of town. In 1753, he was in New England for over two months and at Carlisle, Pennsylvania, for two weeks. Of the eleven 1753 meetings, he missed four. In 1754, he was gone for eight months, missing seven of the nine meetings. In view of that record, it is surprising that he was reelected president on 10 June 1755. At that meeting, however, there was opposition to him, and he was elected by a "majority vote." During 1755, he missed two of the eight meetings. Then, in 1756, he attended no meetings before the election on 11 May, when Richard Peters was chosen president of the Board of Trustees. Indeed, of the thirteen meetings in 1756, he only attended two (14 and 27 December). He lost his influence on the board and was replaced by Peters primarily because he had too many duties that took him out of town for extended periods, especially the position of joint deputy postmaster general of North America. His absences hindered the duties of the trustees. When Peters was elected in his stead, the trustees voted that if the president could not attend an important meeting where an immediate decision must be made, the senior trustee would be vested with all the president's powers.

Though Franklin was replaced because of his numerous absences, three other factors contributed. First, he had emerged as the leader (after Isaac Norris) of the Pennsylvania Assembly and wrote all of its most important and inflammatory messages. Consequently, proprietary partisans like William Allen, Richard Peters, Alexander Stedman, and Joseph Turner had, to some degree, become personal, as well as political, enemies. Second, Franklin thought several subjects, including English, science, accounting, and engineering, should be more important than Greek and Latin. Most of the college-educated trustees disagreed. They believed the traditional study of the classics and theology were the main subjects that colleges should teach. Third, Richard Peters and some other trustees, as well as Provost William Smith, wanted the college to become an Anglican institution. Franklin believed that it should be non-sectarian.

Partially because the college was non-sectarian but mainly because Franklin founded and supported it, the college received its first donation from a private person living at some distance from Philadelphia. The planter Philip Ludwell III, whom Franklin had met in Virginia in the spring of 1756, passed through Philadelphia as the representative of Virginia's governor Robert Dinwiddie to Lord Loudoun. Ludwell had become a friend and admirer of Franklin. Returning from New York to Virginia in September 1756, Ludwell stopped in Philadelphia, where he donated £10 sterling to the Pennsylvania Hospital and £20 sterling to the academy. Franklin took his note on a London banker, submitted the note on 23 September, charging no commission (6:532), and on 30 September 1756 publicized Ludwell's contributions in the *Pennsylvania Gazette*, probably gaining his permission first by saying that the publication would inspire future contributions. Six years later in England, Ludwell commissioned Franklin's 1762 portrait by Mason Chamberlain. The mezzotint by Edward Fisher, reproduced as the frontispiece of this volume, is based on Chamberlain's portrait.[35]

Before being appointed an agent to England for the Pennsylvania Assembly, Franklin attended a final meeting of the trustees on 11 January 1757. The major business was to name a replacement for the deceased Lloyd Zachary. Franklin discovered to his "Mortification" that the majority of the trustees had decided before the meeting to elect the Proprietary Party stalwart Benjamin Chew. Richard Peters reported to Thomas Penn on 14 February that Franklin "blames the Trustees that they did not beforehand consult him on his Election, saying it was a piece of Justice due to him as he was the Father and principal support of the Academy, and this is true, but for all that it was not thought proper to gratify his Pride which now grows insufferable."[36]

During his first mission to England, 1757–62, Franklin purchased equipment for the college and repaid money that Collinson had advanced (7:286). When Deborah Franklin wrote him about the academy, he replied in January 1758, "I am sorry to hear of any Disturbance in the Academy, the rather as by my mistaken Zeal for its Welfare in introducing that imprudent Man [Smith], I think myself in some Degree the Cause of those Misfortunes" (7:368). On 9 September 1758 Kinnersley wrote that he was thinking of resigning. Franklin replied on 28 July 1759 that it would probably be impossible for him to remedy any difficulties that Kinnersley was encountering even if he were present. Before he left Philadelphia, "everything to be done in the Academy was privately preconcerted in a Cabal without my Knowledge or Participation and accordingly carried into Execution. The Schemes of Public Parties made it seem requisite to lessen my Influence."

In perhaps the first occasion when Franklin seemed to feel sorry for himself, he wrote, "The Trustees had reap'd the full Advantage of my Head, Hands,

Heart and Purse in getting through the first Difficulties of the Design, and when they thought they could do without me, they laid me aside. I wish Success to the Schools nevertheless" (8:415–16). Though disappointed that the Academy and College of Philadelphia were not more like his original plan, Franklin nevertheless was proud of the institution. From 1759 to 1763, he patronized and encouraged William Shippen III (1736–1801) and John Morgan (1735–1809), both of whom studied with Franklin's medical friends in Edinburgh and London. After coming home to Philadelphia, the two started the study of medicine at the college.[37]

RETURN TO PHILADELPHIA

After returning to Philadelphia on 1 November 1762, Franklin tried to take an active part as a trustee, but he was swamped with political duties and with post office business. The trustees had agreed on 10 March 1761 to build a dormitory, and Provost Smith was in England raising money for it and the college. Franklin attended a meeting on 9 November 1762, when Smith's success with the proprietor and his appeal to the king were reported. While contractor/carpenter Robert Smith (1722–77) proceeded with construction on the dormitory, Franklin attended six more meetings on 8 February, 2 and 24 March, 12 April, and 17 and 27 May 1763. At the first, on 8 February, Franklin introduced a letter from his social and business friend John Sargent (1714–91), an M.P. and director of the Bank of England, who volunteered to give two gold medals as annual prizes for orations. One should be on the reciprocal advantages arising from "a perpetual Union between Great Britain and her American colonies" and the other "for some Classical Exercise." He asked that Franklin, Isaac Norris, and a third person be in charge of awarding the medals. Franklin shared the letter with Norris, and they agreed that it would be more proper for the college trustees to be in charge. The trustees accepted. They decided that the English prize could go to anyone who had a connection with the college and that the classical prize should go to a graduating senior. Peters and Franklin were appointed to choose the classical subject. For various reasons, the competition for the medals was put off until 1766, when the English prize was awarded to Dr. John Morgan, but the classical prize was not given even then because the contestants' names became known before the prize was awarded.[38]

Despite his numerous other activities, Franklin tried to resurrect the English school. At the same 8 February 1763 meeting, "The State of the English School was taken into Consideration, and it was observed that Mr. Kinnersley's Time was entirely taken up in Teaching little Boys the Elements of the English Language." When Franklin cited this passage in his 1789 "Intentions of the Founders," he explained that the English school had "dwindled into a School similar to those kept by old Women who teach Children their Letters" (S 10:17). The 8 February 1763 minutes reported "that Speaking and Rehearsing in Publick were

Totally Disused, to the great Prejudice of the other Scholars and Students, and contrary to the Original Design of the Trustees in the forming of the School."

At the 12 April meeting, the trustees said that the "Original Design" of the English school should be followed and "that the old Method of hearing them read and repeat in public should be again used." Franklin was appointed to a committee to confer with Ebenezer Kinnersley "as to how this might best be done." In 1789 Franklin explained the 1763 situation. Some of the first trustees "who were Friends to the Scheme of the English Education" were still active, and they called for "a Reformation." Since the original constitution was still in effect, it gave weight to the complaints. The "Latinists," however, decried "the English School as useless." They said, and "indeed they still say," that a school for teaching English should never be joined with a college. The "Latinists looked on every Expence upon the English School as" depriving them of increases in their salaries. The school depended on the English master, when not teaching children, to teach "the Philosophy Classes," which were in "the Latin Part of the Institution." The trustees on 13 June 1763 "did not think proper to lay any further Burthen" upon Kinnersley. Franklin bitterly recalled that the trustees said "no more could be done in the English School than was then done" (S 10:20).

At the 2 March 1763 trustees' meeting, Franklin and others were appointed to examine the nine candidates privately for a college degree. Within the next two weeks they did so, and the boys were judged ready. With Franklin present, on 24 March "The Public Examination of the Students . . . was held in the publick Hall before a large Audience of People & the Students acquitted themselves to the Satisfaction of the Trustees."[39] Then Franklin went off on post office business to Virginia for a month, from mid-April to mid-May, but he returned about 16 May and was present at the 17 May graduation. The last meeting Franklin attended was on 27 May 1763, and he left on 7 June for a six-month post office trip to New England.

AN ANGLICAN INSTITUTION

All other colonial colleges were associated with some religion, and perhaps one reason that the Reverend Samuel Johnson did not want to come to Philadelphia was that its academy was non-sectarian. Franklin wanted to keep it that way, and the Quakers agreed, but many persons feared that it would become an Anglican institution. Peter Collinson had reservations about William Smith in January 1754 partly because he intended to become an Anglican clergyman. That, Collinson thought, might dissuade some Quakers and other dissenters from sending their children to the academy. Franklin had reassured Collinson: "As to his Gown, I think with you that it may not at first be proper to use it frequently in the Academy; tho' if it should prejudice the main design with some, it might perhaps advantage it as much with others" (5:331).

Smith revealed to a few people that he wanted the college to become an

Anglican institution. In November 1756 he wrote that "the Church, by soft and easy Means daily gains ground" in the college. "Of Twenty-four Trustees fifteen or sixteen are regular Churchmen. . . . We have Prayers twice a day, the Children learn the Church-Catecism."[40] Rumors of the increasing Anglican influence in the academy and college circulated. Dr. Samuel Chandler, the non-conformist minister at London's Old Jewry, was a friend of both Smith and Franklin, and Chandler believed in non-denominational colleges (5:211). While in England in 1763 and 1764 collecting money for the college, Smith realized that Chandler and a number of other influential persons preferred that the Philadelphia Academy and College remain non-sectarian. Smith suggested that Chandler call on Thomas Secker, now archbishop of Canterbury, to see if the rumors of the college becoming Anglican could be quieted. Chandler, Smith, and the archbishop "freely debated this Affair for an Hour together."[41] Chandler argued that the academy and college had begun as non-sectarian and had been supported by parties of all denominations. He said that the intentions of the previous donors would be betrayed if the institution became Anglican. The archbishop agreed that it should continue to be non-sectarian.

Smith shrewdly concurred. He suggested that both men send a letter to the trustees stating that position. It would, he said, "be of some Weight to keep Things on their present Footing and prevent all future Jealousies." Chandler wrote the letter on 9 April 1764; he and the archbishop signed it, as did Thomas and Richard Penn and Presbyterian William Allen, who was also in London. Smith brought it back to Philadelphia with a letter from Chandler to Richard Peters of 12 April describing the agreement. At a special trustees' meeting on 14 June 1764, a "fundamental Resolve" passed to keep the institution non-denominational. Though Franklin was not at the meeting, he signed the resolve afterward (before 11 September 1764), as did subsequently elected trustees to 17 August 1790.[42] Shortly after Franklin signed the "fundamental Resolve," the Reverend George Whitefield arrived in Philadelphia on 14 September 1764. As in 1754, Whitefield preached for Franklin's special charitable projects, the Charity School on Wednesday, 17 October 1764, raising £105, and the Pennsylvania Hospital on Sunday, 21 October, raising £170.

Visiting Germany in July 1766, Franklin had several conversations with Gottfried Achenwald, a professor at the University at Göttingen who taught jurisprudence and statistics. Franklin told him about the Philadelphia College and, referring especially to Morgan and Shippen, said that "a medical faculty was established." Franklin hoped soon the university would give doctorates in medicine (13:363). That may have been the first time the college was called a "university," though the word may have been Achenwald's, not Franklin's.

REVIVAL, 1789

During 1776–77, classes were held sporadically. After the British took Philadelphia, the legislature, meeting in Lancaster on 2 January 1778, suspended the powers of the trustees of the college and academy. Assembly members knew that Provost William Smith was a lukewarm patriot—and a devoted Anglican minister who hoped to become a bishop. John Adams met him on 29 August 1774. Adams wrote that Smith "is looking up to Government for an American Episcopate and a Pair of lawn Sleeves." Adams found him "Soft, polite, insinuating, adulating, sensible, learned, industrious, indefatigable."[43] Over a decade later, on 6 March 1789, the Pennsylvania Assembly restored the charter to the University of Philadelphia. The surviving active trustees of the university gathered at Benjamin Franklin's home on 9 March.[44] They unanimously elected Franklin president, resolved to elect six new trustees, and met again on 11 March. For the next several months, in consideration of Franklin's age and illness, the trustees held their meetings at his home. Four more trustees, including Franklin's friend Robert Hare, who had sailed from London to Philadelphia in 1773 with letters of recommendation from Franklin, were elected on 16 March. Provost William Smith, as secretary of the trustees, attended the meetings.

On 2 April 1789, Hare moved that a committee be appointed "to determine,—Whether a Plan can be devised and recommended for carrying on the *English School* (or System of English Education) in such manner, that Youth who have not the Knowlege of the Learned Languages, may acquire the most useful Branches of a liberal Education without them." President Franklin appointed himself, James Wilson, the Reverend William White, D.D., Hare, and Henry Hill "a Committee for this Purpose." Two meetings later, on 18 April, the committee's report was read and ordered to "lie on the Table for further Consideration." Evidently some trustees (no doubt reflecting the opinions of Provost Smith and James Davidson, another classics teacher) asked what would be the implications for the other schools. Franklin appointed a slightly larger committee, excluding himself, "to examine the different Schools, and to enquire what Assistants are further necessary in the said Schools."

The reaction appeared in the 28 April minutes. A possible "Assistant in the English School" was to be hired, if judged qualified, at the same salary as "the other Ushers & Tutors," but at the same meeting it was decided that two ushers in the Latin school were to be continued at a higher salary, £75 each. After that meeting but before late June, Franklin proposed that the English and the Latin schools be separated. In separating the two, he suggested that the money raised for the endowment, land, and buildings of the English school be given to it and that the Latin school keep its own endowment.

The suggestion horrified almost all the trustees.

After Franklin wrote the "Original Intentions" in late June for the trustees who seemed to favor supporting the English school, he gave it to Hare, his main ally. In the "Original Intentions," Franklin declared: "It is therefore that wishing as much good to the Latinists as their System can honestly procure for them, we now demand a Separation, and without desiring to injure them, but claiming an equitable Partition of our joint Stock, we wish to execute the Plan they have so long defeated, and afford the Publick the Means of a compleat English Education" (S 10:28). Even his strongest supporter rejected the idea. Hare wrote him on 14 July 1789: "I fully believe from the discourse of the Trustees, and other persons, on this subject, that such a measure is not practicable at this time."

All the Latinists would rally behind Provost William Smith and oppose giving up any part of the endowment, land, or buildings. Hare continued, "The services rendered by the present Provost, the prejudices entertain'd by many of the trustees in his favor, his active indefatigable character when engag[ing] in measures on which he is intent, and the support he would receive from the friends of the other professors, serve to convince me that this object cannot now be accompli[shed] and that to attempt it in the present state of things, would only add force to the exertions of the adverse party, by giving them two moti[ves] for opposition instead of one." Hare conceded that "such a separation could not now be accomplish'd" but that "it is prudent to hold up" the suggestion "*in terrorem,* and that much benefit has already accrued from the mention of it."[45]

Just two more meetings were held at Franklin's home. On 21 July, only five trustees attended, not including Franklin, who was too ill to attend. The fifteenth and last meeting at Franklin's home was on 27 July 1789. The trustees' minutes noted at the end of the 27 July meeting that they would stop meeting there because of Franklin's "low State of Health." That's no doubt true, but I suspect they also stopped meeting there because he was giving the majority of the trustees a great pain. Franklin continued as president of the trustees until his death. On 17 November 1789 he signed a set of rules for the study necessary before receiving the M.D. degree,[46] but by then his participation was merely formulaic. He presumably took no part in any decision-making process after 27 July 1789. Provost Smith had won the battle for a traditional school during Franklin's life, and he lived to give the eulogy after Franklin's death. (Smith will be mentioned a few times later in the biography.)

At the end of his life, Franklin remained disappointed that the Philadelphia Academy and College had become increasingly like the traditional college, featuring Latin and Greek as the highest attainments. In his June 1789 "Observations Relative to the Intentions of the Original Founders of the Academy," he explained why the "Latinists" preferred the old curriculum. Three or four hundred years ago, "all the Knowledge then contain'd in Books" was in Latin and Greek. Thus it was necessary to learn them in order to learn any field of knowledge. The books that existed were in manuscript and cost so much that only the few wealthy people could purchase them. The common people did not learn to read because, if they did, they would have nothing to read unless they learned Latin or Greek, and if ordinary persons did somehow learn the classical languages, they would still have no money to buy the expensive manuscripts.[47]

Even sixty years after the invention of printing, readers were so few that the printers could not find purchasers for more than three hundred copies of a book. But as printing made books cheap, readers increased, "so much as to make it worth while to write and print Books in the Vulgar Tongues." During the previous two centuries, the various branches of science began to appear in the common languages, "and at this Day the whole Body of Science, consisting not only of Translations, from all the valuable ancients, but of all the new modern Discoveries, is to be met with in those Languages, so that learning the ancient for the purpose of acquiring Knowledge is become absolutely unnecessary" (S 10:30).

Colleges should now, Franklin urged, teach in the modern languages. "But there is in Mankind an unaccountable Prejudice in favour of ancient Customs and Habitudes, which inclines to a Continuance of them after the Circumstances, which formerly made them useful, cease to exist." Franklin said that multitudes of instances proved the point, but he would give just one, the custom of carrying hats. Though they were unknown in Greece and Rome except for helmets, they became common in the Renaissance but went out of fashion as wigs and "Hair nicely dress'd" came to prevail, "lest the curious Arrangements of the Curls and Powdering should be disordered." The custom, however, of carrying a useless hat remained: "there are a multitude of the politer people in all the courts and capital cities of Europe, who have never, nor their fathers before them, worn a hat otherwise than as a *chapeau bras*, though the utility of such a mode of wearing it is by no means apparent, and it is attended not only with some expense, but with a degree of constant trouble" (S 10:31).

Thus Franklin softened his criticisms of the persistence of studying Greek and Latin with a humourous anecdote concerning a foible. The general tone, however, of "The Intentions of the Founders" is bitter, with Franklin acknowledging that the classical school had dominated—and still dominated—the English school.

CONCLUSION

Writing a major biography of Franklin in 1864, James Parton noted that Franklin's hope for "a great school, free from the obstructing nuisance of Latin and Greek, seems as far from realization as ever."[48] No doubt that was true, but American colleges were at that time just beginning to dramatically change. America's first great technological college (Franklin's thirteenth subject) dates from 1861, when William Barton Rogers founded the Massachusetts Institute of Technology. The next year, 1862, Congressman Justin Smith Morrill of Vermont sponsored the Morrill Act, which started the land-grant colleges. That was perhaps the most fundamental change ever in American education. As a result of the Morrill Act, land-grant colleges were founded in every state and territory, and at first they all featured the study of agriculture (Franklin's tenth subject) and to some degree farming technology. Penn finally became a great leader in education in Franklin's eleventh subject, trade and commerce, when Joseph Wharton persuaded the University of Pennsylvania's administration to start a business school, and its first professor was hired in 1883. Franklin's second subject, comparative anthropology, began as a discipline in higher education when Columbia hired Franz Boas as a full professor in 1899.

In Franklin's general approach to education, Harvard led the way. During the forty-year presidency of Charles W. Eliot (1869–1908), Harvard adopted the elective system, and in 1900, Eliot was in great part responsible for the creation of the College Entrance Board Examination, which tested general knowledge rather than simply Latin and Greek for admission to college. But study of the classics continued to dominate higher education until well into the twentieth century. In general, during the first half of the twentieth century, most colleges abandoned requiring Greek and Latin for admission. Not until after World War II, however, did a knowledge of Latin cease to be a requirement for a Ph.D. in engineering and the sciences—and, finally, a few years later, in the liberal arts.

Colleges of the twenty-first century finally offer the range of subjects and the possibilities that Franklin envisioned.

Franklin did not let his disappointment over the failure of the projected English school appear in the *Autobiography*, for he wrote it in great part to encourage people and projects. Besides, the Academy and College of Philadelphia had become, even during his lifetime, a qualified success. Instead of lamenting its failure, Franklin wrote in the *Autobiography*: "The Trustees of the Academy after a while were incorporated by a Charter from the Governor; their Funds were increas'd by Contributions in Britain, and Grants of Land from the Proprietaries, to which the Assembly has since made considerable Addition, and thus was established the present University of Philadelphia. I have been continued one of its Trustees from the Beginning, now near forty Years, and have had the very great Pleasure of seeing a Number of the Youth who have receiv'd their Education in it, distinguish'd by their improv'd Abilities, serviceable in public Stations, and Ornaments to their Country" (A 119).

SIX

Colonial Union, Dumping Felons in America, and Assemblyman, 1751

I would propose to have them [American rattlesnakes] carefully distributed in St. James's Park, in the Spring-Gardens and other Places of Pleasure about London; in the Gardens of all the Nobility and Gentry throughout the Nation; but particularly in the Gardens of the Prime Ministers, the Lords of Trade and Members of Parliament; for to them we are most particularly obliged.
—*Franklin, "Rattlesnakes for Felons," 9 May 1751, 4:132*

THE YEAR 1751 WAS A MOMENTOUS ONE in Franklin's life. After devising the first matching grant and starting the Pennsylvania Hospital, he wrote four of colonial America's most influential writings. The first was his letter to James Parker of 20 March, discussing Archibald Kennedy's manuscript, "The Importance of Gaining and Preserving the Friendship of the Indians to the British Interest." In the letter, Franklin proposed a union of the colonies, which contained the key suggestions later embodied in the 1754 Albany Plan and subsequently in the Constitution of the United States. Second came the April publication in London of *Experiments and Observations on Electricity*. As we have seen, it made Franklin the most famous natural philosopher in the world. The third major publication had two parts: his 11 April editorial, "Jakes on our Tables," castigated the British authorities for treating America like a penal colony; and the follow-up 9 May hoax, "Rattlesnakes for Felons," viciously satirized the British. These two writings contained the most memorable anti-English statements by any American before the Stamp Act. Philadelphians elected Franklin to the Pennsylvania Assembly on 9 May, and in the August session he began his career as the assembly's most active committeeman and chief writer. The fourth major composition of 1751 was his political and demographic study, "Observations Concerning the Increase of Mankind, Peopling of Cities, etc." The next chapter takes up that extraordinary document.

DRAFT OF A UNION OF THE COLONIES

In February or early March, Franklin received Archibald Kennedy's manuscript, "The Importance of Gaining and Preserving the Friendship of the Indians to the British Interest," from James Parker, his former printing partner. Kennedy evidently requested Parker to ask Franklin to review the manuscript. The New York intellectual did not know Franklin well but wanted his thoughts. Replying to Parker on 20 March, Franklin agreed that "securing the Friendship of the Indians is of the greatest Consequence to these Colonies." Franklin wrote that the "surest Means of doing it, are, to regulate the Indian Trade, so as to convince them, by Experience, that they may have the best and cheapest Goods, and the fairest Dealing from the English." He also said that a union of the colonies was desirable because it would "form a Strength that the Indians may depend on for Protection, in Case of a Rupture with the French; or apprehend great Danger from, if they should break with us" (4:117).[1] He faulted, however, previous schemes for unifying the colonies, for they had often been proposed by governors who were "on ill Terms with their Assemblies, and seldom are the Men that have the most Influence among them." Instead, "if you were to pick out half a Dozen Men of good Understanding and Address, and furnish them with a reasonable Scheme and proper Instructions, and send them in the Nature of Ambassadors to the other Colonies, where they might apply particularly to all the leading Men, and by proper Management get them to engage in promoting the Scheme" (4:118), then Franklin believed a union might be made.

Franklin seemed almost naive when he stated, "For reasonable sensible Men, can always make a reasonable Scheme appear such to other reasonable Men, if they take Pains, and have Time and Opportunity for it; unless from some Circumstances their Honesty and good Intentions are suspected." He thought that a "voluntary Union entered into by the Colonies themselves" would be "preferable to one impos'd by Parliament" because it would be easier "to alter and improve, as Circumstances should require, and Experience direct." He said that the English colonies should follow the example of the Iroquois. As Franklin knew, Canasatago, Scarouady, and other Iroquois allies often recommended that the English colonies unite against the French. Franklin wrote: "It would be a very strange Thing, if six Nations of ignorant Savages should be capable of forming a Scheme for such an Union, and be able to execute it in such a Manner, as that it has subsisted Ages, and appears indissoluble; and yet that a like Union should be impracticable for ten or a Dozen English Colonies, to whom it is more necessary, and must be more advantageous; and who cannot be supposed to want an equal Understanding of their Interests" (4:118–19).[2]

Franklin suggested that "a general Council" should be formed "by all the Colonies" and a "general Governor" should be "appointed by the Crown to preside." Everything relating to Indian affairs and the defense of the colonies "might be properly put under their Management." Each colony should be represented in the general council by the amount of money it paid into the common treasury for the common expense. Franklin proposed that the treasury might be supplied by "an equal Excise on strong Liquors in all the Colonies," which would not be applied to the private use of any colony but reserved for the general service. If the council met successively in the different colonies, the members "might thereby become better acquainted with the Circumstances, Interests, Strength or Weakness, &c. of all." Moreover, a rotation of the meeting place would avoid a preference that "might create Jealousy" (4:119).

Kennedy had urged that a strong fort be built at the head of Lake Champlain. Franklin agreed that the location seemed good and added that in peacetime, "Parties of the Garrisons of all Frontier Forts might be allowed to go out on Hunting Expeditions, with or without Indians, and have the Profit to themselves of the Skins they get: By this Means a Number of Wood-Runners would be form'd, well acquainted with the Country, and of great Use in War Time, as Guides of Parties and Scouts, &c." Notably, Franklin used the phrase "Wood-Runners," a literal translation of the French "couriers du bois." In 1751 the English language still did not yet have an apt term for the frontiersman, though America had famous woodsmen for a century before Colonel Thomas Cresap coined the term *frontiersman* in 1755.[3] Franklin praised the Indians' fighting abilities: "Every Indian is a Hunter; and as their Manner of making War, viz. by Skulking, Surprizing and Killing particular Persons and Families, is just the same as their Manner of Hunting, only changing the Object, Every Indian is a disciplin'd Soldier" (4:119–20).

Franklin knew that in the history of America's Indian wars, the Indian experts became major leaders against the Indians: John Mason (1600?–1672) in the Pequot War, 1636–37; Benjamin Church (1639–1718) in King Philip's War, 1675–76; and Sébastien Rale, S.J. (1657–1724), for the French, and Captain John Lovewell (d. 1725) for the English in the Abenaki Indian war (1722–26).[4] Franklin wrote, "Soldiers of this Kind [i.e., frontiersmen who were Indian experts] are always wanted in the Colonies in an Indian War." His next observation anticipated the common American criticism of the reason for the defeat of General Edward Braddock in 1755: "for the European Military Discipline is of little Use in these Woods" (4:20). Franklin also commented on government-sponsored trading posts for Indians and on the increasing German population of Pennsylvania—topics that recur in this volume.[5]

James Parker published Kennedy's pamphlet in early May, which concluded with Franklin's anonymous letter (pp. 28–31). The essay and letter were reprinted in London the following year.[6] Franklin's letter contains most of the basic propositions for the union of the colonies that he advocated in the Albany Plan of 1754 (see appendix 5). Further, his thoughts on how to secure and keep the friendship with the Indians foreshadow the positions advised after the 1753 Carlisle Treaty by Franklin and the Pennsylvania Assembly.

JAKES ON OUR TABLES!

Another imperial concern, the transportation of felons to America, provoked Franklin into writing a series of editorials and a satire. Most felons were thieves, thugs, or murderers, though a small proportion were imprisoned for nonviolent crimes like forgery and some simply for debt. Convicts had been sporadically shipped to America throughout the seventeenth century, but Parliament's Transportation Act of 1718 opened the floodgates. The British government paid merchants to ship convicts to the colonies; and the colonists who bought the criminals' time paid the shipping agents. The criminals were generally condemned to seven years of service, but fourteen years was often imposed on criminals convicted of a charge that carried a death penalty. Colonial assemblies resisted the vastly increased number of transported felons by imposing duties on them (as it did with the importation of slaves), which the purchaser had to pay. That made the felons more costly and thus less salable. The Board of Trade, however, in reviewing the acts of the colonial assemblies, repeatedly recommended that acts imposing duties on the transported felons (or slaves) be disallowed. Indeed, all acts imposing duties on any British imports were vetoed. Colonial assemblies tried to evade that difficulty by making an act expire within a short time, so that by the time the Board of Trade considered it, the act had expired or was about to.[7] Resenting earlier Acts of Trade and Navigation (which Americans thought prejudicial), the Old Charter Party in Massachusetts had passed annual impost bills taxing British goods, but in 1719 Governor Samuel Shute, after receiving direct orders from Britain, refused to pass any further impost bills (*Life* 1:82, 343, 394–96).

Franklin knew that after the Transportation Act of 1718 was passed, Thomas Bordley (1682?–1726), the leader of Maryland's assembly, made the transportation of felons a personal crusade. He published an editorial against the practice in the *American Weekly Mercury* of 14 February 1720/1 and brought before the Maryland courts an amazing series of "pertinacious, unrestrained" legal proceedings against the transportation of felons.[8] Since newspaper editors exchanged and read one another's papers (*Life* 1:243), Franklin at age sixteen had probably read Bordley's editorial. When Franklin arrived in Philadelphia in 1723, he must have heard of Bordley's legal activities. Bordley lived in Bohemia Manor, Maryland, a plantation close to Philadelphia, and visited Philadelphia often. He employed Andrew Bradford on several occasions before bringing the English printer William Parks to Maryland in 1725.[9] Only Bordley's death in 1726 stopped his fight against transported felons.

In 1722, 1729, and 1729/30, the Pennsylvania Assembly imposed a £5 tax on any transported felon who landed in Pennsylvania and required a purchaser to post a bond of £50 for the convict's good behavior. Though the royal colonies were obliged to submit their new acts within three months or as soon as possible to the British authorities for approval or disallowance,[10] Pennsylvania had five years. Once submitted, the British authorities had six months to approve or reject Pennsylvania's acts, but if they were not disallowed within six months, the acts were automatically deemed in effect. Neither Governor William Keith nor Governor Patrick Gordon submitted the acts imposing a tax on transported felons to the Privy Council. It would automatically have referred them to the

Board of Trade, where they would have been disallowed. One presumes that both governors deliberately kept the British authorities ignorant.

By 1731, the Board of Trade had repeatedly struck down acts from various colonies imposing duties on transported felons. Irritated by these attempts to circumvent the transportation of felons, the board issued instructions on 10 December 1731 to all colonial governors that no duties or other taxes could be laid on convicts or slaves shipped to America. Governor Patrick Gordon of Pennsylvania, along with all other colonial governors, received the instructions, but he did not publish them. The governors of Virginia and of Massachusetts, however, circulated copies.[11] Franklin's resentment of the transportation of felons and of the board's action indirectly appeared in his reprinting from Virginia and again from Massachusetts (*Pennsylvania Gazette*, 26 June and 3 July 1732) reports of the instructions against taxing either slaves or felons. Franklin rarely reprinted the same news.

In 1738, the Pennsylvania Assembly passed a "Supplement" to the earlier 1729/30 act. Governor George Thomas submitted it to the Privy Council for enactment.[12] Reviewing the act for the Privy Council, the Board of Trade found that it had no record of the previous acts. The board asked Thomas Penn's attorney who supervised Pennsylvania affairs, Ferdinand John Paris, for evidence that the king had passed the earlier acts. He replied on 13 February 1738/9 that he could not show that they "had ever been laid before this Board or confirmed by His Majesty." On 21 February 1738/9 the board reported to the Privy Council that the acts amounted to "a virtual prohibition of importation of convicts, which render ineffectual the statute relating to the transportation of felons." The board recommended that the act be disallowed, but the dilatory Privy Council did not disallow it within six months, so the act remained in effect.

On 3 February 1742/3, the Pennsylvania Assembly passed another act imposing a duty on transported felons. In England the Privy Council received it on 30 June 1743 and sent it to the Board of Trade on 7 August. On Friday, 2 December 1746, with board members Lord John Monson, Richard Plummer, Hon Baptist Leveson Gower, Lord Thomas Dupplin, and Francis Fane present, the board drafted its report, which was signed on 5 December. Recommending the act's disallowance, these board members sneered: "The Act . . . tends to prevent the introduction of such persons into . . . Pennsylvania who . . . might be of public utility in the improvement and well peopling of the said province." Initiated by the Board of Trade, approved by the Privy Council, and, at least indirectly, by George II, the insult infuriated Franklin. Kevin J. Hayes, who located the source, noted that Franklin often cited the insult "from the early 1750s to the late 1780s to express his indignation with British attitudes toward America."[13]

The board noted that the acts of 1722, 1729, and 1729/30 had "never been laid before His Majesty for his royal approbation or disallowance" and asked whether they, too, should not be disallowed. When Thomas Penn (his brother

Richard left decisions concerning the colony to him) learned of the proposed disallowance of the old acts, he petitioned the king (i.e., the Privy Council, which referred the matter to the Board of Trade). Penn claimed that the three old acts had been submitted to the board and that the last one, of 1730, repealed the former acts of 1722 and 1729. Disallowance of acts that were seventeen or more years old could "affect the most ancient & fundamental Laws of several Colonys." Penn's lawyers argued that to set aside laws passed so long ago would introduce confusion into the legal basis of government. Penn petitioned for "an Opportunity to be heard, by their Counsel" on the subject. Penn probably spoke privately to friends on the board,[14] suggesting that he would see that the old acts of assembly would be struck down by the assembly itself. The petition succeeded. On 17 December 1746 the king in council merely repealed the act of 3 February 1742/3 and made no reference to the old acts.[15] That had the effect of continuing in force the supplemental act of 1738 and the full act of February 1729/30 with its £5 tax and £50 bond.

Two and a half years later, on 19 August 1749, the assembly passed another supplement to the 1730 act. It named Joseph Prichard as collector of the duty in place of the deceased collector. When the act reached England for submission to the Privy Council, Ferdinand John Paris drew up a memorial against it. Penn sent the memorial to Governor James Hamilton in Pennsylvania, who forwarded it to the assembly on 19 January 1750/1. The memorial chastised the assembly, reminded the members that the proprietors had managed to stop the disapprobation of the old acts of 1722, 1729, and 1729/30, and warned that if another supplemental act came before the Board of Trade, it would surely recommend disallowing the former acts.

Neither Penn nor Paris cared about the shipment of felons to Pennsylvania. Penn cared mightily, however, about the precedent of overturning acts that had been in force for years. That, said Paris's memorial, "was a matter of infinite Importance."[16] The memorial asked the assembly to repeal the four acts of 1722, 1729, 1729/30, and 1742. It sugarcoated the request by saying that the new act should be like the old one of 1742 "in all Things save what the Board of Trade objected to in that Act." In other words, the act would no longer be effective in prohibiting the importation of transported felons and slaves into Pennsylvania. The memorial, read to the assembly by Clerk Franklin on 19 January 1750/1, cited the Board of Trade's action of 3 February 1742/3 and evidently made Franklin recall the board's "barbarous *Sarcasm*" (13:79) of 5 December 1746.

When transported felons committed a number of crimes two months later, Franklin revived Thomas Bordley's crusade against transporting felons to America. In the 11 April 1751 *Pennsylvania Gazette*, Franklin published a catalogue of recent crimes. In Virginia six convicts had killed a ship's captain and imprisoned the rest of the crew. When the cabin boy tried to hail a passing ship, they "drove a Spike up thro' his under and upper Jaws, and wound Spun yarn round the End that came out near his Nose, to prevent his getting it out." In

Maryland a "Convict Servant" resolved to kill his mistress but, because she looked so "d——d innocent," he instead cut off his own left hand and said, "Now make me work if you can." From Pennsylvania, Franklin reported two crimes by convict servants. Then he editorialized.

> These are some of thy Favours, BRITAIN! Thou art called our MOTHER COUNTRY; but what good *Mother* ever sent *Thieves* and *Villains* to accompany her *Children*; to corrupt some with their infectious Vices, and murder the rest? What *Father* ever endeavour'd to spread the *Plague* in his Family!—We do not ask Fish; but thou givest us *Serpents*, and worse than Serpents!—In what can *Britain* show a more Sovereign Contempt for us, than by emptying their *Jails* into our Settlements; unless they would likewise empty their *Jakes* on our Tables?—What must we think of that B[oar]d, which has advised the Repeal of every Law we have hitherto made to prevent this Deluge of Wickedness overwhelming us; and with this *cruel* Sarcasm, *That these Laws were against the* Publick Utility, *for they tended to prevent the* IMPROVEMENT *and* WELL-PEOPLING *of the Colonies*!—And what must we think of those Merchants, who for the sake of a little paltry Gain, will be concerned in importing and disposing of these abominable Cargoes? (4:131n5)

Franklin's invective against Britain alluded to Matthew 7:9–11: "what man is there of you, whom if his son ask bread, will he give him a stone? Or if he ask a fish, will he give him a serpent? If ye then, being evil, know how to give good gifts unto your children, how much more shall your Father which is in heaven give good things to them who ask him?" He further impaled Britain's conduct by using the family metaphors that characterized the supposed relationship between Britain and its colonies. Franklin had ironically employed the "mother country" metaphor in an editorial of 9 October 1729 concerning Massachusetts governor William Burnet's demand for a fixed salary (*Life* 1:419) and sarcastically used the comparison in writing the militia "Form of Association" (above, p. 16, 1747). Franklin frequently used it bitterly in later satires of England, though none was stronger than this scatological attack.[17] Here he called up the family metaphor's affectionate connotations to condemn Britain's actions. The "mother country" (which had become the jealous stepmother country), the British authorities, and the merchants concerned in the convict trade were all worse than beasts.

Franklin's strongest language in the editorial complained that sending felons to the colonies was like dumping England's privies on Americans' tables. How perfect was his word *jakes*! He could have said *chamber pots*, but that would not necessarily drown the table with urine and feces. *Privies* or *outhouses* were possibilities, but neither has the low, colloquial connotations of disgust implied by *jakes*. *Dunghill* would do, though *jakes*, being a single syllable with a hard *a* sound, made a better exclamation. The assonance and consonance of "*Jails . . . Jakes*," the hard *a* assonance repeated in "*tables*," and the repeated rhythm of the two clauses all add to the rhetorical effect. The excremental language was shocking—an extraordinary revelation of fury against England and the British authorities.

The reaction? American newspaper editors knew a good thing when they saw it. But that would not entirely account for its reprintings. It touched a nerve. Franklin's catalogue of crimes and his diatribe against the Board of Trade and the "Mother Country" appeared in six of the nine American newspapers being published at the time. Two of the nine have incomplete files and may have published it. After appearing in the *Pennsylvania Gazette*, it was reprinted in the *New York Evening Post* for 15 April; in the *Maryland Gazette*, 17 April; in the *Boston Gazette* and the *Boston Evening Post* for 23 April; and in the *Virginia Gazette* for 24 May. Though the editors of a third Boston paper, the *Post Boy* reprinted the catalogue of crimes that appeared before and after the key insult to Britain ("Jakes on our Tables") on 22 April, they omitted the insult, presumably judging it too daring. Editor William Bradford would not have wanted to print it in his *Pennsylvania Journal*, for he must have been sensitive to the possible charge that his paper merely reprinted pieces from his older, well-established rival. It was the first popular American editorial and, proportionally, the most reprinted one America ever had.[18] In England, the June issue of the *Gentleman's Magazine* reprinted the catalogue of crimes and summarized Franklin's concluding comments, and the July issue of the *London Magazine* reprinted the "Jakes on our Tables" diatribe.[19] Franklin's anti-English invective was—temporarily—famous.

"Rattlesnakes for Felons"

A month later, on 9 May 1751, Franklin reprinted a series of crimes from the *Maryland Gazette* of 27 March through 17 April. A gang of thieves in Chestertown, Maryland, broke into two homes and stole goods; in Baltimore County, a convict servant killed an overseer; in Elk Ridge, another convict servant killed three of his master's children. These and similar reports of crimes occupy more than two of the three columns of the front page. Then came a supposed "Extract of a Letter from Maryland, dated April 26," which I attribute to Franklin. It began with a general indictment of transported felons: "I believe we have every Year three or four Hundred Felons imported here from London; and if, when their Times are out, or before, they were not many of them to move away to the Northward, and elsewhere, we should be over run with them.—Some few may possibly have been transported for small Matters, or thro' false Accusations; but the most well deserve hanging at home." After the "Extract of a Letter from Maryland," Franklin continued with more crime reports, including a forgery committed by a local youth. "No doubt," wrote Franklin, "he had the Advantage of being *improv'd* by the Conversation of some of those Gentry, who are sent over '*for the* IMPROVEMENT *and* WELL PEOPLING *of the Colonies.*'" Another crime report said that a gang of armed thieves in the back country

" When we fee our Papers fill'd continually with Accounts of the moſt audacious Robberies, the moſt cruel Murders, and infinite o- ther Villainies perpetrated by Convicts tranſported from *Europe*, what melancholly, what terrible Reflections muſt it occaſion! What will become of our Poſterity !----Theſe are ſome of thy Fa- vours, BRITAIN ! Thou art called our MOTHER COUNTRY ; but what good *Mother* ever ſent *Thieves* and *Villains* to accompany her *Children* ; to corrupt ſome with their infectious Vices, and murder the reſt ? What *Father* ever endeavour'd to ſpread the *Plague* in his Family !----We do not aſk Fiſh, but thou giveſt us *Serpents*, and worſe than Serpents !-----In what can *Britain* ſhow a more Sovereign Contempt for us, than by emptying their *Jails* into our Settlements ; unleſs they would likewiſe empty their *Jakes* on our Tables ?----- What muſt we think of that B-----d, which has advis'd the Repeal of every Law we have hitherto made to prevent this Deluge of Wic- kedneſs overwhelming us ; and with this *cruel* Sarcaſm, *That theſe Laws were againſt the* Publick Utility, *for they tended to prevent the* IMPROVEMENT *and* WELL-PEOPLING *of the Colonies* !-----And what muſt we think of thoſe Merchants, who for the ſake of a lit- tle paltry Gain, will be concern'd in importing and diſpoſing of theſe abominable Cargoes? "

Figure 26. "Jakes on our Tables!" Pennsylvania Gazette, 11 April 1751. Franklin's "Jakes on our Tables!" was the most widely reprinted American editorial and the most vicious anti-British propaganda before the Stamp Act. After Parliament passed its Transportation Act in 1718, the British began sending numerous convicts to the colonies as indentured servants. The act paid merchants to ship convicts to the colonies, and the ship captains were paid by the colonists who bought the criminals' time. The criminals were generally indentured for seven years of service, but fourteen years was often imposed on those con- victed of a crime that carried a death penalty. Pennsylvania and other colonies resisted the importation of felons (and slaves) by imposing duties on them, but the Privy Council, acting on the recommendation of the Board of Trade, repeatedly disallowed any duty.

When the Pennsylvania Assembly passed another act imposing a duty on transported felons, the Privy Council sent it to the Board of Trade where it too was disallowed on 5 December 1746—but this time with a sneer: "The Act . . . tends to prevent the introduc- tion of such persons into . . . Pennsylvania who . . . might be of public utility in the improvement and well peopling of the said province." The insult infuriated Franklin. After transported criminals committed a series of crimes in Virginia, Maryland, and Pennsylvania in February and March 1751, Franklin published a litany of the crimes— followed by his outraged editorial. Most American newspapers and the July London Mag- azine, reprinted it. The June Gentleman's Magazine summarized it.

Franklin alluded to or quoted the Board of Trade's insult numerous times from 1751 to 1776. Courtesy, Library Company of Philadelphia.

robbed "by Daylight with open Force, greatly molesting and terrifying the In-habitants," and a last news item covered a local robbery.

The crime reports and the letter supplied the context for Franklin's satire that immediately followed, "Rattlesnakes for Felons." Using the patriotic pseud-onym "Americanus," Franklin began in a dispassionate tone, though the words *mistaken* and *kind* were revealed as ironic by the end of the first sentence: "By a Passage in one of your late Papers, I understand that the Government at home will not suffer our mistaken Assemblies to make any Law for preventing or discouraging the Importation of Convicts from Great Britain, for this kind Rea-son, '*That such Laws are against the Publick Utility, as they tend to prevent the* IMPROVEMENT *and* WELL PEOPLING *of the Colonies*'" (4:131).

Employing the family metaphor in the second short paragraph, the irony becomes pervasive as "Americanus" asks for retaliation: "Such a tender *parental* Concern in our *Mother Country* for the *Welfare* of her Children, calls aloud for the highest *Returns* of Gratitude and Duty. This every one must be sensible of: But 'tis said, that in our present Circumstances it is absolutely impossible for us to make *such* as are adequate to the Favour. I own it; but nevertheless let us do our Endeavour. 'Tis something to show a grateful Disposition" (4:131–32).

Then follows the proposition, rattlesnakes for felons: "In some of the unin-habited Parts of these Provinces, there are Numbers of these venomous Reptiles we call RATTLE-SNAKES; Felons-convict from the Beginning of the World: These, whenever we meet with them, we put to Death, by Virtue of an old Law, *Thou shalt bruise his Head.* But as this is a sanguinary Law, and may seem too cruel; and as however mischievous those Creatures are with us, they may possi-bly change their Natures, if they were to change the Climate; I would humbly propose, that this general Sentence of *Death* be changed for *Transportation.*" Besides echoing Genesis 3:15, Franklin alluded to a well-known passage from Horace that contradicted the notion that persons will become different in differ-ent climates.[20] Americanus/Franklin suggested that it was as likely that rattle-snakes would change their natures by being shipped to England as convicts would change their natures by being shipped to America.

The first sentence of the next paragraph claimed that the absurd proposal could actually be undertaken. But the underlying savage authorial voice ridi-culed the proposition. The second sentence, with its extraordinary assault on the English nobility and gentry, the British authorities, the Lords of Trade, and members of Parliament, is amazingly bold. Though the following paragraph anticipates some details in Captain Garrish's letter in Franklin's 1782 fictitious *Supplement to the Boston Independent Chronicle* (the scalps of Americans should be hung "some dark night on the trees in St. James Park, where they could be seen from the King and Queen's Palaces"), "Rattlesnakes for Felons" is not as ghoulish (W 956–60): "In the Spring of the Year, when they [rattlesnakes] first creep out of their Holes, they are feeble, heavy, slow, and easily taken; and if a small Bounty were allow'd *per* Head, some Thousands might be collected annually, and *transported* to Britain. There I would propose to have them carefully distributed in *St. James's Park*, in the *Spring-Gardens* and other Places of Pleasure about *London*; in the Gardens of all the Nobility and Gentry throughout the Nation; but particularly in the Gardens of the *Prime Ministers*, the *Lords of Trade* and *Members of Parliament*; for to them we are *most particularly* obliged" (4:132).

The following paragraph returned to a projector's reasonable voice, only to reveal its inhumanity. Americanus/Franklin noted that the criminals were transported for "private Interests" of some avaricious English merchants rather than for the public welfare of England or America. He satirically repeated the family metaphor for the relationship between the colonies, and travestied that usage with a series of familial relationships ("Son . . . Daughter . . . Wife . . . Husband").

> There is no human Scheme so perfect, but some Inconveniences may be objected to it: Yet when the Conveniencies far exceed, the Scheme is judg'd rational, and fit to be executed. Thus Inconveniencies have been objected to that *good* and *wise* Act of Parliament, by virtue of which all the Newgates and Dungeons in Britain are emptied into the Colonies. It has been said, that these Thieves and Villains introduc'd among us, spoil the Morals of Youth in the Neighbourhoods that entertain them, and perpetrate many horrid Crimes; But let not *private Interests* obstruct *publick Utility*. Our *Mother* knows what is best for us. What is a little *Housebreaking, Shoplifting,* or *Highway Robbing*; what is a *Son* now and then *corrupted* and *hang'd*, a Daughter *debauch'd* and *pox'd*, a Wife *stabb'd*, a Husband's *Throat* cut, or a Child's *Brains beat out* with an Axe, compar'd with this "IMPROVEMENT and WELL PEOPLING of the Colonies!" (4:132–33)

Franklin returned to a seemingly dispassionate voice before again barbarously attacking the British upper classes: "Thus it may perhaps be objected to my Scheme, that the *Rattle-Snake* is a mischievous Creature, and that his changing his Nature with the Clime is a mere Supposition, not yet confirm'd by sufficient Facts. What then? Is not Example more prevalent than Precept? And may not the honest rough British Gentry, by a Familiarity with these Reptiles, learn to *insinuate*, and to *slaver*, and to *wriggle* into Place (and perhaps to *poison* such as stand in their Way)—qualities of no small Advantage to Courtiers! In comparison of which 'Improvement and Publick Utility,' what is a *Child* now and then kill'd by their venomous Bite,—or even a favourite *Lap-Dog*?" The lapdog allusion recalls the common criticism of aristocrats' supposedly valuing lapdogs as much as "Husbands or Children"—a motif that occurs twice in the *Tatler* and that Pope echoed in *Rape of the Lock*: "Not louder Shrieks to pitying Heav'n are cast,/When Husbands or when Lap-dogs breathe their last."[21] Franklin knew both.

The final paragraph recurs to the family metaphor and, in an underlying note, chafes at the Acts of Trade and Navigation: "I would only add, That this Exporting of Felons to the Colonies, may be consider'd as a *Trade*, as well as in the Light of a *Favour*. Now all Commerce implies *Returns*: Justice requires them: There can be no Trade without them. And *Rattle-Snakes* seem the most *suitable Returns* for the *Human Serpents* sent us by our *Mother* Country. In this, however, as in every other Branch of Trade, she will have the Advantage of us. She will reap *equal* Benefits without equal Risque of the Inconveniencies and Dangers. For the *Rattle-Snake* gives Warning before he attempts his Mischief; which the Convict does not. I am, *Yours*, &c. AMERICANUS" (4:133).

The "Water American" (as his fellow printers called Franklin in London) knew from experience the English ignorance and prejudice concerning America and Americans. His resentment against Parliament's Acts of Trade and Navigation appeared in 1729 in both the suppressed addition to "Busy-Body" No. 8 and his pamphlet titled *A Modest Enquiry into the Nature and Necessity of a Paper Currency*. During the 1730s and 1740s, he frequently featured news showing the ignorance and prejudice of the British authorities.[22] Now, however, in 1751, "Jakes on our Tables" and "Rattlesnakes for Felons" vented his fury with the British gentry and authorities—many of whom, of course, did not deserve his outraged disgust.

"Rattlesnakes for Felons" was America's first vicious anti-English satire. More than any earlier American writing, it showed the resentment and outrage caused by the English condescension to and contempt for Americans.[23] The satire was reprinted in the *Boston Gazette*, 21 May; the *Virginia Gazette*, 30 May; and the *Supplement* to Parker's *New York Gazette*, 10 June. Unlike "Jakes on our Tables," "Rattlesnakes for Felons" did not appear in the English magazines; perhaps it was judged too inflammatory.

Franklin's satires on the dumping of transported felons in America changed the American newspaper crime reports. After his 11 April article, most newspapers reported if the criminal was a transported felon; previously, this information was rarely given. Thus the *Maryland Gazette* report of 17 February 1751 of a crime by Newton and Jones did not identify them as transported felons, but after Franklin's 11 April editorial appeared, newspaper editors like Jonas Green of the *Maryland Gazette* called them "Convict Miscreants."

On 5 September 1751, the *Pennsylvania Gazette* printed an "extract" of a letter of 15 August supposedly from Annapolis, which reported that there were "near twenty Persons" currently in the local prison and that "most, if not all of them," were transported felons. The anonymous writer, whom I believe to be Franklin, proceeded with macabre humor: "Our late Law which makes one Convict's Oath good against another Convict, will, I dare say, occasion the Sale of many a Bod-Cord, and the transporting many a Transport into the other World." He mentioned "Perkins and his Gang," an infamous band of criminals on the Virginia frontier, and reported that two recent notorious criminals were going to the frontier to join them. In characterizing the behavior of the frontier

In fome of the uninhabited Parts of thefe Provinces, there are Numbers of thefe venomous Reptiles we call RATTLE-SNAKES ; Felons-convict from the Beginning of the World : Thefe, whenever we meet with them, we put to Death, by Virtue of an old Law, *Thou fhalt bruife his Head.* But as this is a fanguinary Law, and may feem too cruel ; and as however mifchievous thofe Creatures are with us, they may poffibly change their Natures, if they were to change the Climate; I would humbly propofe, that this general Sentence of *Death* be changed for *Tranfportation.*

In the Spring of the Year, when they firft creep out of their Holes, they are feeble, heavy, flow, and eafily taken ; and if a fmall Bounty were allow'd *per* Head, fome Thoufands might be collected annually, and *tranfported* to Britain. There I would propofe to have them carefully diftributed in *St. James's Park,* in the *Spring-Gardens* and other Places of Pleafure about *London* ; in the Gardens of all the Nobility and Gentry throughout the Nation ; but particularly in the Gardens of the *Prime Minifters,* the *Lords of Trade* and *Members of Parliament* ; for to them we are *moft particularly* obliged.

Figure 27. "Rattlesnakes for Felons," Pennsylvania Gazette, 9 May 1751. A month after "Jakes on our Tables!" appeared, Franklin reprinted another series of crimes from other colonial newspapers followed by a "Letter from Maryland," which I suspect Franklin wrote. The letter alluded to the Board of Trade's insult. After the letter, Franklin published a satire, "Rattlesnakes for Felons." The crimes and the letter supplied the context for his vicious satire. In its second paragraph, he burlesqued the common usage of "mother country" to refer to England—an epithet that Franklin transformed into a cruel and evil stepmother. The third paragraph proposed the exchange of rattlesnakes for felons. And the fourth boldly said the snakes should be particularly distributed in the "Gardens of the Prime Ministers, the Lords of Trade and Members of Parliament; for to them we are most particularly obliged." Franklin's ghoulish satire of 12 March 1782, in which he proposed that the scalps taken by the English and their Indian allies be distributed "among both Houses of Parliament: a double Quantity to the Bishops," echoed "Rattlesnakes for Felons."
Like "Jakes on our Tables!," "Rattlesnakes for Felons" was reprinted in the American newspapers. Partially because of "Rattlesnakes for Felons," the rattlesnake became an American icon. Unlike "Jakes on our Tables!," "Rattlesnakes" was evidently considered too outrageous for English periodicals to reprint. Courtesy, Library Company of Philadelphia.

people afraid of Perkins, the author used an unusual comparison—but one that Franklin had voiced twice before: the backwoods people "are forced to humour them, as some *Indians* worship the Devil, for fear he should hurt them."[24]

The 5 September *Pennsylvania Gazette*'s next item reprinted a news notice from the *Boston Weekly News-Letter* of 22 August 1751 that the grand jury there had been discharged because "they have had no Matters of Presentment come before them, so as to offer to the Court." Franklin appended an editorial remark: "*This shews the Difference between Colonies that do not receive Convicts, and those that do.*" Other colonial newspapers reprinted these *Pennsylvania Gazette* items.[25] I speculate that Franklin read the Boston report, thought of reprinting it with an appended note, and then wrote the "Extract of a Letter from Annapolis" to give the Boston piece dramatic effect.

Franklin's reporting of crimes by transported felons, his angry editorial "Jakes on our Tables," the striking satire "Rattlesnakes for Felons," and his follow-up fictitious letters, news reports, and editorial comments all attacked the British authorities for their anti-Americanism. The pieces heightened Americans' awareness of British injustices toward America and of British condescension to and scorn for Americans. Franklin's numerous subsequent sarcastic references in essays and satires to the "IMPROVEMENT *and* WELL PEOPLING" of America prove that the British actions and attitudes continued to infuriate him. The development of Americanism in the colonies received a major impetus from Franklin's writings on transported felons. An immediate influence appeared in William Livingston's long essay against transportation in the New York *Independent Reflector* on 15 March 1753.[26] One might even suspect that by 1751, Franklin believed Britain was driving America to rebellion. His expressions of fury with Britain take on additional importance when read in conjunction with his 1751 essay on demography, trade, and economics— "Observations Concerning the Increase of Mankind."

Assemblyman, 1751

Forming the Association in 1748 made Franklin the most popular person in Pennsylvania. Friends asked him to become a candidate for the Pennsylvania Assembly in 1749, but he declined. The requests continued the next year, Franklin still refusing. When William Clymer, a House of Delegates member from Philadelphia and an Anglican who had worked with Franklin on the militia Association, died just before 26 April 1750, Franklin's supporters again urged him to run. At the beginning of the next session of the Pennsylvania Assembly of 1750–51 (the third session, which met 6–11 May), the sheriff officially informed the assembly on 6 May that Clymer had died. Consequently, the assembly ordered a "Writ for the Sheriff of *Philadelphia*" to conduct an election for a new member.[27]

The 9 May *Pennsylvania Gazette* carried Sheriff Isaac Griffitts's notice that an election to fill the vacancy would be held the next day, 10 May, at the courthouse. Nothing concerning the election is known except that Franklin was elected. Griffitts appeared in the assembly on 11 May to certify Franklin as the new member, but a defect was observed in the form (it had not been signed by a full number of inspectors), and the assembly ordered the sheriff to get the return amended. Since the assembly adjourned that day, Franklin did not take his seat until the fourth and last legislative session, which began on Monday, 12 August, and continued for two weeks through Saturday, 24 August. On 13 August, Franklin "was qualified, and took his Seat in the House accordingly." The same day, William Franklin defeated James Read (who had run against Franklin for clerk in 1748) for the office of clerk of the House and replaced his father.[28] William thus became financially semi-independent, and if he had not done so before, he shortly thereafter moved out of the Franklins' house.

Sessions of Assembly

Except for the two Philadelphia representatives who were elected the following day, elections were held on 1 October (if a Sunday, then 2 October).[29] The first session of the legislature started 14 October (if a Sunday, then 15 October), beginning at 3:00 P.M. Thereafter, meetings were generally held at 10:00 A.M. and 3:00 P.M., and committees met before and after the normal meeting times. The assembly often had just three sessions; in extraordinary years, up to ten sessions. The initial fall session normally lasted only three days. The members were qualified, the clerk and the Speaker of the House were elected, and the governor approved the choice of the Speaker and delivered a short speech calling attention to whatever legislation or problems he wished to present. The Speaker appointed members to the four standing committees and, in some years, to special committees. Then, typically, the assembly, with the concurrence of the governor, adjourned to a specific date during the winter, usually in January or February. If it had pressing business, the assembly would continue in session, and if emergencies occurred before the appointed time for the next session, the governor called an assembly meeting.

The second session of the House considered whatever measures the governor had recommended and took up the petitions to the assembly. Most assembly business originated with a petition. The petitions were read once and then usually ordered "to lie on the Table" for a second reading. After the second reading (on rare occasions immediately after, but usually a day or two later and not infrequently several days later), the petition was sometimes put off "to further Consideration," but often the House took action. The petition might be referred back to the petitioners to bring in a bill, referred to a standing committee to consider and report on it, or referred to a special committee that the Speaker constituted to investigate and to make a recommendation. If the petition presented the possibility of an immediate vote, it might be voted upon. Sometimes a petition was judged not worth considering and dismissed. Except for the brief opening days in October, legislative sessions often concluded with the passage of bills.

The assembly's final session usually occurred in August and attempted to finish whatever business had come before the legislature. It recommended what unfinished business should be taken up by the following assembly. Though the last session entertained new petitions, everyone knew that it was unlikely that new business would be finished in the late summer session. At its end, the assembly made sure that the legislation that had been passed was correctly recorded, and, finally, the assembly settled the year's accounts. After that, the assembly did not dissolve but adjourned until 30 September. That way, it could be recalled if an emergency occurred before the election of the new assembly on 1 and 2 October.

Like today, legislative bodies of colonial governments primarily did their business by committees. The most important person in a colonial (or modern) House of Representatives was the Speaker. He decided what business to take up, in what order, and whom to appoint to the committee. The importance of an individual representative in the legislative processes of government was usually in direct proportion to his number of committee assignments. There were four standing committees. The finance committee oversaw the budget and had more business than any other standing committee. It supervised the Loan Office accounts and the interest arising from them, which was the primary way that the colonial Pennsylvania Assembly financed the government. The finance committee usually had eight members. On the last day of the last session, it presented and settled the accounts for the past legislative year.

The second standing committee was devoted to grievances. It investigated complaints brought before the legislature. Petitions, too, were often referred to it. With considerable business every year, it usually had five members. Third, the committee of correspondence communicated with the assembly's agent in England and with others on behalf of the House. It had three members in the 1750s, always including the Speaker; the other two lived in or near Philadelphia so that they could correspond in a timely manner. The final standing committee, on minutes, had two members. They approved (and sometimes revised) the clerk's minutes before publication. During the early colonial period, the minutes were skimpy; they became fuller as the century moved on. Publication of the "division" (how individual members voted) was still rare in the 1750s.

In addition to the standing committees, the Speaker appointed special ones. The most common special committees in colonial America were those appointed to reply to the governors' messages. A superior writer, Franklin was almost always appointed to those committees. Though most standing and special committees were unexciting, special committees were often responsible for the most important and most disputed pieces of colonial legislation, like the committee on a new paper currency that Speaker Norris appointed in 1751.

Norris appointed Franklin to all four standing committees during his first three years of full service, 1751–54, and then for the three assemblies of 1754–56, he served on three standing committees but not the committee of accounts. Perhaps Franklin told Speaker Norris he would prefer not to continue on it. Though the committee on accounts had the most work of the standing committees, the tasks were in great part routine accounting. The job was exacting, tedious, and time-consuming. And perhaps, since Franklin received money in several different capacities from the assembly (as member, printer, postmaster, plus numerous minor tasks such as translator, purchaser of books, maps, etc.), he preferred not to sit on the committee that approved his pay. Even excluding the standing committees, Franklin served on more committees from 1751 to 1757 than any other representative. Writing Franklin's biographical entry in *Lawmaking and Legislators in Pennsylvania*, Joseph Foster calculated that in these first years as an assemblyman, Franklin had an average of 21.57 committee assignments per term, "nearly twelve and a half more assignments than the average."[30] In 1751, Franklin immediately became, after the Speaker of the House, its most indispensable member.

When the assembly passed a bill, it was sent to the governor for his approval. The governor typically replied that he would consider the bill as soon as he could. Usually within a few days (if the assembly was continuing in session), the governor would either approve it or suggest amendments, though occasionally he would simply reject it. The rare outright rejection killed the bill, for the assembly could not override the governor's veto. If he submitted amendments, the assembly would consider them, sometimes accept some or all of them, and sometimes refuse them. Occasionally, the governor or the Speaker would request a meeting to discuss the bill. A meeting implied that there was room for negotiation. The meeting usually had two persons from the House and two from the governor (usually Secretary Richard Peters and a council member). If they reconciled their differences, both sides approved the result. The governor commonly enacted bills at the end of the session, after a joint committee from the governor and the assembly made sure the engrossed copy was correct. Finally, the approved copy would be deposited in the rolls office, and the governor would send an official copy to England for appraisal—and, hopefully, approval.

Which Party?

Is it a practical question? Were elections in colonial Pennsylvania controlled by political parties? If so, was Franklin in 1750 so popular that he could do without either party? Or was he so popular that both parties claimed him? By the mid-eighteenth century, the Quaker and the Proprietary parties each organized before the elections and put up their strongest candidates. The Quaker intellectual John Smith recorded on 27 September 1750 that he had met with a group of leaders to decide on the "Assembly Ticket." The following day, he recorded that another Quaker Party group had met at Caspar Wistar's and resolved to support him rather than Hugh Roberts for the assembly. Smith, however, refused to try to displace Roberts.

Scholars have differed concerning Franklin's party affiliation when he was elected to the Pennsylvania Assembly.[31] No wonder. He had close friends and associates in both parties and agreed with the Proprietary Party on a key issue of colonial Pennsylvania politics. Led by the proprietaries and the governor, the Proprietary Party included Richard Peters, William Allen, and Franklin's close friends Thomas Hopkinson and William Plumsted. In the 1750s, it had four major positions: (1) it wanted the governor to control the finances, including the interest raised on the lending of paper money; (2) it refused to allow the proprietors' lands to be taxed; (3) it refused to help support the expenses of Indian relations; and (4) it supported giving military aid requested by the crown, though declining to pay a portion of the expense.

The Quaker Party's leaders were Isaac Norris, Speaker of the House, and Israel Pemberton. Not all Quaker Party members were Quakers. Andrew Hamilton, an Anglican and deist, led the Quaker Party as Speaker for all but one year from 1729 through 1749 (*Life* 2:219–26). The Quaker Party differed on the same four positions: (1) the assembly wanted to control the finances, including the interest raised on lending paper currency; (2) it wanted to tax proprietary lands; (3) it wanted the proprietors to support part of the expenses for Indian relations; and (4) on the military, opinion was divided. The moderate majority, led by Isaac Norris, reluctantly supported military expenses when requested but wanted the proprietors to contribute to the cost; the pacifist minority, led by Israel Pemberton, refused to contribute expenses for war—including defensive war.

In contrast to the reluctant moderates and certainly to the pacifists, Franklin believed in defense—and in being prepared for war. As a supporter of defense, he was Pennsylvania's assembly leader, and even its most important leader before becoming an assemblyman. On this crucial issue, he agreed with the Proprietary Party, though some other former and present assemblymen, especially those on the frontier counties, also supported defense. Otherwise, Franklin adhered to the Quaker positions.

His support of defense has caused some scholars to consider him a proprietary partisan. Further, Franklin had a naive streak and wanted to believe that "reasonable, sensible Men can always make a reasonable Scheme appear such to other reasonable Men" (4:118). Consequently he tried to cooperate with proprietary supporters. Before 1751, he had occasionally been disgusted with both parties, writing that each was hypocritically "acting a Farce and playing Tricks to amuse the World" (*Life* 2:350). At various times during the 1730s and 1740s he had expressed contempt for the proprietors and the Proprietary Party.[32] After being elected a member of the House, he hoped that he might be able to bring about agreements between the two parties. He tried to see what a reasonable man might accomplish, but he was almost immediately forced to give it up.

Perhaps more fundamental than specific issues was Franklin's underlying philosophy. The Proprietary Party believed in the prerogatives of the king, the nobility, and other leaders of society, as well as the necessity of hierarchy in society. Its members were generally men of wealth who believed that their rank and class (popular concepts that Franklin scorned) set them apart from the "lower sort." The Proprietary Party was closer to England's Tory Party than to the Whigs. Though the Quaker leaders generally thought that some degree of social hierarchy was necessary, the Quakers were more egalitarian. The Quaker Party was closer to the Whig Party than to the Tories. Franklin's early writings prove that he was heir to the Whig political positions and believed in the "just liberties of the people."[33] A populist, he identified with the common people and sometimes seemed to be prejudiced against not only aristocrats but also extremely wealthy persons.[34] These attitudes, manifested from his earliest writings until his death, revealed that he was more egalitarian than other members of the Quaker Party but far closer to its underlying positions than to those of the Proprietary Party.

Contemporaries who knew Franklin well no doubt realized that he was unsympathetic to the Proprietary Party philosophy. The Proprietary Party leaders, however, had all worked with Franklin on various projects for years, and they knew that people could change. Richard Peters, whom Franklin had ridiculed in 1740 for discriminating between the "better Sort" (the members of the Dancing Assembly) and the "meaner Sort" (the supporters of the Reverend George Whitefield), believed that Franklin would gradually emerge as an administration man. Since Franklin accepted an administrative appointment as justice of the peace for Philadelphia in 1749, the proprietary partisans thought he was changing (*Life* 2:431–32). Thus Peters wrote to Thomas Penn in November 1751 that "Mr. Franklyn I believe woud if it was proper put in his oar but he is naturally very modest & thinks it too soon to open as he is, but a new Member tho' an old Clerk." Peters continued for some time to want to think that Franklin really was "reasonable," that is, held views close to his own, but Peters misjudged.[35] As all Constitutional Convention scholars know, even when he was the oldest delegate, Franklin was more egalitarian than his youngest contemporaries.

Franklin's First Assembly Session, August 1751

Franklin's extraordinary record of service in the Pennsylvania Assembly began the day he took his seat, 13 August 1751. After Franklin was sworn in, the House "took into Consideration the State of the Acts" concerning the transportation of felons to Pennsylvania, and Speaker Isaac Norris assigned Franklin to "a Committee to prepare and bring in a Bill for repealing the Act, entitled, 'A Supplement to the Act, entitled, An Act for imposing a Duty on Persons convicted of heinous Crimes, and to prevent poor and impotent Persons being imported into this Province,' passed in the Year 1749." The future act would be the latest ploy in the cat-and-mouse game that the Pennsylvania legislature had been playing with the British authorities since 1722. The supplemental act merely repealed the act of 2 September 1738, which provided for a successor for the deceased collector of fines. But the underlying motive was to attack the importation of transported felons to Pennsylvania. In view of his ongoing publicity campaign against the transportation of criminals, Franklin was the logical person to assign to the committee.

Since the assembly routinely appointed collectors of the duties without enacting a new bill,[36] why would it bother with this one? A possible reason was, despite the Penns' memorial presented to the assembly in January, to confirm the Pennsylvania act of 1730 imposing a duty on the imported felons. Another possible reason was to have the British strike down all the old acts, as well as this one, which would thereby confirm the British prejudice against America and Americans. That hardly seems to make sense, but it would have repeated Thomas Bordley's actions in Maryland in early 1720s: if the British further revealed scorn and contempt for America, it might so embarrass the British authorities that they might change the policy. On the other hand, if the British reaffirmed the policy, it might outrage all Americans against the British authorities. Perhaps that was what Franklin wanted; or perhaps the policy was just such a festering sore that Franklin and other Americans could not help but scratch.

Franklin acted quickly. The next day, 14 August 1751, the bill was read for the first time; on 15 and 16 August, the second and third times—and unanimously passed. On 21 August, Governor James Hamilton suggested an amendment, which the House agreed to, and on 24 August Hamilton enacted the bill and sent it to Thomas Penn for presentation to the king in council. Penn, however, never presented it.[37] He explained why to Governor Hamilton, who sent Penn's letter to the assembly on 17 October 1752. The letter has not been located (perhaps Penn told Hamilton to allow no copies to be made and to destroy it), but Penn's reasons must have been similar, and perhaps identical to, those he gave when he did not submit the earlier act of 19 August 1749. The act would remind the Board of Trade of the old act of 2 September 1738 imposing a duty on transported felons; the board would repeal the old act; and repealing it would set a precedent for rejecting old acts.

On 15 August 1751, two days after taking his seat in the assembly, Franklin was asked, along with the pacifist Israel Pemberton, to carry a message to Governor Hamilton inquiring whether the proprietaries had agreed to "contribute towards the heavy Charges which are annually brought against the Province, on Account of Indian Affairs." The proprietaries usually controlled the Indian treaties and only they had the right to receive grants of land from Indians, but recently the assembly paid all costs for Indian relations and treaties. Before 1748, the expenses had been small, but they now averaged over £1,000 per year. During the first session of the assembly of 1750–51, on 19 October 1750, the House had pointed out that the benefits the proprietors "reap from the Settlement of their back Lands are very great, and tend peculiarly to the Advancement of their private Properties." The assembly had requested that the proprietors pay a portion of the expense for Indian treaties.[38]

As usual, the proprietors would not part with any money. Governor Hamilton reported their refusal on 16 August 1751: the proprietors "do not conceive themselves under any Obligation to contribute to *Indian* or any other Public Expenses." They claimed that the inhabitants were not taxed "*One Shilling*" for Indian expenses. The proprietors said they were "under no greater Obligation to contribute to the Publick Charges than any other Chief Governor of any of the other Colonies." Trying to get the assembly to drop the issue, they added that "they would have been well pleased to have been freed from the Necessity of giving a disagreeable Answer to any Application upon that Subject." The proprietors did, however, suggest that they would contribute funds toward the support of a "strong trading House" on the frontier.[39]

Franklin must have been outraged by the proprietors' message. He and the assemblymen knew that the comparison to the governors of other colonies was absurd. Royal governors did not purchase land from the Indians for themselves and sell it to the inhabitants. In effect, the proprietors demanded that the assembly pay the cost of making treaties from which the proprietors primarily profited. Of course most of the treaties were also necessary for the frontier settlers, because treaties maintained friendly relations with the Indians. Franklin, along with numerous thoughtful colonists like James Logan, Archibald Kennedy, Cadwallader Colden, and others, knew that the French hoped to dominate the interior of North America. The French wanted to ally themselves with Indian tribes against the English, but the gifts that the English presented to the Indians helped keep the Indians either friendly to the English or neutral in the struggle between France and Great Britain. It was also more convenient and cheaper for most Indian tribes to trade with the numerous English than with the comparatively few French.

The proprietors' refusal angered the assembly. The following day, 17 August, Norris assigned Franklin to a committee "to prepare a Draught of an Answer to the Governor's Messages, and to search the Records and Minutes of the House, and report what they find of the Sentiments of former Assemblies concerning the Expences of *Indian* Affairs," how they have been usually "defrayed, and what Sums" spent "in those Affairs for Twenty Years past." As the former clerk of the House, the printer of its minutes, and the printer of its laws, Franklin knew more about the Pennsylvania Assembly's history than anyone.

Three days later, 20 August 1751, the committee completed the first part of its assignment—the answer to the governor's message. A key position rejected the proprietors' offer of contributing toward building a "strong Trading House" in the Ohio country. Thomas Penn said he would contribute £400 toward its construction and £100 annually toward its maintenance. He did not call it a "fort" because that would have alienated the assembly's pacifist Quakers, but they understood what he intended. Penn had at least two reasons for building a fort. He wanted both to protect the Indian trade and to assert Pennsylvania's possession of the Ohio country from both the French and the Virginians. The French authorities in Canada had sent Captain Céloron de Bienville to the Ohio on 15 June 1751 with more than two hundred men. There he buried lead plates proclaiming the territory part of New France.[40] Virginia's Ohio Company had paid the Indian trader Christopher Gist in 1750 to explore the country. Penn's fort would protect the trade carried on by the Pennsylvania Indian traders and would indirectly claim the western land for the proprietors. Penn specified that, however few men were at the fort, "they should wear an uniform Dress" to look military. Some Quaker Party assemblymen probably suspected that Penn hoped it would be the start of a militia that would become a Penn-controlled military force in the colony—paid for, of course, primarily by the assembly.[41]

Rejecting Penn's offer on behalf of the assembly, Franklin wrote: "we have always found that sincere, upright Dealing with the *Indians*, a friendly Treatment of them on all Occasions, and particularly in relieving their Necessities at proper Times by suitable Presents, have been the best Means of securing their Friendship." The assembly expressed the hope that the proprietors would join them in sharing the cost of Indian expenses. Further, the assembly asserted that some Indian traders were "unfit Persons" and that licenses should not be given to such persons in the future. (Since Pennsylvania's governors charged forty shillings for each license,[42] they sold them to almost anyone who applied.) Finally, the assembly recommended that the next assembly should consider a law for regulating Indian trade and traders "in the Winter Sitting; when the Members are generally most at Leisure to attend closely to publick Business" (4:182–83). Since Franklin had urged fair trade with the Indians in his March 1751 letter to James Parker and Archibald Kennedy, he was probably responsible for the suggestion for a law to regulate the Indian trade.

The committee's second charge was to report on expenses for Indian affairs. Franklin wrote a complete history (not just the previous twenty years) of the House's support, which was read on 22 August. The expenses for Indian relations had been "very inconsiderable" until 1722, when the assembly gave £230 to pay for Pennsylvania's participation in a general treaty at Albany. In 1727, Pennsylvania spent about £70 on Indian affairs, and the assembly paid half, leaving "the rest to be paid by the Proprietary." After that date, the proprietors rarely contributed to Indian expenses. The committee reported that "the generous Allowances" made by the assembly "within four Years past" amounted "to near £5,000." The committee asked the House to determine what proportion of such charges the assembly should pay in the future (4:184–86).

The same 22 August, Franklin presented seven resolutions on Indian expenses, which the House passed unanimously. The second resolve replied to the proprietors' claim that the inhabitants had not been taxed a single shilling for Indian expenses. Franklin contended that though taxes had not been raised "in a formal manner" for defraying "the Charges of Indian Treaties, yet our Excise is really a Tax upon the Province, yielding about *Three Thousand Pounds per Annum* . . . besides the Sums arising upon Licenses, &c. throughout the Province, amounting to very considerable Sums yearly." The assembly had spent a great part of the £3,000 derived annually from the excise taxes on Indian affairs. It also implied that the sums derived from licenses and taken wholly by the proprietors should be partly used for government expenses. The fifth resolve pointed out that the proprietors of Pennsylvania were the "Lords of the Soil" and were more intimately connected with the prosperity of the colony than other governors. The sixth resolve noted that since only the proprietors could buy land from the Indians, they should pay the whole expense of all treaties that were "for Lands only." The seventh resolve said that "the Proprietaries Interests are so constantly intermixt with those of the Province in all Treaties with our Indian Allies" that they should pay "a proportional Part of all such Charges" (4:187–88).

The next day, 23 August, Franklin and a committee urged the proprietors to reconsider their decision. The "Representation" said that though the proprietors were "under no Obligation by Law" to support the Indian treaties, they nevertheless had "Obligations of natural Equity and Justice, to contribute to the Expence." Franklin returned to the Proprietary Party's claim that the inhabitants paid no taxes. While no formal taxes had been paid for the previous several years for the governor's salary or for Indian affairs, "yet the Interest of our Paper Money is a virtual Tax on the People, as it arises out of, and is paid by, their Labour." He repeated that "our Excise is a real Tax, yielding about *Three thousand Pounds per Annum*, which is principally expended in those Services, besides the Tax of Licences of various Kinds, amounting to considerable Sums yearly, which have been appropriated wholly to the support of the Governor" (4:190). Franklin and the assembly had the better arguments, but the proprietors had the power, and Thomas Penn wanted more money from the province. Expenses for Indian treaties would continue to be disputed.

All who knew the actions of individual assemblymen realized that in only two weeks, Franklin had become, after Isaac Norris, the Quaker Party leader. Perhaps Richard Peters and other Proprietary Party members did not at first realize how opposed Franklin was to the proprietors' positions because the "Representation" of 23 August 1751 did not appear in the assembly's *Votes and Proceedings* until 31 December 1754, when it accompanied the first portion of the 1754–55 minutes (4:188n, 5:42). But Franklin's "Resolutions on Expenses for Indian Affairs" of 22 August 1751, published in the *Votes and Proceedings* for 1751, demonstrated his opposition to the proprietors and the Proprietary Party.

SEVEN

The Fundamental Document of the American Revolution, 1751

There is, in short, no bound to the prolific nature of Plants or Animals, but what is made by their crowding and interfering with each others Means of Subsistence. Was the Face of the Earth vacant of other Plants, it might be gradually sowed and overspread with one Kind only; as, for Instance, with Fennel.
—Franklin, "Observations Concerning the Increase of Mankind," 4:233

FRANKLIN'S 1751 MANUSCRIPT "Observations Concerning the Increase of Mankind, Peopling of Countries, &c." (4:227–34) documented the extraordinary population growth in America, portrayed its higher standard of living, and predicted its future greatness. It did not call for independence; it celebrated the British Empire—with America as its future most important part. It showed that the American population, because of the availability of land, was more than doubling every twenty-five years. In contrast, the population of England would not double for more than a thousand years. Franklin predicted that America's population would surpass that of England in a century. It did. In 1850, the United States had a white population of 19,553,068; and in 1851, England and Wales together had a population of 17,900,000.[1]

Despite celebrating the British Empire, "Observations" contained rumblings of discontent with British rule. All who read it carefully realized that if America remained part of the British Empire, the seat of power would move to North America. If it separated from England, it would become a greater empire than Great Britain. "Observations" consists of twenty-four numbered sections, almost all of them short paragraphs of one to three sentences, although one (4:230–31, #13)[2] has six subdivisions. The work has two major theses: (1) people marry and have children when they can afford to do so; and (2) the existence of the American frontier, that is, of land for possible expansion, allowed relatively poor people to start their own farms and possibly to prosper.

BACKGROUND

Educated Americans wanted to believe in the ancient idea of the westward movement of culture and empire. The Greeks liked to think that they were the epitome of civilization, which, they theorized, had begun long ago in the East.

Centuries later, the Romans flattered themselves with the same belief. By the Renaissance, the English had adopted the notion of the westward course of empire (*translatio impereii*), of learning (*translatio studii*), and of religion (*translatio religii*). Sixteenth-century proponents of English colonization—like Richard Eden and Richard Hakluyt—predicted that America would be the next great empire. In "The Church Militant," the seventeenth-century English poet George Herbert wrote the best-known version of the *translatio* idea before the mid-eighteenth century: "Religion stands on tip-toe in our land,/Ready to pass to the *American* strand." Cotton Mather echoed it in the opening of the *Magnalia Christi Americana* (1702).[3]

Franklin used the *translatio* motif in the Library Company directors' address to Thomas Penn in 1733 ("May your Philadelphia be the future Athens of America"), in the "Proposal" for the American Philosophical Society (1743), and in the preface (1744) to James Logan's translation of *Cato Major*. He learned the motif as a boy in Boston. Later, his Junto friend George Webb celebrated the westward movement of civilization in a series of poems written and published in Philadelphia in 1729, 1730, and 1731. Webb's most memorable *translatio* couplet is "Europe shall mourn her ancient Fame declin'd,/And Philadelphia be the Athens of Mankind," which Franklin quoted in August 1753. On 3 September 1730, the *Boston News-Letter* published the "Plymouth Rock Verses," a couplet supposedly found cut into a rock in Plymouth, Massachusetts: "The Eastern World enslav'd, it's Glory ends;/And Empire rises where the Sun descends."[4]

An English minister traveling through the colonies in 1759 and 1760 thought Americans were besotted with the *translatio* idea. He was right. In "Observations" Franklin showed that America was in fact becoming the most populous part of the English-speaking world, thus proving that empire was moving west. Before Walt Whitman's "Passage to India," the greatest expression of the heliotropic movement in the English language was Bishop George Berkeley's "Verses on the Prospect of Planting Arts and Learning in America." Though written in 1726, it was not published until 1752, when the poem immediately became popular, especially in America. Its last stanza said,

> Westward the course of empire takes its way;
> The four first acts already past,
> A fifth shall close the drama with the day;
> Time's noblest offspring is the last.[5]

THE ENGLISH SOURCES OF "OBSERVATIONS"

Six previous English writers on trade and population were especially important sources for Franklin: William Petty (1623–87), whose writings on "political arithmetic" Franklin knew by age sixteen; Edmund Halley (1666–1742), a Renaissance man of his time and a writer on astronomy, population, trade winds, and weather, best known for his discovery of Halley's Comet and his predictions of its return; John Graunt (1620–74), compiler and writer on the bills of mortality; Charles Davenant (1656–1714), writer on trade and mercantilism; Joshua Child (1631–99), writer on trade; and John Cary (d. 1720?), who also wrote on trade and population. At sixteen, Franklin had cited William Petty's 1683 notes on the London bills of mortality in the "Silence Dogood" essay No. 10. Franklin cited Petty again in his 1729 *A Modest Enquiry into . . . a Paper Currency* (*Life* 1:407, 409, 413) and in "The Death of Infants" (*Life* 2:75). After Petty, the major English student of population was Edmund Halley, who began his 1693 "Estimate of the Degrees of the Mortality of Mankind" by noting the shortcomings of Petty's and John Graunt's statistics on the life records of London and Dublin. Halley said that there was no way to estimate how many persons included in the figures immigrated to those cities and that the statistics recorded more deaths than births. He tried to include only natives in his calculations. Franklin followed his recommendation in population studies.[6]

In "Some Further Considerations on the Breslaw Bills of Mortality" (1693), Halley wrote: "the Growth and Encrease of Mankind is not so much stinted by any thing in the Nature of the *Species*, as it is from the cautious difficulty most People make to adventure on the state of *Marriage*, from the prospect of the Trouble and Charge of providing for a Family." As a young man, Franklin made notes on Halley's "Considerations." Franklin's main thesis in "Observations" simply followed Halley (see 4:227, #2). Like Halley, Charles Davenant, *An Essay upon the Probable Methods of Making a People Gainers in . . . Trade* (1699), followed Petty in finding marriage corresponding to the increase of people and celebrated people as "the Strength and Wealth of any Nation."[7]

Halley thought that poor people should not be blamed for their low rate of marriage, since so few "own the Ground that feeds them." Were they able to make a living and marry, "there might well be four times as many Births as we now find." Halley believed that "the Strength and Glory of a King being in the multitude of his Subjects . . . those who have numerous Families of Children [ought] to be countenanced and encouraged by such Laws as the *Jus trium Liberorum* among the Romans."[8] Franklin had copied the Latin phrase in his Junto notes (*Life* 1:344, fig. 23a). An early Junto meeting evidently took up that law and the Roman theories of population. In "Observations," Franklin followed Halley when discussing ownership of land in relation to population and cited the same law, though he denied Halley's belief that laws, without providing additional means, could encourage marriage (4:231, #15).

John Cary's *Essay on the State of England* (1695) contradicted the common notion that emigration had weakened Great Britain. Franklin agreed. Cary argued that colonies benefited Great Britain "as they take off our Product and Manufactures, supply us with Commodities which may be either wrought up here, or Exported again, . . . imploy our Poor, and encourage our Navigation." Cary maintained that "*England* and all its Plantations" were "one great Body, those being so many Limbs or Countries belonging to it, therefore when we consume their Growth we do as it were spend the Fruits of our own Land." Cary is one source of the body/limbs metaphor (a variant of the "Body Politic" metaphor) Franklin often used to represent the whole of the British Empire. The body politic was a common Renaissance political image.[9] Though the metaphor is implicit in the "Mother Country" reference so common in the seventeenth and eighteenth centuries (used in #9; 4:229), it is more fully expressed in the mother/children/ "family" metaphor in #10 (4:229). Franklin's only distinction in using the "Mother Country" imagery is that his usage was so often ironic.

Joshua Child's *New Discourse of Trade* (1698) continued Cary's observation and brought it a step closer to Franklin, for Child claimed that "the employment of those People abroad, do cause the employment of so many more at home in their Mother-Kingdom."[10] Franklin had followed Cary and Child in *A Modest Enquiry into the Nature and Necessity of a Paper Currency* (1729; *Life* 1:404–5). Now in his "Observations," Franklin claimed that "in Proportion to the Increase of the Colonies, a vast Demand is growing for British Manufacturers" (4:229, #10).

THE AMERICAN SOURCES OF "OBSERVATIONS"

In *A Modest Inquiry into the Nature and Necessity of a Paper Currency* (1729), Franklin dealt briefly with population, and during the 1730s, he frequently printed population data in the *Pennsylvania Gazette*. The *General Magazine* for January 1741 carried an "Account of the Export of Provisions from the Port of Philadelphia" from 25 December 1739 to 25 December 1740 and celebrated the Pennsylvanians "who in a few Years have made a Garden of a Wilderness." Because of the food sent from Pennsylvania and the "neighbouring *Provision Colonies*, the British Fleet and Forces in the West-indies are at this Time supplied with Provisions at a moderate Price, while the Enemy is starving . . . which shows that these Colonies give Great Britain a considerable Advantage over its Enemies in an American War, and will no doubt be an additional Inducement to our Mother Country to continue us its Protection" (2:303–4). In "Observations" he repeated the thought about the colonies' help to Britain in its future wars (4:229, #11), and he echoed it on 9 May 1753 (4:486). He knew that the great gains of Parliament had been obtained "by withholding Aids when the Sovereign was in Distress, till the Grievances were removed" (20:280). When he celebrated America's help to England during the 1740s, 1750s, and 1760s, he was covertly suggesting that America could withhold help in the future—until it gained what it wanted from the king and Parliament.

In the spring of 1749, Franklin and his friends surveyed the number of houses in Philadelphia and published the result in the *Pennsylvania Gazette*, where he celebrated Pennsylvania's growth and attributed it to "wholesome Laws with good Government" and to liberty (*Life* 1:242–43). So too, in "Observations," he said that population would increase if there were subsistence and "if the Laws are good" (4:232, #21). During the 1740s, Franklin made

Counties.	Males above 16.	Females above 16.	Males under 16.	Females under 16.	Slaves. Males,	Slaves. Females	Total of Whites,	Total of Slaves,
Middlesex,	1134	1085	1086	956	272	231	4261	503
Essex,	1118	1720	1619	1494	198	177	6644	375
Bergen,	939	822	820	708	443	363	3289	806
Somerset,	967	940	999	867	425	307	3773	732
Monmouth,	1508	1339	1289	1295	362	293	5431	655
Burlington,	1487	1222	1190	996	192	151	4895	343
Gloucester,	930	757	782	676	74	48	3145	122
Salem,	1669	1391	1313	1327	97	87	5700	184
Cape-May,	261	219	271	211	21	21	962	42
Hunterdon,	1618	1230	1270	1170	124	95	5288	219
Totals,	11631	10725	10639	9700	2208	1773	43388	3981
Morris,	1109	957	1190	1087	57	36	4343	93
Hunterdon,	2302	2117	2182	2090	244	216	8691	460
Burlington,	1786	1605	1528	1454	233	197	6373	430
Gloucester,	913	797	786	808	121	81	3304	202
Salem,	1716	1603	1745	1595	90	97	6660	187
Cape-May,	306	272	284	274	30	22	1136	52
Bergen,	721	590	494	585	379	237	2390	616
Essex,	1694	1649	1652	1548	244	201	6543	445
Middlesex,	1728	1659	1651	1695	483	396	6733	879
Monmouth,	2071	1783	1975	1899	513	386	7728	899
Somerset,	740	672	765	719	194	149	2896	343
Totals,	15086	13704	14253	13754	2588	2018	56797	4600

The Number of People in New-Jersey, taken by Order of Government in 1737-8. || Numb. of Ditto, taken in 1745, by Order of Gov. MORRIS.

Note, That Morris and Hunterdon Counties, were both in one, under the Name of Hunterdon, in 1737-8. In 1745, the Number of the People called Quakers in New-Jersey, was found to be 6079 ; no distinct Account was taken of them in 1737-8. Total of Souls in 1737, 47369 ; Ditto in 1745, 61403 ; Increase 14034. Query, At this Rate of Increase, in what Number of Years will that Province double its Inhabitants ?

Figure 28. New Jersey population data, Poor Richard Improved . . . for 1750. *Franklin made notes on population data during the 1730s and 1740s. By 1749, he noted that the American population was growing more rapidly than any other for which he had information. In the fall of 1749, he published some population numbers in the prefatory material to* Poor Richard *for 1750. For New Jersey figures, Franklin gave its total population in 1737 as 47,369; its total in 1745 as 61,403; and the difference as 14,034. He asked, "At this Rate of Increase, in what Number of Years will that Province double its Inhabitants?" Or, how long would it take for the population of 47,369 to become 94,738? For Franklin and other Americans, the population statistics proved that America would become a greater empire than England.*

Most readers would not rise to Franklin's mathematical challenge. The New York intellectual Archibald Kennedy (who lived primarily in Newark, New Jersey) was interested in geopolitics, including population and the American Indian. Kennedy answered the question in his Observations on the Importance of the Northern Colonies *(1750). He said that the New Jersey population would double "in less than twenty-four years."*

Kennedy probably used the simple and naive math that I would have. First, dividing the 14,034 growth in population in eight years by the 1737 figure of 47,369 yields a 29.627 percent population growth. Second, multiplying the 1745 population of 61,403 by 29.627 percent = 18,192, the eight-year increase to 1753. Third, adding the 1745 population of 61,403 to the 18,192 increase gives 79,595 as the population in 1753. Fourth, multiplying the 1753 population of 79,595 by 29.627 percent = 23,582 = the increase to 1761. Fifth, Kennedy added 79,595 and 23,582, which equals 103,177, the projected population in 1761, which meant that the population would more than double in less than twenty-four years.

The better mathematicians among Franklin's readers, however, like Thomas Godfrey or Theophilus Grew (or my consultant, the mathematician Paul C. Pasles), would calculate that the population was growing at 3.297 percent a year, so the 61,403 population would actually double in less than twenty-one and a half years. Courtesy, Library Company of Philadelphia.

manuscript copies of the censuses of New Jersey, and in the fall of 1749 he printed the data in *Poor Richard* for 1750.[11]

Franklin challenged the reader. Most readers, of course, would not attempt to answer. Those who accepted the challenge would probably estimate that in eight years the population had grown by 29 percent, so in less than twenty-four years, it would double. The better mathematicians among his readers, like Thomas Godfrey or Theophilus Grew, would calculate that the population was growing at 1.032 percent a year, so the 61,403 population would double in less than twenty-one and one half years.

In the same *Poor Richard* for 1750, Franklin also gave population statistics from Philadelphia and Boston. Franklin observed that, though the "Colonies on the [European] Continent" doubled in population every thirty years, immigration was the primary cause of their increase: "What the natural Increase of Mankind is, is a curious Question." He cited the population of Breslaw, the same city that Halley used, which had a population of about 34,000 and an annual increase of 64 people. He asked "how long it will be" before the population doubled itself. In settled countries like England, where persons cannot find work, they do not marry. In a pessimistic, Malthusian/Hobbesian note, Franklin said that the "Overplus must quit the Country, or they will perish by Poverty, Diseases, and want of Necessities." Those who find they can barely scrape by, do not marry because they cannot "see how they shall be able to maintain a Family" (3:440, 441).

In 1750, New York's Archibald Kennedy took up the imperial problems facing the British in North America. Though mainly concerned with Indian relations as a key to English power in America, Kennedy's *Observations on the Importance of the Northern Colonies* also considered colonial America's population. Inspired by the 1750 *Poor Richard*, Kennedy used Edmund Halley's statistics and remarks on population and contrasted Halley's population statistics with Franklin's. Kennedy answered Poor Richard's question: in New Jersey, "by an Increase in this Proportion, the Inhabitants will be doubled in less than twenty-four years." Evidently Kennedy used the relatively simple (and inaccurate) math that I would have. Then he estimated that the mainland colonies doubled in population every thirty years: "If this is the Case, we shall soon become powerful States; and the more powerful we grow, still the more People will flock hither." Kennedy echoed Poor Richard's thought and even his diction: "and here is Room, Business, and full Employ for all, and Millions yet unborn."[12] Though Frederick Jackson Turner's frontier thesis has numerous anticipations, Franklin's "Observations" was perhaps the earliest—and the only one more influential.[13]

Like Franklin, Archibald Kennedy criticized the Acts of Trade and Navigation. He said that "all restraining Laws" were "Oppression," especially laws that "the colonists have had "no Hand in the contriving or making." Kennedy predicted that the colonies would soon "interfere in the Manufactures of *Great-*

> It has been computed in *England*, that the Colonies on the Conti-
> nent, taken one with another, double the Number of their Inhabitants
> every Thirty Years. This quick Increase is owing not so much to
> natural Generation, as the Accession of Strangers.----What the natu-
> ral Increase of Mankind is, is a curious Question. In *Breslaw*, the
> Capital of *Silesia*, a healthy inland City, to which many Strangers
> do not come, the Number of Inhabitants was found to be gene-
> rally about 34,000. An exact Register is kept there of the Births and
> Burials, which taken for 30 Years together, amount, as follows,
>
>
>
> Births *per Annum*, - - - - 1238
> Deaths *per Annum*, - - - - 1174
>
> Yearly Increase but - - - 64
>
>
> let the expert Calculator say, how long it will be, before by an In-
> crease of 64 *per Annum*, 34,000 People will double themselves?
>   Yet I believe People increase faster by Generation in these Colonies,
> where all can have full Employ, and there is Room and Business for
> Millions yet unborn. For in old settled Countries, as *England* for In-
> stance, as soon as the Number of People is as great as can be supported
> by all the Tillage, Manufactures, Trade & Offices of the Country, the
> Overplus must quit the Country, or they will perish by Poverty, Dif-
> eases, and want of Neceffaries. Marriage too, is difcouraged, many de-
> clining it, till they can fee how they fhall be able to maintain a Family.

Figure 29. Population growth in Europe and America, Poor Richard Improved . . . *for* 1750. *At the end of the population data from Boston, New Jersey, and Philadelphia, Franklin observed that though the European colonies doubled in population every thirty years, their increase was primarily caused by immigration. He then stated, "What the natural Increase of Mankind is, is a curious Question." He cited the population of Bres-law, the same city that Edmund Halley had used in his 1693 population studies. It had a population of about 34,000 and an annual increase of 64 people. Franklin asked, "let the expert Calculator say, how long it will be" before the Breslaw population doubled itself.*

Franklin's point was that "people increase faster by Generation in these Colonies, where all can have full Employ, and there is Room and Business for Millions yet unborn." In settled countries like England, where persons cannot find work, they do not marry. In a Malthusian comment, Franklin said that the "Overplus must quit the Country, or they will perish by Poverty, Diseases, and want of Necessities." Those who find they can barely scrape by, do not marry because they cannot "see how they shall be able to maintain a Family" (3:440, 441).

Trying to answer Franklin's mathematical question, a naive calculator, like me, will see that since 64 x 500 = 32,000, at that exact rate of increase, it would take a little more than 531 years for the population to reach 68,000. However, after one year the population would be 34,064 and after two, 34,128, and so on. In other words, an "expert Calculator" would take into account the changing base. One way to do this is to find the rate of growth per year: 64 divided by 34,000 = 0.0018824. Using logarithmic tables, which eighteenth-century mathematicians would usually own, one would find that it would take 368.57 years.

But the mathematician Paul C. Pasles pointed out another twist. One does not really know that the population of Breslaw grew at the rate of 64 persons per year, only that it increased over a particular thirty-year period from 32,080 to 34,000, an increase of 1,920 people (64 x 30 = 1920). That is a thirty-year gain of nearly 5.99 percent (1920 divided by 32,080). The annual rate of increase is the thirtieth root of 1.059850374, around 1.00193947. Thus the annual rate of increase is 0.1939 percent. At that rate, it would take 357.74 years, approximately eleven years less than the method a less suspicious "expert Calculator" would choose. Courtesy, Library Company of Philadelphia.

Britain, and supply ourselves." Franklin contradicted Kennedy in "Observations" and denied that America would soon interfere with British manufacturing.[14] Franklin, however, was writing primarily for an English audience. The first known reference to "Observations" shows Franklin sending it to Richard Jackson, the Pennsylvania Assembly's English agent. I suspect Franklin believed that American industry could detract from England's, but an English audience would resent the thought and want to impose more Acts of Trade and Navigation. Later, writing William Shipley of the Royal Society of Arts in 1755, Franklin characterized "Observations" as being written in reply to the English "Jealousies" of the colonies, "which were formerly entertained by the Mother Country." Franklin hoped that these prejudices were subsiding and sent Shipley a copy of his "Observations" because it tended to "show that such Jealousies with Regard to Manufactures, were ill-founded" (6:276).

During the winter of 1750/1, Archibald Kennedy drafted *The Importance of Gaining and Preserving the Friendship of the Indians to the British Interest*. At Kennedy's request, James Parker, who printed the tract later that year, sent Franklin the manuscript. He replied on 20 March 1750/1, agreeing with Kennedy that securing the friendship of Indians was of the greatest importance to the English colonies. Franklin took up several topics including the union of the colonies, the immigration of large numbers of Germans into Pennsylvania, and the population of America. Twice as many immigrants from Great Britain could have come to the colonies, he claimed, "without lessening the Number of People at Home." Following Cary and Child, Franklin claimed that Britain had not lost people by emigration: "When all Employments are full, Multitudes refrain Marriage, 'till they can see how to maintain a Family." The letter to Kennedy anticipated his statement in "Observations": at England's present rate of increase, its population would not double in five hundred years. On the other hand, if half the English population "were taken away and planted in America, where there is Room for them to encrease, and sufficient Employment and Subsistence; the Number of Englishmen [the total number in the colonies and in England] would be doubled in *100 Years*: For those left at home, would multiply in that Time so as to fill up the Vacancy, and those here would at least keep Pace with them" (4:121).

In "Observations" (4:233, #22), Franklin again argued that the increase of American population would also increase Egland's population because of its concomitant increase of trade and manufacturing. Earlier that year (May 1751), Kennedy printed Franklin's letter at the end of his *Importance of . . . the Indians*. Besides anticipating some of Franklin's thoughts in "Observations" on the relation between the American population and the British Empire, Franklin's letter revealed that as of 20 March 1750/1, Franklin had a plan for unifying the colonies.

THE THESES AND IRONIES OF "OBSERVATIONS"

"Observations Concerning the Increase of Mankind, Peopling of Countries, & c." dismissed previous demographic scholarship. Based on cities and established countries, the old studies would not "suit new Countries, as America (4:227, #1). Franklin's basic thesis was that population increased in proportion to marriages, and marriages occurred when persons could afford them (#2). He backed the proposition with two observations. First, the cost of living is more expensive in cities; fewer people there marry and have children (#3). Second, fully settled countries have an abundance of laborers and thus pay less for labor than do new countries. Lower pay means fewer marriages and fewer children (4:227–28, #4).

Following William Petty, John Locke, and Montesquieu, Franklin referred to the socioeconomic theory of the four stages of civilization (the hunter/gatherer, the shepherd/husbandman, the gardener/farmer, and those in trade and manufacturing); each succeeding stage needed less land for subsistence.[15] Persons in the latter three stages occupied Europe, but hunters/gatherers primarily occupied America (#5). Abundant cheap land in America available for farming led to earlier and more marriages and thus more children (4:228, #6). Franklin gave the surprising statistic: "And if it is reckoned there [in Europe], that there is but one Marriage per Annum among 100 Persons, perhaps we may here reckon two; and if in Europe they have but 4 Births to a Marriage (many of their Marriages being late) we may here reckon 8, of which if one half grow up, and our Marriages are made, reckoning one with another at 20 Years of Age, our People must at least be doubled every 20 Years" (4:228, #7). Herein Franklin echoed and explained his statement in *Poor Richard* for 1750—America had "Room and Business for Millions yet unborn" (3:441).

In a second major thesis, Franklin said that since labor was more expensive in America than in England, America could not compete with English manufacturing. Despite the increase of population, "so vast is the Territory of North-America, that it will require many Ages to settle it fully; and till it is fully settled, Labour will never be cheap here, where no Man continues long a Labourer for others, but gets a Plantation of his own." Labor is no cheaper now in Pennsylvania "than it was 30 Years ago, tho' so many Thousand labouring People have been imported" (4:228, #8). Therefore the colonies could not really interfere with the "Mother Country in Trades that depend on Labour, Manufactures, &c." (4:229, #9).

Franklin claimed that as the population increased in the colonies, so did the demand for British manufactures. He had made the point in *A Modest Inquiry* (1729): "And since a Plentiful Currency will be so great a Cause of advancing this Province in Trade and Riches, and increasing the Number of its People; which, tho' it will not sensibly lessen the Inhabitants of Great Britain, will occasion a much greater Vent and Demand for their Commodities here" (1:147). So in "Observations," he wrote that the demand "will increase in a short Time even beyond her Power of supplying, tho' her whole Trade should be to her Colonies." Britain should not, therefore, "too much restrain Manufactures in her Colonies." Franklin implied that if England did "restrain" colonial manufacturing, either the colonies would buy the goods elsewhere (England's longstanding enemy, France, was the obvious alternative) or the future powerful colonies will become independent. Franklin, however, was trying to convince his British audience without threats: "A wise and good Mother will not do it. To distress, is to weaken, and weakening the Children, weakens the whole Family" (4:229, #10).

A major underlying thesis of "Observations" was the future independence of America. It had been predicted several times in the sixteenth century, frequently in the seventeenth, and commonly in the eighteenth, but Franklin, like other politically sensitive Americans, denied that America desired independence.[16] (To say they did would only augment English anti-Americanism.) Instead of suggesting that the British authorities were alienating Americans and driving them to rebellion, he turned the British mercantile argument on its head. If, because of the increasingly large American market, Britain's goods rose higher in price than those of other countries, "Foreigners who can sell cheaper will drive" British merchants and goods from foreign markets. Thus "Foreign Manufactures will thereby be encouraged and increased, and consequently foreign Nations, perhaps her Rivals in Power," will grow "more populous and more powerful; while her own Colonies, kept too low, are unable to assist her, or add to her Strength" (4:229, #11). What a clever stroke! In the future, the dutiful child America would like to be able to continue assisting England but will be kept from doing so by the Acts of Trade and Navigation.

Returning to the statement that labor is more expensive in America, Franklin rejected the "ill-grounded Opinion that by the Labour of Slaves, America may possibly vie in Cheapness of Manufactures with Britain." Slaves, he said, are more expensive in America than laborers in England. Franklin gave the mathematics of purchasing and owning slaves and added two remarks, the latter of which is racist: the first referred to loss by the slaves' "Neglect of Business (Neglect is natural to the Man who is not to be benefited by his own Care or Diligence)" and the second to the pilfering by slaves, "almost every Slave being by Nature a Thief." Why then, Franklin asked, do Americans purchase slaves? "Because Slaves may be kept as long as a Man pleases, or has Occasion for their Labour; while hired Men are continually leaving their Master (often in the midst of his Business,) and setting up for themselves" (4:229–30, #12).

The next three sections, #13, 14, and 15, were not specifically concerned with America, though they were on the topic of the "increase of mankind." Since the increase of people depended on marriages and marriages depended on the possibility of supporting a family, a nation may lose population (#13) in any of six ways:

(1) "Being conquered; for the Conquerors will engross as many Offices, and exact as much Tribute or Profit on the Labour of the conquered, as will maintain them in their new Establishment," thus lowering the standard of living of the natives and consequently discouraging their marriages.

(2) "Loss of Territory." Franklin instanced Wales, where, after being driven out of England, the Welsh were "crowded together in a barren Country insufficient to support such great Numbers" and therefore "diminished 'till the People bore a Proportion to the Produce" (4:230). Gerald Stourzh suggested that, in an undercurrent, Franklin "had in mind . . . the feeling of encirclement, the fear of suffocation by the gigantic French Empire in the back of the colonies."[17]

(3) "Loss of Trade." Exports draw goods from foreign countries, and those in the production and transportation of goods "are thereby enabled to marry and raise Families." If no "Employment is found for the People occupy'd in that Branch," the nation will soon be deprived of so many people.

(4) "Loss of Food." Suppose a "Nation has a Fishery, which not only employs great Numbers, but makes the Food and Subsistence of the People cheaper." If it loses the fishery, "the People will diminish in Proportion as the Loss of Employ, and Dearness of Provision, makes it more difficult to subsist a Family."

(5) "Bad Government and insecure Property. People not only leave such a Country . . . but the Industry of those that remain being discourag'd, the Quantity of Subsistence in the Country is lessen'd, and the Support of a Family becomes more difficult. So heavy Taxes tend to diminish a People" (4:230–31). Franklin implied that the Acts of Trade and Navigation were examples of "Bad Government and insecure Property," but he did not openly say so in "Observations." He did imply, however, that "Bad Government and insecure Property" were reasons for America to become independent.

(6) "The Introduction of Slaves." In the West Indies, poor whites were deprived of employment because of the importation of slaves, "while a few Families acquire vast Estates; which they spend on Foreign Luxuries, and educating their Children in the Habit of those Luxuries; the same Income is needed for the Support of one that might have maintain'd 100." The slaves themselves were ill fed and forced to work excessively, so that "their Constitutions are broken, and the Deaths among them are more than the Births." Franklin commented that "Slaves also pejorate the Families that use them; the white Children become proud, disgusted with Labour, and being educated in Idleness, are rendered unfit to get a Living by Industry."[18] He implied that the same conditions prevailed in the southern mainland colonies, and he next

observed that "The Northern Colonies having few Slaves increase in Whites" (4:231).

From the decrease of mankind, Franklin turned to its increase and indirectly scorned the common celebration of the military hero.[19] "The Prince that acquires new Territory . . . the Legislator that makes effectual Laws for promoting of Trade, increasing Employment, improving Land by more or better Tillage; providing more Food by Fisheries; securing Property, &c.; and the Man that invents new Trades, Arts or Manufactures, or new Improvements in Husbandry, may be properly called Fathers of their Nation, as they are the Cause of the Generation of Multitudes, by the Encouragement they afford to Marriage" (#14). As noted above in discussing Halley's influence, Franklin refuted the possibility of increasing population by "Privileges granted to the married, (such as the *Jus trium Liberorum* among the Romans)." Such laws could help fill a country "thinned by War or Pestilence, or that has otherwise vacant Territory; but cannot increase a People beyond the Means provided for their Subsistence" (4:231, #15).

Franklin had repeatedly opposed the mercantilist principle of colonial subordination as manifested in the Acts of Trade and Navigation, but he had not yet become a thorough supporter of free trade, of the idea of laissez-faire.[20] He wrote that "Foreign Luxuries and needless Manufactures imported and used in a Nation . . . increase the People of the Nation that furnishes them, and diminish the People of the Nation that uses them." Laws that prevent importation and promote exportation of manufactures "may be called . . . generative Laws, as by increasing Subsistence they encourage Marriage. Such Laws likewise strengthen a Country, doubly, by increasing its own People and diminishing its Neighbours" (4:231–32, #16). In "Observations," he did not object to imported goods in general, only to those "Luxuries and needless Manufactures" that made up a considerable part of commerce. The next section made clear one particular objection. Nations should forbid the consumption of East India goods, "for the Gain to the Merchant, is not to be compar'd with the Loss by this Means of People to the Nation" (4:232, #17).

Franklin was inconsistent. Although he objected to the importation of what he considered superfluities, he supported free trade. In 1747 he disapproved of Connecticut's "selfish Law" imposing duties on goods imported from other colonies. Such duties were really a tax on the people of Connecticut, and he suggested that the duties might cause the neighboring colonies to pass their own "selfish" laws, which would hurt Connecticut (3:150–51).

Taking up luxury, Franklin agreed with the Enlightenment thinker Bernard Mandeville,[21] saying that "Home Luxury in the Great, increases the Nation's Manufacturers employ'd by it, who are many, and only tends to diminish the Families that indulge in it, who are few." Then he added an all-important caveat, "The greater the common fashionable Expence of any Rank of People, the more cautious they are of Marriage. Therefore Luxury should never be suffer'd to become common" (4:232, #18). Franklin was right. In the twenty-first century, the American standard of living is comparatively luxurious, and, without immigration, its population would hardly be growing. Franklin also observed that the "great Increase of Offspring in particular Families, is not always owing to greater Fecundity of Nature, but sometimes to Examples of Industry in the Heads, and industrious Education; by which the Children are enabled to provide better for themselves, and their marrying early, is encouraged from the Prospect of good Subsistence" (#19). Finally, if a particular religious sect prizes "Frugality and Industry as religious Duties, and educate their Children therein, more than others commonly do; such Sect must consequently increase more by natural Generation, than other" religious groups (4:232, #20).

Of immigration and emigration, Franklin wrote that immigration "into a Country that has as many Inhabitants as the present Employments and Provisions for Subsistence will bear; will be in the End no Increase of People; unless the New Comers have more Industry and Frugality than the Natives, and then they will provide more Subsistence, and increase in the Country; but they will gradually eat the Natives out." The violent diction "eat the Natives out" suggests cannibalism. It recalls the Hobbesian/Malthusian tone of the 1750 *Poor Richard* on population: the "Overplus must quit the Country, or they will perish by Poverty, Diseases, and want of Necessities." Perhaps he had in mind the Pennsylvania Germans, whom he observed in March 1751 could "under-live, and are thereby enabled to under-work and under-sell the English" (4:120).

Nor was it necessary to bring in immigrants "to fill up any occasional Vacancy in a Country; for such Vacancy (if the Laws are good, #14, 16) will soon be filled by natural Generation." Franklin pointed out that there was now no "Vacancy" in Sweden, France, or other countries "by the Plague of Heroism 40 Years ago"—nor in France by the expulsion of the Protestants; nor in England, by the settlement of her colonies (4:232–33, #21). In this last example, he contradicted most English writers on emigration. In effect, he argued that emigration from a country would not itself decrease population, nor will immigration into a country increase it. Other factors were more important.

The discussion of emigration and immigration ended the essay's logical development. Franklin had introduced pessimistic notes in the two references to war (heroes) and in the reference to famine ("eat the Natives out"), but now he viciously undercut the common theory that "great numbers of people are the riches of a nation." People, like animals and plants, can and will increase until they have ruined themselves: "22. There is, in short, no bound to the prolific nature of Plants or Animals, but what is made by their crowding and interfering with each others Means of Subsistence. Was the Face of the Earth vacant of other Plants, it might be gradually sowed and overspread with one Kind only; as, for Instance, with Fennel; and were it empty of other Inhabitants, it might in a few Ages be replenish'd from one Nation only; as, for Instance, with Englishmen" (4:233, #22). That statement calls humans one more animal species that will multiply until they are so numerous that they will starve (and eat) one another. Nothing like it appeared in any of Franklin's sources, and it does not make entirely good sense in Franklin's "Observations," for he has already shown that luxury, national characteristics, religion, and culture are among the factors that may limit population.

An underlying theme of "Observations" is Franklin's burlesque of the high estate of mankind. People—the riches of the nation? Franklin turns that commonplace on its head. Blindly reproducing until they crowd and interfere with one another's subsistence and starve one another? Franklin ridicules the idea that humans enjoy a special rank between animals and angels. No other eighteenth century writer was so often and so vicious a satirist of the high estate of mankind—and of God. Not only in the great satires from 1765 to 1790, but even in early writings like the *Dissertation on Liberty and Necessity* (1725), "Lying Shopkeepers" with replies by a shopkeeper and a merchant (1730), "On Censure or Backbiting" (1732), "The Death of Infants" (1734), "The Murder of a Daughter" (1734), "Advice to a Pretty Creature and Replies" (1735; see *Life* 2:134–36, 165–66, 75–79, 151–53, 147–48, respectively)—and dozens of later pieces, including "An Apology for the Young Man in Gaol" (1743), and "The Speech of Miss Polly Baker" (1747)—Franklin repeatedly satirizes mankind—and himself. As he concluded the *Dissertation* in 1729: "Mankind naturally and generally love to be flatter'd: Whatever sooths our Pride, and tends to exalt our Species above the rest of the Creation, we are pleas'd with and easily believe, when ungrateful Truths shall be with the utmost Indignation rejected. 'What! bring ourselves down to an Equality with the Beasts of the Field! with the meanest part of the Creation! 'Tis insufferable!' But, (to use a Piece of Sense) our *Geese* are but *Geese* tho' we may think 'em *Swans*; and Truth will be Truth tho' it sometimes prove mortifying and distasteful" (1:71).

Why is fennel chosen as the plant that would overspread the planet? Citing *Hamlet* and *Paradise Lost*, Douglas Anderson has answered: "In the allegorical herbarium, fennel is an emblem of jealousy and flattery."[22] These unsavory characteristics of mankind are not found in other animals, with the probable exception of those closest to human beings, apes and monkeys; and if Franklin thought of that, it only added to the underlying satire.

Franklin returned to the population of America. He had showed that the statistics suggested that the white population was doubling every twenty years (4:228, #7). Now he placed the doubling at twenty-five years (4:233, # 22)[23] but expressed his pleasure in America's increasing numbers—and, consequently, its increasing power. Given its context, one suspects that Franklin may be satirizing himself for his Americanism—and for his anti-English feelings. Though he frequently mocked himself, he delighted in the future glory of America, and he wanted it to excite the reader. He changed the tone from that of a pedagogical treatise to an enthusiastic appreciation: "Thus there are suppos'd to be now upwards of One Million English Souls in North-America, (tho' 'tis thought scarce 80,000 have been brought over Sea) and yet perhaps there is not one the fewer in Britain, but rather many more, on Account of the Employment the Colonies afford to Manufacturers at Home. This Million doubling, suppose but once in 25 Years, will in another Century be more than the People of England, and the greatest Number of Englishmen will be on this Side of the Water. What an Accession of Power to the British Empire by Sea as well as Land! What Increase of Trade and Navigation! What Numbers of Ships and Seamen!" (4:233, #22).[24]

Franklin celebrated the growth of America as part of the British Empire, not as a possible future independent state. Nevertheless, the main underlying thesis of "Observations" suggested a future independent America. After predicting that the population of America would be greater than that of the British Isles in one hundred years, he continued, "We have been here but little more than 100 Years, and yet the Force of our Privateers in the late War, united, was greater, both in Men and Guns, than that of the whole British Navy in Queen Elizabeth's Time." Franklin repeated this observation from the *Pennsylvania Gazette* of 30 August 1744. He was suggesting that when the American population outnumbered that of the English, the American navy, "both in Men and Guns," would be larger than the English navy. America would rule the seas.

At first, the sentence that followed the comment on the British navy seems puzzling: "How important an Affair then to Britain, is the present Treaty for settling the Bounds between her Colonies and the French, and how careful should she be to secure Room enough, since on the Room depends so much the Increase of her People?" (4:233, #22). What was the point of the comment after the British authorities had, to the frustration and chagrin of the Americans, given back Fort Louisbourg, Cape Breton, and other areas of Canada to the French?[25] Franklin was reminding the reader that the British had chosen to keep enemies within easy striking distance of the Americans. The treaty reference implied that the British tried to curtail the growth of the American colonies even though doing so would encourage the growth of a traditional enemy nation. To Franklin, returning Cape Breton, like the Acts of Trade and Navigation (4:229, #9), was an instance of bad government (4:230, #13, parts 2 and 5). The reference to the treaty (4:233, #22) indirectly warned that Americans were disgusted with British policies.

Franklin compared a nation well regulated to "a Polypus; take away a Limb, its Place is soon supply'd; cut it in two, and each deficient Part shall speedily grow out of the Part remaining. Thus if you have Room and Subsistence enough, as you may by dividing, make ten Polypes out of one, you may of one make ten Nations, equally populous and powerful; or rather, increase a Nation ten fold in Numbers and Strength." The polyp seemed to be something between a plant and an animal. The unpleasant connotations of a polyp (which was primarily found in stagnant, stinking waters) undercut the idea of a nation and even, perhaps, the idea of mankind being something between an animal and an angel. And under British rule, America was not "well regulated." Because the proprietors were always eager to sell plots of land (and because their secret instructions hamstrung the governor), Pennsylvania was in a worse political situation than other colonies. Over the previous thirty years the German population had increased from less than 10 percent to perhaps 45 percent of Pennsylvania's population. Franklin next wrote a prejudiced comment about the great number of German emigrants into Pennsylvania: "why should the Palatine Boors be suffered to swarm into our Settlements, and by herding together establish their Language and Manners to the Exclusion of ours? Why should Pennsylvania, founded by the English, become a Colony of Aliens, who will shortly be so numerous as to Germanize us instead of our Anglifying them, and will never adopt our Language or Customs, any more than they can acquire our Complexion" (4:233–34, #23).

Naturally, the ethnocentric remarks would be held against him. They should be, even if he was mocking himself and giving himself as an example of the common prejudice of Pennsylvanians of English descent. Further, one might see in the diction "Anglifying" a reference to angels and to Franklin's ridicule of the high estate of mankind.

Franklin concluded with a racist comment:

the Number of purely white People in the World is proportionably very small. All Africa is black or tawny. Asia chiefly tawny. America (exclusive of the new Comers) wholly so. And in Europe, the Spaniards, Italians, French, Russians and Swedes, are generally of what we call a swarthy Complexion; as are the Germans also, the Saxons only excepted, who with the English, make the principal Body of White People on the Face of the Earth. I could wish their Numbers were increased. And while we are, as I may call it, Scouring our Planet, by clearing America of Woods, and so making this Side of our Globe reflect a brighter Light to the Eyes of Inhabitants in Mars or Venus, why should we in the Sight of Superior Beings, darken its People? why increase the Sons of Africa, by Planting them in America, where we have so fair an Opportunity, by excluding all Blacks and Tawneys, of increasing the lovely White and Red?

The "Superior Beings" are the angels, who are supposedly as far above the estate of mankind as humans are the estate of animals. But, as Douglas Anderson noted, Mars and Venus represent war and lust.[26] Mars recalls the two earlier references to king-heroes as worse than plague and alludes to 2 Samuel 24:12–13.

The "lovely White and Red" could have ended "Observations," but Franklin added one more sentence. He shifted the point of view, just as he did at the end of part 2 of the *Autobiography*, where he changed from a Lockean reality to an Olympian perspective that viewed his own actions, as well as humanity's in general, with irony—and some scorn. The characteristic shift in perspective occurred often, for example in "An Apology for the Young Man in Gaol" (1743),

"The Speech of Miss Polly Baker" (1747), and "The Ephemera" (1778).[27] Here in 1751, the final sentence ended on a note of ironic satire—primarily on himself but also on humans: "But perhaps I am partial to the Complexion of my Country, for such Kind of Partiality is natural to Mankind" (4:234, #24).

Ironic skepticism appeared throughout the essay. "Observations" celebrated America as part of the British Empire, but at the same time Franklin predicted that America's population would be greater than that of the British Isles in a century and that an American city would become the future capital of the empire. But the underlying possibility of American rebellion and independence recurred several times. "Observations" celebrated people as the riches of a nation, but Franklin also suggested that the extraordinary growth of population would ultimately lead to competition for sustenance, widespread famine, and cannibalism. He subtly travestied the idea of people as the riches of a nation when he undercut the idea of the high estate of mankind and suggested negative characteristics of humans. In comparison to Franklin, the eighteenth century's best-known skeptic, David Hume, seems almost naive in discussing demography.[28]

REVISIONS AND INFLUENCE

Concluding a chapter on Franklin's writings (*Life* 2:81–82), I observed that Franklin often wrote for an audience of one—himself.[29] That was the case with the first version of his "Observations." Four years later he allowed it to be printed, and that first version is the text that appears in the *Papers of Benjamin Franklin* and so is reprinted in other collections. But the version that was popular during his life and for the next two hundred years was the text that first appeared in *The Interest of Great Britain Considered* (1760). The satire of humanity and the self-satire were too subtle for a general audience—and the suggestions of rebellion and independence were too bold. Franklin dropped the anti-German remarks in #23, omitted the whole of #24 with its racist sentiments, and changed the racist remark in #12 from "almost every Slave being by Nature a Thief" to "almost every Slave being from the Nature of Slavery a Thief." Franklin's earlier remark on slaves probably had the same meaning. Immediately before it, he had mentioned the "Neglect of Business" by slaves, and explained that "Neglect is natural to the Man who is not to be benefited by his own Care or Diligence."

Franklin also omitted the rumblings of revolt and independence in the last two sentences of #10 and omitted all of #11. Those in #10 said: "Therefore Britain should not too much restrain Manufactures in her Colonies. A wise and good Mother will not do it. To distress, is to weaken, and weakening the Children, weakens the whole Family," and #11: "Besides if the Manufactures of Britain (by Reason of the American Demands) should rise too high in Price, Foreigners who can sell cheaper will drive her Merchants out of Foreign Markets; Foreign Manufactures will thereby be encouraged and increased, and consequently foreign Nations, perhaps her Rivals in Power, grow more populous and more powerful; while her own Colonies, kept too low, are unable to assist her, or add to her Strength" (4:229).

Franklin evidently thought these suggestions of revolt and independence would contradict the primary purposes of the Canada pamphlet, *The Interest of Great Britain Considered*, which argued that Britain should retain Canada rather than the Sugar Islands at the conclusion of the French and Indian War. In the Canada pamphlet, Franklin reassured the English that Americans were loyal and did not envision becoming independent. He said that the growth of the colonies would not "render them *dangerous*." Numerous conflicts and jealousies between the colonies showed that they would not unite with one another. Finally, however, he said in the Canada pamphlet that England might drive the colonies to rebel: "When I say such an union is impossible, I mean without the most grievous tyranny and oppression. People who have property in a country which they may lose, and privileges which they may endanger; are generally dispos'd to be quiet; and even to bear much, rather than hazard all. While the government is mild and just, while important civil and religious rights are secure, such subjects will be dutiful and obedient. The waves do not rise, but when the winds blow" (9:90–91).

Similar warnings concerning bad government occur in "Observations," but Franklin wanted to downplay the implied threat of rebellion in both the 1751 "Observations" and in the 1760 Canada pamphlet. Therefore he omitted the most direct statements of America's unhappiness with the British authorities when reprinting "Observations." He allowed, however, the reference in #22 to the Treaty of Aix-la-Chapelle to remain.

CIRCULATION

Before "Observations" appeared in the summer of 1755, it circulated in manuscript in England and America. Though composed in 1751, the specific day and even the month are unknown. Sometime in 1751, Richard Jackson asked Franklin for an account of the number of Palatines who had come to Pennsylvania during the previous decade. When he replied, Franklin enclosed "a sheet or two on the subject of peopling of countries" (4:388). Neither Jackson's nor Franklin's letters are extant. Jackson loaned the manuscript to Peter Collinson, who wrote Franklin on 3 June 1752 to say that it greatly entertained him and Jackson and that Jackson was writing Franklin about it. Collinson wrote Franklin again on 27 September 1752, wishing that Franklin would oblige "the Ingenious part of Mankind with a publick View of your Observations."

The manuscript circulated widely in New England. Franklin told Dr. John Perkins of Boston on 13 August 1752 about "a small paper of *Thoughts on the peopling of Countries*, which, if I can find, I will send you, to obtain your sentiments." Franklin sent it to him in September (4:319–20, 341, 359). Perkins replied on 16 October 1752 that he thought the essay should be "well considered" by every Englishman who had the "power and Ability to promote the Nation's Interest." Franklin also gave a copy to his brother John Franklin, for on 2 January 1753 he asked John what he thought of the essay (4:358, 409). Before Franklin sent a copy to the Reverend Jared Eliot in Connecticut, he mentioned to Eliot on 3 May 1753 that he hoped to have the comments of both Eliot and the Reverend Jonathan Todd (4:474). Franklin probably did not have time to make the dozen or more copies sent to various people in 1751 and 1752. The logical scrivener was Lewis Evans. He had worked for Franklin for approximately twenty years, had recently copied 155 pages of Franklin's letters on electricity (3:117), and had engrossed the "Articles of Association" for the Philadelphia Contributionship for the Insurance of Homes (4:282). Besides being Franklin's primary clerk in the early 1750s, Evans was as interested in the essay as any Franklin contemporary.

Evidence of its circulation in Philadelphia turns up in an oration given by a teenager at the Philadelphia Academy. In the fall of 1753, young John Morris, Jr., gave a speech on the occasion of the academy's receiving a charter. He praised Franklin as the president of the Board of Trustees and declaimed, "May we not be indulged in the partiality to think that Philadelphia may become an Ornament and Protection to it's Mother Country. How prodigious is it's Growth."[30] Morris echoed Franklin's opinion that America would become more populous than England and that, if America did not become independent, the future capital of the British Empire would be in America. The opinion that the seat of empire would move to America became well-known in the pre-Revolutionary period.[31]

After the New York intellectual and politician Cadwallader Colden heard of "Observations" and requested a copy, Franklin sent it on 6 December 1753. When Colden returned it on 13 February 1754, he said that he agreed with John Bartram: the only criticism he had was the final paragraph concerning the "darkening" of America by the importation of slaves. Colden, however, objected more to the placing of the sentiment at the end than the thought itself and would have preferred that it appear "somewhere in the middle." Only Colden's reference reveals that Bartram had also read the manuscript.

Dr. Perkins or some other Boston friend gave copies to Massachusetts governor William Shirley and to Dr. William Clarke. When Franklin was in Boston at the end of 1754, he and Shirley exchanged letters, and Shirley asked him to read Clarke's manuscript titled "Observations on the late and present Conduct of the French." Like Franklin, Clarke argued that if the French gained control of North America, Great Britain would become a lesser power than France. Shirley requested Franklin to allow his "Observations" to be printed with Clarke's pamphlet. Franklin suggested that Clarke reorganize the contents of his essay and agreed to append his "Observations" (5:456, 6:217).

The Virginian Daniel Fisher, who worked for Franklin as a clerk for several weeks in June 1755, recorded in his diary on 13 and 14 June that he made several copies of "Observations." It circulated among other English savants besides Jackson and Collinson. The anonymous English author of *State of the British and French Colonies in North America* (London: A. Millar, 1755) echoed it in the second section of the second letter of his pamphlet. The pamphlet appeared in London in April, four months before Clarke's pamphlet with Franklin's "Observations" was published in Boston on 21 August and eight months before it was reprinted in London in December.[32] No doubt Dr. John Mitchell (who often saw Peter Collinson at the Royal Society) heard of it before its publication and read it.

EFFECTS

In July 1755, a month before "Observations" was published, Franklin and Hall printed Lewis Evans's *Geographical . . . Essays . . . Containing an Analysis of a General Map of the Middle British Colonies in America.* At the end of his commentary, Evans celebrated the Ohio country, calling it "as great a Prize, as has ever yet been contended for, between two Nations." (The year before, George Washington had surrendered his small force of Virginia militia to the French at Fort Necessity.) Evans understated the size and population of the colonies in order to emphasize that there was no danger of them becoming independent of their "Mother Country." He warned, however, that "repeated and continued ill Usage, Infringements of their dear-bought Privileges, sacrificing them to the Ambition and Intrigues of domestic and foreign Enemies" may provoke the colonies "to do their utmost, for their own Preservation." Like Franklin, he used the body metaphor to describe the relation between the colonies and other parts of Great Britain: "But while they are treated as Members of one Body, and allowed their natural Rights, it would be the Height of Madness for them to propose an Independency, were they ever so strong."[33]

Evans suggested that if the French were not driven out of America, the colonies might, at some time in the future, join with them, which "would be the only Article that would render any Attempt of Independency truly dangerous." For that reason, Evans claimed, "it becomes those who would regard the future Interest of Britain and its Colonies, to suppress the Growth of the French Power, and not the English, in America."[34] The thought echoed Franklin's criticism of the 1748 treaty with France (4:233, #22). The following year, Dr. Samuel Johnson in London reviewed Evans's *Essays.* Johnson quoted Bishop Berkeley's poem on the westward course of empire and conceded that "some great electrical discoveries were made at Philadelphia." Johnson granted that Evans showed the "absurdity" of the suspicions that Americans intended to become independent, but he bristled because Evans "does not omit to hint at something that is to be feared if they are not well used." Johnson found the idea ridiculous: "let us not be frightned by their threats, they must be yet dependent, and if they forsake us, or be forsaken by us, must fall into the hands of France." Johnson was responding to Franklin's thoughts on the future growth of America and its possible future rebellion as they came filtered through the prose of his disciple, Lewis Evans.[35]

Sometime before 1775, Johnson read Franklin's "Observations" and alluded to it in *Taxation No Tyranny*. In a canceled passage at the end of the pamphlet, Johnson wrote that the number of Americans were "at present not quite sufficient for . . . greatness . . . ; but by Dr. Franklin's rule of progression, they will in a century and a quarter be more than equal to the inhabitants of Europe. When the Whigs of America are thus multiplied, let the princes of the earth tremble in their palaces. If they continue to double and double, their own hemisphere will not long contain them." Franklin's "Observations" thus drew forth both Johnson's alarm and his scorn, both indirectly (through Evans) and directly.[36]

Five weeks after the publication of Franklin's "Observations" in Boston, John Adams read it and wrote in a letter of 12 October 1755: "Soon after the Reformation a few people came over into this new world for Conscience sake. Perhaps this (apparently) trivial incident, may transfer the great seat of Empire into America. . . . our People according to the exactest Computations, will in another Century, become more numerous than England itself." Adams's statements on the increase of American population and on American sea power echo Franklin. Adams said that since the colonies had "all the naval Stores of the Nation in our hands, it will be easy to obtain the mastery of the seas, and then the united force of all Europe, will not be able to subdue Us."[37]

Rereading his letter in 1807, Adams claimed that it proved that he made a "declaration of independence in 1755, twenty-one years" before Jefferson's. Adams predicted that the letter would "make a distinguished figure in the memoirs of my life." Had Adams really forgotten that he had read Franklin's famous "Observations" in 1755—and no doubt seen it in print since? Writing Benjamin Rush early in 1807, Adams bragged that he could "boast of my declaration of independence in 1755." Rush, intending no irony, replied on 12 May 1807: "What would not the biographers of Franklin and Washington give for such an early specimen of reflection and foresight? It would have served to elevate them above the rank of prophets. . . . Your letter shall not perish."[38] Rush, too, who had been befriended by Franklin and earlier considered himself a disciple, very probably had read Franklin's "Observations," but by 1800, he had become a bit of a sycophant to Adams.

Another New Englander influenced by Franklin's "Observations" was the Reverend Ezra Stiles, who had honored Franklin with an Latin oration on 5 February 1755. Franklin probably gave him a manuscript copy, but Stiles may only have known it from Clarke's pamphlet or from its periodical publications. It roused Stiles's interest in demography, and he used it in his *Discourse on the Christian Union*, a sermon preached at a convention of the Rhode Island congregational clergy on 23 April 1760. Inspired by Franklin, Stiles noted on his title page that "Four Thousand British Planters settled in New-England, and in

120 Years their Posterity are increased to five hundred thousand Souls." Stiles's purpose was to prove that the New England Congregationalists were increasing faster than persons of other religions and that they would come to dominate America. He cited Franklin's statistic from "Observations" that the population doubled every twenty-five years as well as Franklin's statement from the Canada pamphlet that "in fact there has not gone from Britain to our colonies these 20 years past to settle there, so many as 10 families a year."[39] The quotation proves that Stiles revised his sermon before its publication, for Franklin's Canada pamphlet (*The Interest of Great Britain Considered*) was not published until 17 April 1760. Stiles could not have read it before June 1760.

What was the effect of Franklin's "Observations" on the British authorities? It made them even more concerned about the possible future independence of America than they had been. Unless Britain retarded the growth of America's population and its manufacturing, the colonies would inevitably grow. Therefore, Britain tried to prevent it. One effort was the Proclamation of 1763, which forbade colonial expansion over the Appalachians. The other effort was to impose further Acts of Trade and Navigation. Ironically, in England, "Observations" helped "justify the restrictive policies it sought to eliminate."[40]

In America, "Observations" helped create the Revolution. Numerous historians, from George Bancroft in the pre–Civil War period, to C. W. Alvord in the early twentieth century, to Marc Egnal in the late twentieth century, have argued that most leaders of the American Revolution were expansionists (i.e., persons who believed that America would become a populous and prosperous great empire). Washington, Jefferson, Adams, Franklin, and other Revolutionary War leaders certainly were.[41] Many expansionists, however, remained loyal to Britain. The obvious example in a biography of Franklin is his son William. In the late summer and early fall of 1748, he had journeyed west of Pittsburgh to attend an Indian treaty at Logstown on the Ohio River.[42] He kept a journal and made notes on the longitude and latitude of various towns, which Franklin no doubt read.[43] Franklin's description of the Ohio country as among the "finest" lands in North America for its "extreme richness and fertility" reflected William's admiration for the Ohio (5:457). William Franklin, however, saw that land in the primary way that Franklin presented it in "Observations"—as a part of a great British Empire.

No, it was not necessary to be an expansionist to be a Revolutionary. It helped, however, to sustain one's faith in the American Revolution if one believed that America would become a more populous, more wealthy, and larger empire than England could ever be. Every author of that characteristic poetic genre of the Revolutionary period, "the future glory of America," relied on the *translatio* idea for literary authority and on Franklin's "Observations" for demographic and geographic realities.[44] Benjamin and William Franklin prove that elements of character, personality, personal experience, and ideology had more to do with the decision to be a patriot or a loyalist than expansionism or even politics. I suspect that Franklin's and William's views of the English attitudes toward Americans were as important as demography. What Franklin thought of the English attitudes we have seen in "Jakes on our Tables."

After its publication in the Boston and London editions of William Clarke's *Observations on the Late and Present Conduct of the French* (1755), "Observations" appeared in the *Gentleman's Magazine* (November 1755), the *Scots Magazine* (April 1756), and the *American Magazine* (1758) before being reprinted in revised form in the six editions of Franklin's *Interest of Great Britain Considered* (1760 and 1761). Though the initial printings in Clarke's pamphlet were anonymous, the author was named in the magazines. The revised text also appeared in the *London Chronicle* (20 May 1760), the *Annual Register* (1760), and in the fourth edition of Franklin's *Experiments and Observations on Electricity* (1769). Barbeu Dubourg included it in his translation of John Dickinson's *Letters from a Farmer in Pennsylvania* (1769). Naturally it also appeared in the various collections of Franklin's works, beginning with Dubourg's edition of Franklin's *Oeuvres* (1773) and with Benjamin Vaughan's edition of Franklin's *Political, Miscellaneous and Philosophical Pieces* (1779).

Cerebrel/Visceral: Franklin and the British Empire, 1751

Scholars have often denied that "Observations" had anything to do in Franklin's mind with the future independence of America. That opinion ignores its context in Franklin's life and writings.[45] He composed it only a few months after writing several vicious anti-British editorial notes and a satire on the transportation of felons to America. The differences between the generally detached tone of "Observations" and the angry denunciations of Great Britain's treating America as a penal colony may partially account for the usual scholarly opinion. "Observations" was judicious, restrained, and cerebral; "Jakes on our Tables" and "Rattlesnakes for Felons" were furious, outraged, and visceral. "Observations" proved that America was becoming a great empire and only suggested its discontents; "Jakes" and "Rattlesnakes" proved that America was angry with Great Britain and had reason to rebel. "Observations" was written for intellectuals and sent to England in manuscript in a hope to influence British imperial policy; "Jakes" and "Rattlesnakes" were published in American newspapers to arouse Americans against Britain's unjust treatment of America and against British supercilious condescension toward Americans. "Observations" circulated widely in manuscript between 1751 and 1755 and was published more than a dozen times between 1755 and 1775 and often thereafter; "Jakes" and "Rattlesnakes" were published several times in the 1751 newspapers but not afterward, though Franklin later frequently quoted or alluded to the Board of Trade's insult.[46] "Observations" became Franklin's best-known non-belletristic writing and his most influential political piece; "Jakes" and "Rattlesnakes" were the most direct and savage anti-British expressions by any American before 1765.

Historians have paid far less attention to "Jakes" and "Rattlesnakes" than to "Observations." Nineteenth- and twentieth-century editions of Franklin's writings did not publish "Jakes" before it appeared in volume 4 (1961) of *The Papers of Benjamin Franklin*—and there it is a footnote (4:131). One can understand why most previous historians have ignored it. However, the two vicious anti-British pieces are present implicitly and, to some degree, explicitly in "Observations." The bitter statements concerning the "Mother Country" and the body metaphor in "Jakes" and in "Rattlesnakes for Felons" are echoed in the ironic connotations of the same metaphors in "Observations." The opposition between the two kinds of writings are different sides of the same coin. One attempted to appeal to British intellectuals and political leaders in order to change the British policies peacefully; the other attempted to arouse the American public against the discrimination and condescension of the British policies.

The other important context for "Observations," as Paul W. Connor suggested, was the unity of Pennsylvania and the unity of the colonies.[47] In *Plain Truth* (1747) Franklin argued for the unity of the classes and the regions of Pennsylvania—and made anti-British allusions. In the early 1751 letter to James Parker on Archibald Kennedy's manuscript, Franklin proposed a limited unification of the colonies, which he amplified in the Albany Plan of 1754. Had he no thoughts of the unity of the colonies or of his anti-British writings when composing "Observations"?

Even if one does persevere in the belief that "Observations" was initially (1751) meant only to celebrate the British Empire, one must concede that for many Americans in the pre-Revolutionary period (1765–75), it supplied a fundamental reason for believing that Revolution could be successful. Conversely, for Franklin, who learned from his Uncle Benjamin Franklin that "warres" bring "scars" (1:4), the longer one could put off a possible war of independence, the more one could be certain that America would win the war. And if one could hold off long enough, America would win the war without a life being lost. The future capital of the British Empire would be in America. The facts and the vision expressed in "Observations" allowed Franklin to write the Massachusetts House of Representatives on 7 July 1773: "A little Time must infallibly bring us all we demand or desire, and bring it us in Peace and Safety" (20:283). And on the same day he wrote his old friend Samuel Mather: "*Power* does not infer *Right*; and as the Right is nothing and the *Power* (by our Increase) continually diminishing, the one will soon be as insignificant as the other" (20:288).

But the shots fired at Lexington and Concord ended his hope for peace.

EIGHT

The Pennsylvania Hospital

A Beggar in a well regulated Hospital, stands an equal Chance with a Prince in his Palace, for a comfortable Subsistence, and an expeditious and effectual Cure of his Diseases.
—"Appeal for the Hospital," 8 August 1751, 4:153

FRANKLIN'S FRIEND DR. THOMAS BOND, a fellow Freemason and Library Company member, decided to establish a Pennsylvania hospital early in 1750.[1] Unlike today's hospitals, eighteenth-century ones were primarily "for the Reception and Cure of poor sick Persons, whether Inhabitants of the Province or Strangers." The middle class and wealthy persons paid for care in their own homes. Bond did not, at first, engage Franklin in the project. He "was zealous and active in endeavouring to procure subscriptions for it; but the Proposal being a Novelty in America, and at first not well understood, he met with small Success" (A 122). Several hospitals for the poor had been started in the British Isles but none in America.[2]

Failing to raise sufficient funds, Bond turned to Franklin late in 1750: "he came to me, with the Compliment that he found there was no such thing as carrying a public Spirited Project through, without my being concern'd in it; 'for, says he, I am often ask'd by those to whom I propose Subscribing, Have you consulted Franklin upon this Business? and what does he think of it? And when I tell them that I have not, (supposing it rather out of your Line) they do not subscribe, but say they will consider of it.'" Like Bond, Franklin had read of the public charity hospitals. Twenty years earlier, on 25 March 1731, Franklin had written a newspaper essay, "Compassion and Regard for the Sick," as part of his frequent campaign to do good, and now a possible project might fulfill that desire. He thought Bond's project "very beneficent," resolved to subscribe himself, and joined Bond in soliciting funds.[3] Franklin misremembered the sequence of events. He wrote in the *Autobiography* in 1788 that before making the solicitations, he "endeavoured to prepare the Minds of the People by writing on the Subject in the Newspapers, which was my usual Custom in such cases" (A 122). Bond, however, had already been asking for donations and Franklin at first simply joined him. Franklin's newspaper entreaties appeared later.

Bond and Franklin met with some success, but subscriptions lagged, and Franklin proposed petitioning the assembly for support. Bond agreed, Franklin drew up the petition, had a number of friends (including such wealthy Philadelphians as William Allen and William Branson) sign it, and presented it on 23 January 1751. The petition portrayed the plight of lunatics and the "sick or distempered" poor and requested funds to build a small hospital, "with Power to receive the charitable Benefactions of good People towards enlarging and supporting it" (5:285–86).

The legislators were dubious. Some thought the expenses for physicians would "eat up the whole of any Fund that could be reasonably expected to be raised" (5:286), and others from outside Philadelphia thought it would "only be serviceable to the City, and therefore the Citizens [of Philadelphia] should alone be at the Expence of it." Drs. Thomas and Phineas Bond and Lloyd Zachary overcame the first objection by guaranteeing to attend the hospital *gratis* for three years. Franklin replied to the second, that the proposal "met with such Approbation as to leave no doubt of our being able to raise £2000 by voluntary Donations." The assembly members, however, considered the claim a "most extravagant Supposition, and utterly impossible" (A 122).

The First Matching Grant

"On this," wrote Franklin, "I form'd my Plan." He requested permission from the House to bring in a bill for incorporating the contributors to the hospital and granting it a sum of money. The members agreed because "the House could throw out the Bill if they did not like it." The bill began with the traditional "Whereas" clauses—the first one combining practicality, compassionate humanity, and religion: "Whereas the saving and restoring useful and laborious Members to a Community is a Work of publick Service, and the Relief of the Sick Poor is not only an Act of Humanity, but a religious duty." Franklin wrote the bill "so as to make the important Clause a conditional One, viz. 'And be it enacted by the Authority aforesaid That when the said Contributors shall have met and chosen their Managers and Treasurer, shall have raised by their Contributions *a Capital Stock of £2000 Value* . . . and make the same appear to the Satisfaction of the Speaker *of the Assembly*,'" then the Speaker will "'sign an Order on the Provincial Treasurer for the Payment of Two Thousand Pounds in two yearly Payments, to the Treasurer of the said Hospital, to be applied to the Founding, Building and Finishing of the same'" (A 123).

On 1 February 1750/1, the condition carried the bill through the assembly. Franklin shrewdly, if caustically, judged that "the Members who had oppos'd the Grant, and now conceiv'd they might have the Credit of being charitable without the Expence, agreed to its Passage." On 7 February, the House passed the bill unanimously. Governor James Hamilton reviewed it and returned it with some amendments on 7 May, all but two of which the House accepted; and on 11 May 1751, Hamilton, who had reservations about the bill, nevertheless approved it. Rejecting it would have made him appear to oppose allowing private persons and the government to be charitable.[4]

The *Pennsylvania Gazette* published the proposed matching grant on 6 June 1751. For the next six weeks, Franklin and Dr. Thomas Bond redoubled their efforts. The condition, wrote Franklin, worked both ways, for now "in soliciting Subscriptions among the People we urg'd the conditional Promise of the Law as an additional Motive to give, since every Man's Donation would be doubled. . . . I do not remember any of my political Manoeuvres, the Success of which gave me at the time more Pleasure. Or that in after-thinking of it, I more easily excus'd my-self for having made some Use of Cunning" (A 123).

By 27 June 1751 more than £1,500 had been raised, and the *Pennsylvania Gazette* announced that though it was impossible to apply to everyone for funds, "a Subscription Paper is left at the Post-Office, where Attendance will be given to receive the Subscriptions of all desirous of promoting so good a Work." The *Gazette* also said that the following Monday, 1 July, the hospital managers would be elected at three in the afternoon at the statehouse: "All concerned are desired to attend." Besides Franklin and Thomas Bond, the persons elected managers included Joshua Crosby, a Quaker merchant; Hugh Roberts, Franklin's close friend and a Junto member; Samuel Rhoads, another close friend, builder, and architect; the Quaker intellectual John Smith; and the Proprietary Party stalwart Richard Peters. William Allen, who had subscribed for the largest amount, £150, probably asked not to be elected a manager (5:327).

Those elected managers met at the Widow Pratt's Royal Standard Tavern on 2 July and agreed to ask the proprietors for a plot of ground. On Friday, 5 July, they "viewed several Lots about the town." They liked best "one between 9th and 10th Streets on the south side of Mulberry Street." Calling on Governor Hamilton, the managers told him they intended to appeal to the proprietors for a lot, and asked him to back their request. Hamilton replied that he would not. Later that day, he wrote Thomas Penn that he thought if Penn intended to give them anything, it should be a grant of money. Several subscribers, he said, had each given £100 pounds.[5]

The next day, 6 July, the managers elected the Quaker merchant Joshua Crosby president of the board and elected Franklin clerk "until another shall be appointed." Richard Peters drafted an appeal to the proprietors, "recommending the Hospital to their generosity." At the same time, Israel Pemberton wrote two influential London Quakers, asking them to deliver the appeal to Penn and to back it with their support. The managers met again that afternoon to sign the letter and agreed to meet the first Thursday of every month at 5:00 P.M. Peters, Samuel Hazard, and Pemberton said they would solicit funds from wealthy persons who had not yet contributed.[6]

When the managers met on 12 July, they appointed Franklin and Thomas Bond a committee to prepare a seal for the hospital. In his 1731 "Compassion and Regard for the Sick," Franklin had used the parable of the Good Samaritan and the sick man, and would use it again in his 8 August 1751 "Appeal for the Hospital."[7] Franklin probably suggested the device and the motto and asked the

Figure 30a. *The original seal of the Pennsylvania Hospital. Franklin cited the parable of the Good Samaritan and the sick man in his* Pennsylvania Gazette *essay of 25 March 1731, "Compassion and Regard for the Sick." Twenty years later, when the hospital trustees asked him and Dr. Thomas Bond on 12 July 1751 to have a seal made for the hospital, Franklin thought of the parable of the Good Samaritan. He asked the Boston engraver James Turner, who had engraved the drawings of the Pennsylvania fireplace in 1744, to submit designs for the seal, using the parable. Turner submitted four, and the managers accepted one, with a small alteration. The seal showed the Good Samaritan with a sick man on the Samaritan's horse turning him over to an innkeeper while saying: "TAKE CARE OF HIM AND I WILL REPAY THEE." Courtesy, the Pennsylvania Hospital.*

Boston engraver James Turner,[8] who had engraved the drawings of the Pennsylvania fireplace in 1744, to submit designs for it. Turner submitted four, and the managers accepted one, with a small alteration. It showed the Good Samaritan with a sick man on the Samaritan's horse turning him over to an innkeeper while saying: "TAKE CARE OF HIM AND I WILL REPAY THEE."

Before midsummer, the managers had pledges for £2,000 and presented them on 1 August to the House Speaker, Isaac Norris. They requested the assembly's contribution. Norris, however, said that since he was personally responsible, he must have legal notes that the subscribers who had not yet actually given money would in fact pay. Thereupon the managers called a subscribers' meeting for 8 August. Franklin no doubt had the penal bonds printed for persons to sign who could not immediately pay. On 16 August the speaker informed the House "that the Contributors to the Pennsylvania Hospital, had made it appear to his Satisfaction, that they had complied with the Terms of the late Act of Assembly." The bonds for £2,000 were laid before the House. The Speaker, "with the unanimous Consent of the House, signed an Order on the Trustees of the Loan-Office, for the Payment of Two Thousand Pounds to the Treasurer of the said Hospital, One Thousand Pounds on demand, and the Remainder in Twelve Months."[9]

Figure 30b. A sketch of the original seal. Since the original is worn, cracked, and difficult to decipher, Nian-Sheng Huang has sketched it.

APPEAL FOR THE HOSPITAL

Subscriptions had come in before August from personal solicitations, but now Franklin attempted a public call. On 8 and 15 August 1751 the *Pennsylvania Gazette* featured his "Appeal for the Hospital." After a seemingly classical epigraph that Franklin probably made up ("Good Deeds survive one's death, and Virtue which is eternal, / Does not fear it will be carried off by the Stygian waters") and a biblical one (Matthew 25:36: "I was sick, and ye visited me"), the anonymous author/Franklin said that all species of animals are susceptible to disease. Though everything alive "is liable to Death," humans have the greatest number of illnesses; perhaps "they are the Effects of our Intemperance and Vice, or are given us, that we may have a greater Opportunity of exercising towards each other that Virtue, which most of all recommends us to the Deity, I mean Charity." Christ, "whose Life should be the constant Object of our Imitation . . . always shew'd the greatest Compassion and Regard for the Sick." He visited and comforted "the meanest of the People" and inculcated "the same Disposition in his Doctrine and Precepts to his Disciples" (4:148–49).

Franklin's religious persona, ostensibly a minister, viewed humanitarian acts as, in great part, religious duties. He instanced "that beautiful Parable of the Traveller wounded by Thieves" whom the Samaritan aided. When the Samaritan left him at the inn, he gave the innkeeper money and promised to pay whatever addition the innkeeper spent. Franklin contrasted the Samaritan with Dives, the rich man, who neglected to comfort and assist his helpless neighbor full of sores. As Franklin paraphrased and quoted Luke 16:19–23, he made the text more dramatic by adding a local colloquialism: Dives might have revived and restored his neighbor with "the Crumbs that fell from his Table, or, as we say, *with his loose Corns.*" But Dives did not. Christ consequently saved the Samaritan and condemned the rich man. Franklin wrote: "I was Sick, and ye *Visited me,* is one of the Terms of Admission into Bliss, and the Contrary, a Cause of Exclusion." Help to the needy sick person is, Franklin said, "essential to the true Spirit of Christianity" (4:148–49).

Franklin's well-known saying, "Nothing in life is certain, except death and taxes" has a final, ironic touch. Franklin, however, often voiced the uncertainty of life. In the appeal for the hospital, he used uncertainty as a premise to emphasize the necessity for all men to love one another: "We are in this World mutual Hosts to each other; the Circumstances and Fortunes of Men and Families are continually changing; in the Course of a few Years we have seen the Rich become Poor, and the Poor Rich; the Children of the Wealthy languishing in Want and Misery, and those of their Servants lifted into Estates, and abounding in the good Things of this Life. . . . our present State, how prosperous soever, hath no Stability, but what depends on the good Providence of God" (4:149). That fall, compiling *Poor Richard,* Franklin repeated the thought: "Kings have long Arms, but Misfortune longer: Let none think themselves out of her Reach" (4:247).

Another opinion Franklin often voiced was that a person could do greater good by joining with others: "But the Good particular Men may do separately, in relieving the Sick, is small, compared with what they may do collectively." That was why, in England and Scotland, hospitals for the sick poor have been found "exceedingly beneficial, as they turn out annually great Numbers of Patients perfectly cured, who might otherwise have been lost to their Families, and to Society." They were being established in the larger cities of Europe, "where generally the most skilful Physicians and Surgeons inhabit" (4:150).

In addition to religious and humanitarian appeals, the speaker emphasized the practical benefits of hospitals. Hospitals will make physicians more expert and will help train young ones, which, in turn, would be good for the community: "the Multitude and Variety of Cases continually treated in those Infirmaries, not only render the Physicians and Surgeons who attend them, still more expert and skillful, for the Benefit of others, but afford such speedy and effectual Instruction to the young Students of both Professions, who come from different and remote Parts of the Country for Improvement, that they return with a more ample Stock of Knowledge in their Art, and become Blessings to the Neighbourhoods in which they fix their Residence" (4:150). That reason may well be original. In addition, Franklin here addressed in a minor way the concern that some representatives voiced that the hospital would only benefit Philadelphians.

In "The Appeal, Part Two," Franklin again used a classical epigraph, this one from Cicero, whom he often echoed: "In nothing do men more nearly approach divinity than in doing good to their fellow men." He reinforced it with a Christian thought: "To visit the Sick, to feed the Hungry, to clothe the Naked, and comfort the Afflicted, are the inseparable Duties of a christian Life."

He claimed that Christianity had a "real Effect on the Conduct of Mankind, which the mere Knowledge of Duty without the Sanctions Revelation affords, never produc'd among the Heathens." Only in Christian states were "publick Funds and private Charities . . . appropriated to the building of Hospitals, for receiving, supporting and curing those unhappy Creatures, whose Poverty is aggravated by the additional Load of bodily Pain." Franklin named the locations of a number of "large and commodious Infirmaries" in Great Britain, and quoted Daniel Defoe's praise of hospitals from *A Tour thro' the Whole Island of Great Britain* (4:151).

Dropping the ministerial voice, the anonymous speaker wrote that the increase of "poor diseas'd Foreigners and others" in distant parts of Pennsylvania, "where regular Advice and Assistance cannot be procured, but at an Expence that neither they nor their Townships can afford," has aroused a number of humane persons "to procure some more certain, effectual and easy Methods for their Relief." (Here Franklin again countered the argument that the hospital would benefit only Philadelphia and claimed that the demand originated outside the city.) These humane citizens had presented a memorial to the House of Representatives, which passed a bill, "without one dissenting Voice, giving *Two Thousand Pounds* for building and furnishing a Provincial Hospital, on Condition that two Thousand Pounds more should be rais'd by private Donations." Since then, Philadelphians had heartily promoted the design and raised more than the two thousand pounds necessary. He now hoped that persons living in the country would contribute (4:152–53).

Franklin turned to a practical economic argument. It cost more than ten times as much to nurse and cure the sick in private homes as in a hospital: "For Instance, suppose a Person under the Necessity of having a Limb amputated, he must have the constant Attendance of a Nurse, a Room, Fire, &c. which cannot for the first three or four Weeks be procured at less Expence than *Fifteen Shillings* a Week, and never after at less than *Ten*. If he continues two Months his Nursing will be five Pounds, his Surgeons Fee, and other accidental Charges, commonly amounts to *Three Pounds*, in the whole near *Ten Pounds*; whereas in an Hospital, one Nurse, one Fire, &c. will be sufficient for ten Patients, the extra Expences will be inconsiderable, and the Surgeon's Fees taken off" (4:153).

For the poor sick person, the difference between the private house and the hospital "is still greater." In a hospital, he will be treated by doctors of known abilities in their profession. His lodging will be spacious, clean, and neat, and in healthy situation, and his food will be well chosen and served him. He will have such conveniences "as hot and cold Baths, sweating Rooms, chirurgic Machines, Bandage, &c. which can rarely be procured in the best private Lodgings, much less in those miserable loathsome Holes, which are the common Receptacles of the diseas'd Poor that are brought to this City." Franklin then sounded a strong egalitarian note: "In short a Beggar in a well regulated Hospital, stands an equal Chance with a Prince in his Palace, for a comfortable Subsistence, and an expeditious and effectual Cure of his Diseases." Rhetorically, that radical sentiment may have been a mistake, for most people in the eighteenth century accepted the hierarchical structure of society. The statement, however, testifies to the passion of Franklin's egalitarianism (4:153).

The anonymous author/Franklin returned to his religious persona as he concluded with an appeal: "It is hoped therefore, that whoever will maturely consider the inestimable Blessings that are connected to a proper Execution of the present Hospital Scheme in this City, can never be so void of Humanity and the essential Duties of Religion, as to turn a deaf Ear to the numberless Cries of the Poor and Needy, and refuse for their Assistance, a little of that Superfluity, which a bountiful Providence has so liberally bestowed on them" (4:154).

THE GOAL ACHIEVED

By 20 August 1751, the managers had in cash or in legal guarantees £2,751.16.8, and Speaker Isaac Norris drew upon the trustees of the Loan Office for the £2,000 matching grant, half to be paid immediately and the other half in one year. Two days later, the *Gazette* announced that those who were inclined to subscribe could apply to John Reynell, treasurer. Franklin's publicity for the hospital helped, for on 2 September, Matthias Koplin wrote Christopher Saur, publisher of a Germantown newspaper, saying that he had read about the hospital that was starting in Philadelphia and he was giving it a plot of ground. Franklin translated the German letter for the managers and, on their behalf, wrote Koplin a letter thanking him, which President Crosby signed (4:196–97).

When the managers met on 5 September at the Widow Pratt's Royal Standard Tavern, they decided to open the hospital in a private home until they had a lot and sufficient funds to erect the structure. By October they had settled on John Kinsey's large house on Market Street, near the southwest corner of Fifth (see #4 in endpapers), which had gardens, stables, and a pasture. The managers rented it for £40 a year. They asked that two hundred subscription papers be printed for additional persons who might want to subscribe and ordered the treasurer to advertise that "such as are inclined to subscribe may apply to him and such as have already subscribed may pay." On 12 December, the managers directed Franklin, Crosby, Thomas Bond, John Smith, and Hugh Roberts to prepare rules concerning the election, duties, and powers of the managers. The rules were amended and approved on 16 December and ratified on 13 January 1752.[10] The original document is in Franklin's hand, and he, as clerk of the hospital trustees, testified on 17 January 1752 that it had been passed "by a very great Majority" (5:309). Chief Justice William Allen, Speaker of the House Isaac Norris, and Attorney General Tench Francis approved the rules.

Franklin, no doubt with Thomas Bond and perhaps other physicians, drew up a set of regulations for the admission of patients, which the managers adopted on 23 January. He published the regulations in the *Pennsylvania Gazette* on 24 March 1752 and separately as a broadside. The former was good publicity, and the latter was useful to have for the patients, doctors, and managers. The fifteen rules show Franklin's practical and shrewd sense: "no Patients shall be admitted whose Cases are judg'd incurable, Lunaticks excepted; nor any whose Cases do not require the particular Conveniences of an Hospital." Those with infectious diseases would not be admitted until special housing was built, and mothers with young children must have the children cared for elsewhere (5:310–12).

By 10 February 1752, Kinsey's house had been transformed, and the hospital admitted its first patient. From that date, a committee of managers, together with two physicians, attended the hospital twice a week "to visit the Sick, examine Cases, admit and discharge Patients &c." A physician attended daily. The weekly committee consisted of two managers, appointed for a month at a time, to make the rounds of the hospital twice a week with the physicians. As a member of the weekly committee, Franklin reported on 4 June that in the previous week, three persons had been cured and discharged, that a "dropsical person" was admitted, and that "a Lunatick from New York" was admitted at ten shillings a week. The committee also noted that Dr. Thomas Bond gave them three pounds on account of the board of a patient, which they delivered to the matron (4:320). The forthcoming annual election was announced in the *Gazette* on 2 April, held on 4 May, and the results appeared in the paper on 7 May 1752. Nearly all the former managers were returned, though three resigned (including Richard Peters, possibly because most Proprietary Party members regarded the hospital as primarily a Quaker charity) and were replaced. Shortly afterward, the managers chose six physicians for the following year, each of whom agreed to visit the hospital for six months.[11]

For the first ten months, the physicians supplied the medicines gratis. In December 1752, the hospital received a supply of medicine from London, which cost £112.15.2, and "a Subscription was set on Foot among the charitable Widows, and other good Women of the City." Franklin published the names and the amount donated in *Some Account of the Pennsylvania Hospital*. This first women's auxiliary in America raised more than the amount necessary (5:316).

THE PROPRIETORS' OSTENSIBLE GIFT OF LAND

As Governor Hamilton had foreseen, Thomas Penn was not happy with the proposal for a hospital. Penn wrote Hamilton on 8 September 1751 that it interfered with the proprietors' rights. The projectors "should have represented their intention to us, & submitted their Scheme to our correction here, before they asked for so large a benefaction as Land to the value of perhaps £1500 Sterl'g." Instead the projectors gave every subscriber who donated merely ten pounds "a vote in the settlement of the Scheme." (Franklin's populism contrasts strikingly with Penn's belief in social hierarchy.) Penn told Hamilton that if other such occasions arose, he should not sign a bill until the proprietors had approved it. Penn asserted that the incorporation should not have been enacted by the assembly "without us or our Representative." The incorporation "should have done by Letters Patent under the Great Seal which is always the way here." Therefore "we shall propose the repeal of it in Pennsylvania, with some alteration." If the changes were made, "I shall be very ready to give a piece of Ground of the size proposed for such an hospital and perhaps an handsome benefaction in Money."[12]

Penn offered a plot of land on 28 October 1751 together with a set of instructions for the managers to follow in order to receive it. When Governor Hamilton received the offer, he notified the managers, and Joshua Crosby and Charles Norris came to see him, heard the conditions upon which the land was to be given, and asked for a copy. After several meetings, the managers decided that they could not accept the conditions. Franklin and Israel Pemberton were asked to write Hamilton that they had not yet come to any determination about accepting the land because they could not guarantee that the Pennsylvania Assembly would repeal the Act of Incorporation.

Governor Hamilton informed Penn on 19 June 1752 that he "easily perceived this was a piece of evasion to conceal their intentions from me." He believed that the hospital managers intended to delay until the Act of Incorporation had received the "Royal assent," and after that, "by many smooth Words and Compliments to You, and encomiums on Your Ancestors, endeavour to prevail on You to grant them the Land free from the conditions" proposed. Hamilton also identified the hospital as a Quaker project, no doubt because most of the largest contributions came from Friends. He thought that the Friends would regard the hospital as primarily a Quaker institution and would take credit for it in England, thus using it as propaganda to strengthen the anti-Proprietary Party.[13] Actually, though Dr. Bond had been brought up a Quaker, he had become an Anglican, and Franklin belonged to no church. Although Richard Peters, a Proprietary Party member, supported the hospital and had been elected an original manager, he had resigned. Proprietarian William Allen, who donated generously, did not want to be a manager. Hamilton was right. Most subscribers were Quakers.

Nevertheless, Hamilton may have been wrong in supposing the managers desired to make the hospital primarily a Quaker institution, but he was correct about their intentions concerning the gift and conditions. On 4 June, two weeks before he wrote Penn, the managers had decided to reject the gift and the conditions and had asked Franklin and Pemberton to draft their reasons. The managers would send them to the two influential London Quakers who had already talked to Penn, Thomas Hyam and Sylvanus Bevan. They would present the reasons to Penn.

Franklin's "Remarks"

On 2 July, the managers presented, amended, and approved Franklin's "Remarks," giving their reasons for refusing the land. Franklin tried to be diplomatic. He and the other managers had good reasons for rejecting Penn's conditions, but they still hoped he would give either land or money to the hospital. They had to explain their refusal and ask for Penn's help. The situation was not unlike Franklin's predicament on 17 December 1782, when he apologized to the count of Vergennes for making a treaty with Great Britain without consulting France (contrary to the directions of Congress) and, at the same time, asked to borrow an additional six million livres from France.

Franklin began by saying that, since the "honourable Proprietaries" had "fully express'd their Approbation" of the hospital's beneficent design and had declared "their kind Intentions of aiding and assisting it, by granting a valuable Tract of Land," the managers now had only "to convince our honourable Proprietaries, that the Methods by which they have proposed to aid and assist the Hospital, will by no Means answer these good Intentions, but are really inconsistent therewith." That long, compound, complex sentence mainly consisted of compliments to the proprietaries. Even in refusing the proposed land, it praised the proprietors' "good Intentions" (5:300–301).

Spelling out the reasons for rejecting the gift, Franklin devoted a long paragraph to the proprietors' conditions and a short one to the ground itself. Franklin knew that the proprietors thought that the projectors of the hospital failed in respect to them, but he also thought that the contributors (whose combined subscriptions were far greater than the proprietors' proposed gift) should be respected. His belief rebuked both the proprietors' assumption and the normal eighteenth-century deference. Franklin wrote that a charter granted by an act of assembly "is undoubtedly the best Grant of Incorporation that we can possibly have." The proprietors, however, believed they should be the ones to grant a charter. Franklin said that since "the Representatives of the Freemen of this Province" have "generously contributed" to the hospital, "we should fail of the Respect that is justly due to" the assembly if the managers accepted a different charter, unless it contained "some very great and manifest Advantage." Not only, however, were there no advantages in the proposed charter, but it would restrict the power of the elected managers to make by-laws, and subject the hospital to "Visitors of the Proprietaries Appointment." As for the lot, it, "and of Consequence the Buildings on it," would revert to the proprietaries, "on Failure of a Succession of Contributors." The managers thought it possible that in time "there will cease to be a Succession of Contributors." If that happened, the managers thought it unjust that the lot and buildings on it would become the property of the proprietaries. Ending the paragraph, Franklin, seemingly innocently, wrote, "The Proprietaries, to be sure, have not attended to these Consequences, or they never would have proposed any Thing so inconsistent with the Design they intended to promote."

Franklin's ostensibly respectful attitude toward the proprietors broke down as he gave the reasons for not accepting the "gift." The building lot itself was on swampy ground, next to "the Brick-yards, where there are Ponds of standing

Figure 31. Thomas Penn, mezzotint by David Martin, after Davis. Thomas Penn (1702–75) became the chief proprietor of Pennsylvania in 1746. He lived in Philadelphia for nine years (1732–41) and came to know Franklin as a "sort of Tribune of the People." Avaricious and condescending, Penn believed in a hierarchical society and thought himself superior to all Pennsylvanians. He had resolved to make as much money from Pennsylvania as possible. Since he appointed the lieutenant governor (who was generally called, and functioned as, the governor), whose approval was necessary for any legislation, Penn took a £5,000 bond from every (lieutenant) governor that he would not allow taxation of Penn's property in Pennsylvania. Penn was the only person in Pennsylvania who could buy land from the Indians. He bought large tracts (not always fairly) for little, held them for years, and sold them at expensive prices to settlers, and thereafter charged a small, annual quitrent for the property. Pennsylvanians burned him in effigy in 1741.

The half-length mezzotint portrait of a wealthy gentleman shows Thomas Penn with his face and right shoulder turned toward the viewer. He is wearing a white wig of somewhat more than shoulder length and an elaborately brocaded jacket. The mezzotint artist David Martin (1737–97), who was also an electrician, made portraits of Franklin and of Deborah in 1759.

Although the original clearly reads "Davis, Pinx, 1751," I have not located an English portrait painter of ability named Davis who was active in 1751. (Evidently neither could the editors of the Papers of Benjamin Franklin, *who used the portrait in volume 1, p. 370, with a comment at 1:xx.) The National Portrait Gallery identified him as "Arthur Davis (1711–89)," whom I have not found elsewhere. I suspect that the painter was actually Arthur Devis (1712–87). Perhaps David Martin, the engraver, made an error or perhaps Devis temporarily used the name "Davis." Courtesy, National Portrait Gallery.*

Water, and therefore must be unhealthy, and more fit for a Burying-place (to which Use Part of it is already applied) than for any other Service." Franklin also noted that it was part of a square "allotted by the late honourable Proprietary for publick Uses, as the old Maps of the City will shew." The citizens would think it unjust "if we should accept of this Lot by a Grant from our present Proprietaries, in such Terms as would seem to imply our assenting to their having a Right to the Remainder of the Square" (5:301). Though apparently respectful, Franklin's "Remarks" stated that the proprietors were not really giving a gift of land but doing Philadelphians out of a lot belonging to the citizens. At the same time, they were proposing lord-like privileges for themselves and possibly securing future unjust profits. Franklin's "Remarks" revealed that he considered the proprietors' supposed gift another example of their avariciousness and superciliousness.

The letter to Thomas Hyam and Sylvanus Bevan rehearsed the objections in the "Remarks." Franklin characterized the plot with an ironic contrast: it was "absolutely improper for our Purpose, which is to restore the Sick to Health; and the only proper Use of that Square will be for a Burying-ground" (5:302). The English Friends reported on 31 January 1753 that they had an interview with Thomas Penn, who objected to the "Remarks." He found it disrespectful that the managers esteemed "an Establishment from the Assembly preferable to a Charter from the proprietaries." He also complained about their "questioning" the right of the Proprietaries "to the Square" where they offered the plot. Penn conceded that if the lot reverted to the proprietors, then the buildings on it "should be at the Managers Disposal" (5:304).

Penn could have requested the British authorities to disallow the assembly bill, but he evidently decided that to do so would place him in a bad light not only with the Quaker Party opposition but also with supporters like Richard Peters and William Allen, as well as with charitable-minded persons in general. On 10 May 1753, the hospital act was ratified.[14] Penn apparently still hoped that Franklin would emerge a proprietary supporter. He wrote Richard Peters on 9 January 1753 that he doubted that Franklin intended "to do a thing disagreable to us, by leaving out the Governor from being placed at the head of the Visitation of the Hospital, but no doubt many others had" (5:291n1). Hamilton, however, could hardly have been placed at the head of the managers when he did not support the hospital.

In January 1753 Franklin suggested that charity boxes be prepared to receive small donations for the hospital and that each manager keep one in his place of business or his home. He had come across the idea of such boxes as a boy when he read Cotton Mather's *Bonifacius* or, as the running title had it, "Essays to Do Good." In it Mather celebrated the idea of charity boxes for the poor.[15] At the 1 February meeting, the twelve managers each received a box with the words "Charity for the Hospital" painted on it. By May 1753, Franklin's charity box yielded £1.10.0 (5:317, 318). Though Franklin reported in his 1754 *Some Account of the Pennsylvania Hospital* that the boxes had not raised much money, they were gradually installed elsewhere: one at the entrance to the hospital, one in the assembly, and others in various places of public business. Franklin devised additional ways of raising money. On 5 November 1755, the assembly passed two rules benefitting the hospital. One said that any member who was not present within half an hour after the assembly bell rang must pay a shilling; and a second said that for any absence without a sufficient reason the member would have to forfeit his entire wages for that sitting: "All which Forfeitures shall be paid into the Charity Box for the Use of the Provincial Hospital." Although most charity boxes generated only two or three pounds a year, by 1775, they together had produced more than £900.[16]

SOME ACCOUNT OF THE PENNSYLVANIA HOSPITAL

Franklin wrote a pamphlet history of the hospital describing what had been done and attempting to raise additional money. He completed it on 28 May 1754. The managers asked President Crosby to wait upon Governor James Hamilton with two other managers to tell him about the *Account* and to ask him to add his name to the list of donors that would be printed at the pamphlet's end. Hamilton refused. *Some Account* printed the hospital's founding documents, Franklin's two-part "Appeal for the Hospital," and the financial reports. Franklin's new materials sandwiched these.

The anonymous speaker Franklin chose for the introduction was a humane and religious person reporting the actions of "some Persons." The opening consists of a Faulknerian, compound, complex sentence of nearly four hundred words. The speaker reported that people frequently observed that poor sick persons came to Philadelphia to see physicians but could not find lodging, nurses, and other resources, "for want whereof, many must suffer greatly, and some probably perish, that might otherwise have been restored to Health and Comfort." The same was true of poor persons living in the city "who could not be so well and so easily taken Care of in their separate Habitations, as they might be in one convenient House, under one Inspection, and in the Hands of skilful Practioners." Further, lunatics wandered about, "to the Terror of their Neighbours, there being no Place . . . in which they might be confined, and subjected to proper Management for the Recovery." Therefore, some charitable persons met together and proposed to establish a hospital. The suggestion was "so generally approved: that [considerable subscriptions were made for the purpose], but the Expence of erecting a Building sufficiently large and commodious for the Purpose" was too great, "unless the Subscription could be made general through the Province, and some Assistance could be obtained from the Assembly." Therefore, a petition had been drawn and presented to the House on 23 January 1750/51 (5:284). All that information and appeal was contained in the exhaustive, exhausting, and incontrovertible opening sentence.

The documents and Franklin's commentary constitute the body of *Some*

Account. The speaker is an impartial historian and a statistician. Perhaps the heart of the *Account* is a table near the end that gives an "Abstract of Cases admitted into the Pennsylvania Hospital" from 11 February 1752 to 27 April 1754 (5:324). With its notes and the two following paragraphs, the table was reprinted on the front page of the *Pennsylvania Gazette* on 8 August and reprinted again the following week on 15 August 1754. That was extraordinary. Though Hall now ran the daily business of the printing shop and ostensibly edited the *Gazette*, Franklin often decided what to print. Franklin thought the table was good publicity for the Pennsylvania Hospital.

Following the "Abstract of Cases" of the persons admitted to the hospital and just before the concluding "List of Contributors" with their donations, Franklin wrote a fund-raising appeal. He stated the information yielded in the table: sixty people had been cured, "besides many others that have received considerable Relief, both In and Out-patients; and if so much Good has been done by so small a Number of Contributors, how much more then may reasonably be expected from the liberal Aid and Assistance of the Well-disposed who hitherto have not join'd in the Undertaking?" Experience, he said, "has more and more convinced all concerned, of the great Usefulness of this Charity" (5:325).

In the final paragraphs, Franklin's speaker reverted to a religious person doing good. He said that the sick poor were carefully attended; "the Neatness, Cleanness, and Regularity of Diet" enabled them to recover "much sooner than their own Manner of Living at Home"; and they have the "best Advice, and the best Medicines"—all of which contribute to reclaiming many useful lives. "In short, there is scarce any one Kind of doing Good, which is not hereby in some Manner promoted; for not only the Sick are visited and relieved, but the Stranger is taken in, the Ignorant instructed, and the Bad reclaimed;* present wants are supplied, and the future prevented, and (by easing poor Families of the Burthen of supporting and curing their Sick) it is also the Means of feeding the Hungry, and cloathing the Naked" (5:325–26). The echoes of Isaiah 58:6–8 and Ezekiel 18:7–8, 16–17 reinforced Franklin's Christian persona. The asterisk referred to a footnote saying that the visits and conversation of "some serious Persons" who visit the sick and give them "pious Books" have "been attended with a Blessing." The religious author was presumably among the "serious Persons" who did so (5:325–26). Franklin, like the other hospital managers, visited the hospital on a scheduled basis. If he thought it was good for the patients, he probably gave them religious books.

The anonymous author asked for "additional Benefactions from pious and benevolent Persons" so that the managers would not have to refuse "Admittance to any proper" person because of lack of funds. The speaker then inserted an ostensible quotation which, I suspect, Franklin composed. The speaker said that everyone could contribute something.[17] Echoing Matthew 10:42, the author assured the reader that even those who give the gift of "a Cup of cold Water . . . will not be unrewarded" (5:326).

As earlier in *Poor Richard* and later in his pre-Revolutionary non-importation propaganda, Franklin wrote that every year many people unnecessarily spent money in "vain Superfluities or Entertainments, for mere Amusements or Diversions," and asked if persons "do not wish that Money had been given in the Way now proposed?" The author said that even the "least Mite" can be given without embarrassing the donor, for it can be put into the charity boxes in the managers' homes "or into the Box which is fixed in the Entry of the Hospital." The author also suggested that even if a person had no extra money, goods or products from gardens could be given to the hospital, including "old Linen" and rags, which could be used for "Bandages and other chyrurgical Dressings." All contributions would be thankfully received (5:326–27). Franklin printed the fund-raising appeal twice in the *Gazette*.

One more paragraph, consisting of a single sentence of approximately two hundred words, concluded *Some Account*. Franklin praised the physicians for giving "their Advice and Attendance *gratis*" and the managers for attending the monthly meetings and for faithfully performing the hospital visitations twice a week. The managers have done that service "with greater Readiness and Punctuality than has been usually known in any other publick Business, where Interest was not immediately concerned; owing, no Doubt, to that Satisfaction which naturally arises in humane Minds from a Consciousness of doing Good, and from the frequent pleasing Sight of Misery relieved, Distress removed, grievous Diseases healed, Health restored, and those who were admitted languishing, groaning, and almost despairing of Recovery, discharged sound and hearty, with chearful and thankful Countenances, gratefully acknowledging the Care that has been taken of them, praising God, and blessing their Benefactors, who by their bountiful Contributions founded so excellent an Institution" (5:327). What a wonderful appreciation!

Like modern solicitations, Franklin's pamphlet appended a sentence giving a model for a donor to make a contribution. The last two pages of *Some Account* contain the list of the contributors, among whom neither Governor Hamilton nor the proprietors appear. William Allen gave £150; several wealthy persons gave £100; Franklin gave £25; and most contributors gave less, but even those who gave £1 are recorded. Franklin may have contributed additional goods or cash, for his cumulative total was £66.67.[18] But the hundreds—perhaps thousands—of hours of his efforts for the hospital were more important than his monetary contributions. By 27 July 1754, Franklin and Hall had printed 1,500 copies of *Some Account*. The pamphlet succeeded. In the year before it appeared, only one new donation was recorded; in the year after, new subscribers totaled 186.[19]

Figure 32. Samuel Rhoads, "A South-East Prospect of the Pennsylvania Hospital," 1761. Samuel Rhoads (1711–84), carpenter and master builder, joined Franklin in all of his early civic projects. When Franklin and Dr. Thomas Bond projected a hospital, they naturally turned to Rhoads. He consulted with Bond and other physicians, and then designed a hospital. He presented the plan to the trustees on 25 January 1755, assuring them that one-third of the structure could be built then and the rest added later. Had the entire building been constructed in 1755, it would have been the largest and most impressive building in the colonies. Rhoads and the trustees, however, knew that they could not at first afford so grand a building. A "South-East Prospect of the Pennsylvania Hospital" shows the entire building—which was not completed for another forty years. What Rhoads actually built in 1755 was the hospital's East Wing, the third of the building closest to the observer.

John Winter and Montgomery made a drawing (presumably from Rhoads's architectural design) of the complete plan, which Henry Dawkins and John Steeper engraved for Robert Kennedy, who printed and sold the plate. Kennedy, a mathematics teacher in Philadelphia since at least 1755, advertised in the Pennsylvania Gazette *on 22 October 1761 that a "PROSPECTIVE View of the PENNSYLVANIA HOSPITAL," taken "with the Approbation of the managers of the said Hospital," was "now engraving, and may be expected in two Weeks." By 26 November, it was completed and advertised for sale.*

The cartouche in the bottom center of the engraving portrays a version of the seal of the Pennsylvania Hospital, with the words "TAKE CARE OF HIM & I WILL REPAY THEE." Courtesy, Library Company of Phiadelphia.

Building the Hospital

The managers purchased a lot for the hospital on 11 September 1754. After the carpenter-architect Samuel Rhoads consulted with the physicians, he presented a design for the building to the managers on 25 January 1755, assuring them that one-third of the building, the East Wing, could be built now "with tolerable symmetry" and the rest added later when additional funds were available. The *Pennsylvania Gazette* announced on 25 February 1755 that all contributors should meet on 10 March to consider the design and hear an estimate of its expense. They did, and approved, and Rhoads began to build.[20]

Initially elected president of the managers in 1751, Joshua Crosby was re-elected through 5 May 1755, but died a month later on 27 June. Franklin was elected president on 30 June 1755. He remained in Philadelphia from 12 May to 18 December 1755 and no doubt helped Rhoads negotiate with the tradesmen who donated time, materials, skill, or money to build the hospital. Franklin had done the same in 1748, when the militia Association managers built the battery under Society Hill and again in 1751, when the New Building was transformed into a school. Probably following Franklin's advice, Rhoads hired no tradesman or workman without first obtaining a promise of some free work, a donation, or a discount: "By systematically pursuing methods such as these the Managers were successful in engaging the sympathy and support of almost the entire community for this charitable enterprise."[21]

A high point in the Pennsylvania Hospital's early history occurred on 28 April 1755, when the managers unveiled the building's cornerstone. The city's schools dismissed classes, and the students and public attended the ceremony. President Joshua Crosby, Franklin, the other managers, the physicians, and the subscribers marched from the temporary hospital in Kinsey's house on Market Street to the site of the foundation of the future hospital, on Eighth Street about midway between Spruce and Pine (#1 in the endpapers). To emphasize the historical moment and the progress of Philadelphia, the managers invited John Key, the first person born in the colony after the arrival of William Penn in 1682, to attend. Key proudly did.[22] Years later, Dr. Benjamin Rush recorded an anecdote Dr. Thomas Bond told him: "When . . . Franklin walked out from his house to lay the foundation stone of the Pennsylvania Hospital, he was accompanied by the late Dr. Bond and the managers and physicians of the Hospital. On their way Dr. Bond lamented that the Hospital would allure strangers from all the then provinces in America. 'Then,' said Dr. Franklin 'our institution will be more useful than we intended it to be.'"[23] The original manuscript of the inscription for the cornerstone, in Franklin's hand, survives at the Pennsylvania Hospital (6:61–62).

The *Pennsylvania Gazette* for 29 May reported: "Yesterday Morning the first Stone of the Pennsylvania Hospital was laid by Mr. JOSHUA CROSBY, Presi-

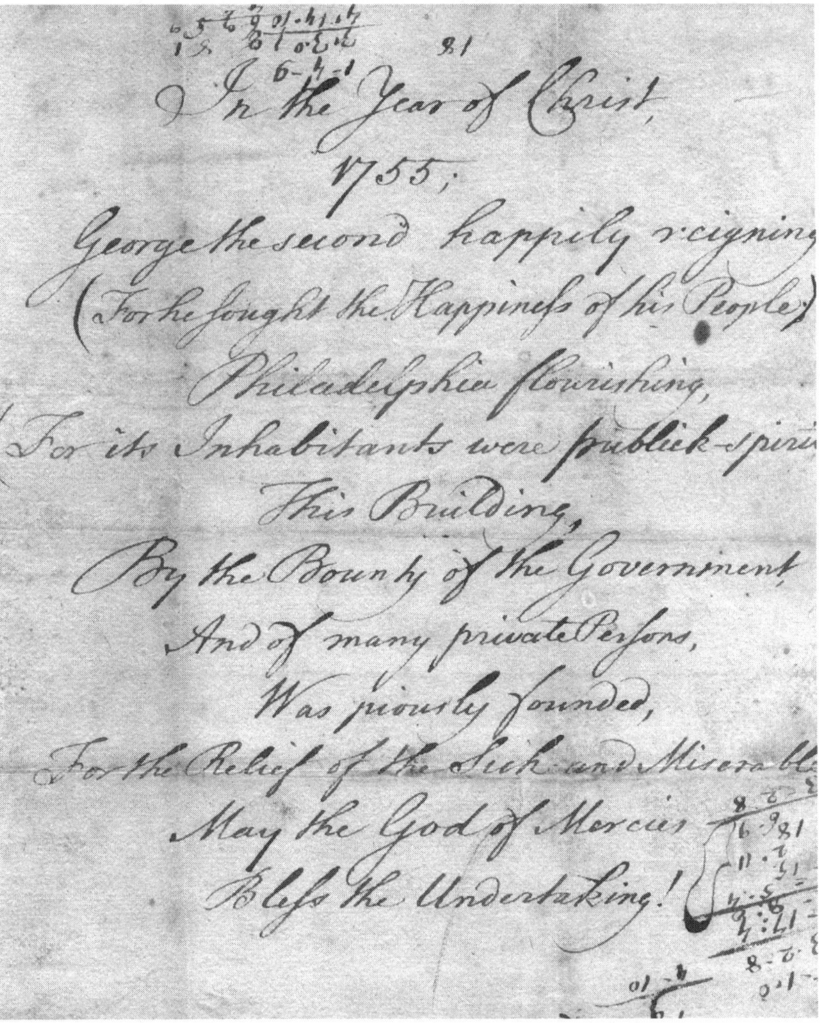

Figure 33. Franklin's draft for the Pennsylvania Hospital cornerstone. At a ceremony on 28 May 1755, Joshua Crosby, president of the Pennsylvania Hospital, attended by the other managers and the physicians of the hospital, laid its cornerstone. Franklin composed the inscription. He used the formal language and roman numerals (in the Pennsylvania Gazette text and in the actual cornerstone) suitable for the inscription. Later, the Library Company directors similarly asked Franklin to write the inscription for the Library Company's new building in 1789. At that time, they thought him too modest and added his name in the inscription (Life 2:123). He was not so famous in 1755.

The reference to King George II is traditional cant, but it may have an indirect purpose. Franklin thanked King George, the public-spirited citizens of Philadelphia, and the Pennsylvania Assembly—all for supposedly being concerned with the project. The latter two referred to groups who had been directly responsible. The reference to King George II indirectly calls attention to the omission of Pennsylvania's proprietors. Naming the king probably implies that the proprietors were not "public-spirited" and did not contribute to or care about "the happiness" of their people. Courtesy, Pennsylvania Hospital.

dent, assisted by the rest of the Managers, and the Physicians of the Hospital.
The Stone is of Pennsylvania Marble, with the following Inscription:

IN THE YEAR OF CHRIST
MDCCLV,
GEORGE THE SECOND HAPPILY REIGNING,
(FOR HE SOUGHT THE HAPPINESS OF HIS PEOPLE)
PHILADELPHIA FLOURISHING
(FOR ITS INHABITANTS WERE PUBLICK-SPIRITED)
THIS BUILDING,
BY THE BOUNTY OF THE GOVERNMENT,
AND OF MANY PRIVATE PERSONS,
WAS PIOUSLY FOUNDED,
FOR THE RELIEF OF THE SICK AND MISERABLE,
MAY THE GOD OF MERCIES
BLESS THE UNDERTAKING!

Perhaps Franklin intimated, if only by omission, that the compliment to George
II for seeking the happiness of his people and to Philadelphians for being public-
spirited contrasted with the actions of Pennsylvania's proprietors. (Later, however, the proprietors did give an annuity and a gift of land.)[24] Construction
proceeded rapidly. At the 27 October managers' meeting, they adjourned for an
hour to watch the raising of the hospital's roof. The craftsmen then began working on the building's interior.

Reelected president on 31 May 1756, Franklin was "requested to agree with
the Engraver to Engrave a Prospect of the New Hospital, on the lowest Terms,
and to make a report, at the next Meeting." But he was absent then, and an
engraving was not produced until 1761. Actually, two engravings were then completed. James Claypoole, Jr., drew and engraved one; and Robert Kennedy
printed another, based on a drawing by Montgomery and John Winter, which
was engraved by John Steeper and Henry Dawkins. Further, Kennedy printed a
second state of his "South-East Prospect of the Pennsylvania Hospital."[25]

After the managers voted to present an address to Governor William Denny,
Franklin wrote it, signed it as president, and presented it on 1 September 1756.
Later that month, Franklin's friend, the Virginia planter Philip Ludwell III, contributed £10 to the hospital, along with his gift of £20 to the Academy and
College of Philadelphia. On 17 December 1756, the patients in Kinsey's home
were moved to the hospital. Since the city primarily grew along the west bank
of the Delaware River, at its founding the hospital was located in an almost
pastoral setting. Franklin attended his last managers' meeting on 27 December
1756, at the hospital building. At the 28 March 1757 meeting, the minutes noted
that he intended "soon to embark for England in the Publik Service of his
Province," and requested his assistance in soliciting donations to the hospital.
Israel Pemberton and Evan Morgan were asked to write Thomas Hyam and

Silvanus Bevan to assist Franklin in any solicitations he made. The managers requested that an announcement of the forthcoming meeting for the election of the managers be printed in the *Gazette*, but no notice appeared. Though news of the hospital and the elections of managers had appeared in the *Pennsylvania Gazette* since the beginning, the announcements nearly ceased altogether after late 1755, when David Hall complained to William Strahan that Franklin had become too busy to help run the press.[26] At the election on 2 May 1757, Franklin was in New York en route to England and not a candidate. The managers elected the Quaker merchant John Reynell the third president of Pennsylvania Hospital.

In England, Franklin performed a number of minor services for the hospital (9:113–14). Though the managers on several occasions asked Franklin to solicit funds for the hospital, he was averse to "begging" and evidently devoted little energy to doing so.[27] He did, however, secure funds for the hospital from the Pennsylvania Land Company. It had been formed in 1699 to sell real estate in Pennsylvania, New Jersey, and Maryland. By 1760 a number of shares in the company were unclaimed and the company was reorganized. The London Quaker Thomas Hyam wrote the managers on 7 June 1760 that he and Dr. John Fothergill had been successful in inserting into the parliamentary act concerning the Pennsylvania Land Company that "all the money which might remain unclaimed in the hands of the land company's trustees on June 24, 1770," would be granted to the Pennsylvania Hospital.[28] The Lord Chancellor ruled on 26 May 1766 that the funds could be invested in 3 percent bank annuities until distributed to the hospital in 1770. With Dr. John Fothergill and the banker David Barclay, Franklin acted as the agent for the hospital managers, receiving the money, investing it, and remitting it when asked.[29]

Dr. Fothergill did another favor for the Pennsylvania Hospital. Though the authors of the standard history of its early years credit Franklin and Drs. Thomas and Phineas Bond with founding its library, on 27 July 1762, Fothergill donated its first book. After that, the managers purchased books for the library. Ordering medical volumes in 1774, they called on Franklin's friend William Strahan, who bought and gave them to the hospital, thereby contributing about £100.[30]

FRANKLIN'S BEQUEST

In his 1788 will, Franklin left the debts owed him in 1757, which were recorded in his Ledger E, to the hospital. He wrote that since the debts had not been collected in so long a time, they had "become in a manner obsolete yet are nevertheless justly due." Although most of them "must inevitably be lost," he nevertheless hoped "something considerable may be recovered." The managers appointed a committee to report on the bequest, and the committee found that the debts totaled £5,508.14.1, in addition to "divers blanks debits and credits, the amounts of which they are not able to ascertain." The committee called on a number of the debtors and their heirs; some said they had accounts against

Franklin greater than those they owed him; some said the estates of the persons named had long since been settled and that they would not admit to any such antiquated claims. The committee concluded that collecting the money would be more trouble than the legacy was worth. At a general meeting of the contributors on 13 July 1790, they noted that many of the debts were small, that some were from persons unknown, that all were thirty to sixty years old, and that some debtors said they had claims against Franklin that the hospital would be accepting if it accepted the bequest. The contributors unanimously voted not to accept it. They nevertheless expressed their gratitude for Franklin's early part in promoting the institution and for his attempt to help it in his will.[31]

NINE

Franklin's First Full Assembly, the Money Bill, and Susanna Wright, 1751–1752

By rendering the Means of purchasing Land easy to the Poor, the Dominions of the Crown are strengthen'd and extended; the Proprietaries dispose of their Wilderness Territory; and the British Nation secures the Benefit of its Manufactures, and increases the Demand for them: For so long as Land can be easily procur'd for Settlements between the Atlantick and Pacifick Oceans, so long will Labour be dear in America; and while Labour continues dear, we can never rival the Artificers, or interfere with the Trade of our Mother Country.
—Franklin's "Report of the State of the Currency," 19 August 1752, 4:350

FRANKLIN AND HUGH ROBERTS were elected Philadelphia representatives on 2 October 1751. The Quaker John Smith recorded that the election was hotly contested and that Franklin received the highest number of votes, 495; that Hugh Roberts received 473; Joseph Fox, 391; and William Plumsted, 303. Smith noted, "A total of 1,662. One half of these being 831, is I suppose a great many more than ever voted for the city before."[1] Of the four, Franklin was apparently regarded as an independent and won votes from members of both parties, though probably not from those absolutely loyal to the Proprietary Party or from the pacifist Quakers. Roberts, Franklin's good friend, and Fox were both Quakers and members of the Quaker Party. Plumsted, another old friend and a former Quaker, had become an Anglican and a Proprietary Party member.

The assembly of 1751–52 had three sessions: the organizing session, 14–16 October 1751; the second session, 3 February–11 March 1751/2, which met for thirty-three days and did most of the year's business; and the third and final session, 10–22 August 1752, which met for twelve days. The major business of the year proved to be the assembly's attempt to pass a paper money bill. In the first session on 14 October, Isaac Norris was unanimously chosen Speaker; and he appointed Franklin to all four standing committees. William Franklin was elected clerk. Then the assembly adjourned to Monday, 3 February.

SECOND SESSION, 3 FEBRUARY–11 MARCH 1751/2

On 3 February 1751/2, Franklin and Evan Morgan performed the formal task of waiting upon the governor and asking if he "hath any Thing to lay before them." Incidently, the use of *hath* rather than *has* probably shows that Clerk William Franklin knew his father's opinion that the English language had too many "s" sounds and that he often preferred the old-fashioned "hath" to "has" (*Life* 2:131–32). For the next several days, the House heard various petitions, several requesting the creation of new counties, so that the persons far from the existing county seats could be represented.

From 1751 to 1757, Franklin served on numerous minor committees. I will present Franklin's minor assignments for the assembly of 1751–52, but subsequent chapters will ignore them.[2] On 6 February 1751/2, a petition claimed that most sales held in public places carried goods similar to those in retail shops and that "Strangers, who contributed nothing towards the Support of Government," imported materials to sell there. After the petition was read for the second time on 7 February, the petitioners were given leave to bring in a bill. They did so on 13 February. On 25 February, it was read the second time and "committed for Amendment to" a committee that included Franklin. But the assembly never returned to it, and therefore, at the end of the third session, 20 August 1752, it was referred, with other bills, to the next assembly. Bills judged of little pressing importance were often put off from one assembly to another. Acts primarily concerned with Philadelphia affairs were usually referred to the Philadelphia Common Council. Neither this bill nor the next was passed during the colonial period.[3]

Another minor committee addressed the issue of stray dogs. The city and county of Philadelphia petitioned against the nuisance on 12 February. Read for the second time the next day, the petition was referred for further consideration. On 24 February Franklin was appointed to "a Committee to prepare and bring in a Bill." The bill for licensing dogs was read on 5 March and for the second time on 10 March. When read for the third time that afternoon, the Speaker referred it to the same committee to be "amended against the next Sessions of Assembly." It, too, dragged on from assembly to assembly before dropping from the record.[4]

NITTY-GRITTY LEGISLATIVE BUSINESS: FOUR EXAMPLES

The laws specified fees for various official functions, but the schedules had been created when the colony had few inhabitants. By 1752 some fees were exorbitant. On 4 February 1752, the assembly read a petition from York County criticizing the high fees that the officers of the courts, especially the county sheriff, collected. The next day, Cumberland County presented a similar petition, and the following day, 6 February, the third article of a long petition from Chester county also complained of high fees. On 18 February, Speaker Norris appointed Franklin to a "Committee to enquire into the State of the Laws of this Province relating to Fees, and report thereon to the House." Reporting on 21 February that the fee structure should be changed, the committee was promptly asked to bring in a bill. The Bill of Fees, read on 27 February, specified fees for the Keeper of the Great Seal, the justices of the Supreme Court, the governor's secretary, the attorney general, the sheriffs of the counties, justices of the peace, justices of the Orphans' Court, the prothonotary or clerk of the Supreme Court, the clerk of the Court of the General Quarter-Sessions, the prothonotary or clerk of the Common Pleas in every county, the register-general of the province, the attorneys, members of juries and inquests, and so forth. Altogether, the committee specified hundreds of minor legal fees. The bill was read for the second time on 2 March and changes were made. After being considered again on 5 March, it was ordered to be transcribed for a third reading, and on 7 March the bill passed the assembly and was sent to Governor Hamilton, who later replied that he would take "the Bill under Advisement till the next Meeting of the Assembly."[5]

At the beginning of the last session of the assembly of 1751–52, the governor's council read and approved amendments to the officers' fee bill on 10 August. The House received the amended bill the next day. On 13 August the assembly accepted some amendments and asked Franklin and Mahlon Kirkbride to confer with the governor. The two reported the next day that Governor Hamilton would take the revisions into consideration. He returned the bill on 18 August with amendments. The House agreed to some, "but in others the House adhered to the Bill." The following day, 19 August, Governor Hamilton replied in writing that the secretary's duties were so various that it was impossible to set a fee that would "be exactly adequate to each Service"; he also believed that the fees specified for the attorney general were "not equal to the Trouble and Skill necessarily required to carry on criminal Prosecutions." The assembly voted not to accept the amendments but declared it "would be glad to have a Conference with the Governor." Franklin attended the 20 August conference. Afterward, the assembly accepted the governor's amendments and had the bill engrossed. Franklin and Secretary Richard Peters compared the bill on the morning of 22 August, and the governor enacted it later that day.[6]

In another case, the Germantown overseers of the poor petitioned the Pennsylvania Assembly for reimbursement. In the early winter of 1750–51, five Nanticoke Indians shot and beat an Albany Indian and left him for dead. After the Nanticoke Indians left, however, the Iroquois was still alive. The overseers of the poor asked Chief Justice William Allen what to do. He instructed them to care for the Indian, who gradually recovered. After ten weeks and four days he was well enough to leave. On 7 February 1751/2, after the Germantown overseers requested reimbursement, the House ordered Franklin and Hugh Roberts to "inspect the said Accounts and report thereon." They replied on 27 February that £12.4.10 should be awarded to the Germantown "Overseers of the Poor," and that £15 should "be allowed to Doctor Charles Bensel, in full of his Account for Medicines and Attendance in the Cure of the wounded Indian." The House ordered payment.[7]

The first act Franklin wrote as an assemblyman that became a law concerned the price of bread. Philadelphia's bakers petitioned the assembly on 7 February 1751/2 to raise the price of bread because flour was so expensive that they could not make the cheaper breads "without manifest Loss to themselves." Consequently, poor people could hardly afford bread. The bakers requested that they be able to make smaller sizes of breads, especially of the "brown bread or good ship stuff," so the poor could afford to buy them. The next day Speaker Norris appointed Franklin to a "Committee to consider the said Petition and the Law of this Province relating to the Assize of Bread, and . . . prepare and bring in a Bill for the Alteration or Amendment of the same."[8]

Perhaps Franklin recalled the cheap "three great Puffy Rolls" he bought when he first entered Philadelphia (A 24), realized how much the price of even the cheapest flour had increased, and reflected that he could not now purchase such a quantity with three pence. The committee agreed that, considering the price of flour, the bakers should be able to charge more. On 21 February the bill was read; five days later it was read again "Paragraph by Paragraph, and ordered to be transcribed for a third Reading." On 28 February it passed and was sent to the governor. Governor Hamilton proposed an amendment on 4 March. It was agreed to, and the bill was ordered to be engrossed. A week later, it was enacted. The king in council approved it on 10 May 1753.[9]

A 4 February 1751/2 petition from New Britain, Bucks County, claimed that different creditors applied for different attachments for small debts, "whereby the Defendant's Effects are consumed in Charges." It asked for a law to prevent more than one attachment, and for each creditor to receive "a proportional share." A similar complaint appeared in a petition from Chester County on 6 February. On 11 February, Franklin and others were assigned to consider the "Attachments for Debts under Forty Shillings" and to "report their Opinion what Amendments may be proper to be made in the said Laws." The committee replied on 14 February that in the case of small debts, legal expenses often consumed "a large part of the debtor's estate, to the great loss and injury of both debtors and creditors." The committee suggested that when a suit was brought and sworn to, the magistrate could take the property of the debtor and publish the proceedings. Only one attachment within a county would be permitted. After officials seized the property of a debtor, there must be a three-month waiting period before its sale, giving the debtor a chance to pay. Following the sale, reasonable charges were paid, then the creditors were to share the attachment "in proportion of their respective debts." The debtor would receive any surplus.[10]

After being read on 26 and 27 February, the House referred the bill for "further Consideration." The next day it was read "Paragraph by Paragraph" and transcribed for a third reading. On 29 February, the bill passed and was sent to the governor, who replied on 10 March that he would amend the bill by the "next Meeting of Assembly." During the third session, on 11 August 1752, the governor returned the bill with amendments, which were accepted on 14 August and ordered to be engrossed with the bill. Members from the assembly and the council compared the bill, and Governor Hamilton enacted it on 22 August. The king in council declared it law on 10 May 1753.[11]

THE MAJOR ISSUE: PAPER MONEY

Ever since the passing of a paper money bill in 1723, the assembly had financed about half of its expenses through interest arising from the Loan Office. Persons could borrow up to £100 on land at an interest rate of 5 percent, which Franklin estimated on 22 August 1751 generated about £3,000 a year (4:187). Pennsylvania's assemblymen all knew that since 1748 Parliament had considered passing an act forbidding colonial paper currency because New England's paper money depreciated so rapidly that the British merchants who accepted it were penalized. But Parliament's currency act of June 1751 only forbade the New England colonies from emitting any further paper currency.[12] The Pennsylvania Assembly believed it could now enact a new paper money bill.

Thomas Penn, however, objected to Pennsylvania's paper currency bills and to the Loan Office because it made the legislature semi-independent. Penn had resolved to control the province's finances. He wrote Governor Hamilton on 29 July 1751: "I am sorry to see every Bill sent up to you calculated to weaken the executive part of the Government, which you are very sensible if complyed with must in the end destroy all order; the only way to prevent it is, not to pass any Bill for raising Money without appropriating the production in the Bill, or leaving it to the Governor & Assembly jointly to do it, & we do not intend to pass any Paper Money . . . but on that Condition—there is nothing but the power of appropriating the publick Money that can give those People [the assemblymen] any weight."[13] Penn's disdain for Pennsylvanians in general and the Pennsylvania legislators in particular naturally increased their contempt for him.

Penn's semi-formal instruction to Governor Hamilton was to be kept secret except from the leading Proprietary Party members. Penn also forbade Hamilton to pass any "Excise Law" without the governor sharing in the decision on how to spend the taxes, but the excise duties were not about to expire. They would have to be repealed—and there was little possibility that the assembly would repeal them.[14]

On 12 February 1751/2, a petition for more paper money was read in the House. The next day it was referred to further consideration. On 14 February, the Speaker ordered that Franklin be one of a "Committee to prepare and bring in a Bill for re-emitting and continuing the Currency of the Bills of Credit of this Province and for striking a further Sum to be made current, and emitted on Loan." The committee brought in its paper money bill on 19 February but left blank the amount to be struck and made current. That meant the committee

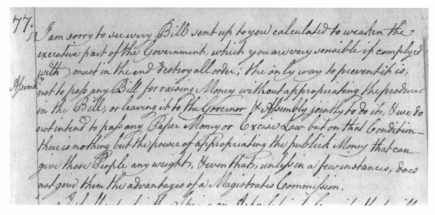

Figure 34a. Thomas Penn's disdain for the legislators of Pennsylvania, Penn to Governor James Hamilton, 29 July 1751. Writing Governor James Hamilton concerning his secret instructions, Thomas Penn ordered him not to pass any money bills or excise taxes unless they specified exactly what the funds would be spent for or unless the governor controlled their disposition. Then Penn superciliously wrote of the Pennsylvania assemblymen: "nothing but the power of appropriating the publick Money . . . can give those People any weight." Courtesy, Historical Society of Pennsylvania.

members disagreed. After being read the second time with the sum still blank, the House resolved itself into a committee of the whole and voted to make the amount £40,000. Read for the third time on 25 February, the bill passed. The next day it was sent to Governor Hamilton.[15]

Hamilton vetoed it on 6 March but did not, of course, cite Penn's instruction. That would have raised an outcry against Penn, the Proprietary Party, and Hamilton. Instead, he said that only by the "strongest Solicitations" were Pennsylvania and the southern colonies exempted from Parliament's currency act of 1751. He reminded the legislators that Pennsylvania had always shown moderation in the past, and that the most recent emission was only £11,110. He claimed it was inadvisable to ask to re-emit "our Present Currency for a long Term of Years" or to ask for "a new Emission of a larger Sum than was ever at one Time made in the Province."[16] The House appointed a committee, including Franklin, to reply. On 7 March, the committee defended its request. Though the bill for £40,000 would have "tended greatly to the Welfare" of the province, the House submitted a bill for only £20,000 in order "to obviate every Objection." Reflecting Franklin's "Observations Concerning the Increase of Mankind" (4:229, #10), the message said that the currency would appear to be to "the Advantage of the Trade of our Mother Country, in full Proportion to what we can expect or hope to reap among ourselves." The committee further stated that the government had only added an inconsiderable sum to the paper currency in the previous twenty years, though "within that Time, the Number of

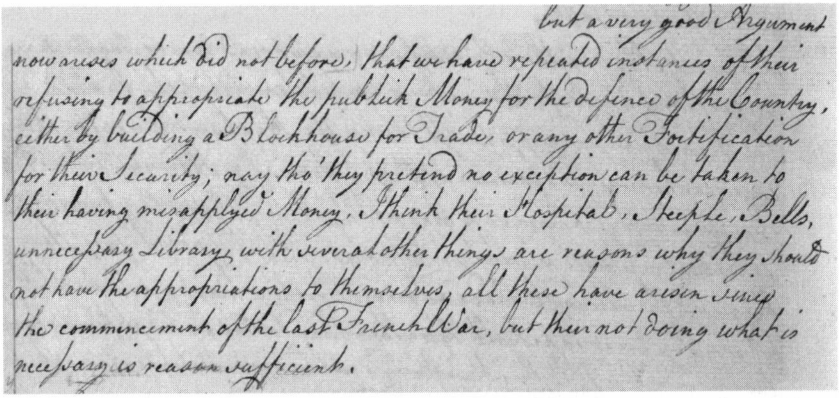

Figure 34b. Thomas Penn's scorn for the Pennsylvania Hospital, Liberty Bell, etc., Penn to Richard Peters, 26 February 1755. To Peters, secretary of the province, Penn complained on 21 February 1755 that the Pennsylvania Assembly spent money frivolously. The assemblymen "pretend no exception can be taken to their having misapplyed Money, I think their Hospital, Steeple, Bells, unnecessary Library, with several other things are reasons why they should not have the appropriations to themselves, all these have arisen since the commencement of the last French War." The items Penn specified were the Pennsylvania Hospital, the statehouse steeple (finished in April 1753), the Liberty Bell (purchased in 1752, recast and hung in the completed statehouse steeple in 1753), the fire bell (also bought in 1752 and hung in the Philadelphia Academy in 1753); and perhaps the Library Company of Philadelphia. The last, however, may refer to the "Books and Maps" that Isaac Norris and Franklin purchased in 1753 for the use of the Pennsylvania Assembly. Courtesy, Historical Society of Pennsylvania.

our Inhabitants and our Trade are greatly increased" (4:273–74). The House approved the committee's message and promptly submitted a revised bill, now requesting £20,000.

Governor Hamilton rejected it on 10 March 1752, claiming that the "present Bills of Credit will continue to be current for more than four Years, without any Diminution, and the Prices of our Export Commodities, in my Opinion, shew we are not in immediate Want of Money as a Medium of Commerce." He again cited the Parliament's act of 1751: "Making the best Judgment I am able of what has lately passed in England, concerning Paper Currencies in America, I cannot see my passing the Bill in the Light the Assembly does, and therefore cannot give my Assent to it." The next day Norris appointed Franklin to a committee "to enquire into the State of our Paper Currency, our foreign and domestick Trade; and the Number of People within this Province, and report thereon to the next Sitting of Assembly."[17] Since the charge described the kinds of concerns that Franklin addressed in his "Observations Concerning the Increase of Mankind," it seems likely that he proposed the committee. The assembly's second session adjourned that afternoon to 10 August. Hamilton knew he would hear from the assembly about the money bill in August. That would traditionally be a short session, but he would have to answer the assembly's renewed request the following winter. Chafing at Penn's instruction of 29 July 1751, Hamilton wrote him on 18 March 1751/2 that the assembly and even some members of the Proprietary Party would never allow the governor to control the money arising from either paper currency or the excise taxes. To emphasize the impossibility of carrying out Penn's desires, Hamilton said he had a "great desire to resign."[18]

Thomas Penn valued Hamilton's service and replied on 30 May 1752: "As soon as I received your Letter I waited on his Lordship as I thought it of great Consequence to know whether there was any room to expect such a Bill would pass here." Penn called upon John Carteret, first Earl Granville, president of the Privy Council. (Granville's former wife, Lady Sophia Fermor, was the sister of Lady Juliana, Thomas Penn's wife.) Penn reported that Granville was "much concerned that Pennsylvania" should ask for a large addition to its paper currency so soon after Parliament had passed a law to prevent the issuing of any more paper money in the New England colonies. According to Penn, Granville "compared our Currency with that of Rhode Island, our People and Trade with theirs," and said "he was sensible there was a great disproportion in the Quantity of Currency in our favor; but much desir'd that if it should be found necessary to increase the Quantity that it should be only a small addition, and that the Bill should not be passed for at least a year, and at the same time that a representative should be sent with it, setting the increase of the Trade of Pennsylvania, and, of its Inhabitants."

Perhaps Penn reported Granville's conversation accurately, but I suspect that Penn supplied him only with select facts. Penn wrote Hamilton: "We then spoke of the Sum, when I proposed Twenty Thousand Pounds, for I found more would not be allowed, and I myself you may be assured did not desire to make the Quantity too great." Penn advised Hamilton to put off the bill and suggested that it could "be done by private Conferences, for this must not be the Subject of a Publick Message, at least no names must be made use of & you will endeavour to do it on the Receipt of this and inform them that I believe a Bill in proper time will be allowed." The latter part of Penn's letter adds to one's suspicion that he made up part of the conversation with Granville, for it has a similar underlying sentiment as the 29 July 1751 letter to Hamilton: "He also said a good deal to me of the great mischief that attended the Assembly having the Power of disposing of the Interest Money, and if any more is issued in the King's Colonys [i.e., the royal colonies, the Privy Council] will give the same Instructions I have sent you."

Despite Hamilton's opinion, Penn continued his campaign to control the colony's funds. He therefore repeated on 30 May 1752 that Hamilton should not pass a currency bill unless the governor controlled the money.[19]

THE LAST ASSEMBLY SESSION OF 1751–52, 10–22 AUGUST 1752

When the Pennsylvania Assembly of 1751–52 met in August, it resolved the pressing business and tried to wind up the session, probably knowing it would be impossible to get Governor Hamilton to approve a currency bill. Perhaps, as Penn had suggested, Hamilton had conferred privately with Speaker Isaac Norris and Franklin and asked that the bill be put off for a year. But Franklin had prepared his "Report on the State of the Currency" on 19 August 1752. Franklin's extraordinary document reflected his "Observations Concerning the Increase of Mankind." He presented a history of the paper money acts since 1723 and pointed out that the £80,000 in paper currency presently in use was to continue less than four years longer, "when it must begin to sink," one-sixth part per year. In six years the province would be left without any currency, "except that precarious One of Silver, which cannot be depended on, being continually wanted to ship Home, as Returns, to pay for the Manufactures of Great-Britain" (4:345). Shipping and commerce in Pennsylvania were falling in the years before 1723 when the first paper money act passed but since then have "flourished and encreased in a most surprizing Manner." Calculating Pennsylvania's population, Franklin cited the bills of mortality and the tax records from Philadelphia through 1751 before considering the population increase in Pennsylvania's other counties, beginning with Bucks and Chester. Next, he turned to the trade with England, quoting from a report to Parliament of 4 April 1749 by the inspector general of the customs. Like the overseas trade, the commerce within Pennsylvania had increased in proportion to the increasing population (4:348).

Both the manner of issuing the paper currency and "the Medium itself" contributed to its success. Loans from no less than £12.10 to no more than £100 per person, to be repaid in yearly quotas, had "put it in the Power of many to purchase Lands . . . and thereby to acquire Estate to themselves, and to support and bring up Families." Without the loans, many "would probably have continued longer in a single State" or remained laborers for others or emigrated. Now the demand for money and for borrowing from the Loan Office had greatly increased, and since more than a thousand applicants were waiting, "a vast Multitude of our Inhabitants have, to procure Settlements, wandered away to other Places." The increase in population, "great as it is, would probably have been much greater" if more paper currency had been issued (4:348–49). With a touch of irony, Franklin conceded that making it easy "for the industrious Poor to obtain Lands, and acquire Property in a Country" could be charged with keeping up "the Price of Labour." That made it "more difficult for the old Settler to procure working Hands, the Labourers very soon setting up for themselves." Thus, despite the number of laborers who have immigrated into Pennsylvania, "Labour continues as dear as ever"—a point made in "Observations" (4:228, #8). Nevertheless, for the old settler, the "Inconvenience is perhaps more than balanced by the rising Value of his Lands, occasion'd by Encrease of People" (4:349–50).

The report ended by paraphrasing the thesis of Franklin's "Observations": "by rendering the Means of purchasing Land easy to the Poor, the Dominions of the Crown are strengthen'd and extended; the Proprietaries dispose of their Wilderness Territory; and the British Nation secures the Benefit of its Manufactures, and increases the Demand for them." Franklin again anticipated Frederick Jackson Turner's frontier thesis as a reason that American manufacturing could not compete with England's: "For so long as Land can be easily procur'd . . . so long will Labour be dear in America; and while Labour continues dear, we can never rival the Artificers . . . of our Mother Country" (4:350).

When Thomas Penn read the report, he may have conceded that these were all good reasons, especially that money available in the Loan Office made his "Wilderness" lands more valuable, but he thought it more important to curb the power of the assembly—which he intended to do by cutting off its funds. Presented to the Pennsylvania Assembly on 20 August 1752, Franklin's report was referred on 22 August to the following assembly of 1752–53 for consideration. Richard Peters reported to Thomas Penn that some members of the assembly had begun to say that Hamilton's excuses were subterfuges and that the proprietors had forbidden him to pass a paper currency bill.[20] Franklin must have heard these rumors and probably believed them true. Like other assembly members, Franklin evidently thought Thomas Penn was more concerned with his own power than with Pennsylvania's welfare. On that same 22 August, the finance committee, which included Franklin, settled the annual accounts, and the session adjourned.

Though Franklin was involved only as an assemblyman, two other acts and a minor item of the assembly of 1751–52 are of interest. On 12 February the assembly requested "That the Superintendants of the State-house do provide a suitable Ink-stand of Silver for the Use of the Speaker's Table." Philip Syng made the elaborate silver inkstand, for which the assembly paid the high price of £25.16 at the session's end. Used in signing both the Declaration of Independence and the Constitution, Syng's ink stand is displayed today at Independence Hall. The two acts created new counties. On 20 February, the House passed the bill forming Berks County and the next day passed a bill creating Northampton County. Governor Hamilton approved them on 11 March 1751/2.[21] Each county, however, was given just one representative, whereas the oldest counties each had eight. Both the boundaries of the two new counties and the number of representatives allowed were a gerrymandering attempt to keep the Quaker Party in power and to restrict the German influence. Years later, the Paxton Boys identified the unfair representation in the Pennsylvania Assembly as a major grievance and, somehow, a partial excuse for the murder of innocent Indians.

SUSANNA WRIGHT

Other than official occasions with the assembly and the other organizations that Franklin belonged to that kept minutes, little is known of Franklin's and Deborah's social life. One tantalizing reference is his thank-you letter to Susanna Wright (1697–1784). She was the daughter of Franklin's friend John Wright, who died in 1749, and sister of John (1711–59) and James (1714–75), both of whom, like their father, served as representatives to the General Assembly. Franklin wrote her on 21 November 1751 that "Your Guests all got well home to their Families, highly pleas'd with their Journey, and with the Hospitality of Hempstead." Franklin, Deborah, and perhaps William and Sarah, together with some other person(s), had all visited Susanna Wright at her home on the Susquehanna, Lancaster County, where she owned a ferry and land. She never married, but Samuel Blunston (1689–1745), another former Lancaster County representative, left her a major part of his vast estate and is known to have asked her to marry him.[22] A feminist, fine poet, active political figure, and an advocate of Americanism, she was probably the most intellectual woman whom Franklin had met to that date.

With his thank-you letter, Franklin sent "Susy" Wright a gift of superior candles, which he said she would especially prize since they were "the Manufacture of our own Country" (4:211). He also gave her a copy of the latest *Gentleman's Magazine* because of its article and illustration of the "Marble Aqueduct" in Portugal. He evidently knew that she would be interested in such engineering feats. Franklin is said to have written an "Ode on Hospitality" about the stay at Hempfield, but it seems not to be extant. Franklin valued her friendship and capabilities. Four years later, Franklin consulted her about securing wagons for General Edward Braddock. Deborah Franklin was among Wright's friends and correspondents.[23]

CONCLUSION

During the assembly of 1751–52, Franklin had thirty-six assignments—the most of any member.[24] In his first full year in the House, he had become, after Speaker Isaac Norris, its most influential member. Though Proprietary Party members still hoped that Franklin would identify with Penn and the administration, he was already the foremost spokesman of the moderate wing of the Quaker Party. Like most assemblymen, Franklin despised Thomas Penn for attempting to deprive Pennsylvanians of the ability to control their own government and the funds it raised.

TEN

Insurance: The Philadelphia Contributionship

On 26 August 1751, Franklin proposed in the Union Fire Company that two members from each Philadelphia fire company attend a meeting on 7 September 1751 "to Consider such Matters as they may think will tend Most to the Utility of the Inhabitants in General."
—Union Fire Company Minutes, p. 136; Historical Society of Pennsylvania

FRANKLIN STARTED THE PHILADELPHIA CONTRIBUTIONSHIP for the Insurance of Houses from Loss by Fire, America's first successful fire insurance company, in 1752. He attempted to do so in late 1749.[1] If he followed his customary practice, he brought up the idea in the Junto, made a brief speech in its favor, and the members discussed it. But there are no minutes of the Junto meetings. The minutes of the Union Fire Company, however, state that on 26 February 1749/50, two new members, Israel Pemberton, Jr., and Philip Benezet, agreed to add six pounds to the Company's stock to make £100 "to put to interest to raise a fund for Insurance for this Company." A motion to spend the Company's money had to be announced in a meeting before the motion was voted, and the company had to be notified that a vote to spend the company's funds would take place at the forthcoming meeting. Therefore, the motion to set aside £88 of the company's stock must have been voted upon at the January (or earlier) meeting, and the motion would have had to be introduced at the December, 1749 (or earlier) meeting. Evidently the new members would not have been required to contribute to the existing fund, so their generosity was recorded.

Later in the same 26 February meeting, the "Company present" agreed "to advance their proportion of one hundred pounds, to be joined with one hundred raised before to make two hundred in order to raise a fund for an Insurance Office to make up the Damage that may Arise by Fire among this Company." The motion was contingent, of course, upon the members at the next meeting agreeing with the proposition.[2]

Franklin was absent from the 26 February 1749/50 meeting, probably because he was suffering with his first attack of gout. He knew, however, what the business of the meeting would be. He had been present at the January meeting. Given his comparatively sporadic attendance at the Union Fire Company during the 1740s, his faithful record in 1750 (when he missed only the February and April meetings) suggests that he had some project he wanted the company to accomplish. Since the company lent an individual £100 that same evening, recording that the bond signed would be "given in the names of Hugh Roberts, Benjamin Franklin, & Philip Syng," that too argues that he previously knew the evening's business.

Fire insurance does not appear in the Union Fire Company minutes again until 24 September 1750 when Franklin was serving as the clerk, but a committee to draw up articles of organization for an insurance scheme had been appointed and done its work. "The Articles relating to the Insurance of Houses were read" at the meeting. The members wanted to read them at their leisure, and it was agreed that no one was "to keep them above 24 Hours." After everyone else had examined them, they were "lastly to be delivered to Benjamin Franklin to be Engrossed." Franklin must have been thoroughly familiar with them before the meeting. There is no absolute proof, but, as I will argue below, he probably wrote them, perhaps modeling them upon the London Amicable Contributionship for Insuring Houses (4:282). No mention of insurance was recorded at the next Union Fire Company meeting, 29 October, but on 26 November, the engrossed copy of the articles was submitted to the company and signed by everyone present except Daniel Benezet. Then the insurance scheme languished, probably because, even if all the members of the Union Fire Company signed, the amount of money they would raise would be insufficient to pay for the destruction of a single moderately expensive house worth, say, £500. Franklin needed a larger base of membership than the Union Fire Company could provide.

At the 26 July 1751 Union Fire Company meeting, the "Succeeding Clerk" was ordered to "give Notice that a Matter of Some Importance is to be Determined at the Next Meeting." Franklin presented on 26 August a proposal "relating to . . . the late Scheme for Insurance of Houses" and requested that the Company appoint two "Members to attend such Persons as may be appointed by the other Several Fire Companies to meet at the Widow Pratt's *Royal Standard* in Market Street on the 7th day of the 7th Month next, to Consider such Matters as they may think will tend Most to the Utility of the Inhabitants in General." Franklin and Philip Syng were appointed. Howard E. Gillingham aptly commented, "How like BF to suggest that which 'will tend Most to the Utility of the Inhabitants in General.' "[3]

Preparing for the 7 September meeting, Franklin printed a *Deed of Settlement of the Society for insuring of Houses.* When the representatives from seven fire companies met, Franklin proposed a fire insurance company. No doubt the printed *Deed* of 1751 had articles similar to those drawn up and circulated in the Union Fire Company on 24 September 1750 and engrossed two months later, 26 November 1750. During the fall and winter of 1751–52, Franklin circulated the *Deed of Settlement* (or "articles of association") until he obtained more than 50 subscribers. Then he announced in the *Pennsylvania Gazette* for 4 February 1752

that "The subscribers to the articles of insurance of houses from fire . . . are
desired to meet on Saturday next, at three a clock in the afternoon, at the Court
house, in order to agree on proper measures for carrying the same into immediate execution."

By Saturday, 8 February 1751/2, Franklin had the map-maker Lewis Evans
engross the articles in the printed *Deed* of 1751 on a sheet of parchment[4] and
asked Governor James Hamilton to be the first subscriber. He signed, then
Franklin and Syng, and then the subscribers who met at the court house that
day. Comparatively few subscribers, however, showed up and signed, so Franklin announced in the *Gazette* of 18 February that someone would be present at
the Court House every Saturday afternoon to sign up subscribers until 13 April
1752, "being the day appointed by the said articles for electing directors and a
treasurer."

The annual general meeting of the subscribers was held on the second Monday in April at the Court House when twelve directors and a treasurer were
elected. Franklin, William Coleman, Philip Syng, Samuel Rhoads, Hugh Roberts, Israel Pemberton, Jr., John Mifflin, Joseph Morris, Joseph Fox, Jonathan
Zane, William Griffitts, and Amos Strettell were elected directors, and John
Smith, treasurer.[5] The directors then met, elected Franklin President, and asked
Joseph Saunders, a young merchant who was writing marine insurance, to serve
as the company's clerk for an annual salary of forty pounds.

The directors next met on 11 May at the Widow Pratt's on Market Street
across from the Court House, the customary meeting place of Franklin's Union
Fire Company. The directors decided to impose a fine on themselves of 1 shilling
for not meeting precisely at the time ordered, and 2 shillings for a total absence.
Philip Syng was asked to provide a Seal for the Company, showing the four
Hands of two persons grasping each other's four wrists (a symbol of strength in
joining together), with the Motto, "Philadelphia Contributionship." The London Hand in Hand Fire Company is generally said to have inspired the seal, but
that simply shows two clasped hands, which is a common symbol of friendship.
A closer source is the Associator flag described in the *Pennsylvania Gazette* of 12
January 1747/8, showing "Three Arms, wearing different Linnen, ruffled, plain,
and checqued; the Hands joined by grasping each the other's Wrist, denoting
the Union of all ranks. Motto, Unita Virtus Valet." But the Philadelphia Contributionship seal has four hands grasping four wrists, suggesting only two persons, not three, which is a fireman's carrying grip, sometimes called the Lady-
to-London grip, a wonderfully suitable symbol that suggests fire, support, and
strength.

Initially, numerous matters required attention, and Franklin called a spate
of meetings, 16, 20, 23, and 30 May 1752. On 16 May, they described the Clerk's
duties and pay, 40£ per year, and settled on the pay for a house survey, 2 shillings and 6 pence. On 20 May, with Franklin absent, Hugh Roberts was asked
to bargain with John Stow about getting lead hand-in-hand signs made. They

would be placed on the insured buildings to advertise the company. On 23 May, the directors specified the form or wording of the policies and asked Franklin "to get a sufficient number" printed.

In June, the directors met on the 2nd, 6th, 13th, 20th and 27th. Joseph Fox and Samuel Rhoads wrote the first policy on treasurer John Smith's house and kitchen (presumably the kitchen was separate), which was on King Street between Mulberry and Sassafrass, valuing it at £1,000. Smith insured £500 of the property for 20 shillings per hundred. The rate of 20 shillings per hundred pounds of value was comparatively low mainly because the house and kitchen were entirely made of brick. Fox and Rhoads evaluatedd Franklin's two houses on the south side of High Street on the 13th. Franklin's house "where Dan'l Swan dwells" (policy # 19), was valued at £200 and insured at 35 shillings per hundred of value. Sarah Read had given the property to her two daughters and their husbands, Deborah and Benjamin Franklin, and Frances and John Croker. The Crokers had sold their half to Franklin on 12 October 1745, for £60. The charge to Franklin was £3.10.0. Franklin's second house, policy # 20, where "Eden Haydock dwells," was valued at £150 and insured at 50s per hundred. The higher cost per hundred pounds of value for the latter was owing to its being "a Painters Shop." Sarah Read had given this property to her son John Read on 12 April 1734, who sold it to Franklin, 15 November 1751, for £390. The insurance on it cost £3.15.0. There was an additional charge for the two policies, marks, and survey fees of £1.00, making Franklin's total cost £8.5.0.

During June, the directors stopped meeting at the Widow Pratt's and started on the 20th to meet at Joseph Saunders's house. In July, the directors met on the 4th (the first time that all the directors were present; usually one to three missed the meeting), 11th, 22nd, and 29th, with Franklin missing meetings on the 11th and 22nd. As the normal routines settled, the necessity for frequent meetings decreased. The regular time for the monthly meeting was on the first Tuesday of the month. There were two meetings in August (on the fourth and eighteenth); with Franklin missing both. At the latter meeting, which Franklin could not attend because the legislature was in session, the clerk recorded that 45 policies had been issued since 22 July. By the end of the summer, more than 84 policies had been issued.[6] In September, Franklin attended the only meeting held, on the first. There were two meetings in October, on the 3rd (which Franklin missed because he was at a Common Council meeting) and the 17th, which he managed to attend after the assembly meeting. Franklin missed the monthly meetings in November on the 7th and in December on the 5th.

By 1753, the minutes of the monthly meetings record little other than a brief listing of the new policies approved or disapproved. Since most of the directors were "engaged at the Mayor's Court," on the 2nd of January, they agreed to meet on the 9th. Franklin missed that meeting but was present on 6 February, 6 and 14 March, and 3 April. At the last, it was "Agreed that Philip Syng, Amos

Strettell, Joseph Trotter, Joshua Crosby, and Evan Morgan be Judges & Managers of the Election for the Directors & Treasurer for the ensuing Year."

The election was held on 9 April 1753 at 3 P.M. at the Court House. Benjamin Franklin, William Coleman, Joseph Morris, Samuel Rhoads, Israel Pemberton, Jr., John Mifflin, Hugh Roberts, Joseph Fox, James Pemberton, Isaac Jones, Abel James, and James Logan were elected directors, and John Smith was again chosen treasurer. The directors reelected Franklin President. He attended the 23 April meeting, but then he was absent on 1 May (he wrote Jared Eliot on 3 May that he had "never been more hurried in Business"), 5 June (he was entertaining William Smith who was visiting the Philadelphia Academy), 3 July and 7 August (on these two dates he was in New England on post office business), 4 September (he was at an Assembly meeting), 2 October (he was at an Indian treaty in Carlisle) , and 6 November. He attended the several December meetings.

During that month, a house, which the Contributionship had insured, burned. The *Pennsylvania Gazette* for 20 December reported that on 18 December, "between Five and Six a Clock, a Fire broke out in the House of Mr. Andrew Reed, Merchant, in this City, which, besides destroying a Quantity of valuable Houshold Goods, and about 150 Barrels of Flour and Bread, belonging to different Persons, did some considerable Damage to the lower Parts of the Building; but by the great Activity and Industry of the People, the Roof and upper Floors were saved; and the House being insur'd, the Damage will be immediately repaired, without Cost to the Owner." The last phrase, which was good advertising for the Contributionship, shows that Franklin evidently wrote the account. The house Reed occupied belonged to the Contributionship member Peter Bard. Union Fire Company members fought the fire, and the company's minutes record that Charles Norris, Richard Hockley, Philip Syng, and Samuel Morris all lost fire-fighting equipment. The recently purchased and installed fire bell at the Academy must have resounded, calling forth the firemen. With others, Franklin must have rushed out to fight the fire.

On the afternoon of the 18th, a special meeting of the Contributionship was called. Though Peter Bard was out of town, the directors roughly evaluated what the repairs would cost and consented to pay to have the house cleaned and the broken windows replaced. They met again on 24 December after Bard's return. They agreed to pay for and supervise the repairing of his house. The cost for repairs came to £145—almost one fourth of the company's assets of £554. At that last meeting of the year, Franklin "produced an Acct. which he had paid to Lewis Evans for Engrosing the Insurance Articles etc, amounting to £2.9.0. which was ordered to be paid by the Treasurer to the said Benj. Franklin." Through the first two years of the Contributionship, he had been its leader, evidently the key founding member as well as President and director.

On 2 January 1754, Franklin left with William Hunter on post-office business for Maryland, and so missed the 3 January and 5 February meetings. At the latter, William Maugridge borrowed £200 from the Contributionship, with

Franklin guaranteeing "that the interest shall be punctually paid."[7] Franklin was present for the 5 March meeting by which time the Contributionship had issued 254 policies. Franklin then missed the meetings on 12 (which conflicted with a meeting of the Academy Trustees), 21 March, and 4 April (when he was at an Assembly meeting). He was present for the 6 April meeting. The Clerk, Joseph Saunders, prepared a statement of the "Fines due from the Directors of Philad.a Contributionship from 9th April 1753 to 8th of April 1754." Franklin had been absent more than any other director and paid £1.5.[8]

Franklin missed the general meeting of the subscribers that elected the directors on 8 April 1754 and was not reelected to the board of directors. Perhaps he asked not to be. The fire insurance company was providing the service that he and his friends had intended and was becoming a successful company. He was frequently out of town, and when present, often could not attend its meetings because of other business. He evidently stopped giving the Philadelphia Contributionship priority once it was up and running. America's first successful insurance company no longer needed him.

ELEVEN

Paper Currency, the Coming of War, and a Trip to New England, 1752–1753

"True Respect is not necessarily connected with Rank, and . . . it is only from a
Course of Action suitable to that Rank" that the proprietors "can hope to obtain"
respect.
—11 September 1753, 5:49

THOUGH THE QUAKER PARTY and the Pennsylvania Assembly tried to avoid the
issue, the invasion of the French and their Indian allies into the frontier was
gradually affecting Pennsylvania. Skirmishes anticipating the French and Indian
War (or Seven Years' War) of 1755–63 occurred with increasing frequency during
1750–55. Pennsylvania fur traders in the Ohio country were seized by French
forces, taken to Canada, and sent to France, from whence, by various routes,
they made their way back to Philadelphia. There, they appeared before the assembly, asking for comparatively small sums to help them return to the frontier.
These were granted. The larger question, however, was funds for military defense. Franklin and most frontier county representatives wanted a supply bill
for defense. The Proprietary Party did too, but refused to have the assembly
control the money, to have the proprietors taxed for defense, or to permit issuing new paper money from the Loan Office. Under pressure, the Quaker Party
moderates were willing to vote for defense—but only if the proprietors contributed some share. Franklin and the frontier county members agreed with the
moderate Quakers. In an emergency, however, Franklin and many members
were finally willing to abandon their principles and to tax themselves while
exempting the proprietors.

Speaker Isaac Norris assigned Franklin to all four standing committees on
17 October 1752: correspondence, minutes, accounts, and grievances. As a member of the last, Franklin devoted considerable time from May through August
1753 to the complaints against William Craig, sheriff of Northampton County,
whom the assembly finally reprimanded on 31 August.[1] Speaker Norris also appointed Franklin on 17 October 1752 to another time-consuming committee:
one that would inspect the laws of the province. Its members were to report

which ones were near expiring and recommend what new laws, renewals, additions, or changes should be made.

THE 1752–53 ASSEMBLY'S SECOND SESSION, 15–27 JANUARY 1753

After James Logan's death in 1751, Franklin was probably the best bookman in Philadelphia. Early in the second session, on 16 January 1753, Speaker Isaac Norris, who was also a major book collector, named Franklin and himself a committee to procure books and maps for the use of the Pennsylvania Assembly.

Paper Currency

The assembly took up paper currency on Franklin's forty-seventh birthday, 17 January 1753. The members heard his report from the previous assembly session and resolved to form a committee of the whole the following morning. On 18 January, three resolutions were made and passed unanimously: (1) the paper currency should be re-emitted; (2) the ragged and torn bills should be replaced; and (3) an addition to the paper money in circulation should be made. Norris assigned Franklin to a committee to bring in a bill "agreeable to the Resolves" (4:496). Reported and read the first time on 19 January, the amount of the "further addition" to be issued was left blank. The next day, the members agreed that it should be £20,000. Governor James Hamilton had presumably passed on to Norris and Franklin Thomas Penn's word that £20,000 was the largest amount the Privy Council would accept. The assembly resolved on 23 January that the borrowers on the former paper money acts should be allowed to renew their mortgages for one year and that the sum to be renewed could not exceed £100. Read for the third time and passed the next day, the bill was carried to Governor Hamilton.[2] It would re-emit the current paper money (£80,000) and make the additional £20,000 current for sixteen years.

Hamilton wrote the proprietors that he either had to veto the bill or "lay before them your Instructions." He preferred to do the latter, but William Allen and Tench Francis advised him that a revelation of the instruction of 30 May 1752 insisting on the governor's control of interest arising from a paper currency bill would "raise such a Flame in the province as would not be quench'd in many Years."[3] So Hamilton tried to evade the decision. He replied to the assembly on Friday, 26 January, that great prejudice still existed in England against any colonial paper currency and that he therefore could not "at present give my Assent." Since the winter session would end the following day, the assembly put off considering the governor's veto to the May session.

The proprietary supporters all knew that the citizens and the members of assembly strongly felt the need for a paper currency. Attorney General Tench Francis wrote to Thomas Penn on 9 February 1753: "The moment this Instruction should be known it would occasion a downright Civil War in the Province . . . In fine it could not be imagined to what Lengths an enraged people might go."[4] Governor Hamilton found himself in an impossible position and resigned on 9 February, effective a year after Penn received the letter. Thomas Penn wrote on 28 March that he had received Hamilton's and Francis's letters and that he was now canceling the 30 May 1752 instruction. He had believed that "Men of Property . . . would assist you" in carrying out the instruction.[5] Several days later on 2 April 1753, Penn wrote Hamilton that he had known that "great opposition would be made," yet he expected that with "several of the most considerable people with us we might in time have gained the point." But since Hamilton found himself deserted by the other proprietary supporters, "I am much pleased you have put of[f] the Bill." Penn was also glad that Hamilton had not made public the instruction to have executive control of any interest arising from a paper currency bill. Penn hoped that "it has been communicated to so few persons, that it will be stil kept secret."[6]

Twenty-three years before, Parliament had demanded that all paper currency acts passed in the colonies should have a clause declaring that the act "shall not take effect" until approved by the British authorities. Now in his 2 April letter, Penn advised Hamilton to accept the paper money bill provided that it had a suspending clause, which would keep the bill in limbo "until the King's pleasure is known."[7] Penn thought the assembly would accept such an act and that the pressure on Hamilton would be relieved. Penn evidently assumed that, if necessary, he could have his friends and relatives on the Board of Trade and the Privy Council disallow the act.

Prelude (1748–52) to the French and Indian War

As shown in Volume 2, Pennsylvania's James Logan foresaw in the 1730s that the French would want to control the western part of Pennsylvania, especially the Ohio country, for it provided a passage by water from near the Great Lakes to New Orleans. He negotiated with the Six Nations to align the Shawnee and other Indians living in the Ohio area with the English. The treaty of Lancaster (1744) ceded Iroquois land to the colonies of Pennsylvania, Maryland, and Virginia and seemingly confirmed the success of Logan's policy (*Life* 2:227–28, 231–32). Three factors, however, ruined Logan's strategy. First, the Ohio Indians became increasingly unhappy with the supposed suzerainty of the Iroquois. Second, different colonies became rivals for the West: in 1747 a group of Virginians formed the Ohio Company, intending to acquire land on both sides of the Ohio River, even though part of the land was in Pennsylvania. Third, the French trade between the Great Lakes and New Orleans dramatically increased.

In July 1748, the Oneida chief Scarouady brought a large group of Miamis (or Twightwee) and Shawnee Indians from the Ohio for a second treaty at Lancaster. After the treaty, Franklin analyzed the economic and imperial situation from an optimistic, anti-French point of view in the *Pennsylvania Gazette* on 28 July 1748: "We are informed that some of the more distant nations wait only to hear what reception the Twightwees meet with, being strongly inclined to throw themselves into the arms of the English, who have since the war furnished goods to their allies cheaper than the French could do. Had the war [King George's War, 1744–48] continued a few years longer, probably the greatest part of the French Indians would have been brought over to the English interest and the trade accordingly have fallen naturally into the hands of the British nation."

THE LOGSTOWN TREATY, 1748

To cement relations with the Ohio Indians, Conrad Weiser—accompanied by a major Pennsylvania Indian trader, George Croghan, by the part-Huron, part-Seneca, part-French trader Andrew Montour, and by William Franklin—took gifts from Pennsylvania and Virginia to Logstown, about twenty miles down the Ohio River from modern-day Pittsburgh. The Logstown treaty (8–17 September 1748) "opened up trade possibilities with the western Indians all the way to the Mississippi and from the Michigan peninsula to the Kentucky region." The treaty with the Delawares, Shawnees, and Iroquois "marks the height of the English influence in the Ohio region until after the peace of 1763." Since the Ohio Indians had previously been under the French influence, the treaty temporarily ended French dominance in the Ohio. George Croghan and a few other Pennsylvania fur traders established posts in the area and confirmed the allegiance of the local Indians.[8]

The French resolved to regain their influence. On 15 June 1749, Canadian authorities sent Captain Céloron de Bienville with more than two hundred men to the Ohio country, where he buried metal plates claiming the country for France.[9] Learning of the French activity, Governor Hamilton asked George Croghan on 30 June 1749 to go to the Ohio and assess the situation. Two months later, Franklin reported in the *Pennsylvania Gazette* for 31 August 1749 that Croghan found French officials in the Ohio area trying to persuade the Indians to side with them. The same year, Virginia's Ohio Company built its first fortified house about sixty miles southeast of Pittsburgh, where Wills Creek flows into the north branch of the Potomac, now the site of Cumberland, Maryland.

Squatters in Pennsylvania had settled on the Indian lands, especially along the Juniata River (which flows from the west into the Susquehanna River about halfway between Philadelphia and Pittsburgh). Several Six Nations tribes intended to come with their allies to Philadelphia to complain about the squatters, but the Seneca and Onondaga Indians grew tired of waiting for the others and came alone, arriving in Philadelphia on 1 July 1749. Responding to their complaints, Governor Hamilton issued a proclamation on 18 July against the Juniata settlers. He also suggested to the Indians in Philadelphia (complying with Thomas Penn's instructions) that Pennsylvania might purchase more Indian land.

Just after the Seneca and Onondaga left, the remainder of the Six Nations delegation, under the old chief Canasatego, showed up at Conrad Weiser's home. Weiser was told to say that the presents had already been given and that there was nothing to discuss. The dismissal insulted Canasatego and the Indians

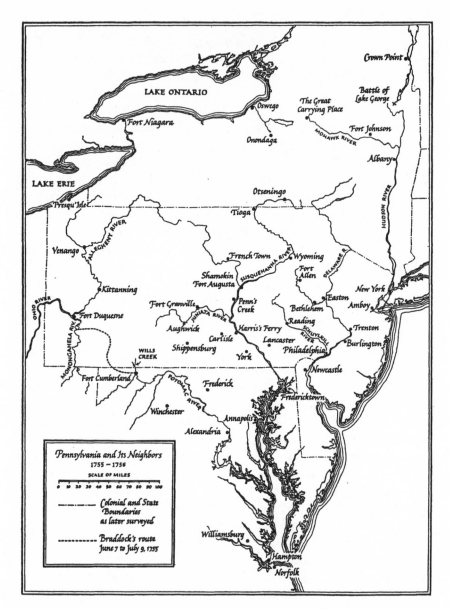

Map 2. Pennsylvania and its neighbors

with him. They came on and arrived in Philadelphia in August where, from 16 to 21 August 1749, they conducted a treaty, full of duplicity on both sides. Later, when the Pennsylvania authorities forced the squatters off the Juniata lands, the officials burned their cabins and alienated a number of the frontiersmen, a few of whom, including the boy Simon Girty, later became famous anti-American frontier fighters.[10]

In 1750, the Pennsylvania traders established a fortified trading house at Pickawillany, a Twightwee/Miami Indian settlement on the Great Miami River (present-day Piqua, Ohio), about two hundred miles west of Pittsburgh. The Miami chief Memeskia ("Old Briton") was a special friend of the English. The settlement, so far into what the French considered their territory, infuriated New France's authorities—who put a price on the head of George Croghan.[11] Alarmed by news of the French incursions down the Mississippi and Ohio, and fearing that Virginia's Ohio Company might make good their occupation of what he considered western Pennsylvania, Thomas Penn urged the Pennsylvania government to build a fort on the Allegheny River. Although Croghan assured Hamilton that the Indians wanted a fort, the assembly consulted Andrew Montour and Conrad Weiser, who contradicted Croghan. On 21 August 1751, Franklin reported that Croghan must have "misunderstood or misrepresented" the Indians (4:182). Thereupon, the Pennsylvania Assembly declined building a fort (4:182).[12]

First Blood

On 21 June 1751, a party of more than two hundred Chippewa and Ottawa Indians with thirty French soldiers commanded by a young cadet, Charles-Michel Mouet de Langlade, attacked the Indians and Pennsylvania traders at Pickawillany. After the outnumbered Twightwees surrendered, the French Indians killed a wounded Pennsylvania trader and ate his heart and then killed, boiled, and ate the Miami chief Memeskia. The French praised young Mouet de Langlade as "very brave," with "much influence on the minds of the Indians," and "very zealous when ordered to do anything."[13] The Indians allied with the English expected the governments of Pennsylvania, New York, and Massachusetts, whose people vastly outnumbered the French, to take some action, but the different American colonies hesitated—and hesitated.

When the Marquis de Duquesne arrived in Quebec as governor-general of New France in July 1752, he dispatched Captain Paul Marin de la Malgue with fifteen hundred soldiers to construct forts to and on the Ohio River.[14] By the spring of 1753, Fort Presqu'ile (Erie, Pennsylvania) on Lake Erie and Fort Le Boeuf on French Creek, a tributary of the Allegheny River at Waterford, Pennsylvania, were under construction (see map 3, p. 369). During the summer of 1753, construction began at Fort Machault, at the junction of French Creek and the Allegheny.[15] The next fort to be built would be Fort Duquesne (Pittsburgh), where the Allegheny met the Monongahela and formed the Ohio River, the strategic key to the Ohio Valley.

May 1753

Replying to Peter Collinson's letter on "Observations Concerning the Increase of Mankind," Franklin disavowed the theory of climate as the primary influence on the different customs of mankind and instead proposed that it was the traditions and culture of the particular people, for the Germans, unlike the English, retained their industry in America, whereas the English laborers seemed to become lazier (4:479). Since the theory that climate created human culture was one idea underlying the supposed inferiority of American Indians (and whites?), he was indirectly replying to English condescension toward America (*Life* 1:297, 2:218). Franklin moved on to the ostensibly puzzling fact that whites who lived with the Indians did not want to return to white civilization, whereas Indians who lived with the whites generally returned as soon as possible to the Indian way of life. The wide-ranging letter of 9 May 1753 also took up ecology and the large numbers of Germans immigrating into Pennsylvania. The letter's conclusion dealt with English-American relations, and Franklin suggested that England was becoming weaker and America stronger. The thought was a staple of the *translatio imperii*, proven by his "Observations." Now he brought up England's oppression of America and warned that England would need America's help in the future (4:486). He had earlier said so in his "Account of the Export of Provisions from Philadelphia" (16 February 1741; 2:303–4) and repeated it in "Observations" (4:229, #11). As I noted above (p. 243), he indirectly suggested that when England needed America's help, America would then (if not before) gain whatever it wanted from England.

Then he called upon the body metaphor that he had earlier applied to the sections and the classes within Pennsylvania in *Plain Truth* (1747): "a Mortification begun in the Foot may spread upwards to the destruction of the nobler parts of the Body" (4:486). In addition to calling for unity, the body metaphor in this context had two implications: one was that the failure of an empire began at its edges; the other was that as the former colonies became separated, they would become independent. He reaffirmed the latter connection in his notes for a pamphlet on the Stamp Act: "The Empire weaken'd, and the Foundation laid of a total Separation. Mortification in the Foot" (P 13:83).

In the spring session (21 May–1 June) of the Pennsylvania Assembly of 1752–53, Governor James Hamilton informed the assembly on 22 May 1753 that a large number of French and Indians were on the way to the Ohio country and that the "Six Nations, with a Mixture of Shawanese and Delawares . . . will be obliged to retire and leave their Country for Want of Means to defend it against this armed Force; as will also the Twightwees." Hamilton asked for funds to help arm and support the Indians. That same morning four frontiersmen from Cumberland County petitioned the assembly for aid, reporting that French Indians with a Frenchman "at their Head" had taken them prisoner in western Pennsylvania, carried them to Quebec, then shipped them to Rochelle, France, where they were released by the English ambassador who sent them to London, "from whence they got Passage" to Philadelphia. They requested money to enable them to return to Cumberland County. After being questioned before the House, they were given £16 to defray their expenses home. On 29 May 1753, the assembly interrogated several traders who had just returned from the Ohio country. The next day, the assembly voted to give £200 to the Twightwee/Miami Indians as a condolence for the loss of fourteen Indians at Pickawillany and an additional £600 for presents to other Indian allies, "or such part thereof as the Governor may think necessary."[16]

Franklin and others were appointed to draft an answer to the governor's 22 May message requesting funds for defense. The committee reported that the government of New York was more immediately concerned with the direction of Indian affairs and that Virginia should also contribute assistance to the Indians, yet, "notwithstanding we have the Misfortune to differ in Sentiments with our Proprietaries in the Part they ought to bear in these Expenses, the Assembly have given liberally to help the Indians" (4:502). Governor Hamilton reported on 29 August that he had not yet sent the £200 to the Twightwees. The French and Indians were on the march to the Ohio, and neither the goods nor the persons conducting them would be safe. Also, Hamilton had not been able to judge how best to spend the £600 and so had sent Conrad Weiser to the Onondaga country to learn the state of affairs. He would follow Weiser's advice.

As if to remind itself that the citizens demanded a paper currency, the assembly on 22 May 1753 read a Lancaster County petition requesting one. The next day, the assembly resumed deliberation on the paper money bill, and the following day Norris appointed Franklin to a committee to comment on the issue. Reporting on 25 May, Franklin stressed that the British merchants trading to Philadelphia had testified to Parliament and to the Board of Trade that the act for £80,000 in 1739 "was not only a reasonable Sum, but absolutely necessary for carrying on the Commerce of the Country." The trade to Britain in the three years before 1739 amounted to £179,654.9.2, whereas during 1749–51, the trade amounted to £647,317.8.8. The population, domestic trade, and the need for a medium of exchange had all similarly increased. Franklin argued that the British merchants would agree that the additional £20,000 funds proposed was indispensable and would probably think it was not as suitable "to our Circumstances as a larger Sum"; £100,000 now was not as proportionable to the trade as £80,000 was in 1739. "As the Money circulating among us diminishes, so must our Trade and Usefulness to Great-Britain, and our Consumption of its Manufactures, diminish" (4:497–98).[17]

The House approved Franklin's message on 25 May 1753. Governor Hamilton replied on 30 May that he assumed the assembly would meet again in August and that he preferred to keep the paper money bill for consideration until that time. Hamilton had evidently received Penn's 2 April instruction telling him to insert a suspending clause. Probably suspecting that the assembly would object, the governor stalled.

Two Letters: (1) Franklin's Religion and (2) Celebrating Philadelphia

Joseph Huey, a religious zealot whom Franklin had "relieved in a paralytic case by electricity" (4:504), wrote him on 2 June 1753 not to pride himself too much on his own achievements but to have faith. When Franklin replied on 6 June with a statement of his religious principles, he kept a copy of the letter and later occasionally sent it to others. It circulated widely. The editors of the *Papers* mentioned that they had located ten contemporary copies and could have found more (4:503–6). Perhaps Franklin simply pretended that there was a person named Joseph Huey. No doubt he helped people who sometimes told him to thank God, have faith, and attend religious services, but we cannot be certain that a person named Joseph Huey did. The letter form was a common literary genre; Franklin used it often; and he not infrequently created addressees.[18]

After a complimentary opening to the ailing Huey giving Franklin's "hope you will continue mending till you recover your former Health and Firmness," he expressed his belief in a version of the Golden Rule: "the only Thanks I should desire is, that you would always be equally ready to serve any other Person that may need your Assistance, and so let good Offices go round, for Mankind are all of a Family" (4:504).

Franklin's third paragraph declared that he regarded his own kindnesses to others as "paying Debts," for he had received "much Kindness from Men, to whom I shall never have any Opportunity of making the least direct Return." He had also received "numberless Mercies from God, who is infinitely above being benefited by our Services." He echoed his sentiment that "Doing good to Men is the only Service of God in our Power" (3:419). In addition, he suggested that prayers were less worthy than doing good: "These Kindnesses from Men I can therefore only return on their Fellow-Men; and I can only show my Gratitude for those Mercies from God, by a Readiness to help his other Children and my Brethren. For I do not think that Thanks, and Compliments, tho' repeated Weekly, can discharge our real Obligations to each other, and much less those to our Creator" (4:504–5).

Though he did not believe that good works would earn him admittance to heaven, he nevertheless suggested that God was good to those who were not evil and implied that perhaps there was no hell—which may have implied that he was denying an afterlife.

> You will see in this my Notion of Good Works, that I am far from expecting (as you suppose) that I shall merit Heaven by them. By Heaven we understand, a State of Happiness, infinite in Degree, and eternal in Duration: I can do nothing to deserve such Reward: He that for giving a Draught of Water to a thirsty Person should expect to be paid with a good Plantation, would be modest in his Demands, compar'd with those who think they deserve Heaven for the little Good they do on Earth. Even the mix'd imperfect Pleasures we enjoy in this World are rather from God's Goodness than our Merit; how much more such Happiness of Heaven. For my own part, I have not the Vanity to think I deserve it, the Folly to expect it, nor the Ambition to desire it; but content myself in submitting to the Will and Disposal of that God who made me, who has hitherto

preserv'd and bless'd me, and in whose fatherly Goodness I may well confide, that he will never make me miserable, and that even the Afflictions I may at any time suffer shall tend to my Benefit. (4:505)

The last sentiment reflected his attitude toward his suffering with gout (he had his first attack in the beginning of 1750) and even, to some degree, anticipated his later attitude toward his bladder stone.

Though the Golden Rule is biblical, Franklin did not invoke Matthew 7:16 or Luke 2:313. He may have thought that Huey, like most devout Christians of the day, would have known those verses: "The Faith you mention has doubtless its use in the World; I do not desire to see it diminished, nor would I endeavour to lessen it in any Man. But I wish it were more productive of Good Works than I have generally seen it: I mean real good Works, Works of Kindness, Charity, Mercy, and Publick Spirit; not Holidaykeeping, Sermon-Reading or Hearing, performing Church Ceremonies, or making long Prayers, fill'd with Flatteries and Compliments, despis'd even by wise Men, and much less capable of pleasing the Deity." Franklin voiced a similar thought in *Poor Richard* for November 1753: "Serving God is Doing Good to Man, but Praying is thought an easier Service, and therefore more generally chosen" (4:406). Later, in "The Levée," Franklin directly ridiculed attempts to flatter God (S 7:431). Continuing to Huey, Franklin wrote: "if Men rest in Hearing and Praying, as too many do, it is as if a Tree should value itself on being water'd and putting forth Leaves, tho' it never produc'd any Fruit" (4:505).

In the letter's last paragraph, Franklin referred to several biblical passages, thereby making it seem as if he were primarily reflecting Christian doctrine: "Your great Master tho't much less of these outward Appearances and Professions than many of his modern Disciples. He prefer'd the Doers of the Word to the meer Hearers" (paraphrasing James 1:22–25); "the Son that seemingly refus'd to obey his Father and yet perform'd his Commands, to him that profess'd his Readiness but neglected the Works" (echoing Matthew 21:28–32); "the heretical but charitable Samaritan, to the uncharitable tho' orthodox Priest and sanctified Levite" (Luke 10:30–36); "and those who gave Food to the hungry, Drink to the Thirsty, Raiment to the Naked, Entertainment to the Stranger, and Relief to the Sick, &c. tho' they never heard of his Name, he declares shall in the last Day be accepted, when those who cry Lord, Lord; who value themselves on their Faith tho' great enough to perform Miracles but have neglected good Works shall be rejected" (partially quoting Matthew 25:35–46, a favorite passage).[19] In the words "tho' they never heard of his Name," Franklin echoed a thought in both his first Hemphill tract and his *Speech Deliver'd by an Indian Chief* (*Life* 2:510–11, 513–14).

Christ, Franklin claimed, profess'd that He came not to call the "Righteous but Sinners to Repentance" (cf. Matthew 9:13, Mark 2:17, and Luke 5:32). Franklin said that those words expressed Christ's "modest Opinion that there were some in his Time so good that they need not hear even him for Improvement; but now a days we have scarce a little Parson, that does not think it the Duty of every Man within his Reach to sit under his petty Ministrations, and that whoever omits them offends God." Franklin closed: "I wish to such more Humility, and to you Health and Happiness, being Your Friend and Servant, B Franklin" (4:506).

Perhaps few persons other than ministers who read the letter would have recognized all the allusions, but almost all its readers would have recognized that the letter frequently used biblical teaching. Thus, as with his advocacy of the Golden Rule near the letter's beginning, Franklin made it seem as if he believed in the Christian virtues—as he generally did. Alfred Owen Aldridge commented that in his attack on "narrow spirits," Franklin was not condemning all ministers, churches, and religious ceremonies.[20] His sending a copy of the letter only weeks before his death to the Reverend Ezra Stiles (W 1180) supports Aldridge's opinion. Though the letter to Huey continues Franklin's youthful animosity toward some clergymen, it primarily affirms his belief in fundamental virtues and supports them with the teachings of Christ.

At about the same time he wrote the letter to Huey, he wrote a "letter" comparing the three major American cities. The *Gentleman's Magazine* for August 1753 contained two articles about Philadelphia. One was called "A Comparative View of Philadelphia, Boston, and New York," and the other, titled "A Description of Philadelphia," accompanied Nicholas Scull and George Heap's "Map of Philadelphia."[21] Franklin may have written both, but I am only certain about the first. In the "Comparative View," the author briefly sketched the history of the three cities and then claimed that Philadelphia, though most recently founded, "exceeds either of the others, in the number of houses and inhabitants." The reason is the "genius and disposition of the inhabitants, rather than to the situation of the place," for New York has the better strategic location. The author gives the numbers: in 1746, Boston had 1,760 dwellings; in 1750, Philadelphia had 2,100 dwellings; and in 1751, New York had "about 2050."

Franklin often used population data and not infrequently generalized about the culture found in different places (both are in his "Observations Concerning the Increase of Mankind," 1751), but the best evidence for the attribution is the conclusion. The author cites a couplet written twenty-five years earlier: "*Rome* shall lament her ancient Fame declin'd. / And *Philadelphia* be the *Athens* of mankind." The writer of the "Comparative View" identified the couplet's author as George Webb. He was an original member of the Junto and a printer who had worked with Franklin for Samuel Keimer. The couplet originally appeared anonymously in Titan Leeds, *American Almanac for 1730*.[22] I doubt that many Philadelphians, even in 1729, knew who wrote the poem. Franklin would have. He printed Webb's fine poem *Batchelors-Hall* in 1731. Like Webb, Franklin not infrequently used the *translatio* motif, but unlike Webb and most believers in the "Westward Course of Empire" before 1751, Franklin allied it with America's population. In 1753, it was extremely unlikely that anyone other than Franklin had the opinions or the knowledge to write "A Comparative View."

NEW ENGLAND, 14 JUNE–25 AUGUST 1753

From 14 or 15 June to 25 August 1753, Franklin visited the colonies north of Pennsylvania as post office comptroller. He hoped to improve the routes, to meet and evaluate the post riders, and to consider possible locations for additional post offices. He had been appointed postmaster of Philadelphia in 1737, and I have speculated that after Elliott Benger became postmaster general in 1744, Benger appointed Franklin comptroller of the post office for North America. Before the summer of 1745, Franklin had designed and printed a form for the colonial postmasters to use (*Life* 2:383, fig. 25). When the Franklins moved early in 1748 from the Grace House at the present 131 Market Street, the post office remained at its convenient location on the Grace property for two years. When Franklin moved to a home owned by John Wister on 325 Market Street in January 1752, he advertised that the post office was now kept there.[23] As before, ship captains often did not deliver the mail to the post office but instead allowed various persons to go through the mail or dropped pieces off at a favorite tavern. The result was that sometimes letters were stolen or simply mislaid.[24]

After Comptroller Franklin heard of the grave illness of Elliott Benger, he wrote his influential London Quaker friend, Peter Collinson, on 21 May 1751 that Benger was thought to be dying and that Franklin's friends advised him to apply for the position of deputy postmaster general. He enclosed for Collinson a letter that Chief Justice William Allen had written to his main London correspondents recommending Franklin for the position. As he typically did, Franklin ended his letter on an ironic and humorous note: the former postmaster general gave £200 for the post and he was willing to pay £300, "Howsoever, the less it costs the better as 'tis an Office for Life only which is a very uncertain Tenure" (4:136). On 13 June 1751, the *Pennsylvania Gazette* reprinted news of Benger's death from the 22 May *Maryland Gazette*.

Before leaving Philadelphia, Franklin learned of Benger's death and appointed William Franklin deputy postmaster of Philadelphia. William Franklin advertised in the 5 July 1753 *Pennsylvania Gazette* that the post office was now kept at his home on "Third Street, next but one above Church Alley," and announced the beginning of a major improvement in the colonial post office—the penny post. (No doubt Franklin had designed the change before he left.) "Whatever Letters, for Persons living in Town, remained uncall'd for, on those Days they are brought to the Post-Office, will, the next Morning, be sent out by a Penny-Post."

The Journey

Perhaps it was on this 1753 trip that Franklin had a mishap. As he was boarding a boat going to New York, "the unskillful management of the Boatman, overset the canoe from whence I was endeavouring to get on board her, near Staten Island." Dumped in the water, the excellent swimmer was in no danger and quickly clambered aboard the boat. When it arrived in New York, he gave every one onboard a liberal entertainment. A passenger named Hayes "never saw me afterwards, at New York, or Brunswick, or Philada. that he did not dun me for Money on the pretence of his being poor, and having been so happy as to be Instrumental in saving my Life, which was really in no Danger." Since Hayes "never incurr'd any Risque, nor was at any Trouble in my Behalf, I have long since thought him well paid for any little Expence of Humanity he might have felt on the Occasion. He seems, however, to have left me to his Widow as part of her Dowry." When Franklin recorded the incident nearly forty years later, he still occasionally gave the widow money for the husband's heroic effort.[25]

Franklin arrived in New York about 16 June, where he spent several days with his former partner James Parker and probably with New York friends like his former physician, Dr. John Bard, and the New York intellectuals James Alexander, Archibald Kennedy, and Cadwallader Colden. Franklin had been in contact with tutor William Smith, later provost of the College of Philadelphia, about a possible role in the Philadelphia Academy, and visited him, too. Smith accompanied Franklin to Connecticut, where they probably spent the night in Stratford with Dr. Samuel Johnson. They rode on to New Haven, where Franklin wrote a letter to Peter Collinson on 26 June recommending Smith.

While in New Haven, Franklin called on the Reverend Thomas Clap, president of Yale, who had a special interest in science, and then went on to Killingworth to see the Reverend Jared Eliot, a natural philosopher and good friend. In Rhode Island, he would have stayed in Newport and spent time with his sister-in-law, Ann Franklin, who was a printer, and with her son, James Franklin, Jr., who, after finishing his apprenticeship with Franklin five years earlier, had returned to Newport. Franklin probably suggested to "Jemmy" that it might be advantageous to start a printing shop in New Haven. While in Newport, Franklin looked up Thomas Vernon, the son of Franklin's early creditor, Samuel Vernon. The following year, Franklin and William Hunter appointed Thomas Vernon the Newport postmaster. From Boston, Franklin wrote to his friend Hugh Roberts on 16 July that he had enjoyed a "delightful Journey hither" over some of the "best punning Ground perhaps in the Universe." Evidently he and Jared Eliot had fun together.

Boston, 1753

Having returned to Boston in 1724, 1733, 1743, and 1746, Franklin was now making his fifth visit. Each time he had spent four to six weeks there, and on this trip, he again stayed about six weeks. He arrived around 2 July and left about 12 August. He may have lodged with his favorite sister, Jane Mecom, who was living at the old family home on Union Street and taking in boarders, but she had seven children living with her. More likely he stayed with his brother John Franklin (1690–1756), who had married Elizabeth Gooch Hubbart and had a large home on Cornhill, rooms to spare, and servants. Besides his youngest sister, Jane, Franklin no doubt saw his other siblings who lived in Boston: his oldest sister, Elizabeth Douse, now age seventy-five, who lived on Unity Street, and his next-to-youngest sister, Lydia Scott. (The houses are identified in the front endpapers of *Life*, Volume 1: Mecom is #5; John Franklin, #7; and Douse, #1.)

Franklin enjoyed brother John's stepchildren. The oldest son, the merchant Thomas Hubbart, had married Judith Ray, whose younger sister Catharine ("Katy") Ray became Franklin's close friend. Franklin appointed the second son, Tuthill Hubbart, postmaster of Boston after John Franklin's death in 1756. The daughter, Elizabeth ("Betsy"), was probably still living in the John Franklin house. Hereafter, Franklin often corresponded with the Hubbarts. While in Boston, Franklin would have called on his nieces Mary Davenport Rogers and her husband, John, and Abiah Davenport Griffith and her husband, John—both daughters of his sister Sarah (Franklin) Davenport. The Boston merchant Jonathan Williams, Sr., the husband of Franklin's niece Grace Harris, became a frequent correspondent. During the Revolution, his son, Jonathan Williams, Jr., assumed the responsibility under Franklin as America's main commercial agent in France. And Franklin's nephew William Homes, a Boston silversmith, was the son of his sister Mary and the sea captain Robert Homes, the first person in the Franklin family to hear of Franklin's whereabouts after he ran away from Boston in 1723.

Ellis Huske (d. 1755), postmaster for Boston and the provinces north of Massachusetts, lived in Portsmouth, New Hampshire, and was its chief justice. Franklin spent considerable time with him. Besides being postmaster, Huske printed the *Boston Weekly Post-Boy* and naturally hired help with his Boston businesses. In 1753 Samuel Holbrook was serving as his deputy postmaster in Boston and publishing the newspaper. Though supposedly retired, Franklin still had financial reasons to call on Boston's printers and book-sellers, for he sold them paper and no doubt offered whatever books and pamphlets David Hall was publishing. On 23 July, he requested William Franklin to send sixty reams of paper, "Law Size, No. 2," to Holbrook (5:15).

Franklin surely called on the engraver James Turner and the bookbinder and book-seller Charles Harrison, for he often had business with both. He also would have looked up Henry Price (1697–1780), formerly the Masonic provincial grand master of New England, whom he had visited on earlier trips and corresponded with in 1734. Records show he attended Masonic meetings in 1743 and 1754. Thomas Oxnard succeeded Price as the provincial grand master of all North America, and, as we have seen, on 10 July 1749 Oxnard appointed Franklin provincial grand master of Pennsylvania's Masons. But William Allen appealed to London, and the English grand master appointed Allen provincial grand master of Pennsylvania, which caused all the officers of the four Boston lodges to protest the action (see above, fig. 21, p. 171). Franklin had many friends among Boston's Freemasons.

John Winthrop, Hollis Professor of Mathematics at Harvard, Dr. John Perkins, whose theories on tornadoes and on epidemic catarrhal fevers Franklin published, and the wealthy merchant James Bowdoin, for whom Franklin had Lewis Evans make the most complete and accurate copy of his early letters on electricity, all were good friends as well as accomplished natural philosophers. Franklin surely enjoyed time with them. Drs. William Clarke and John Perkins were among the Boston intellectuals to whom Franklin sent his 1751 "Observations Concerning the Increase of Mankind." Another old friend of "Half a Century's Standing" (25 July 1773) was Judge Samuel Danforth (1696–1777), an alchemist, politician, and member of the Massachusetts Council. Franklin saw him on the Boston visits.

Franklin called on the Reverends Jonathan Mayhew, Samuel Cooper, Mather Byles, and Samuel Mather. Mayhew's liberal religious views would have appealed to him. Franklin considered Mayhew a friend and in 1764 sent him one of Edward Fisher's mezzotints (see frontispiece). Cooper became a major political correspondent during the pre-Revolutionary period. Byles, a nephew of Cotton Mather and a childhood acquaintance, corresponded with Franklin. No evidence shows that Franklin knew Byles's poetic nemesis, Joseph Green, but they were the same age, and Green may have been a classmate with Franklin in the South Grammar School. Franklin knew Green's writings and echoed at least one in "The Speech of Miss Polly Baker" (*Life* 2:542–43, 553). Samuel Mather, a son of Cotton, was another childhood acquaintance who, like Byles, had been involved in the *New-England Courant* controversies in 1721–23.

Whether or not the Reverend Mather Byles first suggested (as Franklin later said) that Harvard give Franklin an honorary master of arts degree, we can be sure that Professor Winthrop supported the motion.[26] The *Boston Gazette* of 31 July 1753 featured the event: "On Monday last [23 July] the Corporation of *Harvard College* met at *Cambridge*, and taking into Consideration the great Genius of Benjamin Franklin, of *Philadelphia*, Esq; for Learning, the high Advances he has made in *Natural Philosophy*, more especially in the Doctrine and Experiments of Electricity, whereby he has rendered himself justly famous in the Learned World, unanimously voted him a Degree of *Master of Arts*, which Vote was the Day following as fully confirmed by the Overseers of that Society, and on Friday [27 July] the President presented him a Diploma therefor."

John Adams recorded a 1753 incident. Franklin's brother John took him to Braintree to see the glassworks in Germantown, in which he and Franklin had shares. On Sunday, they attended the Reverend Anthony Wibert's service, and afterward "Squire" Edmund Quincy, an old schoolmate from Boston Latin, asked them to take tea. He was the brother of Josiah Quincy, a major partner in the Germantown glass factory. At Edmund Quincy's home, the conversation "turned upon the Qualities of American Soils, and the Different Commodities raised" in America. "Mr. Franklin mentioned, that the Rhenish Grape Vines had been introduced, into Pennsylvania, and that some had been lately planted" in Philadelphia, which "succeeded very well. Quincy said, 'I wish I could get some into my Garden. I doubt not they would do very well in this Province.' Mr. Franklin replied, 'Sir if I can supply you with some of the Cuttings, I shall be glad to.' Within a few Weeks, Mr. Quincy was surprised with a Letter from some of Franklin's friends in Boston, that a Bundle of these Rhenish slips were ready for him. These came by Water. Well, soon afterwards he had another Message that another Parcell of slips were left for him by the Post." Quincy thanked Franklin in 1754 and later told John Adams about Franklin's surprising effort.[27]

Adams mentioned Franklin once earlier in his diary. During a social Sunday evening at James Putnam's on 14 March 1756 he recorded: "Several observations concerning Mr. Franklin of Phyladelphia, a prodigious Genius cultivated with prodigious industry." Four years later, Adams heard the anecdote concerning Quincy and the grapevines, prefacing it with the remark that it was "a remarkable Instance of Mr. Ben. Franklin's Activity, and Resolution, to improve the Productions of his own Country, for from that source it must have sprang, or else from an unheard of Stretch of Benevolence to a stranger." By that time (1756), Adams had noted reading *Reflections on Courtship and Marriage* and had given examples of the prejudice against lightning rods, but on neither occasion mentioned Franklin's name.[28]

Franklin bought two lots in Germantown near the glassworks, evidently during this visit. John Franklin wrote him in the fall that houses were being built on them. Several years later, Franklin told his sister Jane Mecom that he had "never expected much" from the investment, but he bought the lots and built houses on them "in Complaisance to my Brother." Franklin conducted at least two other business dealings with family members. First, though Jane Mecom was living in the main structure on the large lot on Union and Hanover streets, the property had been left equally to all the children of Josiah and Abiah Franklin (she had died the year before). Jane inherited only one-ninth of the property, and most of the other heirs wanted to sell. Though advertised on 6 November 1752, the property had not sold. John Franklin and William Homes, the executors, must have consulted Franklin, and they advertised the property on 23 July while he was in Boston. After it did not sell for another year, William Homes bought it from the other heirs. Franklin gave his share to Jane.

Second, sister Elizabeth Douse's husband had recently died. Franklin had loaned her and her husband £60 Pennsylvania currency in 1748, taking a mortgage on their Boston house as security. Sometime during this 1753 visit he gave Elizabeth an additional sum and took out a new mortgage on the house. He left Boston before executing the deed, which was recorded on 27 September. Thomas Hubbart witnessed the new mortgage. Franklin also arranged with his

brothers John and Peter for each to contribute a small pension toward Elizabeth's support. While he was still in Boston, Franklin's sister Lydia turned 45 on
8 August. Though he and his brother John had a full schedule that day, they
probably made time to visit and give her birthday presents.

A celebration and spectacle began the day before, 7 August, when Governor
William Shirley, the hero of the 1745 Cape Breton victory, returned from Europe
and arrived at Castle William, where he was met by numerous persons, probably
including Franklin. Two days later, Governor Shirley arrived at Boston, landing
at the end of Long Wharf. A crowd of officials and gentlemen met him, and
they walked in procession to the courthouse: "There was the greatest Concourse
of People on the Long Wharff, and in the Streets thro' which he passed, that
was ever seen there at one Time." Franklin no doubt attended the "elegant"
dinner at Faneuil Hall welcoming Shirley and afterward admired the fireworks,
which continued throughout the evening.[29]

The Linen Manufactory

The meeting of the Boston Society for Encouraging Industry and Employing the
Poor on 8 August was a high point of Franklin's 1753 visit. In 1749, Peter Collinson had sent Franklin *A Letter from Sir Richard Cox . . . a sure method to
establish the Linen-Manufacture.* Impressed with it and probably knowing that
his brother and other Boston friends had planned on 10 March 1748 to establish
a linen manufactory, Franklin sent it on to his brother John, who had contributed £50 in Massachusetts currency, Old Tenor, toward the project.[30] The subscribers, led by Andrew Oliver, had the Boston printer John Draper reissue
Cox's letter late in 1750. Oliver added a preface dated 2 November 1750 emphasizing that Massachusetts produced "an abundance of Flax" that was highly
salable, and that a linen manufactory could employ many "young People and
Children." The subscribers concluded by saying that they had raised money for
the manufactory and were reprinting Cox "in Hopes that it will facilitate the
Design . . . and Influence the Practice of all who have a due Regard for the
Prosperity of the Province."[31]

Just over a year after publishing Cox's letter, the Boston Society for Encouraging Industry and Employing the Poor published an advertisement on 15 January 1752 offering a series of premiums for the greatest quantity of flax, for the
largest amount of fine thread for linen cloth, and for the best large quantity of
cloth. John Franklin must have sent a copy to Franklin, who replied with his
own present of ten pistoles (a pistole or doubloon was a Spanish gold coin
worth about 17 shillings sterling) for prizes. The *Report of the Committee* of
the society, dated 12 February 1752, featured Franklin's contribution and gave
information on the society's finances, asking for more funds.[32]

Thomas Fleet published a 1753 pamphlet describing the society's goals titled
*Industry & Frugality Proposed as the surest Means to make us a Rich and Flourish-
ing People* (Andrew Oliver was the likely author). It included praise for "the

generous Donation of an *ingenious Gentleman* in a neighbouring Province, whose Benevolence extends to Mankind in general, and to whom Mankind in general are under the greatest Obligation"—no doubt Franklin.[33] Franklin sent a copy to Collinson, who noted in it that he was in part responsible for the society's organization and "Great Success" (5:233n9). Preparations for the spectacle surely took up some of John Franklin's time in early August. The society met early on the morning of 8 August, and later that morning the Reverend Samuel Cooper "preached an excellent Sermon before . . . a vast Assembly of all Ranks and Denominations, in the Old South Meeting house." The sermon raised £453 "old Tenor."

The society staged a spectacle in the afternoon, which Franklin surely attended: "about 300 Spinners, all neatly dressed, and many of them Daughters of the best Families in Town, appeared on the Common, and being placed orderly in three Rows, at Work, made a most delightful Appearance." John Franklin's stepdaughter Betsy Hubbart was probably among them. "The Weavers also (cleanly dressed in Garments of their own weaving) with a Loom, and a young Man at Work, on a Stage prepared for that Purpose, carried on Mens Shoulders, attended by Musick, preceded the Society, and a long Train of other Gentlemen of Note, both of Town and Country, walking in Procession to view the Spinners; and the Spectators were so numerous, that they were compared, by many, to one of Mr. Whitefield Auditories, when he formerly preached here on the Common." Perhaps Franklin wrote the news report. He no doubt sent it on to David Hall, who reprinted it in the *Pennsylvania Gazette* on 23 August.

Return to Philadelphia

About 12 August 1753, Franklin left Boston, probably before Governor Shirley read Franklin's 1751 "Observations Concerning the Increase of Mankind." (Two years later Shirley persuaded Franklin to publish the "Observations" in a pamphlet by Dr. William Clarke.) On the journey back, the Reverend Thomas Clap entertained Franklin in New Haven, perhaps on 14 August. Clap probably instigated the movement for Yale to grant Franklin an honorary master's degree, which, after approval of the Yale corporation, he received on 12 September; it was his second honorary degree. Since Franklin was by then in Philadelphia, Clap sent it to him. While in New Haven, Franklin had investigated real estate. He was planning to set up his nephew "Jemmy" with a New Haven printing shop. As it turned out, Jemmy preferred to remain with his mother in Providence.

Franklin arrived in New York "about Noon" on Friday, 17 August, where he "had the Pleasure of hearing from my Family, that all were well" (5:21). From New York, he wrote Thomas Clap on 20 August, thanking him for his hospitality and revealing that they had talked about the Susquehanna Company's plan to purchase a large tract of land in the Wyoming Valley from the Six Nations. The area is (and was then considered by most Pennsylvanians to be) in Pennsylvania.

Franklin wrote that he was disappointed to find the proposal "to purchase a large Tract of land," which supposedly lay within the bounds of the charter of Connecticut, printed in the *Boston News-Letter*. The notice said the projectors supposed "it will be in Time a distinct Government."[34] Franklin objected for two reasons: it might give notice to the French and "put them on taking some preventive Measures," or it might arouse some persons in England "to obtain a Patent before we can take Possession and make a Settlement." Then Franklin generalized: "Great Designs should not be made publick untill they are ripe for Execution, lest Obstacles are thrown in the Way; and small Obstacles are sufficient to overset young Schemes, which when grown strong would force their Way over greater." With his letter he sent Clap a description of Pennsylvania's boundaries from its 1682 charter.

Though the British authorities and the governments of the colonies occasionally attempted to control the press, I do not know of a previous example where an individual tried to limit what it would print. Franklin, however, told Clap that he would "endeavour to prevent the reprinting of that Paragraph" here in New York and in the colonies "to the Southward" (5:22). He must have spoken to his former partner James Parker, editor of the *New York Gazette*, and Hugh Gaine, editor of the *New York Mercury*, and written notes to the newspaper editors south of New York. I have not found the report reprinted.

Why would Franklin seemingly encourage the Connecticut settlement? If he was not just trying to please Clap, I suspect that he had two reasons. Like George Washington and numerous others, Franklin wanted to create new colonies, partially because of the wealth they could bring to the original grantees and investors. But perhaps he also wanted to limit the power and possessions of Thomas Penn—who was, in the view of Franklin and others, an enemy of Pennsylvanians' general welfare. When he projected "A Plan for Settling Two Western Colonies" in 1754, he explained to Peter Collinson that one reason was "to divert the Connecticut Emigrants from their Design of invading this Province, and to induce them to go where they would be less injurious and more beneficial" (6:87). A decade later Connecticut settlers did come to Pennsylvania's Wyoming Valley, and warfare broke out between them and the Pennsylvanians. From 1769 through the Revolution, numerous people died in the Wyoming Valley war. The best-known battle occurred in 1778 and became the subject of Thomas Campbell's popular poem *Gertrude of Wyoming*.

HOME AGAIN

Franklin arrived back in Philadelphia on Friday afternoon, 24 August. The next day, he returned to his usual Philadelphia routines, signing a document as justice of the peace and attending a meeting of the Pennsylvania Hospital managers. At the last session of the Pennsylvania Assembly (27 August–11 September), Governor Hamilton presented amendments to the assembly's £20,000 money bill. The main one called for a suspending clause, which said the act would not be in force until approved in England. The Pennsylvania Assembly considered the amendments on 29 and 30 August, accepting some but unanimously rejecting the suspending clause. The revised bill was sent to the governor, who replied on 31 August that he was keeping the suspending clause. He cited an instruction "the Lords of the Regency" sent to the colonies in 1740 that demanded the clause for any paper currency act.[35]

Speaker Isaac Norris assigned Franklin to a committee on 1 September to consider the governor's message, and two days later Franklin reported that the suspending clause was "destructive of the Liberties derived to us by the Royal and Provincial Charters, as well as injurious to the Proprietaries Rights, and without any Precedent." Examining the 1740 suspending clause, Franklin claimed that it was meant to be temporary. Although it applied to the paper money of all the colonies, Parliament had subsequently examined Pennsylvania's paper currency and found no fault with it. Franklin exclaimed: "Unfortunate Pennsylvania, under such Sentiments! If the King should judge all the Purposes of that Instruction answered, upon passing the Paper Money Act, laid upon him by his Parliament in 1751 we must nevertheless for ever continue under the Burden of it, without Redress" (5:23, 26).

Franklin pointed out that Governor Hamilton had made "Objections of different Kinds" to all money bills during the assemblies of 1751–52 and of 1752–53 (5:26). Hamilton's new requirement of a suspending clause had evidently just occurred to him. Franklin and the committee implied that Thomas Penn had instructed Governor Hamilton not to pass any bills of credit and that Hamilton was merely devising reasons to avoid revealing his instructions. Franklin cited the section from the Pennsylvania charter that said the proprietary governors should make laws "according to their best Discretion, by and with the Advice, Assent and Approbation of their Delegates" (5:26, 6:134). He implied that the proprietors violated the charter when they issued instructions to the governors and took bonds to ensure the governors' compliance. He also cited Parliament's defeat of attempts to make royal instructions binding upon the colonies.[36] Franklin concluded, "there has never been one single Instance of the Passing of any Law under the Restrictions now contended for by the Governor, from the first Settlement of this Province to the present Time" (5:28–29).

The next day the assembly unanimously approved the committee's 3 September report. Speaker Norris then assigned Franklin to a committee to answer the governor's 29 August message. The 5 September reply repeated and amplified the information in the 3 September report, argued that the suspending clause was "destructive of the Liberties granted to the People . . . by the Royal and Provincial Charters," and even claimed that it injured "the Proprietaries Rights" (5:29). Later, Thomas Penn had second thoughts about a suspending clause, and before 1755 agreed with the House that it did indeed undercut his position with the British authorities.[37] Governor Hamilton demanded on 7 September that the bill have the clause. The assembly unanimously rejected his amendment. Hamilton reported in a letter to Penn of 8 September that the House claimed that "a Governor here cannot be laid under Instructions, either from the Crown or from the Proprietor."[38] Hamilton's statement accurately presents Franklin's radical opinion and probably reflects private conversation, for it is more straightforward than Franklin's reference to royal instructions in the previous assembly reports (5:28)—and anticipates his assembly statement made on 11 September (5:32–33), which he repeated nine months later in a letter to Peter Collinson (5:332).

THE REPLY TO GOVERNOR HAMILTON, 11 SEPTEMBER 1753

The squabble over the £20,000 money bill continued. The House passed it on 24 January 1753; Governor Hamilton rejected it on 26 January; it was resubmitted to the governor on 25 May with Franklin's rejoinder; he returned it on 29 August, demanding a suspending clause; the House replied on 30 August; Hamilton responded on 31 August; the House replied on 5 September; the governor rejoined on 7 September; and Franklin and the House replied on 11 September, the last day of the assembly of 1752–53.

In the last refutation, Franklin and the committee contended that Governor Thomas had ignored the suspending clause in 1746 (5:35)[39] and that other governors had done so earlier. They charged that Governor Hamilton had decided to follow the outdated and previously ignored clause because of the proprietors' secret instructions. Then, more strongly stating the suspicion introduced on 3 September that Hamilton's "Objections of different Kinds" covered an unacceptable secret instruction given by the proprietors, Franklin said that the governor was evidently "restricted by the Proprietaries from giving his Assent to the Emission of any further Sum in Bills of credit" (5:37).

Royal and proprietary instructions were a longstanding grievance in the colonies. The Old Charter Party in Massachusetts objected to royal instructions, and Franklin had editorialized against them in 1730 (*Life* 1:419–20). As Governor Hamilton repeatedly refused the money bills, the assemblymen came to think, as Richard Peters wrote to Thomas Penn (4 October 1752), that Hamilton was under secret instructions regarding money bills. Penn replied on 9 January 1753 that it was only a surmise, but Hamilton wrote Penn on 8 September 1753 that the delegates believed it.[40]

In its 11 September reply, the House noted, "it may be presumed the Representatives of this Province, when met in their Assemblies, have some valuable Privileges yet left, in framing their Laws, to do Justice between Man and Man, without the Aid of an additional Instruction; and we hope it cannot be expected that we should very easily part with those Rights, and depend on Royal Instructions, over which we are to allow the Governor the Power he is pleased to contend for, and we have no Reason to doubt, all Men of Understanding and Candour will prefer a regular Course of Laws, occasionally suited to the Times, and framed by the Representatives of the People annually chosen, and assented to by their Governor, to a Series of Instructions sent for that Purpose from so great a Distance" (5:38, 40). The claim for a right to self-government, independent not only from the proprietors but also from British authority, was, in 1753, extraordinary, even though it echoed positions taken in Massachusetts and in Virginia in the seventeenth century.

Furthermore, "if the Liberty the Governor contends for can mean that we must allow him to judge for himself, how far he may or may not obey such Royal Instructions, at his own Risk (as his Majesty's highest Displeasure is threatened against him particularly) and at his own Pleasure too, then we must own we are at a Loss to distinguish any great Difference between the mischievous Tendency of an Act to inforce all Orders and Instructions of the Crown whatever, and the Necessity the Governor is pleased to think we are under to allow him the Power of inforcing them whenever he shall think fit" (5:39). In conclusion, Franklin returned to the proprietors: the House "had good Reason to believe" that "private Instructions from our Proprietors" compelled the governor not to approve a money bill (5:41). The House approved the report and recommended the next assembly consider the matter. On that same last day of the assembly of 1752–53, Franklin reported on another issue.

THE REPORT OF 11 SEPTEMBER 1753

In 1749 and again in 1750, the Pennsylvania Assembly requested that the proprietaries contribute to the cost of Indian expenses. As we have seen (above, p. 237), Governor Hamilton delivered the refusal of the proprietors on 16 August 1751. The House had replied on 23 August that though the proprietors were "under no Obligation by Law" to support Indian treaties, the House thought they had a moral responsibility to do so. Hamilton had sent the representation to England. On 23 May 1753, the House asked if the proprietors had answered. Hamilton promptly sent Secretary Peters to the assembly on 24 May. The proprietors' message amplified the previous claim that they were under "no greater Obligation to contribute to the publick Charges than any Chief Governor of another Colony" (5:44). On 30 May 1753, Speaker Norris appointed Franklin to a committee to frame an answer.

Presented on the last day of the fourth session, Franklin's rejoinder was approved unanimously. It did not appear in the assembly's *Votes and Proceedings* for 1752–53, probably because on 24 May 1753 the proprietors had accused the House of printing a representation in August 1751 "just before an Election" as anti-Proprietary Party propaganda (5:46). Since this 11 September rejoinder was also "just before an Election," the assembly refrained from printing it until early 1755. Then it appeared in the assembly's minutes for 31 December 1754 in parallel columns, with the proprietaries' statements on the left and Franklin's rejoinder on the right. Though the proprietor's message said that the "Representation" appeared "just before an Election," Franklin noted that it had not been published "till after the Election was over." He ironically observed that "the Proprietaries" had "of late Years, no formidable Share of the People's Love and Esteem," so that current members of assembly need hardly fear that Proprietary Party adherents would replace them in an election (5:46, 47).

Franklin's report refuted each of the proprietors' reasons for not supporting the Indian trade, usually with irony, sometimes with sarcasm, and occasionally with a dramatic direct address and personification. The proprietors had written that in view of "the Rank which the Crown has been pleased to give us in Pennsylvania," the assembly had not treated them with the respect they deserved (5:47). That irritated the populist Franklin. The proprietors had, wrote Franklin, been treated respectfully: "As to *Rank*, the Proprietaries may remember, that the Crown has likewise been pleased to give the Assemblies of this Province a Rank; a Rank which they hold, *not by hereditary Descent*, but as they are the voluntary choice of a free People, unbrib'd, and even unsollicited. But they are sensible that *true Respect* is not necessarily connected with *Rank*, and that it is only from a Course of Action suitable to that Rank they can hope to obtain it" (5:48–49). In effect, he said the proprietors deserved no respect.

The report mainly has a measured, restrained tone, correcting the proprietors' account and its self-justifying, faulty logic. Toward the end, however, Franklin grew sarcastic about their "utter Contempt" of the people and "how much they are above valuing the Peoples Regard" (5:54). In their last paragraph the proprietors asked the assembly not to send them any "representation" in the future but instead to "be satisfied with such an Answer as the Governor may have Orders to give on our Behalf." That statement outraged Franklin: "No King of England . . . has ever taken on himself such State, as to refuse personal Applications from the meanest of his Subjects, where the Redress of a Grievance could not be obtain'd of his Officers. Even Sultans, Sophys, and other eastern absolute Monarchs" have spent days hearing petitions "of their very slaves, and are the proprietaries of Pennsylvania become too great to be addressed by the Representatives of the Freeman of their Province? If they must not be reason'd with, because they have *given* Instructions, nor their Deputy because he has *receiv'd* them; our Meetings and Deliberations are henceforth useless; we have only to know their Will, and to obey" (5:57).

Ending the extraordinary 11 September report, Franklin and the committee said that the royal colonies were in a "much more eligible Situation" than the proprietary colonies. Franklin then scorned the proprietors and threatened that Pennsylvania would rebel and become a royal colony. With a reference to 1 Kings 12, Franklin wrote that if the proprietors continue to "follow the Advice of Rehoboan's Counsellors, they will, like him, absolutely lose—at least the Affections of their People. A Loss, which however they affect to despise, will be found of more Consequence to them than they seem at present to be aware of" (5:57).[41]

Trying to excuse his sometime friend Franklin from the onus of signing the report, Peters wrote that Franklin had not been on the original committee, that the original had been "excessively malicious," and that Franklin had been added to the committee and softened the report. Franklin, however, had been on the original committee and no doubt drafted the report. Peters was presumably either misinformed or was trying to excuse Franklin to Penn. "My hand should have been burnt rather than sign a Paper against my Judgment," wrote Richard Peters on 27 November to Thomas Penn.[42]

CONCLUSION

At the same time that the proprietors were cutting off the money supply from interest on the loans on paper currency and refusing to pay any proportion of expenses for Indian relations, they were demanding that the assembly give arms and major presents to the Indian tribes. Though Franklin wrote that the proprietors had recently enjoyed little "of the People's Love and Esteem," in fact, they had long been resented—for opposing paper money in the 1720s and for ruthlessly enforcing the quitrents in the late 1730s. The earlier popular anger toward Thomas Penn was best shown when he was hung in effigy at the 1741 election. Now, in the early 1750s, the assembly and Franklin openly and repeatedly stated their contempt for the proprietors, especially Thomas Penn. Informed of the assembly's actions in rejecting Governor Hamilton's amendment, Penn wrote on 1 November 1753 that since he gave his consent to pass the bill, "we cannot now retract by desiring you to incert any Clause, that might put a stop to it, or which is not in the Bill sent back to the House, as that wou'd look disingenuous." Penn therefore gave up the idea of inserting a clause in the bill guaranteeing "the security of our Rents" and instead "agreed to accept a separate Bill" providing £130 for "our" rents. Penn sent along an instruction forbidding Hamilton to pass a re-emitting act, and another instruction allowing him to pass it if it had a clause requiring the permission of both the governor and assembly to approve any expenditures from the interest arising from the bill.

In denying the validity of Thomas Penn's instructions and in challenging the royal instructions, Franklin claimed that Pennsylvania, and indeed, the other colonies had the right to govern themselves. In effect, Franklin claimed the colonies were and should be independendent. Governors Hamilton and later, Robert Hunter Morris,[43] both realized that Franklin and the assembly were in effect denying the authority of Great Britain. Both governors said so. Most of the assemblymen, however, did not realize the full implication of their resentment and rejection of Thomas Penn's secret instructions. They wanted to believe that they were loyal Englishmen, supporters of King George II. Franklin knew that the delegates believed themselves to be loyal English-Americans but also realized the full implications of the rejection of English authority. He probably thought that most delegates would come to realize the logic of their position.[44]

The following assembly of 1753–54, however, had even more pressing concerns.

TWELVE

The Carlisle Treaty, Postmaster General, a Trip to New England, and Assembly Sessions, 1753–1754

Be pleased to cast your Eyes toward this [wampum] Belt, whereon six Figures are delineated, holding one another by the Hands. This is a just Resemblance of our present Union: The five first Figures representing the five Nations, to which you belong, as the sixth does the Government of Pennsylvania; with whom you are linked in a close and firm Union. In whatever Part the Belt is broke, all the Wampum runs off, and renders the Whole of no Strength or Consistency.
—Conrad Weiser, speaking for Franklin and the Pennsylvania commissioners at the Carlisle Treaty, 2 October 1753, 5:94

FRANKLIN AND INDIAN TREATIES

FRANKLIN HAD WITNESSED Indian treaties as a boy in Boston and later in Philadelphia. He knew the rituals of the Iroquois and other Indian tribes along the East Coast from Massachusetts to Delaware and admired their metaphorical language. He published more treaties than any other colonial printer and made them as attractive as possible. Earlier, he wrote the most popular supposed Indian speech before "Logan's Speech" (*Life* 2:509–14), and later he echoed passages from several authentic speeches and praised Indian civility.[1] He had never, however, played a key role in an Indian treaty. That changed. Governor James Hamilton learned on 20 September 1753 that "some Chiefs of the Indians of the Six Nations, of the Shawanese, of the Delawares, and of the Twightwees, living on the Waters" of the Ohio River, had just concluded an unsatisfactory treaty with Virginia at Winchester and were on their way to Carlisle, Pennsylvania, where they would arrive on 22 September. Hamilton called a meeting of the council for 21 September. He also contacted the assembly members in town and asked them to attend. Speaker Isaac Norris, Franklin, and several others did. After hearing the letter that William Fairfax of Virginia had written to Hamilton, the group advised meeting with the Ohio Indians "who might be distressed by the hostile Proceedings of the French." Since the assembly had voted £800 in

May for the Indians, "of which the Governor had the sole Disposal, it might be for the Public Good to take this opportunity of enquiring into their Circumstances and making them a Present of Goods" amounting to £800, "if it should be found necessary." Hamilton appointed Richard Peters, Isaac Norris, and Franklin as commissioners to represent Pennsylvania.[2]

The Carlisle Treaty, 1–4 October 1753

The commissioners must have immediately ordered that goods be purchased and that gifts of wampum belts and strings be made. They set out two days later, 23 September 1753, took the Reading road, arrived at Conrad Weiser's home on 24 September, crossed the Susquehanna at Harris's Ferry (Harrisburg, Pennsylvania), and, with Weiser, arrived at Carlisle two days later. They had made a hard, fast horseback trip in record time. (Reading, Harris's Ferry, and Carlisle are all on map 2, p. 308.) The Iroquois and Twightwee/Miami Indians arrived the same day with four Indian traders: Pennsylvania's George Croghan and Andrew Montour, and Virginia's William Trent and Christopher Gist. Although the wagons bringing presents for the Indians were coming, the treaty could not begin until the "Presents of Condolence should be first made to wipe away Tears" for those persons killed at Pickawillany. The Pennsylvania commissioners exchanged good wishes with Scarouady, the Oneida chief representing the "Mingo" Iroquois, and had small drinks with them that night. The commissioners ordered the tavern-keepers not to sell liquor to the Indians. The Indians complained, and the commissioners replied that there would be plenty to drink at the treaty's conclusion. Franklin ironically noted that the Indians promised not to drink until then, "and they kept their Promise—because they could get no Liquor" (A 121).

The four Indian traders told the commissioners about events in the Ohio since the Pickawillany attack. The French had come into the Ohio territory and the Twightwees had twice warned them away. So the two "Half Kings" of the Mingo Iroquois had split into two parties: Scarouady had come east to try to negotiate with the Virginians at Winchester; and Tanaghrisson, the "Half Brother" at Logstown, had gone to warn the French one last time not to settle on the Ohio. The traders told them that the Winchester treaty had been inconclusive. The Indians had asked the Virginians not to build a fort on the Monongahela River below Pittsburgh; nevertheless, Virginia intended to do so.[3] The Indians had come on to Carlisle because Governor Hamilton had repeatedly asked Andrew Montour to invite the Ohio Indians to Pennsylvania. Now Montour had persuaded them to come. Because of the large number of Indians attending the conference, the commissioners ordered more presents (5:66, 84–85).

Early on 1 October the commissioners received word that the French commander, Paul Marin de la Malgue, had treated Tanaghrisson contemptuously

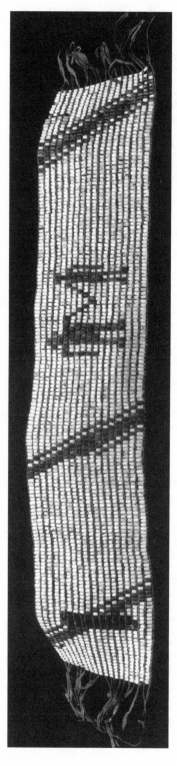

Figure 35. A Penn wampum belt: two figures holding hands. Early American settlers adopted the traditional Indian customs and gifts. Wampum belts and strings marked negotiations between Indian tribes and later between whites and Indians. Franklin attended Indian treaties as a boy in Boston and later in Philadelphia. He took part in the Carlisle Treaty of 1–4 October 1753 with the Ohio Indians and drafted the governor's speeches in the Easton Treaty of 8–17 November 1756 with the Delaware Indians.

This wampum belt, given by the Penn family in 1857 to the Historical Society of Pennsylvania, was often called the "William Penn Belt." The Delaware Indians supposedly gave it to William Penn in the first Pennsylvania peace treaty (1682). No evidence supports the tradition that the belt was given on that occasion, but it is typical of the expressions of alliance and friendship between the Lenni-Lenape or Delaware Indians and the Pennsylvania authorities.

In an icon of friendship and unity, the two figures are holding hands. One wampum belt in the Easton treaty portrayed six figures holding hands. The bulky-looking figure in this belt is a white man wearing the usual European clothing with a broad-brim hat, and the slender figure (who is actually the same size) is an Indian wearing his traditional dress. The diagonal black beads on either side of the two figures probably represent a clean, bright chain or a path/road in good condition (notice especially the attractive line of spaced beads on either side of the black beads), symbolizing frequent exchanges and good relations. Because the third chain or path has a bar through it, I suspect it represents a path to others—outsiders or enemies against whom the two figures are united.

During Indian treaties, the gifts of strings and belts of wampum marked specific points made by the Indians (and by the whites, copying Indian protocol). In general, one can say that the more elaborate the belt, the more important the article, and that the strings denoted comparatively minor points. Courtesy, Atwater Kent Museum of Philadelphia, Historical Society of Pennsylvania Collection.

on 3 September and that, on his return to Logstown, Tanaghrisson "shed Tears, and had actually warned the English Traders not to pass the Ohio, nor to venture either their Persons or their Goods, for the French would certainly hurt them."[4] Scarouady said that he and his brother "Half King" would decide "what is to be done" after he returned home and they conferred (5:90).

The treaty began on 1 October when Conrad Weiser gave the Indians a string of wampum in condolence for their losses. Scarouady replied with a string "that you may hold the antient Union, and strengthen it, and continue your old friendly Correspondence." The commissioners said that they now "dig a Grave for your Warriors . . . and we bury their Bones decently; wrapping them up in these Blankets; and with these [presents] we cover their Graves." They added, "We partake of your Grief, and mix our Tears with yours. We wipe your Tears from your Eyes, that you may see the Sun, and that every Thing may become clear and pleasant to your Sight; and we desire you would mourn no more. *Here a Belt was given.*" The commissioners recalled the old treaties and renewed them: "we rekindle the old Fire, and put on fresh Fuel." Echoing those sentiments, Scarouady said: "Let us keep the Chain from rusting, and prevent every Thing that may hurt or break it, from what Quarter soever it may come" (5:92–93).

The following day, 2 October, the commissioners gave gifts for the Indians to divide "in such Proportions as shall be agreeable to you. You know how to do this better than we." After the gifts, the commissioners gave a belt "whereon six Figures are delineated, holding one another by the Hands." They claimed the belt was a "just Resemblance of our present Union: The five first Figures representing the five Nations, to which you belong, as the sixth does the Government of Pennsylvania; with whom you are linked in a close and firm Union. In whatever Part the Belt is broke, all the Wampum runs off, and renders the Whole of no Strength or Consistency." They must all stay together. "We on our Part shall always perform our Engagements to every one of you. In testimony whereof, we present you with this Belt" (5:94). Unfortunately, this wampum belt does not survive. Figures holding hands was a traditional Delaware Indian symbol of friendship, familiar to the Pennsylvanians from such wampum belts as the one often called the "Penn Treaty Belt."[5]

Since the Iroquois had been the Six Nations for over twenty years, it may seem surprising that five rather than six figures represented them. The alliance, however, had traditionally been called the Five Nations, and tradition was all-important in Indian treaties. Additionally, the total of six figures was easier to make than seven (the Six Nations plus Pennsylvania). Whoever designed the belt had in mind the sentiment that accompanied the gift. Both belt and speech echoed the advice the Onondaga chief Canasatego gave at the 1744 Lancaster treaty—strength lay in unity (*Life* 2:347). The union theme had been frequent in Franklin's writings from at least *Plain Truth* (1747). His best-known statement of the necessity for union occurred in the letter to James Parker of 20 March 1751 on Archibald Kennedy's manuscript titled "The Importance of Gaining . . . the Friendship of the Indians," and Franklin may well have been responsible for the belt.[6] He repeated the advice to join together in the Albany Treaty.

On 3 October, Scarouady echoed the commissioners' speech of the previous day, agreeing with it on behalf of the Indians present: "We shall take Care that it be always remembered by us; and believe it will be attended with suitable Returns of Love and Affection." A Twightwee leader assured the commissioners of their love and, referring to the Pennsylvania trader killed at Pickawillany, covered "the Graves of the English with this Beaver Blanket" (5:95). Scarouady stated that the Indians wanted no more settlers over the mountains. He told the Pennsylvanians that Virginia's governor "desired Leave to build a strong House on Ohio" but that the Indians asked that "Pennsylvania and Virginia would at present forbear settling on our Lands, over the Allegheny Hills." They wanted the English "to call your People back on this Side the Hills, lest Damage should be done, and you think ill of us" (5:96).

In order to keep up trade and the friendly intercourse, the Indians appointed "George Croghan, on our Part, and desire you to appoint another on your Part, by a formal Writing, under the Governor's Hand," to make certain both parties abide by the agreement. "Let none of your People settle beyond where they are now; nor on the Juniata Lands, till the Affair is settled between us and the French. At present, George Croghan's House, at Juniata may be the Place where any Thing may be sent to us." (Aughwick, now Shirleysburg, on the Juniata River, is about thirty miles northwest of Carlisle, Pennsylvania. See map 3, p. 369.) Scarouady remonstrated that too many English traders were on the Ohio and wanted them recalled. Traders should remain in "three Places" only: (1) "LogsTown," now Amboy, Pennsylvania, on the Ohio, about twenty miles northwest of Pittsburgh; (2) "the Mouth of Canawa," the Conemaugh River, which flows into the Allegheny about twenty miles northeast of Pittsburgh; and (3) "the Mouth" of the Monongahela, that is, Pittsburgh. The Indians would come to those places to buy goods, "and no where else. We shall likewise look on them under our Care, and shall be accountable for them" (5:97).

Calling for three trading posts on the Ohio contradicted Scarouady's statements at Winchester that the Virginians should not build a fort on the Ohio. Did the Indians at Carlisle discriminate between a fort and a trading post? Perhaps, though Francis Jennings thought that the minutes of both the Winchester and the Carlisle treaties may have been tampered with. I suspect that the Indians did not object to trading posts and that they may not have objected to trading posts that were also forts. They objected to the influx of farmers and settlers who came out and built homes around the forts.

Scarouady complained that the "English Goods are sold at too dear a Rate to us. If only honest and sober Men were to deal with us, we think they might afford the Goods cheaper." He said that the whiskey traders, who came with thirty or forty kegs, "put them down before us, and make us drink; and get all the Skins that should go to pay the Debts we have contracted for Goods bought of the Fair Traders." The whiskey traders ruined not only the Indians but the fair traders too: "These wicked Whiskey Sellers, when they have once got the Indians in Liquor, make them sell their very Clothes from their Backs. In short, if this Practice be continued, we must be inevitably ruined: We most earnestly therefore beseech you to remedy it" (5:97).

Apologizing for the Shawnees who had acted with the French, Scarouady said the Shawnee regretted that they had "lost all our Sense and Wits, when we slipp'd out of your Arms; however, we are now in one another's Arms again, and hope we shall slip out no more." He asked the commissioners to keep the Onondaga council (i.e., the Six Nations) informed of their treaty and asked for "some Horses to carry our Goods; because you have given us more than we can carry ourselves." That afternoon Andrew Montour translated for the Twightwees who said that they had been hurt but only on one side of the body. On the other side, "Our Arm is entire; and with it we laid hold on our Pipe, and have brought it along with us, to shew you it is as good as ever: And we shall leave it with you, that it may be always ready for us and our Brethren to smoak in when we meet together." Here the chief "delivered over the Calumet, decorated with fine Feathers" (5:98–99).

Franklin had no doubt heard of the calumet and of the figures of speech the Twightwees used, but he had not before witnessed the Twightwees' ceremonies. Our heart, the Twightwees said, "is green, and good, and sound: This Shell, painted green on its hollow Side, is a Resemblance of it. The Country beyond us, towards the Setting of the Sun, where the French live, is all in Darkness; we can see no Light there: But towards Sun-rising, where the English live, we see Light; and that is the Way we turn our Faces. Consider us as your fast Friends, and good Brethren." The chief delivered a large shell, "painted green on the Concave-side." The Twightwees also gave a large beaver blanket "as a Seat for all our Brethren to sit on in Council. In the Middle of it we have painted a green Circle, which is the Colour and Resemblance of our Hearts; which we desire our Brethren may believe are sincere towards our Alliance with them" (5:100–101).

The Twightwees' diction had more color, light and dark, body imagery, and references to shells than did that of the Iroquois, and unlike the East Coast Indians, they characteristically used the calumet or peace pipe decorated with feathers. The next day, 4 October, the commissioners thanked the Twightwees for their "Professions of Love and Esteem," which denoted "a sincere and friendly Disposition." The Twightwees could depend on the English to continue to be friends.[7] The remarks on the traders and on the "vast Quantities of Rum, and its ill Effects" impressed Franklin, Norris, Peters, and Weiser: "Was it now in our Power to rectify these Disorders, and to put Matters on the Footing you propose, we would do it with great Pleasure." But they lacked the authority. They would, however, relay the message to the governor with their "heartiest Representations of the Necessity of these Regulations." The commissioners promised to say that "unless something effectual be speedily done," Pennsylvania could "no longer expect Safety or Profit" in trade with the Twightwees, "nor the Continuance" of their "Affection" (5:102–3).

After assuring the Ohio Indians that they would report the treaty to the Iroquois, the commissioners agreed to "assist you with Horses" to carry away the goods. Scarouady had earlier requested that the broken guns of the Indians be mended, and the commissioners had sent for a gunsmith, "as no One of that Trade lived in the Town." He had said he would come, but broke his word. Therefore, the commissioners apologized and returned the wampum they had accepted with the request (5:103). Reassuring the Twightwees, the commissioners said, "we entertain no hard Thoughts of you; nor in any wise impute to you the Misfortune that befel the English in your Town [Pickawillany]; it was the Chance of War: We were struck together; we fell together; and we lament your Loss equally with our own" (5:104).

Reflecting Indian etiquette, the commissioners were silent for a time (Pennsylvanians readily adopted the Indian protocol, for the Pennsylvania Assembly, influenced by the Quaker meeting, had periods of silence; *Life* 2:324). They said they had heard that the Ohio country was in such disarray they doubted that a large store of goods in addition to those "already given you" could be safely delivered at this time. When, however, it was "safe, seasonable, and likely to do you the most Service," the additional goods would be given. They were left temporarily with George Croghan, who would deliver them whenever the Pennsylvania governor directed (5:105).[8]

The commissioners asked Scarouady for a special favor. At the Winchester treaty he had agreed to go to Charleston, South Carolina, to ask that some Shawnee be released from prison. The commissioners feared, however, that if he did not return to the Ohio and "assist in the Consultations with the Half King, and their other Chiefs . . . all may be irrecoverably lost." They said that they knew he wanted to fulfill his promise, but they intended to secure the Shawnees' permission for him to return now to the Ohio. They could "sooner and more effectually" secure the release of the prisoners "by the joint Interposition of the Governors of Pennsylvania and Virginia" than by Scarouady's personal solicitation. Governor James Hamilton would send "Letters to Carolina" quicker by water "than you can perform the Journey" and an express could be dispatched to Virginia's Governor Robert Dinwiddie, "as soon as we return to Philadelphia."[9] After objecting, the Shawnees at last consented. Scarouady then decided to "go Home, and do every Thing in my Power for the common Good." He informed the whites "that we have set a Horn on Andrew Montour's Head, and that you may believe what he says to be true, between the Six Nations and you, they have made him one of their Counsellors, and a great Man among them, and love him dearly" (5:106). That concluded the treaty on 4 October, except for giving "private Presents at parting, to such of the Chiefs, and others, as were recommended by the Interpreters to their particular Notice" (5:107).

Then the commissioners gave the Indians the promised liquor. "This was in the Afternoon. They were near 100 Men, Women and Children, and were lodg'd in temporary Cabins built in the Form of a Square just without the Town. In the Evening, hearing a great Noise among them, the Commissioners walk'd out to see what was the Matter. We found they had made a great Bonfire in the Middle of the Square. They were all drunk Men and Women, quarrelling and fighting. Their dark-colour'd Bodies, half naked, seen only by the gloomy Light of the Bonfire, running after and beating one another with Firebrands, accompanied by their horrid Yellings, form'd a Scene the most resembling our Ideas of Hell that could well be imagin'd. There was no appeasing the Tumult, and we retired to our Lodging. At Midnight a Number of them came thundering at our Door, demanding more Rum; of which we took no Notice" (A 121).

Comparing the Indians to devils dancing in hellfires perpetuated a trope found in a series of New England histories of Indian wars. It began with William Bradford (whose account Franklin read in Nathaniel Morton's 1669 version); the Indian expert John Mason used it in describing the Pequot War of 1636–37; the engraving of the burning of the Pequots' fort in John Underhill's *News from America* (1638) portrayed it; and Benjamin Church's history and Mary Rowlandson's captivity narrative of King Philip's War (1675–76) repeated it, as did the narratives of the various Indian wars by the New England historians Edward Johnson and Increase and Cotton Mather. Since Franklin's *Autobiography* was better known in the nineteenth century than these earlier New England writers, he was a key figure in continuing a traditional image and personification of the Indians as devils, which the captivity narratives and Nathaniel Hawthorne echoed in the nineteenth century.[10]

"The next Day, sensible they had misbehav'd in giving us that Disturbance, they sent three of their old Counsellors to make their Apology. The Orator acknowledg'd the Fault, but laid it upon the Rum; and then endeavour'd to excuse the Rum, by saying, 'The great Spirit who made all things made every thing for *some Use, and whatever Use he design'd any thing for, that Use it should always be put to; Now, when he made Rum, he said,* Let this be for Indians to get drunk with. And it must be so.'" Then Franklin made a comment that has sometimes been misunderstood: "And indeed if it be the Design of Providence to extirpate these Savages in order to make room for Cultivators of the Earth, it seems not improbable that Rum may be the appointed Means. It has already annihilated all the Tribes who formerly inhabited the Sea-coast" (A 121). Franklin's seemingly racist remark has two primary meanings. First, it satirizes the use of reason to make excuses. His anecdote of abandoning his vegetarianism when he smelled the fresh cod frying has a similar theme. Wanting to eat the cod, he recalled that he saw a small cod taken out of the stomach of a large one. He said to himself, if they eat one another, he did not see why he should not eat them. Then he ironically observed, "So convenient a Thing it is to be a *reasonable Creature*, since it enables one to find or make a Reason for every thing one has a mind to do" (*Life* 1:215–16). Like Franklin, the Indian apologist used logic to excuse and justify the Indians' actions.

Second, Franklin's anecdote covertly satirizes interpreting events as the "Design of Providence." That theory of history and of causation was common throughout Franklin's life. Making rum the "appointed Means" of the "Design of Providence" for annihilating the Indians ironically undercuts the "Design of Providence." As we will see, Franklin's remark anticipated a not dissimilar anecdote concerning religion and rum when, during the construction of Fort Allen, he suggested to the Reverend Charles Beatty that he serve as "Steward of the Rum" (A 148). The recent racist interpretations of Franklin's remark reflect twenty-first-century sensibilities more than either eighteenth-century intellectual history or Franklin's personal beliefs.

Later, concluding their report to Governor Hamilton on 1 November 1753, Franklin, Peters, and Norris emphasized that they agreed with the Indians' complaint about the whiskey traders: "the Quantities of strong Liquors sold to these Indians in the Places of their Residence, and during their Hunting Seasons, from all Parts of the Counties over Sasquehannah, have increased of late to an inconceivable Degree, so as to keep these poor Indians continually under the Force of Liquor, that they are hereby become dissolute, enfeebled and indolent when sober, and untractable and mischievous in their Liquor, always quarrelling, and often murdering one another." The commissioners recommended that the traders should give bonds for their behavior. If the whiskey traders continue to behave in the same way, "their own Intemperance, unfair Dealings, and Irregularities, will, it is to be feared, entirely estrange the Affections of the Indians from the English; deprive them of their natural Strength and Activity, and oblige them either to abandon their Country, or submit to any Terms, be they ever so unreasonable, from the French."

The commissioners apologized for presenting "these Truths" to the governor and asked that they might "stand excused in recommending in the most earnest Manner, the deplorable State of these Indians, and the heavy Discouragements under which our Commerce with them at present labours, to the Governor's most serious Consideration, that some good and speedy Remedies may be provided, before it be too late" (5:107). Franklin quickly printed the treaty and advertised it in the 15 November 1753 *Pennsylvania Gazette*.[11]

POSTMASTER GENERAL

Franklin had asked Peter Collinson and William Allen to help him secure the appointment as postmaster general for North America. They did, but William

Hunter, printer and postmaster of Williamsburg, had also applied and been recommended. The postmaster general of Great Britain, Sir Everard Fawkener, decided to appoint them as joint postmasters general of North America. Before making the decision, he no doubt conferred with the secretary of the post office, George Shelvocke (1702–60), who oversaw the day-to-day running of the London office. Franklin probably learned the news when he arrived back from the Carlisle Treaty on 8 October. In supporting Franklin for the position of deputy postmaster general, William Allen no doubt expected that Franklin would become a Proprietary Party partisan. Though his 1751 letter advocating Franklin for the position is not extant, Allen continued to support Franklin for another two years. He wrote his bankers on 5 November 1753 that Franklin "by Solicitations from me to sundry of my friends has obtained the Office of being joint Post Master." He asked his bankers to call upon "Mr. Shelvock [*sic*], the Secretary of the Post Office (who has been instrumental in obtaining the Office) and give security if it is desired." He concluded, "I beg pardon for giving you this Trouble; but as it is giving the finishing Stroke to an affair I have had much at heart, I beg you would be so good as to excuse it."[12]

The next day Richard Peters wrote Thomas Penn that Franklin had been made deputy postmaster general of the colonies "owing to Mr. Allen's interest" and that Allen had assured Peters that Franklin "would act a fair and good Part in the Assembly tho he would have a difficult time of it, and was not unsuspected, and this last Office would increase the Jealousies of [the Quakers]—but set him aside, and there is not a man who can write in the Assembly." In his reply to Peters, Penn (like Allen) took credit for the appointment: He said that he told Sir Everard Fawkener, secretary to the duke of Cumberland, "I thought Mr Franklin as capable as any man in America to serve the Crown."[13] No doubt Penn intended for Peters to report the words to Franklin, and Penn, like Allen, thought the appointment would make Franklin a thorough proprietarian.

The person whom Franklin most likely thought most influential and responsible, Peter Collinson, seems to be the only one involved who did not claim credit for Franklin's appointment (4:134–36). Collinson probably also enlisted his close friend Dr. John Fothergill—the two had collaborated in publishing the first edition of Franklin's *Experiments and Observations on Electricity* in 1751— but Fothergill's role is merely my guess. Both Collinson and Fothergill would have known George Shelvocke well. He was a fellow member of the Royal Society (elected 10 March 1742/3), which was located near the post office headquarters, and attended the Royal Society meetings. Since he was interested in natural philosophy, he would have known of Franklin's experiments and their spectacular success. I suspect it was Franklin's successes in science, more than Allen's influence, that made Shelvocke "instrumental in obtaining the Office."[14] Proprietary Party leaders, however, chose to believe that Franklin had been bought and paid for by William Allen. Thus William Smith wrote years later that Allen got Franklin appointed "the joint-postmaster of America, by means of his namesake, the worthy Ralph Allen, Esq., of *Bath*, to whom" Franklin was "utterly unknown" (11:506).

Alexander Spotswood's salary had been £300 per annum, plus a commission of 10 percent "out of the clear profits."[15] Franklin and Hunter shared a salary of £600 "to be paid out of the Money arising from the Postage of Letters passing and repassing through the said provinces and Dominions of North America" (5:18). But, as William Allen wrote his banker, David Barclay, on 5 November 1753, in the colonies "the Profits of the Post Office" have "never amounted to so much as has been sufficient to pay the Salaries and Charges." Everyone knew, however, that the colonies were growing, and Allen, a shrewd businessman, recognized Franklin's ability: "I am persuaded that by Mr. Franklin's good Management, matters will be put upon a better footing, and that there will be yearly some Ballance to be remitted to the General Post Office."[16]

In 1753 the existing mail service was slow and uncertain. The mail took several days to get from Philadelphia to New York, and from New York to Boston it usually took more than a week. Since the mail did not adhere to the supposed schedule, it often waited from several days to a week to go to the next destination. So mail from Philadelphia to Boston generally took three weeks, and the return trip another three weeks. If Franklin and Hunter were to make money, they would have to dramatically increase the amount of mail going between the major colonial towns. The service would have to become more frequent and more reliable, and it would have to expand. Franklin intended to make sure the post office did expand—and that it made money. Since he had projected a unified plan for the American colonies in 1751 and had witnessed the extraordinary unifying effect that George Whitefield had on the colonies during the 1740s, he no doubt also thought that frequent and reliable mail service would promote colonial union.

In the fall of 1753, Franklin set about his new duties. As comptroller, Franklin had far more experience with the post offices, especially in the Middle Colonies and New England, than did William Hunter. Franklin evidently drew up a series of *Instructions* and *Directions* for the postmasters, circulated them to Hunter for his approval, and then printed them for the postmasters. Franklin and Hunter had known of one another for years. After the death of Williamsburg's William Parks in the spring of 1750, Hunter published the *Virginia Gazette* and no doubt exchanged newspapers and pamphlets with Franklin. Though Franklin testified after Hunter's death that they had worked together in "the most perfect Harmony" (9:363), Hunter was often ill from 1753 until his death in August 1761, and Franklin did most of the labor in the partnership. The *Instructions* gave regulations for the postmasters: for example, number "18, You are not, out of Friendship or Compliment to any Person whatsoever, to delay his Majesty's Post one Quarter of an Hour, beyond the usual and fixed Times of his Departure" (5:167). The *Directions* illustrated what amounts to charge for postage and gave a convenient method to use (cf. the "Postmaster's waybill," *Life* 2:383, fig. 25). The hypothetical dates given in the *Directions* are from 3 October to 22 December 1753, suggesting that the document was composed about November 1753 (5:161–77).[17]

Franklin wrote his brother John in Boston about the appointment in October and said that any profit from the position was dubious partly because the office had been divided. John replied with information about the post riders from Boston to Portsmouth who took the mail as private commissions and turned over only a few letters to the postmasters (5:118). As Franklin and Hunter increased the frequency and extent of the mail service, it lost more and more money, but by the time Franklin left for England in the summer of 1757, the improvements and changes had finally begun to make the deputy postmastership of the colonies profitable.[18]

THE ASSEMBLY OF 1753–54

The assembly of 1753–54 had five sessions: the organizing session of 15–17 October; a long business session of 4 February–9 March, adjourned until 6 May but recalled by the governor on 2 April; a third session, 2–11 April; a fourth session, 6–18 May, adjourned until 19 August but recalled on 6 August; and a final, fifth session, 6–17 August. In the years before the French and Indian War became official, the governor recalled the assembly because of military crises. The House met for a total of sixty seven days—the longest assembly to that date in Pennsylvania.

On Monday, 15 October 1753, the new assembly unanimously elected Isaac Norris as Speaker. The next day, as in 1752, Norris appointed Franklin to all four standing committees: accounts, correspondence, grievances, and minutes. He was also appointed to "a Committee to inspect the Laws of this Province, and report which . . . are expired or near expiring, and ought to be re-enacted; with their Opinion what Amendments to them or others may be necessary" and also to "a Committee to enquire into the State and Circumstances of the Trade of this Province with regard to the Quantity of our Paper Currency from its first Emission in 1723, to the present Time."[19] The House then adjourned to 4 February 1754. Creating a committee on trade and paper currency announced that the 1753–54 assembly intended to continue the fight for an addition to the paper currency and called on Franklin for facts and arguments.

POST OFFICE BUSINESS, ANNAPOLIS, JANUARY 1754

The joint deputy postmasters general for North America journeyed south from Philadelphia on 2 January 1754 "to regulate and settle the Affairs of the Post Office." Franklin and William Hunter probably took the "ROADS Southwestward" itemized, with mileage, in *Poor Richard* for 1754: "From Philadelphia to Darby 7, to Chester 9, to Brandywine 14 [present-day Wilmington, Delaware, where they may have spent the night], to Newcastle 6 [Newcastle, Delaware, a more important port than Wilmington in the mid-eighteenth century], to Elk River 17, to N. East 7, to Susquehanna 9." They probably spent another night at the Susquehanna ferry.

Continuing south in Maryland "to Gunpowder Ferry 25, to Petapsco Ferry 20," they arrived at Baltimore, Maryland, which had only twenty five houses in 1752.[20] Franklin probably met the lawyer William Young in Joppa, near the Gunpowder River, and appointed him his attorney for Maryland's "Western Shore." Franklin later noted that the newspaper and post office debts that he left with Young totaled £346.16.5 and that Young would receive 15 percent of whatever he collected. Young advertised in the *Maryland Gazette*, on 18 February 1754 that all persons indebted to Franklin on the Western Shore of Maryland must "make speedy payment of their respective debts." Franklin and Hunter may have spent a night at Joppa and another at Baltimore.

From Baltimore, "to Annapolis 30." The *Maryland Gazette* of 17 January announced that Franklin and Hunter had arrived in Annapolis "last Week." They probably arrived on Thursday or Friday, 10 or 11 January (had they arrived before the tenth, editor Jonas Green would have published the note in his paper of the tenth). Though Franklin and Hunter could not have had more than a day or two of business in Annapolis, they probably spent two or three days there. It was the largest Maryland town, and they surely had more social and business contacts there than elsewhere in Maryland. They went on from Annapolis "to Queen Anne's Ferry 13, to Upper Marlborough 9, to Port Tobacco 30, to Southern's Ferry 30." At Southern's Ferry on the Potomac River they evidently parted after making decisions concerning the post office route through Maryland. Hunter went on to Virginia, and Franklin began the return trip to Philadelphia. Before starting for their respective homes, Franklin and Hunter presumably made plans to tour the Middle Colonies and New England after the conclusion of the Pennsylvania Assembly's last session for the year, expected in mid-August.

THE TUESDAY CLUB

Back in Annapolis on Tuesday evening, 22 January, Franklin attended the Tuesday Club at the home of the Scots physician Dr. Alexander Hamilton. Clubs and club life appear throughout Franklin's biography. His own club, the Junto, was exceptional, for its purpose was self-education. Most eighteenth-century clubs were social, usually held in taverns, and accompanied by food, drink, and song. A few had their own clubhouse, and some met in members' homes. Because Dr. Alexander Hamilton kept a journal of the club meetings and then wrote a facetious *History of the Tuesday Club*, it is the best-known colonial

American club. In the *History*, Hamilton assigned mock names (which generally revealed some aspect of the subject's character) to the club members—and to some visitors.

On 22 January eight members and three guests attended. The members were William Lux, merchant, the club's deputy president, whose club name was Crinkum Crankum. The Reverend Alexander Malcolm, rector of St. Anne's, Annapolis, wrote treatises on mathematics and music; his club title was chancellor and his name, Philo Dogmaticus. Jonas Green, who had worked as a journeyman printer in Philadelphia, was editor of the *Maryland Gazette* and postmaster of Annapolis; he was the poet laureate and master of ceremonies of the club, with the club name Jonathan Grog. William Thornton, a merchant and ship owner, was the club's chief musician and attorney general with the club names Solo Neverout and Protomusicus. Walter Dulany, merchant, businessman, and member of the Maryland Council, was the brother of Daniel Dulany, Jr. (1722–97), the leading Maryland lawyer, whom Franklin had employed several times. Walter Dulany's club name was Slyboots Pleasant. (John) Beale Bordley, lawyer, agricultural experimenter, and later a member of the American Philosophical Society, was the posthumous son of Thomas Bordley; he was master of ceremonies with the club name Quirpum Comic. William Cumming, Jr., lawyer and planter, had the club name Jealous Spyplot, Jr. And Dr. Alexander Hamilton, the "life and Soul" of the Tuesday Club, had traveled from Annapolis to Maine in the summer of 1744 and perhaps met Franklin in Philadelphia. Hamilton dubbed himself Loquacious Scribble.

Beside Franklin, two other guests attended, though only one, the Reverend Thomas Thornton, who had recently arrived in Maryland, was given a club name, Nolens Volens. Hamilton dubbed Franklin Electro Vitrifice, or electric glass-rubber. Perhaps the name reflected Kinnersley's 1749 lectures in Annapolis, where he explained that the name for electricity came from the Greek word for amber, and if they had known that glass had the property of generating static electricity better than amber, the name for electricity would have been *vitricity*, from *vitrum* or glass.[21]

The evening was spent in dinner, drinking, singing, and a mock prosecution. As part of its feigned satire of English history, the club had a "Chancellor's Rebellion" or "clubbical Interregnum" on 10 December 1751, in which the president was deposed. Since the occasion supposedly marked the end of the so-called Royalist Club, the triumphant traitors proposed that the "Clubical Ensigns ought to be exposed at public vendue, vizt: the Chair of State, Canopy of State, Mallet of State, Cap of State," and so forth.[22] The monarchy, however, had been restored, and dreadful luxury again reigned. Then, on the night of Franklin's visit, Dr. Alexander Hamilton pretended that one of the former conspirators (Quirpum Comic, alias Beale Bordley) had taken the president's chair of state and exposed it to public sale, but the public rejected it because the seat smelled. Loquacious Scribble (Hamilton) said that Quirpum Comic should be punished by being lowered from the elevated rank of longstanding member to honorary member. Regular members were called longstanding members, with a bawdy allusion to their penises.

Hamilton recorded the following smutty dialogue, which included Franklin's pun. Jonathan Grog (Jonas Green) commented, "Why Mr. Secretary, you would not have us to dock the Gentleman, I suppose the member, however he may stand now at this Juncture is as long as ever." The deputy president (William Lux) laughed, "Ha ha, ha, the longstanding members methinks are waggish." Electro Vitrifice (Franklin) quipped, "Longstanding Members, I think Gentlemen, with Submission, are not so properly waggish, because if they stand they cannot wag." To which the chancellor (Philo Domaticus/Reverend Alexander Malcolm) replied, "Yea, but with your leave Sir,—I say these members must stand before they can wag." Loquacious Scribble concluded his entry for the meeting by recording that "Several new Songs were sung at this Sederunt by the Longstanding members, and mirth was very much Promoted in Club."[23] One wonders if Franklin contributed one of the "new Songs"; he certainly would have enjoyed the mirth.

Returning to Philadelphia, Franklin probably sailed from Annapolis across the Chesapeake Bay to Chestertown, Maryland. He noted in his account book for January that he left a "List of Gazette Debts" with Thomas Ringgold of Chestertown (which is on the Eastern Shore) for collection. The notes on William Young in Baltimore and Ringgold in Chestertown were both written later and only dated January 1754.[24] By 1 February, Franklin was back in Philadelphia, for he witnessed a deed as justice of the peace the next day.

THE SECOND SESSION, 4 FEBRUARY–9 MARCH 1754

The first full day of the second session began on 5 February with the *Pennsylvania Gazette* reporting George Washington's news that the French had built forts toward the Ohio Valley, that they expected an English army to attack them, and that the French intended to fight the English colonists. As Governor James Hamilton had reported, the British secretary of state Robert D'Arcy, fourth earl of Holderness, had advised the governors of the colonies in a circular letter of 28 August 1753 to keep up with developments in the different colonies. In case of an invasion, they should help one another.[25] The assembly expected instructions concerning the French threat, but Hamilton was ill on 5 February and reported that he hoped soon to be better.

THE £40,000 MONEY BILL

During the three months since the first assembly session Franklin had updated the statistics he had compiled for the "Report on the State of the Currency" on 19 August 1752 (4:344–50). He now surveyed the state of Pennsylvania's trade with regard to the quantity of paper currency from its first emission to the present. Imports from Britain amounted to £15,992 in 1723, £56,690 in 1737, and £190,917 in 1751. The wheat, flour, bread, and flax exported in 1729–31 averaged little more than £60,000 a year, but in 1751 they were £187,457. In 1729–31, the amount of paper currency in circulation was about the same quantity as in 1754. Franklin repeated his 19 August 1752 observation that the number of people had increased in proportion to the domestic trade. The 6 February 1754 report concluded that the paper currency must shortly begin to diminish one-sixth annually and said that it was necessary "not only to prolong the Re-emissions, but to strike and emit an additional Sum" (5:195).

That afternoon the House resolved that both were necessary. Norris appointed Franklin to a committee to bring in a bill. The resulting act for £40,000 passed the House on 12 February. (Hugh Roberts, John Smith, Samuel Rhoads, and Israel Pemberton offered to be signers for the bills and to give the money for the service to the Pennsylvania Hospital.) Governor Hamilton was hamstrung by Thomas Penn who had, 1 November 1753, again ordered him not to pass any money bill unless he controlled its funds. Hamilton gave "an absolute Negative" to the £40,000 bill on 19 February. Claiming that sufficient funds were available to the House, Hamilton nevertheless said he wanted the assembly to pass a money bill. Hamilton was prepared to "strike a further Sum in the Bills of Credit, to defray the Charges of raising Supplies for his majesty's Service"—if the House created "a proper Fund or Funds for sinking the same in a few Years."[26] Since the governor would not pass a bill for additional paper currency that could be loaned out at interest, thereby giving the assembly a source of income, the only other possibility for funds came from the excise duties—the House's other source of income. Reluctant to use that inadequate source, the assembly did not reply to the governor until 15 May.

By 13 February, Governor Hamilton had somewhat recovered, met with his council, and prepared a message to the assembly. It included the 18 September 1753 Board of Trade's letter to colonial governors calling for the Albany Treaty; Virginia governor Robert Dinwiddie's letter of 29 January reporting George Washington's account of the French invasion of the northwestern part of Pennsylvania (which Franklin's *Gazette* had reported earlier); New York governor James DeLancey's letter of 11 December 1753 proposing to start the treaty at Albany on 13 or 14 June 1754; and Massachusetts governor William Shirley's letter of 26 November 1753 asking for information concerning the French forces.

Hamilton requested funds to raise "a large number of Men" to fight the French. The situation, he said, was an "extraordinary Emergency" that rendered null the 1740 instruction requiring a suspending clause.[27] He also urged support for the Albany Conference and a union of the colonies. He repeated these recommendations on 4 April and 7 May. But the Quaker-dominated assembly, with many pacifist members, did not want to support a war. Franklin was irritated with their inaction in the face of danger. From Friday to Sunday, 22–24 February 1754, Franklin spent what time he could spare with the Virginian Thomas Walker, a merchant, land speculator, explorer, and frontier expert who had come to Philadelphia to arrange for supplies for General Edward Braddock's army. Deborah and Franklin had him to dinner on Saturday night, 23 February. Probably reflecting information that Walker supplied, Franklin's *Gazette* published news on 26 February of a French party coming down from Canada to Logstown on the Ohio and another coming from New Orleans up the Mississippi to the Miami River. The paper also reported that French Indians had murdered a family on the Virginia frontier. Franklin was trying to influence the assemblymen to vote money for defense.

The members, however, knew that Lord Holderness had said in his circular letter that the colonies were to resort to force only if the French were within their territory. In reply, Governor Hamilton had written on 25 November 1753 that he thought one or more French forts had been built within the western limits of the province, "but as the Western Bounds" of the province "have never been actually run, I cannot speak with Certainty." Answering the governor's request on 27 February, the assembly used this loophole to evade giving money for a military purpose: the members claimed "it would be highly presumptuous" for them to decide the boundaries of Pennsylvania, especially since the governor had not attempted to furnish it with any materials to judge.[28]

Attempting to answer the assembly's question as to whether the French forces were really within Pennsylvania's bounds, Governor Hamilton turned over the various estimates of the location of "Shanoppin's Town" (on the Allegheny River, just a few miles north of present-day Pittsburgh). The same 6 March, Isaac Norris appointed Franklin to a "Committee to take the several Papers sent down by the Governor, concerning the Western Bounds of this Province, into their Consideration, and report thereon to the House To-morrow Morning."[29] The next day, Franklin and the committee reported that Shanoppin probably lay within Pennsylvania but that the information was not certain. I suspect that Franklin had argued that Shannopin's Town was clearly within Pennsylvania's boundaries, but the majority of the committee equivocated. Therefore, the committee referred the information to the House (5:222–29). When Speaker Norris appointed a committee that afternoon to reply to the governor, he omitted Franklin, who was undoubtedly the strongest advocate of defense. On 8 March the "Question was put" whether it was clearly apparent that the French forts were within Pennsylvania's boundaries. The assembly voted it was not.[30]

On 9 March, the assembly judged it "most prudent" to wait until it learned what Virginia intended to do about the French invasion of its territory. On that note, the assembly adjourned to 6 May.[31] While the pacifists and some Quakers who did not want to raise money stalled, the French and French Indians advanced into the frontier of Pennsylvania and Virginia. Everyone on the frontier was in danger, and frontier families were being killed. The assembly would not vote funds because the proprietors refused to allow a paper currency issue. If the governor had approved the paper currency issue or, possibly, if the proprietors would have paid a portion of the expenses for Indian affairs, the majority of the assembly would have voted for defense. As it was, the only way that the assembly could raise money to fight was by imposing taxes—but the bill must exempt the proprietors and yet give the governor the key role in dispensing funds. The assembly's refusal to support defense came down to a struggle for power. Franklin believed that the proprietors should also be taxed, but he was willing to exclude them rather than fail the frontier people in the emergency.

Turning to the governor's request for funds for the Albany Conference and to his suggestion that the commissioners should plan for a union of the colonies, the assembly on 27 February only gave authority for the commissioners to make a treaty with the Indians. Indeed, it expressed skepticism concerning the necessity for a conference. The House noted that the Carlisle treaty (1–4 October 1753) cost £1,400, "which we shall discharge chearfully, notwithstanding our Proprietaries refuse to contribute any Part of our Indian Expences." The assembly conceded to make provision for commissioners to go to Albany and to give "a small Present: but as we have been already at so considerable an Expence at our late Treaty," the assembly saw no good reason for an additional large gift.[32] The assembly obviously cared little about the forthcoming Albany meeting.

During the three-week interval between the second and third assembly sessions, Franklin busied himself with post office and paper merchant business, and with his numerous civic responsibilities: the Library Company, the Philadelphia Academy, the Union Fire Company, the Pennsylvania Hospital, the Philadelphia Contributionship, and with social life, including the Freemasons. He entertained Beale Bordley, whom he had recently seen at the Annapolis Tuesday Club in January, and gave him letters of introduction to friends in New England (5:234–35).

Boston's Dr. William Clarke wrote Franklin on 18 March 1754 asking for statistics concerning the population of the Six Nations and their allies, for information concerning the trade of the English and French with the Indians, for data on the geography of the Great Lakes, the Ohio country, and the Mississippi, for the locations of the forts that the French intended to build, and for the journals of frontiersmen who had ventured west to those areas (5:250–52). It was a tall order—and rather surprising that the answers to many or most of these questions were not available in Boston. A close friend of Massachusetts governor William Shirley, Clarke no doubt had access to the materials that Shirley and other Massachusetts officials possessed. However, he had read Franklin's 1751 "Observations Concerning the Increase of Mankind" and knew, like other contemporaries, that Franklin had long been accumulating information on such questions.[33] As we will see, Franklin replied as soon as he could.

THE THIRD SESSION, 2–11 APRIL

No doubt hoping the assembly would reconsider its refusal to aid Virginia, on 26 March 1754, Franklin printed in the *Pennsylvania Gazette* the letter from Governor Dinwiddie that George Washington delivered to the commander of Fort Le Boeuf. Franklin translated the French commander's intransigent reply, which asserted "the King my Master's Rights to the Lands situated along the Ohio." Governor James Hamilton had presented copies of the letters reporting the French invasion to the assembly on 14 February; subsequently, he had received letters from Governor Dinwiddie dated 23 February and 1 March. The Virginia Assembly had voted £10,000 to defend the colony and Dinwiddie was raising six companies of Virginians to send to the Ohio. He requested that Pennsylvania's forces join the Virginians at Wills Creek, which flows into the Potomac at Cumberland, Maryland (see map 2, p. 308, or map 3, p. 369). Governor Hamilton had also recently received a letter dated 4 March from Massachusetts Governor William Shirley on the necessity of a colonial union and the desirability of accomplishing it at the forthcoming Albany Treaty.[34]

Responding to the worsening situation and to Governor Dinwiddie's appeals, Hamilton recalled the assembly on 2 April. The following morning he asked for funds to support troops to be sent to join Virginia's forces. By a mere two-vote majority (18 to 16) on 5 April, the House voted to give money "to the King's Use"—which, in this case, meant to pay to send troops to Wills Creek to aid Virginia. But how much? After several days of acrimonious debate led by Franklin in favor of support, the House defeated a motion to pass a "Bill for striking the Sum of" £20,000 "for the King's Use" on 9 April by a vote of 8 to 25. Next, "The Sum of Fifteen Thousand Pounds" failed, with Franklin among the 10 persons who voted for it, while 23 voted against it. Then, the sum was reduced to £10,000, but that too failed, with 11 persons voting for it and 22 against.[35]

On 10 April, the House debated all day on the motion. Recounting the events a week later, Isaac Norris wrote on 19 April to the House's English agent, Robert Charles, that "the heat and eagerness" of those who favored the bill put off the moderate members, who were also influenced by the Maryland Assembly's lack of action. Writing with hindsight, Norris said that a bill for £7,500 would have passed. Perhaps so.[36] But after another "long Debate" the assembly voted on 11 April whether to give £5,000. This also failed, now with 10 persons voting for it and 22 against. Amazingly, however, Franklin—the primary spokesman for defense in the government—voted against it. He lost his temper and his normally cool judgment. Franklin, Evan Morgan of Philadelphia County, Griffith Owen of Bucks County, David M'Connaughy of York County, John and Joseph Armstrong, both of Cumberland County, and William Parsons of Northampton County all voted against it. They all had voted in favor on every preceding vote. Except for John Wright of Lancaster County, every supporter of the £20,000

The 11th Day of the Month called *April*, 1754, *A. M.*

The Houfe again refum'd the Confideration of the Sum to be given to the King's Ufe; and after a long Debate, the Queftion was put, *Whether* Five Thoufand Pounds *fhould be the Sum given to the King's Ufe at this Time?* *Paft in the Negative.*

YEAS.	NAYS.	NAYS.
Hugh Evans,	*Edward Warner,*	*Thomas Cummings,*
Jofeph Stretch,	*Evan Morgan,*	*Nathaniel Pennock,*
Mahlon Kirkbride,	*Jofhua Morris,*	*George Afhbridge,*
Derrick Hogeland,	*Jofeph Fox,*	*Nathaniel Grubb,*
William Smith,	*Benjamin Franklin,*	*William Peters,*
Jofeph Gibbons,	*William Callender,*	*Peter Worrall,*
Peter Dicks,	*Jofeph Hamton,*	*David M'Connaughy,*
James Wright,	*Samuel Brown,*	*John Armftrong,*
Calvin Cooper,	*William Hoge,*	*Jofeph Armftrong,*
John Wright.	*Griffith Owen,*	*Mofes Starr,*
	Jonathan Ingham,	*William Parfons.*

Figure 36. Furious Franklin! The Pennsylvania Assembly's Votes and Proceedings for 11 April 1754. On 3 April 1754, by a mere two-vote majority, the Pennsylvania Assembly voted to supply money for arms and troops to defend the frontier, where settlers were being killed. But how much? Franklin led the passionate debate in favor of defense. After several days of arguing, the amount of £20,000 was defeated on 9 April by a vote of 8 to 25; then £15,000 was defeated by a vote of 10 to 23, and finally £10,000 was defeated, 11 to 22. Naturally the Quaker pacifists, led by Israel Pemberton, opposed the bill. But many Quakers, like Speaker Isaac Norris, believed that Pennsylvania should contribute some support for the settlers on the frontier. According to Norris, Franklin's passion alienated some assemblymen who might otherwise have voted for the bill.

After another day of arguing, the assembly proposed and on 11 April voted on an amount of £5,000 pounds. Franklin, in disgust and fury, voted against it. For Franklin, it was a rare and foolish display of pique and anger. (He displayed anger fairly often—but not foolish anger.) It would certainly have been better for the frontier settlers to have had £5,000 for arms and troops than nothing. Franklin lost his temper and carried with him all the members who had voted for every larger sum—except Lancaster County assemblyman John Wright. Had Franklin and his friends who had voted for every previous sum also voted for £5,000, it would have passed. John Wright showed common sense, and Franklin did not. Courtesy, Library Company of Philadelphia.

grant thought that £5,000 was too little to make a significant contribution. If those seven persons (Franklin, Morgan, et al.) had voted for the £5,000 amount, it would have passed, 18 to 15. After a week of debate, Franklin and almost everyone else who favored supporting the military had become so emotional that they lost all spirit of compromise. Only John Wright, the brother of Susanna and James Wright, showed common sense.[37]

The Solomon-like opinion of Isaac Norris that £7,500 would have passed was simply an after-the-fact compromise figure. Norris also seemed to betray a bit of pleasure in Franklin's being defeated and even suggested Franklin may have had some ulterior motive. Norris reported to Robert Charles that Franklin "has much disobliged some of our House and of his Electors without doors by his conduct in our last Sess[io]n in which they think Zeal carryd him too far if he had no Interested Views."[38]

Most of those who voted for the earlier, larger amounts for defense were from the frontier counties. It would be too simple, however, to say that only the frontier inhabitants cared about the threat of a French and Indian war, for many pacifists, both German and Quaker, lived on the frontier. Nevertheless, most pacifist Quakers (and those who did not want to pay taxes) were from Bucks, Chester, and Philadelphia counties or from Philadelphia city. After the £5,000 amount failed, the Speaker appointed a committee including Franklin to reply to the governor's message requesting funds to support the Virginia military and adjourned to 3:00 P.M. The reply to the governor said that the members could not agree on the sum to be granted, "except in such a Sum as, in the Judgment of many of them, is quite disproportionate to the Occasion." They also announced their intention to adjourn to 13 May, giving the hackneyed excuse "of consulting their Constituents on this important Affair."[39]

On 4 April 1754, Governor Hamilton delivered to the assembly letters from New York governor James DeLancey and Massachusetts governor William Shirley urging the commissioners at the forthcoming Albany Treaty to form a union of the colonies. Hamilton requested advice concerning the instructions to the commissioners—again in effect asking the representatives to empower the Pennsylvania commissioners to create a plan for colonial union. When the House considered the governor's message on 6 April, it wanted first to know "what Gentlemen he purposes to appoint as Commissioners." The same day, Governor Hamilton replied that he intended to appoint John Penn and Richard Peters for the council and Speaker Norris and Franklin for the House.[40] (Appointing Norris meant that the House would support the finances of the commissioners.) In the afternoon of 11 April, the House resolved to give £500 for a present to the Indians at the forthcoming treaty and to support the commissioners' expenses. Significantly, the House said nothing about the attempting to form a plan of union at Albany. Replying to the assembly's notice that it intended to adjourn until 13 May, Governor Hamilton said that "so long an Adjournment" would "render any Thing you can then propose to do for his Majesty's Service ineffectual." So the assembly begrudgingly voted to come back a week earlier, 6 May.

PUBLICATION OF THE INDIVIDUAL MEMBERS' VOTES

Just before adjourning, the House "Ordered, That the Minutes of this Sitting be printed with all convenient Speed." That was unusual, but the House had a special reason. For the second time in the history of the Pennsylvania Assembly, the division (i.e., how individual representatives voted) was published. Franklin, being one of the two persons on the assembly's committee for the minutes, was no doubt in part responsible for recording the division. But both sides wanted the votes known. The other member on the committee, Edward Warner, had voted against giving the money. He and no doubt many other members of the assembly wanted the votes published in order to appeal to the pacifist Quakers, and Franklin wanted to appeal to those who favored defense. The assemblymen were beginning to think that the votes should be public. The recording of the five votes of the division (that of 5 April, the three on 9 April, and the final one on 11 April) reveals how passionately the legislators felt about the issue—emotions that only escalated in future sessions.[41] From this time on, publication of the votes by individual assemblymen became frequent. That was a major change in colonial—and world—politics (*Life* 1:83, 2:332).

Thomas Pownall and Dr. William Clarke

Before the end of the current session of the assembly on 13 April, Thomas Pownall, a well-connected young Englishman whose younger brother was the secretary of the Board of Trade, came to Philadelphia. He had arrived in America earlier that year as the secretary of the newly appointed New York governor, Sir Danvers Osborn, who took one look at New York and killed himself. Writing on 17 April, Richard Peters characterized Pownall as "a sensible & well accomplished Gentleman" who had been spending his time seeing the plays in Philadelphia, conducting electrical experiments, and attending sessions of the assembly. Pownall evidently attended Ebenezer Kinnersley's lectures on electricity, which were advertised in the *Pennsylvania Gazette* on 26 March and 4 and 11 April. He later did some electrical experiments with Kinnersley or Franklin. During his Philadelphia visit, Pownall came to know Franklin, and before the end of the year they were good friends.[42]

In April or early May 1754, Franklin wrote Boston's Dr. William Clarke "that although several of the English Governments are singly a Match for the French; yet under their present Circumstances and disposition, all of them together are not able to withstand them" (5:270). Replying on 6 May, Clarke agreed and expressed the fear that the French would ultimately become "sole Masters of this Continent." The union of the colonies, Clarke thought, was "hardly to be expected to be brought about by any confederacy, or voluntary Agreement, among our selves." It would not be done until the British imposed unity upon them. Though the opinion was contrary to Franklin's 1751 view, the colonies' actions (and inaction) during 1752 and 1753 had changed his mind. Clarke was probably reflecting an opinion that Franklin expressed in one of the two letters he wrote to Clarke within the previous month, but neither is extant. Clarke then expressed another Franklin opinion: "how little Attentive those that have the management of this authority are, and have been to the Affairs of the Plantations, we know but too well" (5:270).

Clarke sent Franklin "the heads" of topics for "several small pieces," and asked Franklin "about the nature of the Union, that ought to be established amongst" the colonies. Unfortunately Clarke's topics do not survive, but they probably reflect Franklin's 20 March 1751 letter on colonial union to James Parker. Before Franklin received Clarke's letter, he had designed and printed the most famous American cartoon—urging the unification of the colonies.

THIRTEEN

The Pennsylvania Germans

Methods of great tenderness should be used, and nothing that looks like a hardship be imposed. Their fondness for their own Language and Manners is natural: It is not a Crime.
—Franklin to Peter Collinson, on the Pennsylvania Germans [December 1753 or January 1754], 5:158

BY 1748, THOUSANDS OF GERMANS were immigrating to Pennsylvania annually. The percentage of Germans coming into colonial Pennsylvania between 1740 and 1750 was higher than the percentage of immigrants entering the United States at any later time.[1] Dr. Thomas Graeme, a key Proprietary Party member, wrote Thomas Penn on 6 November 1750 about the "present clamour of a great many people here of all Ranks, Friends as much as others," who feared that the Germans, "by their numbers and Industry, will soon become Masters of the province" and a majority in the legislature. Graeme had talked with Governor James Hamilton about the increasing German population, and they agreed that the best way to prevent the Germans from gaining political control of the province and, at the same time, ostensibly to please them was to create (but gerrymander) two new counties. If Philadelphia County were divided sixteen or eighteen miles south of Reading, if Bucks County were divided about the same distance south of "the Forks" of the Delaware, and if the new counties received only two members each, the German influence "would by this division comprehend to a trifle the whole Body of the Dutch and consequently forever exclude them from becoming a Majority in the assembly." Even if Lancaster and York counties, together with these two new counties, sent only Germans to the Pennsylvania Assembly, "it would make but Ten Members in 38."[2]

The Quaker Party went along with the Proprietary Party's proposals. The Germans had voted for the Quaker Party candidates because of the influence of John Kinsey, the disingenuous Speaker of the House, leader of the Quaker religion, and friend of the Germans. After his death in 1750, the Quakers could no longer be sure of their support. The two parties collaborated to minimize the German vote. The Pennsylvania Assembly created Berks and Northampton counties on 11 March 1752—Berks primarily from northwestern Philadelphia County, and Northampton from northwestern Bucks County. Each new county was assigned only one seat, rather than the two Dr. Graeme suggested.[3]

FRANKLIN'S ROLE

Like other British colonial Americans, Franklin expressed concern about the number of Germans immigrating into Pennsylvania. On 20 March 1751, after reading Archibald Kennedy's manuscript titled "The Importance of Gaining and Preserving the Friendship of the Indians," he wrote that Kennedy's remarks concerning the immigration of Germans into Pennsylvania were "just." If the rate of immigration continued, Pennsylvania would in a few years become a German colony: "Instead of their Learning our Language, we must learn theirs." The English had already abandoned some neighborhoods because almost everyone there spoke German and had different manners and customs. Before long, numbers of English people might leave Pennsylvania for that reason. Laborers, artisans, and farmers were prejudiced against the Germans in part because they "under-live, and are thereby enabled to under-work and under-sell the English; who are thereby extreamly incommoded and consequently disgusted" (4:120–21). The prejudice against recent immigrants who would work for less money than those born in America recurred throughout American history. Though Franklin did not mention Jonathan Swift, he no doubt recalled Swift's objections to the immigration of Palatines into Ireland.[4] Franklin questioned the Germans' loyalty to Britain. The comparatively few numbers of Germans who had joined the Association to fight a possible invasion by the French and Spanish had disappointed him (4:120–21).

Later in 1751, Franklin voiced his reservations concerning German immigration in concluding his "Observations Concerning the Increase of Mankind." It contained both the self-satiric ethnocentric opinions he had expressed elsewhere in the tract concerning negroes and other non-white races. During 1752 he sent manuscript copies to friends in England, including Peter Collinson, who commented on it in a letter of 29 August 1752, which is not extant. In a long letter of 9 May 1753, Franklin replied to him that "I am perfectly of your mind, that measures of great Temper are necessary with the Germans." He was "not without Apprensions, that thro' their indiscretions [those of the Pennsylvania Germans] or Ours, or both, great disorders and inconveniences may one day arise among us." Since few English Pennsylvanians understood German, the English "cannot address them either from the Press or Pulpit." Franklin suggested that a society be formed to aid Germans. Though industrious and frugal, the immigrants were generally uneducated and did not value learning. Most disliked their own clergy. "As Kolben says of the young Hottentots, that they are not esteemed men till they have shewn their manhood by beating their mothers, so these seem to think themselves not free, till they can feel their liberty in abusing and insulting their Teachers." Pennsylvania's Germans were now taking a more active political role and could "carry all before them, except in one or two Counties" (4:483–84).

The German language, Franklin commented, was becoming common in

Pennsylvania. Half the printing houses were German; advertisements were generally printed in both languages; the street signs appeared in both languages, and in some places only in German; and bonds and other legal instruments in German were permitted in the courts "(though I think it ought not to be)." Franklin was nevertheless not against the immigration of Germans to America, for "their industry and frugality is exemplary; They are excellent husbandmen and contribute greatly to the improvement of a Country." He did, however, think that the great stream of German immigration should "be turned from this to other Colonies." In addition, English schools should be established where the Germans are "now too thick settled" (4:485). Franklin even repeated the rumor that the French had established a German settlement in the Ohio region in order to influence the Germans on the Pennsylvania frontier (4:483–85).

In reply, the generally kind and humane Peter Collinson proposed to Franklin on 12 August 1753 seven measures "to Incorporate the Germans more with the English and Check the Increase of their Power." Numbers 2, 3, 4, and 5 were surprisingly severe: (1) to establish more English schools among them; (2) to require that every German and his children speak English in order to be qualified for "any Place of Trust or Profit Civil or Military"; (3) to prohibit accepting as legal any deeds, bonds, and so on in German; (4) to suppress all printing houses that only print German; (5) to prohibit the importation of any German books; (6) to encourage marriages between English and Germans "by some Priviledge or Donation from the Public"; and (7) to discourage sending more Germans to Pennsylvania and to encourage sending them instead to Georgia, North Carolina, and Nova Scotia (5:21).

Franklin replied to Collinson late in 1753 or early in 1754 that "Methods of great tenderness should be used, and nothing that looks like a hardship imposed. Their fondness for their own Language and Manners is natural: It is not a Crime." Commenting on Collinson's seven proposals, he thought the first, establishing English schools, was an excellent idea, provided that they were free. The second, requiring all persons who enjoyed a post of trust, profit, or honor to be able to speak English, was reasonable, but he thought their children should not be included: "If the Father takes pains to learn English, the same Sense of its usefulness will induce him to teach it to his Children." He found the third, requiring all legal writings to be in English "(Wills made on a Man's Death Bed excepted, as an English Scribe may not always be at hand)," was "necessary." He thought the fourth and fifth proposals, concerning printing houses and the importation of German books, too harsh (5:158–59).

The proposal for intermarriage would "either cost too much, or have no Effect." Franklin's comments on German women are surprising, making me wonder about the German women Franklin knew: "The German Women are generally so disagreable to an English Eye, that it wou'd require great Portions to induce Englishmen to marry them." He characterized a German man's idea of a "pretty Girl": "*dick und starcke*, that is, *thick and strong*, always enters into their Description of a pretty Girl: for the value of a Wife with them consists much in the Work she is able to do. So that it would require a round Sum with an English Wife to make up to a Dutch Man the difference in Labour and Frugality." Collinson's last proposal, to discourage more immigration to Pennsylvania and to encourage it to other colonies, echoed Franklin's letter to Collinson (5:159–60). Containing his most sustained expression of opinions on Pennsylvania Germans, Franklin's letter mainly defended them from strictures proposed by a generally benevolent Quaker.

Franklin served on the committee on the laws for the 1753 assembly. In its report of 15 February 1754, the committee said "That for the better Preservation of the English Language, in this Province, it may be proper to require by a Law, that all written Contracts be in English, and to give some Encouragement to English Schools in those Parts of the Province where Foreigners are thick seated" (5:202). The House ignored the recommendation, probably because it would be expensive to implement.

A rumor that Pennsylvanian's Germans would join with the enemy French and Indians was widespread. Trying to dispel the slander, Philadelphia County's German Protestants welcomed Governor Robert Hunter Morris on 20 November 1754 and asserted their loyalty to King George and England. They said that they had been accused "publickly both here and in England, of a Secret Conspiracy against our King and Government." Not a single instance, they said, "can be proved of any Disloyalty, much less of any Conspiracy against our beloved King George and Country we live in." Newspapers generally did not print the numerous addresses welcoming a new governor and never, that I recall, printed such an address several months afterward. This address, however, appeared nearly four months later in the 11 March 1755 *Pennsylvania Gazette*. Evidently, after Franklin returned from New England in late February, he learned of the address and thought its publication might help scotch an unfair rumor.[5]

Franklin praised the Germans for their loyalty and help in the 15 May 1755 *Gazette*: "We hear from the Counties of Lancaster, York and Cumberland, that Notice being given there, that Waggons and Carriage Horses were wanting for the Use of the Army, great Numbers were immediately offered, and 150 Waggons, laden with Oats, Indian corn, and other Forage, were dispatched to the Camp in a few Days, and as many more might have been had if wanted, the People offering with great Readiness and Chearfulness, from a Zeal for his Majesty's Service." Franklin's praise contrasts with the opinions of Provost William Smith and George Washington. Smith suggested that the Pennsylvania Germans provided food and wagons in order to turn them over to the French, and Washington thought they did it only for the money.[6]

Massachusetts governor William Shirley wrote Secretary of State Thomas Robinson on 24 January 1755 that the Germans in Pennsylvania made up half of the population (in 1766, Franklin guessed it was about one-third of the non-Indian population) and were indifferent about the possibility of the country becoming French, "provided they could be eased of their Quitrents, & have their Grants of Land enlarg'd to them."[7] In his *Brief State . . . of Pennsylvania* (1756), William Smith said that one-fourth of the Germans were Catholics— implying that they were in the French interest.[8] Writing the synod in Holland on 8 October 1755, the German Reformed Coetus in Pennsylvania believed that it should deny the rumor that "Papacy" was invading the country. No one, the Coetus said, had become a Catholic.[9]

THE GERMAN SOCIETY

The Reverend Michael Schlatter (1716–90), a German Reformed clergyman, had come to Pennsylvania in 1746 and attempted to organize the scattered German churches from New Jersey to Virginia. He returned to Amsterdam in 1751, reported on the churches' hapless condition, and published in Dutch *A True History of the Real Condition of the Destitute Congregations in Pennsylvania.* Responding to an English translation, the Society for the Propagation of the Knowledge of God among the Germans was formed in London. The Reverend Samuel Chandler (1693–1766), the eminent dissenting minister of London's Old Jewry, served as its secretary. William Smith, in London to receive holy orders, read Collinson's and Franklin's opinions on the Germans. He learned of the society and submitted a plan that included the establishment of free schools to teach English in Pennsylvania's German communities. As he wrote to Peters and Franklin, he had "taken the liberty in some places to make use of" their letters (5:208).

Smith wanted "to have the management of this important Trust devolved upon Men of the first rank of Pennsylvania, and not upon Clergy who depend on Dutch Synods." Those men, of course, would include Franklin and Peters (the most influential persons among the trustees of the Philadelphia Academy, where Smith hoped to be employed). Controlling the money, Smith wrote in February 1754, "will keep their Clergy who are in our pay under proper awe" (5:208). It is doubtful that Franklin or Peters thought such a practice necessary, but they probably supposed the system for dispersing the funds would gradually evolve. They also probably assumed that Smith meant that they were the men "of the first rank." Perhaps they did not believe financial control was of immediate concern, but Smith's attitude and his policy became a key reason for the failure of the German charity schools.

The Reverend Samuel Chandler drew up *A Memorial of the Case of the German Emigrants Settled in the British Colonies* (1754) to appeal for funds.[10] Collinson informed Franklin on 26 January 1754 that the German Society desired his "Correspondence, Advice and Counsel." Chandler asked Thomas Penn for the names of individuals who would be responsible for the society in America, and Penn named a group of proprietary partisans: Governor James Hamilton, Chief Justice William Allen, Secretary Richard Peters, William Smith, and the Indian authority Conrad Weiser, who was German. At Smith's suggestion,

Franklin was also named an American trustee. Chandler wrote them a joint letter on 15 March 1754, which Smith carried back to Philadelphia. Since Franklin, Peters, and Weiser were all about to set out for the Albany Conference, the six trustees could not meet until August. Meanwhile, the German Society appointed Michael Schlatter, who had returned to Pennsylvania two years earlier, as superintendent of Pennsylvania's charity schools.

Working with Schlatter, William Smith established schools at Reading, New Providence, Lancaster, and upper Solfort and projected others to begin a few weeks afterward. The German Reformed Coetus, meeting in Philadelphia on 11 April 1755, called the scheme a "praiseworthy undertaking" and voted to thank the American trustees. One influential Pennsylvania German, however, immediately objected. The Germantown printer Christopher Saur, a Dunkard and pacifist, considered the German Society an insult. The assumption that the Germans were ignorant and poor angered him, and he led a movement against the society's linguistic and cultural English imperialism. The ministers of the Coetus, however, condemned "the unseemly conduct of the journalist" Saur, "who is and remains steadily an enemy of the Protestant Church, and thus also of the new school enterprise."[11] Upon receiving information about the charitable aims of the German Society from Smith on 29 May 1754, Franklin replied to Collinson that he applauded "most sincerely, so judicious, so generous, and so pious an Undertaking." The society could depend "on everything in my Power that may contribute to its Success" (5:333).

The English thought that the intentions of the German Society were altruistic and that no one could object to it. Franklin, however, should have known better. For years the Society for the Propagation of the Gospel (SPG) had been helping support Anglican ministers in New England, but New Englanders widely resented the SPG and its ministers. The Congregational inhabitants believed that they knew the Bible and Christianity better than their Anglican counterparts. Congregationalist New Englanders considered the SPG an imperialist Anglican plot to undermine New England's religion and culture. Similarly, many Pennsylvania Germans viewed the German Society as an imperialist English and American plot to undermine their language and culture.

Saur's anticlericism offended others besides the ministers in the Coetus. The Reverend Henry Melchior Muhlenberg wrote Franklin on 3 August 1754 that Saur "often tells the People that Clergy of all kinds are Rogues and Tools of tyrranical Government to awe the Mob." Some Germans agreed with Saur. Muhlenberg suggested that the society establish a German press to counter Saur. He mentioned that Franklin had a press with German types that had produced German publications in Philadelphia from 1749 to 1752. He thought that such a press would be successful among the Germans. After reading Muhlenberg's letter of 3 August to the American trustees at William Allen's country home at Mt.

Airy on 10 August 1754, Franklin offered to sell the society a press and his German types for £25 less than their market value (5:419–20). The trustees bought them for £109.8.4 sterling and asked Franklin to hire a printer.[12]

Smith wrote Thomas Penn on 2 July 1755 that the press would keep Franklin's name because he was "very popular among the Dutch, by his waggon-project." On Friday, 23 August 1755, the American trustees of the German Society met at Bush Hill, Governor Hamilton's home, where Franklin reported that the German printer he had spoken with, Anton Armbrüster, would rather take the German press at his own risk and simply charge the trustees for printing. The trustees decided, however, that they wanted to have "the sole direction of the press and newspaper" and asked Franklin to inform the printer.[13] Armbrüster accepted the terms, though he had started the *Philadelphische Zeitung* on 12 July 1755.

The appearance of a rival press and newspaper hardened Saur's opposition. By the late spring of 1755 he had no doubt read William Smith's *Brief State* with its attacks on the Germans and on him.[14] He wrote Conrad Weiser on 16 September 1755 that he doubted "whether it is really true that Gilbert Tennent, Schlatter, Peters, Hamilton, Allen, Turner, Shippen, Smith, Franklin, and others . . . do care in the least for the real conversion of the ignorant Germans in Pennsylvania." The scheme for free schools was instead "the foundation for the subjection of this country." The pacifist Saur said that what the German Society really wanted was for "the Germans to stick out their necks by serving in the militia in order to protect the property of these gentlemen."[15]

Franklin and Smith were each partly to blame for the Germans' hostility to the free German schools. Franklin's "Observations Concerning the Increase of Mankind," which had been circulating in manuscript since 1751, was published in Boston and London in 1755 and reprinted in the *Gentleman's Magazine*. Well-informed Germans like Saur read Franklin's comment on the "Palatine boors herding together." Smith had proclaimed his prejudice against the Germans in his *Brief State*. Though primarily Proprietary Party propaganda against the Quakers, *Brief State* also censured the Germans. Smith wanted to deny the Germans, as well as Quakers, the franchise. All voters, he wrote, must take an oath of allegiance and test oath and must understand English and the province's constitution. Further, all legal documents (including wills) must be written in English, and foreign-language printing of periodicals should be forbidden unless accompanied by an English translation.[16] Smith echoed some of Collinson's 1751 suggestions concerning the Pennsylvania Germans. One suspects the London Quaker realized with chagrin that his proposals were too strong when he saw them printed as anti-Quaker, as well as anti-German, propaganda.

Since Smith's *Brief State* was anonymous, many Germans probably did not know he was the author. But Saur may have. Smith's control of the German Society's funds undercut Michael Schlatter, who had initially been responsible for raising the money. Schlatter had intended to give the funds to the Coetus of the German Reformed Congregations and that organization, in turn, would give it to the ministers. Smith, however, now made firm his February suggestion that the American trustees control the money. He wrote to Thomas Penn on 2 July 1755 that the American trustees should be the ones to pay the ministers to teach in the free schools. "This will convince the Ministers of our regard to Religion, & keep them firm to the Interest of the Schools, because they think their Salary depends entirely on the Services among the Children."[17]

Smith thought his scheme would "spawn yet more trustees (three English and three German) for each individual German school," whose teachers Smith would pay from the German Society's charitable funds. The historian Francis Jennings called the German schools "an intricate political machine" of the Proprietary Party. He found it a "formidable" political "apparatus."[18] Though Jennings exaggerated, I agree that Smith and Thomas Penn had hopes that they might use the teachers in their political battle against the Quaker Party. But Smith's control alienated the German Reformed Coetus. On 8 October 1755, it noted that the schools would probably not be of much "public or private" use because their only object was to introduce "the English language among the Germans, which is purely a political matter." They found that the German schools that did not teach English could expect no help, "as examples show." They objected too that some of the English/German teachers were "Moravians, Quakers, Separatists, perchance even Deists and others of this class." When the leaders of the Coetus complained to William Smith that the arrangement was not in accordance with the contributors in Holland, he brusquely responded, "The Fathers in Holland have nothing to do in it."[19]

Despite the worsening frontier conditions, Saur continued to advocate pacifism, writing on 1 August 1755 that "If a man sees Indians coming toward his house he does well to bring them bread and milk (if he has it). If they are enemies they will become friendly."[20] But as the Indians killed Saur's friends and neighbors in 1755 and 1756, the Pennsylvania Germans gradually abandoned his leadership. Some pacifist sects changed their minds and prepared to fight. When Franklin went to the frontier in December 1755 and began building forts in the areas the Germans occupied, he became friends with several German leaders and more popular than ever with the Germans.

Letters from Holland and Amsterdam in 1756 said that the contributors there had "the greatest expectations" of the charity schools and asked the Pennsylvania Coetus to tell them what the "ministers have received from the honorable Society in London as a Supplement to our salaries." The Coetus leaders did not know. They wrote Franklin on 16 June 1756 asking what monies had been given the various ministers and teachers[21] and came to him with their letter. They later explained to the foreign contributors that they wrote Franklin because "of all the Directors, [he] was nearest at hand." Was he actually more convenient? Smith and probably Hamilton were also in Philadelphia. The Coetus leaders evidently trusted Franklin more than the other American managers. Franklin, however, did not know and was just leaving for New York to confer with Lord Loudoun. He sent them to see Smith, the secretary of the trustees. Smith then "showed to us not only more clearly the origin of the schools from the London instruction, but also delivered a certain sum of money to each one of us." He gave them £91, for which they carefully accounted: eight ministers received £10, one received £8, and one £3. The Coetus repeated (17 June 1756) its opinion that Smith's words about the Holland synod's role concerning the funds were "very harsh" and "displeased us."[22]

"Franklin Is Alone"

Franklin signed a joint letter from the American trustees to the German Society on 24 September 1756, which complimented the sponsors and enclosed an accounting of the money spent. He had little further role in the society for several reasons. The most obvious was simply time. He had more duties and responsibilities than ever before. Something had to give. But why the German Society? By late 1755 the other American trustees—Smith, Allen, Hamilton, and Weiser—had all become political opponents. As Franklin became known as the Quaker Party leader, the proprietary partisans became unfriendly. It was uncomfortable to be with them. Further, Smith, with the support of all the American trustees except Franklin, controlled the funds and made the decisions. Perhaps the most important reason was Franklin's changing attitude toward the Pennsylvania Germans. Though he was no doubt still concerned about the great number of Germans immigrating into Pennsylvania, he had evidently come to regret his earlier cultural chauvinism when he saw Smith and the other American trustees displaying their prejudice. (That he wrote the anti-German and racist remarks in the 1751 "Observations" to mock human prejudice in general and his own feelings in particular was no excuse.) Franklin believed that education in German and/or in the English language should be supported. The other American trustees thought only English should be supported. On 26 June 1756, Richard Peters wrote Thomas Penn, "Mr. Franklin is alone in the German Schools."[23]

The project of "Anglifying" the Pennsylvania Germans failed. Muhlenberg's printing project was unsuccessful, and the last known issue of the *Philadelpische Zeitung* was for 31 December 1757. Perhaps the printer Anton Armbrüster was partly to blame, for he was later described as an "idle, drunken good for nothing Fellow" (12:343n). After Franklin left Philadelphia but before he sailed from New York in 1757, the German Reformed Coetus repeated in its report of 24 August 1757 that it could do nothing to support the free schools, "since the Directors try to erect nothing but English schools, and care nothing for the German language."[24]

Michael Schlatter wrote Franklin in England complaining of Smith's haughtiness and of his demand that the students learn English. After receiving Schlatter's letter, Franklin attended one more meeting of the German Society, in early

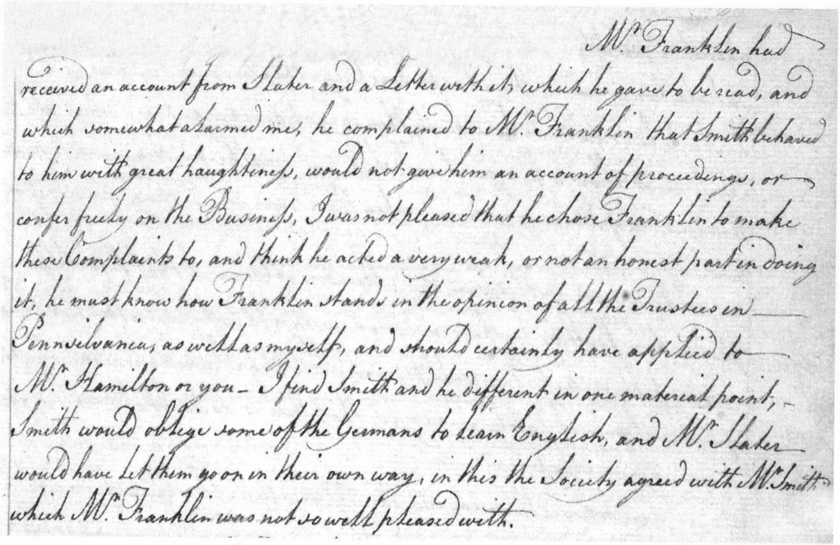
Mr Franklin had
received an account from Slater and a Letter with it, which he gave to be read, and
which somewhat alarmed me, he complained to Mr Franklin that Smith behaved
to him with great haughtiness, would not give him an account of proceedings, or
confer freely on the Business, I was not pleased that he chose Franklin to make
these Complaints to, and think he acted a very weak, or not an honest part in doing
it, he must know how Franklin stands in the opinion of all the Trustees in
Pennsilvania, as well as myself, and should certainly have applied to
Mr Hamilton or you — I find Smith and he different in one material point, —
Smith would oblige some of the Germans to learn English, and Mr Slater
would have let them go on in their own way, in this the Society agreed with Mr Smith
which Mr Franklin was not so well pleased with.

Figure 37. Thomas Penn to Richard Peters, 13 May 1758, on Franklin opposing the other trustees of the German charity schools. As it became clear that the primary purpose of the Pennsylvania German Society was to have the Germans learn English and to win their support of the proprietary government, Franklin gradually withdrew from the society. When the organization of Pennsylvania's German ministers wanted information from the trustees in early May 1756, it appealed to him. Franklin, however, was "alone in the German Schools," as Richard Peters wrote on 26 June 1756. All the other American trustees of the German Society were proprietarians and followed Provost William Smith's decision to limit their support to the teaching of English.

After the Reverend Michael Schlatter, a Pennsylvania German leader, complained to Franklin about the trustees' refusal to pay for education in the German language, Franklin attended one more meeting of the society on 13 May 1758, presented Schlatter's letter, and argued that the society should support education in either German or English. The trustees were meeting in London with James Hamilton, Dr. Samuel Chandler, Thomas Penn, Franklin, and perhaps others. The trustees supported Smith.

Unhappy that Schlatter wrote Franklin, Thomas Penn told Richard Peters that Schlatter "must know how Franklin stands in the opinion of all the Trustees in Pennsylvania, as well as myself." Penn continued: "I find Smith and he different on one material point,—Smith would oblige some of the Germans to learn English, and Mr. Slater would have let them go on in their own way, in this the Society agreed with Mr. Smith, which Mr. Franklin was not so well pleased with." Courtesy, Historical Society of Pennsylvania.

May 1758 with Dr. Samuel Chandler, Thomas Penn, James Hamilton, and no doubt others present. Franklin reported Schlatter's complaints. The only record of the meeting is Thomas Penn's letter to Richard Peters of 13 May 1758. Penn thought Schlatter was "weak" and "dishonest" in writing to Franklin. Why? "He must know how Franklin stands in the opinion of all the trustees in Pennsylvania, as well as myself." Because of their political differences, Penn wanted to hear nothing from Franklin.

Schlatter wrote Franklin rather than Smith, Peters, Allen, or Penn because he thought or knew that Franklin would be sympathetic. Franklin was, but the trustees (at least the American trustees and Thomas Penn) of the German Society no longer welcomed him. Any message delivered through Franklin to the trustees stigmatized the sender. Penn continued: "I find Smith and he different on one material point,–Smith would oblige some of the Germans to learn English, and Mr. Slater would have let them go on in their own way, in this the Society agreed with Mr. Smith, which Mr. Franklin was not so well pleased with."[25] Franklin may have acted naively. He should have foreseen that Penn and all the American trustees would have been against him. What he could possibly have done would have been to pass on the letter to the Reverend Samuel Chandler privately before the meeting and have him present the Pennsylvania Germans' complaint.

The German Society languished. Chandler continued to support the schools, but when he lost his influence at court he gave up the society. His role ended in 1769 when he turned over the remaining funds for the society to the trustees of the College of Philadelphia for its Charity School. Franklin had become the only American trustee whom the Pennsylvania Germans respected. Not until 1787 when George Clymer, Robert Morris, and other of Franklin's friends started Franklin College (to which Franklin contributed £200—twice as much as any other subscriber) was a thorough English and German bilingual education finally offered in Pennsylvania.[26]

FOURTEEN

Assembly Sessions, the Snake Cartoon, and the Albany Conference, 1754

We desire that You will strengthen Yourselves and bring as many into this Covenant Chain as you possibly can.
—Hendrick/Theyanoguin, a Mohawk chief, at the Albany Conference, 1 July 1754, *urging the colonies to unite*

IN THE EARLY SPRING OF 1754, learning of the English fort under construction at present-day Pittsburgh, Captain Claude-Pierre Pécaudy, seigneur de Contrecoeur, traveled from Canada to the fort with more than five hundred men and eighteen cannon and demanded its surrender. Ensign Edward Ward, who had been left in charge with about forty men, had no alternative; he capitulated on 17 April 1754. Then Contrecoeur began building Fort Duquesne.[1]

Before Philadelphians learned the distressing news, Franklin attempted to drum up support for defenses on the Pennsylvania frontier. He printed a letter dated 8 April in the 2 May 1754 *Pennsylvania Gazette* "from a gentleman residing in one of the Colonies to the Northward." Franklin's prefatory editorial note said the letter "contains a more full and exact Account of the Armament sent last summer from Canada, and of the pernicious Consequences that may attend the French settling in Ohio." The anonymous author was "extremely sorry" to hear that Pennsylvania and Maryland had not taken seriously the "imminent Danger." If the French make a settlement on the Ohio, "they will then have great Advantages over the Southern Colonies." During the supposed peace, "they will continually be spiriting on the Indians . . . to murder and scalp the Inhabitants of your back Counties, in order to prevent the Extension of your Settlements." And in wartime, they and their Indian allies will attack the frontiers. Unarmed and disunited, Americans will not "be able to repel the Invaders, or prevent their ravaging and laying waste your Country, or hinder them from committing their too well known Barbarities on such of your Inhabitants as may fall within their Power!"

The correspondent's persona was that of a shrewd old hand who had been active in military and Indian affairs for over a decade: "The evil Day may a while be put off, but sooner or later it will surely come, unless you rouse from the Lethargy you seem at present in, and make Use of those Means to protect yourselves which the Almighty has put in your Power." To prevent the French and their Indian allies from ravishing the frontiers, the English colonies must form "a hearty Union." Then, with "proper Management," the colonists might, "with little Assistance from our Mother Country, not only dislodge the French from Ohio, but from Quebeck itself." But sending "three or four Hundred Men, against five times their Number, can answer no other End than to expose us to the Contempt of our Indian Allies, who will think themselves obliged to quit the Interest of those that seem unable to protect them."

The Pennsylvania Assembly was scheduled to meet four days later on 6 May. It seems likely that Franklin published the letter as propaganda for defense and colonial union. Franklin obviously wrote the prefatory note, and since the letter's sentiments dovetail with Franklin's, he probably wrote it.

On 3 May 1754, Governor James Hamilton received George Washington's letter informing him of Ensign Edward Ward's surrender. With 150 troops, Washington was advancing slowly across the mountains, making a road for the cannon that Colonel Joshua Fry was bringing. Washington's forces came from Wills Creek on the upper Potomac to the Monongahela River at the mouth of Stone Creek (or Redstone Creek), which is about "37 miles above the Fort taken by the French, from whence we have a water Carriage down the River" to the forks of the Ohio. Washington enclosed a speech from the Half King Scarouady, who had been the chief spokesman at the Carlisle Treaty. Scarouady asked the Pennsylvanians and Virginians to join him to fight the French: "if you do not come to our Relief, We are gone entirely, and shall never meet, I believe, which grieves my Heart."[2]

News of the French occupying the strategic location at what is now Pittsburgh alarmed Americans. It meant that the French would control the Ohio and the Mississippi from the Great Lakes to New Orleans—and most of the land between the Alleghenies and the Rockies. On 7 May, Governor Hamilton presented the assembly with Washington's letter, the speech of Scarouady, and a letter from the commanding officer at Oswego.[3] Franklin wrote a news article based on these three items. Published on Thursday, 9 May, the article opened: "Friday last [3 May] an Express arrived here from Major Washington, with Advice, that Mr. Ward, Ensign of Capt. Trent's Company, was compelled to surrender his small Fort in the Forks of Monongahela to the French . . . who fell down from Venago with a Fleet of 360 Battoes and Canoes, upwards of 1000 Men, and 18 Pieces of Artillery, which they planted against the Fort; and Mr. Ward having but 44 Men, and no Cannon to make a proper Defence, was obliged to surrender." All the details (including the exaggerated number of French troops) came from Washington.

UNION OF THE COLONIES

Franklin reported Washington's progress toward the Monongahela and his expectation that Colonel Fry would shortly join him. Franklin also gave the information from the commanding officer at Oswego. In an editorial note, he stressed the need for a union of the colonies: "The confidence of the French in this Undertaking seems well-grounded on the present disunited State of the British Colonies and the extreme Difficulty of bringing so many different Governments and Assemblies to agree in any speedy and effectual Measures for our common Defence and Security; while our Enemies have the very great Advantage of being under one Direction, with one Council, and one Purse."

Combining reports of the worst recent outrages with a prediction of the dire possibilities for the future, Franklin warned: "Hence, and from the great Distance of Britain," the French "presume that they may with Impunity violate the most solemn Treaties subsisting between the two Crowns, kill, seize and imprison our Traders, and confiscate their Effects at Pleasure (as they have done for several Years past), murder and scalp our Farmers, with their Wives and Children, and take an easy Possession of such parts of the British Territory as they find most convenient for them; which if they are permitted to do, must end in the Destruction of the British Interest, Trade and Plantations in America" (5:274–75). Although primarily addressed to Pennsylvanians (especially to the assemblymen), at least the last sentence of the news report seems to have been intended for the British authorities.

Join, or Die

Following his analysis, Franklin dramatically presented the alternatives in America's most famous cartoon—a snake cut into parts labeled with the initials of the colonies, over the words "JOIN, or DIE." It was the first symbol of the unification of the American colonies.[4] Although the idea of the colonial American union recurred repeatedly during the seventeenth and eighteenth centuries, it had a semi-secret existence. British officials knew that the divided colonies were weak and feared that the colonies, if united, would desire independence. Americans realized that the British regarded any suggestion of American independence as traitorous and therefore denied having such thoughts. Nevertheless, writers from Richard Hakluyt in the late sixteenth century to the outbreak of the American Revolution predicted that the colonies would become independent.[5] Franklin knew the earlier writings and expected that America would either become independent or become the most important part of the American-British empire.

Franklin was responsible for the idea of the cartoon, but did he make the woodcut? The date of the news report bears upon the question. He may have had access to the several reports before Governor Hamilton presented them to the assembly on 7 May 1754, but he evidently wrote the news report and designed the cut-snake cartoon on 8 May, the day before they appeared in the Pennsylvania Gazette, when he sent them to Pennsylvania's agent Richard Partridge. Perhaps Franklin foresaw the dramatic appeal of a cartoon calling for a union of the American colonies and had a local woodcarver make the cut. Sev-

Figure 38. America's most famous cartoon: "JOIN, or DIE," Pennsylvania Gazette, 9 May 1754. By May, the unofficial war with France had been under way for several years, with France gradually building forts from Lake Erie to New Orleans. Though the English settlers outnumbered the French, they were not united, and the separate colonies would not help one another. Indeed, they sometimes warred with one another over disputed boundaries. In the 2 May 1754 Pennsylvania Gazette, Franklin published a letter, supposedly from New England (but I suspect it was by Franklin), recommending that the colonies unite. The following week, Franklin reported the defeat of Ensign Edward Ward at the forks of the Ohio and editorialized in favor of colonial unification.

Franklin accompanied the editorial with the most famous cartoon in American history, a snake cut into eight pieces, labeled with the names of the colonies, over the legend "JOIN, or DIE." It was the first symbol of American union.

The idea of the cut snake rejoining its parts reflects folklore about the supposed "joint or glass snake," which could rejoin after being broken or cut into pieces. Franklin no doubt also knew the image from emblem books—a French one portrayed a snake cut into two pieces, above a motto saying, "Un Serpent coupé en deux. Se rejoindre or mourir" (Either join or die). Most 1754 American newspapers printed a version of Franklin's cartoon. He had projected a union of the colonies in 1751 and did so again at the 1754 Albany Conference. Versions of the cut-snake emblem later appeared as propaganda for union in the pre-Revolutionary period. Courtesy, Library Company of Philadelphia.

eral years earlier, on 20 March 1750/1, he had written James Parker that a union was desirable as a bulwark against the French and Indians. It seems more likely, however, that the immediate inspiration for the cartoon, as for Franklin's news report, was Washington's letter.

If Franklin learned the news on 7 May, whom could he have engaged to make the woodcut? Franklin wanted it right away. Perhaps someone locally could do it immediately, perhaps not. Franklin, however, could make the cut; he wanted it immediately; and he probably made it. Had a good artist done it, we might have been able to see the markings on the snake and whether the tail had rattles.[6] As it is, we have a generic snake, with a tail diminishing to a point. The cartoon does not portray a rattlesnake—though Franklin might have wanted it to.

The editorial and cartoon was successful in America: the *New York Gazette*, the *New York Mercury*, the *Boston Gazette*, and the *Boston Weekly News-Letter* all produced their own versions in the next three weeks.[7]

Within a month, Franklin left Philadelphia to attend the Albany Conference. He arrived in New York City on 5 June. On 8 June he circulated among the New York intellectuals a draft of his plan for American unification. The snake cartoon had prepared the way. Since Franklin had even sent a copy to Richard Partridge requesting him to have it reprinted in the "most publick Papers" in England (5:273), we can be sure that he encouraged its reprinting in America.[8] When the *Virginia Gazette*, on 19 July 1754, reported Colonel George Washington's defeat at Fort Necessity, its editor concluded by recalling Franklin's cartoon: "Surely this will remove the infatuation of security that seems to have prevailed too much among the other colonies" and "inforce a late ingenious Emblem worthy of their Attention and Consideration." Reprinting the *Virginia Gazette* article, the *South Carolina Gazette* explained the allusion to the snake device. After examining the different versions of the emblem, the careful scholar Albert Matthews stated in 1907 that "the fame of the snake device had been spread throughout the colonies."[9]

THE SNAKE SYMBOLISM

Though the snake in the Western world primarily symbolized evil, Franklin made the rattlesnake not only a symbol of America but also of American resentment and hostility toward the English. In the most significant previous use of the snake in American culture, Franklin had written in the 9 May 1751 "Rattlesnakes for Felons" hoax that the rattlesnake was the most suitable exchange that America could make for the human serpents (a.k.a. "English convicts") that Britain shipped to the colonies (4:130–33). The satire identified the rattlesnake with America. The slightly earlier vicious news note of 11 April 1751, "Jakes on our Tables," and Franklin's "Rattlesnakes for Felons" were the most biting anti-English writings in the colonial American press before the Stamp Act.[10]

Though not so savage as Franklin's 1751 editorial and satire, his news report of 9 May 1754 again expressed American resentment against Britain. Because of America's "great Distance" from England, the French could make war on the American frontiers without the English bestirring themselves. When Franklin used a cut snake on 9 May 1754 as a symbol of the necessity for American unification, the snake implied patriotic American feelings and recalled the earlier anti-English sentiments. Implicit in the joining of the parts of the snake was not only the union of the colonies but also a hint of America's future independence. That undercurrent became explicit in Franklin's later uses of the snake, both in visual images and in stinging rhetoric.

The serpent is an archetypal symbol with multiple and rich meanings.[11] As a symbol of eternity and unity, it most often appears in circular form with its tail in its mouth. Franklin knew the various symbolic meanings of the serpent, and when he wanted to portray colonial union, he recalled the image of a serpent cut into two that appeared in a seventeenth-century emblem book, Nicolas Verrien's *Recueil d'emblemes* (Paris, 1696), plate 61, no. 7 (figure 4). The accompanying motto reads "Un Serpent coupé en deux. Se rejoindre ou mourir" (A serpent cut in two. Either join or die).[12] Folklore concerning the joint or glass snake, which supposedly can rejoin its parts after being broken or cut into pieces, probably inspired Verrien's emblem. Franklin knew both the folk belief and the French emblem.[13]

Another Franklin inspiration was the recent and amazing discovery of the strange qualities of the polyp. In *Poor Richard* for 1751, Franklin discussed "that most unaccountable of all Creatures the Polype" (4:93). He probably had read Abraham Trembley's 1748 comparison of the regenerating power of the polyp to the "chimerical idea" that a snake cut in half could join its parts together and become "one and the same serpent."[14]

From the cut-snake cartoon of 1754 until the end of the Revolutionary War, the snake, especially the rattlesnake, frequently appeared as a symbol of America. Dr. Samuel Johnson had seen the symbol numerous times, and in his 1775 *Taxation No Tyranny*, he linked it with Franklin's theory of the increase of American population. Condemning Americans, Johnson wrote: "the continent of North America contains three millions, not of men merely, but of Whigs, of Whigs fierce for liberty, and disdainful of dominion; that they multiply with the fecundity of their own rattle-snakes, so that every quarter of a century doubles their numbers."[15] The paper currency of the Continental Congress and of various colonies, the flags, and decorations of war objects (e.g., drums) all commonly featured a snake.[16] General Horatio Gates wrote to John Adams on 23 April 1776 that he did not think that General William Howe intended to make New England, which he called "the Head of the Snake" (alluding to Franklin's labeling the head "N.E." in the "Join, or Die" cartoon), the object of his next campaign.[17] After Loyalists and others like London's Dr. Samuel Johnson satirized the Americans' use of the snake, Franklin replied with "The Rattlesnake as a Symbol of America, by an American Guesser" (27 December 1775), giving sixteen attributes of snakes, the first half dozen of which are standard in heraldry and emblem literature.[18]

In 1778, a rattlesnake appeared in the frame of Franklin's most famous portrait. It is curled around the top half of the frame of Joseph-Siffred Duplessis's

1778 *Benjamin Franklin* (Metropolitan Museum of New York). In the picture's iconographic symbolism, the snake suggested American uniqueness, patriotism, pugnacity, and, because part of the snake makes a circle at the top, unity.[19] Though prefigured by Franklin's 1751 satire "Rattlesnakes for Felons," Franklin's 1754 "Join, or Die" cartoon established the rattlesnake as a symbol of America.

ENGAGEMENTS AT "THE FLATS" AND "FORT NECESSITY"

As Contrecoeur forced Ensign Ward to surrender and then started building Fort Duquesne, George Washington was on his way to the forks of the Ohio. After learning of Ward's surrender, Washington nevertheless continued, hoping that Colonel Joshua Fry (author of the Fry and Jefferson map with Jefferson's father) would catch up to him before he reached the French. Washington's Indian allies, the Mingos under the Half King Chief Tanaghrisson, found the camp of a small French party at "the Flats" and informed Washington, who "marched at the Head of a Company of about 40 Men" with the rain falling so heavily "that they could scarce keep their Ammunition dry." They fought on 28 May.

The *Maryland Gazette* of 13 June 1754 reported that the French "about 36 in Number" fired first and killed one of "Major Washington's Men and wounded another. The English returned the Fire, and killed 7 or 8 of the French, on which the Rest took to their Heels; but the Half King, and his Indians, who lay in Ambush to cut them off in their Retreat, fell upon them, and soon killed and scalped Five of them." Consequently they fled toward the English and "begged for Quarter." Washington protected them, though the Half King wanted to kill and scalp them all, "as it was their Way of Fighting, and he alleged that those People had killed, boiled, and eat his Father, and that the Indians would not be satisfied without all their Scalps." Washington, however, "persuaded him to be content with what Scalps he had already won. One of the five killed and scalped by the Indians was "Monsieur Jumonville, an Ensign, whom the Half King himself dispatched with his Tomahawk." Although there were numerous preceding incidents suggesting the beginnings of an imperil conflict in America, the battle of less than eighty men on 28 May 1754 marked the first engagement between official forces in what became known in America as the French and Indian (or Seven Years') War.[20]

Washington and his men went on, and seven weeks later they found themselves followed by a French force of about five hundred men commanded by Louis Coulon de Villiers, the older brother of Joseph de Villiers de Jumonville, the ensign killed at "the Flats" on 28 May. The *Pennsylvania Gazette* of 25 July reported Washington's surrender: "Washington, with the Virginia Regiment, and Captain [James] MacKay, with the South Carolina Independent Company, together, did consist but of Four Hundred Men, of which a good many were sick, and out of Order. On the third of July the French, with about Nine Hundred Men, and a considerable Body of Indians, came down upon our Incampment, and continued to fire, from all Quarters, from Eleven in the Morning till

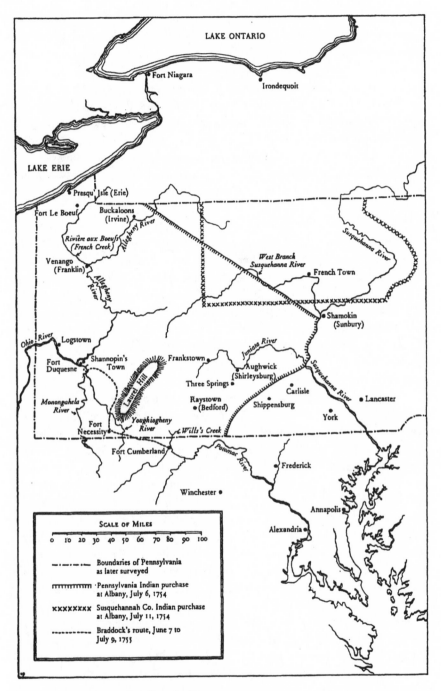

LAKE ONTARIO

Fort Niagara

Irondequoit

LAKE ERIE

Presqu' Isle (Erie)

Fort Le Boeuf

Buckaloons
(Irvine)

Rivière aux Boeufs
(French Creek)

Allegheny River

Venango
(Franklin)

Allegheny River

West Branch
Susquehanna River

French Town

Susquehanna River

Shamokin
(Sunbury)

Ohio River Logstown

Fort
Duquesne

Shannopin's
Town

Frankstown

Juniata River

Aughwick
(Shirleysburg)

Three Springs

Laurel Hill

Carlisle

Susquehanna River

Lancaster

Monongahela
River

Raystown
(Bedford)

Shippensburg

York

Fort
Necessity

Youghiogheny
River

Wills's Creek

Fort Cumberland

Potomac River

Frederick

Winchester

Annapolis

SCALE OF MILES

0 10 20 30 40 50 60 70 80 90 100

Alexandria

— · — · — Boundaries of Pennsylvania
as later surveyed

ΠΤΤΤΤΤΤΤΠ ·Pennsylvania Indian purchase
at Albany, July 6, 1754

xxxxxxxx Susquehannah Co. Indian purchase
at Albany, July 11, 1754

----------- Braddock's route, June 7 to
July 9, 1755

Map 3. *Western Pennsylvania and adjacent parts, 1753–55*

Night, when the French call'd out to our People, they would give them good Conditions, if they would capitulate, a Copy of which I here inclose you." Surrounded by the French at the camp he called "Fort Necessity," Washington surrendered on 4 July 1754.

Villiers, who assuredly had heard of his younger brother's death, behaved like an officer and a gentleman. He allowed the defeated American and Indian forces to leave when he could have massacred them. Washington's defeat presaged disaster for persons living on the frontier. The same news article reporting his surrender said that "many of the Back Inhabitants were coming down to Winchester with their Effects, for fear of being cut off by the Indians; and that in general they were in the utmost Consternation."

THE 1753–54 ASSEMBLY'S FOURTH SESSION, 6–18 MAY

On Tuesday, 7 May, Governor James Hamilton informed the assembly of Ensign Ward's surrender and said that the frontier needed immediate aid. Hamilton and the moderate Quaker Party members had an additional reason for action. The first edition of William Smith's anonymous anti-Quaker pamphlet, *A Brief State of the Province of Pennsylvania,* had appeared in London in February and just reached Philadelphia. It blamed the Quakers and their German supporters for not protecting the Pennsylvania frontier and demanded that British authorities disenfranchise the Germans and Quakers;[21] Pennsylvania's Quaker Party leaders had to counter.

On 9 May 1754, the day that Franklin's cut-snake cartoon appeared in the *Pennsylvania Gazette,* the House met at 10:00 A.M. and considered the same 9 April money bill of a month before: a "Bill for striking the Sum of [blank] Thousand Pounds in Bills of Credit, and for granting [blank] Pounds thereof to the King's Use, &c." Again, the question was: how much? When the members met that afternoon, they argued about the amount to give "for the King's Use" (i.e., for defense) and moved to pay £20,000. Only the same eight persons, including Franklin, who had voted for that sum before, voted in its favor. Next, the vote for granting £15,000 failed, 10 to 22, but then a bill for giving £10,000 scraped through, 17 to 15, and it was passed on 10 May.[22] The bill extended the excise tax on liquor for ten years to repay the £10,000. Since the excise tax would yield between £3,500 and £4,000 a year, it would leave £2,500 to £3,000 a year for the assembly to spend as it deemed necessary. Reporting the vote in the third edition of his *Brief State,* Provost William Smith claimed that the excise tax was for twelve, rather than ten, years and that it "would raise £45,000, viz. 10,000 for the King's Use, and the remaining 35,000 would have been at" the disposal of the assembly "for what Uses they might think fit." Though Smith exaggerated, the bill would indeed have raised more than £25,000 in ten years.[23]

The governor returned the bill on 14 May with several amendments. The House promptly considered it, accepted some amendments, and returned it to the governor.[24] Still bound by Thomas Penn's instruction of 1 November 1753 not to pass any bill in which he did not control the funds, Governor Hamilton again resorted to a subterfuge. On 15 May, he demanded that the assembly make the excise tax good for only four years. At £3,500 a year, that would raise £14,000, leaving £4,000 after paying the £10,000, and leaving nothing after paying the governor £1,000 a year. Hamilton attempted to justify his position by citing the Currency Act of 1751, by which the New England colonies had to sink paper money emissions within five years. Franklin and other members of the assembly thought Hamilton was clutching at straws to conceal the proprietors' secret instructions. The House unanimously rejected the four-year requirement, leaving the province defenseless.[25]

Characterizing the bill in the third edition of his *Brief State* (1756), Smith said that the assembly would have applied the money "to distress all who oppose their Measures, and for building Hospitals, purchasing Lands, Libraries, etc." Smith objected to Franklin's civic programs even though Smith benefited from one of them as provost of the Academy and College of Philadelphia. The sycophantic Smith no doubt adopted these opinions from Thomas Penn. Penn later wrote to Governor Robert Hunter Morris that the assembly had often applied money it raised "to unnecessary purposes" like the Library Company and the hospital (see fig. 34b, p. 293).[26] Naturally Thomas Penn's and William Smith's selfish attitudes disgusted civic-minded and humanitarian Philadelphians—especially Franklin.

On 15 May 1754 Speaker Norris appointed Franklin and others to reply to the governor's demand; that afternoon, the assembly read, approved, and sent the governor its answer: "the Representatives of the People have an undoubted Right to judge, and determine, not only of the Sum to be raised for the Use of the Crown, but of the Manner of raising it." As he had done on 11 September 1753, Franklin cited the actions of Governor George Thomas in 1746 as a precedent (5:351) and claimed that the "representatives are best acquainted with the Circumstances of the People." The 15 May message also noted that Hamilton had pleaded for an immediate supply bill because of the military emergency, but he now rejected it. With sarcasm, Franklin continued that Hamilton must not now "think the Danger so imminent, or the Emergency so great or as real, as he then apprehended it to be." Ending, Franklin said that if Hamilton's amendment limiting the term of the excise to four years was insisted on, "the Bill cannot pass" (5:281–82).

Governor Hamilton answered on 17 May 1754, claiming that Governor Thomas in 1746 had never communicated the act of 1746 "for the Royal Approbation."[27] Norris appointed Franklin and others to reply, and he drew up a series of resolves, adopted the next day, asserting that the House had complete responsibility for taxation. Since 1753, Franklin and the House had had no doubt that secret instructions from Thomas Penn, which, in their opinion, kept the province defenseless, bound Governer Hamilton. Franklin's resolves concluded by saying that "if the Governor is restricted by any Instruction from passing this

Bill," it must be by a private instruction from the proprietaries "which he has never been pleased to lay before this House," and that it could not by the royal instruction that he had cited and that "he hath so effectually invalidated."[28] With that, the assembly adjourned to 19 August but was recalled on 6 August after George Washington's defeat at Fort Necessity.

On 7 May 1754, Governor Hamilton had given the assembly copies of various papers regarding the forthcoming Albany Treaty and reminded them that he had requested its advice on 4 April. The governors of Massachusetts and New York made proposals "so agreeable to my Sentiments, that I earnestly recommend it to your Consideration; and that you will enable me to instruct the Commissioners from this Province to concur with those from the other Colonies, in Case a reasonable Plan shall be offered them for that Purpose."[29] Hamilton no doubt knew of Franklin's 1751 published proposal for unifying the colonies and may have been referring to it. Speaker Norris assigned a committee on 10 May to reply to the governor's message. Because Franklin was to be one of the commissioners receiving the instructions, the committee did not include him. The report was "read and considered and referred to further consideration" on 13 May and again the next morning. That afternoon, "after a considerable Debate thereon," it was "transcribed as it now stands."[30] On 13 and 14 May, Franklin no doubt argued for a colonial union, and he may have used the example of the union of the Six Nations, just as he had in 1751. Unfortunately, the division was not recorded. I suspect that the assemblymen who voted with Franklin on 8 May to give £20,000 for combating the French and Indians on the frontier were the same ones who now supported the idea of a union.[31] But Franklin and those who agreed with him could not overturn the committee report.

No doubt hoping to influence the assembly, Franklin published in the *Gazette* on 16 May Governor Shirley's letter of 4 March to Governor Hamilton advocating colonial union. The letter, however, did not sway the assembly. On 18 May, it begrudgingly agreed to give £500 for the Indians at Albany and to pay for the commissioners to attend the conference. At the same time, the assembly replied to Hamilton's three requests (14 February, 4 April, and 7 May) that it support the idea of a union of the colonies: "no Propositions for an Union of the Colonies, in *Indian* affairs, can effectually answer the good Purposes, or be binding, farther than they are confirmed by Laws, enacted under the several Government comprized in that Union." This adumbration of states rights doomed any possible union. The assembly also took jabs at the governor and proprietor by referring to the secret instructions ("we know not what Restrictions the Governor may lie under in passing our Acts") and disgustedly mentioned the proprietors' refusal to pay any part of the expenses for Indian affairs ("we have very little Reason to depend upon any Assistance in Our *Indian* Expences, where, by a former Assembly, it has been respectfully addressed for, and where we think in justice we have a Right to expect it"). The assembly stated that the sole purpose of their support of the Albany Treaty was to renew the "Covenant-Chain with the Six Nations."[32] With that, the assembly adjourned. Franklin's Albany Plan of Union was dead aborning. Franklin, however, was not one to give up easily.

Franklin had initially thought that "a voluntary Union entered into by the Colonies themselves . . . would be preferable to one impos'd by Parliament" partly because he believed that Americans on the spot would find the union "more easy to alter and improve, as Circumstances should require, and Experience direct" (4:118).[33] The actions of the Pennsylvania Assembly, however, together with the unwillingness of other colonies to help Virginia against the Indian attacks on its frontier, changed Franklin's mind. He saw that the colonies would not voluntarily enter into a union. Therefore, when a few weeks later he wrote his 8 June 1754 "Short Hints towards a Scheme for Uniting the Northern Colonies," he said that after the colonists formed a scheme for union, the plan should be "sent home, and a Act of Parliament obtain'd for establishing it" (5:338). In a complete about-face, Franklin suggested that Parliament should have greater power over the colonies, should be able to override their charters, and should force them into a new relationship with one another and with Great Britain.

Considering the relations between the colonies and Great Britain, Franklin surely thought of the long-term probabilities. As he had shown, the colonies would become more populous and more powerful than Great Britain. If they remained separate and did not cooperate, they might not be strong enough to oppose the French and Indians. But if they unified, the colonies would be too strong for the French and Indians now and would be too strong within three generations for Britain to dominate. Franklin probably had such considerations in mind when he suggested that Parliament enact a scheme to unite the colonies for defense. Perhaps Franklin was trying to woo his fellow members of the assembly. Though Speaker Norris had earlier reported that Franklin was losing his popularity, Norris now thought he had regained his interest with the majority of the Quaker members.[34]

INTERVAL, 19 MAY 2–JUNE 1754

From the assembly's adjournment on 18 May until Franklin left for Albany, he kept up with his usual rush of activities and prepared for the trip, visiting Isaac Norris at his country estate, Fairfield, on 22 May. William Smith, now an Anglican minister, returned from London on 23 May and delivered the Copley medal of the Royal Society to Franklin. The trustees of the academy hired Smith at its meeting the next day, 24 May. Franklin completed the manuscript of "Some Account of the Pennsylvania Hospital" and submitted it on 28 May. That same day, he wrote a long letter to Peter Collinson on atmospheric electricity, on the construction of barometers, and on politics, among other matters.

The letter presented Franklin's view of what should be the relation between

Britain and the colonies: "Britain and her Colonies should be considered as one Whole, and not as different States with separate Interests." After this reasonable and almost commonsensical generalization, Franklin proceeded to castigate Britain's instructions to its governors and its treatment of the colonies: "Instructions from the Crown to the Colonies, should have in View the Common Weal of that Whole, to which partial Interests ought to give way: And they should never Aim at extending the Prerogative beyond its due Bounds, nor abridging the just Liberties of the people: In short, they should be plainly just and reasonable, and rather savour of Fatherly Tenderness and Affection, than of Masterly harshness and Severity. Such Instructions might safely be made publick; but if they are of a different kind, they must be kept secret."

Franklin knew, however, that the mercantilist theories favored a few Englishmen rather than the good of the whole. He also knew that many British authorities wanted to ignore the traditional rights of the colonists and make the crown's instructions to the governors the law (5:332–33). Franklin judged Britain's treatment of the colonies arbitrary and unjust. His criticisms of Britain were all the more surprising since he was writing an Englishman whom he did not personally know. In condemning Parliament's acts and the crown's instructions, Franklin also had in mind Penn's secret instructions. James H. Hutson suggested (and I agree) that Franklin meant for Collinson to show Penn the letter.[35] Governor Hamilton's astute observation of 8 September 1753 that Franklin denied the validity of both proprietary and royal instructions was here confirmed (see above, p. 324).

On 30 May, Franklin wrote Thomas Penn his first and only personal letter. All other correspondence between them occurred in one of Franklin's official positions. Even this letter was semi-official: as noted in chapter 12, Penn had informed Richard Peters that he told the joint postmaster general, Sir Everard Fawkener, that he thought Franklin "as capable as any man in America to serve the Crown." Peters told Franklin that Fawkener had said he would like to see a plan for the possible expansion of the post office in America. Franklin wrote Penn and indirectly Fawkener that after he returned from Albany, he and William Hunter, his co–deputy postmaster for North America, intended to journey through all the northern colonies "to visit all the Post Offices, and see every thing with our own Eyes; after which we may be able to project some Plan of that kind."

Franklin thanked Penn "for your favourable Character of me to Sir Everard, and for the Assurances you are pleas'd to give me of your friendly Offices" (5:334–35). Franklin concluded by offering his services to Penn. Penn may have been sincere concerning Franklin in his letter to Peters, though he may have exaggerated his recommendation of Franklin, which seems to have been made after Franklin had been appointed. On the other hand, Franklin knew Penn's avarice and his belief in prerogative privileges well. Surely Franklin's letter was primarily polite cant; but was it so entirely? Franklin worked with Richard Peters, James Hamilton, and William Allen, all of whom believed in prerogative privileges, and with Israel Pemberton, James Morris, and other pacifists. These people, sometimes friends, sometimes opponents, and all of them neighbors, were constants in the small society of Pennsylvania politics. Franklin worked with any of them whenever he could do so; and he almost always opposed them whenever they disagreed with what Franklin considered an important issue. But, occasionally, to achieve some goal, it was necessary to abandon his beliefs and defer to others—the traditional Latin training at the Philadelphia Academy being one example. It would have been characteristic of Franklin to try to see if he could find some common ground with Penn. The supercilious Penn, however, did not want to try.

Before leaving for Albany, Norris and Franklin, together with the representatives of the council and the proprietors, discussed the forthcoming treaty with Governor James Hamilton. He wrote on 2 June, to Governor James DeLancey of New York the substance of what he said to the commissioners. Though Hamilton could not get the Pennsylvania Assembly to give the commissioners "any specific Powers or Advices," he hoped "that upon a full and free Discussion of the State of the Colonies at the Treaty, something of general Utility may be agreed upon, or that a candid Representation of our Condition may be made to his Majesty, and his Interposition implored for our Protection."[36] Perhaps he was reflecting Franklin's revised position on colonial union.

The Albany Conference

The Journey

Franklin left Philadelphia for Albany, New York, on Monday morning, 3 June 1754, and returned on the evening of 28 or morning of 29 July. Besides Franklin, the Pennsylvania delegation to Albany consisted of John Penn (1729–95, Thomas Penn's nephew), Richard Peters, Isaac Norris, and the Indian expert Conrad Weiser.[37] From a sketchy diary that Peters kept, we know their route and some of their activities.[38] If, as Franklin wrote in the *Autobiography*, he "projected and drew up a Plan for the Union of all the Colonies" as he traveled to New York, it must have been done on the evening of 3 or 4 June. On 3 June the four commissioners and Weiser had lunch at Bristol, Pennsylvania, on the Delaware River, then rode up to the ferry at Trentown, where they crossed the Delaware River and had dinner. On Tuesday, they journeyed through thunderstorms from Kingstown to Brunswick, New Jersey. Because of the weather, they probably stopped a little early; Franklin might have worked that evening on the Albany Plan.

On Wednesday, 5 June, the five went from Woodstock to Staten Island Point, where they crossed the bay to New York in a little over an hour and proceeded to Scotch John's tavern, the Crown and Thistle, on Whitehall Slip. They waited on Acting Governor James DeLancey at John Watts's home and lodged that

Short hints towards a scheme for uniting the Northern Colonies

A Governour General
To be appointed by the King.
To be a Military man.
To have a Salary from the Crown
To have a negation on all acts of the Grand Council, and carry into execution what ever is agreed on by him & that Council

Grand Council
One member to be chosen by the Assembly of each of the smaller Colonies & two or more by each of the larger, in proportion to the Sums they pay Yearly into the General Treasury.

Members Pay
——— Shillings sterling p Diem dewring their sitting & mileage for Travelling Expences ———

Place & Time of meeting
To meet ——— times in every year, at the Capital of each Colony in Course, unless particular circumstances & emergencies require more frequent meetings & Alteration in the Course of places, The Governour General to Judge of those circumstances &c & call by his Writts ———

General Treasury
Its Fund, an Excise on Strong Liquors pretty equally drank in the Colonies. or Duty on Liquor imported ——— or ——— shillings on each Licence of Publick House. or Excise on Superfluities as Tea &c &c. all which would pay in some proportion to the present wealth of each Colony, and encrease as that wealth encreases, & prevent disputes about the Inequality of Quotas ———
To be Collected in each Colony, & Lodged in their Treasury to be ready for the payment of Orders issuing from
the

Figure 39. Franklin's "Short Hints" for the Albany Plan, 8 June 1754. On 8 June, Franklin sent his "Short Hints towards a Scheme for Uniting the Northern Colonies" to James Alexander, asking for his thoughts on the two-page document and requesting him to forward it to Cadwallader Colden for his suggestions. Revising the plan he had put forward to Alexander in 1751, "Short Hints" was the second stage in the composition of the Albany Plan of 10 July 1754. Limiting the organization to "the Northern Colonies" was primarily a suggestion of modesty on Franklin's part; for his first, third, and final version of the Albany Plan included all the existing mainland colonies, except for the two supported by annual grants from Parliament, Georgia and Nova Scotia (Delaware was implicitly considered with Pennsylvania).

The substance of all four plans is similar, but Franklin had thought in 1751 that the colonies should join together voluntarily. Since then, he had realized that they would not; they were jealous of one another, and each prized its own laws and government. So now he suggested that Parliament should create a union of the colonies. The union would only be for defense and for questions concerning the creation of future colonies; the existing colonies would continue with their own legal systems and traditions. Franklin, however, wrote (August 1754) in "Reasons and Motives for the Albany Plan" that any union would be a step toward a future political union of the colonies. He had long thought that England treated the colonies unfairly, and he knew, as he implied in 1751 and and 1754 (and directly stated in 1760), that repeated ill usage would drive the colonies to rebellion. Courtesy, Collection of the New York Historical Society.

night at Edward Willet's Province Arms Inn (formerly the DeLancey mansion) at 115 Broadway.[39]

Since Franklin wrote that he conferred with James Alexander and Archibald Kennedy about his plan while in New York (A 131), he may have done so on Thursday, 6 June, while the other three commissioners and Conrad Weiser purchased presents for the Indians. Franklin probably joined the group for dinner that night with DeLancey at Willet's Province Arms. Richard Peters recorded that on Friday, 7 June, he and the Maryland commissioners went to Peter Livingston's; then "Dined at Phil Livingston's; went to Mr. Wells's Country house, with Mr. Walton, there we drank Cydar." Franklin was evidently not with Peters the next day, Saturday, 8 June. That day, he sent James Alexander a copy of his "Short Hints towards a Scheme for Uniting the Northern Colonies," asked for his suggestions, and requested him to send on the manuscript to Cadwallader Colden for his comments (5:335–38). The "Short Hints" is the second surviving document in the evolution of Franklin's Albany Plan. The first was his letter to James Parker of 20 March 1750/1, which Parker had printed early in May 1751 as an appendix to Archibald Kennedy's *Importance of Gaining and Preserving the Friendship of the Indians* (4:117–21).

On Saturday evening, Franklin may have joined Peters and the other commissioners for supper at the home of the Reverend Henry Barclay of Trinity Church. The Reverend Samuel Johnson, whom Franklin had tried to hire as the head of the Philadelphia Academy and who was now President of King's College, New York, was a fellow guest. Peters recorded that the conversation was about Indians (Barclay had spent eleven years, 1735–46, in Albany and Schenectady, knew the Mohawk language, and translated the litany from the Book of Common Prayer into Mohawk.) They stayed late. Peters noted that Governor DeLancey left at 11 o'clock.

At 7:00 A.M. on Sunday with the Maryland commissioners and "a great number of private gentlemen," Franklin sailed up the Hudson for Albany.[40] James Alexander wrote Colden on 9 June, enclosing Franklin's "Short Hints." Alexander said that he had talked with Franklin and Peters about the difficulty of uniting the colonies, "Whereon Mr. Franklin promised to set down some hints of a scheme that he thought might do which accordingly he sent to me." Alexander's letter to Colden implies that Franklin wrote the "Short Hints" in New York after talking with Peters and Alexander about the union of the colonies, rather than writing the document as he traveled to New York. Since Alexander wrote in 1754 and Franklin in 1788, and since Franklin had more time to write in New York than on the journey, I suspect that Alexander is correct about the date (7 June, plus or minus a day) and place of composition.

Alexander reported to Colden some "difficulties" he found in Franklin's plan: persons skilled in warfare were lacking for the "Grand Council," and persons on the Grand Council might reveal war plans to the enemy. He also thought that a "Council of State" should always be with the governor-general to advise him, and that the governor-general and the Council of State should display both the accounts at every meeting of the "Grand Council" and as much of the business "as is safe to be made Publick." Alexander also said that the "Grand Council with the Governour Generall [should] have power to" increase but not to decrease the "Duties laid by Act of Parliament" and, in emergencies, the council with the governor-general should have the power to issue bills of credit "bearing a small interest but not to be tenders" (5:340–41). If Alexander sent Franklin his comments (which tended to favor prerogative power), Franklin ignored them.

Albany

Franklin and others arrived at Albany on Monday, 17 June. He was among the twenty gentleman who dined with Governor DeLancey and had "a Handsome Entertainment, good wine, and Arrak Punch." A Connecticut commissioner, Theodore Atkinson, kept a brief diary at Albany. He recorded that the Pennsylvania commissioners called on the New Hampshire members after dinner on Tuesday, 18 June. The next morning New Hampshire returned the visit and then they went together to the town hall for the start of the conference.[41]

The Albany Conference began on 19 June 1754, with Governor DeLancey and four of his council, four commissioners from Massachusetts, three commissioners from Connecticut, two from Rhode Island, two from Maryland, and four from Pennsylvania. Three key additional persons were Conrad Weiser, Pennsylvania's Indian expert; William Johnson, Indian agent, who had originally come to New York's Mohawk Valley in 1737 as the representative of his uncle, Admiral Peter Warren, M.P.; and Thomas Pownall, who may have journeyed to New York with the Pennsylvanians. Governor DeLancey probably invited Pownall because Pownall's brother John was the secretary to the Board of Trade. The commissioners met at Albany's city hall and began to prepare the opening speech to the Iroquois. A committee drafted the speech, the assembled commissioners debated it on 21 June, and they agreed on it Saturday, 22 June. A fifth Massachusetts commissioner, Thomas Hutchinson (1711–80), the future governor of Massachusetts, arrived late on 21 June.

On Monday afternoon, 24 June, the representatives discussed a colonial union. They agreed that a "union of all the Colonies is . . . absolutely necessary for their Security and Defence." Each government was asked to appoint one person to a committee "to prepare and receive Plans or Schemes for the Union of the Colonies and to digest them into one general Plan for the Inspection of this Board." Theodore Atkinson (1697–1779) was named from New Hampshire; Hutchinson was named from Massachusetts; William Pitkin (1694–1769) from Connecticut; Stephen Hopkins (1707–85) from Rhode Island; Franklin from Pennsylvania; and Benjamin Tasker (1720–60) from Maryland. DeLancey appointed William Smith (1697–1769) from New York. Usually, the first person listed chaired the committee, but the sequence here is simply in north-to-south order, except for New York, listed last. However, since Franklin's plan seemed to be preferred and since he compiled the final report, he probably chaired the committee.[42]

No one expected the Iroquois to reply that Monday. The Indian protocol, which the whites adopted, was to consider what had been said and to reply the following day. Franklin noted in his *Autobiography*, "The Debates upon" colonial union "went on daily hand in hand with the Indian Business." Rather than switch back and forth, I will first deal briefly with the Indian treaty.

The Treaty

Governor James Hamilton's standing instruction from Pennsylvania's proprietors said to "take all Opportunities of making another Purchase of Lands from the Six Nations." Upon receiving news of a forthcoming treaty, Hamilton sent John Shikellamy/Onkikswathetami, an Oneida chief, in the spring of 1754 to the Six Nations to let the Iroquois know that Thomas Penn wanted to purchase more land at Albany. Shikellamy had been the key negotiator of the alliance that Pennsylvania had formed with the Six Nations in 1736. Before the commissioners left in June, Hamilton relayed Thomas Penn's instructions to John Penn and Richard Peters—purchase additional lands from the Iroquois, "the larger the better."[43]

Governor DeLancey opened the treaty with a speech to the Iroquois on Saturday, 29 June 1754. He promised friendship, gave a large wampum belt, and pledged to renew the Covenant Chain. He also asked whether the Iroquois had allowed or approved of the French building forts "between the Lake Erie and the River Ohio." In addition to the official treaty minutes, we have Thomas Pownall's report of the proceedings addressed to "My Lord," probably the earl of Halifax, president of the Lords of Trade. Pownall recorded that when the Indians received the Covenant Belt, each of the Six Nations "singly after one another, shou'd have sounded the Yoheighish." Instead, they sounded a single cry until, "being reminded that the other was expected of them," they did it in the usual custom.[44] The violation of the usual etiquette indicated that the Iroquois had doubts about the treaty.

That same Saturday, the Stockbridge Indians arrived. Franklin and another commissioner waited on DeLancey to inform him. On Monday, 1 July, Franklin reported that Governor DeLancey said he had not invited the Stockbridge Indians and did not want to contribute to their support. The commissioners examined the records and noted that the Stockbridge Indians usually attended the Iroquois treaties at Albany and were traditionally supported. Thereupon DeLancey agreed to address them and to contribute to their support, but added that he expected the other colonies also to contribute. That afternoon, the famous old Mohawk chief Hendrick/Theyanoguin (ca. 1680–1755)[45] replied to DeLancey for the Six Nations, going through the form of renewing and brightening the Covenant Chain. He encouraged the English colonies to join together against the French: "We desire that You will strengthen Yourselves and bring as many into this Covenant Chain as you possibly can." He accused the English of neglecting the Six Nations for the past three years. "Taking a Stick and throwing it behind his Back," Hendrick said, "You have thus thrown us behind your backs, whereas the French" were "using their utmost Endeavours to seduce and bring our People over to them."[46]

The *Gentleman's Magazine* reprinted his speech: "Look at the French, they are Men; they are fortifying every where. We are ashamed to say it, You are all like Women, bare and open without any Fortifications." He condemned the governors of Virginia and Canada for quarreling about lands that belonged to the Iroquois and for building forts on them. They should have asked permission. Hendrick accused the Albany merchants of trading for furs with the French Indians and paying them with guns and ammunition, which were now being used against the English. In effect, Hendrick accused the Albany merchants of betraying the English and the Iroquois. Reporting on the conference, Thomas Pownall, who had become friendly with Conrad Weiser, reported that in this speech, the Indians "spoke freely from their heart."

Hendrick's brother Abraham reminded the group that three years before he had requested that William Johnson have charge of Indian affairs. Governor George Clinton of New York had promised to have it done. The request, Abraham said, must have "drowned in the sea." Abraham repeated Hendrick's statement of 12 June 1753 that "the Fire here is burnt out."[47] The dramatic statement called an end to the alliance.

After his brother's speech, Hendrick held up two belts that the proprietors of Pennsylvania had sent to the Iroquois to discuss selling land to Pennsylvania. The Pennsylvania commissioners wanted to conduct the negotiations in the open treaty. DeLancey and the representatives of the other colonies, however, judged that the "Matter regarded only the Province of Pennsylvania" and should be conducted in private. The Pennsylvanians objected but were overruled.[48] Peters, John Penn, and Conrad Weiser may have suspected that the Iroquois might sell land and later repudiate doing so.

On Wednesday, 3 July, Governor DeLancey apologized to the Six Nations for the past neglect by the English and declared, "the Covenant is renewed, the Chain is brightened, the Fire burns clear, and We hope all Things will be pleasant on both Sides for the Future." The commissioners called on Weiser to answer the charge that the governors of Virginia and Pennsylvania had just begun sending traders into the Ohio. Weiser reminded them that "The Road to Ohio is no new Road." For the past thirty years Pennsylvania traders had been going to the Ohio. Until the French armies came, there had been no problems. Weiser gave a detailed history of the movements on the Ohio frontier by the English and the French from 1750, claiming that the English had only sent soldiers to the Ohio country at the Indians' request.

Responding to the Six Nations' complaint about the trading at Albany, Governor DeLancey granted that trading took place but denied that anyone at Albany sold guns and ammunition to the French. He promised that in the future the Albany commissioners for Indian affairs would consult with the Iroquois. That afternoon, the mayor and corporation of Albany invited all the commissioners and the many gentlemen in town to the town hall. Atkinson recorded, "Had a great Dinner & wine. . . . Were very merry."⁴⁹ Since Atkinson had a toothache, the occasion must have indeed been merry.

On Thursday, 4 July, the Iroquois accepted the statements made the previous day, agreed to keep the Covenant Chain, but warned that "the French have their Hatchet in their Hands" and that Albany was not safe from a French attack. Pownall, who watched the treaty and heard translations from Indian experts present in addition to the official interpreters, judged that now the Indians spoke "from the Mouth and not from the Heart." Their speeches were only "Political Farce and Compliment." Pownall commented that for "address and management of" such cant, "These People, tho we are apt to think them savages . . . do actually exceed the Europeans." He may well have been reflecting Franklin's opinion of the Indians' civility in waiting till the following day to reply to a speech. From at least the time that he adopted the Socratic method as a teenager in Boston, through his Junto rules, and his comments on humility in his "Plan for moral Perfection" (A 15–16, 61, 89–90), until his old age, when Thomas Jefferson testified that "one of the rules which . . . made Dr. Franklin the most amiable of men in society" was that he never contradicted anybody, Franklin attempted (though he sometimes failed, especially in politics in the 1750s) to preserve a diplomatic politeness and civility in his discourse. Franklin's 1741 "A Speech Deliver'd by an Indian Chief" anticipated the cultural relativism and appreciation of Indian manners that he elsewhere frequently displayed.⁵⁰

Whether or not Franklin shared his appreciation of Indian politeness with Pownall, the Englishman realized that the Indians used their rhetorical ability and politeness to disguise as well as to present positions. Pownall gave three examples of the Indians' disingenuous rhetoric. Concerning DeLancey and New York, Hendrick said: "The Power is the Governors, he has a right to do as he will, 'tis ours to be satisfyed and we submit." That bit of insincerity is found in the official record. The other two examples of the Indians' "Political Farce and Compliment" differ somewhat from the authorized translation. In the official minutes, Hendrick thanked "The governor of Virginia for assisting the Indians at Ohio, who are our Relations and Allies." In Pownall's version, Hendrick said, "Virginia has done well in engageing in the Assistance of our Flesh and Blood against the French." Third, in the official minutes, Hendrick said of Pennsylvania: "We approve of the Governor of Pennsylvania not having yet intermeddled in the Affair. He is a wise, a prudent Man, and will Know his own Time." Pownall's version reported: "Pennsylvania has done well in doing nothing, Onas is wise of head and knows his own time."⁵¹ Perhaps Pownall exaggerated, but after the speeches of 1 July, the Indians' submissive statements on 4 July contradicted their earlier opinions. Though some individual Iroquois were strongly allied with the English and some with the French, the Six Nations as a whole preferred to remain neutral and simply wanted to receive the presents. Pownall, who became "intimately acquainted with a Gentleman who speaks the Language readily" (presumably Conrad Weiser, the only Indian expert Pownall named), said that the Iroquois were afraid of the French and had "no confidence or trust in any measures or promises" that the English made. The Iroquois therefore had resolved "to observe a neutrality." That policy continued a longstanding Six Nations' tradition.[52]

Friday afternoon at 3:00, the commissioners joined together to repay New York's hospitality. Atkinson reported that they entertained "the Govr & Council of York, Mare & Corporation & officers & Gentlemen of the City at Diner in the Town Hall which Turnd out well."[53] The next day, Saturday, 6 July, Governor Clinton told the commissioners that his funds were all spent and that he could no longer support the Indians. The commissioners voted to continue their support. When the delegates reviewed the final speech that DeLancey intended to make to the Indians, they asked Thomas Hutchinson and Franklin to write a message to DeLancey saying that "no Notice is taken of the Complaints of the said Indians relating to their Lands." Since the complaint was a "principal Occasion" of the Albany Treaty, the commissioners asked that DeLancey address the issue. He replied the same day, telling them that he had settled the principal complaint and that he had promised to look further into other complaints about Indian lands when he returned to New York. After hearing DeLancey's speech, the Six Nations agreed on Tuesday, 9 July, to wait another year for DeLancey to look into and put right their claims.

While the main Indian negotiations took place, both Pennsylvania and Connecticut conducted private negotiations with the Iroquois to buy land. On Friday and Saturday, 5 and 6 July, John Penn and Richard Peters, aided by Conrad Weiser, bought a large tract of land from the Iroquois on behalf of the proprietors. The Iroquois thereafter sold a portion of the same land in the Wyoming Valley to Connecticut entrepreneurs. (For the overlapping boundaries, see map 3, p. 369) Chicanery prevailed on all sides. The Iroquois were selling traditional Delaware Indian lands—to which the Delaware Indians thought the Iroquois had no right. Weiser and Peters knew that the Wyoming Valley was traditionally Delaware Indian land. According to the Delaware Indian chief Teedyuscung in 1756, land fraud, including the sale of these lands, was an underlying cause of the Delawares' attacks on the Pennsylvania frontier in 1755. Though Franklin and Norris had no part in the negotiations, they did witness that the signatures on the Pennsylvania deed were real.[54]

The Indian treaty achieved little. Thomas Pownall realized that the Iroquois intended to be neutral in part because the English were "neither able nor willing to defend them. . . . If they were press'd by the English (who themselves took no real and Actual Step) to declare [that they would fight the French], I am told they have spoke, according as they express it, *from the Mouth and not from the Heart.*" If the Iroquois pledged to support the English, the French and their Indian allies would attack and "ruin" them.[55] The Albany Treaty made it obvious that a higher authority than the individual colonies should be in charge of Indian affairs. An indirect result of the treaty was disastrous. Fighting between Connecticut, Pennsylvania, and the Indians living in the Wyoming Valley of Pennsylvania started as a result of the land purchases by the two colonies and continued into the Revolution. The internecine war was an extraordinary example of the jealousies between the various colonies. It was famous at the time and remains so partly because of John Vanderlyn's painting, *The Death of Jane McCrea* (1804), and because of Thomas Campbell's poem *Gertrude of Wyoming* (1809).

Franklin judged that "nothing of much importance was transacted with" the Indians (5:393), but he did not foresee the negative results of the treaty and of the sale of the Wyoming Valley. On the other hand, he had high hopes for the Albany Plan of Union.

The Union of the Colonies

The committee on the union of the colonies was appointed on Monday, 24 June 1754, and met for the first time the next morning. Franklin evidently produced a copy of his "Short Hints" then. The committee next met on Friday morning, 28 June. The committee members must have debated the provisions on both occasions. Though other persons presented plans, "mine happen'd to be prefer'd," recorded Franklin, "and with a few Amendments was accordingly reported" (A 131). Theodore Atkinson noted that the draft was read a first and second time "& then Directed that Each Colloney be Served with a Copy for their Perusal & Consideration." At 5:00 that afternoon, the official minutes reported that the union committee submitted "short hints of a scheme" for union, "of which copies were taken by the Commissioners of the respective Provinces."[56] That document, "the 28 June Short Hints," is the third in the evolution of the Albany Plan (5:357–64). Though it was the first to contain suggestions from other persons, it mainly amplified Franklin's 8 June text (5:335–38).[57]

On Saturday and Monday, 29 June and 1 July, all the delegates debated the "Hints." "We had a great deal of Disputation about it," wrote Franklin, "almost every Article being contested" by someone, "but at length we agreed on it pretty unanimously" (5:394). That same 1 July, the conference decided to "draw up a Representation of the present State of the Colonies" and assigned the task to the committee charged with forming a plan for union. Thomas Hutchinson was the principal author of the "Representation." On the morning of Tuesday, 2 July, the commissioners discussed whether Parliament should impose the union or whether individual colonies should vote on it. On this subject, Franklin had changed his mind after witnessing the inability of the various colonies to act together in face of the French and Indian attacks. Franklin's revised view prevailed.

The group voted "to form a plan of a Union of the Colonies to be established by Act of Parliament." Atkinson noted that two delegates from Pennsylvania and three from Connecticut voted against it. Since Richard Peters had thought union for defense was necessary,[58] John Penn and Isaac Norris were evidently the two Pennsylvania commissioners who voted against Parliament's establishing the union. In hindsight, it could be said that the 2 July vote "to form a plan of Union" was the most significant accomplishment at Albany.

Nearly a week later on Monday, 8 July, the committee debated the plan in the morning and afternoon. The following morning the "plan was debated and agreed upon, and Mr. Franklin was desired to make a draft of it as now concluded." That afternoon Franklin was absent while writing it, and the next morning, he reported the plan of union, "which was read paragraph by paragraph and debated and the further consideration of it deferred to the afternoon." Wednesday afternoon, 10 July, the plan of union was recorded. Had there been any changes in the document that Franklin had prepared the previous day and presented that morning? Perhaps. The record is silent. After further debate, it was "Resolved, That the Commissioners from the several Governments be desired to lay the same before their respective Constituents for their Consideration, and that the Secretary to this Board transmit a Copy with this Vote thereon to the Governor of each of the Colonies which have not sent their Commissioners to this Congress."[59]

So far as I can determine, the Albany Conference neither approved nor adopted the Albany Plan. Instead, "after Debate" on what we know as the Albany Plan of Union, the commissioners merely voted to send it to "the Governor of each of the Colonies which have not sent their Commissioners to this Congress." In effect, the Albany Plan was merely sent to the various colonies "for their Consideration."[60] One could argue that the vote on the morning of 9 July was an approval of the final plan: "The Plan of the Union was debated and agreed upon, and Mr. Franklin was desired to make a Draught of it as now concluded." But if the document had been approved on the ninth, why did the commissioners debate it on the morning of the tenth? And what was the further debate after the plan was recorded on the afternoon of the tenth? The most likely conclusion is that the Albany Conference simply sent the Albany Plan to the colonies "for their Consideration."

One could argue that the decision on 2 July to form a "Plan of a Union . . . to be established by Act of Parliament" meant that the final plan was to be sent to England for Parliament to establish. However, the Albany Conference could not have known on 2 July what the final plan would be. If the commissioners had intended to send the Albany Plan to England and to request Parliament to establish the union, a motion to that effect should have been made and passed on the tenth.[61]

Indeed, for whom could the various delegates be approving the plan? They could not be approving it for their respective colonies. Only the Massachusetts commissioners had an instruction to try to frame a plan of union (which only meant that they would then submit the plan to Governor Shirley and the Massachusetts General Court). The representatives from the other colonies could only be considering the Albany Plan of Union as individuals. Thomas Pownall put the best face on the situation by saying that the delegates "were all the Leading Men in their respective Provinces."[62] He therefore supposed that "their Opinion will be the Sense, in general, of the Provinces they represented." Even Pownall, however, said that the gentlemen from New York (which did not send official commissioners) and Pennsylvania's Isaac Norris opposed the plan. Thomas Hutchinson gave the plan even less chance of implementation than did Pownall. Hutchinson thought that some delegates who voted for the plan did so only because they "doubted whether it would ever be approved of by the king, the parliament, or any of the American assemblies."[63]

On Thursday, 11 July, Franklin attended the final Albany Congress session. William Johnson spoke on the Six Nations and ways to defeat the "Designs of the French," and Thomas Pownall offered "certain Considerations" on the plan of union. The commissioners directed Franklin to thank Johnson and Pownall. The following day, the Pennsylvania commissioners probably started their return to Philadelphia by sailing down the Hudson River. Even at its conclusion at Albany, the Albany Plan of Union was an inconclusive failure.[64] Nevertheless, it was an attempt to make a federal government from the disparate colonies and had major implications for the colonies' future.

Aftermath

Writing "Reasons and Motives for the Albany Plan" in late July 1754, Franklin said that the plan was just sufficient to show the sentiments of the persons present at Albany on "the kind of union that would best suit the circumstances of the colonies, be most agreeable to the people, and most effectually promote his Majesty's service and the general interest of the British empire." The plan was sent "to the assemblies of the several colonies for their consideration, and to receive such alterations and improvements as they should think fit and necessary; after which it was proposed to be transmitted to England to be perfected, and the establishment of it there humbly solicited." Franklin added, "This was as much as the commissioners could do" (5:400), but in fact they had no mandate to do this much.

Franklin devoted a section of "Reasons and Motives" to the "Reasons Against a Partial Union" (401–2). Two are of special interest. Number 5 projects new colonies "westward on the Ohio and the lakes," an anticipation of his "Plan for Settling Two Western Colonies" (late 1754). He claimed that new colonies are "a matter of considerable importance to the increase of British trade and power, to the breaking that of the French, and to the protection and security of our present colonies" (5:491). A unified colonial government could better carry out that task than a partial union.

Number 6 anticipates the gradual development of a stronger union than the one foreseen at Albany: "by the frequent meetings-together of commissioners or representatives from all the colonies, the circumstances of the whole would be better known, and the good of the whole better provided for; and that the colonies would by this connection learn to consider themselves, not as so many independent states, but as members of the same body; and thence be more ready to afford assistance and support to each other, and to make diversions in favour even of the most distant, and to join cordially in any expedition for the benefit of all against the common enemy" (5:401–2). In effect, the partial union planned at Albany was a step toward the colonists' viewing themselves not as Virginians or as New Englanders but as Americans.

The remarks on the "Grand Council" repeat that Franklin considered the colonial assemblies to be comparable in their function to Great Britain's House of Commons. The Grand Council, wrote Franklin, was "intended to represent all the several houses of representatives of the colonies, as a house of representatives doth the several towns or counties of a colony. . . . That a house of commons or the house of representatives, and the grand council, are thus alike in their nature and intention" (5:404). Despite being told later by both England's attorney general and solicitor general that the colonial assemblies were necessarily inferior to the House of Commons, Franklin often restated his belief that their functions were similar.[65]

When Governor DeLancey sent his report on the Albany Conference to the Lords of Trade on 22 July 1754, it included the Albany Plan of Union. After receiving the plan, the Board of Trade passed it on to the Privy Council on 29 October, saying that it "would not presume to make any observations upon it, but transmit it simply for Your Majesty's consideration." The board, however, pointed out that it was immediately necessary to reform the "management and direction of Indian Affairs" and "to build some forts upon the frontiers within the territory of the Six Indian Nations." The board recommended that William Johnson be put in charge of all relations with the Six Nations. That was done in 1755.[66]

After receiving the Board of Trade's report, the Privy Council said it would consider the plan after hearing from the colonies. It never heard from them. The Connecticut Assembly judged that the proposed area was "too large . . . to be in any good manner administred," and that in time such a union "may be dangerous and hurtful to his Majesty's interest, and tends to subvert the liberties and privileges" of Connecticut's citizens. Therefore, the Connecticut Assembly directed its agent to oppose the union if the plan came before Parliament. The New Jersey Assembly also condemned the plan, finding "things in it, which if carried into Practice would affect our Constitution in its very Vitals."[67]

In England, the Albany Plan was dead in the water, partly because the Board of Trade and the Privy Council had previously drawn up a possible plan of union. When they consulted George Onslow, Speaker of the House of Commons, about the plan, he told them on 9 September 1754 that it would cause a major debate in the House, for many members feared that a union, even of just the northern colonies, might lead to independence. The leading minister, Thomas Pelham-Holles, duke of Newcastle, promptly dropped the idea. The historian Alison Gilbert Olson judged that "the feasibility of uniting the colonies had been thoroughly considered before copies of the Albany plan ever arrived in England." Olson pointed out that because of the news of George Washington's defeat, the British authorities had decided to send General Edward Braddock to fight the French in America. Why, in this emergency, would the British leaders stir up a controversy concerning America's possible future independence?[68] They expected that Braddock and his army would end the immediate crisis and then the British authorities could consider other American matters.

For Franklin, perhaps the most significant achievement of the Albany Treaty and Albany Plan was simply getting to know better persons like Thomas Pownall, William Johnson, Stephen Hopkins, Benjamin Tasker, Thomas Hutchinson, and others. Franklin had met most of them casually before, but now he knew them fairly well. He would have numerous dealings with them in the future. And they had come to know the leadership potentialities of Franklin, whom they had known primarily as a printer, businessman, heating engineer, and electrician. He was gradually becoming one of the best-known persons in colonial America. On 22 July the New York Mercury featured his return with that of the other commissioners to the city on 17 July, and a New York diarist recorded on the seventeenth that "Gentlemen have been this hour past going in and coming out from paying their compliments to Mr. Franklin."[69]

Franklin's involvement in the plan of union continued. That December, he exchanged letters on the plan with Governor William Shirley. Franklin remained hopeful for some time that the British authorities would establish the Albany Plan or "something like it." He told Peter Collinson on 29 December that it was unlikely the American assemblies would approve any plan, but he still hoped that one might "be form'd at home by the Ministry and Parliament" (5:454). He wrote Collinson on 26 June 1755 that until a union existed, "an American War" would never be "carried on as it ought to be, nor Indian Affairs properly managed" (6:88). And to Richard Partridge, the Pennsylvania Assembly's English agent, he wrote on 25 October 1755 that he wished the next Parliament would "establish an Union of the Colonies for their common Defense" (6:231–32). Perhaps he still hoped so in 1756. Why? I suspect that he saw a modest military union of the colonies as a first step toward a possible political union of the colonies, with or without Great Britain. Indeed, he implicitly suggested in "Reasons and Motives for the Albany Plan" that the colonies would gradually come to regard themselves as one whole if they formed a military union such as the Albany Plan (5:401–2).[70]

Despite its complete failure, the Albany Plan was the most important design for a union of the colonies before 1775 and the most significant congress of the American colonies before the Stamp Act Congress in 1765. Walter Isaacson noted that a new concept known as federalism underlay its structure: a central government would deal with "national defense and westward expansion, but each colony would keep its own constitution and local governing power." Franklin echoed the Albany Plan in his "Notes for Discourse with Ld. C[hatham]" on 31 January 1775 and used parts of it when he drafted his bold "Proposed Articles of Confederation," 21 July 1775.[71] Along with other members of the 1787 convention, he recalled it when writing the Constitution of the United States. I suspect, too, that he thought the promise of the Albany Plan was finally being fulfilled.

THE 1753–54 ASSEMBLY'S FIFTH SESSION, 6–17 AUGUST

Although the Pennsylvania Assembly had adjourned on 18 May until 19 August, Governor Hamilton recalled it on 6 August. The next day, he informed the delegates that the French and their Indian allies had invaded the English provinces and had defeated Washington and the Virginia forces at Fort Necessity. He said that the delegates must immediately raise a militia to defend the frontier of Pennsylvania, that they should support their Indian allies who had fled into the settled parts of Pennsylvania, and that they must provide the frontier people with arms and ammunition to defend themselves. Reporting the proceedings of the Albany Congress, Hamilton emphasized that the French incursions into the Ohio country were made without the consent of the Six Nations, who "reproach us with supine Negligence, and the defenceless State" of our country. The commissioners at Albany had considered and drawn up "a Representation of the present State of the Colonies." Further, judging that no "effectual Opposition was like to be made to the destructive Measures of the French, but by an Union of them all for their mutual Defence," the commissioners had "devised likewise a general Plan for that Purpose, to be offered to the Consideration of their respective Legislatures." Governor Hamilton gave both Thomas Hutchinson's "Representation" and Franklin's Albany Plan his "Approbation" and recommended them to the assembly.[72]

On 9 August, the House defeated a motion to grant £20,000 for the "King's Use" by a vote of 23 to 11 and a motion for £15,000 by 20 to 12, with Franklin voting for both. On the third roll call, a motion to grant £10,000 passed (the House had previously passed a £10,000 bill on 10 May, which Hamilton rejected on 15 May). Speaker Norris assigned Franklin to a committee to bring in a bill for £30,000, with £10,000 for the "King's Use" and the remainder for exchanging the ragged and torn bills. The following Monday, 12 August, Virginia governor Dinwiddie's letter of 31 July was read, together with a French report (which Franklin probably translated) of the surrender of Washington and the Virginia troops at Fort Necessity. In view of the appalling news, Franklin engineered a motion to enlarge the bill before the House to £20,000, which failed, and another motion to enlarge the amount to £15,000, which passed, 24 to 9.[73]

The House immediately sent Governor Hamilton the bill for striking £35,000. He replied on 15 August with sundry amendments. The key one restricted the sinking of the £15,000 debt from ten to six years. (Hamilton had on 15 May already vetoed a ten-year tax.) Though the House had adamantly refused previously to sinking the debt in four years, Hamilton probably had some hope that it would accept a six-year term. Since, however, his term of office had expired and he considered himself a private citizen, he also would not put his name as governor in the bill. The House returned that it would list the lieutenant governor and "other Gentlemen therein named" in the bill but would not admit any other changes. The following day, Hamilton said that he could not pass the bill but that he expected that his replacement would shortly arrive, "who may possibly think himself more at Liberty" to approve it.[74] In effect, Hamilton admitted to the legislators that his instructions forbade him to pass such a bill. On the afternoon of 16 August, the House proposed to adjourn the next day.

DISPOSAL OF THE ALBANY PLAN

On the assembly's last day, 17 August, "The Part of the Governor's Speech, relating to the Plan of Union among the several British Colonies on this Continent, was read; and, after a considerable Debate whether the said Plan should be either recommended or referred to the Consideration of the succeeding Assembly, the Question was put, upon Motion made, that the said Plan of Union be referred to the Consideration of the next succeeding Assembly?" The motion was defeated.[75] Franklin must have been crushed. Writing about the outcome in 1788, he said that the House, "by the Management of a certain Member, took it up when I happen'd to be absent, which I thought not very fair, and reprobated it without paying any Attention to it at all, to my no small Mortification" (A 132).

Franklin's account is probably incorrect. He was present in the assembly on 13 August when a division was recorded. He knew on 16 August that the following day would be the last of the 1753–54 assembly. So far as any records show, he was present in Philadelphia on both 16 and 17 August. He must have realized that the assembly would consider the Albany Plan on the seventeenth. I suspect he was present and took a leading part in the "considerable Debate." Even if present, Franklin had reason to chafe at the "Management of a certain Member" regarding the Albany Plan. Speaker Isaac Norris took care of minor matters of business during the last session of the assembly of 1753–54 but only allowed the Albany Plan to become a subject for discussion and debate on 17 August. It was a foregone conclusion that the assembly of 1753–54 would do nothing about the Albany Plan on the last day of the session. Franklin could only hope that the plan would be recommended to the consideration of the following assembly, for 1754–55, but the assemblymen knew that their Speaker had been present at Albany and that he opposed the plan.

The Quaker Party objected to the Albany Plan primarily because it was a military plan. A letter of October 1754 by the Anglican Charles Willing, a member of the Union Fire Company, confirms Norris's opposition and that of the Quaker Party: "Our vile broad brims here would not even admit" the Albany Plan "to be read in the house as hearing 'twas destructive of their peaceable rights and therefore condemned it upon the representation of their Speaker who was one of our company at Albany."[76] Speaker Isaac Norris killed the plan in Pennsylvania—perhaps partially because the delegates at Albany preferred Franklin's plan of union to Norris's. Years later, when Joseph Galloway complained to William Franklin that Speaker Norris seemed inconsistent in his support, William replied on 28 December 1759: "I have myself seen several Instances where he [Norris] has given such an Opposition to some Measure propos'd by my Father, as could not be accounted for but from Motives of Jealousy. This, however, never created any personal Difference between them. Whenever the Speaker propos'd any Measure which appear'd to my Father not detrimental to the Public Welfare, he ever gave it all the Assistance in his Power, and whenever the Speaker oppos'd any Measure propos'd by my Father he never showed any Resentment to him on that Account."[77]

Although Pennsylvania's governor James Hamilton supported the Albany Plan, he had resigned and his replacement was due shortly. Governor Robert Hunter Morris arrived in Philadelphia on 3 October 1754. Morris expressed his view of the Albany Plan in a letter to Massachusetts governor William Shirley on 10 November 1755: it was founded "upon such Republican Principles, that I do not wonder it was not relished at home, as it seemed calculated to unite the Colonys in such a manner, as to give the Crown little or no influence in their Councils."[78] In his analysis of the Albany Plan's failure, the Reverend James Maury, Thomas Jefferson's early teacher, partially agreed. Using an Indian metaphor, Maury said, "The Indians . . . tell us that we resemble a chain of sand." Besides appreciating the Indians' advice that the colonists join together, Maury commented on the British fear that the colonists might do so: "A remedy for this evil, though obvious and practicable, and recommended by several of His Majesty's governors here, the great men on your side of the water have not thought proper to apply, from a principle in politics, which we on this side of it think more obvious than wise or just."[79]

Franklin was at least partly right in saying that the "Assemblies did not adopt it, as they all thought there was too much *Prerogative* in it; and in England [and by some persons in America] it was judg'd to have too much of the *Popular*" (A 131).

FIFTEEN

Boston, America and the Empire, and Katy Ray, 1754–1755

Americans "have most contributed to enlarge Britain's empire and commerce, en-
crease her strength, her wealth, and the numbers of her people at the risque of their
own lives and private fortunes in new and strange countries." Therefore Americans,
rather than Englishmen, "ought rather to expect some preference" from the British
authorities.
—*Franklin to Governor William Shirley, 22 December 1754, 5:451*

THE NEW ENGLAND POST OFFICE inspection trip of 2 September 1754 to 21 February 1755 took longer and became more interesting than Franklin had expected. He and William Hunter, joint postmasters general for North America, probably rode horseback,[1] evaluating the routes, riders, and postmasters from Philadelphia northward. They were in New York on 17 September when Franklin wrote a letter recommending a writing master to Richard Peters, secretary of the council. Franklin joked that Pennsylvania was about to have a new governor and a new assembly but that he "did not desire to see a new Secretary: I only think it convenient that what he writes may possibly be read." Since Franklin and Hunter had probably arrived in New York on 4 or 5 September 1754, it seems surprising that they were still there on 17 September. Perhaps Hunter was temporarily ill (he became quite sick in Boston), or perhaps the two sailed up the Hudson to Albany during the twelve-day stay, for it, too, had an important post office. One early change as a result of the trip was announced in the *Pennsylvania Gazette* for 10 October. William Franklin, comptroller, advertised that instead of a weekly post between Philadelphia and New York, the riders would now go three times a week, at 8:00 A.M. on Monday, Wednesday, and Friday. Return letters would arrive in Philadelphia from New York by 5:00 P.M. on Tuesday, Thursday, and Saturday.

Franklin and Hunter were in Boston by early October. After Franklin's nephew William Homes had purchased the Franklins' former Union Street house, Jane Mecom had moved to a house on Hanover Street, near the Orange Street Inn, where she took in boarders. If she had a vacancy, Franklin probably stayed with her. If not, then he stayed with his brother John, who lived nearby on Cornhill Street, near Dock Square. (See front endpapers to *Life,* Volume 1:

the Douse/Mecom house is #1; the Union [at Hanbury] Street House is #5; and John Franklin's house is #7.) Franklin and Hunter intended to go to Piscataqua (i.e., the customs district north of Boston that included Newburyport and Portsmouth, New Hampshire) to see the route and talk with the postmasters. Ellis Huske (d. 1755) was still the postmaster for Boston and the areas north of it and lived in Portsmouth. William Hunter, however, fell ill with a high fever in early October and remained in Boston. In consultation with his brother John, Franklin did extend the post office northward, and after he left Boston, John Franklin advertised on 1 February 1755 that a post office was established "at Providence in Rhode Island Government, and at Marblehead Eastward."

As in his earlier Boston trips, Franklin called on the printers and major merchants, hawking the Franklin and Hall imprints and telling them the prices he charged for various kinds of paper. Among the printers, an old favorite was Thomas Fleet, whom he had known since he was an apprentice working for his brother James. Fleet had been a Couranteer. Franklin knew all Boston's printers and did business with several of them as well as with the bookbinders and booksellers. In 1755 he wrote a brief description of the "Prices of Printing Work in Philadelphia" in 1754, probably during the Boston visit.[2]

Hunter's illness forced Franklin to spend extra time in Boston, where he socialized with old and new friends. On Friday, 11 October, he attended a "Quarterly Communication or Grand Lodge" of the Massachusetts Freemasons held at the Concert Hall. Franklin's Masonic acquaintances present on the occasion included Henry Price, grand master, whom Franklin had met in 1733 and seen again in 1743; Benjamin Hallowell, John Rowe, John Leverett, and the merchant Jeremy Gridley, who may have been a schoolmate. Representatives attended from the four Boston lodges and the New London Lodge (Connecticut). The main business of the meeting was to petition the Grand Lodge of England that the grand master of North America be appointed for a term of three years "and no longer." In place of former grand master Henry Price, the electors chose Jeremy Gridley, who, like all the Boston Masonic leaders, had protested when the Grand Master of England replaced Franklin with William Allen as grand master of Pennsylvania (see above, fig. 22, p. 172).[3]

"A PLAN FOR SETTLING TWO WESTERN COLONIES"

Sometime late in 1754, perhaps while waiting in Boston for Hunter's health to improve, Franklin drew up "A Plan for Settling Two Western Colonies." When he mentioned the "Plan" to Peter Collinson on 26 June 1755, he explained that he drew it up "to divert the Connecticut Emigrants from their Design of Invading this Province, and to induce them to go where they would be less injurious and more useful." That suggests he intended to show it to his Connecticut friends on his return from Boston. Franklin found it "certain, that People enough may be had, to make a strong English Settlement or two in those Parts" (6:87). Such a colony was desirable for at least three reasons that he named.

First, many Americans, like those in Connecticut, wanted new land. Second, the existing colonies needed a strong settlement in the interior to protect them from hostile Indians and from the threat of the French encircling them. Third, in Franklin's idealistic mode, he hoped it would be good for the Indians, for the public, for the British Empire, and for religion. (He had anticipated these reasons in July, writing "Reasons and Motives for the Albany Plan"; 5:411.)

Beginning with an enthusiastic appreciation of the country "back of the Apalachian mountains, on both sides" of the Ohio River, and "between that river and the" Great Lakes, Franklin predicted that it would become a "Populous and powerful dominion" either of France or England. If it became French, the growth of the English colonies would taper off and the French would increase. The English commerce and alliance with the western Indians would halt. If, however, the future colonies became English, the English population would expand dramatically, the coastal colonies would be protected, the joining of the French from Canada to Mississippi would be forestalled, and the Indian nations befriended (5:457–59).

The current boundaries of some colonies from the Atlantic to the Pacific were "too long for their breadth." The Appalachian Mountains should be their limit, and new colonies should be formed in the West. The existing colonies could hardly extend their boundaries; instead, something like the unification of the colonies proposed in the Albany Plan would be an appropriate vehicle for establishing new colonies over the mountains. If some form of colonial union were not created, then the British authorities should deed the land to wealthy British or Americans who contributed to the settlement of the land or to those who went themselves to settle. Franklin left out the details, but either the more money invested or the more persons in a family who emigrated, the more land was to be given. He asserted, however, "That as many and as great privileges and powers of government, be granted to the contributors and settlers, as his Majesty in his wisdom shall think most fit for their benefit and encouragement, consistent with the general good of the British empire: for extraordinary privileges and liberties, with lands on easy terms, are strong inducements to people to hazard their persons and fortunes in settling new countries." Franklin noted that "the support of government in the colonies of Connecticut and Rhode Island, (which now enjoy that and other like privileges)," was "much less expensive, than in the colonies under the immediate government of the crown, and the constitution more inviting" (5:459–60).

Knowing that it was unlikely that the British authorities would grant such major privileges, Franklin shrewdly proposed that they have a time limit: "Such powers of government . . . might be judged unfit when it becomes populous, and powerful; these might be granted for a term only; as the choice of their own governor, for ninety-nine years" (5:460). His private opinion was that separate independent legislatures were superior for distant colonies; otherwise bad governors and lack of good information brought about their dissolution. One suspects that he believed that "extraordinary privileges and liberties" would be difficult or impossible to restrict after a century had passed, and that before then America might well have become independent.

Franklin said that the English should take over the forts the French had built, naming one at Niagara. Evidently he named others, which the earliest editor suppressed.[4] Then he suggested erecting a small fort at "Buffalonic on the Ohio, above the settlement [on the Allegheny, at the time often identified as the Ohio-Allegheny River; "Buckaloons" on map 3, p. 369]; and another at the mouth of Hioaga [Cuyahoga River, the site of Cleveland] on the south end of Lake Erie, where a port should be formed." Franklin evidently thought that the port would be the capital of this colony. The settlers for it could come overland from Carlisle and Harris's Ferry (Harrisburg) in Pennsylvania.

The second colony would be on both sides of the river "Siotha, which runs into the Ohio about two hundred miles below Logs Town." Its seat would be at the mouth of the "Siotha" (Scioto) River, which flows into the Ohio River at Portsmouth, Ohio. "For forty miles on each side of it and quite up to its heads," there was "a body of all rich land; the finest spot of its bigness in all North America." It also had "the particular advantage of sea-coal in plenty (even above ground in two places) for fewel, when the woods shall be destroyed. This colony would have the trade of the Miamis or Twightwees; and should, at first, have a small fort near Hockkockin, at the head of the river; and another near the mouth of Wabash. Sandoski, a French fort near the lake Erie, should also be taken; and all the little French forts south and west of the lakes, quite to the Mississippi, be removed." He thought that settlers of this colony could come from Virginia and take boats down the "navigable branches of the Kanhawa" to the Ohio, "not far above the mouth of Sciota." Or they might "rendezvous at Will's Creek, and go down the Monongahela to the Ohio" (5:461). Franklin was evidently using Lewis Evans's map of 1749, or perhaps a draft of the Evans map of 1755, but he no doubt had copies of John Patten's map of 1752 as well as other manuscript maps.

Franklin thought that the "fort and armed vessels at the strait of Niagara would be a vast security to the frontiers of these new colonies against any attempts of the French from Canada. The fort at the mouth of the Wabash, would guard that river, the Ohio, and Cutava river, in case of any attempt from the French of Mississippi." Ever ready to turn to specific, practical suggestions, Franklin added, "Every fort should have a small settlement round it; as the fort would protect the settlers, and the settlers defend the fort and supply it with provisions" (5:461–62). He recommended strengthening the fort at Oswego, "and some armed half-gallies or other small vessels, kept there to cruise on lake Ontario, as proposed by Mr. Pownall . . . at the Albany treaty." And finally, he also recommended building a fort "at Tirondequat on lake Ontario" (5:463).

As the reference to Thomas Pownall shows, Franklin knew that Pownall would be interested in the "Plan for Settling Two Western Colonies" and he no

doubt sent him and Lewis Evans copies. Franklin's plan may have in turn inspired Pownall, who drew a rough map sometime within the next year, which
added some details for Franklin's proposed colonies. Pownall used many of the
same names and places that Franklin mentioned, but like Franklin, Pownall had
a copy of Evans's and probably of Patten's map. Although Pownall had Lake
Ontario and part of Lake Erie on his map, he devoted almost half of it to Halifax
and Nova Scotia, places that have little to do with Franklin's new colonies.

Franklin returned to the idea of a western settlement in a letter to George
Whitefield of 2 July 1756: "I sometimes wish that you and I were jointly employ'd by the Crown to settle a Colony on the Ohio. I imagine we could do it
effectually, and without putting the Nation to much Expence. But I fear we shall
never be call'd upon for such a Service. What a glorious Thing it would be, to
settle in that fine Country a large Strong Body of Religious and Industrious
People! What a Security to the other Colonies; and Advantage to Britain, by
Increasing her People, Territory, Strength and Commerce." He appealed to
Whitefield—and also to his own sense of what religion should be in the following: "Might it not greatly facilitate the Introduction of pure Religion among the
Heathen, if we could, by such a Colony, show them a better Sample of Christians than they commonly see in our Indian Traders, the most vicious and abandoned Wretches of our Nation?" Then he repeated a fundamental value: serving
God was serving the public good. But was there also a suggestion of a revolutionary note in suggesting that the service of "our gracious King" was also the
"Publick Good"? Did the sentiment not also define the "Public Good" as the
duty of the king? "In such an Enterprize I could spend the Remainder of Life
with Pleasure; and I firmly believe God would bless us with Success, if we undertook it with a sincere Regard to his Honour, the Service of our gracious King,
and (which is the same thing) the Publick Good" (6:468–69). What if the king
did not aim at the "Publick Good" of America and Americans?

When asked by the British authorities (perhaps directly by William Pitt) to
recommend a course of action if the British took Fort Duquesne in the winter
of 1758–59, Franklin and Richard Jackson[5] replied by naming several of these
same forts. The British should go from Fort Duquesne to Fort Le Boeuf, to
Presqu'Isle, on to Venago, and then to Fort Niagara, thereby securing the interest of the Six Nations, peace with the Shawnee Indians, and intercourse with the
Twightwees (8:191–93).

AMERICA AND THE EMPIRE

Franklin wrote his son William on 14 October 1754 that Massachusetts governor
William Shirley was "particularly civil." Still in Boston on 25 November, Franklin explained to friends that Hunter's sickness and "various Accidents" had prevented his return as soon as he had planned. By December 1754 Governor
Shirley abandoned hope that the colonies would voluntarily form a union of
which he could approve. He thought that some features of the Albany Plan were

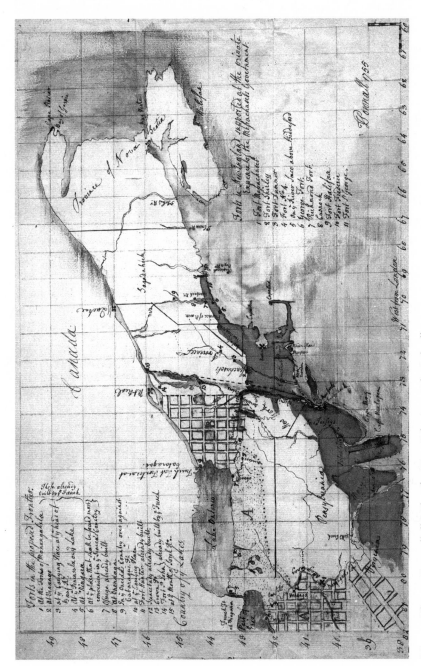

Map 4. Thomas Pownall, "A Plan for New Colonies on the Lakes," 1755

impractical and others were too democratic. Shirley drafted his own plan and asked Franklin for his opinion. Franklin's three letters of 3, 4, and 22 December sounded the boldest note of Americanism that had yet been heard: they complement and advance his 1751 writings on the relations between the American colonies and the British Empire.

As Franklin remembered Shirley's plan in 1766, "the Governors of all the colonies, attended by one or two members of their respective councils, should assemble, concert measures for the defence of the whole, erect forts where they judged proper, and raise what troops they thought necessary, with power to draw on the treasury here for the sums that should be wanted; and the treasury to be reimbursed by a tax laid on the colonies by act of parliament." In his *History of . . . Massachusetts*, Thomas Hutchinson, who was close to Shirley and knew his plans for the union of the colonies, similarly presented Shirley's plan. But Hutchinson's words (written during the Revolution) are so similar to Franklin's (published in 1766) that he must have been echoing Franklin's well-known introduction to the letters to Shirley.[6]

Three specifics of Shirley's plan appear in Franklin's rebuttal. First, Shirley would not give the colonists a vote in choosing the members of the Grand Council. Second, an act of Parliament to support the union would tax Americans. Third, the colonial militia could be ordered to any place where it was needed in the colonies. When Franklin returned "the loose sheets" of Shirley's plan on 3 December 1754, he included a brief letter. He said that excluding the colonists from a role in the choice of the Grand Council would be unsatisfactory. Further, taxing Americans "by Act of Parliament, where they have no Representative," would also give "extreme dissatisfaction." He conceded that the proposed "general Government might be as well and faithfully administer'd" without the vote of the people, but he said that where taxes were to be imposed, "it had been found useful to make it, as much as possible," done by the vote of the people or of their representatives. Colonists, like others, "bear better when they have, or think they have, some share" in the hard decisions. When any public measures are distasteful to the people, "the wheels of Government must move more heavily" if the people themselves have not imposed the measures (5:443).

Later, on 3 December or early the next day, Governor Shirley asked Franklin for more detail concerning the colonists' reactions. From Franklin's reply, we know that Shirley stated that the governors and the councils (at least some of whom were to be the members of the Grand Council)[7] should have the power "to raise such Sums as they shall judge necessary." And the Grand Council would have the power to march the militia into whatever part of America that it was needed. Shirley had evidently argued that the Albany Plan was too democratic. Franklin replied that it was less so than the governments of Rhode Island or Connecticut, which have "never abused" their privileges (5:444–45). Though some scholars have questioned whether Shirley was presenting his own plan or one that had been drawn up in England (5:442, 542n8), Franklin believed at the time that Shirley's outline was a "proposed Alteration of the Albany Plan."

Franklin repeated that excluding the colonists from "all Share in the Choice of the Grand Council" and "Taxing them by Act of Parliament where they have no Representative" would give extreme dissatisfaction. His positions echoed John Wise's declarations of "no taxation without representation," the Old Charter Party positions of Franklin's Boston youth, the sentiments of his *Modest Enquiry into the Nature and Necessity of a Paper-Currency* (1729), and his early writings for the *Pennsylvania Gazette*.[8] He also knew the Reverend Jonathan Mayhew (1720–66) had published in 1750 that King Charles I was an unjust king who deserved to be overthrown because "He levied many taxes upon the people without consent of parliament." Franklin may not have read Mayhew's sermon when it first appeared in print, but the series of attacks on it in Thomas Fleet's *Boston Evening Post* from February to July 1750 would have made Franklin read it. Franklin no doubt placed Mayhew in the tradition of the Old Charter Party. If they had not met before, they did so during Franklin's visits to Boston in 1753 and 1754. As mentioned earlier Franklin considered Mayhew a friend.[9]

In his reply to William Shirley, Franklin continued: "In Matters of General Concern to the People, and especially where Burthens are to be laid upon them, it is of Use to consider as well what they will be apt to think and say, as what they ought to think." Americans would say, "and perhaps with Justice," that the colonists "are as loyal, and as firmly attach'd to the present Constitution and reigning Family, as any Subjects in the King's Dominions." There existed no reason to doubt "the Readiness and Willingness of their Representatives to grant, from Time to Time, such Supplies, for the Defence of the Country, as shall be judg'd necessary, so far as their Abilities will allow" (5:443–44). As Franklin later often said, the proper way to raise money from America was by requisitioning it from the assemblies, which were the parliaments of the colonies.[10]

The people, Franklin stated, "who are to feel the immediate Mischiefs of Invasion and Conquest by an Enemy, in the Loss of their Estates, Lives and Liberties, are likely to be better Judges of the Quantity of Forces necessary to be raised and maintain'd, Forts to be built and supported, and of their own Abilities to bear the Expence, than the Parliament of England at so great a Distance." He had maintained the same position in 1729: "we . . . are the best Judges of our own Necessities"—which, as he knew, had reflected Captain John Smith's statement that "any reasonable man there [in America] may better advise him-selfe, than one thousand of them here [in England] who were never there" (5:444, 1:147; *Life* 1:405).

Instead of consulting Americans, the British authorities listened to the governors, who "often come to the Colonies meerly to make Fortunes, with which they intend to return to Britain." Franklin insulted the American governors (surprisingly, in a letter written to Governor Shirley) as being "not always Men of the best Abilities and Integrity." He also charged that some governors "might possibly be sometimes fond of raising and keeping up more Forces than necessary, from the Profits accruing to themselves, and to make Provision for their Friends and Dependents." Robert Beverley bitterly expressed this old American complaint in his *History of Virginia* (1705).[11] According to Franklin, the councillors were as bad as the governors. In most colonies, the crown appointed them "on the Recommendation of Governors." They were "often of small Estates, frequently dependant on the Governors for Offices, and therefore too much under Influence" (5:444). The governors and councillors, he said, should not have the power "to raise such Sums as they shall judge necessary, by Draft on the Lords of the Treasury, to be afterwards laid on the Colonies by Act of Parliament, and paid by the People here." They might abuse the power "by projecting useless Expeditions, harassing the People, and taking them from their Labour to execute such Projects, and meerly to create Offices and Employments, gratify their Dependants and divide Profits" (5:444).

Since the colonists were not represented in Parliament, "taxing them by Parliament" was unjust. To refuse them the liberty of choosing a representative council to meet in the colonies to consider and judge "the Necessity of any General Tax" and the amount "shews a Suspicion of their Loyalty to the Crown, or Regard for their Country, or of their Common Sense and Understanding, which they have not deserv'd" (5:445). As he had done previously, Franklin chafed at the English assumption of superiority.[12]

Compelling colonists "to pay Money without their Consent would be rather like raising Contributions in an Enemy's Country." It would treat them as a conquered people, not as true British subjects. On the other hand, a tax laid by "Representatives of the Colonies might easily be lessened as the Occasions should lessen." But a tax "once laid by Parliament, under the Influence of the Representations made by Governors, would probably be kept up and continued, for the benefit of Governors, to the grievous Burthen and Discouragement of the Colonies, and preventing their Growth and Increase." Power to march the colonists from one end of the colonies to the other, being a country of at least 1,500 square miles, without the approval or consent of their representatives, "might be grievous and ruinous to the People" (5:445).

Franklin added an interpretation of Shirley's plan that reduced it to absurdity. He claimed that if the colonies could be "well governed by Governors and Councils appointed by the Crown, without Representatives, particular Colonies may as well or better be so governed; a Tax may be laid on them all by Act of Parliament, for Support of Government, and their Assemblies be dismiss'd as a useless Part of their Constitution." The powers proposed in the Albany Plan of Union, Franklin pointed out, were not "so great as those the Colonies of Rhode Island and Connecticut are intrusted with, and have never abused." Franklin alluded to the president-general's power in the Albany Plan: the crown appointed him, and he controlled everything by his veto power, but Rhode Island and Connecticut elected governors who had no veto power (5:445).

The colonies bordering on the French "are properly Frontiers of the British Empire," and frontiers "are properly defended at the joint Expence of the Body of People in such Empire." The citizens of the seacoasts of Britain would think it hard, Franklin wrote, that they should by an act of Parliament be obliged "to maintain the whole Navy, because they are more immediately defended by it." It would be worse if those citizens were not allowed votes in choosing the members of Parliament. If Americans must bear the total expense of defending the frontier, it seems hard not to allow them a share in voting the money and judging of its amount and necessity. Shirley had implied that the colonists paid no taxes to Great Britain. Franklin protested that Americans annually paid great sums to Britain. The taxes that farmers or tradesmen paid in Britain enter into and increase the price of the agricultural and manufacturing products. A "great Part" of the increased price "is paid by Consumers in the Colonies, who thereby pay a considerable Part of the British Taxes" (5:445–46). Though Franklin's argument might be sound, it was too complex to convince many Englishmen.

Britain also imposed taxes on colonists by the Acts of Trade and Navigation. Franklin objected that the colonies were restrained in their trade with foreign nations when they could be supplied with manufactures cheaper from France, Spain, or elsewhere: "The Difference of Price is a clear Tax to Britain." The colonists were obliged to ship a "great Part of our Produce directly to Britain," where the duties laid upon them lessened the price paid to the planter. American goods that sold for less in England than they would in foreign markets were "a Tax paid to Britain." Americans were forbidden to make some manufactures and had to buy them from British merchants; thus "the whole Price of these is a Tax paid to Britain." The colonists increased the consumption and demand for British manufactures, causing their price to rise: "the Advance is clear Profit to Britain, and enables its people better to pay great Taxes; and much of it being paid by us is clear Tax to Britain" (5:446).

Franklin generalized that since the colonists were not allowed to regulate their own trade or to restrain the importation and consumption of British superfluities "as Britain can the Consumption of Foreign Superfluities," their whole wealth centered finally among the merchants and inhabitants of Britain. If the colonists made them richer and enabled them better to pay their taxes, "it is nearly the same as being taxed ourselves, and equally beneficial to the Crown." He claimed that though the Americans "have no Share in the Laying or Disposing" of these secondary taxes found in the Acts of Trade and Navigation, they did not "complain of" them. (Actually, he complained of them throughout the three letters to Shirley, most directly on 22 December.) But "to pay immediate heavy Taxes, in the Laying Appropriation or Disposition of which, we have no Part, and which perhaps we may know to be as unnecessary as grievous, must seem hard Measure to Englishmen, who cannot conceive, that by hazarding their Lives and Fortunes in subduing and settling new Countries, extending the Dominion and encreasing the Commerce of their Mother Nation, they have forfeited the native Rights of Britons, which they think ought rather to have been given them, as due to such Merit, if they had been before in a State of Slavery." Here he voiced the opinion that the Americans, rather than the English, should be favored (5:446–47).

These thoughts would, Franklin predicted, be "said by the People, if the propos'd Alteration of the Albany Plan should take Place." In addition, the colonists would object to the administration of the Board of Governors and council if the British authorities appointed them because the colonists had no role in their election. On the other hand, representatives whom the people elected could attempt to reconcile the people to necessary and even unpopular measures. But if taxes were simply imposed by British authorities, they would "probably become suspected and odious." The result would be "animosities and dangerous Feuds" between the authorities and the people, "and every Thing go into confusion." He concluded his letter of 4 December that he might be too apprehensive about Shirley's projected plan for unification, "but having freely given my Opinion and Reasons, your Excellency can better judge whether there be any Weight in them" (5:447).

John Adams cited Franklin's 4 December letter at length in his "Novanglus" essay of 30 January 1775, calling him a "sagacious gentleman, this eminent philosopher, and distinguished patriot," who refuted "the great design of taxing the colonies by act of parliament." Adams suggested that "the ministry at home" and Governor Shirley were either "discouraged by these masterly remarks" or by some unknown cause, but "the project of taxing the colonies was," in 1754, "laid aside."[13]

FRANKLIN'S AMERICANISM: THE WORLD TURNED UPSIDE DOWN

Between 4 and 22 December 1754, Governor Shirley had another conversation with Franklin on uniting the colonies; now, however, Shirley suggested uniting them with Great Britain by giving the Americans representatives in Parliament. We do not know what Franklin replied in conversation, but he wrote on 22 December that he had considered the matter further, "and am of opinion, that such an Union would be very acceptable to the Colonies" on two conditions. First, the colonists would have to be given "a reasonable number" of representatives. Franklin made it clear that he knew the number would not be in proportion to the population of America; the British authorities would never do it.

Second, Parliament must also revoke "all the old Acts of Parliament restraining the trade or cramping the manufactures of the Colonies . . . and the British Subjects of this side the water put, in those respects, on the same footing with those in Great Britain, 'till the new Parliament, representing the whole, shall think it for the interest of the whole to re-enact some or all of them." Though Franklin had written on 4 December that the colonists did not complain about the Acts of Trade and Navigation, he contradicted himself here. He now revealed what he actually felt. As he had said earlier, the acts were unfair to Americans.[14] Did Franklin really believe that the English Parliament would overturn its past Acts of Trade and Navigation? It seems unlikely. But Franklin could, on occasion, be wonderfully impractical and idealistic.[15]

How many were the minimum number of representatives from America? The number should be sufficient to offset "the private interest of a petty corporation" or of a "particular set of artificers or traders in England." Franklin said that such groups "seem, in some instances, to have been more regarded than all the Colonies, or that was consistent with the general interest, or best national good" (5:449). A government of all the colonies by Parliament, "in which they are fairly represented," would be "vastly more agreeable to the people" than the recent attempts in Parliament to make "Royal Instructions" binding upon them.[16] The idealistic Franklin also hoped that the people of Great Britain and the colonies would "learn to consider themselves, not as belonging to different Communities with different Interests, but to one Community with one Interest, which I imagine would contribute to strengthen the whole" (5:449–50).

Franklin made a series of comparisons showing the absurdity of the Acts of Trade and Navigation—unless one considered the colonies not really a part of the British Empire. For example, he named iron manufacturing, which was taxed or forbidden in America. Did it matter if the manufacturers lived at Birmingham or Sheffield or Philadelphia, since all were within the bounds of the empire, and the wealth generated and the persons employed would stay within the British Empire? If the Goodwin Sands could be laid dry by banks and "land equal to a large country thereby gain'd to England" and filled with English inhabitants, "would it be right to deprive such Inhabitants of the common privileges enjoyed by other Englishmen, the right of vending their produce in the same ports, or of making their own shoes, because a merchant, or a shoemaker, living on the old land, might fancy it more for his advantage to trade or make shoes for them?" Obviously, the answer to the rhetorical question was no. "Would it be right even if the land were gained at the expence of the state?" No. "Would it not seem less right, if the charge and labour of gaining the additional territory to Britain had been borne by the settlers themselves? And would not the hardship appear yet greater, if the people of the new country should be allowed no Representatives in the Parliament exacting such impositions?" (5:450).

Franklin wrote that the colonies were "so many Countries gained to Great Britain." They were actually more advantageous to England than if they had been gained from its coasts, "For being in different climates, they afford greater variety of produce, and materials for more manufactures; and being separated by the ocean, they increase much more its shipping and seamen." Since they are all part of the British Empire, "which has only extended itself by their means; and the strength and wealth of the parts is the strength and wealth of the whole;

what imports it to the general state, whether a merchant, a smith, or a hatter, grow rich in *Old* or in *New* England?" (5:450–51).

The argument and Franklin's comparisons were cogent and undeniably sound—unless, of course, the Americans were somehow considered not really citizens of the British Empire. The opinion that the British Empire should be run for the good of the whole was a centerpiece of Franklin's views—and the basis for his objections to the Acts of Trade and Navigation and to other English discriminations against America (e.g., the transportation of felons). But the argument must have flabbergasted Shirley.

Why, Franklin asked, should a state favor part of its people, "unless it be most in favour of those who have most merit?" If there is any difference between the inhabitants of England and the American colonies, it is the Americans "who have most contributed to enlarge Britain's empire and commerce, encrease her strength, her wealth, and the numbers of her people at the risque of their own lives and private fortunes in new and strange countries." Americans, he concluded, "ought rather to expect some preference" (5:451). For Shirley and other Englishmen, Franklin's statements were heresy. They contradicted the British system of mercantilism—which almost all Englishmen in 1754 thought was the way God intended the world to be.

By this time, Franklin had three basic beliefs concerning the relations between Great Britain and the colonies. These remained fundamental until the outbreak of fighting in 1775. First, he idealistically hoped that British authorities would come to realize that they should be working for the good of the whole English empire, not just for the economic and political advantages that some persons could force upon America. He said in 1751 that Parliament should act for the "general interest" of the whole empire, repeated it in his letters to Shirley, and later illustrated the opposite consequences in his Stamp Act cartoon *Magna Britannia, Her Colonies Reduc'd* (1766).[17] Second, as a prerequisite for the election of American members of Parliament, it would be necessary first that "all the old Acts of Parliament restraining the trade or cramping the manufactures of the Colonies, be at the same time repealed, and the British Subjects of this side the water put, in those respects, on the same footing with those in Great Britain" (5:449). In effect, he championed America's right to economic self-government. He surely knew that this demand would seem outrageous and would never be granted. And third, if Great Britain continued its present treatment of America, colonial government would break down, and America would rebel.

Franklin expressed the sequence of thought from the first to the third position in one sentence on 24 December 1754: "I should hope too, that by such an union, the people of Great Britain and the people of the Colonies would learn to consider themselves, not as belonging to different Communities with different Interests, but to one Community with one Interest, which I imagine would contribute to strengthen the whole, and *greatly lessen the danger of future separations*" (5:449–50; emphasis mine).

Of course Franklin put the suggestion of the future independence of the colonies into the mildest possible language, but from the 1750s to the Revolution, he repeatedly stated that England was driving the colonies to rebellion. Indeed, even the 4 December letter predicted that if England attempted to tax America directly, "Animosities and dangerous Feuds will arise between the Governors and Governed, and every Thing go into confusion" (5:447). That happened in the Stamp Act crisis. He had suggested the possibility of American independence in both "Rattlesnakes for Felons" and "Observations Concerning the Increase of Mankind" in 1751, and in the letter to Peter Collinson in 1753, when he wrote that "a Mortification begun in the Foot may spread upwards to the destruction of the nobler parts of the Body." He did so more directly in the Canada pamphlet in 1760 (9:90–91). To close friends like Joseph Priestley, Jacques Barbeu-Dubourg, and Jan Ingenhousz, Franklin predicted in the mid-1760s that America would finally revolt against England.[18] It would have been foolish—indeed, traitorous—for him publicly to proclaim such positions while he was in England. It would also have ended his possible usefulness in both England and America. Nevertheless, from the 1750s to the start of the American Revolution, no one so often threatened revolution or so often stated that Britain was driving America to revolt.[19]

The bold revolutionary Franklin of the 1750s occasionally seemed to have become a trimmer in the post–Stamp Act era. As war became more than a possibility, Franklin counseled caution and delay. Why? If war started in the 1760s or 1770s, both Americans and British would undergo great suffering and loss of life. But if a war could be delayed for several decades, America would either become independent or would become the center of British Empire without loss of life.[20] Within a few decades, England would realize that it could not win a war with America. Then England would grant fair terms of existence to the colonies. But despite his certainty of the progress of the colonies, Franklin was unwilling for Americans to be oppressed or for Americans not to claim their rights. The boldest revolutionary always underlay the practical conciliator. Considering the rate of growth of America's population, it would become the dominant part of the British Empire—but insults and outrages were not to be borne. Franklin's attitudes outraged his more conservative contemporaries, for he was far ahead of his time.

Assessing the genesis of the U.S. Constitution at the end of his life, James Madison wrote that these 1754 letters of Franklin "repelled with the greatest possible force, within the smallest possible compass," Britain's claim to govern America. Madison said that "volumes" of all succeeding arguments on American rights to self-governance were here expressed "within the compass of a nut shell."[21]

Leaving Boston

By late December William Hunter had recovered sufficiently to return to Virginia. The postmasters general commissioned Thomas Vernon postmaster of Newport, Rhode Island, on 24 December (5:451–52). In the appointment, Franklin was trying to do Vernon a favor because of his father's forbearance. In 1724, Samuel Vernon had asked Franklin to collect a debt for him in Philadelphia. Franklin did and then spent the money in London in 1725. About 1730, when Vernon asked for it, Franklin did not have the money but said that he would shortly repay it with interest. The easygoing Vernon agreed, and Franklin made good on the debt. Now Franklin was again repaying the deceased Samuel Vernon.[22] Hunter left around Christmas day, probably with Captain Campbell, whom Thomas Fleet in the *Boston Evening Post* listed as "Cleared Out" for Virginia during the week before 30 December.

Franklin settled accounts with his brother John on 24 December and, two days later, with Thomas Fleet.[23] Franklin wrote Peter Collinson on 29 December that he intended to set out for home the next day. On Monday morning, 30 December, he wrote James Bowdoin a brief note, thanking him and Mrs. Bowdoin "for your many Civilities" and saying that he intended to spend at least ten days in Rhode Island. Finally, he sent a short letter to Governor Shirley, making suggestions for revising William Clarke's draft of *Observations on the Late and Present Conduct of the French* (Boston, 1755) and giving permission to append his "Observations Concerning the Increase of Mankind" to Clarke's pamphlet (5:455–56). That same day, Fleet's *Boston Evening Post* announced that "the Post-Office is now kept at Mr. *John Franklin*'s in Cornhill."

Katy Ray

During the latter part of Franklin's Boston stay, Catharine Ray came to visit her sister, Judith (Ray) Hubbart, the wife of Thomas Hubbart, John Franklin's stepson. Naturally "Katy" Ray (as Franklin called her) met Franklin, who may have been staying with his brother John. The forty-nine-year-old Franklin and the twenty-three-year-old Katy delighted in one another's company. She talked about her boyfriends to Franklin, and he sometimes guessed her thoughts. They sang and played musical instruments together. When he was about to leave Boston, they agreed to journey together to Westerly, Rhode Island, from whence Katy would sail off to Block Island, her parents' home, which was about twelve miles off the coast. Elizabeth ("Betsy") Hubbart and an unknown "Mr. Best," who may have been a post rider, hired as a servant and guide for the trip, accompanied them at least part of the way. Before they left, Franklin had the four horses "sharp shod, and the Shoes steel'd." Leaving on 30 December, they encountered freezing temperatures and icy roads.

By the time they had gone just a short distance, Franklin realized that the Boston blacksmith had done a poor job horseshoeing. Later, he wrote his brother John about the difficulty. The horses slipped on the ice, "and Betsy and

Mr. Best may remember with what great Difficulty we got them up a little Icy Hill, in the morning of our 2d Day's Journey. We were oblig'd to alight and lead them, and they could no more stand than if they had been shod with Skates, but were upon their Knees and Noses every step." When the group came to a town to spend the night, Franklin had the shoes examined, and the blacksmith there said there was not "a Grain of Steel in all the 16 Shoes." So Franklin had them all well shod there, which cost only £2.8.0, whereas Franklin had paid £8 to the Boston blacksmith. "Now do me the Favour to learn that Smith's Name, and tell all your Friends and mine what a Rogue he is, that no body may trust him for the future."

Franklin had been told that the Boston smith was "*New Light.*" The thought caused Franklin to ironically joke and pun about dishonest religious zealots, using biblical phrases. He did not bother to consult a Bible, and he misremembered, for the "let him that stole steal no more" quotation is not from Revelations but Ephesians 4:28: "I thought that could not well be, he had shown such a strict Regard to the old *moral Law* in the 8th Commandment, *Thou shall not STEEL*. I rather take him to have been a Thief, and if he minds any Scripture, 'tis that in the Revelations, *Let him that hath stole, STEEL no more*; and so the Rascal only cheats" (5:520–21). Despite the icy roads, slipping horses, and later a "wrong Road, and a soaking Shower" (6:183), Franklin and Katy Ray had a wonderful time together and remembered the journey with pleasure.

On their fourth day, they reached Westerly, where Catharine's sister Anna lived with her husband, Samuel Ward. They stayed there for at least a day before Catharine left for her parents' home on Block Island where, she had heard, her father was sick. Franklin "thought too much was hazarded, when I saw you put off to Sea in that very little Skiff, toss'd by every Wave. But the Call was strong and just, a sick Parent. I stood on the Shore, and look'd after you, till I could no longer distinguish you, even with my Glass; then returned to your Sister's, praying for your safe Passage." Franklin had ridden from Anna and Samuel Ward's home at Westerly to the coast to see Katy off. "Towards Evening all agreed that you must certainly be arriv'd before that time, the Weather having been so favourable; which made me more easy and chearful, for I had been truly concern'd for you" (5:502–3).

The letters between Catharine ("Katy") Ray and Franklin testify to the strong affection that the forty-nine-year-old married man and the twenty-three-year-old single woman had for one another. Several scholars have speculated that Katy's early letters to Franklin do not survive because he judged them too affectionate and liable to be misjudged by some persons,[24] and I think the hypothesis is likely. His letters to her are affectionate, and occasionally flirtatious, adding zest to their relationship. At the same time Franklin frequently reminds her of his wife, Deborah, and his family in Philadelphia. He generally adopts the tone and the role of an avuncular older friend, concerned for her well-being and happiness. But as the flirtations are the most fun and interesting to readers, those are the most quoted parts, which is, perhaps, as it should be.

Katy initiated the correspondence with a letter (not found) of 20 January, from Block Island, which Franklin received shortly before 4 March and took the first opportunity to reply: "It gives me great Pleasure to hear that you got home safe and well that Day" you sailed. Having expressed his affection and concern for her, Franklin slowly and subtly introduced the realities of his own situation: "I left New England slowly, and with great Reluctance: Short Days Journeys, and loitering Visits on the Road, for three or four Weeks, manifested my Unwillingness to quit a Country in which I drew my first Breath, spent my earliest and most pleasant Days, and had now received so many fresh Marks of the People's Goodness and Benevolence, in the kind and affectionate Treatment I had every where met with." Thus the letter includes Katy in a circle of affectionate friends whom Franklin was reluctant to leave.

He continued: "I almost forgot I had a Home; till I was more than half-way towards it; till I had, one by one, parted with all my New England Friends, and was got into the western Borders of Connecticut, among meer Strangers: then, like an old Man, who, having buried all he lov'd in this World, begins to think of Heaven, I begun to think of and wish for Home; and as I drew nearer, I found the Attraction stronger and stronger, my Diligence and Speed increas'd with my Impatience, I drove on violently, and made such long Stretches that a very few Days brought me to my own House, and to the Arms of my good old Wife and Children, where I remain, Thanks to God, at present well and happy."

This was a wonderful reminder to an impressionable, evidently infatuated, young woman that Franklin was old (comparatively—he had had his fiftieth birthday in Rhode Island), married, and unavailable. If he had spent his most pleasant days in New England, nevertheless, Deborah and his family were his heaven. Having declared his situation, Franklin then flirted: "Persons subject to the Hyp, complain of the North East Wind as increasing their Malady. But since you promis'd to send me Kisses in that Wind, and I find you as good as your Word, 'tis to me the gayest Wind that blows, and gives me the best Spirits. I write this during a N. East Storm of Snow, the greatest we have had this Winter: Your Favours come mixd with the Snowy Fleeces which are pure as your Virgin Innocence, white as your lovely Bosom,—and as cold:—But let it warm towards some worthy young Man, and may Heaven bless you both with every kind of Happiness." He closed his 4 March 1755 letter with thanks to her and her family for their hospitality, and again reminded her of the realities of their situation: "Let me often hear of your Welfare, since it is not likely I shall ever again have the Pleasure of seeing you. Accept mine, and my Wife's sincere Thanks for the many Civilities I receiv'd from you and your Relations; and do me the Justice to believe me, Dear Girl, Your affectionate faithful Friend and humble Servant" (5:503).

Franklin received a letter from her dated 3 March (not found) and he replied about 31 March. Only a fragment of his reply is extant, but Katy may have asked his advice about a young man Franklin knew, who had been courting her in Boston. She also told him of another young man who was wooing her. Franklin wrote that he had hinted to the one young man not to be "too forward in Professions of Love, till by his Assiduities and little Services he had made some Progress in gaining the Lady's Esteem and Affection." His suggestion was ignored. She wrote him that the young man had "declar'd himself all at once violently in love" with her. Franklin gave a comparison with negative implications: "He seems like a Brand brought flaming to a fresh Hearth; not kindled there, indeed, but it burns nevertheless." That might have seemed like an endorsement of the other suitor, but Franklin continued: "Nobody can judge for you in this Affair, better than you can for yourself; you know both the Gentlemen, and I believe you will determine rightly.[25] I only pray God to bless you in your Choice; whether it be either of them or any other; and you may depend I shall mention nothing of your having communicated the Matter to me."

No one else would see her letters, Franklin said, and he added that "suspicious Minds" could easily mistake her expressions of affection. He implied that the danger of "suspicious Minds" seeing his letters was the reason he was not more affectionate: "You may write freely everything you think fit, without the least Apprehension of any Person's seeing your Letters but myself. You have complimented me so much in those I have already receiv'd, that I could not show them without being justly thought a vain Coxcomb for so doing; and the Hint you give in your last is sufficient for those you may favour me with hereafter. I know very well that the most innocent Expressions of warm Friendship, and even those of meer Civility and Complaisance, between Persons of different Sexes, are liable to be misinterpreted by suspicious Minds; and therefore though you say more, I say less than I think, and end this Letter coolly in the plain common Form, with only Dear Miss, Your humble Servant B Franklin" (5:536–37).

A letter of Katy's, dated 31 March, which is also the probable date that he wrote the above letter, is another one not extant. Perhaps it also contained expressions that Franklin judged too strong for "suspicious Minds" and therefore destroyed. Her letters of 28 April and 1 May are also not extant (cf. 6:182n3). Finally, we have her first extant one, 28 June 1755, written from Block Island. Addressing "Dear, Dear Sir," Katy was upset that he had not replied to her last three letters, causing her to shed "many tears." (She did not know that Franklin was with General Braddock in Maryland and then on the Pennsylvania frontier collecting wagons for Braddock's army from 9 April to 12 May.) "Suerly I have wrote too much and you are affronted with me." She had said "a thousand things that nothing Should have tempted me to [have] Said to any body els." She wanted to hear that he was well. "Forgive me and love me one thousandth Part So well as I do you and then I will be Contented and Promise an amendment." She signed it "your most Sincere affectionate and obliged friend," and then added a postscript, "My Proper Respects to Mrs. Franklin and Daugter." Further, she asked him to accept "the Sugar Plums they are every one Sweetn'd as you used to like" (6:96). Sweetened, no doubt, with her kisses.

Franklin had not received her letter of 28 June when he wrote her on 11 September 1755, apologizing that he had been away for nearly six weeks and then so caught up in public affairs that it was impossible to keep up his "private Correspondencies, even those that afforded me the greatest Pleasure." He assured her he was well and answered her question "whether every body love me yet, and why I make 'em do so." He said that more people loved him now than ever before, explained why, and then switched from the public sphere to a private flirtation: "For since I saw you, I have been enabled to do some general Services to the Country, and to the Army, for which both have thank'd and prais'd me; and say they love me; they *say so*, as you us'd to do; and if I were to ask any Favours of them, would, perhaps, as readily refuse me: So that I find little real Advantage in being belov'd, but it pleases my Humour" (6:182).

It was nearly four months, Franklin complained, since he had heard from her. He assured her that "the Pleasure I receive from one of yours, is more than you can have from two of mine," and recalled the pleasure they had together as "we talk'd away so agreably, even in a Winter Journey, a wrong Road, and a soaking Shower." Was she still living in "that Monastery" (Block Island), or had she "broke into the World again, doing pretty Mischief?" What had become of her suitors, "Mr. B. and Mr. L. and what the State of your Heart is at this Instant? but that, perhaps I ought not to know; and therefore I will not conjure, as you sometimes say I do." Evidently Franklin had sometimes played ESP games with her, guessing her thoughts and feelings.

Katy had presumably told him that she had resolved to be careful in her future courtships and asked him to translate a letter in Spanish that a suitor who signed himself "Laureano" had sent her (perhaps the "Mr. L."). Franklin replied that though he commended her prudence, if he "were courting you, I could not heartily approve such Conduct." In the same letter, Katy requested copies of the songs he had sung. We know that he replied with his own "Wedding Anniversary Song," but it is fun to speculate about what other songs he had sung to her. Sometime during the period of this volume, 1748–57, he came across a poor Scots family in the Allegheny Mountains, where, sitting on the porch after dinner, the wife sang an older popular song in a voice so moving that it brought tears to Franklin's eyes. When he related the anecdote to l'abbé André Morellet about 1780, he used it as a touchstone for the appeal of the Scottish folk songs. So I speculate that Franklin sent Katy one or two traditional folk songs (perhaps the ones celebrated by Joseph Addison in the *Spectator*) and one or two popular songs (like *Sae Merry as We Twa hae Been*—which Ellen Cohn identified as the popular song sung by the wife in the Allegheny Mountains) and perhaps another of his own compositions. Just as his taste in art, literature, moral philosophy, and politics all reflected his egalitarianism, so too did his taste in music, as will appear more fully in the next volume of the biography.[26]

Franklin also translated the Spanish letter. He used a metaphor that may have referred to something she had mentioned that she was making. The metaphor both flirted and implied his love for Deborah: "You have spun a long Thread, 5022 Yards! It will reach almost from Block Island hither. I wish I had hold of one End of it, to pull you to me: But you would break it rather than come. The Cords of Love and Friendship are longer and stronger, and in Times past have drawn me farther; even back from England to Philadelphia. I guess that some of the same kind will one day draw you out of that Island." Actually, he had not returned from England to Philadelphia in 1726 because of Deborah. He may have returned for "Love" for the place and "Friendship" for a number of people, but as we know, Deborah had abandoned him and married another. There is no doubt, however, that he and Deborah were now comfortable in their love for one another.

Katy and Franklin had evidently talked of such diverse topics as the peat on Block Island and different kinds of cheese. She sent him examples of the peat and the several cheeses made on Block Island. Thanking her, Franklin said his Irish friends told him it was "the right Sort" of peat but that the Philadelphia area had nothing like it. He praised the cheeses, one especially that everyone agreed exceeded "any English Cheese they ever tasted." He introduced another reference to Deborah: "Mrs. Franklin was very proud, that a young Lady should have so much Regard for her old Husband, as to send him such a Present. We talk of you every Time it comes to Table; She is sure you are a sensible Girl, and a notable Housewife; and talks of bequeathing me to you as a Legacy; But I ought to wish you a better, and hope she will live these 100 Years; for we are grown old together, and if she has any faults, I am so us'd to 'em that I don't perceive 'em, as the Song says." His "Wedding Anniversary Song" (*Life* 2:271–75) must have been among those he sang in Boston and was now sending her. Here he quoted a stanza from it: "Some Faults we have all, and so may my Joan, / But then they're exceedingly small; / And now I'm us'd to 'em, they're just like my own, / I scarcely can see 'em at all, / My dear Friends, / I scarcely can see them at all." He assured Katy that neither she nor Deborah had any faults. "And since she is willing I should love you as much as you are willing to be lov'd by me; let us join in wishing the old Lady a long Life and a happy" (6:183–84).

Catharine Ray wrote him on 2 August that she was writing a short letter (not found) because she expected to see Franklin soon in Boston. He replied on 26 August that he was so involved in public affairs in Philadelphia that he could not make so long a trip and asked for all her news. He then teased her: "Your Apology for being in Boston, 'that [you must] visit that *Sister once a Year,*' makes me suspect you are there for some other Reason: for why should you think your being there would need an Excuse to me, when you knew that I knew how dearly you lov'd that Sister? Don't [try to hide] your Heart from me.

You know I can [conjure?]. Give my best Respects to your Sister, and tell [her] and all your other Sisters and Brothers, that they must behave very kindly to you, and love you dearly; or else I'll send a young Gentleman to steal and run away with you, who shall bring you to a Country from whence they shall never hear [a] Word of you, without paying Postage." The wry note in the last three words and the deflation of possible extraordinary and spiritual implications of the preceding statement are a Franklin hallmark. He added that he and Deborah join "in Love to you and sincere Wishes for [your] Welfare" (6:494).

A fragment of a Franklin letter playfully and fancifully interpreted a seal on a letter sent him by John Franklin's youngest stepdaughter, Elizabeth (Betsy) Hubbart. The seal showed a cupid with a heart in his hand and in the background a block with two hearts on it.[27] Franklin wrote that the block could be an altar but was presumably an anvil, and the two hearts on it were about to be welded together. They were the hearts of Catharine Ray and Elizabeth Hubbart. When the two hearts had been made one, Cupid would fly with the joined hearts "to Your very affectionate, B. Franklin." Then he added a postscript, presumably giving Deborah's interpretation of the seal, but which I suspect was also Franklin's. Deborah "tells me I have not rightly interpreted the Seal. She agrees that the two Hearts on the Altar represent yours and Katy's, but the Cupid represents her Husband, and the Heart in his Hand is hers [Deborah's heart], which he takes with him wherever he goes, leaving the others for some body else. We are not like to settle this Point between us, so you must determine it" (6:222).

Whether or not Deborah joined in the interpretation of the seal, Franklin's correspondence with Katy Ray shows that he was not keeping his affection for Katy a secret. Deborah knew about it, but Franklin's affection for Katy presumably did not worry her. Franklin may have displayed similar affection previously, perhaps with the older Susanna Wright and perhaps with other women—as he would in the future.

The immediate family and close friends of Catharine Ray must have known of her affection for Franklin and of his affection for her. Elizabeth Hubbart had accompanied them out from Boston and wrote Franklin late in 1756 an anecdote that she found funny about how the blind and feeble eighty-one-year-old Joseph Hubbart started courting younger women within a month of his wife's death (7:69–71). Franklin replied that her story was "well told and entertaining." But his next sentence was surprising: "Only let me admonish you of a small tho' common Fault of Story-tellers." He said that one should not introduce an anecdote by saying how comical it is: "For when the Expectation is rais'd too high, 'Tis a Disadvantage to the Thing expected." What seems surprising is the word *admonish*. It is too strong. Franklin, a great writer, certainly could have chosen something like *critique* rather than a word that suggests Betsy was violating her duties or was doing something wrong. Perhaps the diction was insensitive because he thought Betsy Hubbart might covertly be alluding to his relationship with Katy Ray.

After his surprisingly critical reply, Franklin went on to draw a moral from the tale, one that could be read as an implied defense of his affection for a young lady: "Old Age, we see, is subject to Love and its Follies as well as Youth: All old People *have been* young; and when they were so, they laugh'd, as we do, at the Amours of Age. They imagin'd, 'tis like, that the Case would never be theirs. Let us spare 'em, then; lest the same Case should one day be ours." Franklin became ironically amused at himself, for it was just four days before his fifty-first birthday: "I see you begin to laugh already at my ranking myself among the Young! But you, my Girl, when you arrive at Fifty, will think no more of being old, than does Your affectionate Uncle, B. Franklin" (7:95).

Franklin wrote Katy Ray a farewell letter on 3 March 1757, shortly before leaving for England. He thanked her for her letter of 8 November 1756 (not found), wished her well, told her to give his "best compliments" to all her friends and relations who "love me," and ended with a nice turn: "I should have said all that love you, but that would be giving you too much trouble. Adieu, dear good girl, and believe me ever your affectionate friend, B. Franklin." From Philadelphia on 24 March 1757, Franklin wrote her brother-in-law, Samuel Ward, at Westerly, sending some seeds "of the Grain called Whisk Corn, or Broom Corn." Franklin had brought some back from his trip to Virginia in 1756. He described when and how to plant them, praised the uses of the grain and the whisk, and said to "Give my dear Friend Katy enough of the Tops to make a Whisk for her Mantelet; and with it, if you please, a Kiss from me, and my best wishes" (7:153–54). The next year Katy married William Greene (1731–1809), who served as governor of Rhode Island during 1778–86. Catharine (Ray) Greene and Franklin remained close friends for the rest of his life.

SIXTEEN

Libels on the Assembly, Quincy's Mission, and General Braddock, 1755

Strict Forms ought, in my Opinion, to be disregarded in Cases of Necessity.
—*Franklin to Susanna Wright, 28 April 1755, planning to ask Chief Justice William Allen to urge constables to help raise wagons for General Braddock, 6:23*

THE NEW PENNSYLVANIA GOVERNOR, Robert Hunter Morris (ca. 1700–1764), a "two-bit Thomas Penn" (as James H. Hutson called him), arrived in Philadelphia on 3 October 1754. He was one of the twenty-four proprietors of East New Jersey, who were hated for their quitrents, for holding on to the best lands while prices rose, and for their harsh treatment of squatters. In appointing Morris governor, Thomas Penn affirmed his commitment to the measures that had made Pennsylvanians resent—and even despise—him.[1]

From numerous New Jersey contacts, Franklin knew Morris well. They had seen one another earlier in the fall of 1754 in New York when Franklin was on his way to New England on post office business. Morris had just arrived from England and was going to Pennsylvania. He asked Franklin if he "must expect as uncomfortable an Administration" as the previous governor. "I said, No; you may on the contrary have a very comfortable one, if you will only take care not to enter into any Dispute with the Assembly. 'My dear Friend, says he, pleasantly, how can you advise my avoiding Disputes. You know I love Disputing; it is one of my greatest Pleasures: However, to show the Regard I have for your Counsel, I promise you I will if possible avoid them.'" Franklin conceded that Morris "had some Reason for loving to dispute, being eloquent, an acute Sophister, and therefore generally successful in argumentative Conversation." Franklin added: "these disputing, contradicting and confuting People are generally unfortunate in their Affairs. They get Victory sometimes, but they never get Good Will, which would be of more use to them." Returning to Pennsylvania in the late winter, Franklin found that Morris "and the House were already in high Contention, and it was a continual Battle between them, as long as he retain'd the Government" (A 132–33).

Governor Morris informed Thomas Penn on 26 October 1754 that the assembly's agent, Robert Charles, had somehow secured a copy of Penn's secret instructions "to Mr. Hamilton and myself, and I am well informed that a paper from him was read by the Speaker to a number of the members, containing the Substance of your Instructions relating to the Appropriation." Penn, however, wrote Richard Peters on 21 February 1755 that he did not think Speaker Norris or anyone in the assembly had really secured a copy of the instructions. He said that assemblymen "often pretend to know what they only suspect in order to draw it out of others." A few days later, Penn wrote Governor Morris on 25 February that he had mentioned "in conversation" the instruction regarding money to Lord Halifax, who chaired the Board of Trade from 1748 to 1761. Penn speculated that Halifax might, in turn, have mentioned it at the Board of Trade, "whence Mr. Charles may have got it."[2]

Penn was probably correct in judging that the assemblymen did not really know his instructions. Speaker Norris had heard from Robert Charles a rumor that the proprietors had bound the governors not to pass any money bill in which the governor did not control the expenditures. But a year and a half later, after Governor Morris revealed his instruction concerning money bills to the assembly on 30 June 1756, Franklin and the committee of correspondence wrote Charles about them. Charles replied on 12 August 1756 that he was glad "that we are no longer to Combat in the Dark Instructions Secreted yet enforced under different appearances." He added that "The Instructions Govr. Morris has at last communicated speaks out the Matter which has been always apprehended" (6:482).

In the assembly's second session (2 December 1754 to 10 January 1755), Governor Morris informed the members on 3 December 1754 of the French and Indian incursions on the frontier, said that the Virginia House of Burgesses had voted £20,000 for defense, and asked the Pennsylvania Assembly for funds. The assembly appropriated £20,000 "for the King's use" on 12 December, but Morris rejected the bill on the eighteenth, supposedly because it did not have a suspending clause.[3] Since the assemblymen believed that the real reason was Thomas Penn's instruction that the governor control the funds, they were furious with him. On 19 December, Morris further informed the House that General Edward Braddock was on his way to America and the British authorities expected Pennsylvania to contribute to his support. Replying to Morris's message of 18 December, the House asked "whether he has any further Instructions from our Proprietaries, which influence him in refusing his Assent to our Bill?"[4]

On 24 December, Morris repeated former governor James Hamilton's argument that any money bill must have a suspending clause. The House said no suspending clause was necessary: Governor Thomas had approved a supply bill in 1746 that did not have the clause and had been approved in England. But Morris, like Hamilton, maintained that Governor Thomas had not, in fact, submitted it to the English authorities. The delegates voted on 3 January 1755 to circumvent the governor and borrow £5,000 on the House's credit for provisions for the king's troops, appointed a commission for that purpose, and then adjourned until 12 May (5:527–28).[5]

Before General Edward Braddock left England to take command of the British forces in America, Thomas Penn called on him on 7 November 1754 with "informations and advices . . . for the good of the Cause." No doubt Penn's "Cause" was mainly to say that the Quaker-controlled assembly was averse to British authority and was financially able but unwilling to contribute to defense.[6] Governor Morris and Provost William Smith sang the same song; Morris wrote Sir Thomas Robinson, secretary of state, on 30 January 1755 that the assembly had passed a bill for £20,000, which he "could not agree to consistent with my duty," and then he condemned the House for borrowing £5,000 for support of the army because "they may hereafter use that Power in a manner inconsistent with the publick good & the Just dependence of this Province upon the Crown." (The Proprietary and Royal parties in the colonies often raised the specter of rebellion and independence to justify themselves and to alarm the British authorities.) To Sir John St. Clair, quartermaster general for Braddock's army, Morris stressed the wealth of Pennsylvania and the disobedience of the assembly and only vaguely referred to the £20,000 bill that he had refused. He did not mention the £5,000 that the assembly had raised to aid the army. Morris said he had "no Money at my Command" because the Quakers were unwilling to support the military and were "extremely unwilling to part with Money upon any Terms."[7]

Reelected to the assembly in October, Franklin had been appointed to all four standing committees. He arrived back in Philadelphia about 20 February. The Virginia frontiersman and entrepreneur Thomas Walker came to Philadelphia on Saturday, 22 February, and called on Franklin "for his assistance." Sir John St. Clair had asked Walker to help in arranging supplies for Braddock's army. Franklin evidently contacted Speaker Isaac Norris, who was one of the commissioners appointed on 3 January 1755 to oversee the £5,000 from the Loan Office, and set up a meeting of the commissioners for Monday. On Sunday, 23 February, after Walker attended Christ Church, he "Dined with Mr. Franklin." On Monday, Franklin took him to the state house. Though not yet sworn in as a member of the assembly for 1755–56 and though he had not been named a commissioner, Franklin joined them to consider Walker's request. They agreed to purchase 14,000 bushels of wheat, have it ground and bolted by Walker's directions, and packed in casks "ready to be delivered on the first advice from Governor Dinwiddie" that Braddock's army had arrived. The committee also promised to engage "a Sufficient Number of Waggons or other Carriages for transporting the same to the mouth of the Conegochig [Conogogee]."[8]

After General Braddock arrived, St. Clair told him Morris's account of Pennsylvania's inaction. Angry, Braddock wrote Morris on 28 February a blistering indictment of the Pennsylvania Assembly. Braddock condemned the "pusillanimous and improper Behaviour in your Assembly" and its "Faction and Opposition where Liberty and Property are invaded." He accused the Pennsylvanians of "an absolute Refusal to supply either Men, Money, or Provision for their own

Defence while they furnish the Enemy with Provision." The assembly, he charged, had taken "no Measures" to repair or make roads, or "to provide Horses and Carriages to transport the Stores." Pennsylvanians have not even provided "Subsistence for those Troops who are come to restore and preserve that Property which their factious Councils have suffered to be invaded."[9]

Delighted with Braddock's threats, Morris wrote him on 12 March, further condemning the Pennsylvania Assembly. He celebrated the fort ("strong House") that Thomas Penn had said in 1751 he would support with £400. Had the House spent £1,000 then, Morris said, it "would have been sufficient" to forestall the French. He claimed the province had nearly 300,000 people, mostly wealthy farmers, and could furnish food and other supplies for an army of 100,000 men. The assembly had a "Revenue of Seven Thousand a Year and Fifteen Thousand Pounds in Bank, all at the Disposal of the House," but the representatives would contribute nothing. To his previous lies, Morris added that the Pennsylvania merchants were traitors: Pennsylvania supplied the flour and other food shipped by New York and by New England to Louisbourg where it enabled the French to support their army on the frontier. After condemning the assembly and the province, Morris praised himself and his supposed efforts to aid Braddock.[10]

The Assembly's Third Session, 17 March–9 April

Recalled by Governor Morris, the Pennsylvania Assembly met on 17 March and Clerk William Franklin swore in Franklin as a member. The next day, Morris informed the House that General Edward Braddock and his army had arrived in Virginia. Morris gave the assembly a copy of Braddock's letter, which said that he could winter-quarter his troops wherever he pleased and threatened: "you may assure your Assembly I shall have Regard to the different Behaviour of the several Colonies and shall regulate their Quarters accordingly." Braddock would use "unpleasant Methods" with the Pennsylvanians if necessary. Morris expected that Braddock's letter, written in a "high stile," would have an effect on the assembly.[11] The governor requested on 18 March that the Pennsylvania Assembly vote funds for "Men, Provisions and Money" for Braddock. He also said that the New England colonies were preparing a fort at Crown Point on Lake Champlain and that he expected Pennsylvania to help.

That same afternoon, 18 March, Morris objected to the assembly's including in their minutes two letters from Secretary of State Sir Thomas Robinson. Morris claimed that the letters might furnish the enemy with intelligence. Speaker Norris appointed Franklin to a committee to answer. The next morning, 19 March, Franklin said that the intelligence in the letters previously appeared in both England and America and contained nothing not known to the French. He also ridiculed the governor's "charge against us, of taking a very extraordinary and unconstitutional Measure to keep" the House minutes "a Secret from him." Remarking on the difference between the important issues in Morris's morning request of 18 March and the trivial ones he introduced in the afternoon, Franklin asked Morris "to suspend these irritating Accusations, and novel Demands, till a Season of more Leisure, and permit us to proceed, without any further Interruption of that Kind, on the Business for which he has been pleased to call us together, and the very important Matters he has recommended to our Consideration" (5:531).

On receiving the House's letter, Morris became furious and dashed off a note to printers Franklin and Hall saying that it would be "prejudicial to his Majesty's Service to publish those Letters." He forbade them to do so (5:532). Franklin promptly called on Secretary Richard Peters "with an earnest Request that it might not at this Time be insisted on." Franklin was "apprehensive" that he would have to produce it in the House, which would order him "to publish the Votes, and that he should as Printer to the Assembly be obliged to do it." Franklin said he feared "the Differences would encrease between the Two Branches of the Legislature and the King's Business be thereby exceedingly retarded."

Peters presented Franklin's request to the governor and council. The council members said that although the governor was right, it would be better to put off the matter until the end of the session. Morris, however, "was clear that this and no other Time was the proper one, and thought it would have a good Effect on public Business and make the Assembly more careful in their other Proceedings." He also demanded a copy of their proceedings each day. The council again urged him to delay such issues until the immediate requests for funds had been taken care of. Morris, however, insisted the printers comply.[12]

On 20 March, Speaker Norris appointed Franklin to a committee to answer the governor's demand. Franklin laid before the House the message Governor Morris had sent David Hall and him forbidding them to print Robinson's letters. As Franklin predicted, the order irritated the assemblymen. The letters belonged in the minutes, they said, and the House was the sole judge of what should appear there. Franklin and Hall therefore wrote Governor Morris that as "the immediate Servants of the House," they were "oblig'd . . . to obey their Orders" (5:535). Just as Franklin feared, Morris obstinately persevered. He next insisted that the assembly clerk, William Franklin, should attend him with the minutes every night, but the assembly refused, saying Morris should have the minutes when they were printed. Then Morris ordered Secretary Peters to inspect the journals, but the assembly would not allow it.[13]

After hearing from Morris, Thomas Penn wrote that he hoped the English authorities would censure the printer "for not observing the Governor's order." Hoping to have Franklin removed as joint deputy postmaster general of America, Penn told Secretary of State Robinson about Franklin's printing the letters and signing "that vile Report" of 11 September 1753, but Robinson merely replied that "General Braddock had represented him as having done considerable Services." The foolish non-issue was brought up nearly two years later, when Governor William Denny suggested to Lord Loudoun that he should issue orders that Franklin and other newspaper printers not be allowed to publish "Articles of Intelligence" unless they had Denny's or Loudoun's permission.[14]

News of Braddock's anger with Pennsylvania spread. Edward Shippen (1729–1806) wrote his father in Lancaster about Braddock's "most alarming letter" on 19 March 1755. He reported that Braddock said "he is determined to obtain by unpleasant Methods what it is their Duty to contribute with the utmost Chearfulness" and that "the Assembly know not how to stomach" it. The letter will "frighten them into some reasonable measures, as it must be a vain thing to contend with a General at the head of an army . . . especially as in all probability he will be supported in every Thing at home."[15] On 20 March, Franklin was appointed to a committee to reply to the governor's request for aid. That afternoon, the committee said the assembly would "immediately" comply and contribute "such Sums of Money as may be consistent with our Circumstances." In addition to the supply bill, Governor Morris had requested a law to prevent war materials, flour, and other provisions from being shipped to the French. On Saturday, 22 March, Speaker Norris appointed Franklin to a committee to provide that law.[16]

JOSIAH QUINCY'S MISSION

On 13 February 1755, Massachusetts governor William Shirley proposed that a joint colonial force commanded by Sir William Johnson attack the French fort at Crown Point (see map 2, p. 308, upper right). The Massachusetts House of Representatives agreed on 18 February and asked Pennsylvania "to contribute a Quantity of Provisions to be transported to Albany for the Service of the Army."[17] Trying to win Pennsylvania's support, Governor Shirley sent Colonel Josiah Quincy to Philadelphia to solicit assistance. Quincy was a partner with Franklin's brother John in the Germantown, Massachusetts, glassworks. Shirley knew that Franklin and Quincy were friends, and he no doubt advised Quincy to consult Franklin. Quincy called on him when he arrived in Philadelphia and perhaps stayed with the Franklins.

Franklin advised Quincy first to appeal to the governor and Pennsylvania Council. Quincy appeared before them on 20 March "to consult and agree on the Method" of requesting the Pennsylvania Assembly for help. Governor Morris and the council suggested that he write a request, which Morris would lay before the House. Franklin may have drafted it for him, and on 21 March, Quincy presented it, asking for "a quantity of Provisions sufficient for the subsistence of the men proposed to be raised." From 20 to 22 March and again on Monday, 24 March, the House debated the governor's request for funds, including supplies for the Crown Point expedition. Governor Morris recorded that Franklin labored "hard to prevail with them to give Forty Thousand Pounds for the general Service, and to sink it by a Tax in Five Years, but even he despairs of Success and thinks they will only offer me a Bill of the same Nature of that I refused to pass the last Sessions."[18] Franklin had evidently checked with Morris to see if he would pass a bill that would be sunk within a shorter time than the usual ten years the assembly demanded. Presumably, Morris had said that he would pass it if the time were limited to five years. Franklin was trying to find a way to support the war effort, but Morris consistently, childishly, and foolishly sought to have his own way in minor matters. Perhaps Morris hoped that the assembly would pass a bill that he could not enact and thereby put the Quaker-controlled assembly in an unfavorable light with the British authorities. Morris wrote Braddock on 25 March that he had pressed the assembly to vote for aid for the army, but "I have no hopes of their acting reasonably."[19]

The House resolved on 25 March to prepare a money bill for £25,000, of which £5,000 would be to repay the members who had borrowed that amount on the credit of the House on 3 January; £10,000 would be for provisions for the Crown Point expedition; £5,000 for General Braddock; and £5,000 for clearing roads, payments of posts, and so forth. Franklin served on the committee that prepared the bill. Brought in on 26 March, it passed two days later. A "ten years continuance of the Excise at £2,500 per annum" would raise the funds. Franklin recorded that "Mr. Quincy laboured hard with the Governor to obtain his Assent, but he was obstinate" (A 135). Morris's instructions would not allow him to pass the bill.[20] Morris declared to the assembly on 1 April: "his Majesty and his Ministers, a British Parliament, your own Constituents, and the neighbouring Governments, will be at no Loss on whom to lay the Blame."[21]

Customarily, the governor kept a bill if he was giving it further consideration but returned a rejected bill. The spiteful Morris, however, kept the vetoed bill. When two members of the House called on him for its return, he said on 3 April that it was "of so extraordinary a Nature, that he thinks it his Duty to lay the same before his Majesty, and he keeps it for that Purpose." When Morris finally gave the assembly his reasons for vetoing the bill on 16 May, he charged that the assembly's "Resolutions are and have been to take Advantage of your Country's Danger, to aggrandize and render permanent your own Power and Authority, and to destroy that of the Crown." And he raised the usual slander that the Americans intended to revolt and become independent: "That it is for this Purpose and to promote your Scheme of future Independency You are grasping at the Disposition of all the Publick Money and at the Power of filling all the offices of Government."[22]

Writing of the bill in the *Autobiography*, Franklin incorrectly recalled that it would tax the proprietary estate along with other lands (A 135), but that attempt was made later, in November 1755. Expecting Morris to reject it, Franklin prepared a memorial for Quincy to submit to the Pennsylvania Assembly. When Governor Morris vetoed the bill, Quincy immediately presented the memorial (6:4–5). In it, Quincy (actually, Franklin) lamented that Governor Morris vetoed the bill to aid New England. The memorial's preface pleased the assembly, for it would make the assembly look good in the English press.[23] Franklin recalled in the *Autobiography*: "the Assembly, tho' very desirous of making their Grant to New England effectual, were at a Loss how to accomplish it. I then suggested a Method of doing the Business without the Governor, by Orders on the Trustees of the Loan-Office, which by Law the Assembly had the Right of Drawing. There was indeed little or no Money at that time in the Office, and therefor I propos'd that the Orders should be payable in a Year and to bear an Interest of Five per Cent. With these Orders I suppos'd the Provisions might easily be purchas'd. The Assembly with very little Hesitation adopted the Proposal" (A 135). The pacifist Quaker leader Israel Pemberton begrudgingly conceded that Franklin "perfected the Scheme," though he added "some others had projected" it (6:53).

Franklin, however, wrote his account in 1788, thirty-three years later. The idea of adding 5 percent interest to the notes may not have been part of his original proposal. Governor Morris, writing on 9 April 1755, said that when he rejected the bill, the assembly "resolved to borrow ten thousand pounds upon their own credit, and apply it to the eastern expedition, but upon tryal they found the mony'd people not inclinable to Lend any money upon so precarious a security, whereupon they agreed to Issue notes payable to the Bearer in a year, with five percent Interest, and lest these notes should not obtain a currency, I am told they are forming an association to circulate them."[24] But one can hardly trust Morris's reports. The assembly actually voted £15,000 (not the £10,000 Morris reported) on 2 April, £5,000 of which was to repay the money the assembly borrowed for Braddock's troops on 3 January and £10,000 to support the New England troops going to attack Crown Point.[25] Franklin was on the committee "directed to sign and dispose" of the notes: "They obtain'd instant Credit, and were not only receiv'd in Payment for the Provisions, but many money'd People who had Cash lying by them, vested it in those Orders, which they found advantageous, as they bore Interest while upon hand, and might on any Occasion be used as Money: So that they were eagerly all bought up, and in a few Weeks none of them were to be seen" (A 135–36).

In the *Autobiography*, Franklin remembered, "Mr. Quincy return'd Thanks to the Assembly in a handsome Memorial, went home highly pleas'd with the Success of his Embassy, and ever after bore for me the most cordial and affectionate Friendship" (A 136). Franklin had reason to be proud; his maneuver deserves to be ranked with the idea of a matching grant for the Pennsylvania Hospital. Israel Pemberton reported to Dr. John Fothergill that Governor Morris was "extreamly mortifyed by the Success of this Proceeding." Morris represented the Pennsylvania Assembly and especially the Quakers as rich, selfish traitors, but Franklin had come up with a way to finance defense without the governor's "Concurrence and against his Designs" (6:53–54).

Governor Morris had taken Thomas Penn's instruction to heart: no money bill should pass that the governor did not control. Morris fumed to Penn on 9 April 1755 that "in Effect" the assembly was "making paper money without the

Consent of the King or Governor." Morris hyperbolically said that the action was a step toward rebellion: "for if an Assembly who claim a right of sitting when & as long as they Please, of keeping their proceedings a secret from the government, can borrow & dispose of money, & circulate their notes without the knowledge or Consent of government, and that without Limitation of sum, they may, whenever they Please, employ that Power against the Government." On the same day, he wrote similarly to Sir Thomas Robinson of the danger "such powers" posed in the hands of an assembly "annually chosen by a People, a great Part, if not the Majority of whom, are Foreigners unattached to an English Government, either by Birth or Education." In effect, inspired by Smith's *Brief State*, Morris asked that Germans as well as Quakers be disenfranchised and suggested that the Germans in Pennsylvania were traitors.[26]

SCAROUADY

On 31 March 1755, the Oneida chief Scarouady, leader of the Mingo Iroquois and (in his own opinion) a supervisor of the Shawnee and other Ohio Indians, reported to the Pennsylvania Council his conversation with the "Principal Man" of the Caughnawaga (an Indian tribe and town on the St. Lawrence River, below Quebec). The Caughnawaga leader said: "Brother, the French and the English are quarrelling about our Lands and want to engage Us in their Quarrel, but why should We meddle on either side; the English, You see, buy our Lands from Us, piece after piece, and tho' they pay Us for it and so get it from Us with our own Consent, yet what they give Us is soon spent and gone, and We much straitned for want of our Lands. The French take whole Countrys from Us by Force, never asking Us for our Consent, and so between both We shall in a little Time have no Lands." The Caughnawagas were "determined to stand Neuters and let the French and English fight it out together, and the more they destroy one another the better." The chief assured Scarouady that the Caughnawaga would not fight for the French and beseeched "them not to fight for the English."[27]

As Scarouady knew, the policy of pitting the English and the French against one another had been the strategy of Teganissorens, the Onondaga chief and chief spokesman of the Iroquois Indians, who flourished from ca. 1680 to ca. 1718. Though some individual Indians and groups identified with the English (especially the Mohawks and other eastern tribes) and some with the French (especially the Senecas and other western tribes), most Iroquois chiefs preferred to stand aside and allow the French and English to fight one another. The major chiefs only feared that either the French or the English would grow too great and completely subjugate the other. In his 5 September 1745 message to the House, Governor George Thomas had recalled that at the 1744 Lancaster Treaty, the Iroquois had said they would remain neutral in the war between the French and the English. In 1745, Conrad Weiser reported to him that "one of the most politick" of the Iroquois "Sachems" (probably the Oneida chief Canasatego) said their "true interest" would be not to join with either the French or the English. Thomas thought that, in view of the English victory at Cape Breton, the Iroquois might join the French "in order to preserve the Balance."[28]

Scarouady, however, identified with the English and intended to fight the French, but he complained to Morris and the council on 31 March 1755 that the English gave few and cheap presents in comparison to the French (he later contradicted this statement when asking for more presents). He and the warriors with him wanted clothes and supplies. The next day, Governor Morris gave the minutes of this council meeting to the assembly and asked them to support Scarouady and other Indian allies. The governor also requested funds "for the ensuing Treaty." Speaker Norris appointed Franklin to a committee "relating to Indian Affairs" on 5 April, and he wrote its report. The assembly provided for Scarouady and his party but suggested that they settle near French Town (on the west branch of the Susquehanna River) where the Indians could farm the cleared land. The committee also said that the assembly had not previously heard of "the ensuing Treaty." Until the members had information about it, they presumed the governor would not expect the House to take any action.[29]

In his initial message of 18 March 1755, Governor Morris had informed the assembly that General Braddock requested postal service be established between Philadelphia and Winchester, Virginia. Consequently, on 22 March, the House asked Franklin to consider the proposal and "report to the House his Opinion of the best Method of establishing and supporting such Post." Franklin reported on 9 April that he would establish a "regular Post from this City to *Winchester*." He would "keep an Account of the Expences attending the Maintaining such Post, and the Produce from the Letters conveyed thereby, and exhibit the same Account to the Assembly at the End of the Year, if the House shall think fit to agree to make good the Deficiency, in case the Produce should not prove equal to the Expence." The House "unanimously agreed . . . and ordered that all Letters sent by the said Post to and from the Army should pass free of all Charge." On 9 April, the assembly adjourned until 12 May.[30]

GENERAL EDWARD BRADDOCK

General Braddock arrived in Virginia on 19 February and reached Williamsburg on 23 February. After conferring with Virginia's governor Robert Dinwiddie, he called a meeting of the colonial governors at Alexandria, Virginia, to discuss the war effort and obtain their aid. Governor William Shirley of Massachusetts, Colonel William Johnson, and Governor James DeLancey of New York arrived in Philadelphia on the evening of 8 April. Speaker Isaac Norris had asked Franklin "to wait upon" Braddock, not as from the assembly "but as Postmaster General, under the guise of proposing to settle with him the Mode of conducting with most Celerity and Certainty the Dispatches between him and the Governors of the several Provinces, with whom he must necessarily have continual

Correspondence, and of which they propos'd to pay the Expence" (A 136). Franklin had planned to go to Winchester to set up the post and then to wait upon General Braddock, but when Governor Shirley arrived in Philadelphia on 8 April, he "insisted on B. Franklin going with" the governors toward Williamsburg the next day. That night, Franklin must have hurriedly prepared.

The pacifist Israel Pemberton, Jr., wrote Dr. John Fothergill that Franklin "with some difficulty undertook the Journey tho' he had scarce perfected the Scheme . . . to raise a Sum of Money legally without the Governor's concurrence" (6:53). After the assembly adjourned on the morning of 9 April, Franklin and his son William (now about twenty-seven years old) accompanied governors Shirley, DeLancey, and Morris for three days, until they reached Annapolis, Maryland, where they arrived about 8:00 P.M. on 12 April. The next day, the governors went on to meet General Braddock at Alexandria. Franklin and William remained in Annapolis and probably conferred with printer and postmaster Jonas Green about the post service. When Franklin wrote Deborah on 13 April, he said that on the trip home he would go from Winchester to Carlisle in order to arrange the mail route from Philadelphia. After Braddock met with the governors in Alexandria on 14 April, he went to Frederick, Maryland, to wait for the horses and wagons that governors Robert Dinwiddie of Virginia and Horatio Sharpe of Maryland had promised. Franklin and his son made the trip to Winchester and arranged for a post there. Traveling from Winchester toward Carlisle, they passed through Frederick about 18 April, where they met General Edward Braddock. (See map 3, p. 369.)

Braddock was "waiting impatiently for the Return of those he had sent thro' the back Parts of Maryland and Virginia to collect Waggons." Franklin stayed "with him several Days, Din'd with him daily, and had full Opportunity of removing all his Prejudices, by the Information of what the Assembly had before his Arrival actually done and were still willing to do to facilitate his Operations" (A 136). Israel Pemberton further reported to Fothergill that Braddock and his officers "had been told that we had refused to supply them with Provisions and carriages, tho' the pay for it had been offered us." Braddock had also been told that the assembly "would not agree to open a Road from their Camp to our Settlements and it was very constantly insinuated that we were at the same time supplying the French with Provisions." According to Pemberton, Franklin assured Braddock that the Pennsylvania Assembly "had voted £5,000 to be laid out in Provisions and made ready before their Arrival, that no Notice had ever been given of their wanting any more Carriages than the Virginians and Marylanders had undertaken to Furnish and that a Committee was then Surveying the Ground in Order to lay out the Road" (6:54). In the *Autobiography*, Franklin did not mention that he told Braddock of the £20,000 bill that the assembly voted on 12 December 1754 and the £25,000 bill voted on 28 March 1755, both of which Morris rejected—but Franklin surely did.

Gifts for the Junior Officers

At the camp, while Franklin was "supping one Evening with the Officers of Col. Dunbar's Regiment, he represented to me his Concern for the Subalterns, who he said were generally not in Affluence, and could ill afford in this dear Country to lay in the Stores that might be necessary in so long a March thro' a Wilderness where nothing was to be purchas'd." Sympathizing with their situation, Franklin thought he saw a way to help them and to help secure the good opinion of General Braddock and the other officers. The next morning he wrote the "Committee of Assembly, who had the Disposition of some public Money, warmly recommending the Case of these Officers to their Consideration, and proposing that a Present should be sent them of Necessaries and Refreshments." William Franklin, "who had had some Experience of a Camp Life, and of its Wants," drew up a list for Franklin, which he enclosed. The committee approved, and sent twenty horses, each with a parcel of food and drink for the junior officers. Beside the essential food, the drink included two dozen bottles of "old Madeira Wine" and two gallons of "Jamaica Spirits." One suspects that all junior officers drank toasts to the Pennsylvania Assembly. As Franklin foresaw, the presents "were very thankfully receiv'd, and the Kindness acknowledg'd by Letters to me from the Colonels of both Regiments in the most grateful Terms" (A 137–38).

Wagons

On 22 April, when Franklin was about to leave Braddock's camp, "the Returns of Waggons to be obtain'd were brought in, by which it appear'd that they amounted only to twenty-five, and not all of those were in serviceable Condition. The General and all the Officers were surpriz'd, declar'd the Expedition was then at an End, being impossible, and exclaim'd against the Ministers for ignorantly landing them in a Country destitute of the Means of conveying their Stores, Baggage, &c. not less than 150 Waggons being necessary." Franklin said that "it was a pity they had not been landed rather in Pennsylvania, as in that Country almost every Farmer had his Waggon." General Braddock "eagerly laid hold of my Words, and said, 'Then you, Sir, who are a Man of Interest there, can probably procure them for us; and I beg you will undertake it.'" Franklin asked "what Terms were to be offer'd the Owners of the Waggons?" Braddock asked what terms were necessary. Franklin listed those he deemed appropriate, and Braddock agreed to them and immediately had "a Commission and Instructions" prepared for Franklin (A 137). The following morning, 23 April, Braddock gave Franklin £795.15.6 for the wagoners and the use of the horses and wagons (6:17).

Franklin took off for Wright's Ferry on the Susquehanna River, where he consulted with his friends Susanna Wright and her brother James on 24 or 25 April. Susanna suggested that Franklin call citizens from the local townships together to present them with his wagon proposal. On the way to Lancaster, Franklin remembered that Chief Justice William Allen would be at the court at

Lancaster. He wrote Susanna Wright on the morning of 28 April that he intended to ask Allen to recommend "from the Bench that the Constables should immediately call the Inhabitants of their respective Townships together." The pragmatic Franklin added that he did not know whether Allen "will think a Person in his Station, can, in Court, regularly intermeddle in such Affairs; but I shall endeavour to persuade him to it, as strict Forms ought, in my Opinion, to be disregarded in Cases of Necessity." (As we will see, Franklin held the same belief when minister to France and when negotiating the peace treaty with Great Britain.) In his last important act of collaboration with Franklin, Allen made the request from the bench, "setting forth . . . in the warmest Terms, the Duty" the people "owed to their Sovereign, who had graciously undertaken this expensive Expedition for their immediate Safety." Allen's speech, together with Franklin's broadside advertisement, was successful.

While at Wright's Ferry, Franklin no doubt heard of Sir John St. Clair's treatment of the Pennsylvania road builders. On 16 April 1755, St. Clair had arrived at their camp and roundly cursed George Croghan, James Burd, and John Armstrong, among others. He "stormed like a Lyon Rampant." He said that they should have started building the road in January, that it was too late to do it now. "That instead of marching to the Ohio he would in nine days march his Army into Cumberland County to cut the Roads, press Horses, Wagons, etc. and that he would not suffer a Soldier to handle an Axe, but by Fire and Sword oblige the Inhabitants to do it." Ranting and raving, he said he would "burn the Houses" of the farmers, "kill all kind of Cattle and carry away the Horses." He swore he did not care for anything the assembly did and would "hang an arse (as he phrased it) on the occasion, and told Us to go to the General if We pleased, who wou'd give Us ten bad words for one that he had given."[31]

The Wagon Advertisement, 26 April 1755

Franklin composed the wagon advertisement at Lancaster on 26 April, giving the terms that he had earlier suggested to Braddock, which, besides good pay, guaranteed that no wagoners would be "called upon to do the Duty of Soldiers, or be otherwise employ'd than in conducting or taking Care of their Carriages and Horses." The advertisement also contained Franklin's personal address to the citizens. At the camp at Frederick "a few Days since," Franklin found General Braddock and his officers "extreamly exasperated, on Account of their not being supply'd with Horses and Carriages, which had been expected from this Province as most able to furnish them; but thro' the Dissensions between our Governor and Assembly, Money had not been provided nor any Steps taken for that Purpose." Franklin's statement was not true, for Braddock expected horses and wagons from Virginia and Maryland, not Pennsylvania, but it made the following appeal and threat more effective: "It was proposed to send an armed Force immediately into these Counties, to seize as many of the best Carriages

and Horses as should be wanted, and compel as many Persons into the Service as would be necessary to drive and take care of them." Franklin's statement preyed upon the farmers' fears of the army, for the soldiers had, from their first landing in Virginia "till they got beyond the Settlements . . . plundered and stript the Inhabitants, totally ruining some poor Families, besides insulting, abusing and confining the People if they remonstrated" (A 141). Franklin also knew that many inhabitants had heard of Sir John St. Clair's threats to the Pennsylvania road builders.

The advertisement continued, "I apprehended that the Progress of a Body of Soldiers thro' these Counties on such an Occasion, especially considering the Temper they are in, and their Resentment against us, would be attended with many and great Inconveniencies to the Inhabitants; and therefore more willingly undertook the Trouble of trying first what might be done by fair and equitable Means." Franklin said that the hire of the horses and wagons would altogether amount to more than £30,000, "which will be paid you in Silver and Gold of the King's Money," thereby relieving the area's chronic shortage of currency. He suggested that farmers who could not spare four horses, a wagon, and a driver from their farms "may do it together, one furnishing the Waggon, another one or two Horses, and another the Driver, and divide the Pay proportionably between you." He threatened that if they did not volunteer to help "when such good Pay and reasonable Terms are offered you," their loyalty would be suspected. (The Pennsylvania Germans knew that some Britons thought they were not loyal to Britain.)[32] Further, "the King's Business must be done. . . . Waggons and Horses must be had; violent Measures will probably be used; and you will be to seek for a Recompence where you can find it, and your Case perhaps be little pitied or regarded" (A 194–95).

Franklin said he had "no particular Interest in this Affair; as (except the Satisfaction of endeavouring to do Good and prevent Mischief) I shall have only my Labour for my Pains." Franklin recalled Governor George Thomas's letter to the Lords of Trade of 20 October 1740 (which Franklin surreptitiously published in 1741 to influence the election; *Life* 2:337, fig. 20). According to Governor Thomas, the Quakers secured victory by deceiving the Germans "into a Belief, that a Militia will bring them under as severe a Bondage to Governors as they were formerly under to their Princes in *Germany*; that the Expence would impoverish them; and that if any other than *Quakers* should be chosen upon the Assembly, they would be dragg'd down from their Farms, and obliged to build Forts, as a Tribute for their being admitted to settle in the Province." Franklin echoed the earlier threat. If he could not obtain the wagons, horses, and drivers, "I am oblig'd to send Word to the General in fourteen Days; and I suppose Sir John St. Clair the Hussar, with a Body of Soldiers, will immediately enter the Province, for the Purpose aforesaid, of which I shall be sorry to hear, because *I am, very sincerely and truly your Friend and Well-wisher*, B. Franklin" (A 195).

Contemporaries attested that Franklin's threat was effective. The advertisement was celebrated, and the reference to St. Clair was well-known. William Shirley, Jr., secretary to General Braddock, wrote Governor Morris on 14 May: "I can but honour Franklin for the last Clause of his Advertisement." Reports concerning the advertisement appeared in the English periodicals. The *Gentleman's Magazine* praised Franklin's conclusion: "Mr. *Franklin* observed that General St. Clair's dress was of the *Hussar* kind, and this gave him a hint which he immediately improved: He caused a report to be propagated among the *Germans*, that except 150 wagons could be got ready, and sent to the general within a certain time, *St. Clair*, who was a *Hussar*, would come among them, and take away what he found by force: The *Germans* having formerly lived under despotic power, knew the *Hussars* too well to doubt their serving themselves, and believing that General *St. Clair* was indeed a *Hussar*, they provided, instead of 150, 200 wagons, and sent them within the time that Mr. *Franklin* had" named.[33]

Sir John St. Clair must have been unhappy at being called a "hussar" and angry that Franklin used and publicized his foolish threats to the road builders. St. Clair no doubt grated his teeth when he read in the *Gentleman's Magazine* that he was a military authoritarian, ready and willing to violate civilian rights.[34] As we will see in Volume 4, after Franklin sailed for England in 1757, St. Clair retaliated—by insulting Deborah Franklin. Though Franklin falsely created the identification of St. Clair as a hussar, the man's reputation helped. Israel Pemberton, writing on 19 May (no doubt after reading Franklin's advertisement), said that Franklin providentially avoided the "Effects which might reasonably be expected from a Madman such as Sinclair . . . coming with an Armed Force" (6:54).

About the time that Franklin hired the Lancaster printer William Dunlap (who had married Deborah Coker, the daughter of Deborah Franklin's sister, Frances)[35] to print the advertisement, he also had him print a contract between Franklin (or his deputy) and the person(s) hiring out the horses or wagons. Two days later on Monday, 28 April, Franklin signed the first contracts in Lancaster. He advertised that he would sign contracts in Lancaster until 30 April, and in York, which was southwest across the Susquehanna, beginning on 1 May. Meanwhile, William Franklin had gone on to Carlisle to sign contracts there. In about a week, Franklin had arranged for 150 wagons and wagoners and 600 horses for Braddock. Israel Pemberton wrote Dr. John Fothergill that Franklin was "the only person" who was equal to the task (6:54).

Franklin put himself at financial risk: "I receiv'd of the General about £800 to be disburs'd in Advance money to the Waggon-Owners &c.: but that Sum being insufficient, I advanc'd upwards of £200 more, and in two Weeks, the 150 Waggons with 259 carrying Horses were on their March for the Camp. The Advertisement promised Payment according to the Valuation, in case any Waggon or Horse should be lost. The Owners however, alledging they did not know General Braddock, or what dependence might be had on his Promise, insisted on my Bond for the Performance, which I accordingly gave them" (A 137).

"The General too was highly satisfied with my Conduct in procuring him the Waggons, &c. and readily paid my Account of Disbursements; thanking me repeatedly and requesting my farther Assistance in sending Provisions after him" (A 138). As the Pennsylvania wagons rolled in, Braddock read Franklin's advertisement and learned of St. Clair's treatment of the Pennsylvania road builders. William Shirley, Jr., reported that the general gave St. Clair "what is called, in the Language of the Camp, a *Set down* upon this Affair." Braddock wrote Secretary of State Thomas Robinson on 5 June 1755 from Fort Cumberland, Wills Creek, commending Franklin's "great punctuality and Integrity," calling him "almost the only Instance of Ability and Honesty I have known in these Provinces. His Waggons and Horses . . . are indeed my whole Dependence."[36] Braddock asked if he could do anything for Franklin. Franklin took the opportunity to request that the army enlist no more indentured servants and discharge those who had been recruited. "This he readily granted, and several were accordingly return'd to their Masters on my Application" (A 142).

Franklin had more to do. The horses and wagons had to be appraised, and forage for the 600 horses provided. The broadside concerning appraisals was dated from Lancaster, 6 May (6:26). Franklin was still there on 8 May but returned to Philadelphia on 12 May for the opening of the assembly's fourth session. Two days later, Governor William Shirley wrote concerning the supplies for the Crown Point expedition to Speaker Isaac Norris. Since Norris was out of town, Franklin, who was on the committee to purchase the supplies and was a member of the assembly's committee of correspondence, replied on 22 May, giving details of what had been purchased and shipped. As usual, Franklin displayed extraordinary knowledge. He gave evaluations of the excellence of the beef, pork, rum ("good Barbados, instead of New England"), peas, meal, flour, rice, and bread. He also commented on the possibilities of trading part of it, "Connecticut Pork being plenty at New York, and Bread wanting." Franklin also noted that all the supplies could not, as requested, be sent directly to Albany "without re-shipping some at New York: our Vessels of any Burthen drawing too much Water for that River" (6:58).

THE 1754–55 ASSEMBLY'S FOURTH SESSION, 12–17 MAY

On the afternoon of Monday, 12 May, "The House taking into consideration the great Service done to the King's Forces, and to this Province, by *Benjamin Franklin*, a Member of this House, in his late Journey through *Maryland*, and our Back Counties, it was unanimously, *Resolved*, That the Thanks of this House be now given to the said Member for those Services."[37] Resuming his usual routines, Franklin attended a meeting of the Library Company directors that evening. At a meeting of the trustees of the Philadelphia Academy on 13 May, they discussed the additional charter that would add a college to the existing academy (6:28–37). On 15 May, the *Pennsylvania Gazette* announced that Franklin had accomplished his ostensible reason for the trip to Winchester: "The new Post between Philadelphia and Winchester, in Virginia, set out from the Post Office in Philadelphia this Morning, to continue his weekly Stages, setting out every Thursday Morning, during the Summer. Letters for Lancaster, York, or Cumberland Counties, in Pennsylvania, for the back Parts of Virginia, or for the Army, should be brought to the Office before Nine a Clock on Thursday Mornings." Franklin earlier had decided to create a central dead letter office at Philadelphia, and he heard from Boston that the post had been extended north from Boston to Halifax. He sent news of both developments to David Hall.[38]

In the assembly session of 12–17 May, Franklin served on several committees and wrote their messages. One message concerned the numerous sick and poor German immigrants brought into Philadelphia to be sold as indentured servants who were so ill that no one would buy their time. Ship captains simply turned them out to starve and die on the streets. The assembly had passed an act concerning the abandoned, sick immigrants on 31 December; Governor Robert Hunter Morris had replied on 2 April with numerous amendments; the assembly accepted some and refused others. On 14 May, Governor Morris sent down a bill "adhering" to his earlier amendments and saying that rather than have a committee of the assembly wait upon him, he wanted them to meet with members of the council. Norris appointed Franklin to a committee to reply. On 15 May Franklin said that the assembly wished Morris would have "exercised his own Judgement upon this our Bill, without referring . . . to a Committee of his Council, most of them such, as we are informed, who are, or have lately been, concerned in the Importations, the Abuses of which this Bill was designed to regulate and redress." Franklin itemized a number of abuses the law had intended to correct, but which the governor refused, with the result that if the assembly passed the "Bill as it comes down from the Governor, we should be more exposed to the Abuses and Grievances it was intended to redress, than we are at present by the Laws now in Being" (6:40, 41). Norris also appointed Franklin to a committee on 14 May "to prepare a State of the Bills" before the governor and the assembly.

THE DESPICABLE MORRIS

On 16 May, Governor Morris charged the assembly with doing nothing for the king's service, refusing to furnish Braddock's army with provisions and necessary carriage, "though your Country is full of both." Morris knew better. His speech was intended not for the legislators but for the English who presumably would not know of the £15,000 the assembly had raised through Franklin's clever plan, or of the gifts of horses and supplies to the junior officers, or of Franklin's securing 150 wagons and 600 horses from Pennsylvania for Braddock's march, or of Morris's rejection of the bill for £25,000. Though he had not yet received Thomas Penn's letter of 10 May 1755, wherein Penn said of the Pennsylvania Assembly, "the more indecent their behaviour is the better, as it may be attended with good consequences here,"[39] Morris nevertheless knew Penn's position. Morris's lying speeches for the British authorities would please the equally despicable Thomas Penn.

Morris's chicanery riled the assembly. Speaker Norris appointed Franklin to the committee to reply; he wrote the rejoinder; and the House approved and delivered it on Saturday, 17 May. Franklin pointed out that the assembly had approved a bill for £25,000 for the king's use on 28 March and that Morris had vetoed it on 1 April, though the entire amount was for the king's service. Morris, however, falsely represented that only £5,000 of the total was for Braddock. Franklin and the committee said that Morris systematically misrepresented, distorted, and lied in reporting the assembly's actions. He obviously had an audience other than the assembly in mind when he wrote the address. Morris pretended that the governor and proprietor had tried to assist the king's forces in America, but in fact they only obstructed the assembly's attempts to help. Franklin wrote that "Subtility and Dexterity appear in this Manner of disguising Truths, and changing Appearances." He summed up: "while we find the Governor transforming our best Actions into Crimes; and endeavouring to render the Inhabitants of Pennsylvania odious to our gracious Sovereign and his Ministers, to the British Nation, to all the neighbouring Colonies, and to the Army that is come to protect us; we cannot look upon him as a Friend to the Country" (6:48, 49). Then the assembly adjourned to 1 September.

Delighted by Franklin's denunciation of Morris, Israel Pemberton wrote Dr. John Fothergill that Morris's speech, with its "Falsehoods and the most malicious Representations," had angered Franklin. Pemberton hoped that Franklin would "act Steadily and Zealously in our Defence." Knowing that Morris's real audience was the British authorities, Pemberton asked Fothergill to use his influence to counter Morris's lies (6:55).

Though he held Morris in contempt, Franklin was surprisingly gentle in his recollections of Morris, emphasizing his frequent good nature in personal relations and his humor. Franklin wrote in the *Autobiography*: "I was put on every Committee for answering his Speeches and Messages, and by the Committees always desired to make the Drafts. Our Answers as well as his Messages were often tart, and sometimes indecently abusive. And as he knew I wrote for the Assembly, one might have imagined that when we met we could hardly avoid cutting Throats. But he was so good natur'd a Man, that no personal Difference between him and me was occasion'd by the Contest, and we often din'd together" (A 133). In conversation with John Jay in Paris, Franklin recalled Morris's pride in his messages—and his expected chagrin at Franklin's rejoinders: "Morris after having sent a Message to the assembly, met Saml. Rhoades and asked him what he thought of it—Rhoads said he thought it very smart—ah, sd Morris I thought so too when I had finished it—but tomorrow we shall see Benj. Franklin's answer and then I suspect we shall both change our minds."[40]

THE ROAD TO FORT DUQUESNE

In the spring, Governor Morris had asked James Burd (1726–93), a Lancaster County militia captain, to survey a road from Shippensburg, Pennsylvania, to the Monongahela, just south of Fort Duquesne. On 10 May General Braddock wrote Morris that he "found it absolutely necessary" to send the assistant quartermaster general Matthew Leslie to Pennsylvania to buy supplies for the horses and men. He asked for Morris's assistance.[41] On Sunday, 18 May, Morris turned to Franklin, who immediately replied to Morris that if he wrote to Speaker Norris and the assembly committee on spending funds for defense and recommended the affair, they would act promptly. Franklin said he would "convene the Committee early to-morrow, deliver your Letter, and do my utmost to forward the Business" (6:50). Since he was in Philadelphia and Norris was evidently at his country estate, Franklin acted as chair of the committee.

The next day, the assembly committee wrote the governor that it had expended all the money and had no way to procure any more, since "the Assembly is risen and gone home," but if the governor approved, they would, as private persons, "advance the Money that may be necessary on this Occasion" and carry out the business "upon the most reasonable terms, that can be obtain'd; Not doubting but that General Braddock will duly reembruse us" (6:51). Morris wrote Braddock on 20 May, saying the committee had no money and "could only assist as private Persons." The governor told Braddock that he had "supplied" Leslie with £500 and told Edward Shippen at Lancaster to furnish the deputy quartermaster general with "any greater Sum he may want."[42] I suspect that the £500 Morris "supplied" was not from him but from the committee. On 17 May 1755, Richard Peters learned at Shippensburg that Burd had only sixty men working with him on the road and that they had cut just seven miles in ten days. At that rate, it would take more than six months to make a road to the Monongahela. Peters said that the neighboring area could supply no more men and requested that Governor Morris write Edward Shippen at Lancaster to, if possible, raise more.

Morris turned to Franklin, asking him to write an advertisement for men to build the road. Franklin promptly did, promising that the assembly would pay the laborers and "that they shall not be press'd" into military service. The ad succeeded. On 26 May, Governor Morris wrote Robert Orme, General Braddock's aide-de camp, that two hundred men were now at work cutting the road to the Monongahela. Morris was somewhat fearful that Braddock would not approve the terms Franklin had advertised: "If for the King's Service Mr. Franklyn & myself give to any persons for their encouragement reasonable promises, as well for just pay as that they shall not be press'd into Service than that they engage for, I hope these will be well taken."[43] Edward Shippen, Burd's brother-in-law, wrote Governor Morris on 13 June that "Labourers come in but slow, having sent away only 40 since the Advance Money came; however, as I imagine,

Mr. Burd has now upwards of 200 men at Work [building the road to Monon-
gahela], the General I hope will have no reason to complain, for I am informed
they proceed very briskly."⁴⁴

On 30 May, Franklin issued passes to two men to go to Shippen in Lancaster.
Unfortunately, when they arrived he had no money to pay them, and they returned to Philadelphia. Franklin, on the committee to disperse the £15,000 that
the assembly had voted on 2 April, wrote Shippen on 2 June that the committee
had given the governor 100 dollars to send Shippen (6:67). The hypocritical
Morris was unhappy that the Pennsylvania Assembly was helping the war effort
and sneered in a letter to Thomas Penn: "How consistent the furnishing of
cannon and stores of war may be with the non-resisting principals of my quak-
ing Assembly, I cannot pretend to say."⁴⁵

One hundred soldiers joined James Burd's two hundred road builders in
June to guard them, but the soldiers brought along only two days' provisions,
and the laborers were running out of supplies. Braddock requested Franklin's
help. He undertook the task "and was busily employ'd in it" in June and early
July 1755. Franklin advanced "for the Service, of my own Money, upwards of
£1000 Sterling, of which I sent him an Account. It came to his Hands luckily for
me a few Days before the Battle, and he return'd me immediately an Order on
the Paymaster for the round Sum of £1000 leaving the Remainder to the next
Account. I consider this Payment as good Luck; having never been able to obtain that Remainder" (A 138–39).

FRANKLIN SLANDERED AND PRAISED

Though William Shirley, Jr., wrote Governor Morris that Franklin "has been of
the greatest Service in procuring Horses & Waggons," Morris suppressed that
information when he wrote Thomas Penn reporting that Pennsylvania had supplied 150 wagons and 600 horses to Braddock.⁴⁶ William Smith likewise tried
to assail Franklin. In his account to Penn, Smith talked of Franklin's "wicked
insinuation that the Germans would perhaps be obliged sometime to plough
the Lord Proprietor's Manors, as in Germany."⁴⁷ Smith knew or believed that
the Reverend Samuel Chandler, a leading London dissenting minister, had a
high opinion of Franklin. Therefore, not long before he wrote Penn defaming
Franklin, the hypocrite Smith wrote Chandler, "You do me great Honor in
mentioning my Name in the same Line, & in the same advantageous Light, with
the name of my much admired Friend, Mr. Franklin."⁴⁸

Replying to the information from Governor Morris and Richard Peters that
they had been helpful in assisting General Braddock in securing wagons and in
supplying his army with forage and provisions, Thomas Penn regretted that he
had praised Franklin for these efforts. Penn wrote Peters on 13 August: "We are
very well pleased to hear the Commiss'rs appointed by the Governor have laid
out the Road so well, and that the Ground is so good, as to admit of the dispatch
you have made in the making of it, which is a work of great importance, and as

such I have spoke of it here, for I think such a Service should not be conceal'd, and tho' the Assembly do not agree to the several matters recommended to them by the Governor, yet justice should be done them, where they do anything for the publick Service." Evidently Peters had also celebrated Morris for helping with materièl after Franklin secured the wagons. "We are also much pleased to find you have been able to supply the General with the Forage and Provisions he wanted, which I wish I had known, with more exactness before, as I gave all the merit of supplying both Wagons and Forage to Mr. Franklin, when he did it, I apprehend, by direction of the Governor, and in concert with you at least, tho' I suppose the latter part after you had been at the Camp was done by yourself."[49]

After Thomas Oxnard of Boston appointed Franklin grand master of Pennsylvania on 10 July 1749, William Allen revealed that he was easily made jealous. When the colonels of the two regiments wrote the Pennsylvania Assembly thanking Franklin and, in consequence, when the House voted him its thanks on 12 May, I suspect that Allen felt overlooked. He had helped Franklin secure the wagons in Lancaster by recommending the cause from the bench to the constables. Then Franklin received high praise from General Braddock and key British officials, with no mention of Allen. Franklin's emergence as the major writer and the second (if not the) most important leader for the main Quaker Party was the primary reason that Allen became Franklin's enemy after mid-1755, but a resentment over the neglect of his role in helping secure transportation for Braddock perhaps added personal jealousy to the political reasons for his antipathy. Despite his probable discontentment with Franklin, Allen attended the ceremony at the Pennsylvania Hospital on 28 May when the founders laid its cornerstone containing Franklin's inscription. For several days thereafter, Franklin was ill and confined to his home (6:88).

THE 1754–55 ASSEMBLY'S FIFTH SESSION, 13–28 JUNE

Responding to General Braddock's call for supplies for the march from Fort Cumberland, Maryland, to Fort Duquesne, Governor Morris reconvened the Pennsylvania Assembly on 13 June. He immediately showed a childish pique by saying that the assembly had not informed him that William Franklin had been chosen "Clerk of Assembly, and had a Right to certify the Proceedings of the House." Of course Morris knew and had been dealing with William Franklin as clerk in the previous sessions of the current assembly and for the past four years. Morris simply was asserting his importance—and irritating the assembly.[50] The next day Morris addressed the assembly, asking for supplies for Braddock's army and a guard to protect them. He also requested that the assembly enact a militia bill and pass a law regulating the prices that could be charged for the army's supplies.

Because of his resentment with the assembly over its publication of letters in April, Morris did not include a copy of Braddock's letter requesting aid.

Behaving in kind, the assembly immediately asked for it. Morris refused on 14 . June, saying that it "contained many matters which were not proper to be made public." The committee/Franklin answered the governor on 16 June: the delegates "cannot take the Letter into Consideration without seeing it." They hoped the governor would not, by starting "New Methods of Proceeding" and engaging "us in trivial Disputes, any longer obstruct or delay the Publick Service" (6:74). Perhaps it was after reading Franklin's reply that Morris wrote on the same day to Massachusetts governor William Shirley: "Franklin tho' a man of extraordinary ability and most extensive genius, Has very out of the way notions of the power of the People, and is as much a favourer of the unreasonable claims of American Assembly as any man whatever, he is indeed against the Quakers in opinion in point of defence, and would wish them less in power in this Province than they are, but you are sensible that will be only changing hands."[51]

On 21 June 1755 Morris replied to the assembly, blaming it for not accepting his demands and repeating the bugbear of Pennsylvania's treason for the English authorities: a future assembly could use its "Powers against the Government."[52] Just before the close of the session, the assembly rejoined on 27 June that if the "Letters and Papers" were to be the basis of the assembly's conduct, then the House should have copies of them, which it "may publish or not according to their own Prudence" (6:73–74, 91–93).

Governor Morris evidently hoped the legislators would be so angry that they would take no action and that he could then condemn them to the British authorities. Despite Morris's insults, Speaker Norris and the assembly proceeded to business, no doubt knowing Morris wanted an excuse to condemn them. On 17 June, Norris assigned Franklin to a committee to prepare "a Bill for the better and more regular Provision of Carriages and Pack-horses, for his Majesty's Service." He drafted it on Saturday, 18 June. Two days later, the assembly passed a bill for £15,000 (the same voted on 2 April). The bill began by recalling that the governor had in April refused a bill for granting £25,000. The House had then passed a bill on 2 April for £15,000, which was "paid out of the Monies in the Disposition of the House." The assembly noted that it was sending money that it had raised in interest on former notes, and that the proprietors, as usual, had contributed nothing. It said that the £15,000 it had given could not answer all the purposes intended by the bill for granting £25,000. Now on 21 June, the treasury was "almost exhausted" (6:83). Therefore the assembly was enacting a further bill for £15,000 for "cutting of Roads the better to supply the King's Troops, paying for Carriages, Expresses, and other contingent Expences in the King's Service."

Trying not to reveal Thomas Penn's instructions, Governor James Hamilton on 11 September 1753 and Governor Morris on 24 December 1754 had both claimed that a suspending clause was necessary in money bills. They repeatedly denied that Governor Thomas ever sent the 1746 bill to London. Thus it could not be a precedent for ignoring the suspending clause. But the original confirmation of the 1746 act by the Privy Council had been found in the papers of John Kinsey sometime before 5 April 1755, when a certified copy of it had been presented to the governor and council. Morris must have known about it since at least that date, though he had continued to pretend that the suspending clause was necessary.[53] The message to Governor Morris pointed out that the bill "carefully followed the Act passed by Governor *Thomas*" on 24 June 1746, for granting" money "for the King's Use," and with its current bill, the assembly sent the "Original Confirmation" of that bill dated 20 October 1748.[54] Morris again followed Penn's secret instructions and demanded on 25 June the same amendments that the House would not accept in April.

FRANKLIN'S OPINION

Franklin wrote his friend James Wright (Susanna Wright's younger brother) on 26 June that Governor Morris proposed to pass the bill "with about 30 Amendments, of which one is that the Commissioners named in the Act to dispose of the £5,000 for Roads, Indian Expenses &c. shall lay out none of the Money without his Consent. Another that the £10,000 given to General Braddock with the £5,000 be sunk in 5 years. Another that the Money arising from the Excise during the remaining 5 years be not disposed of without the Governor's Consent. Another that the Treasurer S. Preston Moore, be named in the Bill to continue till another be appointed by Act of Assembly &c. &c. &c." Franklin predicted that the House would "adhere to their Bill, and will send it up again tho' without any Hopes of its Passing." Franklin seemed ironically pleased with Morris's message concerning the bill, for "the Mask is now forc'd off." He wrote that now Governor Morris mentioned "not one word" of the "King's Instructions [the suspending clause] which have long been made a Pretense to harass us." Morris was willing to pass a paper money bill "without a reclaiming Clause &c. provided we comply with the Proprietary Instructions, and agree not to chuse our own Officers nor make use of our own Money without his Consent." Franklin added that "We should not have had this Clearing up of Things, if we had not sent him the original Royal Approbation of Governor Thomas's Act, which deprived him of all the old Subterfuges" (6:90–91).

In another letter of 26 June, Franklin wrote in a different strain to his London Quaker friend Peter Collinson. Franklin represented himself as a failed mediator: "In yours of Aug. 4. you express your Concern that such trifling Punctilio's in our Publick Affairs should obstruct necessary Measures. You will see more of the same Trifling in these Votes, on both sides. I am heartily sick of our present Situation: I like neither the Governor's Conduct nor the Assembly's, and having some Share in the Confidence of both, I have endeavour'd to reconcile 'em, but in vain." His only consolation was that he could "now and then" influence a "Good Measure." He complained that "both Sides expect more from me than they ought, and blame me sometimes for not doing what I am not able to do, as well as for not preventing what was not in my Power to prevent." He was probably referring to his known advocacy of armed forces as something the Proprietary Party hoped that he could effect.

He concluded: "The Assembly ride restive; and the Governor, tho' he spurs with both Heels, at the same time reins-in with both Hands, so that the Publick Business can never move forward; and he remains like St. George in the Sign, always a Horseback, and never going on. Did you never hear this old Catch?

> There was a mad Man, He had a mad Wife
> And three mad Sons beside;
> And they all got upon a mad Horse
> And madly they did ride.[55]

'Tis a Compendium of our Proceedings, and may save you the Trouble of reading them" (6:86–87). Franklin's prediction to James Wright proved true. After a final flourish of exchanges with the governor, the assembly, unwilling to tax if the governor would control the funds, adjourned until 1 September.

The Masonic Lodge

Near the end of the fifth session of the assembly, the Philadelphia Freemasons staged one of those public performances in which early modern Europe and America abounded. Ironically, it marked what was probably the last time that Franklin and William Allen cooperated and perhaps the last time that Franklin heard a sermon by the Reverend William Smith. In the elaborate ceremony interspersed with bells pealing, music playing, and cannon firing, the first Masonic lodge building in America opened on St. John's Day, 1755. Planning for the structure began when the Grand and the First (St. John's) Lodge agreed on 12 March 1752 to appoint a committee to find a suitable site for a Masonic building that could also contain a space for Philadelphia's Dancing Assembly. Dr. Thomas Bond chaired the lodge committee, which included William Franklin. Six weeks later, the committee reported recommending a lot on the south side of Norris (Lodge) Alley (now Sansom Street) between Chestnut and Walnut streets. Norris Alley then ran from Second Street to Dock Street. William Allen and James Hamilton each pledged £50 for the site and building; William Plumsted, £25; Franklin and Alexander Huston, £20; and William Franklin and all the other members (except four) of the St. John's Lodge pledged £15 each.[56]

The work proceeded apace and was finished by the summer of 1755. The *Pennsylvania Gazette* announced on 20 June 1755: "The Grand Annual Feast and general Communication" of Philadelphia's Freemasons would be held on St. John the Baptist's Day, Tuesday, 24 June. The Masons were to meet at 8:00 A.M. at the Lodge Building (#15 in the endpapers), parade to Christ Church (#27) for a sermon, and return to the lodge for a feast. Though few Quakers were Freemasons, Speaker Isaac Norris canceled the usual Tuesday morning meeting in consideration of the several Masons who would not be attending that morning.

Visiting from Virginia, young Daniel Fisher turned out for the spectacle and recorded: "the greatest Procession of Free Masons to the Church and their Lodge, in Second Street that was ever seen in America. No less than 160 being in the Procession in Gloves, Aprons, etc., attended by a band of Music. Mr. Allin [Allen], the Grand master, honoring them with his company, as did the Deputy Grand Master, Mr. Benjamin Franklin and his son, Mr. William Franklin, who walked as the next Chief Officer. A sword-Bearer with a naked sword drawn headed the Procession. They dined together elegantly, as it is said at their hall upon Turtle, etc."[57] The list of officers of the Grand Lodge shows that there had been no changes in its officers since William Allen received an appointment from William, Lord Byron, in 1751.[58]

The *Pennsylvania Gazette*, 3 July, reported the procession.

    I. The *Sword Bearer*, carrying a drawn sword.

   II. Six Stewards with white rods.

        Bro. William Moore, Bro. John Swift, First Lodge.

        Bro. Emanuel Rouse, Bro. Jacob Viney, Second Lodge.

        Bro. Walter Shea, Bro. Hugh Donaldson, Tun Tavern Lodge.

        Walking two and two.

  III. The Grand Secretary William Franklin, who bore a crimson damask cushion, on which was laid an open Bible.

        The Grand Treasurer William Plumsted, Esq., also with a crimson damask cushion upon which was the Book of Constitutions.

  IV. Grand Chaplain Rev. William Smith.

   V. The Grand Master William Allen, Esq., supported by Bros. Hon. Robert Hunter Morris, Esq. and James Hamilton, two brethren of Rank and Distinction.

  VI. The Deputy Grand Master Benjamin Franklin Esq., supported in like manner by Bros. Dr. Thomas Cadwalader Esq. and Thomas Boude.

 VII. The two Grand Wardens.

        Dr. Thomas Bond, Senior Grand Warden.

        Joseph Shippen, Junior Grand Warden.

VIII. His Excellency John Tinker, Esq., Governor of Providence [in the Bahamas].

        John Penn, Esq.

  IX. Three Tylers—Carrying Columnes of the three orders—Doric, Ionic and Corinthian.

Next came the wardens, secretaries, and treasurers of the three Philadelphia lodges, then visiting Freemasons (in addition to John Tinker) and the members of the three lodges. The final display in the procession was "The *Grand Master's*, Governor *Morris's*, Governor *Tinker's* and others of the Brethren Coaches and Chariots, empty." The Masons in the parade were "all new cloathed with Aprons, white Gloves and Stockings, and the Officers in the proper Cloathing and Jewels of their respective Lodges, with their other Badges of Dignity. When the procession arrived at *Market Street*," it was saluted "by a Discharge of *Nine* Cannon from a Brother's Vessel, handsomely ornamented with Colours, which lay opposite the said Street, for that Purpose." One assumes that the ship belonged to Allen.

At Christ Church, William Smith preached and then the parade returned to the new Masonic lodge, with "the Band of Musick before them . . . playing the *Enter'd Apprentice's Song.*" After dinner, the Masons drank fourteen toasts, including one to William Allen; a penultimate one to "General BRADDOCK, and Success to His Majesty's Forces"; and finally, "Prosperity to Pennsylvania, and a Happy Union to His Majesty's Colonies." (Though the "Union" was primarily meant to refer to a military one against the French, it is suggestive. One wonders if Franklin proposed it.) The ceremony ended at 5:00 P.M., though Franklin and some others may have left at 3:00 for the assembly. Knowing that his sermon would be published, Smith immediately turned it over to Franklin and Hall who brought it out, together with the news of the procession, on 3 July. Since Smith "inveighed against those who held a doctrine of non-resistence," Franklin had Hall reprint that part after Braddock's defeat in the 31 July *Pennsylvania Gazette.*[59]

BRADDOCK'S DEFEAT, 9 JULY 1755

The colonists thought that Braddock's large, well-equipped army would have little trouble taking Fort Duquesne and wiping out the other French forts from the Great Lakes through the Ohio country. Franklin had doubts. A day or two before 22 April, Franklin had a conversation with Braddock that gave him pause. He judged Braddock to be a brave man who "might probably have made a Figure as a good Officer in some European War. But he had too much self-confidence, too high an Opinion of the Validity of Regular Troops, and too mean a One of both Americans and Indians." Though the Pennsylvania Indian expert and trader George Croghan joined Braddock on his march with one hundred Indians, "who might have been of great Use to his Army as Guides, Scouts, &c. if he had treated them kindly," Braddock "slighted and neglected them, and they gradually left him" (A 139). Evidently Franklin thought that if Braddock had kept the scouts, the French and their Indian allies would not have surprised him and his army. Of course Franklin was writing long after Braddock's defeat and could be falsifying his earlier position. But his published criticism in 1751 of the normal European military discipline as unsuitable for fighting in the American forests (4:120) and Susanna Wright's letter (fig. 40, p. 429) show he had reservations concerning Braddock's presumed forthcoming success.

Franklin further reported that in conversation, Braddock gave him "some Account of his intended Progress. After taking Fort DuQuesne, says he, I am to proceed to Niagara; and having taken that, to Frontenac, if the Season will allow time; and I suppose it will; for Duquesne can hardly detain me above three or four Days; and then I see nothing that can obstruct my March to Niagara." (See map 3 for Braddock's route and Fort Niagara.) Franklin had some doubt: "Having before revolv'd in my Mind the long Line his Army must make in their March, by a very narrow Road to be cut for them thro' the Woods and Bushes; and also what I had read of a former Defeat of 1500 French who invaded the Iroquois Country, I had conceiv'd some Doubts and some Fears for the Event of the Campaign. But I ventur'd only to say, To be sure, Sir, if you arrive well before Duquesne, with these fine Troops so well provided with Artillery, that Place, not yet compleatly fortified, and as we hear with no very strong Garrison, can probably make but a short Resistance."

But there was the matter of getting his army to Fort Duquesne. "The only Danger I apprehend of Obstruction to your March, is from Ambuscades of Indians, who by constant Practice are dextrous in laying and executing them. And the slender Line near four Miles long, which your Army must make, may expose it to be attack'd by Surprize in its Flanks, and to be cut like a Thread into several Pieces, which from their Distance cannot come up in time to support each other. He smil'd at my Ignorance, and reply'd, 'These Savages may indeed be a formidable Enemy to your raw American Militia; but upon the King's regular and disciplin'd Troops, Sir, it is impossible they should make any Impression'" (A 139–40).

Like Franklin, William Shirley, Jr., also had reservations about Braddock, though the fact that his father (Governor William Shirley) was second, not first, in command of the British army in America may have influenced him. Writing Governor Morris on 23 May 1755, young Shirley found General Braddock "most judiciously chosen for being disqualified for the Service he is employed in, in almost every respect; he may be brave for ought I know, and he is honest in pecuniary Matters. But as the King said of a neighbouring Governor of yours when proposed for the Command of the American Forces about a Twelfth month ago, and recommended as a very honest Man tho' not remarkably able, 'a little more Ability and a little less Honesty upon the present Occasion might serve our Turn better.'"[60]

In May or June, Drs. Thomas and Phineas Bond came to Franklin "with a Subscription Paper, for raising Money to defray the Expence of a grand Fire Work, which it was intended to exhibit at a Rejoicing on receipt of the News of our Taking Fort DuQuesne." Franklin, however, was not so positive of Braddock's victory. "I looked grave and said, 'it would, I thought, be time enough to prepare for the Rejoicing when we knew we should have occasion to rejoice.'" The Bonds were surprised at Franklin's reaction. "'Why, the D——l,' says one of them, 'you surely don't suppose that the Fort will not be taken?' 'I don't know that it will not be taken; but I know that the Events of War are subject to great Uncertainty.'" Franklin gave his reasons for doubting and "The Subscription was dropt. . . . Dr. Bond on some other Occasions afterwards said, that he did not like Franklin's forebodings" (A143, 139).

On Friday, 18 July 1755, at 3:05 P.M., Philadelphia learned the shocking news.[61] The Virginian Daniel Fisher, who was working part-time as Franklin's secretary, recorded that "the Forces under General Braddock were entirely defeated by the French on the ninth, on the River Monongahela, the General, Lieutenant John St. Clair and a number of the officers killed, and all our fine Artillery taken. The Consternation of this City upon the occasion is hardly to be expressed." For the next two days Philadelphia received conflicting accounts, but on Sunday, 20 July, Fisher recorded: "'It is now reduced to a certainty that our army under General Braddock, is defeated. The General and Lieutenant John St. Clair dangerously wounded, about a Thousand men lost with the Train of Artillery and Baggage. The remaining part of the Army, under Colonel Dunbar, have destroyed all their baggage except two six-pounders and Provisions necessary for their Retreat to Will's Creek."

Robert Orme, aide-de-camp to Braddock, confirmed the disaster. Fisher noted: "The Mob here upon this occasion were very unruly, assembling in great numbers, with an intention of demolishing the Mass House belonging to the Roman Catholics, wherein they were underhand excited and encouraged by some People of Higher Rank. But the peaceable Quakers insisting that the Catholics as well as Christians of other denominations were settled upon the faith of the Constitution and William Penn's Charter, and that the Government were bound to protect them so long at least, as they remained inoffensive and paid dutiful regard to the Establishment; the Magistrates met and with a good deal of difficulty prevailed with the Mob to desist." One suspects that Franklin was among those opposing the mob.[62]

Franklin briefly spoke of Braddock's defeat in the *Autobiography*: "The Enemy however did not take the Advantage of his Army which I apprehended its long Line of March expos'd it to, but let it advance without Interruption till within 9 Miles of the Place; and then when more in a Body, (for it had just pass'd a River where the Front had halted till all were come over) and in a more open Part of the Woods than any it had pass'd, attack'd its advanc'd Guard, by a heavy Fire from behind Trees and Bushes; which was the first Intelligence the General had of an Enemy's being near him." Most historians today believe that both parties were surprised and that the French and Indians had the better ground and made better use of trees and other shelter. Franklin continued that the "Guard being disordered, the General hurried the Troops up to their Assistance, which was done in great Confusion thro' Waggons, Baggage and Cattle; and presently the Fire came upon their Flank; the Officers being on Horseback were more easily distinguish'd, pick'd out as Marks, and fell very fast; and the Soldiers were crowded together in a Huddle, having or hearing no Orders, and standing to be shot at till two thirds of them were killed, and then being seiz'd with a Pannick the whole fled with Precipitation."

Franklin was of course concerned with what happened to the wagoners, horses, and wagons: "The Waggoners took each a Horse out of his Team, and scamper'd; their Example was immediately follow'd by others, so that all the Waggons, Provisions, Artillery and Stores were left to the Enemy." The fleeing British regulars "arriv'd at Dunbar's Camp, and the Pannick they brought with them instantly seiz'd him and all his People. And tho' he had now above 1000 Men, and the Enemy who had beaten Braddock did not at most exceed 400, Indians and French together; instead of Proceeding and endeavouring to recover some of the lost Honour, he order'd all the Stores Ammunition, &c. to be destroy'd, that he might have more Horses to assist his Flight towards the Settlements." Franklin sarcastically reported that Dunbar and his troops hastily retreated, "not thinking himself safe till he arriv'd at Philadelphia, where the Inhabitants could protect him."

Braddock's defeat and Dunbar's flight, wrote Franklin, "gave us Americans the first Suspicion that our exalted Ideas of the Prowess of British Regulars had not been well founded" (A 141). Franklin's comment might seem surprising, since the rivalry between the British regulars and the colonial militia was long-standing and since the Americans generally and Franklin particularly thought that the American militia had proved its mettle in the 1745 battle of Louisbourg. He was, however, writing this part of the *Autobiography* in 1788, when most of his prospective readers would no longer remember the amazing victory at Cape Breton. Many, however, would know of the common English charge in the pre-Revolutionary period and in the Revolutionary War that Americans were cowards (*Life* 2:353).

In 1755, Americans commonly blamed the English defeat on their not knowing how to fight in the woods. William Allen wrote his English bankers on 21 July, "General Braddock with an advanced part of his Army was attacked by one Third of his Number of Indians & French & put to the Rout; one half of his party either killed or wounded; his Military Chest with £25,000 Sterling, all his Artillery, Baggage, Paper &c. lost to the Enemy. And what is scarce to be credited, the Remainder of his Army was in such a pannick, that they retreated after having destroyed all the Ammunition & Provisions, and brought off only with them two Six Pounders of all the fine Train, Sent out of England." He said that "if the Train or Ammunition had been preserved, the Americans were so enraged, that they would of themselves, have raised Sufficient Number of men to dislodge the French men."

But Allen was, of course a proprietary partisan and condemned the Quaker Party: "Could our Assembly be prevailed on to raise the Money, not less than 3000 men would have gone out of this Province; who as they fight for their Country, and are more used to the Woods & have a better notion of the Indian method of Fighting, would behave in another manner than the English Troops have done." Like the now deceased William Shirley, Jr., Allen had a low opinion of Braddock: "The General sent over (who is now dead of his wounds) was quite an improper man, of a mean Capacity, obstinate and self-sufficient, above taking advice, & laughed to scorn all such as represented to him that in our

Wood Country, war was to be carried on in a different manner from that in Europe. Nothing, he thought could stand his Veterans."[63]

Franklin's report in the *Pennsylvania Gazette* of 24 July also stressed that the French and Indians "fought in the Indian Manner from behind Trees, taking Aim, firing and retiring; but the English kept together in a Body, firing in the European manner; and after an Engagement of near three Hours, they were obliged to retreat, with the Loss of Part of the Artillery and the Baggage; a great Number of Officers and Soldiers being killed and wounded." Several weeks later, on 21 August, the *Gazette* reported that the Virginia "Officers and Troops behaved like Men, and dy'd like Soldiers; for out of three Companies that were there that Day, scarce 30 came safe out of the Field; Capt. Peyroney, and all his officers down to a Corporal were killed. Captain Polson's Company (who was himself killed) shared almost as hard a Fate, for only one of his escaped. Capt. Stewart, and his Light Horse, behaved gallantly, having 25 killed out of 29, which he brought into the Field." The British "Regulars," however, were "seized with such Pannick, that their Officers lost all Command of them, and they would gather in a Body 10 or 12 deep, contrary to orders, and then in their Confusion would level, fire and shoot down the Men before them, so that many of those killed and wounded received their Shots from our own Soldiers." Washington was not mentioned, though he had two horses killed under him and his clothes were shot through several times, but he came through the battle unscathed.[64]

According to the road builder James Burd, however, General Braddock, rather than the troops, prevented the British from fighting Indian-style. From Dunbar's camp at Shippensburg, Burd wrote on 25 July: "The Enemy kept behind Trees and Loggs of Wood, and cut down our Troops as fast as they cou'd advance. The Soldiers then insisted much to be allowed to take to the Trees, which the General denied and stormed much, calling them Cowards, and even went so far as to strike them with his own Sword for attempting the Trees; Our Flankers and many of our Soldiers that did take to the Trees were cut off from the Fire of our own Line, as they fired their Platoons wherever they saw a Smok or Fire." George Washington wrote in disgust, "We have been most scandalously beaten by a trifling body of men."[65]

Scarouady agreed with the other American assessments. On 22 August, Conrad Weiser delivered at a council meeting a speech that Scarouady had made to him in private, but Scarouady, Andrew Montour, and other key Indians were present at the council. The Iroquois chief blamed the general for the defeat: "it was the pride and ignorance of that great General that came from England. He is now dead; but he was a bad man when he was alive; he looked upon us as dogs, and would never hear any thing what was said to him. . . . that was the reason that a great many of our Warriors left him & would not be under his Command."

Franklin and the other commissioners had given an Indian treaty belt to Scarouady and his allies at the Carlisle Indian treaty two years before that stressed unity between Pennsylvanians and their Indian allies. Now, in an example of the Iroquois thesis, Scarouady urged the English to unite to fight the French and the French Indians. Like many Americans, he thought that Americans were better frontier fighters than the English. He advised the English "not to give up . . . let us unite our Strength. You are very numerous, and all the English Governors along your Sea Shore can raise men enough; don't let those that come from over the great Seas be concerned any more; they are unfit to fight in the Woods. Let us go ourselves, we that came out of this Ground, We may be assured to conquer the French." But no American troops or even guns for their Indian allies were forthcoming.[66]

Franklin's "full Account of our shameful Defeat on the Ohio" is not extant, but he summarized his thoughts to Collinson on 27 August: "The General presum'd too much, and was too secure. This the Event proves; but it was my opinion from the Time that I saw and convers'd with him" (6:170). Franklin's assessment of Colonel Dunbar was more unkind, for Braddock was evidently a man of courage and of honor. Dunbar, however, was suspect: "He Being at Philadelphia on his Retreat, or rather Flight, I apply'd to him for the Discharge of the Servants of three poor Farmers of Lancaster County that he had inlisted, reminding him of the late General's Orders on that head. He promis'd me, that if the Masters would come to him at Trenton, where he should be in a few Days on his March to New York, he would there deliver their Men to them. They accordingly were at the Expence and Trouble of going to Trenton, and there he refus'd to perform his Promise, to their great Loss and Disappointment" (A 142).

As soon as the defeat was generally known, the owners of the horses and wagons called on Franklin "for the Valuation which I had given Bond to pay." Franklin assured them that "the Money was ready in the Paymaster's Hands, but that Orders for paying it must first be obtained from General Shirley." Franklin had written Shirley and asked for the orders but "he being at a Distance an Answer could not soon be receiv'd." Some owners began suing Franklin. "General Shirley at length reliev'd me from this terrible Situation, by appointing Commissioners to examine the Claims and ordering Payment. They amounted to near twenty Thousand Pound, which to pay would have ruined me" (A 142–43).

DUNBAR FLEES TO PHILADELPHIA

Colonel Dunbar wrote Governor Morris on 16 July that he was on his way to Philadelphia to go into winter (!) quarters. Governor Morris informed the assembly on 28 July that Dunbar was retreating to Philadelphia, leaving the frontier defenseless. The French, "flushed by their late Victory . . . will . . . penetrate deep into the Province, and the People being defenceless, will immediately quit their Habitations." He asked for measures to protect the frontier and said, "you may assure yourselves my best Assistance shall not be wanting." Speaker Norris appointed Franklin and James and John Wright to reply to Governor Morris. They requested the governor to ask Dunbar to place his forces on the frontier, "as there are yet several Months in which the Weather . . . is commonly such as that it is not absolutely necessary Men should go into Quarters." Morris sent the message to Dunbar, adding his appeal to keep the troops west of the Susquehanna River, where they could easily be supplied.[67]

Franklin was perhaps unfair to Colonel Dunbar in the *Autobiography*. Franklin echoed the popular opinion that John Shirley (another son of Governor William Shirley) wrote Governor Morris on 12 August: Dunbar's retreat was thought by many to be a "Dishonour" to the British army.[68] In the *Autobiography* Franklin added that though the governors of Virginia, Maryland, and Pennsylvania asked Dunbar to remain on the frontier, he continued his "hasty March" through the country. Actually, Governor William Shirley, upon whom command devolved upon Braddock's death, ordered Dunbar on 6 August 1755 to go to New York in order to make his army available for the attacks on Niagara and Crown Point. That was, however, four weeks after Braddock's defeat, and by then Dunbar was outside Philadelphia, not on the frontier. On 12 August, Shirley wrote Dunbar again, now saying to attack Fort Duquesne or, if that was impractical, to guard the Pennsylvania frontier or, if that was impractical, to return to New York. At a conference, however, Maryland's governor Horatio Sharpe and all Dunbar's military advisors agreed that a new offense against Fort Duquesne was unlikely to succeed.[69] Franklin surely knew of the orders and the council of war but does not mention them. It was unfair of Franklin to suppress information that tended to exonerate Dunbar's actions, and the posting of troops in Boston in the early 1770s (20:399) no doubt influenced his judgment in the *Autobiography*. Nevertheless, Franklin had cause to be angry. Dunbar had immediately run away from a force less than one-third as large as his and had been responsible for the loss of cannons, wagons, and other supplies left for the enemy when he retreated—and for the subsequent loss of the lives of numerous frontier settlers.

SEVENTEEN

Assembly Crises, Crown Point, Parables, and Glimpses of Deborah, 1755

Vassals must follow *their Lords to the Wars in Defence of their Lands; our Lord Proprietary, though a Subject like ourselves, would send us out to fight for him, while he keeps himself a thousand Leagues remote from Danger! Vassals fight at their Lords Expence, but our Lord would have us defend his Estate at our own Expence! This is not merely Vassalage, it is worse than any Vassalage we have heard of; it is something we have no adequate Name for; it is even more slavish than Slavery itself.*
—*Franklin to Governor Morris, 8 August 1955, 6:138*

THOUGH THE HOUSE HAD ADJOURNED on 28 June until 1 September, Governor Robert Hunter Morris issued writs for the assembly to meet on Wednesday, 23 July, because of Braddock's defeat. Writing from Fort Cumberland, Maryland, Colonel James Innes of Virginia asked for troops. He reported that not "one single Person came here as Militia from either Virginia or Maryland" and swore that "3,000 or 4,000 Men will absolutely carry Victory before us, when 5 Times their Number in a little Time hence will not do."[1] On Thursday morning, 24 July, Governor Morris summoned the assembly to the council chamber, reported Braddock's defeat, and said: "There are Men enough in this Province to protect it against any Force the French can bring, and Numbers of them are willing and desirous to defend their Country . . . but they have neither Arms, Ammunition, nor Discipline." He asked for both provisions and for a militia and cautioned the assembly not to revive "any Matters that have been in Dispute" over previous money bills. Reflecting Innes's plea, Morris said that "If something very effectual be not done at this Time for the Safety and Security of the Province, the Enemy . . . will strengthen themselves in such a Manner that it will be next to impossible for us to remove them."[2]

Despite his message, Morris knew that he must refuse any bill that taxed the proprietors or that gave control to the assembly over any money that they raised. He proposed on Friday, 25 July, to the council to raise £20,000 or £30,000 by private subscription "for the King's Service." In consultation with William

Allen, however, "so many Difficulties and Objections were made" that the proposal was dropped. Naturally Franklin, the most active House member on defense, was extraordinarily busy. Focusing on Franklin's activities in the assembly, Joseph S. Foster summarized: "from 28 July to 25 September 1755, Franklin was appointed to 11 committees, all of which dealt with the crisis."[3]

THE SUPPLY BILL FOR £50,000

In unusually quick time, the assembly decided at the opening of the session to raise £50,000 for the king's use. The next morning, 26 July, the House resolved itself into a committee of the whole "to consider of the Ways and Means" to raise the money. By 29 July, the House was ready to act: "Resolved, That a Tax be now laid upon all Estates, Real and Personal, within this Province." This was a different way to raise money. Not since 1717 had there been a general land tax in Pennsylvania, but that tax had exempted the proprietor and the lieutenant governor.[4] A tax was harder on the people than enacting an excise bill or a paper money bill—but governors had recently rejected all such bills. In the emergency, the assembly was willing to tax the people, but it was unwilling to exclude the proprietors from taxation. The bill specified that it would tax "all" estates. Franklin served on the committee to draft the bill, which presented it on Thursday, 31 July.[5]

The preamble to the £50,000 tax bill stressed that the assembly had already given money "for purchasing Provisions for the King's Forces, erecting and maintaining Posts, clearing Roads, maintaining of Indians, and other heavy Charges," but that now the treasury was "exhausted." Since Thomas and Richard Penn, "our Proprietaries, may, and we presume will, consider it their highest Duty and Interest to contribute chearfully their Part for the common Good of themselves and all other . . . Inhabitants of this Province," the assembly enacted a tax on all the estates, real and personal, within the province "(the estates of the Honourable Thomas Penn and Richard Penn . . . not excepted)," twelve pence for every pound, "clear Value of the said Estate, yearly, for the Space of Two Years."[6] Since persons whose estates (real and personal) were worth less than thirty pounds had not been taxed in previous tax bills, the assembly added that every single freeman age twenty-one who "hath[7] been out of his Apprenticeship or Servitude for the Space of Six Months" shall be taxed twenty shillings. The law enjoined the commissioners and assessors to take an oath that the "Rates and Sums" of the tax would be "equally assessed" without favor or prejudice. Any commissioner who refused the duty must pay twenty pounds and any assessor, ten pounds, to the provincial treasurer.

Aiming especially at the proprietors, the bill also taxed unimproved lands: "And forasmuch as large Tracts of valuable Land have been located and held in this Province without Intention of Improvement, but merely in Expectation of receiving hereafter higher Prices for private Advantage, by Means whereof those Lands remain uncultivated, and great Numbers of People have been necessitated to leave this Province and settle in other Colonies," therefore "it is thought reasonable on this Occasion" to tax "such unlocated and unimproved lands . . . according to their Situation and Value at any Prices not exceeding *Fifteen Pounds*, nor under *Five Pounds*, for every Hundred Acres."[8] Since many persons simply settled on land without legally owning it or paying rent on it, these persons must "give a true Account of the particular" lands they claim, "both clear and Wood-land," and pay taxes "just as the Freeholders do." Further, the money raised would be at the disposal of a committee including Franklin, "with the Consent and Approbation of the Governor of this Province, or with the Consent and Approbation of the Commander in Chief of the King's Forces in America."[9] On Saturday, 2 August, the assembly approved the £50,000 bill and sent it to the governor.

The following Tuesday, 5 August, Governor Morris proposed several amendments to the bill, including exempting "the Proprietary Estate from contributing any Thing towards the Sum to be raised for the common Security of the Province." The same day, Franklin and others replied that taxing the proprietors' estates seemed "so perfectly equitable and just" that the assembly was surprised. The committee entreated the governor to "acquaint us explicitly" whether he was "restricted" by instructions from doing so (6:130). The next day Morris finally disclosed his instructions: "in the Proprietary Commission appointing me to this Government, there is a Proviso that nothing therein contained shall extend, or be construed to extend, to give me any Power to do or consent to any Act whereby the Estate or Property of the Proprietaries may be hurt or incumbered." Speaker Norris ordered that Franklin and others reply.[10] Two days later, 8 August, Franklin's long message to the governor questioned his motives and the constitutionality of the governor's amendments. Since Morris had claimed that it was his duty to do nothing to hurt or encumber the proprietors' estates, Franklin replied: "As Representatives of the People we think it as much our bounden Duty to do nothing that may *hurt or encumber* the Estates of our Constituents . . . yet we never conceived that giving a Part to save the Whole, and not only to save it, but to render it of double or treble Value (which must the Case with Proprietary Lands) could properly be called *hurting* or *encumbering* an Estate" (6:131–32).

Franklin claimed that taking a bond from the governor for the performance of his secret instructions violated section 4 of the Royal Charter of 1682, which stipulated that the governors had the power to make laws "according to their best Discretion" (6:134), a claim that Franklin had made earlier (3 September 1753; 5:26). Franklin cited the council meeting held on 23 May 1704 by "his son and heir [William Penn, Jr.], [by] the learned Judge [Roger] Mompesson, and several others distinguished for their Ability." They all affirmed and signed the opinion.[11]

To the governor's argument that the proprietors could not be taxed by the assembly, Franklin replied, "we do not propose to tax the Proprietary as Governor, but as a Fellow Subject, a Landholder and Possessor of an Estate in Pennsylvania; an Estate that will be more benefited by a proper Application of the Tax, than any other Estate in the Province" (6:135). Franklin excoriated Thomas Penn: "How odious must it be to a sensible manly People, to find *him* who ought to be their Father and Protector, taking Advantage of Publick Calamity and Distress, and their Tenderness for their bleeding Country, to force down their Throats Laws of Imposition, abhorrent to common Justice and Reason!"

From Penn, Franklin turned to Governor Morris: "Why will the Governor make himself the hateful Instrument of reducing a free People to the abject State of Vassalage; of depriving us of those Liberties, which have given Reputation to our Country throughout the World, and drawn Inhabitants from the remotest Parts of Europe to enjoy them?" Franklin turned to what had become, since his 22 December 1754 letter to Governor Shirley, a favorite theme—Americans had created the civilization that they enjoyed and ought to be rewarded for it: "Liberties not only granted us of Favour, but of Right; Liberties which in Effect we have bought and paid for, since we have not only performed the Conditions on which they were granted, but have actually given higher Prices for our Lands on their Account; so that the Proprietary Family have been double paid for them, in the Value of the Lands, and in the Increase of Rents with Increase of People." Franklin concluded by conceding that the message contained "some Appearance of Warmth" (6:138). The assembly's message appeared in the *Pennsylvania Gazette* on 14 August.[12]

Addressing the assembly on Tuesday, 12 August, Governor Morris defended his actions and the proprietors, and claimed that he should be the one to determine how the tax money was spent. He objected "to be thus injuriously treated, and represented as the hateful Instrument of reducing a Free people to the abject State of Vassalage."[13] Franklin printed his speech in the same *Pennsylvania Gazette*, 14 August, that carried the original charge. William Plumsted, William Allen, and other Proprietary Party members knew that the assembly would not agree to the governor's demands and offered £500 on Saturday, 16 August, if the assembly would pass the £50,000 bill exempting the proprietors' lands (6:141; cf. 240, 240n8). The proprietarians took the £500 figure from Franklin's speech of 8 August where he had suggested that the proprietor's tax might not be "a Hundredth Part" of the £50,000 tax (6:136). Affronted that the proprietors would not contribute toward defense in the emergency, the assembly replied that it would be improper to accept such a proposal concerning unevaluated estates. Further, the representatives probably believed that the proprietors' proportional tax would be larger than £500. But the assembly was also showing its pique—while frontier settlers were being killed.

On Friday, 19 August, the assembly approved Franklin's reply. He quoted Morris's argument with his statement that Pennsylvanians had the "Rights of the Freeborn Subjects of England" but claimed that Morris had violated those rights. The money bills of an assembly must be "accepted as they are tendered, if at all accepted, and that without any Proposal of Amendments" (6:141). Franklin denied that Pennsylvanians and their representatives were, as the governor suggested, "ungovernable or rebellious." In a direct insult, Franklin wrote that Morris could not govern: "he has not that *Spirit of Government*, that *Skill*, and those *Abilities*" to qualify as a governor (6:150). Making a rare appeal to natural rights,[14] Franklin wrote: "The Right of disposing of our own Money, we think is a natural Right, and we have enjoyed it ever since the Settlement of the Province, and constantly been in the Exercise of it in every Instance, expect perhaps in a few, where, on extraordinary Occasions, we have chosen to make special Appropriation by a particular Law. . . . This natural and legal Right, as we contend it is, was never denied us, or called in Question, as we know of, but by our present proprietaries" (6:154–55).

Turning the knife in Morris at his objection to his being "injuriously treated and represented as the hateful Instrument of reducing a free People to the abject State of Vassalage," Franklin charged that the proprietors and Morris, acting for them, claimed privileges exceeding those of feudal lords: "Vassals must *follow* their Lords to the Wars in Defence of their Lands; our Lord Proprietary, though a Subject like ourselves, would *send* us out to fight *for* him, while he keeps himself a thousand Leagues remote from Danger! Vassals fight at their Lords Expence, but our Lord would have us defend his Estate at our own Expence! This is not merely Vassalage, it is worse than any Vassalage we have heard of; it is something we have no adequate Name for; it is even more slavish than Slavery itself." From bashing Thomas Penn, Franklin turned to Morris: "if the Governor can accomplish it, he *will* be deemed the hateful Instrument (how much soever he is disgusted with the Epithet) as long as History can preserve the Memory of his Administration" (6:161–62). Franklin published this assembly message in the *Pennsylvania Gazette* on 21 August.[15]

On some afternoon following a bitter exchange with Franklin and the assembly, Morris encountered Franklin in the street.

> Franklin, says he, you must go home with me and spend the Evening. I am to have some Company that you will like; and taking me by the Arm he led me to his House. In gay Conversation over our Wine after Supper he told us Jokingly that he much admir'd the Idea of Sancho Panza, who when it was propos'd to give him a Government, requested it might be a Government of *Blacks*, as then, if he could not agree with his People he might sell them. One of his Friends who sat next me, says, Franklin, why do you continue to side with these damn'd Quakers? had not you better sell them? the Proprietor would give you a good Price for them. The Governor, says I, has not yet *black'd* them enough. He had indeed labour'd hard to blacken the Assembly in all his Messages, but they wip'd off his Colouring as fast as he laid it on, and plac'd it in return thick upon his own Face. (A 133–34)

Morris proposed on 16 August that if the assembly passed a paper money bill, he would approve it, providing that the term for repayment was limited to

As to myfelf, I think it neceffary to fay, that for the Difpatch
of the publick Bufinefs at this critical Conjuncture, when every
Heart fhould be concerned for the publick Service, I ftudioufly a-
voided every Thing that could renew the Difputes that fubfifted
between us, and earneftly recommended the fame Temper of Mind
to you, and cannot therefore but be exceedingly furprized in Return to be thus injurioufly treated, and reprefented as the hateful
Inftrument of reducing a free People to the abject State of Vaffalage. What Grounds have you, Gentlemen, for this heavy Charge?
What Laws of Impofition abhorrent to common Juftice and common Reafon, have I attempted to force down your Throats?
Have I propofed any Thing to you, during the Courfe of my fhort

Figure 41a. Governor Robert Hunter Morris protests that he is not a "hateful Instrument" trying to reduce "a free People to the abject State of Vassalage." Pennsylvania
Gazette, 14 August 1755. Despite the slaughter of Pennsylvanians by the French and hostile
Indians on the frontier, Governor Robert Hunter Morris abided by Thomas Penn's secret
instructions not to pass any money bill that taxed his estates or that did not put the
governor in control of the expenditures. Thus Morris vetoed every assembly bill to raise
money to defend the frontier. On behalf of the assembly, Franklin charged on 8 August
1755 that the governor was making himself "the hateful Instrument of reducing a free
People to the abject State of Vassalage." In a message of 12 August, Morris complained to
the assembly that he was not a "hateful Instrument." The messages of 8 and 12 August
both appeared in the 14 August Gazette. Courtesy, Library Company of Philadelphia.

five years. The House asked on the morning of 21 August if he would assent to
the £50,000 bill; he replied that the question surprised him, and he would not.
Franklin and the committee pointed out that on 14 August Morris wrote that
he could not then "pass our Bill without his Amendments, whatever he might
be when he heard our Arguments." From that phrase, the assembly believed that
he might, after hearing their arguments, assent to the assembly's £50,000 bill.
Morris therefore had no reason for his surprise. The House said that it had no
funds to sink so great a sum as £50,000 in five years "without . . . an equitable
Tax" to which he would not agree. In disgust, Franklin said that the assembly
did not have "the least Reason to think he was sincerely desirous of having any
Thing done for the Defense of the Province" (6:166).

Indirectly attacking Morris and Thomas Penn, Franklin published in the
same 21 August Gazette a letter dated from Albany in which the author proposed
that the New York legislature release the frontier people from paying their quitrents for "some Years" in view of their distress. The news item reminded Pennsylvanians of the avariciousness with which Penn collected his quitrents. When
Thomas Penn read it, he suspected that Franklin made up the letter. Penn wrote
Richard Peters on 25 October that Franklin had "published what he calls a Letter
from Albany in his paper of the 21st of August in which it is proposed to the

The Governor thinks himfelf injurioufly treated by our Requeft, "that he would not make himfelf the hateful Inftrument of re- "ducing a free People to the abject State of Vaffalage," and afks, "What Grounds have you, Gentlemen, for this heavy Charge? "What Laws of Impofition abhorrent to common Juftice and com- "mon Reafon have I attempted to force down your Throats?" &c. A Law to tax the People of *Pennfylvania* to defend the Proprietary Eftate, and to exempt the Proprietary Eftate from bearing any Part of the Tax, is, may it pleafe the Governor, a Law *abborrent to common Juftice, common Reafon*, and *common Senfe*. This is a Law of Impofition that the Governor would force down our Throats, by taking Ad- vantage of the Diftrefs of our Country, the Defence of which he will not fuffer us to provide for, unlefs we will comply with it.--- Our Souls rife againft it. We cannot fwallow it.---What other Inftance would the Governor defire us to give, of his endeavouring to reduce us to a State of Vaffalage? He calls upon us for an In- ftance. We give him the very Law in Queftion, as the ftrongeft of Inftances. Vaffals muft *follow* their Lords to the Wars in Defence of their Lands; our Lord Proprietary, though a Subject like our- felves, would *fend* us out to fight *for* him, while he keeps himfelf a thoufand Leagues remote from Danger! Vaffals fight at their Lords Expence, but our Lord would have us defend his Eftate at our own Expence! This is not merely Vaffalage, it is worfe than any Vaf- falage we have heard of; it is fomething we have no adequate Name for; it is even more flavifh than Slavery itfelf. And if the Go- vernor can accomplifh it, he *will be* deemed the hateful Inftrument (how much foever he is difgufted with the Epithet) as long as Hiftory can preferve the Memory of his Adminiftration.

Figure 41b. Franklin compounds the earlier attack on Governor Morris, Pennsylvania Gazette, 21 August 1755. Franklin redoubled his charge on 19 August: Morris (and Thomas Penn) demanded a vassalage "worse than any Vassalage we have heard of . . . it is even more slavish than Slavery itself." Two days later, Franklin printed the message in the 21 August Gazette and reprinted both the 8 and 19 August charges in the House's Votes and Proceedings . . . for 1754–1755, which was for sale by 25 December 1755. Courtesy, Library Company of Philadelphia.

Assembly of New York to ease the people of their Quit rents for some years."[16] Like Penn, I also think that Franklin composed the "Letter from Albany."

On 29 July 1755, Governor Morris had presented a scheme to grant two hundred acres of trans-Appalachian land to every soldier who enlisted, and more to every officer, without any purchase money and with an exemption from quitrent for the following fifteen years; the condition was that the land would be settled upon within three years after the removal of the French.[17] Morris had Richard Peters consult Franklin about it before making the proposal, and Franklin rejected it, giving the reasons listed below. Morris nevertheless introduced it, writing Thomas Penn on 31 July: "This offer, which I do not expect will be accepted from what pass'd with Mr. Franklin previous to the making it, will, I think, put" the assembly "in the wrong at home."[18] When Morris presented his proposal to the legislature, Speaker Norris appointed Franklin to the committee to reply. Franklin had already drafted it. The assembly adjourned for half an hour, Franklin presented his draft to the committee, which quickly accepted it, and the assembly reconvened.

For the assembly, Franklin ridiculed the governor's offer on 8 August: "We are sorry . . . that the Proposal is made in such Terms as that it may be fully complied with, and yet nothing in Reality be granted. First, because Lands West of the Allegheny Mountains differ greatly in their Quality, and though some are exceeding good, there are many Hundred Thousand Acres that are not worth accepting; and *good Land* is not so much as mentioned in the Proposal." Second, the best lands east of the mountains are not better than those in Virginia, which are available "without Purchase Money, at Two Shillings Sterling Quitrent, and none to be paid for Fifteen Years." But in Pennsylvania, the quitrent was 4s, 6d sterling. Therefore "an Offer even of the best Lands" in western Pennsylvania "would be neither more nor less than this, That for the Encouragement of such as shall, with the Hazard of their Lives, recover the Proprietaries Country from the Enemy, he will graciously sell them a Part of the Lands so recovered, at twice the Price demanded by his Neighbour" (6:133). Thomas Penn wrote Morris on 4 October that he should not have consulted Franklin beforehand "without you could have followed his advice," and commented that Franklin "has in resentment made the same observation that he did to Mr. Peters."[19]

When it appeared that the army was going into winter quarters in Philadelphia, Speaker Norris appointed Franklin on 11 August to a committee to draft a bill "for providing Quarters for such of his Majesty's Officers and Soldiers as may arrive in this Province." In the act, passed 15 August, Franklin cleverly adopted sections of a British act that regulated the quartering of soldiers in England, hoping that since it had been a British law, it would be acceptable in the colonies. To make it obvious that it followed the British act, Franklin announced in the title that it simply adopted the British act. But the act said that no one could "presume to place, quarter or billet any soldier" upon any British person "without his consent." Franklin also made the act expire in a year. Franklin's intent, of course, was to prevent Colonel Dunbar from billeting his soldiers in Philadelphia for the winter. Governor Morris approved the act, no doubt because it copied a British act. In London, however, the British authorities found that the "tendency" of the act "must unavoidably be to Cramp the Publick Service, and obstruct the defence of the Province." The English act was made in times of peace "when soldiers were kept up without Consent of Parliament" during Charles I's and Charles II's time, but it was inappropriate in the colonies during a "time of War." The Privy Council disallowed it on 7

July 1756.[20] Though the act was about to expire anyway, the repeal meant that the governor would reject any future similar act.

In a brief message of 16 August, Governor Morris asked the assembly to create a law to prevent supplies from reaching the French at Louisbourg. Since he knew that the assembly had passed and he had approved such a law at the last assembly, the message was meant to suggest to the British authorities that Philadelphians were supplying Louisbourg. Franklin and another member replied on 20 August, pointing out that the assembly had passed such a bill and the governor had approved it at its last session (16 and 18 June). Since the governor had not "pointed out . . . any Defect in that Act" and none has occurred to the members of the assembly, "we cannot at present think what" further action should be taken (6:163–64). Morris wrote other governors that if the assembly did nothing, he would "lay an embargo on Philadelphia and New Castle." He did so but predicted that it would be ignored. Morris wrote New York's governor James DeLancey that "we have got to such . . . disobedience in this Province, that Orders of the Government have very little weight" (6:164n1).

On the last day of the session, 22 August, replying to petitions from the frontier townships for arms, the assembly appointed Franklin and five others to a committee to spend up to £1,000 "(with the Consent and Approbation of the Governor of this Province) for the King's Use." When Morris was out of town and frontiersmen came in for weapons, Franklin, who acted as the executive of the committee, distributed them. Despite the emergency and the immediate necessity for action, Morris charged that Franklin's action infringed "the rights of Government."[21]

Though Governor Morris refused to pass a tax to pay for a militia, he repeatedly demanded the assembly enact a militia bill.[22] The record does not say which members of the House were appointed to draft the reply to Morris, but they no doubt included Franklin, not only because all other major writing committees of the assembly of 1754–55 did but also because the result was a message so similar to his earlier ones.[23] In the last address of the session, 22 August, the assembly said that since Morris refused the bill for granting £50,000 unless the proprietors' holdings were not taxed, it would merely be a waste of time to send Morris a militia bill. There was no money to support a militia. Franklin and the committee said that "we now wait the Determination of our Superiors what Powers he has, or ought to have, as our Governor under the Royal and Provincial Charters, and what exclusive Rights our Proprietaries may be justly intitled to in the Laying and Levying of Taxes for the common Security and Defence of their Estates with all the other Estates within this Province."[24] The reference to the "Royal and Provincial Charters" especially alluded to Franklin's citations on 8 August both to section 4 of the Charter of Pennsylvania and to the commission of Lieutenant Governor John Evans in 1704 (6:133–35).

When it sent the message to Morris, the House also said that it intended to adjourn to 15 September. Even before reading the assembly's message, Morris threatened that "if he found that the House had not given him a satisfactory Answer to his Messages relating to a Militia, he should call them again immediately."[25] The House promptly adjourned.

Overview of Pennsylvania Politics, 1755

Franklin wrote Peter Collinson on 27 August 1755 his summary thoughts on the recent politics, including a defense of the Quaker majority (but not the pacifists) in the assembly. Since at least 1741, the Proprietary Party wanted the English authorities to disenfranchise Pennsylvania's Quakers. Franklin confided to Collinson: "To me, it seems that if *Quakerism* (as to the Matter of Defence) be excluded the House, there is no Necessity to exclude *Quakers*, who in other respects make good and useful Members." He said that Quakers had now shown that they would give money to defend the lives of Pennsylvanians. "I know the Quakers now think it their Duty, when chosen, to consider themselves as Representatives of the *Whole People*, and not of their own Sect only; . . . and therefore, tho' they can neither bear Arms themselves, nor compel others to do it, yet very lately, when our Frontier Inhabitants, who are chiefly Presbyterians or Churchmen, thought themselves in Danger, and the Poor among them were unable to provide Arms, and petitioned the House, a Sum was voted for that purpose, and put into the Hands of a Committee to procure and supply them."

Franklin knew that Morris and perhaps other proprietary partisans were willing to sacrifice the interests of Pennsylvania and the lives of the frontier citizens to discredit the Quakers. He reported that since he "had a principal Share" in securing the "late generous Grants," the governor and friends "are angry" at the success of his scheme, because it denied the Proprietary Party the possibility "of a fresh Accusation against Quakers." Governor Morris had behaved childishly, wrote Franklin, in order to anger the House and make the members unwilling to vote funds to prosecute the war. Had his ploy succeeded, Morris could have claimed that the members had not voted funds because they were Quakers; subsequently he could have demanded that Quakers be forbidden to be assemblymen (6:170–71). William Smith attempted to disenfranchise the Quakers just months before in his *Brief State* (6:52n5).

Richard Hockley, receiver-general of Pennsylvania, had written Thomas Penn on 22 March 1755 that Franklin "was always of a Republican disposition and levelling Principles and has been the chief instrument in everything that has been illnaturdley said or wrote." Hockley again blasted Franklin on 25 August, reporting that Franklin's "crony" Tench Francis, formerly the attorney general, said that "the Proprietors ought to be burn'd in Effegy in every square in Town." Though the two were "men of parts," they were "rottenhearted" and had "poison'd the people Against your Family to a great degree and if they had their Deserts should suffer as Incendiarys."[26]

To the same effect, Governor Morris wrote Secretary of State Thomas Robinson on 28 August that the assembly messages are "intended to heat and inflame the minds of the people and to set them against the Government . . . these Messages will make them Jealous of the Government they live under, backward in assisting it, and more inclinable to submit to the French, & accept of the offers they will doubtless make them." Morris attempted to discredit Franklin: "I think it my duty to observe to You that Mr. Benjamin Franklin, who holds an office of profit under the General post office, is at the head of these extraordinary measures taken by the Assembly, writes their Messages and directs their motions."[27] This was the first of the numerous times to 1774 that persons suggested that Franklin should be removed as joint deputy postmaster general of America because he was not supporting the British authorities. (These persons were presumably ignorant of the fact that the position of joint deputy postmaster general for North America had not yet paid Franklin and Hunter anything, but that the postal service was, in fact, becoming ever more indebted to them.) Morris also wrote Governor DeLancey that the principles of Franklin's messages were "Republican, and they are calculated to heat & inflame the people, to infuse into the minds of the Germans and others—that their rights & Liberties are invaded, & that they are to be made slaves & vassells."[28]

Alarmed by the July act of assembly that attempted to raise £50,000 to defend the province (the first such tax since 1711), pacifist Friends were especially concerned because the assembly appointed members to oversee the expenditure, rather than simply turning it over to the government. Thus, Friends such as Isaac Norris II and Joseph Fox would be directing the war effort. Though that position was consistent with the major Quaker tradition (referring to Matthew. 22:21: "Render unto Caesar the things which are Caesar's; and unto God the things that are God's"), the Pennsylvania Quakers were becoming more pacifist. The Philadelphia Quaker Yearly Meeting, held at the end of September and early October, took up the military defense of Pennsylvania. The best-known conscientious Quaker of the day, John Woolman, described the debate over pacifism as "the most weighty that ever I was at." Though Friends disagreed among themselves, the Yearly Meeting appointed a committee to consider the question of paying taxes to support war. After the tax was passed, the pacifists within the committee issued a pamphlet on 16 December 1755 that urged members not to pay taxes for military supplies, *An Epistle of Tender Love and Caution to Friends in Pennsylvania*. The Philadelphia Yearly Meeting of 1755 had also appointed a standing committee called the Philadelphia Meeting for Sufferings. A political action committee, it attempted to act "in all Cases, where the Reputation & Interest of Truth and our Religious Society are concerned."[29]

THE 1754–55 ASSEMBLY'S SEVENTH SESSION, 15–30 SEPTEMBER

Though Governor Morris and the assembly knew that neither would concede and that almost no business would be done, a few new matters called for attention. A petition of 19 September complained that Colonel Dunbar was enlisting servants and apprentices, thus depriving the masters of indentured servants

whose time had been purchased. The petitioners had applied to the commanding officers without success. The House asked Franklin "to endeavor to prevail
upon Colonel Dunbar to discharge the said Servants and Apprentices, or take
such other Steps for that Purpose as the said Member shall judge necessary."[30]
Franklin had already written Governor William Shirley concerning the enlistments (doubtlessly reminding him of General Braddock's promise). He replied
on 17 September, in a letter that Franklin had not yet received, that he had
instructed Colonel Dunbar to return such enlisted men to their owners (6:190).

In addition to minor committees, Franklin served on one answering Governor Morris's recriminations of 24 August, where he argued that the assembly's
claim to "a natural exclusive Right to the Disposition of publick money . . . is
against reason." Morris charged the assembly with wanting "to set up a Democracy at once." Franklin replied on 29 September, pointing out Morris's inconsis-
tences and his final admission to following "*private Instructions*," which had
never been "mentioned before; of which none can judge till he shall think fit to
produce them." Franklin claimed that Morris's messages agreed with those of
"a late famous Libel, intituled, *A Brief State of Pennsylvania*." Franklin still believed that Morris, rather than Provost William Smith, had written the tract,
but since both Morris and Smith advocated Thomas Penn's positions, it is not
surprising that Franklin initially attributed it to Morris.[31]

Franklin again used the natural rights philosophy to justify the people's "exclusive Right" to dispose of the money they raised. Echoing his 8 August ridicule
of Morris's offer of western lands to those who served in the militia, while
simultaneously foreshadowing his later arguments in favor of a royal rather than
a proprietary government, he wrote: "That the Proprietaries are intitled to the
Character of the *best Landlords*, we can by no Means presume to say with the
Governor; since his Majesty's Lands are granted without Purchase Money, on
Half the Quitrent, and the Quitrents are applied to the Support of Government
and Defence of the Country: We cannot therefore but be of Opinion, that the
King is a much better Landlord." Franklin also condemned the proprietors'
claim to "that invidious and odious Distinction, of being exempted from the
common Burdens of their Fellow Subjects" (6:197, 199).

As the former clerk of the House and the printer of its *Votes and Proceedings*
and its *Laws*, record-keeper Franklin knew the history of the assembly's debates
better than anyone. "That there is a Design in the Proprietaries and Governor,
to abridge the People here of their Privileges, is no Secret. The Proprietaries
have avowed it in their Letter to the House, dated London, March 2, 1741[/2].[32]
The Doctrine that it is necessary, is publickly taught" in their *Brief State*. Further, "the Governor himself has told us, that we have more" privileges "than is
suitable for a dependent Colony." Such statements "do not . . . alienate their
[Pennsylvanians'] Affections from *his Majesty's* Government, though they may
from *the Proprietaries*." The assembly's "Confidence in the Crown" is as great
as ever; but when the proprietors' governors "are continually abusing and cal-

umniating the People," the people must lose all confidence in the governors (6:203). Governor Morris says that "we stir up his Majesty's Subjects against his Majesty's Government, forgetting all Duty to our Sovereign," but if we reply that the difficulties he meets with "are not owing to those Causes, which indeed have no Existence, but to his own Want of Skill and Abilities for his Station, he takes it extreamly amiss, and says, 'we forget all Decency to those in Authority.' We, however, think there is likewise 'some Decency due to the Assembly, as a Part of the Government'" (6:203).

Through Franklin's and Josiah Quincy's efforts, the Pennsylvania Assembly had voted £10,000 for the Crown Point expedition in April. On 8 September 1755, provincial militia and Indian allies under William Johnson attacked a French stronghold on Lake George. The English won the hard-fought battle and took the French commander prisoner, but Johnson was wounded and did not immediately go on to Crown Point. Franklin and others heard that the colonial militia needed further supplies. Governor Morris, however, did not present the assembly with that information, and the assembly asked him on 17 September "if any Application had been made to him by the Eastern Governments for a farther Supply of Provisions." The next day Morris replied that he had received a letter from Governor Spencer Phips of Massachusetts requesting more supplies for the additional men raised for the Crown Point expedition and asked for more funds. The assembly immediately requested that the letter be sent to it. Morris said that he had orders from Sir Thomas Robinson, secretary of state, that Morris's messages to the assembly should suffice to do business.[33] (Perhaps Robinson did so order, but I doubt it.) Without the letter, the House refused to act.

The House said that "great Inaccuracies and Want of Exactness" were so frequent in Governor Morris's messages that it could not act upon them without "the Papers therein referred to." Therefore it had taken no action. Thomas Hutchinson of Massachusetts, however, had written to Franklin, urging an immediate supply of the provisions that Massachusetts had requested of Pennsylvania. Franklin evidently talked to Speaker Norris about it and suggested the assembly endorse a private loan—which would be repaid by the next assembly. In the session's penultimate day, 29 September, Speaker Norris called upon Franklin, who presented Hutchinson's letter. The House promptly resolved that a voluntary subscription of up to £10,000 should be raised for the troops at Crown Point and that the next assembly would repay the funds. Norris, Franklin, and whoever else was involved in advancing the money showed an almost surprising trust in the voters to elect an assembly that would repay them. It happened. The accounts reported on 3 December 1755 that Speaker Norris had advanced £179.3.3 and Franklin had advanced £80.2.2½ for the Crown Point expedition, which, along with other disbursements, the House agreed to pay. Despite the financial assistance, no further advance toward Crown Point was attempted because of the replacement of Governor Shirley as commander in chief and the consequent refusal of the American militia to serve under British, rather than American, officers.[34]

FRANKLIN'S STRATEGY

Knowing that Governor Morris was trying to put the Pennsylvania Quakers in as bad a light as possible in order to have them disenfranchised, the publicity expert Franklin countered him. At the end of the assembly's sixth session on 22 August, Franklin, as a member of the assembly's committee of correspondence, wrote the assembly's agent Richard Partridge an account of the £50,000 supply bill. Franklin emphasized the assembly's efforts to pass previous bills to support the military in America and indirectly castigated the subterfuges the Proprietary Party had made to defeat all supply bills. Franklin listed the ways that the assembly's £50,000 bill attempted to avoid all the governor's past supposed reasons for not passing a money bill: to avoid all former disputes about suspending clauses, the members chose to make no paper money. To avoid all disputes about control of the funds raised, the members agreed "to put it into the hands of commissioners, to be disposed of by them for the king's service, *with the consent and approbation of the governor,* or of the commander in chief of the king's forces in *N. America.*" Since collecting the tax would require some time, the assembly "impowered the commissioners to draw orders on the treasurer, (not exceeding the sum granted) payable out of the tax as it should come into his hands." To secure the money quickly and to give the creditor compensation, the bills of credit were to bear an interest rate of 5 percent for no more than two years. Lest issuing bills of credit be considered as making money, the act said that they were not legal tender. Finally, to avoid all possibility of violating an act of Parliament made for other colonies whereby money bills must be sunk within five years, the assembly voted to have these bills of credit sunk in two years.

Partridge had Franklin's account read in the Board of Trade on 6 December and printed in the *Gentleman's Magazine* for November 1755.[35] Although failed bills were rarely printed, Franklin (who had been appointed with Joseph Fox on 15 October 1754 as a committee to revise the minutes) made sure that this bill, with Governor Morris's proposed changes exempting the proprietors from paying any significant money for the defense of their large holdings, appeared in the legislature's *Votes and Proceedings* for 1754–55.[36] During September, William Smith wrote Thomas Penn about Franklin: "Though I flatter myself with having as much of his [Franklin's] Confidence as he gives any Body, I can neither learn nor conjecture what he means. . . . he always did and still does treat me as his Bosom-friend" (6:211). Franklin was no doubt beginning to suspect Smith. For his part, Smith probably thought that Franklin was, like him, committed to the main chance. Franklin, however, meant what he wrote for the assembly.

At the end of the assembly of 1754–55, the frontier was defenseless and rapidly being abandoned. The French and their Indian allies were killing the frontier settlers, who demanded help that neither the governor nor the assembly was willing to give. On at least two occasions, frontiersmen carted bodies of the killed and scalped settlers to Philadelphia and put them on the state house steps.[37] Nevertheless, in the election on 1 and 2 October, the voters elected the same Quaker Party members by a large majority. Two conscientious Quakers from frontier areas (Moses Starr of Berks County and Peter Worrall of Lancaster County)[38] chose not to run again, but most frontier delegates had been and were for defense. But because of the number of assemblymen assigned to different counties, the Quakers controlled the assembly. The three older counties where Quakers predominated each had eight representatives, for a total of twenty-four members, whereas the newer, frontier counties with primarily German and Scots-Irish populations had a total of ten.

FRANKLIN'S PARABLES

Franklin did not date his best-known parables or publish them himself, and their times of composition are unknown. Some evidence, however, suggests that he had the "Parable against Persecution" with him during his trip to New England in the fall and winter of 1754–55. Lacking specific dates, I arbitrarily discuss the two parables here. Franklin himself said that the "Parable on Brotherly Love" was written at about the same time as the "Parable against Persecution."

"A Parable against Persecution"

Franklin's "Parable against Persecution" is among his best-known hoaxes. He wrote his friend Benjamin Vaughan about it on 2 November 1789, confessing that it gave him a good deal of amusement when he recited it "by heart" out of a Bible. In conversation, Franklin would sometimes allude to the "Chapter" in Genesis that contained the moral against persecution. He would then call for a Bible and read the chapter aloud. Actually, he had composed and memorized the supposed "Chapter." Then he and his acquaintances would sometimes discuss its moral. He wrote Vaughan that the remarks that the "Scripturians" made on it were "sometimes very diverting" (S 10:53). Since eighteenth-century manuscript and printed copies in English and in French survive, we know the hoax was popular. Franklin and others testify that it was successful, fooling most people who heard it into thinking that it actually was from Genesis in the King James Bible.

The earliest known reference to "A Parable against Persecution" is in a retained draft of a letter by Ezra Stiles dated 2 August 1755. The editors of the *Papers of Benjamin Franklin* speculate that Franklin may have given it to Stiles while visiting New Haven in early February 1755 or may have sent it to him after returning to Philadelphia (6:115–16). Franklin and his joint deputy postmaster general, William Hunter, left Philadelphia in September 1754 and were in Boston until 31 December 1754. On his way back to Philadelphia, Franklin visited President Thomas Clap of Yale in New Haven. Since Franklin and Hunter probably rode through New Haven on the way to Boston in late September, it is also possible that Franklin gave it to Stiles then. I doubt that he would simply have sent the piece to Stiles but hypothesize that Franklin read it to him either in September 1754 or in January 1755. I also suspect that Stiles, who was a brilliant minister, smoked the hoax as Franklin recited it.

Later, Franklin read the "Chapter" from Genesis while visiting Scotland in the summer of 1759 and at least two Scots friends asked for and received copies. Lord Kames, a leading Scottish intellectual, printed it in 1761 (6:116). After Franklin had returned to Philadelphia in 1762, the successful printer William Strahan, who had been Franklin's best friend in London during 1757–62, printed it in his popular London newspaper, the *London Courant*, for 17 April 1764. Franklin was ambivalent about its printings. He wrote Strahan on 24 September 1764 that he "was always unwilling to give a Copy of the Chapter, for fear it should be printed, and by that means I should be depriv'd of the Pleasure I often had in amusing People with it. I could not however to two of the best men in the World, Lord Kames and Mr. Small, and should not to the third, if he had not been a Printer. But you have overpaid me for the Loss of that Pleasure, by the kind things you have so handsomely said of your Friend in the Introduction" (11:354).

Franklin's parable tells the story of Abraham and the stranger: When a weary, elderly stranger passed by Abraham's tent at sundown, Abraham persuaded him to spend the night and served him a meal. But when the stranger ate without thanking God for the food, Abraham became angry and "drove him forth with Blows into the Wilderness." At midnight, God asked Abraham, "where is the Stranger?" When Abraham told God, He replied, "Have I not borne with him these hundred ninety and eight Years . . . and couldst not thou, that are thyself a Sinner, bear with him one Night?" Abraham went and found the Stranger, brought him back to his tent, treated him kindly, and in the morning sent him away with gifts. God told Abraham that for his sin, his descendants would be "afflicted four Hundred Years in a strange Land. But for thy Repentance will I deliver them; and they shall come forth with Power, and with Gladness of Heart, and with much Substance" (6:123–24).

Franklin evidently sometimes simply called it "The Chapter of Abraham and the Stranger," but at other times identified it as chapter 22, 25, 27, 39, or 51 of Genesis (6:115). Franklin gave it a chapter number merely to make the parable seem more authentic, and those who knew their King James Bible fairly well would perhaps recall that the chapters on Abraham began around chapter 17 and continued through chapter 25. Of course if they knew the Bible thoroughly, like Ezra Stiles, they probably recalled that Abraham was killed off in chapter 25 and that chapter 27 told of Jacob's obtaining Isaac's blessing.

The opening imitates the style and diction of the King James Bible: "And it came to pass." The clause recurs hundreds of times in the King James Bible—so much so that Mark Twain burlesqued it in *Roughing It*. The phrase in the second line, "and behold a Man," is also biblical, appearing in Luke 9:38, Acts 8:27, and Zechariah 1:8 and 2:1. In addition to specific verbal echoes, the setting (tent, staff, "unleavend Bread,"), style ("Zeal was kindled," "abideth alway," "from before my Face," and "Bowed with Age" and the use of the second person singular), and contents ("wash thy Feet," "at Midnight God called," "these hundred ninety and eight Years") all seem biblical.

The moral, however, is more typical of Franklin than of Genesis or the Old Testament. He thought that no one should be punished for any speculative opinion, unless it harmed others. As he argued in Samuel Hemphill's trial, Philadelphians should allow believers in Mohammad to live among them and to preach Mahometanism (2:32). What should be done with persons who disagreed with you on spiritual matters? Nothing, for "he *may* be in the right" (*Life* 2:238, 250). As John Adams commented in 1811, Franklin "was a friend to unlimited toleration in matters of religion." Throughout his life, in numerous writings, Franklin suggested that no one could be certain of the ultimate truths of theology.[39]

Franklin's impish streak appeared in the parable. Christians generally assumed that it was a Christian document, despite the numerous centuries of religious warfare between Catholics and Protestants in Ireland, France, and elsewhere in the Western world. For thoughtful contemporaries, the parable had ironic overtones in view of Christianity's history. On another level, some few persons recognized that it was not biblical, and they probably believed it to be Franklin's creation. Close acquaintances knew that toleration was a doctrine that Franklin "most assiduously cultivated."[40]

But evidently almost no one before 1781 knew Franklin's underlying ironic joke. The source was the Persian poet Sa'di, whose text reflected Mohammedanism (6:121). That would have surprised most of his auditors and horrified some. But the relativist Franklin believed in theological diversity and happily celebrated the fine expression of toleration in a religious, though non-Christian, text. He had become interested in Islam early, and at age 23 wrote in his Busy-Body essay series (# 3) that in ancient times, Persians taught virtue in their schools (1:118–19). In the following Busy-Body, as Kevin J. Hayes pointed out, Franklin quoted and artfully adapted Henry Maundress's celebration of Islamic civility in *Travel from Aleppo to Jerusalem* (1:125–26). Among other later writings, Franklin cited Mohammad in his 1764 *Narrative of the Late Massacres in Lancaster* (11:58–59).[41] He may have thought that few Christian contemporaries would want to acknowledge that Mohammedanism could outdo Christianity, especially in such a Christian virtue as toleration.

Franklin claimed in 1789 that his only contribution to the parable was the biblical style "and the addition of the concluding threatening and promise" (S 10:53). James Madison knew that some persons charged Franklin with plagiarism, but he thought that a phrase Franklin evidently inserted (God telling Abra-

Poſtſcript.

To the Editor of the London Chronicle.

SIR,

SOME time ago, being in company with a friend from North America, as well known throughout Europe for his ingenious diſcoveries in natural philoſophy, as to his countrymen for his ſagacity, his uſefulneſs, and activity, in every public-ſpirited meaſure, and to his acquaintance for all the ſocial virtues ; the converſation happened to turn on the ſubject of Perſecution. My friend, whoſe underſtanding is as enlarged as his heart is benevolent, did not fail to urge many unanſwerable arguments againſt a practice ſo obviouſly repugnant to every dictate of humanity: At length, in ſupport of what he had advanced, he called for a Bible, and turning to the Book of GENE-SIS, read as follows :

I own I was ſtruck with the aptneſs of the paſſage to the ſubject, and did not fail to expreſs my ſurpriſe, that in all the diſcourſes I had read againſt a practice ſo diametrically oppoſite to the genuine ſpirit of our holy religion, I did not remember to have ſeen this chapter quoted ; nor did I recollect my having ever read it, tho' no ſtranger to my Bible. Next morning, turning to the Book of Geneſis, I found there was no ſuch chapter, and that the whole was a well-meant invention of my friend, whoſe ſallies of humour, in which he is a great maſter, have always an uſeful and benevolent tendency.

With ſome difficulty I procured a copy of what he pretended to read, which I now ſend you for the entertainment of your readers ; and you will perhaps think it not unſeaſonable at a time when our Church more particularly calls upon us to commemorate the amazing love of HIM, who poſſeſſing the divine virtue of Charity in the moſt ſupreme degree, laid down his life EVEN FOR HIS ENEMIES. I am, &c.

April 16, 1764. W. S.

Figure 42. William Strahan on Franklin's mock-biblical parables, the London Chronicle, *17 April 1764. William Strahan (1715–85), a leading London printer, started corresponding with Franklin in 1743 and became a favorite source of information for Franklin before 1748. He was Franklin's closest friend during Franklin's first English agency, 1757–62. Although Franklin did not want to publish "A Parable against Persecution," Strahan knew that Franklin had given copies to Scottish friends and that Lord Kames had printed it. Strahan prefaced its publication with a note "To the Editor of the* London Chronicle" *and concluded the hoax with his own reaction. Strahan was at first taken in and thought it was a biblical text, then believed that Franklin made it up. Later, he enjoyed the comments of those who did not smoke the joke. Strahan did not know the final twist: Franklin's parable was not only not biblical, it was not really entirely Franklin's original creation. It actually adapted a passage from the Persian poet Sa'di, a Mohammedan semi-sacred text. Franklin would have been privately amused at Strahan and others who thought that its moral was good—and uniquely Christian.*

Though the two printers had much in common, they gradually grew apart during Franklin's second English agency (1764–75), for after 1765, the Scottish-born Strahan revealed he, too, had some of the prevailing anti-American sentiments. Courtesy, Library of Congress.

ham, "who are thyself a sinner") improved the original.⁴² Though the parable is copied, it is also original. Without the King James style and without the pointed conclusion, it would have been much less effective. And for some of the few who later knew its source, a part of its originality and its effect lay in the ostensibly contradictory fact that "A Parable against Persecution" was in great part copied from a non-Christian text. As James N. Green and Peter Stallybrass pointed out in discussing Franklin's epitaph, its "originality can only be understood in relation to the tradition that it imitates and creatively deforms." They are right. So too with Franklin's adaptation of Sa'di, a sacred text of Mohammedanism.⁴³

Like Franklin's "Speech Deliver'd by an Indian Chief, in Reply to a Swedish Missionary," the "Parable Against Persecution" presents the theses of "A Dialogue between Two Presbyterians" (1735; *Life* 2:510–11) in a subtle and artful form. Further, Franklin may have wanted to use the Indian speech and Sa'di as sources precisely because they are based upon supposedly actual happenings. The Christian ideal of toleration reflected actions and beliefs of persons in other cultures as well as Christianity. Thus the truth of Christian ideals was reinforced. The underlying imitation also raises the parable to a complex hoax—one that partially satirizes the provincial assumptions of good friends like Kames and Strahan, that satirizes the self-complaisance of mankind, and that satirizes Franklin. As in the conclusion of *A Dissertation on Liberty and Necessity*, Franklin undercuts the estate of mankind—humans are animals who use their mental abilities to fool themselves (*Life* 1:286).

A Parable on Brotherly Love

Like the "Parable against Persecution," the "Parable on Brotherly Love" pretends to be from the Bible. The annotations of "A Parable on Brotherly Love" in the *Papers of Benjamin Franklin* cite eleven biblical echoes: seven to Genesis, one to Samuel, one to Kings, one to Chronicles, and one to Jeremiah. This parable was actually based on another great religious writing, the Jewish Code of Maimonides, perhaps from a translation into Latin by Georgius Gentius (6:125).⁴⁴ Franklin's "chapter" begins with the scarcity of iron, echoing 1 Samuel 13:19–20, and with the Ishmaelites bearing "spicery and balm and myrrh" (Gen. 37:25). His version tells of a selfish brother named Reuben, who buys an ax, but when the three brothers, Simeon, Levi, and Judah, separately ask to borrow the ax, Reuben refuses each one. Then, as he hewed timber on a riverbank, the ax fell in the water, and he could not find it (6:126).

By this time, however, the three brothers had all sent away and purchased axes. Reuben tried to borrow Simeon's ax and was refused. Then he approached Levi, who said he would lend him the ax but shamed him for his earlier conduct. Reuben approached Judah, "And as he drew near, Judah beheld his Countenance as it were confused with Grief and shame; and he prevented him, saying, My Brother, I know thy Loss, but why should it grieve thee? Lo, have I not an

Ax that will serve both thee and me? take it I pray thee, and use it as thine. . . . And Joseph saw these Things, and reported them to his Father Jacob." After hearing the account, Jacob said that "Judah hath the Soul of a King. His Fathers Children shall bow down before him, and he shall rule over his Brethren, nor shall the Sceptre depart from his house, nor a Lawgiver from between his Feet, until Shiloh" (6:127–28).

Franklin's "Parable on Brotherly Love" is less dramatic than "A Parable against Persecution." "Brotherly Love" introduces a previously unknown person, Joseph, son of Jacob (an additional biblical reference, Genesis 37ff.), late in the parable. Its moral, the Golden Rule, is more obvious than the moral of toleration. The "Brotherly Love" parable has never been widely popular. The moral was certainly among Franklin's personal beliefs, but he presented the Golden Rule in other, more interesting ways, including the letter to Joseph Huey of 2 June 1753.[45]

GLIMPSES OF DEBORAH

Deborah Franklin appeared several times in two diaries of 1755. The first diarist found her to be an obstinate, outspoken, shrewish, and jealous stepmother who was loyal and faithful to her husband. The second diarist discovered in her a gracious, friendly, wealthy, intelligent, and kind leader of Philadelphia's society.

The Jealous Stepmother

On 22 May 1755, Daniel Fisher, a well-connected young Virginian who knew Colonel William Hunter, joint deputy postmaster general of North America with Franklin, came to Philadelphia, having some intimation from the merchant William Nelson (1711–72) of Yorktown, Virginia, that William Allen might hire him in a mercantile position. Fisher took lodging at the Indian King, on Market Street, near Third. William Allen, however, said he could not use him. Fisher meant to ask Colonel William Hunter for his advice, but before Fisher could speak with Hunter, he left on 3 June for Virginia. Not knowing what to do, Fisher decided to write Franklin, though they were unacquainted. "The next morning" Fisher delivered the letter to Franklin's home and "without reserve laid the whole of my affairs before him, requesting his aid, if such a thing might be without inconvenience to Himself." The same day, 4 June, Fisher received a note in reply: "Mr. Franklin's compliments to Mr. Fisher and desires the favor of his Company to drink Tea at 5 o'clock this afternoon."[46]

Fisher went to the Franklins' house and "met with a humane, kind reception." Franklin "expressed concern" for Fisher's situation "and promised to assist me into some business provided it was in his power." As he left, "a Silversmith in the neighborhood of Mr. Franklin seeing me come out of that Gentleman's House, spoke to me as I was passing his door and invited me to sit down. . . . I had been several times in his company at my Inn and considered him as a very inquisitive person, craving a knowledge of other People's affairs, though noways concerning himself." Sure enough, silversmith Samuel Soumien "soon began to fish for my business with Mr. Franklin by asking whether I had any previous knowledge or acquaintance with him." Soumien offered Fisher "a private Lodging . . . at Twelve shillings a week," which Fisher accepted (F271). That was eight shillings less than Peter Kalm had been paying at the Indian Queen seven years earlier (*Life* 2:567).

The next day, 5 June, Fisher met Deborah Franklin: "As I was coming down from my chamber this afternoon a Gentlewoman was sitting on one of the lowest stairs, which were but narrow, and there not being room enough to pass, she arose up and threw herself upon the floor and sat there. Mr. Soumien and his Wife greatly entreated her to arise and take a chair, but in vain; she would keep her seat, and kept it, I think, the longer for their entreaty. This Gentlewoman, whom, though I had seen before, I did not know, appeared to be Mrs. Franklin. She assumed the airs of extraordinary Freedom and great Humility, Lamented heavily the misfortunes of those who are unhappily infected with a too tender or benevolent disposition, said she believed all the world claimed a privilege of troubling her Pappy (so she usually calls Mr. Franklin) with their calamities and distress, giving us a general history of many such wretches and their impertinent applications to him" (F271–72). One suspects Deborah Franklin meant to include Fisher among those who made "impertinent applications" to Franklin. Fisher may have thought so and become prejudiced against Deborah. He only noted, however, that "Mr. Franklin's moral character is good, and he and Mrs. Franklin live irreproachably as man and wife." That Sunday, 8 June 1755, he dined with the Franklins, and during the next week he worked occasionally for Franklin copying letters and documents. On 28 July he began lodging and boarding with them, acting as Franklin's clerk (F272).

Fisher reported that the silversmith Mr. Soumien had often told him of the "great uneasiness and dissatisfaction in Mr. Franklin's family." Fisher recorded in his diary that he "was unwilling to credit" the report, "but as Mrs. Franklin and I . . . began to be Friendly and sociable, I discerned too great grounds for Mr. Soumien's Reflections, arising solely from turbulence and jealousy and pride of her disposition." Deborah was jealous of William Franklin. She suspected, wrote Fisher, that Franklin had greater "esteem for his son in prejudice of herself and daughter, a young woman of about 12 or 13 years of age." To Fisher's eye, however, "it was visible Mr. Franklin had no less esteem" for Sarah "than for his son" (F276). Franklin often saw William "pass to and from his father's apartment upon Business (for he does not eat, drink or sleep in the House) without the least compliment between Mr[s]. Franklin and him or any sort of notice taken of each other." One day, however, as Fisher "was sitting with her," William Franklin went by, and "she exclaimed to me (he not hearing), 'Mr. Fisher, there goes the greatest Villain upon the Earth.'" Fisher wrote that the words "greatly confounded and perplexed me, but did not hinder her from pursuing her Invectives in the foulest terms I ever heard from a Gentlewoman. What to say or do I could not tell, till luckily a neighbor of her acquaintance coming in I made my escape" (F276).

Thereafter, Fisher "industriously avoided being alone with her and she appeared no less cunning in seeking opportunities of beginning the subject again in so much that I foresaw a very unpromising situation." The respect that Fisher thought due to William, "which his father always paid him and which I was determined he should receive from me, would not, I perceived clearly, be endured by a woman of her violent spirit." (When he wrote "Elysian Fields," Franklin praised Deborah for having "as much good Sense, a little more of Spirit" than Madame Helvétius; W 924.) Fisher found his situation increasingly uncomfortable and "began to wish" he was not living with the Franklins (F276–77).

Though Deborah surprises us by appearing to be a jealous stepmother in Fisher's eyes, Franklin is the same well-meaning person who appears so often: "Having as yet made no settled agreement with Mr. Franklin, I was not certain that he had any real occasion for my services, having Several Days together nothing for me to do." Captain James Coultas, who expected to be elected Philadelphia's sheriff, suggested that he might be able to employ Fisher. He "immediately flew to my friend, Mr. Franklin, with the news, that he might participate in my satisfaction, but was somewhat surprised that he did not consider what I had done in the same view with myself." He said Coultas was "a very worthy man" who would perform everything he promised, "but could not apprehend that anything he could do for me would be worthy my acceptance; that he had himself thought of several ways of serving me, and has rejected them only because he esteemed them too mean." Franklin said he could secure for him a teaching position in "the academy, in the capacity of English school master, a place of £60 a year, with some other advantages, but refrained mentioning it to me in hopes of having it soon in his power of doing better for me." Since Ebenezer Kinnersley was the English school master at a salary of £150 a year, Franklin was evidently thinking of offering Fisher a job as Kinnersley's assistant. Fisher told Franklin that he was diffident about his ability to do "justice to his recommendations, a thing which he said, he was not in the least apprehensive of. However, presuming it gave him no offense, I craved his leave to decline the kind offer, and he declared himself very well satisfied" (F275).

On 7 August 1755, Fisher heard about an opportunity in Virginia and recorded in his diary that "The uncertainty of my situation" and his "apprehensions of Mrs. Franklin's turbulent temper" were considerations affecting his decision to leave Philadelphia. He showed Franklin the letter from Williamsburg and "craved his opinion, who very readily came into mine." On Saturday night, 9 August, he stayed up with Franklin until 11:00 and then left the following morning for Williamsburg (F277).

Fisher knew the Franklins for just over two months and only lived with them for a week and a half. He was a young man, about twenty-one years old, and evidently regarded Deborah as an older woman whom he did not especially like or respect.

The Gracious Social Leader

A different Deborah Franklin emerges from the journal of Charlotte Brown, the matron of the hospital for General Edward Braddock's forces who came to America in 1755. Her diary entries are intermittent, sometimes only one in two weeks and sometimes entries every day for several days. She arrived in Philadelphia on 18 October, just over two months after Fisher left. Like him, she took lodgings at the Indian King. She noted on 24 October that seven ladies of the town, evidently including Deborah Franklin, came to see her.[47] On 17 November, Charlotte Brown again recorded that several ladies came to call upon her, but the only one she named was Deborah Franklin, whom she obviously regarded as the most important. Deborah was then about forty-nine and evidently attractive. Mr. Black, the clerk of the hospital, joined the company "very much elevated" and said "he must pay them the Scotch Compliment and kiss all round he said they were all very handsome" (B191).

The next entry in Brown's diary, Thursday, 27 November, recorded: "Mrs. Franklin sent her Chaise for me and I was receiv'd with great politeness." Deborah and, presumably Franklin, received Brown and whoever else was with her. The assembly, however, was in session and Franklin was busy. Israel Pemberton mentioned that he talked with Franklin that day.[48] When Brown returned home that evening, she noted that Deborah "did me the favour to drive me home herself." Since Franklin wrote several letters that day, perhaps he was writing them while Deborah drove Brown home. Brown attended the Philadelphia Fair the following day with a number of unidentified ladies, probably including Deborah, and watched the dancing there that night (B191).

A few entries later, Charlotte Brown recorded that Deborah came to see her on 24 January 1756. Franklin was then on the frontier at Gnadenhütten, building Fort Allen. On Sunday, 25 January, Brown noted that she went to Christ Church to hear a sermon by "Mr. Jinnings" (Robert Jenney), "dined at Mr. Franklins and drank Tea with Dr. Loyds" (perhaps Dr. Lloyd Zachary). On 12 February, she went with Deborah to the Philadelphia Academy "and was agreably entertain'd by hearing the Boys speak." Franklin had returned to Philadelphia late on 5 February, and since he was still the president of the academy's Board of Trustees, he may have managed to attend the performance, but the assembly was in session, meeting at 10:00 A.M. and at 3:00 P.M., and he no doubt was present. The same day, the Philadelphia Regiment elected him colonel, and somehow he also found time to write his sister Jane Mecom. Charlotte Brown recorded dining with Provost William Smith later that day, and it is unlikely that Franklin and Deborah were present (B192). Preparing to leave for New York, Charlotte Brown "Took Leave of all my Friends" on 14 February, but the next day, she "Took Leave of Mrs. Franklin who was so kind as to give me

Figure 43. Deborah Franklin by Benjamin Wilson. Wilson's portrait presents Deborah as a well-dressed, slightly plump woman in her forties (Franklin was also becoming stout in his forties) with an expensive pearl clip in her hair. The diary of Charlotte Brown (the matron of the British army's hospital) reveals that Deborah Franklin was by 1754 a leading member of Philadelphia's society. Since Wilson painted the portrait from a miniature by an unknown American artist, he may have imagined the dress. Linda Eaton and Anne Verplanck, curators at the Winterthur Museum, noted that Deborah was wearing "standard portraiture clothes, not necessarily a real/genuine outfit," and that the drapery over the shoulder hides the dress.

Franklin had the portrait painted about the same time that he had Wilson do his own in 1759, intending to hang them together after he returned to Philadelphia. He shipped his portrait to Philadelphia about 1760 and kept Deborah's with him until he left London in 1762. When he returned to London (1764–75), he took Deborah's portrait with him, and in 1775 brought it back to Philadelphia where they hung side by side. During the Revolution, however, the British occupying Philadelphia took away his picture and left Deborah's. It had remained there "as a kind of widow," he wrote on 23 October 1788, until Madame Marie-Anne Lavoisier (the wife of the chemist) sent him her copy of Duplessis's great portrait. Franklin hung it next to Deborah's, "and the lady," he wrote in thanks for the gift of the portrait, "seems to smile, as well pleased." Courtesy, American Philosophical Society.

Letters to New York she waited on me to the Boat . . . and at 10 I set sail for New York." In New York on 18 February, Brown "Delivered the Letters Mrs. Franklin gave me" to Dr. John Bard "and was kindly received, staid and dined" (B192–93).

Are the Opposite Opinions Valid?

In the opinion of one important unmarried woman visiting America, Deborah Franklin was Philadelphia's leading lady. Since Charlotte Brown held a responsible position, I would guess that she was considerably older than Daniel Fisher. Brown may have been younger than Deborah, though probably well over thirty. She never specifically mentioned Benjamin Franklin, who was on the frontier most of the time that she was in Philadelphia, but she was impressed with Deborah, who evidently liked her and looked out for her. To Brown, Deborah was a friendly and generous patron and a major figure in Philadelphia society.

Charlotte Brown's opinion contrasts with the usual scholarly view. Carl Van Doren fixed the twentieth-century opinion of Deborah in his 1938 biography: "The more formal gentry of Philadelphia long looked, condescendingly if approvingly, on Franklin as a tradesman, and never accepted his wife or included her in invitations to their houses."[49] Van Doren cited no evidence, and I believe Daniel Fisher's account and post-Victorian social attitudes influenced his opinion more than Deborah's correspondence or the social attitudes of eighteenth-century Philadelphians. In many ways, colonial American society was more stratified than early twentieth-century society, but it was also more fluid than any other Western society.[50]

No Philadelphians enjoyed higher social standing than Franklin's two important friends and patrons, James Logan and Andrew Hamilton. Logan came to Pennsylvania as William Penn's secretary and rose to be the dominant social and intellectual leader of Pennsylvania.[51] Hamilton's origins are obscure, but Franklin told John Jay in 1783 that it was said that he came to America "as a Servant. Mr. Brooke who in those Days was an old Man told Dr. Franklin that he had seen Hamilton who then lived at Lewis Town studying the Law in an Osnabrigs Shirt and Trowsers, that he observed often, and that from his great application he predicted that he would one Day make a Figure in that Profession—He was a man of exceeding good Talents & ready Elocution."[52] Hamilton became the most famous American lawyer of his day and the dominant political leader of Pennsylvania in the early 1730s.[53] They both, along with their wives and children, became social leaders. Hamilton's son married William Allen's daughter and became governor of Pennsylvania. James Logan and Andrew Hamilton were exceptional persons, but so was Franklin. By 1740, Philadelphians of the time regarded James Logan and Andrew Hamilton as among the highest class in their society. By 1755, I suspect that Franklin and Deborah, William, and Sarah were also regarded as among Philadelphia's social leaders.

The gender and different relations to Deborah of Daniel Fisher and Charlotte Brown may partially explain their contrasting reports. Fisher saw her in more familiar and intimate situations and witnessed her interactions within her family and with her neighbors. He did not identify with Deborah and did not seem to like her. As I suggested, Fisher may have thought that Deborah ranked him with the "wretches" who made "impertinent applications" to Franklin. That probably prejudiced him against her. He respected Benjamin Franklin and perhaps identified with William Franklin, who was about twenty-seven years old in 1755—not too much older than Fisher. Although Charlotte Brown never mentioned Franklin, she must have met him on occasion, for she had financial dealings with him.[54] She identified with Deborah, and Deborah's attentions flattered her. Brown saw Deborah in fairly formal social situations and benefited from Deborah's kindnesses. Just as Franklin patronized Fisher, so Deborah patronized Brown. Both views of Deborah Franklin are valid. Other sources support each.[55] Like most people, Deborah had many qualities—most of which neither diarist revealed. (Consider, for example, Chapter 19's incidental discussions of the relations between Franklin and Deborah while he was on the frontier.) Each diarist, however, is uniquely valuable: Fisher for confirming Deborah's temper and her jealousy of William Franklin; Brown for her view of the kindly matron prominent in Philadelphia society.

What is the reader to think? One scholar finds Deborah "loud and lowly and scarcely literate," then says she was never invited to the homes of Philadelphia's gentry and therefore Franklin did not want to take her abroad; the scholar then condemns Franklin for having "completely forgotten" Deborah within half a year of her death. Another calls her "plodding but useful" and condemns Franklin for being more engaging to his readers than to "poor Deborah." Still another accuses him of ignoring his engagement to Deborah while in London in 1725, only writing her once, and not writing his friends about her after her death.[56] Though Carl Van Doren is partially responsible for the myth that Philadelphia society never accepted Deborah or invited her to their homes, he celebrates the friendship and love between Franklin and Deborah. In my opinion, none of the slanders against her is just—nor is the claim that Franklin was indifferent. Scores of loving letters between Franklin and Deborah testify to their mutual affection.

The French and Indians Attack and Pennsylvania Responds, 1755

Those who would give up essential Liberty, to purchase a little temporary Safety, deserve neither Liberty nor Safety.
—Franklin for the Pennsylvania Assembly, 11 November 1755, 6:242

THE ASSEMBLY'S FIRST SESSION, 14–18 OCTOBER 1755

ON 16 OCTOBER, Pennsylvania's governor Robert Hunter Morris received letters reporting Indian massacres on the Virginia and Maryland frontiers. He did not, however, inform the assembly or request any support for Pennsylvania's frontier. Shocked by his keeping the House ignorant, Richard Peters wrote Conrad Weiser that "the lives of people were not to be plaid with nor thrown away because the two parts of the legislature differ." Peters vowed he would not "be accessory to such a step."[1] On the morning of 18 October, Peters met with Speaker Norris and put the letters on Indian affairs in his hands. Norris read them and asked if he should not lay them before the House. Peters replied that the governor "had given him no Orders or Authority for that Purpose" and took them back. Norris told the House about the letters but said that he "could not presume to charge his Memory with the Particulars, so as to lay them before the House for the Foundation of their Consideration." The House then sent two members to the governor, asking if he "had any thing to lay before them, particularly any matter relating to Indian affairs." If not, the members proposed adjourning to 1 December. Morris condescendingly replied "that if he had any Business to lay before the House, he should have done it before now." Obviously Norris had told members of the House about the frontier news. Normally, the House would have adjourned to January or February, but instead it set the date for the next session at 1 December.[2]

What could Governor Morris have been thinking? Did he hope the assembly would do nothing and frontier settlers would be killed—so that the British authorities would therefore want to remove Quakers as members of the assembly? Was he willing to sacrifice the lives of the frontier settlers in order to accomplish this purpose? Evidently Richard Peters thought so. Morris must also have believed that he was doing what Thomas Penn wanted.

Why did not Speaker Isaac Norris request funds for defense of the frontier?

He and other members of the assembly had probably heard rumors of the attacks before Peters showed Norris the information about them. Why did Norris not appoint a committee to investigate the matter and to report to the House? Norris probably knew how the members would react. Franklin and most frontier county delegates would want to raise money to support a militia. The pacifist assemblymen would vote against doing so, and some Quaker members would be confident that their past fair dealings with the Indians would make Pennsylvania immune from frontier attacks. Norris probably believed that there was not yet any point in asking the assembly for action. Despite knowing of frontier attacks in the neighboring areas of Virginia and Maryland, neither the governor nor the assembly prepared for defense.

THE FRENCH AND INDIANS ATTACK

On 16 October 1755, the day that Governor Morris received word of the earlier onslaughts in Virginia and Maryland, the French and Indians attacked the settlement at Penn's Creek and the Susquehanna River, just fifteen miles north of where the Juniata River meets the Susquehanna The Iroquois had sold the area to Pennsylvania at Albany just the year before (see the area indicated in map 3, p. 369), but the Delaware Indians who assaulted Penn's Creek may not have known or cared what the Iroquois did. They resented the supposed suzerainty of the Iroquois over them and may even have attacked partly for that reason.[3]

News reached Philadelphia on 24 October when diarist Charlotte Brown recorded, "An Express is arriv'd from Lancaster with an Account that the Indians are scalping all before them."[4] After Governor Morris learned the news in New Castle, Delaware, the hypocrite wrote Conrad Weiser on 29 October that "If the Assembly had paid any the least regard to my Recommendations, . . . the people would not at this time have remained without protection or such a quantity of innocent Blood have been spilt." Morris called the assembly to meet "next Monday" and hoped they would "now (tho' late) make some Provision for the safety of the Province." He told Weiser that he could assure "the people that whenever the Assembly enables me to act vigorously in their defense I shall most readily do it." He ended by complaining that he had "neither Arms nor Ammunition at my disposal or I should have sent" them earlier.[5]

Though Franklin was ill on 25 October when the news came to Philadelphia, he immediately contacted Evan Morgan, who was also a commissioner, and the two ordered "600 good Arms" and ammunition to be sent to the frontier. When Governor Morris learned of Franklin's quick action, he objected that the assembly had sent arms to the frontier without his permission, contrary to the act empowering the law. Though he realized that Pennsylvania public opinion would turn against him if he tried to condemn Franklin for sending off the weapons in the emergency, Morris knew that Thomas Penn would agree. Morris wrote him on 22 November that Franklin's action was "a very extraordinary measure, as the people will be thereby taught to depend upon an Assembly for what they should only receive from the Government, and if it is not criminal I am sure it ought to be so."[6]

Franklin informed assembly agent Richard Partridge on 25 October that the enemy surprised eight families at Penn's Creek: "13 grown Persons were killed and scalped, and 12 Children carried away." He lamented that Morris had rejected the defense bill for £50,000 of 2 August (6:231). The Proprietary Party and William Smith reacted to the disaster by drafting a petition asking the king to ensure that Pennsylvania could be "put into a *Posture of Defence.*" In effect, they requested that Quakers should not be assemblymen. On the same day that Franklin wrote Partridge, William Allen, who had been circulating Smith's anti-Quaker petition, sent it to the proprietary agent Ferdinand J. Paris (6:231).

On Wilderness Fighting

Despite being ill and confined to his "Room and Bed" for the previous eight days, Franklin replied on 2 November to a letter received "just now per Express" from James Read, his former neighbor now living in Reading, Pennsylvania. Franklin sent him fifty muskets, which, in case the men were on horses, were "all furnish'd with Staples for Sling Straps" so that "the Piece may be slung at the Horseman's back." The next morning Franklin added advice on using dogs in fighting: "If Dogs are carried out with any Party, they should be large, strong and fierce; and every Dog led in a Slip-String, to prevent their tiring themselves by running out and in, and discovering the Party by Barking at Squirrels, &c. Only when the Party come near thick Woods and suspicious Places, they should turn out a Dog or two to search them." If they discovered enemy Indians, then the dogs should all be turned loose "and set on. They will be fresher and fiercer for having been previously confin'd, and will confound the Enemy a good deal, and be very serviceable." He explained that this was the Spanish method (6:235).[7]

Franklin further advised that to avoid being tracked and then surprised at night, a party that encountered a stream could travel up or down the stream "in the Water a Mile or two, and then encamp." He also suggested that troops going to a normal night's camp should not go directly to it but pass it by at some distance, then turn and come to it from the other side. Franklin illustrated this advice with a simple sketch. "Or suppose a Party marching from A intends to halt at B; they do not go strait to B, and stop there, but pass by at some little distance, and make a Turn which brings them thither. Then between B and C two or three Centinels are plac'd to watch the Track, and give immediate Notice at B. if they perceive any Party pass by in Pursuit, with an Account of their Number, &c. which enables the Party at B to prepare and attack them if they judge that proper, or gives them time to escape" (6:236).

A------------------------------ C------
　　　　　　　　　　　　　　　　B -----

THE ASSEMBLY'S SECOND SESSION, 3 NOVEMBER–3 DECEMBER 1755

Governor Morris recalled the assembly for 3 November 1755. He said he was "ready and willing" to sign a bill for "any Sum in Paper-Money the present Service may require" if the funds would be sunk within five years. He warned, however, that he would not "pass any Bills of the same or a like Tenor of those I have heretofore refused."[8] Replying to the governor's appeal for funds to defend the frontier, the assembly debated a paper money bill on 5 November and resolved to strike £60,000 in bills of credit to be "sunk by a Tax of *Six-pence per Pound*, and *Ten Shillings* per Head, yearly, for Four Years, on all the Estates, Real and Personal, and Taxables, within this Province." Speaker Norris appointed Franklin to the committee to draft the bill.[9]

With a vengeance, Franklin turned the suspending clause against the proprietors. Since 29 August 1753, the governors had demanded that money bills have a suspending clause, which, they argued, a royal instruction of 21 August 1740 demanded of Pennsylvania. Then the members had found in the deceased John Kinsey's papers that the British authorities had approved the currency act of 7 March 1745/6, which had not contained a suspending clause, thereby ruining that proprietary dodge for not approving money bills.[10]

Now Franklin resurrected the old idea of the suspending clause—and reversed it to use against the proprietors. The £60,000 bill taxed the proprietors' estates but submitted to "his Majesty's Royal Determination" the question of whether the estates of the proprietors should be exempted from taxation. It provided, "that if at any Time, during the Continuance of the Act, the Crown should think fit to declare, that the Estates of the Proprietaries in this Province ought to be exempted, in such Case the Tax, tho' assessed, shall not be levied, or if any Part has been levied, the same shall be refunded" (6:240). What a clever maneuver! Morris had repeatedly claimed that he could not pass such a bill, because the British authorities would veto it. Here the assembly invited the British authorities to overturn the Pennsylvania legislature, but Franklin and the Quaker Party assemblymen believed that the British authorities would allow the taxation to stand. (In England, lords' holdings were taxed.) On 6 November, the day that Franklin submitted the bill to the assembly, Governor Morris learned its terms and discussed it with his council, who unanimously agreed that he could not assent to it. Nevertheless, the House passed it on Saturday 8 November, with seven pacifist Quakers dissenting because it was for military purposes.[11]

As soon as the governor received it, he sent an irate message admonishing the assemblymen for passing a bill they knew he could not accept. In effect, he said that his commission forbade him to tax the proprietors. He did not, however, return it. Subsequently, when an assembly committee asked him whether he would or would not pass it, he displayed his pique by replying that if the assembly asked him that in writing, he would reply. Many persons, especially Proprietary Party members, faulted the Quaker Party more than the governor for the lack of defense. On 8 November 1755, a contemporary noted that "the Indians have burnt a Town within 30 Miles of us," but the news "had no Effect on the Quakers. . . . The Assembly met but to no purpose for they will not do any thing to defend themselves."[12]

After the House's morning session on 8 November, the assembly adjourned, and that afternoon, in the state house, Scarouady dramatically addressed the governor, Pennsylvania Council, House, magistrates, and citizens: "I want you to open your hearts, I want to look into their insides. I must now know if you will stand by us; to be plain, if you will fight or not. . . . if you will not fight with us, we will go somewhere else." He asked for an immediate answer. The governor replied that he had to consult others but that as soon as he knew what he could do, he would inform Scarouady. Then the governor asked the Speaker and assembly to return to their meeting, and to "strengthen my Hands and enable me to" answer. In the opinion of the historian Julien P. Boyd, Scarouady's speech was the most dramatic spectacle in the state house before the Revolution.[13] The House considered the governor's speech and "*Ordered*, That *Joseph Stretch, Benjamin Franklin, Joseph Hamton, George Ashbridge, James Webb, David M'Connaughy* and *William Edmonds* be a Committee to prepare a Draught of a Message to the Governor, in Answer thereto" and then adjourned to the following Monday at 3:00 P.M. When the council met that Saturday night, Richard Peters informed them that the House had adjourned. The governor immediately prepared to set out for the frontier.[14]

FRANKLIN'S MESSAGE, 11 NOVEMBER

Appointed to a committee on the afternoon of 10 November to answer the governor's veto, Franklin immediately drafted a message, which the assembly approved the next day. He ridiculed Morris's claim that it was a "just Right" that the proprietors should not be taxed: "If it be one of the '*just Rights of Government*' that the Proprietary Estate should be exempted in a Tax for the common Defence of all Estates in the Province, those *just Rights* are well understood in England; the Proprietaries are there upon the Spot, and so can the more easily sollicit their own Cause, and make their Right of Exemption appear, if such a Right there be." Even if the proprietors had been at as great a distance from London as the assembly, "they might nevertheless safely confide in his Majesty's known Wisdom and impartial Justice, that all their just Rights would be duly preserved" (6:240). Franklin used the usual cant about the king's "Wisdom and impartial Justice" to make the assembly seem dutiful members of the British Empire and to lampoon the proprietors.

Franklin's rhetoric was superior to the weak reasons that the governor used in reply. Franklin claimed that even the Proprietary Party members believed that such a tax was equitable, for on 16 August they had "entered into a voluntary Subscription to pay . . . what they supposed the Tax might amount to, being assured, as they said, that if the Proprietaries were present, it would be *altogether* unnecessary." Franklin sarcastically added that if the proprietarians' belief were true, the proprietors could solicit "the King's Approbation to the Law" and refuse "to petition for the Exemption" (6:240–41).

Franklin had itemized for Richard Partridge the various pretenses by Governors Hamilton and Morris for rejecting previous supply bills in his 28 August 1755 letter, which would shortly appear in the *Gentleman's Magazine.*[15] Now on 11 November he added to them. Referring to the suspending clause and Governor Thomas's passing of a supply bill in 1746, Franklin said Morris rejected "some" supply bills "for not complying with obsolete occasional Instructions (tho' other Acts exactly of the same Tenor had been past since those Instructions, and received the Royal Assent)." Second, alluding to the act of 7 March 1745/6 forbidding the New England colonies to print paper money, he wrote, "Some for being inconsistent with the supposed *Spirit of an Act of Parliament*, when the Act itself did not any way affect us, being made expresly for other Colonies" (6:241). Third, "Some for being, as the Governor was pleased to say [16 May 1755], '*of an extraordinary Nature*,' without informing us wherein that extraordinary Nature consisted."[16]

Franklin finished by charging that Governor Morris vetoed other bills for "disagreeing with new discovered Meanings, and forced Constructions of a Clause in the Proprietary Commission." The House was consequently "at a Loss to divine what Bill can possibly pass" (6:241). The word *divine* is perfect for the context: the denotative meaning "to perceive intuitively" is clear, while the connotation suggests that the assemblymen would have to have God-like omniscience to fathom the governor's possible objections.

Franklin charged that since the proprietary instructions were secret, the assembly spent time and money preparing and framing bills that proved abortive. He portrayed the absurdity of the situation the secret instructions caused. The assembly was driven from bill to bill without a valid reason and could raise no funds unless "we fortunately hit on the only Bill the Governor is allowed to pass, or till we consent to make such as the Governor or Proprietaries direct us to make." He said that "we might as well leave it to the Governor or Proprietaries to make for us what Supply Laws they please, and save ourselves and the Country the Expence and Trouble" (6:241). He sarcastically added that all debates and reasonings were in vain "where Proprietary Instructions, just or unjust, right or wrong, must inviolably be observed. We have only to find out, if we can, what they are, and then submit and obey." In his attack, Franklin again mentioned the proprietors' 1751 refusal to bear any part of Indian expenses. Their "Conduct, whether as Fathers of their Country, or Subjects to their King, must appear extraordinary, when it is considered that they have not only formally refused to bear any Part of our yearly heavy Expences in cultivating and maintaining Friendship with the Indians, tho' they reap such immense Advantages by that Friendship; but they now, by their Lieutenant, refuse to contribute any Part towards resisting an Invasion of the King's Colony, committed to their

Care; or to submit their Claim of Exemption to the Decision of their Sovereign."
Franklin asserted that the House had "taken every Step in our Power" for the
"poor distressed Inhabitants of the Frontiers." The members believe that even
"in the Midst of their Distresses" the people on the frontier "do not wish us to
go farther."

Concluding the message Franklin wrote a sententia that summed up the
assembly's position and became a resounding statement of its principle: "Those
who would give up essential Liberty, to purchase a little temporary Safety, deserve neither Liberty nor Safety" (6:242, 21:498). Franklin knew and may slightly
echo Francis Bacon's expression in his essay "Of Great Place": "It is a strange
desire, to seek power and to lose liberty."[17]

ASSEMBLY MANEUVERS, 17–25 NOVEMBER

Governor Morris suggested on 17 November that the House pass two different
£60,000 tax bills, one exempting the proprietors from taxation, the other taxing
them, with the commissioners, the governor, and the assembly assessing the tax.
(I assume, as no doubt the assembly did, that if both bills otherwise had the
same conditions as the bill previously rejected, the governor would accept the
bill exempting the proprietors.) Speaker Norris appointed Franklin and others
to reply. The House resolved that if, after receiving its reply, the governor did
not approve the tax bill, the assembly "would respectfully remonstrate to our
Sovereign, and humbly beseech that he would be graciously pleased to cause
our present Governor to be removed from this Province, or take such other
Measures as may prevent the fatal Consequences that are likely to ensue from
his Conduct." The longstanding threat to request a royal government was becoming a reality.[18]

On 18 November, the committee answered Morris. Rephrasing his 19 August
speech, Franklin again claimed that "one of the most valuable Rights of British
Subjects" was "to have their Bills granting Money to the Crown, accepted without Amendments; a Right that cannot be given up, without destroying the Constitution, and incurring greater and more lasting Mischiefs than the Grant of
Money can prevent" (6:251).[19] The present assembly had considered the twenty
amendments the governor had proposed to the bill granting £50,000 in the last
assembly, and though it did not see "the Necessity or Use of many of those
Amendments," the assemblymen nevertheless wanted to avoid all disputes and
so "admitted *every one of them* that was of any Consequence into the present
Bill; except that of exempting the Proprietary Estate." With Franklin's reverse
suspending clause, which invited the king in council to rescind the bill, the
assembly "imagined no farther Objection could remain" (6:252).

But the assembly had learned "how little is to be gained by such Compliance,
and how endless it is to admit any Change in such Bills; for now the Governor
proposes to amend his own Amendments, adds to his own Additions, and alters
his own Alterations; so that tho' we should accede to these, we are not sure of

being ever the nearer to a Conclusion." After those rhetorical strokes, Franklin ended, "as it is a Money Bill, as the whole Sum is granted to the Crown, and to be paid by Tax on the Subjects in this Province, we cannot receive any Amendment to it." The message pointed out that in England, the estates of the lords were taxed and concluded that if Morris did not pass the bill, the House would make "an immediate Application and Complaint against him to our Sovereign" (6:253). Shortly after reading Franklin's message, Secretary Peters wrote to Thomas Penn on 20 November that Franklin was a dangerous person, for he "has an excellent Understanding and can think well under the Force of very violent Passion."[20]

On Saturday morning, 22 November 1755, Governor Morris sent the assembly a message that Franklin characterized as little more "than a Collection of the Governor's former groundless Charges and Calumnies against the Assemblies and People of this Province, which have been repeatedly refuted" (6:256). Speaker Norris appointed Franklin to a committee to consider the message and to decide whether to answer it. The committee prepared an answer, which was read on 25 November.[21]

The reply had two parts. First, Franklin and the committee said that though they had written a full rebuttal, they recommended that it be suppressed in view of the promising development of a major contribution from the proprietors. (Franklin probably proposed this moderating possibility.) There were, however, new charges to refute. Franklin rebutted the new charge that the assembly had "contemptuously treated" the proprietors' offer of £400 to build a fort on the Ohio and dismissed the accusation that the assembly denied the "French Encroachments were within the King's Dominions" (6:258–59). Governor Morris on 22 November had justified his numerous proposed amendments by listing twenty-one past actions granting money to the crown that contained amendments by Pennsylvania's governors, but Franklin and the assembly rebutted and ridiculed the supposed justification with ten comments, for example: "Thirdly, Where the Governor proposed Amendments to Bills, which not being agreed to, the Bills never passed at all, yet these are recited as Bills amended by the Governor" (6:260).

The second part replied to the governor with what the editors of the *Papers of Benjamin Franklin* called a "masterpiece of invective" (6:262). Though read in the assembly on 25 November, Franklin, on the committee on the minutes, "laid [it] aside" for the time being but resurrected and printed it as a supplement to the votes for the second session of the assembly.[22] The message repeated Franklin's argument (first made in December 1754 in letters to Governor William Shirley) that Americans had all the rights of Englishmen—and more: "the Freeborn Subjects of England do not lose their essential Rights by removing into the King's Plantations, extending the British Dominions at the Hazard of their Lives and Fortunes, and encreasing the Power, Wealth, and Commerce of their Mother Country; they have, on the contrary, particular Privileges justly granted and added to their native Rights, for their Encouragement in so useful and meritorious an Undertaking."

Franklin and the assembly claimed that the Pennsylvania assembly was similar to Great Britain's House of Commons, as could be proved by their charter and laws (6:264). Franklin again echoed Robert Beverley in attacking colonial governors: "Governors are frequently transient Persons, of broken Fortunes, greedy of Money, without any Regard to the People, or natural Concern for their Interests, often their Enemies, and endeavouring not only to oppress but defame them, and render them obnoxious to their Sovereign, and odious to their Fellow Subjects." While continuing the attack on Morris, he segued into an assault on Thomas Penn: "Our present Governor not only denies us the Privileges of an English Constitution, but would, as far as in his Power, introduce a French one, by reducing our Assemblies to the Insignificance of their Parliaments, incapable of making Laws, but by Direction, or of qualifying their own Gifts and Grants, and only allowed to register his Edicts. He would even introduce a worse; he requires us to defend our Country, but will not permit us to raise the Means, unless we will give up some of those Liberties that make the Country worth defending." Franklin introduced a biblical comparison that impressed the Virginia lawyer and litterateur John Mercer, who echoed Franklin in his Stamp Act protest. Franklin wrote: "this is demanding *Bricks without Straw*, and is so far *similar* to the Egyptian Constitution. He has got us indeed into *similar* Circumstances with the poor Egyptians, and takes the same Advantage of our Distress; for as they were to perish by Famine, so he tells us we must by the Sword, unless we will become Servants to our Pharaoh, and make him an *absolute Lord*, as he is pleased to stile himself *absolute Proprietary*."[23]

The assembly's investigation of possible reasons for the Indians to attack the frontier proceeded concomitantly with the supply bill. On 4 November, Speaker Norris had assigned a committee composed in part of Quaker pacifists to inquire into the "Dissaffection." A message to the governor was submitted and approved on 5 November asking whether he knew of any "Disgust or Injury the *Delawares* or *Shawnees* have received" from Pennsylvania. If so, the assembly hoped to "regain" their affection. On 7 November, Franklin was assigned to a committee to create a bill for supplying Indian allies with goods "at more easy Rates, supporting an Agent or Agents among them, and preventing Abuses in the *Indian* Trade."[24] Franklin and Norris knew that in their report on the Carlisle Treaty in 1753, they, along with Secretary Peters, had recommended to the governor and council that the Indian trade be regulated (5:107). At that time Franklin had written James Bowdoin about the Massachusetts laws dealing with the Indian trade. He had replied on 12 November 1753, sending along the law and some comments on it. Now in 1755, Franklin and the committee brought in a bill on 11 November which the assembly passed and the governor immediately put off. Richard Peters explained in a letter to Thomas Penn of 13 November that the act was modeled on the "New England Plan" and would exclude the governor from power in the trade. On 3 December, 1755, the House warned that such a bill was necessary, but the governor introduced a number of amendments that the assembly would not accept. The assembly passed another version of the bill two years later, with Speaker Isaac Norris writing Franklin on 7 April 1757 that the governor "adheres to his Amendments" and that the assembly would not agree.[25]

On Saturday, 8 November 1755, Governor Morris censured the assembly for sending him a message talking of "regaining the Affections of the Indians now employed in laying waste the Country and butchering the Inhabitants." He said the Indians had never complained "of any Injury done them." He claimed that he despaired of the assembly "doing any thing, and shall, therefore, immediately set off for the Back Counties, and if they have not all the Assistance their present Distresses make necessary, it will not be for want of Inclination in me but Power." Morris added that if any bills were brought to him that he could assent to, he would promptly deal with them. Showing his usual childish temper, he did not return the bill, and when the House asked him to do so, he refused.[26]

That Saturday afternoon, Norris assigned Franklin to a committee to answer the governor. When the House met on Monday, 10 November 1755, the reply was read, approved, and ordered to be transcribed. The House then received another message from Morris, informing it that Scarouady and his Indians were the only Indian allies in the area. They asked for arms and ammunition and for a number of troops to act in concert with them against the French and Indians. Norris appointed Franklin and others to answer them.[27] In addition to touching on the reasons the Indians might have for making war against Pennsylvanians, who were their longtime friends (6:239), the committee sent a separate message replying to Morris's demands of 10 November. Franklin and the committee reminded him that he had the authority to raise men, and if he approved the money bill, he had the necessary funds (6:243–44).

Being informed that the Shawnees complained that the proprietors had not paid for a large tract of land on the west side of the Susquehanna River across from Harris's Ferry, the House created another committee led by Franklin to investigate the charge.[28] Since Governor Morris had sarcastically replied on 11 November to the assembly's previous request of 5 November, the assembly was now more specific. Franklin and Speaker Norris had been present at the Carlisle Treaty in 1753 and Franklin made notes that the Shawnees had complained that they had not been paid for the land (6:288n1). Richard Peters had said he would bring up the matter to the proprietors. The committee modestly inquired on 18 November if the Shawnees had not been promised "that Application should be immediately made to the Proprietaries." The committee hoped that "Satisfaction" had been given, "But we desire, if the Governor pleases, to be informed of the Particulars" (6:254–55).

Governor Morris asked a council committee to report on Pennsylvania's treatment of the Indians. On 22 November, it replied that Pennsylvania's conduct toward the Indians had always been "just, fair, and generous." Two days later Governor Morris and the council answered that they had examined "all the proper Persons," inspected the "Council Books, *Indian* Treaties, and other Books and Papers that could furnish us with any Lights into" Indian relations, especially the treaty at Carlisle, in October 1753. They found no record of the Indians making any complaint "of their not having received Satisfaction for the said large Tract of Land." They had also asked Richard Peters, who had been present at the treaty, "to know whether he remembered any such Complaint to have been made." Not only did Peters answer that he did not remember to have heard at Carlisle or anywhere else "of any such Complaint," but he also had never heard of "any Promise to make an Application" on behalf of the Indians "to the Proprietaries for such Satisfaction." Further, he did not believe that the Shawnees had "any Right to" any land in Pennsylvania.[29]

At the end of the session, Speaker Norris appointed Franklin to a committee to reply. He did so on 3 December, praising the proprietors in general for their Indian policy. He added, however, that the Shawnees complained after "the Publick general Business of the Treaty was over." The complaint was not "inserted in the printed Account of the Treaty," and Richard Peters had evidently forgotten it. The assembly recorded that it regretted the claims were not investigated and settled, even though the "present Situation and Power of the French, might have been sufficient nevertheless to have engaged those Indians in the War against us" (6:288). Though mild, the words implied that the proprietors had been indirectly responsible for the Indian attacks. No doubt Franklin and the anti-proprietary assemblymen, especially the pacifists, wanted to believe it was true. As we will see, the Delaware chief Teedyuscung thought it was at least partially true.

Morris and William Smith on Franklin

Governor Morris wrote Penn on 22 November that since "Franklin has put himself at the head of the Assembly they have gone to greater lengths than ever, and have not only discovered the Warmth of their Resentment against your Family but are using every means in their Power, even while their Country is invaded, to wrest the Government out of your hands, and to take the whole powers of it into their own." Morris's accusation echoed his attempt to portray Franklin as a traitor because he sent arms to the besieged frontiersmen. Morris further charged that Franklin was merely using the Quakers and "has views that they know nothing of." The pacifists generally opposed Franklin, who was, and had been throughout his time in Pennsylvania, a supporter of defense. But Morris seemed to say that other Quaker leaders opposed Franklin. Naturally some Quaker leaders did occasionally, for example, Speaker Norris versus Franklin on the Albany Plan. Morris wrote, "the more sensible part of them are not heartily satisfied with his attachment to them." Indeed not, since Franklin opposed the pacifists. Morris explained Franklin's motivations as hatred for the Penn family and a desire for power: "he is courting them in order to distress you, and at the same time leading them into measures that will in the end deprive them of any share in the administration." One might think that if that were so, Morris would approve of it, for he knew that Penn and the Proprietary Party wanted to "deprive" the Quakers "of any share in the administration."[30]

Not to be outdone by Morris, the Reverend William Smith wrote Thomas Penn on 27 November that Pennsylvanians were "a giddy and feeble mob . . . a levelling and licentious Race of Republicans" led by Franklin. In his *Brief View*, Smith pretended that a "Gentleman in the Back Counties" wrote a friend in town about the Quakers' inquiry into the causes of the Indians' disaffection. To many readers, the damning analogy must have seemed appropriate: "suppose some of these Assembly-Men's Houses in Town, to be on Fire, and they come to you, in breathless Haste, calling for Buckets and Water: Then, instead of affording them what Help you can, suppose you should proceed leisurely and calmly to enquire of them, how the House catched Fire? Was it by Design or any malicious Person? If so, pray who was he? And what was the supposed Rise of his Malice? Did he receive any Affront: And what was it? And when?"[31]

THE PROPRIETORS' £5,000

On Saturday, 22 November 1755, Governor Morris received Thomas Penn's letter of 4 October, giving £5,000 from arrears on quitrents toward defense. Public opinion and the British authorities were responsible for Penn's contribution. Dr. John Fothergill, Thomas Penn's physician and the person partly responsible for publishing Franklin's *Experiments and Observations on Electricity* in 1751, had spoken to Penn about his refusal to contribute to Pennsylvania's defense. Fothergill wrote the Philadelphia pacifist James Pemberton on 4 October that he had read in the Boston papers that Governor Morris had refused a £50,000 tax bill because it also taxed the proprietors' estates. Fothergill had told Penn that he should "consider in what light such conduct at such a time must appear."[32]

Penn wrote Governor Morris that same 4 October that Thomas Robinson, secretary of state, told him in the morning that "he has heard several people express a dislike to your refusal on our part to assist the publick at such a time as this." Robinson had also said that he was sorry to see the long messages between the governor and the assembly. He suggested "that these disputes will cause an enquiry to be made by Parliaments, which may be dangerous at this Conjuncture, when all persons ought to engage against the common Enemy." As a result, Penn wrote Morris that he was offering £5,000 as a "free gift" (his words) to help in the crisis. He wanted it done quickly, for "the times are critical, and every body's Eyes are upon us."[33]

Franklin knew of Thomas Penn's letter to Morris and judged that English public opinion and officials had "intimidated" him. After Morris received Penn's letter on Saturday, 22 November, he presented it to the council on Monday, 24 November, and sent the House a message announcing the proprietors' gift.[34] He did not mention that the funds were to be collected from past-due quitrents. The unpopular quitrents would have to be collected, and some were uncollectible. The devious Thomas Penn thus put the assembly in the position of collecting his quitrents while at the same time announcing that he was freely giving a sum larger than the tax that he would have had to pay.

After learning of the proprietors' gift, the House passed a tax bill but first asserted its privileges. The House resolved on Tuesday, 25 November, that "the Right of granting Supplies to the Crown . . . is alone in the Representatives of the Freemen met in Assembly, being essential to an *English* Constitution. And the Limitation of all such Grants, as to the Matter, Manner, Measure and Time, is in them only." Despite its rhetoric, the assembly resolved to accept the proprietors' gift in lieu of their share of taxes and ordered Franklin and others to bring in a supply bill for £60,000. Even if the assemblymen knew that the money from Penn would come from his quitrent arrears, they had little choice but to accept the supposedly "free gift" in lieu of Penn's estate being taxed. The frontier people were being killed, and they were furious with both Penn and the assembly. Had the assembly not voted money for defense, it would have seemed to care less about the lives of the settlers than did the proprietors. On 26 November, the committee brought in the supply bill, of which £55,000 was to be in bills of credit. The £60,000 bill quickly passed the House. Though Governor Morris thought the money should have been ordered into his hands and though the council thought the bill should have several amendments, in view of the emergency they advised the governor on 26 November to pass it without amendments. He did so on 27 November.[35]

Writing the assembly's London agent Richard Partridge on 27 November, Franklin reported the bill had passed and "That the Proprietaries Estate is exempted from the Tax, in Consideration of their Gift of Five Thousand Pounds to the Publick." He then expressed his disgust for the proprietors: "Thus by their senseless Refusal of the first Bill granting Fifty Thousand Pounds, and mean selfish Claim of a Right to Exemption from Taxes, they have brought on themselves infinite Disgrace and the Curses of all the Continent" (6:273). From a different point of view, the pacifist leader Israel Pemberton objected to the act: passing it was "very imprudent & a violation of the Trust reposed" in the Quaker assemblymen. Their driving force was to gain "some Advantage over the Governor & Proprietor, for the sake of which every other Consideration seem'd to be little regarded." Pemberton said that no Quaker assemblyman should vote for "measures to be carried into Execution by a Committee of their own Nomination." It was a "manifest inconsistency and not to be reconciled to our Profession." No doubt he especially had in mind the two Quaker members who had been appointed provincial commissioners—Speaker Isaac Norris and the Quaker carpenter Joseph Fox. After Franklin, Fox was the most active commissioner appointed from the assembly. The Friends disowned him in 1756 for supporting defense.[36]

The Mob and the Militia Bill

After Governor Morris reported on 18 November 1755 that Indians had attacked Tulpehocken (the Tulpehocken Creek flows into the Schuylkill River a few miles north of Reading; see map 2, p. 308) and killed many inhabitants, he asked for an immediate supply of money "to afford the necessary and timely Assistance to the distressed Inhabitants in the Back Counties" and requested the assembly to pass a militia act. "Without a Law of this Kind, it will be impossible to keep up, or govern any Troops that may be raised." The next morning, 19 November, Franklin brought in a bill titled "An Act for the better ordering and regulating the Military Force of this Province."[37] The editors of the *Papers of Benjamin Franklin* commented that it was a rare occasion "during these years when an important bill originated with an individual." A committee, including Franklin, was appointed to revise the bill (at least it changed its title), and on Friday afternoon, 21 November, it passed with four pacifist Quakers voting against it: "An Act for the better Ordering and Regulating such as are willing and desirous to be united for Military Purposes within this Province."[38]

Earlier that Friday morning, Speaker Norris appointed Franklin to a committee to reply to the governor's message of the previous day. After noon, the committee did so, saying the assembly had no money, but if the governor would pass the £60,000 money bill, the assembly could immediately borrow the amount needed to support the frontier settlers.[39]

After receiving Franklin's militia bill on Friday afternoon, Governor Morris told the House on Saturday morning, 22 November, that it contained provisions (repeating his charge of 16 May) "of a very extraordinary Nature," and that it would fail to defend the province. Nevertheless, he would assent to it in the emergency.[40] He passed the bill on Tuesday, 25 November, in the remarkably short time of five legislative days after its introduction. He had written Thomas Penn on 22 November that he knew the bill would "do no good yet I believe I must consent to it . . . if it be only to shew that I am willing to do any thing that has even a chance of contributing to the defence of the Province." He also confessed that he hoped by his approval "to avoid the resentment of a Mob that I am informed will be in Town from the back Countys in a few days." He judged that "these people, when they come, notwithstanding any thing I can do, may think me the cause of all their sufferings and act accordingly."[41]

The older scholarship claimed the governor and assembly passed the militia bill because a mob of frontiersmen appeared in Philadelphia and demanded action. The 1963 editors of the *Papers of Benjamin Franklin*, however, noted that "official word of the intended march did not reach the governor and Council until Monday," 24 November, and that by the time the mob appeared before the governor on Monday night and the assembly on Tuesday morning, the passage was already a fait accompli, with only the procedural steps remaining. That is true, but it ignores that the governor and the assembly had heard by Saturday,

22 November, if not before, that on Wednesday, 19 November, a number of Chester and Philadelphia county citizens had met and signed a petition to the assembly. They were coming en masse to present it in Philadelphia.

Both the numbers and the demands of the supposed "mob" are contradictory. Governor Morris wrote Thomas Penn on 28 November that 700 persons came to town on Monday night, 24 November (6:280). William Smith gave three different estimates: in *A Brief View*, his estimate was 400; in the *Philadelphische Zeitung*, 600; and in his letter of 27 November to Thomas Penn, 300. Several years later, Joseph Galloway wrote that 200 people came to town.[42] It seems doubtful that there could have been as many as even 200 people, for Franklin's routine activities were undisturbed. He attended the legislature that Monday afternoon and went to the usual Union Fire Company meeting that evening, 24 November.

Though Morris's letter to Penn of 22 November documents his supposed fear of the mob (and indirectly asserts to Penn his bravery and shrewd political dealings), Joseph Galloway, who became Franklin's political lieutenant, wrote that Governor Morris and the Proprietary Party organized the protest in order to force the assembly to submit. Galloway charged that letters from Proprietary Party leaders condemned the assembly, extolled the governor's measures, and called for the people to come down in multitudes and demand supplies on the governor's terms. According to Galloway, John Hambright, a tavern-keeper, with "others of that Business, who hold their Licenses under the Governor," led the mob. William Moore, chief justice of Chester County (and a proprietary partisan), was another leader. He wrote Governor Morris on 23 November that two thousand people from Chester County were coming to town to demand that the government protect the frontier settlements.[43] According to Galloway, when the mob came to Philadelphia, "the Governor's Faction dispersed amongst them" and "maliciously endeavoured to inflame their Minds against the Assembly," but others (no doubt members of the Quaker Party) "gave a fair and impartial Representation of the Assembly's Conduct" and undeceived the majority. Since Galloway wrote in 1759 and seems to have been prejudiced against Moore, his testimony is suspect. Many frontier people were angry with both parties and wanted action, though some were members of each party—and some of neither.

Richard Hockley's letter to Thomas Penn of 16 December repeats Governor Morris's fear of the mob: Morris "with some others about him were excessively frightned upon hearing of a number of Country People being come to town as they imagined in a Clamourous manner, and it was with much Intercession he was prevailed upon not to go into the Jerseys that night. . . . I presumed to mention the disadvantage that might accrue on such a Step both with respect to himself and the Government . . . as it woud have given the Populace some reason to suspect he had acted such a part as he cou'd not stand by. . . . Mess.rs Allen, Miflin, Lardner and myself told him we woud arm and stand by him if there was a necessity for it."⁴⁴ In his report to Penn, Morris made himself the hero of the occasion. He wrote that on Tuesday evening, 25 November, two of the mob's leaders "in a very humble manner, begg'd of me to do every thing in my power to preserve the People." They hoped "that no unreasonable Disputes . . . wou'd hinder us from providing for the Safety of the People." Morris claimed he was sorry "they were laid under a necessity to come down to this City to ask for what it was the Duty of the Legislature to afford without asking." He expressed his sympathy for the people, said he had repeatedly called on the legislature to grant money for defense, and reported that the only result had been "to draw upon myself, and the Proprietarys, reflections, and the worst of Language" (6:280).

The governor told the mob's leaders that as soon as the proprietors learned of Braddock's defeat they had sent £5,000 as a free gift to support the defense of the province. (He of course did not tell them that Thomas Penn only contributed after the English public and the British authorities expressed their disapproval of Penn's position.) Morris reported to Penn that the leaders were "perfectly satisfied" and asked if they could go to the assembly. Assenting, Morris said that he recommended they behave "in the same peaceable manner they had done to me" (6:281).

The *Votes and Proceedings of the Assembly* record that on Tuesday morning, a group of inhabitants of Philadelphia and Chester counties asked to speak to the assembly. They were admitted and presented a paper to the speaker, which twenty-nine persons had signed on 19 November, requesting that the governor and House take "Measures . . . for our Preservation in this Time of imminent Danger." The assembly minutes record that Speaker Norris replied that the members of the House represented the people and that their powers "were derived from the People." He asked them "Whether they desired that the House should give up any Rights, which, in the Opinion of the House, the People were justly entitled to." They answered no. They only sought that the province "might be relieved from its present unhappy situation." The Speaker reported that since the proprietors were now willing to contribute to "the common Security of the Province," the representatives would speedily relieve the current distress. Then the petitioners withdrew.⁴⁵

Morris wrote Penn a different account of the meeting. He said that the frontier people were unhappy with the assembly because it "sent for a few of them only into the House." He claimed the assembly members "took greater state upon them than the Governor, though they" represented the people. He added that Franklin "harrang'd them, telling them the Assembly had done every thing that was consistent with the Liberties and Privileges of the People, for which they, the House, were contending, some of the People answered that they did not know that their Liberties were invaded, but they were sure their Lives and Estates were." Franklin's "harangue," said Morris, "had not therefore the effect he desir'd, and I suppose expected, for great pains had been taken by some of the Members, and all their numerous Emissarys to sow sedition in the minds of all these Country People, who were however proof against all their Lies." Morris told Penn that the country people returned home "quite satisfied" with the proprietors and governor, "but very much otherwise with that of the Assembly" (6:281).

Morris's seven hundred mob members and Smith's three hundred were probably written to supply Penn with material to use against the assembly (and probably also to gain Penn's sympathy for his ostensibly poor, beleaguered Pennsylvania lieutenants). I suspect that more people would have signed the petition in Chester and Philadelphia counties than would make the trip to Philadelphia. No reliable evidence exists, but I doubt that the supposed "mob" consisted of even twenty-nine people. If there were two hundred people (the smallest number otherwise given), why would they present a petition that only twenty-nine persons signed? Could they have wanted to keep their identities secret? And what about Franklin's role when the mob appeared in the assembly? Would he, rather than Speaker Norris, have replied to the petitioners? It would have been a breach of etiquette for him to do so—unless it was done at the Speaker's request. It seems unlikely that Norris would have asked him to. Further, Franklin was not an especially good public speaker. Morris probably made up the story. The pusillanimous Morris was evidently continuing to portray Franklin as the real leader of the assembly and as an implacable opponent of Thomas Penn. I suspect the "mob" consisted of about a dozen people.

On 28 November, Morris wrote Thomas Penn, again attempting to justify passing the militia bill. He realized that Penn and the British authorities would find it objectionable: Penn because the governor did not control the militia, and the British authorities because its terms were so lenient. Morris was right: Penn objected and the British authorities vetoed it. Morris told Penn that the assembly did not expect him to pass it; the bill was only intended "to raise a clamour against me." He claimed that by passing it, he had outfoxed the assembly. He further asserted that now the people have "in great measure turned upon" the assembly. The bill would be "impossible to carry" into "execution, and is therefore no more than waste Paper" (6:282).

THE BILL'S PROVISIONS

In part, Franklin's militia bill reflected the terms of Franklin's 1747–48 Association. The militia was to be voluntary, and the enlisted men would elect the company officers. The great difference was that the militia was "for the first time in Pennsylvania history, to be established by formal legislative act" (6:268–69). As in 1747, the troops would vote for officers, whom the governor would commission. Further, the company officers would meet and elect officers for the regiment. If the governor approved them, he would commission them. If the governor refused to grant a commission to any officer, two other persons would be presented in his stead, "one of whom, at his Pleasure, shall receive his Commission" (6:271). After the companies and regiments were formed, the governor or commander in chief, with the advice and consent of the regimental officers, would form articles of war to govern the forces and to bring offenders to justice. The company officers must volunteer to be bound by the articles.

The articles of war would be "as near as possible" to the military laws of Great Britain, considering "the different Circumstances of this Province compared with Great-Britain, and of a voluntary Militia of Freemen, compared with mercenary standing Troops." No persons who had not voluntarily signed the articles would be subject to them. No servants or youths under twenty-one could join without the consent in writing of his parents, guardians, or masters. No militia member would be protected in any suit or action brought against him in court "except during his being in actual Service in Field or Garrison." Without his signed consent, no one in the militia could be compelled or led to go more than "three Days March beyond the inhabited Parts of the Province; nor detained longer than three Weeks in any Garrison." Finally, the militia act was to continue in force only until 30 October 1756 (6:272–73). The king in council, however, rejected it on 7 July 1756,[46] as Philadelphians learned by 15 October—fifteen days before the bill was due to expire (6:411n3).

TROUBLESOME PETITIONS

More than a dozen petitions came to the November assembly from the frontiers asking for help against the French and Indian attacks, but three additional ones were especially challenging. One from Justice William Moore and thirty-five additional citizens of Chester County, presented on 5 November, castigated both the assembly's disputes with the governor and the pacifist members' voting against all military expenses. Another, from Anthony Morris and twenty-two other Quakers addressed to the assembly on 7 November, claimed that raising sums of money to be spent conducting war "appears to us in its Consequences to be destructive of our religious Liberties" and said that many conscientious Quakers must refuse to pay taxes for such purposes. The third (written by William Smith), from William Plumsted, mayor, and 133 other Philadelphians, was presented on 12 November and demanded a stronger militia law and appropriations for defense.[47] Franklin, Speaker Isaac Norris, and other assemblymen knew that the proprietors would use these three petitions against the assembly.

Realizing that the pacifist petition would inflame the frontier people, the assembly tried to keep it a secret, but, the doorkeeper, Edward Kelly (presumably disgusted by the pacifists), spread word of the petition. Consequently, on 11 November the assembly dismissed him. When Governor Morris wrote Thomas Penn about the petition, he made it seem as if it represented the view of all Quakers: "their address will shew whatever their pretences and professions have been that they never intended to do any thing in defence of their Country, and that the [currency] Bill they now propose and insist on, is intended only to save appearances." Morris, however, well knew that the majority of Quaker assemblymen, like Speaker Isaac Norris, disapproved of the pacifists' address and had voted to support an expensive tax for defense. Seven pacifist assemblymen recorded their vote against the bill.[48]

Speaker Norris appointed Franklin to a committee on 13 November to reply to the three petitions. The committee reported on the next day, but some assemblymen objected, so the message was recommitted to committee, and the same happened on 15 November.[49] Debated on the last day of the session, 3 December, it was ordered to be recorded without being approved (6:246–48). Since the date on the report was 14 November, it may be that the original report was the one entered in the minutes. The committee said that William Moore had written his petition before the House "entered on any Business," and it assumed that the House kept up "unnecessary Disputes with the Governor, when as yet there were none begun." Founded on mistakes and misrepresentations, it was "improper to be presented to the House." The third petition, from Anthony Morris and twenty-two other pacifist Quakers, insinuated that numerous additional Quakers would refuse to pay taxes and thereby assumed that it spoke for others unnamed, which the assembly committee doubted, and "is therefore an unadvised and indiscreet Application to the House." Four pacifist Quaker members of assembly, James Pemberton, William Callender, Joseph Gibbons, and Peter Worral, dissented to this part of the message.[50] The petition from Mayor William Plumsted and 133 others who called themselves the "principal Inhabitants" of Philadelphia, contained many signatures of "*Strangers* or *obscure Persons* and some of them *under Age.*" Mayor Plumsted, instead of behaving with good intentions, had drawn on "many indiscreet or unwary Persons" through the influence of his office and thereby "failed greatly in the Duty of his Station" (6:246–48).

An Attempt to Heal the Wounds

While Governor Morris was libeling Franklin to Penn and while Provost William Smith was attacking him and the Pennsylvania Quakers,[51] Franklin tried to get the opposing partisans in Pennsylvania to work together. In a 27 November 1755 *Pennsylvania Gazette* editorial, he wrote,

> It is said that a Bill for giving Sixty Thousand Pounds to the King's Use, sent up Yesterday by the Assembly, will this Day be passed by the Governor, to the great Joy of all that wish well to this of late unhappy Province. The honourable Proprietaries have, on their Part, made a free Gift of Five Thousand Pounds for the Defence of the Country. By the Militia Law, passed on Tuesday, those who bear Arms, may be formed into regular Bodies, with due Order and Discipline, and thereby become better able to serve their Country, more secure in themselves, and more terrible to their Enemies. And by the Act for giving Sixty Thousand Pounds (which Sum is immediately to be struck in paper Bills) Money will be furnished to buy Arms, and Ammunition, and pay such as shall bravely go forth

in Defence of their Country. It is hoped that the cruel Spirit of Party, which has for some time past raged so violently among us, will now subside; and that we shall no longer, by our Dissentions, continue Enemies to our Friends, or Friends to our Country's Enemies.

With its concluding chiasmus, the brief editorial is another minor rhetorical gem.

Franklin was trying to put the best face on the situation. He must have known that Penn's £5,000 was in overdue quitrents and that it could not be used to strike the paper money bills, but he tried to reassure the frontier settlers and to help calm both parties. His militia bill of 25 November and the supply bill of 27 November were symbiotic. Neither could have made a difference by itself. Without the money, the men would not enlist, but together, Franklin hoped that they would provide the men and money to defend the frontier.

Franklin's Summary

Writing in 1787, Franklin recalled that on 17 November the governor had proposed a series of amendments to the £60,000 tax bill,[52] all of which the assembly rejected. Franklin summed up the 1755 quarrels between the assembly and the governor in his *Autobiography* and concluded with a reference to one of these amendments: "Governor Morris who had continually worried the Assembly with Message after Message before the Defeat of Braddock, to beat them into the making of Acts to raise Money for the Defence of the Province without Taxing among others the Proprietary Estates, and had rejected all their Bills for not having such an exempting Clause, now redoubled his Attacks, with more hope of Success, the Danger and Necessity being greater. . . . In one of the last, indeed, which was for granting £50,000 his propos'd Amendment was only of a single Word; the Bill express'd that all Estates real and personal were to be taxed, those of the Proprietaries *not* excepted. His Amendment was; for *not* read *only*. A small but very material Alteration!" (A 143–44).[53]

Franklin added that when the news of Braddock's defeat reached England, "our Friends there whom we had taken care to furnish with all the Assembly's Answers to the Governor's Messages, rais'd a Clamour against the Proprietaries for their Meanness and Injustice in giving their Governor such Instructions, some going so far as to say that by obstructing the Defence of their Province, they forfeited their Right to it. They were intimidated by this, and sent Orders to their Receiver General to add £5000 of their Money to whatever Sum might be given by the Assembly, for such Purpose" (A 144). Franklin was probably reading between the lines when he wrote in 1788 that some persons in England believed the proprietors forfeited their right to Pennsylvania.[54]

"A Dialogue between X, Y, and Z," 18 December 1755

The forthcoming meetings on Monday, Tuesday, and Wednesday, 22–24 December 1755 of militia volunteers to elect officers of the companies occasioned

Franklin's "Dialogue."[55] Franklin knew the Proprietary Party's scorn for the militia act and feared that the British authorities would "negative" the bill. He defended it in his 18 December *Pennsylvania Gazette* "Dialogue" and sent a copy to London, where the *Gentleman's Magazine* acknowledged receiving it from "Americanus" in its February issue and published it in March.[56] "A Dialogue" featured three speakers: a reasonable advocate of the militia (X), a doubter that the militia could be effective (Y), and a Proprietary Party spokesman (Z). The setting is X's home, where Y and Z are calling on him. When Z asked what he thought of the militia bill, X replied that the more he considered it, the better he liked it (6:297).

Z objected that the bill did not specify the time and place to meet or the person(s) to call the volunteers together. X replied that the words "as heretofore they have used in Time of War" referred to the 1747–48 militia Association and that "we may now *lawfully do* in this Affair, what we then did *without law*." Y agreed and suggested that the "Officers of the old Companies call the old Associators together" and that additional new companies may be formed "as the associated Companies were." Z said that the Quakers could show up and elect officers. X conceded the possibility but said they did not do so in the former Militia Association. Z then claimed that the governor should appoint the officers because the people might choose an unworthy, though popular, man. That's possible, X said, but if all officers appointed by governors were "always Men of Merit," it would be "wrong ever to hazard a popular Election." X agreed that the governor should not have officers forced upon him who were incompetent. On the other hand, people would "engage more readily in the Service" and face danger with more intrepidity if they knew and respected the ability and courage of the person leading them (6:297–98).

X, the reasonable advocate, said that the act was a "proper Medium" between the two modes. The troops choose, and if the governor approves, he appoints the choice; if not, the governor passes on to a second choice and even a third. X added that "This Mode of Choice is moreover agreeable to the Liberty and Genius of our Constitution," being similar to the laws whereby sheriffs and coroners "are chosen and approved." Y, the doubter that the militia could be effective, asked if it were "agreeable to the English Constitution." Echoing Franklin's earlier statements of Americanism (5:447, 451, 6:264), X replied that "by removing into America, cultivating a Wilderness, extending the Dominion, and increasing the Wealth, Commerce and Power of their Mother Country, at the Hazard of their Lives and Fortunes," the emigrants "ought not, and in Fact do not thereby lose their native Rights. There is a Power in the Crown to grant a Continuance of those Rights to such Subjects, in any Part of the World, and to their Posterity born in such new Country" (6:299).

The colonists had and deserved greater rights and liberties than the English. To encourage and reward those who ventured to the new lands, England had in some cases granted "Liberties and Privileges, not used in England, but suited to the different Circumstances of different Colonies." These "additional Liberties and Privileges" were not regularly enjoyed "under an English Constitution." So, too, Americans could have a different militia law (6:299).

When Z, the Proprietary Party spokesman, argued in favor of a universal draft, X replied that cowards rather weakened than strengthened a militia. Perhaps thinking of Braddock's defeat and Colonel Dunbar's army fleeing, Franklin wrote: "Fear is contageous, and a Pannick once begun spreads like Wildfire, and infects the stoutest Heart." But, objected Z, wise governments have compelled "all Sorts of Persons to bear Arms, or suffer heavy Penalties." Demonstrating his thorough knowledge of the Bible, X/Franklin replied that the wisest legislator, God, exempted the cowards, and cited Deuteronomy 20:8 and Judges 7:4–6. Z abruptly declared, "I am no Coward; but hang me if I'll fight to save the Quakers." In the most effective passage in "A Dialogue," Franklin adopted the colloquial, downright, tough language and attitudes that he frequently displayed. Bluntly, X/Franklin rejoined, "That is to say, you won't pump Ship, because 'twill save the Rats, as well as yourself" (6:305).

The doubting Y said that the method of forming the militia companies seems "so round-about" that we will not have "the Benefit of it in any reasonable Time." X, however, explained that citizens could elect company officers within a week, that the company officers could choose regimental officers in another week, and the whole "may be in Order in a Month." X then urged speed and considered the war's international context: "as the Colonies are at present the Prize contended for between Britain and France, and the latter, by the last Advices, seems to be meditating some grand Blow, Part of which may probably fall on Pennsylvania, either by Land or Sea, or both, it behoves us, I think, to make the best Use we can of this Act, and carry it immediately into Execution both in Town and Country" (6:306).

If the militia act worked, demanded Z, "what shall we have to say against the Quakers at the next Election?" X/Franklin concluded, "O my Friends, let us on this Occasion cast from us all these little Party Views, and consider ourselves as Englishmen and Pennsylvanians. Let us think only of the Service of our King, the Honour and Safety of our Country, and Vengeance on its Murdering Enemies. If Good be done, what imports it by whom 'tis done? The Glory of serving and saving others, is superior to the Advantage of being served or secured. Let us resolutely and generously unite in our Country's Cause (in which to die is the sweetest of all Deaths) and may the God of Armies bless our honest Endeavours" (6:306).

Recalling the militia bill in his *Autobiography*, Franklin said that when the £60,000 bill passed, he was appointed one of the commissioners for disposing of the money. "I had been active" in writing the act, "and procuring its Passage: and had at the same time drawn a Bill for establishing and disciplining a voluntary Militia, which I carried thro' the House without much Difficulty, as Care was taken in it, to leave the Quakers at their Liberty. To promote the Association necessary to form the Militia, I wrote a Dialogue, stating and answering all the Objections I could think of to such a Militia, which was printed and had as I thought great Effect" (A 144). But, as we will see, the pacifist Quakers objected, and the Proprietary Party members sabotaged the militia.

NINETEEN

General Franklin on the Frontier, 1755–1756

Franklin will at least deserve a Statue for his Prudence Justice Humanity and above all for his Patience.
—*Dr. Thomas Lloyd on Franklin, 6:381–82*

"**With the consent and approbation** of the governor," the commissioners controlled the £60,000 supply bill that had passed on 27 November 1755. When the assembly recessed on 3 December, Franklin and the other commissioners started meeting daily, "Sundays not excepted."[1] Governor Robert Hunter Morris and the commissioners decided to build a fort at Shamokin, which was near the meeting of the east and north branches of the Susquehanna River (see maps 2 and 3). From there the English could "carry the warr into the Enemy's Country and hunt them in all their Fishing, Hunting, Planting, and dwelling places" (6:455). On 5 December, Franklin informed his former Junto friend William Parsons, who was at Easton, Northumberland County, that the commissioners had "a good Agreement with the Governor." Franklin also wrote Parsons that "300 Men are ordered to be immediately raised on pay, to range the Frontiers, and Block-houses for Stages to be erected at proper Distances" (6:290).

Parsons had written Franklin on 25 and 27 November about Indian attacks. Replying on 5 December, Franklin said that he had sent one hundred arms to Easton, with a pound of powder and four pounds of lead for each gun. Parsons should loan them to poor families on the frontier who had no arms or money to buy weapons. Since Parsons was a Proprietary Party leader, Franklin wrote, "All Party laid aside, let you and I use our Influence to carry this Act into Execution." Franklin signed, "Your affectionate Friend" (6:290–91).

Devastating attacks occurred northwest of Philadelphia in Northumberland County's Moravian settlements. Pennsylvania lacked an organized system of defense. Though Franklin's militia bill had passed on 25 November, the troops did not elect the militia company officers until 22–24 December, and Governor Morris did all he could to hinder the formation of the companies (6:383–89). In the same *Pennsylvania Gazette* of 27 November, where Franklin tried to heal the wounds between the Proprietary and Quaker Party members, he reported the massacre at the Moravian settlement at Gnadenhütten. Few people escaped.

When the nearby Easton residents learned the news, they "sent over to the Jerseys to Colonel Anderson," requesting help. He quickly came with a "Company, and marched in Pursuit of the Enemy, as he did most readily on a late Occasion of the same Kind." At the same time, a number of Northampton inhabitants took up arms and "went likewise in Search of the Indians."[2]

Franklin published a detailed account of the massacre in the 4 December *Gazette*. A Gnadenhütten teenager managed to escape by jumping out a second-story window and running into the woods. He said that about twelve Indians had attacked the house, killed five people in it, and then burned it. In addition, "One Man that got out of the House was shot in the Back, and had also three or four Blows in his Body by a Tomahawk, him they also scalped." The Indians burned "all the Grain and Hay," the "Meeting house," and all the houses in the settlement. They took "the Horses, and more than forty Head of fat Cattle." The early report was partially inaccurate, but as more information came in, Franklin was presumably too busy with various duties, including preparing to go off to Easton, to write a fuller account. Perhaps, however, he did not want to publish the facts that the Indians killed only the white missionaries, that the attackers consisted of only twelve Indians, and that the entire group of seventy Moravian Indians around the settlement made their way safely to Bethlehem.[3]

THE DEFENSE STRATEGY CHANGES

After Governor Morris left on 8 December for a meeting with General William Shirley and the other colonial governors in New York to plan for mutual defense, further marauding on the Pennsylvania frontier made the commissioners reconsider their plan. The Indian trader George Croghan and others advised that they should secure the frontier with a chain of forts before assaulting the Indians. That advice, in conjunction with the continuing Indian depredations, convinced them that they should first protect the settled areas along Pennsylvania's frontier (6:455). Three commissioners—Franklin, former governor James Hamilton, and Joseph Fox—went to Northampton County to organize defenses. Morris had given Hamilton the authority to commission officers.

Franklin wrote Parsons again on 12 December, acknowledging his letters of 6 and 9 December, informing him that he or Hamilton or both would be with Parsons at Easton "in a few days to establish Ranging or Watching Parties, Blockhouses, &c." Franklin's letter came in a wagon with 56 arms, 50 pounds of gunpowder, 200 pounds of lead, 50 blankets "and a Hogshead of Rum." Since the supplies were intended for the rangers, they should be kept until "our Arrival. . . . I do not enlarge, as I expect soon to see you, and the Waggoner waits" (6:292). On Monday, Parsons dramatically wrote Franklin and Hamilton, "it is not unlikely that it may be the last time." The frontier settlers west of Easton had fled, and Easton was now the frontier: "Our poor people of this Town have quite expended their Little substance and are quite wearied out with watching and were all along in hopes the Government would have taken some

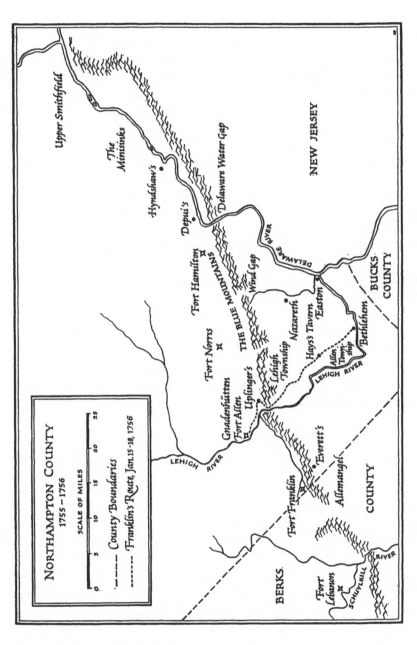

Map 5. *Northampton County*

measures for their Relief and for the security of the Town. But now seeing themselves, as well as the Town neglected, they are moving away as fast as they can.
So that if we have not help nor no orders from the Commissioners to use means
to get help in a day or two, We shall every one of us be obliged to leave the
Town and all we have in it to the Fury of the Enemy, who there is no reason to
doubt are lurking about within sight of us." Parsons had spent "what little stock
of Cash I had in publick Services, so that I am obliged to send this by a private
hand, not being able to pay a person to go Express with it. Pray do something
or give some order for our speedy relief, or the whole Country will be entirely
ruined."

Parsons wrote that if only the commissioners "had but given encouragements to some Persons, that you could have confided in [one assumes he meant
himself], for their Employing people just for our present Defence, 'till you could
have agreed upon a general Plan, all this part of the Country might have been
saved which is now entirely lost and the Enemy are still perpetrating further and
further, and if immediate measures are not taken they will very soon be within
sight of Philadelphia" (6:293–94). Arms and supplies arrived later that day. That
same Monday, 15 December, Franklin wrote him that three companies of troops
would be with him shortly and that he and Hamilton would set out on Thursday
"to visit you, erect Blockhouses," and enlist officers. Since neither he nor Hamilton knew many people in Northampton County, he asked Parsons to think of
suitable persons to be commissioned "for raising and commanding Men to be
kept in the Province Pay." Franklin enclosed £20 toward buying food for the
Easton refugees. Though Franklin had not received the desperate letter Parsons
wrote that same day, he knew the state of mind that Parsons must have been
in and wrote "Be of good Courage. . . . Your Friends will never desert you"
(6:292–93).

Franklin and three other commissioners wrote George Croghan on 17 December requesting him to go to Cumberland County and erect three "Stockadoes" (6:294–95). The assemblymen had realized on 28 November that they
would need the expertise of Croghan and William Trent in the crisis and had
relieved them from the threat of "restraint or arrest" for debt. Their finances
had collapsed during "the defection of our Indian allies from their former
friendship."[4] David Hall informed William Strahan on 17 December 1755 that
Franklin was setting out for the frontier tomorrow "in order to erect Forts, six
Blockhouses, and appoint Rangers, &c. for the Protection of the Country. God
grant something may be done effectually for our Defence; for if it is not done
soon, we shall all be ruined and many will be slaughtered in the most cruel
Manner." Though Franklin had turned over the day-to-day printing business to
Hall in the beginning of 1748, he had written and selected materials for the
Pennsylvania Gazette, compiled *Poor Richard*, and recommended certain pam-
phlets and books—none of which was called for in the terms of the partnership.
Hall now lamented to Strahan that the war "employs Mr. Franklin so much that

he has no Time to think any Thing about our particular Business, which gives me the more to do."[5]

QUAKER PACIFISTS

John Churchman, a leading Quaker pacifist, had spoken to the Pennsylvania assembly on 7 November 1755 against giving any support for defense, but the assembly nevertheless passed the supply bill on 27 November, naming as commissioners the Quakers Isaac Norris and Joseph Fox in addition to Franklin. Churchman denounced the supply bill at a Philadelphia Quaker meeting in December. He and John Woolman, the most talented Quaker spiritual leader of the day, prepared a remonstrance against the measure and a call for Quakers to refuse to pay taxes to support defense. Since Quakers were a majority in the assembly, Churchman and Woolman charged that many Quaker assemblymen must have supported the bill, which would tax other persons, including pacifists, to support the war. Churchman wrote that "many friends thought they could not be clear as faithful watchmen, without communicating to their brethren, their mind and judgment concerning the payment of such a tax; for which purpose an Epistle was prepared, considered, agreed to, and signed by twenty one friends."[6]

John Woolman drafted the "Epistle of Tender Love and Caution to Friends in Pennsylvania" on 16 December. It said that the Friends were "painfully apprehensive, that the large sum granted by the late Act of Assembly for the King's use, is principally intended for purposes inconsistent with our peaceable testimony; we therefore think, that as we cannot be concerned in wars and fightings, so neither ought we to contribute thereto, by paying the tax directed by the said act, though suffering be the consequence of our refusal, which we hope to be enabled to bear with patience." The authors proclaimed "our fidelity to the present government, and our willingly paying all taxes for purposes which do not interfere with our consciences" but suggested that all those who were truly meek and humble should have the "true fortitude and patience to bear" the sufferings they might have to endure.[7]

On the day that "The Epistle of Tender Love and Caution" circulated in Philadelphia, a group of frontiersmen, disgusted with the Pennsylvania assembly's inaction, placed on the stairs of the state house (i.e., Independence Hall) two men and a boy whom Indians had killed and scalped. Although the experienced hospital matron Charlotte Brown must have witnessed many deaths, she pronounced the sight "the dismallest . . . I ever saw."[8]

It did not persuade the pacifists. Israel Pemberton wrote London's Dr. John Fothergill the next day, 17 December, that the assembly's passing the November money bill was "very imprudent & a violation of the Trust reposed in them, especially as they had reason to believe they might have raised the mony in another manner not liable to the same exceptions but this would not gratify their Darling scheme of gaining some Advantage over the Governor & Proprie-

tor, for the sake of which every other Consideration seem'd to be little regarded." Pemberton particularly objected to the assembly members' "entring
into these measures to be carried into Execution by a Committee of their own
Nomination." He proclaimed it a "manifest inconsistency and not to be reconciled to our Profession—it not appearing to be done in Consequence of any
Demand of Tribute from the King."[9]

The "Epistle," like the pacifists' 7 November objections to the assembly,
delighted the Proprietary Party. Provost William Smith obtained a copy, wrote
a preface flogging the Quakers and sent it off to London where it appeared as
anti–Quaker Party propaganda. The "Epistle" strengthened the hand of those
who wanted to rid the Pennsylvania assembly of Quakers by requiring that all
assemblymen take oaths.[10]

To the Frontier

To organize defenses, Franklin set out for the frontier on Thursday, 18 December 1755, the day his militia dialogue appeared in the *Pennsylvania Gazette*. Accompanying him were his son William, possibly dressed in the scarlet uniform
of the Grenadiers to which he belonged,[11] his fellow commissioners James Hamilton and Joseph Fox, and Captain James McLaughlin with fifty provincial caval-
rymen. That night, the commissioners stayed at a poor inn. Franklin wrote
Deborah that the lady in charge was "about to put very damp sheets on the
bed," but "we desired her to air them first; half an hour afterwards, she told us
the bed was ready, and the sheets *well aired*. I got into bed, but jumped out
immediately, finding them as cold as death, and partly frozen. She had *aired*
them indeed, but it was out upon the *hedge*. I was forced to wrap myself up in
my great coat and woollen trowsers, every thing else about the bed was shock-
ingly dirty" (6:365).

The next evening, Friday, 19 December, they reached Bethlehem, up the
Lehigh River about ten miles from Easton, and spent the night there, perhaps
at the Crown Inn. William Edmonds, the Moravian who represented Northampton County in the Pennsylvania Assembly, joined them the next day for the
trip to Easton. Writing Morris on Monday evening, 22 December, James Hamilton reported that "every thing that has been said of the distress of the Inhabitants" was "more than verified upon our own view." He asked the governor to
recruit more men from the Philadelphia area, for there were few at Easton, and
"the terror that has seized them, is so great, or their Spirits so small, that unless
men come from other parts of the Province, I despair of getting such a number
here as will be sufficient." Hamilton added that they had intended to set out the
next day but the wagons with the provisions had not yet arrived, nor did they
yet have sufficient troops. The commissioners remained at Easton until 30 December.

Hamilton advised Morris: "I heartily wish you were at Liberty to declare
Warr . . . and offer large rewards for Scalps, which appears the only way to clear

our Frontiers of those Savages, & will, I am persuaded be infinitely cheapest in the end." With no militia law, the troops "join and leave their Captains at their own humour."[12] On Christmas day, 1755, someone at Easton (almost certainly Franklin) wrote the *Pennsylvania Gazette*, detailing the situation and listing many of the houses destroyed and the persons killed. Most survivors had fled across the Susquehanna into New Jersey. The only stronghold north of Easton was the farm of Samuel and Aaron Dupuy, about twenty-five miles up the Delaware River, just beyond the Delaware Water Gap and the Blue Mountains. Two days later, on 27 December, Franklin wrote Deborah from Easton that "We all continue well, but much harrass'd with business; after many Difficulties and Disappointments, we march'd two Companies, yesterday, over the Mountains." As soon as the soldiers received "Shoes, Arms and Blankets," which were "expected hourly," he would "move towards Berks County" (6:312).

Since the commissioners were about to leave Easton, Franklin gave detailed instructions to William Parsons, whom Hamilton had commissioned a major. The draft is in Franklin's holograph; the editors of the *Papers* speculated that the fair copy was probably in William Franklin's hand and signed by Hamilton. Parsons should immediately "raise and take into Pay for one Month a Company of Foot consisting of 24 Men, to be employ'd as a Garrison, Guard and Watch for the Town of Easton, who shall be allow'd at the Rate of 6 Dollars per Month, with Arms and Ammunition, and 15 lb. of Bread and Meat per Week and a Gill of Rum per Day for each Man." Parsons was to keep "a constant regular Watch" every Night, with "4 Sentinels being plac'd at the outer Ends of the four principal Streets, and one near the Guard Room, to be relieved every Hour." During the day, Parsons should post at least one sentinel on the hill, "to be relieved every 2 Hours, or oftener if you shall judge expedient." He should also "send out a Scout to range some Miles round the Town, to examine all Thickets and Places capable of concealing Parties of the Enemy, and take Notice if any Tracks appear, or Marks of their Approach." When the troops had time, Franklin charged them to "clear the Bushes away that are within and round the Town to the Distance of Musket Shot at least from the Town." Parsons would oversee these tasks and report to the governor (6:313–14).[13]

CALLED TO READING

Governor Morris summoned the commissioners to meet him at Reading on 1 January 1756, whence they intended to ride to Carlisle for an Indian treaty. Having left Easton in the morning, the commissioners arrived at Bethlehem before nightfall on 30 December. Evidently Captain William Hayes and James McLaughlin and their Northampton County troops accompanied them. The commissioners had a long meeting with "Brother Joseph," that is, Bishop Augustus Gottlieb Spangenberg, the Moravians' spititual leader. After the commissioners left for Reading, Captain William Hayes and his soldiers set out from Bethlehem for the deserted settlement at Gnadenhütten. There, on 2 January, about twenty of the troops Hayes had sent ahead were killed by "at least" 250 Indians. Outnumbered and short of ammunition, he retreated (6:341).

Franklin, Hamilton, Fox, and William Franklin arrived at Reading in the midafternoon on New Year's Day 1756. Just a couple of hours earlier, Governor Morris and Richard Peters had come. Peters noted the "intolerably great" panic of the inhabitants: "The Country People expect the Indians in ten Days to fall on some part of the Country, that being their time of the Moon, but I hope they are not true prophets. What may be I cant say but for any thing I see at present five hundred Indians may lay as far Waste before them as they please." At Morris's order, the *Pennsylvania Gazette* of 1 January advertised an award of "Seven Hundred Pieces of Eight . . . for any Person or Persons who shall bring into this City the Heads of Shingas, and Captain Jacobs, Chiefs of the Delaware Indian Nation; or Three Hundred and Fifty Pieces of Eight for each." The two had "received many Favours from this Government, and now treacherously deserted our Interest."

The Bethlehem Moravians learned on 2 January that the Indians had routed Captain William Hayes at Gnadenhütten and held the site. A party brought back some wounded troops. "An express was sent . . . to the Commissioners at Reading." The Moravians noted that "Towards evening upwards of one hundred fugitives were received at Bethlehem and in the Crown Inn—We scarcely know how to provide for them." The next day Hayes wrote the governor and commissioners of the defeat. Governor Morris, Franklin, and the other commissioners received news of the fresh disaster on 3 January, and Morris immediately wrote Bethlehem that he would again send out a force to take Gnadenhütten and cover the frontiers. He also informed the militia that they would receive "forty Pieces of Eight for every Indian they shall kill and scalp in any action they may have with them"—paid upon delivery of the scalps. Morris proposed that one commissioner "return to Bethlehem and Easton, and there give fresh Directions to the Troops and post them in the best Manner for the Protection of the remaining Inhabitants."[14] The governor may have asked who would do it. Perhaps all three volunteered, perhaps only Franklin did, perhaps Morris simply asked Franklin. Franklin was the most popular commissioner, and choosing him made good sense. Perhaps, however, Morris hoped that it might be an easy way to get rid of Franklin—permanently.

COMMANDER OF NORTHAMPTON COUNTY

Morris commissioned Franklin on 5 January 1756 to take charge of all defenses in Northampton County. He could dismiss any officers previously appointed, commission any that he wanted, charge any necessary expenses to the government, and order all civil authorities in the county. The commission had no title. Historians call him either "General" or "Colonel" during his stay in Northampton. Since most contemporaries called him "General" (e.g., 6:381), I will use that title. In the *Autobiography*, Franklin remarked, "My Son who had in the preceding War been an Officer in the Army rais'd against Canada, was my Aid de Camp, and of great Use to me" (A 145). William's rank is also unknown, but James Hamilton probably commissioned him a captain before the commissioners departed from Philadelphia.

Having left Reading on 5 January with William and twenty soldiers from Captain James McLaughlin's company, Franklin spent the night at either Levan's or Trexler's tavern and arrived at Bethlehem on 7 January, where the Moravians called him "General Lieutenant and Captain in chief of our Country." Bishop Spangenberg visited him "in the name of the congregation."[15] Franklin "was surprized to find" Bethlehem "in so good a Posture of Defence." Alarmed by the destruction of the Moravians at Gnadenhütten, the brethren had built a stockade around the main buildings, "had purchased a Quantity of Arms and Ammunition from New York, and had even plac'd Quantities of small Paving Stones between the Windows of their high Stone Houses, for their Women to throw down upon the Heads of any Indians that should attempt to force into them." Franklin, whose air baths and his writing about his "Pennsylvania Fireplace" emphasized the benefit of fresh air (*Life* 2:469–72), noted that the Moravians' large dormitories had "Loopholes at certain Distances all along just under the Cieling, which I thought judiciously plac'd for Change of Air." The armed Moravians kept guard, "and reliev'd as methodically as in any Garrison Town."

Surprised because he knew the Moravians "had obtain'd an Act of Parliament exempting them from military Duties in the Colonies," Franklin had assumed they "were conscienciously scrupulous of bearing Arms." He asked Bishop Spangenberg if they were not pacifists. He answered "That it was not one of their establish'd Principles; but that at the time of their obtaining that Act, it was thought to be a Principle with many of their People. On this Occasion, however, they to their Surprize found it adopted by but a few." Franklin, who believed in self-defense, commented, "It seems they were either deceiv'd in themselves, or deceiv'd the Parliament." Then Franklin wrote one of the sententiae for which he had a genius: "But Common Sense aided by present Danger, will sometimes be too strong for whimsicall Opinions" (A 145).

On Thursday, 8 January, having talked with the survivors, Franklin wrote accounts of the disasters at Gnadenhütten on 1 January and at Allemangle on 4 January. They appeared in the *Pennsylvania Gazette* (6:349–52). Four hundred whites and seventy Indians had fled to Bethlehem. Franklin arranged for soldiers and two wagons belonging to the Moravians to take provisions to Nazareth, and for teams from Nazareth to take provisions to the soldiers "north of the Blue Mountains."[16]

Saturday night, 10 January, he dined with the Moravians and heard their musicians play. On Sunday he attended a Moravian church service, "where I was entertain'd with good Musick, the Organ being accompanied with Violins, Hautboys, Flutes, Clarinets, &c." Brother Reinke's text was 1 John 3:8: "He that committeth sin is of the devil; for the devil sinneth from the beginning. For this purpose the Son of God was manifested, that he might destroy the works of the devil." The Moravian Record noted that Franklin was "very attentive." He reported in the *Autobiography* that "their Sermons were not usually preached to mix'd Congregations, of Men Women and Children, as is our common Practice; but that they assembled sometimes the married Men, at other times their Wives, then the Young Men, the young Women, and the little Children, each Division by itself." The sermon Franklin heard was preached to the children, "who came in and were plac'd in Rows on Benches, the Boys under the Conduct of a young Man their Tutor, and the Girls conducted by a young Woman. The Discourse seem'd well adapted to their Capacities, and was delivered in a pleasing familiar Manner, coaxing them as it were to be good. They behav'd very orderly, but look'd pale and unhealthy, which made me suspect they were kept too much within-doors, or not allow'd sufficient Exercise" (A 149–50).

We are fortunate to have several views of Bethlehem from the 1750s and 1760s. One was by Franklin's friend Thomas Pownall, who visited Bethlehem in 1754, perhaps at Franklin's suggestion, and the others are by Nicholas Garrison, Jr., a local Moravian artist who lived in Bethlehem. It seems likely that Franklin met him sometime during his stay there. Less than three years later (29 July 1758), Garrison married a daughter of Franklin's old friend William Parsons.[17]

During the week at Bethlehem, Franklin "enquir'd a Little into the Practices of the Moravians. . . . I found they work'd for a common Stock, eat at common Tables, and slept in common Dormitorys, great Numbers together." Was it true, Franklin asked, that Moravian marriages "were by Lot?" Bishop Spangenberg said "that Lots were us'd only in particular Cases. That generally when a young Man found himself dispos'd to marry, he inform'd the Elders of his Class, who consulted the Elder Ladies that govern'd the young Women. As these Elders of the different Sexes were well acquainted with the Tempers and Dispositions of their respective Pupils, they could best judge what Matches were suitable, and their Judgments were generally acquiesc'd in. But if for example it should happen that two or three young Women were found to be proper for the young Man, the Lot was then recurr'd to." Franklin objected: "If the Matches are not made by the mutual Choice of the Parties, some of them may chance to be very unhappy. And so they may, answer'd my Informer, if you let the Parties chuse for themselves.—Which indeed I could not deny" (A 149–50).

At Bethlehem, Franklin issued orders to the captains of the first companies that he commanded. Order No. 6 concerned scalping: "You are to acquaint the Men, that if in their Ranging they meet with, or are at any Time attack'd by the Enemy, and kill any of them, Forty Dollars will be allow'd and paid by the Government for each Scalp of an Indian Enemy so killed, the same being produced with proper Attestations" (6:353). James Hamilton had, on 22 December, stressed the necessity of offering bounties for scalps, and Governor Morris had made it official policy on 3 January.

Before marching for Gnadenhütten on Thursday, 15 January, Franklin wrote

Figure 44. Nicholas Garrison, Jr., "A View of Bethlehem, one of the Brethren's Principal Settlements in Pennsylvania." Nicholas Garrison, Jr. (fl. 1740–80), came to Pennsylvania with his father, a Moravian ship captain, in 1740 and later settled in Bethlehem. He drew several views of Bethlehem, and at least two were engraved and printed in London. The engraver Isaiah Noual (1725–post 1763), who joined the Moravian church in London in 1750, executed this "View of Bethlehem" on 27 November 1757. Other states of the same view were listed for sale by Robert Sayer on 53 Fleet Street, London.

The Lehigh River is in the foreground, with the Crown Inn on the left and perhaps the ferry house on the right. The large buildings in the center were the dormitories. Franklin especially admired their loopholes near the ceiling for air circulation (A 149). The buildings in the rear left were farms, and the building in the background was the community store, run for a time by William Edmonds, the Northhampton County representative who served in the assembly with Franklin and accompanied him to Gnadenhütten.

On 29 July 1758, Garrison married Johanna Grace Parsons, a daughter of Franklin's old Junto friend William Parsons. They lived in Philadelphia, where he did his best-known painting and drawing, A View of the House of Employment, Almshouse, Pennsylvania Hospital, and Part of the City of Philadelphia (1767?), engraved in London by James Hullett. When the British occupied Philadelphia, the Garrisons fled to Bethlehem and subsequently to Berks County. Courtesy, Moravian Church Archives.

Deborah that he would have about 130 men with him and would act cautiously, "so as to give the Enemy no Advantage thro' our Negligence. Make yourself therefore easy" (6:361). He left Bethlehem about noon with seven wagons, five of which he had bought from the Moravians, "for our Tools, Stores, Baggage, &c."[18] With him were about 47 soldiers, William Franklin, the Reverend Charles Beatty, and Dr. Thomas Lloyd.

"Just before we left Bethlehem, Eleven Farmers who had been driven from their Plantations by the Indians, came to me requesting a supply of Fire Arms, that they might go back and fetch off their Cattle. I gave them each a Gun with suitable Ammunition." Franklin detached several soldiers and sent them with the farmers. During that day, "We had not march'd many Miles before it began to rain, and it continu'd raining all Day." He and his party were lucky. The farmers and soldiers were attacked as they crossed a creek. All but two were killed. A survivor named John Adam Huth told of the action in the *Pennsylvania Gazette* of 29 January. Since the report was well written, I suspect Franklin took an oral report from Huth and sent it on. Either Huth or the other survivor told Franklin that "his and his Companions Guns would not go off, the Priming being wet with the Rain" (A 146). Along the road, 75 men joined them, bringing the total to 122—pretty close to the 130 he told Deborah.

Franklin's party marched all afternoon in a cold rain: "There were no Habitations on the Road, to shelter us, till we arriv'd near Night, at the House of a German [John Hays's Tavern], where and in his Barn we were all huddled together as wet as Water could make us." Recalling the fate of the farmers, he wrote in the *Autobiography*, "It was well we were not attack'd in our March, for Our Arms were of the most ordinary sort and our Men could not keep their Gunlocks dry. The Indians are dextrous in Contrivances for that purpose, which we had not" (A 146). At Hays's Tavern, they found Ensign Sterling with twenty-three men. The next day, Friday, 16 January "we moved cautiously" through the Lehigh Water Gap, "a very dangerous Pass." Dr. Thomas Lloyd recorded in his diary that "the Rocks overhang the roads on each Side and render it practicable for a very small Number to destroy a Thousand" (6:380). Franklin had the area "reconnoitred" and "took possession of the Passes" before the main body proceeded. That night they reached Uplinger's "but twenty one Miles from Bethlehem, the Roads being bad, and the Waggons moving slowly" (6:370).

The next morning, Franklin's fiftieth birthday, another twenty troops reinforced them. Dr. Lloyd reported that they were now, on 17 January, "in the Country of an Enemy, against whom all possible Caution is absolutely necessary, and scarce sufficient to prevent Surprizes." Lloyd described the scene in the morning.

the Several Companies were drawn up on a Parade, and attended with orderd Firelocks in the most solemn Manner, to an excellent Prayer and animating Exhortation, delivered by the Revd Mr. Beatty; and immediately after began their March, which was conducted by Mr. William Franklin with great Order and Regularity. . . . First the Scouts ranged the Woods and Mountains in the Front, in a Semi Circular Line. Lieutenant Davis, of McLaughlin['s company], led the advanced Guard of 22 men, the Van follow'd at about 200 paces' distance, commanded by Wetherhold; Captain Wayne led the Centre, where marched the General, the Chaplain, and all the Waggons, Baggage, etc., which Capt. Foulke with 47 Men followed; and the Rear Guard was brought up by Ensign Sterling. We had besides Scouts out, on each Flank, and Spies on every Hill. In this Manner our Line of March extended a full Mile and made a pretty appearance from the Hills.

And so they set out, but a hard, cold rain wet their guns so thoroughly that Franklin ordered their return to Uplinger's. That night, the firing of shots alarmed them. Two sentinels had seen two Indians who quickly disappeared.[19] On Sunday, 18 January, the party passed through "the worst Country" that Dr. Lloyd ever saw: "Hills like Alps on each Side and a long narrow Defile where the Road scarcely admitted a single Waggon." At the bottom of the gorge, there was "a rapid Creek with steep Banks." Across from the road, a "Bridge made of a single Log" provided a path that led into the rocks "so that the Indians might with Safety to themselves from the Caverns in the Rocks have cut us all off notwithstanding all Human Precaution" (6:381).

GNADENHÜTTEN

Franklin and the soldiers arrived at Gnadenhütten about noon on Sunday, 18 January 1756. Dr. Lloyd reported that Franklin "immediately employd our Men in forming a Camp and raising a Breast Works to defend it. Here all round appears Nothing but One continued Scene of Horror and Destruction. Where lately flourished a happy and peaceful Village is now all silent and desolate the Houses burnt the Inhabitants buttchered in the most Shocking Manner their mangled Bodies . . . exposd to Birds and Beasts of Prey and all Kinds of Mischief perpetrated that wanton Cruelty can invent" (6:381).

In a *Pennsylvania Gazette* article, Franklin said that it rained all Monday, "with so thick a Fog, that we could not see round us, so as either to chuse a Place for a Fort, or find Materials to build it." The weather cleared that night, and on Tuesday morning, 20 January, he selected the best place for the fort, "marked out the Ground, and at Ten o'Clock set the Men to work." The circumference of the fort measured 455 feet. In the *Autobiography*, he recalled that the men had 70 axes and "were immediately set to work, to cut down Trees; and our Men being dextrous in the Use of them, great Dispatch was made. Seeing the Trees fall so fast, I had the Curiosity to look at my Watch when two Men began to cut at a Pine. In 6 Minutes they had it upon the Ground; and I found it of 14 Inches Diameter. Each Pine made three Palisades of 18 Feet long, pointed at one End" (A 146). Writing in 1788, Franklin exaggerated; in the contemporary news account, he said they were each 15 feet long (6:363).

While the men were cutting trees for the palisade, "our other Men dug a Trench all round of three feet deep in which the Palisades were to be planted." The body of the wagons "being taken off, and the fore and hind Wheels separated by taking out the Pin which united the two Parts of the Perch, we had 10 Carriages with two Horses each, to bring the Palisades from the Woods to the Spot" (A 147). Franklin said in his news report that the men worked "with such Spirit, that now, at Half past Three in the Afternoon, all the Logs for the Stockade are cut, to the Number of 450, being most of them more than a Foot in Diameter, and 15 Feet long. The Trench to set them in, being three Feet deep, and two wide, is dug; 14 Pair of Wheels are drawing them together; some are erected, and we hope to have the whole up, and to be quite inclosed tomorrow. The Fort will be about 125 Feet long, and 50 broad" (6:362–63).

Franklin reported the practicalities: "There was a Saw Mill near, round which were left several Piles of Boards, with which we soon hutted ourselves; an Operation the more necessary at that inclement Season, as we had no Tents. Our first Work was to bury more effectually the Dead we found there, who had been half interr'd by the Country People." The troops also built "a strong Breast work, Musquet Proof" (6:381, 366).

A news report of Tuesday, 20 January (no doubt by Franklin), said that the Reverend Charles Beatty "is with us, and we have regular Prayers Morning and Evening. We went to Prayer before we began to work, all the Men being drawn up to receive Orders and Tools" (6:363). Franklin suppressed at least one reason why the men were all "drawn up." In the *Autobiography*, he wrote: "We had for our Chaplain a zealous Presbyterian Minister . . . who complain'd to me that the Men did not generally attend his Prayers and Exhortations." Impishly, Franklin observed to Beatty that the men received half a gill of rum in the morning and half in the evening and were "punctual in attending to receive it." Franklin said: "It is perhaps below the Dignity of your Profession to act as Steward of the Rum. But if you were to deal it out, and only just after Prayers, you would have them all about you." Beatty knew it was true, "lik'd the Thought, undertook the Office, and with the help of a few hands to measure out the Liquor executed it to Satisfaction; and never were Prayers more generally and more punctually attended" (A 148). "Steward of the Rum"! I doubt that Franklin actually said those words to Beatty, but their use in the 1788 anecdote when Franklin wrote about the event shows that he still found the incident humorous and ironic.

On Wednesday, 21 January 1756, it rained hard most of the day and delayed the work (6:366). The alternating days of work and idleness because of heavy rain gave Franklin "occasion to observe, that when Men are employ'd they are best contented. For on the Days they work'd they were good-natur'd and chearful; and with the consciousness of having done a good Days work they spent the Evenings jollily; but on the idle Days they were mutinous and quarrelsome, finding fault with their Pork, the Bread, &c. and in continual ill-humour; which put me in mind of a Sea-Captain, whose Rule it was to keep his Men constantly

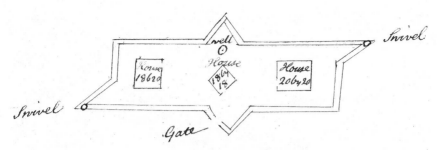

Figure 45a. Franklin's sketch of Fort Allen at Gnadenhütten, 25 January 1756. Franklin's holograph letter and sketch are not extant, but a copy made on 30 January 1756 was inserted in the journal of the Pennsylvania Provincial Council. Franklin wrote in his 25 January letter that the fort was complete and that the troops had hoisted the British flag. Then they "made a general Discharge of our Pieces, which had been long loaded, and of our two Swivels, and named the Place Fort Allen in Honor of our old Friend." He added that the fort was "125 Feet long, 50 wide, the Stockadoes most of them a Foot thick, they are 3 Foot in the Ground and 12 Feet out, pointed at the Top" (6:367).

The sketch shows the location of the two swivel guns, the gate, the well, and the three structures within it, the center one measuring 18 x 18, the left one 18 x 20, and the right one 20 x 20. Courtesy, Pennsylvania Historical and Museum Commission.

at Work; and when his Mate once told him that they had done every thing, and there was nothing farther to employ them about; O, says he, *make them scour the Anchor"* (A 147). One suspects Franklin created the anecdote partly to clinch the moral.

By Thursday, 22 January, most of the stockade was up, and on Friday morning it was finished. He recalled in the *Autobiography* that work began on the "Stage of Boards all round within, about 6 Feet high, for the Men to stand on when to fire thro' the Loopholes. We had one swivel Gun which we mounted on one of the Angles; and fired it as soon as fix'd, to let the Indians know, if any were within hearing, that we had such Pieces; and thus our Fort, (if such a magnificent Name may be given to so miserable a Stockade) was finished in a Week" (A 147). Franklin made another minor mistake above, for the sketch of the fort he drew at the time (Sunday, 25 January), in addition to the walls, gate, the well, and three houses within the fort, one 18 *x* 20, one 18 *x* 18, and one 20 *x* 20, it showed the location of not one, but two swivel guns. Franklin added, "This kind of Fort, however contemptible, is a sufficient Defence against Indians who have no Cannon" (A 147).

More soldiers were gradually joining those at Gnadenhütten, and Franklin planned two more forts, each about fifteen miles from Gnadenhütten, one to the southeast, "between this and Fort Lebanon in the Forks of Schuylkill," later called Fort Franklin; and the other to the northwest, which would be called Fort Norris. Franklin intended "to remain here between them till both are finished

Figure 45b. A swivel gun. A swivel gun is a small anti-personnel cannon, less than three feet long, usually mounted so that it could swivel 360°. A muzzle-loader, it had to swivel around to be loaded. Common from the sixteenth until the end of the nineteenth century, swivel guns were typically placed on the rails of warships to repel boarders. They fired musket balls, grapeshot, or other small-diameter bits of metal—even nails. Whalers adapted them as harpoon guns.

The two that Franklin took with him were probably similar to the one that Lewis and Clark mounted on the bow of their keel boat in 1804. They loaded it with sixteen musket balls. The one at Fort Ticonderoga is a standard eighteenth-century swivel gun. Like almost all surviving ones, it lacks the wooden tiller/handle used to aim the gun. Courtesy, Fort Ticonderoga Museum.

. . . that I may be able to Supply and Assist on either Side, as Occasion requires" (6:307–8).

The same day, Sunday, 25 January 1756, the Reverend Charles Beatty preached a thanksgiving sermon. Then Franklin's troops hoisted the British flag, "made a general Discharge of our Pieces, which had been long loaded, and of our two Swivels, and named the Place *Fort Allen* in Honor of our old Friend" (6:366–67, 372–73). No doubt the gesture pleased Allen, but it did little to lessen the increasing antipathy, resentment, and jealousy he felt for Franklin. The same day Franklin wrote Deborah that every day brought him and his companions "more convenient living." He thanked her for the food she had sent: "all agree" that the roast beef and the roast veal "are both the best that ever were of the kind." He added a humorous note: "Your citizens, that have their dinners hot and hot, know nothing of good eating; we find it in much greater perfection when the kitchen is four score miles from the dining room" (6:364–65). When he wrote Governor Morris on Monday, 26 January, he said that they were erecting a third structure within Fort Allen and that as soon as a new convoy of stores and provisions arrived, he was sending more troops to join those building Fort Norris. He hoped "in a week or ten Days, weather favouring, those two Forts may be finished and the Line of Forts compleated and garrisoned, the Rangers in Motion, and the internal Guards and Watches disbanded, as well as some other Companies; unless they are permitted and encouraged to go after the Enemy to Sasquehannah." Franklin itemized the companies and the numbers of men, 522, in pay (6:370–71).

After completing Fort Allen, Franklin sent troops to "scour the adjacent Country. We met with no Indians, but we found the Places on the neighbouring Hills where they had lain to watch our Proceedings." Franklin went out with the scouts and observed where the Indians had spied on them: "There was an Art in their Contrivance of these Places that seems worth mention. It being Winter, a Fire was necessary for them. But a common Fire on the Surface of the Ground would by its Light have discover'd their Position at a Distance. They had therefore dug Holes in the Ground about three feet Diameter, and some what deeper. We saw where they had with their Hatchets cut off the Charcoal from the Sides of burnt Logs lying in the Woods. With these Coals they had made small Fires in the Bottom of the Holes, and we observ'd among the Weeds and Grass the Prints of their Bodies made by their laying all round with their Legs hanging down in the Holes to keep their Feet warm, which with them is an essential Point." Franklin admired their technique: "This kind of Fire, so manag'd, could not discover them either by its Light, Flame, Sparks or even Smoke." He judged that "their Number was not great, and it seems they saw we were too many to be attack'd by them with Prospect of Advantage" (A 147–48).

Franklin wrote Deborah on Friday, 30 January, that "Every other day, since we have been here, it has rained more or less, to our no small hindrance. It rained yesterday, and now again to day." Franklin, no complainer, assured Deborah that "our living grows every day more comfortable." He had intended to write her a long letter, but a number of people have come "from different parts, that have business with me and interrupt me." Since the one room he and others lived in was "quite public," he had to close quickly (6:378). Another opportunity occurred the next day, and he again wrote Deborah that all were well at the fort "and much the better from the refreshments you have sent us." He mocked his usual standard of living: "though there are a great number of things, besides what we have, that used to seem necessary to comfortable livings, yet we have learnt to do without them." The social Franklin was enjoying his companions. The Reverend Charles Beatty "is a useful man here," and Dr. Thomas Lloyd "another." They, with William Franklin, Captain William Clapham, and the Moravian political leader William Edmonds were among Franklin's usual messmates. They all "present their hearty respects to you for the goodies" (6:382–83).

Dr. Thomas Lloyd, who had been with Franklin since early that month at Bethlehem, wrote an appreciation of him at the end of January: "We have omitted Nothing since our Arrival that can contribute to the Happiness and Security of the County in General. Mr. Franklin will at least deserve a Statue for his Prudence Justice Humanity and above all for his Patience." Hinting at the avariciousness and double dealing that accompanied purchasing supplies for the militia, Lloyd continued his praise of Franklin: "It is impossible to convey to you an Idea of the Temper of these People who are daily endeavouring to impede all Measures for their own Safety and studious of Nothing but to improve the general Calamity to their own private Interest" (6:381–82).

SUMMONED HOME

On Sunday, 1 February, Franklin sent troops to build Fort Norris (6:368n). That day, he heard from Philadelphia. Governor Morris wrote that "he had called the Assembly, and wish'd my Attendance there, if the Posture of Affairs on the Frontiers was such that my remaining there was no longer necessary." Franklin also heard from friends in the assembly, "pressing me by their Letters to be if possible at the Meeting." Franklin wrote in the *Autobiography* that since the "three intended Forts" were "being now compleated, and the Inhabitants contented to remain on their Farms under that Protection, I resolved to return" (A 148). He also heard that the militia and other persons intended to "come out and meet me at my Return, to express their thankful Sense of my (small) Services" (7:13). For the next two days, Franklin prepared to leave Fort Allen: "The more willingly as a New England Officer, Col. Clapham, experienc'd in Indian War, being on a Visit to our Establishment, consented to accept the Command." Franklin "gave him a Commission, and parading the Garrison had it read before them, and introduc'd him to them as an Officer who from his Skill in Military Affairs, was much more fit to command them than myself; and giving them a little Exhortation took my Leave" (A 149).

On 4 February, Franklin, his son, and William Edmonds, with an escort of thirty men, rode to Bethlehem. He had his horse shod and his saddle repaired that night.[20] "The first Night being in a good Bed, I could hardly sleep, it was so different from my hard Lodging on the Floor of our Hut at Gnadenhütten, wrapt only in a Blanket or two" (A 149). Since Franklin had learned of the planned demonstrations in his honor, and since he was "above all things averse to making Show and Parade, or doing any useless Thing that can serve only to excite Envy or provoke Malice," he made a hard horseback trip (it had taken two days to go from Philadelphia to Bethlehem in December) and arrived back in one day, late Friday night, 5 February 1756 (7:13).

In the military emergency, Franklin rose to the occasion.

TWENTY

Rival Militias, Colonel Franklin, Virginia, New York, and Frontier Fighting, 1756

*Though the proprietors "pretend to be 'most ready and willing to bear a just Pro-
portion along with their Tenants in any necessary Tax for the Defence of the Prov-
ince,' yet this appears clearly to be a mere Pretence, since they absolutely except
their Quitrents, and their located unimproved Lands, their Fines, and the Purchase-
Monies they have at Interest; that is, in a Manner, their whole Estate, as your
Committee know of little they have left to be taxed, but a Ferry-house or two, a
Kitchen, and a Dog Kennel."*
—Franklin's committee report, 23 September 1756, 6:526

RIVAL MILITIAS

THE MILITIA COMPANIES held elections 22–24 December 1755 while Franklin
was on the frontier. Governor Robert Hunter Morris tried to sabotage the elections. The inspectors submitted to him the nine sets of officers for the Philadelphia militia companies on 29 December, but he refused to certify the officers
except for one company. The other lists did not include the names of the men
(who had volunteered to become soldiers) who had voted for the officers.
Rumor had it that Morris wanted the names to turn them over to the officers
of the British army coming from New York. The volunteer troops would then,
supposedly, be drafted into the regular army.[1] At a council meeting that afternoon, Morris commissioned a number of Proprietary Party partisans who had,
with his encouragement, organized a rival militia organization. His actions angered many persons who supported the assembly's militia. That night, they hung
Morris in effigy "in several places" around the city. One strawman was "put in
the pillory and underneath it the Governors Name wrote at full length." The
next day Richard Peters, secretary of the council, requested the one captain who
had been certified to come with his officers and receive his commission, but he
refused to accept it unless it was on the same terms with the other company
captains (6:384).

That evening, 29 December, a group of academy trustees met at a coffee-
house and the conversation turned to the governor's refusal to sign the commis-

sions. The group included Richard Peters, Dr. Thomas Cadwalader, Thomas Lawrence, and William Allen, all proprietarians, as well as William Masters, the Philadelphia assemblyman with Franklin, and Dr. Thomas Bond, who had taken "Pains . . . to spread a general good Liking" to the militia bill (A 150). Masters knew that the volunteers generally had refused to have their names listed. He took his brother-in-law Thomas Lawrence aside and suggested that the governor would probably sign the commissions if given "a Certificate signd by two or three persons of each ward" testifying to the election of the named officers. The group sent a messenger to Governor Morris asking if he would sign the commissions under those terms. He replied that he would consult the council tomorrow.

Dr. Bond and the officers met the next morning at the Three Crowns tavern, on Second and Walnut streets. Certificates were "drawn up and signed by two or three persons of each ward" testifying to the elections and sent to the governor. The council urged him to sign, and so on Tuesday, 30 December, Morris reluctantly did, except for two officers of whom he disapproved (6:385–86). Five weeks later, on 4 February, Franklin, his son William, and William Edmonds left Fort Allen for Philadelphia and arrived at Bethlehem with an escort of thirty men. The next day the two Franklins made a hard, forced march from Bethlehem to Philadelphia to avoid a reception planned in Franklin's honor. They arrived home late Thursday night, 5 February 1756.

Assemblyman Franklin and Clerk William Franklin had missed the first four days of the House's third session but attended the fifth day, Saturday, 7 February. On 4 February, Governor Morris had requested more money to carry on the war and informed the assemblymen "that a Chain of Forts and Block-houses, extending from the River *Delaware*, along the *Kittatinny* Hills, to the *Maryland* Line, is now almost complete." He did not mention Benjamin Franklin, George Croghan, or any of those who actually risked their lives building the forts. The locals all knew them, but he no doubt hoped the English authorities who read his speech would suppose he had been directly involved. The forts, he informed the English public, were "placed at convenient Distances from each other, and at the most important Passes through the Mountains."[2]

That Saturday afternoon, 7 February, George Washington, journeying from Alexandria, Virginia, to Boston, arrived in Philadelphia. He remained there nearly a week, leaving on Thursday or Friday, and reached New York on Sunday night, 15 February.[3] Franklin and Washington met during that period, perhaps several times. Dr. John Morgan wrote on Monday, 9 February, that "Major Washington is now in Town & has some Business with our Assembly, but what it is, I can't say." Washington would have sought out Franklin, not only because he was the most important assembly member who believed in defense but also because Washington would have wanted to learn firsthand about Pennsylvania's frontier conditions. Later in 1756, the two met at least twice and corresponded (6:488).

The army again enlisted indentured servants and apprentices. Earlier, when General Braddock asked Franklin if there were anything he could do for him, Franklin requested that he enlist no more servants and return those who had been enlisted. Braddock did so. Colonel Dunbar, however, began enlisting servants after Braddock's defeat. Franklin appealed to General William Shirley, who instructed Dunbar and other officers on 19 September 1755 to stop (6:227). Four months later, when it became obvious that not enough freemen were joining, Shirley countermanded those orders on 21 January 1756. Consequently on Saturday, 7 February, the Pennsylvania Assembly received a petition complaining of "the Inlistment of Servants and Apprentices."[4] Speaker Norris appointed Franklin to a committee to write Shirley. Franklin's address was brought in on Tuesday afternoon, 10 February, and agreed to. Franklin asserted that masters "have as true and as just a Property in the Servant bought, as they had before in the money with which he was purchased. That the taking the Servants from us either by open Force or private Practice, is a Violation of that Property and our Rights, a manifest and grievous Injustice and Oppression" (6:399).

On the same subject, Franklin had printed *The Speech of John Wright, Esq; One of the Magistrates of Lancaster County, to the Court and Grand-Jury . . . in 1741*, in which his friend Wright (Susanna Wright's father) protested against Governor George Thomas's enlisting servants. Now, fifteen years later, Franklin echoed Wright. But General Shirley believed he had no alternative and that necessity and tradition sanctioned the acceptance of apprentices and indentured servants into the army. He wrote Franklin a personal letter to that effect on 9 February, which Franklin laid before the House on 19 February. Ironically, it accompanied another letter from Shirley to Franklin, thanking the House for the clothing and supplies sent "as a Present from the Assembly for the Use of the Army" in the Crown Point expedition. In a third letter of 9 February, Shirley wrote the president and council of Pennsylvania that the enlistment of servants was necessary; it was read to the House on 20 February.[5] The issue would become still more irksome after John Campbell, fourth earl of Loudoun, took over as North American commander in chief in March 1756.

What were Pennsylvanians to do? Some Indians were aligned with the French, some with the English. Until 1755, the Indians on the Pennsylvania frontier had been friendly to the English, but now French power was growing. More Indians were moving into the French sphere. The Six Nations or Iroquois had long pretended to be overlords to the Delaware, Shawnee, and other Indians along the Pennsylvania frontier, and the Iroquois tried to remain neutral, their eastern tribes, especially the Mohawks, had traditionally been allied with the English, while the Seneca and other western tribes of the Iroquois identified with the French. Many whites in the frontier towns and farms viewed all Indians as enemies. Some Quakers who wanted to believe that all the depredations were caused by unfair treatment of the Indians took just the opposite point of view. Franklin and others (especially the frontier representatives) believed that if attacked, Pennsylvanians should fight. Like most Pennsylvania leaders, however, Franklin thought that the best possible course of action was to woo the Indians back to an English alliance.

That proved difficult. Traditionally, the whites made friendly overtures to the Indians by inviting them to treaties and giving them presents, including powder, lead, and guns. Such gifts, which the Indians could use to kill whites, were sure to outrage the frontier settlers. Some persons wanted a declaration of war against the Indians, but that would alienate the Indians who remained in the English interest and risked their lives fighting against the French. A declaration of war would also drive most neutral Indians into the French interest. One possible solution was to pretend that the Indians who were attacking whites on the Pennsylvania frontier had defied their Iroquois overlords and to have the Six Nations reprimand them, but some of the Six Nations Indians were among those attacking the Pennsylvanians.

At that point, Governor Charles Hardy of New York asked that Pennsylvania attend a forthcoming treaty with the Six Nations at Albany. Hardy expected Pennsylvania to share the expenses for presents and to reaffirm the traditional friendship. After Governor Morris gave the Pennsylvania Assembly Hardy's request on 16 February, Speaker Isaac Norris appointed Franklin to a committee to reply on 19 February.[6] The next day Franklin and the committee equivocated. Since the treaty was not to be held for more than five weeks; since Sir William Johnson, who had been appointed in charge of relations with the Six Nations and their allies by General Braddock in April 1755, was then negotiating with the Iroquois; and since Pennsylvania's Indian allies, Scarouady and Andrew Montour, were currently meeting with the Delaware and Shawnee Indians in western Pennsylvania, "we apprehend no Inconveniences can ensue from our not giving a determinated Answer" until the House received further information (6:406). The House adjourned for a week.

During the recess, Franklin found time to write a letter about the death of his brother John. After a long and painful illness, John Franklin had died on 30 January 1756. Franklin had written Jane Mecom a note on 12 February, consoling her on the death of "our dear brother." Rushed at the time, Franklin only said, "As our number grows less, let us love one another proportionally more" (6:400). He had lamented the hurry of business: "I find the more I seek for leisure and retirement from business, the more I am engaged in it." He was indeed. The evening of 12 February, the officers of the Philadelphia City Regiment elected him colonel, with William Masters as lieutenant colonel and John Ross, major. Governor Morris knew that Thomas Penn and members of the Proprietary Party would object to the election of Franklin, but in the crisis on the frontier, Morris himself had previously commissioned him the military head of Northumberland County. He realized that numerous citizens, not just good Quaker Party members, would protest if he did not commission Franklin. But Morris put it off while helping organize an independent militia of Proprietary

Party men, based ironically on Franklin's Association of 1747–48. The proprietary militia paraded in Philadelphia on 19 February—while Morris held up the signing of Franklin's commission (6:415–16).

Numerous other duties had occupied Franklin. But finally he had a few hours to spare. On 22 February, in an appreciation of his brother John, he wrote on mortality. He addressed the letter to Elizabeth ("Betsy") Hubbart, John's stepdaughter, who had accompanied him and Katy Ray from Boston at the beginning of 1755: "Dear Child, I condole with you, we have lost a most dear and valuable relation, but it is the will of God and Nature that these mortal bodies be laid aside, when the soul is to enter into real life; 'tis rather an embrio state, a preparation for living; a man is not completely born until he be dead: Why then should we grieve that a new child is born among the immortals? A new member added to their happy society?"

Using the old religious trope of death as a new birth, Franklin transformed the cliché into an appreciation which, for non-Calvinists, makes the message (and almost makes the occasion) attractive: "We are spirits. That bodies should be lent us, while they can afford us pleasure, assist us in acquiring knowledge, or doing good to our fellow creatures, is a kind and benevolent act of God." John Franklin had suffered severely from a bladder stone since before 1752 when Dr. John Perkins (his physician and a family friend) expressed sympathy for "his bad state of health" to Franklin (4:359). Franklin continued: when our bodies "become unfit for these purposes and afford us pain instead of pleasure—instead of an aid, become an incumbrance and answer none of the intentions for which they were given, it is equally kind and benevolent that a way is provided by which we may get rid of them. Death is that way. We ourselves prudently choose a partial death. In some cases a mangled painful limb, which cannot be restored, we willingly cut off. He who plucks out a tooth, parts with it freely since the pain goes with it, and he that quits the whole body, parts at once with all pains and possibilities of pains and diseases it was liable to, or capable of making him suffer."

Franklin concluded with a beautiful invitation: "Our friend and we are invited abroad on a party of pleasure that is to last for ever. His chair was first ready and he is gone before us. We could not all conveniently start together, and why should you and I be grieved at this, since we are soon to follow, and we know where to find him. Adieu" (6:407).

The literary critic William L. Hedges wrote: "The elegance of his final image of death—an invitation to an eternal 'party of pleasure'—has the authentic ring of something he would have liked to believe."[7] I agree; Franklin did not believe it, but he would have liked to. Franklin's letter became well-known. The Reverend Mather Byles of Boston wrote him around the end of 1765 that it was "handed about among us in Manuscript Copies." Byles said he was "charmed with the Easy and Gay Light in which you view this little Earth, as Birth among the Immortals: and as setting out on a Party of Pleasure a little before our

Friends are ready. The Superstition with which we seize and preserve little accidental Touches of your Pen, puts one in mind of the Care of the Virtuosi to
collect the Jugs and Gallipots with the Paintings of Raphael" (12:424).

Colonel Franklin

After the Proprietary Party militia paraded in Philadelphia on 19 February, Morris finally, on 24 February, signed Franklin's commission (6:410–12, 416). Provost
William Smith had supported the extralegal proprietary militia and called for a
meeting at the academy on Saturday, 28 February. Francis Jennings wrote that
Smith had a "rousing oration" prepared for the meeting. Franklin, however,
reviewed the Pennsylvania Regiment that day and then marched to the academy
to hear Smith's proposals relating to the military. Seeing Franklin's regiment
approaching, Smith supposedly shut the academy's doors and hid inside. The
Pennsylvania Gazette celebrated the "fine appearance" of the Philadelphia Regiment.[8]

Several Franklin bills came up during the 1–14 March session of the Pennsylvania Assembly. Asked if he had yet considered the 11 November 1755 bill for
regulating the Indian trade, Governor Morris replied on 3 March 1756 that he
thought it "would be of no Use at this Time." The next day the House disagreed,
said it was important, and requested he consider it.[9] He did so and on 10 March
asked for several amendments. The House replied that the bill was "an Imitation
of the Law for the same Purpose, found so beneficial by long Practice and Experience" in Massachusetts and adhered to the original. From the reference to the
Massachusetts laws, we can be sure that Franklin modeled it on the one James
Bowdoin sent him on 12 November 1753 (5:111–12). Another Franklin bill, "The
Watch and Lamp Bill," was about to expire; a new one was brought in on 5
March, considered the following day, and passed 8 March.[10]

On 3 March, Franklin submitted "A Bill for the better Regulation of such
Soldiers as are or hereafter may be in the Pay of the Province . . . by the Leave
of the House," and read it for the first time. The "Mutiny Act" was in trouble.
Finally considered on 9 March, the act was laid aside by the House. Reconsidered on 10 March, Speaker Norris referred it for amendments to a committee
consisting of John Hughes, Franklin, Griffith Owen, Nathaniel Grubb, James
Webb, John Wright, Jr., and William Edmonds. Four pacifists, James Trotter,
James Pemberton, William Peters, and Peter Worrall, voted against spending
any further time on it. Submitted again on the twelfth, the amended bill failed
by a vote of 17 to 13, with all the committee members except the Chester County
Quaker Nathaniel Grubb voting for it.[11]

Chagrined, Franklin did not accept defeat. He gained the floor on the morning of Saturday, 13 March, and claimed "an absolute Necessity" existed "for
some Law to be speedily passed for the better Regulation of the Soldiers in the
Pay of the Province, or that otherwise they must be disbanded." He argued that
"though the Bills which had already been prepared for that Purpose were not

agreeable to the Mind of the House, yet that the House should meet again this Afternoon, in order to consider if some other measures could not be fallen upon to answer the good End proposed." A number of assemblymen disagreed. A motion to adjourn to Monday was defeated; then a second motion to adjourn to Monday a week later was defeated; a third to adjourn to Monday two weeks later was defeated. Thereupon Speaker Norris adjourned the House to that afternoon.

After discussion, Norris appointed another committee to bring in a bill for regulating the soldiers. To the former committee members Norris added Richard Pearn, William Smith, and Peter Dicks. On Tuesday, 16 March, the revised Mutiny Act was brought in, discussed, and had a second reading. After being debated the next morning, it was transcribed for a third reading. That afternoon, 17 March, the bill, which provided in some cases for the penalty of death, passed, with James Pemberton and Peter Worrall recording their dissent. Franklin and Hughes were ordered to "carry up" the bill to the governor. Then the House adjourned to 5 April. That same day, 17 March, George Washington arrived back in Philadelphia, where he and Franklin probably met again. Since Governor Morris was in New Castle, meeting with the legislature of the Three Lower Counties, Franklin, who was going to Virginia on post office business, was asked to deliver the bill to Morris in New Castle. He did so. Franklin was in Virginia when the governor amended the bill, the assembly revised it, and it finally passed on 15 April.[12]

On 4 March the proprietaries published in the *Pennsylvania Journal* a piece evidently written by Provost William Smith, which sneered at the militia under Colonel Franklin's command, calling them a "pack of men and boys" who knew nothing of military bearing or discipline (6:411n2). Franklin thereupon delayed the appearance of the 4 March *Gazette* and replied to Smith with a series of twenty "Queries." The third and fourth ones epitomize Franklin's position throughout: "3. Whether representing this City in publick Papers, as being, at the same time, both *rich* and *defenceless*, is least agreeable to *Truth* or to *Prudence*, the Way to *deter*, or *invite* an Enemy? 4. Whether a Regiment of Militia, well trained, consisting of near 1000 Men, 50 Pieces of Cannon, and a strong Battery, are to be looked upon as *nothing* towards the Defence of such a Place as this?" (6:418).

In addition to the Queries, Franklin announced, across the bottom of page 2 of the 11 March *Gazette*, that he would hold another review of the Philadelphia Regiment on Society Hill on Tuesday, 16 March, at 2:00 P.M. A late winter snowstorm, however, postponed the review until Thursday. The 25 March *Gazette* reported that "upwards of 1000 able bodied effective Men, besides Officers," formed on Society Hill where Colonel Franklin reviewed them: "Each Company met in the Morning at the Houses of their respective Captains, and march'd down Second Street till they came near the New Market; where the first Company that arriv'd halted, drew up in Platoons, and waited till the Second Company came up; and then each Platoon of the First Company fired retreating, according to the Manner of Street Firing, and the Second Company at the same time Advanced, and fired in like Manner, till they got Possession of the other Ground. The Third Company then advanced, disputed and took the Ground from the Second; and so on, each Company advancing and retreating in their Turns; the Artillery Company, consisting of upwards of 100 Men, with four Neatly painted Cannon, drawn by some of the largest and most stately Horses in the Province, being the Company that last took Possession of the Ground."

Reporting the order of the procession, the article (probably written by Franklin) noted that drummers appeared between the third and fourth ranks of each company. Perhaps most surprising is the note that in the middle of the procession appeared "The Hautboys and Fifes in Ranks." The music historian Raoul F. Camus noted: "a band was present, not restricted to oboes alone. This is the earliest known mention of an actual military band in America."[13] The news report concluded: "When the Regiment came opposite to the Colonel's Door, they were again drawn up in Battalion, and made one general Discharge of Small Arms, and several Discharges of Cannon. Then the several Companies marched off to their respective Places of Rendezvous, and saluted their Captains on being dismissed with a Discharge of their Fire Arms. The whole was conducted with the greatest Order and Regularity, and notwithstanding the vast Concourse of People, not the least Accident happened to any One. It is allowed, on all Hands, that most of the Platoon Firings, the general Fire of the Regiment, and the Discharge of the Artillery, were nearly as well performed as they could be by any Troops whatever. And it is likewise agreed, that so grand an Appearance was never before seen in Pennsylvania." Franklin told of the 18 March 1756 ceremony in the *Autobiography*. Since the ceremony was famous locally, he typically concluded with ironic chagrin about the occasion: "The first Time I review'd my Regiment, they accompanied me to my House, and would salute me with some Rounds fired before my Door, which shook down and broke several Glasses of my Electrical Apparatus" (A 150).

On 19 March, Franklin set out from Philadelphia to confer with the joint deputy postmaster general of North America, William Hunter, in Virginia. To his embarrassment, "the Officers of my Regiment took it into their heads that it would be proper for them to escort me out of town as far as the Lower Ferry. Just as I was getting on Horseback, they came to my door, between 30 and 40, mounted, and all in their Uniforms. I had not been previously acquainted with the Project, or I should have prevented it, being naturally averse to the assuming of State on any Occasion; and I was a good deal chagrin'd at their Appearance, as I could not avoid their accompanying me. What made it worse, was, that as soon as we began to move, they drew their Swords, and rode with them naked all the way." When word of the demonstration reached Thomas Penn, "it gave him great Offence. No such Honour had been paid him when in the Province;

nor to any of his Governors; and he said it was only proper to Princes of the Blood Royal" (A 150–51).

Perhaps Penn also thought it would have been proper for him. Franklin noted, "This silly Affair however greatly increas'd his Rancour against me, which was before considerable, on account of my Conduct in the Assembly, respecting the Exemption of his Estate from Taxation, which I had always op- pos'd very warmly, and not without severe Reflections on his Meanness and Injustice in contending for it." Penn charged that the demonstration was "Proof of my having an Intention to take the Government of the Province out of his Hands by Force" (A 150–51), and on 13 August Penn triumphantly wrote Rich- ard Peters about the demonstration by Franklin's soldiers: "I told my Lord Chancellor the other Day of this extraordinary piece of State, who was much astonished at it."[14] But Franklin simply thought it a "silly Affair."

Virginia, 19 March–9 May 1756

As they journeyed to New Castle, Franklin's slave Peter became ill with a fever and pain, so Franklin had him blooded. Along the way, Franklin gave Governor Morris the assembly's bill passed on 17 March for regulating the soldiers. When Franklin and Peter left for Fredericktown, Cecil County, Maryland, on the Sas- safras River on 20 March, Franklin hired a carriage and put Peter in it, "wrapped up warm, as he could not bear the Motion of the Horse, and got him" to Fredericktown "pretty comfortably." Franklin wrote Deborah the next morning, Sunday, 21 March, that Peter was now "about again and almost well." Franklin went on to Millikin's, Bohemia River, Maryland, where he encountered Colonel George Washington. "Col. Washington . . . proceeded on his Journey by Land" (6:427–28), and Franklin spent the next two nights sailing to Colonel John Hunter's in Hampton, Virginia. There he wrote Deborah a note reporting Peter to be "now quite well" (6:426).

From Hampton, postmasters Franklin and William Hunter rode to Wil- liamsburg on 24 March. There, on 30 March, he reported to Deborah that they were "daily employ'd in Settling our Affairs" (6:429). In the letter, Franklin revealed that he too had been ill but was "quite clear of the Dizziness I com- plain'd of." He was not yet longing for home, "the Worry of perpetual Business being yet fresh in my mind." He praised the countryside, "being now in full Spring." In a few days, he and Hunter would "take a Tour into the Country" (6:429). While he was in Williamsburg, the College of William and Mary voted on 2 April to grant him a master of arts (the first honorary degree it conferred). The postmasters journeyed to Norfolk where, on Saturday, 10 April, "The Mayor, Aldermen and Common-Council of the Borough of Norfolk, in Com- mon Hall assembled, presented the Freedom of the Borough to Marriot Arbuth- not, Esq; Commander of his Majesty's Ship Garland, Benjamin Franklin, Esq of Philadelphia, and John Hunter, Esq, of Hampton." After Franklin returned to Williamsburg, the College of William and Mary held the ceremony on Tuesday,

20 April, awarding him the honorary degree with the Reverend William Preston celebrating him, and "the Reverend Thomas Dawson, A.M., President," conferring the master of arts degree.[15]

While Franklin was in Virginia, the Pennsylvania Assembly met for a fifth session, 5–16 April. Governor Morris declared war on 14 April against the Delaware Indians and others who joined in hostile acts against Pennsylvanians. The proclamation offered rewards for the capture or scalp of hostile Indians.[16] Many Pennsylvanians and all the pacifists objected. Reports of pacifists obstructing the defense of the Pennsylvania frontier circulated in London. The London Quaker physician Dr. John Fothergill was the correspondent from the English Friends' Yearly Meeting to the Philadelphia Yearly Meeting. He wrote Israel Pemberton that Lord Granville, president of the Privy Council, "thought it much better for us, and for the colony likewise, that" pacifists "for the present should decline sitting in the Assembly, rather than be forced out by an Act of Parliament." (In 1747, Franklin had suggested they do so in times of warfare in *Plain Truth*, above, p. 46.) Fothergill also reported on 23 April that "Lord Halifax told a Friend this day, everything was left" to the Pennsylvania pacifists, "in hopes that you would do that of your own accord what they otherwise shall be obliged to do; and not so much perhaps to your satisfaction."[17]

While Franklin was away, Provost William Smith seized the opportunity to attack the regimental parade of 28 February. He wrote in the 15 April *Pennsylvania Journal* that because the Proprietary Party's independent militia "interfered with the aspiring views of a certain mighty Politician [Franklin], who expected that every Person would fall and Worship the Golden-Calf—I had almost said the Golden Bull—which his Hands had just set up, he was determined to pour his whole Fury upon the disobedient. Accordingly, as soon as the [proprietary] *Association* was proposed, he took the alarm, marshall'd his Host, and in due Form marched up with great Guns, and ponderous Axes, and fierce Steeds, and lighted Matches, and all the dreadful Apparatus of War, to lay Siege to—a *poor Half Sheet of Paper*; of which having at last obtained a Copy, altho in a very different Capacity from that of a *General*, he bound and gagged it and threw it into the World, as a Malefactor; stigmatized with his own injurious Remarks before, and impertinent Queries [4 March] behind."[18]

Franklin's son and friends responded in kind, characterizing Smith's writings as "Inveterate Calumny, foul-mouth'd Aspersion, shameless Falsehood, and insatiate Malice."[19] Continuing for several weeks, such exchanges marked a new low in Pennsylvania politics of the mid-eighteenth century, not to be exceeded until the 1764 election.

Franklin returned to Philadelphia about 8 May. Recalled by Governor Morris on 10 May because of frontier Indian attacks, the assembly met and heard the governor's message on 11 May. Writing from Harris's Ferry on the ninth, Morris asked for measures for defense and complained that "nothing good is to be expected from" the existing Militia Act. He asked for a different act in which he would control the troops. The same afternoon, a "Petition from the Officers of the Regiment of Militia, and Artillery Company, of the City of Philadelphia" said that "without Articles or Rules formed for the Government of the Militia," their efforts to create an efficient fighting force were useless. The officers, no doubt with Colonel Franklin as one signer, asked that the assembly enact "additional Provisions" to make the militia act "effectual." On 12 May, Speaker Norris assigned Franklin to one committee to answer the governor's message and to another to draft a bill laying an embargo on provisions and naval stores in Pennsylvania. The latter bill passed the House the next day, 13 May.[20] Franklin's reply stressing the need for "supplementary Amendments" to the militia bill was brought in the same day, agreed to, and ordered transcribed to be sent up to Morris on 14 May.

Though Governor Morris was still at Harris's Ferry, the House received two messages from him on 26 May. One, of 12 May, had arrived half an hour after the House had adjourned on 14 May. It again asked for a new militia act and for an embargo act, the latter of which had been passed. The second letter, of 23 May, requested funds for a joint "Expedition to the Westward" with Maryland troops and funds to encourage seamen to enlist in the navy. The assembly asked Franklin and the other commissioners (i.e., the members of the committee that controlled the expenditures) to find a way to enlist seamen. The commissioners promptly offered a bonus for enlisting and succeeded in sending several dozen volunteers to Captain Richard Spry in Halifax. Norris appointed Franklin on 27 May to a committee to bring a further tax bill "on all the Estates, Real and Personal," to support the war effort, which was presented to the House on 1 June. In a 2 June message, Governor Morris canceled the former declaration of war against the Indians and asked for presents to give them. Replying on behalf of the assembly, Franklin and the committee reported the next day that the commissioners for spending the £60,000 would furnish money for gifts to the Delaware and Shawnee Indians. The reply also reminded the governor that he had kept for "a considerable Time" the bill for regulating Indian trade, which would be "of great Service," and asked that he pass it.[21]

Governor Morris complained to the assembly on 3 June 1756 that he had received no salary for his support since their first sessions, despite the great trouble and expense of government since he had arrived in Pennsylvania. He asked too that the proposed amendments to the bill on Indian trade be sent to him. The House replied that it hoped he might pass the bills concerning "the Excise, Watch and *Indian Trade* bills" before he left for New Castle. The governor said he would again consider the three bills but could not do it immediately. On 4 June, six pacifist Quaker members of the House—James Pemberton, Joshua Morris, William Callender, William Peters, Peter Worrall, and Francis Parvin—requested permission to resign their seats. The House resolved that if those members still wished to resign after the end of the session and gave the

Speaker written notification, he would order the election of new members in their place. Then the House adjourned to 28 June.[22]

British Commanders

Thomas Pownall, whom Franklin had met in Philadelphia early in 1754, had been appointed "secretary extraordinary" to the new military commander in America, Lord Loudoun. Pownall had gradually become an authority on the colonies, and no doubt was appointed Loudoun's secretary partly because officials thought Pownall could advise him. Pownall evidently wrote Franklin in March and suggested that he come to New York to meet Loudoun and arrange for communications between Loudoun's armies, the British government, and the colonial governors. Pownall suggested a scheme whereby eleven express riders in the major towns and others in "intermediate Stages" would deliver letters.

Major General James Abercrombie, Loudoun's second in command in North America, landed in New York on 16 June. If Franklin were still in Philadelphia, he would have heard of Abercrombie's arrival within several days. Franklin arrived in New York on 22 June and presented a memorial on the express riders to Abercrombie that day. The previously suggested plan would be extremely expensive. Instead, Franklin said that "on proper Encouragement," he could easily hire riders and horses nearly anywhere in the colonies. He proposed to pay four shillings per mile for the rider and two per mile for the horse. Abercrombie consulted Governor Charles Hardy of New York and Colonel Daniel Webb (who was briefly in command of the British forces in America after William Shirley left). They agreed to Franklin's proposal but thought that six shillings total for the horse and rider per mile was high. Since Lord Loudoun was expected soon, Abercrombie temporarily approved Franklin's method, but Loudoun would decide when he came (6:463).

While Franklin waited in New York, the Pennsylvania Assembly reconvened on 28 June. Governor Morris revealed on 30 June that the proprietors had instructed him to demand that all money bills must provide that the governor supervise the funds (6:482). Previously, he had been indirectly demanding that he must be given that authority but had not revealed that it was among his instructions from the proprietors. Knowledge that there was such an order from Penn angered the assemblymen—especially Franklin. On 21 July Morris sent the House General William Shirley's 13 July letter announcing Lord Loudoun's appointment as commander in chief of the armed forces in North America. Shirley again thanked Morris and Pennsylvania for their support of the Crown Point expedition and reported that he was being recalled to England. On 22 July the Pennsylvania Assembly approved an address to Shirley, celebrating his services to America and hoping that God would "prosper his further Designs for the Public Welfare." The assembly asked Franklin to present the address to him in New York.[23]

Perhaps at the request of General Abercrombie, Franklin drew up a memorial on 22 July on the state of the Pennsylvania forces for Lord Loudoun. He enumerated the men and armaments, described the project to build a fort at Shamokin (Fort Augusta), and gave the available finances. He concluded by saying that if the troops soon did not receive more money, they would abandon the forts, which must consequently "be destroyed, lest the Enemy take Possession of them." The frontier settlements would then be abandoned (6:470–71).

After Franklin had waited in New York for more than a month, the earl of Loudoun finally landed on Friday, 23 July. That evening "the Mayor and Corporation" of New York entertained him together with "all the Gentlemen in Town."[24] Franklin described the occasion in his *Autobiography*: Governor William "Shirley, tho' thereby superseded, was present also. There was a great Company of Officers, Citizens and Strangers, and some Chairs having been borrowed in the Neighbourhood, there was one among them very low which fell to the Lot of Mr. Shirley. Perceiving it as I sat by him, I said, They have given you, Sir, too low a Seat. No Matter, says he, Mr. Franklin; I find a low Seat the easiest!" (A 162).

During the next two days, 24–25 July 1756, Franklin met several times with Loudoun. He approved Franklin's plan for express riders, and no doubt Franklin explained to him the current impasse in Pennsylvania on further financial support of the war.[25] To Pownall, Franklin probably mentioned the criticisms he was receiving from Thomas Penn, Governor Morris, and others, who said that since Franklin held an appointment from the crown, he should support the government. (Penn and Morris believed that they, not the Pennsylvania Assembly, represented the primary Pennsylvania government.) Perhaps Pownall advised Franklin to write Sir Everard Fawkener, England's joint postmaster general, and suggested to Franklin that if the letter concerned military affairs in America, Fawkener would pass it on to the duke of Cumberland, captain-general of the British army. Franklin wrote Fawkener on 27 July, and mentioned that he might be able to do Loudoun a "Service that he requests of me." The editors of the *Papers of Benjamin Franklin* suggested that Franklin said he would try again to have the Pennsylvania Assembly appropriate money directly for Loudoun's use (6:472); I agree.

Considering the recipient and the probably intended second recipient, the Americanism of Franklin's 27 July letter is surprising. He said that the provincial force moving against Crown Point did not want regulars with them. He explained that the regulars claimed all the "Honour of any Success" and blamed the provincial militia "for every Miscarrage." Franklin reported that the previous year, though there were ten times as many provincials as regulars at the taking of Fort Beauséjour in Nova Scotia on 9 June 1755, the accounts published in England did not mention that "a single New England-Man" was "concern'd in the Affair" (6:473). Franklin's letter mainly explained why enlisting indentured servants into the army was unjust to those who had purchased the servants, even though the recent act of Parliament directed that the masters should be paid a proportional part of the servant's remaining time. He predicted that if the indentured servants could enlist, more slaves would be imported into America (6:472–76). The next day, 28 July, Franklin left for Philadelphia.

Franklin had been in New York during the eighth and ninth sessions (28 June–5 July and 19–22 July) of the 1755–56 Pennsylvania Assembly. The House noted on 3 July that it had received less than £1,000 of the £5,000 "free gift" promised from the proprietors. Penn not only forbade any of his other income from Pennsylvania to be used to pay the £5,000, but even privately requested from Richard Hockley that part of the quitrents be sent to him. On 22 July, the House said that the proprietors still owed £3,940.14. When Thomas Penn learned that the payments were coming in so slowly, he wrote Richard Peters on 10 September that those in arrears must pay: "I expect to hear distresses are made." Former governor James Hamilton, irritated with Thomas Penn for not coming up with the money more quickly, volunteered to give £1,000 of it to Richard Hockley, for him to pay to the assembly, as if from Penn's quitrents. Penn realized that he would have to repay Hamilton and wrote Peters on 9 October that doing so would "distress us beyond measure, if the Money is lent." Of course that was not true; Hamilton advanced the money before hearing about Penn's sniveling; and Penn thanked him in a letter of 8 January 1757.[26]

During the ninth session, on 20 July, the House resolved that an extract of a letter published in London signed "W. Smith" contained "divers wicked Calumnies" against numerous Pennsylvanians and "most infamous, libellous, false and scandalous Assertions against the two Branches of the Legislature." The House called for and questioned Provost William Smith, whose answers the members judged "trifling and evasive." However, since they had pressing matters before them, they discharged Provost Smith "for the present."

Franklin's partner David Hall wrote the academy trustees on 15 July refusing to publish a letter exonerating Provost William Smith from the criticism. Hall said that all the other materials pro and con concerning Smith had appeared in the *Pennsylvania Journal*. Hall had "carefully avoided any concern" with the political issue and therefore would not print this letter. Smith's biographer and grandson, Horace W. Smith, wrote that Franklin was responsible for Hall's refusal. The grandson complained that Franklin "or his known friends were willing to break down the College which he had himself founded, in order to break down a man who in it was now rising into political importance and threatened in that department to become more potential than himself."[27] But Franklin was in New York conferring with General Loudoun from 16 June to 28 July. Since the letter was only presented to David Hall on 13 (or possibly 14) July, and since Hall replied to it on 15 July, Franklin could not have influenced Hall's decision.

Through the agency of Israel Pemberton, a group of wealthy Quakers met with the Oneida chief Scarouady, Captain Newcastle, a Seneca chief, and others at Pemberton's home during 19–23 April 1756 in Philadelphia. The Quakers asked Scarouady and Newcastle to send messages to the Delaware Indians to

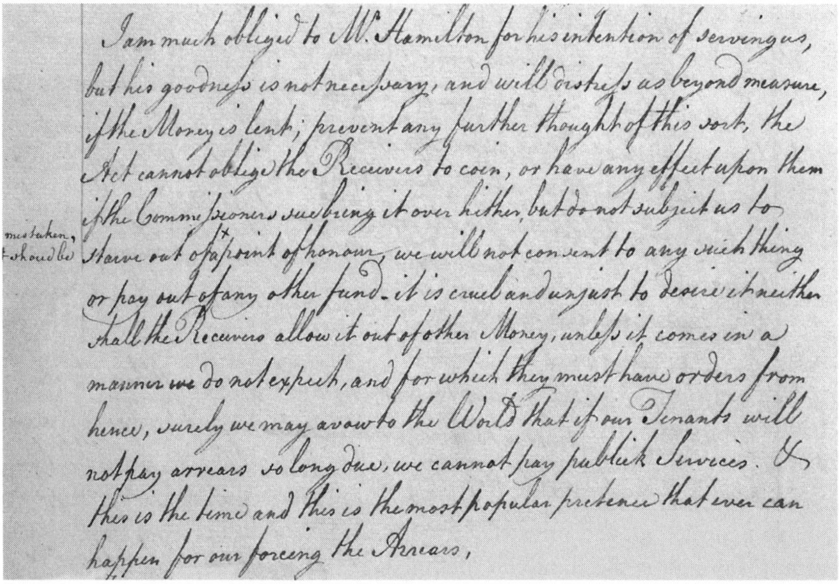
mistaken, +should be

I am much obliged to Mr. Hamilton for his intention of serving us,
but his goodness is not necessary, and will distress us beyond measure,
if the Money is lent; prevent any further thought of this sort, the
Act cannot oblige the Receivers to coin, or have any effect upon them
if the Commissioners such bring it over hither, but do not subject us to
Starve out of a point of honour, we will not consent to any such thing
or pay out of any other fund. it is cruel and unjust to desire it neither
shall the Receivers allow it out of other Money, unless it comes in a
manner we do not expect, and for which they must have orders from
hence, surely we may avow to the World that if our Tenants will
not pay arrears so long due, we cannot pay publick Services. &
this is the time and this is the most popular pretence that ever can
happen for our forcing the Arrears,

Figure 46. Thomas Penn's "free gift" of £5,000: Penn to Richard Peters, 9 October 1756. As the French and Indian War went on, Governor Robert Hunter Morris continued to veto the Pennsylvania Assembly's supply bills because they either taxed Penn's estates or did not make the governor's permission necessary to spend the funds. The dispute became infamous in England, and Thomas Penn found himself criticized. Sir Thomas Robinson, secretary of state, spoke to him on the morning of 4 October 1755 and told him that "several people" had expressed "a dislike to your refusal to assist the publick at such a time as this." Robinson suggested that if the disputes continued, Parliament might make an inquiry into the matter, "which may be dangerous at this Conjuncture, when all persons ought to engage against the common Enemy." Penn therefore wrote Governor Morris that very day, offering £5,000 as what he called a "free gift" toward the war effort.

The "free gift," however, was to be collected from money owed by settlers for the quitrents and for the purchase of lands. Some of the settlers were on the frontier and some had fled their lands. A year later, only £1,000 of the "free gift" had actually been raised, the £55,000 raised by the assembly had been spent, and more money was needed. Disgusted with Penn's parsimony, former governor James Hamilton put up £1,000 of his own money, saying that Penn could repay him later. At this news, Penn wrote Richard Peters 9 October 1756 that giving any of Penn's own money would "distress us beyond measure" and that the time was right to collect the money: "this is the most popular pretence that ever can happen for our forcing the Arrears." Courtesy, Historical Society of Pennsylvania.

come for a peace treaty. The preparatory conferences took place in Easton, Pennsylvania, from 21 July to 7 August, and also from 28 to 31 July. Teedyuscung, a Delaware chief, led the Indians at the conference. Franklin was in New York, but his fellow commissioners Joseph Fox, John Hughes, and William Masters were present, together with Governor Morris, several members of the council, and a number of Quakers. The primary business of the preparatory meetings was to arrange for the treaty at Easton in the fall.[28]

Richard Peters described Teedyuscung to Thomas Penn: Teedyuscung was "near 50 Years Old, a lusty, rawboned Man, haughty and very desirous of respect and Command. He can drink three Quarts or a Gallon of Rum a day without being drunk. He was the Man that persuaded the Delawares to go over to the French and then to attack the Frontiers. He commanded the attacks on Gnadenhütten and he and these with him have been concerned in the Mischiefs done to the Inhabitants of Northampton County."[29]

Franklin knew this information when he secured a copy of the July–August preparatory conference notes and communicated them to Thomas Pownall on 19 August (6:487n7). Perhaps Franklin also knew that Teedyuscung had recently sent off messengers to Niagara to seek French support. He thought that nothing would come of Pennsylvania's conference with Teedyuscung or of Sir William Johnson's June–July treaty with the Six Nations at Onondaga. The Iroquois, Franklin suspected, had privately encouraged the Delawares to attack Pennsylvania. Waiting for the results of the ongoing treaties merely tied the hands of Pennsylvanians while the Indians pillaged the frontier and killed more settlers. Franklin wrote Pownall: "I do not believe we shall ever have a firm Peace with the Indians till we have well drubb'd them." If Loudoun would order the troops of the Royal American Regiment to "take Post on the Frontiers, in the Forts there, where they would find good barracks," they "might be of great Use in defending the Inhabitants, and would be a most acceptable thing to the whole Province." Loudoun, however, ordered the regiment to Albany (6:487–88).

On 17 August, Governor Morris again asked the House for money—for defense, to pay masters whose servants enlisted, and for barracks to accommodate one thousand soldiers. That afternoon, Speaker Norris assigned Franklin to a committee to prepare a supply bill for £40,000 and to answer the governor. The reply, agreed to "with some Alterations," claimed that to raise the money, the proprietors must be taxed along with everyone else (6:485–86). On Thursday, 19 August, however, the House learned that William Denny, who would succeed Robert Hunter Morris as governor, was due to arrive in town the next day; therefore the assembly adjourned until 5:00 P.M., 20 August. No doubt the members knew that festivities would be staged for the new governor's arrival. Accordingly, on Friday, 20 August at 5:00 P.M., Speaker Norris presented an invitation from William Plumsted, mayor, for the members to join the Philadelphia Corporation for dinner at the Freemasons' Lodge that evening. The assembly accepted and ordered "a handsome Dinner" the following Monday at the statehouse. They invited the "present and late Governor, the Governor's Council, Mayor and Corporation, Officers Civil and Military, Clergy, and Strangers, now residing in this City." That same day, Lord Loudoun wrote Governor Denny from Albany that Oswego had fallen to the French and demanded Denny's "Assistance and that of your Province."[30]

Norris assigned Franklin on Saturday, 21 August, to a committee to prepare a "congratulatory Address to the Honourable WILLIAM DENNY." Submitted on Monday, the House approved the address and voted to pay Denny £600 immediately. It had previously paid Governor Morris £500 on his arrival, but nothing since. After voting to pay, the members had second thoughts and withheld the money until 8 April 1757, when Denny finally approved a measure that the House wanted. Denny addressed the House, asking for funds for defense on 24 August and, after receiving Lord Loudoun's request for assistance, again sent a message to the House for funds on 27 August. The same day, the French Acadians whom the British had shipped to Pennsylvania petitioned the House for aid, and Franklin probably made the "literal Translation" of their plea. On 30 August, Franklin was assigned to a committee to answer the governor.[31]

The committee's polite reply ironically concluded that the assembly was confident that the governor (and then, quoting him) "will deny us nothing that he can grant, consistent with his Duty to his Majesty, and the Rights of the Proprietaries." The assembly's message said that "latent Proprietary Instructions" had "rendered ineffectual" former grants of money. Therefore the assembly "humbly" requested that the governor "lay before us full Copies of such of his Instructions as relate to Money Bills," together with the preambles or whatever relates to the "Reasons of such Instruction," so that the assembly could be "informed of the Equity or Necessity of Rules to which a Conformity is required" (6:496). To its surprise, Governor Denny laid before the assembly the eleventh article of the proprietary instruction, which specified that money derived from any money bill must be spent only for the purpose specified in the bill; the twelfth article, which said that no bills for paper currency could exceed £40,000 and that all the interest from money bills must be spent on purposes specified in the bill; and the long twenty-first article, which prohibited any taxation of the proprietary estates.[32]

The information gave Franklin ammunition. On 1 September, he and Joseph Fox requested that the governor say "whether he does not apprehend himself at Liberty, notwithstanding the said Proprietary Instructions, to pass such equitable Bills as we may offer him, if consistent with his own Judgment, and agreeable to such LAWS as have been enacted by his Predecessors, and received the Royal Assent." Denny replied the next day that he could not "recede from my Instructions without risking both my Honour and Fortune."

The assembly then resolved to enact a £60,000 bill, to be sunk by an extension of the excise for twenty years.[33] In the bill itself, passed on 8 September, the House specified the appropriating clauses in the bill, by which £10,000 "shall be a Contribution from this Province towards a general *American* Fund, for the common Service and Defense of the Colonies, and shall be subject to the Orders of Lord Loudoun." Another £15,000 would repay the £15,000 formerly granted for the Crown Point expedition and for General Braddock. The bill named Franklin a commissioner. On 9 September, the assembly sent up a revised version of his old nightly watch bill (*Life* 2:406), which the assembly and Governor Morris had approved but not enacted because Morris had been replaced by Denny. Denny approved it on 13 September and enacted it two days later.[34]

On Saturday, 11 September, Governor Denny asked for a meeting with a committee of the House concerning the £60,000 bill. Speaker Norris appointed Franklin to it. They met Monday morning, 13 September. After hearing Denny's objections, Norris asked Franklin and others to reply. They did so that day, and another conference took place on the following morning. Denny rejected the bill on 14 September and returned it two days later. That afternoon, Norris placed Franklin on a committee to consider the proprietary instructions on money bills "and report their Opinion thereon to the House." They were also requested "(if they find they have sufficient Time during the Sitting of this Assembly)" to "draw up a Representation of the present State of this Province, and report the same to the House." In effect, Norris asked for an updated version of Franklin's 19 August 1752 report on Pennsylvania's trade and population.[35]

In reply to Governor Denny's rejection of the supply bill, Franklin drew up a series of resolves: the first charged that the "Proprietary Instructions are arbitrary and unjust, an Infraction of our Charter, a total Subversion of our Constitution, and a manifest Violation of our Rights, as freeborn Subjects of England." The last resolve stated: "That the Proprietaries encreasing their Restrictions upon the Governor . . . at a Time when the Province is invaded by the King's Enemies, and barbarous Tribes of Indians are ravaging the Frontier Settlements, and their forbidding the Passing of any Bills whereby Money may be raised for the Defence of the Inhabitants, unless those Instructions are strictly complied with, is tyrannical, cruel and oppressive, with Regard to the People, and extremely injurious to the King's Service: Since if the Assembly should adhere to their Rights, as they justly might, the whole Province would be thrown into Confusion, abandoned to the Enemy, and lost to the Crown" (6:514).

Concluding these resolves, Franklin and the House stated that necessity forced them to give up their principles.[36] "The House therefore, reserving their Rights in their full Extent on all future Occasions, and PROTESTING against the Proprietary Instructions and Prohibitions, do, nevertheless, in Duty to the King, and Compassion for the suffering Inhabitants of their distressed Country, and in humble but full Confidence of the Justice of His Majesty, and a British Parliament, waive their Rights on this present Occasion only."

Then the assembly resolved that a new money bill be brought in "conformable to the said Instructions." Norris assigned Franklin to the committee to bring in a £30,000 bill "to be struck in Paper Bills of Credit, and sunk by an Excise on spiritous Liquors within Ten Years" (6:514–15). Franklin quickly wrote the bill. It was read that afternoon, and the House passed it and delivered it to the governor—all on 17 September. Governor Denny met with his council on the morning of 18 September. At first the members urged him to pass the bill because the entire amount was appropriated for the use of the king and to be spent "with the Governor's Approbation and not otherwise." But as they considered the report of the Lords of Trade on the £60,000 passed the previous November, they changed their minds. The council told Denny to reduce the term for sinking the bills of credit from ten to five years. They also noted that the bill stated that fines from the city (which had always been given to the city corporation) would now go to the assembly. This, too, should be changed.

After meeting with Speaker Norris and Franklin, Governor Denny held another meeting of the council that same Saturday, 18 September, announcing that the two said that the House was "determined on this" bill "and no other." The council now pointed out that the bill also took away the governor's right to a fine of five pounds "on Conviction of any one's keeping a publick House without his Lycence." The council members unanimously recommended that the governor insist that those fines remain with the governor and that the other fines remain with the city corporation. At a subsequent meeting with Denny, Franklin with an assembly committee "used a great many Arguments and some precedents in favour of the present Clauses." Since Denny was unfamiliar with the history of the fines, he asked James Hamilton and Benjamin Chew to discuss the issues with the assembly committee. Franklin and Norris agreed to leave the clause appropriating the fines out of the bill. On Monday, 20 September, Speaker Norris informed the House that Governor Denny was ready to pass the bill provided that the House delete the clause giving the assembly monies from fines. The House agreed "on account of the present Exigency of Affairs" and passed the £30,000 bill. Denny approved it the next day, 21 September.[37]

On the session's penultimate day, Franklin submitted the report on the proprietary instructions (6:515–31). Read again the next day and unanimously approved, the report's most telling passage said that though the proprietors claimed in the instruction to Governor Denny that they were "most ready and willing to bear a just Proportion along with their Tenants in any necessary Tax for the Defence of the Province," this was a "*mere Pretence,* since they absolutely except their Quitrents, and their located unimproved Lands, their Fines, and the Purchase-Monies they have at Interest; that is, in a Manner, their *whole Estate,* as your Committee know of little they have left to be taxed, but a Ferry-house or two, a Kitchen, and a Dog Kennel" (6:526).

What a wonderful sarcasm—"a Dog Kennel." The House resolved to draw up a remonstrance and send it "Home to *England* . . . representing the pernicious Consequences to the *British* interest . . . if we are, contrary to our Charters and Laws, to be governed by Proprietary Instructions" (6:516). Since the 1755–56 assembly was about to adjourn and a new assembly for 1756–57 would shortly be elected, the present assembly recommended that the new one take action.

THE COLONISTS ATTACK, 8 SEPTEMBER 1756

John Armstrong, a surveyor and proprietary partisan of Carlisle, had been elected a lieutenant colonel of the militia early in 1756. Leading about 400 troops on 30 August, he left Carlisle to attack Kittanning on the Allegheny River, about 25 miles north of Fort Duquesne (see map 2, p. 308). Home to approximately 100 Indians, the town was the stronghold of the well-known warriors Shingas and Captain Jacobs. On the evening of 7 September, Armstrong's scouts encountered several Indians near Kittanning. Armstrong did not attack them lest one of the supposedly few Indians escaped and warned the town. Instead he left Lieutenant Hogg with twelve men to assault them at daylight. About three in the morning, the provincial troops reached the Allegheny River, rested until dawn, and then assaulted Kittanning.

Armstrong succeeded in burning Kittanning and killing Captain Jacobs. Shingas was evidently away. The *Pennsylvania Gazette* for 23 September reported that "The Indians had a Number of spare Arms in their Houses, loaded, which went off in quick Succession as the Fire came to them; and Quantities of Gunpowder which had been stored in every House blew up from time to time, throwing some of their Bodies a great Height into the Air." When a number of Indians crossed the river at a distance, Armstrong feared they might surround the troops, and he retreated. Armstrong's military victory was a much-qualified success. Though he had the advantage of surprise and outnumbered the Indians about three to one, he recovered only a few prisoners, lost approximately twice as many men as the hostiles, was wounded, and retreated while being attacked.[38] Lieutenant Hogg with his twelve men found that the small party of Indians was actually a larger number than his men, and though he killed several Indians, he lost more men than the Indians did and was himself killed.

Nevertheless, the colonists regarded the fight at Kittanning as a success. The Indians abandoned the town and moved further west. Armstrong's victory, the first engagement against the Indians after Braddock's defeat, raised morale along the Pennsylvania frontier. Moreover, for those who identified with America rather than Great Britain, it reinforced the opinion of many Americans after the Cape Breton victory of 1745 (*Life* 2:350–56) that the American militia were better fighting men than the British regulars.

TWENTY-ONE

The Easton Treaty and Assembly Sessions, 1756–1757

The Spirit that makes them [the Proprietors] so ardently aim at the Disposition of Money not their own, is the same with that which inclines lesser Knaves to rob and pick Pockets. They seem to have no Regard to the Publick Welfare, so the private Point may be gained. 'Tis like Firing a House to have an Opportunity of Stealing a Trencher.
—Franklin to Joseph Galloway, 11 April 1757, 7:179

THE ELECTION OF 1756

THE ELECTION OF 1 OCTOBER 1756 shattered the Quaker dominance of Pennsylvania politics. The preceding summer, because of the war on the frontier, six pacifist Quakers had found themselves in an untenable position and resigned from the assembly on 4 June 1756—just four months before the 1 October 1756 election. Nevertheless, the prospects did not look good for the Proprietary Party. Richard Peters reported to Thomas Penn on 26 June that Thomas Leech, Daniel Roberdeau, and William Masters—all Franklin supporters—had replaced them. Then, on 4 September 1756, Peters reported to Penn that the forthcoming 1 October election would be carried by "the hot-heads" and that Franklin would have the "rule over them." Therefore, after being elected, they "will do all the hurt they can to the Proprietaries." At the 1 October election, four conscientious Quaker delegates who had not resigned were reelected. They resigned on 16 October, just two days into the new assembly of 1756–57. Though the Quaker Party had dominated the assembly from its beginning and though Quakers had almost always constituted the religious majority, they fell to only 33.5 percent during the assembly year of 1756–57 and never again became the majority religious denomination in Pennsylvania's House.[1]

Governor Denny had informed the assembly on 17 August 1756 that the French and their Indian allies had attacked and burned Pennsylvania's Fort Granville on the Juniata River. On 9 September, the *Pennsylvania Gazette* carried the news that the Massachusetts troops under Governor William Shirley and General Pepperill had been defeated at Oswego, New York. More French and Indian attacks on Pennsylvania's frontier would surely follow. On 22 September, Richard Peters reported to Thomas Penn that James Hamilton, William Allen, and Benjamin Chew had two meetings with Franklin, proposing that Franklin support an election "Ticket" for Philadelphia County containing the names of Isaac Norris, Joseph Fox, John Hughes, Daniel Roberdeau, Jacob Duché, William Coleman, Phineas Bond, and Henry Paulin. Peters wrote that Franklin had agreed, but "the Ticket is extreamly disagreable to the Town in general and tho the Gentlemen are bound in honor to support the Ticket yet I do not know that it will be carried."

One wonders if Franklin really agreed and who the other "Gentlemen" were who were supposedly bound to abide by the agreement. Why would Franklin agree? The hard-core pacifists had resigned from the assembly and, as Franklin knew, the chief London Friends had advised that while the war continued, all delegates who opposed defense should resign. Franklin and those who supported defense would surely win the 1756 election on 1 October. The only possibility that might make some sense is that Hamilton, Allen, and Chew promised Franklin that they would convince Governor Denny to support a bill taxing the proprietors if the proprietary supporters like Coleman, Bond, Duché, and the obscure Paulin were delegates. But there is no evidence for that scenario, which, in any case, seems most unlikely.

Peters said that the outcome would "depend on the determination of Friends at their Publick Meeting at Burlington." He suggested that at the meeting, the Friends might decide not to support Isaac Norris. Norris, however, had consistently been the candidate with the most votes in Philadelphia County since the death of John Kinsey in 1750. Although the Friends meeting under the leadership of Israel Pemberton usually contained a number of outspoken pacifists like John Woolman and John Churchman, Pemberton and the majority of Friends knew that the meeting could destroy itself by driving out popular though lukewarm pacifists like Isaac Norris. On 1 October 1756, Norris again had the highest number of votes from Philadelphia County. It seems unlikely that the Friends meeting would agree to back a slate of candidates that contained persons like William Coleman, who was disenfranchised by the Quaker meeting in 1747. And Franklin had no following in the Friends' official meeting. He was regarded as the major war-monger in the colony.

In the same 22 September letter, Peters said that "Franklin is implacable, and Mens Spirits are by his perverse Obstanacy, extreamly embitterd against the Proprietors." If Franklin were "implacable," would he support proprietarians? When Richard Peters reported to Penn on 2 October that the proprietarians had lost the election, he did not mention Franklin's supposed betrayal of Allen, Hamilton, and Chew.[2] I suspect that Peters was mistaken in his 22 September reports concerning meetings that he had not attended. At any rate, on 1 October, the moderate Quakers Norris and Fox placed first and second in Philadelphia County, followed by the Anglicans Leech, Hughes, Roberdeau, Bayton, Galloway, and Pearne.

Crises in the French and Indian War demanded long sessions of the Pennsylvania Assembly of 1756–57. Though the first session of assembly generally lasted only three or four days, the 1756 assembly began on 14 October and continued to 4 November. The assemblymen had dramatically changed. Most pacifist Quaker former delegates chose not to run because they could not support a war. Franklin noted in the *Pennsylvania Gazette* for 7 October that of the thirty-six elected representatives to the House, "we hear there are Sixteen of the People called Quakers, and that the Remainder are of the Church of England, and other Denominations." For the first time in Pennsylvania's history, Quakers did not constitute a majority of the assembly. The Quaker or Popular Party, however, remained strong. It attracted members who sided with Franklin. They were for defense but against the Proprietary Party. Among the new members in 1756, the lawyer Joseph Galloway, with whom William Franklin had studied law, was representative of the new members, except that he had the most meteoric rise of the new members in the assembly—and then, when the Revolution came, the most meteoric fall. On Saturday, 16 October 1756, two days after the assembly met, four of the sixteen elected Quakers resigned because "the Ministry have requested the *Quakers* . . . to suffer their Seats, during the difficult Situation of the Affairs of the Colonies, to be filled by Members of other Denominations."[3]

THE FIRST ASSEMBLY SESSION OF 1756–57

On 19 October Governor Denny requested the House to pass an embargo on materials for French territories; to provide quarters for troops who would be stationed in Pennsylvania; to create a new supply bill for defense; to pass a new militia bill to replace Franklin's of the previous year, which had been disallowed in England; and to raise funds for the forthcoming Easton Indian conference. Denny sent along the Board of Trade's report, dated 3 March 1756, to the Privy Council rejecting the colony's repeated argument against providing for defense and its claim that the proprietor was obliged to defend them. The Board of Trade said that "neither the Charter of Privileges, nor any Laws then existing, gave" the citizens of Pennsylvania "such Right of Exemption from military Service; and it was observed, that the Proprietor was no more obliged to be at the Expence of defending them . . . than the Governors of any other Colonies."[4]

Norris assigned Franklin on 21 October to a committee to prepare a bill to regulate the hire of wagons for the military and the next day to a committee on billeting soldiers. The House resolved on 23 October to support the expenses for a treaty with the Delaware Indians in November. On Tuesday, 26 October, Franklin served on a committee to confer with the governor about the Indians in town. That Thursday, Franklin brought in a bill for "regulating the Forces" of the province. His former "Mutiny Act" would expire on 30 October. Also on Thursday, 28 October, Franklin, as president of the hospital, presented its annual report to the assembly. Richard Peters hopefully reported to Penn at the end of October that the "two Champions" had fallen out and that Norris was now favorable toward the proprietors, but a few days later William Allen saw no signs of "mutual Jealousy" between Franklin and Norris.⁵ If the report had any foundation, it might have been over Franklin's strident support of defense, but Norris was human enough to resent Franklin's increasing popularity and his support by fellow assemblymen.

On 3 November, Franklin's bill for "regulating" the soldiers passed. It primarily updated his previous militia bill (7:8). The governor approved it the next day. That same 4 November, Governor Denny asked the House to appoint members to join him at the Easton Indian conference. Norris appointed Franklin, Joseph Fox, John Hughes, William Masters, and himself to go to Easton, and the House adjourned to Monday, 22 November.⁶

THE EASTON TREATY, 8–17 NOVEMBER 1756

Through Sir William Johnson and the Iroquois allies, Pennsylvania had arranged for a possible peace treaty with the Delaware Indians. Teedyuscung, the primary Delaware spokesman, had conducted a comparatively brief preparatory treaty with Governor Robert Hunter Morris at Easton late in July 1756. The two parties agreed to meet again in November when representatives of the Six Nations and the Ohio Indians would also attend. Franklin was not present at the July meeting, but he secured its minutes and sent a copy to Thomas Pownall, Lord Loudoun's consultant on American affairs. Franklin thought the July meeting with Teedyuscung had been a farce and a waste. Early in August, Bishop Spangenberg of Bethlehem had written Isaac Norris disparagingly of Teedyuscung's behavior. Franklin sent along Spangenberg's letter and said the Iroquois had urged "these Indians to fall upon us; they have taken no Step to defend us, as their Allies, nor to prevent the Mischief done us." He thought it had been a mistake to sue for peace through Sir William Johnson. Pennsylvania had remained defenseless while waiting for some action, "and in the mean while our Frontier People were continually butcher'd." He thought Pennsylvania would never "have a firm Peace with the Indians till we have well drubb'd them."

Franklin proposed, however, another possible course of action: if Lord Loudoun "would order the Recruits, now near 500 to march up and take Post on the Frontiers, in the Forts there, where they would find good Barracks; and might be of great Use in defending the Inhabitants, it would be a most acceptable thing to the whole Province" (6:487–88). But Loudoun ordered the troops to Albany where they waited and waited, while Loudoun planned and planned an attack on Lake George.

On 1 October William Denny, the new governor of Pennsylvania, received a letter from Lord Loudoun of 22 September telling him that Sir William Johnson was in complete charge of Indian affairs and that Pennsylvania was to follow the directions of Johnson and himself. Aghast at the turn of events, Richard Peters wrote Thomas Penn on 2 October that "if Indian affairs are taken out of the hands of this Government so as neither to suffer the Govr to confer or treat with Indians all our friendly Indians will soon turn against us & we shall have a most lamentable winter. Lord Loudoun cannot, will not, spare Men or once think about us."[7] Peters thought that Pennsylvania should proceed with the scheduled November treaty. Denny consulted the Pennsylvania Council on 22 October. It agreed with Peters, saying that the royal charter gave the proprietors the right to treat with the Indians and that the Pennsylvania authorities were obliged to do so by the July preparatory treaty.

Denny asked the House for its opinion. In a rare display of unity, the House concurred. Its message displayed Franklin's diplomatic tact. He began by thanking the British authorities "for the late wise Regulation of putting Indian Affairs . . . under a more general Direction than they have heretofore been." Both the Indians and the colonists would benefit. "However burdensome the present War with the Indians may be to this Province," Pennsylvania did not desire that "a separate Treaty should be concluded on our Behalf." Nevertheless, he and the House disagreed with Lord Loudoun's order, without directly saying so. Their ostensible reason was good. They were merely continuing an exchange made "before Sir William Johnson's Powers were made known," an exchange the Indians justifiably expected. If Pennsylvania turned the Delaware Indians and their allies away, they might well be "disgusted, and the Opportunity of bringing them to a general Peace with all the British Colonies be lost."

With this semi-subterfuge, the assembly advised the governor to meet with the Indians, giving them the "customary Presents . . . to relieve their Necessities, and assure them of our sincere Inclination to take them again into Friendship, forgive their Offences, and make a firm Peace with them." Franklin added that the Pennsylvanians would at the same time "let them know, that the Government of this Province cannot agree to make a Peace with them for itself, and leave them at Liberty to continue the War with our Brethren of the neighbouring Colonies: That we are all Subjects of one great King, and must, for the future, be all at Peace or all at War with other Nations at the same Time." Since Sir William Johnson had the general management of all Indian affairs for the colonies from Virginia to Canada, "we must therefore refer the Indians" to Johnson "for a final Conclusion and Ratification of this Treaty." In concluding the message, Franklin avoided repeating the word *treaty*: an "*Interview* [emphasis mine] of this Kind with the Indians, we apprehend, may at this Time be greatly for His Majesty's Service, and for the Advantage not only of this, but of all the neighbouring Colonies, and not inconsistent with the Intention of Lord Loudoun's Letter: Which we nevertheless submit to your Honour's prudent Consideration" (7:5–7).

On 11 October, the Pennsylvania councillors received a letter from Major William Parsons at Easton advising them that Teedyuscung was at Wyoming but had been repeatedly warned that the Pennsylvanians intended to kill him. The council sent Parsons a message that the warnings had no substance and that he should invite Teedyuscung to Fort Allen at Gnadenhütten, from whence he should supply an escort to Easton.[8] On 3 November, Secretary Richard Peters read Conrad Weiser's letter to Denny concerning the forthcoming treaty. Though irritated that the treaty would be conducted at Easton rather than Philadelphia, Denny said he would leave for Easton the next day. He also received a message from the Quaker Friendly Association for Regaining and Preserving Peace with the Indians, offering to send presents to the Indians and to come to the conference. He agreed (7:9–13).

Isaac Norris, in poor health, did not go. Franklin, Fox, Hughes, and Masters, all provincial commissioners, attended. Israel Pemberton, the leader of the Friendly Association, took with him Charles Thomson, who had left employment as an usher at the College and Academy of Philadelphia to become head of Latin at the Friends Public School. Franklin left on 5 November with the other commissioners, spent that night at Samuel Dean's on Tohicon Creek, Bucks County (about two-thirds of the way to Bethlehem), arrived at Bethlehem, Northampton County, on the sixth and at Easton on Sunday the seventh (7:15). Denny had learned enough of Franklin's ability that he asked Franklin to draft his speeches to the Indians. As we have seen, Franklin had been a key figure in the Carlisle Treaty of 1753 (above, pp. 328–29). He was probably glad to have a chance to participate in another treaty.

The conference began at 11:00 A.M., Monday morning, 8 November. Though Franklin drafted Denny's speeches and though Franklin and Hall printed the treaty, what they printed were the official minutes, written by Richard Peters and no doubt approved by the governor and his council. Other manuscript sources, cited below, valuably supplement the printed treaty. Governor Denny "Marched from his Lodging to the . . . Conference, guarded by a party of the Royal Americans in the Front and on the Flanks, and a Detachment of Colonel Weiser's Provincials in Subdivisions in the Rear, with Colours flying, Drums beating, and Musick playing, which order was always observed in going to the . . . Conference." After Teedyuscung claimed that he had, as agreed upon in the spring, done all he could to bring back captives whom the Indians had taken, he swore to his good faith and said that the bad reports about him should "be no more minded than the whistling of Birds." The governor replied that he looked forward to Teedyuscung's remarks the following morning.[9]

Teedyuscung opened on Tuesday, 9 November, by recalling the former "happy Times," apologized for the behavior of "our Foolish young People," and claimed he disapproved of the attacks. The next day, Conrad Weiser informed the governor that an Indian from Fort Allen said that a group of Indians near there had heard a rumor that Teedyuscung and his party had been killed by the English, and they intended to avenge them. But learning it was false, the Indians waited near Fort Allen. News of the waiting Indians delayed the meetings for two days while Governor Denny sent the interpreter Moses Tatamy to invite them to attend the conference. Since some enemy Indians had recently attacked settlers along the frontier, the Indians near Fort Allen were desired to "keep together, lest they be mistaken for enemy Indians." The Indians near Fort

Allen refused to come further but said that Teedyuscung could speak for them and that they would abide by whatever agreement he made.[10]

At a meeting of the governor and commissioners on Wednesday, 10 November, the commissioners said that the Indians thought "Injustice had been done them in Land Affairs." Governor Denny replied that he would ask Teedyuscung about it "in plain Terms." Richard Peters and Conrad Weiser urged Denny not to do so because it was evident that the French had pressed the Indians to "strike their old friends." Denny, however, chose to follow the recommendation of Franklin and the commissioners.[11] Before the treaty resumed, the governor and others read over Franklin's draft of the governor's speech, made "some Alterations," and sent word that the governor would address the Indians that afternoon.

On Friday, 12 November, Governor Denny thanked the Indians, affirmed Pennsylvania's friendship, and then asked: "As we are now met together, at a Council-Fire, kindled by us both, and have promised, on both Sides, to be free and open, to one another, I must ask you, how that League of Friendship came to be broken? Have we, the Governor, or People, of *Pensilvania,* done you any Kind of Injury? If you think we have, you should be honest and tell us your Hearts; You should have made Complaints, before you struck us; for so it was agreed in our ancient League: However, now the Great Spirit has, thus happily, brought us once more together, speak your Mind plainly, on this Head, and tell us, if you have any just Cause of Complaint, what it is?" Teedyuscung replied that he would answer the next day.[12]

Israel Pemberton wrote of the interaction on 12 November that he had not "for many years been at a treaty" in which the Indians gave "such full and frequent expressions of approbation by their hearty, united 'yeho' after every sentence." At the end the Indians "hurried across the Benches to offer the Governor their hands. One of them cry'd out, 'Oh! He is a good Man, there is no Evil in his Heart.'"[13]

Denny invited Franklin, Pemberton, and several others to have dinner with him that evening. Peters claimed to be happy to have the opportunity to prove that Teedyuscung's complaint was groundless. Groundless or not, Franklin suggested that the surest and quickest way to settle the grievance was to pay the Delaware Indians now. Tatamy, the Indian interpreter, told the Quakers that the Walking Purchase had been a fraud. He later said to Conrad Weiser the major underlying reason for the Indian warfare was that the Iroquois had sold the New England men the Wyoming Valley at the Albany Treaty.[14] Was the underlying problem the Walking Purchase, the sale of Indian land at the Albany Treaty, or both? Teedyuscung seemed to confuse the two. William Penn had presumably initiated the Walking Purchase in 1686 with the Delaware Indians living at the forks of the Delaware (the land between the Lehigh and the Delaware rivers; see map 5, p. 499). In 1736, the Delaware Indian chiefs Nutimus and Tishcohan expressed skepticism to James Logan concerning the purchase, and Logan produced a deed describing an intended cession of land as far as a man could go in a day and a half (it did not say "walk"),[15] and asked the Iroquois (who were supposedly the overlords of the Delaware Indians) to confirm the deed. They did so. The next year Thomas Penn had the "walk" performed. Most authorities agree that even if there had been a "Walking Purchase" in 1686, the 1737 "walk" took in far more land than the Indians intended (*Life* 2:331).

Early Saturday morning, Franklin wrote Deborah a complaining but charming letter about her not writing: "I wrote to you a few days since, by a special messenger, and inclosed letters, for all our wives and sweethearts; expecting to hear from you by his return, and to have the northern newspapers and English letters, per the packet; but he is just now returned without a scrap for poor us. So I had a good mind not to write to you by this opportunity; but I never can be ill-natured enough, even when there is the most occasion. The messenger, says he left the letters at your house, and saw you afterwards at Mr. Dentie's and told you when he would go, and that he lodged at Honey's, next door to you, and yet you did not write. . . . I think I wont tell you that we are well, nor that we expect to return about the middle of the week, nor will I send you a word of news; that's poz. My duty to mother, love to the children, and to Miss Betsey and Gracey, &c. &c. I am, Your *loving* husband, B. Franklin."

"PS. I have *scratched out the loving words*, being writ in haste by mistake, when *I forgot I was angry*" (7:17–18).

About noon on Saturday the thirteenth, Teedyuscung began with the traditional "Condolence Ceremony": "I am sorry for what has happened, and I now take and wipe the Tears from your Eyes, as there is great Reason for Mourning. This I not only do on my own Part, but on the Part of the *Six Nations*, who will put their Seal to it.—I take away the Blood from your Bodies, with which they are sprinkled: I clear the Ground, and the Leaves, that you may sit down with Quietness: I clear your Eyes, that when you see the Day-Light you may enjoy it." After more expressions of solicitude, he concluded, "Your Wound is cured."[16]

Replying to Governor Denny's request of the day before, Teedyuscung proceeded to give a "true Account how I came to strike you." He said he had been accused of attacking the English before he actually did, but "The King of *England*, and of *France*, have settled, or wrought, this Land so as to coop us up, as if in a Pen." The "Foolish and Ignorant Young Men" believed the French who said that it was the fault of the English, so the young Indians attacked the English. But "Some Things that have passed in former Times, both in this and other Governments, were not well pleasing to the *Indians*; indeed, they thought them wrong." Despite some confusing syntax, the several slightly different texts make it clear that Teedyuscung laid the principal cause on the French leading astray the "foolish young Indians." He had said so on Tuesday, 9 November, and again here. The Indians had evidently agreed on this explanation at a preparatory conference. Now, however, he added that past wrongs—in New Jersey as

well as Pennsylvania—made the blow fall heavier. Seeming to end the conference, Teedyuscung said he would let Governor Denny know further about peace
if they met together the following spring; until then, he would notify the Pennsylvanians if he heard of any war parties setting out against the English.

Denny, however, persisted: Teedyuscung had mentioned "Grievances."
What were they? Teedyuscung said he had "not far to go, for an Instance: This
very Ground, that is under me (striking it with his Foot) was my Land and
Inheritance, and is taken from me, by Fraud. When I say this Ground, I mean
all the Land lying between *Tohiccon* Creek and *Wioming*, on the River *Susquehannah*." As Richard Peters well knew, the ground at Easton had been part of
the Walking Purchase. Peters promptly dropped his pen and refused to record
any more of the treaty.[17] Governor Denny then asked Charles Thomson, who
was taking notes of the proceedings, to continue as the secretary.

Teedyuscung claimed that New Jersey had also cheated the Delawares of
"several tracts." He said that "The Proprietaries who have purchased their
Lands from us cheap, have sold them too dear, to poor People, and the *Indians*
have suffered for it." If they had sold them cheaper and asked those who bought
them to treat the Indians with kindness, it would have been better. As it stood,
"you will not allow us to cut a little Wood to make a Fire; nay, hinder us from
Hunting, the only Means left us of getting our Livelihood." He questioned what
was done about the memorandum he gave Governor Morris in April 1755 concerning a tract of New Jersey land. Though Secretary Peters had said that the
governor would look into the matter, Teedyuscung had heard nothing further.
(The minutes of the 14–24 April 1755 meeting contain no reference to the New
Jersey land.)[18]

Governor Denny asked him what he meant by saying land had been taken
from him by fraud. Teedyuscung replied: "When one Man had formerly Liberty
to purchase Lands, and he took the Deed from the *Indians*, for it, and then dies;
after his Death, the Children forge a Deed, like the true One, with the same
Indian Names to it, and thereby, take Lands from the *Indians*, which they never
sold—this is Fraud. Also, when one King has Land, beyond the River, and another King has Land, on this Side, both bounded by Rivers, Mountains and
Springs, which cannot be moved, and the Proprietaries, *greedy* [emphasis mine]
to purchase Lands, buy of one King, what belongs to the other,—this, likewise
is Fraud." Teedyuscung's first example refers to the Walking Purchase and the
documents years later supposedly proving it; and the second refers to the Iroquois at the Albany Treaty selling the Delaware lands in the Wyoming Valley.
As we will see, the use of the word *greedy* upset Peters.[19]

Since the examples seemed general to the new governor, he asked Teedyuscung "whether he had ever been used, in that Manner?" Yes, the chief replied,
Pennsylvania had taken from him "all the Land extending from *Tohiccon*, over
the *Great-Mountain*, to *Wioming*, . . . by fraud; for when I had agreed to sell the
Land to the old Proprietary, by the course of the River, the Young Proprietaries

Figure 47. *The Reverend Richard Peters, attributed to John Wollaston. The half-length portrait of Richard Peters, secretary of the province, shows him in his clerical dress. Though a leading member of the Proprietary Party, Peters cooperated with Franklin on numerous civic and charitable activities. One occasion when Peters rose above party considerations was at the opening of the assembly of 1755–56, when Governor Robert Hunter Morris suppressed the information that the Pennsylvania frontier settlers were being attacked by the French and hostile Indians. Morris wanted the Pennsylvania Assembly to do nothing so he could condemn them to the English authorities for not taking action. Peters, however, informed Speaker Isaac Norris on 18 October 1755 of the letters from the frontier. Peters played an important part in Philadelphia's small society in the 1740s and 1750s.*

Like most people in the eighteenth century, Peters believed in a hierarchical society, whereas Franklin was a radical egalitarian. Peters worked for Thomas Penn and wanted to think that Penn was fundamentally a good man, whereas Franklin held Penn in contempt as an avaricious landlord who considered himself superior to everyone in Pennsylvania. Courtesy, Pennsylvania Academy of Fine Arts.

came and got it run by a straight Course, by the Compass, and by that means took in double the Quantity intended to be sold." Though the reference was clearly to the Walking Purchase, the mention of the Wyoming Valley again confused the issue by also alluding to the 1754 Albany purchase. That Saturday evening, several Quakers met with the interpreter Moses Tatamy and condemned the Walking Purchase.[20]

Sunday morning, 14 November, the discomposed Richard Peters went to the house where several Friendly Association members were staying and demanded to see the minutes that Abel James had made of the Saturday meeting. James replied he would get them. Peters said no, James should just tell him what he understood Teedyuscung to have said which Charles Thomson recorded as "the English Government being greedy in the purchase of lands from the Indians." Peters charged that Thomson implied that the proprietors "had purchased of those who had no right to sell, which was Mr. Franklin's interpretation, to blacken the Proprietors and support a party." Peters claimed that Teedyuscung had not "said any such thing, and that the Proprietaries had always been solicited by the Indians" to purchase more land. Peters claimed "that the Proprietaries could not be charged therewith nor had Teedyuscung said any such thing." Franklin and the Quakers were "putting things in the Indians' Heads."[21]

Abel James replied that he understood "the Indians charged the Proprietaries, as well as others, with unfairness," and that they complained particularly about the Walking Purchase. Peters conceded that the "'walk' could not be vindicated" but that the proprietors had paid several times for the land. Peters left but soon rushed back. "These practices shall not be suffered. You shall be taken proper notice of. You are putting things into the Indians' heads." With that, he "went off in a great passion."[22]

Later that day, Peters and Conrad Weiser attended a meeting with the governor and the members of the Pennsylvania Council present at Easton. Both Peters and Weiser agreed that when the Indians formerly complained about the Walking Purchase, "their complaint was heard in a great Council of the Six Nations, held at Philadelphia in the year 1742."[23] On that occasion the Six Nations examined the documents and declared the complaints of their cousins, the Delawares, to be unreasonable. The Iroquois were "very angry" with the Delawares "for complaining without Cause." Though Peters and Weiser had been "present at the Council when the Delawares' complaints were heard and settled by the Six Nations," neither was officially "concerned in this Transaction." Since the documents were present in Philadelphia, Governor Denny concluded that he would investigate the complaints there, and, "if justly founded," he would amply redress them.[24]

When Denny consulted the commissioners, Franklin and the others said that "such Promises had been frequently made the Indians by the Governors of other Provinces and not performed, and these people might consider them as now made with a Design to evade giving them redress." The commissioners added, "as more Goods were brought, than were proper at this Time to be given to the small Number of *Indians* come down, it would be better, whether the Claim was just or unjust, to offer them immediate Satisfaction, which they, on the Part of the Publick, with the Governor's Approbation, were willing to do; judging this wou'd effectually remove all their Uneasiness." Governor Denny was persuaded by them, and Franklin accordingly drafted the governor's answer.[25]

That evening, rumor had it that a party of whites intended to kill the Indians while they slept. Several days earlier, a peddler was jailed who had offered knives to some soldiers to cut the throats of the Indians and who said he would himself "destroy Teedyuscung." In face of the rumor, Governor Denny had the guards doubled and "all the boats near the town . . . secured, to prevent people coming from New Jersey, as they had threatened to do."

Later, some other Friends called on Peters, who went with them to a house rented by the Friends where Peters found Teedyuscung, the interpreter Tatamy, and several additional Quakers. The Friends told Peters that Teedyuscung "cam to them to communicate his uneasiness, on account of the several threats which had been given them, and that he was apprehensive some of his people were gone, and more would go" because of the previous night's alarm. After further conversation, Peters declared "he was fully satisfied that the Friends spoke truth, and that he had been misinformed." In their own opinion, however, the Quakers thought Peters had "a fixed purpose . . . to confuse, misrepresent, and obstruct an honest, fair inquiry in order to an amicable adjustment."[26]

The Indian treaty restarted on Monday, 15 November, with the governor's repeating parts of the condolence ceremony. He continued with the speech Franklin had prepared. The Indians should have complained to the whites before attacking them: "When the Great Creator made Man, he gave him a Tongue, to complain of Wrongs, two Ears, to hear a Brother's Complaints, and two Hands, to do him Justice, by removing the Cause—All these were made before the Hatchet, and should be first used" (7:20). Governor Denny said that since most persons concerned in the original Walking Purchase of 1686 and even the one run in 1737 were dead, and since the Indians generally did not read, "it may be hard for me to satisfy you, of the Truth, tho' my predecessors dealt ever so uprightly; therefore, to shew our sincere Desire to heal the present Differences, and live in eternal peace with you our Brethren, tell me, what will satisfy you, for the Injustice you suppose has been done you . . . and if it be in my Power, you shall have immediate Satisfaction, whether it be justly due to you or not." Denny then asked again that Teedyuscung bring down all the prisoners from his country and reminded him that Sir William Johnson in the future would be in charge of all Indian relations. Denny concluded by saying that he was giving a large quantity of goods, "a large part of them" given by Quaker descendants of those who came over with William Penn, as a "Testimony of their regards and affection for the Indians, and their earnest desire to promote this good work of Peace."[27]

On Tuesday, 16 November, Teedyuscung opened with two epic similes urging the mutual cooperation of the whites and Indians: "Take Pains therefore, and though you are a Governor, do not put off these Things from Time to Time, as our Forefathers did." When asked for clarification, Teedyuscung said that the quarrel between the French and English and the young Indians being "deluded by the *French*" was "the first and principal Cause" of the Indians attacking the Pennsylvanians, "tho' other Things helped, to make the Blow fall quicker and faster."[28] Teedyuscung further said that the past purchases of Indian lands "was not the main Thing which I cam about" and that he did not intend "to mention it in these difficult Times," for it was not "the first Cause of the Stroke, tho' it was the Foundation of our Uneasiness." He said that he could not give the "true value" of the land taken (presumably referring to the Walking Purchase) and that "many more were concerned" who were not present. Therefore, he would put off any remuneration until their next meeting.

Replying to the governor's repeated request, Teedyuscung added that he only knew of two more white prisoners in his camps, but if Governor Denny could find more and give men to help bring the prisoners down, he would "gather and scoop in as many as I can." He complained that New Jersey officials confined some Indians and asked that they have freedom. Near the end, he said that "in order to prevent Misunderstandings," he would like to have a copy of the minutes from the former conference in April as well as this one: "What is committed to writing will not easily be lost, and will be of great use to all, and better regarded." He asked the governor to take special care of the interpreter Plumpshire, and concluded by giving a gift of deer skins.[29] That seemingly concluded the treaty. But Franklin drafted another speech for the governor, and at six the next morning, the commissioners called on Denny and advised him to fix the "Value of the Damages that the Delawares had suffered in the Purchases of Land." Denny sent Weiser to ask Teedyuscung if this would be agreeable. (Richard Peters wrote Thomas Penn on 22 November that the commissioners were thinking of offering £500.) The chief, however, declared, "he had no power to take any sum." He would try to bring as many persons who were concerned to the next meeting in the spring, "when it might be further considered."

Governor Denny thought of an additional matter he wanted to discuss with Teedyuscung and sent for him and a small group of Indians. He said that he would send two Indians from the Six Nations to help bring back whatever captives the Indians had. Finally, Denny reported that several Indians had sickened and died at Philadelphia, including Captain Newcastle. Using the language of the condolence ceremony, Denny gave a string of wampum, seven black shrouds, and some handkerchiefs to alleviate the Indians' grief. The last meeting concluded on 17 November with further exchanges of goodwill.[30] That afternoon

Figure 48. Indian gorget from the Friendly Association for Regaining and Preserving Peace with the Indians, ca. 1760. Joseph Richardson, silversmith. The gorget portrays a flourishing tree (the archetypal tree of life was a traditional Indian symbol of peace), the sun (a symbol of good weather and good times), and a white man and an Indian at a strong fire (a symbol of good relations). The white man is handing the Indian a calumet or peace pipe decorated with feathers. Except for the calumet, which was mainly used by the Plains Indians, the symbols and ceremony were common throughout the Pennsylvanians' contacts with the Indians. Since future members of the Friendly Association (founded in 1756) knew it from the Twightwees/Miamis at the Carlisle Treaty (1–4 October 1753), this gorget was probably intended for them or for some other Ohio-area Indians.

The silversmith Joseph Richardson was a member of the Friendly Association and is known to have made thirty gorgets, among other objects, as gifts to Indians, at its behest. In 1757 he struck a peace medal for the militia Association, which had the same symbols as this gorget. Israel Pemberton, the primary and wealthiest founder of the Friendly Association, was probably chiefly responsible for having the expensive silver presents made. Courtesy, Atwater Kent Museum of Philadelphia, Historical Society of Pennsylvania Collection.

or perhaps early the next morning, Franklin set out for Philadelphia and arrived Thursday evening, 18 November.

Later that month, the House asked for a copy of the Easton Treaty minutes, and Richard Peters delivered them on 30 November. In January 1757, the Proprietary Party briefly investigated Teedyuscung's charges that the proprietors had unfairly taken the Indians' lands. Nicholas Scull testified before the council on 25 January that he was present at the Walking Purchase, that it had been done fairly during one day and a half, that the walkers never did more than walk, and that the Indians at the time did not complain. However, Franklin and the other House commissioners who had been present at Easton objected to the treaty minutes and, indirectly, to Scull's testimony. They declared that "the Complaints made by the Indians" at Easton, "whether justly founded or not, should be fully represented, and their Sense of them understood." They were weakly represented in the official minutes. "We think it necessary to observe to the House, that we conceive the Warmth and Earnestness with which they insisted on the Wrongs that had been done them in the Purchases of Land, are much too faintly expressed in this Account of the Conference." They also testified that Peters himself said that the Walking Purchase was "(in his own Words) *unworthy of any Government*."

Franklin had changed his mind about Teedyuscung and the Delaware Indians since he wrote Thomas Pownall the previous August. Franklin now believed that the Delawares had been cheated by the Pennsylvania authorities—and probably also by the Iroquois at the Albany Treaty. He boldly printed the commissioners' report to the House of 29 January 1757 as part of its *Votes and Proceedings* and as an appendix to the treaty itself.[31]

THE ASSEMBLY SESSION, 22 NOVEMBER–24 DECEMBER

In the month-long second session of the Pennsylvania Assembly, Speaker Norris appointed Franklin and Joseph Galloway to ask Governor Denny to lay before the House the proprietary instructions that related to "Matters of Legislation." Franklin diplomatically did so (7:29–30). Denny reported one instruction on 26 November that told him "to settle a regular and useful Militia" in Pennsylvania, but other matters intervened. Throughout the entire 1756–57 legislative year, the assembly was bogged down in a dispute over the Northhampton County election between William Plumsted, a Proprietary Party member, and William Edmonds, a Moravian and Quaker Party member. At the end of the assembly year, the House finally decided on 23 September, in favor of Edmonds.[32]

Speaker Norris had referred the troubled question of the quartering of soldiers in Philadelphia to Franklin and a committee on 22 October. He brought in a bill on 2 December, which was passed on 3 December and sent to the governor. The quartering of troops in private and public houses remained an issue in colonial America and was finally listed as the first of a number of grievances in the Declaration of Independence ("quartering large bodies of armed troops among us") and became the third amendment to the U.S. Constitution ("No Soldier shall, in time of peace be quartered in any house, without the consent of the Owner, nor in time of war, but in a manner to be prescribed by law"). Franklin's bill of 3 December anticipated the later position of the United States, but on 7 December, Governor Denny rejected it because the bill demanded citizens' permission before soldiers could be billeted in their homes. On 7 July 1756, the king in council had repealed Franklin's similar act of 15 August 1755. The House now struck out billeting in private houses and sent it back to Denny. He replied on 8 December that not enough public housing existed in Philadelphia for the soldiers, so he found the bill insufficient. Richard Peters, however, added the governor's personal message: if the House refused to change the bill, he would accept it. Franklin reported that Philadelphia alone had 117 public houses. Denny passed the bill.[33]

On 9 December, Philadelphia's mayor, Attwood Shute, informed the Philadelphia Common Council that he had been asked "to provide Winter Quarters" for fifty officers and five hundred soldiers who would shortly be in town. He said that the rooms in the public houses would be insufficient for five hundred soldiers and that the officers would not be satisfied with the public housing. The Philadelphia council advised that the Pennsylvania Assembly's recommendation "should be strictly pursued," but if it proved inadequate, "the Sufferers ought to Apply to the Assembly, where only a Remedy could be provided." Two days later, the mayor and aldermen remonstrated to the assembly that many keepers of public houses were "so poor and indigent" that they could not provide decent housing for any troops. Moreover, Captain John Tulleken of the Royal American Regiment demanded a hospital "with Bedding, Fire and other Necessaries" for the sick troops, among whom smallpox was spreading. The mayor and aldermen could not satisfy the soldiers' needs.[34]

The assembly asked how many soldiers had been provided housing and what was still needed. William Franklin, clerk of the House, reported on the morning of 14 December 1756 that the previous day he had asked the mayor, who replied that because they could not possibly pay the costs, several "Tavern-keepers had already resigned, and he expected that many more would do the same before Night." Therefore, it would be useless to prepare a tally now, but he would do so that night or early the next morning.[35]

Governor Denny reported to the Pennsylvania Council on 15 December that many soldiers were still inadequately housed, the weather was cold, and the smallpox increasing. Colonel Henry Bouquet (1719?–65), who had served in Swiss regiments in Europe before being commissioned lieutenant colonel in the Royal American Regiment in 1756, said he "was loath to take violent Measures, but if something was not instantly done he hoped the Governor would issue a Warrant to the Sheriff to assign him Quarters in private Houses." Bouquet said that a "new Hospital was promised to him by the Managers, but they drew back from their Promises, and he could neither get the new Hospital nor the old one, nor any House for an Hospital."[36] Bouquet applied to the city authorities, who advised him to appeal to the assembly. At this time, the Pennsylvania Hospital trustees were moving the patients from John Kinsey's house on Market Street to the new hospital building at Eighth and Pine streets.

On 16 December, Denny gave Bouquet a warrant to billet the soldiers in private quarters, though he left a space to insert the number of soldiers.[37] Sheriff James Coultas suggested that they spread the word of the warrant. He also said that Philadelphia had a number of empty houses that needed only straw, wood, and a few necessaries to become decent quarters at a small expense. Speaker Norris appointed Franklin on 16 December to a committee to draft a message to the governor concerning quartering soldiers in private houses. Franklin asked that the public housing be inspected. He noted that the provincial commissioners in charge of disposing the £30,000 bill should see that the soldiers had a hospital. Franklin added that a guard house had been provided "at the Expence of the Province." The message was approved and sent to the governor (7:46–47).[38]

Sheriff Coultas asked Colonel Bouquet on Saturday morning, 18 December, to loan him the writ to show "his Friends" who had influence in the assembly. That same morning, the assembly received Denny's message saying the current housing was inadequate, and "The King's Troops must be quartered." Norris immediately appointed Franklin to reply. That afternoon, Franklin presented the reply to the House, which approved it. Governor Denny found the proceedings irregular: instead of a petition being presented to the House, "the Writ itself was laid before the House in a clandestine manner, and very improperly by the Sheriff's Consent, which threw the House into a Ferment and for the first Time since the Charter they sat all Saturday Afternoon and Sunday Morning." On Sunday, 19 December, the assembly entered its reply in the minutes and marched through the streets to deliver it to Governor Denny "when the Streets were full of People going to their respective Places of Worship."[39] Norris also appointed Franklin to a committee to confer with the governor.

The parties met at 12:30 on Monday. According to Governor Denny and the council, Franklin "opened the Conference by making large Professions of the good Disposition of the House for the Army." Denny said that 62 beds are wanted for 124 soldiers "who lie upon Straw" and more for recruits arriving daily. The committee said that it could prepare the laws, but only the governor could enforce them. (That was disingenuous since the commissioners controlled the funds.) The committee stated that public houses in the outskirts of Philadelphia were not used, but the governor replied that the troops must be housed in Philadelphia. Someone (probably Franklin) replied with an extended comparison: "if Necessity warranted Quartering on private Houses by Force, and contrary to Law; and Military Officers were the only Judges of that Necessity, they might say it was necessary to quarter the whole Army, not only in one City, but in one Square, or one Street; and thereby harass the Inhabitants excessively" (7:57).

Richard Peters wrote to Thomas Penn that at the 20 December meeting Franklin "behaved with great rudeness and Insolence to the Governor, declaring he was no Governor, as he did not protect the People and calling him in express Terms a meer Bashaw." Governor Denny "tamely put up with" the insults "in the presence of his Council, without any apparent resentment or Reply. . . . It was likewise insinuated by B. Franklin as if the Council obstructed the publick Business, misrepresented matters to the Governor and inflamed him to take Arbitrary and Tyrannical measures." In the provincial council records, Peters claimed that Franklin and other members of the committee used "offensive, indecent, and rude Expressions."[40] The next day, 21 December, the House reaffirmed that it would provide housing for the troops when it was shown that the public housing was inadequate. Governor Denny immediately replied that in a war, the assembly must furnish adequate quarters, carriages, and other support whenever troops are stationed within or marching through a province.[41]

On a committee to consider the message, Franklin and others reported on 24 December 1756 that the assembly had, in fact, provided money for such purposes and that it had also passed a bill for £60,000, of which £10,000 was for Lord Loudoun, but the governor vetoed the bill because it was larger than £30,000. Franklin charged that Governor Denny, like former governor Morris, wrote messages in great part for the British authorities and attempted to make the assembly look bad. Franklin and the committee concluded that the times called "rather for Action than Altercation" and recommended that the House make no answer to the governor's message but "apply themselves diligently to raising the necessary Supplies for his Majesty's Service, and to perfecting the Militia Bill now under their Consideration."

Meanwhile, the House had resolved on 15 December to grant a £100,000 supply bill for defense, and thereafter met a number of times as a committee of the whole to consider how to raise the money. It finally decided on 23 December that a tax should be laid on "all estates, real and personal, and Taxables within the same, sufficient to raise the said Sum in one Year." The next day, 24 December, Franklin was appointed to a committee to prepare and bring in the bill.[42] Then the assembly adjourned until 3 January.

On Saturday afternoon, Christmas Day, Governor Denny called a meeting of the commissioners in charge of the £30,000 and presented Lord Loudoun's threatening letter: "If the number of troops now in Philadelphia are not sufficient [to command quarters], I will instantly march a number sufficient for that purpose and find quarter to the whole." According to Richard Peters, the commissioners nevertheless intended to do nothing "but on B.F.'s expressing his Sentiments in favour of a total Compliance, the rest immediately Changed their Tone and fell in with the measure."[43] At 10:00 the next morning, Peters wrote the commissioners saying that Loudoun wanted to know immediately whether the lodging Colonel Bouquet demanded will be actually provided "and the Hospital repaired and furnished on or before the first day of January." Peters sent along Lieutenant Lewis Ourry's report that 94 men lay on straw, 73 had not even straw, and that there were no quarters fit for officers, nor any for the recruits coming in daily (7:61–63).

Franklin met with Colonel Bouquet that evening, received a list of what was necessary, met with several of the other commissioners, and then guaranteed Bouquet that "every Thing will be provided agreable to the Memorandums made between us this Evening." In a letter to Penn of 10 January 1757, Richard Peters sourly noted that "Col. Bouquet hinted that had he applied directly to B.F. and not to the Governor, matters would have been done at first to Lord Loudoun's Satisfaction" (7:64, 64n4). The delay was only partially Franklin's fault. Franklin and the assembly had repeatedly asked for specific information and not received it. No single commissioner could make a decision, and the group of commissioners would not want to pay unless they thought the majority of the assembly members would agree.

A surprising result of the dispute over quartering in Philadelphia was that Franklin became good friends with both Colonel Bouquet and Lieutenant Ourry. When Bouquet was leaving Philadelphia in the spring, Franklin gave him, on 14 April, a letter of introduction to Dr. Alexander Garden of Charleston, saying that Garden would be pleased with his conversation and calling him a man "of Learning, Ingenuity and Politeness" (7:183). The Franklins enjoyed and entertained both Bouquet and Ourry, and Ourry later corresponded with Deborah and called on her while Franklin was in England.[44]

THE THIRD SESSION OF THE 1756–57 ASSEMBLY, 3 JANUARY–9 APRIL 1757

The longest Pennsylvania Assembly session in the colonial period began on 3 January and continued through 9 April 1757. On 4 January, Franklin and the commissioners in charge of the £30,000 supply bill laid before the assembly Governor Denny's 29 December letter. He had requested funds for George Croghan's embassy on behalf of Sir William Johnson to the Pennsylvania Indians. Croghan wanted to send messengers to the Delaware Indian spokesman, Teedyuscung, and to the Susquehanna Indians. The three groups would meet at Harris's Ferry, where Croghan would attempt to get a party to visit the Shawnee and Delaware Indians at the Ohio. If the Ohio Indians were "well disposed," the Pennsylvania authorities would invite them to a conference in the spring. The commissioners replied to Denny that the £30,000 had been spent. However, on 6 January the assembly resolved to pay the expenses of messengers in order to have the conference. On 8 January, Israel Pemberton and the Friendly Association added £100 to the assembly's funds.[45]

Franklin and others appointed on 24 December brought in a supply bill on 5 January 1757 for £100,000. The committee submitted two acts the next day—Franklin's bill for regulating soldiers, which passed on 12 January, and a supplement to the nightly watch bill, which passed on 13 January. The governor assented to both on 18 January.[46] When the assembly discussed the supply bill on 5 and 6 January, the members noted that the proprietors still owed £2,840 of the £5,000 "free gift" of November 1755. On 7 January, the House defeated a motion to include a £2,840 charge to the proprietors in lieu of a tax on their estates. The assembly reconsidered the revised £100,000 bill and passed it on 22 January. Since it taxed the proprietors' estates, Governor Denny vetoed it on 25 January. The assembly prepared a remonstrance the next day, and on 27 January, the Pennsylvania Assembly marched through the streets of Philadelphia to the governor's house to deliver it. Richard Peters wrote that the purpose of the assemblymen was "to Alarm everybody with the Sight and the Occasion."[47] The remonstrance asserted that the "Proprietaries professed Willingness to be taxed" was a sham, that they actually were injuring "the Interests of the Crown," and that they behaved tyrannically to Pennsylvanians. The assembly unanimously demanded the governor sign the bill, "as he will answer to the Crown for all the Consequences of his Refusal at his Peril." Governor Denny immediately rejected the remonstrance, saying he would keep it until he had taken a copy, which he would send the king with his reasons for rejecting it.[48]

Benjamin Franklin, Pennsylvania Agent

Without dissent, the assembly resolved on 28 January 1757 to send commissioners to England "to solicit a Removal of the Grievances we labour under by Reason of Proprietary Instructions." The next day, the House resolved that Franklin and Speaker Norris go to England on its behalf. The two requested some time to consider the request. On 1 February Franklin served on a committee to prepare a new £100,000 tax bill that would exempt the proprietors. Brought in on 2 February, it was read the first and second time and, after some alterations, ordered to be transcribed for a third reading. The following day, 3 February, the bill passed. The assembly had given in.

Called on that same day to say whether they would accept the appointment to England, Speaker Norris replied that the state of his health would make the trip difficult for him and that he might be of more service to the House in Pennsylvania, but he would do whatever the members wished. Franklin said that it was a high honor to be asked, but if Speaker Norris would go, he thought an additional person unnecessary. He, too, however, was at "the Disposition of the House, and was ready to go whenever they should think fit to require his Service." The House unanimously thanked both. "Resolved, That this House will make Provision for defraying the Expence that may attend their Voyage, and the Solicitation of the Affairs of the Province in *England*; and that Mr. *Franklin* do first go over."[49] On 8 February, Dr. John Kearsley, Jr., a Proprietary Party partisan, wrote former governor Robert Hunter Morris, who had returned to New Jersey as chief justice, that Franklin "Jumps at going" to England because his office as deputy postmaster general "shakes." Kearsley wrote that although Franklin "would not go but to Support this falling interest of his own, he is artfully Insinuating that he goes on his Countrys Service. Most Certain I am that he will go at his Countrys Expence for he is wicked enough to Blind the People" (7:110n9).

Isaac Norris named a committee on 17 February to list the grievances "necessary to be represented Home to England." Since the summary would serve as a basis for Franklin's actions in the attempt to make Pennsylvania a royal colony, he was not named to the committee. The report, however, enumerated charges that Franklin had made in the quarrel with the proprietary government for the previous several years. The seven committee members who signed the 22 February report included Franklin's close friends Thomas Leech and John Hughes, as well as the new member who became his political lieutenant, Joseph Galloway. The report objected to the "impractical and unconstitutional Instructions" of the proprietors that bound the governors; objected to the governors' control of money bills as contrary to the practice in England where the Commons was the sole judge of the ways and amounts of money granted to the king; and objected to the proprietors' appointing judges and other officers to offices at "their Will and Pleasure" rather than, as in England, "during their good behaviour." The practice supposedly kept judges and other officers "subject to the Influence and Direction of the Proprietaries." In addition, the assembly named the problem of the British army enlisting servants, "without the least Satisfaction being made to the Masters" (7:138–41).

Relief for Innkeepers

The Quartering Act of 8 December required innkeepers to provide soldiers billeted upon them with decent shelter and bedding for four pence a day. They lost money on that allowance and petitioned the assembly for relief on 3 January 1757. Speaker Norris assigned Franklin to a committee to prepare a bill to relieve innkeepers. The bill, which would pay the innkeeper four pence more a day, and be financed by an additional tax of two pence per gallon on all liquor sold in the province, was reported on 18 January, amended three days later, and passed on 24 January. Governor Denny returned it on 3 February with five amendments, four of which the House agreed to. The House sent the bill back to the governor. Denny returned it on 7 February because the bill would supposedly tax the innkeepers whom it was designed to relieve and because it would not raise enough money.

Norris appointed Franklin and John Hughes a committee to reply on 7 February. Answering Denny on 9 February, they pointed out that the bill taxed all the innkeepers, whereas the only ones who had soldiers billeted on them were the Philadelphia innkeepers. The argument implied that the tax paid by the Philadelphia innkeepers who actually had soldiers billeted upon them would be far less than the additional four pence a day that they received. Franklin and Hughes also claimed that no one could be certain whether the tax on liquor would be sufficient, but if it fell short, the assembly could subsequently make an additional provision. The reply concluded that if the governor did not pass the bill, "Affairs of great Importance will not at present admit of our spending more Time" on it (7:120). The governor and council unanimously adhered to their amendment, but on 5 March reconsidered, and on 14 March, the day Lord Loudoun arrived in Philadelphia, the governor approved the law, which became official on 17 March.[50]

The New £100,000 Tax Bill

Framed as a supplement to the £60,000 bill of 27 November 1755, the new £100,000 bill added a 5 percent annual tax on the income from estates in addition to the 2½ percent annual tax of 1755. Like that act, it exempted the estates of the proprietors but retained control of the expenditures by assembly-appointed commissioners. Because of the latter provision, and because it called for four years in which to sink the bills of credit, it was doomed. Passed by the assembly on 3 February, the act was referred by Governor Denny to three council members for objections. Denny rejected the bill, noting seven objections, on 11 February and returned it to the assembly the next day.[51] Speaker Norris promptly appointed Franklin to a committee to reply.

On 17 February, Franklin answered that even if the assembly could convince Governor Denny of the justice of the bill, it could not "change his Instruction," which he was determined to follow. Therefore, the committee chose to report to the House the reasons for the terms of the current bill. Since the governor had previously refused bills for granting £60,000 (September 1756) and another for £100,000 (January 1757),[52] the delegates had chosen to make this bill a supplement to one the king in council had approved on 7 July 1756. The governor, however, objected to various provisions of the act, even though many were identical to the former, approved act.

Franklin refuted the seven objections. The first objection said that Pennsylvania's currency would be in danger of depreciation if £45,000 were struck and expressed concern for the estates of widows and orphans. Franklin replied that, according to Denny's instructions, he was permitted to re-emit the £80,000 current in Pennsylvania and an additional £40,000 for sixteen years, "without any Provision against the Injuries the Estates of the Widows and Orphans might sustain thereby." The governor's third demand would effectually allow no more than £30,000 a year to be collected—at the same time that he said that the entire tax must be collected in one year. But £30,000 was only one-quarter of what the governor said he needed. The real reasons for the governor's rejecting the bill were the proprietors' instructions: they insisted that the quitrents be paid in sterling rather than Pennsylvania currency and that they or their deputies control the disposal of the money. Only "the Want of Compliance with those Proprietary Instructions," Franklin wrote, caused the supply bill not to be approved. The additional supposed reasons—like the concern for widows and children—were "only introduced to save That [the instructions] the Shame of standing alone" (7:123, 127, 132).

A month before Franklin's report of 17 February 1757, it became known that Lieutenant General John Campbell, fourth lord Loudoun, would be arriving in Philadelphia for a council of war with the southern governors. Initially, the proprietary partisans greeted the news with glee. Richard Peters wrote Thomas Penn on 10 January that Governor Denny intended to "lay Franklin's Conduct before Lord Loudoun," who would set Franklin straight, and thereafter "it may be determined what further measures to take with him."[53] But as the time passed, Denny and the Pennsylvania councilmen changed their minds. Perhaps Governors Horatio Sharpe of Maryland, Robert Dinwiddie of Virginia, and Arthur Dobbs of North Carolina influenced the proprietary stalwarts. Governor Sharpe must have met Franklin on one or perhaps all three of his trips to Annapolis (January 1754, April 1755, or March 1756). Likewise, Governor Dinwiddie no doubt had met Franklin during his extended Virginia stay in April 1756, perhaps when the College of William and Mary conferred a master of arts degree on him on 20 April 1756. It seems unlikely that Denny or any of the southern governors knew Loudoun personally, and since Franklin had spent more than five weeks in New York with him during the previous June and July, they probably asked Franklin about the commander in chief. Moreover, once the proprietary partisans considered the advisory role of Thomas Pownall to Lord Loudoun and Pownall's friendship with Franklin, they began to fear that the Proprietary Party, not Franklin and the assembly, might be judged at fault.

The governors, as well as others like George Washington who were gathered in Philadelphia in February to wait for Lord Loudoun, all knew of General Braddock's high opinion of Franklin and his recent praise to the British authorities of Franklin and of Pennsylvania. Even if Denny and his council did not want to admit it, Governors Sharpe, Dinwiddie, and Dobbs must have known that some authorities held Pennsylvania and Franklin in high esteem. Further, the three governors probably knew that almost all members of the Pennsylvania Assembly, not just Franklin, opposed Denny and the proprietors' instructions. No further rumors suggested Lord Loudoun might chastise Franklin. After the 18 February report of the assembly was read at a provincial council meeting on 5 March, the council unanimously decided that the £100,000 supply bill "should be detained till Loudoun's arrival, as something might be said by him on the Subject which might extricate the Governor and Assembly out of the Difficulties attending the passing Such a Bill."[54]

Loudoun in Philadelphia, 14–27 March 1757

Franklin intended to leave for New York in late February 1757 in order to take the packet *Halifax*, Captain Morris, to London in mid-March. David Hall wrote William Strahan on 14 February that Franklin was leaving in a few days, and William Franklin resigned as clerk of the House on Friday, 18 February, to sail with him. Franklin ordered sea stores for William and himself put onboard the packet and had James Parker in New York buy live fowl for the voyage. Though Lord Loudoun had called a council of war to meet in Philadelphia on 17 February, Franklin assumed it did not concern him. Loudoun, however, wrote Franklin that he had heard he intended to sail to England on the next packet, but Loudoun requested that Franklin postpone his voyage until the following packet sailed, which would be about 25 March. He wanted to see Franklin in Philadelphia, "as I know your Presence will be of great Use in forwarding whatever shall be found necessary to be done." News that Loudoun had requested Franklin's presence must have alarmed the proprietarians. Franklin replied on 3 March that he would wait (7:133, 143). Meanwhile, Governors Dinwiddie and Sharpe arrived in Philadelphia on 16 February, and Colonel George Washington came about the same time, but Loudoun was delayed and did not arrive until mid-March. No doubt the Franklins saw the governors and Washington socially several times during their weeks in Philadelphia.

Lord Loudoun arrived in Philadelphia on Monday, 14 March, and immediately conferred with the southern governors and Franklin. That same day, Governor Denny and his council approved the assembly's Quartering Act. Loudoun noted that Colonel John Stanwix, Bouquet's superior, told him of the pay for quarters for officers.[55] The next day, Speaker Norris appointed Franklin to a committee to write the assembly's address to Lord Loudoun. It was Franklin's last official duty in the 1756–57 assembly. Norris presented it on 16 March and Loudoun replied that if the colonies performed "what they ought on their Parts, they might be assured nothing should be wanting on his."[56] On 16 March Franklin met alone with Loudoun on Pennsylvania's possible support for a supply bill. Loudoun noted: "Mr. Frankland. Talked over the Situation of this Country and the deplorable State it appears to be in. He promises to do every thing in his Power that I recommend." Loudoun consulted Governors Dobbs, Dinwiddie, and Sharpe on Pennsylvania's politics and asked Governor Denny if he could not give up any of the proprietors' instructions. Denny turned over the request to Richard Peters and Benjamin Chew. To the assembly bill, they listed eight objections, which the council considered on 17 March.[57] The objections were mainly the ones Franklin and others had rebutted the previous month on 17 February.

On Friday, 18 March, Loudoun reminded Israel Pemberton that Indian relations had been taken out of the control of the different colonies and "more so out of Private Societys"—a warning that the Quakers' Friendly Association must no longer meddle in Indian affairs. That evening, the Philadelphia Corporation entertained Loudoun, the officers, principal inhabitants of Philadelphia, and all visiting dignitaries at the state house. On Saturday, 19 March, Loudoun recorded that "Whilst Mr Frankland and I were talking over the affairs in Dispute between the Governor and the Assembly in order to trie to bring them to an agreement, which the Governor had desired I might trie with Mr Franklin.

When Dinwiddie called and afterward Mr Denny, both of whch were called on at Mr Frankland's desire, and we went throu the dispute on the bill neather of them agreed on the facts which the other aledged, but Mr Frankland was much more acquainted with the affair than the Governor."[58]

Writing about the meeting in the *Autobiography* in 1788, Franklin recalled that he and Denny met with Lord Loudoun and discussed the differences between the House and the governor: "In behalf of the Assembly I urg'd all the Arguments that may be found in the publick Papers of that Time, which were of my Writing, and are printed with the Minutes of the Assembly and the Governor pleaded his Instructions, the Bond he had given to observe them, and his Ruin if he disobey'd: Yet seem'd not unwilling to hazard himself if Lord Loudon would advise it. This his Lordship did not chuse to do, tho' I once thought I had nearly prevail'd with him to do it; but finally he rather chose to urge the Compliance of the Assembly; and he entreated me to use my Endeavours with them for that purpose; declaring he could spare none of the King's Troops for the Defence of our Frontiers, and that if we did not continue to provide for that Defence ourselves they must remain expos'd to the Enemy" (A 158). Franklin was probably recalling the meeting on Saturday, 19 March. The extant evidence supports Franklin thus far.

The 1963 editors of the *Papers of Benjamin Franklin* suggested that on 19 March, Loudoun probably showed Franklin and Norris the propositions that Denny and the council had agreed upon two days before (7:148). Presumably, Franklin asked for a copy and said that he would return it with a summary of the assembly's objections. He did so, probably on Sunday, 20 March, or perhaps the next day (7:149–52). Matters came to a head on Monday, 21 March. Loudoun noted in his diary: "Indian Bill. The Pensilvania Indian bill which Mr Denny des[ires] says the assembly to furnish the mony for the presents to the Indians, they to appoint the commissioners to dispose of it, the supplee to be disposed of by the Assembly, the Governor to have nothing to do with it." He added that "Mr. Frankland has said to Mr Dinwiddy in the presence of the Governor [Denny] that he had the sole disposal of it."

At a meeting of the Pennsylvania Council on Monday morning, 21 March, Governor Denny tried to discredit Franklin. Denny told Lord Loudoun about Franklin's post office income and his powers to appoint postmasters and create routes. (In fact, the post office made no money before 1757.) Denny also criticized Franklin's controlling a newspaper: "Mr. Franklin has in particular the great Advantage of circulating his Papers free, and receiving Intelligence, which he may make the best or worst Use of in the present Situation of Affairs." The governor implied that Franklin was not above publishing secret information in the papers: "Sir Charles Hardie wrote to the late Governor Morris and myself, to prevent the Publication of Improper Intelligence in Newspapers." Denny suggested that Loudoun forbid American newspapers to publish "Articles of

Intelligence" in them unless they first received his permission."⁵⁹ Loudoun ignored the suggestion.

Richard Peters went over the differences between the governor and the assembly at this same 21 March council meeting. He said that the £100,000 bill before the governor had "many things in it which are acknowledged by Mr. Franklin to be unjust." If Peters was correct, Franklin may have had in mind a revised method of property valuation and assessment. Denny reported on 10 April 1757 that as part of the agreement with Lord Loudoun to pass the bill, Franklin promised that "the loose Method of taxing, and the Number and Nomination of the Assessors, should be rectified in another future bill."⁶⁰ In summarizing the differences with the assembly, Peters complained that the Indian trade bill excluded the governor and the council "from any share in the Choice of Officers, or approbation of their Proceedings, or even in the disposal of the Presents that are proposed to be made to the Indians out of the Profits arising from the sale of Goods." Loudoun asked Governor Dinwiddie for his opinion of the Indian trade bill. Dinwiddie replied that the "Bill appears to me very usefull, and may be of great Service in furnishing the Indians with Goods much cheaper than they can be supplied from the French, and in Course may get the Interest of the whole Tribes of Indians." With minor reservations, he approved of the bill.⁶¹

That afternoon, Governor Denny received an express from Fort Augusta that eight hundred French and Indians were at the "Head of the West Branch of Susquehannah . . . making Canoes there" to attack the fort. (See maps 2 or 3, pp. 308, 369.) But in the garrison, the troops "refused to do Duty for want of Pay, and that there was a Scarcity of Provisions and Ammunition." Denny consulted Lord Loudoun, who "advised him by Letter not to make any further Opposition to the Supply Bill, but to pass it directly." Denny promptly informed the assembly that he would pass it the following day, 22 March, at 1:00 P.M., "if it can be engrossed and ready by that time."⁶²

When Franklin wrote about the events in 1788, he misremembered: "I acquainted the House with what had pass'd" during his conference with Denny and Loudoun, "and presenting them with a Set of Resolutions I had drawn up, declaring our Rights, and that we did not relinquish our Claim to those Rights but only suspended the Exercise of them on this Occasion thro' *Force*, against which we protested, they at length agreed to drop that Bill and frame another conformable to the Proprietary Instructions" (A 158). Franklin was recalling the dramatic remonstrance that he drew up three months earlier, when the assembly marched through the streets and presented it to Denny on 26 January. After that, Franklin wrote another bill exempting the proprietary estates from taxation, which passed the House on 3 February. Franklin had already abandoned the high principles that he had announced on 11 November 1755, "Those who would give up essential Liberty, to purchase a little temporary Safety, deserve neither Liberty nor Safety" (6:242). He had done so, however, only after writing an eloquent protest that the assembly was temporarily abandoning its position to save lives on the frontier (above, p. 532).

Loudoun urged Denny to pass the 3 February bill, not a new one. Loudoun found it "absolutely necessary for the Security and Defense of the Southern Provinces that this Province shou'd furnish and keep up their Quota of Forces." Adding that time would not permit preparing a new bill, Loudoun said that "I must, in this Situation of Affairs, desire of You to wave your Instructions for the present, and pass this Bill." Governor Denny did.[63] When Thomas Penn learned the news in May, he was furious with Denny for passing the bill and with Lord Loudoun for interfering in the politics of the province. When Franklin had his first conference with Thomas Penn in London on 13 August, the proprietor was still fuming that Loudoun had put "so much confidence in Franklin" (7:153n6).

Since Franklin and the assembly had exempted Thomas Penn from being taxed on 3 February, what was the sticking point? Denny (and Penn, in turn) may have had five reservations. First, the bill named as commissioners mainly assembly members and friends of Franklin: Lynford Lardner, John Mifflin, Joseph Fox, John Hughes, William Masters, Joseph Galloway, and John Baynton. Lardner (1715–74), though a member of the provincial council, was Franklin's good friend; John Mifflin (1715–59), was the second council member; Joseph Fox (1709–79), a Philadelphia County representative, was allied with Franklin; John Hughes (ca. 1712–72), another Philadelphia County representative, was Franklin's close friend; William Masters (ca. 1710–60), a Philadelphia city representative, was called a "Minion" of Franklin by Richard Peters; Joseph Galloway (ca. 1731–1803), another representative from Philadelphia County, became Franklin's main political heir and Speaker of the House from 1766 through 1773; and John Baynton (1726?–73) was also a member from Philadelphia County. Only two commissioners were members of the provincial council—and one of them was allied with Franklin; the other five were all Quaker Party representatives.

A second possible reservation was that the act said the "governor or commander-in-chief" of the province could authorize the expenditures. Penn probably thought that only the governor should be able to release funds. Loudoun, the commander in chief, was not beholden to Penn. Third, the assembly was to audit the expenses. Penn probably wanted the provincial council, Secretary Richard Peters, or some other proprietary partisans to audit them. Fourth, the bill would repay the money advanced by private individuals (like Isaac Norris and Franklin) for defense of the province. And fifth, if the tax raised in four years should be insufficient, then the tax would be continued; and if there were any funds left over, the House would control the "overplus."[64] It's doubtful that anyone thought there would be more than enough funds, but Morris and Penn no doubt objected to the precedent.

The last time we can be certain that Franklin attended a meeting of the legislature was on 15 March, when he wrote the welcoming address to Lord Loudoun; but he may have attended on 23 March, when Governor Denny passed the £100,000 bill. Franklin spent time with the visiting governors that day, and Governor Sharpe entrusted him with a letter to give Lord Baltimore in London. The governors met with Lord Loudoun for the last time on 24 March. Governors Sharpe and Dinwiddie left for Annapolis the following day (3:51).

On Saturday, 26 March, Franklin met with Lord Loudoun, who asked if the assembly intended to pay for the indentured servants who enlisted in the army: "Mr. Franklin says he knows of no intention they have of paying anything for Indented servants." Loudoun then asked "what was the meaning of the £10,000 he writ to Mr Thomas Pownel the assembly had raised for the King's use." Franklin had written Pownall on 9 September 1756 that £10,000 of the £60,000 supply bill of August–September 1756 would be subject to the orders of Loudoun for a general fund for defense of the colonies. Franklin replied that Governor Denny had rejected the bill. And why, asked Loudoun, did Pennsylvania demand a receipt from the officer who enlisted an indentured servant? Franklin said, so that a committee of the assembly "might be able to make a list of them that they might applie Home for redress." The reply upset Loudoun: "I sade as that affair of Recruiting was immediately under me in the first Instance, I thought it extraordinary they should applie home before they first tried whether I would settel it with them and desired to see the List they had made up." Franklin told him that "it was not finished but I should have a copy as soon as it was made out."[65] The following day, Sunday, 27 March, Loudoun set out for New York.

Writing in the *Autobiography* about Lord Loudoun, Franklin either misremembered his last conversations with him in Philadelphia or he chose to make up an anecdote that revealed Loudoun's character: "He set out for New York before me; and as the Time for dispatching the Pacquet Boats, was in his Disposition, and there were two then remaining there, one of which he said was to sail very soon, I requested to know the precise time, that I might not miss her by any Delay of mine. His Answer was, I have given out that she is to sail on Saturday next, but I may let you know, *entre nous*, that if you are there by Monday morning you will be in time, but do not delay longer. By some Accidental Hindrance at a Ferry, it was Monday Noon before I arrived, and I was much afraid she might have sailed as the Wind was fair, but I was soon made easy by the Information that she was still in the Harbour, and would not move till the next Day" (A 159). As we will see, Franklin actually arrived in New York on a Friday and evidently had not been told that a packet was leaving on Monday.

WINDING UP PHILADELPHIA AFFAIRS

On 28 March Franklin renewed his lease on Robert Grace's Market Street property for seven years at an annual rent of £60. He had evidently first leased it in

1739, though the first extant lease is dated 30 December 1745 (3:51). Franklin signed one last time as a provincial commissioner on 29 March 1757, a bill to pay Lieutenant Lewis Ourry for quartering soldiers. On the next day, he made out a bill to the proprietors for various printing charges from 1734 to 1745, totaling £57.1.6. On the last day of the month, Thursday, 31 March, the House approved the instructions to Franklin for his English mission "to obtain Redress of those several Infractions of the Royal Grant and Proprietary Charter, and other Aggrievances" (7:163). As Franklin knew, the assembly hoped he could have the proprietor's secret instructions struck down or, if not, made public, and that he would be able to have the proprietor's lands taxed in common with other lands.

Deborah Franklin's son-in-law, William Dunlap, had been printing in Franklin's Lancaster office with Franklin's types beginning 1 February 1754, and he was now moving to Philadelphia. On 1 April 1757, Franklin charged him £61.13.4 for the past rent and use of the types in Lancaster. After settling other accounts for the next two days, Franklin appointed Dunlap postmaster of Philadelphia on Monday, 4 April 1757, gave Deborah Franklin his power of attorney (he had first done so as early as 30 August 1733; 1:331), and set out for New York with William, accompanied by his slave Peter and William's slave King and a dozen friends. They stopped at Fairhill, Isaac Norris's estate, and went on to Trenton, New Jersey, where Franklin wrote Deborah the next morning, saying that they all had spent "a very agreable Evening together" (7:175).

One wonders about Franklin's slave Peter. In his will of 28 April 1757, Franklin directed that "my Negro Man Peter, and his Wife Jemima, be free after my Decease." No later references to Peter or Jemima in the Franklin household turn up in Philadelphia. It seems surprising that Franklin would separate a married couple, and the 1963 editors of the *Papers of Benjamin Franklin* speculate that it could have been "a son of the same name" who accompanied Franklin to England (7:203). As we have seen, Franklin cared for Peter when he became ill on the trip to Viriginia in March 1756 (above, p. 523). While in England, Franklin refers to Peter several times, but he is never mentioned again after 10 August 1761 (P 9:338). Peter and Jemima are the last slaves that Franklin evidently purchased, though James Parker in 1763 gave Franklin a slave, George, as part of a debt he owed Franklin (12:65).[66]

On 7 April, Franklin and William arrived at Elizabeth Town, New Jersey, dined with Governor Belcher, and sailed to New York the next day. Franklin called upon Lord Loudoun on Saturday, 9 April. Loudoun noted, "Mr. Frankline arrived last night from Philadelphia. Things remain there as they did."[67] After hearing from Joseph Galloway that the Indian trade bill was lost, Franklin wrote on 11 April, said he was sorry, and expressed contempt with the proprietors and their party: "It is some Advantage that the iniquitous Views of the Proprietor and his Creatures of the Council are so clearly discover'd by their Conduct on this Occasion." He added an extraordinary comparison skewering his opponents: "The Spirit that makes them so ardently aim at the Disposition of Money not their own, is the same with that which inclines lesser Knaves to rob and pick Pockets. They seem to have no Regard to the Publick Welfare, so the private Point maybe gained. 'Tis like Firing a House to have an Opportunity of Stealing a Trencher" (7:179).

TWENTY-TWO

Franklin in New York and at Sea, 1757

I think a Set of Experiments might be instituted, first to determine the most proper Form of the Hull for swift sailing; next the best Dimensions and properest Place for the Masts; then the Form and Quantity of Sails, and their Position as the Winds may be; and lastly the Disposition of her Lading. This is the Age of Experiments; and such a Set accurately made and combin'd would be of great Use.
—A 165

In New York Franklin busied himself writing letters on 11 and 14 April, including a long one on heat and cold to Dr. John Lining. Afterward he called on Lord Loudoun, who talked with Franklin about the Albany post. Loudoun wanted the postal service to be more frequent between New York and Albany, so Franklin investigated. William Franklin had been comptroller but was now about to go to London with him, and his joint postmaster, William Hunter, was in London.

Franklin commissioned his former employee and partner James Parker as comptroller of the post office on 22 April. He designed a series of instructions for Parker, which concluded, "In general, you are to inform yourself from time to time whether the Posts continue to keep their Stages regularly, and whether the respective Postmasters give such due Attendance at their Offices as is satisfactory to the Publick; and to endeavour the Rectification of every thing that you find amiss, so that Correspondence may not be impeded or interrupted by any Neglect or Mismanagement in the Post Office, or Misconduct of the Riders, nor any just Cause of Complaint be given to the Merchants or others who correspond per Post" (7:197). Franklin reported to Loudoun on 30 April that the Albany post would now go twice a week. Over the previous year, Franklin and Hunter had paid the Albany postmaster £35 New York currency, but now they would give him £40 a year. The two post riders were in the future to "have £125 currency a year for which they are to go twice a week for seven months and [during the winter] once a week for five months. Which makes about £4 each journey."[1]

The following Tuesday, 19 April, Franklin wrote his sister Jane Mecom about their older half sister, Elizabeth Douse. Franklin had held a mortgage and bond on her house since 1748, and Jane tried to look out for Franklin's interest. Franklin, however, was not primarily concerned about the money. He had taken the mortgage to support his aged sister. Now he wrote Jane: "As *having their own Way* is one of the greatest Comforts of Life, to old People, I think their Friends should try to accommodate them in that, as well as in any thing else. When they have long liv'd in a House, it becomes natural to them, they are almost as closely connected with it as the Tortoise with his Shell, they die if you tear them out of it. Old Folks and old Trees, if you remove them, tis ten to one that you kill them. So let our good old Sister be no more importun'd on that head. We are growing old fast ourselves, and shall expect the same kind of Indulgencies. If we give them, we shall have a Right to receive them in our Turn."

Franklin asked Jane to see Elizabeth "as often as your Affairs will permit," and observed that "*Old Age, Infirmities,* and *Poverty,* join'd, are Afflictions enough; the *Neglect* and *Slight* of Friends and near Relations, should never be added." Then he added a psychological insight, which he combined with his characteristic perception of the difference between appearance and reality: "People in her Circumstances are apt to suspect this sometimes without Cause; *Appearances* should therefore be attended to, in our Conduct towards them, as well as *Realities.*" He also mentioned that he was writing Jonathan Williams (a Boston merchant married to Franklin's niece Grace Harris) "to continue his care," which no doubt included reports on the situation of Jane as well as Elizabeth. Several years earlier (probably on his 1753 Boston trip) Franklin had set up a small (monthly?) fund for Elizabeth from his brother Peter, his now-deceased brother John, and himself. Evidently Jonathan Williams oversaw the payment (7:190–91).

Besides the Albany post, Franklin had two matters to discuss with Lord Loudoun. In Philadelphia, they had spoken about payment for indentured servants and apprentices who joined the army. Persons whose servants or apprentices had joined the army expected Pennsylvania's Assembly to find some way to reimburse them. William Franklin, as House clerk, had advertised for masters to supply information concerning such enlistments to the assembly. As reported above, Franklin's instructions for his British mission directed him to protest those enlistments (7:141). On 25 April, Franklin received a list of conscripted servants from Joseph Galloway with the note, "This List is not yet compleat, the Claims continuing to come in daily." Franklin gave it to Loudoun that day. Loudoun noted that the "sum it amounts to as it now standes unverified and unfilled up is in Pensilvania currency £3652." Loudoun, who was meticulous in his accounting, added, "¹/₂ which is of dollars 9738 2/3 or in Sterling £2272.7.1."²

Seeming to suspect that everyone was trying to cheat the British army, Loudoun noted that Galloway's account "included recruits raised in Mr Shirley's time for the 44th and 48th Regts, the Nova Scotia Regts, and his 50th and 51st Regts." Repeating his Philadelphia question, Loudoun asked if the Pennsylvania

Assembly did not intend to pay for the servants. Franklin replied no. Loudoun, further repeating his conversation of a month before, "askt him to what purpose they proposed the £10,000 they had proposed a bill for, which was to be put into my handes for the Publick Service." Franklin reminded him that it was to have been a "part of a fund to be raised by all the Provinces," which the British government had requested but which was part of a supply bill that Governor William Denny negatived. Franklin also evidently said that if the bill had been passed, Loudoun could have used the money to reimburse the owners.

Continuing with quibbles and evasions, Loudoun claimed that though a recent act of Parliament specified masters be remunerated for the time left of servants who enlisted, he "did not see that they had any right to charge on that Act of Parliament any of" the servants who had enlisted "before it was made." Franklin "proposed to have this affair settled and that I should appoint some people to look into the manner of making up the accounts and the payment of it" in Pennsylvania. Loudoun replied he could not "now, as the troops were all agoing to the field and I had not officers nor could not have, till the campain was over." Franklin then suggested Loudoun "refer it to the Govr and some people in Philadelphia." But Loudoun told him the "officers must be heard who had enlisted the men." Otherwise, Loudoun would be hearing "the evidence on one side only."[3]

Loudoun also put off Franklin's personal financial repayment. After Franklin had furnished General Braddock with wagons in early June 1755, he had been asked to provide the army with food and supplies. He had done so throughout the rest of June and early July until Braddock's defeat in mid-July. Franklin had assumed that if the province of Pennsylvania did not pay for the supplies (and it did not), Braddock would do so. In New York Franklin received a statement of the accounts, "which could not sooner be obtain'd from the different Persons I had employ'd . . . in the Business, and presented it to Lord Loudoun." He had the accounts examined "by the proper Officer, who, after comparing every Article with its Voucher, certified them to be right, and the Balance due, for which his Lordship promis'd to give me an Order on the Paymaster" (A 162–63).

Franklin called for the payment several times, but Loudoun recorded on 26 April: "there is a ballance of his account still unpaid for waggonage on Mr Braddock's march; I once intended to have cleared. But when he [Franklin] showed me the valuation and that each waggon load cost for carriage £17.12.6, it surprised me and I beged to be excused." Attempting to justify his refusal, Loudoun noted, "This would have been paid and cleared when Mr Leake [Robert Leake, commissary of stores for the army in North America] was at Philadelphia but the accounts and receipts were not then collected."[4] Four days later, 30 April, Loudoun recurred to the debt: "I have told Mr Frankline again that on Considering his accounts for things furnished in M G Braddock's campain, I can not clear them." His reasons were, "First as Mr Shirley has paid them in part and I have no direction about them." The second reason was repeated, "the state of his account surprised me, being £17.12.6 a load for carrying each load of Forrage from Philadelphia to the army." Loudoun added that Franklin answered "that the Country gave near as much more to persuade the people to go."[5] Loudoun told Franklin that he had decided not to mix his accounts with those of his predecessors. "And you, says he, when in England, have only to exhibit your Accounts at the Treasury, and you will be paid immediately" (A 163).

Franklin showed his irritation with Loudoun's decision. He mentioned the "great and unexpected Expence I had been put to by being detain'd so long at New York, as a Reason for my desiring to be presently paid." Loudoun, perhaps smarting at the implied criticism, replied with an affront that Franklin recorded: "On my observing that it was not right I should be put to any farther Trouble or Delay in obtaining the Money I had advanc'd, as I charg'd no Commissions for my Service," Loudoun replied, "O, Sir . . . you must not think of persuading us that you are no Gainer. We understand better these Affairs, and know that every one concern'd in supplying the Army finds means in the doing it to fill his own Pockets." Franklin recorded both the insult and the fact that he was "not paid it to this Day." He added, "of which more hereafter" (A 163), but the *Autobiography* stops shortly after his arrival in England later that year. If Franklin earlier had enjoyed a favorable opinion of Loudoun, he now had reason to change it.

While waiting in New York for a packet to sail, Franklin made out a new "Last Will and Testament," leaving Jane Mecom "the mortgage I have on my Sister Douse's house and lot in Boston, with said Douse's bond, and every demand I have against my said Sister Douse's estate. Only I will that my said Sister Douse be never disturbed in the possession of the said house and lot during her life, though she should not be able to discharge the said mortgage or pay the interest arising on the same. Also I give to my sister Jane Mecom the share of my father's estate and the particular legacy which he left me by his will, and also the debt due me from that estate" (7:199–205).

A high point during Franklin's generally tedious months-long wait in New York occurred on Tuesday evening, 3 May, which William Franklin described in a letter to his fiancée, Elizabeth Graeme: "Parson Campbell and his Wife are here. I spent one *whole Night* in her Company. This you may say wants a little Explanation. You must know then that my Father and I were invited to spend an Evening at Dr. Bard's where she lodges, in Company with several other Gentlemen and Ladies. We were there inform'd that Sir Charles Hardy's Flag was to be hoisted by 4 aClock the next Morn[in]g [4 May] and at Sun Rise to be saluted by all the Vessels in the Harbour; upon which, as we were all in extreme high Spirits, and well pleas'd with each other, we concluded to sit up and be Spectators of the Ceremony."[6] Dr. John Bard and his family were close friends. He had been Franklin's physician before moving to New York, and it was to Dr.

Bard and his wife that Deborah Franklin gave Charlotte Brown a letter of introduction.

Another social occasion shortly followed. Franklin had realized by the end
of April that Loudoun was not soon going to allow a packet boat to sail. He
wrote Deborah and Sally to join him and William for a New Jersey tour. The
women arrived in Woodbridge, New Jersey, about 6 May. On Monday, 9 May,
the Franklins visited Newark where Archibald Kennedy, whose son sailed with
Franklin in the following month to England, entertained them. William Franklin reported that the group on the New Jersey tour "consisted of some Gentlemen and Ladies" from New York "and my Mother and Sister" (7:213n). From
Newark, they rode to Colonel John Schuyler's estate at Plympton, New Jersey.

When Franklin had visited Schuyler in the fall of 1749, he admired Schuyler's
enclosed deer park and his banked meadows. At that time, the copper mine,
which had been extremely profitable, was closed because of flooding, but at this
visit eight years later, a steam engine brought from England in 1753 and in operation by 1755 kept the mine open (3:465). According to Thomas Pownall, who
duplicated Franklin's trip in 1754 (probably at Franklin's suggestion), the park
contained 680 acres and had 300 deer. From Schuyler's, the Franklins and their
friends probably went to the Passaic River and journeyed along it up to the
Great Falls of the Passaic, at present-day Paterson, New Jersey. Pownall sketched
it in 1754 and estimated its height at 90 feet. Later measurements make it approximately 70 feet. Pownall's sketch and his description deserve to be better
known. It is comparable to but, I believe, more effective than Thomas Jefferson's
description of the Natural Bridge of Virginia. William Franklin was also impressed by the views along the Passaic River: "The Face of the Country, its many
Improvements, the Variety of romantic Prospects which almost everywhere
about afforded me far greater Pleasure than any Thing I had ever seen before. I
had not the least Idea that Views so agreeably enchanting were to be met with
in America."[7]

Concluding the trip, 12 May 1757, William Franklin and Sally journeyed to
New York, while Franklin and Deborah stayed in Woodbridge. There, on 18
May, Franklin settled accounts with his nephew James Franklin. About the same
time, Franklin paid for passage and sea stores for himself and his party, which
amounted to £55.0.0.[8] Franklin returned to New York on Monday, 23 May, expecting to sail for London the next day, but again Loudoun delayed. Now it was
rumored that a strong French fleet was nearby (7:217n). Franklin and William
remained in New York, but Sally returned to Woodbridge on 27 May, where she
and Deborah apparently stayed several days before going home to Philadelphia
(7:174).

A letter to Jane Mecom of 30 May 1757 contained the sharpest comment
Franklin ever made to his favorite sister. Her son Benjamin Mecom had abandoned printing in Antigua, received another loan from Franklin, and moved
back to Boston. Isaiah Thomas recorded that Mecom's press did not arrive from

Figure 49a. *View of the Great Falls, Passaic River, by Thomas Pownall, 1754. Engraved by Paul Sandby, 1761. Franklin's friend Thomas Pownall, who was in Philadelphia in 1754 and later that year at the Albany Conference, served as governor of Massachusetts from 1757 to 1760. Geography, art, and scenic landscapes were among Pownall's many interests. In 1754, he traveled to Colonel John Schuyler's copper mines in Plympton, New Jersey, and on to the Passaic Falls at present-day Paterson, New Jersey. Since Franklin had taken this same sightseeing journey in 1749, he may have inspired Pownall's visit. Pownall wrote: "The Falls of Passaik are a very curious natural Phenomenon. The River runnin round the Back of a Rocky Cliff, which by some Accident has been shattered & riven from Top to Bottom about 90 feet, turns short round it & Tumbles head long with an Inconceivable force & Velocity down the horrid chasm foaming with its hoarse stunning roar at its base more like something combustible than Water."*

Pownall's description and Sandby's engraving of his sketch mark an advance toward a romantic appreciation of nature. Pownall had read and been influenced by Longinus's On the Sublime *(translated from the Greek in 1739). If the text in Pownall's* Topographical Description *(1774) accurately copied the notes he made in 1754, they surprisingly anticipate Edmund Burke's* Philosophical Enquiry into . . . the Sublime *(1757). Earlier important American nature descriptions, like those by William Byrd of Westover and Dr. Alexander Hamilton of Annapolis, did not attempt to express the feeling of awe. Later, Thomas Jefferson, influenced by Longinus and Burke, attempted to capture the sublime in writing about the Natural Bridge of Virginia in* Notes on the State of Virginia *(1781), but in eighteenth-century American nature literature, only William Bartram's* Travels *(1791) calls forth the sublime's hallmark of appreciation combined with awe more effectively than does Pownall. Courtesy, British Library.*

Figure 49b. View of the Great Falls, Passaic River, by Thomas Pownall, detail showing two persons on the cliff. The primary purpose of the two tiny figures is to show the height and grandeur of the falls, but the two figures also suggest a shared appreciation of the sublime beauty around and below them. The person closest to the falls seems to be gesturing. The scene anticipates Asher B. Durand's 1849 painting Kindred Spirits.

Antigua for several months, and that Mecom occasionally came and did a little printing where Thomas was an apprentice: "He was handsomely dressed, wore a powdered bob wig, ruffles and gloves; gentlemanlike appendages which the printers of that day did not assume, and thus apparelled, would often assist, for an hour, at the press."[9] His mother, Jane Mecom, thought that after John Franklin's death, Franklin should have made her son Benjamin the Boston postmaster, but Franklin had appointed John's stepson Tuthill Hubbart, no blood relation, to the position. Jane suggested that Franklin take it away from Hubbart and give it to his nephew and namesake. Franklin replied that it was "a rule with me, not to remove any officer that behaves well, keeps regular accounts, and pays duly; and I think the rule is founded on reason and justice. I have not shown any backwardness to assist Benny, where it could be done without injuring another. But if my friends require of me to gratify not only their inclinations, but their resentments, they expect too much of me."

Franklin knew that blunt and direct statement would upset Jane. He continued: "Above all things I dislike family quarrels, and when they happen among my relations, nothing gives me more pain. If I were to set myself up as a judge of those subsisting between you and brother's widow and children, how unqualified must I be, at this distance, to determine rightly, especially having heard but one side. They always treated me with friendly and affectionate regard, you have done the same. What can I say between you, but that I wish you were reconciled, and that I will love that side best that is most ready to forgive and oblige the other. You will be angry with me here, for putting you and them too much upon a footing, but I shall nevertheless be, Dear sister, your truly Affectionate brother" (7:222–23). Franklin did not want to say that Benjamin Mecom had been flighty and not kept good accounts. Mecom would have been a poor choice for the responsibility.

Franklin created an anecdote about Loudoun's delays. Going one morning to pay his respects, Franklin found waiting there an express rider, James Ennis, who was delivering a message from Pennsylvania's governor William Denny to

Lord Loudoun. According to Franklin, Loudoun had told Ennis to wait till the next day to return to Pennsylvania so that he could reply. When Franklin saw Ennis two weeks later, he was surprised to find him so soon returned: "*Return'd*; No, I am not *gone* yet.—How so?—I have call'd here by Order every Morning these two Weeks past for his Lordship's Letter, and it is not yet ready.—Is it possible, when he is so great a Writer, for I see him constantly as his Scritore. Yes, says Innis, but he is like St. George on the Signs, *always on horseback, and never rides on*" (A 160). Franklin had used the same words and image twice previously (2:195 and 6:87), and it seems unlikely to me that Ennis really said them. On occasion, Loudoun undoubtedly kept the express riders and the regular post riders waiting, but he would not have kept one waiting for two weeks. Every week, the normal post riders would have gone back and forth twice. Any one of them could be kept waiting, but after three or four days, another mail rider would arrive.

Franklin, however, had good reason to be disgusted with Lord Loudoun for keeping the packet boats interminably waiting and for his implied insult to Franklin, and better reason (as we will see in Volume 4, because of his future treatment of Deborah Franklin) to cast Loudoun in an unfavourable light in the *Autobiography* in 1788. Franklin concluded his account of Loudoun with a general remark on his character and on politics: "On the whole I then wonder'd much, how such a Man came to be entrusted with so important a Business as the Conduct of a great Army: but having since seen more of the great World, and the means of obtaining and Motives for giving Places and employments, my Wonder is diminished" (A 161).

AT SEA

Franklin wrote Deborah on 2 June that he expected to sail the next day and he did finally board the ship *General Wall*, Captain Walter Lutwidge, on 5 June. Even then, however, the convoy, including the packets, anchored off Sandy Hook for fifteen days because Loudoun feared a French fleet might be lurking off the coast. Finally, on 20 June, the convoy sailed.

On 21 or 22 June, while still with the fleet, the ever-curious Franklin "observed the Wakes of two of the Ships to be remarkably smooth, while all the others were ruffled by the Wind, which blew fresh. Being puzzled with this differing Appearance I at last pointed it out to our Captain, and asked him the meaning of it? 'The Cooks, says he, have I suppose, been just emptying their greasy Water thro' the Scuppers, which has greased the Sides of those Ships a little;' and this Answer he gave me with an Air of some little Contempt, as to a Person ignorant of what every Body else knew." No doubt all old sailors had repeatedly observed the phenomenon. Franklin considered it: "In my own Mind I at first slighted his Solution, tho' I was not able to think of another." Then he remembered what he had read in Pliny about stilling the waters with oil and "resolved to make some Experiment of the Effect of Oil on Water when I should have Opportunity." As we shall see, Franklin did so over the course of the next fifteen years and finally gathered together his data on 7 November 1773 (20:463–74).

Another incident during the two days that the packet sailed with the fleet caused Franklin to speculate. Captain Lutwidge "had boasted much before we sail'd, of the Swiftness of his Ship. Unfortunately when we came to Sea, she proved the dullest of 96 Sail, to his no small Mortification." When another ship "almost as dull as ours," came near and was passing the packet, Lutwidge "order'd all hands to come aft and stand as near the Ensign Staff as possible. We were, Passengers included, about forty Persons. While we stood there the Ship mended her Pace, and soon left our Neighbour far behind, which prov'd clearly what our Captain suspected, that she was loaded too much by the Head." He rearranged the placement of the casks of water, "on which the Ship recover'd her Character, and prov'd the best Sailer in the Fleet" (A 163).

That experience caused Franklin to advocate testing and analyzing shipbuilding: "It has been remark'd as an Imperfection in the Art of Shipbuilding, that it can never be known 'till she is try'd, whether a new Ship will or will not be a good Sailer; for that the Model of a good sailing Ship has been exactly follow'd in the new One, which has prov'd on the contrary remarkably dull. I apprehend this may be partly occasion'd by the different Opinions of Seamen respecting the Modes of lading, rigging and sailing of a Ship." Franklin explained that each captain had his own system: "The same Vessel laden by the Judgment and Orders of one Captain shall sail better or worse than when by the Orders of another." So the position of the freight, as well as the amount, affected the sailing. Franklin continued: "Besides, it scarce ever happens that a Ship is form'd, fitted for the Sea, and sail'd by the same Person. One Man builds the Hull, another riggs her, a third lades and sails her. No one of these has the Advantage of knowing all the Ideas and Experience of the others, and therefore cannot draw just Conclusions from a Combination of the whole. Even in the simple Operation of Sailing when at Sea, I have often observ'd different Judgments in the Officers who commanded the successive Watches, the Wind being the same, One would have the Sails trimm'd sharper or flatter than another, so that they seem'd to have no certain Rule to govern by."

Then the disciple of Francis Bacon, Isaac Newton, and experimental philosophy observed: "Yet I think a Set of Experiments might be instituted, first to determine the most proper Form of the Hull for swift sailing; next the best Dimensions and properest Place for the Masts; then the Form and Quantity of Sails, and their Position as the Winds may be; and lastly the Disposition of her Lading. This is the Age of Experiments; and such a Set accurately made and combin'd would be of great Use. I am therefore persuaded that erelong some ingenious Philosopher will undertake it: to whom I wish Success" (A 164–65). Modern ship designers, whether for the navy or merchant ships, undertake such experiments. But Franklin's advice is often still ignored.[10]

Captain Lutwidge's repositioning the freight was fortunate, for after the packet left the convoy, it was chased "several times" by French ships "but out-sail'd every thing" (A 165).

THE WAY TO WEALTH

For twenty-six consecutive years Franklin wrote *Poor Richard's Almanac*, twenty of which contained an entertaining prefatory skit. As he sailed to England, he thought that he might never write another. The "preface" to the 1758 almanac was more than ten times as long as any previous one, beginning on the prefatory page, occupying a page throughout the twelve months of the year and continuing for an additional one. The setting was an auction, with persons waiting for the sale to begin. Over a year later, when first published separately, Benjamin Mecom titled it *Father Abraham's Speech to a Great Number of People, at a Vendue of Merchant Goods* (Boston: Mecom, 1758). The title *The Way to Wealth* superseded it.[11] The piece gathered together nearly all of Poor Richard's former sayings on industry and frugality and added others. Franklin put them into a connected and dramatic context in a speech by Father Abraham within a framework supplied by that vain, pompous naif, Richard Saunders, a.k.a. Poor Richard.

As literature, *The Way to Wealth* is extraordinary. Despite almost four-fifths of it consisting of proverbs and sententiae—literary forms memorable in themselves and ones that tend to dominate their contexts—Franklin managed to make *The Way to Wealth* a unified whole. He wedged the hundreds of proverbs within a speech and wedged the speech within a framework containing an introduction and a conclusion. The sayings are thus doubly imprisoned and controlled. Father Abraham's speech itself contains two major divisions—a section on industry and one on frugality—plus a brief conclusion which, on an underlying level, undercuts the speech's materialism. Then Poor Richard reappears in the framework's conclusion, and, in the last sentence, the ostensibly foolish naif turns the tables on the reader.

At the time, Franklin was fifty-one, America's best-known writer, and the world's best-known living scientist. *Poor Richard's Almanac* had continued to be a major source of income for the printing firm of Franklin and Hall and was read by thousands of barely literate people as well as by America's scientists and literateurs, like Archibald Kennedy. As everyone knew, almanacs were discarded at the year's end. Some authors despised proverbs and scorned Franklin (*Life* 2:191–93). But Franklin loved proverbs and was proud of his almanac. He thought his almanacs of possible use to the poor and inexperienced as well as interesting for their intellectual content.

The almanac for 1758 opened with Poor Richard speaking: "I have heard that nothing gives an Author so great Pleasure, as to find his Works respectfully quoted by other learned Authors." Franklin burlesqued the naive philomath Poor Richard, for "learned Authors" despised most almanac writers and would hardly—and not with respect—quote an almanac writer. The contemporary English writer whom Franklin most admired when an adolescent and young man was Jonathan Swift, who spurned proverbs and almanac writers (*Life* 1:108, 170, 2:173–79, 191–92). But *The Way to Wealth* used and controlled the attitude that condescended to the almanac maker. Poor Richard said: "This Pleasure I have seldom enjoyed; for tho' I have been, if I may say it without Vanity, an *eminent Author* of Almanacks annually now a full Quarter of a Century, my Brother Authors in the same Way, for what Reason I know not, have ever been very sparing in their Applauses; and no other Author has taken the least Notice of me, so that did not my Writings produce me some solid *Pudding*, the great Deficiency of *Praise* would have quite discouraged me" (7:340).

Reading the above, one may recall Franklin's observation in the *Autobiography*: "Indeed I scarce ever heard or saw the introductory Words, *Without Vanity I may say* &c. but some vain thing immediately follow'd" (A 2). Franklin italicized *eminent Author* to emphasize its oxymoronic quality when referring to a philomath. And the clause "for what Reason I know not," while continuing the naif pose of Poor Richard, reminds the reader that the almanac writers are jealous of one another's financial success—which is their only measure of excellence, as the last part of the quotation indirectly affirms. The second brief paragraph brings the opening framework of the pompous, vain naif to a climax with the ridiculous portrayal of Poor Richard quoting himself "with great Gravity."

The third paragraph introduces the speech of a "plain clean old Man, with white Locks" called "Father Abraham," who cites numerous Poor Richard's proverbs. After the speech, Poor Richard is surprised to observe the people gathered for the sale buying extravagantly. However, Poor Richard himself benefited: "though I had at first determined to buy Stuff for a new Coat, I went away resolved to wear my old One a little longer" (7:350). Poor Richard's "old" coat may be autobiographical. When Franklin returned home to Boston in 1724, he was dressed in a "genteel new suit from head to foot," wore a watch, and gave his brother's journeymen money to drink to his health. But as he sailed back to Philadelphia from England in 1726, Franklin resolved to live frugally until he had paid his debts and had become to some degree financially secure. Evidently he abided by the resolve. His 1728 competitor, Samuel Keimer, wrote that Franklin's "Merits" were "as threadbare as his Great Coat." Since it seems unlikely that any coat purchased new that fit the twenty-year-old Franklin in 1726 would have been "threadbare" by 1728, the twenty-two-year-old Franklin apparently bought a cheap, secondhand coat when he returned from England (*Life* 1:382, 388).

Few people like to hear economic realities about themselves, and Franklin constructed *The Way to Wealth* so that the moral is not addressed to the reader (except in its final sentence) but to those gathered at "a Vendue of Merchant Goods" who are complaining of the economy, the taxes, and their own finances but who nevertheless demonstrate their prodigality by buying "extravagantly."

Idleness and Wealth Versus the Work Ethic

In the eighteenth century, aristocrats did not work. Work was scorned. Even in the early nineteenth century, aristocrats commonly despised those who worked. William Cavendish, fifth duke of Devonshire (1748–1811), said of a cousin, "He is not a gentleman; he works." In the Western world's hierarchical society, only the aristocrats and the upper classes had liberty and freedom. The historian Gordon S. Wood observed, "Unlike ordinary people, gentlemen, or the better sort, traditionally were not defined or identified by what they did, but by who they were. . . . The gentry's distinctiveness came from being independent in a world of dependencies, learned in a world only partially literate, and leisured in a world of labourers."[12]

The Way to Wealth subverted the aristocratic and hierarchical bases of eighteenth-century society. It assumed that a person was not born into a fixed station in life but existed in a fluid society and could change. The sententiae and other materials in *Poor Richard* from 1733 to 1758 praised work and lampooned aristocrats. When Franklin gathered together the sayings on industry and frugality for the 1758 *Poor Richard*, he advocated a revolutionary idea that redefined which persons were actually the most valued members of society. They were not the kings or the aristocrats or the gentlemen who lived in leisure but *homo economicus*, the farmers, artisans, tradesmen, and merchants who worked. An underlying message of *The Way to Wealth* dismantled the old social system and announced the coming of a new age of egalitarian values where people were prized not for what they were or for what their ancestors did but for what *they* did. Franklin reaffirmed that radical idea in his 1784 "Information to Those Who Would Remove to America." The question put to a stranger in America, Franklin said, was not "*What is he*? But *What can he do?*" (W 977).

Before and during the Revolution, John Adams was frequently amazed at what he considered Franklin's prejudice against kings.[13] He was right. Franklin satirized the idea of aristocracy when he was a boy writing for the *New-England Courant* in 1721 and 1722 and later in *Poor Richard*. In the 1737 almanac, Franklin wrote: "The greatest monarch on the proudest throne is obliged to sit upon his own arse" (2:166). When Franklin replied to Sir Michael Foster's defense of the impressment of seamen in 1770, he idealistically claimed that "Inconvenience to the whole Trade of a Nation will not justify Injustice to a single Seaman" (35:492, 495); he lampooned Judge Foster's favoring the rich over the poor (35:498–99, 501); he suggested that judges (including Foster), rather than seamen, should be impressed (35:499–500); and he concluded that the king should be impressed rather than a poor seaman, for "I am not quite satisfied of the Necessity or Utility" of the "Office" of king (35:500). Franklin's 1770 protest against impressment circulated in England, but it was not published then, for of course it was treason.[14]

Franklin was the most radical as well as the oldest Revolutionary. In age, he

could have been the father of Washington, Adams, or Jefferson, or the grandfather of Alexander Hamilton, Charles Carroll, or James Madison. On 7 and 10
August 1787 in the Constitutional Convention, the eighty-one-year-old Franklin
made the most forceful argument for extending the right to vote as widely as
possible, specifically condemning property qualification as necessary either for
the franchise or for officeholding.[15] Franklin saw no innate difference between
the rich and the poor. Others, however, did, and scorned those who worked. In
reply, Franklin praised the work ethic.

From the Romantics to the present, the celebration of industry and frugality
in *The Way to Wealth* has bothered some persons. Usually, they have no idea of
its liberating social philosophy for the ordinary person in the eighteenth century. It was a radical, new vision of a future society, but the society everyone
actually lived in was highly stratified and primarily valued only those who were
considered the upper class. That was true even in eighteenth-century America,
which was the most democratic society that existed.[16] But *The Way to Wealth*
envisioned a better and more egalitarian world.

Max Weber's *The Protestant Ethic and the Spirit of Capitalism* shares with
D. H. Lawrence's essay on Franklin the dubious distinction of being the best-
known criticism of Franklin. Having written about Lawrence's view of Franklin
previously (*Life* 2:57–58), I'll here briefly discuss Weber. He does not cite *The
Way to Wealth* but two short pieces: the "Hints for those that would be Rich"
and "Advice to a Young Tradesman" (2:165–66, 3:306–8). Both celebrate industry and frugality as being, according to the words in "Advice," "the Way to
Wealth" (3:308).

Though Weber found the "thirst for gold" omnipresent from the ancient to
the modern world, he thought that the concepts of duty and calling were more
common in Puritanism than in Anglicanism,[17] and that in its purest form, the
idea appeared in Benjamin Franklin. According to Weber, Franklin announced
capitalism's obedience to duty and to a calling: "the *summum bonum* of this
ethic, the earning of more and more money, combined with the strict avoidance
of all spontaneous enjoyment of life, is above all completely devoid of any eu-
daemonistic, not to say hedonistic, admixture. It is thought of so purely as an
end in itself, that from the point of view of the happiness of, or utility to, the
single individual, it appears entirely transcendental and absolutely irrational.
Man is dominated by the making of money, by acquisition as the ultimate purpose of his life." Obviously this caricature has no similarity to the life or to the
actual characteristics of Benjamin Franklin. Weber further says that capitalism
flourished in New England during Franklin's day and that it is "undoubted that
capitalism remained far less developed" in the other colonies, especially in the
South.[18] That view is just the opposite of the opinions of such contemporary
historians as Jack P. Greene and David Hackett Fischer.[19] Weber's thesis as applied to Franklin is supported by only a few sentences—and by a complete

ignorance or disregard of his biography and of his writing, except for those few sentences.

Franklin lists thirteen virtues in part 2 of the *Autobiography*. The first two are particularly adopted for his faults—or what he considered his faults. The other eleven virtues are more general (*Life* 2:43–47) and include the two major ones in *The Way to Wealth*—industry and frugality. Frugality is a seemingly practical, capitalistic-oriented virtue. It was one of the qualities that Franklin resolved upon in his "Plan of Conduct" formulated at sea in 1726 (1:100). Writing a plan for self-discipline about six years later, he had finally cleared himself from the debt—though just barely. But Franklin's definition of what he meant by frugality was unselfish and humanitarian: "Make no Expense but to do good to others or yourself: i.e. Waste nothing" (A 79). "To do good to others" contradicts the supposedly selfish capitalistic implications of frugality. Instead, it suggests the Christian doctrine of loving one's fellow human beings. That was the generous philanthropy that Franklin, even as a young man, practiced. His definition of frugality included the Christian doctrine of charity—a virtue that Franklin practiced throughout his life, perhaps most notably in helping found the Pennsylvania Hospital, of which he was the second president. Like almost all hospitals of the day, the Pennsylvania Hospital was primarily a charitable institution.

The other major virtue in *The Way to Wealth* was industry, #6 in the list of virtues. Though the word suggests a time- and machine-oriented value pointing to success in a modern society, industry is a necessary discipline in farming and all endeavors. Franklin's gloss on the word was: "Lose no Time.—Be always employ'd in something useful.—Cut off all unnecessary Actions" (A 79). "Something useful"—what does that mean? We naturally think of something useful personally, but is it also something useful to others, to one's city, to mankind? In Franklin's life, it had those inclusive meanings. Even in the questions for the Junto members, Franklin made service "to mankind" part of formulaic ritual (*Life* 1:341).

Franklin's three pages on industry in *The Way to Wealth* use several rhetorical devices to make the piece progress. The first two paragraphs conclude with the most striking (and now the best known) of the Poor Richard proverbs. Thus, the first paragraph has "*God helps them that help themselves*" (7:341). The second one ends with "*Early to Bed, and early to rise, makes a Man healthy, wealthy and wise*" (7:342). The third paragraph piles on three proverbs: "*constant Dropping wears away Stones, and by Diligence and Patience the Mouse ate in two the Cable; and little Strokes fell great Oaks*" (7:343). The fourth paragraph states that "Industry gives Comfort, and Plenty, and Respect," and concludes with three proverbs: "*Fly Pleasures, and they'll follow you. The diligent Spinner has a large Shift; and now I have a Sheep and a Cow, every Body bids me Good morrow*" (7:343). The next two brief paragraphs advocate constancy. In writing them, Franklin must have thought of his favorite sister's son, Benjamin Mecom, and his recent letter concerning him to Jane Mecom. Mecom's "flighty Unsettledness of Temper" and his "Fickleness" made him impossible. Franklin had written his parents in 1752, "Without some share of steadiness and perseverance, he can succeed no where" (4:385).[20]

The final paragraph on industry maintains that paying attention to detail is necessary: "*For want of a Nail the Shoe was lost; for want of a Shoe the Horse was lost; and for want of a Horse the Rider was lost*, being overtaken and slain by the Enemy, all for want of Care about a Horse-shoe Nail" (7:344).

Poverty, Debt, Imprisonment

Part 2 of "Father Abraham's Speech" advocates frugality and begins with the commonsensical observation that if one does not live within one's means, debt will surely follow. Sir William Keith, the Pennsylvania governor who duped the eighteen-year-old Franklin with promises to help him start a printing business, was a cautionary example. In the late 1720s, the former governor was imprisoned for debt in England and spent the remainder of his life in and out of debtor's prison, finally dying in London's Old Bailey in 1749.

In *The Way to Wealth*, Franklin observed, "Your Creditor has Authority at his Pleasure to deprive you of your Liberty, by confining you in Gaol for Life, or to sell you for a Servant, if you should not be able to pay him!" (7:348). Franklin was once in such a position. In 1724, Governor Keith said that he would support Franklin as Pennsylvania's official printer if Franklin set up his own printing house. Franklin did not have the money, so Keith suggested he borrow it from his father. Keith wrote a letter praising him to his father. Although Franklin did not comment on the incongruity of a letter of recommendation to his own father, surely he found it amusing. His father, however, had no extra money either (*Life* 1:250–52). On the way back from Boston in 1724, Franklin visited his brother John in Newport, Rhode Island. John's friend Samuel Vernon gave him a note for about £35 to collect in Philadelphia. Franklin did so but gradually loaned the money to his friends John Collins in Philadelphia in 1724 and James Ralph in London in 1725. He noted in the *Autobiography*, "This afterward occasion'd me a good deal of Uneasiness" (A 31).

To judge by the number of times Franklin mentioned the debt in the *Autobiography* (A 31, 33, 34, 55, 58, 65), this erratum bothered him more than any other. When, about 1729, Vernon asked Franklin to remit the money, he was unable to do so. Franklin asked for more time and said that he would pay interest on the debt. Vernon could have had Franklin jailed (*Life* 1:308, 324–25, 376, 457).

Debt and the specter of imprisonment influenced Franklin's newspaper publications in late 1729. In the 20 November 1729 *Gazette*, Franklin described the economic conditions in Ireland. In a preface Franklin stressed the "Poverty, Wretchedness, Misery, and Want" among the Irish, their high taxes, and "their griping avaricious Landlords" who exercised over them "the most merciless Racking Tyranny and Oppression." As I pointed out in Volume 1 (*Life* 1:427–28),

Franklin's editorial note anticipated his 13 January 1772 observations on Ireland and Scotland when he said that "the Bulk of the People" were "extreamly poor, living in the most sordid Wretchedness in dirty Hovels of Mud and Straw, and cloathed only in Rags." He claimed that the American Indians lived better lives than the ordinary Scots or Irish. The *Pennsylvania Gazette*'s next issue, 24 November 1729, began a series of reprinted articles on the abysmal conditions in British jails. Then on Tuesday, 9 December, Franklin editorialized that he was "glad to observe, that those Papers have been more generally entertaining than some others which were only fill'd with Paragraphs of common Foreign Occurrences." The series on prisons did not appear in any other colonial newspaper, and Franklin's editorial note prefigures his later concern about the plight of the poor.

After being elected clerk of the Pennsylvania Assembly in 1736, Franklin read to the Pennsylvania Assembly the petitions of persons imprisoned for debt. Usually they asked to be released, sometimes even as indentured servants, in order to work to pay off their debts. Fifteen years later, after being elected an assemblyman, Franklin served on committees to resolve petitions from jailed debtors. In the spring of 1753, Speaker Norris assigned him to a committee to consider the petition of Benjamin Bagnall, Jr., who had been imprisoned for debt over a year before. Bagnall, his wife, and two children had been given three shillings a week for their subsistence, which was the most allowed by the Insolvent Act, but which was insufficient for a person with three dependents. Three weeks later Norris assigned Franklin to consider a petition from Robert Sitlinton, who had been in the Philadelphia jail for the previous fourteen months, "without the least legal Allowance having been made for his Support."[21] Imprisonment for debt and the resulting destitution were omnipresent in Franklin's day.

Franklin warned against debt in *The Way to Wealth*. In a passage that Franklin made more dramatic by referring to the forthcoming auction, Father Abraham said, "We are offered, by the Terms of this Vendue, *Six Months Credit*; and that perhaps has induced some of us to attend it, because we cannot spare the ready Money, and hope now to be fine without it. But, ah, think what you do when you run in Debt; *You give to another Power over your Liberty*" (7:347–48). After lamenting the condition of the debtor, Franklin recalled the sumptuary laws, which, though not altogether repealed, eighteenth-century Americans had generally ignored. "What would you think of that Prince, or that Government, who should issue an Edict forbidding you to dress like a Gentleman or a Gentlewoman, on Pain of Imprisonment or Servitude." Such laws had been common in the sixteenth and seventeenth centuries and were still enforced in many European countries. Father Abraham continued: "Would you not say, that you are free, have a Right to dress as you please, and that such an Edict would be a Breach of your Privileges, and such a Government tyrannical?" Of course the reader, like the supposed audience at the auction, agreed with the rhetorical question. "And yet," Father Abraham said, "you are about to put yourself under that Tyranny when you run in Debt for such Dress!" (7:348).

Franklin said that though the end of six months may seem far away, "The Day comes round before you are aware, and the Demand is made before you are prepared to satisfy it." Franklin's words and thought echo the verses on the end of the world in the Bible and in the New England poet Michael Wigglesworth's best-seller, *The Day of Doom*. (Franklin had used these same awe-inspiring touchstones in his Junto speech, "On the Providence of God in the Government of the World"; *Life* 1:349.) After the chilling and dreadful allusion, Franklin added an original saying on debt: "*The Borrower is a Slave to the Lender, and the Debtor to the Creditor*, disdain the Chain, preserve your Freedom; and maintain your Independency: Be *industrious* and *free*; be *frugal* and *free*" (7:349).

Religious Satire

Besides undercutting the semi-feudal, hierarchical basis of society, *The Way to Wealth* satirized the religiously centered eighteenth-century worldview. We do not know whether Franklin was responsible for the title *The Way to Wealth*, though he used the words in his 1748 "Advice to a Young Tradesman" (3:308).[22] The title is, however, apt. Numerous works appeared in the seventeenth and eighteenth centuries with a similar name. Most earlier ones, including Cotton Mather's *Way to Prosperity* (1690), urged spiritual salvation.[23] Franklin's *Way to Wealth* focused on this world, not the next. In view of the common similar titles, even the name "The Way to Wealth" mocks the religiously centered world of the past.

The persona, "Father Abraham," has biblical suggestions. We recall that in Genesis 22, Abraham becomes the father of his country and God tests him by asking that he kill his only son, Isaac. Abraham was about to do so when an angel told him to desist (Gen. 22:1–14). As Franklin knew, many deists condemned Genesis 22, saying that a morally wrong action (e.g., human sacrifice) could not really be divinely inspired. The idea of human sacrifice to God seemed characteristic of a primitive, atavistic religion. For eighteenth-century literati, Father Abraham called to mind the deists' attacks on the biblical passage and its numerous defenders.[24] Franklin applied the suggested fanaticism and literalness of the biblical Abraham to his fictive character.

In addition, Father Abraham's speech parodied the structure and repetitive "logical proofs" of the typical puritan sermon. To Father Abraham, the sayings of Poor Richard are the Bible. James N. Green and Peter Stallybrass agree that Father Abraham quotes "Poor Richard's sayings . . . like biblical verses in a sermon."[25] As Poor Richard tells the reader at the end of *The Way to Wealth*, the assembled crowd behaved, "just as if it had been a common sermon" (7:350). Evidently the Théophilantropes, a deistic French society that reprinted and celebrated the piece, recognized its religious irony.[26]

Satire of Materialism

Ultimately, Franklin did not celebrate *homo economicus*. On another underlying level, he burlesqued both Father Abraham and Poor Richard for the single-minded view of a world in which the greatest values are the frugality and economy that lead the way to material wealth. The followers of Max Weber took the suggested fanaticism and literalness of the biblical Abraham to absurd heights. Franklin, however, lampoons the pursuit of fashion, superfluities, and wealth. Materialism was not the worst fault of Franklin's time, but it was becoming a characteristic of the increasingly consumeristic eighteenth-century middle class.[27] Franklin, however, scorned the pursuit of wealth. After he retired as a printer at age forty-two, he wrote his mother that for his epitaph, he "would rather have it said, *He lived usefully,* than *He died rich*" (3:475). In a letter of 10 June 1771, Franklin judged that "The Love of Money is not a Thing of a certain Measure, so as that it may be easily filled and satisfied, Avarice is infinite" (18:124). Poor Richard and Father Abraham are fools who have replaced spiritual, moral, and humanitarian values with materialism.

When Father Abraham ends his speech and combines the two sections on industry and frugality, Franklin lightly mocks popular beliefs in astrology and magic. Father Abraham preaches "*Get what you can, and what you get hold;* / *'Tis the Stone that will turn all your Lead into Gold,* as *Poor Richard* says. And when you have got the Philosopher's Stone, sure you will no longer complain of bad Times, or the Difficulty of paying Taxes." Franklin's underlying irony is that materialism is ultimately as illusory as the philosopher's stone.

Franklin even has Father Abraham condemn materialism: "This Doctrine, my Friends, is *Reason* and *Wisdom*; but after all, do not depend too much upon your own *Industry,* and *Frugality,* and *Prudence,* though excellent Things, for they may all be blasted without the Blessing of Heaven; and therefore ask that Blessing humbly, and be not uncharitable to those that at present seem to want it, but comfort and help them. Remember *Job* suffered, and was afterwards prosperous" (7:349). Thus, at the end of Father Abraham's speech, Franklin recurs to the Golden Rule and charity, which he used in 1731 to define the fifth virtue, frugality ("Make no Expence but to do good to others or yourself: i.e. Waste nothing"). As we have seen, Franklin believed charity to be a fundamental virtue. He had good company in his belief, for the best-known passage in Paul's first epistle to the Corinthians said: "And now abideth faith, hope, and charity, these three; but the greatest of these *is* charity" (1 Cor. 13:13; one can argue, however, that the word is more properly *caritas,* or love, not charity). In *The Way to Wealth*'s secondary ironic underlying level, Franklin satirizes Poor Richard and Father Abraham for their fanatically literal devotion to materialism. Franklin's life, as well as his writings, prove that although he had great common sense, he was not devoted primarily to the goods of this world.

Though the penultimate short section of Father Abraham's speech itself has a spiritual and Christian message, the final paragraph returns to the practical materialistic world of everyday life, where *"Experience keeps a dear School, but Fools will learn in no other, and scarce in that"* (7:349). What, then, is the ultimate message of *The Way to Wealth?*

The Society of the Free and Easy

Franklin hoped that *The Way to Wealth* would lead people into a condition where they could join the "Society of the Free and Easy." He projected such a society around 1730, when he drew up his plan of thirteen virtues and the discipline for the working hours of the day. It was a more ambitious scheme than the Junto, which he had formed three years earlier. Of the Society of the Free and Easy, he wrote: "That the Members should engage to afford their Advice Assistance and Support to each other in promoting one another's Interest Business and Advancement in Life: That for Distinction sake we should be call'd the Society of the *Free and Easy*; Free, as being by the general Practice and Habit of the Virtues, free from the Dominion of Vice, and particularly by the Practice of Industry & Frugality, free from Debt, which exposes a Man to Confinement and a Species of Slavery to his Creditors" (A 93). He echoed that early plan in *The Way to Wealth* when he wrote: "Be *industrious* and *free*; be *frugal* and *free*" (7:347).

But for what purpose will one be free and easy? What ideals animated Franklin's projected society? He knew "that the hope of becoming at some time of Life free from the necessity of care and Labour, together with fear of penury, are the mainsprings of most peoples industry" (4:481), but Franklin also recognized that "when Men are employ'd they are best contented" (A 147). To do nothing is to be nothing. When he retired, Franklin wanted to pursue science, and, after a brief military career, he did. Several years later, he became caught up in politics. He changed his goals. Jefferson wrote during the American Revolution that Franklin belonged to that "order of geniuses above" the "obligation" to public service and was "therefore exempted from it. No body can conceive that nature ever intended to throw away a Newton upon the obligations of a crown."[28] Franklin disagreed. Over twenty-five years earlier, 11 October 1750, he had pronounced: "Had Newton been Pilot but of a single common Ship, the finest of his Discoveries would scarce have excus'd, or atton'd for his abandoning the Helm one Hour in Time of Danger; how much less if she had carried the Fate of the Commonwealth" (4:67).

Franklin wanted people to become free and easy so that they could create themselves. He wrote in his 1749 *Proposals Relating to the Education of Youth in Pennsylvania* that the purpose of the academy was to prepare the eighteen-year-old graduates to be trained for *"Any* business, *any* calling, *any* profession!" that they then wished to begin.[29] He believed that the position of the retiring person who was free and easy should be at least as open. A person may not want to pursue science or politics, and his or her goals might be entirely different from

Franklin's. Franklin's own ideals included egalitarianism, opportunity for everyone, and doing good. Franklin's ideals underlay the *Autobiography*'s thirteen virtues and the chart of the hours of the day. They are the morning and evening questions in Franklin's chart: "What Good shall I do this day?" and "What good have I done today" (A 83). In the peroration to his 1749 *Proposals Relating to the Education of Youth*, Franklin, the serious projector, wrote: "*Doing Good to Men* is the *only Service of God* in our Power" (3:419). The cheeky Franklin, however, noted in *Poor Richard* for 1753: "Serving God is doing good to Man, but praying is thought an easier Service and therefore more easily chosen" (4:406).

Because of the sound economic advice and the simple, naive, and familiar style, the French philosophes all praised *The Way to Wealth*. Brissot de Warville, abbé Claude Fauchet, Melchier Grimm, Jean Baptiste Say, the physiocrats (including du Pont de Nemours), and Jacques Barbeu Dubourg are among the French intellectuals who perceived that Franklin's text was a radical social and economic doctrine, while at the same time they thought it a masterpiece of popular literature. Like Jill Lepore, they appreciated that it was "a parody, stitched and bound between the covers of a sham."[30]

Franklin sent the long preface dated 7 July off to Philadelphia in late July or August. David Hall published it in *Poor Richard* for 1758 on 6 October (7:327). During the next quarter of a millennium, it was republished thousands of times and became, after the *Autobiography*, the best known of Franklin's writings.

LAND!

On 16 July 1757, at the voyage's end, the packet encountered a greater danger than the French privateers:

> the Captain judg'd himself so near our Port, (Falmouth) that if we made a good Run in the Night we might be off the Mouth of that Harbour in the Morning, and by running in the Night might escape the Notice of the Enemy's Privateers, who often cruis'd near the Entrance of the Channel. Accordingly all the Sail was set that we could possibly make, and the Wind being very fresh and fair, we went right before it, and made great Way. The Captain after his Observation, shap'd his Course as he thought so as to pass wide of the Scilly Isles: but it seems there is sometimes a strong Indraught setting up St. George's Channel which deceives Seamen. . . . This Indraught was probably the Cause of what happen'd to us. We had a Watchman plac'd in the Bow to whom they often call'd, *Look well out before, there*; and he as often answer'd, Aye! But perhaps had his Eyes shut, and was half asleep at the time: they sometimes answering as is said mechanically: For he did not see a Light just before us, which had been hid by the Studding Sails from the Man at Helm and from the rest of the Watch; but by an accidental Yaw of the Ship was discover'd, and occasion'd a great Alarm, we being very near it, the light appearing to me as big as a Cart Wheel. It was

Midnight, and Our Captain fast asleep. But Capt. Kennedy jumping upon Deck, and seeing the Danger, ordered the Ship to wear round, all Sails standing, an Operation dangerous to the Masts, but it carried us clear, and we escap'd Shipwreck, for we were running right upon the Rocks on which the Lighthouse was erected. This Deliverance impress'd me strongly with the Utility of Lighthouses, and made me resolve to encourage the building more of them in America, if I should live to return there. (A 165)

The following morning, the sounding showed "we were near our Port, but a thick Fog hid the Land from our Sight." Franklin then gave one of his comparatively rare appreciations of scenery: "About 9 aClock the Fog began to rise, and seem'd to be lifted up from the Water like the Curtain at a Play-house, discovering underneath the Town of Falmouth, the Vessels in its Harbour, and the Fields that surrounded it. A most pleasing Spectacle to those who had been so long without any other Prospects, than the uniform View of a vacant Ocean!" Franklin wrote Deborah that as they landed at Falmouth on Sunday, 17 July, "The bell ringing for church, we went thither immediately, and with hearts full of gratitude, returned sincere thanks to God for the mercies we had received: were I a Roman Catholic, perhaps I should on this occasion vow to build a chapel to some saint; but as I am not, if I were to vow at all, it should be to build a *lighthouse*" (7:243).

TWENTY-THREE

Assessing Franklin, Age 42 through 51

*It was also thought, that by the frequent meetings-together of commissioners or
representatives from all the colonies, the circumstances of the whole would be better
known, and the good of the whole better provided for; and that the colonies would
by this connection learn to consider themselves, not as so many independent states,
but as members of the same body; and thence be more ready to afford assistance
and support to each other, and to make diversions in favour even of the most
distant, and to join cordially in any expedition for the benefit of all against the
common enemy.*
—Franklin, "Reasons and Motives for the Albany Plan," 5:401

DURING 1748–57, Franklin continued to write on religion and theology, but
he increasingly devoted his energies to natural philosophy rather than moral
philosophy and to physics rather than metaphysics. To a large degree, he had
achieved the economic independence that would allow him to pursue his multi-
farious interests. He loved his children and his wife, and Deborah continued to
be an essential partner and helpmate, though she sometimes behaved like a
jealous stepmother to William—and so, too, thought Franklin, did England
toward America.

Franklin took part in Pennsylvania politics almost as soon as he arrived in
Philadelphia, but after his election to the Pennsylvania Assembly in 1751 he became immersed in it. At the same time, his Americanism became more obvious,
and he began writing frequently about the relations between America and the
British Empire. In the latter part of this assessment, I will attempt to show how
Franklin's writings on America and the British Empire during the period
1748–57 prove he had, so far as surviving evidence shows, the most outspoken
Americanism of anyone at that time. Concluding the assessment, I will discuss
what effect the increasing recognition of Franklin's extraordinary abilities had
on him and his contemporaries.

Just as, from his knowledge of Chinese history and culture, and especially
from his publication of "The Morals of Confucius" in the *Pennsylvania Gazette*
of 7 and 21 March 1737/8, one could argue that Franklin was America's first
Confucian and Sinologist,[1] so too from his knowledge of Middle Eastern history
and culture, and especially from his artful and subtle advocacy of a Mohammedan sacred text in "A Parable Against Persecution," one could argue that he

was America's first Islamicist, though not a Mohammedan (see p. 463). Though he may deserve these descriptions, numerous Europeans knew more of the Middle and Far East than he. Knowledge of these cultures is an interesting aspect of his general curiosity about people and cultures and reflects something akin to his recommending such subjects as comparative anthropology as projected subjects for his Academy of Philadelphia (see pp. 183–84), but it does not compare with his original contributions in natural philosophy, like his work as a weatherman or a heat engineer. Nevertheless, his interest in and extensive knowledge of Near and Far Eastern cultures are relatively unknown and appear in these years (as they do earlier and later) and seem noteworthy, as well as characteristic of his extraordinary curiosity, range of interests, and cosmopolitanism.

Though Franklin's "Parable against Persecution" might be considered an exception, Franklin finally had dropped his smart-aleck comments on ministers and religion. In part, the change came simply from greater maturity and from becoming good friends with a series of worthy ministers like George Whitefield, Jared Eliot, Ezra Stiles, and several in Boston. At the same time, he realized that he had a religion, one that he increasingly identified as an absolute, that is, as a version of God. As he wrote in *Poor Richard* for 1757, "At the Day of Judgment, we shall not be asked, what Proficiency we have made in Languages or Philosophy; but whether we have liv'd virtuously and piously . . . For then the Constellations themselves shall disappear, the Sun and Moon shall give no more Light, and all the Frame of Nature shall vanish. But our good or bad Works shall remain forever, recorded in the Archives of Eternity" (7:89). In a letter of 6 June 1753 to Joseph Huey and in writing about religion in the Academy of Philadelphia, he repeated his belief in the Golden Rule and in fundamental Christian virtues. As we have seen in his essay "What is True?" (*Life* 2:520–21), he regarded that classic metaphysical question with skepticism. As a "Comfortable Pyrrhonist" (*Life* 2:295–98), he even burlesqued absolute skepticism. Now, however, in asserting his beliefs in traditional Christian virtues (which are in great part the same as those of other religions), he identified them with religion. Franklin commented to his religious friend Dr. John Perkins that rainwater is sweet because "It has pleased the Goodness of God so to order it, that the Particles of Air will not attract the Particles of Salt: though they strongly attract water" (4:440). For the rest of his life, Franklin frequently expressed such beliefs, even though I am sure, as Jake says to Brett in Hemingway's *A Farewell to Arms*, that Franklin thought it was "pretty to think so."

Franklin still devoted time and effort to his old projects, especially to the Union Fire Company and the Library Company of Philadelphia, and he undertook several new ones, the Academy and College of Philadelphia, the Pennsylvania Hospital, and an insurance company. By the end of 1756, he had become Philadelphia's most civic-minded and essential citizen. His best-known production of literature during this period came at the very end, written while on the voyage to England in the summer of 1757. *The Way to Wealth* ostensibly describes how to make and accumulate money, but its underlying message, which was similar to the ideals of the Library Company and the revisionist program of the Philadelphia Academy, is possibility. *The Way to Wealth* repudiates the existing hierarchical society of the eighteenth century. Instead, it claims that the individual can and should have the opportunity to create himself. Like the *Autobiography*, *The Way to Wealth* is based on egalitarianism and the American Dream of a better world, and it posits that the individual may help in making himself and the world better.

Franklin's character and ideals remained generally the same. He still hoped to attain the status of a friend to humankind and, for some contemporaries, came to be regarded as an *amicus humani generis* before 1757. He remained a fun, good friend to his favorite companions—and even to some enemies, as he indirectly testified in praising Governor Robert Hunter Morris for his ability to put aside politics and be convivial. Franklin continued his regime of self-discipline and study, as his achievements testify—and so too, does his criticism of Governor James Hamilton for having "a decent Share of Talents but not much improved."[2] But the strong passion and foolish anger that he sometimes displayed concerning local and imperial politics startlingly refute a common major previous image, that of the calm, cool, deliberate man of reason (which appears frequently in every volume of the *Life* and is strikingly presented in this frontispiece).

The power of the press recurs frequently herein. The first chapter, on the militia Association, demonstrated it best. For seven months, from November 1747 to May 1748, Franklin printed pamphlets, broadsides, and literally hundreds of items in the *Pennsylvania Gazette* concerning the Association. Nothing else in colonial America before the Stamp Act had as much publicity within so short a period. Although the Reverend George Whitefield has been justly treated as a print media phenomenon, the *Pennsylvania Gazette* devoted almost three times as much space in a seven-month period to the Association (from November 1747 to May 1748) as it did to Whitefield in a seven-month period during his heyday in the Great Awakening (March through September 1740).[3] Although Whitefield was the subject of the material about him, he created only a portion of the coverage. Franklin created the Association and all its news coverage. As James Logan wrote, Franklin was "the very soul of the whole." Richard Peters repeated that phrase about Franklin as the founder of the Academy and College of Philadelphia, which also received major publicity from Franklin. When he decided to support Thomas Bond's project for the Pennsylvania Hospital, he wrote that he first attempted "to prepare the Minds of the People by writing on the Subject in the Newspapers, which was my usual Custom" (A 122).

Previous volumes of the *Life* pointed out that Franklin's writings and publications influenced local Pennsylvania politics, but they did not emphasize that the *Pennsylvania Gazette* published far more local political news than any other colonial American newspaper. As clerk of the assembly from 1734 to 1751, Franklin copied the speeches of the assembly to the governor, and as printer of the assembly's *Votes and Proceedings,* he printed them in the official record. He must have asked for and secured permission (though the permission is rarely recorded) to also print these messages and other political material in the *Pennsylvania Gazette.* As Franklin knew better than any contemporary, and as he wrote in *Proposals Relating to the Education of Youth in Pensylvania* (1749), "Modern Political Oratory" is "chiefly performed by the Pen and Press." Newspapers copied from one another, so the other colonial newspapers often reprinted Pennsylvania's political news. Pennsylvania politics became the best-known American politics. I hypothesize that Franklin's political reporting caused other colonial assemblies to want to publish their proceedings—and such materials appeared ever more frequently from the 1730s to the Revolution.

From 1748 to 1757, Pennsylvania's politics dominated colonial news. The opposing parties (the governor and the Proprietary Party versus Franklin and the Quaker Party) pleaded their cases before the Pennsylvania populace and, simultaneously, the British authorities. Indeed, reporting itself became an issue in Pennsylvania, with governors Robert Hunter Morris and William Denny trying—and failing—to control it. Franklin continued to be the most important person in Pennsylvania's political reporting when he became an assemblyman, for he moved from serving as the assembly's clerk who took down the minutes to serving on the House committee that decided what to include in the minutes. The minutes became fuller and recorded more "divisions" (the votes of individual representatives on specific issues). Volume 1 noted that James Franklin published the first division in the English-speaking world, and volume 2 pointed out that Franklin recorded the second (*Life* 1:83, 2:332). In this volume, Franklin reported the several divisions of 5, 9, and 14 April 1755. After that, the record of the Pennsylvania divisions became common. No other colony—and certainly not England, where political reporting was cloaked in secrecy—had anything approaching Pennsylvania's political newspaper coverage. Franklin believed that the public needed specific information in order to determine for whom to vote.

Reviewing a book on the Albany Treaty, a distinguished scholar wrote, "No serious historian would argue that in 1754 Franklin was an American patriot."[4] But as a literary historian, I am sometimes not altogether serious. The best-known example of American resentment of British authority is "No Taxation without Representation"! Franklin expressed that sentiment several times during these years, and, as he well knew, the Reverend John Wise, the hero of the Old Charter Party, had done so in 1687 (*Life* 1:76–77). John Adams wrote Thomas Jefferson on 24 August 1815: "What do we mean by the Revolution? . . . The Revolution was in the Minds of the People, and this was effected, from 1760 to 1775, in the course of the fifteen Years before a drop of blood was drawn at Lexington." Three years later, 25 July 1818, writing James Madison, Adams said that "the first Settlers brought Independence with them." Madison agreed on 7 August 1818: "Our forefathers brought with them the germ of Independence, in the principle of self-taxation."[5]

The British, however, believed in mercantilism, whereby colonies and colonists existed for the good of England. Most British authorities thought colonies were meant to be exploited. Many assumed that Britain had settled America at Britain's expense in order to exploit it. Many Americans, however, rejected that view. They objected to the British appointment of royal governors, to the British instructions to governors, and to the Acts of Trade and Navigation. Like the Reverend John Wise, James Franklin, Nathaniel Gardner, and numerous other Americans of his own day, Franklin argued that the colonists had all the same rights (trial by jury, habeas corpus, etc.) as Englishmen (*Life* 1:164, 343)—most notoriously, no taxation without representation.

Dumping Shit and Piss on our Dining Tables!—In "Jakes on our Tables!," the most widely reprinted editorial before the Stamp Act, Franklin pilloried Parliament for transporting criminals to America. The Board of Trade, the official group in charge of American affairs and, presumably, most knowledgeable about America, declared, in what Franklin called a "barbarous *Sarcasm*," that transporting felons to the colonies was for "the better peopling of America." Franklin exposed English contempt and scorn for Americans in two additional 1751 writings: "Rattlesnakes for Felons" and "Observations Concerning the Increase of Mankind"—boldly and savagely in the first, and subtly in the second. He did so earlier in writings for the Association (1747–48); later in his remarks of 9 May 1753 on climate and human characteristics; and in three letters to Massachusetts governor William Shirley in December 1754.

Franklin's objections in 1755–57 to the quartering of troops in private homes and to the enlistment of indentured servants belong in the subset of objections to British authority covered by "no taxation without representation." Those two measures also stole money or property from Americans. As he wrote to Governor Shirley on 4 December 1754, "it is suppos'd an undoubted Right of Englishmen not to be taxed but by their own Consent given thro' their Representatives" (5:445). In reply to Governor Shirley's suggestion of American representation in Parliament, Franklin said that first, all the anti-American acts of Parliament must be repealed (5:449, 16:243). He knew that Parliament would never do so. Was he then implying that America would and must rebel? Franklin thought the only acceptable way to raise money in America was by requesting it from the colonies. Each had an assembly, and Franklin believed the colonial assemblies were American versions of the English Parliament.

In his more conciliatory arguments, Franklin said that the British Empire should be run not for the good of England to the disadvantage of America but for the good of the whole British Empire. He wrote his English friend and patron Peter Collinson on 28 May 1754 that Britain and her colonies should be considered as "one Whole, and not as different States with separate Interests"

(5:332–33). In a 22 December 1754 letter to Governor Shirley, he wrote that in the past, "the private interest of a petty corporation or of . . . a set of artificers or traders in England" have sometimes been more important than "the best national good" (5:449). Franklin did not say to Collinson that Americans should be preferred to Englishmen (Franklin was more honest to Shirley than to his good friend and generous patron Collinson), but he could reasonably claim that the empire should be run for the good of the whole.

The future glory of America was a longstanding idea, connected with the *translatio* theme, or the westward movement of arts and sciences (*Life* 1:58, 228, 2:103, 286, and above, pp. 240–41, 314). Franklin gave the ancient idea a factual basis in his population studies. "Observations Concerning the Increase of Mankind" (1751) showed that by natural increase (i.e., excluding emigrants), the population of whites in America was doubling within every twenty-five years, whereas the population in Europe was not doubling within a thousand years. Because of the existence of large amounts of uncultivated land in America, its population would continue to increase exponentially for longer than the following century. America would become a stronger, more populous empire than England. And if America remained within the British Empire, its center would move to America. But the occasion for his population study was to condemn the Acts of Trade and Navigation, most immediately the Iron Act of 1750, not to assert (though it is certainly implied) the inevitable dominance of America in the future English-speaking empire.

Franklin again used population data in a Pennsylvania Assembly message of 19 August 1752. He stressed the necessity of a paper currency for Pennsylvania while he simultaneously argued that the availability of land in America meant that English manufacturers would, without any taxes imposed on trade and navigation, be able to undersell any possible American competition: "In fine, by rendering the Means of purchasing Land easy to the Poor, the Dominions of the Crown are strengthen'd and extended; the Proprietaries dispose of their Wilderness Territory; and the British Nation secures the Benefit of its Manufactures, and increases the Demand for them: For so long as Land can be easily procur'd for Settlements between the Atlantick and Pacifick Oceans, so long will Labour be dear in America; and while Labour continues dear, we can never rival the Artificers, or interfere with the Trade of our Mother Country" (4:350). The Americanism is clear, though Franklin primarily wanted to convince the British authorities that American manufactures were no threat to England. Thus the British authorities should allow the act increasing Pennsylvania's paper money to pass.

Additional Americanist motifs that recur in the pre-Revolutionary period turn up before 1757. In *Plain Truth*, he claimed that the English cared little and knew less about America: "we are *far from* ZIDON, *and there is no Deliverer near*" (3:193, 202). He condemned Parliament's and the king in council's instructions to colonial governors and assemblies—especially Thomas Penn's instructions to the Pennsylvania governors. He claimed that the defense of the frontiers of an empire should be at the cost of the entire empire, not just those parts that happen to be on the frontiers. Making this point, he used the body metaphor (sacrificing a part of the body wounds the whole), which reappeared frequently in his writings.

The most certain evidence that the Americanization of Benjamin Franklin was fully formed before the end of this period is his claim that Americans deserved greater liberties and privileges than the English. Many Americans in the seventeenth and eighteenth centuries had taken pride in America and in its achievements, but no one, before Franklin, argued that Americans had more merit than the English and that, "if there be any difference" between the English and the Americans, Americans deserved preference. Americans, wrote Franklin on 22 December 1754, "have most contributed to enlarge Britain's empire and commerce, encrease her strength, her wealth, and the numbers of her people, at the risque of their own lives and private fortunes in new and strange countries." Therefore, Americans "methinks ought rather to expect some preference" (5:451). He repeated the claim a year later. "*Additional* Liberties and Privileges, not used in *England*, but suited to the different Circumstances of different Colonies" should be granted to Americans (6:299).

In view of Franklin's Americanism, I believe that his quest for a military union of the colonies is actually a first step toward a federal union. The usual interpretation of the "Join, or Die" campaign and the 1751–54 plans of union is that the colonies would join together only militarily and only as part of the British Empire. That seems to be true of these selected documents. But even within them, Franklin directly reveals that a primarily military union would gradually become something else: as representatives of all the colonies met together, "the circumstances of the whole would be better known, and the good of the whole better provided for; and . . . the colonies would by this connection learn to consider themselves, not as so many independent states, but as members of the same body" (5:401–2). That "body" was not the British Empire, but the American colonies. Franklin expected that even a limited military union would prepare the way for a federal political union. Further, when one considers Franklin's writings concerning the union of America together with his anti-English writings of 1751, the interpretation emerges that a unified federal American government will revolt against Great Britain.

James Madison did not know Franklin's anti-British writings of 1751 or practically any of his other writings on British-American relations of 1748–57. Nevertheless, as I noted when concluding the discussion of Franklin's December 1754 letters to Governor William Shirley, Madison judged that Franklin's letters expressed in "a nut shell" the succeeding arguments of the American "patriots." If an American patriot existed in 1754, it was Benjamin Franklin.

Major themes in other writings also suggest Franklin's Americanism: his scorn for the idea of kings, of aristocracy, and of hierarchical social and political structures; and his resentment of "strangers," English governors and placemen. These motifs suggest that he envisioned a more egalitarian world. He hoped that a society of more possibilities for more people could be created in America. As I have stressed in this and the previous two volumes, egalitarianism was a fundamental Franklin principle. In Chapter 5, on the Academy and College of Philadelphia, I did not ask a fundamental question: who should receive a higher education? Franklin's attitudes toward education, like his views on politics, are a subset of his beliefs concerning what is and should be the social structure of society. Franklin was a radical egalitarian—an uncommon, even rare, position in the eighteenth century. John Adams's views were typical of those who considered themselves among the colonial gentry, and Jefferson's opinions were about halfway between those of Franklin and Adams.

John Adams argued in court in 1761 that the separation between yeoman and gentleman was "the most ancient and universal of all Divisions of People." Adams said of the defendant: "he is not a gentleman in any Respect, neither by Birth, Education, Office, Reputation, or Employment: and indeed I have no reason to think him one in Thought, Word, or Deed. He springs from ordinary Parents, he can scarcely write his Name, his Business is Boating, he never had any Commissions, and therefore to call him Gentleman is an arrant Prostitution of the Title." Writing Thomas Jefferson on 2 September 1813, Adams defined the "five Pillars of Aristocracy" as "Beauty, Wealth, Birth, Genius, and Virtues." Adams believed that persons who possessed most of these qualities should be educated and should be society's leaders.[6]

Jefferson replied on 28 October 1813 that he agreed "there is a natural aristocracy among men. The grounds of this are virtue and talents." The artificial aristocracy existed based on birth and wealth. The "natural aristoi" who possessed virtue and talents should, in Jefferson's opinion, be educated and should become the leaders of society. In *Notes on the State of Virginia*, he presented his scheme of education toward the end of Query XIV. All boys would receive a basic education in reading, writing, and arithmetic. At the end of three years of free schooling, the "best genius" in the school would be sent on to a traditional grammar school. There, "Greek, Latin, geography, and the higher branches of numerical arithematic" would be taught. After one or two years, about half of the scholarship boys would be selected to continue on for the full six years of grammar school. "By this means twenty of the best geniuses will be raked from the rubbish annually." At the end of six years, half of the scholarship boys would be selected to continue on to "William and Mary college."

Jefferson's scheme provided for the education of boys who would not otherwise be able to go beyond home education—and for the education of the "best geniuses" among the boys. His belief that the majority were intellectual "rubbish" was typical of the eighteenth-century western world. The thought that the "better sort" or "upper classes" were distinguished by virtue and talents from the vast majority of people was not uncommon among members of the Third

Estate. Every careful observer of society realized that a few individuals who were not wealthy or aristocrats achieved distinction in business, politics, or moral or natural philosophy.[7] Like Jefferson, other philosophes thought there was a "natural aristoi," and Jefferson seemed rather proud of his method for discovering and cultivating them.

Unlike Adams and Jefferson, Franklin believed in the possibility of higher education for everyone. He wrote that the Library Company of Philadelphia was partly responsible for major changes in American society: "The Institution soon manifested its Utility, was imitated by other Towns and in other Provinces, the Librarys were augmented by Donations, Reading became fashionable, and our People having no publick Amusements to divert their Attention from Study became better acquainted with Books, and in a few Years were observ'd by Strangers to be better instructed and more intelligent than people of the same Rank generally are in other Countries" (A 74).

The use of the word *intelligent* is especially interesting, for its primary meaning is "having the faculty of understanding." Franklin, a literary genius sensitive to denotations as well as connotations of words, hereby asserted that no difference existed between the "common Tradesmen & Farmers" in America and "most Gentlemen" in other countries. Some philosophes of Franklin's day, like Thomas Jefferson, had discredited wealth and/or family as the basis for social distinction. What remained, for most eighteenth-century students of social organization, was not just acquired ability but a profound difference in the degree of ability. They thought intelligence distinguished the upper from the lower classes.

Franklin attacked the supposed distinction. There is no difference in ability, in fundamental intelligence, he claimed, between the "common Tradesmen & Farmers" of Philadelphia and "most Gentlemen." He annihilated the basis of social hierarchy as it existed in most Enlightenment thinkers. Given the opportunity, common tradesmen and farmers were as intelligent as gentlemen. Franklin also linked education and politics. He wrote that the availability of books "contributed in some degree to the Stand so generally made throughout the Colonies in Defence of their Privileges" (A 72). The Library Company contained especially the classic Whig writings[8]—and, as we have seen, the Academy and College of Philadelphia used those classics as models of the English language.

In a letter to Lord Shelburne, England's prime minister during the peace treaty negotiations in 1782, Franklin's disciple Benjamin Vaughan explained Franklin's radical attitudes toward class and intellectual differences: Franklin "thinks that the lower people are as we see them, because oppressed; and then their situation in point of manners, becomes the reason for oppressing them." Education would largely wipe out the difference between the "upper" and "lower" sort. Franklin believed that education should and would characterize the future American society. Franklin's vision of the Third Estate became the egalitarian wave of the future, though it may never be entirely fulfilled.

A major personal change came about during this period in Franklin's relations with his contemporaries. We have seen that William Allen became jealous when Franklin was named grand master of Pennsylvania and have encountered suggestions that Speaker Isaac Norris was sometimes unfriendly as Franklin became the most important leader of the Quaker Party. One supposes that most contemporaries who had the normal amount of pride and frequent contact with Franklin accepted that he was friendly and liked him, despite the knowledge that he knew more, wrote better, had more ideas, and worked harder than they did. Most of his good friends, like John Bartram, Hugh Roberts, Ebenezer Kinnersley, and others in New York and New England, seemed comfortable with his genius and his industry. When Provost William Smith belittled Franklin for plagiarizing from Ebenezer Kinnersley's work in electricity, Kinnersley denied it and selflessly celebrated Franklin.

Nevertheless, if one had the normal amount of self-respect and self-delusion, it must have sometimes been difficult to be with or work with Franklin. How would one like to be a good, hardworking commissioner at the Easton Treaty in November 1756 and to realize that Charles Thomson inadvertently wrote in the minutes, "Franklin and the other commissioners"? Thomson did not consider the other commissioners as important. They were not, either at the conference or back in Philadelphia—or anywhere except in their own families and, possibly, in their own opinions. Further, as the joint deputy postmaster general, Franklin had the power to give places of profit to postmasters throughout the colonies. In addition, he had become, in 1752, the most famous living natural philosopher in the world.

Fame has two sides. On the one hand, if one had more than the normal amount of pride, then one could not help but be jealous and perhaps, at least a little, hate Franklin. On the other, it could be flattering to spend time with the most famous American. And he was a fun companion. A wonderful young lady like Catharine Ray could easily become infatuated with him. Franklin seemed to accept the admiration of his contemporaries comfortably and, not quite so comfortably, the hostility of persons like William Allen or Provost William Smith. From the time he was a boy writing the "Silence Dogood" letters, he demonstrated an ironic distance toward himself. He needed it now and would need that self-mocking stance more so when more persons became his admirers and more persons became his jealous enemies.

As I suggested in the beginning of this chapter, the changes in Franklin's life partly mirrored and partly anticipated the major shifts in society from the early seventeenth to the late eighteenth centuries. Religion was the most widely and hotly debated topic of the seventeenth century, and though it remained a key issue in all subsequent years, politics had become the most widely debated topic by the late eighteenth century. Following the general shift from religion to politics, education began shifting from classical emphases and religious control to modern subjects and secular control. As we have seen, Franklin led in that change. So, too, in the adumbrations of a future American empire that he projected in 1751 and in 1754, religion had little official role. The government and its ideals would be secular, not religious. Franklin satirized reason, the Enlightenment, and the idea of the perfectability of mankind, yet for numerous contemporaries and later persons, he embodied progress, the Enlightenment, and the amelioration of the condition of humans. For every person who read Hume, Voltaire, the skeptics, deists, or atheists of the Enlightenment, hundreds knew its dominant symbol—the lightning rod—and its creator, Benjamin Franklin.

APPENDIX 1. *New Attributions*

20 November 1729, *PG*. Editorial at end of article on the wretched conditions in parts of the British Isles. Above, p. 579; see also *Life* 1:427.

9 December 1729, *PG*. Editorial on the misery of prisoners in jails for debt. Above, p. 580; see also *Life* 1:427–28.

5 November 1747, *PG*. Anonymous article (p. 1, col. 1) addressed to "Mr. Franklin" on Barclay's *Apology*. Cf. P 3:183–84, and *Canon* 111. Above, p. 42.

19 November 1747, *PG*. Advertisement, supposedly by rich persons and Proprietary Party members, defending themselves from the calumnies of BF in *Plain Truth*. Above, p. 42.

3 December 1747, *PG*. Associator propaganda describing the English sacking of Portobello. Above, p. 24.

28 July 1748, *PG*. Editorial note on the forthcoming Lancaster treaty with Scarouady and the Miamis and Swawnese Indians. Above, p. 306–7.

18 May 1749, *PG*. A report on the number of houses in Philadelphia "from a Motive of Curiosity, by twelve careful persons." Above, p. 314; see also *Life* 1:242–43.

12 June 1751, *PG*. News notes from Philadelphia on crimes by transported felons, and a supposed "Extract of a Letter from Maryland, dated April 26." Above, p. 224.

5 September 1751, *PG*. "Extract" of a letter supposedly from "Annapolis, 15 August" together with news notes on crime. Above, p. 225.

August 1753. "A Comparative View of Philadelphia, Boston, and New York." *Gentleman's Magazine* 23:372–73. Above, p. 314.

18 May 1754, V 5:3713–17. Franklin's "Resolves" in reply to Governor Andrew Hamilton's message of 17 May 1754. In his memorandum of services for the Pennsylvania Assembly, Franklin noted for 18 May 1754, "A Number of Resolves drawn up by him and agreed to" (4:161, 161n13). Above, chap 14, n. 28, p. 682.

1754. "Prices of Printing Work in Philadelphia, 1754." Mss. American Antiquarian Society. This is not really a new attribution, just a piece so far not printed in P. See Douglas C. McMurtrie, *The Price of Printing in Philadelphia, 1754* (Chicago: Privately Printed, 1928).

21 March 1755, CR 6:329–30. Governor Morris and the council suggested that Josiah Quincy write a letter, which Morris would lay before the House. Franklin evidently wrote it for him and on 21 March, Quincy presented it. Above, pp. 419–21.

21 June 1755, V 5:3915–16. Bill for raising an additional £15,000 for "cutting of new Roads for the better supplying the King's Troops, Hiring of Carriages, Payment of Expresses, and other contingent Charges for the King's Service." Franklin's draft of a preamble for the bill is printed in P 4:83, but the description of it on 21 June (V 5:3915–16), which Franklin seemed proud of (P 6:90–91), is not in the *Papers*. Hutson, "BF" 326, 358n145, believed that Franklin wrote every important assembly message from the spring of 1755 to the spring of 1757. Above, p. 436.

21 August 1755, *PG.* In an indirect attack on Morris and on Thomas Penn, Franklin published a letter from Albany in which the author proposed that the New York legislature ease the people of their quitrents for several years in view of their taxes supporting the war effort. The news item reminded Pennsylvanians of the avariciousness with which Penn collected his quitrents. Penn suspected that Franklin wrote it. Cf. V5:4006–7. Above, pp. 452–53.

29 January 1756, *PG.* News report of Indians attacking and killing farmers, signed by John Adam Huth. Probably written by Franklin from Huth's oral testimony. Above, p. 505.

APPENDIX 2. *Franklin's Residences and Real Estate to 1757*

When Franklin arrived in Philadelphia on 6 October 1723, he spent the first night at the Crooked Billet Tavern (endpapers #39), the site of the present 35 South Front Street; then lived for about a month at Andrew Bradford's home on South Second Street (endpapers #12), close to the great Quaker Meeting House at the corner of Market and Second streets. When he went to work for Samuel Keimer, he rented a room from John Read, at 318 Market Street (endpapers #12), where he lived until leaving for London in September 1724. After returning in mid-1726, he lodged with Thomas Denham at 39 South Front Street (endpapers #38). No records indicate where he lived during or after his illness in February 1727, but about 1 June 1728, he rented a house from Simon Edgell (endpapers #35), at the site of the present 139 Market Street. He remained there until 11 January 1738/9, when he rented a building and lot owned by Robert Grace, at the present 131 Market Street (endpapers #36). (See A 25, 27, 59–60, 124; and DH under the appropriate date.)

PHILADELPHIA RESIDENCES, 1748–1757

1748–50, 200 North Second Street: Sarah Dillwyn (endpapers #28), ca. 1 January

The Franklins left their residence owned by Robert Grace at 131 Market Street and moved to a three-story house on the northwest corner of Sassafras (Race) and Second streets, owned by Sarah Dillwyn, where Dr. Cadwalader Evans had recently lived (DH, 13 November 1748). The Franklins probably thought the location, away from the busy market, would be more attractive. It evidently proved inconvenient, and two and a half years later, they moved back to Market Street, next door to their former residence (DH, 31 May 1750).

1750–51, 141 Market Street: Timothy Matlack (endpapers #34)

The 31 May 1750 *Pennsylvania Gazette* advertised: "TO BE LETT, The house at the corner of Sassafras and Second-streets, in which Benjamin Franklin now dwells. Enquire of Sarah Dillwyn." The Franklins were moving. Shortly after 31 May 1750, the Franklins moved to 141 Market Street, next door to their former residence at 129 Market Street (1728–39) and just a few houses north of their former residence at 131 Market Street (1739–48).

1751–61, 325 Market Street: John Wister (end papers # 14)

Before October 1751, the Franklins moved to the site of the present 325 Market Street, renting from John Wister at £38 per year. They stayed there until October 1755. The location was two blocks closer to the state house where Franklin often had business. John Wister, a Philadelphia wine merchant, was the brother of Caspar Wistar [sic], who founded a glassworks in Salem, New Jersey, in 1738. In September 1752, BF installed a lightning rod in the Wister house, which tested whether or not the atmosphere was charged with electricity (fig. 15b, p. 115, above).

Real Estate (Excluding Residences) Owned by Franklin

1733, Lampblack House, Philadelphia

On 21 March 1733, Franklin bought a lampblack house from Nathaniel Jenkins for £35, thus assuring himself of a constant supply of a primary ingredient for making ink. It probably was located within several blocks of Market and Second streets ("Accounts," 21 March 1733). Franklin likely sold it to David Hall sometime after they became partners in 1748.

9–11 April 1734: Read Property on [318] High/Market Street (endpapers, between #10 and #12)

Sarah Read, Deborah's mother, gave her two daughters and their husbands the western half lot of what is now 318 Market Street. Thus Deborah and Benjamin Franklin and Frances and John Croker jointly owned a half lot. The two owners gave Sarah Read lifelong use of the house and halflot on 11 April (1:362–70). BF bought out John Croker and his wife on 12 October 1745 (3:44–45, 4:208–9). In his 28 April 1757 will, BF left these lots to Deborah and—after her decease—to their daughter, Sarah (7:201). This was the first of the several lots that became the Franklin property; see below, endpapers #10, 11, and 12.

31 July 1741, Pasture, Philadelphia

BF purchased a lot from the brick maker William Coats on 31 July 1741, evidently as a place to keep a pony for William. The ground rent due on 2 August annually was £3.4.0 (2:310.). A Philadelphia historian located it at Hickory Lane, which ran west from the present Fifth Street and Fairmont Avenue to Ridge Avenue. I speculate above (p. 108) that Franklin performed his kite experiment there in June 1752. In his 28 April 1757 will, BF left the lot to his son William (7:200).

1 August 1741, Arch (Mulberry) Street Property, Philadelphia

BF purchased a house and lot from the bricklayer Christopher Thompson and his wife, Mary, located on the north side of Mulberry or Arch Street, between Fourth and Fifth streets. Franklin paid ground rent on it (£3.17.0, due 21 March) until 13 December 1771, when he bought it for £64.3.4 (2:311; 18:262). In his 28 April 1757 will, BF left it to his son William (7:200). It might be the site of BF's "Pattern House" (7:320–21). In his last will, BF left the property to his daughter, Sarah Franklin Bache.

12 October 1745, Read Property on High/Market Street, Philadelphia

BF purchased the eastern half of the Read lot on High (Market) Street, with the dwelling house on it, from John Croker and his wife, Elizabeth, of Staten Island,

New York. BF was buying out the interest of John Croker, whose former wife, Frances Read Croker, had died (1:363, n.6; 3:44–45). In his 28 April 1757 will, BF left these lots (C2 and C5) to Deborah and—after her decease—to their daughter, Sarah (7:201). This was the second of the several lots that became the Franklin property— see above, 9–11 April 1734.

22 August 1748. Douse House, Unity Street, Boston, Massachusetts

BF's sister Elizabeth Douse and her husband, Richard, mortgaged their home and lot on Unity Street, Boston, to BF on 22 August 1748 for £60 Pennsylvania currency. On 27 September 1753, Elizabeth Douse renewed the mortgage, now for £100 in her own name (5:66–67). In his 28 April 1757 will, BF left it to his sister Jane, together with the bond and "every demand" against Elizabeth Douse's estate. BF specified, however, that she should never be disturbed in her possession of the house (7:199). After Elizabeth Douse's death in 1759, BF gave the income from it to Jane. She occupied it in 1784, and he left it to her in his 1788 will (5:66–67).

8 August 1750: Two Tenements in Germantown, Near Boston, Massachusetts

At the urging of his brother John Franklin, who wanted to start a glassworks, BF joined in partnership with him, Norton Quincy, Peter Etter, and Joseph Crellius, buying land at Braintree, Massachusetts. The glassworks "did not prosper," and John Franklin died on 30 January 1756. BF wound up owning "two small tenements" in what was then called Germantown, near Boston. He left them to his nephew James Franklin in his 28 April 1757 will (7:199). For John Franklin's letter concerning the investment, see 26 November 1753 (5:118–19). What happened to the two small tenements is unknown (5:118–19). Franklin does not mention them in his 1788 will.

15 November 1751: John and Martha Read, High/Market Street, Philadelphia

John Read, Deborah's brother, sold the lot he had inherited from his mother, Sarah Read, to BF for £390 Pennsylvania currency (4:208–9). It had been part of Deborah's father's property and bordered those mentioned above ("Read Property"). In his 28 April 1757 will, BF left these lots to Deborah and—after her decease—to their daughter, Sarah (7:201). This was the third of several lots that became the Franklin property.

25 March 1752, Moore Property, High/Market Street, Philadelphia

Samuel Preston Moore and Hannah Moore sold the adjoining lot next to John Read's (which BF had bought on 15 November 1751) to BF (4:209n3, 295–96). He left it to his daughter, Sarah, in his 28 April 1757 will (7:201). This was the fourth of several lots that became the Franklin property.

8 November 1753: Lot in New Haven, Connecticut

Franklin intended to help his nephew James Franklin, Jr., start his own printing business in New Haven and thus bought a well-located plot of land near Yale College in 1753. "Jemmy" Franklin, however, preferred to remain in Newport, Rhode Island, with his mother. BF's former partner, James Parker, set up a printing house in New Haven late in 1754 (he printed Nathaniel Ames's almanac for 1755; E 7144). Sometime around 1757, possibly on 22 April 1757, when Franklin commissioned Parker comptroller of the post office (7:194–98), Franklin sold him the lot for $90 (5:109–10).

APPENDIX 3. *Electrical Terminology*

FRANKLIN'S CONTRIBUTIONS TO ELECTRICAL TERMINOLOGY

In an essay titled "Franklin's Vocabulary," David Yerkes concluded with a list of the words that Franklin had contributed to the English language, according to the information available (1990) in the second edition of the *Oxford English Dictionary*. The following list gives the electrical terms found in Yerkes's article, their earliest occurrence, and a few additions. I point out instances where I have noticed earlier uses of the terms.

In addition to the primary sources, the following contain key information: David Yerkes, "Franklin's Vocabulary," *Reappraising Benjamin Franklin: A Bicentennial Perspective*, ed. J. A. Leo Lemay (Newark: University of Delaware Press, 1993) 396–414; Haller; and Peter Collinson to Cadwallader Colden, 30 March 1745, Colden 3:110.

FRANKLIN'S NEW (?) TERMS

armateur, 29 April 1749; P 3:357, ¶ 17. Franklin used the word in his first description of a plate battery.

brush, 29 April 1749; P 3:366, ¶ 5. A brush-like discharge of electric sparks.

charge, charged, discharge, uncharged (*OED* 5), 25 May 1747; P 3:134; *charged*, 29 July 1750; P 4:15; *uncharged*, 1 July 1773; P 20:265.

condense (*OED* 1.c.), 21 December 1751; P 4:217.

electrical atmosphere, 28 July 1747; P 3:157; Yerkes 405; in Haller 196A and B. The earlier definition is the immediate area around an electrified object that contains the electrical "effluvia" from it (illustrated by the figure at the bottom of the first plate in Franklin's *Experiments and Observations on Electricity* [1751]). Defined at P 4:11, no. 7 and no. 9. Franklin's second definition is the electricity in clouds that can cause thunder and lightning. He suggested the latter definition in his comments on the Lewis Evans map prepared in 1748 (*Life* 2:483) and presented it in his long letter to Kinnersley of 29 April 1749 (P 3:396).

electrical battery, 29 April 1749; P 3:357; Yerkes 405.

electrical fire, 25 May 1747; P 3:127; Yerkes 405; in Collinson to Colden, 30 March 1745.

electrical fluid, 29 July 1750; P 4:10; Yerkes 405.

electrical shock, 29 April 1749; P 3:365; Yerkes 406.

electric blast, 29 June 1751; P 4:144; Yerkes 406.

electric fire, 29 April 1749; P 3:366; Yerkes 406; "this new fire," Haller 194A.

electrician, 29 April 1749; P 3:365; Yerkes 406.

impermeability, 29 June 1755; P 6:98; Yerkes 406.

Leyden bottle, 29 July 1750; P 4:30; Yerkes 407.

Leyden phial, 18 March 1755; P 5:522; Yerkes 407.

minus, 25 May 1747; P 3:131. Online *OED* (2006), *minus* as adjective, "C," cites Franklin from his 1751 pamphlet as earliest usage.

negative, 25 May 1747; P 3:131. Online *OED* (2006), *negative* as adjective, "6a," citing B. Martin 1755 as earliest usage.

non-conductor, 31 October 1751; P 4:203. See *non-electric* (below).

plus, 25 May 1747; P 3:131. Online *OED* (2006), *plus* as "Electr. 1," cites Franklin from his 1751 pamphlet as earliest usage.

positive, 25 May 1747; P 3:131. Online *OED* (2006), *positive* "10 Electr. a" cites B. Martin 1755 as earliest usage.

repellency, 25 May 1747; P 3:127; Yerkes 407.

strike blind, (strike people blind), 29 July 1750; P 4:20; Yerkes 408.

striking distance, 29 July 1750; P 4:19; Yerkes 408.

A FEW COMMON ELECTRICAL TERMS IN 1748

conductor. OED #11. *Physics:* W. Watson, *PT* 43 (1745): 482, note "I call *non-electrics* or Conductors of Electricity those bodies, such as wood, animals living or dead, Metals, etc." Priestley, *History of Electricity* (1775) 1:82, says that Desaguliers "first applied the term *conductor* to that body to which the excited tube conveys its electricity; which term has since been extended to all bodies that are capable of receiving that virtue." See also Heilbron *E* 292n12.

dangling boy. Stephen Gray's popular experiment, ca. 1730, a human being could function as a prime conductor by being suspended with silken ropes and charged with electricity. Heilbron's *E* 247, 293.

electric per se. Priestley defined it as "those bodies in which electricity may be excited by heating or rubbing"; *History of Electricity* (1775) 1:82. Franklin said it should be replaced by *conductor* (31 October 1751; P 4:203).

glass tube. Used by Hauksbee to generate sparks by rubbing.

Leyden jar. In English, news of the "Leyden experiment" and the "Leyden jar" began to appear in the *Gentleman's Magazine* and the *Philosophical Transactions* in 1746.

non-electric. Introduced by Desaguliers in *PT* 41 (1742): 205. The *OED* defined it as "A thing or substance that does not generate static electricity when rubbed." Franklin replaced it with the word *non-conductor* (31 October 1751; P 4:203).

prime conductor. A suspended iron rod hanging by silk ropes. The "dangling boy" experiment used a boy as a prime conductor. Bose, 1743; Heilbron *E* 265.

resinous. 5. Electr. OED = 1742 J. T. Desaguliers, *Diss Electr,* 41 "The Air being electrical of a vitreous Electricity, and sulphur of a resinous Electricity." (The electric charge obtained from amber by rubbing.)

sulphur ball. The ball in Von Guericke's rudimentary electric machine.

suspenders. Non-conducting strings or ropes (especially silk) used to hold a conducting substance. See *prime conductor.*

vitreous electricity. Positive electricity obtained from glass by rubbing. Dufay, *Memoirs, Académie des Sciences* (Paris, 1733), 467–69; Heilbron *E* 257. *OED* lists *PT* 51 (1759): 308.

The Influence of Benjamin Franklin's "Observations Concerning the Increase of Mankind" (1751) on Ezra Stiles, Richard Price, and Adam Smith; on Thomas Malthus; and on Alfred Russel Wallace and Charles Darwin

Scholars have noted the influence of Franklin on Malthus and of Malthus on Darwin, but they usually date the influence on Malthus after he wrote the first edition (1798) of his *Essay on the Principle of Population*. This appendix proves Franklin's influence on Ezra Stiles, Richard Price, and Adam Smith, whose population studies Franklin inspired and who cite Franklin's work. It further proves that through these three sources, Franklin's "Observations Concerning the Increase of Mankind" inspired the basic thesis of the first edition of Malthus's *Essay* (1798). In conclusion, it mentions the key citations showing that Malthus's use of Franklin in turn inspired Wallace and Darwin.

EZRA STILES

Yale's Reverend Ezra Stiles was a friend, disciple, and admirer of Franklin. Inspired by the population data in Franklin's "Observations," Stiles collected additional data for his *Discourse on the Christian Union* (1761). On its title page, Stiles announced "Four thousand British Planters settled in New England, and in 120 Years their Posterity are increased to five hundred thousand."[1] In his version of *translatio religii*, Stiles intended to prove that Congregationalists would increasingly outnumber the Episcopalians, Friends, and Baptists in New England. Stiles sent Franklin at least one copy of the sermon. Stiles added specific population statistics to those in Franklin's "Observations" but advanced no new theories for the rapid increase of colonial America's population.

RICHARD PRICE

Richard Price (1723–91), like Franklin and Joseph Priestley, belonged to the "Club of Honest Whigs" that met at St. Paul's Coffeehouse on Thursday nights from the 1760s to 1775. A precursor of life insurance actuaries, Price sent the first version of his *Observation on Reversionary Payments* to Franklin with a letter of 3 April 1769. He asked Franklin to submit it to the Royal Society for publication if Franklin thought it worthy. He did. It appeared as "Observations on the Expectations of Lives, the Increase of Mankind, the Influence of Great Towns on Population," *PT* 59 (for 1769): 89–125.[2] Price's title, especially the phrase "Increase of Mankind," alludes to

Franklin's "Observations." In the letter itself, Price cites Franklin's figure of the American colonies' population doubling every twenty-five years and Ezra Stiles's estimate of the persons on the frontier doubling every fifteen years. Price repeated the twenty-five-year figure for all the American colonies and predicted that in seventy years, the United States would have twice the number of inhabitants as Great Britain (P 16:103–5). No doubt Franklin had sent Price a copy of Stiles's sermon.

Citing the New Jersey population figures for 1738 and 1745, Price concluded that the colony's population doubled in twenty-two years (10:103–4). Franklin had paid special attention to the New Jersey statistics in *Poor Richard* for 1750 and 1754, and he no doubt supplied Price with both the New Jersey figures and Ezra Stiles's sermon. Price ended the long letter with an extravagant compliment to Franklin. Price's later *Observation on Reversionary Payments*, which contains the earlier letter to Franklin, has notes on the socioeconomic stage theory and on the population of the American colonies—topics also found in Franklin's "Observations."[3] The fundamental statistic on American population cited by both Ezra Stiles and Richard Price was Franklin's observation that the English population in America doubled every twenty-five years.

ADAM SMITH

Previous scholarship showing that Franklin's "Observations" influenced Adam Smith's *Wealth of Nations* (1777) has been inconclusive.[4] Smith met Franklin in Edinburgh in mid-September 1759, and no doubt saw him in Glasgow later that year (one early Smith biographer suggests that Franklin and his son William stayed with Smith).[5] Smith knew Franklin's Scottish friends, David Hume and Lord Kames, very well. Moreover, the Glasgow economist was a close friend of William Strahan (Franklin's best friend during his first mission to England, 1757–62). Smith read Franklin's writings as well as works by others who reflected Franklin, like Richard Jackson, Thomas Pownall, Richard Price, and Joseph Priestley.[6] Smith probably read Franklin's "Observations Concerning the Increase of Mankind" in the *Gentleman's Magazine* in 1755 or in the *Scots Magazine* in 1756, but he also had two copies in his library: one in Franklin's *Interest of Great Britain Considered* (1760), and the other in Franklin's *Experiments and Observations on Electricity* (1769 edition).[7]

Franklin and Smith had many sources in common; therefore, the fact that something in Smith's *Wealth of Nations* appeared previously in Franklin's "Observations" does not prove that Smith echoed Franklin. Nevertheless, I believe that Franklin's "Observations" influenced Smith. I will cite Smith by page and then section number and Franklin similarly. Since Franklin's essay has been discussed in Chapter 7 ("The Fundamental Document of the American Revolution"), I quote it comparatively little.

Various instances in Smith's *Essay* directly mirror Franklin's "Observations." For example, Smith distinguished between the population of "new Colonies" and older settled countries (564–66; IV.vii.b.1–3); Franklin began "Observations" with the same point (4:227, #1). Smith commented that "The wages of labour . . . are much higher in North America than in any part of England" (87; I.viii.22; in P 4:228,

#6). Smith observed that "The liberal reward of labour encourages marriage" (565; IV.vii.b.2; in P 4:227, #2). He wrote: "Compare the slow progress of those European countries of which the wealth depends very much upon their commerce and manufactures, with the rapid advances of our North American colonies, of which the wealth is founded altogether in agriculture" (422–23; III.iv.19; cf. P 4:227, #3). He reflected Franklin's same thesis later: "The plenty and cheapness of good land . . . are the principal causes of the rapid prosperity of new colonies" (573; IV,vii.b. 19).[8]

Like Franklin, Adam Smith commented on the different socioeconomic stages of mankind when considering colonies: "the natives of every part of America, except Mexico and Peru, were only hunters; and the difference is very great between the number of shepherds and that of hunters whom the same extent of equally fertile land can maintain" (634; IV.vii.c.100; and 691; V.1.a.5; cf. P 4:228, #5). Annotating Smith on the socioeconomic stage theory, the editors of *Wealth of Nations* cite Montesquieu, Cantillon, and Sir James Steuart; Smith certainly knew them all, but he also knew Franklin, whose "Observations" more closely dovetails with Smith's train of thought.[9]

Adam Smith said that marriage depended on one's ability to foresee making a living: "The most decisive mark of the prosperity of any country is the increase of the number of its inhabitants." And then Smith echoed Franklin's estimates of population: "In Great Britain, and most other European countries," the population is "not supposed to double in less than five hundred years," but "in the British colonies in North America," the population doubles "in twenty or five-and-twenty years" (87–88, I.viii.23; repeated at 423, III.iv.19). Franklin gave the doubling as twenty years in 4:228, #7, and as twenty-five years in 4:233, #22. Most writers whom Franklin influenced cite the twenty-five-year figure. Smith is the only one I recall who gives *both* Franklin figures. Smith wrote that because Americans had so much land, they were eager to employ laborers and paid them well: "But those liberal wages, joined to the plenty and cheapness of land, soon make those labourers leave him in order to become landlords themselves, and to reward, with equal liberality, other labourers, who soon leave them for the same reason that they left their first master. The liberal reward of labour encourages marriage" (565; IV.vii.b.2; cf. P 4:228–29, #8, and 4:227, #2).

Smith wrote: "To prohibit a great people . . . from making all that they can of every part of their own produce, or from employing their stock and industry in the way that they judge most advantageous to themselves, is a manifest violation of the most sacred rights of mankind." Smith nevertheless claimed that America's economy had fared well: "Unjust, however, as such prohibitions may be, they have not hitherto been very hurtful to the colonies. Land is still so cheap, and consequently, labour so dear among them, that they can import from the mother country, almost all the more refined or more advanced manufactures cheaper than they could make them for themselves." Smith condemned the Acts of Trade and Navigation: "those prohibitions . . . are only impertinent badges of slavery imposed upon them, without any sufficient reason, by the groundless jealousy of the merchants and manufacturers of the mother country" (582; IV.vii.b.44). These statements show that Smith is more direct than Franklin in "Observations," who primarily tried to convince his English readers that Americans could not compete with them in manufacturing (P 4:229, #9, also #10, #11). But Franklin wrote dozens of pieces in the English press between 1751 and 1776 against the Acts of Trade and Navigation: for example, Franklin's letters to Governor Shirley written at the end of 1754 appeared in the *London Chronicle*, 8 February 1766, and were reprinted several times (P 5:443–47, 449–51, 13:118–20). Though most of Franklin's objections to the Acts of Trade and Navigation were relatively muted, Smith must have read many of them between 1760 and 1775.

America, Smith claimed, opened a new market for the manufactured goods of Europe: "In new colonies, agriculture either draws hands from all other employments, or keeps them from going to any other employment. There are few hands to spare for the necessary, and none for the ornamental manufactures. The greater part of the manufactures of both kinds, they find it cheaper to purchase of other countries than to make for themselves. It is chiefly by encouraging the manufactures of Europe, that the colony trade indirectly encourages its agriculture. . . . The manufacturers of Europe, to whom that trade gives employment, constitute a new market for the produce of the land; . . . the home market [for agricultural products] . . . is thus greatly extended by means of the trade to America" (609; IV.vii.c.51). Smith argued that the colonization of America has resulted "in the augmentation of its [Europe's] industry" (591; IV.vii.c.4). All countries that trade to America directly and indirectly have "gained a more extensive market for their surplus produce, and must consequently have been encouraged to increase its quantity" (591; IV.vii.c.6). Most, but not all, earlier writers on trade had said that America drained Britain of its wealth, resources, and people, but Franklin had contradicted them, briefly in a *Modest Enquiry* (1729) and forcefully in "Observations." Smith agreed with Franklin, who claimed that "in Proportion to the Increase of the Colonies, a vast Demand is growing for British Manufactures, a glorious Market wholly in the Power of Britain, in which Foreigners cannot interfere, which will increase in a short Time even beyond her Power of supplying, tho' her whole Trade should be to her Colonies: Therefore Britain should not too much restrain Manufactures in her Colonies. A wise and good Mother will not do it. To distress, is to weaken, and weakening the Children, weakens the whole Family" (P 4:229, #10). Franklin's opinions on the colonial trade were well-known when Smith wrote the *Wealth of Nations*.

Smith said that slaves were "commonly managed by a negligent master or careless overseer" and did not manifest "the strict frugality and parsimonious attention" of poor whites. Smith consequently found that "the work done by freemen comes cheaper in the end than that performed by slaves," and claimed that it was even true in Boston, New York, and Philadelphia, "where the wages of common labour are so very high" (99; I.viii.41; cf. P 4:229, #12). In *Lectures on Jurisprudence*, Smith was even closer to Franklin's statement: "the advantage gained by the labours of the slaves, if we deduce their originall cost and the expence of their maintenance, will not be so great as that which is gain'd from free tenants."[10]

In addition to the availability of good land, the "liberty to manage their own affairs" in their own way was, wrote Smith, a major cause of "the prosperity of all new colonies" (572, IV.vii.b.16). He added that the "political institutions of the English colonies have been more favourable" than those of France, Spain, or Portugal (572; IV.vii.b.17; cf. P 4:230, #13). Smith also wrote that "in consequence of the moderation" of taxes in the English colonies, the citizens have been better able to support themselves and to increase in number (573; IV.vii.b.20; cf. P 4:230, #13).

Of taxes, Smith wrote: "Upon the sober and industrious poor, taxes upon such commodities [superfluities] act as sumptuary laws, and dispose them either to moderate, or to refrain altogether from the use of superfluities which they can no longer easily afford." Smith thought such taxes were generally good (872; V.ii.k.7; also 894–96). Here Smith echoed Hume as well as Franklin (P 4:232, #17). Hume's "Of Taxes" (published in 1752, so neither Franklin nor Hume could have influenced the other), said "the best taxes are such as are levied upon consumptions, especially those of luxury. . . . They naturally produce sobriety and frugality, if judiciously imposed."[11] Smith believed that "Small property holders view their holdings with "affection," take pleasure "not only in cultivating but in adorning it," and are "generally of all improvers the most industrious, the most intelligent, and the most successful." Like Franklin, Smith repeatedly turned to the availability of land as key to prosperity: "In North America . . . the purchase and improvement of uncultivated land, is there the most profitable employment . . . and the most direct road to . . . fortune" (423–24; III.iv.19). Franklin, too, had introduced cultural/psychological reasons into "Observations" (P 4:232, #19).

Both Smith and Franklin stated that the present rate of increase of population in North America was not "owing to the continual importation of new inhabitants, but to the great multiplication of the species" (88; I.viii.23; cf. P 4:232–23, #21). Like Franklin, Smith wrote, "Every species of animals naturally multiplies in proportion to the means of their subsistence, and no species can ever multiply beyond it" (97; I viii.39; cf. P 4:233, #22, #23). As in Franklin, the thought has a Hobbesian, even Malthusian, note. What happens when one reaches the limit of subsistence?

Adam Smith predicted that the future center of the British Empire would be in America: "Such has hitherto been the rapid progress of that country in wealth, population and improvement, that in the course of little more than a century, perhaps, the produce of America might exceed that of British taxation. The seat of empire would then naturally remove itself to that part of the empire which contributed most to the general defence and support of the whole" (625–26; IV.vii.c.79). Franklin had implied that, because of the increase of American population and the size of America, it would become more populous and powerful than the British Empire (P 4:233, #22), but he did not say it as directly in 1751 as Smith did in 1776.

The most convincing bit of evidence that Smith directly used Franklin's "Observations" is his citation of Franklin's two different rates of growth of the American colonies. Even without it, the evidence proves beyond a reasonable doubt that when Smith wrote of the increase of the colonial American population, he was indebted to Franklin.

Thomas Robert Malthus

Thomas R. Malthus cited Franklin a number of times in the second edition, 1803 (followed by later editions), of *Essay on the Principle of Population*, but in the preface to the 1803 edition, Malthus said that he had not read Franklin's "Observations" when he originally published the *Essay* in 1798. Therefore, I. Bernard Cohen and many other scholars have thought that Malthus only used Franklin to "bolster an argument which Malthus had already made."¹² Malthus acknowledged, however, that the Reverend Ezra Stiles, Dr. Richard Price, and Adam Smith influenced the first edition.¹³ As I have shown, all three read and reflected Franklin's "Observations." All three cite Franklin's figure for the population of America doubling every twenty-five years. From these three sources, Malthus gave the same figure in chapter 1 of his first edition (p. 20) and commented on the next page that the population of America, "when unchecked, goes on doubling itself every twenty-five years, or increases in a geometrical ratio." In chapter 2, p. 37, he gave Franklin's observation that "population does invariably increase, where there are the means of subsistence."¹⁴

Malthus began the first edition of chapter 3 (39–40) with a discussion of the socioeconomic stage theory of civilization, similar to that in Franklin, Smith, and Price. He later observed that the population of the American Indian "is thin from the scarcity of food" and that the second stage cannot support as many people as farming (39–40, 45–46). Both Franklin and Smith, among others, made the same remark. In chapter 4, he wrote that "population constantly bears a regular proportion to the food that the earth is made to produce" (55)—a basic Franklin thesis, repeated by Smith. In chapter 6, Malthus cited Ezra Stiles's statistics from Richard Price, and generalized that the growth of population in America "was a rapidity of increase, probably without parallel in history" and again stated that the population in America doubles every twenty-five years (105). He questioned why it did not do so in England, and answered, "the want of room and food" (109)—the fundamental factors given by Franklin for the increase of population, which Price and Smith repeated. In chapter 10, he again cited Stiles from Price, saying that in the "back country" of America, the population has doubled every fifteen years, but then he returned to the American population doubling every twenty-five years (185–86).

No doubt other persons after Franklin would have come up with the twenty-five-year geometrical rate of increase, but Franklin made the observation first and the persons read by Malthus copied Franklin's data. After the publication of his first edition, Malthus read Franklin, and in his second and all subsequent editions, Malthus emphasized his statement that the availability of land and a sufficient food supply were the greatest encouragement to population (in 1803, 1:293; in 1798, 27), just as Franklin and Adam Smith did earlier (P 4:227–28, #2, #4, #6). Malthus also pointed out that hunting and gathering food required an enormous amount of land, which agriculture did not (1803, 1:30; 1798, 43–46). Franklin, Price, and Smith had similarly argued the economic stage theory of civilization before him (P 4:228, #5). Though Malthus made these points, he need not have been even indirectly influenced by Franklin. But in his "General Deductions," Malthus twice echoed Franklin's "Observations": "The only true criterion of a real and permanent increase in the population of any country is the increase of the means of subsistence," and "in America . . . the reward of labour is at present so liberal" (1803, 1:302; 1798, 27; cf. P 4:233, #22; and 4:228, #6, #8). Malthus may not have read these opinions in Franklin but had read them in Richard Price and Adam Smith before writing the first edition of his *Essay*. He also read them in Franklin's "Observations" before writing the second edition.[15]

Patricia James, the editor of the best annotated edition of Malthus's *Essay*, said that Franklin's short essay prefigured "the gist of Malthus's principle of population" (2:285). A recent demographer wrote that the growth of the American population as reported by Richard Price "became the primary piece of empirical evidence cited by Malthus in support of his belief that population would increase geometrically in the presence of benevolent political institutions and abundant fertile land that together held at bay the great checks of misery and vice."[16] Just a few paragraphs into the first chapter of the second and the later editions of his *Essay*, Malthus wrote: "It is observed by Dr. Franklin that there is no bound to the prolific nature of plants or animals but what is made by their crowding and interfering with each other's means of subsistence. Were the face of the earth, he says, vacant of other plants, it might be gradually sowed and overspread with one kind only; as, for instance, with fennel: and were it empty of other inhabitants, it might in a few ages be replenished from one nation only; as, for instance, with Englishmen." Malthus commented that Franklin's observation was "incontrovertibly true"[17] and then went on to discuss its implications.

I conclude that, through Stiles, Price, and Smith, Franklin provided Malthus with key statistics and generalizations for his first edition, and that after he read Franklin, Malthus acknowledged Franklin's data and reasoning as a foundation of his *Essay on the Principle of Population* (1803).

Alfred Russel Wallace and Charles Darwin

Wallace and Darwin came up with the theory of natural selection at about the same time and independently of one another. Though the theory of natural selection had many antecedents, both Wallace and Darwin identified Thomas Malthus as the primary single influence on their thinking. Alfred Russel Wallace testified in his autobiography that Malthus inspired his theory that "the best fitted live." He had read Malthus as a young man and wrote that "Its main principles remained with me as a permanent possession, and twenty years later gave me the long-sought clue to the effective agent in the evolution of organic species." He also said that if he had never read Malthus, "I should probably not have hit upon the theory of natural selection and obtained full credit for its independent discovery."[18]

Charles Darwin knew that Franklin was a good friend of both his grandfathers, Josiah Edgewood and Erasmus Darwin, and of his father, Robert Waring Darwin. In his short biography of Erasmus Darwin, Charles Darwin quoted a snippet from a letter by Erasmus to Franklin. Neither Darwin nor Wallace, however, directly quoted from Franklin's demographic treatise, though Darwin cited from Malthus Franklin's figure of the doubling of population in the United States every twenty-five years.[19]

Darwin described the most important influence on the origin of his theory of natural selection in his *Autobiography*: "In October 1838, that is, fifteen months after I had begun my systematic enquiry, I happened to read for amusement Malthus on *Population*, and being well prepared to appreciate the struggle for existence which everywhere goes on from long-continued observation of the habits of animals and plants, it at once struck me that under these circumstances favourable variations would tend to be preserved, and unfavourable ones to be destroyed. The result of this would be the formation of new species. Here then I had at last got a theory by which to work."[20] Darwin again credited Malthus with the fundamental insight that he applied to natural selection in his *Variation of Plants and Animals*. After studying the plants and animals on the Galapagos Archipelago, Darwin wrote, "it long remained to me an inexplicable problem how the necessary degree of modification could have been effected, and it would have thus remained for ever, had I not studied domestic productions, and thus acquired a just idea of the power of selection. As soon as I had fully realized this idea, I saw, on reading Malthus on population, that Natural Selection was the inevitable result of the rapid increase of all organic beings."[21]

In one passage of his *Descent of Man*, Darwin echoed Malthus echoing Franklin: "Civilized populations have been known under favourable conditions, as in the United States, to double their numbers in twenty-five years. . . . The present population of the United States (thirty millions), would in 657 years cover the whole terraqueous globe so thickly, that four men would have to stand on each square yard of surface. The primary or fundamental check to the continued increase of man is the difficulty of gaining subsistence, and of living in comfort. We may infer that this is the case from what we see, for instance, in the United States, where subsistence is easy, and there is plenty of room."[22] Since Darwin himself cited Malthus as his primary inspiration, all writers on Darwin's inspiration at least mention Malthus. To give one example, Silvan S. Schweber emphasizes that Malthus's "*quantitative mathematical*" scheme of the American population doubling every twenty-five years "crystallized various aspects of his formulation and helped fit the separate elements into a coherent whole."[23]

I conclude that Franklin's 1751 "Observations Concerning the Increase of Mankind, Peopling of Cities, etc." influenced Ezra Stiles's *Discourse on the Christian Union* (1761), Richard Price's *Observations on Reversionary Payments* (1771), and Adam Smith's *Wealth of Nations* (1776); from these, it became an inspiration for Thomas Malthus's *Essay on the Principle of Population* (1797 [indirectly], 1803 [directly] and all later editions); and through Malthus, it influenced Alfred Russel Wallace and Charles Darwin's theory of natural selection.

APPENDIX 5. *Franklin's Plan of Union and the Albany Plan*

The Albany Plan of Union was the fourth version of a plan that Franklin had suggested in 1751. The first two were entirely his creation. He drew up the third and fourth at the Albany Conference in the summer of 1754, incorporating the suggestions of others on the committee appointed to formulate a plan of union. This appendix analyzes the differences between the four versions and assesses Franklin's role in the Albany Plan.

The four versions are: (1) the 1751 sketch in a letter addressed to James Parker, 20 March 1750/1 (4:117–19); (2) the 8 June 1754 "Short Hints towards a Scheme for Uniting the Northern Colonies" (5:337–38); (3) the Albany Conference document of 28 June 1754, "Short Hints towards a Scheme for a General Union of the British Colonies on the Continent" (5:361–64); and (4) the Albany Plan, written by Franklin on the afternoon of 9 July 1754 (5:387–92), though it may have been slightly revised on 10 August. The last document incorporated the positions the union committee agreed on.[1] The texts of the first, second, and fourth versions are reliable, but the 28 June document, evidently written on the afternoon of 28 July by the New Hampshire delegate to the union committee, Meshech Weare (1713–85), is less so. One difference between Franklin's first two versions is the seven-part structure that he imposed on the 8 June text (# 2). The 28 June document (# 3) probably had a similar structure, though the unique and careless copy that survives only lists the last three sections under separate headings. Its title and overall structure, however, are close to those of the 8 June document.

To compare the four, I take the headings from the 8 June document, quote the pertinent passage from # 1, 2, and 3, note the differences and similarities between them, and contrast them with # 4, the Albany Plan. Each section judges whether the Albany Plan merely amplified or substantively changed the first three versions. Before taking up the seven headings, I discuss the title, preamble, and a remark on the separate colonies, none of which is included within the seven headings.

For the 1751 sketch, the words "Union of the Colonies" (4:117) are present but not as a title. The title of the 8 June document (# 2) is "Short Hints towards a Scheme for Uniting the Northern Colonies" (5:337), and in the 28 June piece (# 3), "Short Hints towards a Scheme for a General Union of the British Colonies on the Continent" (5:361).

The title of the second document suggests that Franklin was limiting the plan of union to the colonies that would be present at the Albany Conference. The other two suggest that he intended to include all the colonies. I suspect that in the second document, which Franklin gave to friends in New York for their suggestions, he was merely being modest. During the Albany debates on the plan of union, he opposed schemes that would make the union less than inclusive of all the well-established colonies. He argued that "by the frequent meetings-together of commissioners or representatives from all the colonies, the circumstances of the whole would be better known, and the good of the whole better provided for; and that the colonies would by this connection learn to consider themselves, not as so many independent states, but as members of the same body" (5:401–2).[2]

The Albany Plan was titled "Plan of a Proposed Union of the Several Colonies of Massachusetts-bay, New Hampshire, Coneticut, Rhode Island, New York, New Jersey, Pensilvania, Maryland, Virginia, North Carolina, and South Carolina, For their Mutual Defence and Security, and for Extending the British Settlements in North America" (5:387). In contrast to the previous three titles, the Albany Plan specified which colonies would be included. Delaware, Georgia, and Nova Scotia were omitted. Delaware had its own legislature but shared the same governor and council with Pennsylvania. Governor James Hamilton had not appointed commissioners from Delaware, perhaps thinking that Pennsylvania's commissioners were also representing it or that, since Delaware was in no danger from enemy Indians, it would not care to spend money attending a treaty. Assuming that Pennsylvania's representation included Delaware, Franklin wrote to Cadwallader Colden three days after the conclusion of the Albany Plan that the commissioners had agreed on a union of the colonies, "from N Hampshire to So. Carolina inclusive" (5:393). Georgia and Nova Scotia had small populations, and Parliament supported them. Presumably they would be included in the union when they became populous and self-sufficient.

The Albany Plan's title specified that its purpose was for "Mutual Defence and Security" (the assumed though unspecified purpose of the earlier three documents) and for extending "the British Settlements in North America." The latter was new only in the title, for Franklin's 8 June document (#2) said that a duty and power of the "Governor General and Grand Council" was to "make and support new settlements" (5:338). In one or more of the debates on the proposed plan, Franklin probably argued that settling future colonies should be planned and deliberate, not just the inadvertent result of individuals moving into the frontier. Both the rival land negotiations between Connecticut and Pennsylvania during the Albany Conference and the rival settlements of Virginia companies and Pennsylvanians in the Ohio country from 1748 to 1754 demonstrated the desirability, even the necessity, of a unified approach to colonial expansion. Thus, in the title and its implications, the Albany Plan merely amplifies Franklin's earlier proposals.

The preamble to the 28 June document (# 3) sets forth the necessity of balancing the prerogative of the crown and the liberties of the people: "In Such a Scheme the Just Prerogative of the Crown must be preserved or it will not be Approved and Confirmed in England. The Just liberties of the People must be Secured or the Several Colonies will Disapprove of it and Oppose it. Yet Some Prerogative may be abated to Extend Dominion and Increase Subjects and Some Liberty to Obtain Safety" (5:361). Though the rationale does not appear in the two earlier plans or in the Albany Plan itself, they all attempt to balance a central prerogative power and the existing liberties of the various colonies. I speculate that Franklin spelled out the reason for compromise to try to convince other members of the union committee that concessions were necessary. In the *Autobiography*, Franklin blamed the plan's failure on the unwillingness of either the British authorities or the colonies to compromise: "The Assemblies did not adopt it, as they all thought there was too much *Prerogative* in it; and in England it was judg'd to have too much of the Democratic" (A 131).

I conclude that although Franklin specified the compromise between British prerogative and colonial rights in the third document, he implied it in #1, 2, and 4.

The 28 June text (# 3) specified a federalist structure in which the colonies would retain their individual constitutions: "Suppose then that One General Government be formd Including all the Brittish Dominions on the Continent Within and Under which Government the Several Colonies may Each Enjoy its own Constitution Laws Liberties and Priviledges as so many Separate Corporations in one Common Wealth" (5:361). The Albany Plan, which specified that the military and civil establishments of each colony would "remain in their present State, this General Constitution Notwithstanding" (5:392), repeated the same statement. In the 8 and 28 June texts (# 1 and 2), Franklin no doubt assumed that the colonies would keep their own charters and would function in their wonted ways, only superimposing a unified government for defense and expansion. He knew that the colonies would not want a drastic change. Nevertheless, some commissioners, especially the Connecticut representatives, thought that the president-general was given too much power. That was part of their reason for rejecting the Albany Plan.[3] Thus, the version of "states' rights"/federalism specified in the latter two versions are also in the first two.

THE GOVERNOR GENERAL

The 1751 sketch (# 1) said, "A general Governor appointed by the Crown to preside in that Council, or in some Manner to concur with and confirm their Acts, and take Care of the Execution" (4:119). The 8 June 1754 (# 2) text said, "A Governor General To be appointed by the King, To be a Military man, To have a Salary from the Crown, To have a negation on all acts of the Grand Council, and carry into execution what ever is agreed on by him and that Council" (5:337). The 28 June 1754 (# 3) text said, "A President General to be appointed by the Crown to Receive his Salary from Home. His assent to Render valid all Acts of the Grand Councill. His Duty to Carry them into Execution" (5:361).

The difference between the titles "Governor-General" and "President-General" seems minor. To the first document, Franklin added in the second that the governor-general should be a military man and have a salary from the crown. The first document, however, more specifically than the second, charged the governor-general with the "execution" of the decisions of the Grand Council. The third document reaffirmed the previous two statements (only putting the negative on all acts in a positive manner) but dropped the second document's requirement that the governor-general be a military man. The Albany Plan said the appointment and support of the "President-General" is the same as that in the second document, though the Albany Plan added that in case of the death of the president-general, the Speaker of the Grand Council would assume the same position "until the King's Pleasure be known" (5:387, 389, 391). The addition is a common-sense supplement.

Since the supposed primary purpose of the union was defense, Franklin may have thought the governor-general should be a military man, but he would hardly have been committed to that position. He knew that the most successful military expedition in recent American history had been the conquest of Louisbourg in 1745: Massachusetts governor William Shirley instigated it and militia general William Pepperrell, whom the British would not have considered a "military man,"carried it out. Dropping the "military man" requirement may have been suggested by someone else at the Albany Conference, but Franklin would readily have agreed.

Grand Council

The 1751 sketch said, "Each Colony should be represented by as many Members as it pays Sums of [blank] Hundred Pounds into the common Treasury for the common Expence" (4:119). The 8 June text (# 2) said "One member to be chosen by the Assembly of each of the smaller Colonies and two or more by each of the larger, in proportion to the Sums they pay Yearly into the General Treasury" (5:337). The 28 June text (# 3) said, "To this End Suppose there be a Grand Council to Consist of two members at least Chosen by the Representatives of each Colony in Assembly. The larger Colonies to Choose more in Some Proportion to the Sums they Yearly Contribute to the General Treasury. The Elections may be every three years and the members of each Colony to Continue till a new Choice. Assemblies to be Called for that purpose in each Colony once in three years in the month of May" (5:361).

Though similar to the 1751 sketch, the 8 June draft makes certain that every colony is included in the common treasury. It also says that the colonies would choose the members of the Grand Council. The 28 June text (# 3) requires that each colony have at least two members and adds the term of service: members were to be elected in May for three-year terms. That the colonial assemblies would choose the members of the Grand Council makes sense; otherwise, a separate popular election (which required more time and money) would have to be held.

The election of the "Grand Council" members by the assemblies of each colony is the same as in the Albany Plan (5:387) in # 2 and 3. The number of delegates from each colony is now specified, with New Hampshire and Rhode Island each having the minimum two representatives. After three years, the representatives chosen will be in proportion to the amount of money given (as in the first three documents above), though with every colony having at least two members (as in the third document) and none more than seven members. The length of the term of election, three years, is the same as in the third document (5:388). In addition, the Albany Plan added that in case of the death or resignation of a member, his successor would be elected "at the next Sitting of the Assembly of the Colony he represented" (5:388).

The 28 June version (# 3) indicated at its end that the question of a quorum should be decided. The Albany Plan usefully spelled out what would constitute a quorum: twenty-five members, "among whom there shall be one, or more from a Majority of the Colonies" (5:391). The Albany Plan added the desirability that the laws should be "as near as may be agreeable to the Laws of England" (a standard statement in colonial laws, no doubt silently assumed in the earlier plans). The laws must be submitted to the king in council "for Approbation, as Soon as may be after their Passing and if not disapproved within Three years after Presentation to remain in Force." All the colonies except Connecticut, Rhode Island, and Maryland required approval of the laws by the British authorities. Without this clause subjecting the unified colonial government to Britain, Franklin knew that not even America's best friends in England would have considered creating a union of the colonies. The editors of the *Papers of Benjamin Franklin* pointed out that the transmittal to England ("as soon as may be") and the time specified for the king's approval followed the Massachusetts charter of 1691 and therefore suggested that Thomas Hutchinson supplied the schedule (5:391n3). Though Franklin would have known the Massachusetts requirements, I suspect that he knew the 1754 Board of Trade would have regarded the Pennsylvania arrangement (five years to report the law but only six months for the Privy Council to act) as too liberal. Thus, the Albany Plan's additions usefully spell out details but do not essentially alter the earlier substance.

Members Pay

Not in Franklin's 1751 letter. His 8 June plan has "[blank] Shillings sterling per Diem during their sitting and mileage for Travelling Expences" (5:338). The 28 June text has: "Members Pay ten shillings Sterling per Diem. During their Siting and Journey twenty miles to be Reckond a Days Journey" (5:362). Though omitted from the 1751 statement, pay was expected by members of colonial assemblies, and Franklin included the fact, though not the sum in the 8 June document (# 2). (The Pennsylvania Assembly paid six shillings per diem, Pennsylvania currency.) Rough roads and ferry crossings slowed one down, but twenty miles a day seems almost leisurely. The Albany Plan (5:389) was identical to the 28 June text (# 3). Thus, the latter two versions merely explain payments implied in the earlier ones.

Place and Time of Meeting

Franklin's 1751 letter said, "Perhaps if the Council were to meet successively at the Capitals of the several Colonies, they might thereby become better acquainted with the Circumstances, Interests, Strength or Weakness, &c. of all, and thence be able to judge better of Measures propos'd from time to time: At least it might be more satisfactory to the Colonies, if this were propos'd as a Part of the Scheme, for a Preference might create Jealousy and Dislike" (4:119). The 8 June (# 2) proposal: "To meet——times in every Year, at the Capital of each Colony in Course, unless particular circumstances and emergencies require more frequent meetings and Alteration in the Course, of places. The Governour General to Judge of those circumstances &c. and call by his Writts" (5:338). The 28 June (# 3) version: "Meetings of the Grand Councill once in every year And at Such other times As the President General shall think proper to Call them having first been Applied to or obtained the Consent in writing of Seven of the Members for that purpose. At any annual Meeting the Councill to Determine where the next meeting is to be, to Sit by their own adjournments not Subject to Prorogations or Dissolutions by the President General without their own Consent. No Sessions to Continue longer than Six weeks without the Consent of the Councill" (5:361–62).

The 1751 text gives a rationale for different meeting places, and the 8 June text agrees and may suggest normally meeting more than once a year. The 28 June text avoids the question of where to meet. In addition, the two June 1754 texts allow for the governor-general to call a council meeting, just as the governor of Pennsylvania could call a meeting of the Pennsylvania legislature.

The Albany Plan is similar to the 28 June text, but the first meeting is to be held at Philadelphia, with no mention of the venues of succeeding meetings (5:388, 388–89). The Albany Plan also specified that the "Grand Council" would choose its own Speaker, though the earlier versions no doubt assumed it would. The president general's calling a meeting upon an emergency was in the 8 June text, and the annual meeting and its duration (no longer than six weeks) was similar to that in the 28 June text. The ability to "sit by their own adjournments not Subject to Prorogations or Dissolutions by the President General" was an addition to the previous drafts. Since it was a privilege the Pennsylvania Assembly enjoyed, Franklin may have intended to insert it in any formal plan and was probably responsible for its addition.

Except for the place of meeting, the Albany Plan followed Franklin's earlier three plans. The commissioners present at Albany evidently did not want to meet south of Philadelphia. Franklin later called for different places of meeting in his 1775 "Proposed Articles of Confederation" (22:122); therefore he was presumably outvoted at Albany.

General Treasury

The 1751 text read, "Which Treasury would perhaps be best and most equitably supply'd, by an equal Excise on strong Liquors in all the Colonies, the Produce never to be apply'd to the private Use of any Colony, but to the general Service" (4:119). The 8 June text (# 2) read, "Its Fund, an Excise on Strong Liquors pretty equally drank in the Colonies or Duty on Liquor imported, or——shillings on each Licence of Publick House or Excise on Superfluities as Tea &c. &c. all which would pay in some proportion to the present wealth of each Colony, and encrease as that wealth encreases, and prevent disputes about the Inequality of Quotas. To be Collected in each Colony, and Lodged in their Treasury to be ready for the payment of Orders issuing from the Governour General and Grand Council jointly" (5:338). The 28 June text (# 3) read, "It is a difficult Matter to fix Quotas to be paid by each Colony that would be Equal to the ability of Each, or if Really Equal to Perswade the Colonys to think so or if Equal now that would long Continue so Some Colonies Growing faster than Others. Therefore Let the Money arise from somewhat that may be nearly proportionable to Each Colony and Grow with it, Such as from Excise upon Liquors Retailed or Stamps on all Legal Writings Writs &c. or both to be Collected in Each Province and Paid to a Treasurer to be Appointed in each Colony by the Grand Councill to be Ready on Orders from the President General and Grand Councill.

. . . "Their Accompt to be yearly Settled and Reported to the Several Assemblies of each Colony" (5:362).

All three are concerned with an "equitable" way of raising money and suggest a tax on liquor, but the 8 June text (# 2) adds the possibility of taxes on licensing taverns, coffeeshops, and so forth, and "superfluities" such as tea, while the 28 June text (# 3) adds a tax on "stamps on all Legal Writings." It also specified that the °accounts should be reported and settled annually, which was routine in Pennsylvania and other colonies. It had an explanatory preamble not dissimilar to its introductory preamble, stressing the need for ensuring that the tax would not bear harder on one colony than on others. It added other possibilities to Franklin's suggestion in the 1751 text for a tax on liquor and in the 8 June text (# 2) for other "superfluities." One major difference in the 28 June text (# 3) is that the Grand Council would appoint a treasurer in each colony; in the earlier versions, the colonial treasurers of the individual colonies would serve.

In contrast to the earlier three texts, the Albany Plan was vague about taxes, merely saying that the council would have the "Power to make Laws And lay and Levy such General Duties, Imposts, or Taxes, as to them shall appear most equal and Just." It echoed Franklin's opinion that the taxes should "rather discourage Luxury, than Loading Industry with unnecessary Burthens" (5:390). The Albany Plan spelled out the addition in the 28 June text (#3) concerning the treasurer: the council "may Appoint a General Treasurer and a Particular Treasurer in each Government, when Necessary." The change continued the tendency introduced in that text to unify the collection of funds and to make it more efficient. In addition, the Albany Plan spelled out safeguards that Franklin probably assumed in his earlier drafts: no money was to be dispersed without the "joint Orders of the President General and Grand Council Except where Sums have been Appropriated to particular Purposes, And the President General is previously impowered By an Act to draw for such Sums" (5:390–91).

Evidently, the Albany commissioners could not agree on what to tax. Unwilling to give up their existing liquor taxes or to specify any other tax, they nevertheless paid lip service to Franklin's view that only luxuries should be taxed. Twenty-one years later, Franklin's 1775 "Proposed Articles of Confederation" said that each colony should be taxed "in proportion" to its population but it, too, evaded the question of what to tax by saying that taxes should be "laid and levied by the Laws of each Colony" (22:123).

Duty and Power of the Governor-General and Grand Council

The 1751 sketchbook said, "Every Thing relating to Indian Affairs and the Defence of the Colonies, might be properly put under their Management" (4:119). The 8 June text (#2) read, "To order all Indian Treaties.——make all Indian purchases not within proprietary Grants——make and support new settlements by building Forts, raising and paying Soldiers to Garison the Forts, defend the frontiers and annoy the Ennemy.——equip Grand Vessels to scour the Coasts from Privateers in time of war, and protect the Trade——and every thing that shall be found necessary for the defence and support of the Colonies in General, and encreasing and extending their settlements &c. For the Expence they may draw on the fund in the Treasury of any Colony" (5:338). The 28 June text (# 3) "To hold or order all Indian Treaties, Regulate all Indian Trade, make Peace and Declare war with the Indian Nations, Make all Indian Purchases of Lands not Within the Bounds of Perticuler Colonies, Make new Settlements on Such Purchases by Granting Lands Reserving a Rent for the General Treasury Raise and Pay Soldiers and build forts to Defend the frontiers of Any of the Colonies, Equip Guardships to Scour and Protect the Coasts from Privateers and Pyrates, Appoint all Military officers that are to Act Under the General Command, the President General to Nominate and the Councill to approve. But all Collectors or farmers of the Duties Excise &c. for the General Treasury and other Civil officers necessary, are to be Chosen by the Grand Councill And Approved by the President General. They shall not Impress men in any Colony without the Consent of its Legislature. Acts or Laws made by them to Regulate Indian Trade or new Settlements of Lands to be Sent home to the King and Councill for approbation within blank months. They may Draw on the General Fund in any Colony for Defraying all General Expences. Their Accompt to be Yearly Settled and Reported to the Several Assemblies of Each Colony, Each Colony may Defend it Self on any Emergency. The Accompts of Expence to be laid before the Grand Councill and Paid as far as Reasonable" (5:362–63).

The two June texts included support for "encreasing and extending" the settlements. The 28 June text added that the council will make "all Indian Purchases of Lands not Within the Bounds of Perticuler Colonies," which protected the interest of the existing colonies (except those whose charters went from the Atlantic to the Pacific). A new provision in this text was the idea of raising money from the new settlements by "Reserving a Rent for the General Treasury." A difference in this text is that the treasury was to be centralized, whereas it would exist separately in each colony in the 8 June text. Franklin's 1751 letter said nothing about impressment. Since he objected to impressment, it's surprising that the 28 June text would allow it—even with the permission of the local legislature.[4]

The Albany Plan changed "Reserving a Rent" derived from new settlements to granting "Lands in the Kings Name, reserving a Quit Rent to the Crown, for the use of the General Treasury." Making and supporting new settlements was part of the June texts, but the Albany Plan added that the Grand Council would "make Laws for regulating and Governing . . . new Settlements, till the Crown shall think fit to form them into Particular Governments" (5:390).[5] The Albany Plan specified that the president-general was to nominate all military officers but that they needed the approbation of the Grand Council, and that the Grand Council was to nominate all civil officers but that they needed the approbation of the president-general. The balance of prerogative and democratic has Franklin's earmarks. In case of vacancies among the military or civil officers, the governor of the province could appoint the replacement until "the Pleasure of the President General and the Grand Council can be known" (5:392).

Finally, as in the 28 June version (# 3), the Albany Plan said that any colony could defend itself in an emergency and later submit the expenses to the president-general and Grand Council "who may allow and order payment of the same As far as they Judge such Accounts Just and reasonable" (5:392).

I conclude that the Albany Plan usefully supplemented Franklin's first two texts but did not substantially change them. It evaded the question, as did Franklin's versions, of the boundaries of the colonies whose charters went from sea to sea. It continued to forbid impressment without the consent of the colony's legislature (# 3).[6]

Manner of forming this Union

The 1751 text read, "A voluntary Union entered into by the Colonies themselves, I think, would be preferable to one impos'd by Parliament; for it would be perhaps not much more difficult to procure, and more easy to alter and improve, as Circumstances should require, and Experience direct" (4:119). The 8 June text (# 2) read, "The scheme being first well considered corrected and improved by the Commissioners at Albany, to be sent home, and an Act of Parliament obtain'd for establishing it" (5:338). The 28 June text (# 3) read, "When the Scheme is well Considered Corrected and Improved a Temporary Act of Parliament to be Obtained for Establishing of it" (5:363).

Franklin changed his mind between the writing of the first two texts. He had learned that a voluntary union was impractical. The colonies whose frontiers were not immediately threatened (e.g., New Jersey) and those that were far away from Albany did not support a war effort against the French and Indians and did not bother to send delegates to the Albany Conference. The later June text repeated the earlier one, except for the key word *temporary*. Does that mean that the union would cease when and if the threat from the French and Indians ceased? Or does it mean that the act would be temporary until all the affected colonies approved it? Colonial legislation was usually passed for a limited period, but a good act could be renewed comparatively easily. Perhaps Franklin included the word *temporary* to reassure those who had doubts that the act would be reviewed in five or so years.[7]

The Albany Plan says nothing about the manner of forming the union. However, as I pointed out in discussing the plan, the Albany commissioners resolved on 10 July: "That the Commissioners from the several Governments be desired to lay the same before their respective Constituents for their Consideration, and that the Secretary to this Board transmit a Copy with this Vote thereon to the Governor of each of the Colonies which have not sent their Commissioners to this Congress."[8] The Albany Plan asked for the different colonies to consider the plan and to send on their revised versions to Parliament. No colony did.

The Albany Plan did not agree on a way to form the union, nor did it ask Parliament to form it. The lack of clear direction concerning the "manner of forming the union," as well as the failure to agree on how to finance the union, indicated that the plan was doomed.

3 Postscripts

At the conclusion of the 28 June text (# 3), there are three notes, all evidently meant for further discussion: First note: "*Perticuler Colonies not to Declare Warr*" (5:363).

Since individual colonies could defend themselves in an emergency, the commissioners were presumably differentiating between a defensive position (resisting an attack) and an offensive one (declaring war). The Albany Plan reaffirmed that individual colonies could defend themselves from attack and was silent about individual colonies declaring war. The second note was: "*Quere Whether the Duties Excise &c. are best Established by the Grand Councill or by the Act of Parliament that forms the Constitution*" (5:364). The Albany Plan evaded this question (cf. "General Treasury") and the third note asked: "*Quorum of the Councill how many*" (5:364). This query depended upon the number of delegates. The Albany Plan settled the question (see "Grand Council").

The numerous differences that exist between Franklin's original plans and the Albany Plan can be categorized as amplifications of the original plans, as additions to them, or as changes to or reversals of Franklin's plans. Amplifications to the earlier topics are common. For example, in case of the death of the president-general, the Speaker of the Grand Council would assume that position "until the King's Pleasure be known." Another amplification is the specification of the number of representatives and the election of successors. More significant are the additions to Franklin's original proposals: the president was given the power to call a meeting upon an emergency, and there could be no impressment in a colony without the legislature's consent.

The key changes are, at most, only four. (Since Franklin was alone responsible for the change in the second version to having Parliament impose the union, I do not count it.) Franklin on 8 June required that the governor-general be a military man. Though dropping that requirement was a major change, Franklin probably suggested it only because he thought it would appeal to the British authorities. The second change regarded the place of meeting. Franklin thought the congress should meet in the different colonies so that the representatives would come to know the different parts of the country. He was outvoted. The third change was the unification of the treasury. In Franklin's plans, the treasurer of each colony was responsible for the funds raised and spent. The Albany Plan called for a treasurer of all the colonies. The fourth important change was the Albany Plan's failure to agree upon what to tax.

Setting aside the reasons in England for the failure of the plan, one could argue that the commissioners at Albany never resolved its finances or the "Manner of forming this Union"—either would itself have doomed the Albany Plan. Sending the plan to the colonies meant little. It could be interpreted as merely informational, not as a call for each colony to report to the others on the plan and not as a call to approve or disapprove it and send it on to the British authorities.

Franklin "heartily" wished that "the Union may be approv'd of by the Assemblies of the several Colonies, and confirm'd by the King and Parliament, with some Improvements that I think necessary, but could not get inserted in the Plan" (5:393). The Albany Plan of Union was significant in part because it was the most important attempt to create a union of the colonies before Franklin's "Proposed Articles of Confederation" (1775) and before the 1782 Articles of Confederation. Though the

Albany Plan differed from what Franklin originally wrote and from what he wanted, it was nevertheless, in most essential points, *his* plan. As Franklin wrote Cadwallader Colden on 14 July 1754, "The Commissioners agreed on a Plan of Union, viz. From N Hampshire to So. Carolina inclusive: the same with that of which I sent you the Hints, some few Particulars excepted" (5:393).

APPENDIX 6. *Franklin's Saying: "Essential Liberty . . . Temporary Safety"*

Those who would give up essential Liberty, to purchase a little temporary Safety, deserve neither Liberty nor Safety.
—Franklin, 11 November 1755, in a Pennsylvania Assembly address to the governor
(P 6:238–43, at 242)

Franklin delivered this rallying cry in reply to Governor Robert Hunter Morris's veto of an act to raise money to defend Pennsylvania's frontier. Morris had rejected the act because it went against his secret instruction not to tax the proprietors' lands along with everyone else's. Pennsylvania was in a crisis. Sixteen months earlier, the French and their Indian allies had defeated George Washington at Fort Necessity, 3 July 1754, and a year later, they defeated General Edward Braddock's army on its march to Fort Duquesne, 9 July 1755. Despite the desperate situation, Governor Morris repeatedly vetoed the legislature's tax bills to finance Pennsylvania's defenses. Franklin replied for the assembly with the resolute "essential Liberty" sententia.

Franklin and the majority of Pennsylvania's legislators believed that the proprietors would benefit more financially from peace in Pennsylvania than anyone actually living in Pennsylvania; in peacetime, more immigrants came to Pennsylvania, and the proprietors sold them land. The assembly also believed that if it raised the money, it should have the sole right of disposing of it. But the frontier raids continued. Ten months after the "essential Liberty" speech, Franklin advanced a series of resolves in the Pennsylvania Assembly on 16 September 1756 condemning the proprietors and their instructions to the governor as well as the governor's constantly shifting subterfuges for refusing to pass another money bill. Franklin and the House conceded that practical necessity was forcing them to abandon their principles. The last resolve stated: "That the Proprietaries encreasing their Restrictions upon the Governor . . . at a Time when the Province is invaded by the King's Enemies, and barbarous Tribes of Indians are ravaging the Frontier Settlements, and their forbidding the Passing of any Bills whereby Money may be raised for the Defence of the Inhabitants, unless those Instructions are strictly complied with, is tyrannical, cruel and oppressive, with Regard to the People, and extremely injurious to the King's Service."

Because of the deaths on the frontier, Franklin and the assembly gave in: "Since if the Assembly should adhere to their Rights, as they justly might, the whole Province would be thrown into Confusion, abandoned to the Enemy, and lost to the Crown, the House therefore, reserving their Rights in their full Extent on all future Occasions, and PROTESTING against the Proprietary Instructions and Prohibitions, do, nevertheless, in Duty to the King, and Compassion for the suffering Inhabitants of their distressed Country, and in humble but full Confidence of the Justice of His Majesty, and a British Parliament, waive their Rights on this present

Occasion only; and do further *Resolve*, That a new Bill be brought in for granting a Sum of Money to the King's Use, and that the same be made conformable to the said Instructions, &c." (6:514–15).

On 3 February 1757, Franklin and the Pennsylvania Assembly passed a bill exempting the proprietors' property from taxation. They would not, however, concede entirely and allow the governor to control the money raised. Governor William Denny (who took office on 20 August 1756) refused to pass the bill. In March 1757, Lord Loudoun, commander in chief of the British army in America, came to Philadelphia and attempted to negotiate with Pennsylvania's governor and the assembly. On 21 March 1757, Iroquois Indian allies reported that a large body of French and Indians was about to attack Fort Augusta. The Pennsylvania militia there had not been paid and was abandoning the fort. General Loudoun consequently urged Governor Denny to ignore his instructions and pass the assembly's bill. He did so on 23 March 1757.

In the end, both sides buckled. Franklin and the Pennsylvania Assembly abandoned their lofty position of 11 November 1755: "Those who would give up essential Liberty, to purchase a little temporary Safety, deserve neither Liberty nor Safety." They surrendered, but refused to surrender entirely; subsequently, pressured by Lord Loudoun, the governor gave in, partially.

But, as we shall see, Pennsylvanians later revived Franklin's rallying cry.

APPENDIX 7. *Post Office Expansion,* 1753–1757

When Franklin and William Hunter were appointed joint deputy postmasters general in 1753, there were thirteen post offices in the colonies. By 1757, they had transformed the colonial postal system. Service was faster, more frequent, and covered a larger area. In 1753, New England had three post offices: one in Portsmouth, New Hampshire; one in Boston; and one in Newport, Rhode Island. By mid-1757, it had eleven; Massachusetts had added Newbury, Salem, and Marblehead; and Connecticut built offices in Providence, Newport, New London, New Haven, and Norwalk.

The Middle Colonies had six offices in 1753: two in New York (Albany and New York); one in Pennsylvania (Philadelphia); and three in New Jersey (Brunswick, Burlington, and Trenton). By 1757, they had ten: three more in New Jersey (at Elizabeth Town, Prince Town, and Woodbridge) and one more in Pennsylvania (at Lancaster).

In 1753, the South had four offices: New Castle, Delaware; Annapolis, Maryland; Williamsburg, Virginia; and Charleston, South Carolina. By 1757, it had ten: Delaware had added Wilmington; Maryland had added Baltimore; and Virginia had added four: Alexandria, Dumfrees (south of Mt. Vernon), Fredericksburg (at the upper end of the Rappahanock River), and Norfolk.

In addition to the post offices, mail could be picked up at any tavern or house along the post rider's route; thus, in 1753, Franklin also listed a letter from Boyd's Hole, Virginia (a tavern on the Potomac south of Mt. Vernon). During General Edward Braddock's time in America, the post office expanded to keep in touch with the army. In May 1755, Franklin therefore established post offices at Fredericksburg and Winchester, Virginia, and at Lancaster. The Lancaster office continued after Braddock's defeat in midsummer 1755. In three years, Franklin and Hunter added eighteen post offices.

APPENDIX 8. *Franklin's Wealth, 1756*

Most Franklin biographers have overestimated his wealth. One excellent twenty-first-century scholar thought he was "perhaps one of the richest colonists in the northern parts of the North American continent." In fact, eight years after he retired, he was nowhere close to being in the top 5 percent of Philadelphia's wealthiest persons. More than two hundred Philadelphians had greater estates than he. He was at about the tenth percentile in wealth.

For the years 1748–57, the partnership with Hall paid Franklin about £620 annually (P 3:276). The earliest measure of Franklin's "sufficient tho' moderate Fortune" (A 119) that may have some value is the 1756 tax evaluation of Philadelphia property: Franklin was assessed at £60. The evaluation measures only the Philadelphia property (building[s] and/or contents) and not the subject's income nor any assets outside Philadelphia. It thus has limited usefulness, but it provides one indication of Franklin's standing among his neighbors in 1756. The tax list does not include all Philadelphians; persons whose estates were less than £8 were not taxed.

People were taxed at 4d per pound on their estates. On an estate of £60, one was taxed 240d (20s or £1). Franklin's wealth gradually increased, and, as we come to other sources giving his comparative wealth, I will discuss them in later volumes. Perhaps in the last volume, an overview of Franklin's changing wealth may be possible.

To show that Franklin's wealth was comparatively modest among his contemporaries, I print four lists: first, the Junto members and close friends; second, the fifty Philadelphians whose estates were ranked highest; third, those appraised (with Franklin) at £60 in all wards; and fourth, those whose holdings were appraised at above £60 in the North Ward (Franklin's ward). At the end I give the percentages of those persons in Philadelphia whose assessment was the same or larger than Franklin's in all wards, and then those in Franklin's North Ward.

The source for all data is Hannah B. Roach, "Taxables in the City of Philadelphia, 1756" (originally published in the *Pennsylvania Genealogical Magazine* 22, no. 1 [1961]: 3–41); I use it from Roach, *Colonial Philadelphians*, Monograph Series no. 3 (Philadelphia: Genealogical Society of Pennsylvania, 1999) 105–46. The following lists all include the name, ward, pagination in Roach, and value of the estate (not necessarily in that order).

FRANKLIN'S JUNTO COMPANIONS AND OTHER CLOSE FRIENDS

In alphabetical order, I list Franklin's close friends who were alive in 1756 and lived in Philadelphia. I give the birth and death dates and the identification found in the tax list (there are many John Joneses, but only one cordwainer).

If we limit the list to friends who were Junto members (*), only Stephen Potts was poorer than Franklin. Another, John Jones, was taxed at the same rate. The list makes it clear that Franklin was not especially wealthy within the circle of his good friends. Of the sixteen listed here, five had taxes less than his: Stephen Potts, at £16; Nicholas Scull, at £24; Ebenezer Kinnersley and Lynford Lardner, at £30; and partner David Hall, at £36. Two of the six whose estates were valued at less, Nicholas Scull and Lynford Lardner, had property elsewhere, so the Philadelphia tax is not a good indication of their wealth. Robert Grace lived in New Jersey and is mentioned here only because David Hall occupied his Philadelphia property. In fact, only three people in the list were poorer than Franklin: Stephen Potts, Ebenezer Kinnersley, and David Hall. Ten were wealthier. Of the sixteen, William Masters was by far the wealthiest.

Bond, Dr. Thomas (1713–84) 143 (Walnut Ward, £80)

*Coleman, William, merchant (1704–11 January 1769) 117 (Lower Delaware Ward, £140)

Francis, Tench, Esq. (1722–58) 126 (Middle Ward, £120)

Galloway, Joseph, lawyer (ca. 1731–1803) 126 (Middle Ward, £70), plus 127 (Petty John's Estate, for which Galloway was rated, £160)

*Grace, Robert (1709–66) 122 (High Street Ward)—David Hall was rated £36 for his estate

Hall, David (ca. 1714–72) 122 (see Grace)

*Jones, John, Jr., cordwainer (d. 1761) 141 (South Ward, £60)

Kinnersley, Ebenezer (1711–78) 127 (Middle Ward, £30)

Lardner, Lynford (1715–74) 133 (Mulberry Ward, £30)

*Masters, William (ca. 1710–60) 118 (Lower Delaware Ward, £400)

*Plumsted [Plumstead], William, Esq. (1708–65) 115 (Dock Ward, £250)

*Potts, Stephen, bookbinder (1704–58) 139 (North Ward, £16)

*Rhoads, Samuel, carpenter (1711–84) 116 (Dock Ward, £100)

*Roberts, Hugh, ironmonger (1706–86) 139 (North Ward, £150), plus 138 (John Kinsey's Estate, for which Roberts was rated £50)

*Scull, Nicholas, surveyor (1687–1761) 135 (Mulberry Ward, £24)

*Syng, Philip (1703–89) 123 (High Street Ward, £24), plus 124, the Widow Waits's estate, for which Syng was rated (High Street Ward, £60)

The Fifty Philadelphians Who Paid the Most Taxes in 1754

The information is arranged in descending order. First is the amount of the tax; second, the numerical ranking followed by the name(s), arranged alphabetically; then the ward in which he or she lived; and last, the page in Roach where the information may be found.

£600. 1. Allen, William, Esq. (Lower Delaware), 117.

£500. 2. Branson, William, Mercht. (Mulberry), 129.

£400. 3–4. 3. Masters, William, Esq. (Lower Delaware), 118; 4. Pemberton, Israel, Mercht. (South), 142.

£350. 5–6. 5. Emlin, George, Gentleman (Middle), 125; 6. Morris, Anthony, Brewer (Mulberry), 133.

£300. 7–11. 7. Powell, Sam'l Senr's Est. for which Rob't Strettell is rated (Dock), 115; 8. Moore, Preston Samuel, Doctor (North), 138; 9. Morris, Anthony's Est. for wch John Rowen is rated (Dock), 115; 10. Powells Est. for wch the Wido is rated (Dock), 115; 11. Stamper, John Esq. (Dock), 116.

£250. 12–16. 12. Griffitts, William, Mercht. (Dock), 113; 13. Moore, William, Mercht. (Chestnut), 111; 14. Plumstead, Wm Esq. (Dock), 115; 15. Turner, Joseph, Mercht. (Chestnut), 111; 16. Warner, Wido for the Est. (Mulberry), 136.

£240. 17–20. 17. Meredith, Reese, Mercht. (Lower Delaware), 118; 18. Mifflin, Samuel, Mercht. (Chestnut), 111; 19. Norris, Isaac's Est. for wch Samuel McCall is rated (Lower Delaware), 118; 20. Shute, Attwood, Esq., Mercht. (Dock), 116.

£225, 21. Goodman, Walter, Mercht. (Upper Delaware), 120.

£220. 22. Fox, Joseph, Carpenter (North), 137.

£180. 23–25. 23. Benezett, Daniel, Mercht. (Mulberry), 129; 24. Emlin Samuel, Shopkeeper (Middle), 125; 25. Wister, John, Mercht. (North), 140.

£170 26–27. 26. Pemberton, James, Mercht. (South), 142; 27. Reynolds, John, Mercht. (Walnut), 144.

£160. 28. Petty, Joseph's Est for wch Joseph Galloway is rated (Middle), 125.

£150. 29–34. 29. Hamilton, James's, Est for wch Plunkett Fleeson is rated (Middle), 126; 30. Maddox, Joshua, Mercht. (Chestnut), 111; 31. Mifflin, John, Mercht. (Chestnut), 111; 32. Norris, Charles, Esq. (South), 141; 33. Roberts, Hugh, Ironmonger (North), 139; 34. Warder, Jeremiah, Hatter (North), 140.

£140. 35–38. 35. Coleman, William, Mercht. (Lower Delaware), 117; 36. Kearsley, John, Doctor (Chestnut), 110; 37. Keen, Peter, Mercht. (Middle), 127; 38. King, Joseph, Flour Brander (Dock), 114.

£135. 39. Peel, Oswald's Est for wch Thos Richie is rated (Upper Delaware), 120.

£130. 40–42. 40. Mickle, Samuel (North), 138; 41. Pemberton, Rachell (South), 142; 42. Willing, Charles's, Est for wch Thos Willing is rated. (Dock), 117.

£125. 43. Morris, James's Est for wch Anthony Morris is rated (Mulberry), 133.

£120. 44–50. 44. Bingham, Wm, Mercht. (Dock), 112; 45. Bullock, George, Tanner (Dock), 11; 46. Francis, Tench Esq. (Middle), 126; 47. Lawrence, Thos, Mercht. (High Street), 123; 48. Logan, James, Mercht. (Mulberry), 133; 49. Richardson, Joseph, Mercht. (Dock), 116; 50. Sims, Joseph, Mercht. (Dock), 116.

THOSE APPRAISED (WITH FRANKLIN) AT £60 IN ALL WARDS

Allen, Nathanel Senr, Cooper (*Lower Delaware Ward*) 117

Baker, Joseph, Hatter (*High Street Ward*) 122

Bayley, Richrd, Carpenter (*Dock Ward*) 112

Bayley, John, Silversmith (*Dock Ward*) 112

Burge, Samuel, Mercht (*North Ward*) 136

Carpenter, Wido (*Lower Delaware Ward*) 117

Chevalear, Peter, Distiller (*Mulberry Ward*) 130

Chew, Benjn, Attorney (*Dock Ward*) 113

Clampfer, William (*Mulberry Ward*) 130

Coutlas, James, Sheriff (*South Ward*) 140

Coxe, William, Mercht (*South Ward*) 140
Cresson, James's, Est. for wch John Atkinson is rated (*Middle Ward*) 125
Drason, Matthew's, Est. for wch Wm Hill is rated (*Middle Ward*) 125
Edwards and Wishart, Merchts (*Lower Delaware Ward*) 117
Elliot, Andrew, Mercht (*Lower Delaware Ward*) 117
Farmer, Richard, Doctor (*Middle Ward*) 126
Fisher, William, Mercht (*Upper Delaware Ward*) for wch Philip Syng is rated, (*Lower Delaware Ward*) 119
Franklin, Benja, Esq, (*North Ward*) 137
Fussell, Solomon, Shopkeeper (*High Street Ward*) 122
Gray, George's, Est. for wch Wm Shute is rated (*Walnut Ward*) 143
Grimes, Thos, Doctor (*Dock Ward*) 113
Hamilton, Mary (*South Ward*) 141
Harrison, Cahrles (*North Ward*) 138
Harrison, Henry, Mercht (*High Street Ward*) 122
Hassell, Ann, Wido (*Chestnut Ward*) 110
Holton Wido (*Mulberry Ward*) 132
Hous's, Est. for wch the Wido is rated (*Dock Ward*) 114
Howell, Samuel, Hatter (*Middle Ward*) 126
Huston, Alexr., Mercht (*High Street Ward*) 122
Inglis, John (*Dock Ward*) 114
Jones, Charles, Gentleman (*Middle Ward*) 127
Jones, Humphrey (*Mulberry Ward*) 132
Jones, John, Cordwainer (*South Ward*) 141
Kendell, Benja, Shoemaker (*South Ward*) 141
McCullough, James, Carpenter (*North Ward*) 138
McIllvaine, Wm, Mercht (*Dock Ward*) 115
McMutry, David and Co, Merchts (*Lower Delaware Ward*) 118
Melchoir, Leond, Tavernkeeper (*Mulberry Ward*) 133
Murgatroyd's Est. for wch the Wido is rated 133
Nicholas, Jane, Wido (*North Ward*) 139
Parrock's Est. for wch the Wido is rated (*Mulberry Ward*) 134
Prior, Silas, Baker (*Walnut Ward*) 144
Pyewell, William, Mercht (*Lower Delaware Ward*) 118
Redman, John, Doctor (*North Ward*) 139
Redman, Joseph (*North Ward*) 139
Richardson, Frances, Mercht (*Chestnut Ward*) 111
Rollinson, Robert, Butcher (*Mulberry Ward*) 134
Sayre, John, Distiller (*Middle Ward*) 128
Searles, John, Mercht (*Dock Ward*) 116
Sheraswood, George, Shoemaker (*South Ward*) 142
Standley, Valentne, Potter (*North Ward*) 139
Steadman, Alexander, Mercht (*Middle Ward*) 128
Stedman, Chas, Mercht (*Dock Ward*) 116

Stretch, Thomas, Clockmaker (*South Ward*) 142
Swift, John, Mercht (*Chestnut Ward*) 111
Vanderspreigel, Wm, Mercht (*Upper Delaware Ward*) 121
Waits Wido's Est (*High Street*), for which Philip Syng was rated, 124
White, Thomas, Mercht (*North Ward*) 140
Wooley, Edmond, Carpenter (*Mulberry Ward*) 136

PERSONS (ALPHABETICALLY ARRANGED) EVALUATED AT OR ABOVE £60 IN
FRANKLIN'S NORTH WARD

1. Cambell, Thos, Shopkeeper, 137	80
2. Chappell, John, Shopkeeper, 137	90
3. Fox, Joseph, Carpenter, 137	220
4. Franklin, Benja, Esq, 137	60
5. Greenleafe, Isaac, Mercht, 137	80
6. Harts Est. for wch Mary Hart is rated, 138	80
7. Hockley, Richard, Mercht., 138	90
8. Lawrence, John, Lawyer, 138	100
9. Mickle, Samuel, 138	130
10. Moore, Preston Samuel, Docter, 138	300
11. Paschall, Wido, 139	80
12. Roberes, Hugh, Ironmonger, 139	150
13. Shippen Est. for wch Edw. Shippen Jr. is rated, 139	100
14. Shippin, William, Docter, 139	90
15. Standley, Valentne, Potter, 139	60
16. Wister, Richard, Buttonmaker, 140	90
17. Wister, Wido, 140	100
18. Wister's Est. for wch the Wido Wister is rated, 140	100
18. Warder, Jeremiah, Hatter, 140	150
19. Wister, John, Mercht., 140	180

Total number of persons enumerated in all wards: 2,381
    Those assessed over £60:   221 (9.28%)
    Assessment at or over £60   281 (11.80%)

Total number of persons in North Ward: 277
    Assessment over £60:   18 (6.49%)
    Assessment at or over £60   27 (9.74%)

APPENDIX 9. *The Americanization of Benjamin Franklin*

When did it begin? Biographers have had different opinions. But first, what does *Americanization* mean? By *Americanization* I mean primarily, when did Franklin reject the idea of Britain's control of the colonies through Parliament or through the king in council? Concomitantly, when did he start taking special pride in American culture and in the achievements of the American colonists? If one defines Franklin's Americanization as the time when he believed that Americans and Englishmen *should* (as opposed to *would*) fight one another, the answer is never.

Franklin's biographers date his Americanization to the pre-Revolutionary period, that is, sometime between 1765 and 1775. Carl Van Doren, Verner W. Crane, and Esmond Wright all did so. In 1996, Robert Middlekauf reflected the twentieth-century view: "Before the American Revolution, he loved England and the British Empire more than anything else and probably more than anyone else. They were the great loves that stirred him the most deeply" (116).

The twenty-first-century biographers say the same. W. H. Brands (2000) found that on 13 March 1768, "Franklin reached what seemed the Rubicon of relations between Britain and the American colonies. Either Parliament was supreme in all areas pertaining to the provinces or it was supreme in none. 'I think the arguments for the latter more numerous and weighty than those for the former.'" Yet Brands added that "Franklin, still the British imperialist, favored a transatlantic union" (403). His final judgment was that, until the Cockpit ordeal in 1774, Franklin had been "Britain's most loyal subject, its best friend among the Americans" (7). Edmund S. Morgan (2002) argued that Franklin's position shifted from British imperialism to intransigent Americanism during 1768 and 1769 (168–71). James Srodes (2002) said Franklin changed in the late 1760s (217ff.). Walter Isaacson (2003) quotes Gordon Wood's *Radicalism* (1992) with approval: "Once we fully accept the fact that Franklin between 1760 and 1764 was an enthusiastic and unabashed royalist who did not and could not foresee the breakup of the Empire, then much of the surprise, confusion and mystery of his behavior in these years falls away." Later, Isaacson writes that Franklin was "still a committed royalist" in 1765 (193–94, 219). In *The Americanization of Benjamin Franklin*, Gordon S. Wood (2004) finds Franklin an "imperialist and royalist" in the early 1760s, "ambivalent" about America in the late 1760s, and "ultimately . . . a patriot" after the Cockpit affair on 29 January 1774 (91, 124, 141). Jerry Weinberger (2005) found that Franklin "remained a staunch imperialist" until "the beginning of 1774" (220, 288). Joyce E. Chaplin (2006) judged him "no longer conciliatory" after the Cockpit hearing (238). And Lorraine Smith Prangle (2007) wrote that he stopped being a royalist in the early 1770s, added that he became a thorough American in the last decade before the Revolution, and concluded that the key change began in 1768 (132, 140, and 145).

I disagree with the judgments just cited. When a boy in Boston, Franklin imbibed the political beliefs of the Reverend John Wise, Nathaniel Gardner, James Franklin, and, in general, those of the Old Charter Party. The Old Charter Party denied the right of the English authorities to change the Massachusetts charter; it rallied around Wise's cry of "no taxation without representation"; and it taxed English imports in a stout reply to the Acts of Trade and Navigation. The Old Charter Party stalwarts believed they had all the rights and liberties of Englishmen, and they scorned the "strangers" sent to govern them. They took pride in America and in their achievements in New England. Biographers of Franklin have ignored the existence of the Old Charter Party and the adherence to it by James Franklin, Nathaniel Gardner, and other Couranteers and politicians Franklin knew as a boy. None has commented that Franklin's "'Hints' or Terms for a Durable Union," between 4 and 6 December 1774 (21:365–68), reprise the Old Charter Party's positions—but they do.

Only a little direct evidence of these attitudes can be found in the adolescent Franklin, but Silence Dogood (a.k.a. Franklin, age sixteen) declared herself "a mortal Enemy to arbitrary Government and unlimited Power. I am very jealous for the Rights and Liberties of my Country" (1:13). Throughout his life as a young man (age twenty to forty-two), Franklin frequently revealed his adherence to the Old Charter Party's ideals. Nevertheless, not until the period from 1748 to 1757 do we have sufficient evidence to prove that Franklin had all the fundamental beliefs of an American rebel. I bring together the main topics that support that opinion in Chapter 23, and put them in the index under those headings. Franklin demonstrated a thorough Americanism before 1757. But of course he said and wrote different things as the occasion demanded or permitted. He was attempting to help the American cause—not trying to be hung as a traitor.

Clark, *Public Prints*	Charles E. Clark. *The Public Prints: The Newspaper in Anglo-American Culture, 1665–1740.* New York: Oxford University Press, 1994.
Cohen, *BF'sE*	I. Bernard Cohen. *BF's Experiments and Observations.* Cambridge, Mass.: Harvard University Press, 1941.
Cohen, *BF's Science*	I. Bernard Cohen. *BF's Science.* Cambridge, Mass.: Harvard University Press, 1990.
Cohen, *Founding Fathers*	I. Bernard Cohen. *Science and the Founding Fathers.* New York: Norton, 1995.
Cohen, *F&N*	I. Bernard Cohen. *Franklin and Newton.* Philadelphia: APS, 1956.
Colden	Cadwallader Colden. *Letters and Papers* 9 v. New York: New York Historical Society, 1918–37.
Connor	Paul W. Connor. *Poor Richard's Politics: BF and His New American Order.* New York: Oxford University Press, 1965.
Corner and Booth	*Chain of Friendship: Selected Letters of Dr. John Fothergill.* Ed. Betsy C. Corner and Christopher C. Booth. Cambridge, Mass.: Harvard University Press, 1971.
CR	Colonial Records. *Minutes of the Provincial Council of Pennsylvania.* 16 v. Harrisburg, Pa., 1852–53.
Crane	Verner Winslow Crane. *BF and a Rising People.* Boston: Little, Brown, 1954.
DAB	*Dictionary of American Biography.* 11 v. Ed. Dumas Malone. New York: Scribner's, 1958–64.
Davidson	Robert L. Davidson. *War Comes to Quaker Pennsylvania, 1682–1756.* New York: Columbia University Press, 1957.
DCB	*Dictionary of Canadian Biography.* 4 v. [those who died from 1100 to 1800] Ed. George W. Brown et al. Toronto: University of Toronto Press, 1966–79.
DF	Deborah Franklin.
DH	J. A. Leo Lemay. "A Documentary History of BF." http://www.english.udel.edu/lemay/franklin.
Diamondstone	Judith M. Diamondstone. "The Philadelphia Corporation, 1701–1776." Ph.D. diss., University of Pennsylvania, 1969.
Dray	Philip Dray. *Stealing God's Thunder.* New York: Random House, 2005.
E (followed by a number)	Charles Evans, *American Bibliography: A Chronological Dictionary . . . to 1820.* 14 v. Chicago and Worcester, Mass.: Evans and American Antiquarian Society,

1903–59. [The Evans online edition contains additional materials.]

EA	John Alden et al., eds. *European Americana: A Chronological Guide to Works Printed in Europe Relating to the Americas.* 6 v. New York: Readex, 1980–97.
Egnal	Marc Egnal. *A Mighty Empire: The Origins of the American Revolution.* Ithaca, N.Y.: Cornell University Press, 1988.
ESTC	English Short Title Catalogue [to 1800]. http://estc.ucr.edu.
Finger	Stanley Finger. *Dr. Franklin's Medicine.* Philadelphia: University of Pennsylvania Press, 2006.
Fleming	Thomas J. Fleming. *The Man Who Dared the Lightning.* New York: Morrow, 1971.
Ford	Paul Leicester Ford. *Franklin Bibliography: A List of Books Written by, or Relating to Benjamin Franklin.* Brooklyn, New York, 1889.
Foster	Joseph S. Foster. "Benjamin Franklin." In Horle 3:531–72.
Freeman, *GW*	Douglas Southall Freeman. *George Washington: A Biography.* 7 v. New York: Scribner's, 1948–57.
FRS	Fellow of the Royal Society of London.
Gegenheimer	Albert Frank Gegenheimer. *William Smith Educator and Churchman 1727–1803.* Philadelphia: University of Pennsylvania Press, 1943.
GM	*Gentleman's Magazine.* London, 1731–.
Gipson	Lawrence Henry Gipson. *The British Empire before the American Revolution.* 15 v. New York: Knopf, 1936–70.
Gipson, *Evans*	Lawrence Henry Gipson. *Lewis Evans.* Philadelphia: HSP, 1939.
Green	James N. Green. *Poor Richard's Books: An Exhibition of Books Owned by BF Now on the Shelves of the Library Company of Philadelphia.* Philadelphia: Library Company, 1990.
Green and Stallybrass	James N. Green and Peter Stallybrass. *BF: Writer and Printer.* New Castle, Del.: Oak Knoll Press, 2006.
GT	*The Autobiography of Benjamin Franklin: A Genetic Text.* Ed. J. A. Leo Lemay and P. M. Zall. Knoxville: University of Tennessee Press, 1981.
GWP	George Washington. *Papers, Colonial Series.* Ed. W. W. Abbot et al. Charlottesville: University Press of Virginia, 1983–.

Hackmann	W. D. Hackmann. *Electricity from Glass: The History of the Frictional Electrical Machine, 1600–1850*. Alphen aan den Rijn, Netherlands: Sijthoff and Noordhoff, 1978.
Haller	Albrecht von Haller. "An historical account of the wonderful discoveries made in Germany, &c. concerning Electricity." *GM* 15 (April 1745): 193–97.
Hamilton	Alexander Hamilton. *The Itinerarium.* Ed. Carl Bridenbaugh. Chapel Hill: University of North Carolina Press, 1948.
Hanna	William S. Hanna. *BF and Pennsylvania Politics.* Stanford, Calif.: Stanford University Press, 1964.
Hawke	David Freeman Hawke. *Franklin.* New York: Harper and Row, 1976.
Hays	I. Minis Hays. *Calendar of the Franklin Papers* [v. 2–6 of *The Record of the Celebration of the Celebration of the Two Hundredth Anniversary of the Birth of Benjamin Franklin*]. Philadelphia: APS, 1906–8.
Heilbron, *E*	J. L. Heilbron. *Electricity in the 17th and 18th Centuries.* Berkeley: University of California Press, 1979.
Heilbron, *Elements*	J. L. Heilbron. *Elements of Early Modern Physics.* Berkeley: University of California Press, 1982.
Henderson	Archibald Henderson. "Dr. Thomas Walker and the Loyal Company of Virginia." *PAAS* 41 (1931): 77–178.
Horle	Craig W. Horle et al., eds. *Lawmaking and Legislators in Pennsylvania: A Biographical Dictionary.* Vol. 2, *1710–1756.* Vol. 3, *1757–1775.* Philadelphia: University of Pennsylvania Press, 1997–2005.
HSP	Historical Society of Pennsylvania.
Hutchinson	Thomas Hutchinson. *History of . . . Massachusetts-bay.* 3 v. Ed. Lawrence Shaw Mayo. Cambridge, Mass.: Harvard University Press, 1936.
Hutson	James H. Hutson. *Pennsylvania Politics, 1746–1770.* Princeton, N.J.: Princeton University Press, 1972.
Hutson, "BF"	James H. Hutson. "BF and Pennsylvania Politics, 1751–1755: A Reappraisal." *PMHB* 93 (1969): 303–71.
H. W. Smith	Horace Wemyss Smith. *Life and Correspondence of the Rev. William Smith.* 2 v. Philadelphia: Ferguson Bros., 1880.
Isaacson	Walter Isaacson. *BF.* New York: Simon and Schuster, 2003.
JA	John Adams.

JAD   John Adams. *Diary and Autobiography.* 4 v. Ed.
                              Lyman H. Butterfield et al. Cambridge, Mass.: Har-
                              vard University Press, 1961–62.
JAP   John Adams. *Papers.* Ed. Robert J. Taylor. Cam-
                              bridge, Mass.: Harvard University Press, 1977–.
Jennings   Francis Jennings. *BF, Politician.* New York: Norton,
                              1996.
Jennings, *Empire*   Francis Jennings. *Empire of Fortune: Crowns, Colo-
                              nies, and Tribes in the Seven Years War in America.*
                              New York: Norton, 1988.
Karu   Stuart Karu. *The Intellectual World of Benjamin
                              Franklin.* Philadelphia: University of Pennsylvania
                              Press, 1990.
Kelley   Joseph J. Kelley. *Pennsylvania, the Colonial Years.*
                              Garden City, N.Y.: Doubleday, 1980.
Ketcham   Ralph Ketcham. *BF.* New York: Washington Square
                              Press, 1965.
Ketcham, "BF and Smith"   Ralph Ketcham. "BF and William Smith." *PMHB* 88
                              (1964): 142–63.
Krider   E. Philip Krider. "BF's Science," in Talbott 162–97.
Lemay, "American Aesthetic"   J. A. Leo Lemay. "The American Aesthetic of BF."
                              PMHB 111 (1987): 465–99.
Lemay, *EK*   J. A. Leo Lemay. *Ebenezer Kinnersley, Franklin's
                              Friend.* Philadelphia: University of Pennsylvania
                              Press, 1964.
Lemay, "Frontiersman"   J. A. Leo Lemay. "The Frontiersman from Lout to
                              Hero: Notes on the Significance of the Comparative
                              Method and Stage Theory in Early American Litera-
                              ture and Culture." *PAAS* 88 (1979): 187–223.
Lemay, "Lockean Realities"   J. A. Leo Lemay. "Lockean Realities and Olympian
                              Perspectives: The Writing of Franklin's *Autobiogra-
                              phy.*" In *Writing the American Classics*, ed. James
                              Barbour and Tom Quirk. Chapel Hill: University of
                              North Carolina Press, 1990, 1–24.
Lemay, *Men of Letters*   J. A. Leo Lemay. *Men of Letters in Colonial Mary-
                              land.* Knoxville: University of Tennessee Press, 1972.
Lemay, *Reader*   J. A. Leo Lemay. *An Early American Reader.* Wash-
                              ington, D.C.: U.S. Information Agency, 1989.
Lemay, *Renaissance Man*   J. A. Leo Lemay. *Renaissance Man in the Eighteenth
                              Century.* Los Angeles: Clark Memorial Library, 1978.
Lemay, "Robert Beverley"   J. A. Leo Lemay. "Robert Beverley's *History and Pres-
                              ent State of Virginia* and the Emerging American Po-
                              litical Ideology." In *American Letters and the*

	Historical Consciousness: Essays in Honor of Lewis P. Simpson, ed. J. Gerald Kennedy and Daniel Mark Fogel. Baton Rouge: Louisiana State University Press, 1987, 67–111.
Lemay, "Vanity"	"The Theme of Vanity in F's *Autobiography.*" In *Reappraising* 372–87.
LCP	Library Company of Philadelphia.
Mandeville	Bernard Mandeville. *Fable of the Bees.* Ed. F. B. Kaye. 2 v. Oxford: Clarendon Press, 1966.
Marietta	Jack D. Marietta. "Conscience, the Quaker Community, and the French and Indian War." *PMHB* 95 (1971): 3–27.
Mather, *Bonifacius*	Cotton Mather. *Bonifacius* (running title, "Essays to do Good"). Ed. David Levin. Cambridge, Mass.: Harvard University Press, 1966.
McAnear	Beverley McAnear. "Personal Accounts of the Albany Congress of 1754." *Mississippi Valley Historical Review* 39 (1952–53): 727–46.
McMaster	John Bach McMaster. *BF as a Man of Letters.* Boston: Houghton, Mifflin, 1887.
Middlekauf	Robert Middlekauf. *BF and His Enemies.* Berkeley: University of California Press, 1996.
Miller	C. William Miller. *BF's Philadelphia Printing.* Philadelphia: APS, 1974.
Minutes, Phila.	*Minutes of the Common Council . . . of Philadelphia.* Philadelphia, 1847.
Morgan	Edmund S. Morgan. *BF.* New Haven, Conn.: Yale University Press, 2002.
NCE	*The Autobiography of BF: A Norton Critical Edition.* Ed. J. A. Leo Lemay and P. M. Zall. New York: Norton, 1986.
Newman	Eric P. Newman. *Early Paper Money of America.* 4th ed. Iola, Wisc.: Kraus Publications, 1997.
NYCD	*Documents relative to the Colonial History of the State of New York.* Ed. John Rowman Brodhead and E. B. O'Callaghan, 15 v. Albany, N.Y.: Reed, Parsons, 1856–87.
OED	*Oxford English Dictionary.* 2nd ed., online.
Oldest Revolutionary	*The Oldest Revolutionary: Essays on BF.* Ed. J. A. Leo Lemay. Philadelphia: University of Pennsylvania Press, 1976.
P	*The Papers of BF.* Ed. Leonard W. Labaree. 38 v. New Haven: Yale University Press, 1959–.

PA   Pennsylvania Archives.
PAAS   *Proceedings of the American Antiquarian Society.*
Pangle, *Political Philosophy*   Lorraine Smith Pangle. *The Political Philosophy of
                                    BF.* Baltimore: Johns Hopkins University Press,
                                    2007.
Pangle and Pangle   Lorraine Smith Pangle and Thomas L. Pangle. *The
                                    Learning of Liberty: The Educational Ideas of the
                                    Founding Fathers.* Lawrence: University Press of
                                    Kansas, 1993.
PAPS   *Proceedings of the American Philosophical Society.*
Parton   James Parton. *Life and Times of BF.* 2 v. Boston: Os-
                                    good, 1864.
Pascal   Blaise Pascal. [Pensées.] *Monsieur Pascall's Thoughts,
                                    Meditations, and Prayers.* Tr. Joseph Walker. Lon-
                                    don: J. Tonson, 1688.
Pasles   Paul C. Pasles. *BF's Numbers.* Princeton, N.J.:
                                    Princeton University Press, 2007.
PG   *Pennsylvania Gazette.*
PHS   Pennsylvania Historical Society.
PLB   The Penn Letter Books, formerly commonly called
                                    PPOC, and available on the TPP microfilm from
                                    HSP.
PMHB   *Pennsylvania Magazine of History and Biography.*
PPOC   Penn Papers Official Correspondence, HSP. Now
                                    also commonly called PPL, the Penn Letter Books,
                                    available on the TPP microfilm from HSP.
PT   *Philosophical Transactions of the Royal Society of
                                    London.*
Reappraising   *Reappraising BF.* Ed. J. A. Leo Lemay. Newark: Uni-
                                    versity of Delaware Press, 1993.
Roach   Hannah B. Roach. "BF Slept Here." *PMHB* 84
                                    (1960): 127–74.
Rothermund   Dietmar Rothermund. *Layman's Progress: Religious
                                    and Political Experience in Colonial Pennsylvania.*
                                    Philadelphia: University of Pennsylvania Press, 1961.
Rush, *Letters*   Benjamin Rush. *Letters.* 2 v. Ed. Lyman H. Butter-
                                    field. Philadelphia: APS, 1951.
Sabin   Joseph Sabin, Wilberforce Eames, and R. W. G. Vail,
                                    eds. *Bibliotheca Americana.* 29 v. New York: Sabin,
                                    1868–1936.
Sachse   Julius F. Sachse. *BF as a Freemason.* Philadelphia,
                                    1906.

Sappenfield	James A. Sappenfield. *A Sweet Instruction: Franklin's Journalism as a Literary Apprenticeship.* Carbondale: Southern Illinois University Press, 1973.
Schiffer	Michael Brian Schiffer. *Draw the Lightning Down.* Berkeley: University of California Press, 2003.
Schutz, *William Shirley*	John A. Schutz. *William Shirley.* Chapel Hill: University of North Carolina Press, 1961.
Sellers	Charles Coleman Sellers. *BF in Portraiture.* New Haven, Conn.: Yale University Press, 1962.
Sewell	Philadelphia Museum of Art. *Philadelphia: Three Centuries of American Art.* Ed. Darrel Sewell. Philadelphia: Philadelphia Museum of Art, 1976.
Shaftesbury	Anthony Ashley Cooper, third earl of Shaftesbury. *Characteristics of Men, Manners, Opinion, Times.* Ed. Lawrence E. Klein. Cambridge: Cambridge University Press, 1999.
Shields, *Civil Tongues*	David S. Shields. *Civil Tongues & Polite Letters in British America.* Chapel Hill: University of North Carolina Press, 1997.
Shields, *Oracles*	David S. Shields. *Oracles of Empire: Poetry, Politics, and Commerce in British America, 1690–1750.* Chicago: University of Chicago Press, 1990.
Shields, "Wits"	David S. Shields. "The Wits and Poets of Pennsylvania: New Light on the Rise of Belles Lettres in Provincial Pennsylvania." *PMHB* 109 (1985): 99–144.
Shipton	Clifford K. Shipton. *Sibley's Harvard Graduates.* Boston: Harvard University Press, 1933–.
Shirley, *Correspondence*	*Correspondence of William Shirley.* Ed. Charles Henry Lincoln. 2 v. New York: Macmillan, 1912.
Smith, *Brief State*	William Smith. *A Brief State of the Province of Pennsylvania.* 3rd ed. London: Griffiths, 1756.
Smith, *Brief View*	William Smith. *A Brief View of the Conduct of Pennsylvania, for the Year 1755.* London: R. Griffiths, 1756.
Smith, *Hannah*	John Smith. *Hannah Logan's Courtship.* Philadelphia: Ferris and Leach, 1904.
Sparks	Jared Sparks. *Works of BF.* 10 v. Boston: Hilliard, 1836–40.
Statutes	James T. Mitchell and Henry Flanders, eds. *The Statutes at Large of Pennsylvania from 1682–1801.* Harrisburg, Pa.: State Printer, 1896–1915.
Stourzh	Gerald Stourzh. *BF and American Foreign Policy.* Chicago: University of Chicago Press, 1954, 1969.

Swift, ed. Davis

Jonathan Swift. *Prose Works*. Ed. Herbert Davis. 14 v. Oxford: Blackwell, 1939–68.

Talbott

Page Talbott. *BF in Search of a Better World*. New Haven, Conn.: Yale University Press, 2005.

Thayer

Theodore Thayer. *Pennsylvania Politics and the Growth of Democracy*. Harrisburg: Pennsylvania Historical and Museum Commission, 1953.

Thayer, *Pemberton*

Theodore Thayer. *Israel Pemberton*. Philadelphia: Historical Society of Pennsylvania, 1943.

Thomas

Isaiah Thomas. *History of Printing in America*. Ed. Marcus A. McCorison. New York: Weathervane Books, 1970.

TJ

Thomas Jefferson.

TJP

Thomas Jefferson. *Papers*. Ed. Julian P. Boyd et al. Princeton, N.J.: Princeton University Press, 1950–.

Tocqueville

Alexis de Tocqueville. *Democracy in America*. Tr. George Lawrence, ed. J. P. Mayer. New York: Doubleday, 1969.

TPP

Thomas Penn Papers [microfilm]. Philadelphia: HSP, 1968.

v.

volume(s).

V

Pennsylvania Archives. 8th ser. [*Votes and Proceedings of the Pennsylvania Assembly*].

VD

Carl Van Doren. *BF*. New York: Viking, 1938.

Wallace

Paul A. W. Wallace. *Conrad Weiser*. Philadelphia: University of Pennsylvania Press, 1945.

Wallace, *Teedyuscung*

Paul A. W. Wallace. *King of the Delawares: Teedyuscung, 1700–1763*. Philadelphia: University of Pennsylvania Press, 1949.

Walters

Kerry S. Walters. *BF and His Gods*. Urbana: University of Illinois Press, 1999.

Weinberger

Jerry Weinberger. *BF Unmasked*. Lawrence: University of Kansas Press, 2005.

Wolf and Hayes

Edwin Wolf 2nd and Kevin J. Hayes. *Library of BF*. Philadelphia: APS, 2006.

Wolff

Mabel Pauline Wolff. *The Colonial Agency of Pennsylvania, 1712–1757*. Philadelphia: Intelligencer Printing Company, 1933.

Wood, *Americanization*

Gordon S. Wood. *The Americanization of BF*. New York: Penguin Press, 2004.

Wood, *Radicalism*

Gordon S. Wood. *The Radicalism of the American Revolution*. New York: Knopf, 1992.

Wright	Esmond Wright. *Franklin of Philadelphia*. Cambridge, Mass.: Harvard University Press, 1986.
WF	William Franklin.
WMQ	*William and Mary Quarterly*, 3rd ser.
WN	Adam Smith. *An Inquiry into the Nature and Causes of the Wealth of Nations*. Ed. R. H. Campbell and A. S. Skinner. 2 v. Indianapolis: Liberty Fund, 1981.
Zall	P[aul] M. Zall. *BF, Laughing*. Berkeley: University of California Press, 1980.

NOTES

CHAPTER 1

1. Davidson 50–63; Salley F. Griffith, "'Order, Discipline, and a Few Cannon: Benjamin Franklin, the Association, and the Rhetoric and Practice of Boosterism," *PMHB* 116 (1992) 131–55; and Anderson 188–99.

2. CR 5:91.

3. V 4:3138–44, 3144–48.

4. CR 5:113–14.

5. Miller 420.

6. CR 5:145–47.

7. CR 5:149–52.

8. "The first American political cartoon" is defined here as a cartoon used in an American political situation. Franklin may have made the woodcut himself, though not for *Plain Truth* but for the children's reader he published earlier in 1747, Thomas Dilworth's *New Guide to the English Tongue*; E40424, Miller 415. It contained twelve Aesop fables, illustrated with woodcuts containing such American details as the Conestoga wagon and Franklin's Pennsylvania fireplace (*Life* 2: figs. 26a and 26b, pp. 396–97). Lemay, "American Aesthetic" 466–71.

9. W 223; *Canon* #55, pp. 82–83.

10. BF had used the proverb earlier: "Englishmen feel but cannot see; as the Italian says of us" (P 2:14). He evidently adapted it from James Harrington, "Political Aphorisms," #5: "The People cannot see, but they can feel." "The Italian" is probably Machiavelli, in *The Prince*, end of chapter 18, who contrasts seeing and feeling, though without reference to Englishmen.

11. There were two English priests in Philadelphia and two German priests on the frontier. Joseph L. J. Kirlin, *Catholicity in Philadelphia* (Philadelphia: McVey, 1909) 55.

12. Franklin used the body metaphor in his anti-Stamp Act cartoon, "Magna Britannia, her Colonies Reduc'd," which satirized Britain for sacrificing its own arms and legs (13:66). Wilmarth S. Lewis, followed by the editors of the *Papers* (13:67), attributed Franklin's use of the body metaphor to earlier English cartoons of 1749 and 1756, but the body politic metaphor is common, and Franklin may or may not have known those cartoons. David George Hale, *The Body Politic: A Political Metaphor in Renaissance English Literature* (The Hague: Mouton, 1971).

13. "Accounts," 13 July 1748.

14. Alan Tully, "Politics and Peace Testimony in Mid-Eighteenth-Century Pennsylvania," *Canadian Review of American Studies* 13 (1982): 159–77, at 176–77n29.

15. Green and Stallybrass 81, fig. 6, say that the brief letter "is written in support of Franklin's position."

16. *Treatise Shewing the Need we Have to rely upon God as the soul Protector of this Province* (Philadelphia: Armbruster, 1748) 18, 19, 23; E6254.

17. Franklin wrote about this petition in the *Gazette*, 8 September 1743; *Life* 2:340–42.

18. Wood, *Americanization* 55–60, suggested that by the beginning of 1748, Franklin had become, philosophically as well as financially, a member of the upper class, a gentleman. Isaacson, 124, however, remarked on BF's "populist insistence that there be no class distinctions."

19. *Minutes*, Phila. 489–90.

20. Wolff 114–15; Thayer 22; and Sappenfield 117.

21. CR 5:158–59.

22. CR 5:158.

23. Green and Stallybrass 86–87.

24. Gilbert Tennent, *The Late Association for Defense, Encourag'd* (Philadelphia: Bradford, [1748]) 35; E6244.

25. Not in P; see *Canon* 111–13.

26. Theodore Dwight Bozeman, *To Live Ancient Lives: The Primitivist Dimension in Puritanism* (Chapel Hill: University of North Carolina Press, 1988).

27. *Cicero*, Loeb Classical Library, v. 14, *Pro T. Annio Milone*, tr. N. H. Watts (Cambridge, Mass.: Harvard University Press, 1979) 16–17.

28. V 4:3042.

29. Richard B. Morris, ed., *John Jay, the Winning of the Peace: Unpublished Papers, 1780–1784* (New York: Harper and Row, 1975) 716–17.

30. Union Fire Company Minutes, 90, HSP.

31. Smith, *Hannah* 141–42.

32. Lemay, "Vanity."

33. The discussion echoes Lemay, "American Aesthetic" 471–75.

34. Franklin's joke of 26 January 1784 asserting his preference for the turkey rather than the eagle as a symbol of the United States had a serious undercurrent. It ridiculed the traditional European values of military prowess, aristocracy, and feudalism with which the eagle was associated and asserted the rise of domestic, democratic, and middle-class values associated with the turkey. Lemay, "American Aesthetic" 497–99.

35. C. N. Elvin, *A Handbook of Mottoes* (1860; Detroit: Gale, 1971). I thank Nicholas P. Gross for correcting my high school Latin.

36. Chester County Historical Society, #1987.857. Dr. Patricia J. Keller called the quilt to my attention in 1997.

37. Bartram, *Correspondence* 292.

38. Richard Peters to Thomas Penn, 25 March 1748, TPP, reel 6, frame 101.

39. CR 5:158–59.

40. CR 5:198, 187 respectively.

41. Ibid.; P 3:222n. Cf. Isaacson 125.

42. CR 5:215.

43. Thomas Penn to Lynford Lardner, 29 March 1748, TPP, reel 1, frames 311–13.

44. CR 5:320–23.

45. *PG,* 19 January 1748.

46. Smith, *Hannah* 189–93.

47. John Churchman, *An Account of the Gospel Labours* (Philadelphia: Crukshank, 1779) 68–73; E16223. Though the printed account says Churchman visited Philadelphia in the spring of 1748, Churchman's notes, as copied by John Woolman, reported that it was "In the 4th month" (March was still the traditional Quaker "first" month—and there were no meetings in April). John Woolman, *Journal and Major Essays,* ed. Phillips P. Moulton (New York: Oxford University Press, 1971) 78. Herman Wellenreuther, "The Political Dilemma of the Quakers in Pennsylvania, 1681–1748," *PMHB* 94 (1970): 168–69, dates the speech to 9 June; Bauman, 12, seems to date it to "late in 1748." I follow Woolman and Wellenreuther in dating the month to June and my own estimate in dating the speech to 10 or 11 June.

48. Churchman 72–73.

49. Richard Peters Letterbook, 313–14, PHS; V 4:3194.

50. Penn to Peters, 9 June 1748, TPP, reel 1, frames 314–16; *PG,* 18 August 1748.

51. For the author, see *Calendar* #886.

52. Following J. Bennett Nolan, *Printer Strahan's Book Account* (Reading, Pa.: Bar of Berks County, 1939) 33, the editors of the 1961 *Papers,* 3:39n, 329–30, supposed that Read warned Franklin in 1747 not to run again. But that was before Franklin organized the voluntary Pennsylvania militia Association, to which Franklin refers as the reason some members were dissatisfied with him. I believe the date was before the clerk's election on 15 October 1748. In 1997, I gave reasons in the DH, under 14 October 1747, for believing that it was in 1748 that Read tried to supplant Franklin.

53. Penn to Jonathan Belcher, 21 February 1748/9, TPP, reel 1, frame 330.

CHAPTER 2

1. Daniel Boorstin makes this myth the foundation of his Franklin discussion in *The Americans: The Colonial Experience* (New York: Random House, 1958) 251–59.

2. Joseph Priestley, *History and Present State of Electricity* (London: Dodsley, 1767) 158; in 1775 edition, 1:192, 225; all references are to the 1775 edition unless otherwise noted.

3. Actually, Franklin met Dr. Archibald Spencer in Boston in 1743. J. A. Leo Lemay, "Franklin's 'Dr. Spence': The Reverend Archibald Spencer (1698?–1760), M.D.," *Maryland Historical Magazine* 59 (1964): 199–216.

4. Cohen, *F&N* 431; Lemay, *EK* 54, 59; J. L. Heilbron, "Franklin, Haller, and Franklinist History," *Isis* 68 (1977): 539–44; Heilbron, *E* 325. Studies on Franklin

have continued to say so: Schiffer 48; Tom Tucker, *BF and His Electric Kite Hoax* (New York: Public Affairs, 2003) 12–13; Dray 45–46. Haller's essay was reprinted in the *Scots Magazine* 7 (June 1745): 277–83, and in the Boston *American Magazine* 2 (December 1745): 530–37.

5. The same issue of the *GM*, 15 (April 1745): 224, advertised "*Acta Germanica. No. VI. Vol. II*, (in which is a large account of electricity, with copper plate representations) pr. 6d. Robinson." I have searched in vain for a copy of the pamphlet. The Library Company's 1746 catalogue was actually printed in 1747 and titled *The Charter of the Library Company of Philadelphia* (Philadelphia: Franklin, 1746); E5853.

6. Haller 194a. Collinson's letter accompanying his presents to the Library Company is not extant; Colden 3:110. Lemay, *EK* 57n28, pointed out that Collinson echoed Haller's language; Cohen, *Founding Fathers* 54, Cohen, *BF's Science* 62, makes a similar observation.

7. Rene Descartes, *Discourse on the Method . . . a Bilingual Edition*, ed. George Heffernan (Notre Dame: University of Nortre Dame Press, 1994) 35.

8. Cohen, *BF'sE* 409–21. The manuscript is in HSP. References to Lecture One cite pagination from *BF'sE*.

9. J. A. Leo Lemay, "Franklin and Kinnersley," *Isis* 52 (1961): 575–81.

10. Cohen, *BF'sE* 71n28.

11. Pliny was in the *New-England Courant* Library; *Life* 1:162–63.

12. Cohen, *BF'sE* 410.

13. Heilbron, *Elements* 165–66; Cohen, *BF's Science* 29.

14. The article on "electricity" in Ephraim Chambers, *Cyclopaedia* (London: Knapton, 1728), described electrical research through Hauksbee. The Library Company had a copy before 1741 (1741 *Catalogue* 9). Franklin no doubt had his own copy; he reprinted its article on earthquakes in the 15 and 22 December 1737 *PG*.

15. Priestley 1:31; Heilbron, *Elements* 171.

16. J. T. Desaguliers, *A Course of Mechanical and Experimental Philosophy* (London, 1725) 3; ESTC T1882.

17. Hackman 4.

18. *PT*, abridged by Lowthrop and Jones, 5 v.; Edwin Wolf 2nd, "First Books and Printed Catalogues," *PMHB* 78 (1954): 58.

19. Edwin Wolf 2nd, "Franklin and His Friends Choose Their Books," *PMHB* 80 (1956): 24.

20. *PT* 37 [1731–32]: 399–404; Heilbron, *Elements* 172–32.

21. Isaac Greenwood, *A Course of Philosophical Lectures* [Boston, 1739]; E39848. In *Life* 2:489 and 604n45, I mentioned Greenwood's earlier and fuller (twelve pages) *Experimental Course of Mechanical Philosophy* (Boston, 1726), E2746. I did not note this later, four-page syllabus, which Greenwood no doubt followed in his Philadelphia lectures in 1740. David C. Leonard, "Harvard's First Science

Professor," *Harvard Library Bulletin* 29 (1981): 168, showed that it was printed in 1739.

22. Cohen, *BF'sE* 410–11.

23. Dufay, *PT* 38 (1733–34): 258–60; Haller 194a; Heilbron, *Elements* 174; Priestley 1:59.

24. Heilbron, *Elements* 174; Gray, *PT* 39 (1735–36): 16–24.

25. *PT* 38 (1733): 263; Priestley 1:61; Cohen, *BF'sE* 43.

26. Haller 193b.

27. Cohen, *F&N* 243–60, surveyed Desaguliers's influence on Franklin. For Desaguliers's terminology, see Hackmann 64–65.

28. J. T. Desaguliers, *Course of Experimental Philosophy* (1734–44) 2:335; Heilbron, *Elements* 174; Wheler, *PT* 41:1 (1739–40): 98–117; Priestley 1:82; Paul Fleury Mottelay, *Bibliographical History of Electricity* (London: Griffin, 1922) 168; Hackmann 82.

29. *PT* 38: 435 (1733–34): 441–50.

30. St. George Leakin Sioussat, "The *PT* in the Libraries of William Byrd of Westover, BF, and the APS," *PAPS* 93 (1949): 99–113, at 105; Wolf and Hayes #2950.

31. Library Company Minute Book, 1:124; Library Company of Philadelphia.

32. Arlene Palmer, "BF and the Wistarburg Glassworks," *Antiques* (January 1974): 207–10.

33. Heilbron, *E* 312–14.

34. Humphrey Davy, *Collected Works*, ed. John Davy (London: Smith, Elder, 1840) 8:263.

35. *London Magazine* 15 (July 1746): 352; *Scots Magazine* 8 (December 1746): 577. The Franklin/Kinnersley lecture said that Bose "first found in 1744, the method of kindling Spirits by the Electric Spark." Cohen, *BF'sE* 412.

36. Bartram, *Correspondence* 287.

37. In March 1747, Collinson sent Franklin the last four issues of *PT*, William Watson's *Experiments and Observations . . . of Electricity* (1746), and Watson's *Sequel to Experiments and Observations* (1746). P 3:134, 141.

38. John Farley, *The Spontaneous Generation Controversy from Descartes to Oparin* (Baltimore: Johns Hopkins University Press, 1977).

39. Priestley 1:142–44, 194.

40. Aphorism #95 in Francis Bacon, *Novum Organum*; quoted from *Philosophical Works* 288. For an analysis of Newton's methods in the *Optics*, see Cohen, *F&N* 151–201.

41. For Franklin's "new Terms" in electricity, see appendix 3.

42. Robert A. Millikan, "BF as a Scientist," in *Meet Dr. Franklin* (Lancaster, Pa.: Franklin Institute, 1943) 11–26, at 16.

43. John Freke, *An Essay to Shew the Cause of Electricity* (1746), abstracted in *GM* 16 (October 1746): 521–22. J. L. Heilbron suggested to me that others took up Freke's ideas later in approximations to field theory.

44. *London Magazine* 15 (November 1746): 594, #27.

45. *GM* 16 (November 1746): 569–70.
46. Cohen, *F&N* 459–60.
47. Heilbron, *E* 330.
48. Quoted in Alfred Owen Aldridge, "BF: The Fusion of Science and Letters," in *American Literature and Science*, ed. Robert J. Scholnick (Lexington: University Press of Kentucky, 1992) 53, citing Duane, *Life and Writings* 2:387 (Ford #585).
49. Cohen, *BF'sE* 412.
50. Duane Roller and Duane H. D. Roller, *The Development of the Concept of Electric Charge* (Cambridge, Mass.: Harvard University Press, 1954) 59.
51. Priestley 1:195–96.
52. Ibid. 1:196–97; Cohen, *BF'sE* 65–66.
53. Edward Shippen to Joseph Shippen, 16 May 1751, Shippen Papers APS.
54. Priestley 1:201.
55. Marquis de Condorcet, *Eloge de M. Franklin* (Paris: Chez Pyre, 1791) 12; Ford #841. See also in Condorcet, *Oeuvres* 3:372.
56. *OED*, s.v. *"battery"*: "III. A combination of simple instruments, usually to produce a compound instrument of increased power; applied originally with a reference to the *discharge* of electricity from such a combination." In 1801 Sir Humphrey Gilbert adapted Franklin's term to voltaic electricity. *OED*, 10a. See also appendix 3.
57. Priestley 1:198.
58. Lemay, *EK* 58–61.
59. Wolf and Hayes # 1336, p. 555.
60. Lemay, *EK* 61.
61. Lemay, *EK* 88, 112.
62. Edward Shippen to Joseph Shippen, 11 September 1751, Shippen Papers, APS.
63. Gipson, Evans 4–10; Walter Klinefelter, *Lewis Evans and His Map* (Philadelphia: American Philosophical Society *Transactions* 61, pt. 7, 1971) 33.
64. Hauksbee, cited in Clark, *BF* 79.
65. Dr. Samuel Wall, *PT* 26 (1708): 69–76; Heilbron, *E 236*; Clark, *BF* 79; Gray, *PT* 39 (1735–36): 16–24, at 24.
66. Haller 193b.
67. Cohen, *BF'sE* 419.
68. *GM* 21 (April 1751): 190, #14.
69. Krider 186.
70. P 3:365–76. The editors of the *Papers* thought that Dr. John Mitchell was the addressee, but Franklin stated in the *Autobiography* that he wrote it for Kinnersley and sent a copy to Mitchell (A 153).
71. The reason for the mistaken notion that Franklin at first intended to have insulated lightning rods rather than grounded ones was that early Franklin students relied primarily on the materials published in Franklin's *Experiments and Observations on Electricity* (1751). Though the pamphlet described both grounded and insulated lightning rods, Franklin's proposed test for determin-

ing whether electricity existed in thunderclouds called for an insulated rod. Franklin's first suggestion of lightning rods, however, was in a letter to Collinson of 2 March 1750. It hypothesized that lightning rods would protect structures and ships from lightning. To protect them, the lightning rods would have to be grounded. Cohen, *BF's Science* 87, thought that it was obvious that BF was speaking of grounded lightning rods (P 3:472–73).

72. *GM* 20 (December 1750): 537n.

73. Immanuel Kant, "Was ist Äufklarung?" (1784).

74. Heilbron, *E* 336.

75. I. Bernard Cohen, *Some Early Tools of American Science* (Cambridge, Mass.: Harvard University Press, 1950), nos. 17, 18, and 19 following p. 154, with commentaries on pp. 161–62. Since these houses demonstrated a difference between pointed lightning rods and those with a sphere, they probably date from the period of the American Revolution, when pointed rods were identified with Franklin and America, whereas ones with knobs or spheres at the top were identified with King George III and British authority. They must date from after 1773, when the controversy between the points and knobs started. See also Brandon Brame Fortune and Deborah J. Warner, *Franklin & His Friends* (Washington, D.C.: Smithsonian National Portrait Gallery, 1999) 77 (figs. 5–10).

76. Lemay, *EK*, frontispiece.

77. Royal Society Journal Book (entries are chronological), 275.

78. The 1961 editors of the *Papers* followed Cohen, *BF'sE* 77–100, and have, in turn, influenced subsequent scholarly opinion, e.g., Raymond Phineas Stearns, *Science in the British Colonies of America* (Urbana: University of Illinois Press, 1970) 628–29; Heilbron, *E* 335, 346n10; and Dray 60. Tucker, 106–7, is an exception.

79. Cohen, *BF'sE* 84–85, 88; Heilbron, *E* 346n10, and subsequent scholars have not realized that the first notice merely reprinted Kinnersley's advertisement—and quite possibly did not guess until months later that the anonymous advertisement had anything to do with Franklin.

80. Franklin assured Benjamin Gale that the mistakes made in his piece as printed in the *GM* were not worth correcting, for the paper was accurately printed in the *PT*, and nobody paid any attention to the careless notices in the popular magazines (P 14:60).

81. William Watson, "Some Further Inquiries into the Nature and Properties of Electricity," *PT* 45 (1748): 93–120. Watson quoted Franklin on pp. 98–100.

82. Identified only as "a Gentleman at Paris to his Friend at Toulon" in *GM* 22 (June 1752): 263–64, but Franklin specified the author (A 155). Edward Wright (b. ca. 1729; d. 20 August 1761), M.D., Edinburgh, 1753. Admitted FRS, 5 April 1759, with Peter Collinson as his primary sponsor. P 7:24 n3, biog. note; 7:51; Wolf and Hayes #3720.

83. Commenting on the chapter by email on 2 January 2007.

84. William Stukeley, "On the Causes of Earthquakes," *PT* 46 (1749–50): 641–46,

with the reference to Franklin on p. 643. By the time this number (#497) of the *PT* appeared, Stukeley, who corresponded with Collinson, knew that Franklin's writings on electricity were going to be published. He cited it as edited "by Mr. Collinson, F.R.S. London, 1750.8vo."

85. Royal Society, "Journal Books of Scientific Meetings, 1660–1800," reel 8, pp. 205–6, 213, 214–16. For BF's reply of 27 July 1750, see reel 4, pp. 7–8.

86. I suspect that the date of the letter should be 6 December 1749. It would be extraordinary for a letter written in Philadelphia to reach Collinson in London and then be transmitted to the Royal Society within five weeks. Furthermore, the two experiments recounted in the letter are much less significant than the account in section 24 of Franklin's major summary of 29 July 1750.

87. *PT* 47 (1751–52): 202–11, reprinted in P 4:136–42.

88. Stearns, 628, says that after hearing Watson's "Account," the society "immediately and unanimously voted to publish all of Franklin's communications in the *PT*." I could not find this vote in the minutes nor did the Royal Society publish them.

89. Royal Society, "Journal Books of Scientific Meetings, 1660–1800," reel 8, p. 159.

90. "A Letter from Mr. Franklin to Mr. Peter Collinson . . . concerning the Effects of Lightning," *PT* 47 (1751–52): 289–91; P 4:143–44.

91. Franklin called him "Delor" (A 155). As the translator of Giambatista Beccaria's *Lettre sur l'électricité* (Paris: Ganeau, 1754), he is "M. De Lor."

92. P 4:363 has February; I follow the date in Heilbron, *E* 348.

93. Priestley 1:382–83; and Dr. Wright's letter of 14 May 1752, *GM* 22 (June 1752): 263–64.

94. E. Philip Krider, email correspondence with the author, 20 December 2005.

95. *GM* 22 (May 1752): 229, and *London Magazine* 21 (May 1752): 238, printed the French report of 26 May confirming BF's hypothesis.

96. Benjamin Wilson, "Memoir," transcribed by J. W. Hulton, 26–27, National Portrait Gallery Archives; John Bevis, *GM* 22 (August 1752): 383.

97. *Monthly Review* 9 (August 1753): 103–13, at 104.

98. Dalibard wrote in the advertisement to the second edition of his translation that "as soon as the first edition . . . was completed, I sent a copy of it to M. Franklin, which put me into direct correspondence with him." Franklin, however, could not have received the book before 14 September 1752, when he wrote Cadwallader Colden that he saw in the May issue of the *GM* that a French translation of his *Experiments and Observations* had appeared and said he hoped Collinson would send him a copy.

99. Cohen, *BF's Science* 66–109, is the best discussion. According to the lists in the *Pennsylvania Gazette*, no ships from France entered into Philadelphia in June or July, but from "Bourdeaux, the ship *Greyhound*" entered sometime during the week ending 7 August, and the *Pembroke*, 13 August. From Great Britain, the ship *Crawford* entered sometime during the week ending 11 June; *Samson* entered from Bristol, 2 July; the ship *Dursey* entered from Belfast and the ship

Bendall entered from Liverpool, 13 August; and the ship *Beaver* from Dublin, 20 August. Evidently the success of the French experiments was unknown in New York until the week ending 2 October, when James Parker, Franklin's former partner, printed in the *New York Gazette or Weekly Post Boy* news of BF's sentry box experiments from the *GM* for June.

100. Edward M. Riley, "The Independence Hall Group," *Transactions of the APS* 43, pt. 1 (1953): 7–42, at 17; Martin P. Snyder, *City of Independence* (New York: Praeger, 1975) 37–38.

101. Priestley wrote that the key was fastened to the end of the hemp string, "that the electric virtue might stop when it came to the key." Cohen, *BF's Science* 230n10.

102. Priestley 1:216.

103. Priestley 1:80. A[lexander] McAdie, "The Date of Franklin's Kite Experiment," *PAAS* 34 (1924): 195, noted that when the string became wet and acted as a conductor, the fibers no longer stood out.

104. Penrose R. Hoopes, "Cash Dr. to BF," *PMHB* 80 (1956): 46–73, at 50, 50n7; Henry Stuber, "Life of Franklin," *Universal Asylum and Columbian Magazine* 5 (September, 1790): 142; Parton 1:290; I. Minis Hays, *PAAS*, n.s., 34 (1924): 202; Clark, *BF* 85, following Edwin J. Houston, "Franklin as Man of Science," *Journal of the Franklin Institute* 161 (1906): 282.

105. Franklin, who had been asked for a detailed account of the death of Richmann by James Bowdoin, printed the report of his death in the *PG*, 5 March 1754. Heilbron, *E* 352n36, cites the statistical possibility. Priestley 1:106, 107–8.

106. Krider's estimates were given in response to my query of 16 January 2006.

107. Pierre Eugène DuSimitiér's notes (Library of Congress) record it from the paper, which is not extant.

108. Cohen, *BF's Science* 83, wrote that after Franklin performed the kite experiment in June, he "had no further reason to delay the introduction of lightning rods to protect buildings in Philadelphia," but Cohen ignored the necessity of having others approve of erecting rods on the statehouse and the academy. Cf. Tucker 191–92.

109. McAdie 194.

110. Cohen, *BF's Science* 99; at 82, Cohen argues that BF erected the lightning rods in June or July 1752.

111. *PT* 47 (1751–52): 565–67. The editors of the *Papers* (4:364–66) compare the letter to Collinson with the account Franklin printed in the 19 October *PG*.

112. William E. Lingelbach, "BF and the Scientific Societies," *Journal of the Franklin Institute* 261 (1956): 9–31.

113. In *PT* 44 (1746–47): 704–49, with the description of the German's ringing the bells with his electrical machine on pp. 735–36.

114. Reviewing part III (1754) of Franklin's *Experiments and Observations on Electricity*, William Bewley gave a theory that also attributed the luminous appearance of seawater to microscopic "animalcules" as observed by Dr. Vianelli of Chiog-

gia, Italy. *Monthly Review* 11 (December 1754): 417. Benjamin Christie Nagle, *Monthly Review . . . Indexes of Contributors and Articles* (Oxford: Clarendon, 1934) 110. Evidently Bowdoin's and Vianelli's hypotheses were independent, though Vianelli's were more conclusive.

115. E. Philip Krider, email correspondence with the author, 29 January 2006. The *OED* defines "leader" in meteorology: "a leader stroke is a preliminary stroke of lightning that ionizes the path taken by the much brighter return stroke that follows."

116. Cohen, *BF's Science* 118–58.

117. Cotton Mather, *The Christian Philosopher*, ed. Winton U. Solberg (Urbana: University of Illinois Press, 1993) 72–73.

118. Jonathan Edwards, paragraph 9 of "Personal Narrative."

119. Cohen, *BF'sE* 421.

120. Lemay, *EK* 77–79.

121. *PT* 48 (1753–54): 201–16, at 202, 205, 206.

122. JAD 1:60.

123. Stephen Hales, "Some Considerations on the Causes of Earthquakes," *PT* 46 (1749–50): 669–81.

124. John Winthrop, *A Lecture on Earthquakes* (Boston: Edes and Gill, 1755) 6, 9–10; E7597. An abbreviated version of the same information is in *PT* 50 (1757): 1–18, at 2–3, 12.

125. JAD 1:61–62.

126. Cohen, *BF's Science* 139.

127. *London Magazine* 16 (June 1747): 273, (July 1747): 312, 314; *GM* 22 (August 1752): 363–64; Finger 89–109.

128. For more on Logan and Belcher, see Finger 92–95.

129. Cadwalader Evans, "A Relation of a Cure Performed by Electricity," *Medical Observations and Inquiries* (1757): 83–86; Randolph Shipley Klein, "Dr. Cadwalader Evans (1716–1773)," *Transactions of the College of Physicians of Philadelphia* 35 (1967–68): 30–36; Finger 106–7.

130. Priestley 1:220.

131. Priestley 1:221, citing Johan Carl Wilcke Des Hern Bf's Esq. Briefe von der Elektricität (Leipzig: Gottfried Kiesewetter, 1758) 351.

132. Despite I. Bernard Cohen's refutation of this myth in 1945, subsequent observers still maintain its truth. Cohen, "How Practical Was Benjamin Franklin's Science?" *PMHB* 69 (1945): 284–93; reprinted in Cohen, *BF's Science* 31–39. Boorstin, 243–65.

133. Cohen, *BF's Science* 32.

134. Cohen, *F&N* 110; see also Chapter 3.

135. Adrienne Koch, *Power, Morals, and the Founding Fathers* (Ithaca, N.Y.: Cornell University Press, 1961) 16.

136. J. L. Heilbron has pointed out flaws in Priestley's reasoning and denied that the experiment demonstrated the law of squares. Heilbron, *E* 464.

137. Priestley 2:15–16.

138. Ibid. 2:39.

139. Ibid. 1:196, 197, 220.

140. Poe's review of Hawthorne's *Twice-Told Tales*, in *Edgar Allan Poe: Essays and Reviews*, ed. G. R. Thompson (New York: Library of America, 1984) 572.

141. Samuel Briggs, *Nathaniel Ames* (Cleveland, 1891) 257–58.

142. Aldridge, *French* 124, citing Schelle, ed., *Oeuvres de Turgot* 5:647.

143. Alexander von Humboldt, *Cosmos*, v. 2 (1849) 727.

144. Robert A. Millikan, "Benjamin Franklin as a Scientist," *Journal of the Franklin Institute* 232 (1941): 407–23, esp. 409.

145. Ibid. 417.

146. Albert Parry, ed. and trans., *Peter Kapitsa on Life and Science* (New York: Macmillan, 1968) 34, 49.

CHAPTER 3

1. E6783; Miller 546. The preface and appendix are reprinted in Bartram, *Correspondence* 780–83.

2. Cohen, *BF's Science* 185–93, contains a revised version of "BF and the Transit of Mercury in 1753," *PAPS* 94 (1950): 222–32. Cohen's 1950 version contained a facsimile of *Letters Relating to the Transit of Mercury over the Sun* [Philadelphia: Franklin and Hall, 1753]; E7038; Miller 574.

3. For the hydrographer Bonnécamps, see *DCB* 4:76–77.

4. Cohen, *BF's Science* 190, notes that after 1761 and 1769, there were transits in 1874 and 1882, and that the next ones would be 2004 and 2012.

5. Cohen, *BF's Science* 193.

6. Krider, 169, citing Gisela Kutzbach, *The Thermal Theory of Cyclones* (Boston: American Meterological Society, 1979) 63–117.

7. George Hadley, "Concerning the Cause of the General Trade-Winds," *PT* 39 (1935–36): 58–62. Franklin annotated the Royal Society's 1769 edition, p. 197, with the following holograph note: he had "formerly, in some Magazine, met with the foregoing Manner of explaining the Trade Winds; but at the Time of Writing this Paper did not recollect to whom he was indebted for it. He now finds that it was first communicated to the Royal Society by a very ingenious Member, Mr. Geo. Hadley, in 1737." The printed footnote in the 1774 edition is on p. 197. E. Philip Krider to J. A. Leo Lemay, 4 April 2007.

8. Krider, 327 n9, pointed out that Herman von Helmholtz, who analyzed what happened mathematically, also used the "bathtub" analogy. Kutzbach 96–99.

9. Alexander Stuart, "Part of a Letter . . . concerning some Spouts," *PT* 23 (1702–3): 1077–80.

10. Franklin's plate had a magic square where I have inserted the cross-section. Lesser-known but, in the opinion of Paul C. Pasles, more interesting magic squares will be illustrated in *Life*, Volume 5: a magic square of 16 from the

Canton Papers, and a magic square of 8 from Barbeu-Dubourg's *Oeuvres* (Ford 315). Pasles 202 (fig. 8.5) and 207 (fig. 8.7).

11. Krider 170.

12. For additional examples, see pp. 110, 183, and 189. Cohen, *F&N* 387; J. L. Heilbron, "BF as Natural Philosopher," in *Reappraising* 212; Patricia Fara, *An Entertainment for Angels: Electricity in the Enlightenment* (New York: Columbia University Press, 2002) 107–8; and Jessica Riskin, *Science in the Age of Sensibility* (Chicago: University of Chicago Press, 2002) 74–76, 76n16.

13. P 9:297, 308, 28:213. *The Journals of Captain James Cook*, ed. J. C. Beaglehole, 3 v. in 4 (Cambridge: Hakluyt Society 1755–74) 2:142.

14. It could have been his father, also Colonel Benjamin Tasker (1690–68), though the son (1722–60) seems more probable. P 6:167n2.

15. Glyn Williams, *Voyages of Delusion: The Northwest Passage in the Age of Reason* (London: Harper/Collins, 2002), sets the De Fonte narrative within its eighteenth-century contexts. For the text, see *Voyages to Hudson Bay in Search of a Northwest Passage, 1741–47*, 2 v., ed. William Barr and Glyndwr Williams (hereafter Barr and Williams)(London: Hakluyt Society, 1994–95) 2:20–27.

16. Petiver (1665?–18) published the De Fonte hoax in his *Monthly Miscellany*, January 1707/8, 123–26, 183–86. Henry R. Wagner, "Apocryphal Voyages to the Northwest Coast of America," *PAAS* 41 (1931): 190–96 reprinted it, 179–234. On pp. 202–3, Wagner showed that the author took background information for the early part of his account from William Dampier's *New Voyage* (London, 1697) and suggested that Daniel Defoe might be the author. For eighteenth-century reprintings, see Barr and Williams 2:353–56.

17. Barr and Williams 2:357–63.

18. "Effects of Cold," *PT* 42: 464 (1742–43): 157–71; the portions Franklin used are in Barr and Williams at 1:225–28. John Harris, *Navigatium atque Itinerantium Bibliotheca*, ed. John Campbell, 4 v. (London, 1744–48) 2:1028, BF's ownership of books concerning the northwest passage is confirmed by his lending Swaine the "Journals of the last voyage" (4:466).

19. Percy Adams, "The Case of Swaine versus Drage," *Essays . . . Presented to Stanley Pargellis* (Chicago: Newberry Library, 1965) 157–68; Adams, "The Man Who Married Hannah Boyte," *Soundings* 82 (1999): 183–203, at 201.

20. Lemay, *Men of Letters* 270–74; Howard N. Eavenson, *Map-Maker & Indian Traders* (Pittsburgh: Univiversity of Pittsburgh Press, 1949) 72.

21. For Dobbs, see Wolf and Hayes 872. BF had been following the Dobbs versus Middleton arguments since at least 1744 (P 2:410). Barr and Williams 2:355. For BF's copy of Swaine's *Account of a Voyage*, see Wolf and Hayes 3299.

22. [Charles Swaine], *The Great Probability of a Northwest Passage* (London: T. Jefferys, 1768) 65ff., 142–45.

23. For the maps illustrating Admiral De Fonte's supposed voyage, see Kenneth A. Kershaw, *Early Printed Maps of Canada*, 4 v. (Ancaster, Ont.: Kershaw, 1993–

98) 4:170–206. Charles Swaine's map is plate 942, entry 1197 (4:172); also in Wagner, facing 204, and in Williams, facing 198.

24. Lemay, *Men of Letters* 270–74. It may have been the enmity of Franklin and his friends that caused Sterling later to identify with Provost William Smith and to celebrate Smith in a 1758 iambic pentameter poem of 156 lines. William Smith Papers, v. 6, formerly at HSP, now at the University of Pennsylvania.

25. [Swaine], *Great Probability*, preface.

26. Edwin Swift Balch, "Arctic Expedition sent from the Colonies" 427, gives the pay for the "Draughtsman & Mineralist" and Eavenson proves that Pattin made the "Trader's Map" (a map of the Ohio country in December 1752), 28–47 and the map to Shannopintown (1753–54), 156–64, before setting out on the second voyage of the *Argo*. Eavenson reproduces both maps.

27. BF sent at least twelve copies to William Franklin. WF noted under the date of 11 July 1769: "Ten of *Drage's* Books were likewise delivered to J. Davenport for Sale, and are to be accounted for. One I kept, & one I sold to Mr. Odell." Franklin Papers, v. 67, no. 24, Mss, APS, *The Two Hundredth Year Anniversary United Brethren Missions Year Book* (Bethlehem, Pa.: Church of the Brethren, 1931); Eavenson, *Map-Maker* 48–49.

28. *PG* 29 November 1753. I find no other references to a "Bull's-Head Tavern" and suspect it was the "BoarHead" Tavern in Pewter Platter Alley (*PG*, 22 August 1751, 30 July 1752, and 21 August 1755).

29. P 4:413n5. *GM* 24 (1754), map facing p. 123. Entry 1213, plate 952, in Kershaw (4:183, 186).

30. [Swaine], *Great Probability* xii.

31. The small anthropological collection of Eskimo materials had disappeared from the Library Company by 1828. Balch 425n4.

32. John Adams, "Dr. Franklin once gave to Lord Bute his Reasons in Writing for believing this a genuine Voyage." JAD 3:140.

33. Jefferys Del'Isle/Delisle; Kershaw, plate 957 (4:189), and entry 1218 (4:190).

34. John Green (d. 1757), *Remarks in Support of the New Chart of North and South America* (London: For Thomas Jefferys, 1753); Sabin 28538; ESTC T146626. Warren Heckrotte and Edward H. Dahl, "George Louis Le Rouge, Vitus Bering, and Admiral de Fonte: A Cautionary Tale about 'Cartographic Firsts,'" *Map Collector* 64 (Fall 1993): 18–23, at 20.

35. Franklin and Swaine/Drage remained friends. On 26 March 1769, BF wrote Daniel Burton, secretary of the Society for the Propagation of the Gospel in Foreign Parts, and secured Swaine an appointment as an Anglican minister; P 16:70–71. On 2 March 1771, Theodorus Swaine Drage wrote BF about his troubles as an Anglican priest during the Regulator movement in North Carolina; P 18:38–50.

36. JAD 3:108–9.

CHAPTER 4

1. CR 5:277–80.

2. V 4:3198, 1 September 1748. Peters to Penn, 16 June 1748, TPP, reel 6.

3. V 4:3194; *PG*, 18 August 1748.

4. V 4:3197–3203, at 3198.

5. CR 5:339–40; in *PG*, 8 September 1748.

6. V 4:3206; *PG*, 15 September 1748.

7. V 3:3225. Peters Letter Book, 1747–50, 2r–3v, HSP; in the photocopy of Peters Letter Book, p. 339. William Wade Hinshaw, *Encyclopedia of American Quaker Genealogy*, 7 v. (Baltimore: Genealogical Publishing Company, 1969–77) 2:386.

8. Saturday, 12 May; Smith, *Hannah* 286; Edwin B. Bronner, "The Disgrace of John Kinsey," *PMHB* 75 (1951): 400–415; Gipson, *Evans* 135.

9. Smith, *Hannah* 298.

10. *PG*, 20 February 1753.

11. Ibid.; *Minutes*, Phila. 565.

12. *PG* 20 February 1753.

13. Rohr Family, Society Miscellaneous Collection, PHS.

14. When Oxnard died in 1754, the *PG* reprinted a long obituary on 11 July 1754.

15. Sachse 86 and facsimile, 87.

16. Sachse 83–84; Melvin M. Johnson, *Beginnings of Freemasonry in America* (New York: Doran Company, 1924) 124–32.

17. For William, Baron Byron of Rochdale (1722–98), the great-uncle of the poet, see G. E. C[okayne], *Complete Peerage*, 14 v., ed. Vicary Gibbs (London: St. Catherine Press, 1910–98) 2:456. Julius Friedrich Sachse, *Old Masonic Lodges of Pennsylvania* (Philadelphia, 1912), 53–56; Johnson 359, 369.

18. A few notes on the various officers are in the DH, under 7 October 1751.

19. Johnson 359, 370. For members of the Philadelphia St. John's lodges at this time, see P 5:236–37, and *PMHB* 20 (1896): 121. *Proceedings in Masonry: [Boston] St. John's Grand Lodge, 1733–1792* (Boston: Grand Lodge, 1895) 20; for Hugh McDaniel's offices, see pp. 7, 10.

20. Hanna 45, 49; Rothermund 71. Governor James Hamilton wrote Thomas Penn that he had put several members of the assembly in the "commission of the peace, yet they will not qualify for fear of losing their popularity"; Hanna 45. Hutson, however, 307n13, argued that it was "not until after the provincial elections of October, 1764" that the Proprietary Party began to use the magistrate's position as patronage.

21. Peters to Penn, TPP, reel 7, frames 0579–80. The letter is only dated 1752.

22. David Paul Brown, *The Forum: Or Forty Years Full Practice at the Philadelphia Bar* (Philadelphia: Small, 1856) 236–37, 582–88.

23. CR 5:572.

24. John Hill Martin, *Martin's Bench and Bar of Philadelphia* (Philadelphia: Rees Welsh, 1883) 68. At Isaac Norris's Fairfield, BF proved a deed of sale on 22 May

1754 from Hannah Harrison (sister of Isaac Norris II) to her brother Charles Norris. Montgomery County Historical Society. Cited by W. T. Parsons, "Isaac Norris II, the Speaker" (Ph.D. diss., University of Pennsylvania, 1955) 162.

CHAPTER 5

1. *Life* 1:151–53, 207–8. Thomas H. Montgomery, *History of the University of Pennsylvania . . . to 1770* (Philadelphia: Jacobs Company, 1900); Edward Potts Cheyney, *History of the University of Pennsylvania, 1740–1940* (Philadelphia: University of Pennsylvania Press, 1940); William L. Turner, "The College, Academy, and Charitable School of Philadelphia . . . 1740–1779" (Ph.D. diss., University of Pennsylvania, 1952); and Turner, "The Charity School, the Academy, and the College: Fourth and Arch Streets," APS *Transactions* 43 (1953): 179–86. Horle 3:43–44 provides a valuable synopsis.

2. P 1:320; *Life* 2:103, 492.

3. Franklin's commonsensical opinion on spelling contrasts markedly with his phonetic interests: he said, "I think the worst Spelling the best" (P 28:422; see also 15:174–78, 218–19).

4. Bernard Bailyn, *Education in the Forming of American Society* (Chapel Hill: University of North Carolina Press, 1960) 35.

5. A recent biographer claimed that Franklin attempted to appear like a gentleman by 1745 and therefore called himself a "Typographer," but it was Robert Grace, not Franklin, who did so. I thank Ellen Cohn for identifying the document's handwriting (P 3:51).

6. *Life* 1:227–33. For several responses to criticism of America and the American Dream, see J. A. Lemay, *An Early American Reader* (Washington, D.C.: U.S. Information Agency, 1988) 140–72.

7. For additional misrepresentations of authorities than those cited by the *Papers*, see Pangle & Pangle on Locke, 75, 80 and n. 11, 83–86 and nn. 17–22; and on Milton, 78 and n. 8, 80–81 and n.13, 86. Francis Bacon, *Philosophical Works*, ed. John M. Robertson (London: Routledge, 1905) 79.

8. For the stage theory, see Lemay, "Frontiersman," and chapter 7, p. 249.

9. Shaftesbury, 50, on public spirit; on the usefulness of virtue, see *Life* 2:67–69, 207–9 and Tocqueville 525–30; see also *Life* 2:42.

10. Tocqueville also makes the point, 482–87.

11. For Locke/Hobbes, see *Life* 2:286. On associations, Tocqueville 513–20.

12. Richard Foster Jones, *Ancients and Moderns* (St. Louis: Washington University Press, 1936).

13. BF praised the *Universal History* in the 1746 Library Company *Catalogue*; *Life* 2:117.

14. William Douglass, *Historical Summary . . . of the British Settlements in North America* (1749, 1751). Lengthy earlier ones were Captain John Smith's *History of Virginia* and John Oldmixon's *History of the British Empire in America*. Oldmixon had been in the *New-England Courant*'s library; *Life* 1:162.

15. When I wrote a master's thesis on Kinnersley in 1962, I looked in the University of Pennsylvania Archives for an invoice of the instruments or any surviving ones in vain. Lemay, *EK* 103, 112.

16. Karu fig. 42.

17. Philip G. Nordell, "The Academy Lotteries," *University of Pennsylvania Library Chronicle* 19 (Spring 1953): 51–76, at 57.

18. *Minutes*, Phila. 524–25.

19. Ibid. 527–29.

20. Ibid. 524–25.

21. I suspect that Peters knew James Logan had used this phrase just three months earlier to describe Franklin's role in the militia Association.

22. Samuel Johnson, *Ethices Elementa* (Boston: Rogers and Fowle, 1746) E5794; for Martin, see Bell 1:105–8.

23. Herbert W. Schneider and Carol Schneider, eds., *Samuel Johnson . . . His Career and Writings*, 4 v. (New York: Columbia University Press, 1929); Richard Peters to Samuel Johnson, 6 August 1750; Montgomery 509.

24. BF's edition of Johnson is E6859; Miller 554.

25. Richard Peters, *A Sermon on Education* (Philadelphia: Franklin and Hall, 1751) 22–25; E6754; Miller 541.

26. William Smith, *A General Idea of the College of Mirania* (New York: Parker and Weyman, 1753) 15, 14; E7121.

27. Gegenheimer 31.

28. H. W. Smith 1:39.

29. Though Peter and Jemima are generally assumed to be the slave couple that Franklin referred to in a letter to his mother on 12 April 1750 (3:474), it is not certain. Franklin's relations with Peter in 1756 (6:425) seem almost the opposite of those with the earlier unnamed slave. The only mention of Jemima occurs in Franklin's will of 28 April 1757, where Peter and his wife, Jemima, are to be freed after BF's death (7:203).

30. Jennings 69–70.

31. Peters 21. The information is repeated in "a brief account of the Academy in the City of Philadelphia," *GM* 23 (December 1753): 552–53. Gegenheimer, 40, suggested that Smith wrote the "brief account," but Peters did.

32. *Statutes* 4:144.

33. Nordell, "The Academy Lotteries."

34. *Minutes*, Phila. 585.

35. Sellers 57–58, 219.

36. *Minutes of the Trustees of the College, Academy and Charitable Schools . . . Volume 1 1749 to 1768* (Wilmington, Del.: Scholarly Resources, 1974) 78. The *Minutes* are chronological, but the page is sometimes useful. Hereafter, College Minutes.

37. Finger 138–41.

38. Montgomery 366–69. Four of the submissions (by Morgan, Stephen Watts,

Joseph Reed, and Francis Hopkinson) for the English prize were published: *Four Dissertations on the Reciprocal Advantages of a Perpetual Union between Great Britain and Her American Colonies* (Philadelphia: W. & T. Bradford, [1766]); Evans 10400.

39. College Minutes 194.

40. H. W. Smith 1:143.

41. Ibid. 1:355.

42. College Minutes.

43. JAD 2:115.

44. The story of the college during the Revolutionary period has little to do with Franklin's life. The second volume of the *Minutes of the Trustees*, pp. 165–80, records the meetings in Franklin's home in 1789. I thank Mark Frazier Lloyd, archivist of the University of Pennsylvania, for photocopies of those pages.

45. Quoted from the CD ROM of *The Papers of Benjamin Franklin*, Packard Humanities Institute, Los Altos, California.

46. H. W. Smith 2:312–13.

47. S 10:29. WN 765 (V.i.f.20) also objected to the common Latin education and likewise complained that people continued in "the established forms and ceremonies."

48. Parton 1:308.

CHAPTER 6

1. Richard Peters asked Thomas Penn on 15 October 1750 about his sentiments on a union of the colonies in Indian affairs. Peters evidently thought a union of the colonies, at least in Indian affairs, would be beneficial. Peters to Penn, 15 October 1750, TPP, reel 6; PPOC, 5:73, last page.

2. *Life* 2:348, 248n32.

3. Lemay, "Frontiersman" passim, especially 189–90.

4. For Mason and Church, see *ANB*; for Rale, *DCB* 2:542–45; and for Lovewell, Lemay, *Early American Reader* 480–84. More on the Abenaki war is found in the entry for Mog, *DCB* 2:476–77.

5. See below, ch. 13, trade (post Carlisle Treaty).

6. E6699. Lawrence C. Wroth, *An American Bookshelf, 1755* (Philadelphia: University of Pennsylvania Press, 1934) 12–15, 118–21.

7. Standard overviews include Abbot Emerson Smith, *Colonists in Bondage* (Chapel Hill: University of North Carolina Press, 1947) 89–135; A. Roger Ekirch, *Bound for America* (Oxford: Clarendon, 1987); and Kenneth Morgan, *Slavery and Servitude in Colonial North America* (New York: New York University Press, 2001). Cheesman A. Herrick traces the history of Pennsylvania's attempts to evade the Transportation Act of 1718 in *White Servitude in Pennsylvania* (Philadelphia: McVey, 1926) 119–34.

8. Clark, *Public Prints* 119, celebrated the editorial as "the first American newspaper statement critical of British colonial policy." Clark thought it was by An-

drew Bradford or a close associate. He found it a "rare statement for the first half of the century, if not unique . . . preceding by thirty years Benjamin Franklin's famous" satire, "Rattlesnakes for Felons." Bradford, however, was neither bold nor a good writer. Bordley wrote the editorial. Judge Carroll T. Bond characterized Bordley, noting that he brought "eight suits, seven writs of error or appeals within the province and five appeals to the King in Council" against the transportation of felons. *Proceedings of the Maryland Court of Appeals, 1695–1729* (Washington, D.C.: American Historical Association, 1933) 241. See also Aubrey C. Land, *The Dulanys of Maryland* (Baltimore: Maryland Historical Society, 1955) 88–97, and J. A. Leo Lemay, "The Namierizing of Early American History," *Virginia Magazine of History and Biography* 88 (1980): 94–103.

9. Lemay, *Men of Letters* 112.

10. Leonard W. Labaree, *Royal Instructions to British Colonial Governors, 1670–1776*, 2 v. (1935; rpt. New York: Octagon Books, 1967) 1:133–40, at #213–14.

11. Kevin J. Hayes, "The Board of Trade's 'Cruel Sarcasm': A Neglected Franklin Source," *Early American Literature* 28 (1993): 171–76, at 172; Oliver Norton Dickerson, *American Colonial Government, 1696–1765: A Study of the British Board of Trade* (Cleveland: Clark, 1912) 244–47; Labaree, *Royal Instructions* 2:673–74, #939.

12. For the act of 14 February 1729/30, see *Statutes* 4:164–71; for the supplement of 2 September 1738, see 320–21; and for the act of 3 February 1742/3, 360–70.

13. BT *Journal* 8:215–17; *Statutes* 4:509–10; *Acts PC*, 4:20–21; PA 1:721; Hayes 171.

14. *Acts PC* 4:21; PA 1:716–21. Through his brother-in-law John Carteret, first Earl Granville (1690–1763), a member of the Privy Council from 1720, and its president during 1751–63, Thomas Penn had excellent contacts with the Privy Council and with the board.

15. *Statutes* 4:503–4.

16. CR 5:500.

17. P 1:161, 3:205. Melvin Yazawa, *From Colonies to Commonwealth: Familiar Ideology and the Beginnings of the American Republic* (Baltimore: Johns Hopkins University Press, 1985) 87–89, 248–49.

18. I blithely made this up. If I am ever proven wrong, my ghost will be awed by the amount of work that went into the effort.

19. *GM* 21 (June 1751): 279 *London Magazine* 20 (July 1751): 293.

20. Horace, *Epistles* 1:xi, 27: *Caelum non animum mutant, qui trans mare currunt*; they who cross the sea change their climate, not their natures. Cf. *Life* 1:297nn65–70. Samuel Purchas partly echoed and partly quoted Horace in his dedicatory poem for Smith's *General History of Virginia* (1624), in John Smith, *Complete Works*, ed. Philip Barbour, 3 v. (Chapel Hill: University of North Carolina Press, 1986) 2:47, line 4. George Mason later alluded to the idea, "To the committee of Merchants in London," June 6, 1766; Robert A. Rutland, ed., *The Papers of George Mason*, 3 v. (Chapel Hill University of North Carolina Press, 1970) 1:68.

21. Alexander Pope, *Rape of the Lock*, ed. Geoffrey Tillotson (London: Methuen, 1940) 180 (canto 3, ll. 157–58), where *Tatler* Nos. 47 and 121 are cited.

22. *Life* 1:82, 394–96, 404–5, 413, 2:215–18. On 17 and 24 June 1731 Franklin published "the mortifying News" of the imminent passage of the Molasses Act. In the following *Gazette*, 1 July 1731, he reprinted an article against the bill "for Restraining our Northern Colonies from carrying Horses and Lumber to the Foreign Colonies." On 31 July, he reprinted an attack on New England manufactures from the London *Daily Post Boy*, together with a refutation. In 1732, notes on mercantile acts against the mainland colonies appeared on 27 April and 11 May. The 8 June 1732 *Gazette* noticed several anti-American mercantilist acts: one forbidding the importation of hops into Ireland from America; another against exporting any hats from America; another for limiting the number of hat apprentices in the colonies; and another about the progress of the Molasses Act. Such news appeared in the *PG* every year. When Franklin noticed essays in other papers condemning the Acts of Trade and Navigation, he reprinted them. Thus, on 20 December 1748 the *PG* reprinted an essay from the Boston *Independent Advertiser* giving American grievances against England.

23. *Life* 1:296–97, 2:158–60. Robert A. Rutland, ed., *The Papers of George Mason*, 3 v. (Chapel Hill: University of North Carolina Press, 1970).

24. P 1:121; W 54; cf. P 20:395.

25. The *Boston Gazette* of 17 September is one example.

26. William Livingston, *The Independent Reflector*, ed. Milton M. Klein (Cambridge, Mass.: Harvard University Press, 1963) 164–69, at 165. In turn, it influenced William Smith, Jr., *History of the Province of New York*, ed. Michael Kammen, 2 v. (Cambridge, Mass.: Harvard University Press, 1972) 1:223.

27. Horle 2:285; V 4:3423.

28. V 4:3432.

29. I describe only the time that Franklin was serving, 1751ff. For an overview of the colonial period, 1710–56, see "Election Procedures" in Horle 2:20–23.

30. Foster 3:537A.

31. Hanna 51; cf. Hutson, "BF" 312–17; Jennings 81–83; Foster 3:537–43.

32. *Life* 2:214–15, 226, 331–33, 356, 559.

33. Silence Dogood; Junto ("15. Have you lately observed any encroachment on the just liberties of the people?" [1:258]); *PG* editorial, 24 September 1730, Nicholas Scull's Junto poem, ca. 1732; Franklin's poem, "The Rats & the Cheese," etc. *Life* 1:148, 334, 341, 418–19, 420–21, and especially 459.

34. *Life* 1:397–413; 2:193–213, 358–75, 429–35.

35. Foster 3:538.

36. Herrick, *White Servitude* 127n44.

37. *Statutes* 5:131–32.

38. V 4:3363.

39. V 4:3437–38.

40. "Céloron de Blainville, Pierre Joseph," *DCB* 3:99–100.

41. CR 5:515.

42. *Statutes* 2:62.

CHAPTER 7

1. Conway Zirkle, "BF, Thomas Malthus and the United States Census," *Isis* 48 (1957): 58–62, at 62. For the "thousand year" figure, see P 4:121; WN, 88, has the population double in five hundred years "in Great Britain and other European countries." Discussions of "Observations" include Cary, *F's Economic Views* 46–60; VD 216–18; A. Owen Aldridge, "F as Demographer," *Journal of Economics* 9 (1949): 25–44; Crane 68–70, 95–96; Connor 69–79; Drew R. McCoy, *Elusive Republic: Political Economy in Jeffersonian America* (Chapel Hill: University of North Carolina Press, 1980) 48–75; Cohen, *Founding Fathers* 156–64; Anderson 159–68; and Pasles 6–8. For Franklin's later major uses of the ideas in the "Observations," see P 8:340–56, 9:47–100, esp. 78–79, 14:131, 17:7, 18:27, 123, 20:10, 10 n1.

2. "Observations" (P 4:227–34), hereafter cited by volume, page, and section number.

3. On the popularity of Herbert's lines in early New England, see Abram E. Cutter, "Poetical Prognostics," *New England Historical and Genealogical Register* 27 (1873): 347–51. For BF's use of the *translatio* idea, see *Life* 1:58 58n19 (478), 286 286n15 (492–93), 2:103, 103n10 (584), 286, 286n15 (593).

4. Lemay, *Reader* 37–50, at 39. P 1:321, 2:380, 405. Franklin later used the motif at P 9:7, 10:215, 232, and 18:163. Uncle Benjamin Franklin used the *translatio* idea in a poem sent "To My Name 1713"; P 1:6.

5. R. S. Crane, *A Collection of English Poems, 1660–1800* (New York: Harper, 1932) 340; Andrew Burnaby, *Travels through North America* (1904; rpt. New York: A. M. Kelley, 1970) 149.

6. For young Franklin as a statistician, see *Life* 1:448–50.

7. For BF's notes on Halley, see APS ms: BF84, v. 68, fol. 83. Edmund Halley, "An Estimate of the Degrees of the Mortality of Mankind," and "Some Further Considerations on the Breslaw Bills of Mortality," *PT* 17:196, 198 (1693): 596–610, 654–56; Charles Davenant, *An Essay upon the Probable Methods of Making a People Gainers in the Balance of Trade* (London, 1699) 33. See also Charles M. Andrews, *Colonial Period of American History*, v. 4: *England's Commercial and Colonial Policy* (New Haven, Conn.: Yale University Press, 1938) 412–24.

8. Halley 655–56. Since Franklin quoted the Latin phrase in his notes for topics to take up in the Junto, he evidently had read Halley by 1732.

9. See Chapter 1.

10. Joshua Child, *New Discourse of Trade* (London, 1698) 195.

11. *Poor Richard Improved . . . for 1750* (Philadelphia: Franklin and Hall, [1749]) [p. 3]; E6320; Miller 469. See I. Hays 4:173; New Jersey censuses of 1737, 1738, and 1745. P 3:439n2. BF returned to the New Jersey census in *Poor Richard* for 1754

(P 5:182–83). For various mathematical questions in *Poor Richard*, see Pasles 67–74.

12. Archibald Kennedy, *Observations on the Importance of the Northern Colonies* (New York: James Parker, 1750) 3–4.

13. Frederick Jackson Turner knew Franklin's writings and reviewed Edward E. Hale, *Franklin in France*, v. 1 and 2 in the *Dial* 8 (May 1887): 7–10, and 9 (1888): 204–6. See also Gilbert Chinard, "Looking Westward," in *Meet Dr. Franklin* (Philadelphia: Franklin Institute, 1943) 135–50; Stourzh 48–82; and James H. Hutson, "BF and the West," *Western Historical Quarterly* 4 (1973): 425–34.

14. Kennedy 10. Franklin, "Observations" 4:229, #9.

15. Sir William Petty, *Economic Writings*, ed. Charles Henry Hull, 2 v. (Cambridge: Cambridge University Press, 1899) 2:469, 473–74; John Locke, *Two Treatises of Government*, ed. Peter Laslett, 2nd ed. (Cambridge: Cambridge University Press, 1970) 312; Montesquieu, *Spirit of the Laws*, tr. Thomas Nugent (New York: Hafner, 1949) 275 (bk. 18, 10). See also Lemay, "Frontiersman."

16. Charles Sumner, *Prophetic Ideas Concerning America* (Boston: Lee and Shepard, 1874); Bumsted.

17. Stourzh 58.

18. David Hume made a similar comment in his essay "Of the Populousness of Ancient Nations" (1752), in *Essays, Moral, Political, and Literary*, ed. Eugene F. Miller, rev. ed. (Indianapolis: Liberty Fund, 1987) 383–84, where the editor notes that "Hume anticipates the arguments of many . . . [who opposed] slavery." The sentiment was not uncommon. William Byrd of Westover, a major slave owner, wrote a similar statement in a letter of 12 July 1736 in which he also opposed the slave trade. Byrd, *Correspondence*, 3 v. (Charlottesville: University Press of Virginia, 1977) 2:487–89.

19. *Poor Richard* for 1748 claimed that "There are three great destroyers of mankind, *Plague, Famine,* and *Hero,*" and the worst was hero. Echoing 2 Samuel 24:12–13, BF said that war, generally created by hero-kings, was the greatest plague. In *Poor Richard* for 1750, he used Charles XII of Sweden as an example of one such hero (3:249–50, 253–54, 453–54).

20. See P 21:175 for BF's use of the phrase; See P 16:34 (31 January 1769) for adopting the idea of free trade.

21. Mandeville.

22. Anderson 164.

23. The best single indication that Adam Smith directly used Franklin in WN (1776) is that he cited both of Franklin's figures. See appendix 4.

24. Morgan, 76, wrote: "Did Franklin recognize that he was making an unspoken threat . . . power could move across the ocean and there would be no more senseless regulations of America by officials who knew nothing of America? He gave no indication that he thought so, but he must have seen deeper implications than he specified." Others who believe that Franklin's underlying message

was the future revolt and independence of the colonies are Connor 72–73 and Anderson 158–67.

25. In *Poor Richard* for July 1749, he had remarked critically, "The Preliminaries of the new Peace are copied from those of the old one [the 1713 Peace of Utrecht]: 'tis to be hoped the Peace itself will be better" (P 3:342).

26. Though many scholars have pointed out that "Palentine boors" meant nothing more than German peasants, the connotations of "boors" are, to my mind, negative. Farley Grubb noted that "Pennsylvanians of German Ancestry accounted fo 50 to 60 percent of Pennsylvania's population in 1760 and 33 percent in 1790." Grubb, "German Immigration to Pennsylvania, 1790 to 1820," *Journal of Interdisciplinary History* 20 (1990):417–36, at 417. Anderson 163.

27. Lemay, "Lockean Realities" 16–18. See also Lemay, "Polly Baker," in *The Oldest Revolutionary* 112–14; and *Life* 1:362–64, 2:48, 526, 549, 530, 560.

28. "Wherever there are the most happiness and virtue, and the wisest institutions, there will also be the most people." Hume, *Essays* 382.

29. See also *Life* 1:431–34, 2:76–79, 509–14, 522–26.

30. On or after 13 July 1753, short orations praising the proprietors for granting a charter were made by Francis Hopkinson, Josiah Martin, John Morris, Jr., and William Masters. Montgomery, *History* 178–79. Morris's praise of Franklin and of Franklin's civic improvements, especially his reflection of Franklin's attitudes concerning the future of America, irritated Thomas Penn. P 5:213, 213n6. Cf. William Smith to BF, February 1754, P 5:213.

31. P 5:213, and see above, note 10; P 4:486, 17:375.

32. Fisher in *PMHB* 17 (1893): 273; the anonymous *State* is ESTC T45619. The *London Magazine* announced its publication, 24 (April 1755): 191, #24, whereas the *Boston Weekly News-Letter* advertised Clarke's pamphlet as "Just Published" on 21 August 1755; it was reprinted in London in December (*London Magazine* 24 [1755]: 630, #62). See also Wroth, *An American Bookshelf* 41n54, 138.

33. For another BF use of the body metaphor, see BF to Collinson, 9 May 1753 (4:486).

34. Lewis Evans, *Geographical . . . Essays* 31, 32. E7411; Miller 605.

35. Samuel Johnson, *Political Writings,* ed. Donald J. Greene (New Haven, Conn.: Yale University Press, 1977) 201, 211–12. Johnson, a reviewer for the *British Magazine,* may have been responsible for reprinting a large section of Franklin's hypothesis for explaining thunder from *Experiments and Observations* in the *British Magazine* for April 1751, pp. 196–201; cf. P 3:367–76.

36. Johnson, ed. Greene, 455n. Johnson canceled the word "should." Neither Paul J. Korshin nor Neill R. Joy knew of Franklin's strong connection with Lewis Evans: Korshin, "BF and Samuel Johnson: A Literary Relationship," in *BF: An American Genius,* ed. Gianfranca Balestra and Luigi Sampietro ([Rome]: Bulzoni Editore, 1993) 33–49; Neill R. Joy, "Politics and Culture: The Dr. Franklin–

Dr. Johnson Connection, with an Analogue," *Prospects* 23 (1998): 59–105, at 67–69.

37. Adams to Nathan Webb; the editors of JAP noted that after reading Franklin's "Observations," the prospect of America's succeeding England as the seat of empire, or becoming itself a powerful independent empire, was "a natural inference." JAP 1:5, 7n2.

38. The Adams-Rush correspondence editors noted that the letter "was hardly intended to support American independence. It was rather an argument for empire, the enlarged position of America in the future British empire." *The Spur of Fame: . . . John Adams and Benjamin Rush,* ed. John A. Schutz and Douglass Adair (San Marino, Calif.: Huntington Library, 1966) 82, 82n16, 84.

39. Ezra Stiles, *Discourse on the Christian Union* (Boston: Edes and Gill, 1761) 108–9; E9018; quotation from Canada pamphlet (P 9:95n) on 111.

40. Hawke 95; see also Aldridge 107; Fleming 32.

41. Egnal; George Washington wrote William Crawford on 21 September 1767: "I offered in my last to join you in attempting to secure some of the most valuable lands in the King's part, which I think may be accomplished after awhile, notwithstanding the proclamation that restrains it at present, and prohibits the settling of them at all; for I can never look upon that proclamation in any other light (but this I say between ourselves) than as a temporary expedient to quiet the minds of the Indians. It must fail, of course, in a few years, especially when those Indians consent to our occupying the lands." *The Washington-Crawford Correspondence,* ed. C. W. Butterfield (Cincinnati: R. Clarke and Company, 1877) 3.

42. William Franklin's trip took place from 11 August to mid-October 1748. Sheila L. Skemp, *WF* (New York: Oxford University Press, 1990) 11–12.

43. Thomas Pownall cites WF's journal in *Topographical Description of the . . . United States,* ed. Lois Mulkearn (Pittsburgh: University of Pittsburgh Press, 1949) 125.

44. For the genre, see Kenneth Silverman, *A Cultural History of the American Revolution . . . 1763–1789* (New York: Crowell, 1976), index, s.v. "Rising Glory of America," and *translatio studii.* Representative lines may be found in David Humphries, "Address to the Armies," *American Museum* 1:3 (March 1787): 230–40.

45. VD 217–18, 289; Fleming 31; Hawke 333; Wood, *Americanization* 71; and Chaplin 142. When considering the same facts, Franklin combines the same emotional and intellectual elements in his letter to Peter Collinson on 30 April 1764. The metaphors of the cat's skin and the monopoly of the carrion are violent. But the references to America's growth are comparatively abstract: "for as to our being always supply'd by you, 'tis a Folly to expect it. Only consider *the Rate of our Increase,* and tell me if you can increase your Wool in that Proportion, and where, in your little Island you can feed the Sheep." P 11:183.

46. Hayes, "The Board of Trade's 'Cruel Sarcasm.'" An especially effective allusion, the only one that repeats the "Jakes on our Tables" insult, was Franklin's "A Defense of the Americans," 9 May 1759; P 8:351.

47. Connor 247n3.

CHAPTER 8

1. The three essential records are the "Managers Minutes," Archives of the Pennsylvania Hospital, Philadelphia; Thomas G. Morton and Frank Woodbury, *History of the Pennsylvania Hospital* (Philadelphia: Times, 1897), hereafter cited as Morton and Woodbury; and William H. Williams, *America's First Hospital* (Wayne, Pa. Haverford House, 1976), hereafter Williams. I am indebted to Stacey Peeples, archivist of the Pennsylvania Hospital, for permission to use the minutes, and to Robert Cox, formerly manuscript librarian of the American Philosophical Society, for copying them from a microfilm in its possession. For a synopsis, see Horle 3:44.

2. Williams 12–15; also Williams, "The 'Industrious Poor' and the Founding of the Pennsylvania Hospital," *PMHB* 97 (1973): 431–43.

3. *Canon* 53; W 169–71.

4. *Statutes* 5:128–31.

5. "Managers Minutes" 2–3; Smith, *Hannah* 308; Morton and Woodbury 13–14.

6. "Managers Minutes" 3–4.

7. Martha Gandy Fales, "Heraldic and Emblematic Engravers of Colonial Boston," *Boston Prints and Printmakers, 1670–1775, Proceedings of the Colonial Society of Massachusetts* 46 (1973) 197–98, illustration on 198, fig. 88, from Pennsylvania Hospital. P 4:149; "Compassion and Regard for the Sick," *PG* 25 March 1731, W 169–70.

8. On Turner, see Peter J. Parker, in Sewell 64–65. Franklin had met Turner at Masonic meetings in Boston in 1743 (*Life* 2:311, where I mistakenly gave James Turner's first name as Lewis).

9. Morton and Woodbury 25; V 4:3436.

10. P 4:110, 255, and 5:306 n8 say 17 January—the date that Franklin noted the contributors approved the law (5:309).

11. P 5:315; the *PG* for 7 May 1752 noted that "Monday last [4 May] the Contributors to the Pennsylvania Hospital met at the Court-house" and voted for the directors. P 4:111 has the correct date, but P 5:314 is incorrect.

12. Penn to James Hamilton, 8 September 1751, TPP, reel 1, frames 0406–07.

13. Morton and Woodbury 14–15.

14. V 3569; *Statutes* 5:131, 502–3.

15. Mather, *Bonifacius* 114.

16. Morton and Woodbury 263–64; Williams 32.

17. Compare Franklin's statements concerning the ability of even the old and infirm to help with fire fighting (P 2:12–14); or the appeal that women as well as old men could help the militia Association (P 3:211, A 109–10).

18. P 5:327–30; Morton and Woodbury 384.

19. Williams 32.

20. Edward B. Krumbhaar, "The Pennsylvania Hospital," *Transactions of the APS* 43 (1953): 237–46; Ellen S. Jacobowitz in Sewell 77–78.

21. Morton and Woodbury 37.

22. Ibid. 39.

23. Rush, *Letters* 2:1063.

24. Thomas and Richard Penn gave an annuity of £40 a year in 1762, together with a promise of a building lot adjoining the hospital, which was legally donated on 10 November 1767. Morton and Woodbury 270, 273, 321.

25. "Managers Minutes" 211. Martin P. Snyder, *City of Independence: Views of Philadelphia Before 1800* (New York: Praeger, 1975) 53–57, 65, and notes, 285. See also *The Art of Philadelphia's Medicine* (Philadelphia: Philadelphia Museum of Art, 1965) 105–6.

26. "Managers Minutes" 233. Hall to Strahan, 17 December 1755, David Hall Letterbooks, APS.

27. P 8:82n7, 9:255, 280, 33:354.

28. Morton and Woodbury 250n.

29. The amount was £8,543.12.5 sterling. P 13:274n1, 19:289, 339–40, 20:3–4.

30. Morton and Woodbury, 346 for Fothergill, 347 for Strahan.

31. S 10:500; Morton and Woodbury 68–69.

CHAPTER 9

1. Smith, *Hannah* 312.

2. All his committee assignments are in V; many are mentioned in his "Record of Service in the Assembly, 1751–64" (P 4:154–80), in DH, and in Foster. The committees are also indexed in Work Projects Administration, *Pennsylvania Archives: Eighth Series, Index of Votes . . . Daily Sessions* (mimeographed, Harrisburg, Pa., 1963) 114–15.

3. V 4:3476, 3493.

4. V 4:3493, 3503.

5. V 4:3490, 3492, 3504.

6. V 4:3511, 3513, 3514; *Statutes* 5:161–78.

7. V 4:3481, 3495.

8. V 4:3480, 3481; *Statutes* 5:48.

9. V 4:3494; *Statutes* 5:147–50.

10. V 4:3473, 3482.

11. V 4:3496, 3504; *Statutes* 5:179–83.

12. Parliament's colonial currency act, 24 George II, c. 53.

13. Penn to Hamilton, 29 July 1751, TPP, reel 1, frame 401; Hanna 40–44; Hutson, "BF" 322.

14. Hutson, "BF" 322.

15. V 4:3483, 3487, 3490, 3493, 3494.

16. V 4:3500–3501.

17. V 4:3503–4, 3506–7.

18. Hamilton to Penn, 18 March 1751/2, TPP, reel 1, frame 423; Hanna 43.

19. Penn to Hamilton, 30 May 1752, TPP, reel 1, frame 0432; Hutson, "BF" 324.

20. Peters to Penn, 4 October 1752; Hutson, "BF" 321n42.

21. *Statutes* 5:133–47.

22. Horle 2:230; all four representatives have biographical sketches in Horle.

23. Marion Wallace Reninger, "Susanna Wright," *Journal of the Lancaster County Historical Society* 63 (1959): 183–89; Willis L. Shirk, Jr., "Wright's Ferry: A Glimpse into the Susquehanna Backcountry," *PMHB* 120 (1996): 61–87; and the poems in Milcah Martha Moore, *Commonplace Book*, ed. Catherine La Courreye Blecki and Karin A. Wulf (University Park: Pennsylvania State University Press, 1997). Richard Peters called her "Susy" in a letter of 17 November 1742 cited in "Women and Provincial Elections," Horle 2:27.

24. Horle 2:895.

CHAPTER 10

1. The best accounts are *At the Sign of the Hand-in-Hand* (Philadelphia, 1926); Harrold E. Gillingham, "Philadelphia's First Fire Defences," *PMHB* 56 (1932): 355–77, at 368–72; Nicholas B. Wainwright, *A Philadelphia Story: The Philadelphia Contributionship* (Philadelphia, 1952); and *The Philadelphia Contributionship: 250th Anniversary* (Philadelphia, 2002). Horle 3:44 contains a valuable brief account. I thank Carol Smith, Archivist, Philadelphia Contributionship, for permission to use its early minutes and thank the American Philosophical Society for a copy of its microfilm of the minutes..

2. Contributionship minutes are in chronological order. I cite the dates in the text.

3. Contributionship minutes; Gillingham 368.

4. The official engrossed "Deed" of 25 March 1752 (P 4:283–93) adds legalese and corrects several mistakes in the earlier printed *Deed* of 1751 (E6757, Miller 542).

5. For sketches of the directors, see Wainwright 29–33, and *250th Anniversary* 14–17.

6. Wainwright 39.

7. J. Bennett Nolan, "Ben Franklin's Mortgage on the Daniel Boone Farm," *PAPS* 87 (1944): 394–96, at 395.

8. Saunders's account is reproduced in *At the Sign of the Hand in Hand* 18.

CHAPTER 11

1. V 4:3475.

2. V 4:3548; P 4:158, 158n11, citing Peters to Penn, 7 February 1753.

3. James Hamilton to the proprietors, 9 February 1753, TPP, reel 7 (PPOC, 6:9–13).

4. Hutson, "BF" 324.

5. Penn to Hamilton, 28 March 1753, TPP, reel 7, frame 619.

6. Penn to Hamilton, 2 April 1753, TPP, reel 1, frame 0474.

7. Ibid.

8. Boyd, *Treaties* li. Jennings, *Empire* 28–33, stresses that the Shawnee and Miami Indians were really outside of the Iroquois Covenant Chain.

9. "Céloron de Blainville, Pierre Joseph," *DCB* 3:99–100; CR 5:510–11.

10. Consul Willshire Butterfield, *History of the Girtys* (Cincinnati: R. Clarke and Company, 1890); Boyd, *Treaties* lxi and n136.

11. Anderson, *Crucible* 25.

12. At a council meeting on 9 February 1749/50, Governor James Hamilton read an extract of a letter from Thomas Penn offering to give £400 for building a fort and £100 annually for a fort to keep some men: "However few the Men are they should wear an uniform Dress, that tho' very small it may look Fort like" (CR 5:514–15). Cf. Boyd, *Treaties* liv–lv.

13. "Mouet de Langlande, Charles-Michel," *DCB* 4:563.

14. "Marin de la Malgue, Paul," *DCB* 3:431–2.

15. Anderson, *Crucible* 32.

16. V 5:3553–56, 3563.

17. Franklin echoed his 19 August 1752 "Report on the State of the Currency" and anticipated his 6 February 1754 "Report on the State of the Trade." P 4:344–50, 5:193–95.

18. Though I would have the same opinion if persons with the surname Huey were common, they are not. No Huey turns up in Horle, in the index to *PMHB* through 1999, or in the wills of Philadelphia city and county through the first quarter of the nineteenth century—with one exception: an "Ann Huey" is listed in the *Abstracts of Philadelphia County Wills, 1820–1825* (Westminster, Md.: Family Life Publications, 1998) 192. Franklin's letter of 13 December 1757, against attacking religion, has no addressee (P 7:294–95) and will be discussed in Volume 4.

19. A favorite passage, cited also in the letter to his parents; *Life* 2:299.

20. Aldridge, *Nature's God* 126–27.

21. *GM* 23 (August 1753): 372–73, 373–74. Martin P. Snyder, *City of Independence* (New York: Praeger, 1975), fig. 15.

22. *Calendar* #1151.

23. *Life* 2:380–87; the form, on 383, is fig. 25. *PG*, 14 January 1752.

24. See *PG* 5 December 1751, 27 August 1752, 17 May 1753.

25. 19 December 1789; S 10:74–75.

26. BF credited Byles with his "first Academical Honours." BF to Byles, 1 June 1788 (S 8:656).

27. JAD 1:125.

28. JAD 1:13, 61–62, 72, 125–26.

29. Schutz, *William Shirley* 168.

30. Edward Winslow, "The Early Charitable Organizations of Boston," *New England Historical and Genealogical Register* 44 (1890): 100–103.

31. *A Letter from Sir Richard Cox . . . a sure method to establish the Linen-Manufactory* (Dublin, printed; London, reprinted; Boston, reprinted and sold by J. Draper in Cornhill); E6481. Title page reproduced in Nian-Sheng Huang, "Financing Poor Relief in Colonial Boston," *Massachusetts Historical Review* 8 (2006): 73–103, at 85.

32. The ad is E40671 (reproduced in Huang 81); the report of the committee announcing Franklin's gift and giving a brief account of the society's finances is E40672.

33. [Andrew Oliver?], *Industry & Frugality Proposed,* E7027, quotation on p. 11.

34. *Boston News-Letter,* 9 August 1753.

35. V 4:3576. Hutson, "BF" 328n67, traces Thomas Penn's reasons for gradually abandoning the demand for a suspending clause.

36. Winfred Trexler Root, *The Relations of Pennsylvania with the British Government, 1696–1765* (1912; rpt New York: Burt Franklin, 1970) 371, 388; Leonard Woods Labaree, *Royal Government in America* (New Haven: Yale University Press, 1930) 33–35.

37. Hutson, "BF" 327, 328n67.

38. Hamilton to Penn, 8 September 1753, TPP, reel 7, v. 6, p. 99. See also Hutson, "BF" 321.

39. Hamilton attempted to refute the precedent in his speech of 1 March 1754; V 5:3657–58.

40. Peters to Penn, 4 October 1752, TPP, reel 1, frame 0459; Penn to Peters, 9 January 1753, reel 7, v. 5, p. 285; and Hamilton to Penn, 8 September 1753, reel 7, v. 6, p. 99. For previous beliefs that governors acted on secret instructions, see *Life* 2:508, 509.

41. For the 1741–43 threats to become a royal colony, see *Life* 2:345, 596n27.

42. Peters to Penn, 27 November 1753, TPP, reel 7, frames 804–5; PPOC 6:141.

43. Hutson 39n66 gave four 1755 instances of Gov. Morris charging the assembly with treason for objecting to proprietary instructions.

44. Penn to Hamilton, 1 November 1753, TPP, reel 1, frame 0499.

CHAPTER 12

1. *Life* 1:16, 2:231–32, 347–49, 378–79. For BF's mock captivity narrative, which contains another imagined Indian speech, see P 15:145–57.

2. CR 5:657–58. Franklin misremembered and wrote that the House nominated the members of the assembly who would attend the treaty; A 120.

3. Jennings, *Empire* 56–58.

4. "Tanaghrisson," *DCB* 3:613–14.

5. It was celebrated as such when HSP originally received it. In the guessing game of what the belts mean, I follow my own ignorant impressions. Cf. Frank G. Speck, *The Penn Wampum Belts* (New York: Museum of the American Indian, Heye Foundation, 1925) 12–13.

6. Stourzh 47–54.

7. Sometime during the conference Franklin asked the Twightwees about the possibility of an English colony in the Ohio. They said they "would gladly encourage and protect an infant English settlement"; P 5:458.

8. Jennings, *Empire* 59, believed that the £800 worth of goods was withheld from the Indians. Perhaps, but it seems to me more likely that the reference is to the additional gifts the commissioners ordered.

9. Jennings, *Empire* 57–58, argued that Scarouady actually intended to make certain that the Shawnee Indians remained prisoners until and unless the Iroquois asked that they be released.

10. For Franklin's use of the tradition, see Lemay, "Frontiersman" 207, 207n54. See also Kenneth Silverman, *The Life and Times of Cotton Mather* (New York: Harper and Row, 1984) 238–39 and notes on p. 448; and Karen Schramm, "The 'Devil's Territories' or 'Preservation of the World': Thoreau's Subversion of Puritan Wilderness Discourse," in *Finding Colonial Americas*, ed. Carla Mulford and David S. Shields (Newark: University of Delaware Press, 2001) 403–14.

11. *A Treaty Held with the Ohio Indians at Carlisle in October 1753* (Philadelphia: Franklin and Hall, 1753); E7026; Boyd, *Treaties* 123–34, with notes on the text, 305.

12. *The Burd Papers: Extracts from Chief Justice Allen's Letter Book*, ed. Lewis Walker Burd (n.p., 1897) 10.

13. Peters to Penn, 6 November 1753, TPP, reel 7, frames 779–84; Penn to Peters, 1 February 1754, TPP, reel 1, frames 181–82.

14. Royal Society of London, online library and archive catalogue, record of members. He was the son of a famous privateer, author, and explorer of the same name. In 1757, the son edited a second edition of his father's *Voyage Round the World*.

15. Fairfax Harrison, "The Colonial Post Office in Virginia," *William and Marry Quarterly*, 2 ser., 4 (1924): 71–92, at 81n18.

16. *The Burd Papers* 10.

17. *Instructions to Deputy Post Masters* [Philadelphia: Franklin and Hall, 1753]; E1604; Miller 571; and *Instructions to the Deputy Post-Masters for Keeping Their Accounts* [Philadelphia: Franklin and Hall, 1753]; E11239; Miller 572.

18. See Appendix 7.

19. V 5:3622–24; P 4:159.

20. Sherry H. Olson, *Baltimore* (Baltimore: Johns Hopkins University Press, 1997) 1.

21. For biographical sketches, see Dr. Alexander Hamilton's *History of the Tuesday Club*, 3 v., ed. Robert Micklus (Chapel Hill: University of North Carolina Press, 1990) 1:lxxix–cv; hereafter cited as Micklus. For Kinnersley's lecture, see Lemay, *EK* 63–71.

22. Micklus 2:372.

23. For the Chancellor's Rebellion, see Micklus 2:357–72, quotation at 372; for Franklin's visit, 3:214–15. Micklus pointed out that the club's mock revolt marked a supposed return to the "heroic times of Innocence & Simplicity"

that existed before luxury asserted itself and conquered. Robert Micklus, *Comic Genius of Dr. Alexander Hamilton* (Knoxville: University of Tennessee Press, 1990) 192–97, quotation at 195.

24. Ledger D 83, 183, Franklin MSS, APS.

25. CR 5:689–90; Gipson 4:289–92.

26. V 5:3649–50.

27. CR 5:711–22; V 5:3637–38.

28. Henderson 94–95; V 5:3653–54.

29. V 5:3676–77.

30. V 5:3680–81.

31. V 5:3652–3656; CR 5:748.

32. V 5:3654–55.

33. Penn to Peters, 9 March 1754, postscript, TPP, reel 1, frame 0519.

34. CR 5:765–66, 767, 6:16–20.

35. Horle 3:955A; V 5:3692–93.

36. Isaac Norris Letter Book 9:50, HSP.

37. V 5:3694. In Franklin's original printing of the *Votes and Proceedings* (Philadelphia: Franklin and Hall, 1754); E7287; this last vote is on p. 49.

38. Isaac Norris Letter Book, 9:50, HSP.

39. V 5:3695.

40. V 5:3691.

41. V 5:3696, 3697; 5 April 1754 (V 5:3690), 9 April (V 5:3692–93), 11 April (V 5:3694). Perhaps the vote on the tobacco inspection law in Virginia was published. The *PG* for 22 February 1738/9 reprinted from the *Virginia Gazette* gives the numbers in the division but not the names. Neither the *Virginia Gazette* nor Virginia's *Journals of the House of Burgesses* is extant for the original dates.

42. Julian P. Boyd, ed., *Susquehanna Company Papers* (1930; rpt. Ithaca, N.Y.: Cornell University Press, 1962) 1:85.

Chapter 13

1. Farley Grubb, a colleague in economics, confirmed the hypothesis and provided the following: The ratio of German immigrants in the decade of the 1740s to the Pennsylvania population in 1750 was 17.4 percent. Between 1820 and 1960, the number of immigrants per decade for the whole United States was never over 10 percent, peaking at 9.52 percent for the decade 1901–10.

2. Thomas Graeme to Thomas Penn, 6 November 1750, TPP, reel 6. "Dutch" referred to the Pennsylvania Germans; online *OED*, s.v. "Pennsylvania Dutch." Discussions of BF and the Germans include Arthur D. Graeff, *The Relations between the Pennsylvania Germans and the British Authorities, 1750–1776* (Norristown: Pennsylvania German Society, 1939); Whitfield J. Bell, Jr., "BF and the German Charity Schools," *PAPS* 99 (1955): 381–87; Glenn Weaver, "BF and the Pennsylvania Germans," *WMQ* 14 (1957): 536–59; Dietmar Rothermund, "The German Problem of Colonial Pennsylvania," *PMHB* 84 (1960): 3–21.

3. Horle 2:53.

4. *The History of the Last Four Years of the Queen*, in Swift, ed. Davis, 7:167.

5. PA, 1st ser., 2:183–86.

6. Smith, *Brief State* 17; GWP 1:299; *PG*, 15 May 1755.

7. Gipson 6:14; PA, 1st ser., 2:9. Testifying before Parliament in 1766, Franklin estimated that Germans constituted about one-third of the population (somewhat more than 53,000), and that the total non-Indian population was about 160,000, but in conversation later that year with Gottfried Achenwall, he supposedly estimated the German population to be 90,000 to 100,000; P 13:132, 353–54.

8. Smith, *Brief State* 38. Actually, there seems to have been a total of 606 Catholic Germans out of a population of more than 50,000. PA, 1st ser., 3:144–45.

9. *Minutes and Letters of the Coetus of the German Reformed Congregations in Pennsylvania* (Philadelphia: Reformed Church, 1903) 137–38, hereafter *Coetus.*

10. Mistakenly attributed to Franklin by Sabin 25554 and Wroth, *American Bookshelf* 26, 82n65.

11. William Smith to Thomas Penn, 10 April 1755, TPP, reel 8, frames 53–54; *Coetus* 130.

12. H. W. Smith 1:72–73.

13. Ibid. 70–72.

14. Smith, *Brief State* 28, 35.

15. Rothermund, "German Problem" 14. Swift had earlier said that the Irish were lured to America to provide the older settlers there with "a Screen against the Assaults of the *Savages*." *Intelligencer* no. 19 (1728) and *Answer to the Craftsman* in Swift, ed. Davis, 12:60, 176.

16. Smith, *Brief State* 28–31, 39–42.

17. William Smith to Penn, 2 July 1755, TPP, reel 8, frame 199.

18. Jennings 79.

19. *Coetus* 138.

20. Graeff 56.

21. *Coetus* 148, 143.

22. Ibid. 143, 148.

23. Richard Peters Letter Book, 1755–57, bottom paragraph on p. 61 (modern numbering in pencil), HSP (formerly in Gratz Collection, now with Peters mss).

24. *Coetus* 157.

25. Penn to Peters, 13 May 1758, TPP, reel 8, frames 156–61; P 8:68n2.

26. Rush, *Letters* 1:420–27.

CHAPTER 14

1. Anderson, *Crucible* 45–49.

2. CR 6:31.

3. Ibid. 28–34.

4. Sinclair Hamilton, "'The Earliest Device of the Colonies and Some Other Early Devices," *Princeton University Chronicle* 10 (1948–49): 117–23, at 118.

5. In 1732, James Logan wrote (the manuscript exists in Benjamin Franklin's holograph) that Great Britain kept "the several Colonies under distinct and independent Commands, the more effectually to Secure them from a Revolt from the Crown." Joseph C. Johnson, ed., "A Quaker Imperialist's View of the British Colonies in America: 1732," *PMHB* 60 (1936): 97–130, at 127. Charles Sumner, *Prophetic Voices Concerning America* (Boston: Lee and Shephard, 1874); Richard Frothingham, *Rise of the Republic of the United States* (Boston: Little, Brown, 1872) 101–57; Justin Winsor, *Narrative and Critical History of America*, 6 v. (Boston: Houghton, 1887) 6:231–74, esp. 255n; Frederick D. Stone, "Plans for the Union of the British Colonies of North America, 1643–1776," in Hampton L. Carson, *History of the Celebration of the One Hundredth Anniversary of the Constitution of the United States*, 2 v. (Philadelphia: Lippincott, 1889) 2:439–503; and Bumsted. See also A 113–14; and *Canon* 132–33.

6. McMaster, 162, thought "both the design and the cutting were the work of Franklin." VD, 220, thought BF "probably" drew it. Martha G. Fales speculated that James Turner made the woodcut; Fales, "Heraldic and Emblematic Engravers of Colonial Boston," *Boston Prints and Printmakers, 1670–1775, Proceedings of the Colonial Society of Massachusetts* 46 (1973): 218. Turner is known to have moved about 1754 to Philadelphia (P 3:144n). If he were in Philadelphia and made the woodcut, it's not one of his best efforts.

7. Albert Matthews, "The Snake Devices, 1754–1776, and the *Constitutional Courant*, 1765," *Publications of the Colonial Society of Massachusetts* 11 (1906–7): 409–53, at 416–17; Lemay, "American Aesthetic" 475–80; Lester C. Olson, *Emblems of American Community in the Revolutionary Era* (Washington, D.C.: Smithsonian Institution Press, 1991) 21–73, and Olson, *BF's Vision of American Community* (Columbia: University of South Carolina Press, 2004) 27–76.

8. I only examined the *Gentleman's Magazine, London Magazine,* and *Scots Magazine* for the period. Olson, *BF's Vision* 46–53, showed that the device became well-known to British authorities and that a few allusions to it appeared in the English newspapers reprinting the *Virginia Gazette* essay, 49–50, but Olson did not find the device itself in a contemporary English publication.

9. Matthews 418, 419. See also Olson, *Emblems* 21–73, 236–38.

10. No general study exists of colonial American responses to English condescension. When such a study is made, Franklin will be the key figure. See *Life* 2:158–60.

11. J. E. Cirlot, *A Dictionary of Symbols*, tr. Jack Sage (New York: Philosophical Library, 1962), s.v. "serpent," 272–77; Ad de Vries, *Dictionary of Symbols and Imagery* (Amsterdam: North Holland Publishing Company, 1974), s.v. "serpent," 410–15. See also E. McClung Fleming, "Symbols of the Young Nation, 1765–1790," in William Vincent Shannon et al., eds., *Symbols and Aspiration, 1776–1976* (Cleveland: Western Reserve Historical Society, 1976) 25–62, at 47–48;

and Fleming, "Seeing Snakes in the American Arts," *The Delaware Antiques Show 1969* (Wilmington, 1969) 75–85 (odd-numbered pages only), where the serpent is portrayed in various American arts as temptation, as evil, as wisdom, as disunity (the cut-snake cartoon), as eternity, as the United States, and as a folk character.

12. One example of the snake as unity that Franklin probably knew is George Wither, *A Collection of Emblemes* (1635; fac. ed., Columbia, S.C.: University of South Carolina Press, 1975) 102. Frank Sommer, "Emblem and Device," *Art Quarterly* 24 (1961): 56–76, at 63, 65, first pointed out Franklin's probable source. Olson, *BF's Vision* 38, 266n30, added two other editions of Verrien as possible sources.

13. Ernest W. Baughman, *Type and Motif-Index of the Folktales of England and North America* (The Hague: Mouton, 1966) B765.7 (p. 86) and X1321.3 (p. 526).

14. Cohen, *Founding Fathers* 52–53.

15. Samuel Johnson, *Political Writings*, ed. Donald J. Greene (New Haven, Conn.: Yale University Press, 1977) 414.

16. Edward W. Richardson, *Standards and Colors of the American Revolution* (Philadelphia: University of Pennsylvania Press, 1982), e.g., 14, 67 ("Don't Tread on Me"), 110, 115, 116, 119, 121, 129, 136; William Rea Furlong et al., *So Proudly We Hail: The History of the United States Flag* (Washington, D.C.: Smithsonian Institution Press, 1981) 51, 70–77; Newman, 40, 142, 318 (3), 417. Olson, *BF's Vision* 53–68, devotes special attention to the uses of the cartoon during the Stamp Act controversy, and Olson, *Emblems* 21–74, gives numerous later uses.

17. JAP 4:142.

18. "Ye sons of Sedition, how comes it to pass that America's typ'd by a Snake in the grass." *Rivington's NY Gazetteer*, 25 August 1774, reprinted in Furlong et al., *So Proudly We Hail* 72. Canon 124–26.

19. Though the snake in the cut-snake cartoon is not a recognizable rattlesnake (the tail tapers to a point and has no rattles), the snake in the frame of the Duplessis portrait is. See Ellen G. Miles, "The French Portraits of BF," 283, in *Reappraising*. Keith Arbour believes that Franklin was personally responsible for details in the picture and the frame. Arbour, "One Last Word: BF and the Duplessis Portrait of 1778," *PMHB* 118 (1994): 183–208.

20. Anderson, *Crucible* 5–7, 51–59, gives a version of the battle in which Tanaghrisson tomahawked Jumonville after the surrender. W. J. Eccles, "Coulon de Villiers de Jumonville, Joseph," *DCB* 3:150–51, notes that the French force was an embassy and has Jumonville struck down while trying to read the formal summons calling upon the English to withdraw. See also GWP 1:110–15.

21. Bauman 23–25.

22. V 5:3701–2.

23. Hutson, "BF" 332. Smith, *Brief State* 21.

24. V 5:3702, 3704.

25. V 5:3705, 3706; Hutson, "BF" 333–34.

26. Smith, *Brief State* 22. Penn to Morris, 26 February 1755, TPP, reel 1, frames 0584–85. See also Thayer, *Pemberton* 38n55; and Jennings 98, 213n9.

27. V 5:3710.

28. In his memorandum of services for the Pennsylvania Assembly, Franklin noted for 18 May 1754, "A Number of Resolves drawn up by him and agreed to." P 4:161, 161n13. At n. 13, the editors wrote, "See below under this date," but the resolves are not printed there; instead in the headnote to 15 May 1754 (P 5:281), only one resolve appears (it is the top one at V 5:3714).

29. V 5:3698.

30. Ibid. 3704, 3705.

31. They were Evan Morgan, Philadelphia County; Griffith Owen, Bucks County; John Wright, York County; David M'Connaughy, York County; John Armstrong, Cumberland County; Joseph Armstrong, Cumberland County; and William Parsons, Northampton County. V 5:3701.

32. Ibid. 3717–18.

33. As BF wrote in 1729, the colonists "are the best Judges of our own Necessities" (*Life* 1:405); see also BF to William Shirley, 4 December 1754, P 5:444.

34. Foster 549b.

35. Hutson, "BF" 334, believed that Collinson showed all the letters he received concerning Pennsylvania to Thomas Penn and "was certain to show him" this one.

36. CR 6:48–49.

37. P 5:344–53 discusses and chronicles the Albany Plan. Besides CR 6:57–110, basic documents are found in *NYCD* and McAnear. Discussions are found in Gipson 5:120–42; Robert C. Newbold, *The Albany Congress and Plan of Union of 1754* (New York: Vantage Press, 1955); and Timothy J. Shannon, *Indians and Colonists at the Crossroads of Empire: The Albany Congress of 1754* (Ithaca, N.Y.: Cornell University Press, 2000).

38. Peters, Diary, PA, 1st ser., 2:145–46.

39. References to places mentioned in Peters's diary are located from Isaac Newton Phelps Stokes, *Iconography of Manhattan Island, 1498–1909*, 6 v. (reprint of 1906–28; New York: Arno Press, 1967).

40. *New York Mercury*, 10 June 1754.

41. McAnear 730–31.

42. CR 6:66–67.

43. Ibid. 110.

44. Ibid. 70; McAnear 741; Jennings, *Empire* 99.

45. McAnear 736; CR 6:72, 73; *DCB* 3:622–24.

46. CR 6:80; McAnear 741. *GM* reprinted the speech: 25 (June 1755): 252–54, at 253a.

47. CR 6:81–82; P 5:348–49; Shannon 186–87. Cf. 12 June 1753.

48. CR 6:114.

49. Ibid. 83, 84–85; McAnear 737.

50. Thomas Jefferson, *Writings*, ed. Paul L. Ford, 12 v. (New York: Putnam, 1893–99) 9:232; *Life* 2:509–14.

51. CR 6:88; McAnear 741.

52. CR 6:89; Pownall, in McAnear 741, 743, 742, 740, respectively; Wallace 357–58; Anderson, *Crucible* 1–21; Shannon 143. See also below, s.v. "Teganissorem."

53. McAnear 738.

54. CR 6:123, 7:324, 326, 431–33. Wallace 359–60; Newbold 137–40; Jennings, *Empire* 101–6, 276–78; Anderson, *Crucible* 78; Jennings 89; and Foster 541a all seem to hold Franklin and Norris partly responsible for the purchases, but their only role was to witness the signatures. For the Wyoming Valley warfare, see Horle 3:24–27.

55. McAnear 740–41.

56. Ibid. 735; CR 6:71.

57. For a comparison of the four documents resulting in the Albany Plan of Union, see Appendix 5.

58. PA, 1st ser., 2:197–99; P 5:336n1. Peters had proposed a union of the colonies in 1750: see T. Penn to Peters, 24 February 1750/1: "I think it would be of great advantage to the English Interest, for several Colonys to join in the management of Indian Affairs, and appoint as you suggest, Deputys from each of them to manage the whole agreeing upon a proportion that each Colony will bear of the expence." TPP; reel 1, frame 0387. Peters's "Plan for a General Union of the British Colonies of North America" was printed in Carson, 2:472–74; characterized in Gipson 5:128.

59. CR 6:105, 109.

60. Ibid. 109.

61. Ibid. 105, 109. Newbold, 115, says that "the congress approved the revised plan." The conflicting statements of contemporaries are given at P 5:374–76.

62. McAnear 744. Thomas Hutchinson wrote, "This was an assembly the most deserving of respect of any which had been convened in America, whether we consider the colonies which were represented, the rank and characters of the delegates, or the purposes for which it was convened." Hutchinson 3:15.

63. McAnear 744; Hutchinson 3:17.

64. P 5:352–53; PA, 2nd ser., 6:214–17, 209–14, respectively; CR 6:110.

65. BF presented the colonial assemblies as versions of the British Commons at P 6:141–42, 530; 7:138, and in the examples cited below. The attorney general and solicitor general denied their comparability in Provost William Smith's case (*Acts PC* 4:383–84).

66. *NYCD* 6:917, 919; Alison Gilbert Olson, "The British Government and Colonial Union, 1754," *WMQ* 17 (1960): 22–34, at 33.

67. *The Public Records of the Colony of Connecticut*, 15 vols., v. 1–3 ed. J. H. Trumbull, v. 4–15 ed. C. J. Hoadly (Hartford, Conn.: Case, Lockwood and Brainard Company, 1850–90), v. 10, *1751–1757*, 292; William A. Whitehead, ed., *Docu-*

ments Relating to the Colonial History of the State of New Jersey, 1st ser. (Newark, N.J.: Daily Advertiser Printing House, 1882), 16:492.

68. Olson 34; Shannon 211; see also Herbert L. Osgood, *American Colonies in the Eighteenth Century*, 4 v. (New York: Columbia University Press, 1924) 4:324–28; Newbold 135–78; Gipson 143–66; and Shannon 205–33.

69. Parton 1:339, citing George Bancroft, *History of the United States*, 6 v. (Boston: Little, Brown, 1854) 4:125n.

70. Cf. Shannon 198.

71. L. K. Mathews, "BF's Plans for a Colonial Union, 1750–1775," *American Political Science Review* 8 (1914): 393–412; P 21:462, 22:120–25; Isaacson 160.

72. V 5:3719, 3721, 3722.

73. Ibid. 3726–28.

74. Ibid. 3730–31.

75. Ibid. 3733.

76. Charles Willing and son to Thomas Willing, October 1754, Willing Letterbook, HSP.

77. Newcomb 63n, citing WF's letter to Galloway at Yale.

78. PA, 1st ser., 2:499.

79. *Memoirs of a Huguenot Family*, ed. Ann Maury (New York: Putnam's, 1853) 382.

CHAPTER 15

1. BF did in 1763, when he fell, dislocating his shoulder (10:338, 338n5).

2. See Appendix 1.

3. *Proceedings in Masonry: [Boston] St. John's Grand Lodge, 1733–1792* (Boston: Grand Lodge, 1895) 34–35.

4. Benjamin Vaughan first published the "Plan" during the Revolution: Franklin, *Political, Mikscellaneous, and Philosophical Pieces* (London: J. Johnson, 1779) 133–43; Ford 342.

5. Since the "omniscient" Jackson was not an authority on the American frontier, perhaps BF was simiply consulted through Jackson.

6. P 13:120. Hutchinson 3:17. Shirley's letter of 24 December 1754 to Sir Thomas Robinson said that a president-general appointed by the crown should be the chief executive and that the Grand Council, rather than being elected by the assemblies of the colonies, should also be appointed by the British authorities. Shirley, *Correspondence* 2:114–17. Perhaps Shirley was more democratic in expressing his views to Franklin. At any rate, Franklin objected to funding the union by Parliament's taxing the colonies, rather than by the colonists' taxing themselves. Schutz, *William Shirley* 181–84, finds Shirley reluctant to present his own views to the Massachusetts legislature. I suspect he knew that it too would judge his opinions to smack of prerogative. Shannon, 226–32, discriminates the "provincial and imperial perspectives" of Franklin and Shirley.

7. Shirley, *Correspondence* 2:96.

8. *Life* 1:79–84, 94, 343, 396, 398, 405, 413, 460, 2:215–18, 509.

9. Reverend Jonathan Mayhew, *A Discourse Concerning Unlimited Submission* (Boston: Fowle and Gookin, 1750) 42; E6549; Charles W. Akers, *Called unto Liberty: A Life of Jonathan Mayhew* (Cambridge, Mass.: Harvard University Press, 1964) 254n16, for the newspaper controversy. P 11:89.

10. BF referred to the assemblies as America's "Parliaments" in 1744 (2:411).

11. Lemay, "Robert Beverley" 74–78, 94–95.

12. *Life* 2:158–60, 215–18, and Chapter 6.

13. JAP 2:234–35.

14. Franklin's "'Short Hints' or Terms for a Durable Union," 4–6 December 1774, P 21:365–68, contains the provision: "All the Acts restraining Manufacturers in the Colonies to be reconsider'd." The last word was originally "repealed," but Franklin was persuaded to substitute the less definite verb; P 21:366n7.

15. BF made similar comments as preconditions to any possible plan of colonial union in both his "'Short Hints' or Terms for a Durable Union" and BF to Joseph Galloway, 25 February 1775. P 21:365–68, 509–10.

16. He had objected to "Royal Instructions" earlier: *Life* 2:217–18, 508–9; see above, pp. 323–27.

17. The last two sentences of #10 in "Observations" read: "Therefore Britain should not too much restrain Manufactures in her Colonies. A wise and good Mother will not do it. To distress, is to weaken, and weakening the Children, weakens the whole Family." These Franklin judged too bold in context for the English audience, and he deleted them in the 1760 and later reprinting of "Observations." See also P 13:84, 21:417.

18. Joseph Priestley, *Autobiography*, ed. Jack Lindsay (Teaneck, N.J.: Fairleigh Dickinson University Press, 1970) 116. P 19:177–78n8; P 25:288.

19. Cf. *Canon* 132–33; P 9:90–91.

20. On BF as a trimmer, see especially the early pages of Jack P. Greene, "The Alienation of BF, British American," in *Understanding the American Revolution: Issues and Actors* (Charlottesville: University Press of Virginia, 1995) 247–84.

21. *The Records of the Federal Constitution of 1787*, ed. Max Farrand, plus *Supplement*, ed. James H. Hutson, 4 v. (New Haven, Conn.: Yale University Press, 1987) 3:540.

22. *Life* 1:252, 261, 308, 376; 2:50, and the discussion above, p. 316.

23. BF's accounts in Ledger D 347, 205, APS.

24. VD 235: "She later thought them indiscreet, and he may have thought so too." Isaacson 163: "Franklin didn't save most of her letters, perhaps out of prudence." See also Aldridge 118–20; Hawke 122; Brands 259.

25. William G. Roelker, ed., *BF and Catharine Ray Greene: Their Correspondence* (Philadelphia: American Philosophical Society, 1949), theorized that some young Boston man asked BF about courting and BF advised him, only to find that the young man ignored his advice and declared his passion to Katy Ray (P 5:536n7).

26. André Morellet, *Mémoires . . . de l'académie Français*, 2 v. (Paris: Ladvoccat,

1821) 1:289; and Ellen Cohn, "BF and Traditional Music," in *Reappraising* 290–318, at 290–91. For the songs and ballads BF wrote, see *Life* 1:59, 62–66, 2:271–75, 280–85; for his art, see Lemay, "American Aesthetic"; for literature, see the discussion of BF's prose style, journalism, and proverbs in *Life* 1:108, 414–56, esp. 455–56; 2:192–213, esp. 192–93, 212–13; and for moral philosophy, see "On Simplicity" (13 April 1732), *Life* 2:63–66.

27. The 1963 editors of the *Papers* theorized that the recipient was Elizabeth Hubbart and described how the seal must have looked (P 6:222nn6,7).

CHAPTER 16

1. Hutson, "BF" 335–36; Wolff 157. On Morris, see Horle 2:75–77, 1120–21; *ANB*; *DAB*; Bell 1:94–100.

2. Morris to Penn, 26 October 1754, TPP, reel 8, frame 83; PA, 1st ser., 2:254; Wolff 168–69.

3. V 5:3768, 3771–72.

4. Ibid. 3791.

5. Ibid. 3796, 3841.

6. Gratz Collection, Papers of the Governors, Thomas Penn mss., HSP; Jennings 100.

7. PA 1st ser., 2:249–50; CR 5:299–300.

8. Henderson 95, 122. Henderson was uncertain whether the month was February or March, but the references to Walker in CR 6:301, 303, and PA, 1st ser., 2:253, 257, prove it was February. Conogogee Creek flows from Pennsylvania into the Potomac River, Maryland, between Winchester, Virginia, and Frederick, Maryland.

9. CR 6:307–8.

10. Ibid. 336–37.

11. Ibid. 307–8; PA, 1st ser., 2:286.

12. CR 6:327–28.

13. Ibid. 327; Morris to T. Penn, 9 April 1755, PA, 1st ser., 2:287–89.

14. PA, 1st ser., 2:420; T. Penn to Morris, 19 September 1755, TPP, reel 1, frame 202; CR 7:447.

15. [Thomas Balch], *Letters and Papers Relating Chiefly to the Provincial History of Pa* (1855) 35; Wallace 381.

16. V 6:3866, 3872, 3873; P 4:162, 162n20.

17. CR 6:317.

18. Ibid. 329–30, 335.

19. Ibid. 338.

20. V 5:3870–71; PA 1st ser., 2:189.

21. V 5:3874; PA 1st ser., 2:287.

22. V 5:3878–79; CR 6:387.

23. Foster 542b.

24. PA, 1st ser., 2:288.

25. P 6:6–7; V 5:3877.

26. PA, 1st ser., 2:288; Morris to Robinson, in Gipson 6:69.

27. On Scarouady, see DH 1747; CR 6:343. The policy of neutrality was a longstanding Iroquois position, though some Iroquois, especially the Mohawks, were allied with the English and some with the French. Cf. DH, 5 September 1745. As we have seen, Thomas Pownall commented on this Iroquois policy in Chapter 4, "Albany Treaty" (above, 383, citing McAnear 740–41). See also Scarouday (DH, 31 March 1755) and "Secret Intelligence from Shippensburgh" (DH, late 1755).

28. V 4:3053; CR 4:772–73; Wallace 225. See also just above, n. 27, and Jennings, BF 123.

29. V 5:3874, 3884, 3886; P 6:8–9. The treaty the governor had neglected previously to specify was held more than three months later with Teedyuscung at Easton; see below, Chapter 21.

30. V 5:3885–86. P 4:163, 163n6.

31. CR 5:368–69.

32. See Chapter 13.

33. GM 25 (August 1755): 378. Parton wrote that Franklin appealed "to each of the great motives that induce men to depart from the routine of their lives—self-interest, fear, pride, and generosity" (1:351).

34. Richard Peters to the Proprietors, 17 May 1755, Peters mss. III, HSP; Israel Pemberton to John Fothergill, 755, Etting Collection, Pemberton Papers, II, HSP; Hanna 213n7.

35. P 5:199n8, 7:158.

36. PA, 1st ser., 2:317; P 6:14.

37. P 4:163, 163n7, 6:54–55, 59; V 5:3889.

38. PG, 17 and 28 April 1755.

39. CR 6:386–88; V 5:3893–96; Thomas Penn to Morris, 10 May 1755, Catherine Barnes, Autographs, Catalogue 18 (Philadelphia: Barnes, 1996), p. 32.

40. NCE 209.

41. CR 6:383.

42. CR 6:394.

43. PA, 1st ser., 2:329.

44. PA, 1st ser., 2:359.

45. Quoted in J. Bennett Nolan, General BF (Philadelphia: University of Pennsylvania Press, 1936) 10.

46. PA, 1st ser., 2:311, 330; cf. P 6:61.

47. Smith to Penn, no date (ante 27 November 1755), TPP, reel 8, frames 296–302.

48. Smith to Chandler, dated only April 1755, below. See DH, 31 January and 5 February, 1756; H. W. Smith 1:102.

49. Penn to Peters, 13 August 1755, TPP reel 1, frame 0621.

50. V 5:3904.

51. PA, 1st ser., 2:362; Hutson, "BF" 311.

52. CR 6:387.

53. V 5:3710, 3796, 3910, 3913, 3915–16; CR 6:356; Statutes 5:45–49; confirmed 29 October 1748, Statutes 5:49, 470–71.

54. CR 6:437–38.

55. The "old Catch" is an abbreviated version of a Mother Goose rhyme. Iona and Peter Opie, *Oxford Dictionary of Nursey Rhymes* (London: Oxford University Press, 1973) 292.

56. P 5:235–37. Sachse 90; on p. 4, Sachse mistakenly lists BF rather than WF as a member of the planning committee; and the mistake recurs in *PMHB* 30 (1906): 289. Sachse published a later list of those who donated money for the building in *PMHB* 20 (1896): 120–21, which also lists the members of St. John's Lodge who did not subscribe; it has some omissions and differences from the original list of pledges at P 5:235–37.

57. *PMHB* 17 (1893): 273. According to the *Gazette*, the number was 127, not 160.

58. The lack of change in the Pennsylvania's Grand Lodge of the "Moderns" may have been one reason that the "Moderns" Masonic organization became moribund and the "Ancients" replaced it (*Life* 2:92).

59. *PG*, 3 July 1755, p. 3; William Smith, *A Sermon Preached in Christ-Church, Philadelphia . . . the 24th of June, 1755* (Philadelphia: Franklin and Hall, 1755); E7571; Miller 627.

60. William Shirley, Jr., to Morris, 23 May 1755, CR 6:404–5.

61. CR 6:477, mistakenly printing "10 instant," rather than 18 instant.

62. "Extracts from the Diary of Daniel Fisher," *PMHB* 17 (1893): 263–78, at 273–74.

63. *Burd Papers* (1897) 22–23. See also Elain G. Breslaw, "'Dismal Tragedy': Drs. Alexander and John Hamilton Comment on Braddock's Defeat," *Maryland Historical Magazine* 75 (1980): 118–44.

64. Freeman, *GW* 2:73.

65. CR 6:501; Freeman, *GW* 2:88.

66. CR 6:589; Wallace 390.

67. P 6:112; V 5:3931.

68. PA, 1st ser., 2:387.

69. Shirley, *Correspondence* 2:215–16, 218, 231–34; Gipson 6:132–33; P 4:164, 164n1; V 5:3951.

CHAPTER 17

1. CR 6:478–79.

2. Ibid. 486–87; V 5:3926–28.

3. CR 6:492; Foster 543–44.

4. *Statutes* 3:128.

5. V 5:3928; P 6:129.

6. V 5:4072–73.

7. The use of "hath" rather than "has" is one minor indication of Franklin's authorship. *Life* 2:131–32, 132n19. See section 2 of "An Act for Granting . . . £60,000"; and a "Supplement" to the bill passed 23 March 1757; *Statutes* 5:202, 295.

8. V 5:4074–75. The entire bill is printed at ibid. 4072–78.

9. V 5:4077. Governor Morris's proposed amendments of 5 August are printed at ibid. 4078–80.

10. V 5:3936–37, 3938; P 4:164, 164n19, 6:130–31.

11. P 6:134, citing the original, CR 2:146.

12. *PG*, 14 August 1755, p. 2, col. 1, for "hateful Instrument." In the *Votes and Proceedings* for 1754–55 (E7532), 126.

13. P 4:164, 164n2; V 5:3964–65; CR 6:537–46, *vassalage* at 544–45; in E7532 at 135.

14. For Franklin's epistemological skepticism, see *Life* 2:520–21.

15. E7532 at 151–52.

16. *PG*, 21 August 1755, p. 3, col. 2; see DH. Penn to Peters, 25 October 1755, TPP, reel 1, frame 642.

17. V 5:3932.

18. CR 6:518.

19. Ibid. 732.

20. *Acts PC* 4:338; *Statutes* 5:194–95; Kelley 331.

21. V 5:4004; CR 6:663.

22. Morris did so on 24 July, 9, 21, and 22 August; V 5:3927, 3949, 4003, 4006, 4008.

23. Hutson, "BF" 326n, said Franklin "wrote every important Assembly message from the spring of 1755 until his departure for England in the spring of 1757."

24. V 5:4006.

25. Ibid. 4006, 4008.

26. Richard Hockley to Thomas Penn, 22 March 1755, TPP, reel 8, frames 230–31.

27. CR 6:600. Egnal, 79n41, also cites John Smith to R. Wells, 22 August 1755, John Smith Correspondence, HSP.

28. PA, 1st ser., 2:396.

29. Bauman 44–45, 72–73.

30. V 5:4014.

31. CR 6:619; P 6:195. At first Isaac Norris also believed that Smith was not the author; Horle 3:956b.

32. The proprietors' 2 March 1741/2 letter was evidently not printed in CR or V, but references to it are in V 4:2739, 2748. On 19 May 1742, Isaac Norris, Thomas Leech, Robert Jones, Oswald Peele, Israel Pemberton, and Samuel Blunston were appointed to be a committee to prepare an answer to the proprietors' letter; V 4:2749. The previous summer, Thomas Penn promised Jeremiah Langhorne, William Allen, Lawrence Growdon, John Kearsley, William Clymer, Septimus Robinson, William Plumsted, and James Hamilton that he would support a petition to prohibit Quakers from being assemblymen. Horle, "Jeremiah Langhorne" 2:647, "Harmanus Alrichs" 2:196; and *PMHB* 23 (1899): 383, 499. See also *Life* 2:336–40.

33. V 5:4010, 4012, 4013.

34. P 4:165, 165n9; V 5:4041; Gipson 6:174–76, 205–6.

35. The reading is confirmed by the 6 December 1755 entry in *Board of Trade Journals* (also transcripts) 63:363, HSP. BF's letter to Partridge was printed without

attribution in the *GM*, 25 (November 1755): 486–87. Francis Jennings, "An Early Political Paper of Benjamin Franklin," *American Journal of Legal History* 8 (1964): 264–66.

36. V 5:4072–80, at 4077.

37. Charlotte Brown's diary in Isabel M. Calder, *Colonial Captivities, Marches, and Journeys* (1935; rpt. Port Washington, N.Y.: Kennikat Press, 1967) and Smith, *Brief State* postscript.

38. Horle 3:944–50, 1078–83.

39. In addition to the references to the Hemphill tracts, see the letter to his parents (*Life* 2:295–98), "A Speech Delivered by an Indian Chief" (*Life* 2:510–13), "What is True?" (*Life* 2:520–24), and "The Speech of Miss Polly Baker" (*Life* 2:545–48). For Adams, see *NCE* 247.

40. Donald H. Meyer, *Democratic Enlightenment* (New York: Putnam, 1976) 218.

41. Maundress, *Travel from Aleppo* (Oxford: at the Theater, 1703); Kevin J. Hayes, "Franklin," in *Oxford Handbook of Early American Literature*, ed. Hayes (New York: Oxford University Press, 2008) 434–35.

42. "Madison's 'Detached Memoranda,'" ed. Elizabeth Fleet, *WMQ* 3 (1946): 540. Madison has "who" whereas Franklin had "that."

43. Green and Stallybrass 17–23; see also my review in the American Antiquarian Society, *The Book*, no. 69 (July 2006): 7–9, at 7.

44. P 6:125, 125nn5–7. If he used the translation of the Code of Maimonides by Georgius Gentius, Franklin may have recalled, with some private amusement, the name of another person, "the learned *Greutzius*" (*Life* 1:437).

45. The Golden Rule also appears in the *Proposals Relating to the Education of Youth in Pennsylvania* (1749; Chapter 5) and the 8 August 1751 "Appeal for the Hospital" (Chapter 8).

46. "Extracts from the Diary of Daniel Fisher, 1755," *PMHB* 17 (1893): 263–78, at 271. Page references for the next several paragraphs (F plus page) are all to Fisher's diary.

47. Charlotte Brown, in Calder, *Colonial* 190. Page references for the next several paragraphs (B plus page) are to Brown's diary.

48. Pemberton to Dr. John Fothergill, 27 November 1755, Pemberton Papers, HSP.

49. VD 125.

50. Ibid. 231–32.

51. Frederick B. Tolles, *James Logan and the Culture of Provincial America* (Boston: Little, Brown, 1957).

52. *NCE* 209–10.

53. Horle 3:416–49, at 417.

54. Franklin's Ledger D, 249, APS, records two accounts with Brown: 1755, "Mrs. Charlotte Browne's Acct. Rec'd of her Money in Trust Being Province Orders, 180.0.0. [120.0.0?]," and 1756, "Mrs. Charlotte Browne's Acct. Rec'd & added the Interest of one Year, 6.0.0."

55. Examples of her responsible partnership in business dealing (passim), her social

standing (611), her temper (611), and her reputation as a stepmother (612, 612n13) may also be found in J. A. Leo Lemay, "Deborah Franklin, Lord Loudoun, and Franklin's *Autobiography,*" *Huntington Library Quarterly* 67 (2004): 607–66. See also Jennifer Reed Fry, " 'Extraordinary Freedom and Great Humility': A Reinterpretation of Deborah Franklin," *PMHB* 127 (2003): 167–96.

56. Wood, *Americanization* 33, 83, 154; Weinberger 106, 290; and Isaacson 44, 300–301; cf. *Life* 1:265–67 for a differing interpretation of Franklin's and Deborah's actions in 1725.

CHAPTER 18

1. CR 6:641–44; P 6:230n8; Boyd, *Treaties* lxx.

2. P 6:229, 230n8; V 5:4091–92; CR 6:645–46.

3. P 6:229n2; CR 6:647.

4. Charlotte Brown, in Isabel M. Calder, *Colonial Captivities, Marches, and Journeys* (1935; rpt. Port Washington, N.Y.: Kennikat Press, 1967) 190; hereafter Brown.

5. CR 6:652.

6. Ibid. 663, 679; P 6:229n3; CR 6:739; P 6:234n3, 237.

7. Kevin J. Hayes suggested that Franklin may have been alluding to Jean Baptiste Labat's four-volume *Voyage du chevalier Des Marchais en Guinée* (1731).

8. V 5:4097.

9. Ibid. 4100.

10. V 4:3579; Hutson, "BF" 327–28; *Statutes* 5:7–15.

11. The editors of the *Papers* noted that it was the assembly's first proposal "to refer the tax dispute to the King" (6:240). V 5:4104.

12. CR 6:680; V 5:4104; Brown 190–91.

13. CR 6:686–87; Boyd, *Treaties* lxix.

14. V 5:4107; CR 6:688.

15. Francis Jennings, "An Early Political Paper of Benjamin Franklin," *American Journal of Legal History* 8 (1964): 264–66; *GM* 25 (November 1755): 486–87.

16. CR 6:386.

17. See appendix 6. Francis Bacon, *Philosophical Works*, ed. John M. Robertson (London: Routledge, 1905) 747.

18. V 5:4121; *Life* 2:345, 345n27.

19. Earlier versions are at 6:141, 194; later ones are at 6:263–64, 513 and 7:262, 381–82.

20. Richard Peters Letter Book, 1755–57, formerly in Gratz Collection, now housed with the Peters Papers, HSP.

21. V 5:4144, 4153.

22. Ibid. 4157, 4175–79.

23. For Beverley, *Life* 1:79, 79nn1, 2, 2:216. For Mercer's echo of Franklin, see J. A. Lemay, "John Mercer and the Stamp Act in Virginia, 1764–1765," *Virginia Magazine of History and Biography* 91 (1983): 3–38, at 34.

24. V 5:4096, 4099, 4103.

25. P 4:166, 166n12, 5:79 (to Bowdoin), 107 (end of Carlisle Treaty), 154 (to Bowdoin); 7:175, 175n9.

26. CR 6:684–85.

27. V 5:4109.

28. Ibid. 4121.

29. CR 6:726; V 5:4146.

30. CR 6:739–40; P 7:173n4, 376n9.

31. William Smith to Penn, 27 November 1755, TPP, reel 8, frames 275–76; Smith, *Brief View* 54, 56.

32. Corner and Booth 167.

33. CR 6:731.

34. Ibid. 733; V 5:4150–51.

35. V 5:4159–60; CR 6:737–38; *Statutes* 5:201–12, 531.

36. Israel Pemberton to John Fothergill, 17 December 1755, Pemberton Papers, 2:8, Etting Collection, HSP; Marietta 16–17.

37. V 5:4122, 4130.

38. The four pacifists who voted against it were James Pemberton, Joshua Morris, Joseph Trotter, and Peter Worrall; Horle 2:746. P 6:267, 269; *Statutes* 5:197–201, 530–44.

39. V 5:4132.

40. CR 6:724.

41. P 6:267; CR 6:741.

42. Smith, *Brief View* 81; Arthur D. Graeff, *The Relation between the Pennsylvania Germans and the British Authorities, 1750–1776* ([Norristown]: Pennsylvania German Society, 1934) 136–37; and William Smith to Penn, 27 November 1755, TPP, roll 8, frames 275–76; [Joseph Galloway], *A True and Impartial State of . . . Pennsylvania* (Philadelphia, 1759) 143.

43. CR 6:729.

44. Richard Hockley to Thomas Penn, 16 December 1755, TPP, reel 8, frames 0279–80.

45. V 5:4157–58.

46. *Statutes* 5:201, 532.

47. V 5:4099, 4103, 4115–17.

48. Ibid. 4109–10; CR 6:739.

49. V 5:4117, 4118, 4119.

50. Ibid. 4173–74.

51. In 1755, Smith attacked the Quaker Party and Franklin in *Brief State*; P 6:52n5. He renewed his Proprietary Party propaganda with *Brief View*; P 6:213n8.

52. CR 6:702.

53. In the *Autobiography*, Franklin alluded to the "essential Liberty . . . temporary Safety" when he stressed the assembly's "essential Right" years later (A 144).

Franklin probably recalled Morris's change of a single word (also on A 144) when he proposed in 1765 the change of a single number when the Stamp Act should be enacted, from 1765 to 2765; P 13:132n1.

54. Since Franklin wrote this part of the *Autobiography* in 1788, he may have been attempting to justify his failed attempt in the1760s to make Pennsylvania a royal province.

55. *PG*, 25 December 1755, 1 January 1756.

56. *GM* 26 (February 1756): 83–84, (March 1756) 122–26.

CHAPTER 19

1. *Statutes* 5:201–12, at 211. GWP 2:226. J. Bennett Nolan tells an engaging story of Franklin's military service in late 1755 and early 1756 in *General BF* (1936; rpt. Philadelphia: University of Pennsylvania Press, 1936).

2. Lieutenant Colonel John Anderson lived on a farm just across the Delaware River from Easton. The previous occasion was on 2 November: after an alarm from Easton, he gathered his troops and marched to help on 3 November. William Nelson, ed., *Documents Relating to the Colonial History . . . of New Jersey*, 32 v. (Patterson, N.J.: Press Printing Company, 1897) 19:552–54; Joseph R. Klett, *Genealogies of New Jersey Families*, 2 v. (Baltimore: Genealogical Publishing Company, 1996) 2:375–76.

3. Joseph Mortimer Levering, *A History of Bethlehem, Pennsylvania, 1741–1892* (Bethlehem, Pa.: Times Publishing Company, 1903) 315.

4. V 5:4165; *Statutes* 5:212–15.

5. Hall to Strahan, 17 December 1755, David Hall Letterbooks, APS.

6. Churchman, *An Account of the Gospel Labours* (1779) 172.

7. Churchman 173–74.

8. "Journal of Charlotte Brown," in Calder, *Colonial* 191.

9. Pemberton to Fothergill, 17 December 1755, Pemberton Papers, 2:8, Etting Collection, HSP. Marietta, "Conscience" 16–17.

10. I have not found a copy of Smith's edition of the epistle, but Fothergill's letter to Israel Pemberton of 2 August 1756 refers to its London publication; Corner and Booth 184.

11. Following Nolan 17, biographers commonly say so, but I looked in vain for any evidence that William was wearing his former uniform. Sheila L. Skemp, 10, writes that William returned to Philadelphia in May 1747 "with the rank of captain" and that he "quickly returned to his regiment." But neither the 7 May or the 28 May ads for deserters gives any rank. I have found no evidence that he was promoted from an ensign. Isaacson, 170, has Benjamin Franklin putting on a military uniform before setting out for the frontier, but the commissioners had no uniforms.

12. CR 6:763–64. Cf. P 6:307n4, where the editors correct the misdating of Hamilton's letter.

13. P 6:343–47 gives biographical notes on the captains BF commissioned.
14. "Moravian Record," *PMHB* 18 (1894): 377–78; PA, 1st ser., 2:543; P 6:349n7; CR 6:771–72; Peters to Penn, 1 January 1756, TPP, reel 8, frames 304–5.
15. "Moravian Record" 377.
16. Ibid. 377–78.
17. For Garrison and his *View of the House of Employment . . . and Part of the City of Philadelphia*, see Ellen S. Jacobowitz, in Sewell 91–93. For Pownall's *View of Bethlehem*, see P 6:xvi, 358.
18. "Moravian Record" 377; P 6:369, 380.
19. Nolan 72.
20. William C. Reichel, *The Crown Inn . . . 1745* (Philadelphia: Wilbur, 1872) 56–57.

CHAPTER 20

1. CR 6:766.
2. V 5:4181; Horle 3:846a.
3. *PG,* 12 February 1756 noted he arrived "last week"; Freeman, *GW* 2:158.
4. V 5:4185.
5. *Speech of John Wright,* E4872; Miller 272; *Life* 2:333–35; V 5:4198–4201.
6. CR 7:41–42; V 5:4196, 4200; P 6:405.
7. William L. Hedges, "From Franklin to Emerson," in *Oldest Revolutionary* 139–56, at 152.
8. *PG,* 4 March 1756; Jennings 136.
9. V 5:4203, 4206.
10. Ibid. 4208, 4209, 4207; *Statutes* 5:224–43.
11. V 5:4204, 4207, 4208, 4210.
12. Ibid. 4211, 4212, *PG,* 18 March 1756, said Washington arrived in Philadelphia "yesterday."
13. Raoul François Camus, "Military Music of Colonial Boston," in *Music in Colonial Massachusetts, 1630–1820 I: Music in Public Places* (Boston: Colonial Society of Massachusetts, 1980) 81.
14. Penn to Peters, 13 August 1756, TPP; reel 1, frames 0722–24.
15. *Pennsylvania Journal,* 6 May 1756, reprinting from a *Virginia Gazette* of 23 April. *A Historical Sketch of the College of William and Mary* (Richmond, Va.: Gary and Clemmitt, 1866) 42.
16. E7754; Miller 650. Text in *PG,* 22 April 1756, and in CR 7:74–76, 88–90.
17. Corner and Booth 179.
18. Ketcham, "BF and Smith" 148–49; P 6:420–22n5.
19. *Pennsylvania Journal,* 15 April 1756; Ketcham, "BF and Smith" 148–50.
20. V 5:4232, 4233, 4234.
21. Ibid. 4245, 4240–41, and 4242–43, respectively.
22. Ibid. 4243–44, 4245.
23. Ibid. 4283–84.
24. Stokes 4:682.

25. Loudoun Diary and Notes, Huntington Library, San Marino, California.

26. V 5:4263–4264; Penn to Hockley, 27 May 1756 (TPP, reel 1, frame 706); to Peters, 9 October 1756 (TPP, reel 2, frame 16); to Hamilton, 8 January 1757 (PPOC, 5:68–69).

27. H. W. Smith 1:128.

28. *Minutes of Conferences Held with the Indians, at Easton, in the Months of July and November, 1756* (Philadelphia: Franklin and Hall, 1757); E7923; Miller 676; Boyd, *Treaties* 141–49. BF's copy, with his annotations, is at the University of Pennsylvania. Talbott 202, fig. 6.1.

29. Peters to Penn, 4 August 1756, TPP, reel 8, frames 418–28.

30. CR 7:234.

31. V 5:4289, 6:4561, 5:4291–92, 4293–95, respectively.

32. Ibid. 4298–4306.

33. Ibid. 4307–8.

34. Ibid. 4313–14, 4325; *Statutes* 5:224–43.

35. V 5:4319, 4320–24, 4326; P 5:344–50.

36. See Appendix 6.

37. CR 7:256–57, 264; V 5:4329; *Statutes* 5:243–62.

38. William A. Hunter, "Victory at Kittanning," *Pennsylvania History* 23 (1956): 376–407; "Shingas," *ANB*.

CHAPTER 21

1. Peters to Penn, 26 June, 4 Sept 1756, TPP reel 8, frames 127–29,134; Horle 2:132 and graph at 133.

2. For Franklin's supposed betrayal, see Newcomb 32–34 and the previous scholars he cites. Peters to Penn, 22 September, 2 October 1756, reel 8, frames 138–39, 139–40.

3. V 6:4385; P 7:10n4.

4. V 6:4387–88, 4390.

5. Ibid. 6:4407, 4409–19; Horle 3:959b.

6. V 6:4427.

7. *PMHB* 31:247.

8. CR 7:267.

9. Richard Peters, secretary, *Minutes of Conferences, Held . . . at Easton* (Philadelphia: Franklin and Hall, 1757) 16–17 (hereafter *Minutes/Easton*); E7923; Miller 676. Boyd, *Treaties* 305, noted that the copy he reproduced had underscoring, marginal marks, and "abundant commas" added by Ferdinand J. Paris. The Evans online text reproduced this copy. Since I could not always be sure that the commas were Paris's manuscript additions, I have included them in my quotations. *PG*, 10 March 1757, advertised that the treaty was just published, and two corrections to the treaty's text appeared in the next *PG*, 17 March 1757. I collated the texts of the November treaty in Franklin's 1757 imprint with that in CR 7:313–38. They are the same, except for thirteen substantive differences:

one typo in *Minutes/Easton*, and several careless mistakes in CR. The few important differences (like the conference starting in the "Forenoon" at 3:00 P.M. rather than 11:00 A.M. in CR) seem not to be intended to alter the substance of what *Minutes/Easton* reported. But for reservations by Franklin and the other commissioners concerning the official minutes, see the remarks (discussed below) they made in the assembly on 29 January 1757. Franklin printed them as an appendix, p. 36, to *Minutes/Easton*. Boyd, 305–6, discusses the texts. James T. Merrill, "'I desire all that I have said may be taken down aright': Revisiting Teedyuscung's 1756 Treaty Council Speeches," *WMQ* 63 (2006): 777–826, studies the textual differences. He has a more complete survey of the "Easton Treaty Texts, July and November 1756," together with a comparison of the versions of Teedyuscung's words, at the *William and Mary Quarterly* Web site, <Merrill, Easton Treaty Texts>; Jennings, *Empire* 276–81.

10. *Minutes/Easton* 18; Samuel Parrish, *Some Chapters in the History of the Friendly Association* (Philadelphia: Friends Historical Association, 1877) 31.

11. *Minutes/Easton* 19; CR 7:318; Parrish 32–33.

12. P 7:16–17; *Minutes/Easton* 19–20; CR 7:320.

13. Parrish 33.

14. CR 7:431–33; Parrish 34–35; Wallace, *Teedyuscung* 133. For Peters's thoughts on the Walking Purchase, see Peters to T. Penn, 22 November 1756, DH.

15. William A. Hunter, "Moses (Tunda) Tatamy," in *Northeastern Indian Lives*, ed. Robert S. Grumet (Amherst: University of Massachusetts Press, 1996) 260.

16. *Minutes/Easton* 21; CR 7:321–22.

17. *Minutes/Easton* 23; CR 7:324; Parrish 35–39; Jennings, *Empire* 279.

18. *Minutes/Easton* 23; CR 7:325. Governor Morris was only present at the meeting in Philadelphia on 23 and 24 February; CR 6:364–65, 370–72.

19. "Greedy" is in *Minutes/Easton* 23.-10 (i.e., ten lines from the bottom of p. 23).

20. *Minutes/Easton* 23; CR 7:326; Hunter, "Tatamy," 265; Matthew C. Ward, *Breaking the Backcountry: The Seven Years' War in Virginia and Pennsylvania, 1754–1765* (Pittsburgh: University of Pittsburgh Press, 2003) 139.

21. Ward, *Breaking the Backcountry* 139. "Minutes of the Friendly Association," Gratz Collection, 20–21, HSP. The call number is "Am 525." The information concerning the November Easton Treaty begins in the unpaginated minutes on a verso page (p. 32), easily recognized because it has a paragraph heavily crossed out. The top of the page begins, "On the 9th about 11 o'clock."

22. Parrish, 35–37, dates Peters's angry outburst on Monday morning, 15 November.

23. *Minutes/Easton* has 1743, a typo for 1742; CR 327 has it right. Boyd, *Treaties* xxxi–xxxii, 15–39, 303–4.

24. *Minutes/Easton* 24.

25. Ibid. 25; CR 7:327–28.

26. Parrish 37 and n37.

27. *Minutes/Easton* 25–27; CR 7:330–32.

28. *Minutes/Easton* 28; CR 7:333, which has an error.

29. *Minutes/Easton* 29–30; CR 7:334–35.

30. R. Peters to T. Penn; 22 November, 1756, p. 7, TPP, reel 8, pp. 201–5; P 7:22–23; CR 7:336.

31. CR 7:400; P 7:111–12; E7998, pp. 75–76; E7923, p. 31.

32. V 6:4429, 4442; Horle 3:459.

33. V 6:4404–5, 4440, 4442–43, 4448–50; CR 7:346, 348–50; *Statutes* 5:269–78.

34. *Minutes*, Phila. 601–2; V 6:4457–58.

35. V 6:4458.

36. CR 7:358. For the quartering problems, see *The Papers of Henry Bouquet*, ed. S. K. Stevens et al., 6 v. (Harrisburg: Pennsylvania Historical and Museum Commission, 1952–94) 1:30–45.

37. CR 7:358, 361–62; P 7:46n5.

38. P 7:47n5; CR 7:357, 361–62; V 6:4461.

39. P 7:48n7, 49n2; PA, 1st ser., 3:111, 112.

40. R. Peters to T. Penn, 26 December 1756, TPP, reel 8, frames 510–15 (p. 4 of the letter); CR 7:374.

41. V 6:4475.

42. Ibid. 4459, 4477.

43. Peters to Penn, 26 December 1756, TPP, reel 8, frames 510–15 (p. 6 of letter); P 7:62n9.

44. Donald Cornu, "Captain Lewis Ourry, Royal American Regiment of Foot," *Pennsylvania History* 19 (1952): 249–61.

45. CR 7:382–83, 384–85; V 6:4485; Nicholas D. Wainwright, *George Croghan: Wilderness Diplomat* (Chapel Hill: University of North Carolina Press, 1959) 120–21; Parrish, 54–55.

46. *Statutes* 5:281–83, 284–87.

47. P 7:107; cf. Horle 3:960a, n124.

48. P 7:107–9; V 6:4501; *Statutes* 5:597–607.

49. V 6:4506.

50. CR 7:416, 431, 436; *Statutes* 5:288–90.

51. *Statutes* 5:303.

52. CR 6:504–15; 7:106–7.

53. TPP, reel 8, frame 154.

54. CR 7:430–31.

55. Loudoun Notebooks, Huntington Library, HM 1717, v. 2, p. 42b; P 7:146–47.

56. V 6:3548.

57. CR 7:442–43.

58. HM 1717, v. 2, p. 43b; also P 7:148.

59. HM 1717, v. 2, p. 45a; CR 7:447. Cf. 18–20 March 1755; P 5:527–35.

60. PA, 1st ser., 3:118. On the assessment of property values, see P 5:251n4, 7:106, 126n5, 128n7, 149n8.

61. CR 7:450.

62. CR 7:453.
63. CR 7:454, 470–72; *Statutes* 5:294–302.
64. Richard Peters called Masters, Franklin's "Minion"; Horle 3:845b. The first three possible reasons are from section 10 of the act, *Statutes* 5:301–2; the fourth is section 11, p. 302; and the fifth is section 12, p. 302.
65. HM 1717, v. 2, pp. 48b–49a. For a slightly different transcription, see P 7:224n6.
66. DF mentioned George later several times (P 5 and 6); he died on 19 June 1781 (P 35:185n7).
67. HM 1717, v. 2, p. 55a.

CHAPTER 22

1. Huntington Library mss., HM 1717, 2:57a, 66a–b.
2. Huntington Library mss., LO 3415.
3. HM 1717, 2:62a–b.
4. Ibid. 2:63a.
5. Ibid. 2:66a–b; also P 7:226n9.
6. WF to Eliza Graeme, 5 May 1757; in the grangerized copy at Lily Library, Indiana University, of Washington Irving, *Life of George Washington*, 8:396. The Reverend Colin Campbell is in Frederick Lewis Weiss, "The Colonial Clergy of the Middle Colonies," *PAAS* 66 (for October 1956): 167–351, at 193–94.
7. WF in *PMHB* 39 (1915): 262. Thomas Pownall kept a journal while traveling in 1754. Pownall, *Topographical Description of . . . the United States of America*, ed. Lois Mulkearn (Pittsburgh: University of Pittsburgh Press, 1949) 98. John Seelye, *Beautiful Machine: Rivers and the Republican Plan 1755–1825* (New York: Oxford University Press, 1991) 47–56, has the best appreciation of Pownall. William Nelson, "Josiah Hornblower, and the First Steam Engine in America," *Proceedings of the New Jersey Historial Society*, 2nd ser., 7 (1883): 177–247, at 192.
8. BF, "Account of Expences of My Voyage to England Disbursm't &c. 1757–62," p. 2. APS mss: B/F85f/6/1; P 7:164–65. Hays 3:555 is microfilm SR 3, no. 42, printed by Eddy, *PMHB* 55 (1931): 97–133.
9. Thomas 141–42.
10. A water taxi in Baltimore's Inner Harbor turned upside down in a squall on 6 March 2004, drowning several passengers.
11. I use the popular title and comment on its possible authenticity near the end of the chapter. The original *Poor Richard* for 1758 is E7899; Miller 657. The following discussion amplifies the section on *The Way to Wealth* in J. A. Leo Lemay, "Benjamin Franklin," *Major Writers of Early American Literature*, ed. Everett Emerson (Madison: University of Wisconsin Press, 1972) 214–17. I ignore the argument that *The Way to Wealth* was particularly appropriate to America as a young country; Clinton Rossiter and others have done justice to that thesis. Rossiter, *Seedtime of the Republic* (New York: Harcourt, Brace, 1953) 304.
12. Wood, *Americanization* 40, 38.
13. JAD 1:198, 4:150–51.

14. For the date of Franklin's reply to Foster, see also J. A. Leo Lemay, "Recent Franklin Scholarship," *PMHB* 126 (2002):327–40.

15. VD 752.

16. J. G. A. Pocock, "The Classical Theory of Deference," *American Historical Review* 81 (1976): 516–23; Richard E. Beeman, "Deference, Republicanism, and the Emergence of Popular Politics in Eighteenth-Century America," *WMQ* 49 (1992): 401–30.

17. Other scholars find the pursuit of wealth common in the writings of the Jesuits, common in Renaissance Italy, and generally common in Christianity. H. M. Robertson, *Aspects of the Rise of Economic Individualism* (New York: Kelley and Millman, 1959), esp. 160–67.

18. Max Weber, *The Protestant Ethic and the Spirit of Capitalism*, tr. Talcott Parsons (London: Allen and Unwin, 1930) 53, 55.

19. Jack P. Greene, *Pursuits of Happiness: The Social Development of Early Modern British Colonies and the Formation of American Culture* (Chapel Hill: University of North Carolina Press, 1988); David Hackett Fischer, *Bound Away: Virginia and the Westward Movement* (Charlottesville: University Press of Virginia, 2000).

20. "On Constancy," W 225–28; *Life* 2:261–62.

21. V 5:3687–88, 3697, 3703. As usual, private negotiations freed the prisoner; no further mention of Bagnall or Sitlinton occurs in the records. During Franklin's assembly service from 1751 to 1757, only one person imprisoned for debt was officially granted relief, Joseph Yeates (21 September 1756); *Statutes* 5:262–65. The Indian traders George Croghan and William Trent were granted relief for ten years, but the king in council struck down the act on 16 June 1758: V 5:4161–62, 4165, 4166–67; *Statutes* 5:212–15.

22. In *The Library Company of Philadelphia 1996 Annual Report* (Philadelphia: Library Company, 1997) 8–11, James N. Green argued that Franklin chose the name. Green and Stallybrass, 130, point out that the title evidently appeared before 1773 when a French translation appeared as "Le Moyen de s'Enricher."

23. A best-seller in the genre was Gervase Markham's *A Way to Get Wealth*, with more than eighteen editions from 1625 through the early eighteenth century. Some similar titles were G. B., *Way to be Rich* (1662); Robert Crowley, *Way to Wealth* (1550); John Gore, *Way to Prosper* (1636, 1646); John Trusler, *Way to be Rich*, at least six editions, with one in 1750; and his childhood favorite, Thomas Tryon, *Way to Health, Wealth, and Happiness* (see *Life* 1:68, 215).

24. Günter Gawlick, "Abraham's Sacrifice of Isaac Viewed by the English Deists," *Studies on Voltaire and the Eighteenth Century* 56 (1967): 577–600.

25. Green and Stallybrass 124.

26. Aldridge, *French* 52–53.

27. Richard Bushman, *The Refinement of America* (New York: Knopf, 1992).

28. TJP 2:202–3.

29. Bailyn, 35.

30. Jill Lepore, "What Poor Richard Cost Benjamin Franklin," *New Yorker*, 28 Jan 2008, 78–81, at 79. Aldridge, *French* 45–52, 54–59.

CHAPTER 23

1. *Life* 1:424; and A. Owen Aldridge, *The Dragon and the Eagle* (Detroit: Wayne State University Press, 1993) 24–30, 66–92.
2. *NCE* 209, 210.
3. Frank Lambert, *"Pedlar in Divinity": George Whitefield* (Princeton, N.J.: Princeton University Press, 1994). The great difference was that Whitefield was a national and international press celebrity (though news about him primarily appeared in the places where he was currently preaching), while the Association was a local Pennsylvania event.
4. Edward Countryman's review of Timothy Shannon, *Indians and Colonists at the Crossroads of Empire: The Albany Congress of 1754*, in *WMQ* 57 (2000): 862. For scholarship on the question, see Appendix 9.
5. Cappon 2:455; Adams Papers, Massachusetts Historical Society, microform, reel 123; *Writings of James Madison*, ed. Gaillard Hunt (New York: Putnam's, 1908) 8:413. Madison, Adams, and all the key Old Charter Party members knew that previous legal attempts to refuse taxation without representation were confirmed by the first article in the 1628 "Petition of Right."
6. JAD 1:198; Cappon 2:371.
7. Cappon 2:388; TJ, *Notes on the State of Virginia*, ed. Frank Shuffleton (New York: Penguin, 1999) 153. On the rise of some individuals in society, see BF, p 3:400n.
8. Jack P. Greene, *The Intellectual Heritage of the Constitutional Era: The Delegares Library* (Philadelphia: Library Company, 1986).

APPENDIX 4

1. Ezra Stiles, *Discourse on the Christian Union* (Boston: Edes and Gill, 1761); E9018.
2. P 16:81–107; Richard Price, *Correspondence*, 3 v., ed. W. Bernard Peach and D. O. Thomas (Durham, N.C.: Duke University Press, 1983–93) 1:58–79.
3. Campbell and Skinner, WN 2:325, show that Malthus used the fifth edition (2 v. [London: T. Caldell, 1792]) of Price's *Observations on Reversionary Payments* when originally writing his essay.
4. For the early suggested similarities between Franklin's 1729 *Modest Enquiry* and Smith, see Parton 1:186–87, who at the same time disclaimed the necessity of seeing any direct influence. Franklin's influence upon Adam Smith's references to paper currency and to Pennsylvania are obvious and will not be discussed here. For the influence of Franklin's "Observations" on Smith, see Parton 1:418–19; Lewis J. Carey, *Franklin's Economic Views* (Garden City, N.Y.: Doubleday, 1928) 123–27; Verner W. Crane, *Benjamin Franklin, Englishman and American* (Providence, R.I.: Brown University, 1936); John Ray, *Life of Adam Smith*

[1895], ed. Jacob Viner (New York: Augustus Kelley, 1965) 42–47; and Tracy Mott and George W. Zinke, "BF's Economic Thought: A Twentieth-Century Appraisal," *Critical Essays on BF*, ed. Melvin H. Buxbaum (Boston: G. K. Hall, 1987) 111–28, at 114, 118.

5. Ray, *Smith* [1895], ed. Viner, 151. Viner doubted that Smith consulted Franklin during the writing of the *Wealth of Nations* and doubted too that BF and WF stayed with Smith in Glasgow in 1759. I agree with Viner, but I think it likely that Smith would have entertained them during their 1759 visit to Glasgow. J. Bennett Nolan, *BF in Scotland and Ireland, 1759 and 1771* (Philadelphia: University of Pennsylvania Press, 1938) 62–63.

6. References to Pownall's and Price's writings are identified in WN 1066. The books of Pownall and Price are in James Bonar, *A Catalogue of the Library of Adam Smith*, 2nd ed. (1932; rpt. New York: Augustus M. Kelley, 1966), 150; and in Hiroshi Mizuta, *Adam Smith's Library: A Supplement to Bonar's Catalogue with a Check-List of the Whole Library* (Cambridge: Cambridge University Press, 1967) 131. References to Richard Jackson (*Historical Review . . . of Pennsylvania*, compiled from materials that Franklin supplied) are in Bonar 140 and Mizuta 95. References to Priestley are in Bonar 151 and Mizuta 131–32.

7. On Franklin in Smith's library, see Bonar 72, 148; Mizuta.

8. At WN 572 (IV.vii.b.16), Smith wrote, "Plenty of good land, and liberty to manage their own affairs their own way, seem to be the two great causes of the prosperity of all new colonies." Though his examples come in part from Greece and Rome (566–67), Smith also contrasts the growth of the contemporary English colonies with those of other countries in America, finding that the relatively independent political system of the English colonies was in great part responsible for their greater increase in population than the colonies of the Spanish, Portugese, or French.

9. The editors of WN discuss the significance of the stage theory for Smith, 11–16.

10. WN 99n39.

11. WN's editors, 896n, cite Hume, *Essays, Moral, Political, and Literary*, ed. Green and Grose, 1:358. In the Liberty Press edition of Hume, *Essays, Moral, Political, and Literary*, ed. Eugene F. Miller, rev. ed. (Indianapolis: Liberty Fund, 1985) 345.

12. Cohen, *Founding Fathers* 161.

13. Thomas Robert Malthus, *An Essay on the Principle of Population*, ed. Patricia James, 2 v. (New York: Cambridge University Press, 1989) 1:1.

14. Thomas Robert Malthus, *An Essay on the Principle of Population* (London: J. Johnson, 1798).

15. Malthus used the edition of Franklin's *Political, Miscellaneous and Philosophical Pieces*, ed. Benjamin Vaughan (London: J. Johnson, 1779).

16. David W. Galenson, "The Settlement and Growth of the Colonies," in *The Cambridge Economic History of the United States*, v. 1: *The Colonial Era*, ed.

Stanley L. Engerman and Robert E. Gallman (New York: Cambridge University Press, 1996), 135–208, at 169.

17. Malthus 1:10.

18. Alfred Russel Wallace, *My Life: A Record of Events and Opinions*, 2 v. (New York: Dodd, Mead, 1905) 1:362–63, 32, 240, respectively.

19. *The Works of Charles Darwin*, ed. Paul H. Barrett and R. B. Freeman, 29 v. (London: Pickering, 1986–89), v. 21 (*Descent of Man*) 48, citing Malthus.

20. *Works*, v. 29 (*Autobiography*) 144; cf. 10:xiv.

21. *Works* 19:8–9.

22. *Works*, 21 (I):48.

23. Silvan S. Schweber, "The Origin of *The Origin* Revisited," *Journal of the History of Biology* 10 (1977): 229–316, at 232.

Appendix 5

1. The 1962 editors of the *Papers* argue convincingly that Jonathan Trumbull wrote his Short Plan and Long Plan, printed in the Connecticut Historical Society *Collections* 17 (1918): 20–29, after the Albany Plan of Union was recorded on 10 July. P 5:382–86.

2. PA, 1st ser., 2:197. Shannon 183, 181.

3. Theodore Atkinson in McAnear 738. Shannon 192 explains their objection.

4. P 35:491–502, and see my review in *PMHB* 126 (2002): 327–29.

5. The 1962 *Papers* editors found the procedure "a pale foreshadowing of the scheme adopted in the Northwest Ordinance of 1787 for the creation of 'territorial' governments as a transitional step in the evolution of new states" (P 5:378).

6. According to Thomas Hutchinson, the council was to have power "to purchase from the Indians, for the crown, such lands as are not within the bounds of any colony, or which may be within such bounds, *when some of the colonies shall be reduced to more convenient dimensions.*" Hutchinson appended a footnote: "I am not now able to ascertain the colonies to which Mr. Franklin had a special reference. Probably Connecticut was one, and perhaps Virginia another. This reduction could be made only by authority of parliament." Hutchinson 3:16.

7. Shannon 190.

8. CR 6:109.

Appendix 7

The information in this appendix is compiled mainly from newspapers; from the information at P 5:171–72; from the post office accounts for 1757 at the APS, mss: BF85/F6/no. 13; and from an account described at P 7:158–60, 160–62.

INDEX

Page numbers in italics indicate illustrations and captions.

ACKNOWLEDGMENTS

Deborah Fox in the English Department office has repeatedly found the time to type difficult manuscripts, to index, and to help in many ways. My research assistants for the years 2005–8, Andreea Fodor, Mike McGeehee, and Melanie Scriptunas, have carried out numerous tasks, including reading drafts of chapters. To meet deadlines, I have also had the help of Michelle Smock and Michael Steier. My friend John Quintus, now retired from the State Department, has read the entire manuscript. Kimberley DePaul has also done me that great favor.

Colleagues at the University of Delaware who have taken time and answered my questions are Farley Grubb, economics; Nicholas P. Gross, classics; Robert P. Gilbert and Robert Stark, mathematics; and David Johnson, physics. I am greatly indebted to Susan Brynteson, May Morris Director of Libraries; Linda L. Stein, humanities librarian; and the interlibrary loan librarians at the University of Delaware.

Since I am ignorant concerning electricity, I called upon J. L. Heilbron, whose book on electricity in the seventeenth and eighteenth centuries is the standard study. He generously read the long electricity chapter. John Aubrey Adams, who is also writing about Franklin and electricity, gave me a number of suggestions. I have repeatedly questioned E. Philip Krider, an authority on lightning, who has invariably replied with authoritative information. Paul C. Pasles of Villanova University corrected my numbers and provided a mathematician's expertise to some of Poor Richard's tantalizing arithmetical questions. The book would have been better if I had been knowledgeable enough in science to follow all their suggestions.

Friends at the Winterthur Museum, Library, and Gardens have answered my inquiries: Don Fenimore, curator emeritus of metals; Linda Eaton, curator of textiles; and Ann Verplanck, curator of prints and photographs. Writing the chapter on General Benjamin Franklin, I consulted Kate Clark Engel, a historian at Texas A&M University; James Talareco, Bethlehem Digital History Project; and Paul Peucker, archivist, and Lanie Williamson, assistant archivist, of the Moravian Church Archives.

Roy E. Goodman and Valerie-Anne Lutz at the American Philosophical Society, and John Van Horn, James N. Green, and Charlene Peacock at the Library Company of Philadelphia have all been consistently helpful. At the University of Pennsylvania, Mark Fraser Lloyd, director of archives, Nancy Miller, archivist, and John Pollack, of the Van Pelt Library, gave friendly aid, especially with the chapter on the Philadelphia Academy and College.

It has been fun to come to know and spend social time with a number of Franklinists: Keith Arbour, Nian-Sheng Huang, Stuart Karu, Stacy Schiff, James Srodes, and Jay Robert Stiefel. Former students who are experts whom I correspond with often and consult on Franklin are Carla Mulford and Kevin J. Hayes. And occasionally, someone with expertise in an entirely different field has a sidelight to share on Franklin that I may or may not be able to use but whose enthusiasm and knowledge I enjoy: for example, microbiologist Douglas E. Eveleigh, of Rutgers University, who loves the bayberry plant and suggests that Abiah Folger Franklin introduced her husband, Josiah, to its superior wax for candles. I am grateful to the Packard Humanities Institute for giving me a copy of its CD ROM containing the texts of *The Papers of Benjamin Franklin*.

The University of Pennsylvania Press has been a pleasure to work with. Jennifer Backer, the copyeditor for Volume 3, is the same person who copyedited the first two volumes. She has corrected, revised, and transformed my messy manuscript into something far better than it was. I am most grateful to her. Erica Ginsburg, Associate Managing Editor of the University of Pennsylvania Press, has been superb.

My greatest obligation is to Ellen Cohn and the other editors, past and present, at *The Papers of Benjamin Franklin*. I have constantly relied upon their excellent work. Among them, good friends of long standing are Whitfield J. Bell, Jr., Claude-Anne Lopez, Barbara Oberg, and Ellen Cohn.

Franklin's Philadelphia 1723–1776

Property owned by Benjamin Franklin shown in solid black

1. Pennsylvania Hospital, opened 1756

2. Loganian Library, opened 1754–55

3. State House (Independence Hall), occupied 1735

4. Pennsylvania Hospital, 1752–56

5. Graves of Francis Folger Franklin, 1736, and Deborah Franklin, 1774, in Christ Church Burying Ground

6. "New Building," erected 1740; acquired for Academy and College 1750

7. Carpenters' Hall, erected 1770

8. Andrew Hamilton's residence, 1718–c.1727; Israel Pemberton's residence, 1745–54

9. Indian Queen Tavern

10. Franklin's residence, 326 Market St., 1761–65

11. Franklin's house, completed 1765

12. John Read's residence; Samuel Keimer's printing office was next door, 1723–26

13. Prison, erected 1723

14. Franklin's residence, 325 Market St., 1751–61; Post Office(?), 1752–53

15. Masonic Lodge, erected 1755

16. City Tavern, erected 1773

17. James Logan's residence, c.1720–c.1730

18. Indian King Tavern, a meeting place for Junto and Masonic lodge

19. First Presbyterian Church, erected 1704; enlarged 1752

20. Probable site of Samuel Keimer's printing office, 1726–30

21. Andrew Bradford's printing office, 1724–38; William Bradford's printing office, 1742–43

22. Andrew Bradford's printing office, c.1717–24

23. Friends' Meeting Houses: Great Meeting House, 1696–1755; Greater Meeting House, 1755–1804

24. Court House, erected c.1709

25. William Franklin's Post Office, 1753–57

26. Union Fire Company engine probably kept here, 1743

27. Christ Church, erected 1695; enlarged 1727–44

28. Franklin's residence, 1748–50

29. Budd's Buildings

30. William Bradford's printing office, 1743–54

31. Andrew Bradford's printing office, 1738–42

32. London Coffee House, opened 1754

33. William Bradford's printing office, 1754–77

34. Franklin's residence, 141 Market St., 1750–51

35. Franklin's residence, 139 Market St., 1728–39

36. Franklin's residence, 131 Market St., 1739–48; printing office, 1739–65; Post Office, 1739–52

37. Site of early meetings of Library Company

38. Thomas Denham's shop, where Franklin was clerk, 1726–27

39. Crooked Billet Tavern, where Franklin spent his first night, 1723

40. Association Battery (Atwood's Wharf), 1747

41. Tun Tavern, a Masonic meeting place

42. Market Street wharf, where Franklin landed, 1723

43. William Allen's residence

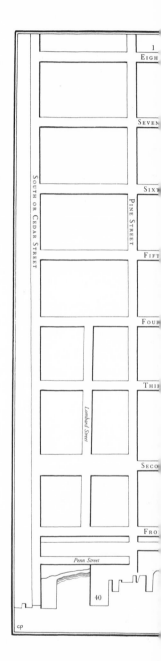